TOLKIEN'S LIBRARY
An Annotated Checklist

Oronzo Cilli

Foreword
Tom Shippey

Text Copyright © 2019 Oronzo Cilli
Cover Illustration © 2019 Jay Johnstone

First published by Luna Press Publishing, Edinburgh, 2019

Tolkien's Library: An Annotated Checklist ©2019. All rights reserved. No part of this publication may be reproduced, stored in a retrieval system, or transmitted in any form or by any means, electronic, mechanical, photocopy, recording or otherwise, without prior written permission of the copyright owners. Nor can it be circulated in any form of binding or cover other than that in which it is published and without similar condition including this condition being imposed on a subsequent purchaser.

The quotations from Tolkien's writings and the unrestricted Tolkien Papers in the Bodleian Library, University of Oxford, have been made available with the kind permission of the Tolkien Estate, and are acknowledged in detail in the Bibliography.

www.lunapresspublishing.com

ISBN-13: 978-1-911143-67-3

To Christopher and Priscilla Tolkien,
from the depth of my heart, for everything,
for every single day of these past forty years
spent in sharing your father with us.

Contents

Acknowledgements	vii
Foreword by Tom Shippey	xi
Preface	xvii
Tolkien's Library	1
The published writings of J.R.R. Tolkien 1910 - 1972	328
Interviews & Reviews	340
J. R. R. Tolkien: Supervisor and Examiner 1929-1960	345
Tolkien and Early English Text Society 1938-1972	354
Tolkien's Lectures 1920-1959	357
Bibliography	369
Index	386

Acknowledgements

This present work is the result of research which started in 2015. It grew in the process of writing as numerous suggestions were kindly given to me by friends and scholars whom I can but only respectfully thank.

First of all, though, I should thank you, my reader friend, not simply out of courtesy, but for dedicating your time to my work and for trusting me enough to follow this reconstruction of mine.

If the present book started with a simple search, it soon became something more, in the first place, because of John Garth, who first believed in its purpose and to whom I am thankful for his friendship.

With all my heart, I would also like to thank all the people who were so kind as to share information, and pictures, related to Tolkien's books: Mahdî Brecq, Pieter Collier, Ryszard Derdziński, Jeremy Edmonds, Eduardo Ferreira, Bradford Lee Eden, Wim Meeuws (Thornton's Bookshop) and Elena Rossi. I feel the same gratitude to friends who own some of them in their private collections: Christina Scull, Wayne G. Hammond, Aaron O'Brien, Charles Styles, Claudio Testi, Alan Reynolds and Carl F. Hostetter. I should also mention the writers and editors who update their websites daily, including all the information they have gathered on Tolkien's life and works: the Tolkien Library of Pieter Collier, the Tolkien Collector's Guide of Jeremy Edmonds, and the Tolkien Gateway. In each of these, I found precious information which was, most importantly, thoroughly documented.

I owe special thanks to Douglas A. Anderson, Pieter Collier, Dimitra Fimi, Jason Fisher, Peter Gilliver, Wayne G. Hammond, John Garth, Carl F. Hostetter, Jeremy H. Marshall, Neil Holford and Christina Scull, who kindly read most of this book in typescript and gave me valuable advice and words of encouragement.

I'm deeply grateful to the highly knowledgeable staff of many libraries and archives, because I would not have had the opportunity to mention many books in my list if I had not received the invaluable lists of volumes preserved by them. I would particularly like to thank: Colin Harris, former Superintendent, Special Collections Reading Rooms, the Department of Special Collections, Bodleian Libraries, University of Oxford; Judith Priestman, Curator, Modern Literary Manuscript Collections, Bodleian Library; Jocelyn English, Deputy Librarian, English Faculty Library; Sandra Nisin, Pour les fonds patrimoniaux, Bibliothèque ALPHA, Université de Liège; Alan Vaughan Hughes, Head of Special Collections and Archives and Alison Harvey, Archivist, Cardiff University; Aaron M. Lisec, Research Specialist, Special Collections Research Center Morris Library Southern Illinois University; Catherine McIlwaine,

Tolkien Archivist at the Bodleian Library, University of Oxford, for sending me information on books consulted by Tolkien at the Bodleian and for allowing me to study the Tolkien manuscripts preserved in the Weston Library in June 2018. Also, Julia Walworth, Fellow Librarian at the Merton College, Oxford, for availability and kindness; Penelope Baker, College Archivist at the Exeter College (Archives and Special Collections), Oxford, for sending me information on books consulted by Tolkien at Exeter College when he studied there (1911-1915), books which were listed by John Garth during his research, leading to the excellent works *Tolkien and the Great War: The Threshold of Middle-earth* (2003) and *Tolkien at Exeter College: How an Oxford Undergraduate Created Middle-earth* (2014).

I cannot forget Christina Scull and Wayne G. Hammond with their monumental and indispensable work *J.R.R. Tolkien: Companion & Guide* (HarperCollins 2017, 3 vols). And to Jason Fisher, for allowing me to read an excerpt from his unpublished and not quite finished paper, 'The J.R.R. Tolkien Collection in the Cushing Memorial Library and Archives at Texas A&M University'.

This present work has also been enriched by precious suggestions from my friend, and Tolkien scholar, Giovanni Carmine Costabile, especially concerning Medieval Studies related to *Sir Gawain and the Green Knight*; Giovanni has been thoroughly researching the influence of the Middle English romance on Tolkien for quite a while. I owe a lot to Giovanni, with whom I shared many facets of my research, as much as he shared his own with me. In fact, he helped me by making available some of the information gathered in June 2018 throughout his consultation of Tolkien's unpublished manuscripts related to the Gawain-Poet, at Weston Library in Oxford. In this research, in fact, he had collected precious information about circa a hundred books which Tolkien had consulted, many of which had never previously been included in the list.

For my work becoming a book in its own right, I owe this to Francesca Barbini and Tom Shippey. Francesca was immediately enthusiastic about this project, and warm-heartedly welcomed me into the wonderful Luna Press family. Tom was the one who read what was then but a disorganised draft and assured me that it should absolutely be published. It was September 2016 and, since then, the great scholar, whom I have always viewed as my role-model in Tolkien Studies, has always been by my side with suggestions and advice to motivate me and substantially contribute to the shaping of my work, improving it. I hope I deserve Tom's kind words in his invaluable *Foreword*.

I would like to thank the friends who listened to my reflections on this work and, even if they could not yet read it at the time, appreciated the very idea of it: Enrico Introini, Gabriele Marconi, Dario Saderi, Giuseppe Scattolini, Gianluca Comastri, and Guglielmo Spirito O.F.M. To my wife Filomena, who supported me through various moments of doubt and uncertainty, and to my little children, Nicola and Raffaella. I hope that one day they will, by reading this book, understand my love for the Oxford Professor and the reason for so many hours spent in my studio among notes, books, and scattered papers.

I am also deeply grateful to the Tolkien Estate for their kind permission to quote from Tolkien's published works. Special thanks are due to Cathleen Blackburn, legal representative of the Tolkien Estate, for her reading of my work, for her support and her replies to my queries.

A special thanks to Priscilla, Professor Tolkien's daughter, for her words of encouragement and for the unexpected and moving gift that was sent to me a few days before this work was finished: the book *Pageant of the Popes* (1943) by John Farrow, was a gift from her father, and features her name written on its pages in his own handwriting.

Last, but not least, to John Ronald Reuel Tolkien, for believing, and for allowing so many of us to wander through lands we feel we belong to, where we will never grow tired of traveling, ever Westwards, in the light of the Evenstar.

Oronzo Cilli
Barletta, Italy
3 January 2019

Foreword

Tom Shippey

A combination of circumstances means that we know more about Tolkien than about almost any other author, from any period. The devoted editorial work carried out over more than forty years by his son and literary executor, Christopher Tolkien; Tolkien's own habit of retaining drafts and documents of all kinds; his well-recorded public life as a teacher and professor (the latter a rank which in his time involved considerable administrative responsibility); and most of all, the intense interest he aroused during his lifetime and soon after it: all these factors brought it about, that much of what was known about him was retained, and little was forgotten. Published results include the early authorised biography by Humphrey Carpenter, the *Tolkien Encyclopedia* edited by Michael Drout, and the three very substantial volumes of *The J.R.R. Tolkien Companion and Guide*, prepared by Christina Scull and Wayne Hammond, which offer among much else a "*Chronology*" of Tolkien's life, recording events often day by day.

Nevertheless, in spite of all the efforts above (and many more, few of them so well directed), there remains a certain opacity about Tolkien, both professionally and personally. Although there is still living memory of him, his background sometimes appears far removed from contemporary experience, especially as regards academic critics, and especially as regards American academic critics. Attempts continue to be made to force him into a role acceptable to modern academia: as a subversive, as an 'outsider' because of his Catholicism (or some other cause), as a 'post-modernist' before his time. Conversely, he continues in the same circles to be criticised for *not* holding views acceptable to modern academia, strange though such views would have seemed in his own time and milieu. Too often there is a wide cultural gap between the author and his professional critics – though much less of one between him and his international legion of fans.

As this book shows, there is a way to bridge that gap which has not been previously attempted: a fact which makes this work by Oronzo Cilli arguably the work with most potential for giving us a truer understanding of Tolkien; a work which, besides its own immediate effect, points the way for many further studies. What Oronzo has done is, quite simply, to collect what is known about the books Tolkien owned and read.

Much material comes from Tolkien's own notes and references. More comes from the way much of his own personal library has survived, bequeathed to institutional libraries like the English Faculty Library and the Taylorian

Library at Oxford, or held by libraries such as those at Marquette University in Milwaukee, Wisconsin, and the Marion E. Wade Center in the United States. Still more has survived because of the fact that Tolkien's books were very soon regarded as collectors' items, and were duly collected by people with no academic connections, like the astute Mr Stanley Revell, an Oxford butcher: strong literary interests are not the sole preserve of professional critics. All such matters, now assembled, provide a substantial corpus of knowledge which is hard to match within literary history.

It is an old adage (too often ignored by literary biographers) that, "if you want to understand a man, read his books", and this is usually taken to mean, "read the books he wrote". The adage is certainly true in that sense, but it is just as true if applied to the books he read – and even more, those he owned and retained. They tell us about an author's personal interests, literary and cultural horizons, formative assumptions, one might say, his "mental furniture".

What, then, do Tolkien's books tell us? A great many of them, indeed the majority, are the tools of his trade. What they tell us is what a trade it was! Very few academic disciplines can match both the rigour and the range of philology, as it was in Tolkien's lifetime. There can be few English-speakers now living who have mastered, or even looked into, Karl Brugmann's *Kurze vergleichende Grammatik*, or "Short Comparative Grammar of the Indo-Germanic Languages" – a mere 853 pages including foreword and appendices. Still fewer have worked through Hermann Hirt's seven-volume *Indogermanische Grammatik*. Yet Tolkien not only owned the books, and read them, but had strong feelings about them, writing (as Oronzo notes) "probably wrong ... most unlikely ... nonsense" in the margins of the latter.

Who nowadays would be fit to have an opinion on such matters? Only someone who had mastered the scholarly literature. One might note that the word "Indo-Germanisch" occurs 46 times in Oronzo's list, always in German, with "Indo-Germanic" once – and that is in a description of Hirt's German book. The whole concept of language-families, and the description of languages on which it rests, and the awareness of languages as evolving entities, was the main quasi-Darwinian achievement of the humanities in the nineteenth century, but English-speakers were not major contributors to it. Tolkien's deep awareness of it made him something of an anomaly within the English-speaking world, even in Oxford. Nevertheless, that awareness lies behind the immense efforts he made to create not only his imagined languages (as many others have done, often as a result of Tolkien's example) but also to give them consistent inner relationships and a complex history – which is, of course, also the history of their speakers. Scholars like Brugmann, and Hirt as well, and the whole argumentative intellectual movement of which they were part, helped to make *The Lord of the Rings* what it is.

So much for rigour, but what of range? In his "Preface", Oronzo points out that, for all Tolkien's modesty about his ability as a Celticist, his books show that he spent considerable time and money on acquiring and reading books in or about Celtic languages. Nor were these only related to the major modern survivors, Irish and Welsh, but also to Scots Gaelic, Breton, Cornish, Manx and even Gaulish (of which very little indeed is known, though this would not deter a philologist, accustomed to "reconstructing" words and languages on comparative evidence). But Celtic and Germanic languages form only a fraction of the whole "Indo-Germanic" family and, in any case, Tolkien stretched out to other branches of that family, and even beyond it. He had books on Gallego and Finnish and Lithuanian and Assyrian, as well as a substantial knowledge (much of it going back to his schooldays, and showing up in the prizes awarded by King Edward's School) of the Classical languages, Latin and Greek. It was all part of his professional equipment, like the many Icelandic sagas and Old and Middle English texts he owned – though it was only the latter which he had to teach. But he was not a man restricted to "set books".

Nor was his linguistic range only geographical. Notoriously, all was grist that came to the philological mill: no discipline was inherently more democratic, for information could be and was gained from many forms of language regarded by the *literati* as "sub-standard". Tolkien owned and used many works in and about English dialects, including his tutor Joseph Wright's 6-volume *English Dialect Dictionary*. They explain some of the words that appear in his fiction (though some remain obscure, like Sam Gamgee's "ninnyhammer"). Perhaps it was a word used by Derbyshire lead-miners, for which see Oronzo's entry under "Williamson, F.". The resources of English vocabulary go even beyond the vast extent of the *Oxford English Dictionary*.

Tolkien's work for the *OED* project nevertheless makes the point once again about range of reading. Tolkien's investigation of the word "Walrus" led him to works on Arctic exploration. "Wampum" led him to the history of early America (in which he seems to have had also a non-lexicological interest). "Wait-a-bit" took him into Africa, though once again – see entry on "Kingsley, Mary" – his interest there was not just in words. As for England itself, one should note Tolkien's continuing interest in place-names, works about which occur some forty times among his books, all of them crammed with historical and linguistic information, much of it unprocessed by and unknown to the world at large. One of the silliest accusations levelled against Tolkien by the dictators of literary culture is that he was "half-educated". What can one say but, "What a large half that was!". Few even among Oxford professors could match the range and volume of his reading.

Tolkien's books do, moreover, show a great deal of standard literary culture. It's often not possible to say which edition he used, but he refers familiarly to Coleridge, Donne, Dryden, Milton, Shakespeare, Skelton, Spenser, Swift, and less-known authors such as Nashe and Rowe. It is interesting, in view of his reputation as an anti-modernist, that he owned a copy of the fragments of Joyce's *Finnegans Wake*, including the fragment *Anna Livia Plurabelle*, published in 1930. (We might remember that Joyce was a sort of philologist too: he had at least taken a course in the subject, and remembered it in his "Oxen of the Sun" section of *Ulysses*.)

Yet Tolkien's educational focus, at least – much of which fed through very evidently into his fiction – was in the early literature of England (which by the convention of the University of Leeds, still alive to this day, was allowed to include Old Norse / Icelandic literature, on the grounds that much of Yorkshire had at one time been Norse-speaking, with profound effects even on modern English). Tolkien owned more than seventy volumes of the E.E.T.S. (Early English Text Society), that we know of, but in addition he had editions, sometimes many editions, of works he studied, taught and learned from all his life: seventeen editions or translations of *Beowulf*, for instance, including his own, posthumously published in 2014. Other works of continuing fascination are the romances of *Sir Orfeo* and *Sir Gawain*, the Finnish *Kalevala*, the Welsh *Mabinogion*, the Old Norse poems of the *Poetic Edda*. These are well-known as influences on Tolkien, but one should note also seven editions of the Old English poem *Exodus* (including Tolkien's own), and nine of the different versions of the "Rule for Anchoresses" or *Ancrene Riwle* (again including Tolkien's own). Tolkien certainly devoted much time and attention not only to reading these works, but to wondering what they meant, and what they revealed, sometimes, of the lost culture of medieval England. These and similar works led him to balrogs and dwimmerlaiks, as *Sir Gawain* had to woses.

Perhaps the most unexpected avenue into Tolkien's mind revealed by Oronzo's book is, however, the popular contemporary literature Tolkien read. It was known that Tolkien (like his friend C.S. Lewis) took a certain interest in science fiction, but there was rather more of this than one might think. Tolkien mentions not only some of the early British classics of "scientific romance", a kind of proto-science fiction (Lindsay, O'Neill, Stapledon, and the major game-changer for the field, H.G. Wells); not only familiar British writers of fantasy, such as Dunsany and Eddison; but also several writers of commercial twentieth-century science fiction or fantasy, such as John Christopher, Frank Herbert, Sterling Lanier, Lyon Sprague de Camp. He did not like all of them, but one he mentions with mild approval is Robert E. Howard, creator of the "Conan" cycle. This is something of a surprise, given that Conan is the pre-eminent example of hairy-chested macho barbarian heroism, so very un-hobbitical. Perhaps Tolkien appreciated Howard's efforts to create a sense of age, of lost civilisations? Once again, though, his range of sympathies and interests was greater than one would have guessed.

There are other avenues which could be followed. Some works may perhaps live on in memory only because they were owned by Tolkien, as has been the case with Edward Wyke-Smith's *Marvellous Land of Snergs*, recovered for us by Douglas Anderson. Some will no doubt search out copies of Amanda McKittrick Ros's *Irene Iddesleigh*, to find out what the Inklings thought was so irresistibly funny; or Horace Vachell's *The Hill* (a school story, if memory serves me, about cricket). Other works may explain Tolkien's casual allusions to things once familiar, long-since forgotten. In a note of 1956 Tolkien disclaimed ever having had a "With-the-flag-to-Pretoria" spirit, but what spirit was that? It is explained by a forgotten book by one Herbert Wingley Wilson: it must have been popular when Tolkien was a child of eight or ten, popular enough for people to know what he meant fifty years later (but not now). Many will recognise some similar allusion, some piece of cultural history.

One has to recognise, finally, that there are inevitably some gaps, and some uncertainties. It is important to note Oronzo's careful use of P.s. (Primary source), S.s. (Secondary source), and *NED* (*New English Dictionary*). Thus, I remain persuaded that Tolkien very probably read Michael Aislabie Denham's pamphlets on folklore – one of them is the only work to use the word "hobbit" before Tolkien – on the grounds of Tolkien's interest in folklore and in Yorkshire dialects. This, however, is only a supposition, and so recorded very properly as only "S.s". As for gaps, Tolkien had a high regard for the writer John Buchan (as reported by C.S. Lewis), but actually mentions only one of his books, and that not the likeliest, the spy-story *Greenmantle*. One might "infer" knowledge of several others (one of Buchan's highly Tolkien-esque stories is printed by Douglas Anderson in his *Tales Before Tolkien*), but the connection would be a guess.

Similarly, Oronzo has found evidence of Tolkien's knowledge of many works by William Morris, and sometimes the evidence is incontrovertible: Tolkien bought three of them with his Skeat Prize money in April 1914; he lectured at Oxford on Morris's *Sigurd the Volsung* in 1941, while his son Christopher records the bequest to him of three of Morris's seven late romances. Did Tolkien read the other four? It seems very likely, given his interest in Morris, but direct proof is lacking: though, once again, Oronzo has found an interesting and suggestive connection to what was by all accounts the best-known of the seven, *The Well at the World's End*, in a painting by Tolkien which seems to illustrate a moment in Morris's story. Direct evidence of ownership may be lacking, but books get lost, or are read in borrowed copies. Who can list all the books they have owned or read?

We have here, then, only a sample of Tolkien's reading. But it is a large, significant, well-organised and often revealing sample. It deserves detailed and careful study. Such study will throw up many new insights into Tolkien's thoughts, his life-experience, and the way that experience expressed itself in his fiction.

The best guide to an author's mind is through his books, and in the work of

Oronzo Cilli we have now the best and most valuable guide to Tolkien's books. It is a devoted, enduring, and above all inspirational work of scholarship, but not, as Oronzo knows, a final one. It joins that very select group of works, the most useful of all: a book we should keep, update, and write notes in the margin of, for the rest of our lives.

Preface

Then the Frost his songs recited,
And the rain its legends taught me;
Other songs the winds have wafted,
Or the ocean waves have drifted;
And their songs the birds have added,
And the magic spells the tree-tops.

Kalevala I, 65-70, translated by W. F. Kirby

Amongst several pictures portraying Professor Tolkien, I have always been particularly fascinated by the photographs taken by Leslie Stanley and Pamela Chandler. By Leslie Stanley, "a devoted fan and amateur photographer" (Scull-Hammond 2017a, p. 558), I prefer the pictures taken in July 1958 in Tolkien's study at Merton College and, by Pamela Chandler, "a well-known portrait photographer" (Ivi 2017a, p. 607), those showing him in his study-garage in August 1961 (in black and white and, in September 1966, in colour). While I look at those pictures, I always wonder about the books on the shelves behind the Professor. He attributed the foundation of his personal library to his tutor at Oxford, Kenneth Sisam: "Incidentally the foundation of my library was laid by Sisam. He taught me not only to read texts, but to study second-hand book catalogues, of which I was not even aware. Some he marked for me."[1] Considering that he was an Oxford Professor and a highly educated man, I was not surprised to find out how many books he owned. What I often wondered about, instead, was: *Which titles precisely did John Ronald Reuel Tolkien read?*

I always imagined myself being there, in his studio at Merton, or in the studio-garage, observing by what criterion, if any, he had placed these books on the shelves, and maybe also those which could be found on his table at that particular moment. If he had allowed me, I would have closely examined the titles and maybe even asked him about a specific novel, or handbook, or the reason for a note; or perhaps I would have simply watched in amazed silence as he spent his day among those books. Mine is, obviously, a mere fancy, but the photographs I earlier mentioned inspired me to give it a sense of "reality". That fancy would then become a wish: to reconstruct Tolkien's library or, better still, to be able to name the titles housed on his shelves.

Because of this, the desire to finally be able to take a look at those bookshelves and get lost in the myriad of records, corrections and notes never left me: my

---

1. Letter from Tolkien to Neil Ker, 22 November 1970 [*Letters* 318]

curiosity was constantly stimulated by new acquisitions for my studies and collection, consisting of various titles, both academic and fiction, which once belonged to the Professor.

As any experienced reader would expect, his library changed as the years passed: some titles were given away to others, some new titles were added, both as purchases and gifts. Nevertheless, there were also titles that never left him; ones that Tolkien would never part with.

Nowadays, even if the titles from Tolkien's library were scattered, and no trace is left of much of its contents, nonetheless it is possible to "reconstruct" the library itself, chiefly due to the Professor's habit of signing his name in many of his books.

Throughout his life, Tolkien would sign as: "Tolkien" (with three dots below); "JRRT"; "J.R.R.T."; "J. R. T."; "JRR Tolkien"; "Ronald Tolkien"; "John Ronald Reuel Tolkien"; "John Reuel Tolkien"; "John Ronald Tolkien"; "J. R. Reuel Tolkien", or "J.R.R. Tolkien". Tolkien often noted the date of the signature. For example: "mcmxiii"; "March 24", "1920"; "Jan. 1922"; "1923" or "22.2.20". In many cases, mostly while he was a student, he also noted the place of signature. Furthermore, he used to write notes, corrections and records in a lot of books.

But what was he interested in? As a Professor, of course, his most focused interests were General Philology, dialects, and place-names: he owned many grammar guides and dictionaries of the languages he studied and taught (Old English, Middle English, Welsh, Finnish, Old Norse, Gothic, but also Latin, Greek and Spanish). Obviously, he was also interested in Medieval English literature, while Classics might come as a surprise to many people, although it is worth mentioning that Tolkien first studied Classics (Greats) at Oxford before turning to English, as well as learning that he read many authors of the 20th century. For example, one may cite his note regarding James Joyce's *Finnegan's Wake*, which was written on two sheets of paper and is now preserved in the Bodleian Library in Oxford, as well as many of his writings.

But, today, you may well ask yourself: Where are all of Tolkien's books nowadays?

Oxford: Faculty of English and Weston Library

After his death, on 2nd September 1973, his personal library was inherited by his third son, and literary executor, Christopher, who worked as a scholar in the same field as his father and merged the bulk of his father's library with his own (Anderson 2006a, p. 361). When Christopher Tolkien decided to forsake his former career and dedicated himself fully to the task of editing his father's works, also moving to France, he retained most of his father's library while donating some of the volumes to Oxford libraries. About three hundred titles were given to the English Faculty Library at Oxford University, a portion of which is described as "Tolkien's Celtic Library" (more than two hundred and fifty titles were primary and secondary sources concerning Celtic languages and literature).

The language of the books is not limited to English (and its varieties throughout the ages), but there are also books in Latin, French, Welsh, German, Norwegian, Danish, Old Norse, Icelandic, Irish (Old, Middle and Modern), Gaulish, Scottish, Celtic, High Celtic, and Breton (Old and Middle).

The volumes were bought by Tolkien in the period between 1920 and 1926, with over a third marked by him with the date "1922". Dimitra Fimi writes: "It is, of course, not easy to determine what percentage of the whole body of Tolkien's books they comprise. [...] Still, this data is both valuable and significant for Tolkien scholarship, especially in terms of his involvement with Celtic Studies. Tolkien's "Celtic Library" consists of books on Celtic languages (including Welsh, Old and Middle Irish, Gaelic, and Breton), and also an important number on Irish and Welsh medieval literature, together with translations, editions and even facsimiles of manuscripts of original texts" (Fimi 2007, p. 51). Carl Phelpstead states that the collection of Tolkien's books in the English Faculty Library in Oxford certainly bears witness to the vigour and determination with which he attempted to learn Irish (and it must be recognised that he very possibly had a better command of the language than his modest comments to Rang [August 1967] and Mitchison [18 December 1949] suggest) (Phelpstead 2011, p. 27).

Today, Tolkien's personal Celtic library is preserved at the Weston Library under the auspices of the English Faculty Library in Oxford, as was confirmed to me by Jocelyn English, Deputy Librarian of the Library of the Faculty of English.

Besides the above-mentioned three hundred, about forty-five, and also many manuscripts previously owned by Tolkien, went to the New Bodleian Library in Oxford in July 1982.

The registration of the books and the manuscripts was executed by the Archive Manager, Judith Priestman, in two periods, 1994 and 2003: the whole collection was stored in the section "Western Manuscripts", split into the subsections: "MSS. Tolkien 1-25" (published academic and literary works, 1936-1968), "MSS. Tolkien Drawings" (Artwork, c. 1900-1973), "MSS. Tolkien A 1-39 and A-61" (academic papers, c. 1913-1971), "MSS. Tolkien E 16/1-45" (annotated volumes from Tolkien's library), along with another section for reserved and not available.

Marquette University, Marion E. Wade Center and others

While some volumes of Tolkien's library are preserved in Marquette University, Milwaukee, which acquired them after his death, it is vital to remember that this important University also owns the original manuscripts of some of Tolkien's works (*The Hobbit*, *Farmer Giles of Ham* and *The Lord of the Rings*) which were sold by the author himself. This acquisition was due to the foresight of William B. Ready, Library Director from 1956 to 1963, who, immediately after the publication of *The Lord of the Rings*, gained permission from the administration of the University and, thanks to Bertram Rota, a noted London antiquarian bookseller, managed to contact Tolkien. After some negotiation, Tolkien sold the manuscripts for £1,500 (a little less than $5,000 at the time of sale). The first manuscripts were delivered to the University in 1957. A year later, it was the turn of *The Lord of the Rings*. Marquette University hosts one of the most important Tolkien collections in the world, both in terms of its quantity and the value of its components. In 1957, the University managed to acquire the original manuscript of *Mr Bliss*.

The Marion E. Wade Center at Wheaton College (Illinois) is a special research collection of manuscripts, books and papers, primarily relating to seven British authors: C.S. Lewis, J.R.R. Tolkien, G.K. Chesterton, Dorothy L. Sayers, Charles Williams, Owen Barfield, and George MacDonald. The Center holds a variety of materials related to Tolkien and his work and was conceived in 1965 by Clyde S. Kilby, professor of English at the college, who started by collecting letters from Tolkien's colleague and friend, C.S. Lewis. In 1974, the family and business associates of Marion E. Wade, founder of the ServiceMaster Company, established the center in the businessman's memory. In 2001, the Marion E. Wade Center moved to its current location in a faux English manor house. The main display room of the collection features Tolkien's writing desk, the one that he used for the entire process of writing *The Hobbit*. Among the valuable pieces of the collection are manuscripts, books and letters that belonged to him.

The Cushing Memorial Library and Archives at Texas A&M University owns sixteen books from Tolkien's personal library on the subject of philology, and in German (a private gift in the late 1970s). The exact provenance of these items is not documented but a few have small penciled prices in the neighborhood of £1, suggesting they passed through the hands of second-hand booksellers. The books date from a relatively early period in Tolkien's life, from roughly 1920 through 1927 (Jason Fisher).

In my research, I found books that had belonged to Tolkien at the Boston College (Chestnut Hill, Massachusetts), British Library (London), Indiana University (Bloomington), Jesus College (Oxford), Liverpool Hope University (Liverpool), Morgan Library & Museum (New York), Oratory of Saint Philip Neri (Birmingham), University of St Andrews Library (St Andrews), and at the Université de Liège (Liège) in the special collection with the books that Tolkien gave to Simonne d'Ardenne.

Books in private collections

When Tolkien retired from his Oxford chair in 1959, he vacated his college rooms, and had insufficient space in his home for all the books that he had kept in Merton. He was therefore forced to give up some books from his personal library (Scull-Hammond 2017b, p. 249). Several other books were sold in the second-hand market after his death, in 1973. Some of them were acquired by Thornton's Bookshop (also known, more briefly, simply as Thornton's), the oldest University bookshop in Oxford, founded by Joseph Thornton in 1835, located at 11 Broad Street, in 1973, the year Tolkien died. A man called Stanley Revell, owner of a butcher's shop in Abingdon Road, Oxford, bought many volumes and placed a label on them reading, 'From the Library of J. R. R. Tolkien'. Revell was not a great fan of Tolkien but, from selling those books, many of them signed and annotated by the author, he earned enough money to buy first editions of works written by his true literary hero, Thomas Stearns Elliot (Blackwell's Rare Books 2012, pp. 81-2).

Revell was not the only one. Desmond Morris, an English ethologist, zoologist, surrealist painter, author of children's fiction (e.g. *The Naked Ape*, 1967), and known for his television programmes such as *Zoo Time*, was surprised to discover that Tolkien's collection of books had been sent to Thornton's to be sold. He was shown them, arranged in a back room at Thorntons. Although Tolkien's specialist subjects were outside Morris's range of interests, he noticed that he had written his name in pencil in each of the volumes and so decided to acquire one as a memento of the great author [A. 166].

Tolkien's daughter Priscilla also owned some academic publications which used to belong to her father. Years later, she sold some of them to Glen Howard GoodKnight II (one of the founders of the Mythopoeic Society) for a good cause: "The origin of this project began in 1975, when I visited England primarily to visit people and places known to the Inklings. During one of the visits with Priscilla Tolkien, she was holding a book sale for charity of many books that belonged to her father. I was able to obtain a good number of these, the majority of which were translations of his various works." (GoodKnight 1982, p. 22). More books, especially editions of titles by Tolkien in translation, were given by Priscilla to a bookshop in Oxford.

Still further, there were books by Tolkien preserved by his son John which, after his death, were sold to a bookshop near Christ Church College in Oxford.

Therefore, the books you might find on sale which used to belong to Tolkien, or were signed by him, usually come from one or another of these sources and, as one can easily guess, they are sought after by collectors and scholars.

For example, there's the case of Sister Maura O' Carroll (Sisters of Notre Dame), who went to Blackwell's to buy a Latin dictionary in the first half of the 1970's, while she was studying the 13th century manuscript Laud Misc. 511, for her doctoral research in Oxford.

"When I was rooting in Blackwell's' second hand books I found a Latin Dictionary – just the job for a weak Latinist. Only when I looked at it more closely did I realize that Professor Tolkien had bought this book when he was a schoolboy in Birmingham before WW1. I later discovered that many of his books had been sold after his death in 1973 and this Dictionary was among them. So sometime between 1976 and 1978 I took it back to London with me and it sat on my book shelves until 2016. I don't think I consulted it much in any of the Latin texts I laboured over."
(Liverpool Hope University, 2017)

The dictionary was the *Latin-English Dictionary: Based Upon the Works of Forcellini and Freund* by William Smith, printed in 1857 in London by John Murray [A. 2147]. On the frontpiece, one may find the signature "John Ronald Reuel Tolkien" and the initials K.E.S. (King Edward's School), with the apposition of the date 1908, just below. The dictionary and other volumes were donated by Sister Maura to Liverpool Hope University, and were placed in the library's Special Collections, available to the public.

It should be noted that the authenticity of some items is questionable, while some others bear excised signatures from less marketable signed works in Tolkien's library. (Scull-Hammond 2017b, p. 249)

I think it is interesting for many scholars to know which titles were read by, or belonged to, Tolkien, as noted by Tom Shippey: "Tolkien cannot be properly discussed without some considerable awareness of the ancient works and the ancient world which he tried to revive" (Shippey 2000, p. xxvii). This question has been the most important for me and my studies. How can I help provide other scholars with the same information about these titles?

Therefore, I compiled a list (which is obviously partial) of his books, working on three different levels. In the first place, I collected all information on the books kept in the above-mentioned libraries. Secondly, I collected all information available on line (from auctions, private collections and specialised websites). Thirdly and lastly, I looked at all his academic writings, taking note of any mention of books he had analysed and studied.

This book is the result of that research, and I hope it will be useful for scholars and researchers, looking for any further information concerning Tolkien's library which might be subsequently collected, thereafter perhaps resulting in updated editions which could potentially be enriched and expanded in all of its aspects.

Research Methodology

The purpose of this work, as I mentioned earlier, is to gather information about what Tolkien read during his life. As you will observe, the material herein collected is quite abundant (but I am aware that the research does not end here). In order to ease the reading I have chosen to divide the work into six sections:

[A] Tolkien's Library
It is certainly the most important section and includes the list of books we know with absolute certainty Tolkien read, consulted, bought or borrowed. Furthermore, I include the books he read as cited by scholars in some of their works.

This section took its present form after research in three distinct phases: checking primary sources, secondary sources and *NED*.

Primary sources
This phase involved checking books we know for sure to have constituted a part of Tolkien's personal library, books he is known to have owned, borrowed from libraries, or cited in his writings (and not just in his academic writings, but also in his letters). Those include books preserved in University archives, not only in England, and also ones which are preserved in private collections and whose origin is confirmed. The second step in this process was to check Tolkien's writings by analysing his works published between 1922, the year of publication of his first academic work, *A Middle English Vocabulary*, and 2016, when *The Lay of Aotrou & Itroun*, edited by Verlyn Flieger, was published. Guided by this, I consulted all of the academic and fictional works written by Tolkien, a total of 5,082 pages (see Bibliography). All of his correspondence, addressed to readers, friends, colleagues and relatives, both included and in Humphrey Carpenter's collection of Tolkien's *Letters*, and otherwise known, should also be added. I searched all explicit references to any text which he read, studied, or simply was aware of, as well as many quotes and citations by him. A hard task, which I hope has been worth the effort, although I have to say it was also fascinating because it allowed me to learn previously unknown aspects of Tolkien's interests and passions. The examples I could present are almost enough to fill another book but, for sake of brevity, I shall only cite one, which I think is useful in displaying the unique sense of *gramarye* of my research.

In *The Fellowship of the Ring*, Book Two, one finds this sentence from Elrond during his council: "Time was when a squirrel could go from tree to tree from what is now the Shire to Dunland west of Isengard". One might also find a parallel in an ancient saying quoted by Tolkien and Gordon in their 1925 first edition of *Sir Gawain and the Green Knight*, on page 94, in the endnote to line 701, "þe wyldrenesse of Wyrale". The endnote reads: "Wirral was made into a forest by Randle Meschines, third earl of Chester, and remained wild as late as the sixteenth century. There was an old saying that: From Blacon Point to Helbree | A squirrel may leap from tree to tree." Through further research, I observed that, in *The Golden Bough: a study in comparative religion*, the anthropologist James George Frazer writes: "In the forest of Arden it was said that down to modern times a squirrel might leap from tree to tree for nearly the whole length of Warwickshire" (Frazer 1890, p. 57). A very interesting observation, although, as Giovanni C. Costabile, whom I thank, and I agreed, the forests of Arden and Wirral were not exactly one and the same place, and Tolkien could never have derived a saying on the latter from one concerning the former. By taking into account the fact that Frazer himself, in footnote 3 to page 57, cites the 1922 *The Origins of English History* by Charles Isaac Elton as a source, one might read: "In the Warwickshire Arden it was said that even in modern times a squirrel might leap from tree to tree for nearly the whole length of the county" (p. 224). This saying can also be found in earlier works than Frazer's and Elton's. For example, in the 1855 *Journal of the Royal Agricultural Society of England* by Henry Evershed, one may read: "Timber and coppice, still abundant, were formerly much more so; the forest of Arden extended through the middle of the county, and to describe how thick the timber stood, it was said that a squirrel might leap from tree to tree nearly the whole length of the county" (p. 490). Furthermore, in the 1813 *General View of the Agriculture of the County of Warwick: With Observations on the Means of Its Improvement* by Adam Murray, one reads: "I have heard it mentioned by some of the old people, that this forest of wood or timber trees stood so thick at one period, that a squirrel might leap from one tree to another, nearly the whole length of the county" (p. 140). The saying which we are interested in is also found in *The land we live in, a pictorial and literary sketch-book of the British Empire* (Vol. I, 1856, p. 160); it was mentioned by G. Busk in his article "An Account of the Discovery of a Human Skeleton beneath a Bed of Peat on the Coast of Cheshire", published in the *Transactions of the Ethnological Society of London* (Vol. IV, 1866, pp. 101-4). J. A. Harvie-Brown also mentions it in "Mr Harvie-Brown on the Squirrel in Great England", in *Proceedings of the Royal Physical Society of Edinburgh*, (Vol. VI, 1881, p. 33); Alfred Rimmer quotes it in *Ancient Streets and Homesteads of England* (1877, p. 221), and George Morley, citing Elton, copies it in *Shakespeare's greenwood* (1900, p. 203). In all of the aforementioned works, one may find the same saying, which the wise men still loved to recall and which was told both about Arden Forest and Wirral. In Tolkien's and Gordon's *Sir Gawain*, the rhyming couplet is found also in *The History of the County Palatine and City of Chester* by George Ormerod (Vol. II, 1819, p. 190); in the ballad "The Old Times of Cheshire", included in *Ballads and Legends of Cheshire*, a collection edited by Egerton

Leigh (1867, pp. 312, 314) and in *A perambulation of the Hundred of Wirral in the county of Chester* by Harold Edgar Young (1909, p. 11). Tolkien might have read all of these three works, and perhaps particularly the ballads but, lacking a surer confirmation, I preferred not to include any of them in the present work. After all, he might also have simply overheard the saying somewhere.

Secondary sources
Secondary sources are related to the input of many scholars who greatly advanced our knowledge of Tolkien and whose works represent real touchstones in Tolkien Studies: Douglas A. Anderson, Michael D. C. Drout, Raymond Edwards, Jason Fisher, Dimitra Fimi, Verlyn Flieger, John Garth, Wayne G. Hammond, Carl Hostetter, Stuart D. Lee, Carl Phelpstead, John Rateliff, Christina Scull, Tom Shippey, Christopher Tolkien, and Arden R. Smith. From reading their monographies and articles, I was able to find many works cited that I suspected Tolkien might have read, as well as many others I did not suspect, and all of these have been included in my list.

New English Dictionary
From Tolkien's involvement in editing the *New English Dictionary*[1] (later *Oxford English Dictionary*), in the period of time between 1919 and 1920, I was able to gather information about works which Tolkien read. Through his work there, he had met Henry Bradley, the second of the four editors of the first edition of the dictionary, working with him on the "W" entries.[2] A first reference book for my research was *The Ring of Words: Tolkien and the Oxford English Dictionary* by Peter Gilliver, Edmund Weiner and Jeremy H. Marshall; according to them, he was involved in editing about 60 words. I chose to take into account those entries from the Oxford University Press Archives, rather than reporting Tolkien's signed drafts. For each entry, I searched in *A New English Dictionary on Historical Principles* (Vol. X, Pt. II V-Z, 1928) and, for any single quote, I identified all the references of the edition cited. This was also thanks to precious support from the platform www.archive.org, a useful tool to consult for hard to access works.

Work on the *NED* is described by the words of Peter M. Gilliver: "After some little time spent in learning his job, then, Tolkien at last started work on the drafting of Dictionary entries. This central task seems to have been organised much as it is today: each assistant was allocated an alphabetical range by his

---
1. It was in 1884 that it began to be published in unbound fascicles under the name of *A New English Dictionary on Historical Principles* (*NED*). In 1895, the title *The Oxford English Dictionary* (*OED*) was first used unofficially on the covers of the series, and in 1928 the full dictionary was republished in ten bound volumes. In 1933, the title *The Oxford English Dictionary* fully replaced the former name in all occurrences. Here I chose to use the acronym *NED* because the volume used for my research is the 1928 edition.
2. In *Farmer Giles of Ham* (1949), the 'Four Wise Clerks of Oxenford' to whom the question was put as to what a blunderbuss was. are clearly the *OED*'s four first editors, James Murray, Henry Bradley, William Craigie, and Charles Onions.

or her Editor, and would deal with all aspects of the final text – pronunciation, spelling variants, and etymology, as well as the defining of the various senses and the selection and copy-editing of illustrative quotations. The text prepared in this way would eventually be revised by the Editor, who frequently made substantial changes such as reclassifying the senses (and rewriting the definitions accordingly), choosing different quotations, and even deciding to reject a word entirely, often because of a paucity of quotation evidence." (Gilliver 1995, p. 175).

In the following, you may find the list of books that were read by, or belonged to, Tolkien, specifying their authors, publishers, year of printing and, where applicable, what the Professor noted on them. Each book reports the source, which falls into one of the below three categories:

P.s. (*Primary source*) Where Tolkien himself mentioned the book.
S.s. (*Secondary source*) Where the book is mentioned by a scholar who has had access to Tolkien's writings or is a scholar whose scientific rigor is recognised by all.
NED (*New English Dictionary*) This type includes works cited in the *OED*, when Tolkien worked as a member of Bradley's editorial staff between 1919 and 1920. His contribution to the *OED* was in the range from "waggle" to "wold". Jeremy H. Marshall, co-author of *The Ring of Words*, suggested: "In connection with his work for the *NED*, he may have had no knowledge of the book beyond the excerpt that had been written on a dictionary slip and selected for quotation in the dictionary." Also: "In a very few cases it might be reasonable to suppose that a cited book was actually in the collection of the Dictionary Department for him to consult. For example, the *OED* Archives still hold a copy of Badcock's *Slang* (1823) (cited at 'wallop'), so Tolkien could well have used it; and the Department has a working collection of E.E.T.S. volumes, many of which must date back to Tolkien's time. In some instances, there does seem circumstantial evidence to support the inference: if he knew S. R. Crockett's *Black Douglas* (1899), for example, it is not impossible that he had also read *The Lilac Sunbonnet* (1894). However, it seems to me fairly unlikely that he had actually looked at copies of such disparate books such as Grant Allen's *For Maimie's Sake* (1886), Jane Aster's *Habits of Good Society* (1859), and William Tennant's *Papistry Storm'd* (1827), or the issue of *The Garden* for 16 Sept. 1882 (cited at 'walnut'): the quotations taken by the reader would have been sufficient for his purpose. For older works such as Blundeville's book on horsemanship, he would also have relied chiefly on information supplied by a reader." It was, however, considered correct, for the sake of completeness, to include the texts that are mentioned in the *OED* entries on which Tolkien worked.

[B]   The published writings of J. R. R. Tolkien 1910-1972

I decided to provide readers with a comprehensive list of all the writings published by Tolkien during his lifetime, as this work was limited to that period.

[C]   Interviews & Reviews

In addition to Tolkien's interviews, the list also presents the reviews of his books that he certainly read, cited or commented on in his letters or elsewhere.

[D]   J. R. R. Tolkien: supervisor and examiner 1929-1960

This section lists the student dissertations of which Tolkien was an examiner and supervisor. Several of those works were subsequently published in full or in revised form.

[E]   Tolkien and Early English Text Society 1938-1972

The Early English Text Society (E.E.T.S.) 'was founded in 1864 by Frederick James Furnivall, with the help of Richard Morris, Walter Skeat, and others, to bring the mass of unprinted Early English literature within the reach of students. Most of the works attributed to King Alfred or to Aelfric, along with some of those by Bishop Wulfstan, and much anonymous prose and verse from the pre-Conquest period, are to be found within the Society's three series (O.S. = Original Series; S.S. = Supplementary Series; E.S. = Extra Series); all of the surviving medieval drama, most of the Middle English romances, much religious and secular prose and verse, including the English works of John Gower, Thomas Hoccleve, and most of Caxton's prints, all find their place in the publications.' (Hudson 2015). On 6 December 1938, Tolkien was appointed a member of the Early English Text Society Committee – from April 1949, the Early English Text Society Council (Scull-Hammond 2017a, p. 238) – he attended meetings as his other duties permitted until 12 May 1973, when he took part in his last E.E.T.S. Council meeting at Lady Margaret Hall at 2.15 p.m. (Ivi 2017a, p. 811). Like all Council members, Tolkien received proofs of works the Society published, and any comments that were made – by any members – were sent to the editor of the particular work (Scull-Hammond 2017c, p. 1238). This list contains books published in the time when Tolkien was a member.

[F]   Tolkien's Lectures 1920-1959

Tolkien was first of all a Professor, and many of the books he read are closely connected with his profession. Here I list his lectures in Leeds and Oxford and date them, also specifying the Term and the topic dealt with. I am sure that it will be very useful for those who want to compare the books listed in section A with his lectures.

I conclude by noting that the present work doesn't "reconstruct" a physical library that once existed, but rather an imaginary collection which includes books or other printed items which Tolkien once owned (and may or may not have read), and works he did not own but is known to have read or consulted (such as the run of Andrew Lang fairy books he used at the Bodleian), along with works he referred to in his writings but might not have owned or consulted directly. Even for those items he owned, he may not have owned them all at the same time, as he had to dispose of some of his books – at least when he left Merton, when he moved to Poole, and when he returned to Oxford – according to changing circumstances. In addition, there were other books in the Tolkien household which were not, strictly speaking, part of Tolkien's personal library, but owned variously by his children, though Tolkien sometimes consulted them.

*

In the following, I include a few cross references to specific sources recurring within the main list. The reason for doing so, besides avoiding repetition, lies in the fact that these sources require special consideration.

P.s. #1 Tolkien, J. R. R. *Tolkien: On Fairy-stories*. Expanded edition, with commentary and notes. Edited by Verlyn Flieger & Douglas A. Anderson. London: HarperCollinPublishers, 2008, pp. 320

> **a.** Verlyn Flieger & Douglas A. Anderson wrote: "Works consulted or cited by J.R.R. Tolkien [Some of the items listed below are mentioned only in Tolkien's research notes or draft materials, and not in the finished essay]."

S.s. #1 Germany and Britain agreed in 1941 to allow prisoners of war to sit examinations, and an international inter-library loan system was organised by the Bodleian Library. Several institutions were involved, including the University of Oxford, which instituted a special Honours Examination in English Literature and Language, granting a certificate or diploma. The "course has been specially prepared by Professor Tolkien and Mr. C. S. Lewis of Magdalen which would bring a student up to Honours standard if carefully studied." (British Red Cross Society, 1942). "The Educational Books Department sent out the necessary library of 300 books covering the whole range of English Literature. The examiner had the choice of the Medievel, Middle or Modern Periods and had to take about ten papers. This was without precedent in the history of the University" (Gunston 1943, p. 305). In March 1943, Tolkien, C. S. Lewis, and Leonard Rice-Oxley were appointed to be examiners of Allied prisoners of war in Germany who had worked on the Board's set syllabus. From the "Result of Examinations - Prisoners of War Camps", 1st July to 31st December 1943, "the Examiners appointed by the Board of the Faculty of English Language and Literature have made the following awards:" [they were reported in the form of the names, prison camp and the classes: I (2), II A (4), II (8) and III (3)]. Under the awards, we find the signatures of C. S. Lewis, J.R.R. Tolkien, and Leonard Rice-Oxley (Red Cross and St. John War Organisation 1944, p. 32).

The examination schemes prepared by Tolkien and Lewis were published in: Holland, Robert W. (Compiled and Edited by). *Adversis Major. A Short of the Educational Books Scheme of the Prisoners of War Department of the British Red Cross Society and Order of St. John of Jerusalem.* London: Staples Press Limited, 1949.

NED #1 [Tolkien, J. R. R. *The Book of Lost Tales*, Vol. II. Edited by Christopher Tolkien. Boston: Ballantine Books, 1992]

a. [*The Fall of Gondolin*, p. 149] "Subsequently my father took his pencil to *Tuor B*, emending it fairly heavily, though mostly in the earlier part of the tale, and almost entirely for stylistic rather than narrative reasons; but these emendations, as will be seen, were not all made at the same time. Some of them are written out on separate slips, and of these several have on their reverse sides parts of an etymological discussion of certain Germanic words for the Butcher-bird or Shrike, material which appears in the Oxford Dictionary in the entry *Wariangle*. Taken with the fact that one of the slips with this material on the reverse clearly contains a direction for the shortening of the tale when delivered orally (see note 21), it is virtually certain that a good deal of the revision of Tuor B was made before my father read it to the Essay Club of Exeter College in the spring of 1920."

NED #2 [Gilliver, Peter; Marshall, Jeremy H.; Weiner, Edmund. *The Ring of Words. Tolkien and the Oxford English Dictionary.* Oxford: University Press, 2009.]

a. [p. 12] *Waggle*: "Bradley also completely rewrote Tolkien's etymology of the verb. Tolkien's division of the verb into senses and subsenses was also revised slightly, although this must have taken place at the proof stage: two quotations which he had grouped together as illustrating a sense 'to shake the body or any part of the body' were subsequently split up, one of them (the quotation dated circa 1826) being inserted in the more general sense 2a, and the other (dated 1852) identified as a distinct construction (sense 1d as published, where it is described as a 'nonce' use, i.e. a one-off use of a word)."

b. [p. 15] *Waist-cloth, Waistband & Waistcoat*: "Tolkien proceeded to write full entries for *waist-cloth* (3 senses), *waistband* (2 senses) and – after considerable deliberation (surely to be expected of a future connoisseur of the garment) – *waistcoat*. After waistcoat follow several other waist-compounds and derivatives (*waisted, waist-rail* and the like)."

c. [pp. 17-8] *Waiting, Waiting-room, Waiting-woman, Wait-a-bit & Waiter*: "'The complex word *wait* was dealt with by Bradley, but he once again allowed Tolkien to 'mop up' the related words, including *waiting* (along with *waiting-room* and *waiting-woman*), *wait-a-bit* (a South African plant, whose variability of spelling received comprehensive treatment before the simplifying touch of Bradley's pen), and waiter, whose eleven senses were left much as Tolkien drafted them."

d. [pp. 18-9] *Waiterage, Waiterdom, Waiterhood & Waitering*: "In a dictionary the size of the *OED* even nonce-words can find room; however, at this stage in the project the Editors were under considerable pressure to keep the volume of text down as much as possible, and so Tolkien's original full-scale entries for *waiterage* ('the performance of a waitefs duties'), *waiterdom* ('Waiters considered as a class, or collectively'), *waiterhood* ('the state or condition of a waiter'), and *waitering* ('the occupation of a waiter') were subsequently condensed into a sub-entry under waiter."

e. [p. 20]. "Once again Tolkien's impulse was to say more about the history of the word and its connotations than Bradley could allow space for: a small-type note in his final draft of the published sense 3, deleted before publication, represents the last stage in a long struggle to convey a sense of the word's overtones."

f. [pp. 22-3] *Walnut, Walrus, Wampum & Wampumpeag*: "Tolkien was not assigned a continuous range of words, but instead worked on four individual entries, for the words *Walnut, Walrus, Wampum*, and *Wampumpeag* (the less familiar word from which wampum derives). [...] *Wampumpeag* was an etymological challenge of a rather different kind, in that it derives from an Algonquian Indian word; frustratingly, the slips for the entry are missing from the archives, but the surviving materials for wampum suggest that Tolkien enjoyed tackling these exotic imports from the New World."

g. [pp. 22-3] *Wallop & Walm*: "Tolkien's next substantial word was *wallop*: both the relatively straightforward noun, and the verb, concerning the etymology of which Tolkien provides a full five paragraphs of scholarly speculation, hardly altered at all by Bradley, who by this stage clearly had considerable confidence in him – sufficient confidence to entrust him with the Old English word *walm* (synonymous in some senses with wallop, which is perhaps why Tolkien was given both to do)."

h. [p. 23] *Walnut & Walrus*: "*Walnut* and *walrus* were known to have unusually troublesome Germanic etymologies, which is probably why they were assigned to Tolkien. [...] There is considerably more evidence of the struggles he had with the etymologies of *walnut* and *walrus* which gave him such trouble that he even discussed them at home with his family. Bradley was obviously pleased with the result, for when the fascicle *W-Wash* was published in October 1921, *walnut*, *walrus*, and *wampum* were among the few entries singled out in a prefatory note as containing 'etymological facts or suggestions not given in other dictionaries'."

i.   [p. 42] "Entries in the *OED* worked on by Tolkien: *Waggly*, *Waggling*, *Walloper*, *Walloping* (noun & adjective)."

Tolkien's Library

1. Aasen, Ivar Andreas. *Norsk ordbog med dansk forklaring af Ivar Aasen. Omarbeidet og forøget udg. af en ældre "Ordbog over det norske folkesprog"*. Christiana: P.T. Mallings boghandel, 1873.
   NED : #2 h. | 'W' (1928), p. 53 'Wallop'.

2. Adamnan, Saint. *Vita S. Columbae*. Edited by Joseph Thomas Fowler and James Reeves. Oxford: At the Clarendon Press, 1920.
   Description: Contains loose notes on pp. 1, 6, 28, signed: 'W.R.C.' Autographed a front flyleaf, dated: 'March 1921'.
   Collection: Tolkien's personal Celtic library, preserved at the Weston library under the auspices of the English Faculty Library (Oxford).

3. Adams, Joseph Quincy. *Joseph Quincey Adams memorial studies*. Edited by James Gilmer McManaway. Washington: Folger Shakespeare Library, 1948.
   P.s.: *Sir Gawain and the Green Knight* (1967) 'Select Bibliography', p. 155. (pp. 639-40).

4. Adshead, Gladys L. and Annis Duff. *An Inheritance of Poetry*. With decoration by Nora S. Unwin. Boston: Houghton Mifflin Company, The Riverside Press, 1948.
   Notes: Contains *Goblin Feet* (66), Riddles from *The Hobbit* (79), *Roads Go Ever Ever On* (318) and *Sing All Ye Joyful…* (364).

5. Ælfric, Abbot of Eynsham. *Ælfric's Catholic homilies. The first series: text*. Series: E.E.T.S. (Early English Text Society), SS 17. Edited by Peter Clemoes. London: Published for the Early English Text Society by the Oxford University Press, 1997.
   S.s.: Scull-Hammond (2017c), p. 1238. 'On 26 March 1957 R.W. Burchfield, Secretary of EETS, asked Tolkien if he had had time to examine and comment on P. Clemoes's specimen homily (i.e. *Ælfric: Catholic Homilies*, ed. P. Clemoes, still forthcoming in 1962)'.

6. _____. *Ælfric's Lives of Saints, being a set of Sermons on Saints' Days formerly observed by the English Church*, Vol. I. Series: E.E.T.S. (Early English Text Society), OS 76. Edited by Walter William Skeat. London: Published for the Early English Text Society by Kegan Paul, Trench, Trübner and Co., 1881.
   P.s. 1: MS. Tolkien A 21/13 fol. 119. Note by Tolkien, 'Books in Exeter Library useful', with shelfmarks, on back of photostat reading list dated October 1913. Tolkien writes: 'All EETS publications'. [Tolkien Papers, Bodleian Library, Oxford]
   P.s. 2: *Sigelwara land* (1932), p. 188. Tolkien cites *Passion of St Julian and his Wife Basilissa*, 'Þa cwæþ se geeadcucoda. me coman to sil-herwan. … Þas þyllice me tugon to þære sweartan helle.' (iv, 285-290).

7. _____. *Ælfric's Lives of Saints, being a set of Sermons on Saints' Days formerly observed by the English Church*, Vol. II. Series: E.E.T.S. (Early English Text Society), OS 76. Edited by W. W. Skeat. London: Published for the Early English Text Society by Kegan Paul, Trench, Trübner and Co., 1900.
   P.s. 1: MS. Tolkien A 21/13 fol. 119. Note by Tolkien, 'Books in Exeter Library useful', with shelfmarks, on back of photostat reading list dated October 1913. Tolkien writes: 'All EETS publications'. [Tolkien Papers, Bodleian Library, Oxford]
   P.s. 2: 'Chaucer as a Philologist: *The Reeve's Tale*' (1934), p. 164 n. 46. Tolkien cites *St Mary of Egypt* 'ic … þa wangas mid tearum ofergeát' (556).

P.s. 3: *Beowulf* (2002) 'Version A', p. 67 n. †.
S.s.: Ollscoil na h-Éireann G 260 (1949). Tolkien quotes: 'Sēo ylce rōd siððan ðe Ōswold ... ārwurðne bisceop, Aidan gehāten' (XXVI. 30-53, p. 126-8).

8. _____. *Exameron Anglice. Or the Old English Hexameron*. Edited by Samuel Crawford. Series: Bibliothek der angelsächsischen Prosa, 10. Hamburg: Henri Grand, 1921.
    Description: Autographed on front flyleaf.
    Collection: Tolkien's personal Celtic library, preserved at the Weston library under the auspices of the English Faculty Library (Oxford).

9. _____. *The Homilies of the Anglo-Saxon Church*, Vol. I. Series: Cambridge library collection. Edited by Benjamin Thorpe. Cambridge: The University Press, 1844.
    P.s.: *Sigelwara land* (1932), p. 187 n. 5; 188.
    S.s.: Scull-Hammond (2017a), p. 46. April 1913: Tolkien will need to become familiar with a range of literary and philological subjects and set texts as prescribed in the Oxford Regulations of the Board of Studies, knowing that he may be examined on them in ten papers at the end of *Trinity Term 1915*: Old English texts. *The Assumption of St John the Apostle* and *The Nativity of the Innocents*.

10. _____. *The Homilies of the Anglo-Saxon Church*, Vol. II. Series: Cambridge library collection. Edited by Benjamin Thorpe. Cambridge: The University Press, 1844.
    P.s.: *Sigelwara land* (1932), p. 188.

11. _____. *The Old English version of the Heptateuch Ælfric's treatise on the Old and New Testament and his preface to Genesis*. Series: E.E.T.S. (Early English Text Society), OS 160. Edited by Samuel Johnson Crawford. London: Oxford University Press, 1922.
    P.s.: *Sigelwara land* (1932), p. 183 n. 1 Tolkien quotes: *Elipoleas, þæt is on Englisc 'Sunnan Burh,'* Gen. lxi 45 (p. 185).

12. _____. *A Saxon treatise concerning the Old and New Testament. Written about the time of King Edgar (700 yeares agoe) by Ælfricus Abbas, thought to be the same that was afterward Archbishop of Canterburie*. Edited by William Lisle *et alii*. London: Printed by Iohn Hauiland for Henrie Seile, dwelling in Pauls Church-yard at the signe of the Tygers head, 1623.
    P.s.: *Sigelwara land* (1932), p. 187 n. 4.

13. Aeschylus. *The Agamemnon of Aeschylus*. With a metrical translation, and critical and illustrative notes by Benjamin Hall Kennedy. Cambridge: The University Press, 1882 (2nd ed.).
    P.s.: *Exeter College library register*. Tolkien's borrowing record: *Hilary Term 1913* from 17 January to 4 March.

14. _____. *The 'Agamemnon' of Aeschylus*. With an introduction, commentary and translation by Arthur Woollgar Verrall. London: Macmillan and Co., 1889.
    P.s.: *Exeter College library register*. Tolkien's borrowing record: *Hilary Term 1913* from 17 January to 4 March.
    S.s. 1: Garth (2014), p. 23. Garth writes: [1913] 'With a mere six weeks left before the exams, a flurry of library borrowings – Sophocles' *Oedipus Tyrannus* and *Electra* and Aeschylus' *Eumenides*, *Agamemnon* and *Choephoroe* - suggest he was far from familiar with the set texts'.
    S.s. 2: Scull-Hammond (2017a), p. 34. *Michaelmas Term 1911*: Tolkien begins to read Literae Humaniores or Classics, mainly Greek and Latin authors but also Philosophy and Classical History. During his first five terms at Oxford he will attend lectures and classes to prepare for his

Section A

first examination, Honour Moderations (popularly 'Hon. Mods'), which he will take in February 1913. During this term he almost certainly attends lectures by L.R. Farnell on *Agamemnon* by Aeschylus in translation, a set text, on Wednesdays and Fridays at 10.00 a.m. at Exeter College, beginning 18 October; p. 40. *Michaelmas Term 1912*: Tolkien possibly attends Gilbert Murray's lectures on Aeschylus' *Agamemnon* and Euripides' *Electra* on Tuesdays and Thursdays at 12.00 noon in the Examinations School, beginning 15 October; p. 44. 27 February 1913: The First Public Examination for the Honour School of Greek and Latin Literature (Honour Moderations) begins. He is also examined on four Greek plays, *Oedipus Tyrannus* and *Elektra* by Sophocles, *Agamemnon* by Aeschylus, and the *Bacchæ* by Euripides, with special attention to *Oedipus Tyrannus*.

15. _____. *The Choephoroi*. Greek text with English translation, introduction, commentary and indices by Arthur Woollgar Verrall. London: Macmillan, 1893.
    P.s.: *Exeter College library register*. Tolkien's borrowing record: *Michaelmas Term 1912* from 16 November to 5 December.
    S.s.: Garth (2014), p. 23. Garth writes: [1913] 'With a mere six weeks left before the exams, a flurry of library borrowings - Sophocles' *Oedipus Tyrannus* and *Electra* and Aeschylus's *Eumenides*, *Agamemnon* and *Choephoroe* - suggest he was far from familiar with the set texts'.

16. _____. *Choephoroi*. Series: Clarendon press. With introduction and notes by Arthur Sidgwick. Oxford: At the Clarendon Press, 1892 (new ed.).
    P.s.: *Exeter College library register*. Tolkien's borrowing record: *Michaelmas Term 1912* from 16 November to 5 December.

17. _____. *Eumenides Of Aeschylus*. With an introduction, commentary, and translation by Arthur Woollgar Verrall. London: Macmillan and Co., 1908.
    P.s.: *Exeter College library register*. Tolkien's borrowing record: *Michaelmas Term 1912* from 16 November to 5 December.
    S.s.: Garth (2014), p. 23. Garth writes: [1913] 'With a mere six weeks left before the exams, a flurry of library borrowings - Sophocles' *Oedipus Tyrannus* and *Electra* and Aeschylus's *Eumenides*, *Agamemnon* and *Choephoroe* - suggest he was far from familiar with the set texts'.

18. Ahlqvist, August. *De Fem första sångerna af Kalevala med svensk ordbok* (The Kalevala: National Epic of the Finnish People). Helsingfors: Öhmanska Bokhandeln, 1853.
    Description: Inscribed in pencil on the title page: 'J.R.R. Tolkien'. Includes a label added by Stan Revell to books owned by Tolkien, 'From the Library of J.R.R. Tolkien', on inside front cover.
    Collection: Marion E. Wade Center, Wheaton College (Wheaton, Illinois).

19. Albrecht, William Price. *The Loathly Lady in 'Thomas of Erceldoune. With a text of the poem printed in 1652*. Albuquerque: Uni. New Mexico, 1954.
    Description: Inscribed on front flyleaf: 'for Professor J.R.R. Tolkien | with best regards and thanks, | A. p. Albrecht'.
    Collection: Tolkien's personal Celtic library, preserved at the Weston library under the auspices of the English Faculty Library (Oxford).

20. Alighieri, Dante. *De Monarchia*.
    S.s.: Scull-Hammond (2017a), p. 445. 16 February 1954: Tolkien attends a meeting of the Oxford Dante Society. Dr Lorenzo Minio-Paluello reads a paper on the philosophical background of Dante's *De Monarchia*.

21. _____. *De Vulgari Eloquentia*.
    S.s. 1: University of Leeds (1921), p. 154. English Language and Literature - Scheme A. Texts and Period selected for 1921-22. (e) History of Criticism: Special Texts suggested for study. Ordinary Degree of B.A. with Honours. Final Examinations.
    S.s. 2: Scull-Hammond (2017a), p. 400. 13 November 1952: Tolkien attends a meeting of

the Oxford Dante Society and Professor Alfred Ewert reads a paper on Dante's '*De Vulgari Eloquentia*, l. II, c. 7'.

22. _____. *Divina Commedia*.
Notes: The Bodleian Library has notes for a talk, *A Neck-verse*, [MS. Tolkien A 13/1], that Tolkien gave to the Oxford Dante Society about the word *lusinga* (July 1947).
P.s. 1: MS. Tolkien A 13/1 *Draft of talk to the Oxford Dante Society: A neck-verse* (1947), fol. 171. Tolkien quotes: 'Lo giorno se n 'andava, e l'aere bruno toglieva li animai che sono in terra da le fatiche loro' (*Inferno*, II, 1-3); fol. 172. Tolkien quotes: 'Perché d'Amaro Senta il sapor della pietade acerba' (*Purgatorio*, XXXIII, 80-1); fol. 173. Tolkien quotes 'ma se donna del ciel ti move o regge, | come tu dì, non c'è mestier lusinghe' (*Purgatorio* I, 92-93). [Tolkien Papers, Bodleian Library, Oxford].
P.s. 2: MS. Tolkien A 35 *Pearl* fol. 112. [Tolkien Papers, Bodleian Library, Oxford].
P.s. 3: *Sir Gawain and the Green Knight* (1975), p. 21. Tolkien writes: 'In the *Divina Commedia* the *Nel mezzo del cammin di nostra vita* of the opening line, or *la decenne sete of Purgatorio xxxii*, are held to refer to real dates and events, the thirty-fifth year of Dante's life in 1300, and the death of Beatrice Portinari hi 1290'.
S.s.: Scull-Hammond (2017c), p. 1233. *Michaelmas Term 1947*: Tolkien read a paper *A Neck-Verse* at meeting of the Oxford Dante Society possibly during this Term, as he placed a draft of it in an envelope postmarked 4 July 1947. Tolkien began the paper by quoting a rhyme [*Miserere mei, Deus* …] by which, if he could recite it, an accused in the Middle Ages might be granted 'benefit of clergy' and be spared the hangman. The paper was on *Lusinga* with reference to the canto XVIII of the *Inferno* and to the canto I of the *Purgatorio* (Tolkien was a member from 1945 to 1955); p. 365. 9 November 1948: Tolkien attends a meeting of the Oxford Dante Society and C.S. Lewis reads a paper on the imagery of the last ten cantos of Dante's *Paradiso*; p. 370. 24 May 1949: Tolkien attends a meeting of the ODS and Professor Ernst Fraser Jacob reads a paper on the feudal hierarchy in Dante's *Paradiso*; p. 406. 27 May 1952 Tolkien hosts a meeting of the ODS at Merton College. Professor W.J. Entwistle reads a note on Dante's *Convivio* II.iv, on his *Paradiso*, Cantos 27, 30, 100, and 114, and on his letter to his patron, Cangrande della Scala on the motion (in medieval astronomy) of the sphere of the fixed stars. Professor A.P. d'Entrèves reads Dante's *Paradiso*, Canto XXXIII; p. 422. 26 May 1953 Tolkien attends a meeting of the ODS. Professor A.P. d'Entrèves reads Dante's *Inferno*, Canto XXVIII, and Dr Lorenzo Minio-Paluello reads Dante's *Paradiso*, Canto III; p. 455. 25 May 1954: Tolkien attends a meeting of the ODS. Professor A.P. d'Entrèves reads Dante's *Purgatorio*, Canto VIII.

23. _____. **La Divina Commedia di Dante Alighieri**, commentata da Attilio Momigliano. Vol. I Inferno. Firenze: Sansoni, 1945.
P.s.: MS. Tolkien A 13/1 *Draft of talk to the Oxford Dante Society: A neck-verse* (1947) fol. 173. Tolkien refers to 'vegetazione parassitaria'.

24. _____. **La Divina Commedia di Dante Alighieri**, commentata da Attilio Momigliano. Vol. II Purgatorio. Firenze: Sansoni, 1946.
P.s.: MS. Tolkien A 13/1 *Draft of talk to the Oxford Dante Society: A neck-verse* (1947) fol. 173.

25. _____. **La Divina Commedia di Dante Alighieri**, commentata da Attilio Momigliano. Vol. III Paradiso. Firenze: Sansoni, 1947.
P.s.: MS. Tolkien A 13/1 *Draft of talk to the Oxford Dante Society: A neck-verse* (1947) fol. 173.

26. _____. *La Vita Nova*.
S.s.: Scull-Hammond (2017a), p. 383. 23 May 1950: Tolkien attends a meeting of the Oxford Dante Society and Colin Hardie reads a paper on Dante's first mention of Virgil in Canto 25 of *La Vita Nuova*; p. 455. 25 May 1954: Tolkien attends a meeting of the ODS. Dr Lorenzo Minio-Paluello reads from Dante's *Vita Nuova*.

27. _____. *Le Rime*.
S.s.: d'Entréves (1952), p. 111. 20 February 1945: Colin Hardie reads a paper on the lyrics poems '*Amor, da che convien…*' (CXVI) at meeting of the Oxford Dante Society (Tolkien was a member from 1945 to 1955).

SECTION A

28. _____. *The Epistle to Cangrande*.
   S.s.: Scull-Hammond (2017a), p. 374. 9 November 1949: Tolkien attends a meeting of the ODS and Professor William James Entwistle reads a paper *Quante Commedie: The Epistle (X) to Con Grande*.

29. Allen, Hope Emily (Edited by). *Writings ascribed to Richard Rolle: Hermit of Hampole and Materials for his Biography*. New York: Mod. Lang. Assoc., 1927.
   Description: Autographed in pencil on front flyleaf. Notice to reviewers used as bookmark between the pages 106-7.
   Collection: Tolkien's personal Celtic library, preserved at the Weston library under the auspices of the English Faculty Library (Oxford).

30. Alois, Brandl. *Anglica: Untersuchungen zur englischen Philologie: Alois Brandl zum 70. Geburtstage überreicht*, Vol. I Sprache und Kulturgeschichte. Series: Palaestra 147. Leipzig: Mayer and Müller, 1925.
   Description: Autographed on frontispiece: 'J.R.R. Tolkien'. Inscribed in pencil and ink.
   Collection: Private [Sold by Loome Theological Booksellers, formerly 'David Miller collection'].
   P.s.: *Philology: General Works* (VI 1927, for 1925), p. 32 n. 1, 33-35, 50.

31. _____. *Anglica: Untersuchungen zur englischen Philologie: Alois Brandl zum 70. Geburtstage überreicht*, Vol. II Literaturgeschichte. Series: Palaestra 148. Leipzig: Mayer and Müller, 1925.
   Description: Autographed on frontispiece: 'J.R.R. Tolkien'. Inscribed in pencil and ink.
   P.s.: *Philology: General Works* (VI 1927, for 1925), p. 32 n. 1.

32. Ammianus, Marcellinus. *The Roman Historie, containing such acts and occurrents as passed under Constantius, Julianus, Jovianus, Valentinianus, and Valens, Emperours*. Translated by Philemon Holland. 1609.
   P.s.: MS. Tolkien A 11 *Notes on Pearl* fol. 59. [Tolkien Papers, Bodleian Library, Oxford]
   NED 1: #2 c., d. | 'W' (1928), p. 27 'Waiter, 7. c. esp.' 1609 – 'Butlers, carvers, yeomen of the cellar, wayters at the table'.
   NED 2: #2 h. | 'W' (1928), p. 56. 'Walm, v. Obs. 1. c.' –1609 'They saw afarre off a mightie deale of smoke waulming up into the aire' (xvii, i, 80).

33. Amours, François Joseph. *Scottish Alliterative Poems in Riming Stanzas*. Series: Scottish Text Society. Edinburgh and London: Printed for the Society by W. Blackwood and Sons, 1897.
   P.s. 1: *Sir Gawain and the Green Knight* (1925), p. xxvi. Tolkien and Gordon write: 'For bibliography of the Irish and French analogues of *Sir Gawain*, see the bibliography in Kittredge's study'. In Kittredge's study, this article is mentioned in 'XIII. Rauf Coilyear' (p. 306); p. 100, line 1139 ff. Tolkien and Gordon cite *The Awntyrs off Arthure at the Terne Wathelyne* (pp. 115-71) lines 33-67 (118-21).
   P.s. 2: *Sir Gawain and the Green Knight* (1967) 'Select Bibliography: editions of texts quoted more than once in the notes', p. 156. 'The Wntyrs off Arthure'., 'Rauf Coilȝear'.

34. _____ (Edited by). *The Original Chronicle of Andrew of Wyntoun: Printed on Parallel Pages from the Cottonian and Wemyss Mss., with the Variants of the Other Texts*, Vol. IV Texts: Books V [Ch. xiii, xiv], VI, VII [Ch. i-vii]. London: Printed for the Society by W. Blackwood and sons, 1906.
   P.s.: 'Chaucer as a Philologist: *The Reeve's Tale*' (1934), p. 138. Tolkien quotes: 'Quliill wepyt, quhill scho wongys wete' (v, ix, 1968).
   NED: #2 h. | 'W' (1928), p. 53 'Wallop v. I. 1. b.' – c 1420 'þe cursoure he straik wibe þe spuris, And walapande our floyis and furis Al befor þe ost he rade' (iv, 234).

35. *Ancrene Riwle | Ancrene Wisse* [Middle English rule for anchoresses].
    For editions and translations of the various versions of this work, see d'Evelyn, Day, Herbert, Mack, Morton, Salu, Tolkien, Trethewey, Wilson R. M.
    S.s.: Scull-Hammond (2017a), p. 122. Leeds academic year 1920-1921. While at Leeds Tolkien will produce various duplicated or mimeographed pages to give to his students. The topics of such pages include the *Ancrene Riwle* (October 1920).

36. Andler, Charles. *Mélanges de Littérature et de philologie germaniques offerts á Ch. Andler. Par ses amis et anciens éleves*. Publications de l'Université de Strasbourg, fasc. XXI. Paris: Librairie Istra, Maison d'Edition, 1924.
    P.s.: *Philology: General Works* (V 1926, for 1924), p. 34 n. 4.

37. Andrews, Albert Le Roy. *Hálfs saga ok Hálfsrekka*. Halle: Max Niemeyer, 1909.
    P.s.: *Beowulf* (2002) 'Version A', p. 69 [p. 234-5]. Tolkien quotes: 'æ mun uppi' (stanza 31, p. 108).

38. *Anglo-Saxon Chronicle* 1137-54. [Old English collection of annals, see Thorpe].
    P.s. 1: MS. Tolkien A 21/13 *The English MSS*. fol. 203. [Tolkien Papers, Bodleian Library, Oxford]
    P.s. 2: *The Fall of Arthur* (2013), p. 225.
    S.s.: #1 Holland (1949), p. 139. Appendix XI: Oxford Examinations for Prisoners of War. B.1 Old English: 'Þa on morgenne gehierdun ... cyninge ofslægene wærum'

39. Anwyl, Edward. *A Welsh grammar for Schools*, Pt. I, Accidence. Series: Parallel Grammar Series. London: Swan Sonnenschein, 1907 (3rd ed.).
    Description: Autographed and dated in pencil on front flyleaf: 'Summer 1919'. Annotated linguistic note in pencil on inside front cover and on text.
    Collection: Tolkien's personal Celtic library, preserved at the Weston library under the auspices of the English Faculty Library (Oxford).
    S.s. 1: Phelpstead (2011), p. 118.
    S.s. 2: Scull-Hammond (2017a), p. 116.

40. Appel, Carl. *Provenzalische Chrestomathie: mit Abriss der Formenlehre und Glossar*. Leipzig: O. R. Reisland, 1920 (5th ed. rev.).
    Description: On front flyleaf in ink: 'J.R.R. Tolkien'.
    Collection: Private [Sold by Loome Theological Booksellers, formerly 'David Miller collection'].

41. Appelöf, Jakob Johan Adolf and Karl Gustav Westman. *Sveriges förkristna konungalängd. Inbjudningsskrift till åhörande af de offentliga föreläsningar med hvilka*. Uppsala: Alqvist & Wiskells, 1910.
    Description: Tolkien's signature to front endpaper.
    Collection: Private [Sold by Simon Finch Rare Books Ltd.].
    S.s.: Finch (2002), p. 54.

42. Apuleius. 'Eros and Psyche' in *The Golden Ass*.
    P.s. 1: *On Fairy-stories* (1947), p. 48.
    P.s. 2: *Tolkien On Fairy-stories* (2008), p. 38.
    S.s.: Scull-Hammond (2006b), p. 820.

43. _____. *The Most Pleasant and Delectable Tale of the Marriage of Cupid and Psyche*. Series: Bibliothéque de Carabas. Translated by William Adington and with a discourse on the fable by Andrew Lang. London: David Nutt, 1887.
    P.s.: #1 a. | *Tolkien On Fairy-stories* (2008), p. 306. Tolkien refers to Lang introduction.

44. Arber, Edward. *Shorter Elizabethan Poems*. Series: An English Garner. Introduction by Arthur Henry Bullen. Westminster: A. Constable and Co., 1903.
    S.s.: University of Leeds (1920), p. 147. English Language and Literature - Scheme A. Texts and

Period selected for 1920-21. (b) Special period: 1557-1637. (c) Texts suggested for study with Special Period. Ordinary Degree of B.A. with Honours. Final Examination.

45. Aristophanes. *The Birds of Aristophanes*.
    Notes: In July 1910 Tolkien played the part of the Inspector.
    S.s. 1: *King Edward's School Chronicle* (October 1911), p. 72.
    S.s. 2: Scull-Hammond (2017a), p. 24.
    S.s. 3: Scull-Hammond (2017b), pp. 315, 622.

46. _____. *The Peace of Aristophanes*.
    Notes: In July 1911 Tolkien played 'a spirited Hermes'.
    S.s. 1: *King Edward's School Chronicle* (October 1911), p. 72.
    S.s. 2: Scull-Hammond (2017a), p. 32.
    S.s. 3: Scull-Hammond (2017b), p. 315.

47. Armstrong, Edward Cooke. *Le chevalier à l'Épée; an old French poem* (Johns Hopkins University Dissertation). Baltimore: J. Murphy, 1900.
    P.s. 1: *Sir Gawain and the Green Knight* (1925), p. xxvi. Tolkien and Gordon write: 'For bibliography of the Irish and French analogues of *Sir Gawain*, see the bibliography in Kittredge's study'. [*NED*] In Kittredge's study, this article is mentioned in 'X. Le Chevalier à l'Épée' (pp. 302-03), 'XI. The Canzoni' (p. 305).
    P.s. 2: *Sir Gawain and the Green Knight* (1967) 'Select Bibliography', p. 154.

48. Arngrimur Jónsson. *Arngrimi Jonae Opera Latine conscripta*, Vol. I. Series: Bibliotheca Arnamagnaeana, 9. Edited by Jakob Benediktsson. Hafniae: Ejnar Munksgaard, 1950.
    P.s.: *Finn and Hengest* (1982), pp. 55 n. 46; 58 n. 53; 77 n. 83.

49. _____. *Arngrimi Jonae Opera Latine conscripta*, Vol. II. Series: Bibliotheca Arnamagnaeana, 10. Edited by Jakob Benediktsson. Hafniae: Ejnar Munksgaard, 1951.
    P.s.: *Finn and Hengest* (1982), pp. 55 n. 46; 58 n. 53; 77 n. 83.

50. _____. *Arngrimi Jonae Opera Latine conscripta*, Vol. III. Series: Bibliotheca Arnamagnaeana, 11. Edited by Jakob Benediktsson. Hafniae: Ejnar Munksgaard, 1952.
    P.s.: *Finn and Hengest* (1982), pp. 55 n. 46; 58 n. 53; 77 n. 83.

51. _____. *Arngrimi Jonae Opera Latine conscripta*, Vol. III. Series: Bibliotheca Arnamagnaeana, 12. Edited by Jakob Benediktsson. Hafniae: Ejnar Munksgaard, 1957.
    P.s.: *Finn and Hengest* (1982), pp. 55 n. 46; 58 n. 53; 77 n. 83.

52. Ascham, Roger. *The Scholemaster*. Edited by Edward Arber.
    S.s.: University of Leeds (1920), p. 147. English Language and Literature - Scheme A. Texts and Period selected for 1920-21. (b) Special period: 1557-1637. (c) Texts suggested for study with Special Period. Ordinary Degree of B.A. with Honours. Final Examination.

53. Ásmundarson, Valdimar (Edited by). *Eiríks saga Rauða ok Graenlendinga þattr*. Series: Íslendinga sögur, 34. Reykjavík, S. Kristjánsson, 1902.
    P.s.: *The Story of Kullervo* (2016), pp. 246, 251. Tolkien cites the Icelandic explorers, Thorfinn and Skraeling, who appear in Ásmundarson's book.

54. _____ (Edited by). *Fóstbrœðra saga*. Íslendinga sögur 26. Rejkyavik: Sigurður Kritjansson, 1899.

Description: Annotated in pencil on front flyleaf and text. Autographed in pencil inside front cover.
Notes: Five volumes bound together: spine marked 19 [A. 60], 26, 31 [A. 57], 35 [A. 59]. Also contains 32 [A. 58].
Collection: Tolkien's personal Celtic library, preserved at the Weston library under the auspices of the English Faculty Library (Oxford).
P.s.: *Beowulf* (2002) 'Transcription of Legibile Portions of Folios 71-81: Notes and Jottings', p. 410.

55. _____ (Edited by). *Gunnlaugs saga Ormstungu.* Íslendinga sögur 9. Rejkyavik: Sigurður Kritjansson, 1911.
    Notes: Four volumes bound together: spine marked 6 [A. 2250], 8 [A. 56], 9, 17 [A. 2252].
    Collection: Tolkien's personal Celtic library, preserved at the Weston library under the auspices of the English Faculty Library (Oxford).
    P.s.: *The Legend of Sigurd & Gudrün* (2009), pp. 87, 199 Christopher Tolkien writes: 'The sources for this section of the Lay [Dauði Sinfjötla (The Death of Sinfjötli)] are the Saga and a short prose passage in the Edda entitled *Frá dauða Sinfjötla (Of Sinfjötli's death).*'

56. _____ (Edited by). *Hrafnkels saga freysgoða.* Íslendinga sögur 8. Rejkyavik: Sigurður Kritjansson, 1911 (2 copies).
    Notes: Four volumes bound together: spine marked 6 [A. 2250], 8, 9 [A. 55], 17 [A. 2252].
    Collection: Tolkien's personal Celtic library, preserved at the Weston library under the auspices of the English Faculty Library (Oxford).
    S.s. 1: Scull-Hammond (2017a), p. 46. April 1913: Tolkien will need to become familiar with a range of literary and philological subjects and set texts as prescribed in the Oxford Regulations of the Board of Studies, knowing that he may be examined on them in ten papers at the end of *Trinity Term 1915*. In addition, Tolkien will have to choose a Special Subject on which he will be examined separately. He will choose Scandinavian Philology, which according to the *Regulations* will have special reference to Icelandic.
    S.s. 2: Scull-Hammond (2017a), p. 56. *Hilary Term 1914*: Tolkien also attends this year (or, less probably, in 1915) W.A. Craigie's lectures on Hrafnkel's Saga on Thursdays at 5.00 p.m. in the Taylor Institution, beginning 22 January.

57. _____ (Edited by). *Hallfreðar saga.* Íslendinga sögur 31. Rejkyavik: Sigurður Kritjansson, 1901.
    Description: Annotated in pencil on front flyleaf and text. Autographed in pencil inside front cover.
    Notes: Five volumes bound together: spine marked 19 [A. 60], 26 [A. 54], 31, 35 [A. 59]. Also contains 32 [A. 58].
    Collection: Tolkien's personal Celtic library, preserved at the Weston library under the auspices of the English Faculty Library (Oxford).
    S.s.: Scull-Hammond (2017a), p. 46. April 1913: Tolkien will need to become familiar with a range of literary and philological subjects and set texts as prescribed in the Oxford Regulations of the Board of Studies, knowing that he may be examined on them in ten papers at the end of *Trinity Term 1915*. In addition, Tolkien will have to choose a Special Subject on which he will be examined separately. He will choose Scandinavian Philology, which according to the *Regulations* will have special reference to Icelandic.

58. _____ (Edited by). *þorfinns saga Hvita.* Íslendinga sögur, 32. Rejkyavik: Sigurður Kritjansson, 1902.
    Description: Annotated in pencil on front flyleaf and text. Autographed in pencil inside front cover.
    Notes: Five volumes bound together: spine marked 19 [A. 60], 26 [A. 54], 31 [A. 57], 35 [A. 59]. Also contains 32.
    Collection: Tolkien's personal Celtic library, preserved at the Weston library under the auspices of the English Faculty Library (Oxford).

59. _____ (Edited by). *þorfinns saga Karlsefnis.* Íslendinga sögur 35. Rejkyavik:

Sigurður Kritjansson, 1902.
> Description: Annotated in pencil on front flyleaf and text. Autographed in pencil inside front cover.
> Notes: Five volumes bound together: spine marked 19 [A. 60], 26 [A. 54], 31 [A. 57], 35. Also contains 32 [A. 58].
> Collection: Tolkien's personal Celtic library, preserved at the Weston library under the auspices of the English Faculty Library (Oxford).
> S.s.: Scull-Hammond (2017a), p. 46. April 1913: Tolkien will need to become familiar with a range of literary and philological subjects and set texts as prescribed in the Oxford Regulations of the Board of Studies, knowing that he may be examined on them in ten papers at the end of *Trinity Term 1915*. In addition, Tolkien will have to choose a Special Subject on which he will be examined separately. He will choose Scandinavian Philology, which according to the *Regulations* will have special reference to Icelandic.

60. _____ (Edited by). *Vigá-Glúms saga*. Íslendinga sögur 19. Rejkyavik: Sigurður Kritjansson, 1897.
> Description: Annotated in pencil on front flyleaf and text. Autographed in pencil inside front cover.
> Notes: Five volumes bound together: spine marked 19, 26 [A. 54], 31 [A. 57], 35 [A. 59]. Also contains 32 [A. 58].
> Collection: Tolkien's personal Celtic library, preserved at the Weston library under the auspices of the English Faculty Library (Oxford).

61. Asser, John. *Asser's life of King Alfred: together with Annals of saint Neots erroneously ascribed to Asser*. Edited by William Henry Stevenson. Oxford: At the Clarendon Press, 1904.
> P.s. 1: *English and Welsh* (1963), p. 29.
> P.s. 2: *Finn and Hengest* (1982), p. 56.

62. Assmann, Bruno (Edited by). *Die Handschrift von Exeter, Metra des Boetius, Salomo und Saturn, die Psalmen*, Vol II. Series: Bibliothek der Angelsächsischen Poesie. Begründet von Christian Wilhelm Michael Grein. Leipzig: Kassel George H. Wigand, 1894.
> P.s.: *Exeter College library register*. Tolkien's borrowing record: *Long vacation 1914* from 19 January to 14 October.

63. _____ (Edited by). *Homilien und Heiligenleben*. Series: Bibliothek der angelsächsischen Prosa, 3. Hamburg: Henri Grand, 1889.
> Description: Autographed, dated: '1919' and annotated in pencil on front flyleaf.
> Collection: Tolkien's personal Celtic library, preserved at the Weston library under the auspices of the English Faculty Library (Oxford).

64. *Atlakviða*. [heroic poems of the Poetic Edda, see Jónsson]
> P.s. 1: Gordon-Tolkien Collection, University of Leeds MS 1952/2/2 (1920s). Poem written in pen and ink: *Gunnars End*. The composition is inspired by the Norse heroic poem 'Atlakviða', in the medieval Icelandic manuscript the 'Codex Regis'.
> P.s. 2: *Beowulf* (2002) 'Textual Notes A-Text', p. 328.
> P.s. 3: *The Legend of Sigurd & Gudrún* (2009), pp. 311-12. Christopher Tolkien writes: 'My father devoted much time and thought to *Atlakviða*, and prepared a very detailed commentary (the basis for lectures and seminars) on this extraordinarily difficult text. It is a poem that he much admired. Despite its condition, 'we are in the presence (he wrote) of great poetry that can still move us as poetry. Its style is universally and rightly praised: rapid, terse, vigorous – while maintaining, within its narrow limits, characterization. The poet who wrote it knew how to produce the grim and deadly atmosphere his theme demanded. It lives in the memory as one of the things in the Edda most instinct with that demonic energy and force which one finds in Old Norse verse'.'

65. Auden, Wystan Hugh. *About the House*. London: Faber & Faber Ltd., 1966.

Description: A copy was sent to Tolkien by the author, with dedication.
P.s.: *Letters* 284 (1966). To W.H. Auden.
S.s. 1: Scull-Hammond (2017a), p. 686.
S.s. 2: Scull-Hammond (2006b), p. 820.

66. _____. *Making, Knowing and Judging*. Oxford: At the Clarendon Press, 1956.
Description: Auden writes (p. 13): 'I remember one I attended, delivered by Professor Tolkien. I do not remember a single word he said but at a certain point he recited, and magnificently, a long passage of *Beowulf*. I was spellbound. This poetry I knew was going to be my dish. I became willing, therefore, to work at Anglo-Saxon because, unless I did, I should never be able to read this poetry. [...] Anglo-Saxon and Middle English poetry have been one of my stronger, most lasting influences.'

67. _____. *The Shield of Achilles*. New York: Random House, 1955.
Description: Auden sent an inscribed copy of the book to Tolkien.
P.s.: Tolkien's unpublished letter to Elizabeth Jennings, 2 December 1955. Tolkien congratulates Jennings on the publication of her poetry book *A Way of Looking* and discusses the merits of W. H. Auden's *Shield of Achilles*, and mentions the review of both books in *Time and Tide*.
S.s.: Scull-Hammond (2017a), p. 506.

68. Auerbach, Erich. *Mimesis: The representation of reality in Western literature*. Princeton: Princeton University Press, 1953.
P.s.: *Letters* 183 (1956). Notes on W.H. Auden's review of *The Lord of the Rings*.

69. Augustine, Saint, Bishop of Hippo. *King Alfred's Old English version of St. Augustine's Soliloquies*. Edited by Henry Lee Hargrove. New York: Henry Holt and Co., 1902.
P.s.: MS. Tolkien A 12/3 *Rough text of a lecture on Sir Gawain*, 1965 fols. 17-59. [Tolkien Papers, Bodleian Library, Oxford].

70. Aulnoy, Madame d' (Marie-Catherine). *The Fairy Tales of Madame d'Aulnoy, newly done into English*. London: Lawrence and Bullen, 1892.
P.s.: *On Fairy-stories* (1947), p. 40. Tolkien writes: '…as in France it went to court and put on powder and diamonds'; 177.

71. Austin, Thomas (Edited by). *Two fifteenth-century cookery-books. Harleian ms. 279 (ab. 1430), & Harl. ms. 4016 (ab. 1450), with extracts from Ashmole ms. 1429, Laud ms. 553, & Douce ms. 55*. Series: E.E.T.S. (Early English Text Society), OS 91. London: Published for the Early English Text Society by Kegan Paul, Trench, Trübner and Co., 1888.
P.s.: MS. Tolkien A 21/13 fol. 119. Note by Tolkien, 'Books in Exeter Library useful', with shelfmarks, on back of photostat reading list dated October 1913. Tolkien writes: 'All EETS publications'. [Tolkien Papers, Bodleian Library, Oxford]
NED: #2 i. | 'W' (1928), p. 57 'Walnut, 1.' c 1430 – 'Take curnylles of walnotys' (*Ashmole MS. 1439. Sauces*., p. 109).

72. Avicenna. *Canon medicinae*, Vol. I.
P.s.: MS. Tolkien A 13/2 *Notes and drafts of lectures on Chaucer: Pardoner's Tale* fol. 178.
S.s.: Carpenter (1979), p. 124 n. 1. Tolkien's poem about Charles Williams ('*Our dear Charles Williams many guises show…*' pp. 123-26). Tolkien quotes *fen*: the name of a section in Avicenna's *Canon of Medicine*; also used by Chaucer in *The Pardoner's Tale*.

73. *Awntyrs off Arthure at the Terne Wathelyne*. [Middle English alliterative verse, see Amours].
P.s. 1: MS. Tolkien A 12/2 *Commentary on Sir Gawain, lines 1999-2523* fol. 2. Tolkien quotes 'snetarand' (v. 82). [Tolkien Papers, Bodleian Library, Oxford]

P.s. 2: *Sir Gawain and the Green Knight* (1925), p. 100, line 1139 ff. Tolkien and Gordon cite *The Awntyrs off Arthure at the Terne Wathelyne* (pp. 115-71) lines 33-67 (118-21).

74. *Ayenbite of Inwyt* (or *Prick of Conscience*). [Middle English confessional prose work, see R. Morris, Rolle, Senff and Wallenberg].
    P.s. 1: MS. Tolkien A 13/2 *Notes and drafts of lectures on Chaucer: Pardoner's Tale* fol. 141. [Tolkien Papers, Bodleian Library, Oxford].
    P.s. 2: MS. Tolkien A 21/13 *The English MSS*. fol. 203. [Tolkien Papers, Bodleian Library, Oxford].
    P.s. 3: *Oxford University Press Archives* (Oxford). In an 'office copy' of the OED (Vol. VII, O-P, first edition), Tolkien writes a marginal note about a sense pass (verb) on page 524: '1347 *Ayenbite vor to pasi þet*' (Of þe yfþe of red and virtue of merci). His quotation being added as an antedating '. (*Cfr* Gilliver-Marshall-Weiner 2006, pp. 34-35).

75. *Babes in the Wood*. [Traditional children's tale].
    P.s.: *Tolkien On Fairy-stories* (2008) 'Manuscript A. [MS Tolkien 4, fols. 59-77]', p. 177.

76. Bach, Adolf. 'Deutsche Siedlungsnamen in genetisch-wortgeographischer Betrachtung'. *Beiträge zur Germanischen Sprachwissenschaft: Festschrift für Otto Behaghel*. Heidelberg: Carl Winter, 1924. [A. 1045].
    P.s.: *Philology: General Works* (V 1926, for 1924), p. 36.

77. Bach, Herbert Ernest. *Cheddar, its gorge and caves*. Boston: John Wright, 1947.
    P.s.: *Letters* 321 (1971). From a letter to P. Rorke, S.J.

78. Bacon, Francis. *Of the Advancement of Learning*. London: Joseph Malaby Dent, 1915.
    S.s. 1: University of Leeds (1920), p. 147. English Language and Literature - Scheme A. Texts and Period selected for 1920-21. (b) Special period: 1557-1637. (c) Texts suggested for study with Special Period. Ordinary Degree of B.A. with Honours. Final Examination.
    S.s. 2: University of Leeds (1921), p. 155. English Language and Literature - Scheme B. Texts for 1921-22. (d) Outlines of the History of English Literature. Ordinary Degree of B.A. with Honours. Final Examinations.

79. Baillie-Grohman, William Adolph (Edited by). *The Master of Game: the oldest English book on hunting (by Edward, second Duke of York, written 1406-13)*. London: Chatto and Windus, 1904.
    P.s. 1: *Sir Gawain and the Green Knight* (1925), p. xxvi; p. 100, line 1150; p. 101 line 1156-7.
    P.s. 2: *Sir Gawain and the Green Knight* (1967) 'Select Bibliography', p. 155.

80. _____ (Edited by). *The Master of Game: the oldest English book on hunting (by Edward, second Duke of York, written 1406-13)*. London: Chatto and Windus, 1909 (2nd ed.).
    P.s. 1: *Sir Gawain and the Green Knight* (1925), p. xxvi.
    P.s. 2: *Sir Gawain and the Green Knight* (1967) 'Select Bibliography', p. 155.

81. Baist, Gottfried. 'Das germanische Suffix –ingô'. *Zeitschrift für romanische Philologie*, Vol. XXXI. [A. 887]. Halle: Max Niemeyer, 1907.
    P.s.: 'Middle English 'Losenger'' (1953), p. 67 n. 1.

82. Baker, Augustine and Justine McCann. *The Cloud of unknowing and other treatises* [The Epistle of Privy Counsel, Mystica theologia of Saint-Denis], by an English mystic of the 14th century, with a commentary on the 'Cloud' [Secretum sive mysticum]. London: Burns Oates, 1952 (6th ed. rev.).
    S.s.: Scull-Hammond (2017a), pp. 412, 414.

83. Baker, George P. *The Fighting Kings of Wessex*. London: Bell, 1931.
    P.s.: *Finn and Hengest* (1982), p. 72 n. 74.

84. Banks, Mary Macleod. *An alphabet of tales: an English 15th century translation of the Alphabetum Narrationum of Étienne de Besançon, from Additional MS. 25,719 of the British Museum*, Vol. I, Pt. A-H. Series: E.E.T.S. (Early English Text Society), OS 126. London: Published for the Early English Text Society by Kegan Paul, Trench, Trübner, 1904.
    P.s. 1: MS. Tolkien A 11 *Notes on Pearl* fol. 124. [Tolkien Papers, Bodleian Library, Oxford]
    P.s. 2: MS. Tolkien A 21/13 fol. 119. Note by Tolkien, 'Books in Exeter Library useful', with shelfmarks, on back of photostat reading list dated October 1913. Tolkien writes: 'All EETS publications'. [Tolkien Papers, Bodleian Library, Oxford]

85. _____. *An alphabet of tales: an English 15th century translation of the Alphabetum Narrationum of Étienne de Besançon, from Additional MS. 25,719 of the British Museum*, Vol. II, Pt. I-Z. Series: E.E.T.S. (Early English Text Society), OS 127. London: Published for the Early English Text Society by Kegan Paul, Trench, Trübner, 1904.
    P.s. 1: MS. Tolkien A 11 *Notes on Pearl* fol. 124. [Tolkien Papers, Bodleian Library, Oxford]
    P.s. 2: MS. Tolkien A 21/13 fol. 119. Note by Tolkien, 'Books in Exeter Library useful', with shelfmarks, on back of photostat reading list dated October 1913. Tolkien writes: 'All EETS publications'. [Tolkien Papers, Bodleian Library, Oxford]

86. Barbier, Paul. *English Influence on the French Vocabulary*, Pt. I. Series: Society for ure English Tract no. VII. Oxford: At the Clarendon Press, 1922.
    P.s.: *Philology: General Works* (IV 1924, for 1923), p. 21.

87. _____. *English Influence on the French Vocabulary*, Pt. II. Series: Society for ure English Tract no. XIII. Oxford: At the Clarendon Press, 1923.
    P.s.: *Philology: General Works* (IV 1924, for 1923), p. 22.

88. Barbour, John. *The Bruce*. [Early Scots narrative poem, see Skeat].
    P.s. 1: MS. Tolkien A 11 *Notes on Pearl* fols. 38-9. [Tolkien Papers, Bodleian Library, Oxford].
    P.s. 2: MS. Tolkien A 21/7 fol. 35. [Tolkien Papers, Bodleian Library, Oxford].
    P.s. 3: MS. Tolkien A 21/13 *Chronological Library Table of Middle English* fol. 202. [Tolkien Papers, Bodleian Library, Oxford].
    S.s. 1: Ollscoil na h-Éireann G 259 (1949).
    S.s. 2: Scull-Hammond (2017a), p. 46. April 1913: Tolkien will need to become familiar with a range of literary and philological subjects and set texts as prescribed in the Oxford Regulations of the Board of Studies, knowing that he may be examined on them in ten papers at the end of *Trinity Term 1915*: Middle English texts.
    NED: #2 h. | 'W' (1928), p. 53 'Wallop v. I. 1. b.' – 1375 'To this word thai assentyt all, And fra thaim walopyt owyr mar' (II, 440).

89. _____. *Barbour's Des schottischen Nationaldichters Legendensammlung nebst den Fragmenten seines Trojanerkrieges*, Vol. I. Edited by Carl Horstmann. Heilbronn: Henninger, 1881.
    P.s.: *Sir Gawain and the Green Knight* (1925), p. 95 line 774 *Sayn Gilyan*. Tolkien and Gordon cite 'XXV. Julian' (p. 219).

90. _____. *Die Fragmente des Trojanerkrieges*, Vol. II. Edited by Carl Horstmann. Heilbronn: Verlag von Gebr. Henninger, 1882.
    P.s.: *Sir Gawain and the Green Knight* (1967) 'Select Bibliography: editions of texts quoted more than once in the notes', p. 156. '*Scottish Troy Fragments*'.

Section A

91. Barfield, Owen. *Poetic Diction. A Study in Meaning.* London: Faber and Faber, 1928.

> P.s. 1: *Letters* 15 (1937). To Allen & Unwin. Tolkien writes to Mr Furth (Allen & Unwin): 'The only philological remark (I think) in *The Hobbit* is on p. 221 (lines 6-7 from end): an odd mythological way of referring to linguistic philosophy, and a point that will (happily) be missed by any who have not read Barfield (few have), and probably by those who have'. The passage in *The Hobbit* (1937) is: 'There are no words left to express his staggerment, since Men changed the language that they learned of elves in the days when all the world was wonderful' and remember the Barfield's concept 'that of the 'metaphorical period', a wonderful age when a race of anonymous and mighty poets took hold of a bald inventory and saturated it with poetic values' (ch. iv, 'Meaning and Myth').
> P.s. 2: *On Fairy-stories* (2008), p. 38.
> P.s. 3: *A Secret Vice* (2016), p. 67.
> S.s. 1: Carpenter (1979), p. 42. Not long after the book's publication, Lewis reported to Barfield: 'You might like to know that when Tolkien dined with me the other night he said a propos of something quite different that your conception of the ancient semantic unity had modified his whole outlook and that he was always just going to say something in a lecture when your conception stopped him in time. 'It is one of those things,' he said 'that when you've once seen it there are all sorts of things you can never say again.' Perhaps it was as a result of reading Barfield's book that Tolkien made an inversion of Miller's remark. 'Languages', he declared, 'are a disease of mythology.'
> S.s. 2: Anderson (2002), p. 271 n. 2.
> S.s. 3: Lewis (2009b), p. 1509. Letter to Barfield – 1928. Lewis writes: 'You might like to know that … We went on to observe on the paradox that tho' you knew much poetry and little philology the philological part of your book was much the sounder'.
> S.s. 4: Scull-Hammond (2017a), p. 153
> S.s. 5: Scull-Hammond (2017b), pp. 99, 101, 575, 701, 1059.

92. _____. *The Silver Trumpet.* London: Faber and Gwyer, 1925.

> S.s. 1: Anderson (2002), p. 271 n. 2.
> S.s. 2: Lewis (2009a), p. 198. Letter to Barfield – 28 June 1936. Lewis writes: 'I lent *The Silver Trumpet* to Tolkien and hear that it is the greatest success among his children that they have ever known. His own fairy-tales, which are excellent, have now no market: and its first reading– children are so practical!– led to a universal wail 'You're not going to give it back to Dr Lewis, are you?' All the things which the wiseacres on child psychology in our circle said when you wrote it turn out to be nonsense. 'They liked the sad parts', said Tolkien 'because they were sad and the puzzling parts because they were puzzling, as children always do.' The youngest boy liked Gamboy because 'she was clever and the bad people in books usually aren't.'
> S.s. 3: Scull-Hammond (2017a), p. 197. May-June 1936 C. S. Lewis lends Tolkien his copy. It is much appreciated by the Tolkien children.
> S.s. 4: Scull-Hammond (2017b), pp. 99, 517.

93. Barners, Juliana and William Blades (Edited by). *The Boke of Saint Albans.* London: Elliot Stock, 1901.

> P.s. 1: *Sir Gawain and the Green Knight* (1925), p. xxvii; p. 101, line 1169 *þe wratteȝ*. Tolkien and Gordon cite: 'For two causes the hert … hym sewen to begyle'.
> P.s. 2: *Sir Gawain and the Green Knight* (1967) 'Select Bibliography', p. 155.
> P.s. 3: *Beowulf* (2002) 'Textual Notes A-Text', p. 330.

94. Barrie, James Matthew. *Peter and Wendy.* New York: Scribner, 1912.

> P.s. 1: *On Fairy-stories* (1947), p. 65.
> P.s. 2: *Tolkien On Fairy-stories* (2008), p. 58.
> P.s. 3: *Tolkien On Fairy-stories* (2008) 'Manuscript A. [MS Tolkien 4, fols. 59-77]', p. 190.
> P.s. 4: *Tolkien On Fairy-stories* (2008) 'Manuscript B [MS. Tolkien 4, fols. 73-120]', p. 237.

95. _____. *Peter Pan in Kensington Gardens.*

> P.s. 1: *On Fairy-stories* (1947), pp. 65, 87.
> P.s. 2: *Tolkien On Fairy-stories* (2008), pp. 58, 82.

P.s. 3: *Tolkien On Fairy-stories* (2008) 'Manuscript B [MS. Tolkien 4, fols. 73-120]', p. 237.

96. Barth, Karl. 'Dr Karl Barth and The War, A Letter to a French Pastor'. *The Guardian*, 15 March 1940.
    S.s.: Lewis (2009a), p. 404. Letter to his brother Warren – 28 April 1940. Lewis writes: 'In the evening we had the first weekly Inklings. (By the way, Williams brought back the *Guardian* and I have read the article you mentioned on Karl Barth).'

97. Baskervill, William Malone (Edited by). *Andreas. The legend of St Andrew*. Boston: Ginn, 1885.
    Collection: Taylor Institution Library, Bodleian Libraries (Oxford).
    P.s. 1: MS. Tolkien 16/2 *Notes and drafts concerning Andreas*. [Tolkien Papers, Bodleian Library, Oxford]
    P.s. 2: *Beowulf* (2014), p. 277.
    NED: #2 h. | 'W' (1928), p. 54. 'Walm *sb.*[1] *Obs.* 1. a. (In OE. only.).' – a 1000 He yðum stilde, wæteres wælmum' (452).

98. Bateson, H. (Edited by). *Patience, a West Midland poem of the fourteenth century*. Series: Publications of the University of Manchester. English series, III. Manchester: University Press, 1912.
    P.s. 1: *Sir Gawain and the Green Knight* (1925), p. xxv.
    P.s. 2: *Sir Gawain and the Green Knight* (1967) 'Select Bibliography', p. 153.

99. _____ (Edited by). *Patience, a West Midland poem of the fourteenth century*. Manchester: University Press, 1918 (2nd ed.).
    P.s.: Sir Gawain and the Green Knight (1925), p. xxv. [Tolkien and Gordon indicate '1915', corrected only in the edition edited by Norman Davis (1967)]

100. Battle of Brunanburh [Old English poem, see Sedgefield]
    P.s.: *The Fallo of Arthur* (2013), p. 224.

101. Battle of Maldon [Old English poem, see E.V. Gordon, Laborde and Sweet].
    P.s. 1: *The Homecoming of Beorhtnoth Beorhthelm's Son* (1953).
    P.s. 2: *Finn and Hengest* (1982), p. 32.
    S.s.: #1 Holland (1949), p. 138. Appendix XI: Oxford Examinations for Prisoners of War. B.1 Old English: vv. 91-118.

102. Bauer, Harry C. 'Words with a bibliographic provenience'. *Library Review*, Vol. XX, no. 6, June 1966, pp. 372-79.
    P.s. Tolkien's unpublished letter to Bauer, 24 November 1966. Tolkien thanks Bauer for an article or reprint Bauer had sent him.

103. Baynes, Thomas Spencer. *The Encyclopaedia Britannica; a Dictionary of arts, sciences, and general literature*, Vol. XXIV. New York: Charles Scribner's sons, 1888.
    P.s.: MS. Tolkien A 19/3 *Etymologies or history of Walrus* fols. 162-195. [Tolkien Papers, Bodleian Library, Oxford].
    S.s.: Tolkien, *Family Album* (1992), p. 42.
    NED: #2 i. | 'W' (1928), p. 58 'Walrus, 1.' 1888 – 'The tusks are formidable weapons of defence, but their principal use seems to be digging, for the molluscs and crustaceans on which the walrus feeds' (p. 337).

104. Beaumont, Francis and John Fletcher. *Philaster*.
    S.s.: University of Leeds (1923), p. 81. Ordinary Degree of B.A., Intermediate Course and Examination: English Literature. Text selected for 1923-24 (ii) Texts suggestes as part of a course of general rending in the period 1579-1645.

NED: #2 c., d. | 'W' (1928), p. 27 'Waiter, 7. *a.*' *Obs.* 1611 (1620) – 'What sawcy groome knocks at this dead of night, Where be our waiters?' (Act. II).

105. Bede, the Venerable Saint. *Baedae Opera Historica*. Edited by Charles Plummer. Oxford: At the Clarendon Press, 1896.
P.s. 1: *English and Welsh* (1963), p. 24.
P.s. 2: *Finn and Hengest* (1982), p. 14 n. 12; p. 69 n. 66.

106. _____. *The Ecclesiastical History of the English People*. London: Oates & Washbourne, 1935.
Collection: Private [Dominic Winter, 5 December 2014]

107. _____. *Historia ecclesiastica gentis Anglorum*, Vol. I. Plummer, C. Oxonii: Typographeo Clarendiano, 1896.
P.s.: *Finn and Hengest* (1982), 14; n. 11. Tolkien quotes: '*Ut ergo conualuit, uendidit eum Lundoniam Freso cuidam* (p. 251)., 69 n. 69.

108. _____. *Historia Ecclesiastica Gentis Anglorum*, Vol. II Commentarium et indices continens. Plummer, C. Oxonii: Typographeo Clarendiano, 1896.
P.s.: *Finn and Hengest* (1982), p. 69 n. 69.

109. _____. *The Old English version of Bede's Ecclesiastical history of the English people*, Vol. I, Pt. I. Series: E.E.T.S. (Early English Text Society), OS 95. Edited by Thomas Miller. London: Published for the Early English Text Society by Kegan Paul, Trench, Trübner and Co., 1890.
P.s. 1: MS. Tolkien A 21/13 fol. 119. Note by Tolkien, 'Books in Exeter Library useful', with shelfmarks, on back of photostat reading list dated October 1913. Tolkien writes: 'All EETS publications'. [Tolkien Papers, Bodleian Library, Oxford]
P.s. 2: *Finn and Hengest* (1982), p. 61 n. 59.

110. _____. *The Old English version of Bede's Ecclesiastical history of the English people*, Vol. I, Pt. II. Series: E.E.T.S. (Early English Text Society), OS 96. Edited by Thomas Miller. London: Published for the Early English Text Society by Kegan Paul, Trench, Trübner and Co., 1891.
P.s. 1: MS. Tolkien A 21/13 fol. 119. Note by Tolkien, 'Books in Exeter Library useful', with shelfmarks, on back of photostat reading list dated October 1913. Tolkien writes: 'All EETS publications'. [Tolkien Papers, Bodleian Library, Oxford]
P.s. 2: *Finn and Hengest* (1982), p. 61 n. 59.

111. _____. *The Old English version of Bede's Ecclesiastical history of the English people*, Vol. II, Pt. I. Series: E.E.T.S. (Early English Text Society), OS 110. Edited by Thomas Miller. London: Published for the Early English Text Society by Kegan Paul, Trench, Trübner and Co., 1897.
P.s. 1: MS. Tolkien A 21/13 fol. 119. Note by Tolkien, 'Books in Exeter Library useful', with shelfmarks, on back of photostat reading list dated October 1913. Tolkien writes: 'All EETS publications'. [Tolkien Papers, Bodleian Library, Oxford]
P.s. 2: *Finn and Hengest* (1982), p. 61 n. 62.
NED: #2 h. | 'W' (1928), p. 54. 'Walm *sb.*¹ *Obs.* 1. a. (In OE. only.).' – c900 'Ʒestilde seo sæ fram ðam wylme' (p. 200).

112. _____. *The Old English version of Bede's Ecclesiastical history of the English people*, Vol. II, Pt. II. Series: E.E.T.S. (Early English Text Society), OS 111. Edited by Thomas Miller. London: Published for the Early English Text Society by Kegan Paul, Trench, Trübner and Co., 1897.
P.s. 1: MS. Tolkien A 21/13 fol. 119. Note by Tolkien, 'Books in Exeter Library useful', with

shelfmarks, on back of photostat reading list dated October 1913. Tolkien writes: 'All EETS publications'. [Tolkien Papers, Bodleian Library, Oxford]
P.s. 2: *Finn and Hengest* (1982), p. 61 n. 62.

113.   Belfour, Algernon Ikey (Edited by). *Twelfth Century Homilies in MS. Bodley 343.* Series: E.E.T.S. (Early English Text Society), OS 137. London: Published for the Early English Text Society by Kegan Paul, Trench, Trübner and Co., 1909.
Collection: Tolkien's personal Celtic library, preserved at the Weston library under the auspices of the English Faculty Library (Oxford).
P.s. 1: MS. Tolkien A 12/1 *Commentary on Sir Gawain*, lines 37-1987 fol. 9. [Tolkien Papers, Bodleian Library, Oxford]
P.s. 2: MS. Tolkien A 21/13 fol. 119. Note by Tolkien, 'Books in Exeter Library useful', with shelfmarks, on back of photostat reading list dated October 1913. Tolkien writes: 'All EETS publications'. [Tolkien Papers, Bodleian Library, Oxford]

114.   Bell, Charles. *The Hand: its mechanism and vital endowments as evincing design.* London: William Pickering, 1834.
P.s.: MS. Tolkien A 19/3 *Etymologies or history of Walrus* fols. 162-195. [Tolkien Papers, Bodleian Library, Oxford]
S.s.: Tolkien, *Family Album* (1992), p. 42.
NED: #2 i. | 'W' (1928), p. 58 'Walrus, 1.' 1833 – 'The bones of the morse or walrus ... are remarkably complete, if we consider the peculiar appearance of the feet in the living animal' (pp. 109-10).

115.   Belloc, Hilaire. *Characters of the reformation. Twenty-Three Portraits By Jean Charlot.* London: Sheed & Ward, 1936.
Description: A birthday gift from J.R.R. Tolkien to his son Michael. With the home-made bookplate of Michael Tolkien to the front pastedown bearing the presentation inscription of his father J.R.R. Tolkien: 'Michael H. R. Tolkien | from his father | J.R.R.T | 22 October 1945'. On the next page 'Michael H. R. Tolkien | Oxford. | February 1946'.
Collection: Private.
S.s.: Scull-Hammond (2017a), p. 313.

116.   _____. *The Crisis of Our Civilization.* London: Cassell and Co., 1937.
Description: A birthday gift from J.R.R. Tolkien to his son Michael. With the home-made bookplate of Michael Tolkien to the front pastedown bearing the presentation inscription of his father J.R.R. Tolkien: 'Michael Tolkien| from his father | October 22nd | 1945'. 22 October is the date of Michael Tolkien's birthday. With the recipient's earlier ownership inscription on the front free endpaper. On the next page 'Michael H. R. Tolkien | 20 Northmoor Road. | Oxford. | Summer 1945'.
Collection: Private.
S.s.: Scull-Hammond (2017a), p. 313.

117.   _____. *Danton: a study.* London: James Nisbet & Co., 1899.
Description: Signed by JRRT and Michael Tolkien. Ownership: 'Michael H.R. Tolkien, Oxford, February 15th, 1946'. Bookplate: 'Study with books' and 'Michael H.R. Tolkien, from his father, 22nd October, 1945' in JRRT's hand. Inserts: 1) 'Michael H.R. Tolkien' pasted insert below. 2) 'If you would like a signature from The Lord of the Rings, you can insert this with my good wishes. J.R.R.T.' in JRRT's hand.
Collection: Private.

118.   Bellows, Henry Adams (Edited by). *The Poetic Edda.* New York: The American Scandinavian Foundation 1923.
S.s.: Anderson (2002), pp, 73-75.

119.   Benedict, Saint Abbot of Monte Cassino. *Der Winteney-Version der Regula S. Benedicti.* Edited by Arnold Schröer. Halle: Max Niemeyer, 1888.

P.s.: *Finn and Hengest* (1982), p. 100 n. 37.

120. Bennett, Jack Arthur Walter. *The History of Old English and Old Norse studies in England from the time of Francis Junius till the end of the eighteenth century.* Oxford: University Press, 1938.
   S.s.: Scull-Hammond (2006b), p. 83. In 1938 Bennett was awarded a D.Phil, for this examined by Tolkien and David Nichol Smith.

121. Benson, Larry Dean. *Art and tradition in Sir Gawain and the Green Knight.* New Brunswick: Rutgers University Press, 1965.
   P.s.: *Sir Gawain and the Green Knight* (1967) 'Select Bibliography', p. 154.

122. Bentcliffe, Eric (Edited by). *Triode*, no. 18 Stockport: Stockport and Intake Dog and Cake Walking Society, May 1960.
   S.s.: Scull-Hammond (2017a), p. 587. April 1960 Tolkien writes to the editor of the fanzine Triode, who had sent him a copy of the issue for January 1960, which contained an article, 'No Monroe in Lothlorien', on the possibility of a film of *The Lord of the Rings*.

123. Benz, Richard. *Historia von D. Johann Fausten dem weitbeschreyten zauberer und schwarzkünstler.* Series: Deutsche volksbücher, 2. Jena: E. Diederichs, 1911.
   Collection: Taylor Institution Library, Bodleian Libraries (Oxford).

124. *Beowulf* [Old English epic poem].
   For editions and translations of this poem, see entries under: Dobbie, Earle, Grein, Grundtvig, Hall, Heyne, Holder, Holthausen, Kemble, Klaeber, Sedgefield, Strong, Thorkelin, Tolkien (2014), Wrenn, Wright D., Wyatt.
   P.s. 1: *Holy Maidenhood* (1923), p. 281.
   P.s. 2: *Tolkien On Fairy-stories* (2008), pp. 34n, 38,
   P.s. 3: *Tolkien On Fairy-stories* (2008) 'Manuscript B [MS. Tolkien 4, fols. 73-120]', p 216, 268.
   P.s. 4: *Tolkien On Fairy-stories* (2008) 'Manuscript B [MS. Tolkien 6, fol. 17]', p. 268.
   P.s. 5: *Tolkien On Fairy-stories* (2008) 'Manuscript B [MS. Tolkien 14, fol. 25]', p. 280n.
   P.s. 6: *Beowulf* (2014)
   S.s. 1: University of Leeds (1923), pp. 135-37. Hb4. (Scheme A and B) Third Year: Monday-Wedsneday 12.00: Old English Heoric Poetry, with special study of *Beowulf.*
   S.s. 2: #1 Holland (1949), pp. 137-38. Appendix XI: Oxford Examinations for Prisoners of War. B.1 Old English: vv. 791-804, 1605-1616, 2406-2419; p. 139.
   NED: #2 h. | 'W' (1928), p. 54. 'Walm sb.[1] Obs. 2.' – 'Wæs ðære burnan wælm heaðofyrum bhat' (2546).

125. *Beowulf, The Fight at Finnesburg* [Portion of an Old English heroic poem, see Grein, Hall, Klaeber, R. Morris, Wrenn, Wyatt].
   P.s. 1: *Beowulf* (1937)
   P.s. 2: *Prefatory Remarks on Prose Translation of 'Beowulf'* (1940).
   P.s. 3: *Finn and Hengest* (1982), p. 9 n. 1.
   P.s. 4: *Beowulf* (2002).
   P.s. 5: *Beowulf* (2014)
   S.s. 1: University of Leeds (1920), pp. 182-84. H2. (Scheme A and B) Second Year: Monday 10.00: Old English Verse with a special study of *Beowulf, The Fight at Finnesburg*.
   S.s. 2: University of Leeds (1921), pp. 192-94, (1922), pp. 133-35, and (1923), pp. 133-35. H2. (Scheme A and B) Second and Third Year: Monday 10.00: Old English Verse with a special study of *Beowulf, The Fight at Finnesburg*.
   S.s. 3: Scull-Hammond (2017a). Leeds academic years 1920-1921 (p. 122); 1921-22 (p. 125) and 1923-24 (p. 131). Lists several lectures or classes to take place during the year for which Tolkien may have responsibility: *Beowulf, The Fight at Finnesburg* on Mondays at 10.00 a.m.

126. Bergin, Osborn Joseph (Edited by). *Sgéalaigheacht Chéitinn. Stories from Keating's History of Ireland, edited with introduction, notes, and vocabulary.*

Dublin: Hodges, Figgis and Co., 1930 (3rd ed.).
>Description: Annotations in pencil and ink on text and inside back cover.
>Collection: Tolkien's personal Celtic library, preserved at the Weston library under the auspices of the English Faculty Library (Oxford).

127.   Bernardi, Theodor von. *Volksmährchen und epische Dichtung*. Leipzig: Verlag von S. Hirzel, 1871.
>P.s.: *Tolkien On Fairy-stories* (2008), p. 306.

128.   Berry, Wendell. *The Hidden Wound*. Boston: Houghton Mifflin and Co., 1970.
>Description: Christmas 1970: A copy was sent to Tolkien by the publisher Austin Olney. Tolkien (through Joy Hill) thanked with a letter (18 December 1970).
>Collection: Private [Oronzo Cilli].

129.   Bertelsen, Henrik. *Dansk Sproghistorisk Læsbog. Første del, Oldtid og middelalder (400-1500),* Vol. I – Tekster og sproghistoriske oversigter (unbound part). København: Gildendalske Boghandel, 1905.
>Collection: Tolkien's personal Celtic library, preserved at the Weston library under the auspices of the English Faculty Library (Oxford).

130.   _____. *Dansk Sproghistorisk Læsbog. Første del, Oldtid og middelalder (400-1500),* Vol. II – Kommentar og ordliste (unbound part). København: Gildendalske Boghandel, 1905.
>Collection: Tolkien's personal Celtic library, preserved at the Weston library under the auspices of the English Faculty Library (Oxford).

131.   Best, Richard Irvine. 'Notes on the script of Labor na hUidre'. *Ériu: The Journal of the School of Irish Learning*, Dublin, Vol. VI, 1912, pp. 161-74.
>P.s.: *Sir Gawain and the Green Knight* (1925), p. xxvi. Tolkien and Gordon write: 'For bibliography of the Irish and French analogues of Sir Gawain, see the bibliography in Kittredge's study'. [NED] In Kittredge's study, this article is mentioned in 'I. Fled Bricrend' (p. 290 n. 3, 292).

132.   _____. 'The Tragic Death of Cúrói mac Dári'. *Ériu: The Journal of the School of Irish Learning*, Dublin, Vol. II, 1905, pp. 18-35.
>P.s.: *Sir Gawain and the Green Knight* (1925), p. xxvi. Tolkien and Gordon write: 'For bibliography of the Irish and French analogues of *Sir Gawain*, see the bibliography in Kittredge's study'. [NED] In Kittredge's study, this article is mentioned in 'II. Gawain and the Green Knight' (p. 293).

133.   *Bestiary, A* 1240-50. [Middle English Bestiary, see Mätzner, R. Morris and Th. Wright *Rel. Ant.*].
>P.s. 1: MS. Tolkien A 21/13 *The English MSS*. fol. 203. [Tolkien Papers, Bodleian Library, Oxford]
>P.s. 2: 'Chaucer as a Philologist: *The Reeve's Tale*' (1934), p. 133.

134.   Beveridge, Erskine. *The 'Abers' and 'Invers' of Scotland*. Edinburgh: W. Brown, 1923.
>P.s.: *Philology: General Works* (IV 1924, for 1923), 30.

135.   *Bevis of Hampton* 1320. [Middle English romance, see Zupitza].
>P.s.: MS. Tolkien A 21/13 *The English MSS*. fol. 203. [Tolkien Papers, Bodleian Library, Oxford]

136.   Binz, Gustav. 'Zeugnisse zur germanischen Sage in England'. *Beiträge zur Geschichte der deutschen Sprache und Literatur*, Vol. XX. Halle: Max Niemeyer, 1895, pp. 141-223.
>P.s.: *Finn and Hingest* (1982), p. 16 n. 17.

137. Birch, Walter de Gray (Edited by). *Cartularium Saxonicum: A Collection of Charters Relating to Anglo-Saxon History,* Vol. I A.D. 430-539. London: Whiting & Co. Ltd., 1885.
   Description: Signed by Tolkien and Rev. John Silvester Davies. Contains the letter from the lay historian to Tolkien requesting assistance translating charters, which Tolkien has annotated with the help of these tomes. The set also includes an examination regulation notice from the Oxford University Board of Examiners.
   Collection: Private [Sold by Simon Finch Rare Books Ltd.]./
   P.s.: *Finn and Hengest* (1982), p. 39 n. 15; p. 52 n. 39; p. 77 n. 84.
   S.s.: Finch (2002), p. 52.

138. _____ (Edited by). *Cartularium Saxonicum: A Collection of Charters Relating to Anglo-Saxon History,* Vol. II A.D. 840-947; Appendix A.D. 601-947. London: Whiting & Co. Ltd., 1887.
   Description: Signed by Tolkien on endpapers and dated '1927'.
   Collection: Private [Sold by Simon Finch Rare Books Ltd.].
   P.s.: *Finn and Hengest* (1982), p. 39 n. 15; p. 52 n. 39; p. 77 n. 84.
   S.s.: Finch (2002), p. 52.

139. _____ (Edited by). *Cartularium Saxonicum: A Collection of Charters Relating to Anglo-Saxon History,* Vol. III A.D. 948-975; Appendix. London: Whiting & Co. Ltd., 1893.
   Description: Signed by Tolkien on endpapers and dated '1927'.
   Collection: Private [Sold by Simon Finch Rare Books Ltd.].
   P.s.: *Finn and Hengest* (1982), p. 39 n. 15; p. 52 n. 39; p. 77 n. 84.
   S.s.: Finch (2002), p. 52.

140. _____ (Edited by). *Cartularium Saxonicum: A Collection of Charters Relating to Anglo-Saxon History,* Vol. IV Index. London: Whiting & Co. Ltd., 1889.
   Description: Signed by Tolkien on endpapers and dated '1927'.
   Collection: Private [Sold by Simon Finch Rare Books Ltd.].
   P.s.: *Finn and Hengest* (1982), p. 39 n. 15; p. 52 n. 39; p. 77 n. 84.
   S.s.: Finch (2002), p. 52.

141. Birney, Earle. 'English Irony before Chaucer'. Offprint from *University of Toronto Quarterly*, Vol. 6, no. 4, July 1937, pp. 538-87.
   Description: Annotated by Tolkien on four pages. Includes a label added by Stan Revell to books owned by Tolkien, 'From the Library of J.R.R. Tolkien'
   Collection: Private [Christina Scull & Wayne G. Hammond].
   S.s. Scull-Hammond (2018a).

142. Bishop, Ian. *Pearl in Its Setting. A Critical Study of the Structure and Meaning of the Middle English Poem.* Oxford: B. H. Blackwell, 1968.
   Notes: Contains an acknowledgement to Gervase Mathew and Tolkien: 'To both of these scholars I am indebted for their great kindness and encouragement at that time [when Bishop was working towards his B.Litt.]; had it not been for the interest which they took in my work then, the present study would probably never have been begun (p. vii).'
   S.s.: Scull-Hammond (2017a), p. 777. Early March 1969, Bishop had been a B.Litt. student working on Pearl in the early 1950s, supervised first by Gervase Mathew and then by Tolkien. He sends a copy of his book.

143. _____. 'The Significance of the 'Garlande Gay' in the Allegory of Pearl'. *The Review of English Studies*, Vol. VIII, no. 29. London: Oxford University Press, 1957, pp. 12-21.
   S.s.: Scull-Hammond (2017a), p. 777.

144. Bjarnarson, Birkir (Edited by). *Sturlunga saga* I (unbound part). Rejkyavík: Sigurður Kritjánsson, 1908.
   Description: Contains invoice for purchase: '5/12/1929' | '14/11/1929'.
   Collection: Tolkien's personal Celtic library, preserved at the Weston library under the auspices of the English Faculty Library (Oxford).

145. _____ (Edited by). *Sturlunga saga* II (unbound part). Rejkyavík: Sigurður Kritjánsson, 1909.
   Description: Contains invoice for purchase: '5/12/1929' | '14/11/1929'.
   Collection: Tolkien's personal Celtic library, preserved at the Weston library under the auspices of the English Faculty Library (Oxford).

146. _____ (Edited by). *Sturlunga saga* III (unbound part). Rejkyavík: Sigurður Kritjánsson, 1913.
   Description: Contains invoice for purchase: '5/12/1929' | '14/11/1929'.
   Collection: Tolkien's personal Celtic library, preserved at the Weston library under the auspices of the English Faculty Library (Oxford).

147. _____ (Edited by). *Sturlunga saga* IV (unbound part). Rejkyavík: Sigurður Kritjánsson, 1915.
   Description: Contains invoice for purchase: '5/12/1929' | '14/11/1929'.
   Collection: Tolkien's personal Celtic library, preserved at the Weston library under the auspices of the English Faculty Library (Oxford).

148. Björkman, Erik (Edited by). *Morte Arthure mit Einleitung, Anmerkungen und Glossar*. Heidelberg: Carl Winter, 1915.
   Description: signed by J.R.R. Tolkien on front free end-paper with occasional annotations.
   Collection: Private [Pieter Collier, sold by Sotheby's, 12 July 2002].
   P.s. 1: MS. Tolkien A 12/2 *Commentary on Sir Gawain, lines 1999-2523* fol. 31. Tolkien quotes 'þe renke relys abowte and rusches to þe erthe' (v. 2795). [Tolkien Papers, Bodleian Library, Oxford].
   P.s. 2: *Sir Gawain and the Green Knight* (1925), p. 979. Tolkien and Gordon quote: 'Thane spyces vnspayly þay sepndyde thereaftyre' (v. 235, p. 8).
   P.s. 3: *Sir Gawain and the Green Knight* (1967) 'Select Bibliography: editions of texts quoted more than once in the notes', p. 156.

149. _____. *Zur Englischen Namenkunde*. Series: Studien zur englischen Philologie, Vol. 47. Halle: Max Neimeyer, 1912.
   Description: Tolkien's calligraphic signature, dated '1926' and, 'from E.V.G.' on the front free endpaper.
   Notes: Bound with [A. 150].
   Collection: Private [Sold by Simon Finch Rare Books Ltd.].
   S.s.: Finch (2002), p. 51.

150. _____. *Nordische Personennamen in England in alt- und frühmittel-englischer Zeit: ein Beitrag zur englischen Namenkunde*. Series: Studien zur englischen Philologie, Vol. 37. Halle: Max Neimeyer, 1910.
   Description: Tolkien's calligraphic signature, dated '1926' and, 'from E.V.G.' on the front free endpaper.
   Notes: Bound with [A. 149].
   Collection: Private [Sold by Simon Finch Rare Books Ltd.].
   S.s.: Finch (2002), p. 51.

151. Blackburn, Francis Adalbert. *Exodus and Daniel. Two Old English Poems Preserved in MS. Junius 11 in the Bodleian Library of the University of Oxford, England*. Boston and London: D. C. Heath, 1907.

P.s. 1: *Sigelwara land* (1932), p. 193 n. 4.
P.s. 2: *The Old English Exodus* (1982), p. ix.
P.s. 3: *Beowulf* (2014), p. 226.

152. Blackwood, Algernon. *The Education of Uncle Paul.* London: Macmillan, 1909.
S.s.: Anderson (2002), p. 90 n. 6.

153. _____. *The Extra day.* London: Macmillan, 1915.
S.s.: Anderson (2002), p. 90 n. 6.

154. _____. *The Glamour of the Snow.*
S.s. 1: Lobdell (1981), p. 10.
S.s. 2: Nelson (2004), p. 177.

155. _____. *The Wendigo*, 1910.
P.s.: 'Nomenclature of *The Lord of the Rings*' (1966), p. 768 '*Crack of Doom.*' Tolkien writes: 'In this story crack is here used in the sense 'fissure', and refers to the volcanic fissure in the crater of Orodruin in Mordor. (I think that this use is ultimately derived from Algernon Blackwood, who as my memory seems to recall used it in this way in one of his books read very many years ago.)'. Probably Tolkien refers to this novel because Blackwood wrote: 'his white and terrified face peeping through the crack of the tent door flap' (p. 125).
S.s. 1: Lobdell (1981), p. 10.
S.s. 2: Nelson (2004), p. 177.

156. _____. *The Willows*, 1907.
S.s. 1: Lobdell (1981), p. 10.
S.s. 2: Nelson (2004), p. 177.

157. _____ and Violet A. Peorn. *Through the crack.* (1925].
S.s.: Anderson (2002), p. 90 n. 6.

158. Blake, William. *The poetical works of William Blake: including the unpublished French Revolution, together with the Minor prophetic books, and selections from the Four Zoas, Milton & Jerusalem.* Series: Oxford edition. Edited by John Sampson. London: Oxford University Press, 1913.
Notes: We know that in 1919 Tolkien read some of William Blake's prophetic books, as he himself admitted, but unfortunately we do not know which of the twelve books. I chose to insert a book that contains them all and perhaps Tolkien could have read.
S.s. 1: Hammond-Scull (2014), p. 25. 'In regard to the use of orc by both Tolkien and the poet William Blake, Tolkien wrote on 29 December 1968 to Sigrid Fowler that according to a note in one of his old diaries, dated 21 February 1919, he had then just been reading part of Blake's prophetic books, which I had never seen before, and discovered to my astonishment several similarities ol nomenclature (though not necessarily in function) e.g. *Tiriel, Vala, Orc*. Whatever explanation of these similarities – few: most of Blake's invented names are as alien to me as his 'mythology''.
S.s. 2: Scull-Hammond (2017a), pp. 69, 115, 407, 773, 774 '31 December 1968, Tolkien writes to Joy Hill, [...] he answered the query to prevent his being associated with Blake, whose works he detests.'

159. Blakeley, Lesley. 'The Lindisfarne s/ð Problem'. Offprint from *Studia Neophilologica* XXII, no. 1, 1949-50, pp. 15-47.
Description: Inscribed by Tolkien 'The Lindisfarne s/ð Problem, Blakeley (B'ham [Birmingham])'. Includes a label added by Stan Revell to books owned by Tolkien, 'From the Library of J.R.R. Tolkien'
Collection: Private [Christina Scull & Wayne G. Hammond].
S.s. Scull-Hammond (2018a).

160. Blanch, Robert J. *Sir Gawain and Pearl. Critical Essays.* Series: A Midland book, MB 93. Bloomington: Indiana University Press, 1966.
P.s.: *Sir Gawain and the Green Knight* (1967) 'Select Bibliography', p. 154.

161. Bliss, Alan J. (Edited by). *Sir Orfeo.* Series: Oxford English Monographs, 4. London Oxford University Press, 1954.
Notes: Tolkien was one of the General Editors for the series. On p. vi: 'It is a pleasure to record the debts which I have incurred in preparing this edition of *Sir Orfeo*: to Professor J.R.R. Tolkien, whose penetrating scholarship is an inspiration to all who have worked with him.' [C: 4]
Collection: Tolkien's personal Celtic library, preserved at the Weston library under the auspices of the English Faculty Library (Oxford).

162. _____. *Sir Orfeo.* Oxford: At the Clarendon Press, 1966 (2nd ed.)
P.s.: *Sir Gawain and the Green Knight* (1975), p. 24.

163. Blöndal, Sigfús. *Islandsk-dansk ordbog*, Vol. I. Reykjavik: I kommission hos verslun Þ. B. Þorlákssonar og hos H. Aschehoug, KØbenhavn, 1920.
P.s.: 'Middle English 'Losenger" (1953), p. 73 n. 1.

164. _____. *Islandsk-dansk ordbog*, Vol. II. Reykjavik: I kommission hos verslun Þ. B. Þorlákssonar og hos H. Aschehoug, KØbenhavn, 1920.
P.s.: 'Middle English 'Losenger" (1953), p. 73 n. 1.

165. Blöndal, Sigfús and Sigurður Sigtryggson. *Myndir úr Menningarsögu Íslands á Lidnum Öldum.* Reykjavík: Bokaverzlun Sigfúsar Eymundssonar, 1929.
Description: Inscribed on page after front flyleaf: 'Til herra professor J.R.R. Tolkien. | Glaðileg Tóe 1929. | Ben S. Þhórarinsson.' Card between the pages of ill. 64 and 65.
Collection: Tolkien's personal Celtic library, preserved at the Weston library under the auspices of the English Faculty Library (Oxford).

166. Bloomfield, Morton Wilfred and Leonard Newmark. *A linguistic introduction to the history of English.* New York: Alfred A. Knopf, 1963.
Description: Signed by Tolkien on front free endpaper 'Tolkien | 4/64' with bookplate of Desmond Morris.
Collection: Private [Sold by Invaluable Auction, Lot. 208, April 2018].

167. Blümel, Rudolf. 'Grundbedingungen der quantitierenden und der akzentuierende Dichtung'. *Streitberg-Festgabe* [A. 2228]. Leipzig: Market und Petter, 1924.
P.s.: *Philology: General Works* (V 1926, for 1924).

168. *Blyssen (The Five Joys of the Virgin).* [Old English Sermon, see R. Morris].
P.s.: MS. Tolkien A 21/7 fol. 47. [Tolkien Papers, Bodleian Library, Oxford]

169. Boccaccio, Giovanni. *Filostrato.*
P.s. 1 In the edition of *Troilus and Criseyde* (1935) [A. 410] belonged to Tolkien, he wrote near the title *Il Filostrato*, 'to taken' (p. xxiii).
P.s. 2: MS. Tolkien A 34/3 Texts for the BBC radio presentation of the translation of *Sir Gawain and the Green Knight*, 1953 fol. 221. [Tolkien Papers, Bodleian Library, Oxford].
P.s. 3: *Sir Gawain and the Green Knight* (1975), p. 17.

170. Böddeker, Karl. *Altenglische Dichtungen des MS. Harley 2253: Mit grammatik und glossar.* Berlin: Weidmann, 1878.
P.s. 1: MS. Tolkien A 12/1 *Commentary on Sir Gawain, lines 37-1987* fol. 1. [Tolkien Papers, Bodleian Library, Oxford].
P.s. 2: MS. Tolkien A 12/2 *Commentary on Sir Gawain, lines 1999-2523* fol. 33. [Tolkien Papers, Bodleian Library, Oxford].

P.s. 3: MS. Tolkien A 11 *Notes on Pearl* fol. 124. Tolkien quotes 'IV. Des Dichters Reue. (Eine Ironie)' on page 151 and refers to *Specimens of lyric poetry* by Wright [A. 2555]. [Tolkien Papers, Bodleian Library, Oxford].
P.s. 4: *Sir Gawain and the Green Knight* (1925), p. 88 line 327 *bayþen*; p. 107, line 1495 *meré*.
P.s. 5: *Sir Gawain and the Green Knight* (1930, 2nd ed.), p. 88 line 477 *heng vp þyn ax*. Tolkien and Gordon cite p. 134.

171. Bodley, John Eduard Courtenay. *France*. London: Macmillan and Co., 1907 (new and revised edition).
Description: Inscribed in back of flyleaf: 'J.R.R. Tolkien. | (from G. B. Smith)'. Rebound with the crest to the front board of the King Edward's School that the two of them attended together.
Collection: Private [Oronzo Cilli].

172. Bodmer, Frederick. *The Loom of Language: A Guide to Foreign Languages for Home Students*. Edited by Lancelot Hogben. London: George Allen & Unwin, 1943.
S.s.: Scull-Hammond (2017a), p. 216. 2 October 1937 Susan Dagnall writes to Tolkien. The idea for *The Loom of Language* originated apparently at a weekend party by a group including one of Allen & Unwin's authors, and the synopsis was passed to them for possible development.

173. Boer, Richard Constant (Edited by). *Grettis saga Ásmundarsonar*. Series: Altnordische Saga-Bibliothek, 8. Halle: Max Niemeyer, 1900.
Description: Contains invoice for purchase: '5/12/1929' & '14/11/1929'.
Collection: Tolkien's personal Celtic library, preserved at the Weston library under the auspices of the English Faculty Library (Oxford).
P.s.: *Beowulf* (2014), p. 210.

174. Boethius. *King Alfred's Old English of Boethius De Consolatione Philosophiae*. Edited by Walter John Sedgefield. Oxford: At the Clarendon Press, 1899.
S.s.: Scull-Hammond (2017a), p. 46. April 1913: Tolkien will need to become familiar with a range of literary and philological subjects and set texts as prescribed in the Oxford Regulations of the Board of Studies, knowing that he may be examined on them in ten papers at the end of *Trinity Term 1915*: Old English texts.

175. Bohnenberger, Karl. 'Zur den Ortsnamen'. *Germanica: Eduard Sievers zum 75. Geburtstage*. [A. 2088] Halle: Max Niemeyer, 1925.
P.s.: *Philology: General Works* (VI 1927, for 1925), p. 52.

176. Boileau Despréaux, Nicolas. *L'Art poétique*. Edited by David Nicol Smith. Cambridge: The University Press, 1919.
S.s.: University of Leeds (1921), p. 154. English Language and Literature - Scheme A. Texts and Period selected for 1921-22. (e) History of Criticism: Special Texts suggested for study. Ordinary Degree of B.A. with Honours. Final Examinations.

177. Bolingbroke, Henry Saint-John. *Letters on the Spirit of Patriotism and on the Idea of a Patriot King*. Edited by Arthur Hassall. Oxford: At the Clarendon Press, 1917.
S.s.: University of Leeds (1921), pp. 144-45. English Literature, text selected for 1921-22. Ordinary Degree of B.A.; p. 191 English Language and Literature. F1. Final Course (English Literature) (ii) The History of English Literature from 1700 to 1765.

178. Bonjour, Adrien. *The Disgression in Beowulf*. Series: Medium Ævum monographs, 5. Oxford: Published for the Society for the Study of Mediæval Languages and Literature by Basil Blackwell, 1950.
Notes: On page vii, Bonjour thanks Tolkien: 'Finally, I express my gratitude to the many Beowulfian scholars cited in the notes, and particularly to three of the greatest, Prof. Fr. Klaeber, Prof. J. R. R. Tolkien, and the late Prof. R. W. Chambers'. Bonjour writes in the Conclusions:

'We therefore think it necessary to point out that we adopt Professor Tolkien's views concerning the general structure of *Beowulf* ... Professor Tolkien admirably shows in fact "the universal significance which is given to the fortunes" of the hero.' (p. 70).

179. _____. 'Monsters Crouching and Critics Rampant: Or the *Beowulf* Dragon Debated'. Offprint from PMLA (*Publications of the Modern Language Association of America*), Vol. LXVI, no. 1. New York: Modern Language Association, March 1953, pp. 304-12.
   S.s.: Scull-Hammond (2017a), p. 421. 29 April 1953: A copy was sent to Tolkien by the author.

180. *Book of Proverbs* [Hebrew Bible | Christian Old Testament, see Wycliffe III].
   P.s.: MS. Tolkien A 13/2 *Notes and drafts of lectures on Chaucer: Pardoner's Tale* fol. 160. [Tolkien Papers, Bodleian Library, Oxford]. Tolkien refers to *Pardoner's Tale* ('What was comaunded unto Lamuel | Nat Samuel, but Lamuel, seye I', 584-5) and he quotes in Latin '*noli regibus o Lamuhel ... non recordentur amplius*' and English 'It is not for kings, O Lemuel ... his misery no more' (xxxi, 4-7).

181. Boorde, Andrew. *The Fyrst boke of the introduction of knowledge made by Andrew Boorde; or A dietary of Health*. Series: E.E.T.S. (Early English Text Society), ES 10. Edited by Frederick James Furnivall. London: Published for the Early English Text Society by Kegan Paul, Trench, Trübner and Co., 1870.
   P.s. 1: MS. Tolkien A 21/13 fol. 119. Note by Tolkien, 'Books in Exeter Library useful', with shelfmarks, on back of photostat reading list dated October 1913. Tolkien writes: 'All EETS publications'. [Tolkien Papers, Bodleian Library, Oxford]
   P.s. 2: *Letters* 241 (1962). From a letter to Allen & Unwin.
   P.s. 3: *English and Welsh* (1963), p. 3. Tolkien quotes 'caws bobi' from 'The Welshman and Wales', v. 15 p. 26 'I do loue cawse boby'.
   NED: 'W' (1928), p. 23 'Waistcoat, *colloq.* or *vulgar*. 4. a.' 1557 – 'I cause a man to lye in his doublet, and a woman in her waste cote.'

182. Borgström, Edward (Edited by). *The Proverbs of Alfred*. Lund: Hakan Ohlsson, 1908.
   Description: Bookmark at pp. 40-41.
   Collection: Tolkien's personal Celtic library, preserved at the Weston library under the auspices of the English Faculty Library (Oxford).

183. Borowski, Bruno. *Lautdubletten im Altenglischen*. Series: Sächsische forschungsinstitut in Leipzig. Forschungsinstitut für neuere philology, III. Halle: Max Niemeyer, 1924.
   P.s.: *Philology: General Works* (VI 1927, for 1925), p. 41.

184. Borroff, Marie. *Sir Gawain and the Green Knight; a stylistic and metrical study*. London: E. Ward, 1962.
   P.s.: *Sir Gawain and the Green Knight* (1967) 'Select Bibliography', p. 153.

185. *Bósa saga ok Herrauds* [*The Saga of Bósi and Herraud*].
   P.s.: *Dragons* (1938), pp. 44-45.

186. Boswell, James. *The Life of Samuel Johnson*, Vol. I.
   S.s.: Lewis (2009a), p. 222. Letter to Owen Barfield – 28 March 1938: Lewis writes: 'I have written to Tolkien. 'Omit no manly degree of importunity' towards Harwood' (letter to Joseph Simpson, p. 347: 'Omit no decent nor manly degree of importunity').

187. _____. *The Journal of a Tour to the Hebrides with Samuel Johnson*. Series: Temple Classic. London: Joseph Malaby Dent, 1920.

S.s.: University of Leeds (1921), p. 141. English Literature, text selected for 1921-22. Ordinary Degree of B.A.; p. 190 English Language and Literature. Int. 1 Intermediate Course (Literature).

188. _____. *Selections from James Boswell's Life of Samuel Johnson*. Edited by Robert William Chapman. Oxford: At the Clarendon Press, 1919.
- S.s. 1: University of Leeds (1920), p. 135 English Literature. Texts Selected for 1920-21; p. 181. English Language and Literature. Int. I Intermediate Course (Literature).
- S.s. 2: University of Leeds (1921), p. 145. English Literature, text selected for 1921-22. Ordinary Degree of B.A.; p. 156. English Language and Literature - Scheme B. Texts for 1921-22. (d) Outlines of the History of English Literature. Ordinary Degree of B.A. with Honours. Final Examinations; p. 191 English Language and Literature. F1. Final Course (English Literature) (ii) The History of English Literature from 1700 to 1765.

189. Bosworth, Joseph. *An Anglo-Saxon Dictionary, based on the manuscript collections of the late Joseph Bosworth*. Edited and enlarged by T. Northcote Toller. Oxford: At the Clarendon Press, 1897.
- Description: Tolkien corrects the *Beowulf* entry by crossing it out entirely and with telling exclamation marks. The *Dictionary* describes *Beowulf* as an ancient Swedish saga re-worked and Christianized by an Anglo-Saxon poet, a laughable notion for Tolkien who had definitively argued against any earlier, Swedish version.
- Collection: Private [Sold by Simon Finch Rare Books Ltd.].
- P.s.: *English and Welsh* (1963), p. 27 n. 1. Tolkien quotes: 'Reht Romwala *jus Quiritum*' from 'Riht, II.' p. 796.
- S.s.: Finch (2002), p. 51.

190. _____. *An Anglo-Saxon Dictionary, based on the manuscript collections of the late Joseph Bosworth. Supplement*. Edited and enlarged by T. Northcote Toller. Oxford: At the Clarendon Press, 1921.
- Description: Extensively annotated. This volume shows Tolkien's interest in mythical creatures: the entry for *hol*, which is annotated, is the root form of 'Hobbit'. The first sentence of Tolkien's *The Hobbit* begins: 'In a hole in the ground lived a hobbit...'. *Ge-smeágan* is also annotated; its definition (to pat, caress, soothe) must bear relation to Gollum (Smeágal) in *The Hobbit* and *The Lord of the Rings*.
- Collection: Private [Sold by Simon Finch Rare Books Ltd.].
- P.s. 1: MS. Tolkien A 11 *Notes on Pearl* fol. 114. [Tolkien Papers, Bodleian Library, Oxford].
- P.s. 2: *Some Contributions to Middle-English Lexicography* (1925), p. 210.
- P.s. 3: *The Devil's Coach-Horses* (1925), p. 332.
- P.s. 4: *Philology: General Works* (V 1926, for 1924), p. 46.
- P.s. 5: *The Old English Exodus* (1982), p. ix.
- S.s.: Finch (2002), p. 51.

191. Bouterwek, Heinrich. 'Angelsächsische glosse'. *Zeitschrift fur deutsches Alterthum*, Vol. IX, 401-529. Leipzig: Weidmannsche Buchhandlung, 1853.
- S.s.: *Sigelwara land* (1932), p. 189 n. 3. Tolkien writes 'Bonterwek' instead of 'Bouterwek'.

192. Bouterwek, Karl Wilhelm. *Cædmon's des Angelsachsen biblische Dichtungen*. Iserlohn: J. Bädeker, 1849.
- Notes: Bound together with *Ein angelsächsisches Glossar* (1851) [A. 193].
- Description: On inside cover inscribed: 'Cædmon'. Twice in pencil and in ink: 'O. W. Tancock. | Sherbone. February 1877 | [From B. Quaitch from Dr Bosworth's Library.]'. Autographed and dated on front flyleaf in pencil: 'Oxford | 1926'. Annotated by both owners in pencil, and once in ink by OWT.
- Collection: Tolkien's personal Celtic library, preserved at the Weston library under the auspices of the English Faculty Library (Oxford).
- P.s.: *The Old English Exodus* (1982), p. ix.

193. _____. *Cædmon's des Angelsachsen biblische Dichtungen, 2. Ein Angelsächsisches Glossar*. Iserlohn: J. Bädeker, 1851.

Notes: Bound together with *Cædmon's des Angelsachsen biblische Dichtungen* (1849) [A. 192].
Description: On inside cover inscribed: 'Cædmon'. Twice in pencil and in ink: 'O. W. Tancock. | Sherbone. February 1877 | [From B. Quaitch from Dr Bosworth's Library.]'. Autographed and dated on front flyleaf in pencil: 'Oxford | 1926'. Annotated by both owners in pencil, and once in ink by OWT.
Collection: Tolkien's personal Celtic library, preserved at the Weston library under the auspices of the English Faculty Library (Oxford).

194. _____. *Cædmon's des Angelsachsen biblische Dichtungen*. Gütersloh: Bertelsmann, 1854 (3rd ed.).
Notes: Contains *Erläuterungen*.
P.s.: *The Old English Exodus* (1982), p. ix.

195. Bowcock, Elijah Wood. *Shropshire place-names*. Shrewsbury: Wilding and Son, 1923.
P.s.: *Philology: General Works* (IV 1924, for 1923), p. 30.

196. Bradley, Andrew Cecil. *Oxford Lectures on Poetry*. London: Macmillan and Co., 1909 (2nd ed.).
P.s.: *Exeter College library register*. Tolkien's borrowing record: *Trinity Term 1915* from 31 May to 16 June.

197. _____. *Shakespearean Tragedy. Lectures on Hamlet, Othello, King Lear, Macbeth*. London: Macmillan and Co., 1904 (2nd ed.).
P.s.: *Exeter College library register*. Tolkien's borrowing record: *Trinity Term 1915* from 31 May to 16 June.

198. Bradley, George Granville (Edited by). *Latin Prose Composition*. London, 1902.
Description: 'King Edward's School. Dated: '27 Nov. 1910'. Notes and doodles throughout (see pp. 49, 56, 129), most Tolkien's hand (but see 169, 193)' [Judith Priestman 1994, rev. 2016].
Collection: Weston Library, Bodleian Libraries (Oxford).
S.s.: Zettersten (2011), p. 78 'During my last visit to the Tolkien Collection at the Bodleian Library, Oxford, I went through Tolkien's books in his private library from his school time, which his family had donated to the Bodleian in July 1982.'

199. Bradley, Henry. *The Making of English*. London: Macmillan, 1904.
P.s.: *Henry Bradley* (1923), p. 4
S.s. 1: University of Leeds (1920), p. 182. English Language and Literature. F2. Final Course (English Literature and Language). Books reccomended.
S.s. 2: University of Leeds (1921), p. 192 English Language and Literature. F2. Final Course (English Literature and Language). Books recommended; p. 193 English Language and Literature. Honours and M.A. Courses. A. Language. H1. First Year. Books Recommended.

200. _____. *The numbered sections in Old English poetical MSS*. Offprint from the proceedings of the British Academy, Vol. VII. London: Published for the British Academy by Humphrey Milford, Oxford University Press, 1915.
Description: Lacks signature, but on page 23 there are substantial corrections in ink in Tolkien's hand.
Collection: Private [Pieter Collier].

201. _____. 'Psalm LXXXV 9'. Offprint from *The Journal of Theological Studies*, Vol. 21, no 83, April 1920, pp. 243-44.
Collection: Private [Christina Scull & Wayne G. Hammond].

202. _____ and Robert Seymour Bridges (Edited by). *On the Terms 'Briton'*,

'British', 'Britisher'; Preposition at end by Henry Watson Flower. Series: Society for Pure English, Tract, no. XIV. Oxford: Clarendon Press, 1923.
>P.s. 1: *Philology: General Works* (IV 1924, for 1923), p. 34.
>P.s. 2: *Philology: General Works* (V 1926, for 1924), p. 30.

203. Brady, Caroline. 'The Old English Nominal Compounds in -*rád*'. Offprint from PMLA (*Publications of the Modern Language Association of America*), Vol. LXVII, June 1952, pp. 538-71.
>Description: Inscribed by the author 'To Professor Tolkien, with highest esteem'. Two corrections by the author. Includes a label added by Stan Revell to books owned by Tolkien, 'From the Library of J.R.R. Tolkien'.
>Collection: Private [Christina Scull & Wayne G. Hammond].
>S.s.: Scull-Hammond (2018a).

204. Bramley, Henry Ramsden (Edited by). *The Psalter, or Psalms of David and certain canticles*. Translated by Richard Rolle of Hample. Oxford: At the Clarendon Press, 1884.
>Collection: Tolkien's personal Celtic library, preserved at the Weston library under the auspices of the English Faculty Library (Oxford).

205. Brandl, Alois. 'Englische Literatur'. *Grundriss der germanischen Philologie*, Vol. II [A. 1841]. Heldensage, Literaturgeschichte, Metrik. Strassburg: Karl J. Trübner, 1893.
>P.s.: *Beowulf* (2002) 'Version B', p. 103.

206. Brate, Erik. *Nordische lehnwörter im Orrmulum*. Halle: Druck von E. Karras, 1884
>Description: Signed on front and includes a label added by Stan Revell to books owned by Tolkien, 'From the Library of J.R.R.Tolkien'.
>Collection: Private [Pieter Collier].

207. Braune, Wilhelm. *Althochdeutsches Lesebuch*. Halle: Max Niemeyer, 1921.
>Description: Signed in the front by J.R.R. Tolkien and annotations in pencil.
>Collection: Private [Sold by Peter Harrington Antiquarian Bookseller].
>P.s.: Mythopoeic Society, *Parma Eldalamberon* 20 (2012), Q26 'Otfrid Excerpt' pp. 108-09. Tolkien writes a transliterations into the Qenya from the *Liber euangeliorum* (*Evangelienbuch*).
>S.s.: Peter Harrington (2003), p. 25.

208. Brehier, Louis (Translated and edited by). *Histoire Anonyme de la Première Croisade*. Series: Classiques de l'histoire de France au Moyen Âge, 4. Paris: Libraire Ancienne Honore Champion, 1924.
>Description: Presentation copy from L. Stampa to Tolkien, signed by Tolkien on front free endpaper and with a few scattered annotations.
>Collection: Private [Sold by Simon Finch Rare Books Ltd.].
>S.s.: Finch (2002), p. 52.

209. Bremer, Otto. *Ethnographie der germanischen Stämme*. Strassburg: Trübner, 1904 (2nd unchanged impression).
>Description: Autographed on frontispiece: 'John Reuel Tolkien | e. coll. exon. | oxon. | mdccccxiv'. Annotations on pages 20, 122.
>Collection: Taylor Institution Library, Bodleian Libraries (Oxford).

210. Brett, Cyril. 'Notes on *Sir Gawayne and the Green Knight*'. MLR (*The Modern Language Review*), Vol. 8, no. 2. April 1913, pp. 160-64.
>P.s.: *Sir Gawain and the Green Knight* (1925), p. 105, line 1440.

211. _____. 'Notes on "Cleanness" and "Sir Gawayne"'. MLR (*The Modern Language Review*), Vol. 10, no. 2. April 1915, pp. 188-95.
   P.s.: Tolkien's unpublished letter to Cyril Brett, 24th August 1924. Concerning his (and Gordon's) edition of *Sir Gawain and the Green Knight*: 'All that you have published on the matter, I may say we have considered most carefully.' [Special Collections and Archives - Cardiff University, GB 1239 401/16].

212. _____. 'Notes on Passages of Old and Middle English'. MLR (*The Modern Language Review*), Vol. 14, no. 1. January 1919, pp. 1-9.
   P.s.: Tolkien's unpublished letter to Cyril Brett, 24th August 1924. Concerning his (and Gordon's) edition of *Sir Gawain and the Green Knight*: 'All that you have published on the matter, I may say we have considered most carefully.' [Special Collections and Archives - Cardiff University, GB 1239 401/16].

213. Breuer, Hermann (Edited by). *Jaufre: ein altprovenzalischer Abenteuerroman des XIII. Jahrhunderts ; nach Wendelin Foersters Kollationen auf Grund sämtlicher bekannter Handschriften mit Einleitung, Inhaltserzählung, Anmerkungen, Namen- und Wortverzeichnis*. Series: Gesellschaft für Romanische Literatur, 18. jahrg. 1925, l. bd.; der ganzen reihe, bd. 46. Göttingen: Gedruckt für die Gesellschaft für Romanische Literatur; Halle : M. Niemeyer, 1925.
   Description: In ink, on front free endpaper, in Tolkien's hand: "J.R.R. Tolkien"
   Collection: Private [Pieter Collier].

214. Brewster, William Tenney. *Specimens of Modern English Literary Criticism*. London: Macmillan, 1919.
   S.s.: University of Leeds (1921), p. 141. English Literature, text selected for 1921-22. Ordinary Degree of B.A.; p. 154. English Language and Literature - Scheme A. Texts and Period selected for 1921-22. (e) History of Criticism: Special Texts suggested for study. Ordinary Degree of B.A. with Honours. Final Examinations. Pt. suggested: *Charles Lamb*.

215. Bright, James Wilson. *An Outline of Anglo-Saxon grammar: published as an appendix to "An Anglo-Saxon reader"*. Published as an appendix to *An Anglo-Saxon Reader*. London: Swan Sonnenschein, 1911 (4th ed.).
   Description: Inscribed on front cover: 'J.R.R. Tolkien'. Includes a label added by Stan Revell to books owned by Tolkien, 'From the Library of J.R.R. Tolkien', on inside front cover.
   Collection: Marion E. Wade Center, Wheaton College (Wheaton, Illinois).

216. _____. 'Notes on the Cædmonian *Exodus*'. MLN (*Modern Language Notes*), Vol. 17, no. 7. Baltimore: Johns Hopkins Press, January 11, 1902, pp. 424-25.
   P.s.: *The Old English Exodus* (1982), p. ix.

217. _____. 'On the Anglo-Saxon Poems *Exodus*'. MLN (*Modern Language Notes*), Vol. 27. Baltimore: Johns Hopkins Press, April 1912, pp. 13-19.
   P.s.: *The Old English Exodus* (1982), p. ix.

218. Brock, Edmund (Edited by). *Morte Arthure Or, the death of Arthur* [alliterative version from Thornton MS.]. Series: E.E.T.S. (Early English Text Society), OS 8. London: Published for the Early English Text by H. Milford, Oxford University Press, 1865.
   Description: Tolkien bought the book in September 1919.
   P.s. 1: MS. Tolkien A 21/13 fol. 119. Note by Tolkien, 'Books in Exeter Library useful', with shelfmarks, on back of photostat reading list dated October 1913. Tolkien writes: 'All EETS publications'. [Tolkien Papers, Bodleian Library, Oxford]
   P.s. 2: *A Middle English Vocabulary* (1922). Tolkien refers to the *Morte Arthure* on the term

'Rescowe, Rescoghe' (*make reschewes*, 433).
P.s. 3: *The Fall of Arthur* (2013), p. 80n. Christopher Tolkien writes: 'My father used a copy of the Early English Text Society edition, as revised by Edmund Brock, 1871, which he acquired in September 1919, and which I have used for the quotations in this book.'
P.s. 4: *Beowulf* (2014), p. 190.
NED: #2 1. | 'W' (1928), p. 54. 'Walloping, *ppl. a.*' – a 1400 'Sweltand knyghtez Lyes wyde opyne welterande one walopande stedez' (2147).

219. Bromwich, Rachel. *Trioedd Ynys Prydein; The Welsh triads*. Cardiff: University of Wales Press, 1951.
P.s.: *Sir Gawain and the Green Knight* (1967) 'Select Bibliography', p. 155.

220. Brooke, Rupert. *The Old Vicarage, Grantchester*. London: Sidgwick & Jackson Ltd., 1916.
P.s.: *Letters* 96 (1945). To Christopher Tolkien. Tolkien writes: 'stands the clock at ten to three, and is there honey still for tea' but in Brooke's poem is: 'stands the Church clock at ten to three? And is there honey still for tea?'

221. Brook, George Leslie. *The Harley lyrics: the Middle English lyrics of Ms. Harley 2253*. Series: Old and Middle English texts, 302. Manchester: The University Press, 1956 (2nd ed.).
P.s.: *Sir Gawain and the Green Knight* (1967) 'Select Bibliography: editions of texts quoted more than once in the notes', p. 156.

222. _____. *1914 and other poems*. London: Sidgwick & Jackson, 1915.
S.s. 1: Scull-Hammond (2006b), p. 819. 'If he followed G.B. Smith's advice in July 1915, he bought and read all of Rupert Brooke's poems, and at least one of the volumes of *Georgian Poetry*' [A. 1520].
S.s. 2: Scull-Hammond (2017a), p. 77.

223. Brooks, Harold. F. (Translated from the Old English by). *Dream of the Rood*. Dublin: Sign of the Three Candles, 1942.
Description: Inscribed on front cover by JRRT: 'A very poor and inaccurate affair'.
Collection: Tolkien's personal Celtic library, preserved at the Weston library under the auspices of the English Faculty Library (Oxford).
S.s.: #1 Holland (1949), p. 138. Appendix XI: Oxford Examinations for Prisoners of War. B.1 Old English: vv. 60-73.

224. Brooks, Kenneth Robert (Edited by). *Andreas and the Fates of the Apostles*. Oxford: At the Clarendon Press, 1961.
Description: A copy was sent to Tolkien by the author, with dedication. Autographed and marked on front title page: 'from K. R. B.' Contains loose copy of letter, JRRT to the author, 13.11.1961, the author's reply and his inscription, which JRRT requested and never stuck into the book. Annotated in pencil.
Collection: Tolkien's personal Celtic library, preserved at the Weston library under the auspices of the English Faculty Library (Oxford).
S.s.: Scull-Hammond (2017a), p. 612. Brooks had worked on the text as a D. Phil, student under Tolkien. Tolkien asks Brooks for a signed slip to insert in his copy. He will buy one or two copies for presents [C. 7].

225. Brown, Arthur C. 'The Knight of the Lion'. PMLA (*Publications of the Modern Language Association of America*), Vol. XX, no. 13. New York: Modern Language Association, 1905, pp. 673-706.
P.s.: *Sir Gawain and the Green Knight* (1925), p. xxvi. Tolkien and Gordon write: 'For bibliography of the Irish and French analogues of *Sir Gawain*, see the bibliography in Kittredge's study'. [*NED*] In Kittredge's study, this article is mentioned in 'VI. La Mule sanz Frain' (p. 299).

226. _____. 'Iwain: A Study in the Origins of Arthurian Romance'. *Harvard studies and notes in philology and literature*, Vol. VIII, 1903.
> P.s.: *Sir Gawain and the Green Knight* (1925), p. xxvi. Tolkien and Gordon write: 'For bibliography of the Irish and French analogues of *Sir Gawain*, see the bibliography in Kittredge's study'. [*NED*] In Kittredge's study, this essay (particularly 'The Combat Motive', pp. 51-56) is mentioned In Kittredge's study, this article is mentioned in 'I. Fled Bricrend' (p. 293), 'VI. La Mule sanz Frain' (p. 299).

227. Brown, Carleton (Edited by). *Religious Lyrics of the Fourteenth Century*. Oxford: At the Clarendon Press, 1923.
> Notes: Kenneth Sisam sent a copy to him in January 1924.
> P.s.: MS. Res. e. 308 *Sir Gawain and the Green Knight*. [Tolkien Papers, Bodleian Library, Oxford]
> S.s.: Scull-Hammond (2017a), p. 133.

228. _____. 'Somer soneday'. Offprint from *Studies in English Philology: a miscellany in honor of Frederick Klaeber*. Minneapolis: University of Minnesota Press, 1929, pp. 362-74.
> Description: In manuscript on front: 'To J.R.R.T with sincere regards C.B.' Includes a label added by Stan Revell to books owned by Tolkien, 'From the Library of J.R.R. Tolkien'.
> Collection: John J. Burns Special Collections Library, Boston College (Chestnut Hill, Massachusetts).

229. _____. 'The text of The Canterbury tales by John M. Manly and Edith Rickert'. Offprint from MLN (*Modern Language Notes*), Vol. 55, no. 8, December 1940, pp. 606-21.
> Description: In manuscript on front: 'To J.R.R.T an essay in MS. relationships C.B.' Includes a label added by Stan Revell to books owned by Tolkien, 'From the Library of J.R.R. Tolkien'.
> Collection: John J. Burns Special Collections Library, Boston College (Chestnut Hill, Massachusetts).

230. _____. 'A Thirteenth-Century Manuscript from Llanthony Priory'. Offprint from *Speculum*, Vol III, no.4, October, 1928, pp 588-595. Cambridge, MA: The Mediaeval Academy of America, 1928
> Description: Inscribed by the author 'To J.R.R.T with Kindest regards C.B.'
> Collection: Private [Pieter Collier]

231. _____ and Geoffrey Victor Smithers, (Revised and edited). *Religious Lyrics of the XIVth century*. Oxford: At the Clarendon Press, 1952 (2nd ed.).
> Description: Annotated in pencil. Bookmark at pp. 32, 33.
> Collection: Tolkien's personal Celtic library, preserved at the Weston library under the auspices of the English Faculty Library (Oxford).

232. Browne, Thomas. *Hydriotaphia, Urn Burial, or, a Discourse of the Sepulchral Urns lately found in Norfolk*.
> S.s. 1: University of Leeds (1920), p. 135 English Literature. Texts Selected for 1920-21. Text suggested: *Urn Buriali*; p. 139 English Language and Literature: English Literature. Text selected for 1920-21. Texts Selected for 1920-21. Ordinary Degree of B.A. with Honours. Final Course and Examination; p. 181. English Language and Literature. Int. I Intermediate Course (Literature).
> S.s. 2: Scull-Hammond (2017a), p. 77.

233. _____. *Pseudodoxia Epidemica or Enquiries into very many received tenets and commonly presumed truths* [*Vulgar Errors*].
> P.s.: *Letters* 240 (1962). To Mrs Pauline [Baynes] Gash. Tolkin writes: 'the hanging up of a kingfisher to see the way of the wind, which comes from Sir T. Browne' (Book III).
> S.s.: University of Leeds (1921), p. 154. English Language and Literature - Scheme A. Texts and Period selected for 1921-22. (d) Texts suggested for study with Special Period 1637-1700.

Ordinary Degree of B.A. with Honours. Final Examinations. Text suggested: *Pseudodoxia Epidemica*, Book I.

234. _____. *Religio medici*.
S.s. 1: University of Leeds (1921), p. 154. English Language and Literature - Scheme A. Texts and Period selected for 1921-22. (d) Texts suggested for study with Special Period 1637-1700. Ordinary Degree of B.A. with Honours. Final Examinations. Text suggested: *Religio Medici*.
S.s. 2: Scull-Hammond (2017a), p. 77.

235. _____. *Religio medici, Letter to a friend &c., and Christian morals*. Series: Golden treasury series. Edited by William Alexander Greenhill. London and New York: Macmillan and Co., 1889.
Description: Includes a label added by Stan Revell to books owned by Tolkien, 'From the Library of J.R.R. Tolkien'.
Collection: Private [Aaron O'Brien].

236. _____. *The Works of Sir Thomas Browne*, Vol. III. Pseudodoxia Epidemica, Books IV-VII, or, Enquiries into Very Many Received Tenets and Commonly Presumed Truths. Edited by Geoffrey Keynes. London: Faber & Gwyer Ltd., 1928.
Description: Borrowed 2 June 1949. From archives book Tues. Oct. 26, 1948 – Friday March 9th 1956.
Collection: Library & Archives, Merton College (Oxford).

237. Browne, William Hand. *The taill of Rauf Coilyear: a Scottish metrical romance of the fifteenth century*. Baltimore: The Johns Hopkins Press, 1903.
P.s.: *Sir Gawain and the Green Knight* (1925), p. xxvi. Tolkien and Gordon write: 'For bibliography of the Irish and French analogues of *Sir Gawain*, see the bibliography in Kittredge's study'. [NED] In Kittredge's study, this article is mentioned in 'XIII. Rauf Coilyear' (p. 306).

238. Browning, Robert. *The Pied Piper of Hamelin*. London, New York: F. Warne, 1845.
P.s.: *Letters* 234 (1961). To Jane Neave. Tolkien writes: 'I am sorry about *The Pied Piper*. I loathe it. God help the children! I would as soon give them crude and vulgar plastic toys. Which of course they will play with, to the ruin of their taste. Terrible presage of the most vulgar elements in Disney.'
S.s. 1: Anderson (2002), p. 253 n. 8.
S.s. 2: Scull-Hammond (2017a), p. 6.
S.s. 3: Scull-Hammond (2006b), p. 815.
Reading period: 1900 – 1906 (S.s.: Scull-Hammond (2017c), p. 1053).

239. _____. *Pocket volume of selections from the poetical works of Robert Browning*. London: Smithe, Elder & Co., 1898.
S.s.: University of Leeds (1921), p. 156. English Language and Literature - Scheme B. Texts for 1921-22. (d) Outlines of the History of English Literature. Ordinary Degree of B.A. with Honours. Final Examinations.

240. Brown, Ursula (Edited by). *Þorgils Saga ok Hafliða*. Series: Oxford English Monographs, 3. London: Oxford University Press, 1952.
Notes: Tolkien was one of the General Editors for the series. In the Introduction: 'valuable criticism and advice'.
S.s.: Scull-Hammond (2006b), p. 728: was originally a thesis produced under Tolkien's supervision.

241. Bruce, Douglas, J. *The evolution of Arthurian romance from the beginners down to the year 1300*, Vol. I. Series: Hesperia, Erganzungsreihe: Schriften zur englischen philologie, 8. Gottingen: Vandenhoeck & Ruprecht, 1928 (2nd ed.).

P.s.: *Sir Gawain and the Green Knight* (1967) 'Select Bibliography', p. 154.

242. _____. *The evolution of Arthurian romance from the beginners down to the year 1300*, Vol. II. Series: Hesperia, Erganzungsreihe: Schriften zur englischen philologie, 9. Gottingen: Vandenhoeck & Ruprecht, 1928 (2nd ed.).
P.s.: *Sir Gawain and the Green Knight* (1967) 'Select Bibliography', p. 154.

243. Brugmann, Karl. *Kurze vergleichende Grammatik der indogermanischen Sprachen. Auf Grund des fünfbändigen Grundrisses der vergleichenden Grammatik der indogermanischen Sprachen von K. Brugmann und B. Delbrück verfasst*. Strassburg: Karl J. Trübner, 1904.
Description: Signed on flyleaf along with the signatures of other previous and later owners: 'JRR Tolkien'.
Collection: Private [TolkienLibrary.com].

244. _____. *Die Syntax des Einfachen Satzes im Indogermanischen*. Berlin and Leipzig: De Gruyter, 1925.
Description: Signed and annotated by Tolkien. There are annotations, corrections and linguistic musings throughout the book, for example on p. 135 'E. he went & did it, he has been and gone and done it'.
Collection: Private [Sold by Simon Finch Rare Books Ltd.].
P.s.: *Philology: General Works* (VI 1927, for 1925), p. 54 n. 10.
S.s.: Finch (2002), p. 52.

245. _____ and Whilelm Streitberg, (Edited by). *Festschrift für Berthold Delbrück. Special issue of Indogermanische Forschungen*. Strassburg: Verlag von Karl J. Trübner, 1912–1913.
Collection: Taylor Institution Library, Bodleian Libraries (Oxford).

246. _____ and Hermann Osthoff. *Morphologische Untersuchungen auf dem Gebiete der indogermanischen Sprachen*, Vol. I. Leipzig: S. Hirzel, 1878.
Description: Bound together with tomes II and III, inscribed in a delicate hand on the inside cover, 'JRR Tolkien | 1926' (Jason Fisher, unpublished).
Collection: The Science Fiction and Fantasy Research Collection of the Cushing Memorial Library and Archives at Texas A&M University.

247. _____ and Hermann Osthoff. *Morphologische Untersuchungen auf dem Gebiete der indogermanischen Sprachen*, Vol. II. Leipzig: S. Hirzel, 1879.
Description: Bound together with tomes I and III, inscribed in a delicate hand on the inside cover, 'JRR Tolkien | 1926' (Jason Fisher, unpublished).
Collection: The Science Fiction and Fantasy Research Collection of the Cushing Memorial Library and Archives at Texas A&M University.

248. _____ and Hermann Osthoff. *Morphologische Untersuchungen auf dem Gebiete der indogermanischen Sprachen*, Vol. III. Leipzig: S. Hirzel, 1880.
Description: Bound together with tomes I and II, inscribed in a delicate hand on the inside cover, 'JRR Tolkien | 1926' (Jason Fisher, unpublished).
Collection: The Science Fiction and Fantasy Research Collection of the Cushing Memorial Library and Archives at Texas A&M University.

249. _____ and Hermann Osthoff. *Morphologische Untersuchungen auf dem Gebiete der indogermanischen Sprachen*, Vol. IV. Leipzig: S. Hirzel, 1881.
Description: Bound together with tome V, inscribed in a delicate hand on the front free endpaper, 'JRR Tolkien | 1926' (Jason Fisher, unpublished).
Collection: The Science Fiction and Fantasy Research Collection of the Cushing Memorial

Section A

Library and Archives at Texas A&M University.

250. _____ and Hermann Osthoff. *Morphologische Untersuchungen auf dem Gebiete der indogermanischen Sprachen*, Vol. V. Leipzig: S. Hirzel, 1890.
Description: Bound together with tome IV, inscribed in a delicate hand on the front free endpaper, 'JRR Tolkien | 1926' (Jason Fisher, unpublished).
Collection: The Science Fiction and Fantasy Research Collection of the Cushing Memorial Library and Archives at Texas A&M University.

251. Buchan, John. *The Blanket of the dark*. London: Hoder, 1931.
S.s.: Shippey (2007), p. 78.

252. _____. *Castle Gay*. Series: Dickson McCunn, 2. London: Hodder & Stoughton, 1930.
S.s.: Shippey (2007), p. 77. Shippey writes: 'the best [Buchan's novel] and funniest centring on the Glasgow grocer Dickson MacCunn. Like Bilbo Baggins, Dickson is a figure of the greatest bourgeois respectability – Gloin says disparagingly of Bilbo "looks more like a grocer than a burglar!"

253. _____. *The Dancing Floor*. London: Hodder & Stoughton, 1926.
S.s.: Shippey (2007), p. 78.

254. _____. 'The Far islands'. *Blackwood's Magazine*, November 1899.
S.s.: Shippey (2007), p. 78.

255. _____. *Greenmantle*. London: T. Nelson and Sons, 1925.
P.s.: *Philology: General Works* (VI 1927, for 1925), p. 63.

256. _____. *The House of the Four Winds*. Series: Dickson McCunn, 3. London: Hodder & Stoughton, 1935.
S.s.: Shippey (2007), p. 77. Shippey writes: 'the best [Buchan's novel] and funniest centring on the Glasgow grocer Dickson MacCunn. Like Bilbo Baggins, Dickson is a figure of the greatest bourgeois respectability – Gloin says disparagingly of Bilbo "looks more like a grocer than a burglar!"

257. _____. *Huntingtower*. Series: Dickson McCunn, 1. London: Hodder & Stoughton, 1922.
S.s.: Shippey (2007), p. 77. Shippey writes: 'the best [Buchan's novel] and funniest centring on the Glasgow grocer Dickson MacCunn. Like Bilbo Baggins, Dickson is a figure of the greatest bourgeois respectability – Gloin says disparagingly of Bilbo "looks more like a grocer than a burglar!" But like Bilbo he also has a buried romantic streak, and in the first of the MacCunn novels, *Huntingtower* (1922), he finds himself an illicit guardian of rescued jewels, and committed to storming "the Dark Tower" to rescue a princess.

258. _____. *Midwinter: certain travellers in old England*. London & New York: Hodder and Stoughton Ltd., 1923.
S.s.: Shippey (2007), p. 77. Shippey writes: 'It is, however, Buchan's relatively little-known historical novels which seem most likely to have roused Tolkien's admiration. The most strikingly Tolkienian is *Midwinter*. Among many connections, it uses the word "halfling" in chapter 1, where we also meet characters strongly reminiscent of Bill Ferny and Tom Bombadil, while a volunteer corps of "Rangers" appears near the end ... There are obvious parallels with the Ring, the Sammath Naur, Gollum, and even Gollum's way of speaking.'

259. _____. *The novel and the fairy tale*. Series: The English association pamphlet, 79. London: Oxford University Press, 1931.
S.s.: Shippey (2007), p. 78.

260. _____. *The Path of the King*. London: T. Nelson & Sons, 1923.
S.s.: Shippey (2007), p. 78.

261. _____. *Witch Wood*. London: Hodder & Stoughton, 1927.
S.s.: Shippey (2007), p. 78.

262. Buckhurst, Helen T. MacMillan. *An Elementary Grammar of Old Icelandic*. London: Methuen and Co. Ltd. 1925.
P.s.: *Philology: General Works* (VI 1927, for 1925), p. 57 n. 13.

263. Buckingham, George Villiers, Duke of. *The Rehearsal*. Stratford-upon-Avon: Shakespeare Head Press, 1914.
S.s. 1: University of Leeds (1920), p. 139 English Language and Literature: English Literature. Text selected for 1920-21. Texts Selected for 1920-21. Ordinary Degree of B.A. with Honours. Final Course and Examination.
S.s. 2: University of Leeds (1921), p. 154. English Language and Literature - Scheme A. Texts and Period selected for 1921-22. (d) Texts suggested for study with Special Period 1637-1700. Ordinary Degree of B.A. with Honours. Final Examinations. In particular *Address to the Reader*.

264. Budge, E. A. T. Wallis. *The Babylonian story of the Deluge and the Epic of Gilgamish*. With an account of the Royal Libraries of Nineveh. London: British Museum, 1920.
Description: Signature on the firt page: 'J.R.R. Tolkien'. Includes a label added by Stan Revell to books owned by Tolkien, 'From the Library of J.R.R. Tolkien'.
Collection: Private [Chris Carroll]

265. _____. *An Egyptian Reading Book for Beginners. Being a Series of Historical, Funereal, Moral, Religious and Mythological Texts Printed in Hueroglyphic Characters Together with a Transliteration and a Complete Vocabulary*. London: Kegan Paul Trench Trübner & Co Ltd., 1896.
Description: Inscribed by Tolkien on front flyleaf: 'JRR Tolkien | 1923'.
Collection: Private [Pieter Collier, sold by Dominic Winter, 6-7 November 2013].
P.s. 1: *On fairy-stories* (1947), p. 4. Tolkien quotes: '*I shall enchant my heart ... and in very truth I shall live*' (p. xxi).
P.s. 2: *Tolkien On Fairy-stories* (2008), p. 37 n. 1,
P.s. 3: *Tolkien On Fairy-stories* (2008) 'Manuscript B [MS. Tolkien 4, fols. 73-120]', pp. 179, 218. Tolkien cites: 'The Tale of the Two Brothers' (pp. 1-40).
S.s. 1: Scull-Hammond (2006b), p. 820.

266. _____. *The chapters of coming forth by day or the Theban recension of the Book of the dead: the Egyptian hieroglyphic text ed. from numerous papyri*, Vol. I. Series: Books on Egypt and Chaldaea, 28. London: Kegan Paul, Trench, Trübner, 1910.
Description: Tolkien's ink inscription to front free end paper. Small paper label of subsequent owner adhered just below Tolkien's inscription.
Collection: Private [Pieter Collier].

267. _____. *The chapters of coming forth by day or the Theban recension of the Book of the dead: the Egyptian hieroglyphic text ed. from numerous papyri*, Vol. II. Series: Books on Egypt and Chaldaea, 29. London: Kegan Paul, Trench, Trübner, 1910.
Description: Tolkien's ink inscription to front free end paper. Small paper label of subsequent owner adhered just below Tolkien's inscription.
Collection: Private [Pieter Collier].

268. _____. *The chapters of coming forth by day or the Theban recension of the Book of the dead: the Egyptian hieroglyphic text ed. from numerous papyri*, Vol. III. Series: Books on Egypt and Chaldaea, 30. London: Kegan Paul, Trench, Trübner, 1910.
   Description: Tolkien's ink inscription to front free end paper. Small paper label of subsequent owner adhered just below Tolkien's inscription.
   Collection: Private [Pieter Collier].

269. Buga, Kazimieras. 'Die Vorgeschichte der aistischen (baltischen) Stömme in Lichte der Ortsnamenforschung'. *Streitberg-Festgabe*. Leipzig: Market und Petter, 1924. [A. 2228].
   P.s.: *Philology: General Works* (V 1926, for 1924).

270. Bugge, Sophus and Magnus Olsen. *Norges Indskrifter med de aeldre Runer: udgivne for Det Norske historiske Kildeskriftfond ved Sophus Bugge*, Vol. I. Kristiania: A. W. Broggers Bogtrykkeri, 1891.
   Description: Signed by Tolkien on front free endpaper.
   Collection: Private [Sold by Simon Finch Rare Books Ltd.].
   S.s.: Finch (2002), p. 52.

271. _____ and Magnus Olsen. *Norges Indskrifter med de aeldre Runer: udgivne for Det Norske historiske Kildeskriftfond ved Sophus Bugge*, Vol. II. Kristiania: A. W. Broggers Bogtrykkeri, 1903.
   Description: Signed by Tolkien on front free endpaper.
   Notes: Bound with [A. 272].
   Collection: Private [Sold by Simon Finch Rare Books Ltd.].
   S.s.: Finch (2002), p. 52.

272. _____ and Magnus Olsen. *Norges Indskrifter med de aeldre Runer: udgivne for Det Norske historiske Kildeskriftfond ved Sophus Bugge*, Vol. III. Kristiania: A. W. Broggers Bogtrykkeri, 1924.
   Description: Signed by Tolkien on front free endpaper.
   Notes: Bound with [A. 271].
   Collection: Private [Sold by Simon Finch Rare Books Ltd.].
   S.s.: Finch (2002), p. 52.

273. Bülbring, Karl Daniel. *Altenglisches Elementarbuch*. Heidelberg: Carl Winter, 1902.
   Description: 'Exeter College. Inscriptions on flyleaf and front endpaper on pastedown: 'John Reuel Tolkien | Coll. exon. Oxon de litt. phil. germ. mcmxiii | EB'. Annotations throughout' [Judith Priestman 1994, revd. 2016].
   Collection: Weston Library, Bodleian Libraries (Oxford).

274. _____. 'E and Æ in the Vespasian Psalter'. *An English Miscellany: Presented to Dr Furnivall in Honour of His Seventy-fifth Birthday*. Oxford: At the Clarendon Press, 1901, pp. 34-45.
   P.s.: *Sir Gawain and the Green Knight* (1925), p. 123 n. 2.

275. Bulwer-Lytton, Edward. *The Pilgrims of the Rhine*. London: Saunders and Otley, 1834.
   P.s.: *Letters* 319 (1970). From a letter to Roger Lancelyn Green. Tolkien writes: 'I can now remember was that (I think) it was by Bulwer-Lytton, and contained one story I was then very fond of called *Puss Cat Mew*'. Probably it was *The Wooing of Master Fox*, chapter XII of this book.

276. Bunyan, John. *Grace abounding to the chief of sinners*. Boston: American tract society, 1905.
   S.s. 1: University of Leeds (1920), p. 139 English Language and Literature: English Literature. Text selected for 1920-21. Texts Selected for 1920-21. Ordinary Degree of B.A. with Honours. Final Course and Examination.
   S.s. 2: University of Leeds (1921), p. 154. English Language and Literature - Scheme A. Texts and Period selected for 1921-22. (d) Texts suggested for study with Special Period 1637-1700. Ordinary Degree of B.A. with Honours. Final Examinations. In particular *Address to the Reader*.

277. _____. *The Holy War*. London: Joseph Malaby Dent, 1901.
   P.s.: *Tolkien On Fairy-stories* (2008) 'Manuscript A. [MS Tolkien 4, fols. 59-77]', p. 191.

278. _____. *Life and death of Mr. Badman*. Cambridge: The University Press, 1905.
   S.s.: University of Leeds (1921), p. 154. English Language and Literature - Scheme A. Texts and Period selected for 1921-22. (d) Texts suggested for study with Special Period 1637-1700. Ordinary Degree of B.A. with Honours. Final Examinations. In particular *Address to the Reader*.

279. _____. *Pilgrim's progress*. London: Ginn and Co., 1917.
   S.s.: University of Leeds (1921), p. 141. English Literature, text (Pt. I) selected for 1921-22. Ordinary Degree of B.A.; p. 189 English Language and Literature. Int. 1 Intermediate Course (Literature) (Pt. I).

280. Burchfield, Robert William. 'A Source of Scribal Error in Early Middle English MSS.' Offprint from *Medium Ævum*, Vol. 22, no. 1, 1953, pp. 10-17.
   Description: Inscribed by JRRT: 'Burchfield | Ormulum | Scribal Confusion of t and gh. Based | on G with (illegible) stroke | omitted'.
   Collection: Tolkien's personal Celtic library, preserved at the Weston library under the auspices of the English Faculty Library (Oxford).

281. Burke, Edmund. *Reflections on the French Revolution*. London: Joseph Malaby Dent, 1910.
   S.s.: University of Leeds (1921), p. 156. English Language and Literature - Scheme B. Texts for 1921-22. (d) Outlines of the History of English Literature. Ordinary Degree of B.A. with Honours. Final Examinations.

282. _____. *Speech on American Taxation*. London: Ginn & Company, 1905.
   S.s.: University of Leeds (1921), p. 135 English Literature. Texts Selected for 1920-21; p. 181. English Language and Literature. Int. I Intermediate Course (Literature).

283. Burkitt, Miles Crawford. Prehistory: *A Study of Early Cultures in Europe and the Mediterranean Basin*. Cambridge: The University Press, 1925 (2nd ed.).
   S.s.: Scull-Hammond (2017b), p. 492. 'We have since been informed by Christopher Tolkien that all of the 'Father Christmas' cave images appear in a book which had once belonged to his father, *Prehistory: A Study of Early Cultures in Europe and the Mediterranean Basin* by M.C. Burkitt (2nd ed. 1925): the single mammoth and the dark bear, from the cave of Les Com-barelles, Dordogne, and the horse, from La Pasiega, Cantabria, appear in plate XI; the bison, from Altamira, Cantabria, in plate XII; the line of three mammoths, based on a mammoth from Font-de-Gaume, Dordogne, in plate XV; the woolly rhinoceros with a glint in its eye, from La Colombiere, and the galloping boar and stag below it to the left, from Altamira, in plate XXVII; the stag at middle left, from Valltorta (Castellon), and the human figure to the right of the bison, from the rock shelter of Tortosilla in south-eastern Spain, in plate XXXIV. Many of the human figures and stylized derivatives (from various Spanish sites) are reproduced in plate XXXVIII. Other human figures on horseback come from Bronze Age sites in Sweden, and the multi-oared boat at top left from a site near Lake Onega in Russia.'

284. Burnet, Gilbert. *History of His Own Time*.
   S.s.: University of Leeds (1921), p. 154. English Language and Literature - Scheme A. Texts

and Period selected for 1921-22. (d) Texts suggested for study with Special Period 1637-1700. Ordinary Degree of B.A. with Honours. Final Examinations. Books suggested IV-VI.

285. Burnham, Josephine May. *Concessive Constructions in Old English Prose*. Series: Yale Studies in English, XXXIX. New York: Henry Holt and Co., 1911.
P.s.: *Finn and Hengest* (1982), p. 122 n. 64.

286. Burrow, John Anthony. *A Reading of Sir Gawain and the Green Knight*. London: Routledge and Kegan Paul, 1965.
P.s.: *Sir Gawain and the Green Knight* (1967) 'Select Bibliography', p. 154.

287. Burton, Robert. *The Anatomy of Melancholy*. London: George Bell and Sons, 1912.
S.s.: University of Leeds (1921), p. 154. English Language and Literature - Scheme A. Texts and Period selected for 1921-22. (d) Texts suggested for study with Special Period 1637-1700. Ordinary Degree of B.A. with Honours. Final Examinations. In particular *Address to the Reader*.

288. Butcher, Samuel Henry. *Aristotle's theory of poetry and fine art: with a critical text and translation of the Poetics*. London: Macmillan, 1920.
S.s.: University of Leeds (1921), p. 154. English Language and Literature - Scheme A. Texts and Period selected for 1921-22. (e) History of Criticism: Special Texts suggested for study. Ordinary Degree of B.A. with Honours. Final Examinations.

289. Butler, Florence Ruth and Mabel Henrietta Prichard. *The Society of Oxford Home-Students: retrospects and recollections (1879-1921)*. Oxford: The Oxonian Press, Queen Street, Printed for private circulation [1930].
Description: Tolkien gives the book, with a dedication, to Simonne d'Ardenne.
Collection: Fonds J.R.R. Tolkien, Bibliothèque ALPHA principale, Université de Liège (Liège), Tol/058.

290. Butler, Samuel. *Erewhon, or, Over the range*. London: Trübner and Co., 1872.
P.s. 1: *Letters* 75 (1944). To Christopher Tolkien.
P.s. 2: *The Notion Club Papers* (1945), p. 172.
S.s.: Scull-Hammond (2006b), p. 818.

291. _____. *Hudibras. Written in the time of the late wars*. Cambridge: The University Press, 1905.
S.s. 1: University of Leeds (1920), p. 139 English Language and Literature: English Literature. Text selected for 1920-21. Texts Selected for 1920-21. Ordinary Degree of B.A. with Honours. Final Course and Examination. Extracts cantos 1, 2.
S.s. 2: University of Leeds (1921), p. 154. English Language and Literature - Scheme A. Texts and Period selected for 1921-22. (d) Texts suggested for study with Special Period 1637-1700. Ordinary Degree of B.A. with Honours. Final Examinations. In particular *Address to the Reader*.

292. Byrne, Evelyn B. and Otto Penzler. *Attacks of taste*. New York: The Gotham Book Mart & Gallery, 1971.
Notes: 100 copies numbered and signed by the editors for presentation. One of these copies was probably sent to Tolkien [e.g. Number 43 presented to Irwin Shaw who was one of the contributors.]
S.s.: Scull-Hammond (2017a), p. 796.

293. Cabrol, Fernand (Compiled by). *The Roman Missal in Latin and English, According to the Latest Roman Edition*. Tours: A. Mame and Sons, 1921.
S.s.: Mythopoeic Society, *Parma Eldalamberon* 20 (2012), Tolkien's transliterations into the Qenya: Q7 p. 41 nn. 7-8 'Pater Noster, Our Father, and Draft Statute'; Q8 (a/b) p. 46 nn. 9-11 'Our Father, Hail Mary, Gloria in Excelsis Deo, and Credo'; Q 18 p. 91 n. 24 'Te Deum Excerpt

('Formal style')'; Q19 p. 93 n. 25 'Te Deum Excerpt'; Q20 p. 96 nn. 26-28 'Te Deum Excerpt'; Q. 25 p. 107 n. 29 'Excerpts from the Mass'.

294.   Cædmon. *Cædmon's Hymn*.
> Notes: In the Bodleian Library, Oxford, is preserved the note with analysis of Old English religious terms and their pagan associations, dated 'Oct. 1927'. Extract from Tolkien's notes: [MS. Tolkien A 29(a) *Lecture notes, 1920s-1930s, on prose extracts and poems from Sweet's* fol. 93:] 'It is remarkable how many of the primary words of the Christian religion were in Germanic, but especially in Old English (the earliest after Gothic to be Christianized) of nature, and therefore ultimately 'heathen' origin. In OE the words for God, heaven, hell, sin, redeemer, saviour, cross, paradise, Easter, Lent, holy, saint, eucharist, baptism, and so on, are all native.'
> Collection: Taylor Institution Library, Bodleian Libraries (Oxford).
> P.s.: 'Chaucer as a Philologist: *The Reeve's Tale*' (1934), p. 135.
> S.s.: Kerry (2011), p. 132.

295.   Caesar, Julius. *Caesar's Gallic war.* Edited by James Bradstreet Greenhough et alii. Boston: Ginn, 1898.
> Description: King Edward's School. Inscribed: 'J.R.R. Tolkien II - KEHS. February 1907' [Judith Priestman 1994, revd. 2016].
> Collection: Weston Library, Bodleian Libraries (Oxford).
> S.s.: Zettersten (2011), p. 78 'During my last visit to the Tolkien Collection at the Bodleian Library, Oxford, I went through Tolkien's books in his private library from his school time, which his family had donated to the Bodleian in July 1982.'

296.   Calder, George (Translated by). *Auraicept Na N-éces. the scholars' primer*. Edinburgh: J. Grant, 1917.
> Description: Autographed: 'John Reuel Tolkien'. Dated on front flyleaf: 'Leeds 1922'.
> Collection: Tolkien's personal Celtic library, preserved at the Weston library under the auspices of the English Faculty Library (Oxford).

297.   Callaway, Canon [Henry]. *Nursery tales, traditions, and histories of the Zulus, in their own words with a translation into English, and notes*. Springvale: Natal, John A. Blair, 1868.
> P.s.: # 1 *Tolkien On Fairy-stories* (2008), p. 306.

298.   Campbell, Alistair. *Old English Grammar*. Oxford: At the Clarendon Press, 1959.
> P.s.: MS. Tolkien A 11 *Notes on Pearl* fol. 114. [Tolkien Papers, Bodleian Library, Oxford].
> S.s.: Edwards (2014), p. 244. Tolkien is thanked in his acknowledements; he had been one of the examiners of Campbell's B.Litt. thesis.

299.   _____. *Frithegodi monachi Breviloquium vitae Beati Wilfredi et Wulfstani cantoris Narratio metrica de Sancto Swithuno*. Series: Thesaurus mundi, 1. Turici: Omslaget påklæbet Padova, 1950.
> Description: On the flyleaf Campbell has inscribed: 'J.R.R.T. editoris observantiae pignus'.
> Collection: Private.

300.   _____ and Fryske Akademy. *Thet Freske Riim en Tractatus Alvinus*. The Hague: Nijhoff, 1952.
> Description: Inscribed by the editor in ink, on front free endpaper: 'J.R.R. T. | with the editor's | kind regards.' Corrections by Tolkien in pencil on three pages (pp. 2, 39, 194). The editor, Alistair Campbell, was one of Tolkien's friends, and often visited him at his Merton Street flat in Oxford, where Tolkien spent his last years following Edith's death in 1971.
> Collection: Private [Pieter Collier].

301.   Campbell, Joseph Francis. *Popular Tales of the West Highlands*, Vol. I.

Edinburgh: Edmonston and Douglas, 1890.
    P.s. 1: *On Fairy-stories* (1947), p. 47 n. 2, 48 n. 1.
    P.s. 2: *Tolkien On Fairy-stories* (2008), p. 37 n. 1, p. 38 n. 1.
    P.s. 3: *Tolkien On Fairy-stories* (2008) 'Manuscript B [MS. Tolkien 4, fols. 73-120]', p. 217 [*The Sea-Maiden*], p. 218 [*The Battle of the Birds*].
    S.s.: Shippey (1992), p. 298.

302. _____. *Popular Tales of the West Highlands*, Vol. II. Edinburgh: Edmonston and Douglas, 1890.
    P.s.: *Tolkien On Fairy-stories* (2008), p. 37 n. 1.
    S.s.: Shippey (1992), p. 298.

303. _____. *Popular Tales of the West Highlands*, Vol. III. Edinburgh: Edmonston and Douglas, 1892.
    P.s.: *Tolkien On Fairy-stories* (2008), p. 98.
    S.s.: Shippey (1992), p. 298.

304. _____. *Popular Tales of the West Highlands*, Vol. IV. Edinburgh: Edmonston and Douglas, 1893.
    P.s. 1: *On Fairy-stories* (1947), p. 47 n. 2, p. 80 n. 2.
    P.s. 2: *Tolkien On Fairy-stories* (2008), p. 37 n. 1, p. 74 n. 3.
    S.s.: Shippey (1992), p. 298.

305. Campbell, Killis. *The Seven Sages of Rome*. London: Ginn & Co., 1907.
    P.s.: MS. Tolkien A 21/13 *The English MSS.* fol. 203. [Tolkien Papers, Bodleian Library, Oxford].

306. Campbell, Roy. *The Flaming Terrapin*. London: Jonathan Cape, 1924.
    P.s.: *Letters* 83 (1944). From a letter to Christopher Tolkien.
    S.s.: Scull-Hammond (2006b), p. 819.

307. _____. *Flowering Rifle*. London: Longmans, 1939.
    P.s.: *Letters* 83 (1944). From a letter to Christopher Tolkien.
    S.s.: Scull-Hammond (2006b), p. 819.

308. Campbell, Thomas and John Watkinson. *A Philosophical Survey of the South of Ireland, in a series of letters to John Watkinson*. Dublin: W. Whitestone, 1778.
    P.s.: *Oxford University Press Archives* (Oxford). A slip written by Tolkien on the etymology of 'Wake' used ('W' p. 31) [A. 1721].
    NED: #2 f. | 'W' (1928), p. 31 'Wake, 3.' 1778 – 'The series of ceremonies used on the night, … that the corpse remains unburied, is what they call a wake' (Letter XXIII, p. 210).

309. 'Cannibalism and Arctic Exploration'. *Pall Mall Gazette*, 16 August, 1884.
    P.s.: MS. Tolkien A 19/3 *Etymologies or history of Walrus* fols. 162-195. [Tolkien Papers, Bodleian Library, Oxford].
    S.s.: Tolkien, *Family Album* (1992), p. 42.
    NED: #2 i. | 'W' (1928), pp. 57-58 'Walrus, 3. *attrib.* and *comb.*' 1884 – 'Each walrus-boat carried six men' (p. 6).

310. Capes, William Wolfe. *Roman History*. London, 1879.
    Description: King Edward's School (with seal stamp on upper board). Inscribed: 'J.R.R. Tolkien | (Prize for 1st in 6th Class K.E.S Birm. | Midsummer 1905 under G. Brewerton)'. Loose leaf (Elvish) [Judith Priestman 1994, revd. 2016].
    Collection: Weston Library, Bodleian Libraries (Oxford).
    S.s. 1: Priestman (1992), p. 16 no. 18.
    S.s. 2: Zettersten (2011), p. 78 'During my last visit to the Tolkien Collection at the Bodleian Library, Oxford, I went through Tolkien's books in his private library from his school time, which his family had donated to the Bodleian in July 1982.'

S.s. 3: Scull-Hammond (2017a), p. 13.

311. Capgrave, John. *The Chronicle of England*. Series: Rerum Britannicarum Medii Ævi Scriptores, or Chronicles and Memorials of Great Britain and Ireland during the Middle Ages, Vol. I. Edited by the Rev. Francis Charles Hingeston. London: Longman, Brown, Green, Longmans, and Roberts, 1858.
    Description: Signed 'JRR Tolkien' on the front flyleaf.
    Collection: Private [Pieter Collier].

312. _____. *The Life of St Katharine of Alexandria*. Series: E.E.T.S. (Early English Text Society), OS 100. Edited by Frederick James Furnivall and Carl Horstmann. London: Published for the Early English Text Society by Kegan Paul, Trench, Trübner and Co., 1893.
    Description: Autographed and dated on front flyleaf:'sept. 1920.' Penciled annotations on p. 463 and on verso of blue page.
    Collection: Tolkien's personal Celtic library, preserved at the Weston library under the auspices of the English Faculty Library (Oxford).
    P.s.: MS. Tolkien A 21/13 fol. 119. Note by Tolkien, 'Books in Exeter Library useful', with shelfmarks, on back of photostat reading list dated October 1913. Tolkien writes: 'All EETS publications'. [Tolkien Papers, Bodleian Library, Oxford].

313. Carducci, Giosué. *Rime di m. Cino da Pistoia e d'altri del secolo XIV*. Firenze: G. Barbera, 1852.
    P.s.: *Sir Gawain and the Green Knight* (1925), p. xxvi. Tolkien and Gordon write: 'For bibliography of the Irish and French analogues of *Sir Gawain*, see the bibliography in Kittredge's study'. [*NED*] In Kittredge's study, this article is mentioned in 'XI. The Canzoni' (p. 304).

314. Carlyle, Robert Warrand and James Alexander Carlyle. *A history of mediaeval political theory in the West*, Vol. I Second century to the ninth. Edinburgh: Blackwood, 1903.
    P.s.: *Philology: General Works* (VI 1927, for 1925), p. 35.

315. _____ and James Alexander Carlyle. *A history of mediaeval political theory in the West*, Vol. II Political theory of the Roman lawyers and the canonists, from the tenth century to the thirteenth century. Edinburgh: Blackwood, 1909.
    P.s.: *Philology: General Works* (VI 1927, for 1925), p. 35.

316. _____ and James Alexander Carlyle. *A history of mediaeval political theory in the West*, Vol. III Political theory from the tenth century to the thirteenth. Edinburgh: Blackwood, 1916.
    P.s.: *Philology: General Works* (VI 1927, for 1925), p. 35.

317. _____ and James Alexander Carlyle. *A history of mediaeval political theory in the West*, Vol. IV Theories of the relation of the empire and the papacy from the tenth century to the twelfth. Edinburgh: Blackwood, 1922.
    P.s.: *Philology: General Works* (VI 1927, for 1925), p. 35.

318. Carlyle, Thomas. *Sartor resartus*. London: Ginn & Co., 1905.
    S.s.: University of Leeds (1921), p. 156. English Language and Literature - Scheme B. Texts for 1921-22. (d) Outlines of the History of English Literature. Ordinary Degree of B.A. with Honours. Final Examinations.

319. Carmichael, Alexander. *Deirdire, and Lay of the Children of Uisne*. Paisley: A. Garner, 1914 (2nd ed.).

Description: Decoratively autographed and dated on front flyleaf: '1922'.
Collection: Tolkien's personal Celtic library, preserved at the Weston library under the auspices of the English Faculty Library (Oxford).

320. Carroll, Lewis. *Alice's Adventures in Wonderland*. London: Macmillan.
P.s. 1: *Letters* 15 (1937). To Allen & Unwin.
P.s. 2: *On Fairy-stories* (1947), pp. 45, 84.
P.s. 3: *Smith of Wootton Major* (2005), p. 73.
P.s. 4: *Tolkien On Fairy-stories* (2008), pp. 36, 55, 60, 79.
P.s. 5: *Tolkien On Fairy-stories* (2008) 'Manuscript B [MS. Tolkien 4, fols. 73-120]', p. 249.
S.s. 1: Scull-Hammond (2017a), p. 6.
S.s. 2: Scull-Hammond (2017c), p. 1053.
Reading period: 1900 – 1906 (S.s.: Scull-Hammond (2017c), p. 1053).

321. _____. *Alice through the Looking Glass* [*Through the Looking Glass and What Alice Found There*]
P.s. 1: [Mythopoeic Society, *Parma Eldalamberon* 20 (2012), Q5 pp. 27-30] 1931. Tolkien writes a transliterations into the Qenya of the first eleven stanzas of 'The Walrus and the Carpenter' by Lewis Carroll. Arden Smith writes: 'Tolkien clearly wrote it from memory, since it differs in several respects from the published version' (p. 29); Q6a, Q6b, Q6c, Q6d pp. 31-38. 1931. And 'Tolkien has written the fourth and fifth stanzas of 'The Walrus and the Carpenter' in different styles of script, with alternate spellings of clear and tear between the second and third blocks of text. The wording matches Lewis Carroll's original, though Tolkien has not punctuated his texts as fully; see the commentary on Q5' (p. 38).
P.s. 2: *Letters* 15 (1937). To Allen & Unwin.
P.s. 3: *Beowulf* (1937), p. 8. Tolkien cites: 'For it is of their nature that the jabberwocks of historical and antiquarian research burble in the tulgy wood of conjecture, flitting from one tum-tum tree to another'. *Jabberwocky* is a nonsense poem about the killing of a creature named 'the Jabberwock included in this novel.
P.s. 4: *Tolkien On Fairy-stories* (2008) 'Manuscript B [MS. Tolkien 4, fols. 73-120]', p. 249.
S.s.: Scull-Hammond (2006b), p. 815
Reading period: 1900 – 1906 (S.s.: Scull-Hammond (2017c), p. 1053).

322. _____. *Rhyme? and reason?* New York: Macmillan and Co.
P.s.: *Letters* 15 (1937) To Allen & Unwin. Tolkien quotes *Hiawatha's Photographing*.

323. _____. *Sylvie and Bruno Concluded*. London: Macmillan.
S.s.: Scull-Hammond (2006b), p. 815.
Reading period: 1900 – 1906 (S.s.: Scull-Hammond (2017c), p. 1053).

324. _____. *Sylvie and Bruno*. London: Macmillan.
P.s.: *Letters* 15 (1937). To Allen & Unwin.
S.s. 1: Scull-Hammond (2006b), p. 815.
S.s. 2: Drout (2007), p. 367.
Reading period: 1900 – 1906 (S.s.: Scull-Hammond (2017c), p. 1053).

325. Carryl, Edward Charles. *The walloping window-blind*. 1885.
P.s.: *Letters* 91 (1944). To Christopher Tolkien. Tolkien writes: 'Very trying having your chief audience Ten Thousand Miles away, on or off The Walloping Window-blind.'

326. Cartellieri, Alexander. 'Richard Löwenherz'. *Probleme der Englischen Sprache und Kultur. Festschrift Johannes Hoops zum 60* [A. 1169]. Heidelberg: Carl Winter, 1925.
P.s.: *Philology: General Works* (VI 1927, for 1925), p. 45. Tolkien writes: 'is good'.

327. Casson, Leslie Frank (Edited by). *The Romance of Sir Degrevant*. Series: E.E.T.S. (Early English Text Society), OS 221. London: University Press, 1949.

P.s.: *Sir Gawain and the Green Knight* (1967) 'Select Bibliography: editions of texts quoted more than once in the notes', p. 156.

328.   Castrén, Matthias Alexander. *M. Alexander Castrén's Ethnologische Vorlesungen über die altaischen Völker: nebst samojedischen Märchen und Tatarischen Heldensagen*. Kaiserliche Akademie der Wissenschaften, 1857.
P.s.: # 1 *Tolkien On Fairy-stories* (2008), p. 306.

329.   Cato, Dionysius. *Disticha de moribus ad filium*.
P.s.: *A Middle English Vocabulary* (1922). Tolkien refers in the Index of names under 'Caton'.

330.   Cawley, Arthur C. (Edited with an introduction). *Pearl. Sir Gawain and the Green Knight*. Series: Everyman's library, 346. Romance. London: Dent, 1962.
P.s.: *Sir Gawain and the Green Knight* (1967) 'Select Bibliography', p. 153.

331.   Caxton, William. *Caxton's Blanchardyn and Eglantine* c. 1489. Series: E.E.T.S. (Early English Text Society), OS 58. Edited by Leon Kellner. London: Published for the Early English Text Society by Kegan Paul, Trench, Trübner and Co., 1890.
P.s.: MS. Tolkien A 21/13 fol. 119. Note by Tolkien, 'Books in Exeter Library useful', with shelfmarks, on back of photostat reading list dated October 1913. Tolkien writes: 'All EETS publications'. [Tolkien Papers, Bodleian Library, Oxford].
NED: #2 h. | 'W' (1928), p. 53 'Wallop v. 2. *trans.*' – c 1489 'Blanchardyn wyth a glad chere waloped his courser as bruyauntly as he coude' (xi, 42).

332.   _____. *Caxton's Eneydos*. Series: E.E.T.S. (Early English Text Society), OS 57. Edited by Matthew Tewart Culley and Frederick James Furnivall. London: Published for the Early English Text Society by Kegan Paul, Trench, Trübner and Co., 1890.
P.s.: MS. Tolkien A 21/13 fol. 119. Note by Tolkien, 'Books in Exeter Library useful', with shelfmarks, on back of photostat reading list dated October 1913. Tolkien writes: 'All EETS publications'. [Tolkien Papers, Bodleian Library, Oxford].
NED: #2 h. | 'W' (1928), p. 53 'Wallop v. 2. trans.' – 1490 'A kayghte … came ayenste hym as faste as he myghte spore and waloppe his horse' (lxi, 161).

333.   _____ (Translated by). *The Right Pleasant and Goodly Historie of the Foure Sonnes of Aymon*, Pt. I. (The English Charlemagne Romances Pt. X) Series: E.E.T.S. (Early English Text Society), ES 44. Edited by Octavia Richardson. London: Published for the Early English Text Society by Kegan Paul, Trench, Trübner and Co., 1884.
P.s.: MS. Tolkien A 21/13 fol. 119. Note by Tolkien, 'Books in Exeter Library useful', with shelfmarks, on back of photostat reading list dated October 1913. Tolkien writes: 'All EETS publications'. [Tolkien Papers, Bodleian Library, Oxford].
NED 1: #2 h. | 'W' (1928), p. 53 'Wallop sb. 1. a."' – c 1489 'Foulques of morillon cam afore all the other, well horsed., the grete valop agenste Reynawde' (p. 229).
NED 2: #2 h. | 'W' (1928), p. 53 'Wallop v. I. 1. a.' – c 1489 'Cam there kyng charlemagn, as fast as his horse myghte wallop' (xiv, 346).

334.   Cecil, David. *Two Quiet Lives: Dorothy Osborne, Thomas Gray*. Indianapolis: Bobbs-Merrill Co., 1948.
S.s. 1: Carpenter (1979), p. 186. Cecil read aloud to the Inklings from his book Two Quiet Lives which he was writing.
S.s. 2: Scull-Hammond (2017a), p. 347.

335.   Chadwick, Hector Munro. *The Origin of the English Nation*. Cambridge: The University Press, 1907.

P.s.: *Finn and Hengest* (1982), p. 69 n. 66.

336. Chadwick, Nora Kershaw. (Edited and translated by). *Anglo-Saxon and Norse poems*. Cambridge: The University Press, 1922.
P.s.: *Finn and Hengest* (1982), p. 134 n 76.

337. _____. *An Early Irish Reader. Being edition and translation of: Scél Mucci Mic Datho, Story of Mac Datho's Pig*. Cambridge University Press, 1927.
Collection: Tolkien's personal Celtic library, preserved at the Weston library under the auspices of the English Faculty Library (Oxford).

338. Chambers, Edmund Kerchever and Arthur Sidgwick (Edited by). *Early English Lyrics: Amorous, Divine, Moral & Trivial*. London: Sidgwick & Jackson Ltd. 1921 (Reprint).
S.s.: University of Leeds (1923), p. 81. Ordinary Degree of B.A., Intermediate Course and Examination: English Literature. Text selected for 1923-24 (i) for detailed study. Tolkien cites *Amorous, Divine Moral and Trivial* (pp. 1-200); p. 93. English Language and Literature. Scheme A. Degree of B.A. with Honours.

339. _____. *English Literature at the Close of the Middle Ages*. Series: Oxford History of English Literature, II.2. Oxford: At the Clarendon Press, 1945.
P.s. 1: MS. Tolkien A 12/1 *Commentary on Sir Gawain, lines 37-1987* fol. 1. [Tolkien Papers, Bodleian Library, Oxford].
P.s. 2: *Research v. Literature* (1946).
S.s.: Scull-Hammond (2017a), p. 318.

340. Chambers, Raymond Wilson. *Beowulf. An introduction to the study of the poem with a discussion of the stories of Offa and Finn*. Cambridge: The University Press, 1921.
P.s. 1: *Beowulf* (1937), p. 47 n. 2.
P.s. 2: *Finn and Hengest* (1982), p. 15 n. 14; p. 45 n 27; p. 48 n. 36; p. 61 n. 58; p. 95 n. 22; p. 98 n. 24; p. 115 n. 58; p. 135 n. 78; p. 137 n. 83.
P.s. 3: *Beowulf* (2002) 'Transcription of Legibile Portions of Folios 71-81: Notes and Jottings', p. 432.Tolkien cites: §8 Questions of Literary History, Date, and Authorship; Beowulf in the Light of History, Archaeology, Heroic Legend, Mythology, and Folklore.
P.s. 4: *Beowulf* (2014), p. 154 n. 1.
S.s. 1: Scull-Hammond (2017a), p. 128. 28 July 1922. By this date Tolkien has agreed to review, for *The English Historical Review, Beowulf* by Chambers. He will make several pages of notes, but will not complete the task.
S.s. 2: Anderson (2006), p. 144 n. 4. "Christopher Tolkien has informed me that his father kept some papers with his copy of the 1921 edition, including a clipping of the anonymous *Times Literary Supplement* review, dated 12 January 1922" (was written by Bruce Dickins).

341. _____. *Beowulf. An introduction to the study of the poem with a discussion of the stories of Offa and Finn*. Cambridge: The University Press, 1932 (2nd ed.).
P.s.: *Beowulf* (2002) 'Version A', p. 46.
S.s.: Scull-Hammond (2017a), p. 128.

342. _____. *Concerning Certain Great Teachers of the English Language*. London: Edward Arnold and Co., 1923.
Notes: A copy was sent to Tolkien by the author.
P.s.: *Philology: General Works* (IV 1924, for 1923), p. 37 n. 17. Tolkien writes: 'Not only does he pay a fitting tribute to many great names among nineteenth-century philologists—but for whose enthusiasm there would yet be little enough 'English' in English universities—but he examines current attacks upon philology which involve injustice to these scholars, or an ignorance of their work which does not excuse the injustice'.
S.s.: Scull-Hammond (2017a), p. 133. 14 January 1924.

343. _____. *England before the Norman Conquest*. Series: University of London

Intermediate Source-Books of History, 7. London: Longmans & Co., 1926.
Description: Written on M.H.R. personal book label (on the front flyleaf) 'Michael H.R. Tolkien | West Hanney | July 3rd, 1975 | (formerly the property of my father. | Professor J.R.R. Tolkien)'. Many sentences and words underlined throughout the book, notes in margin and end paper in J.R.R. Tolkien's hand.
Collection: Private [Pieter Collier].
P.s.: *Finn and Hengest* (1982), p. 69 n. 67, n 72.

344. _____. *Man's Unconquerable Mind. Studies of English Writers, from Bede to A. E. Housman and W. P. Ker*. London: Jonathan Cape Ltd., 1939.
Notes: Tolkien had two copies of this book. The second, he was sent by Chambers between April and May 1939.
P.s.: *Prefatory Remarks on Prose Translation of 'Beowulf'* (1940), p. xxviii n. 1.
S.s.: Scull-Hammond (2017a), p. 242.

345. _____. *The Jacobean Shakespeare and Measure for Measure*. London: The British Academy, 1937.
Notes: A copy was sent to Tolkien by the author.
S.s.: Scull-Hammond (2017a), p. 221.

346. _____. '*Sir Gawayne and the Green Knight*, Lines 697-702'. MLR (*The Modern Language Review*), Vol. 2, no. 2, p. 167, January 1907.
P.s.: *Sir Gawain and the Green Knight* (1925), p. 93, line 691 ff.

347. _____. *Thomas More*. London: Cape, 1935.
S.s.: Scull-Hammond (2017a), p. 190. Chambers send to him two copies.

348. _____. *Widsith. A study in Old English heroic legend*. Cambridge: The University Press, 1912.
P.s. 1: *English and Welsh* (1963), p. 27 n. 1.
P.s. 2: *Finn and Hengest* (1982), p. 10 n. 5; p. 16 n. 17; p. 61 n. 58; p. 67 n. 65.
P.s. 3: *The Legend of Sigurd & Gudrún* (2009), p. 340.
P.s. 4: *Beowulf* (2002) 'Version A', pp. 46, 53.
P.s. 5: *Beowulf* (2014), pp. 239, 327, 337 n. 1.
S.s. 1: University of Leeds (1921), p. 192 English Language and Literature. Honours and M.A. Courses. A. Language. H2. (Scheme A and B) Second and Third Year.
S.s. 2: Shippey (1992), p, 301.

349. Chambers, Robert. *Cyclopædia of English literature. A history, critical and biographical, of authors in the English tongue from the earliest times till the present day, with specimens of their writings*, Vol. I. A history, critical and biographical, of authors in the English tongue from the earliest times till the present day, with specimens of their writings. London: W. & R. Chambers, 1906.
S.s.: University of Leeds (1921), p. 191 English Language and Literature. F1. Final Course (English Literature) Books recommended.

350. _____. *Cyclopædia of English literature. A history, critical and biographical, of authors in the English tongue from the earliest times till the present day, with specimens of their writings*, Vol. II. A history, critical and biographical, of authors in the English tongue from the earliest times till the present day, with specimens of their writings. London: W. & R. Chambers, 1906.
S.s.: University of Leeds (1921), p. 191 English Language and Literature. F1. Final Course (English Literature) Books recommended.

351. _____. *Cyclopædia of English literature. A history, critical and biographical,*

of authors in the English tongue from the earliest times till the present day, with specimens of their writings, Vol. III. A history, critical and biographical, of authors in the English tongue from the earliest times till the present day, with specimens of their writings. London: W. & R. Chambers, 1906.
 S.s.: University of Leeds (1921), p. 191 English Language and Literature. F1. Final Course (English Literature) Books recommended.

352. _____. *Popular rhymes of Scotland.* London: W. & R. Chambers, 1874.
 P.s. 1: *Tolkien On Fairy-stories* (2008) 'Manuscript A. [MS Tolkien 4, fols. 59-77]', p. 179. Tolkien cites 'Milk White Doo'.
 P.s. 2: # 1 *Tolkien On Fairy-stories* (2008), p. 306.

353. Chant, Joy (E. J. Rutter). *Red Moon and Black Mountain.* London: Allen and Unwin, 1970.
 S.s.: Scull-Hammond (2017a), p. 787. 10 June 1970: Rayner Unwin sent Tolkien a proof of *Red Moon and Black Mountain* by Joy Chant and asks him to write a sentence of commendation if he likes it. 22 July 1970 Rayner Unwin's secretary sent a second copy as Tolkien has not received the first.

354. Chapman, Coolidge Otis. 'Numerical Symbolism in Dante and the Pearl'. Offprint from MLN (*Modern Language Notes*), Vol. 64, no. 4, April 1939, pp. 256-59.
 Description: Inscribed by the author 'To Professor Tolkien with the writer's compliments'. Annotated by Tolkien on one page.
 Collection: Private [Christina Scull & Wayne G. Hammond].
 S.s. Scull-Hammond (2018a).

355. Chase, Stanley Perkins. *The Pearl: the fourteenth century English poem rendered in modern verse with an introductory essay.* London: Oxford University Press, 1932.
 P.s.: *Sir Gawain and the Green Knight* (1967) 'Select Bibliography', p. 153.

356. Chaucer, Geoffrey. *The Boke of the Duchesse.*
 P.s. 1: MS. Tolkien A 13/2 *Notes and drafts of lectures on Chaucer: Pardoner's Tale* fol. 163. [Tolkien Papers, Bodleian Library, Oxford].
 P.s. 2: MS. Tolkien A 21/13 Chronological Library Table of Middle English fol. 202. [Tolkien Papers, Bodleian Library, Oxford].
 P.s. 3: MS. Tolkien A 35 *Pearl* fol. 111. [Tolkien Papers, Bodleian Library, Oxford].
 P.s. 4: *A Middle English Vocabulary* (1922). Tolkien refers to *The Boke of the Duchesse* on the term 'Draw(e)' (*make no move against us, play us no trick*).
 P.s. 5: *Sir Gawain and the Green Knight* (1975), p. 21. Tolkien quotes: 'And goode faire White she het … She hadde not hir name wrong' (948-51)

357. _____. *The Cambridge MS. (University library, Gg. 4.27) of Chaucer's Canterbury Tales.* Edited by Frederick James Furnivall. London: Published for the Chaucer society by Nicholas Trübner & co., 1879.
 P.s.: 'Chaucer as a Philologist: *The Reeve's Tale*' *(1934)*, p. 116. Tolkien writes: 'For lack of time and opportunity it is based solely on the facsimile of the Ellesmere MS.; and on the Six-Text and the Harleian MS. 7334 (Hl) printed by the Chaucer Society'.
 S.s.: Fitzgerald (2009), p. 53 n. 10. [In the notes for the Chaucer's conference (1931)] Tolkien admits, the MSS. of the Canterbury Tales exhibit a great degree of dialectal and orthographic variation and he adds that 'for lack of time and opportunity [this study] is based solely on the facsimile of the Ellesmere MS. [A. 374]; and on the Six-Text (Hengwrt (H) [A. 380], Cambridge University Library Gg.4.27 (C), Corpus Christi College, Oxford (O) [A. 372], Petworth (P) [A. 395], Landsdown 851 (L) [A. 382]) and the Harleian MS. 7334 (H1) [A. 378] printed by the Chaucer Society. Furthermore he writes that 'the copyists must, of course, usually have perceived

that the clerks' lines were abnormal in language'.

358. _____. *Canon's Yeoman's Tale* [From *The Canterbury Tales*, Vol. II].
S.s. 1: University of Leeds (1921), p. 145. English Language, text selected for 1921-22 (*Canon's Yeoman's Tale*). Ordinary Degree of B.A.; p. 192 English Language and Literature. F2. Final Course (English Literature and Language) (*The Canon's Yeoman's Tale*).
S.s. 2: Hammond-Scull (2014), p. 160. Hammond and Scull write: 'All that is gold does not glitter' [FoTR, X] In his 'Canon's Yeoman's Tale' in *The Canterbury Tales* Chaucer says: 'But al thyng which that shyneth as the gold | Nis nat gold, as that I have heard told.'

359. _____. *Canterbury Tales*, Vol. I. Edited by Alfred William Pollard. London: Macmillan, 1907.
P.s. 1: MS. Tolkien A 13/2 *Notes and drafts of lectures on Chaucer: Pardoner's Tale*. [Tolkien Papers, Bodleian Library, Oxford].
P.s. 2: *Beowulf* (2014), pp. 163, 281.
S.s.: University of Leeds (1921), p. 153. English Language and Literature - Scheme A. Text selected for 1921-22. Ordinary Degree of B.A. with Honours.

360. _____. *Canterbury Tales*, Vol. II. Edited by Alfred William Pollard. London: Macmillan, 1907.
P.s. 1: MS. Tolkien A 12/1 *Commentary on Sir Gawain, lines 37-1987* fol. 109. Tolkien cites 'Manciple's Tale' vv. 218-220. [Tolkien Papers, Bodleian Library, Oxford].
P.s. 2: *Letters* 182 (1956). From a letter to Anne Barrett, Houghton Mifflin Co.
P.s. 3: *Beowulf* (2014), pp. 163, 281.
S.s.: Ollscoil na h-Éireann G 259 (1949).

361. _____. *Chaucer's Canterbury Tales: The Prologue*. Edited by Alfred William Pollard. London: Macmillan, 1920.
P.s. 1: *Beowulf* (1937), p. 4. Tolkien quotes:'swich a lewed mannes wit to pace the wisdom of an heep of lerned men' (vv. 574-5)
P.s. 2: *Sir Gawain and the Green Knight* (1953), p. 107 n. 17. Tolkien quotes: 'he neueryet no vileinye ne sayde ... unto no maner wight'.
S.s. 1: University of Leeds (1920), p. 135 English Literature. Texts Selected for 1920-21; p. 180. English Language and Literature. Int. I Intermediate Course (Literature).
S.s. 2: University of Leeds (1921), p. 189 English Language and Literature. Int. 1 Intermediate Course (Literature); p. 192 English Language and Literature. Honours and M.A. Courses. A. Language. H1. First Year.
S.s. 3: Scull-Hammond (2017a), p. 122. Leeds academic year 1920-1921. Tolkien might also be responsible for the first few lectures in an introductory course on English Literature which begins with the Prologue to the Canterbury Tales, Mondays and Wednesdays at 11.00 a.m.
S.s. 4: Ollscoil na h-Éireann G 259 (1949).

362. _____. *Chaucer: The Pardoner's Tale*. Series: University Tutorial. Edited by Charles Maxwell Drennan and Alfred John Wyatt. London: W.B. Clive, University Tutorial Press, 1911.
P.s.: MS. Tolkien A 13/2 *Notes and drafts of lectures on Chaucer: Pardoner's Tale* fol. 91. [Tolkien Papers, Bodleian Library, Oxford].

363. _____. *Clerk's Tale* [From *The Canterbury Tales*, Vol. II].
P.s. 1: MS. Tolkien A 13/2 *Notes and drafts of lectures on Chaucer: Clerk's Tale*. [Tolkien Papers, Bodleian Library, Oxford].
P.s. 2: *Holy Maidenhood* (1923), p. 281. Tolkien cites: *Clerk's Tale*.
S.s. 1: University of Leeds (1921), p. 153. English Language and Literature - Scheme A. Texts and Period selected for 1921-22. (b) Chaucer, with a special study (*The Frankeleyns Tale; The Clerk's Tale*). Ordinary Degree of B.A. with Honours. Final Examinations; p. 192 English Language and Literature. Honours and M.A. Courses. A. Language. H1. First Year (*The Clerk's Tale*).
S.s. 2: Scull-Hammond (2017a), p. 46. April 1913: Tolkien will need to become familiar with a

range of literary and philological subjects and set texts as prescribed in the Oxford Regulations of the Board of Studies, knowing that he may be examined on them in ten papers at the end of *Trinity Term 1915*: Middle English texts. *The Franklin's Tale* and *The Clerk's Tale*.

364. _____. *The Clerkes Tale of Oxenford*. Edited by Kenneth Sisam. Oxford: At the Clarendon Press, 1923.
> P.s.: MS. Res. e. 308 *Sir Gawain and the Green Knight*. [Tolkien Papers, Bodleian Library, Oxford].

365. _____. *The complete works of Geoffrey Chaucer*, Vol. I. *Romaunt of the Rose*. Edited by Walter William Skeat. Oxford: At the Clarendon Press, 1894 (2nd ed.).
> P.s. 1: MS. Res. e. 308 *Sir Gawain and the Green Knight*. [Tolkien Papers, Bodleian Library, Oxford].
> P.s. 2: *Sir Gawain and the Green Knight* (1925), p. 81, line 43 *caroles*.

366. _____. *The complete works of Geoffrey Chaucer*, Vol. II. *Boethius and Troilus*. Edited, from numerous manuscripts by Walter William Skeat. Oxford: At the Clarendon Press, 1894.
> P.s. 1: *Exeter College library register*. Tolkien's borrowing record: *Michaelmas Term 1914* from 14 November to 16 January 1915; from 19 January to 15 May 1915; *Hilary Term 1915* from 19 January to 1 March 1915.
> P.s. 2: MS. Res. e. 308 *Sir Gawain and the Green Knight*. [Tolkien Papers, Bodleian Library, Oxford].

367. _____. *The complete works of Geoffrey Chaucer*, Vol. III. The house of fame, The legend of good women. The treatise on the astrolabe; with an account of the sources of The Canterbury Tales. Edited, from numerous manuscripts by Walter William Skeat. Oxford: At the Clarendon Press, 1894.
> P.s. 1: *Exeter College library register*. Tolkien's borrowing record: *Michaelmas Term 1919* from 14 October to 21 January 1920.
> P.s. 2: MS. Res. e. 308 *Sir Gawain and the Green Knight*. [Tolkien Papers, Bodleian Library, Oxford].
> P.s. 3: MS. Tolkien A 12/1 *Commentary on Sir Gawain, lines 37-1987* fol. 102. [Tolkien Papers, Bodleian Library, Oxford].
> P.s. 4: MS. Tolkien A 12/2 *Commentary on Sir Gawain, lines 1999-2523* fol. 7. [Tolkien Papers, Bodleian Library, Oxford].
> P.s. 5: *Sir Gawain and the Green Knight* (1925), p. 81, line 43 *caroles*; p. 93, line 774 *Sayn Guyan*. Tolkien and Gordon quote 'seynt ulyan, lo, bon hostell!' (v. 1022).

368. _____. *The complete works of Geoffrey Chaucer*, Vol. IV. The Canterbury Tales: Text. Edited, from numerous manuscripts by Walter William Skeat. Oxford: At the Clarendon Press, 1894.
> P.s.: MS. Res. e. 308 *Sir Gawain and the Green Knight*. [Tolkien Papers, Bodleian Library, Oxford].

369. _____. *The complete works of Geoffrey Chaucer*, Vol. V. The Canterbury Tales: Notes. Edited, from numerous manuscripts by Walter William Skeat. Oxford: At the Clarendon Press, 1894.
> P.s. 1: *Exeter College library register*. Tolkien's borrowing record: *Michaelmas Term 1919* from 14 October to 21 January 1920.
> P.s. 2: MS. Tolkien A 34/3 Texts for the BBC radio presentation of the translation of *Sir Gawain and the Green Knight*, 1953 fol. 221. [Tolkien Papers, Bodleian Library, Oxford].
> P.s. 3: MS. Res. e. 308 *Sir Gawain and the Green Knight*. [Tolkien Papers, Bodleian Library, Oxford].
> P.s. 4: 'Chaucer as a Philologist: *The Reeve's Tale*' (1934), p. 141. Tolkien writes: 'The joke was probably a current one and was still alive later: Skeat in his note on this passage quotes from the

Arte of Poesie the tale of the tanner of Tamworth, who said "I hope I shall be hanged" (p. 122, 4029).

370. _____. *The complete works of Geoffrey Chaucer*, Vol. VI. Introduction, glossary, and indexes. Edited, from numerous manuscripts by Walter William Skeat. Oxford: At the Clarendon Press, 1894.
P.s. 1: *Exeter College library register*. Tolkien's borrowing record: *Michaelmas Term 1919* from 14 October to 21 January 1920.
P.s. 2: MS. Res. e. 308 *Sir Gawain and the Green Knight*. [Tolkien Papers, Bodleian Library, Oxford].

371. _____. *The complete works of Geoffrey Chaucer*, Vol. VII Chaucerian and other pieces: supplement to the complete works of Geoffrey Chaucer. Edited, from numerous manuscripts by Walter William Skeat. Oxford: At the Clarendon Press, 1897.
P.s.: MS. Res. e. 308 *Sir Gawain and the Green Knight*. [Tolkien Papers, Bodleian Library, Oxford].

372. _____. *The Corpus MS. (Corpus Christi Coll., Oxford) of Chaucer's Canterbury Tales*. Edited by Frederick James Furnivall. London: Published for the Chaucer society by Nicholas Trübner & co., 1868.
P.s.: 'Chaucer as a Philologist: *The Reeve's Tale*' (1934), p. 116. Tolkien writes: 'For lack of time and opportunity it is based solely on the facsimile of the Ellesmere MS.; and on the Six-Text and the Harleian MS. 7334 (Hl) printed by the Chaucer Society'.
S.s.: Fitzgerald (2009), p. 53 n. 10. [see A. 357, S.s.].

373. _____. *The Ellesmere MS. of Chaucer's Canterbury Tales*. Edited by Frederick James Furnivall. London: Published for the Chaucer society by Nicholas Trübner & co., 1879.
P.s.: 'Chaucer as a Philologist: *The Reeve's Tale*' (1934), p. 116. Tolkien writes: 'For lack of time and opportunity it is based solely on the facsimile of the Ellesmere MS.; and on the Six-Text and the Harleian MS. 7334 (Hl) printed by the Chaucer Society'.
S.s.: Fitzgerald (2009), p. 53 n. 10. [see A. 357, S.s.].

374. _____. *The Ellesmere Chaucer reproduced in facsimile*. Preface by Alix Egerton. Manchester: The University Press, 1911.
S.s.: Scull-Hammond (2017a), p. 345. [13 November 1947] 'Tolkien hosts an Inklings meeting at Merton College. Tolkien reads 'a rich melancholy poem on autumn' […], and displays a facsimile of the Ellesmere Chaucer manuscript (of *The Canterbury Tales*) he has bought for £ 55.'

375. _____. *Frankeleyns Tale* [From *The Canterbury Tales*, Vol. II].
S.s. 1: University of Leeds (1921), p. 153. English Language and Literature - Scheme A. Texts and Period selected for 1921-22. (b) Chaucer, with a special study (*The Frankeleyns Tale*; *The Clerk's Tale*). Ordinary Degree of B.A. with Honours. Final Examinations.
S.s. 2: Scull-Hammond (2017a), p. 46. April 1913: 'Tolkien will need to become familiar with a range of literary and philological subjects and set texts as prescribed in the Oxford Regulations of the Board of Studies, knowing that he may be examined on them in ten papers at the end of *Trinity Term 1915*: Middle English texts. *The Franklin's Tale* and *The Clerk's Tale*; p. 53. *Michaelmas Term 1913*: Tolkien probably attends G.K.A. Bell's course on Chaucer's *The Franklin's Tale* on Wednesdays at 5.45 p.m. at Christ Church, beginning 15 October.'

376. _____. *Friar's Tale* [From *The Canterbury Tales*, Vol. II].
P.s.: 'Chaucer as a Philologist: *The Reeve's Tale*' (1934), p. 134.
NED: #1 a. | | 'W' (1928), p. 98 'Wariangle, 1.' c 1386 – 'This Somonour, that was as ful of Iangles, As ful of venym been thise waryangles' (1407-8).

377. _____. *Gentilesse*.

S.s.: University of Leeds (1921), p. 145. English Language, text selected for 1921-22. Ordinary Degree of B.A.; p. 192 English Language and Literature. F2. Final Course (English Literature and Language).

378. _____. *The Harleian MS.7334 of Chaucer's Canterbury Tales*. Edited by Frederick James Furnivall. London: Published for the Chaucer society by Nicholas Trübner & co., 1885.
    P.s.: 'Chaucer as a Philologist: *The Reeve's Tale*' (1934), p. 116. Tolkien writes: 'For lack of time and opportunity it is based solely on the facsimile of the Ellesmere MS.; and on the Six-Text and the Harleian MS. 7334 (Hl) printed by the Chaucer Society'.
    S.s.: Fitzgerald (2009), p. 53 n. 10. [see A. 357, S.s.]

379. _____. *The House of Fame in three books*. Edited by Walter William Skeat. Oxford: At the Clarendon Press, 1893.
    P.s. 1: MS. Res. e. 308 *Sir Gawain and the Green Knight*. [Tolkien Papers, Bodleian Library, Oxford].
    P.s. 2: 'Chaucer as a Philologist: *The Reeve's Tale*' (1934), p. 135.

380. _____. *The Hengwrt MS. of Chaucer's Canterbury Tales*. Edited by Frederick James Furnivall. London: Published for the Chaucer society by Nicholas Trübner & co., 1868.
    P.s.: 'Chaucer as a Philologist: *The Reeve's Tale*' (1934), p. 116. Tolkien writes: 'For lack of time and opportunity it is based solely on the facsimile of the Ellesmere MS.; and on the Six-Text and the Harleian MS. 7334 (Hl) printed by the Chaucer Society'.
    S.s.: Fitzgerald (2009), p. 53 n. 10. [see A. 357, S.s.].

381. _____. *The Knight's Tale*.
    S.s. 1: University of Leeds (1920), p. 139 English Language and Literature: English Language. Text selected for 1920-21. Texts Selected for 1920-21. Ordinary Degree of B.A. with Honours. Final Course and Examination. Extracts ii (*On the State of Learning in England*), viii (*Alfred's Wars with the Dunes*) and xxv (*Selections from the Riddles of Cynewulf*; p. 182. English Language and Literature. F2. Final Course (English Literature and Language).
    S.s. 2: #1 Holland (1949), p. 141. Appendix XI: Oxford Examinations for Prisoners of War. English B.2 Chaucer and his Contemporaries: vv. 1638-1657.

382. _____. *The Lansdowne MS. (No. 851) of Chaucer's Canterbury Tales*. Edited by Frederick James Furnivall. London: Published for the Chaucer society by Nicholas Trübner & co., 1868.
    P.s.: 'Chaucer as a Philologist: *The Reeve's Tale*' (1934), p. 116. Tolkien writes: 'For lack of time and opportunity it is based solely on the facsimile of the Ellesmere MS.; and on the Six-Text and the Harleian MS. 7334 (Hl) printed by the Chaucer Society'.
    S.s.: Fitzgerald (2009), p. 53 n. 10. [see A. 357, S.s.].

383. _____. *The Legend of Good Women*. Edited by Walter William Skeat. Oxford: At the Clarendon Press, 1889.
    P.s. 1: MS. Tolkien A 13/1 *Draft of talk to the Oxford Dante Society: A neck-verse* (1947), fol. 173. Tolkien quotes: 'For in your court is many a losengeour | And many a queynte totelere accusour' (Prologue, 352-3). [Tolkien Papers, Bodleian Library, Oxford].
    P.s. 2: MS. Res. e. 308 *Sir Gawain and the Green Knight*. [Tolkien Papers, Bodleian Library, Oxford].
    P.s. 3: 'Chaucer as a Philologist: *The Reeve's Tale*' (1934), p. 141.
    P.s. 4: 'Middle English 'Losenger'' (1953), p. 65. Tolkien quotes: 'For in your court is many a losengeour … for hate or fore jelous imagining' (Prologue, 352-5).

384. _____. *The Man of Law's Tale*. Edited by Nevil Coghill and Christopher J. R. Tolkien. London: George G. Harrap, 1969. [Jun 69].

385. _____. *Miller's Tale* [From *The Canterbury Tales*, Vol. I].
P.s. 1: MS. Tolkien A 12/1 *Commentary on Sir Gawain, lines 37-1987* fol. 108. [Tolkien Papers, Bodleian Library, Oxford].
P.s. 2: *Letters* 181 (1956). To Michael Straight [drafts]. Tolkien writes: 'Into the ultimate judgement upon Gollum I would not care to enquire. This would be to investigate 'Goddes privitee', as the Medievals said.' quoting 'Men sholde nat knowe of Goddes pryvetee.' (3454)

386. _____. *The Minor Poems*. Edited by Walter William Skeat. Oxford: At the Clarendon Press, 1888.
P.s.: MS. Res. e. 308 *Sir Gawain and the Green Knight*. [Tolkien Papers, Bodleian Library, Oxford].
S.s.: University of Leeds (1921), p. 153. English Language and Literature - Scheme A. Texts and Period selected for 1921-22. (b) Chaucer, with special study. Ordinary Degree of B.A. with Honours. Final Examinations; p. 192 English Language and Literature. Honours and M.A. Courses. A. Language. H1. First Year.

387. _____. *Monk's Tale* [From *The Canterbury Tales*, Vol. I].
P.s.: 'Chaucer as a Philologist: *The Reeve's Tale*' (1934), p. 136.

388. _____. *The Nun's Priest's Tale*. Edited by Alfred William Pollard. London: Macmillan and Co., 1915.
P.s. 1: *On Fairy-stories* (1947), p. 46.
P.s. 2: *Beowulf* (2014), p. 163
S.s.: University of Leeds (1923), p. 81. Ordinary Degree of B.A., Intermediate Course and Examination: English Literature. Text selected for 1923-24 (i) For detailed study; p. 93. English Language and Literature. Scheme A. Degree of B.A. with Honours.

389. _____. *The Nun's Priest's Tale*. Edited by Nevil Coghill and Christopher J. R. Tolkien. London: George G. Harrap, 1959 [28 Feb 60].

390. _____. *The Pardoner's Prologue and Tale*. Series: Chaucher Society's, S.S. 35. Edited by John Koch. London: Published for the Chaucer Society by K. Paul, Trench, N. Trübner & Co., Limited, 1902.
P.s. MS. Tolkien A 13/2 *Notes and drafts of lectures on Chaucer: Pardoner's Tale* fol. 91. [Tolkien Papers, Bodleian Library, Oxford].

391. _____. *The Pardoner's Tale*. [From *The Canterbury Tales*, Vol. I].
P.s. 1: MS. Tolkien A 13/1 *Draft of talk to the Oxford Dante Society: A neck-verse* (1947), fol. 173. Tolkien quotes: 'I haue … the popes hond' (920-23). [Tolkien Papers, Bodleian Library, Oxford].
P.s. 2: MS. Tolkien A 13/2 *Notes and drafts of lectures on Chaucer: Pardoner's Tale*. [Tolkien Papers, Bodleian Library, Oxford].
S.s. 1: University of Leeds (1921), p. 153. English Language and Literature - Scheme A. Texts selected and Period for 1921-22. (b) Chaucer, with special study (*Tale of Sir Thopas*; *The Pardoner's Tale*). Ordinary Degree of B.A. with Honours. Final Examinations; p. 154. English Language and Literature - Scheme A. Texts and Period selected for 1921-22. (d) Texts suggested for study with Special Period 1637-1700 (*The Pardoner's Tale*). Ordinary Degree of B.A. with Honours. Final Examinations.
S.s. 2: Carpenter (1979), p. 124 n. 1. Tolkien's poem about Charles Williams ('*Our dear Charles Williams many guises show…*' pp. 123-26). Tolkien quotes *fen*: the name of a section in Avicenna's *Canon of Medicine*; also used by Chaucer in *The Pardoner's Tale*.
S.s. 3: Scull-Hammond (2017a), p. 46. April 1913: Tolkien will need to become familiar with a range of literary and philological subjects and set texts as prescribed in the Oxford Regulations of the Board of Studies, knowing that he may be examined on them in ten papers at the end of *Trinity Term 1915*: Middle English texts. the *Prologue to The Canterbury Tales* and *The Pardoner's Tale*.

392. _____. *The Pardoner's Tale*. Edited by Nevil Coghill and Christopher J. R. Tolkien. London: George G. Harrap, 1958 [29 Oct 58].

393. _____. *The Parlement of Foules*.
P.s. 1: MS. Tolkien A 13/1 *Draft of talk to the Oxford Dante Society: A neck-verse* (1947), fol. 171. Tolkien quotes: 'The day gan failen, and the darke night, That reveth beastes from hir businesse, Beraft me my book' (XIII, 85-7). [Tolkien Papers, Bodleian Library, Oxford].
P.s. 2: MS. Tolkien A 35 *Pearl* fol. 113. Tolkien quotes: 'The wery hunter … his lady wonne' (vv. 99-106). [Tolkien Papers, Bodleian Library, Oxford].
P.s. 3: 'Chaucer as a Philologist: *The Reeve's Tale*' (1934), p. 109. Tolkien quoting: '*litel erthe that heer is … so ful of torment and of harde grace …*' from lines 56-7.
P.s. 4: *Beowulf* (2002) 'Version A', p. 42. Tolkien writes 'The lyf so schort, the craft so long to lerne so hard the assay so scharp the conquerving as Chaucer says; long study has its rewards' from first verse of Chaucer's Poem '*The lyf so short, the craft so longe to lerne. Th'assay so hard, so sharp the conquerynge, The dredful joye, alwey that slit so yerne; Al this mene I be love.*' The original verse of Hippocrates (Aphorisms 1:1).

394. _____. *Parson's Tale* [From *The Canterbury Tales*, Vol. II].
P.s. 1: MS. Tolkien A 13/1 *Draft of talk to the Oxford Dante Society: A neck-verse* (1947), fol. 169. Tolkien writes: '*For trusteth wel I am northern man*' which refers 'But trusteth wel, I am a southren man' (Prologue, 42).
P.s. 2: *Beowulf* (2014), pp. 280-81. Tolkien quotes: 'But trusteth wel, I am a Southren man, … but litel bettre;' (42-4).

395. _____. *The Petworth MS. of Chaucer's Canterbury Tales*. Edited by Frederick James Furnivall. London: Published for the Chaucer society by Nicholas Trübner & co., 1868.
P.s.: 'Chaucer as a Philologist: *The Reeve's Tale*' (1934), p. 116. Tolkien writes: 'For lack of time and opportunity it is based solely on the facsimile of the Ellesmere MS.; and on the Six-Text and the Harleian MS. 7334 (Hl) printed by the Chaucer Society'.
S.s.: Fitzgerald (2009), p. 53 n. 10. [see A. 357, S.s.]

396. _____. *The Prioresses Tale, Sir Thopas, the Monkes Tale, the Clerkes Tale, the Squieres Tale, from the Canterbury Tales*. Edited by Walter William Skeat. Oxford: At the Clarendon Press, 1880.
P.s. 1: MS. Tolkien A 13/1 *Draft of talk to the Oxford Dante Society: A neck-verse* (1947), fol. 170. Tolkien quotes the close of Hugelin of Pise in the Monkes Tale: 'Redeth the grete poete of Itaille, | That highte Dante, for he can al deuyse, | Fro point, nat o word wol he faille'. [Tolkien Papers, Bodleian Library, Oxford].
P.s. 2: MS. Res. e. 308 *Sir Gawain and the Green Knight*. [Tolkien Papers, Bodleian Library, Oxford].

397. _____. *The Prioress's Tale, The tale of Sir Thopas*. Edited by Lilian Winstanley. Cambridge: The University Press, 1922.
Description: Autographed on front flyleaf: 'J.R.R. Tolkien'. Annotations in pencil pp. lxv, 25.
Collection: Private (Carl F. Hostetter).

398. _____. *Prologue to the Canterbury Tales* [From *The Canterbury Tales*, Vol. I].
S.s. 1: University of Leeds (1921), p. 145. English Language, text selected for 1921-22 (*The Prologue*; *Tale of Sir Thopas*). Ordinary Degree of B.A.; p. 192 English Language and Literature. F2. Final Course (English Literature and Language) (*The Prologue*; *Tale of Sir Thopas*).
S.s. 2: Scull-Hammond (2017a), p. 46. April 1913: Tolkien will need to become familiar with a range of literary and philological subjects and set texts as prescribed in the Oxford Regulations of the Board of Studies, knowing that he may be examined on them in ten papers at the end of *Trinity Term 1915*: Middle English texts. the *Prologue to the Canterbury Tales* and *The Pardoner's Tale*; p. 53. *Michaelmas Term 1913*: Tolkien probably attends G.K.A. Bell's course on Chaucer's *Prologue to the Canterbury Tales* on Wednesdays at 5.45 p.m. at Christ Church, beginning 15 October.

399. _____. *The Prologue to the Canterbury Tales*. Edited by Walter William Skeat.

Oxford: At the Clarendon Press, 1897.
>P.s.: MS. Res. e. 308 *Sir Gawain and the Green Knight*. [Tolkien Papers, Bodleian Library, Oxford].
>S.s.: #1 Holland (1949), pp. 141-42. Appendix XI: Oxford Examinations for Prisoners of War. English B.2 Chaucer and his Contemporaries: vv. 249-268.

400. _____. *The Prologue, The Knights Tale, The Nonne Preestes Tale*. Edited by Richard Morris. Oxford: At the Clarendon Press, 1885.
>P.s.: MS. Res. e. 308 *Sir Gawain and the Green Knight*. [Tolkien Papers, Bodleian Library, Oxford].

401. _____. *The Prologue and Three Tales. The prologue to the Cantebury Tales, the Prioress Tale, the Nun's Priest's Tale, the Pardoner's Tale*. Edited by Harry Walter Cowling. London: Ginn, 1934.
>P.s. 1: Tolkien's unpublished letter to Cowling, 23 December 1934. Tolkien writes: 'I should long ago have thanked you for your admirable Chaucer — marvellously got up too for the price. It was good of you to think of me'.
>P.s. 2: Tolkien. J.R.R. Two Page Manuscript Letter to G. H. Cowling. explaining his procrastination and horror of letter writing. Thanking him for a copy of Chaucer and wishing him Happy Christmas. dated December 23, 1934 from 20 Northmoor Road Oxford. [Sold by Bay East Auctions, 27 November 2011].
>S.s.: Scull-Hammond (2017a), p. 188.

402. _____. *Reeve's Tale* [From Canterbury Tales, Vol. I].
>P.s.: 'Chaucer as a Philologist: *The Reeve's Tale*' (1934), p. 109.

403. _____. *Romaunt of the Rose* [Attributable to Chaucer. see A. 383].
>P.s. 1: MS. Tolkien A 21/13 *Chronological Library Table of Middle English* fol. 202. [Tolkien Papers, Bodleian Library, Oxford].
>P.s. 2: MS. Tolkien A 35 *Pearl* fol. 113. Tolkien quotes: 'Of good and harme ... after al openly' (vv. 16-20). [Tolkien Papers, Bodleian Library, Oxford].
>P.s. 3: 'Middle English 'Losenger"' (1953), p. 65 n. 1.
>*NED*: #2 h. | 'W' (1928), p. 56. 'Walm, *v. Obs.* 1. *intr.* a.' – a 1366 'The water is evere fresh & newe, That welmeth up with wawis bright' (1561).

404. _____. *Sir Thopas* [From *The Canterbury Tales*, Vol. I].
>S.s.: University of Leeds (1921), p. 145. English Language, text selected for 1921-22 (*The Prologue*; *Tale of Sir Thopas*). Ordinary Degree of B.A.; p. 153. English Language and Literature - Scheme A. Texts selected and Period for 1921-22. (b) Chaucer, with special study (*Tale of Sir Thopas*; *The Pardoner's Tale*). Ordinary Degree of B.A. with Honours. Final Examinations; p. 192 English Language and Literature. F2. Final Course (English Literature and Language) (*The Prologue*; *Tale of Sir Thopas*).

405. _____. *To Rosemounde. A Balade*.
>S.s.: University of Leeds (1921), p. 145. English Language, text selected for 1921-22. Ordinary Degree of B.A.; p. 192 English Language and Literature. F2. Final Course (English Literature and Language).

406. _____. *The Squire's Tale*.
>P.s. 1: MS. Tolkien A 12/1 *Commentary on Sir Gawain, lines 37-1987* fol. 106. [Tolkien Papers, Bodleian Library, Oxford].
>P.s. 2: *Sir Gawain and the Green Knight* (1925), p. 97, line 916 ff. Tolkien and Gordon quote: 'This strange knight ... amende with a word'.
>P.s. 3: *Sir Gawain and the Green Knight* (1953), p. 108 n. 30. Tolkien quotes: 'Gawayn, with his olde curteisye ... fairye' (vv. 95-6).

407. _____. *The student's Chaucer being a complete edition of his works*. Edited,

from numerous manuscripts by Walter William Skeat. London: Macmillan and Co., 1894.
> P.s.: MS. Res. e. 308 *Sir Gawain and the Green Knight*. [Tolkien Papers, Bodleian Library, Oxford].
> S.s.: #1 Holland (1949), p. 143. Appendix XI: Oxford Examinations for Prisoners of War. English B.2 Chaucer and his Contemporaries. It is cited 'Chaucer that is floure of rethoryk In englisshe tong' by John Walton of Osney.

408. _____. *The Tale of the Man of Lawe; The Pardoneres Tale; The Second Nonnes Tales; The Chanouns Yemannes Tale, from The Canterbury Tales*. Edited by Walter William Skeat. Oxford: At the Clarendon Press, 1897.
> P.s.: MS. Res. e. 308 *Sir Gawain and the Green Knight*. [Tolkien Papers, Bodleian Library, Oxford].

409. _____. *Troilus and Criseyde*.
> P.s. 1: MS. Tolkien A 21/6 fol. 1. [Tolkien Papers, Bodleian Library, Oxford].
> P.s. 2: MS. Tolkien A 34/3 Texts for the BBC radio presentation of the translation of *Sir Gawain and the Green Knight*, 1953 fol. 221. [Tolkien Papers, Bodleian Library, Oxford].
> P.s. 3: 'Chaucer as a Philologist: *The Reeve's Tale*' (1934), p. 109.
> P.s. 4: *Sir Gawain and the Green Knight* (1953), p. 105.
> P.s. 5: *Sir Gawain and the Green Knight* (1975), p. 17.
> S.s. 1: University of Leeds (1921), p. 153. English Language and Literature - Scheme A. Texts selected and Period for 1921-22. (b) Chaucer, with special study. Ordinary Degree of B.A. with Honours. Final Examinations.
> S.s. 2: #1 Holland (1949), p. 143. Appendix XI: Oxford Examinations for Prisoners of War. English B.2 Chaucer and his Contemporaries.
> S.s. 3: Scull-Hammond (2017a), p. 46. April 1913: Tolkien will need to become familiar with a range of literary and philological subjects and set texts as prescribed in the Oxford Regulations of the Board of Studies, knowing that he may be examined on them in ten papers at the end of *Trinity Term 1915*: Middle English texts.

410. _____. *Troilus and Criseyde*. Edited by Raymond Cullis Goffin. Oxford: The University Press, 1935.
> Description: Autographed on back flyleaf: 'J.R.R. Tolkien'. Annotations and corrections in pencil; p. xxiii: Tolkien writes 'to taken' in the margin of the sentence 'Giovanni Boccaccio, the author of *Il Filostrato* or 'The Love-stricken'.' emphasizing the word'stricken'; p. 27: Tolkien corrected a word of the verse 27, Book two, 'y-see who com 'the here ryde!' with 'y-see who cometh here ryde!; p. 123: Tolkien's long annotation on the passage from'such description of hero' to 'alluded to by Chaucer himself'.
> Collection: Private [Oronzo Cilli].
> P.s.: *Sir Gawain and the Green Knight* (1953), p. 105.

411. _____. *Truth*.
> S.s.: University of Leeds (1921), p. 145. English Language, text selected for 1921-22. Ordinary Degree of B.A.; p. 192 English Language and Literature. F2. Final Course (English Literature and Language).

412. _____. *Wife of Bath's Tale* [From *The Canterbury Tales*, Vol. II].
> P.s.: *Letters* 43 (1941). From a letter to Michael Tolkien. Tolkien quotes '*Allas! Allas! That ever love was sinne!*' (Prologue, 614).

413. _____. *The Works of Geoffrey Chaucer*. Edited by Fred Norris Robinson. Boston: Houghton Mifflin Co., 1957 (2nd ed.).
> Notes: Tolkien has given extensive commentary on Robinson's edition on Mroczkowski's criticism [A. 1693].
> P.s.: *Sir Gawain and the Green Knight* (1967) 'Select Bibliography: editions of texts quoted more than once in the notes', p. 156.

414.   Chesterton, Gilbert Keith. *The Ballad of the White Horse*. London: Methuen and Co. Ltd. 1911.
> P.s. 1: *Letters* 80 (1944). From an airgraph to Christopher Tolkien. Tolkien found the poem 'not as good'As he had remembered. 'The ending is absurd. The brilliant smash and glitter of the words and phrases (when they come off, and are not mere loud colours) cannot disguise the fact that G.K.C. knew nothing whatever about the 'North' heathen or Christian'.
> P.s. 2: *Letters* 312 (1969). From a letter to Amy Ronald.
> S.s.: Scull-Hammond (2006b), p. 821.

415.   _____. *Charles Dickens*. New York: Dood, Mead & Co, 1906.
> S.s.: Flieger, *Tolkien On Fairy-stories* (2008), p. 114.

416.   _____. *The Coloured Lands*. London: Sheed and Ward, 1938.
> P.s.: *Tolkien On Fairy-stories* (2008) 'Manuscript A. [MS Tolkien 4, fols. 59-77]', pp. 109, 189 [*The Wild Goose Chase at the Kingdom of the Birds*], 190 [*On Household Gods and Goblin*], 192-193.
> S.s. 1: Scull-Hammond (2017a), p. 238.
> S.s. 2: Scull-Hammond (2017b), p. 227: Tolkien's famous description of 'Mooreeffoc, or Chestertonian Fantasy', to give only one example, was undoubtedly drawn from the introduction to *The Coloured Lands* in which Maisie Ward summarizes an article by Chesterton in The New Witness for 10 June 1915; p. 1060: Priscilla Tolkien told Donald O'Brien in a letter in August 1992 that her father 'Was steeped in the works of Chesterton and [Hilaire] Belloc' (*Beyond Bree*,September 1992, p. 8). Tolkien bought Chesterton's *The Coloured Lands* soon after its publication late in 1938, and used material from it several times in his lecture *On Fairy-Stories* delivered on 8 March 1939.

417.   _____. *The Everlasting Man*. London: Hodder and Stoughton, 1925.
> S.s.: Scull-Hammond (2006b).

418.   _____. *The Flying Inn*. London: Methuen & Co. Ltd, 1914.
> S.s.: Scull-Hammond (2017b), p. 226-7: according to his friend George Sayer, Tolkien knew poems from Chesterton's *The Flying Inn* (1914) well enough to recite them.

419.   _____. *St Francis of Assisi*. London: Hodder and Stoughton Ltd., 1923.
> S.s.: Scull-Hammond (2017b), pp. 226-27.

420.   _____. *George Bernard Shaw*. New York: John Lane Company, 1909.
> P.s.: *Dragons* (1938), p. 43. Tolkien writes: 'Mr Bernard Shaw might say as he did of the calculations of the astronomers that 'the magnitude of the lie seemed inartistic' (from the chapter 'The Progressive', 'the magnitude of the lie seems to me inartistic', p. 61).
> S.s. 1: Scull-Hammond (2017a), p. 38: 24 February 1912 The Apolausticks meet at 8.00 p.m. in O.O. Staples' rooms to discuss G.K. Chesterton and George Bernard Shaw.
> S.s. 2: Scull-Hammond (2017b), pp. 226-27.

421.   _____. *Heretics*. London: John Lane, 1908.
> S.s. 1: Scull-Hammond (2006b), p. 159.
> S.s. 2: Scull-Hammond (2017a), p. 16. During the 1908-9 school year Ronald will present to the School library two books by G. K. Chesterton, *Orthodoxy* (1908) and *Heretics* (1905).

422.   _____. *The Man Who Was Thursday: A Nightmare*. New York: Dodd, Mead and Company, 1908.
> P.s.: *Tolkien On Fairy-stories* (2008) 'Manuscript A. [MS Tolkien 4, fols. 59-77]', p. 109.
> S.s.: Scull-Hammond (2017b), pp. 226-27.

423.   _____. *The Napoleon of Notting Hill*.
> P.s.: *Tolkien On Fairy-stories* (2008) 'Manuscript A. [MS Tolkien 4, fols. 59-77]', p. 192.

SECTION A

424. _____. *Orthodoxy*. London: John Lane, 1908.
    S.s. 1: Scull-Hammond (2017a), p. 16. During the 1908-9 school year Ronald will present to the School library two books by G. K. Chesterton, *Orthodoxy* (1908) and *Heretics* (1905).
    S.s. 2: Scull-Hammond (2006b), p. 820.

425. _____. *The Outline of Sanity*. London: Methuen & Co. Ltd., 1926.
    P.s.: *Tolkien On Fairy-stories* (2008), p. 116.
    S.s.: Scull-Hammond (2017b), p. 227.

426. _____. *The Wild Goose Chase*.
    P.s.: *Tolkien On Fairy-stories* (2008) 'Manuscript A. [MS Tolkien 4, fols. 59-77]', p. 189.

427. Child, Francis James. *The Debate of the Body and the Soul*. Cambridge: John Wilson, University Press, 1888.
    P.s.: MS. Tolkien A 35 *Pearl* fol. 11. [Tolkien Papers, Bodleian Library, Oxford].

428. _____ (Edited by). *The English and Scottish popular ballads*, Vol. I, Pt. I. Boston and New York: Houghton, Mifflin and Company, 1882.
    P.s.: *Sir Gawain and the Green Knight* (1925), p. xxvi. Tolkien and Gordon write: 'For bibliography of the Irish and French analogues of *Sir Gawain*, see the bibliography in Kittredge's study'. Kittredge's study, this article is mentioned in 'III. The Green Knight' (p. 296), 'V. Le Livre de Caradoc' (p. 298), 'IX. The Carl of Carlisle' (p. 301).
    S.s.: Shippey (1992), p. 298.

429. _____ (Edited by). *The English and Scottish popular ballads*, Vol. I, Pt. II. Boston and New York: Houghton, Mifflin and Company, 1884.
    P.s.: *Sir Gawain and the Green Knight* (1925), p. xxvi. Tolkien and Gordon write: 'For bibliography of the Irish and French analogues of *Sir Gawain*, see the bibliography in Kittredge's study'. In Kittredge's study, this article is mentioned in 'III. The Green Knight' (p. 296), 'V. Le Livre de Caradoc' (p. 298), 'IX. The Carl of Carlisle' (p. 301).
    S.s.: Shippey (1992), p. 298.

430. _____ (Edited by). *The English and Scottish popular ballads*, Vol. II, Pt. I. Boston and New York: Houghton, Mifflin and Company, 1885.
    S.s.: Shippey (1992), p. 298.

431. _____ (Edited by). *The English and Scottish popular ballads*, Vol. II, Pt. II. Boston and New York: Houghton, Mifflin and Company, 1886.
    S.s.: Shippey (1992), p. 298.

432. _____ (Edited by). *The English and Scottish popular ballads*, Vol. III, Pt. I. Boston and New York: Houghton, Mifflin and Company, 1888.
    P.s.: *Sir Gawain and the Green Knight* (1925), p. xxvi. Tolkien and Gordon write: 'For bibliography of the Irish and French analogues of *Sir Gawain*, see the bibliography in Kittredge's study'. In Kittredge's study, this article is mentioned in 'XIII. Rauf Coilyear' (p. 306).
    S.s.: Shippey (1992), p. 298.

433. _____ (Edited by). *The English and Scottish popular ballads*, Vol. III, Pt. II. Boston and New York: Houghton, Mifflin and Company, 1889.
    P.s.: *Sir Gawain and the Green Knight* (1925), p. xxvi. Tolkien and Gordon write: 'For bibliography of the Irish and French analogues of *Sir Gawain*, see the bibliography in Kittredge's study'. In Kittredge's study, this article is mentioned in 'XIII. Rauf Coilyear' (p. 306).
    S.s.: Shippey (1992), p. 298.

434. _____ (Edited by). *The English and Scottish popular ballads*, Vol. IV, Pt. I. Boston and New York: Houghton, Mifflin and Company, 1894.

S.s.: Shippey (1992), p. 298.

435. _____ (Edited by). *The English and Scottish popular ballads*, Vol. IV, Pt. II. Boston and New York: Houghton, Mifflin and Company, 1898.
S.s.: Shippey (1992), p. 298.

436. _____ (Edited by). *The English and Scottish popular ballads*, Vol. V, Pt. I. Boston and New York: Houghton, Mifflin and Company, 1890.
P.s.: Sir Gawain and the Green Knight (1925), p. xxvi. Tolkien and Gordon write: 'For bibliography of the Irish and French analogues of *Sir Gawain*, see the bibliography in Kittredge's study'. In Kittredge's study, this article is mentioned in 'XIII. Rauf Coilyear' (p. 306).
S.s.: Shippey (1992), p. 298.

437. _____ (Edited by). *The English and Scottish popular ballads*, Vol. V, Pt. II. Boston and New York: Houghton, Mifflin and Company, 1892.
P.s.: *Sir Gawain and the Green Knight* (1925), p. xxvi. Tolkien and Gordon write: 'For bibliography of the Irish and French analogues of *Sir Gawain*, see the bibliography in Kittredge's study'. In Kittredge's study, this article is mentioned in 'XIII. Rauf Coilyear' (p. 306).
S.s.: Shippey (1992), p. 298.

438. Chrétien de Troyes. *The Continuations of the Old French Perceval of Chrétien de Troyes*, Vol. I. Edited by William Roach and Robert H. Ivy. Philadelphia: University of Pennsylvania Press, 1949.
P.s.: *Sir Gawain and the Green Knight* (1967) 'Select Bibliography', p. 154. (*Le Livre de Caradoc*, pp. 89-97).

439. _____. *The Continuations of the Old French Perceval of Chrétien de Troyes*, Vol. II. Edited by William Roach and Robert H. Ivy. Philadelphia: University of Pennsylvania Press, 1950.
P.s.: *Sir Gawain and the Green Knight* (1967) 'Select Bibliography', p. 154. (*Le Livre de Caradoc*, pp. 209-19).

440. _____. *The Continuations of the Old French Perceval of Chrétien de Troyes*, Vol. III, Pt. I. Edited by William Roach and Robert H. Ivy. Philadelphia: University of Pennsylvania Press, 1952.
P.s.: *Sir Gawain and the Green Knight* (1967) 'Select Bibliography', p. 154. (*Le Livre de Caradoc*, pp. 141-56).

441. _____. *The Continuations of the Old French Perceval of Chrétien de Troyes*, Vol. III, Pt. II. Edited by William Roach and Robert H. Ivy. Philadelphia: University of Pennsylvania Press, 1955.
P.s.: *Sir Gawain and the Green Knight* (1967) 'Select Bibliography', p. 154.

442. _____. *Perceval le Gallois ou le Conte du Graal*, Vol. I. Published by Charles Potvin. Mons: Dequesne-Masquillier, 1866.
P.s.: *Sir Gawain and the Green Knight* (1925), pp. xiii, xxvi. Tolkien and Gordon cite p. 117 f., p. 84 line 110 *Agrauayn a la dure mayn*. Tolkien and Gordon cite 'Et li secons est Agrevains | Li orguelleus as durens mains' (9309-10).

443. _____. *Perceval le Gallois ou le Conte du Graal*, Vol. III. Published by Charles Potvin. Mons: Dequesne-Masquillier, 1866.
P.s.: *Sir Gawain and the Green Knight* (1925), pp. xiii, xxvi. Tolkien and Gordon cite p. 117 f., p. 84 line 110 *Agrauayn a la dure mayn*. Tolkien and Gordon cite 'Et li secons est Agrevains | Li orguelleus as durens mains' (9309-10).

SECTION A

444. _____. *Der Percevalroman*: (Li Contes de Graal). Series: Sämtliche erhaltene Werke / Christian von Troyes, 5. Halle: Max Niemeyer, 1932.
P.s.: *Sir Gawain and the Green Knight* (1967) 'Select Bibliography', p. 154.

445. Christie, Agatha. *At Bertram's Hotel*. London: Collins Crime Club, 1965.
Description: Gift from his wife Edith. Autographed on front flyleaf: '* | from E | J.R.R. Tolkien'. Collection: Private [Fr. Richard Aladics].
S.s. 2: Michael G.R. Tolkien (1995). Michael G.R. Tolkien writes: [On Agatha Christie books] 'It's not surprising that he read detective fiction for relaxation and went out of his way to praise Agatha Christie.'

446. Christopher, John. [Sam Youd] *The Death of Grass*. London: Michael Joseph, 1956.
P.s.: *Letters* 294 (1967). To Charlotte and Denis Plimmer. Tolkien writes: 'was greatly taken by the book that was (I believe) the runner-up when *The L. R.* was given the Fantasy Award *Death of Grass*'.
S.s. 1: Scull-Hammond (2017a), p. 539.
S.s. 2: Scull-Hammond (2006b), p. 818. Tolkien was also 'greatly taken by' *The Death of Grass*.

447. Cibber, Colley. *An Apology for the life of Mr. Colley Cibber*, Vol. I. London: J. C. Nimmo, 1889.
S.s.: University of Leeds (1921), p. 154. English Language and Literature - Scheme A. Texts and Period selected for 1921-22. (d) Texts suggested for study with Special Period 1637-1700. Ordinary Degree of B.A. with Honours. Final Examinations. chapters suggested: I-VIII.

448. Cicero, Marcus Tullius. *The four orations of Cicero against Catiline*. Translated by Roscoe Morgan. London: James Cornish & Sons, 1879.
Description: Tolkien requested the book on 6 October 1913 (MS. Library Records b. 606). Weston Library (Oxford), 29463 e.1.

449. _____. *De Natura Deorum* [*On the Nature of the Gods*]
P.s.: *Dragons* (1938), p. 46. Tolkien writes: 'already the Roman Latin *draco* appeared in military standards and was fond of treasure. Cicero mentioned it'. Tolkien cites the second book.

450. Clarendon, Edward Hyde. *The History of the Rebellion and civil wars in England begun in the year 1641*, Vol. I. Edited by William Dunn Macray. Oxford: At the Clarendon Press, 1888.
S.s.: University of Leeds (1921), p. 154. English Language and Literature - Scheme A. Texts and Period selected for 1921-22. (d) Texts suggested for study with Special Period 1637-1700. Ordinary Degree of B.A. with Honours. Final Examinations.

451. _____. *The History of the Rebellion and civil wars in England begun in the year 1641*, Vol. II. Edited by William Dunn Macray. Oxford: At the Clarendon Press, 1888.
S.s.: University of Leeds (1921), p. 154. English Language and Literature - Scheme A. Texts and Period selected for 1921-22. (d) Texts suggested for study with Special Period 1637-1700. Ordinary Degree of B.A. with Honours. Final Examinations.

452. Clark, Cecily (Edited by). *The Peterborough Chronicle 1070-1154*. Series: Oxford English Monographs, 5. London Oxford University Press, 1958.
Notes: Tolkien was one of the General Editors for the series.

453. Classen, Ernest and Florence Elizabeth Harmer. *An Anglo-Saxon chronicle from the British Museum, Cotton MS., Tiberius B. IV*. Series: Modern Languages texts, English series. Manchester: The University Press, 1926.

P.s.: *Philology: General Works* (VI 1927, for 1925), p. 50.

454. Clawson, William Hall. *The gest of Robin Hood*. Toronto: University of Toronto Library, 1909.
P.s.: *Sir Gawain and the Green Knight* (1925), p. xxvi. Tolkien and Gordon write: 'For bibliography of the Irish and French analogues of *Sir Gawain*, see the bibliography in Kittredge's study'. [*NED*] In Kittredge's study, this article is mentioned in 'XIII. Rauf Coilyear' (p. 306).

455. Clutton-Brock, Arthur. *William Morris: his work and influence*. London: Williams and Norgate, 1914.
S.s.: Mathews (2002), p. 87. Richard Mathews writes: '[Christopher Tolkien] In a subsequent letter, he listed 11 titles of Morris's books of poems, translations, and fantasies that his father bequeathed to him, including *The House of the Wolfings*, *The Roots of the Mountains*, and *The Sundering Flood*, plus J. W. Mackail's two-volume *Life of William Morris* and A. Clutton-Brock's *William Morris: His Work and Influence*. Tolkien had begun collecting and reading Morris–even reading Morris aloud to his son–at a time when his popularity and critical reputation were at an all-time low and his work had been eclipsed by World War I and the onward rush of technology and current events.' (Christopher Tolkien to the author).

456. Cockayne, Thomas Oswald (Edited by). *The Liflade of St Juliana*. London, 1882.
Description: Inscribed: 'J R R Tolkien'. A few annotations.
Collection: Weston Library, Bodleian Libraries (Oxford).

457. _____. *Leechdoms, wortcunning, and starcraft of early England*, Vol. I. London: Longman, Green, Longman, Roberts, and Green, 1864.
P.s.: *Sigelwara land* (1934), p. 97. Tolkien refers to pp. 24, 52, 152, 254.

458. _____. *Leechdoms, wortcunning, and starcraft of early England*, Vol. II. London: Longman, Green, Longman, Roberts, and Green, 1865.
P.s.: *Sigelwara land* (1934), p. 97. n. 1. Tolkien refers pp. 94, 108, 326.

459. _____. *Leechdoms, wortcunning, and starcraft of early England*, Vol. III. London: Longman, Green, Longman, Roberts, and Green, 1866.
P.s.: *Sigelwara land* (1934), p. 97.

460. _____. *Narratiunculae Anglice conscriptae. De pergamenis exscribebas notis illustrabat eruditis copiam*. London: I. R. Smith, 1861.
P.s. 1: [Mythopoeic Society, *Parma Eldalamberon* 15 (2004), ER1 p. 97] 1918-1920, on a sheet of ruled paper Tolkien writes: 'Cockayne. *Narratiuncula*. 25/18 | Óþer ðara is wæpned cynnes, sunnan trio, óþer wifcynnes, ðæt mónan trio.'
P.s. 2: *Sigelwara land* (1932), p. 189 n. 1.

461. _____ (Edited by). *Seinte Marherete the meiden ant martyr, in Old English*. Series: E.E.T.S. (Early English Text Society), OS 13. Pub. for the Early English text society, by Trübner & co. London, 1866.
Description: Annotations throughout.
Collection: Weston Library, Bodleian Libraries (Oxford).
P.s.: *Sigelwara land* (1932), p. 192 n. 2.

462. _____. *The Shrine: a collection of occasional papers on dry subjects*. London: Williams and Norgate, 1864.
P.s. 1: *Beowulf* (1937), p. 3.
P.s. 2: *Beowulf* (2002) 'Version A', p. 31.

Section A

463. Colborn, A. F. (Edited by). *Hali meiðhad*. Copenhagen: Einar Munksgaard and London: H. Milford, Oxford University Press, 1940.
   Notes: On page 3, Colborn thanks Tolkien: 'I must, at the beginning, thank Professor Tolkien most sincerely for this invaluable help and direction in the original prepration of the work, then calculated to be a part of that examination of the West Midland dialect which he has made one of his special concerns'.
   P.s.: Tolkien's unpublished letter to A. F. Colborn, 21 July 1938.
   S.s.: Millett (1996), p. 108. '[Based on: 'A critical text of Hali Meidhad, together with a grammar and glossarial notes.' [C. 13] B.Litt. diss. U of Oxford, 1934, Dir. J.R.R. Tolkien.]'. And [Colborn] 'There follows a description (47-59) of the MSS, their relationship, and their dialectal features (drawing heavily on Tolkien [Ancrene Wisse and Hali Meidhad (1929)])'.

464. Coleridge, Samuel Taylor. *Biographia literaria*. Oxford: At the Clarendon Press, 1905.
   P.s. 1: *On Fairy-stories* (1947), p. 60.
   P.s. 2: *Tolkien On Fairy-stories* (2008), p. 107. Tolkien quotes the passage 'Willing suspension of disbelief' (p. 144).
   S.s.: University of Leeds (1921), p. 141. English Literature, text selected for 1921-22. Ordinary Degree of B.A.; p. 154. English Language and Literature - Scheme A. Texts and Period selected for 1921-22. (e) History of Criticism: Special Texts suggested for study. Ordinary Degree of B.A. with Honours. Final Examinations.

465. _____. *The Poems of Samuel Taylor Coleridge*. Edited by Ernest Hartley Coleridge. London: Humphrey Milford for Oxford University Press, 1927.
   P.s.: *Beowulf* (2002), p. 38. Tolkien quotes 'Kubla Khan'.

466. Collingwood, Robin George. *The Archæology of Roman Britain*. London: Methuen and Co., 1930.
   Collection: Tolkien's personal Celtic library, preserved at the Weston library under the auspices of the English Faculty Library (Oxford).

467. _____ and John Nowell Linton Myres. *Roman Britain and the English Settlements*. Series: The Oxford History of England. Oxford: At the Clarendon Press, 1936.
   Description: On p. vii: 'Four special debt must be mentioned. My colleague Professor J.R.R. Tolkien has helped me untiringly with problems of Celtic philology'; p. 264, on the deity worshipped at the thermal spring of Bath:'she is traditionally called Sul; but Professor Tolkien points out to me that the Celtic nominative can only be Sulis, and our authority for believing that even the Romans made a nominative Sul on the analogy of their own word sol — perhaps meaning the same — is not good. The Celtic sulis may mean 'the eye', and this again may mean the sun.'
   P.s.: Finn and Hengest (1982), p. 168 n15.

468. Collins, William. *Odes*.
   S.s.: University of Leeds, *Calendar 1921-22*, p. 145. English Literature, text selected for 1921-22. Ordinary Degree of B.A.; p. 191 English Language and Literature. F1. Final Course (English Literature) (ii) The History of English Literature from 1700 to 1765.

469. Collitz, Hermann. *Das Schwache Präteritum und seine Vorgeschichte*, Vol. I. Series: Hesperia, Schriften zur germanischen Philologie, 1. Göttingen: Vandenhoeck and Rupprecht, 1912.
   Description: Autographed: 'JRR Tolkien'. Is written in pencil on the dark green coloured first end paper and the name Tolkien is repeated in orange below that.
   Collection: Private [TolkienLibrary.com].

470. Colvin, Sidney. *Keats*. Series: English Men of Letters. London: Macmillan and Co., 1887.

P.s.: *Exeter College library register*. Tolkien's borrowing record: *Trinity Term 1915* from 15 May to 16 June.

471. *Complaynt of Scotland*, 1548. [Scottish propaganda book, see Laneham].
P.s.: *Philology: General Works* (IV 1924, for 1923), p. 21.

472. Compton-Ricket, Arthur. *A History of English Literature*. London: T.C. & E.C., 1912.
P.s.: *Beowulf* (2002) 'Version A', p. 34 n. 4.

473. Conan Doyle, Arthur. *The Sign of Four*. London: Spencer Blackett, 1890.
P.s.: *Beowulf* (2002) 'Version A', p. 33.

474. _____. *The White Company*. London: Smith, Elder and Co., 1895.
P.s.: Tolkien's unpublished 1920s letter to Edith Bratt. In an interesting group of early Tolkien letters providing a highly detailed account of the tragedy that bestruck him while serving as a tutor to two young Mexican boys and their aunt in 1913. 'Rushing about sight-seeing or any obvious form of enjoyment is of course out of the questions for a while so I have tried to find out what the best, most readable, and best palpable 'instructive' of boys books they haven't read. Many of these I have got in cheap editions ... such as *King Solomon's Mines*, Kim and so forth ... [Jose] is now reading *The White Company*.' [Sold by Christie's, 8 April 2003].
S.s. 1: Scull-Hammond (2017a), p. 52.
S.s. 2: Scull-Hammond (2006b), p. 816.
Reading period: 1913 (S.s.: Scull-Hammond (2017c), p. 1054).

475. Congreve, William. *The Complete Plays of William Congreve*. Series: Mermaid. Edited by Alexander Charles Ewald. New York: American Book Co., 1912.
S.s.: University of Leeds (1921), p. 154. English Language and Literature - Scheme A. Texts and Period selected for 1921-22. (d) Texts suggested for study with Special Period 1637-1700. Ordinary Degree of B.A. with Honours. Final Examinations.

476. _____. *The Way of the World*.
S.s.: University of Leeds (1920), p. 139 English Language and Literature: English Literature. Text selected for 1920-21. Texts Selected for 1920-21. Ordinary Degree of B.A. with Honours. Final Course and Examination.

477. Conway, Robert Seymour. *The Italic dialects*, Vol. I. The records of Oscan, Umbrian and the Minor dialects, including the Italic glosses in ancient writers and the local and personal names of the dialect areas. Cambridge: The University Press, 1897.
Description: Signed in the front by J.R.R. Tolkien and annotations in pencil.
Collection: Private [Sold by Peter Harrington Antiquarian Bookseller].
S.s.: Harrington (2003), p. 25.

478. _____. *The Italic dialects*, Vol. II. An outline of the grammar of the dialects, appendix, indices and glossary. Cambridge: The University Press, 1897.
Description: Signed in the front by J.R.R. Tolkien and annotations in pencil.
Collection: Private [Sold by Peter Harrington Antiquarian Bookseller].
S.s.: Harrington (2003), p. 25.

479. Conybeare, John Josias. *Illustrations of Anglo-Saxon*. Edited by William Daniel Conybeare. London: Harding and lepard, 1826.
P.s.: *Beowulf* (2002) 'Version A', p. 44. Tolkien cites the note on page 33.

480. Cook, Albert Stanborough. *A Glossary of the Old Northumbrian Gospels. Lindisfarne Gospels or Durham book*. Halle: Max Niemeyer, 1894.

SECTION A

Description: Autographed in pencil on front flyleaf.
Collection: Tolkien's personal Celtic library, preserved at the Weston library under the auspices of the English Faculty Library (Oxford).
P.s.: 'Chaucer as a Philologist: *The Reeve's Tale*' (1934), p. 135. Tolkien writes: '*Til* is found in Old English, only in Northumbrian (Ruthwell Cross, Cædmon's Hymn, Lindisfarne glosses: in senses *to*, *for*, and before infinitive)' [p. 185]

481. _____. *A Literary Middle English Reader*. London: Ginn and Co., 1915.
S.s.: University of Leeds (1921), p. 153. English Language and Literature - Scheme A. Texts and Period selected for 1921-22. (a) Selected Texts in Old and Middle English. Ordinary Degree of B.A. with Honours. Final Examinations. 'With special reference to the extracts beginning on pp. 219, 235, 237, 269, 316, 321, 334.

482. Corelli, Marie. *Ziska; the problem of a wicked soul*. Series: Collection of British authors. Leipzig, B. Tauchnitz, 1897.
P.s.: *Oxford University Press Archives* (Oxford). In a slip written by Tolkien on the etymology of 'Waistcoated' not used, and reads: '(waistcoated) | 2. Comb. esp. white-waistcoated: | Weaning a white waistcoat, also applied to | birds with white plumage on the beast'.
NED: #2 b. | 'W' (1928), p. 23 'Waistcoated, *a*.' 1897 – 'His paunch, a kind of waistcoated air balloon.'

483. *Corpus Christi College Cambridge MS. 402*. [Contains *Ancrene Wisse*, Middle English rule for anchoresses].
P.s.: MS. Tolkien A 21/13 *The English MSS*. fol. 197. [Tolkien Papers, Bodleian Library, Oxford].

484. Cosijn, Pieter Jacob. 'Anglosaxonica I'. Beiträge zur Geschichte der deutschen Sprache und Literatur, Vol. XIX. Halle: Max Niemeyer, 1894, pp. 441-61.
P.s.: *The Old English Exodus* (1982), p. ix.

485. _____. 'Anglosaxonica II'. *Beiträge zur Geschichte der deutschen Sprache und Literatur*, Vol. XX. Halle: Max Niemeyer, 1895, pp. 98-106.
P.s.: *The Old English Exodus* (1982), p. ix.

486. Cotgrave, Rande. *A Dictionarie of the French and English Tongues*. Series: Archives de la linguistique française, 92. London; Adam Islip, 1611.
P.s.: MS. Tolkien A 11 *Notes on Pearl* fol. 59. [Tolkien Papers, Bodleian Library, Oxford].
NED 1: 'W' (1928), p. 98 'Wariangle, 1.' 1611 – '*Ancrouelle, pie. an. a Shrike, Ninmurder, Wariangle*'. (p. 40)
NED 2: #2 h. | 'W' (1928), p. 53 'Wallop *sb*. 2. b.' – 1611 '*Onde, Bouillir vne onde*, to boyle a wbyle, or but for one bubble, or a wallop or two'.

487. *Cotton MS Cleopatra C. vi.* [Contains *Ancrene Riwle*].
P.s.: MS. Tolkien A 21/13 *The English MSS*. fol. 197. [Tolkien Papers, Bodleian Library, Oxford].

488. *Cotton MS. Nero A xiv.* [Contains *Ancrene Wisse*].
P.s.: MS. Tolkien A 21/13 *The English MSS*. fol. 197. [Tolkien Papers, Bodleian Library, Oxford].

489. *Cotton MS. Titus D. xviii.* [Contains *Sawles Warde, Seinte Katherine* and *Hali Meiðhad* (Katherine Group)].
P.s.: MS. Tolkien A 21/13 *The English MSS*. fol. 197. [Tolkien Papers, Bodleian Library, Oxford].

490. Coulton, George Gordon. *Chaucer and his England*. London: Methuen & Co., 1909.
S.s. 1: University of Leeds (1920), p. 182. English Language and Literature. F2. Final Course (English Literature and Language). Books reccomended.
S.s. 2: University of Leeds (1921), p. 193 English Language and Literature. F2. Final Course

(English Literature and Language). Books recommended.

491. _____. 'In defence of *Pearl*'. MLR (*The Modern Language Review*), Vol. 2, 1907, pp. 39-43.
P.s.: MS. Tolkien A 35 *Pearl* fol. 114. [Tolkien Papers, Bodleian Library, Oxford].

492. Courthorpe, William John. *History of English Poetry*, Vol. I The Middle Ages: influence of the roman empire; The encyclopædic education of the church; The feudal system. London: Macmillan and Co., 1895.
P.s. 1: *Exeter College library register*. Tolkien's borrowing record: *Summer 1919* from 22 May to 16 June; *Hilary Term 1920* from 21 January to 12 March.
P.s. 2: MS. Tolkien A 21/13 fol. 119. Note by Tolkien, 'Books in Exeter Library useful', with shelfmarks, on back of photostat reading list dated October 1913. [Tolkien Papers, Bodleian Library, Oxford].

493. _____. *History of English Poetry*, Vol. II The Renaissance and the Reformation: influence of the court and the universities. London: Macmillan and Co., 1897.
P.s. 1: *Exeter College library register*. Tolkien's borrowing record: *Summer 1919* from 22 May to 16 June.
P.s. 2: MS. Tolkien A 21/13 fol. 119. Note by Tolkien, 'Books in Exeter Library useful', with shelfmarks, on back of photostat reading list dated October 1913. [Tolkien Papers, Bodleian Library, Oxford].

494. _____. *History of English Poetry*, Vol. III Decadent influence of feudal monarchy, growth of the national genius. London: Macmillan and Co., 1903.
P.s: MS. Tolkien A 21/13 fol. 119. Note by Tolkien, 'Books in Exeter Library useful', with shelfmarks, on back of photostat reading list dated October 1913. [Tolkien Papers, Bodleian Library, Oxford].

495. _____. *History of English Poetry*, Vol. IV Development and decline of the poetic drama: influence of the court and the people. London: Macmillan and Co., 1903.
P.s.: MS. Tolkien A 21/13 fol. 119. Note by Tolkien, 'Books in Exeter Library useful', with shelfmarks, on back of photostat reading list dated October 1913. [Tolkien Papers, Bodleian Library, Oxford].

496. _____. *History of English Poetry*, Vol. V The constitutional compromise of the 18. century. Effects of the classical Renaissance: its zenith and decline, the early romantic Renaissance. London: Macmillan and Co., 1905.
P.s.: MS. Tolkien A 21/13 fol. 119. Note by Tolkien, 'Books in Exeter Library useful', with shelfmarks, on back of photostat reading list dated October 1913. [Tolkien Papers, Bodleian Library, Oxford].

497. _____. *History of English Poetry*, Vol. VI The romantic movement in English Poetry effects of the French Revolution. London: Macmillan and Co., 1910.
P.s.: MS. Tolkien A 21/13 fol. 119. Note by Tolkien, 'Books in Exeter Library useful', with shelfmarks, on back of photostat reading list dated October 1913. [Tolkien Papers, Bodleian Library, Oxford].

498. Coverdale, Miles. *Biblia: the Bible, that is, the holy Scripture of the Olde and New Testament, faithfully and truly translated out of Douche and Latyn in to Englishe*. S.l.: Printed by E. Cervicornus and J. Soter, 1535.
P.s.: MS. Tolkien A 12/1 *Commentary on Sir Gawain, lines 37-1987* fol. 103. [Tolkien Papers, Bodleian Library, Oxford].

SECTION A

499. Coward, Thomas Alfred. *The Birds of the British Isles and their eggs*. London: F. Warne, 1919.
   S.s.: Drout (2007), p. 37

500. Cowley, Abraham. *Essays*. London: Cassell, 1886.
   S.s.: University of Leeds (1920), p. 139 English Language and Literature: English Literature. Text selected for 1920-21. Texts Selected for 1920-21. Ordinary Degree of B.A. with Honours. Final Course and Examination.

501. _____. *The Mistress*. Cambridge: The University Press, 1905.
   S.s.: University of Leeds (1921), p. 154. English Language and Literature - Scheme A. Texts and Period selected for 1921-22. (d) Texts suggested for study with Special Period 1637-1700. Ordinary Degree of B.A. with Honours. Final Examinations.

502. Cowper, William. *The Task: A Poem, in Six Books*.
   P.s.: *Letters* 61 (1944). From a letter to Christopher Tolkien.

503. Cox, Marian Roalfe (Edited by). *Cinderella; three hundred and forty-five variants of Cinderella, Catskin, and Cap o'Rushes, abstracted and tabulated, with a discussion of mediaeval analogues, and notes*. Series: Publications of the Folklore Society, 31. Introduction by Andrew Lang. London: The Folklore Society, 1893.
   P.s. 1: *Tolkien On Fairy-stories* (2008) 'Manuscript B [MS. Tolkien 4, fols. 73-120]', p. 214.
   P.s. 2: #1 a. | Tolkien On Fairy-stories (2008), p. 309. Tolkien refers to Lang introduction.

504. Craigie, William Alexander. 'A Rare Use of the Preposition 'to''. MLR (*The Modern Language Review*), Vol. 20, no. 2, April 1925, pp. 184-85.
   P.s.: Postcard to W. A. Craigie 'apropos of your collection in MLR April 1925'. Date: 5 May [19]26; addressed 22 Northmoor Road, Oxford (Special Collections, James Joyce Library, University College Dublin).

505. *Crist, The*. [A three-part poem in Old English, the first of those in the *Exeter Book*, see Krapp and Dobbie.]
   Notes: Cynewulf is now accepted as the author only of the second part. The word *earendel* appears in the first part, line 104.
   P.s. 1: Tolkien's copy of *Studien zu den Skalden des 9. und 10. Jahrhunderts* (1928) by Konrad Reichardt, contains a page of notes on the verso of Tolkien's dining expenses from Pembroke College during the week of 29 November 1928; the notes refer to the *Genesis* and *Exodus* poems – Old English poetry which Tolkien would used while working on Cynewulf's *Crist*.
   P.s. 2: *Beowulf* (2014), p. 184.
   S.s.: Scull-Hammond (2017a), p. 48. Trinity Term 1913.

506. Crockett, Samuel Rutherford. *The Black Douglas*. London: Smith, Elder, 1899.
   P.s.: *Letters* 306 (1968). From a letter to Michael Tolkien. Tolkien writes: 'Through the episode of the 'Wargs' (I believe) is in part derived from a scene in S. R. Crockett's *The Black Douglas*, probably his best romance and anyway one that deeply impressed me in school-days, though I have never looked at it again.'
   S.s. 1: Anderson (2002), p. 149 n. 10.
   S.s. 2: Scull-Hammond (2006b), p. 816.
   S.s. 3: Drout (2007), p. 367.
   Reading period: 1908 – early 1910 (S.s.: Scull-Hammond (2017c), p. 1054).

507. _____. *The men of the Moss-Hags: being a history of adventure taken from the papers of William Gordon of Earlstoun in Galloway*. London, Macmillan and Co., 1895.
   P.s.: *Letters* 306 (1968). From a letter to Michael Tolkien. Tolkien writes: 'We lay more doggo than 'men of the moss-hags' for some time'.

508. Croker, Bithia Mary. *Babes in the wood: a romance of the jungles*. 1910.
   P.s.: *Letters* 211 (1958). To Rhona Beare. Tolkien writes '[Elrond and Elros] The infants were not slain, but left like 'babes in the wood', in a cave with a fall of water over the entrance. There they were found: Elrond within the cave, and Elros dabbling in the wate'.

509. Crombie, Max. *The Infidel Grape: An Anthology in Miniature in Praise of Wine*. Series: Lute, lyre and lotus minithologies, 2. Northwood: Knights Press, 1940.
   Description: Presentation copy to J.R.R. Tolkien inscribed in pen on inside front cover: 'With every good wish for Christmas- H.T.McM.B.' [Helen Therese McMillan Buckhurst]. And in ink on front free endpaper: 'J.R.R.T.' Includes a label added by Stan Revell to books owned by Tolkien, 'From the Library of J.R.R. Tolkien'.
   Collection: Marion E. Wade Center, Wheaton College (Wheaton, Illinois).

510. Crossley-Holland, Kevin. *Beowulf*. London: Macmillan, 1968.
   S.s.: Scull-Hammond (2017a), pp. 765-66. 25 July 1968: A proof copy was sent to Tolkien by the publisher, encloses the letter from Macmillan & Co. and the proof copy of Crossley-Holland's translation of *Beowulf*, and asks Joy [Hill] to explain that he cannot deal with it because of his accident (3 August 1968).

511. *Cuckoo Song* 1240. [Middle English song, see Ellis].
   P.s.: MS. Tolkien A 21/13 The English MSS. fol. 203. [Tolkien Papers, Bodleian Library, Oxford].

512. *Cursor Mundi* 1320. [Middle English historical and religious poem, see R. Morris].
   P.s. 1: MS. Tolkien A 21/7 fol. 30. [Tolkien Papers, Bodleian Library, Oxford].
   P.s. 2: MS. Tolkien A 21/13 *The English MSS*. fol. 203. [Tolkien Papers, Bodleian Library, Oxford].

513. Cynewulf. *Cynewulf's Elene*. Translated by Ferdinand Holthausen. Heidelberg: Carl Winter, 1914.
   Collection: Taylor Institution Library, Bodleian Libraries (Oxford).
   P.s. 1: MS. Tolkien 16/2 *Notes and drafts concerning Elene*. [Tolkien Papers, Bodleian Library, Oxford].
   P.s. 2: *Beowulf* (2014), pp. 175, 192, 239, 310.
   S.s.: Scull-Hammond (2017a), p. 46. April 1913: Tolkien will need to become familiar with a range of literary and philological subjects and set texts as prescribed in the Oxford Regulations of the Board of Studies, knowing that he may be examined on them in ten papers at the end of Trinity Term 1915: Old English texts.

514. _____. *The Juliana of Cynewulf*. Translated by William Strunk. London: D. C. Healt and Co., 1904.
   P.s.: *Beowulf* (2014), p. 226.
   NED: #2 h. | 'W' (1928), p. 54. 'Walm *sb.*[1] *Obs*. 3. a.' – 'In ðæs leades wylm scufa' (583).

515. d'Alòs-Moner, Ramon *et alii*. *Abhandlungen aus dem Gebiete der mittleren und neueren Geschichte und ihrer Hilfswissenschaften. Eine festgabe zum siebzigsten geburtstag geh. rat prof. dr. Heinrich Finke gewidmet von schülern und verehrern des 'in-' und 'Auslandes'*. Series: Vorreformationsgeschichtliche forschungen. Supplementband. Münster: W. Aschendorff, 1925.
   P.s.: *Philology: General Works* (VI 1927, for 1925), p. 46.

516. D'Ancona, Alessandro. *Sacre rappresentazioni dei secoli XIV, XV e XVI*, Vol. II. Firenze: Successori Le Monnier, 1872.
   P.s.: MS. Tolkien A 13/2 *Notes and drafts of lectures on Chaucer: Pardoner's Tale* fol. 77. [Tolkien Papers, Bodleian Library, Oxford]. Tolkien refers to page 50.

517. d'Arbois de Jubainville, Henry. *Les Celtes. Depuis les temps les plus anciens*

Section A

jusqu'en l'an 100 avant notre ère: étude historique. Paris: A. Fontemoing, 1904.
Collection: Tolkien's personal Celtic library, preserved at the Weston library under the auspices of the English Faculty Library (Oxford).
P.s. 1: *Philology: General Works* (IV 1924, for 1923), p. 23.
P.s. 2: *The Name 'Nodens'* (1932), p. 133.

518. _____. 'Festin de Brigriu: Notice préliminaire; Traduction (Ms. Lebor na hUidre, vers 1100, editeur M.E. Windisch); Note finales'. *Cours de littérature celtique*, Vol. V, 1892, pp. 81-148.
P.s.: *Sir Gawain and the Green Knight* (1925), p. xxvi. Tolkien and Gordon write: 'For bibliography of the Irish and French analogues of *Sir Gawain*, see the bibliography in Kittredge's study'. [*NED*] In Kittredge's study, this article is mentioned in 'I. Fled Bricrend' (p. 292 n. 4).

519. _____. *Introduction a l'etude de la litterature celtique*. Paris: E. Thorin, 1883.
Description: Decoratively autographed and dated on front flyleaf: '1923'. Annotated in red and blue crayon.
Collection: Tolkien's personal Celtic library, preserved at the Weston library under the auspices of the English Faculty Library (Oxford).

520. _____. 'Saint Denis portant sa téte sur la potrine'. *Revue Celtique*, Vol. XII, 1891, pp. 166-67.
P.s.: *Sir Gawain and the Green Knight* (1925), p. xxvi. Tolkien and Gordon write: 'For bibliography of the Irish and French analogues of *Sir Gawain*, see the bibliography in Kittredge's study'. [*NED*] In Kittredge's study, this article is mentioned in 'I. Fled Bricrend' (p. 292 n. 3).

521. _____ and Emilie Ernault. *Glossaire Moyen-Breton*, Vol. II. Des Langues Celtiques. Paris: E. Bouillon, 1895 (Deuxiéme Édition).
Description: Autographed on page after front flyleaf: 'JRR Tolkien. 1922'.
Collection: Tolkien's personal Celtic library, preserved at the Weston library under the auspices of the English Faculty Library (Oxford).
S.s.: Scull-Hammond (2017a), p. 126.

522. D'Arcy, Martin Cyril. *The nature of belief*. London: Sheed & Ward, 1931.
Description: Inscribed, 'To Prof. Tolkien with every good wish from Rene & Jack Eccles Christmas 1931' from Fr. John Tolkien's library.
Collection: Private.

523. d'Ardenne, S. R. T. O. (Simonne Rosalie Thérèse Odile). 'The Devil's Spout'. *Transactions of the Philological Society*, Vol. 45 n 1, November 1946, pp. 31-55.
P.s.: 'Middle English 'Losenger'' (1953), p. 65. Tolkien writes: 'The *totelere* has been brought to book elsewhere; for Professor d'Ardenne has studied this creature, his name, and its connexions, in *The Devil's Spout* with a wealth of learning and illustration which (even if I could emulate it) would not on this occasion be possible.'

524. _____. 'The Old English inscription on the Brussels cross'. *English Studies*, Vol. 21, Nos. 1-6. Abingdon: Routledge, 1939, pp. 145-64.
S.s.: Scull-Hammond (2017a), p. 237.

525. _____ and J.R.R. Tolkien. *An Edition of Þe Liflade ant Te Passiun of Seinte Iuliene*. Liége and Paris: Bibliothéque de la Faculté de Philosphie et Lettres de l'Université de Liége (Fasc. LXIV) Faculté de Philosphie et Lettres and Librarie E. Droz; Printed at the University Press, Oxford, 1936.
Description: The book is dedicated to him: 'TO | PROFESSOR J.R.R. TOLKIEN | THIS SMALL CONTRIBUTION TO THE STUDY OF | THE 'ANCRENE WISSE' LANGUAGE | IS RESPECTFULLY | DEDICATED'. Tolkien is also acknowledged by d'Ardenne in the prefatory note on p. vii. 'To Professor J.R.R. Tolkien I am deeply indebted for assistance from the beginning

of my work on this text, and especially during the revision of the glossary and grammar.'
P.s. 1: *Sir Gawain and the Green Knight* (1967) 'Select Bibliography: editions of texts quoted more than once in the notes', p. 156.
P.s. 2: '*Iþþlen' in Sawles Warde* (1947), p. 169.

526. _____. and J.R.R. Tolkien. *Þe Liflade ant Te Passiun of Seinte Iuliene* [An Edition of the Life and the Passion of Saint Juliana]. Series: E.E.T.S. (Early English Text Society), OS 248. London: Oxford University Press, 1961.
Description: [A. 525].
P.s.: *Sir Gawain and the Green Knight* (1967) 'Select Bibliography: editions of texts quoted more than once in the notes', p. 156.

527. _____ and Eric John Dobson. *Seinte Katerine*. Series: E.E.T.S. (Early English Text Society), SS 7. London: Oxford University Press, 1981.
Description: In their Preface, S.R.T.O.d'A. and E. J. Dobson thank Tolkien: 'When S.R.T.O. d'A. first planned this edition, over forty years ago, she had hoped to have the collaboration of J.R.R. Tolkien, the academic supervisor of her work on *Seinte Iuliene* [A. 525], but in the event (initialy because of the war of 1939-45) he took no part in ti; nevertheless she and her eventuale co-editor wish to express their great sense of obligation to and their admiration of his teaching and inspiration.' (p. vi)
S.s.: Scull-Hammond (2017a), p. 587. 1 May 1960 Robert Burchfield, Early English Text Society, writes to Tolkien. While discussing with Professor d'Ardenne her companion volume to the facsimile of Bodleian MS 34, the Society asked her if she still intended to offer one day what they had understood to be her edition of *St Katherine*. She replied 'that certain parts are ready ... But then she speaks of it as *your* edition: 'You should enquire whether Prof. Tolkien is still contemplating an edition of *St Katherine*' (Tolkien Papers, Bodleian Library, Oxford). He asks if *St Katherine* is to be edited jointly by Professor d'Ardenne and Tolkien, or by Tolkien alone.

528. _____. and J.R.R. Tolkien. '*Iþþlen* in Sawles Warde'. Offprint from *English Studies*, Vol. 28, no. 6. Amsterdam: Swets and Zeitlinger, December 1947, pp. 168-70.
Collection: Private [Tolkien Books].

529. d'Entréves, Alessandro Passerin. 'Gratiosum lumen rationis' (1951). Published in *Dante as a Poltical Thinker*. Oxford: At the Clarendon Press, 1952, pp. 76-97.
S.s.: d'Entréves (1955), p. 38. 17 February 1951: Tolkien attends a meeting of the Oxford Dante and Professor A.P. d'Entréves reads a paper on Dante's political theory.

530. D'Evelyn, Charlotte (Edited by). *The Latin Text of the Ancrene Riwle*. Series: E.E.T.S. (Early English Text Society), OS 216. London: Published for the Early English Text by H. Milford, Oxford University Press, 1944.
Description: Autographed in ball-point on front flyleaf. Text underlined in green crayon. Annotated in pencil. Contains notes made on both sides of a printed letter of reply for writing about *The Lord of the Rings* at front flyleaf, and shopping list as bookmark at pages 96, 97.
Collection: Tolkien's personal Celtic library, preserved at the Weston library under the auspices of the English Faculty Library (Oxford).

531. Dal, Ingerid. 'Zur Entstehung des englischen Participium Praesentis auf -ing'. Offprint from *Norsk Tidsskrift for Sprogvidenskap* 16, 1952, pp. 5-116.
Description: Inscribed by Tolkien: 'English Participial ending *–ing*'. Includes a label added by Stan Revell to books owned by Tolkien, 'From the Library of J.R.R. Tolkien'.
Collection: Private [Christina Scull & Wayne G. Hammond].
S.s. Scull-Hammond (2018a).

532. Dalton, Ormonde Maddock. *A guide to the mediaeval antiquities and objects of later date in the department of British and mediaeval antiquities*. London: Printed

SECTION A

by order of the Trustees, 1924.
    P.s.: *Sir Gawain and the Green Knight* (1925), p. 86 line 168. Tolkien and Gordon cite the illustrations on pages 5-6.

533.   Dares Phrygius. *Daretis Phrygii de excidio Trojae historia.*
    P.s.: *A Middle English Vocabulary* (1922). Tolkien refers in the *Index of Names* under 'Dares'.

534.   Darmesteter, Arséne. *La vie des mots étudiée dans leurs significations.* Paris: Librairie Delagrave, 1887.
    P.s.: 'Middle English 'Losenger'' (1953), p. 64.

535.   Dasent, George Webbe. *A Collection of Popular Tales from the Norse and North German.* London: Norrœna Viking, 1906.
    P.s.: *Letters* 297 (1967). Drafts for a letter to 'Mr Rang'.
    S.s.: Flieger (2003), p. 28. Flieger writes: '[In *On Fairy-stories*] 'From Dasent's introduction to his translation, Tolkien took an extended metaphor, the soup of story and the *bones of the ox* from which it is boiled'.

536.   _____. *Popular Tales from the Norse.* Edinburgh: Edmonston and Douglas, 1859 (2nd ed.).
    P.s. 1: *On Fairy-stories* (1947), p. 47 n. 1, 49. . Tolkien writes: 'In Dasent's words I would say: "We must be satisfied with the soup that is set before us, and not desire to see the bones of the ox out of which it has been boiled [p. xviii]".'
    P.s. 2: *Tolkien On Fairy-stories* (2008), p. 37 n. 1, p. 39.
    P.s. 3: *Tolkien On Fairy-stories* (2008) 'Manuscript A. [MS Tolkien 4, fols. 59-77]', pp. 179, 180, 181, 189.
    P.s. 4: *Tolkien On Fairy-stories* (2008) 'Manuscript B [MS. Tolkien 4, fols. 73-120]', p. 217.
    S.s. 1: Shippey (1992), p. 298.
    S.s. 2: Scull-Hammond (2006b), p. 815.
    Reading period: 1900 – 1906 (S.s.: Scull-Hammond (2017c), p. 1053).

537.   _____. *The story of Burnt Njal: or, Life in Iceland at the end of the tenth century: from the Icelandic of the Njals saga.* Edinburgh : Edmonston and Douglas, 1861.
    S.s.: *King Edward's School Chronicle* (March 1911), p. 19. The Völsunga Saga is but one of many: for instance, the story of Burnt Njal, the longest of them all and one of the very best; and "Howard the Halt," the best of the shorter ones.' (*Cfr.* Anderson, The Annotated Hobbit 2002, p. 3).

538.   Davis, Henry William Carless and John Reginald Homer Weaver (Edited by). *The Dictionary of National Biography* 1912-1921. London: Oxford University Press, 1927.
    P.s.: *Tolkien On Fairy-stories* (2008) 'Manuscript A. [MS Tolkien 4, fols. 59-77]', p. 181. Tolkien cites the biography *Andrew Lang* (1844-1913) written by George S. Gordon on pages 319-323.

539.   Dawson, Christopher. *Progress & Religion: An Historical Enquiry.* London: Shead and Ward, 1929.
    P.s. 1: *On Fairy-stories* (1947), p. 55 n. 1, p. 78 n. 1.
    P.s. 2: *Tolkien On Fairy-stories* (2008), p. 44 n. 1, p. 72 n. 1, pp. 104, 130.
    P.s. 3: *Tolkien On Fairy-stories* (2008) 'Manuscript A. [MS Tolkien 4, fols. 59-77]', pp. 182, 183
    P.s. 4: *Tolkien On Fairy-stories* (2008) 'Manuscript B. [MS. Tolkien 4, fols. 73-120]', p. 239.
    S.s.: Scull-Hammond (2006b), p. 820.

540.   Day, Mabel (Edited by). *The English Text of the Ancrene Riwle, BM MS. Cotton Nero A. xiv.* Series: E.E.T.S. (Early English Text Society), OS 225. London: Published for the Early English Text by Geoffrey Cumberlege, Oxford University

Press, 1952.
> Description: Text underlined in green crayon. Annotated in pencil. Bookmark on pages 150, 151.
> Collection: Tolkien's personal Celtic library, preserved at the Weston library under the auspices of the English Faculty Library (Oxford).

541. de Camp, Lyon Sprague. *Swords & Sorcery: Stories of Heroic Fantasy*. Pyramid Books, 1963.
> Description: Signed and inscribed by the recipient: 'JRR Tolkien | from L. Sprague de Camp | July 1964'. Annotated by Tolkien: 'found [the anthology] interesting but did not much like the stories in it'. On the reverse of a folded sheet of Hotel Miramar writing paper, he wrote a critique of Lord Dunsany's 'Distressing Tale of Thangobrind the Jeweler', one of the contributions to the collection.
> Collection: Private [Bonhams, 28 Mar 2006, London].
> S.s.: Scull-Hammond (2017a), p. 655.

542. De la Mare, Walter. *Broomsticks & Other Tales*. London: Constable & Co., 1925.
> Collection: Private [Sold by Dominic Winter, 5 December 2014]

543. de Saint-Amand, Imbert. *The Duchess of Berry and the Revolution of 1830*. Translated by Elizabeth G. Martin. London: Hutchinson & Co., 1892.
> Description: Tolkien requested the book on 2 March 1912 (MS. Library Records b. 606). Weston Library (Oxford), 2377 e.25.

544. *Debate of the Body and the Soul* a. 1300. [Middle English poem, see Child, Mapes].
> P.s.: MS. Tolkien A 21/13 *The English MSS*. fol. 203. [Tolkien Papers, Bodleian Library, Oxford].

545. Defoe, Daniel. *The Life and Strange Surprising Adventures of Robinson Crusoe*.
> P.s.: *Tolkien On Fairy-stories* (2008) 'Manuscript A. [MS Tolkien 4, fols. 59-77]', p. 177.

546. Dekker, Thomas. *The Guls Hornbook: and The belman of London in two parts*. London: Joseph Malaby Dent & Sons, 1905.
> S.s. 1: University of Leeds (1920), p. 147. English Language and Literature - Scheme A. Texts and Period selected for 1920-21. (b) Special period: 1557-1637. (c) Texts suggested for study with Special Period. Ordinary Degree of B.A. with Honours. Final Examination.
> S.s. 2: University of Leeds (1923), p. 81. Ordinary Degree of B.A., Intermediate Course and Examination: English Literature. Text selected for 1923-24 (ii) Texts suggestes as part of a course of general rending in the period 1579-1645.

547. Demosthenes. *Select Private Orations of Demosthenes*. Pt. I. Edited by Frederick Apthorp Paley and John Edwin Sandys. Cambridge: The University Press, 1885.
> S.s.: Scull-Hammond (2017a), p. 39. Trinity Term 1912: Tolkien attends lectures on the authors set for Honour Moderations: the Private Orations of Demosthenes, on Wednesdays and Fridays at 10.00 a.m., beginning 1 May.

548. _____. *Select Private Orations of Demosthenes*. Pt. II. Edited by Frederick Apthorp Paley and John Edwin Sandys. Cambridge: The University Press, 1886.
> S.s.: Scull-Hammond (2017a), p. 39. Trinity Term 1912: Tolkien attends lectures on the authors set for Honour Moderations: the Private Orations of Demosthenes, on Wednesdays and Fridays at 10.00 a.m., beginning 1 May.

549. Deneke, Helena Clara. *Grace Hadow*. Oxford: University Press, G. Cumberlege, 1946.
> Description: Tolkien gives the book, with a dedication, to Simonne d'Ardenne.
> Collection: Fonds J.R.R. Tolkien, Bibliothèque ALPHA principale, Université de Liège (Liège),

Tol/061.

550. Denham, Michael Aislabie. *The Denham Tracts*, Vol. I. A collection of folklore, reprinted from the original tracts and pamphlets printed by Denham between 1846 and 1859. Edited by James Hardy. London: David Nutt, 1895.
   S.s.: Shippey (2014), p. 3.

551. _____. *The Denham Tracts*, Vol. II. A collection of folklore, reprinted from the original tracts and pamphlets printed by Denham between 1846 and 1859. Edited by James Hardy. London: David Nutt, 1895.
   S.s. 1: Shippey (2014), p. 3. 'It is *possible* that Tolkien read *The Denham Tracts*, and picked up the word *hobbit*'.
   S.s 2 *The Lay of Aotrou & Itroun* (2016), p. 29 n. 16. Verlyn Flieger writes: 'It is a coincidence worth noting that the word *korigans* appears in the 1891 compendium of folklore known as *The Denham Tracts* (Vol. II, p. 79), where it is in the same word-list as the first known recorded use of the word *hobbits*, another term which Tolkien put to good use in his own work.'

552. *Déor's Lament* [Old English poem preserved in the *Exeter Book*, see Krapp and Dobbie.]
   P.s. 1: *Beowulf* (2002) 'Version A', p. 35.
   P.s. 2: *Tolkien On Fairy-stories* (2008) 'Manuscript B [MS. Tolkien 4, fols. 73-120]', p. 240. Tolkien quotes: 'Sæt secg monig sorgum gebunden | wean on wenan wyscte geneahhe | þæt þæs cynerices ofercumen wær [23-25]' that he translates 'Many a man sat chained in sorrow, | with no hope by woe, and wished ofte | that an end had come of that domain'.
   S.s 1: University of Leeds (1920), pp. 182-84. H2. (Scheme A and B) Second Year: Monday 10.00: Old English Verse with a special study of *Deor's Lament*.
   S.s. 2: University of Leeds (1921), pp. 192-94, (1922), pp. 133-35, and (1923), pp. 133-35. H2. (Scheme A and B) Second and Third Year: Monday 10.00: Old English Verse with a special study of *Deor's Lament*.
   S.s. 3: *The Book of Lost Tales*, Vol. II (1992), pp. 328-29. Christopher Tolkien writes: 'In this narrative ... Alfwine is still placed in the context of the figures of ancient English legend: his father is Déor the Minstrel. In the great Anglo-Saxon manuscript known as the *Exeter Book* there is a little poem of forty-two lines to which the title of *Déor* is now given. It is an utterance of the minstrel Déor, who, as he tells, has lost his place and been supplanted in his lord's favour by another bard, named Heorrenda. ... I do not think that my father's Déor the Minstrel of Kortirion and Heorrenda of Tavrobel can be linked more closely to the Anglo-Saxon poem than in the names alone—though he did not take the names at random. He was moved by the glimpsed tale (even if, in the words of one of the poem's editors, "the autobiographical element is purely fictitious"); and when lecturing on Beowulf at Oxford he sometimes gave the unknown poet a name, calling him *Heorrenda*.'
   S.s. 4: Shippey (1992), p. 287. More philologically I would say that what hangs over the end of all Tolkien's fiction is not 'And so they all lived happily ever after', but the line from the Old English poem *Déor*, *Þæs ofereode, þisses swa mæg*. This could be translated bluntly, 'That passed, this can too', but Tolkien translated it – see BLT 2, p. 323, for its importance to him and his writing – 'Time has passed since then, this too can pass'.
   S.s. 5: Flieger (2004), p. 64 n. 16.

553. Deulin, Charles. *Johnny Nut and the Golden Goose* [*Les Trente-six rencontres de Jean du Gogué*]. Done into English by Andrew Lang from the French of Charles Deulin. London: Longmans & Co., 1887, p. 113.
   P.s.: #1 a. | *Tolkien On Fairy-stories* (2008), p. 307. Tolkien refers to Lang translation.

554. Dibelius, Wilhelm. 'Die Selbastándigkeitsbewegung in den englischen Kolonien'. *Anglica: Untersuchungen zur englischen Philologie: Alois Brandl zum 70. Geburtstage überreicht*, Vol. I [A. 30], 1925.
   P.s.: *Philology: General Works* (VI 1927, for 1925), p. 33. Tolkien writes: 'which belongs to a class of writing for which there appears to be an astonish- ing appetite in Germany to~day'

555. Dickens, Charles. *Great Expectations*.
   S.s.: Lewis (2009b), p. 983. Letter to Tolkien – 28 October 1958. Lewis writes: 'It wd. be nicer still if he were accompanied by his Aged P.' (chapter 37, Wemmick takes Pip to meet 'the aged P' or 'the aged Parent').

556. _____. *Oliver Twist*. [London: Richard Bentley, 1898].
   P.s.: *Oxford University Press Archives* (Oxford). In a slip written by Tolkien on the etymology of 'Waistcoated' not used, and reads: '(waistcoated) | 2. Comb. esp. white-waistcoated: | Weaning a white waistcoat, also applied to | birds with white plumage on the beast'.
   NED: #2 b. | 'W' (1928), p. 23 'Waistcoated *b*.' 1898 – 'As I purpose to show in the sequel whether the white-waistcoated gentleman was right or not.'

557. _____. *The Posthumous papers of the Pickwick club*. London: Oxford University Press, 1837.
   P.s.: *Letters* 257 (1964). To Christopher Bretherton. Tolkien writes: 'I have never been able to enjoy *Pickwick*'.
   NED 1: #2 b. | 'W' (1928), p. 23 'Waistcoat' colloq. or vulgar. 1.' 1837 – 'He was habited in a coarse-striped waistcoat, with black calico sleeves, and blue glass buttons.' (chapter X, p. 118); p. 27 'Waiter' 8. 1837 – 'The White Hart hotel ... where the waiters, from their costume, might be mistaken for Westminster boys' (chapter xxxv).

558. Dictys Cretensins. *De Bello Troiano*.
   P.s.: *A Middle English Vocabulary* (1922). Tolkien refers in the Index of names under 'Dites'.

559. Diefenbach, Lorenz. *Celtica*, Vol. I. Sprachliche Documente zur Geschichte der Kelten; Zugleich als Beitrag zur sprachforschung überhaupt. Stuttgart: Imle und Liesching, 1839.
   Description: Decoratively autographed and dated on front flyleaf: '1922'.
   Collection: Tolkien's personal Celtic library, preserved at the Weston library under the auspices of the English Faculty Library (Oxford).

560. _____. *Celtica*, Vol. II. Versuch einer genealogischen Geschichte der Kelten. Stuttgart: Imle und Liesching, 1840.
   Description: Decoratively autographed and dated on front flyleaf: '1922'.
   Collection: Tolkien's personal Celtic library, preserved at the Weston library under the auspices of the English Faculty Library (Oxford).

561. Dieter, Ferdinand; Richard Bethge; Otto Bremer; Friedrich Hartmann; Wolfgang Schlüter, (Edited by). *Laut- und Formenlehre der Altgermanischen Dialekte. Zum Gebrauch für Studierende dargestellt. Erster Halbband: Lautlehre des Urgermanischen, Gotischen, Altnordischen, Altenglischen, Altsächsichen und Althochdeutschen*. Leipzig: O. R. Reisland, 1898.
   Description: 'It has been very sparsely annotated in pencil by Tolkien, normally with corrections or with marginal additions of a Germanic cognate or two, occasionally with lengthier notes on phonology or morphology (e.g., p. 276)'. (Jason Fisher. unpublished).
   Collection: The Science Fiction and Fantasy Research Collection of the Cushing Memorial Library and Archives at Texas A&M University.

562. Dietrich, Franz Eduard. 'Zu Cädmon'. *Zeitschrift für deutsches Alterthum*, Vol. X, 310-367. Berlin: Weidmannsche Buchhandlung, 1865.
   P.s.: *The Old English Exodus* (1982), p. ix.

563. Dillon, Myles (Edited by). *The Cycles of the Kings*. London: Oxford University Press, 1946.
   Description: Decoratively autographed and dated on front flyleaf in pencil: 'Nov. 1946'.
   Collection: Tolkien's personal Celtic library, preserved at the Weston library under the auspices of

the English Faculty Library (Oxford).

564. Dinneen, Patrick Stephen. *Irish-English Dictionary*. Series: The Irish Texts Society. Dublin: Gill, 1904.
    Collection: Tolkien's personal Celtic library, preserved at the Weston library under the auspices of the English Faculty Library (Oxford).
    S.s.: McIlwaine (2018), no. 84.

565. Diodorus, Siculus. *The Bibliotheca Historica of Diodorus Siculus translated by John Skelton*, Vol. I. Series: E.E.T.S. (Early English Text Society), OS 233., Edited by Frederick Millet Salter. London: Published for the Early English Text Society by Geoffrey Cumberlege, Oxford University Press, 1956.
    S.s.: Scull-Hammond (2017a), p. 477. 16 April 1955 The Committee of the Early English Text Society, in Tolkien's absence but with the assistance of a report by him, discuss an edition of the *Bibliotheca Historica* of Diodorus Siculus.

566. _____. *The Bibliotheca Historica of Diodorus Siculus translated by John Skelton*, Vol. II. Series: E.E.T.S. (Early English Text Society), OS 239., Edited by Frederick Millet Salter. London: Published for the Early English Text Society by Geoffrey Cumberlege, Oxford University Press, 1963.
    S.s.: Scull-Hammond (2017a), p. 477. 16 April 1955 The Committee of the Early English Text Society, in Tolkien's absence but with the assistance of a report by him, discuss an edition of the *Bibliotheca Historica* of Diodorus Siculus.

567. Dixon, Richard Watson. *History of the Church of England*, Vol. I. Henry VIII, A.D. 1529-1537. London and Oxford: Smith, Elders, & Co.; G. Routledge and Sons and At the Clarendon Press, 1895.
    P.s.: *Letters* 113 (1948). To C.S. Lewis.

568. _____. *History of the Church of England*, Vol. II. Henry VIII, A.D. 1538-1547: Edward VI, A.D. 1547, 1548. London and Oxford: Smith, Elders, & Co.; G. Routledge and Sons and At the Clarendon Press, 1895.
    P.s.: *Letters* 113 (1948). To C.S. Lewis.

569. _____. *History of the Church of England*, Vol. III. Edward VI, A.D. 1549-1553. London and Oxford: Smith, Elders, & Co.; G. Routledge and Sons and At the Clarendon Press, 1895.
    P.s.: *Letters* 113 (1948). To C.S. Lewis

570. _____. *History of the Church of England*, Vol. IV. Mary A.D. 1553-1558. London and Oxford: Smith, Elders, & Co.; G. Routledge and Sons and At the Clarendon Press, 1891.
    P.s.: *Letters* 113 (1948). To C.S. Lewis.

571. _____. *History of the Church of England*, Vol. V. Elizabeth. A.D. 1558-1563. London and Oxford: Smith, Elders, & Co.; G. Routledge and Sons and At the Clarendon Press, 1902.
    P.s.: *Letters* 113 (1948). To C.S. Lewis.

572. _____. *History of the Church of England*, Vol. VI. Elizabeth. A.D. 1564-1570. London and Oxford: Smith, Elders, & Co.; G. Routledge and Sons and At the Clarendon Press, 1902.
    P.s.: *Letters* 113 (1948). To C.S. Lewis.

573. _____. *Poems*. London: Smith Elder, 1909.
   P.s.: *Letters* 113 (1948). To C.S. Lewis.

574. Dobbie, Elliott Van Kirk. *Beowulf, and Judith*. Series: The Anglo-Saxon Poetic Records, 4. London: Routledge and Kegan Paul, 1953.
   P.s.: *Beowulf* (2002) 'Version A', p. 50.

575. _____. *The Anglo-Saxon Minor Poems*. Series: The Anglo-Saxon Poetic Records, 6. London: Routledge and Kegan Paul, 1942.
   P.s.: *Finn and Hengest* (1982), p. 131 nos. 70, 71; p. 164 n. 7.

576. Dobson, Eric John. *English pronunciation 1500-1700*, Vol. I. Survey of the sources. Oxford: At the Clarendon Press; London: Oxford University Press, 1957.
   S.s.: Scull-Hammond (2006b), p. 211: His thesis, *English Pronunciation 1500-1700 According to the Evidence of the English Orthoepists* (i.e. those who study the correct pronunciation of words), was examined by Tolkien and C. L. Wrenn and later published (1957; 2nd ed. 1968).

577. _____. *English pronunciation 1500-1700*, Vol. II. Phonology. Oxford: At the Clarendon Press; London: Oxford University Press, 1957.
   S.s.: Scull-Hammond (2006b), p. 211: His thesis, *English Pronunciation 1500-1700 According to the Evidence of the English Orthoepists* (i.e. those who study the correct pronunciation of words), was examined by Tolkien and C. L. Wrenn and later published (1957; 2nd ed. 1968).

578. _____. 'The Hymn to the Virgin'. Offprint from *Transactions of the Honourable Society of Cymmrodorion session 1954*. London: Hon. Society of Cymmrodorion, 1955, pp. 70-124.
   Description: Inscribed on front cover: 'With compliments | E. J. D.'
   Collection: Tolkien's personal Celtic library, preserved at the Weston library under the auspices of the English Faculty Library (Oxford).
   S.s.: Phelpstead (2011), p. 118.

579. Donne, John. *Donne's Sermons: selected passages*. Oxford: At the Clarendon Press, 1919.
   S.s.: University of Leeds (1921), p. 154. English Language and Literature - Scheme A. Texts and Period selected for 1921-22. (d) Texts suggested for study with Special Period 1637-1700. Ordinary Degree of B.A. with Honours. Final Examinations.

580. _____. *The Poems of John Donne*, Vol. I. The text of the poems with appendixes. Edited by Herbert John Clifford Grierson. Oxford: At the Clarendon Press, 1912.
   S.s.: University of Leeds (1921), p. 154. English Language and Literature - Scheme A. Texts and Period selected for 1921-22. (d) Texts suggested for study with Special Period 1637-1700. Ordinary Degree of B.A. with Honours. Final Examinations.

581. _____. *The Poems of John Donne*, Vol. II. Introduction and commentary. Edited by Herbert John Clifford Grierson. Oxford: At the Clarendon Press, 1912.
   S.s.: University of Leeds (1921), p. 154. English Language and Literature - Scheme A. Texts and Period selected for 1921-22. (d) Texts suggested for study with Special Period 1637-1700.

Section A

Ordinary Degree of B.A. with Honours. Final Examinations.

582. _____. *The Poems of John Donne*, Vol. II. Series: Muses Library. Edited by Edmund Kerchever Chambers. London: A. H. Bullen, 1901.
   S.s.: University of Leeds (1923), p. 81. Ordinary Degree of B.A., Intermediate Course and Examination: English Literature. Text selected for 1923-24 (ii) Texts suggestes as part of a course of general rending in the period 1579-1645. Text suggested: *Progress of the Soul.*

583. _____. *The School of John Donne*. Edited by Herbert John Clifford Grierson. London: Oxford University Press, 1912.
   S.s.: University of Leeds (1921), p. 154. English Language and Literature - Scheme A. Texts and Period selected for 1921-22. (d) Texts suggested for study with Special Period 1637-1700. Ordinary Degree of B.A. with Honours. Final Examinations.

584. Dottin, Georges. *Les Anciens peuples de l'Europe*. Series: Collection pour l'étude des antiquités nationales, 1. Paris: C. Klincksieck, 1916.
   Description: Autographed in pencil on front flyleaf.
   Collection: Tolkien's personal Celtic library, preserved at the Weston library under the auspices of the English Faculty Library (Oxford).

585. _____. *La Langue gauloise: grammaire, textes et glossaire*. Paris: C. Klincksieck, 1920.
   Description: Autographed in pencil on front flyleaf.
   Collection: Tolkien's personal Celtic library, preserved at the Weston library under the auspices of the English Faculty Library (Oxford).

586. _____. *Manuel d'Irlandais Moyen*, Vol. I. Grammar. Paris: Librairie ancienne H. Champion, 1913.
   Collection: Tolkien's personal Celtic library, preserved at the Weston library under the auspices of the English Faculty Library (Oxford).

587. _____. *Manuel d'Irlandais Moyen*, Vol. II. Textes et glossaire. Paris: Librairie ancienne H. Champion, 1913.
   Collection: Tolkien's personal Celtic library, preserved at the Weston library under the auspices of the English Faculty Library (Oxford).

588. Doutrepont, Auguste. *La Clef d'Amors: texte critique avec introduction, appendice et glossaire*. Halle: Max Niemeyer, 1890.
   Description: Autographed on front flyleaf: 'J.R.R. Tolkien'.
   Collection: Private [Sold by Loome Theological Booksellers, formerly 'David Miller collection'].

589. Dowden, Edward. *Transcripts and Studies*. London: Kegan Paul, Trench, Trübner & Co., 1896 (2nd ed.).
   P.s.: *Beowulf* (2002), 'Version A', p. 41.

590. Draak, Maartje. 'Virgil of Salzburg versus *Aethicus Ister*'. Offprint from *Dancwerc: Opstellen Aangeboden aan Prof. Dr. D. Th. Enklaar ter Gelegenheid*

van Zijn 65. Groningen: Verjaardag, 1959.
>Description: Annotated by Tolkien on three pages. Includes a label added by Stan Revell to books owned by Tolkien, 'From the Library of J.R.R. Tolkien'.
>Collection: Private [Christina Scull & Wayne G. Hammond].
>S.s.: Scull-Hammond (2018a).

591. Drayton, Michael. *Nymphidia.*
>P.s. 1: *On Fairy-stories* (1947), p. 40.
>P.s. 2: *Tolkien On Fairy-stories* (2008), pp. 29-30
>P.s. 3: *Tolkien On Fairy-stories* (2008) 'Manuscript A. [MS Tolkien 4, fols. 59-77]', p. 177
>P.s. 4: *Tolkien On Fairy-stories* (2008) 'Manuscript B [MS. Tolkien 4, fols. 73-120]', pp. 210, 214.
>S.s.: Scull-Hammond (2006b), p. 820.

592. _____. *Poly-Olbion.*
>P.s.: MS. Tolkien A 12/2 *Commentary on Sir Gawain, lines 1999-2523* fol. 5. [Tolkien Papers, Bodleian Library, Oxford].

593. Dryden, Henry Edward Leigh (Edited by). *The Art of Hunting.* Daventry: Thomas Barrett, 1843.
>P.s.: *Sir Gawain and the Green Knight* (1925), p. xxvi.

594. _____. *The art of Hunting, or, Three Hunting MSS.* Revised by Alice Dreyden. Northampton: William Mark, 1908.
>P.s. 1: *Sir Gawain and the Green Knight* (1925), p. xxvi.
>P.s. 2: *Sir Gawain and the Green Knight* (1967) 'Select Bibliography', p. 155.

595. Dryden, John. *An Essay of dramatic poesy.* Edited by Thomas Arnold. Oxford: At the Clarendon Press, 1918.
>S.s. 1: University of Leeds (1920), p. 139 English Language and Literature: English Literature. Text selected for 1920-21. Texts Selected for 1920-21. Ordinary Degree of B.A. with Honours. Final Course and Examination.
>S.s. 2: University of Leeds (1921), p. 154. English Language and Literature - Scheme A. Texts and Period selected for 1921-22. (e) History of Criticism: Special Texts suggested for study. Ordinary Degree of B.A. with Honours. Final Examinations; p. 156. English Language and Literature - Scheme B. Texts for 1921-22. (d) Outlines of the History of English Literature. Ordinary Degree of B.A. with Honours. Final Examinations.

596. _____. *Dryden.* Edited by William Dougal Christie and Charles Harding Firth.
>S.s. 1: University of Leeds (1920), p. 139 English Language and Literature: English Literature. Text selected for 1920-21. Texts Selected for 1920-21. Ordinary Degree of B.A. with Honours. Final Course and Examination. Extracts *Absalom and Achitophel* (part. I).
>S.s. 2: University of Leeds (1921), p. 154. English Language and Literature - Scheme A. Texts and Period selected for 1921-22. (d) Texts suggested for study with Special Period 1637-1700. Ordinary Degree of B.A. with Honours. Final Examinations; p. 156. English Language and Literature - Scheme B. Texts for 1921-22. (d) Outlines of the History of English Literature. Ordinary Degree of B.A. with Honours. Final Examinations. Text suggested: *Religio Laici*

597. _____. *Dryden's Plays.* Edited by George Saintsbury. London: Unwin, 1904.
>S.s.: University of Leeds (1921), p. 154. English Language and Literature - Scheme A. Texts and Period selected for 1921-22. (d) Texts suggested for study with Special Period 1637-1700. Ordinary Degree of B.A. with Honours. Final Examinations.

598. _____. *Dryden's Poems.* Edited by John Sargeaunt. London: Henry Frowde, Oxford University Press, 1913.
>P.s.: *Oxford University Press Archives* (Oxford). A slip written by Tolkien on the etymology of 'Wake' used ('W' p. 31) [A. 1721].
>*NED*: #2 f. | 'W' (1928), p. 31 'Wake, 3.' 1700 – The warlike Wakes continu'd all the Night, And

Fun 'ral Games were played at new-returning Light' ('Palamon and Arcite: or, The Knight Tale', book III, vv. 998-999, p. 313).

599. _____. *John Dryden*, Vol. I. Series: The Mermaid series. Edited by George Saintsbury. London: T. Fisher Unwin, 1920.
S.s.: University of Leeds (1921), p. 141. English Literature, text selected (*Aureng-zebe*) for 1921-22. Ordinary Degree of B.A.; p. 190 English Language and Literature. Int. 1 Intermediate Course (Literature) (*Aureng-zebe*).

600. _____. *Mac Flecknoe; or, A satyr upon the True-Blew-Protestant Poet.*
S.s.: University of Leeds (1920), p. 139 English Language and Literature: English Literature. Text selected for 1920-21. Texts Selected for 1920-21. Ordinary Degree of B.A. with Honours. Final Course and Examination; p. 181. English Language and Literature. Int. I Intermediate Course (Literature).

601. _____. *Preface to the Fables.* Cambridge: The University Press, 1912.
S.s. 1: University of Leeds (1920), p. 139 English Language and Literature: English Literature. Text selected for 1920-21. Texts Selected for 1920-21. Ordinary Degree of B.A. with Honours. Final Course and Examination; p. 181. English Language and Literature. Int. I Intermediate Course (Literature).
S.s. 2: University of Leeds (1921), p. 156. English Language and Literature - Scheme B. Texts for 1921-22. (d) Outlines of the History of English Literature. Ordinary Degree of B.A. with Honours. Final Examinations.

602. _____. *The Poetical Works of John Dryden.* Series: The Globe edition. London: Macmillan, 1920.
S.s. 1: University of Leeds (1920), p. 135 English Literature. Texts Selected for 1920-21. Texts suggested: *Preface to 'Fables'* and *Mac Flecknoe*.
S.s. 2: University of Leeds (1921), p. 141. English Literature, text selected (*Annus mirabilis; Songs, Odes, and Lyrical Pieces*) for 1921-22. Ordinary Degree of B.A.; p. 189 English Language and Literature. Int. 1 Intermediate Course (Literature) (*Annus mirabilis; Songs, Odes, and Lyrical Pieces*).
S.s. 3: Ollscoil na h-Éireann G 257 (1949): Tolkien cites *All for love.*

603. Du Bellay, Joachim. *La Deffence et illustration de la langue francoyse.* Paris: A. Fontemoing, 1904.
S.s.: University of Leeds (1921), p. 154. English Language and Literature - Scheme A. Texts and Period selected for 1921-22. (e) History of Criticism: Special Texts suggested for study. Ordinary Degree of B.A. with Honours. Final Examinations.

604. Du Méril, Édélestand Pontas. *Poésies populaires latines antérieures au douzième siècle.* Paris: Broekhaus et Avenarius, 1843.
Description: Tolkien, in his copy of *The Dark Ages* (1955) by W. P. Ker [A. 1179], corrected a mistake in the title printed in that edition.

605. Dumas, Alexander. *The Three Musketeers.*
S.s. 1: Lewis (2009b), p. 102-3. Letter to Arthur Greef – 25 March 1933. Lewis writes: 'While having a few days in bed recently I tried, at W's earnest recommendation, to read *The Three Musketeers*, but not only got tired of it but also found it disgusting ... I was talking about this to Tolkien who, you know, grew up on Morris and Macdonald and shares my taste in literature to a fault.'
S.s. 2: Scull-Hammond (2017a), p. 179. 'c. 25 March 1933 Tolkien and C. S. Lewis discuss the latter's response to *The Three Musketeers* by Alexandre Dumas as a work with no background behind the plot.'

606. Dunne, John William (Edited by). *The Ancient Irish epic tale Táin bó Cúalnge.* 'The Cualnge cattle-raid,' now for the first time done entire into English out of the

Irish of the Book of Leinster and allied manuscripts. London: David Nutt, 1914.
Description: Autographed and dated on front flyleaf: '1922'.
Collection: Tolkien's personal Celtic library, preserved at the Weston library under the auspices of the English Faculty Library (Oxford).

607. _____. *An Experiment with Time*. London: Faber and Faber, 1934 (3rd ed.).
S.s. 1: Flieger (2001), p. 47. 'contains his interleaved notes and comments, jotted in the course of reading, on Dunne's ideas [on time and dreams] and the theory he derived from them ... not always in complete agreement with Dunne '
S.s. 2: Scull-Hammond (2017c), p. 1056.

608. Dunn, Joseph (Edited by). *La Vie de Saint Patrice: mystère Breton en trois actes*. Paris: Honoré Champion, 1909.
Collection: Tolkien's personal Celtic library, preserved at the Weston library under the auspices of the English Faculty Library (Oxford).

609. Dunsany, Lord (E. J. M. D. Plunkett). *The Book of Wonder*. London: William Heinemann, 1912.
P.s. 1: *Letters* 294 (1967) To Charlotte and Denis Plimmer. Tolkien writes: 'If I attributed meaning to boo-hoo I should not in this case be influenced by the words containing bū in many other European languages, but by a story by Lord Dunsany (read many years ago) about two idols enshrined in the same temple: Chu-Bu and Sheemish.'
P.s. 2: *Letters* 336 (1972). From a letter to Sir Patrick Browne. Tolkien cites 'Chu-Bu and Sheemish'.
S.s. 1: Scull-Hammond (2006b), p. 816.
S.s. 2: Drout (2007), p. 375.
S.s. 3: Edwards (2014), p. 44.

610. Duval, Amaury. 'La Mule sans Frein, par *Paiens de Maisières*'. *Histoire littéraire de la France*, Vol. XIX, 1838, pp. 722-29.
P.s.: *Sir Gawain and the Green Knight* (1925), p. xxvi. Tolkien and Gordon write: 'For bibliography of the Irish and French analogues of *Sir Gawain*, see the bibliography in Kittredge's study'. [*NED*] In Kittredge's study, this article is mentioned in 'VI. La Mule sanz Frain' (p. 299), 'X. Le Chevalier à l'Épée' (p. 303).

611. Dyche, Lewis Lindsay. 'Walrus Hunting in the arctic'. *The Cosmopolitan*, Vol. XX. Irvington-on-the Hudson: Cosmopolitan Press, Aprile 1896, pp. 347-59.
P.s. 1: MS. Tolkien A 19/3 *Etymologies or history of Walrus* fols. 162-195 [Tolkien Papers, Bodleian Library, Oxford].
P.s. 2: *Oxford University Press Archives* (Oxford). In a slip written by Tolkien on the etymology of 'Walrus' not used, and reads: '1896 *Cosmopolitan* xx. 356/2 Near Herbert Island I secured a goodly number of walruses – cows, calves, yearlings and two-year-olds.' Tolkien had added a note at the bottom of the slip: '(see cutting walrus-calf)'. Curiosity: In *The siege and conquest of the North Pole* (London: Gibbings & Co., 1910, 334) by George Bryce, there is written: 'On the 12th August the Falcon left the bay on a cruise for the winter's meat-supply. Near Herbert Island they were successful in obtaining twenty-four walruses.' (Peary's Expedition 1891, p. 293).
S.s.: Tolkien, *Family Album* (1992), p. 42.
NED: #2 i. | 'W' (1928), pp. 57-58 'Walrus, 3. *attrib.* and *comb.*' 1896 – 'Old Ickwa put his hand on me, at the same time pointing to the walrus calf, and said'pee-yuk!'.

612. Earle, John. *The Deeds of Beowulf. An English epic of the eight-century done into modern prose*. Oxford: At the Clarendon Press, 1892.
P.s. 1: *Exeter College library register*. Tolkien's borrowing record: *Hilary Term 1914* from 26 January to 10 March; *Long vacation 1914* from 19 January to 14 October.
P.s. 2: *Prefatory Remarks on Prose Translation of 'Beowulf'* (1940), p. xv.
P.s. 3: *Beowulf* (2002) 'Version A', p. 46.
P.s. 4: *Beowulf* (2002) 'Transcription of Legibile Portions of Folios 71-81: Notes and Jottings',

p. 432.

613. _____. *Microcosmography*.
S.s.: University of Leeds (1921), p. 154. English Language and Literature - Scheme A. Texts and Period selected for 1921-22. (d) Texts suggested for study with Special Period 1637-1700. Ordinary Degree of B.A. with Honours. Final Examinations.

614. _____. *Two of the Saxon Chronicles: parallel with supplementary extracts from the others*, Vol. I. Text, appendices and glossary. Edited by Charles Plummer. Oxford: At the Clarendon Press, 1929.
Description: Autographed on front flyleaf. Annotated in red crayon and pencil pp. 356, 357.
Collection: Tolkien's personal Celtic library, preserved at the Weston library under the auspices of the English Faculty Library (Oxford).

615. _____. *Two of the Saxon Chronicles: parallel with supplementary extracts from the others*, Vol. II Text, appendices and glossary. Edited by Charles Plummer. Oxford: At the Clarendon Press, 1929.
Description: Autographed on front flyleaf.
Collection: Tolkien's personal Celtic library, preserved at the Weston library under the auspices of the English Faculty Library (Oxford).
P.s.: *English and Welsh* (1963), p. 27 n. 1. Tolkien quotes: 'of Weallande … *waelisce men*' (p. 220) and '*Weal-lande … þa Frencyscan*' (p. 237)

616. _____ and Charles Plummer (Edited by). *Two of the Saxon Chronicles Parallel (787-1001 A.D.). With supplementary extracts from the others*. Oxford: At the Clarendon Press, 1920.
S.s.: University of Leeds (1921), p. 145. English Language, text selected for 1921-22. Ordinary Degree of B.A.: p. 153. English Language and Literature - Scheme A. Texts and Period selected for 1921-22. (a) Selected Texts in Old and Middle English. Ordinary Degree of B.A. with Honours. Final Examinations; p. 192 English Language and Literature. F2. Final Course (English Literature and Language).

617. *Edda: Poetic Edda or Sæmundar Edda or the Elder Edda* [Old Norse collection of poems] | *Prose Edda, or the Younger Edda or Snorri's Edda* [Old Norse manual of poetics].
For editions and translations of the *Elder* or *Poetic Edda*, see Auden, Bellows, Gering, Hauser, Hildebrand, Jónsson, W. Morris, Nerman, Ranisch, Sigfusson, Sturluson, Taylor, Wilken, Wimmer.
P.s. 1: MS. Tolkien A 13/1 *Draft of talk to the Oxford Dante Society: A neck-verse* (1947), fol. 171. Tolkien translates from Völuspá, verses 32-41 'Broeðr munu berjask … áðr veröld steypisk'. [Tolkien Papers, Bodleian Library, Oxford].
P.s. 2: *The Notion Club Papers* (1945), p. 214 n. 21. JRRT cites *Skifbladnir* (p. 174) and in Christopher's note 'In the 'Prose Edda' the Icelander Snorri Sturluson tells of Skidbladnir:'skiðblaðnir is the best of ships and made with great skill … and kept in one's pouch' ($42).
P.s. 3: 'Middle English 'Losenger'' (1953), p. 73. Tolkien cites *Hávamál* (Edda Poetic), 74 Tolkien cites *Elder Edda*.
P.s. 4: *Letters* 297 (1967). Drafts for a letter to 'Mr Rang'. Tolkien writes: '*Gandalfr* is a dwarf-name in Völuspá!'
P.s. 5: *Letters* 25 (1938) To the editor of the *Observer*. Tolkien writes: 'The dwarf-names, and the wizard's, are from the Elder Edda'.
P.s. 6: #1 a. | *Tolkien On Fairy-stories* (2008), p. 311. Tolkien cites Þrymskviða (Elder Edda).
P.s. 7: The Legend of Sigurd & Gudrún (2009).
P.s. 8: Beowulf (2014), p. 330 n. 3
S.s.: Scull-Hammond (2017a), p. 46. April 1913: Tolkien will need to become familiar with a range of literary and philological subjects and set texts as prescribed in the Oxford Regulations of the Board of Studies, knowing that he may be examined on them in ten papers at the end of Trinity Term 1915. In addition, Tolkien will have to choose a Special Subject on which he will be

examined separately. He will choose Scandinavian Philology, which according to the *Regulations* will have special reference to Icelandic, together with a special study of the *Snorra Edda* (i.e. the *Prose* or *Younger Edda*).

618.   Eddison, Eric Rücker (Edited by). *Egil's saga, done into English out of the Icelandic*. Cambridge: The University Press, 1930.
P.s.: *Letters* 294 (1967). To Charlotte and Denis Plimmer. Tolkien writes: 'I have read all that E. R. Eddison wrote, in spite of his peculiarly bad nomenclature and personal philosophy'.

619.   _____. *A Fish Dinner in Memison*. Boston: Dutton, 1941.
P.s.: *Letters* 294 (1967). To Charlotte and Denis Plimmer.
S.s.: Scull-Hammond (2006b), p. 818.

620.   _____. *The Mezentian Gate*. London: Curwen Press, 1958.
P.s. 1: *Letters* 73 (1944). From a letter to Christopher Tolkien. Tolkien writes: 'of undiminished power and felicity of Expression'.
P.s. 2: *Letters* 199 (1957). From a letter to Caroline Everett.
P.s. 3: *Letters* 294 (1967). To Charlotte and Denis Plimmer.
S.s. 1: Carpenter (1979), p. 191.
S.s. 2: Scull-Hammond (2006b), p. 818.
S.s. 3: Lewis (2009b), p. 988. Letter to Tolkien – 10 November 1958. Lewis writes: 'You know there is a new E. R. Eddison out? Christopher has my copy at present'.

621.   _____. *Styrbjörn the Strong*. London: Jonathan Cape, 1926.
P.s.: *Letters* 294 (1967). To Charlotte and Denis Plimmer. Tolkien writes: 'I have read all that E. R. Eddison wrote, in spite of his peculiarly bad nomenclature and personal philosophy'.

622.   _____. *Mistress of Mistresses*. London: Faber and Faber, 1935.
P.s. 1: Letters 199 (1957). From a letter to Caroline Everett
P.s. 2: *Letters* 294 (1967). To Charlotte and Denis Plimmer.
S.s.: Scull-Hammond (2006b), p. 818.

623.   _____. *The Worm Ouroboros*. London: Jonathan Cape, 1922.
P.s. 1: *Letters* 73 (1944). From a letter to Christopher Tolkien.
P.s. 2: *Letters* 199n (1955). From a letter to Caroline Everett
P.s. 3: *Letters* 294 (1967). To Charlotte and Denis Plimmer. Tolkien writes: 'You may like or dislike his invented worlds (I myself like that of *The Worm Ouroboros* and strongly dislike that of *Mistress of Mistresses*) but there is no quarrel between the theme and the articulation of the story'.
S.s. 1: Scull-Hammond (2006b), p. 818.
S.s. 2: Gilliver-Marshall-Weiner (2009), p. 102.

624.   Edeyrn, Davod Aur. *Dosparth Edeyrn Davod Aur. Or, the Ancient Welsh Grammar*. Series: The Welsh MSS. Society. Translated by John Williams (Ab Ithel). Llandovery: W. Rees, 1861.
Description: Dated: '1922'.
Collection: Tolkien's personal Celtic library, preserved at the Weston library under the auspices of the English Faculty Library (Oxford).
S.s. 1: Phelpstead (2011), p. 119.
S.s. 2: Scull-Hammond (2017a), p. 126.

625.   Edwards, John Morgan (Edited by). *Hanes A Chan* (Story and Song). Newport: Southall, 1908 (5th ed.).
Description: Signature (erased) on front flyleaf: 'Geoffrey Smith'. Text annotated in pencil by JRRT.
Collection: Tolkien's personal Celtic library, preserved at the Weston library under the auspices of the English Faculty Library (Oxford).
S.s. 1: Garth (2003), p. 357.

S.s. 2: Fimi (2007), p. 67 n. 6.
S.s. 3: Phelpstead (2011), p. 118.
S.s. 4: Scull-Hammond (2017c), p. 1212.

626. _____. *Mabinogion (or Lyfr Coch Hergest)*. Wrecsam: Hughes and Son, Cyhoeddwyr, 1921.
Collection: Tolkien's personal Celtic library, preserved at the Weston library under the auspices of the English Faculty Library (Oxford).
S.s. 1: Fimi (2007), p. 51.
S.s. 2: Phelpstead (2011), p. 118.

627. Edwards, Thomas. *Gwaith Twm o 'r Nant*. Series: Cyfres y fil. Edited by Thomas Evan. Llanuwchllyn: Ab Owen, 1909.
Description: Autographed on back of frontespice: 'Geoffrey Bache Smth'. And in JRRT's writing: 'left by will | to | J.R.R. Tolkien.'
Collection: Tolkien's personal Celtic library, preserved at the Weston library under the auspices of the English Faculty Library (Oxford).
S.s. 1: Garth (2003), p. 357.
S.s. 2: Fimi (2007), p. 67 n. 6.
S.s. 3: Phelpstead (2011), p. 118.
S.s. 4: Scull-Hammond (2017c), p. 121.

628. Egilsson, Sveinbjörn. *Lexicon poëticum antiquæ linguæ Septentrionalis*. Hafniæ: Typis J. D. Qvist, 1860.
P.s.: *Some Contributions to Middle-English Lexicography* (1925), p. 212.

629. _____. *Lexicon Poeticum Antiquæ Linguae Septentrionalis*. Ordbog Over det Norsk-Islandske Skjaldesprog. Edited by Finnur Jónsson. København: Møller 1931.
P.s.: *Finn and Hengest* (1982), p. 52 n. 41; p. 142 n. 92.

630. Einenkel, Eugen. (Edited by). *Anglia: Zeitschrift für englische Philologie*, Vol. XX. Tübingen: Max Niemeyer, 1898.
Notes: Includes 'A contribution towards the study of the Scandinavian elements in Modern English dialects' by Arnold Wall (pp 45-135); and 'London Lickpenny' edited by Eleanor Hammond (pp. 404-20).
P.s.: *Exeter College library register*. Tolkien's borrowing record: *Michaelmas Term 1914* from 5 November to 11 November.

631. _____. *Geschichte der Englischen Sprache*, Vol. II. Historische Syntax. Series: Grundriss der germanischen Philologie, 6. Strassburg: K. J. Trübner, 1916.
Collection: Taylor Institution Library, Bodleian Libraries (Oxford).

632. _____ (Edited by). *Life of Saint Katherine*. Series: E.E.T.S. (Early English Text Society), OS 80. London: Published for the Early English Text Society by Kegan Paul, Trench, Trübner and Co., 1884.
Description: Decoratively autographed and dated: '1920'. Annotated ion red crayon and pencil. Contains empty envelope addressed to JRRT, postcard J. E. Marne to JRRT, 1935, letter E. M. Wright to JRRT, 30.10.1957 and two page of notes, inside front cover.
Collection: Tolkien's personal Celtic library, preserved at the Weston library under the auspices of the English Faculty Library (Oxford).
P.s. 1: MS. Tolkien A 21/13 fol. 119. Note by Tolkien, 'Books in Exeter Library useful', with shelfmarks, on back of photostat reading list dated October 1913. Tolkien writes: 'All EETS publications'. [Tolkien Papers, Bodleian Library, Oxford].
P.s. 2: *Ancrene Wisse and Hali Meiðhad* (1929), p. 108.

633. Ekwall, Eilert. 'Englische Ortsnamenforschung'. *Anglica: Untersuchungen zur*

englischen Philologie: Alois Brandl zum 70. Geburtstage überreicht, Vol. I [A. 30], 1925.
   P.s.: *Philology: General Works* (VI 1927, for 1925), p. 35.

634. _____. *English place-names in '–ing'*. London: Milford, 1923.
   P.s.: *Philology: General Works* (IV 1924, for 1923), p. 30 n. 12.
   S.s.: Zettersten (2011), p. 139 'But in spite of his respect for Ekwall's work, Tolkien proposes a number of discreet corrections to his book from 1923, *English place-names in –ing*.

635. _____. *Historische neuenglische Laut- und Formenlehre*. Series: Sammlung Göschen, 735.Berlin: W. de Gruyter, 1914 (2nd ed.).
   P.s.: *Philology: General Works* (IV 1924, for 1923), p. 32 n. 13.

636. _____. 'A few notes on English etymology and word-history'. *Beiblatt zur Anglia*, Vol. XXIX. Halle: Max Niemeyer, 1918, pp. 195-201.
   P.s.: *Sir Gawain and the Green Knight* (1925), p. 110, line 1710 *strothe*.

637. _____. *Historische neuenglische Laut- und Formenlehre*. Series: Sammlung Göschen, 735. Berlin and Leipzig: W. de Gruyter, 1922.
   P.s.: *Philology: General Works* (IV 1924, for 1923), p. 32 n. 13.

638. _____. *The Place-names of Lancashire*. Manchester: The University Press, 1922.
   P.s. 1: *Philology: General Works* (IV 1924, for 1923), p. 30.
   P.s. 2: *Sir Gawain and the Green Knight* (1925), p. xxiii.
   P.s. 3: 'Chaucer as a Philologist: *The Reeve's Tale*' (1934), p. 163 n. 41.

639. Eliot, Charles Norton Edgecumbe. *A Finnish Grammar*. Oxford: At the Clarendon Press, 1890.
   P.s. 1: *Exeter College library register*. Tolkien's borrowing record: *Michaelmas Term 1911* from 25 November to 5 December; *Michaelmas Term 1912* from 25 October to 5 December. *Michaelmas Term 1914* from 14 November to 16 January 1915.
   P.s. 2: *Letters* 163 (1955). To W.H. Auden. Tolkien writes: 'Most important, perhaps, after Gothic was the discovery in Exeter College library, when I was supposed to be reading for Honour Mods, of a Finnish Grammar. It was like discovering a complete wine-cellar filled with bottles of an amazing wine of a kind and flavour never tasted before. It quite intoxicated me; and I gave up the attempt to invent an 'unrecorded' Germanic language, and my 'own language' – or series of invented languages – became heavily Finnicized in phonetic pattern and structure.'
   P.s. 3: *A Secret Vice* (2016), p. 33.
   P.s. 4: *The Story of Kullervo* (2016), p. xii.
   S.s. 1: Priestman (1992), p. 34.
   S.s. 2: Scull (1993), p. 50. Scull writes: 'The exhibition displayed books from Tolkien's library which showed his interest in languages, including C.N.E. Eliot's *A Finnish Grammar*'.
   S.s. 3: Garth (2003), p. 26.
   S.s. 4: Garth (2014), p. 21.
   S.s. 5: Scull-Hammond (2017a), p. 35.

640. Elliott, Ralph Warren Victor. *Runes. An introduction*. Manchester: The University Press, 1959.
   P.s.: Tolkien's unpublished letter to Jane T. Sibley, 30 May 1959. Tolkien writes: 'There is a book about the historical English and related Runes (which incidentally quotes from the L.R. on its page 33): RUNES, by R.W.V. Elliott, Manchester University Press, 1959 (30/-)'.

641. Ellis, Alexander John. *On early English pronunciation*, Pt. III, *with especial reference to Shakespeare and Chaucer, containing an investigation of the correspondence of writing with speech in England from the Anglosaxon period to*

the present day. Series: E.E.T.S. (Early English Text Society), ES 14, 23. London: Published for the Philological Society by Asher & Co., and the Chaucer Society by Trübner & Co., 1871.
>P.s. 1: MS. Tolkien A 21/13 fol. 119. Note by Tolkien, 'Books in Exeter Library useful', with shelfmarks, on back of photostat reading list dated October 1913. Tolkien writes: 'All EETS publications'. [Tolkien Papers, Bodleian Library, Oxford].
>P.s. 2: *English and Welsh* (1963), p. 41 n. 1. Tolkien writes:'so, hoping that with such words I may appease the shade of Charles James O'Donnell, I will end – echoing in rejoinder the envoi of Salesbury's Preface: Dysgwn y lion Frythoneg!! Doeth yw ei dysg, da iaith deg'. [n. 1] 'Dyscwch nes oesswch Saesnec | Doeth yw e dysc da iaith dec' (from'salesbury's Preface, p. 774).

642. _____. *The only English proclamation of Henry III., 18 October 1258, and its treatment by former editors and translators, considered and illustrated; to which are added editions of The Cuckoo song and The Prisoner's prayer, lyrics of the XIIIth century.* Series: Oxford movement., Halifax and Church sub-collections, 14. London: Asher and Co., 1868.
>P.s.: 1 MS. Tolkien A 21/7 fols. 31-2. [Tolkien Papers, Bodleian Library, Oxford].
>P.s. 2: MS. Tolkien A 21/13 *The English MSS.* fol. 203. [Tolkien Papers, Bodleian Library, Oxford].

643. Ellis, Thomas Peter and John Lloyd. *The Mabinogion, a new translation.* Oxford: Clarendon Press, 1929.
>P.s.: *Sir Gawain and the Green Knight* (1930, 2nd ed.), p. xxvi.

644. Emerson, Oliver Farrar. *A Middle English Reader.* London: The Macmillan Co., 1905.
>S.s.: Lapidge (2002), p. 103. [Napier] A course on Emerson's *Middle English Reader*, first published in 1905 – runs right through from 1887-8 to 1913-14.

645. _____. *A Middle English Reader.* New York: The Macmillan Co., 1919.
>Description: Inside the book is a card from University Press of Oxford that states: 'To Professor Tolkien May 27, 1930'. On the first page is Tolkien's signature in ink, and some more notes in pencil i.e. on page x, next to 'V. Robert of Gloucester's…' Tolkien writes 'N. Owl of | Nightingale'. Collection: Private [Tolkien Collector's Guide].
>S.s.: University of Leeds (1923), p. 94. English Language and Literature. Scheme A. Degree of B.A. with Honours. Texts and Period selected for 1923-24 (a). General reading. Especially Pt. I, A I, ii, Bi, vi; Pt. II, Bii, iv, v.

646. _____. 'Notes on Sir Gawain and the Green Knight'. *Journal of English and Germanic Philology*, Vol. XXI. Urbana: Published Quarterly by the University of Illinois, 1922, pp. 363-410.
>P.s.: *Sir Gawain and the Green Knight* (1925), p. 106, line 1467 *schafted*. Tolkien and Gordon cite p. 389; p. 108, line 1634 *let lodly þerat*.

647. Endter, Wilhelm (Edited by). *König Alfreds des Grossen Bearbeitung der Soliloquien des Augustinus.* Hamburg: Henri Grand, 1922.
>Description: Autographed on front flyleaf.
>Collection: Tolkien's personal Celtic library, preserved at the Weston library under the auspices of the English Faculty Library (Oxford).

648. England, George and Alfred William Pollard (Edited by). *The Towneley plays.* Series: E.E.T.S. (Early English Text Society), ES 71. London: Published for the Early English Text Society by Kegan Paul, Trench, Trübner and Co., 1907.
>P.s. 1: MS. Tolkien A 12/1 *Commentary on Sir Gawain, lines 37-1987* fol. 144. [Tolkien Papers, Bodleian Library, Oxford].
>P.s. 2: MS. Tolkien A 12/2 *Commentary on Sir Gawain, lines 1999-2523* fol. 12. Tolkien refers

to the verse: 'ffor, as eu*er* ete I brede' (v. 395, tr. 'as sure as I have ever enten bread'). [Tolkien Papers, Bodleian Library, Oxford].

P.s. 3: MS. Tolkien A 21/13 fol. 119. Note by Tolkien, 'Books in Exeter Library useful', with shelfmarks, on back of photostat reading list dated October 1913. Tolkien writes: 'All EETS publications' [Tolkien Papers, Bodleian Library, Oxford].

P.s. 4: *Beowulf* (2014), p. 283 n. 1. Tolkien quotes the passage: 'This forty dayes has rayn beyn; it will therefor abate full lele', it is on page 36 of this book.

649. English Association (Edited by). *Poems of To-day*. London: Sidgwick & Jackson, 1916.
> S.s. 1: University of Leeds (1920), p. 180. English Language and Literature. Int. I Intermediate Course (Literature).
>
> S.s. 2: University of Leeds (1921), p. 156. English Language and Literature - Scheme B. Texts for 1921-22. (d) Outlines of the History of English Literature. Ordinary Degree of B.A. with Honours. Final Examinations.

650. Enlart, Camille (Edited by). *Manuel d'Archeologie francaise depuis les temps erovingiens jusqu 'a la renaissance* III - *Le Costume*. Paris: Auguste Picard, 1916.
> P.s.: *Sir Gawain and the Green Knight* (1925), p. xxvii.

651. Erhardt-Siebold, Erika von. *Die Lateinischen Rätsel der Angelsachsen*. Heidelberg: Carl Winter's Universitätsbuchhandlung, 1925.
> Description: Autographed on front flyleaf.
>
> Collection: Tolkien's personal Celtic library, preserved at the Weston library under the auspices of the English Faculty Library (Oxford).

652. Ernault, Emilie. *L'Ancien vers Breton. Exposé sommaire, avec examples et pièces en vers bretons anciens et moderns*. Series: La Bretagne et les Pays Celtiques. Paris: Champion, 1912.
> Description: Autographed: 'John Reuel Tolkien'. Dated on page before half-title page: '1922'.
>
> Collection: Tolkien's personal Celtic library, preserved at the Weston library under the auspices of the English Faculty Library (Oxford).
>
> S.s.: Scull-Hammond (2017a), p. 126.

653. _____. 'Sur l'Étymologie Bretonne'. *Revue Celtique*, Vol. XXV, no. 51, pp. 263-97; no. 83, pp. 405-19. Chartres: Durand, 1914.
> Collection: Tolkien's personal Celtic library, preserved at the Weston library under the auspices of the English Faculty Library (Oxford).

654. Euripides. *The Bacchae of Euripides*. Translated by Gilbert Murray. London: George Allen & Company, Ltd. 1913 (12th ed.).
> S.s.: Scull-Hammond (2017a), p. 43. *Hilary Term 1913*: From 14 January, Tolkien will attend Gilbert Murray' lectures on Euripides' *Bacchae* (a set text) on Tuesdays and Thursdays at 10.00 a.m. in the Examination Schools; p. 44. 27 February 1913: The First Public Examination for the Honour School of Greek and Latin Literature (Honour Moderations) begins. He is also examined on four Greek plays, *Oedipus Tyrannus* and *Elektra* by Sophocles, *Agamemnon* by Aeschylus, and the *Bacchæ* by Euripides, with special attention to *Oedipus Tyrannus*.

655. _____. *The Electra of Euripides*. Translated by Gilbert Murray. London: George Allen & Sons, 1910.
> S.s.: Scull-Hammond (2017a), p. 40. *Michaelmas Term 1912*: Tolkien, possibly attends Gilbert Murray's lectures on Aeschylus' *Agamemnon* and Euripides' *Electra* on Tuesdays and Thursdays at 12.00 noon in the Examinations School, beginning 15 October; p. 44. 27 February 1913: The First Public Examination for the Honour School of Greek and Latin Literature (Honour Moderations) begins. He is also examined on four Greek plays, *Oedipus Tyrannus* and *Elektra* by Sophocles, *Agamemnon* by Aeschylus, and the *Bacchæ* by Euripides, with special attention to *Oedipus Tyrannus*.

Section A

656. Evans, Daniel Silvan. *An English and Welsh Dictionary*, Vol. I. Denbigh: Thomas Gee, 1852.
> Description: Inscribed on front flyleaf: 'Rupert H. Morris. | with his father's best wishes. | October, 1861. 'Also on front flyleaf:'see after page 48'.
> Collection: Tolkien's personal Celtic library, preserved at the Weston library under the auspices of the English Faculty Library (Oxford).
> S.s.: Phelpstead (2011), p. 118.

657. _____. *An English and Welsh Dictionary*, Vol. II. Denbigh: Thomas Gee, 1858.
> Description: Inscribed on front flyleaf: 'Rupert H. Morris. | with his father's best wishes. | October, 1861.'
> Collection: Tolkien's personal Celtic library, preserved at the Weston library under the auspices of the English Faculty Library (Oxford).

658. Evans, Joan. *Dress in mediaeval France*. Oxford: At the Clarendon Press, 1952.
> P.s.: *Sir Gawain and the Green Knight* (1967) 'Select Bibliography', p. 155.

659. Evans, John Gwenogvryn (Edited by). *Chirk codex of the Welsh laws* (Facsimile). Series: Old Welsh Texts, 6. Llanbedrog: N. Wales, 1909.
> Description: Decoratively autographed on front flyleaf.
> Collection: Tolkien's personal Celtic library, preserved at the Weston library under the auspices of the English Faculty Library (Oxford).
> S.s.: Phelpstead (2011), p. 118.

660. _____ (Edited by). *The Black Book of Carmarthen*. Series: Old Welsh Texts, V. Llanbedrog: Evans, 1907.
> Description: Autographed on back of front flyleaf.
> Collection: Tolkien's personal Celtic library, preserved at the Weston library under the auspices of the English Faculty Library (Oxford).
> S.s.: Phelpstead (2011), p. 118.

661. _____ (Palæogr. note). *Black Book of Carmarthen* (Facsimile). Series: Old Welsh Texts. Oxford: Evans, 1888.
> Notes: Facsimile, subscription limited edition of 250. Copy no. 129.
> Description: Contains bookplate of Meyrick Library, Jesus College, Oxford inside front cover, overprinted:'sold by authority | Librarian | Jesus College'. Autographed on the back of front flyleaf.
> Collection: Tolkien's personal Celtic library, preserved at the Weston library under the auspices of the English Faculty Library (Oxford).
> S.s.: Phelpstead (2011), p. 118.

662. _____ (Edited by). *Book of Taliesin* (Facsimile and text). Series: Old Welsh Texts, 9. Llandbedrog: N. Wales, 1910.
> Description: Decoratively autographed and dated on before half title page: '1922'.
> Collection: Tolkien's personal Celtic library, preserved at the Weston library under the auspices of the English Faculty Library (Oxford).
> S.s. 1: Carpenter (1979), p. 124 n. 2. Tolkien's poem about Charles Williams ('*Our dear Charles Williams many guises show...*' pp. 123-26). Tolkien quotes *king or pope, wizard or emperor*: Arthur, the Pope, Merlin, and the Emperor are four of the principal figures in the *Taliessin* poems.
> S.s. 2: Phelpstead (2011), p. 118.

663. _____ (Edited by). *Pedeir Kainc y Mabinogi, Breuddwyd Maxe, Lludd a Llevelys*. Oxford and Pwllheli, 1905.
> Description: King Edward's School, with seal stamp on upper board. Inscribed [by G. B. Smith?]: 'Geoffrey Bache Smith. | (J. T. B. Eng. Essay, 1914)'. Inscribed by Tolkien 'killed in France 1916, bequeathed to J.R.R. Tolkien'. Annotations by Tolkien [Judith Priestman 1994, revd. 2016].

Collection: Weston Library, Bodleian Libraries (Oxford).
S.s. 1: Garth (2003), p. 357.
S.s. 2: Fimi (2007), p. 51.
S.s. 3: Zettersten (2011), p. 78 'During my last visit to the Tolkien Collection at the Bodleian Library, Oxford, I went through Tolkien's books in his private library from his school time, which his family had donated to the Bodleian in July 1982.'
S.s. 4: Phelpstead (2011), p. 117.

664. _____ (Edited by). *The Poetry in the Red Book of Hergest*. Series: Old Welsh Texts, 11. Llanbedrog: N. Wales, 1911.
Description: Autographed on front flyleaf.
Collection: Tolkien's personal Celtic library, preserved at the Weston library under the auspices of the English Faculty Library (Oxford).
S.s.: Phelpstead (2011), p. 118.

665. _____. *The White Book of Mabinogion: Welsh tales [and] romances produced from the Peniarth manuscripts*. Series: Old Welsh Texts, 7. Pwllheli: Evans, 1907.
Description: Decoratively autographed on front flyleaf.
Collection: Tolkien's personal Celtic library, preserved at the Weston library under the auspices of the English Faculty Library (Oxford).
S.s. 1: Fimi (2007), p. 51.
S.s. 2: Phelpstead (2011), p. 118.

666. Evans, Sebastian (Translated by). *High History of the Holy Graal*, Vol. I. London: J. M. Dent and Co., 1898.
P.s.: *Sir Gawain and the Green Knight* (1925), p. xxvi. Tolkien and Gordon write: 'For bibliography of the Irish and French analogues of *Sir Gawain*, see the bibliography in Kittredge's study'. [*NED*] In Kittredge's study, this article is mentioned in 'VII. Perlesvaus' (p. 300).

667. _____ (Translated by). *The High History of the Holy Graal*, Vol. II. London: J. M. Dent and Co., 1898.
P.s.: *Sir Gawain and the Green Knight* (1925), p. xxvi. Tolkien and Gordon write: 'For bibliography of the Irish and French analogues of *Sir Gawain*, see the bibliography in Kittredge's study'. [*NED*] In Kittredge's study, this article is mentioned in 'VII. Perlesvaus' (p. 300).

668. _____ (Translated by). *High History of the Holy Graal*. Series: Everyman's library, 445. London: J. M. Dett, 1913 (Reprint).
Collection: Tolkien's personal Celtic library, preserved at the Weston library under the auspices of the English Faculty Library (Oxford).

669. Evans-Wentz, Walter Yeeling. *The Fairy-Faith in Celtic Countries*. London: H. Frowde, 1911.
S.s.: *The Lay of Aotrou & Itroun* (2016), pp. 22, 32.

670. Ewert, Alfred. *Technicalities*.
S.s.: Scull-Hammond (2017a), p. 319. 28 May 1946: Ewert reads this paper at meeting of the Oxford Dante Society (Tolkien was a member from 1945 to 1955). The paper will be published in *Centenary Essays of Dante* (1965), as *Art and Artifice in the Divina Commedia* (77-90).

671. *Exodus* [Old English heroic poem].
For editions and translations of this Old English poem, see Blackburn, Irving, and further (as part of the Cædmon or Junius Manuscript) Bouterwek, Gollancz, Krapp, Thorpe, Tolkien.
S.s.: Scull-Hammond (2017a), p. 46. April 1913: Tolkien will need to become familiar with a range of literary and philological subjects and set texts as prescribed in the Oxford Regulations of the Board of Studies, knowing that he may be examined on them in ten papers at the end of Trinity Term 1915: Old texts.

SECTION A

672. Falconer, John A. 'Modern Languages and the Recent Reform in Dutch Universities'. *Anglica: Untersuchungen zur englischen Philologie: Alois Brandl zum 70. Geburtstage überreicht*, Vol. I [A. 30], 1925.
    P.s.: *Philology: General Works* (VI 1927, for 1925), p. 33. Tolkien titles the essay 'The reform of modern language teaching in the Dutch universities' and he writes: 'which is interesting and instructive'.

673. Falk, Hjalmar. *Betydningslær (Semasiologi)*. Oslo: H. Aschehoug and Co., 1920.
    P.s. : *Philology: General Works* (IV 1924, for 1923), p. 20.

674. _____ and Alf Torp. (Edited by). *Wortschatz der Germanischen Spracheinheit*. Series: Vergleichendes Wörterbuch der indogermanischen Sprachen, 3. Göttingen: Vandenhoeck und Ruprecht, 1909.
    P.s. 1: MS. Tolkien A 11 *Notes on Pearl* fol. 143. [Tolkien Papers, Bodleian Library, Oxford].
    P.s. 2: *The Name 'Nodens'* (1932), p. 136.

675. Faral, Edmond. *La légende arthurienne: études et documents*, Vol. I. Des origines a Geoffroy de Monmouth. Series: Bibliothèque de l'École des Hautes Études, Sciences Historiques et Philologiques, 255. Paris: Librairie Honoré Champion, 1929.
    P.s.: *Sir Gawain and the Green Knight* (1967) 'Select Bibliography', p. 154.

676. _____. *La légende arthurienne: études et documents*, Vol. II. Geoffroy de Monmouth: la légende arthurienne à Glastonbury. Series: Bibliothèque de l'École des Hautes Études, Sciences Historiques et Philologiques, 256. Paris: Librairie Honoré Champion, 1929.
    P.s.: *Sir Gawain and the Green Knight* (1967) 'Select Bibliography', p. 154.

677. _____. *La légende arthurienne: études et documents*, Vol. III. Documents. Series: Bibliothèque de l'École des Hautes Études., Sciences Historiques et Philologiques, 257. Paris: Librairie Honoré Champion, 1929.
    P.s.: *Sir Gawain and the Green Knight* (1967) 'Select Bibliography', p. 155. 'Historia Brittonum'.

678. Farrow, John. *Pageant of the Popes*. London: Sheed & Ward, 1943.
    Description: Book given by Tolkien to his daughter Priscilla. Tolkien wrote on the first blank page 'P.M.R. Tolkien'.
    Collection: Private (Oronzo Cilli)

679. Fauriel, Claude Charles. *Chants Populaires de la Grece Moderne*, Vol. I Chants Historiques. Paris: Chez Firmin Didot, pére er fils, 1824.
    P.s.: *Tolkien On Fairy-stories* (2008), p. 307.

680. _____. *Chants Populaires de la Grece Moderne*, Vol. II Chants Historique, Romanesques et Domestiques. Paris: Chez Firmin Didot, pére er fils, 1825.
    P.s.: # 1 *Tolkien On Fairy-stories* (2008), p. 307.

681. Fehr, Bernhard (Edited by). *Die Hirtenbriefe Ælfrics in altenglischer und lateinischer Fassung*. Hamburg: Henri Grand, 1914.
    Description: Autographed, with one penciled annotation on front flyleaf.
    Collection: Tolkien's personal Celtic library, preserved at the Weston library under the auspices of the English Faculty Library (Oxford).

682. Feist, Sigmund. *Einführung in das Gotische. Texte mit Übersetzungen und*

Erläuterungen. Series: Teubners philologische studienbücher. Leipzig: B. G. Teubner, 1922.
    Collection: Taylor Institution Library, Bodleian Libraries (Oxford).

683. _____. *Etymologisches Wörterbuch der gotischen Sprache: mit Einschluss des sog. Krimgotischen*. Halle: Max Niemeye, 1909.
    Description: Inscribed on front cover: 'John Reuel Tolkien |: E: | Coll: Exon: Oxon: | ann · dom | mcmxiii | ex · libris · de · litteris: et | philologia: germanica: collectis | tom'. Years after, Tolkien gives the book, with a dedication, to Simonne d'Ardenne: (before his name) 'à Mlle S. d'Ardenne | de'.
    Collection: Fonds J.R.R. Tolkien, Bibliothèque ALPHA principale, Université de Liège (Liège), Tol/053.
    P.s.: MS. Tolkien A 11 *Notes on Pearl* fol. 143. [Tolkien Papers, Bodleian Library, Oxford].

684. _____. *Etymologisches Wörterbuch der gotischen Sprache: mit Einschluss des Krimgotischen und sonstiger gotischer sprachreste*. Halle: Max Niemeye, 1923.
    P.s.: *Sigelwara land* (1934) p. 102 n. 5. Tolkien writes that for the term *sigillum* s.v. *sigljo*; p. 105 n. 3; p. 110 n. 4.

685. _____. *Germanen und Kelten in der antiken Überlieferung*. Halle: Max Niemeyer, 1927.
    Description: Autographed in blue crayon on front cover.
    Collection: Tolkien's personal Celtic library, preserved at the Weston library under the auspices of the English Faculty Library (Oxford).

686. _____. *Indogermanen und Germanen. Ein beitrag zur europäischen urgeschichtsforschung*. Halle: Max Neimeyer, 1924 (3rd ed.).
    Description: A few annotations. Note page 59: 'Vollends im Unklaren bleiben wir über den Grund, weshalb Das Urgermanische morire indogermanischen Medien zu Tenues verschoben cappello, obwohl es doch stimmhafte Verschlußlaute besaß, die wenigstens teilweise (Wortanfang, nach Nasalen usw.) an die Stelle der indogermanischen aspirierten Medien (bh, dh, gh) traten.' Note page 43: 'He lists three languages, 'Paiśācī' (an Indian dialect), 'Tokhar' (Tokharian), and 'Armen' (Armenian). He has also written '(p > ht > t') … p < kh,' and 'p 43' next to all the names. These references are to page forty-three of Indogermanen und Germanen. Feist is again discussing sound shifts (that is, 'p' becomes 'h' and 't' becomes aspirated't' as an example of a sound shift in Armenian) in different languages.'
    Collection: The Science Fiction and Fantasy Research Collection of the Cushing Memorial Library and Archives at Texas A&M University.
    P.s.: *Philology: General Works* (V 1926, for 1924), p. 44 n. 6.

687. Felix of Crowland. *The Anglo-Saxon version of the life of St Guthlac, hermit of Crowland*. Translation and notes by Charles Wycliffe Goodwin. London: John Russell Smith, 1848.
    P.s.: *English and Welsh* (1963), p. 25. Tolkien quotes: 'Bryttisc sprecende', chapter vi, p. 42.

688. _____. *Felix's Life of Saint Guthlac: Texts, Translation and Notes*. Edited by Bertram Colgrave. Cambridge: The University Press, 1956.
    P.s.: *English and Welsh* (1963), p. 24 n. 2. Tolkien quotes: 'What follows occurred in the days of Coenred, king of the Mercians … seemed to burst into flames' (chapter xxxiv, pp. 108-10).

689. Ferri, Ferruccio. *La poesia popolare di Antonio Pucci*. Bologna: Libreria L. Beltrami, 1909.
    P.s.: *Sir Gawain and the Green Knight* (1925), p. xxvi. Tolkien and Gordon write: 'For bibliography of the Irish and French analogues of *Sir Gawain*, see the bibliography in Kittredge's study'. [*NED*] In Kittredge's study, this article is mentioned in 'XI. The Canzoni' (p. 304).

690. Fick, August (Edited by). *Vergleichendes Wörterbuch der indogermanischen Sprachen*, Vol. III Wortschatz der germanischen Spracheinheit mit einem Begleitwort von A Bezzenberger. Göttingen: Vandenhoeck & Ruprecht, 1874 (3rd ed.).

P.s.: *Exeter College library register.* Tolkien's borrowing record: *Michaelmas Term 1912* from 25 October to 5 December.

691. Fiedler, Hermann George. 'Two Problems of the German Preterite-Present Verbs'. Offprint from MLR (*The Modern Language Review*), Vol. XXIII, no. 2. Cambridge University Press, April 1928, pp. 188-96.
Description: Inscribed on front cover: 'Professor Tolkien | with kind regards | from H. G. Fiedler'. Collection: Private [Pieter Collier].

692. Fielding, Henry. *The History of the Adventures of Joseph Andrews, and his friend Mr. Abraham Adams*. London: 1920.
S.s.: University of Leeds (1921), p. 145. English Literature, text selected for 1921-22. Ordinary Degree of B.A.; p. 191 English Language and Literature. F1. Final Course (English Literature) (ii) The History of English Literature from 1700 to 1765.

693. Finch, Rowland George (Translated by). *The Saga of the Volsungs*. London: Nelson, 1965.
P.s.: *Letters* 237 (1962). From a letter to Rayner Unwin. Tolkien writes 'I am afraid it largely tickles my pedantic fancy, because of its echo of the Norse Niblung matter (the otter's whisker)' quoting the Finch's translation, 'The Æsir handed over the treasure to Hredimar, stuffed the otterskin full and set it on its feet. Then the Æsir had to pile the gold alongside and cover it up. When that was completed, Hredimar went up and saw a single whisker, and told them to cover that' (p. 26).

694. Findlater, Andrew (Edited by). *Chambers's Etymological Dictionary of the English language*. London: W. and R. Chambers, 1882.
Description: King Edward's School. Inscribed Notes: 'Feb. 1973. This book was the beginning of my interest in Germanic Philology (& Philol. in general) [about 1904]. Unfortunately, the 'introduction' giving me my first glimpse of 'Lautverschiebung' etc. became so well-worn and tattered that it has become lost.' A few annotations (see note and entry for 'dwarf') [Judith Priestman 1994, revd. 2016]. Tolkien's edition is missing the following pages: Title page; 'Contents', p. iii; 'Preface', pp. v-vi; 'Explanations to the student', pp. vii-viii and 'Abbreviations used in the work', p. viii. Collection: Weston Library, Bodleian Libraries (Oxford).
S.s. 1: Priestman (1992), p. 16 number 19.
S.s. 2: Scull (1993), p. 51. Scull writes: 'The exhibition displayed books from Tolkien's library which showed his interest in languages, including Chambers' Etymological Dictionary'.
S.s. 3: Garth (2003), p. 15.
S.s. 4: Zettersten (2011), p. 78 'During my last visit to the Tolkien Collection at the Bodleian Library, Oxford, I went through Tolkien's books in his private library from his school time, which his family had donated to the Bodleian in July 1982.'
S.s. 5: Scull-Hammond (2017a), p. 10.
S.s. 6: McIlwaine (2018), p. 242.

695. Firth, Charles Harding. *English History in English Poetry, from the French Revolution to the Death of Queen Victoria*. London: H. Marshall and Sons, 1911, p. 308.
S.s.: University of Leeds (1920), p. 181. English Language and Literature. Int. I Intermediate Course (Literature).

696. _____. *Stuart Tracts 1603-1693*. Series: An English Garner. Westminster: A. Constable and Co., 1903.
S.s.: University of Leeds (1920), p. 147. English Language and Literature - Scheme A. Texts and Period selected for 1920-21. (b) Special period: 1557-1637. (c) Texts suggested for study with Special Period. Ordinary Degree of B.A. with Honours. Final Examination. Extracts pp. 106-34.

697. Fisher, Herbert Albert Laurens. *A History of Europe*. London: Edward Arnold & Co, 1938.
Description: Inscribed 'Michael H. R. Tolkien | From | Daddy | October 22nd. 1939' Collection: Private [Sold by Thornton & Sons Booksellers].

698. Fletcher, Jefferson Butler. 'The Allegory of the Pearl'. J.E.G.Ph. (*The Journal*

of English and Germanic Philology), Vol. XX, no. 1, pp. 1-21, 1921.
> P.s.: MS. Tolkien A 35 *Pearl* fol. 114. [Tolkien Papers, Bodleian Library, Oxford].

699. Flom, George T. 'Place-name Tests of Racial Mixture in Northern England'. MLN (*Modern Language Notes*), Vol. 39. Baltimore: Johns Hopkins Press, April 1924, pp. 203-12.
> P.s.: *Philology: General Works* (V 1926, for 1924), p. 55.

700. Foncieux, Georges. 'La Maitresse volage et le chien fidèle, romance et conte'. *Revue des traditions populaires*, Vol. VIII, no. 11, 1893, pp. 513-18.
> P.s.: *Sir Gawain and the Green Knight* (1925), p. xxvi. Tolkien and Gordon write: 'For bibliography of the Irish and French analogues of *Sir Gawain*, see the bibliography in Kittredge's study'. [*NED*] In Kittredge's study, this article is mentioned in 'X. Le Chevalier à l'Épée' (p. 304).

701. Foote, Peter Godfrey and John Townsend. *Northern research: a guide to the library holdings of University College London*, Vol. II. Icelandic. London, Viking Society for Northern Research, University College, 1968.
> Collection: Tolkien's personal Celtic library, preserved at the Weston library under the auspices of the English Faculty Library (Oxford).

702. Forbes, Alexander Robert. *Place-names of Skye and adjacent Islands*. Paisley: Gairdner, 1923.
> P.s.: *Philology: General Works* (IV 1924, for 1923), p. 30.

703. Forchhammer, Jörgen. *Die Grundlage der Phonetik. Ein Versuch, die phonetische Wissenschaft auf fester sprachphysiologischer Grundlage aufzubauen*. Series: Indog. Bibliothek III, 6. Heidelberg: Carl Winter, 1924.
> Description: Signed in the front by J.R.R. Tolkien and annotations in pencil.
> Collection: Private [Sold by Peter Harrington Antiquarian Bookseller].
> P.s.: *Philology: General Works* (V 1926, for 1924), p. 53 n. 12.
> S.s.: Harrington (2003), p. 25.

704. Förstemann, Ernst Wilhelm. *Altdeutsches Namenbuch*, Vol. I. Personennamen. Nordhausen: Ferd. Förstemann, and Brussels & Ghent: Muquart; London: Williams & Norgate, 1856.
> Description: Signed, with flourishes, 'John Reuel Tolkien 1922' on front free endpaper.
> Collection: Private [Sold by Simon Finch Rare Books Ltd.].
> S.s.: Finch (2002), p. 53.

705. ———. *Altdeutsches Namenbuch*, Vol. I. Personennamen. Bonn: P. Hanstein, 1900.
> P.s.: *Finn and Hengest* (1982), p. 39 n. 16; p. 52 n. 39.

706. Förster, Max. 'Ablaut in Flussnamen'. *Streitberg-Festgabe* [A. 2228]. Leipzig: Market und Petter, 1924.
> P.s.: *Philology: General Works* (V 1926, for 1924).

707. ———. *Bêowulf-Materialien zum Gebrauch bei Vorlesungen*. Braunschweig, 1900.
> Description: Tolkien's signature and inscription are on the title page below the ownership stamp of Oxford Professor H.G. Fiedler.
> Collection: Private [Pieter Collier, purchased from Ulysses Books, London, in 2000]

708. ———. *Der Flussname Themse und seine Sippe; Studien zur Anglisierung keltischer Eigennamen und zur Lautchronologie des Altbritischen*. Series: Bayerische Akademie der Wissenschaften. München: In Kommission bei C.H. Beck, 1941.
> P.s.: *English and Welsh* (1963), p. 33 n. 1.

SECTION A

709. _____. 'Die Französierung des Englischen Personennamenschatzes'. Offprint from *Germanica*: Eduard Sievers zum 75. Geburtstage. Halle: Max Niemeyer, 1925.
   Description: This copy is signed by Tolkien at the top of the front page. Tolkien has also added a notation in pencil under his signature, indicating the origin of the article. Interestingly enough, there are a few further pencilled corrections within the pamphlet, which would seem to indicate Tolkien had corrected the German in the pamphlet.
   Collection: Private [Pieter Collier].

710. _____. 'Keltisches Wortgut im Englischen'. Offprint from *Texte und forschungen zur englischen kulturgeschichte; festgabe für Felix Liebermann zum 20. juli 1921* [A. 1379]. Halle: Max Niemeyer, 1921, pp. 119-242.
   Description: Inscribed on front cover: 'JRR Tolkien: from' 'K. Sisam | (autograph) | 1922'. Annotated in pencil. Given by K. Sisam, so autographed. Reprinted and revised from *Texte und forschungen zur englischen kulturgeschichte*.
   Collection: Tolkien's personal Celtic library, preserved at the Weston library under the auspices of the English Faculty Library (Oxford).
   P.s. 1: *Philology: General Works* (IV 1924, for 1923), p. 22.
   P.s. 2: *English and Welsh* (1963), p. 7.
   P.s. 3: *The Old English Exodus* (1982), p. 56.

711. _____. 'Proben eines englischen Eigennamen-Wörterbuches'. *Germanisch-Romanische Monatsschrift*, Vol. XI. Heidelberg: Carl Winter, March-April 1923, pp. 86-110.
   P.s.: *Philology: General Works* (IV 1924, for 1923), p. 22.

712. _____. 'Die spätaltenglische Übersetzung der Pseudo-Anselmschen Marienpredigt'. Offprint from *Anglica: Untersuchungen zur englischen Philologie*, Vol. 1. Series: Palaestra. Leipzig: Mayer and Müller, 1925, pp. 147-48.
   Description: Inscribed in Tolkien's handwriting on the upper cover in red pencil: 'Marienpredigt. | Forster.' Inscribed in pencil and ink.
   Collection: Private [Pieter Collier].

713. _____ (Edited by). *Die Vercelli-Homilien*, Vol. I. Halfte. Hamburg: Henri Grand, 1932.
   Description: Autographed on front cover.
   Collection: Tolkien's personal Celtic library, preserved at the Weston library under the auspices of the English Faculty Library (Oxford).

714. _____. 'War Nennius ein Ire?'. *Eine festgabe zum siebzigsten geburtstag geh. rat prof. dr. Heinrich Finke* [A. 515]. Münster: W. Aschendorff, 1925.
   P.s.: *Philology: General Works* (VI 1927, for 1925), p. 46.

715. _____ and Arthur Sampson Napier. 'Englische Cato und Ilias-Glossen des 12. Jahrhunderts'. Offprint from *Archiv für das Studium der neueren Sprachen und Literaturen*, Vol. CXVII. Braunschwig: George Westermann, 1906.
   Description: Inscribed on front cover: 'With kind regards | from A. S. Napier'. Followed by: '(to H. C. Wyld)'. Written by JRRT in pencil. JRRT has also written: 'Cato and Ilias glosses | Forster and Napier'.
   Collection: Tolkien's personal Celtic library, preserved at the Weston library under the auspices of the English Faculty Library (Oxford).

716. Fowler, Alastair. *Readers of Literature: Inaugural speech as Regius Professor of Rhetoric and English Literature at the university, given on 27th November 1972*. University of Edinburgh, 1973.
   Description: Inscribed by the author on front cover: 'With best wishes 3.8.73 from | Alaistar Fowler'. Includes a label added by Stan Revell to books owned by Tolkien, 'From the Library of J.R.R. Tolkien'.
   Collection: Private.

717. Fowler, Francis George and Henry Watson Fowler. *The Pocket Oxford Dictionary of Current English*. London: Oxford University Press, 1924.
P.s.: *Philology: General Works* (V 1926, for 1924), p. 49 n. 9.

718. Fowler, Henry Watson. *The Split Infinitive*. Series: Society for Pure English, Tract, no. XV. Oxford: At the Clarendon Press, 1923.
P.s. 1: *Philology: General Works* (IV 1924, for 1923), p. 34.
P.s. 2: *Philology: General Works* (V 1926, for 1924), p. 30.

719. _____ and Francis George Fowler. *The King's English. Abridged for School Use*. Oxford: At the Clarendon Press, 1920.
S.s. 1: University of Leeds (1920), p. 180. English Language and Literature. Int. 2 Intermediate Course (Composition). Text-books recommended.
S.s. 2: University of Leeds (1921), p. 190 English Language and Literature. Int. 2 Intermediate Course (Composition).

720. Fowler, Joseph Thomas. *The metrical life of St Cuthbert*. Newcastle upon Tyne: A. Reid, 1910.
P.s.: MS. Tolkien A 12/1 *Commentary on Sir Gawain, lines 37-1987* fol. 144. [Tolkien Papers, Bodleian Library, Oxford].

721. Fox, Adam. *English Poem on a Sacred Subject*. Oxford: Privately printed by John Johnson at the University Press, 1929.
Description: Signed in ink, on upper right corner of the cover, in Tolkien's hand, "JRR Tolkien." Unfortunately the signature has been somewhat compromised by a chip in the cover that has taken out the "olk" in Tolkien. Also included is a printed sheet that reads, "Sent with the Author's compliments and in | accordance with the conditions of the prize. | Magdalen College, | Dec., 1929."
Collection: Private [Pieter Collier].

722. _____. *Old King Coel: A Rhymed Tale in four Books*. London: Oxford University Press, 1937.
P.s. 1: *Letters* 28 (1938). To Stanley Unwin.
P.s. 2: *Farmer Giles of Ham* (2014), p. 196.
S.s.: Scull-Hammond (2006b), p. 819.

723. _____. *Poetry for pleasure. An inaugural lecture delivered before the University of Oxford, 2 November, 1938*. Oxford: At the Clarendon Press, printed at the University Press Oxford by John Johnson printer to the university, 1938.
Description: Signed on the title page "J.R.R.T"
Collection: Private [Pieter Collier].

724. Franck, Johannes and Nicolaas van Wijk. *Etymologisch woordenboek der Nederlandsche taal*. 'S-Gravenhage: M. Nijihoff, 1912 (2nd ed.).
P.s.: *Sigelwara land* (1934), p. 102 n. 5. Tolkien writes that for the term *sigillum* s.v. *Zegel*; p. 103 n. 2; p. 110 n. 4.

725. Freston, Hugh Reginald. *The Quest of Beauty and Other Poems*. Oxford: B. H. Blackwell, 1915.
S.s. 1: Scull-Hammond (2017a), p. 72: 28 May 1915 Tolkien gives a paper on *The Quest of Beauty and Other Poems* by H.R. Freston.
S.s. 2: Scull-Hammond (2006b), p. 819.

726. Friedrich, Johannes; Johannes Batipsta Hofmann, and Wilhelm Horn (Edited by). *Stand und Aufgaben der Sprachwissenschaft. Festschrift für Wilhelm Streitberg*. Series: Germanische Bibliothek, II, 15. Heidelberg, Carl Winter, 1924.
P.s.: *Philology: General Works* (V 1926, for 1924), p. 34 n. 2; pp. 44, 45.

727. Friedwagner, Mathias. *La vengeance Raguidel: altfranzösischer Abenteurroman*.

Series: His Sämtliche Werke, 2. Halle: Max Niemeyer, 1909.
> P.s.: *Sir Gawain and the Green Knight* (1925), p. xxvi. Tolkien and Gordon write: 'For bibliography of the Irish and French analogues of *Sir Gawain*, see the bibliography in Kittredge's study'. [*NED*] In Kittredge's study, this article is mentioned in 'V. Le Livre de Caradoc' (p. 298), 'X. Le Chevalier à l'Épée' (p. 303).

728.   Fry, Donald (Edited by). *Beowulf Poet. A Collection of Critical Essays*. Prentice Hall, 1968.
> Notes: Fry write: 'Beowulf criticism did not begin in 1936. Although J.R.R. Tolkien's '*Beowulf: The Monsters and the Critics*,' first read in that year, completely altered the course of Beowulf studies, he built upon a broad foundation reaching back 121 years to Thorkelin's editio princeps in 1815. That this anthology excludes those pre-Tolkien efforts not so much on their quality as on their emphases, for with Tolkien critical attention turned to the poem considered primarily as a work of art rather than as an artifact' (p. ix).
> S.s.: Scull-Hammond (2017a), p. 738.

729.   Fuller, Thomas. *Wise words and quaint counsels of Thomas Fuller. Selected and arranged, with a short sketch of the autor's life*. Edited by Augustus Jessopp. Oxford: At the Clarendon Press, 1892.
> S.s.: University of Leeds (1921), p. 154. English Language and Literature - Scheme A. Texts and Period selected for 1921-22. (d) Texts suggested for study with Special Period 1637-1700. Ordinary Degree of B.A. with Honours. Final Examinations.

730.   Funke, Otto. *Innere Sprachform. Eine Einführung in A. Martyrs Sprachphilosophie*. Reichenberg: Kraus, 1924.
> P.s.: *Philology: General Works* (VI 1927, for 1925), p. 45.

731.   _____. 'Zur Definition des Begriffes 'Eigenname'. *Probleme der Englischen Sprache und Kultur. Festschrift Johannes Hoops zum* 60 [A. 1171]. Heidelberg: Carl Winter, 1925.
> P.s.: *Philology: General Works* (VI 1927, for 1925), p. 45.

732.   Furnivall, Frederick James. *The Babees Book: Early English Meals and Manners: with some forewords on education in Early England*. Series: E.E.T.S. (Early English Text Society), OS 32. London: Published for the Early English Text Society by H. Milford, Oxford University Press, 1868.
> P.s. 1: MS. Tolkien A 21/13 fol. 119. Note by Tolkien, 'Books in Exeter Library useful', with shelfmarks, on back of photostat reading list dated October 1913. Tolkien writes: 'All EETS publications'. [Tolkien Papers, Bodleian Library, Oxford].
> P.s. 2: *Sir Gawain and the Green Knight* (1925), p. 94, line 762 *Kros Kryst me spede*; p. 97 line 897 *pis penaunce*. Tolkien and Gordon cite 'John Russel's *Boke of Nurture*'; p. 98 line 979. T. and G. cite *hippocras* (p. 123).
> P.s. 3: *Sir Gawain and the Green Knight* (1967) 'Select Bibliography: editions of texts quoted more than once in the notes', p. 156.

733.   _____. *An English Miscellany. Presented to Dr [Frederick James] Furnivall in honour of his seventy-fifth birthday*. Oxford: At the Clarendon Press, 1901.
> P.s.: *Exeter College library register*. Tolkien's borrowing record: *Hilary Term 1914* from 29 January to 10 March; *Hilary Term 1915* from 19 January to 1 March 1915.

734.   _____, Brock; Edmund and Clouston, William Alexander. *Originals and analogues of some of Chaucer's Canterbury tales*. Series: Chaucher Society's, S.S. 7, 10, 15, 20, 22. London: Published for the Chaucer Society by N. Trübner & Co., Limited, 1888.
> P.s.: MS. Tolkien A 13/2 *Notes and drafts of lectures on Chaucer: Pardoner's Tale* fol. 91. [Tolkien

Papers, Bodleian Library, Oxford].

735. _____ and Thomas Oswald Cockayne. *Hali Meidenhad: An Alliterative Homily of the Thirteenth Century*. Series: E.E.T.S. (Early English Text Society), OS 18. London: Oxford University Press, 1922.
> Description: Annotated in pencil and ink. Contains loose letters, A. F. Colborn to JRRT, 14/11/1933.
> Collection: Tolkien's personal Celtic library, preserved at the Weston library under the auspices of the English Faculty Library (Oxford).
> P.s. 1: MS. Tolkien A 21/13 fol. 119. Note by Tolkien, 'Books in Exeter Library useful', with shelfmarks, on back of photostat reading list dated October 1913. Tolkien writes: 'All EETS publications' [Tolkien Papers, Bodleian Library, Oxford].
> P.s. 2: *Holy Maidenhood* (1923), p. 281.
> P.s. 3: *Some Contributions to Middle-English Lexicography* (1925), p. 212.
> P.s. 4: *The Devil's Coach-Horses* (1925), p. 331.
> P.s. 5: *Pearl* (1953), p. xx n. 1.

736. Furuskog, Ragnar. 'A Collation of the Katherine Group (MS Bodley 34)'. *Studia Neophilologica*, Vol. XIX. Uppsala: A.-B. Lundequistska Bokhandeln (1947), pp. 119-66.
> P.s. 1: '*Iþþlen*' *in Sawles Warde* (1947), p. 169.
> P.s. 2: *Studia Neophilologica* (1948), p. 65.

737. Gamillscheg, Ernst. 'La colonisation germanique dans la Gaule du Nord'. *Essais de philologie moderne (1951): Communications présentées au Congrès International de Philologie Moderne, réuni à Liège du 10 au 13 septembre 1951, à l'occasion du LXe Anniversaire des Sections de Philologie germanique et de Philologie romane de la Faculté de Philosophie et Lettres de l'Université de Liège*. Series: Bibliothèque de la Faculté de Philologie et Lettres de l'Université de Liège; 129. Paris: Les Belles Lettres, 1953, pp. 47-62.
> P.s.: 'Middle English 'Losenger'' (1953), p. 64.

738. Gard, Joyce. *Woorroo*. London: Victor Gollancz Ltd., 1961.
> Notes: A copy was sent to Tolkien by the author.
> P.s.: *Letters*, 232 (1961). From a letter to Joyce Reeves.
> S.s.: Scull-Hammond (2017a), p. 612.

739. Gardner, Helen. *The Horn Book Magazine*. Boston: June 1971.
> Description: Autographed: 'J.R.R. Tolkien'. Includes a label added by Stan Revell to books owned by Tolkien, 'From the Library of J.R.R. Tolkien'.
> Collection: Marion E. Wade Center, Wheaton College (Wheaton, Illinois).

740. _____. *The Limits of Literary Criticism. Reflections on the interpretation of poetry and scripture*. London: Oxford University Press, 1956.
> Description: Inscribed in ink on title page: 'J.R.R. Tolkien'. Includes a label added by Stan Revell to books owned by Tolkien, 'From the Library of J.R.R. Tolkien', on inside front cover.
> Collection: Marion E. Wade Center, Wheaton College (Wheaton, Illinois).

741. Garner, Alan. *The Weirdstone of Brisingamen: A Tale of Alderley*. London: William Collins & Sons, 1960.
> S.s.: Lewis (2009b), p. 404. Letter to Roger Lancelyn Green – 15 September 1960. Lewis writes: 'Have you seen Allan Garner's *The Wierdstone of Brisingamen*? Not bad, tho' too indebted to Tolkien. He seems to be a fairly near neighbour of yours–Alderley, Cheshire.'

742. Garrett, Robert Max. *The Pearl: an interpretation*. Series: University of Washington publication in English, Vol. IV, No. 1. Seattle: University of Washington,

1918.
    P.s.: MS. Tolkien A 35 *Pearl* fol. 114. [Tolkien Papers, Bodleian Library, Oxford].

743.   Gasquet, Francis Aidan (Abbot) and Edmund Bishop. *The Bosworth Psalter: an account of a manuscript formerly belonging to O. Turville-Petre, esq. of Bosworth hall, now Addit. MS. 37517 at the British museum*. London: G. Bell and Sons, 1908.
    Description: Attached to the front pastedown and ffep are two newspaper reviews of the book, along with ink annotations dating their publication in 1908. There are also several other ink annotations in the same hand. A bookstore stamp on the flep reads: 'Thornton & Son, Booksellers, 11 The Broad, Oxford.' Several penciled notes, especially on two of the final blank pages, in Tolkien's handwriting. Tolkien obviously bought this book second-hand.
    Collection: Private [Pieter Collier].

744.   Gaston Paris, Bruno Paulin. 'Gauvain et le Vert Chevalier'. *Histoire littéraire de la France*, Vol. XXX Suite du Quatorziéme siécle. Paris: Imprimerie nationale, 1888, pp. 71-78.
    P.s.: *Sir Gawain and the Green Knight* (1925), p. xxvi. Tolkien and Gordon write: 'For bibliography of the Irish and French analogues of *Sir Gawain*, see the bibliography in Kittredge's study'. [NED] In Kittredge's study, this article is mentioned in 'I. Fled Bricrend' (p. 292); 'II. Gawain and the Green Knight' (p. 294), 'X. Le Chevalier à l'Épée' (p. 303), 'XI. The Canzoni' (p. 305).

745.   _____ (Edited by). *La Littérature française au Moyen Âge: 11e-14e siècle*. Paris: Hachette, 1905 (3rd ed.).
    P.s.: *Sir Gawain and the Green Knight* (1925), p. xxvi [In the text, Tolkien and Gordon indicate '1915']. Tolkien and Gordon write: 'For history and bibliography of Old French romances'.

746.   _____ (Edited by). *La Littérature française au Moyen Âge: 11e-14e siècle*. Paris: Hachette, 1914 (5th ed.).
    P.s.: *Sir Gawain and the Green Knight* (1930, 2nd ed.), p. xxvi.

747.   Gay, John. *The Beggar's opera*. London: M. Secker, 1920.
    S.s.: University of Leeds (1921), p. 144. English Literature, text selected for 1921-22. Ordinary Degree of B.A.; p. 191 English Language and Literature. F1. Final Course (English Literature) (ii) The History of English Literature from 1700 to 1765.

748.   Gelzer, Heinrich. *Der altfranzösische Yderroman*. Halle: Verlag von Max Niemeyer; Dresden, Gesellschaft für romanische Literatur, 1913.
    P.s.: *Sir Gawain and the Green Knight* (1967) 'Select Bibliography', p. 155.

749.   Geoffrey of Monmouth, Bishop of St Asaph. *Geoffrey of Monmouth*. Translated by Sebastian Evans. London: Dent, 1903.
    P.s.: *Sir Gawain and the Green Knight* (1967) 'Select Bibliography', p. 154.

750.   _____. *Galfredi Monumetensis Historia Britonum. Nunc primum in Anglia, novem codd. msstis collatis*, Series: Publications of the Caxton Society. Londini, apud D. Nutt 1844. Edited by John A. Giles. London: Caxton Society, 1844.
    P.s. 1: MS. Tolkien A 12/1 *Commentary on Sir Gawain, lines 37-1987* fol. 24. [Tolkien Papers, Bodleian Library, Oxford].
    P.s. 2: MS. Tolkien A 21/13 *The English MSS*. fol. 203. [Tolkien Papers, Bodleian Library, Oxford].
    P.s. 3: *Sir Gawain and the Green Knight* (1925), p. xxvi; p. 83 line 109 Gawan. Tolkien and Gordon cite the name Walgainus (x, 9, 10, 11).
    P.s. 4: *Dragons* (1938), p. 59.
    P.s. 5: *The Notion Club Papers* (1945), pp. 192, 216.
    P.s. 6: *Famer Giles of Ham* (2014), p. 194.

751. _____. *Gottfried's von Monmouth Historia regum Britanniae mit literarhistorischer Einleitung und ausführlichen Anmerkungen*. Edited by Albert Schultz. Halle: Anton 1854.
   P.s. 1: MS. Tolkien A 12/1 *Commentary on Sir Gawain, lines 37-1987* fol. 24. [Tolkien Papers, Bodleian Library, Oxford].
   P.s. 2: MS. Tolkien A 21/13 *The English MSS*. fol. 203. [Tolkien Papers, Bodleian Library, Oxford].
   P.s. 3: *Sir Gawain and the Green Knight* (1925), p. xxvi [In the text, Tolkien and Gordon indicate '1853', corrected from second edition (1930)].

752. _____. *Histoiries of the Kings of Britain*. Series: Everyman's library. Translated by Sebastian Evans. With an introduction by Lucy Allen Paton. London and New York: J.M. Dent and E.P. Dutton & Co., 1912.
   P.s. 1: MS. Tolkien A 12/1 *Commentary on Sir Gawain, lines 37-1987* fol. 24. [Tolkien Papers, Bodleian Library, Oxford].
   P.s. 2: MS. Tolkien A 21/13 *The English MSS*. fol. 203. [Tolkien Papers, Bodleian Library, Oxford].
   P.s. 3: *Sir Gawain and the Green Knight* (1925), p. xxvi.

753. _____. *The Historia regum Britanniæ*. Edited by Acton Griscom. London: Longmans, Green and Co., 1929.
   P.s.: *Sir Gawain and the Green Knight* (1967) 'Select Bibliography', p. 154.

754. _____. *Histoiries of the Kings of Britain*. Series: Everyman's library, 577. Revisioned by C. W. Dunn. London: J.M. Dent, 1958.
   P.s.: *Sir Gawain and the Green Knight* (1967) 'Select Bibliography', p. 154.

755. Geoghegan, Joseph B. (Written and composed by) 'Ten Thousand Miles away'. Published in *The Scottish students' song book*. London: Published for the Scottish Students Song Book Committee by Bayley & Ferguson, 1897, pp. 126-27.
   P.s.: *Letters* 91 (1944). To Christopher Tolkien. Tolkien writes: 'Very trying having your chief audience Ten Thousand Miles away, on or off The Walloping Window-blind.'

756. Gepp, Edward. *An Essex Dialect Dictionary*. London: George Routledge and Sons, 1923 (2nd ed. revised and enlarged).
   P.s.: *Philology: General Works* (IV 1924, for 1923), p. 25 n. 8.

757. Gerbert, de Montreuil. *La continuation de Perceval*, Vol. I. Series: Classiques français du Moyen Age, 28. Edited by Mary Rhionnan Williams. Paris: H. Champion, 1922.
   P.s.: *Sir Gawain and the Green Knight* (1925), p. 112, line 1979 ff. Tolkien and Gordon cite lines 1159 ff.

758. Gering, Hugo. *Glossar zu den Liedern der Edda* (Saemundar Edda). Paderborn: F. S. Schöningh, 1896 (2nd ed.).
   Description: Inscribed on front flyleaf: 'L. H. Perkes | Sept: 1915'. Autographed and dated on front flyleaf: 'sept. 1920'.
   Collection: Tolkien's personal Celtic library, preserved at the Weston library under the auspices of the English Faculty Library (Oxford).

759. _____. *Glossar zu den Liedern der Edda* (Saemundar Edda). Bd. 8 Aufl 5. Series: Bibliothek der ältesten deutschen Literatur-Denkmäler, 8. Paderborn: F. S. Schöningh, 1923 (5th ed.).
   Collection: Tolkien's personal Celtic library, preserved at the Weston library under the auspices of the English Faculty Library (Oxford).

760. Gerrod, H. W. (Collected by). *Essays and Studies by Members of the English*

Association, Vol. XIV. Oxford: At the Clarendon Press, 1929.
   Description: Tolkien gives the book, with a dedication, to Simonne d'Ardenne.
   Collection: Fonds J.R.R. Tolkien, Bibliothèque ALPHA principale, Université de Liège (Liège), Tol/060.
   Notes: Contains Tolkien's essay *Ancrene Wisse and Hali Meiðhad* (pp. 104-26).

761. Gessler, Jean. *Le Livre des mestiers de Bruges et ses dérivés: Quatre anciens manuels de conversation*. Bruges: Fondation universitaire de Belgique, 1931.
   Notes: Set contains six parts. Two introductions (French and Flemish) and four books: 1. *Livre des métiers du XIVth siècle*; 2. *Gesprüchbüchlein romanisch und flamish*; 3. *Caxton's Dialogues in French and English*; 4. *Vocabulaer pour apprendre roman et flameng*.
   Collection: Taylor Institution Library, Bodleian Libraries (Oxford).

762. Gibb, Jocelyn (Edited by). *Light on C. S. Lewis*. London: Geoffrey Bles, 1965.
   Notes: October 1965, a copy was sent to Tolkien by the author.
   P.s.: *Letters* 278 (1965). From a letter to Clyde S. Kilby.
   S.s.: Scull-Hammond (2017a), p. 649.

763. Gibbon, Edward. *The Decline and Fall of the Roman Empire*, Vol. I. Thomas Y. Crowell & Co., 1900.
   S.s.: Shippey (1992), p. 301.

764. _____. *The Decline and Fall of the Roman Empire*, Vol. II. Thomas Y. Crowell & Co., 1900.
   S.s.: Shippey (1992), p. 301.

765. _____. *The Decline and Fall of the Roman Empire*, Vol. III. Thomas Y. Crowell & Co., 1900.
   S.s.: Shippey (1992), p. 301.

766. _____. *The Decline and Fall of the Roman Empire*, Vol. IV. Thomas Y. Crowell & Co., 1900.
   S.s.: Shippey (1992), p. 301.

767. _____. *The Decline and Fall of the Roman Empire*, Vol. V. Thomas Y. Crowell & Co., 1900.
   S.s.: Shippey (1992), p. 301.

768. _____. *The Decline and Fall of the Roman Empire*, Vol. VI. Thomas Y. Crowell & Co., 1900.
   S.s.: Shippey (1992), p. 301.

769. _____. *The Decline and Fall of the Roman Empire*, Vol. VII. Thomas Y. Crowell & Co., 1900.
   S.s.: Shippey (1992), p. 301.

770. _____. *The Decline and Fall of the Roman Empire*, Vol. VIII. Thomas Y. Crowell & Co., 1900.
   S.s.: Shippey (1992), p. 301.

771. _____. *The Decline and Fall of the Roman Empire*, Vol. IX. Thomas Y. Crowell & Co., 1900.
   S.s.: Shippey (1992), p. 301.

772. _____. *The Decline and Fall of the Roman Empire*, Vol. X. Thomas Y. Crowell

& Co., 1900.
:::
S.s.: Shippey (1992), p. 301.
:::

773. _____. *The Decline and Fall of the Roman Empire*, Vol. XI. Thomas Y. Crowell & Co., 1900.
:::
S.s.: Shippey (1992), p. 301.
:::

774. _____. *The Decline and Fall of the Roman Empire*, Vol. XII. Thomas Y. Crowell & Co., 1900.
:::
S.s.: Shippey (1992), p. 301.
:::

775. Gibbs, Henry H. *The romance of Cheuelere Assigne*. Series: E.E.T.S. (Early English Text Society), ES 6. London: Published for the Early English Text Society by N. Trübner and Co., 1868.
:::
P.s. 1: MS. Tolkien A 21/13 fol. 119. Note by Tolkien, 'Books in Exeter Library useful', with shelfmarks, on back of photostat reading list dated October 1913. Tolkien writes: 'All EETS publications'. [Tolkien Papers, Bodleian Library, Oxford].
P.s. 2: MS. Tolkien A 12/2 *Commentary on Sir Gawain, lines 1999-2523* fol. 5. [Tolkien Papers, Bodleian Library, Oxford].
:::

776. Gildas. *De excidio et conquestu Britanniae*.
:::
P.s.: *English and Welsh* (1963), p. 21
:::

777. Gilson, Julius Parnell. 'The Library of Henry Savile of Banke'. Transactions of the Bibliographical Society, Vol. IX, 1908, pp. 127-210.
:::
P.s.: *Sir Gawain and the Green Knight* (1925), p. xxvi. Tolkien and Gordon write: 'For bibliography of the Irish and French analogues of *Sir Gawain*, see the bibliography in Kittredge's study'. [*NED*] In Kittredge's study, this article is mentioned in 'II. Gawain and the Green Knight' (p. 293 n 3).
:::

778. Giovene, Andrea. *The Book of Sansevero*. Boston: Houghton Mifflin and Co., 1970.
:::
Description: Christmas 1970, a copy was sent to Tolkien by the publisher, Austin Olney. Tolkien thanked with a letter December 18, 1970.
Collection: Private [Oronzo Cilli].
:::

779. Giraldus, Cambrensis [Gerald of Wales]. *Annales Cambriæ*.
:::
S.s.: Rhys Roberts (1925), p. 58-9. Tolkien translate 'Gravari quidem ... pro hoc terrarum angulo respondebit' in late twelfth-century English of the South-West Midlands 'þis uolc nu ase monie siðes ear ... iþen deie þes rihtwise domes biuoren þen heste Deme'; p. 59 n. 20. Rhys Roberts writes: 'Professor Tolkien suggests that "senior quidam" may be the Welsh *henddyn*, the typical wise old man; and, following Morris-Jones's *Welsh Grammar*, § 155 iii (2), p. 261, he would identify with *henddyn* the *Hending* who is represented as the author of a collection of traditional proverbial wisdom in South-West Midland Middle English, each proverb ending with "quoth Hending".
:::

780. _____. *Itinerarium Cambriae: seu laboriosae Balduini* [Contains *Cambriæ Description*]. Annotated by Davidis Powell. London: W. Bulmer, 1804.
:::
P.s.: *Sir Gawain and the Green Knight* (1925), p. 93 line 692 ff. Tolkien and Gordon cite Cap. XI, 'De crinium tonsura, dentium cultu, et barbæ rasura' (p. 195).
:::

781. _____. *Giraldi Cambrensis Opera*, Vol. IV. Speculum ecclesiæ, De vita Galfridi archiepiscopi Eboracensis: sive Certamina Galfridi Eboracensis archiepiscopi. Series: Cambridge library collection. Rolls. Edited by John S. Brewer. Cambridge The University Press, 1873.
:::
P.s.: *Sir Gawain and the Green Knight* (1925), p. 115, line 2452 *Morgne þe goddess*. Tolkien and
:::

Gordon quote: 'Propter hoc enim fabulosi britones … ad eius vulnera sanandum' (chapter IX 'De Sepulchro regis Arthuri … adjunctis', p. 51).

782. Girvan, Ritchie. *Beowulf and the seventh century: language and content.* London: Methuen and Co., 1935.
    Notes: Contains *Folk-tale and History in Beowulf.*
    P.s.: *Beowulf* (1937), p. 12.

783. Gislason, Konrad (Edited by). *Fóstbrædra saga. Første hefte.* Kjöbenhavn: Berlingske bogtrykkeri, 1852.
    P.s.: *Beowulf* (2002) 'Version B', p. 137.

784. Goates, Margery (Edited by). *The Pepysian Gospel Harmony.* Series: E.E.T.S. (Early English Text Society), OS 157. London: Published for the Early English Text by H. Milford, Oxford University Press, 1922.
    Description: On front flyleaf: 'Mar. 24/157'. Annotated in pencil. Contains printed label as bookmark, pp. 126, 127.
    Collection: Tolkien's personal Celtic library, preserved at the Weston library under the auspices of the English Faculty Library (Oxford).

785. Goethe, Johann Wolfgang von. *Goethes Faust. Erster und zweiter Teil.* Stuttgart: Carl Krabbe Verlag Erich Gussmann, 1900 (2nd ed.).
    Description: Includes a label added by Stan Revell to books owned by Tolkien, 'From the Library of J.R.R. Tolkien', on front cover. Inscribed in back of flyleaf: 'G. B. Smith. | Sept. 1909.'
    Collection: Private [Elena Rossi].

786. *Golagros and Gawain.* [Scottish poem, 1580].
    P.s.: MS. Tolkien A 12/1 *Commentary on Sir Gawain, lines 37-1987* fol. 11. [Tolkien Papers, Bodleian Library, Oxford].

787. Golding, William. *Lord of the Flies.* London: Faber and Faber, 1954.
    P.s.: Resnik (1967), p. 38 Tolkien refered to Henry Resnik: 'dreary stuff'.
    S.s.: Scull-Hammond (2017c), p. 1055.

788. Goldsmith, Oliver. *Essays* (1765).
    S.s.: University of Leeds (1921), p. 145. English Literature, text selected for 1921-22. Ordinary Degree of B.A.; p. 191 English Language and Literature. F1. Final Course (English Literature) (ii) The History of English Literature from 1700 to 1765; p. 181. English Language and Literature. Int. I Intermediate Course (Literature).

789. _____. *The Life of Richard Nash.*
    S.s.: University of Leeds (1921), p. 145. English Literature, text selected for 1921-22. Ordinary Degree of B.A.; p. 191 English Language and Literature. F1. Final Course (English Literature) (ii) The History of English Literature from 1700 to 1765.

790. _____. *The Vicar of Wakefield.* London: Macmillan & Co., 1910.
    S.s.: University of Leeds (1921), p. 135 English Literature. Texts Selected for 1920-21.

791. _____. *The Works of Oliver Goldsmith*, Vol. II. *Poems.* Series World's Classics, 123. London: Henry Frowde, 1907.
    S.s.: University of Leeds (1921), p. 145. English Literature, text selected for 1921-22. Ordinary Degree of B.A.; p. 191 English Language and Literature. F1. Final Course (English Literature) (ii) The History of English Literature from 1700 to 1765. Text suggested: *The Traveller.*

792. Goldthorpe, John. *The Same Scourge.* London: Longmans, Green and Co, 1954.

Description: Christmas gift from 1963. Inscribed by Michael H.R. Tolkien: 'recommended to me by my father J.R.R. Tolkien, with particular reference to the passages on pages 308 and 353'. On these pages are notes, fe. 'one of the most infinitely moving passages in an infinitely moving book'. On the end paper in the hand of M.H.R. Tolkien notes on 4 reading sessions of the book, fe. Begun: 8.0 p.m. Wednesday, March 29th 1972 (Stonyhurst) // Finished: 1.45 p.m. Thursday April 6th 1972 (A greater aid to firm and real belief then ever).
Collection: Private [Pieter Collier].

793. Gollancz, Israel (Edited by). *The Cædmon Manuscript of Anglo-Saxon Biblical Poetry, Junius XI in the Bodleian Library.* London: Published for the British academy by H. Milford, Oxford University Press, 1927.
P.s.: *The Old English Exodus* (1982), p. ix.

794. _____ (Edited by). *Cleanness: an alliterative tripartite poem on the deluge, the destruction of Sodom, and death of Belshazzar.* Series: Select early English poems, 7. London: H. Milford, Oxford University Press, 1922.
P.s. 1: *Sir Gawain and the Green Knight* (1925), p. xxv.
P.s. 2: *Sir Gawain and the Green Knight* (1967) 'Select Bibliography', p. 153.

795. _____ (Edited by). *A good short debate between Winner and Waster: an alliterative poem on social and economic problems in England in the year 1352 with modern English rendering.* London: H. Milford, Oxford University Press, 1920.
P.s.: *Sir Gawain and the Green Knight* (1967) 'Select Bibliography: editions of texts quoted more than once in the notes', p. 156. '*Summer Sunday*'.

796. _____ (Edited by). *A good short debate between Winner and Waster: an alliterative poem on social and economic problems in England in the year 1352 with modern English rendering.* Revised by M. Day. London: H. Milford, Oxford University Press, 1931.
P.s.: *Sir Gawain and the Green Knight* (1967) 'Select Bibliography: editions of texts quoted more than once in the notes', p. 156. '*Summer Sunday*'.

797. _____ (Edited by). *The Exeter Book. An Anthology of Anglo-Saxon Poetry.* Series: E.E.T.S. (Early English Tex Society), OS 104. London: Oxford University Press, 1864.
P.s. 1: MS. Tolkien A 21/13 fol. 119. Note by Tolkien, 'Books in Exeter Library useful', with shelfmarks, on back of photostat reading list dated October 1913. Tolkien writes: 'All EETS publications'. [Tolkien Papers, Bodleian Library, Oxford].
P.s. 2: *Beowulf* (2014), p. 260. Tolkien refering at this book, cites *Saint Guthlac* and quotes, '*Wyrd ne meahte in fægum leng feorh gehealdan ... þonne him gedémed wæs*' on page 168 of the book by Gollancz.

798. _____. 'Gringolet, Gawain's, Horse'. *Saga-Book of the Viking Society*, Vol. V. London: Printed privately for the Viking Club, 1907-8, pp. 104-09.
P.s.: *Sir Gawain and the Green Knight* (1925), p. 90 line 597 *Gryngolet*.

799. _____ (Edited by). *Patience: an alliterative version of Jonah.* Series: Select early English poems, 1. London: H. Milford, Oxford University Press, 1913.
Description: Inscribed on half-title page: 'To | Professor Wylde | with sincerest regards | 31.X.1913 | Gollancz'.
Collection: Tolkien's personal Celtic library, preserved at the Weston library under the auspices of the English Faculty Library (Oxford).
P.s. 1: *Sir Gawain and the Green Knight* (1925), pp. vii, xxv, xxvi. Tolkien and Gordon write: 'For bibliography of the Irish and French analogues of *Sir Gawain*, see the bibliography in Kittredge's

800. _____ (Edited by). *Patience: an alliterative version of Jonah.* Series: Select early English poems, 1. London: H. Milford, Oxford University Press, 1924 (2nd ed.).
    P.s.: *Sir Gawain and the Green Knight* (1967) 'Select Bibliography', p. 153.

801. _____ (Edited by). *Pearl: An English Poem of the 14th Century.* London: David Nutt, 1891.
    P.s. 1: *Sir Gawain and the Green Knight* (1925), pp. xxv; xxvi. Tolkien and Gordon write: 'For bibliography of the Irish and French analogues of *Sir Gawain*, see the bibliography in Kittredge's study'. In Kittredge's study, this article is mentioned in 'II. Gawain and the Green Knight' (p. 296).
    P.s. 2: *Sir Gawain and the Green Knight* (1967) 'Select Bibliography', p. 153.

802. _____ (Edited by). *Pearl: an English poem of the 14th century.* Together with Boccaccio's *Olympia*. Printed or the author, 1897 (revd.).
    Notes: The bibliographic information on this edition was not initially found (worldcat, SOLO, archive.org). The reason is explained by Gollancz himself, in the new edition of 1921: 'In 1897 I prepared a revised edition of the text, which was privately printed' (1921, p. 1).
    P.s.: *Sir Gawain and the Green Knight* (1967) 'Select Bibliography', p. 153.

803. _____ (Edited by). *Pearl: an English poem of the 14th century.* Together with Boccaccio's *Olympia*. Series: Medieval Library, 13. London: Chatto and Windus, 1921 (new ed.).
    Description: Inscribed: 'J.R.R. Tolkien | Jan. 1922'. A few annotations. Loose leaves [Judith Priestman 1994, revd. 2016].
    Collection: Weston Library, Bodleian Libraries (Oxford).
    P.s. 1: *Sir Gawain and the Green Knight* (1925), p. xxv. Tolkien and Gordon write: 'Good text, the apparatus somewhat out of date'.
    P.s. 2: *Sir Gawain and the Green Knight* (1967) 'Select Bibliography', p. 153.

804. _____ (Edited by). *Pearl, Cleanness, Patience and Sir Gawain, reproduced in facsimile from the unique MS. Cotton Nero A. x in the British Museum.* Series: E.E.T.S. (Early English Text Society), OS 162. London: Oxford University, 1923.
    P.s. 1: *Sir Gawain and the Green Knight* (1925), p. xxv; p. 104, line 1334 *and lere of þe knot.*
    P.s. 2: *Sir Gawain and the Green Knight* (1967) 'Select Bibliography', p. 153.

805. _____ (Edited by). *Saint Erkenwald: an alliterative poem, written about 1386, narrating a miracle wrought by the Bishop in St Paul's Cathedral.* Series: Select early English poems, 4. London: H. Milford, Oxford University Press, 1922.
    P.s. 1: *Sir Gawain and the Green Knight* (1925), p. xxv.
    P.s. 2: *Sir Gawain and the Green Knight* (1967) 'Select Bibliography', p. 153.

806. _____ (Edited by). *Sir Gawain and the Green Knight.* Series: E.E.T.S. (Early English Text Society), OS 210. Edited by Mabel Day and Mary S. Serjeantson. London: Geoffrey Cumberlege, Oxford University Press, 1940.
    P.s. 1: MS. Tolkien A 11 *Notes on Pearl* fols. 38-9. [Tolkien Papers, Bodleian Library, Oxford].
    P.s. 2: MS. Tolkien A 12/2 *Commentary on Sir Gawain, lines 1999-2523* fol. 16. Tolkien cites the *Introduction*, page xxxvi. [Tolkien Papers, Bodleian Library, Oxford].

P.s. 3: *Sir Gawain and the Green Knight* (1953). Tolkien cites p. 123, v. 1880.
P.s. 4: *Sir Gawain and the Green Knight* (1967) 'Select Bibliography', p. 153.
S.s.: Ollscoil na h-Éireann G 259 (1949).

807. _____ and M. Weale. (Edited by). *The Qautrefoil of Love*. Series: E.E.T.S. (Early English Text Society), OS 195. Edited by H. Harnelius. London: Published for the Early English Text Society by Kegan Paul, Trench, Trübner and Co., 1935.
P.s.: *Sir Gawain and the Green Knight* (1967) 'Select Bibliography: editions of texts quoted more than once in the notes', p. 156.

808. Golther, Wolfgang. *Nordische Literaturgeschichte*, Vol. I. Die isländische und norwegische Literatur des Mittelalters (Sammlung Göschen). Berlin: Walter de Gruyter Verlag, 1921.
Description: Annotations in ink, p. l.
Collection: Tolkien's personal Celtic library, preserved at the Weston library under the auspices of the English Faculty Library (Oxford).

809. Gonçalves Viana, Aniceto dos Reis. *Portugais; phonétique et phonologie, morphologie, texts*. Leipzig: B. G. Teubner, 1903.
Description: Tolkien bought this from Blackwell's Booksellers in Oxford (their label is on the inside of the cover) to study. As an *ex libris* Tolkien signed this book at the top of the first page. Inside the books are seven annotations in pencil in the margins (usually corrections!). Tolkien donated this book to the U.S. Catholic University.
Collection: Private.

810. Gonville and Caius College MS. 234/120 [Contains *Ancrene Riwle*, see R. Wilson].
P.s.: MS. Tolkien A 21/13 *The English MSS.* fol. 197. [Tolkien Papers, Bodleian Library, Oxford].

811. Goolden, Peter (Edited by). *The Old English Apollonius of Tyre*. Series: Oxford English Monographs, 6. London: Oxford University Press, 1958.
Notes: Tolkien was one of the General Editors for the series. Contains a one paragraph prefatory note by Tolkien explaining the delay in publishing Goolden's edition and justifying its publication despite the appearance of Dr Josef Raith's edition in 1956. Goolden says in his introduction: 'I am also indebted to the editors of the Oxford English Monographs for undertaking the publication, especially Professor J.R.R. Tolkien who kindly suggested revisions in presentation and style, and these improvements are highly valued.' [C. 20]

812. Gordon, Eric Valentine (Edited by). *The Battle of Maldon*. London: Methuen and Co., 1937.
Description: on p. ix: 'But I owe my greatest debt of gratitude to Miss F. E. Harmer and Professor J.R.R. Tolkien, who read the proofs of my edition and made many corrections and contributions. In the assessment of evidence from historical documents especially Miss Hamrmer's guidance has been invaluable; and Professor Tolkien, with characteristic generosity, gave me the solution to many of the textual and philological problem discussed in the following pages'.
S.s.: Scull-Hammond (2017a), p. 206.

813. _____. *An Introduction to Old Norse*. London: Oxford University Press, 1927.
Notes: On p. viii: 'For help in preparing the apparatus of the book I am indebited especially to Professor J.R.R. Tolkien, who read the proofs of the Grammar and made valuable suggestions and corrections'.
Description: Autographed and dated on front flyleaf in pencil: '1927 | from Press'. Two bookmars at p.v. Annotated in pencil and ink.
Collection: Tolkien's personal Celtic library, preserved at the Weston library under the auspices of the English Faculty Library (Oxford).
P.s.: *Beowulf* (2002) 'Version A', p. 38.

S.s. 1: Gilliver-Marshall-Weiner (2009), p. 96.
S.s. 2: Scull-Hammond (2017a), p. 204. *Beorn's Hall* is adapted from an earlier picture by Tolkien, *Firelight in Beorn's House*, which had been inspired by a drawing of a Norse hall in this book by Gordon (chapter III, *Hrólf Saga Kraka*).

814. _____ (Edited by) *Pearl*. Oxford: At the Clarendon Press, 1953.
Description: Extensively annotated, with note in the preface about help to Ida Gordon. Loose leaves [Judith Priestman 1994, revd. 2016].
Collection: Weston Library, Bodleian Libraries (Oxford).
P.s. 1: *Sir Gawain and the Green Knight* (1975), p. 24.
P.s. 2: *Sir Gawain and the Green Knight* (1967) 'Select Bibliography', p. 153.

815. Gordon, George Stuart and Arthur Montague d'Urban Hughes (Edited by). *Charles Lamb: Prose & Poetry*. Series: Clarendon series of English literature. Oxford: At the Clarendon Press, 1921.
S.s.: University of Leeds (1921), p. 141. English Literature, text selected for 1921-22. Ordinary Degree of B.A.; p. 156. English Language and Literature - Scheme B. Texts for 1921-22. (d) Outlines of the History of English Literature. Ordinary Degree of B.A. with Honours. Final Examinations; p. 190 English Language and Literature. Int. 1 Intermediate Course (Literature).

816. Gordon, Ida L. (Edited by). *The Seafarer*. (with J.R.R. Tolkien). London: Methuen and Co. Ltd. 1960.
Description: It contains the text of Gordon, edited by his widow with the collaboration of Tolkien. On p. vii: 'When my husband, Professor E. V. Gordon, died in 1938 he left an uncompleted draft of an edition of *The Wanderer* and *The Seafarer*, on which he had been working in collaboration with Professor Tolkien's. And my first intention, with Professor Tolkien's approval, was to bring into final form that edition. […] I wish to thank Professor Tolkien for some notes given me with his usual generosity.'

817. Gordon, Robert Kay. *Anglo-Saxon Poetry*. Series: Everyman's library, 794. London: Joseph Malaby Dent, 1926 (2nd ed.).
Description: Signed on title page: 'J.R.R. Tolkien'.
Collection: Private [Worthpoint].

818. Gottfried, von Strassburg. *Tristan* [Middle High German courtly romance].
P.s.: 'Middle English 'Losenger'' (1953), p. 66 n. 1.

819. Götze, Alfred. 'Weingarten und Weinberg in deutschen Ortsnamen'. *Beiträge zur Germanischen Sprachwissenschaft: Festschrift für Otto Behaghel* [A. 1045]. Heidelberg: Carl Winter, 1924.
P.s.: *Philology: General Works* (V 1926, for 1924), p. 36.

820. Gover, John Eric Bruce. *The place-names of Devon*, Pt. I. Series: English Place-Names Society, 8. Cambridge: The University Press, 1931.
S.s.: Scull-Hammond (2017a), p. 184. c. 1934-1935 Tolkien writes a review of the Devonshire [A. 820, 821] volumes published by the English Place-Name Society in 1931 and 1932. This also mentions the Northampton [A. 822] and Surrey [A. 823] volumes, which appeared in 1933 and 1934, but not the 1935 Essex volume. In the event, the review is never published.

821. _____. *The place-names of Devon*, Pt. II. Series: English Place-Names Society, 9. Cambridge: The University Press, 1932.
S.s.: Scull-Hammond (2017a), p. 184. [see A. 820, S.s.].

822. _____, Allen Mawer and Frank Merry Stenton. *The place-names of Northamptoshire*, Series: English Place-Names Society, 10. Cambridge: The University Press, 1933.

S.s.: Scull-Hammond (2017a), p. 184. [see A. 820, S.s.].

823. _____, Allen Mawer, Frank Merry Stenton and Arthur Bonner. *The place-names of Surrey*, Series: English Place-Names Society, 11. Cambridge: The University Press, 1934.
S.s.: Scull-Hammond (2017a), p. 184. [see A. 820, S.s.].

824. Gower, John. *The Complete works of John Gower*, Vol. I. French works. Edited by George Campbell Macaulay. Oxford: At the Clarendon Press, 1899.
P.s. 1: MS. Res. e. 308 *Sir Gawain and the Green Knight*. [Tolkien Papers, Bodleian Library, Oxford].
P.s. 2: *Tolkien On Fairy-stories* (2008), p. 92.

825. _____. *The Complete works of John Gower*, Vol. II. English works (*Confessio amantis, prol.-lib. v. 1970*). Edited by George Campbell Macaulay. Oxford: At the Clarendon Press, 1901.
P.s. 1: MS. Res. e. 308 *Sir Gawain and the Green Knight*. [Tolkien Papers, Bodleian Library, Oxford].
P.s. 2: *Tolkien On Fairy-stories* (2008), p. 92.

826. _____. *The Complete works of John Gower*, Vol. III. English works (Confessio amantis, lib. v. 1971-lib. VIII; and in praise of peace). Edited by George Campbell Macaulay. Oxford: At the Clarendon Press, 1901.
P.s. 1: MS. Res. e. 308 *Sir Gawain and the Green Knight*. [Tolkien Papers, Bodleian Library, Oxford].
P.s. 2: *On Fairy-stories* (1947), p. 41. Tolkien quotes: 'His croket kembd and thereon set ... He scheweth him tofore here yhe' (*Confessio Amantis*, vv. 7065 ff.).
P.s. 3: *Tolkien On Fairy-stories* (2008), p. 92.

827. _____. *The Complete works of John Gower*, Vol. IV. Latin works. Edited by George Campbell Macaulay. Oxford: At the Clarendon Press, 1902.
P.s. 1: MS. Res. e. 308 *Sir Gawain and the Green Knight*. [Tolkien Papers, Bodleian Library, Oxford].
P.s. 2: *Tolkien On Fairy-stories* (2008), p. 92.

828. _____. *Confessio Amantis*. 1393. [Middle English poem].
P.s.: MS. Tolkien A 21/13 *Chronological Library Table of Middle English* fol. 202. [Tolkien Papers, Bodleian Library, Oxford].
S.s.: #1 Holland (1949), p. 142. Appendix XI: Oxford Examinations for Prisoners of War. English B.2 Chaucer and his Contemporaries: Book IV vv. 1306-1332.

829. _____. *Mirour de l'Omme*. Edited by George Campbell Macaulay. Oxford: At the Clarendon Press, 1899.
P.s. 1: *On Fairy-stories* (1947), p. 55.
P.s. 2: *Tolkien On Fairy-stories* (2008), p. 44.

830. _____. *Selections from Confessio Amantis*. Edited by George Campbell Macaulay. Oxford: At the Clarendon Press, 1903.
Description: Decoratively autographed and dated on front flyleaf:'sept. 1919'.
Collection: Tolkien's personal Celtic library, preserved at the Weston library under the auspices of the English Faculty Library (Oxford).
P.s. 1: *On Fairy-stories* (1947), p. 41.
P.s. 2: *Tolkien On Fairy-stories* (2008), p. 31 n. 1.
P.s. 3: *Tolkien On Fairy-stories* (2008) 'Manuscript A. [MS Tolkien 4, fols. 59-77]', p. 175.
P.s. 4: *Tolkien On Fairy-stories* (2008) 'Manuscript B [MS. Tolkien 4, fols. 73-120]', p. 211.

Section A

831. Gow, James. *A companion to school classics*. London: Macmillan and co., 1896.
Description: With school sticker from King Edward's School, in Tolkien's handwriting "J.R.R. Tolkien. | Class (i) | 1907 September 25. On fly-leafs a long piece of 'ancient phoenician inscription', a signature 'Ronald Tolkien' and in back "J.R.R. Tolkien | John Ronald Reuel Tolkien | 1900" and "King Edward's School. | 1900 - 1908 [Class I. 1907]"
Tolkien was practising his autograph inside this textbook.
Collection: Private [Pieter Collier].

832. Graetz, Heinrich. *Les Juifs d'Espagnes 945 – 1205*. Paris: Michel Lévy, 1872.
Description: Bound in contemporary calf. Signed in pencil on the end paper, with an additional Notes: 'purchased at now forgotten dealer, prob. in 1920s'. Tolkien's annotations on pages ii, iv, v, 1, 3, 4, 5, 16, 17, 130 and 131.
Collection: Private [TolkienLibrary.com; Sold on Ebay 17 July 2012]

833. Graf, Leopold. *Landwirtschaftliches im altenglischen Wortschatze*. Breslau: Fleischmann, 1909.
P.s.: *English and Welsh* (1963), p. 27 n. 1. Tolkien quotes: 'jus quiritium weala sunderriht' (p. 28).

834. Grahame, Kenneth. *First Whispers of 'The Wind in the Willows'*. London: Methuen and Co. Ltd. 1944.
P.s.: *Letters* 77 (1944). From a letter to Christopher Tolkien.
S.s.: Scull-Hammond (2006b), p. 1009.
Reading period: 1944 – 1950 (S.s.: Scull-Hammond (2017c), p. 1053)

835. _____. *The Wind in the Willows*. New York: Charles Scribner's Sons, 1908.
P.s. 1: *On Fairy-stories* (1947), p. 46 n. 1.
P.s. 2: *Letters* 51 (1943). From a letter to Christopher Tolkien. Tolkien writes: 'At 91 went to Magdalen and saw the Joad. He is (except in face) not only very like a toad, but is in character v. like Mr Toad of Toad Hall'.
P.s. 3: *Tolkien On Fairy-stories* (2008), p. 36n.
P.s. 4: *Tolkien On Fairy-stories* (2008) 'Manuscript B [MS. Tolkien 4, fols. 73-120]', pp. 217, 247, 249.
P.s. 5: *Tolkien On Fairy-stories* (2008) 'Manuscript B [MS. Tolkien 14, fol. 25]', p. 281.
S.s.: Scull-Hammond (2006b), p. 815.
Reading period: 1908 – 1910 (S.s.: Scull-Hammond (2017c), p. 1053).

836. *Grammar of Basque*.
P.s.: MS. Tolkien A 21/13 fol. 119. Note by Tolkien, 'Books in Exeter Library useful', with shelfmarks, on back of photostat reading list dated October 1913. [Tolkien Papers, Bodleian Library, Oxford].

837. *Grammar of Danish*.
P.s.: MS. Tolkien A 21/13 fol. 119. Note by Tolkien, 'Books in Exeter Library useful', with shelfmarks, on back of photostat reading list dated October 1913. [Tolkien Papers, Bodleian Library, Oxford].

838. *Grammar of Hungarian*.
P.s.: MS. Tolkien A 21/13 fol. 119. Note by Tolkien, 'Books in Exeter Library useful', with shelfmarks, on back of photostat reading list dated October 1913. [Tolkien Papers, Bodleian Library, Oxford].

839. *Grammar of Irish*.
P.s.: MS. Tolkien A 21/13 fol. 119. Note by Tolkien, 'Books in Exeter Library useful', with shelfmarks, on back of photostat reading list dated October 1913. [Tolkien Papers, Bodleian Library, Oxford].

840. *Grammar of Japanese*.
P.s.: MS. Tolkien A 21/13 fol. 119. Note by Tolkien, 'Books in Exeter Library useful', with shelfmarks, on back of photostat reading list dated October 1913. [Tolkien Papers, Bodleian Library, Oxford].

841. *Grammar of Polish*.
P.s.: MS. Tolkien A 21/13 fol. 119. Note by Tolkien, 'Books in Exeter Library useful', with shelfmarks, on back of photostat reading list dated October 1913. [Tolkien Papers, Bodleian Library, Oxford].

842. *Grammar of Roumanian*.
P.s.: MS. Tolkien A 21/13 fol. 119. Note by Tolkien, 'Books in Exeter Library useful', with shelfmarks, on back of photostat reading list dated October 1913. [Tolkien Papers, Bodleian Library, Oxford].

843. *Grammar of Sanskrit*.
P.s.: MS. Tolkien A 21/13 fol. 119. Note by Tolkien, 'Books in Exeter Library useful', with shelfmarks, on back of photostat reading list dated October 1913. [Tolkien Papers, Bodleian Library, Oxford].

844. *Grammar of Swedish*.
P.s.: MS. Tolkien A 21/13 fol. 119. Note by Tolkien, 'Books in Exeter Library useful', with shelfmarks, on back of photostat reading list dated October 1913. [Tolkien Papers, Bodleian Library, Oxford].

845. *Grammar of Turkish*.
P.s.: MS. Tolkien A 21/13 fol. 119. Note by Tolkien, 'Books in Exeter Library useful', with shelfmarks, on back of photostat reading list dated October 1913. [Tolkien Papers, Bodleian Library, Oxford].

846. Grammont, Maurice. 'L'interversion'. *Streitberg-Festgabe* [A. 2228]. Leipzig: Market und Petter, 1924.
P.s.: *Philology: General Works* (V 1926, for 1924), p. 37.

847. Grant, David. *Waes*. London: George Allen and Unwin, 1968.
Notes: A copy was sent to Tolkien by Joy Hill.
S.s.: Scull-Hammond (2017a), p. 764. 4 July 1968.

848. Grattan, John Henry Grafton and P. Gurrey. *Our Living Language: a new guide to English grammar*. London: Nelson, 1925.
P.s.: *Philology: General Works* (VI 1927, for 1925), p. 60 n. 20.

849. Gray, Thomas. *Poems*.
P.s.: *Letters* 288 (1966). To Professor Norman Davis. Tolkien writes 'I feel much honoured [...] by the Faculty's wish to place the bust of me in the English Library in some prominent position – if on second thoughts you do not think a storied urn would be better' quoting 'Can storied urn or animated bust | Back to its mansion call the fleeting breath?' from *Elegy written in a Country Churchyard* (p. 113)'.
S.s.: University of Leeds (1921), p. 145. English Literature, text selected for 1921-22. Ordinary Degree of B.A.; p. 191 English Language and Literature. F1. Final Course (English Literature) (ii) The History of English Literature from 1700 to 1765.

850. Graz, Friedrich. 'Beiträge zur textkritik der sogenannten Cædmon's-chen Dichtungen'. *Englische Studien*, Vol. XXI. Leipzig: O. R. Reisland, 1895, pp. 1-27.
P.s.: *The Old English Exodus* (1982), p. ix; 65.

SECTION A

851. Great Britain Royal Commission on Historical Manuscripts. *Report on Manuscripts in the Welsh Language*, Vol. I. The Welsh manuscripts of Lord Mostyn, at Mostyn Hall, Co. Flint; The Welsh manuscripts at Peniarth, Towyn, Merioneth; the property of William Robert Maurice Wynne. Series: Historical Manuscripts Commission London: Eyre and Spottiswoode, 1898.
    Collection: Tolkien's personal Celtic library, preserved at the Weston library under the auspices of the English Faculty Library (Oxford).
    S.s.: Phelpstead (2011), p. 118.

852. _____. *Report on Manuscripts in the Welsh Language*, Vol. II, Pt. I. Jesus College, Oxford: Free Library, Cardiff; Havod; Wrexham; Llanwrin; Merthyr; Aberdâr. Series: Historical Manuscripts Commission. London: Eyre and Spottiswoode, 1902.
    Collection: Tolkien's personal Celtic library, preserved at the Weston library under the auspices of the English Faculty Library (Oxford).
    S.s.: Phelpstead (2011), p. 118.

853. _____. *Report on Manuscripts in the Welsh Language*, Vol. II, Pt. II. Plas Llan Stephan; Free Library, Cardiff. Series: Historical Manuscripts Commission. London: Eyre and Spottiswoode, 1902.
    Collection: Tolkien's personal Celtic library, preserved at the Weston library under the auspices of the English Faculty Library (Oxford).

854. Green, Arthur Robert. *Sundials: Incised Dials or Mass-Clocks*. Series: Historic monuments of England. London: Society for Promoting Christian Knowledge, 1926.
    P.s.: *Ancrene Wisse and Hali Meiðhad* (1929), p. 120 n. 1.

855. Green, John Richard. *Essays of Joseph Addison*. London: Macmillan, 1920.
    S.s.: University of Leeds (1921), p. 144. English Literature, text selected for 1921-22. Ordinary Degree of B.A.; p. 191 English Language and Literature. F1. Final Course (English Literature) (ii) The History of English Literature from 1700 to 1765.

856. _____. *A Short History of the English People*. London: Macmillan, 1907.
    S.s.: University of Leeds (1921), p. 191 English Language and Literature. F1. Final Course (English Literature) Books recommended.

857. Green, Roger Lancelyn. *Andrew Lang: a critical biography*. Leicester: Edmund Ward, 1946.
    Notes: In his preface, R.L. Green thanks Tolkien: 'And my gratitude to Professor D. Nichol Smith and Pofessor J.R.R. Tolkien for their unfailing guidance and encouragement leaves with me a debt that can never adequantely be repaid' (p. x).
    S.s.: Scull-Hammond (2006b), p. 352. In March 1944 Tolkien and Nichol Smith approved Green's resubmitted thesis *Andrew Lang as a Writer of Fairy Tales and Romances* (March 1943). It was published as *Andrew Lang: A Critical Biography* in 1946.

858. _____. *A Book of Dragons*. [London: Hamish Hamilton, 1970].
    S.s.: Anderson (2002), p. 338 n. 2.

859. _____. *Tellers of Tales*. London: Edmund Ward, 1953 (New enlarged edition).
    Notes: Green writes about Tolkien and his two books, *The Hobbit* and *Farmer Giles of Ham* (pp. 255-56).

860. Greene, Walter Kirkland. *The Pearl: a new interpetation*. PMLA (*Publications of the Modern Language Association of America*), Vol. XL, 1925, pp. 814-27.

P.s.: MS. Tolkien A 35 *Pearl* fol. 114. [Tolkien Papers, Bodleian Library, Oxford].

861.   Gregory of Tours. *The History of the Franks*, Vol. I. Text. Translated by Ormond Maddock Dalton. Oxford: At the Clarendon Press, 1927.
> P.s.: *Beowulf* (2002) 'Version A', p. 51. Tolkien writes: 'the battle of the sixth century (mentioned by Gregory of Tours)'.

862.   Gregory, Pope. *The dialogues of Saint Gregory, surnamed the Great*. Edited by Bevan Edwyn, Edmund Gardner and George Francis Hill. London: Philip Lee Warner, 1911.
> P.s.: MS. Tolkien A 12/3 *Rough text of a lecture on Sir Gawain*, 1965 ff. 17-59. [Tolkien Papers, Bodleian Library, Oxford].
> S.s.: Scull-Hammond (2017a), p. 46. April 1913: Tolkien will need to become familiar with a range of literary and philological subjects and set texts as prescribed in the Oxford Regulations of the Board of Studies, knowing that he may be examined on them in ten papers at the end of *Trinity Term 1915*: Old English texts.

863.   Grein, Christian Wilhelm Michael (Edited by). *Älfrik de Vetere et Novo Testamento: Pentateuch, Iosua, Buch der Richter und Hiob*, Vol. I. Series: Bibliothek der angelsächsischen Prosa, 1. Cassel & Göttingen: Georg Wigand, 1872.
> Description: Inscribed on back of front flyleaf: 'J. Earle | with J. Barer's kind | regards.| Easter Tuesday 1878'. Beneath this autographed and dated '1926'.
> Collection: Tolkien's personal Celtic library, preserved at the Weston library under the auspices of the English Faculty Library (Oxford).

864.   _____. *Beovulf nebst den fragmenten Finnesburg und Valdere in kritisch*. Cassel & Göttingen: G. H. Wigand, 1867.
> P.s.: *Finn and Hengest* (1982), p. 84 n. 4; p. 88 n. 14.

865.   _____. 'Zur Textkritik der angelsächsischen Dichter'. *Germania*, Vol. X. Wien: C. Geroldssohn, 1865, pp. 416-29.
> P.s.: *The Old English Exodus* (1982), p. ix.

866.   _____ and Johann Jakob Köhler (with Ferdinand Holthausen) (Edited by). *Sprachschatz der Angelsächsischen Dichter*. Heidelberg: Carl Winter 1912.
> P.s. 1: *Philology: General Works* (VI 1927, for 1925), p. 57.
> P.s. 2: *Sigelwara land* (1932), p. 195 n. 1.
> P.s. 3: *Sigelwara land* (1934), p. 95 n. 1.
> P.s. 4: *The Old English Exodus* (1982), p. ix.
> P.s. 5: *Finn and Hengest* (1982), p. 83 n. 2.
> P.s. 6: *Beowulf* (2002) 'Version A', p. 45.
> P.s. 7: *Beowulf* (2002) 'Version B', p. 101.

867.   _____ and Richard Paul Wülker. *Bibliothek der Angelsächsischen Poesie*, Vol. I. Leipzig: Georg H. Wigand, 1857.
> Description: Signed by Tolkien in blue crayon on front free endpaper, pencil annotations, and emphases.
> Collection: Private [Sold by Simon Finch Rare Books Ltd.].
> Notes: Bound with [A. 868].
> P.s.: *The Old English Exodus* (1982), p. ix.
> S.s. 1: Finch (2002), p. 52.
> S.s. 2: Garth (2003), p. 44.

868.   _____ and Richard Paul Wülker. *Bibliothek der Angelsächsischen Poesie*, Vol. II. Leipzig: Georg H. Wigand, 1894.

Description: Signed by Tolkien in blue crayon on front free endpaper, pencil annotations, and emphases.
Collection: Private [Sold by Simon Finch Rare Books Ltd.].
Notes: Bound with [A. 867].
P.s.: *The Old English Exodus* (1982), p. x.
S.s. 1: Finch (2002), p. 52.
S.s. 2: Garth (2003), p. 44.

869. _____ and Richard Paul Wülker. *Bibliothek der Angelsächsischen Poesie*, Vol. III. Leipzig: Georg H. Wigand, 1898.
Description: Signed by Tolkien in blue crayon on front free endpaper, pencil annotations, and emphases. Contains one page shows Tolkien's criticism of Cynewull's 'Crist', and provides fascinating evidence of his sustained interest In the ideas and language of 'Crist'.
Description: Signed by Tolkien in blue crayon on front free endpaper, pencil annotations, and emphases.
Notes: Bound with [A. 870].
Collection: Private [Sold by Simon Finch Rare Books Ltd.].
P.s.: *Sigelwara land* (1932), p. 184, n 2.
S.s. 1: Finch (2002), p. 52.
S.s. 2: Garth (2003), p. 44.

870. _____ and Richard Paul Wülker. *Bibliothek der Angelsächsischen Poesie*, Vol. IV. Leipzig: Georg H. Wigand, 1900.
Description: Signed by Tolkien in blue crayon on front free endpaper, pencil annotations, and emphases.
Collection: Private [Sold by Simon Finch Rare Books Ltd.].
Notes: Bound with [A. 869].
S.s.: Finch (2002), p. 52.

871. _____ and Richard Paul Wülker. *Bibliothek der Angelsächsischen Poesie*, Vol. V. Leipzig: Georg H. Wigand, 1921.
Description: Signed by Tolkien in ink on front free endpaper, pencil annotations, and emphases. Contains on page of notes Tolkien has indexed the titles of all the poems cited.
Collection: Private [Sold by Simon Finch Rare Books Ltd.].
S.s.: Finch (2002), p. 52.

872. Grigson, Geoffrey (Edited by). *Concise Encyclopaedia of Modern World Literature*. London: Hutchinson, 1963.
S.s.: Scull-Hammond (2017a), p. 704.

873. Grimm, Jacob Ludwig. *Teutonic Mythology*, Vol. I. Translated by James Steven Stallybrass. London: George Bell, 1882.
P.s.: *Beowulf* (2014), p. 267.
S.s. 1: Shippey (1992), p, 301.
S.s. 2: Anderson (2002), p. 293 n 1.

874. _____. *Teutonic Mythology*, Vol. II. Translated by James Steven Stallybrass. London: George Bell, 1883.
P.s.: *Beowulf* (2014), p. 267.
S.s. 1: Shippey (1992), p, 301.
S.s. 2: Anderson (2002), p. 293 n. 1.

875. _____. *Teutonic Mythology*, Vol. III. Translated by James Steven Stallybrass. London: George Bell, 1883.
P.s.: *Beowulf* (2014), p. 267.
S.s. 1: Shippey (1992), p, 301.
S.s. 2: Anderson (2002), p. 293 n. 1.

876. _____. *Teutonic Mythology*, Vol. IV. Translated by James Steven Stallybrass. London: George Bell, 1888.
    P.s.: *Beowulf* (2014), p. 267.
    S.s. 1: Shippey (1992), p, 301.
    S.s. 2: Anderson (2002), p. 293 n 1.

877. _____ and Wilhelm Karl Grimm. *Kinder- und Hausmärchen*, Vol. I. Berlin: Whilelm Hertz, 1888.
    P.s. 1: *On Fairy-stories* (1947), p. 55.
    P.s. 2: *Tolkien On Fairy-stories* (2008), pp. 45, 197 [*Little Red Riding Hood (Rotkäppchen)*].
    S.s.: *The Lay of Aotrou & Itroun* (2016), pp. 32, 38.

878. _____ and Wilhelm Karl Grimm. *Kinder- und Hausmärchen*, Vol. II. Berlin: Whilelm Hertz, 1888.
    P.s. 1: *On Fairy-stories* (1947), p. 55.
    P.s. 2: *Tolkien On Fairy-stories* (2008), p. 45.
    S.s.: *The Lay of Aotrou & Itroun* (2016), pp. 32, 38.

879. _____ and Wilhelm Karl Grimm. *Geschichte der Deutschen Sprache*, Vol. I. Leipzig: Weidmannsche Buchhandlung, 1848.
    Description: Various names including that of Tolkien and L. Seiffert on first pastye-down.
    Collection: Private [Thornton's Bookshop].

880. _____ and Wilhelm Karl Grimm. *Geschichte der Deutschen Sprache*, Vol. II. Leipzig: Weidmannsche Buchhandlung, 1848.
    Description: Various names including that of Tolkien and L. Seiffert on first pastye-down.
    Collection: Private [Thornton's Bookshop].

881. _____ and Wilhelm Karl Grimm. *Grimm's Household Tales*, Vol. I. Translated by Marguerite Hunt and Foreword by Andrew Lang. London: G. Bell and sons, 1884.
    P.s. 1: *On Fairy-stories* (1947), p. 48 [*Dat Erdmänneken (The Elves)*], pp. 56, 228 [*Von dem Machandelboom (The Juniper Tree)*], pp. 80, 86 [*Der Froschkönig (Frog King)*].
    P.s. 2: *Tolkien On Fairy-stories* (2008), pp. 38 [*Dat Erdmänneken (The Elves)*], 65, 74, 80 [*Der Froschkönig (Frog King)*], 48,
    P.s. 3: *Tolkien On Fairy-stories* (2008) 'Manuscript A. [MS Tolkien 4, fols. 59-77]', pp. 184, 185.
    P.s. 4: *Tolkien On Fairy-stories* (2008) 'Manuscript B [MS. Tolkien 4, fols. 73-120]', p. 228 [*Von dem Machandelboom (The Juniper Tree)*].
    Reading period: 1900-1904 (S.s.: Scull-Hammond (2017c), p. 1053).
    S.s.: Flieger (2003), p. 29.

882. _____ and Wilhelm Karl Grimm. *Grimm's Household Tales*, Vol. II. Translated by Marguerite Hunt and Foreword by Andrew Lang. London: G. Bell and sons, 1884.
    P.s. 1: *On Fairy-stories* (1949), p. 47 n. 2, p. 55 [*Die Gänsemagd (The Goosegirl)*].
    P.s. 2: *Tolkien On Fairy-stories* (2008), p. 37 n. 1, p. 45.
    P.s. 3: *Tolkien On Fairy-stories* (2008) 'Manuscript A. [MS Tolkien 4, fols. 59-77]', p. 179 [*Die Gänsemagd (The Goosegirl)*].
    P.s. 4: *Tolkien On Fairy-stories* (2008) 'Manuscript B [MS. Tolkien 4, fols. 73-120]', p. 217 [*Die Kristalkugel (The Crystal Ball)*].

883. Gröber, Gustav. *Grundriss der romanischen philologie, unter mitwirkung*, Vol. I. Strassburg: K. J. Trübner, 1886.
    P.s.: MS. Tolkien A 21/13 fol. 119. Note by Tolkien, 'Books in Exeter Library useful', with shelfmarks, on back of photostat reading list dated October 1913. [Tolkien Papers, Bodleian Library, Oxford].

884. _____. *Grundriss der romanischen philologie, unter mitwirkung*, Vol. II, Pt. I. Strassburg: K. J. Trübner, 1902.
    P.s.: MS. Tolkien A 21/13 fol. 119. Note by Tolkien, 'Books in Exeter Library useful', with shelfmarks, on back of photostat reading list dated October 1913. [Tolkien Papers, Bodleian Library, Oxford].

885. _____. *Grundriss der romanischen philologie, unter mitwirkung*, Vol. II, Pt. II. Strassburg: K. J. Trübner, 1902.
    P.s.: MS. Tolkien A 21/13 fol. 119. Note by Tolkien, 'Books in Exeter Library useful', with shelfmarks, on back of photostat reading list dated October 1913. [Tolkien Papers, Bodleian Library, Oxford].

886. _____. *Grundriss der romanischen philologie, unter mitwirkung*, Vol. II, Pt. III. Strassburg: K. J. Trübner, 1902.
    P.s.: MS. Tolkien A 21/13 fol. 119. Note by Tolkien, 'Books in Exeter Library useful', with shelfmarks, on back of photostat reading list dated October 1913. [Tolkien Papers, Bodleian Library, Oxford].

887. _____ (Edited by). *Zeitschrift für romanische Philologie*, Vol. XXXI. Halle: Max Niemeyer, 1907.
    P.s.: 'Middle English 'Losenger'' (1953), p. 67 n. 1.

888. Grote, George. *The History of Greece*, Vol. V. London: John Murray, 1851.
    P.s.: *Exeter College library register*. Tolkien's borrowing record: *Michaelmas Term 1911* from 25 November to 5 December.
    S.s. 1: Scull-Hammond (2017a), p. 36. '25 November 1911: Tolkien borrowed this volume from Exeter College library register'.
    S.s. 2: Garth (2003), p. 26.
    S.s. 3: Garth (2014), p. 21.

889. Groth, Ernst Johann. *Composition und Alter der altenglischen (angelsächsischen) Exodus. Inaugural-dissertation*. Berlin: Druck von Franz Ebhardt, 1883.
    P.s.: *The Old English Exodus* (1982), p. ix.

890. Grundtvig, Nicolai Frederik Severin. *Bjowulfs Drape. Et Gothisk Helte-Digt fra forrige Aar-Tusinde af Angel-Saxisk paa Danske Riim*. Kjøbenhavn: A. Seidelin, 1820.
    P.s.: *Beowulf* (2002) 'Version A', p. 43.

891. Gualteruzzi, Carlo (Edited by). *Le ciento nouelle antike*. Bologna: Girolamo Benedetti, 1525.
    P.s.: MS. Tolkien A 13/2 *Notes and drafts of lectures on Chaucer: Pardoner's Tale* fol. 78. [Tolkien Papers, Bodleian Library, Oxford].

892. _____. *Libro di nouelle, et di bel parlar gentile. Nel qual si contengono Cento Nouelle altrauolta mandate fuori da messer Carlo Gualteruzzi da Fano*. In Fiorenza: Nella Stamperia de i Giunti, 1572.
    P.s.: MS. Tolkien A 13/2 *Notes and drafts of lectures on Chaucer: Pardoner's Tale* fol. 78. Tolkien cites 'Novella LXXXII' on page 86 'Qvi conta d'vno romito che andando per un luogo forest trovo molto grande Tesoro'. [Tolkien Papers, Bodleian Library, Oxford].

893. Guðrundsson, Einar. *Skotlands Rímur: Icelandic Ballads on the Gowrie Conspiracy*. Edited by William Alexander Craigie. Oxford: At the Clarendon Press, 1908.
    Description: Autographed and dated in pencil on front flyleaf: '1920'.

Collection: Tolkien's personal Celtic library, preserved at the Weston library under the auspices of the English Faculty Library (Oxford).

894. Guest (Lady), Charlotte (Translated by). *The Mabinogion*, Vol. I. From the Llyfr Coch o Hergest, and other ancient Welsh manuscripts. London: Longman, Brown, Green, and Longmans, 1849.
   P.s.: *Sir Gawain and the Green Knight* (1925), p. xxvi.

895. _____ (Translated by). *The Mabinogion*, Vol. II. From the Llyfr Coch o Hergest, and other ancient Welsh manuscripts. London: Longman, Brown, Green, and Longmans, 1849.
   P.s.: *Sir Gawain and the Green Knight* (1925), p. xxvi.

896. _____ (Translated by). *The Mabinogion*, Vol. III. From the Llyfr Coch o Hergest, and other ancient Welsh manuscripts. London: Longman, Brown, Green, and Longmans, 1849.
   P.s.: *Sir Gawain and the Green Knight* (1925), p. xxvi.

897. _____ (Translated by). *The Mabinogion. From the Welsh of the Llyfr Coch o Hergest* (The Red Book of Hergest). London: Quaritch, 1877.
   P.s.: *Sir Gawain and the Green Knight* (1925), p. xxvi.
   S.s.: Fimi (2007), p. 51.

898. _____ (Translated by). *The Mabinogion.* Series: Everyman's library, 97. London: Joseph Malaby Dent and Sons Ltd., 1913.
   Description: Decoratively autographed and marked on front flyleaf: 'Exeter Coll. | Oxford | May 1st: 1913'. Tolkien bought the book May 1st, 1913.
   Collection: Tolkien's personal Celtic library, preserved at the Weston library under the auspices of the English Faculty Library (Oxford).
   S.s. 1: Fimi (2007), p. 51.
   S.s. 2: Scull-Hammond (2006b), p. 816.
   S.s. 3: Phelpstead (2011), p. 118.
   Reading period: 1913 ca. (S.s.: Scull-Hammond (2017c), p. 214).

899. _____ and Alfred Trubner Nutt (Edited by). *The Mabinogion. Mediaeval Welsh romances.* London: Long Acre, David Nutt, 1910 (3rd ed.).
   P.s.: *Sir Gawain and the Green Knight* (1925), p. xxvi, p. 84 line 109 Gawan. Tolkien and Gordon quote 'He was called Gwalchmai because be never ... the son of his sister, and his cousin' (p. 116); p. 113, line 2136 *paȝe he be a sturn knape To stiȝtel*. T. and G. cite p. 170.

900. Guido delle Colonne. *The 'Gest hystoriale' of the destruction of Troy: an alliterative romance tr. from Guido de Colonna's 'Hystoria troiana'*, Vol. I. Series: E.E.T.S. (Early English Text Society), OS 39. Edited by David Donaldson and George A Panton. London: Trübner, 1869.
   P.s. 1: MS. Tolkien A 12/3 *Rough text of a lecture on Sir Gawain*, 1965 fols. 62-74. [Tolkien Papers, Bodleian Library, Oxford].
   P.s. 2: MS. Tolkien A 21/13 *The English MSS.* fol. 203. [Tolkien Papers, Bodleian Library, Oxford].
   P.s. 3: MS. Tolkien A 11 *Notes on Pearl*, fol. 59. [Tolkien Papers, Bodleian Library, Oxford].
   P.s. 4: MS. Tolkien A 21/13 fol. 119. Note by Tolkien, 'Books in Exeter Library useful', with shelfmarks, on back of photostat reading list dated October 1913. Tolkien writes: 'All EETS publications'. [Tolkien Papers, Bodleian Library, Oxford].
   P.s. 5: *A Middle English Vocabulary* (1922). Tolkien refers to the Destr. Triy on the term 'Text' (407).
   P.s. 6: *Sir Gawain and the Green Knight* (1925), p. 79.
   P.s. 7: 'Chaucer as a Philologist: *The Reeve's Tale*' (1934), p. 136.
   P.s. 8: *Sir Gawain and the Green Knight* (1967) 'Select Bibliography: editions of texts quoted

more than once in the notes', p. 156.

901. _____. *The 'Gest hystoriale' of the destruction of Troy: an alliterative romance tr. from Guido de Colonna's 'Hystoria troiana'*, Vol. II. Series: E.E.T.S. (Early English Text Society), OS 56. Edited by David Donaldson and George A Panton. London: Trübner, 1874.
    P.s. 1: MS. Tolkien A 11 *Notes on Pearl,* fol. 59. [Tolkien Papers, Bodleian Library, Oxford].
    P.s. 2: MS. Tolkien A 21/13 *The English MSS.* fol. 203. [Tolkien Papers, Bodleian Library, Oxford].
    P.s. 3: MS. Tolkien A 12/3 *Rough text of a lecture on Sir Gawain,* 1965 fols. 62-74. [Tolkien Papers, Bodleian Library, Oxford].
    P.s. 4: MS. Tolkien A 21/13 fol. 119. Note by Tolkien, 'Books in Exeter Library useful', with shelfmarks, on back of photostat reading list dated October 1913. Tolkien writes: 'All EETS publications'. [Tolkien Papers, Bodleian Library, Oxford].
    P.s. 5: *Sir Gawain and the Green Knight* (1925), p. 79.
    P.s. 6: 'Chaucer as a Philologist: *The Reeve's Tale'* (1934), p. 136.
    P.s. 7: *Sir Gawain and the Green Knight* (1967) 'Select Bibliography: editions of texts quoted more than once in the notes', p. 156.

902. Gummere, Francis Barton. *Old English Ballads*. Boston: Ginn & Company, 1899.
    S.s.: University of Leeds (1923), p. 85. Ordinary Degree of B.A., Final Course and Examination. Vol. I. Principal Subjects, studied for Two Years. English Language and Literature: English Literature. Period selected for 1923-24: 1579-1645. Texts selected for 1923-24.

903. Güntert, Hermann. *Grundfrage der Sprachwissenschaft*. Series: Wissenschaft und Bildung. Leipzig: Quelle & Meyer, 1925.
    P.s.: *Philology: General Works* (VI 1927, for 1925), p. 56 n. 11.

904. Güterbock, Bruno G. and Rudolf Thurneysen. *Indices glossarum et vocabulorum hibernicorum quae in Grammaticae celticae editione altera explanantur.* Lipsiae: Hirzel, 1881.
    Description: Inscribed on front cover in pencil: 'Zeuss'.
    Collection: Tolkien's personal Celtic library, preserved at the Weston library under the auspices of the English Faculty Library (Oxford).

905. Gutheil, Heinrich and Wilhelm Horn. *Sprachkörper und sprachfunktion im englischen*. Series: Giessener beiträge zur erforschung der sprache und kultur Englands und Nordamerikas, Vol. I. Giessen: Im Verlag des Englischen seminars der Universität Giessen, 1923.
    P.s.: *Philology: General Works* (V 1926, for 1924), p. 34.

906. *Guy of Warwick* 1330. [Middle English romance, see Zupitza].
    P.s.: MS. Tolkien A 21/13 *The English MSS.* fol. 203. [Tolkien Papers, Bodleian Library, Oxford].

907. Haggard, H. Rider. *Ayesha: the return of She*. London: Ward Lock, 1905.
    S.s. 1: Rateliff (1981), pp. 6-8.
    S.s. 2: Drout (2007), p. 369.

908. _____. *Eric Brighteyes*. Leipzig: Heinermann and Balestier Ltd., 1891.
    P.s. 1: *Beowulf* (2002) 'Version A', p. 55.
    P.s. 2: *Beowulf* (2002) 'Transcription of Legible Portions of Folios 71-81: Notes and Jottings', p. 426. Tolkien writes 'Eric Brighteyes (R. Haggard) is as good as most sagas and as heroic'.
    S.s. 1: Drout (2007), p. 369. For Tolkien 'as good as most sagas and as heroic'.
    S.s. 2: Scull-Hammond (2017c), p. 1054.
    Reading period: 1913 ca. (S.s.: Scull-Hammond (2017c), p. 1054).

909. _____. *Heu-Heu or the Monster*. Series: Collection of British and American

authors, 4627. Leipzig: B. Tauchnitz, 1924.
S.s.: Drout (2007), p. 369.

910. _____. *King Solomon's Mines*. London: Cassell and Company, 1886.
P.s.: Tolkien's unpublished 1920s letter to Edith Bratt. In an interesting group of early Tolkien letters providing a highly detailed account of the tragedy that bestruck him while serving as a tutor to two young Mexican boys and their aunt in 1913. 'Rushing about sight-seeing or any obvious form of enjoyment is of course out of the questions for a while so I have tried to find out what the best, most readable, and best palpable 'instructive' of boys books they haven't read. Many of these I have got in cheap editions ... such as *King Solomon's Mines*, *Kim* and so forth ... [Jose] is now reading *The White Company*.' [Sold by Christie's, 8 April 2003].
S.s. 1: Scull-Hammond (2017a), p. 51.
S.s. 2: Scull-Hammond (2006b), p. 816.
Reading period: 1913 (S.s.: Scull-Hammond (2017c), p. 1054).

911. _____. *She: A history of adventure*. London: Longmans, 1887.
P.s.: *The Book of Lost Tales*, Vol. I (1992) p. 335 n. 14.
S.s. 1: Rateliff (1981), pp. 6-8.
S.s. 2: Garth (2003), p. 78.
S.s. 3: Scull-Hammond (2006b), p. 816.
S.s. 4: Drout (2007), p. 369.
Reading period: 1908 – early 1910 (S.s.: Scull-Hammond (2017c), p. 1054).

912. _____. *She and Allan*. London: Hutchinson, 1921
S.s.: Rateliff (1981), pp. 6-8.

913. _____. *The Wanderer's Necklace*. London: Cassell, 1914.
S.s. 1: R. L. Green (1980), p. 7. 'An author whom he, like C.S. Lewis and myself, ranked very high was Rider Haggard; and I was able to lend him at least one, *The Wanderer's Necklace* [1914], which he had never read. But we failed to agree on its merits—probably Tolkien did not like Haggard's treatment of the Viking background in the earlier parts of the story.'
S.s. 2: Rateliff (2012), p. 147.

914. _____. *Wisdom's daughter the life and love story of she-who-must-be-obeyed*. London Hutchinson, 1923 (2nd ed.).
S.s.: Rateliff (1981), pp. 6-8.

915. Hahn, Johann Georg von. *Griechische und Albanesische Märchen*. Leipzig: W. Engelmann, 1864.
P.s.: # 1 *Tolkien On Fairy-stories* (2008), p. 307.

916. Haigh, Walter Edward. *A New Glossary of the Dialect of the Huddersfield District*. Oxford: University Press, 1928.
Description: Autographed and marked on front flyleaf: 'from W. E. Haigh'. First written in pencil and subsequently inked in.
Collection: Tolkien's personal Celtic library, preserved at the Weston library under the auspices of the English Faculty Library (Oxford).
Notes: Contains a six-page *Foreword* by J.R.R. Tolkien. In his preface, Walter Haigh thanks Tolkien: 'In the first place, I would sincerely thank Professor J.R.R. Tolkien, formerly Professor in Leeds University, now Professor of Anglo-Saxon at Oxford. Not only has he almost from the first shown his warm approval of the work, and befriended me with ever-ready advice and encouragement throughout, but he has also generously contributed a valuable Foreword to the Glossary.' (p. x).
S.s.: McIlwaine (2018), no. 84.

917. Hakluyt, Richard. *Voyages of the Elizabethan seamen. Select narratives from the 'Principal navigations' of Hakluyt*. Edited by Edward John Payne. Oxford: At

the Clarendon Press, 1907.
>S.s.: University of Leeds (1920), p. 135 English Literature. Texts Selected for 1920-21; p. 181. English Language and Literature. Int. I Intermediate Course (Literature).

918. Haldane, John Burdon Sanderson. *My friend Mr. Leakey*. London: Cresset Press, 1937.
>S.s.: Scull-Hammond (2006b), p. 820.

919. Halliwell-Phillipps, James Orchard (Edited by). *The Thornton romances: The Early English Metrical Romances of 'Perceval', 'Isumbras', 'Eglamour' and 'Degrevant' Selected from Manuscripts at Lincoln and Cambridge*. Series: The Camden Society, 30. London: John Bowyer Nichols and Son, 1844.
>P.s. 1: *Sir Gawain and the Green Knight* (1925), p. 84 line 110 *Agrauayn a la dure mayn*. Tolkien and Gordon cite page 289
>P.s. 2: *The Devil's Coach-Horses* (1925), p. 333. Tolkien quotes: *wyght horse for to drow* (p. 183).
>P.s. 3: 'Chaucer as a Philologist: *The Reeve's Tale*' (1934), p. 139.

920. _____. *A dictionary of archaic and provincial words, obsolete phrases, proverbs and ancient customs from the 14. Century*, Vol. I, A-I. London: John Russel Smith, 1847.
>P.s.: *The Devil's Coach-Horses* (1925), p. 333.
>*NED*: #2 l. | 'W' (1928), p. 54. 'Walloping, *ppl. a.*' – 1847 '*Walloping*, great, *var. dial*'.

921. _____. *A dictionary of archaic and provincial words, obsolete phrases, proverbs and ancient customs from the 14 Century*, Vol. II, J-Z. London: John Russel Smith, 1847.
>P.s.: *The Devil's Coach-Horses* (1925), p. 333.

922. _____. *Ludus Coventriæ. A collection of mysteries, formerly represented at Coventry on the feast of Corpus Christi*. Series: Shakespeare Society, 4. London: Printed for the Shakespeare Society, 1841.
>P.s. 1: *A Middle English Vocabulary* (1922). Tolkien refers to the *Coventry Mysteries* on the term 'seede' (*my moder of whom I dede sede*, 393).
>P.s. 2: 'Chaucer as a Philologist: *The Reeve's Tale*' (1934), p. 131. Tolkien writes: '*fonne* 169 … The simple *fon* is found, *Coventry Plays*' (pp. 196, 289, 384).

923. Hall, John R. Clark (Translated by). *Beowulf and the Fight at Finnsburg*. London: Swan Sonnenschein and Company, 1901.
>S.s.: Scull-Hammond (2017a), p. 46. April 1913: Tolkien will need to become familiar with a range of literary and philological subjects and set texts as prescribed in the Oxford Regulations of the Board of Studies, knowing that he may be examined on them in ten papers at the end of Trinity Term 1915: Old English texts.

924. _____ (Translated by). *Beowulf and the Finnesburg fragment*. A translation into modern English prose. London: Sonnenschein & Co., 1911 (2nd ed.).
>P.s.: *Beowulf* (2014), p. 295.

925. _____ (Translated by). *Beowulf and the Finnesburg fragment*. Notes by Charles Leslie Wrenn and prefatory by J.R.R. Tolkien. London: George Allen and Unwin, 1940.
>P.s. 1: *Letters* 37 (1939). To Stanley Unwin. Tolkien writes: 'I will try and collect my weary wits and pen a sufficient foreword to the *Beowulf* translation, at once'.
>P.s. 2: *Finn and Hengest* (1982), p. 161 n. 3.
>P.s. 3: *The Legend of Sigurd & Gudrún* (2009), p. 45.
>P.s. 4: *Beowulf* (2014), pp. 9, 141.

926. _____ (Translated by). *Beowulf and the Finnesburg fragment*. Notes by Charles Leslie Wrenn and prefatory by J.R.R. Tolkien. London: George Allen and Unwin (revised), 1950.
> Description: Inscribed on front flyleaf: 'A small tif | for a great Tat | KF | from | J.R.R. Tolkien'.
> Collection: Private [TolkienLibrary.com].

927. _____. *Concise Anglo-Saxon dictionary for the use of students*. Cambridge: The University Press, 1916 (2nd ed.).
> P.s.: *Philology: General Works* (V 1926, for 1924), p. 45.

928. Hall, Joseph. *King Horn: a Middle English romance*. Oxford: At the Clarendon Press, 1901.
> P.s.: MS. Res. e. 308 *Sir Gawain and the Green Knight*. [Tolkien Papers, Bodleian Library, Oxford].

929. _____ (Edited by). *Selections from Early Middle English, 1130-1250*, Vol. I. Texts. Oxford: At the Clarenden Press, 1920.
> Description: Both volumes inscribed: 'J.R.R. Tolkien. | July 1920 (from Clar. Press)'. Has copious annotations, especially to *Ancrene Wisse* [Judith Priestman 1994, revd. 2016].
> Collection: Weston Library, Bodleian Libraries (Oxford).
> P.s. 1: MS. Res. e. 308 *Sir Gawain and the Green Knight*. [Tolkien Papers, Bodleian Library, Oxford].
> P.s. 2: *Some Contributions to Middle-English Lexicography* (1925), p. 213.
> P.s. 3: *'Iþþlen' in Sawles Warde* (1947), p. 168 n. 1.
> P.s. 4: *Studia Neophilologica* (1948), p. 71.

930. _____ (Edited by). *Selections from Early Middle English, 1130-1250*, Vol. II. Notes. Oxford: At the Clarenden Press, 1920.
> Description: Inscribed: 'J.R.R. Tolkien. | July 1920 (from Clar. Press)'. Has a few annotations.
> Collection: Taylor Institution Library, Bodleian Libraries (Oxford).
> P.s. 1: MS. Res. e. 308 *Sir Gawain and the Green Knight*. [Tolkien Papers, Bodleian Library, Oxford].
> P.s. 2: *Some Contributions to Middle-English Lexicography* (1925), p. 213.
> P.s. 3: *Ancrene Wisse and Hali Meiðhad* (1929), p. 107 n. 3; p. 116.
> P.s. 4: *'Iþþlen' in Sawles Warde* (1947), p. 168.

931. Hamilton, George Livingstone. *The Indebtedness of Chaucer's Troilus and Criseyde to Guido delle Colonne's Historia trojana*. New York: The Columbia University Press, 1903.
> S.s.: Ollscoil na h-Éireann G 259 (1949).

932. *Handlyng Synne* 1303. [Middle English poem, see Furnivall].
> P.s.: MS. Tolkien A 21/13 *The English MSS*. fol. 203. [Tolkien Papers, Bodleian Library, Oxford].

933. *Hansel and Gretel*. [Germanic fairy tale, see Grimm and Lang].
> P.s.: *Tolkien On Fairy-stories* (2008) 'Manuscript B [MS. Tolkien 4, fols. 73-120]', p. 247.

934. Harbour, Jennie. *The Fairy Tale Book*. London: Raphael Tuck & Sons, 1934.
> Description: Signed on first free endleaf recto: 'Priscilla M. R. Tolkien'.
> Collection: Weston Library, Bodleian Libraries (Oxford).

935. Hardie, Colin (Edited by). *Centenary Essays on Dante. By members of the Oxford Dante Society*. Oxford: At the Clarendon Press, 1965.
> Description: Tolkien was elected as the fiftyeighth member on 20 February 1945, and resigned on 15 February 1955.

936. Hardwick, Carles. *A poem on the times of Edward the second: from a ms. preserved in the library of St. Peter's College, Cambridge*. London: Printed for the Percy Society, 1849.
      P.s.: 'Chaucer as a Philologist: *The Reeve's Tale*' (1934), p. 152.

937. Harmer, Florence Elizabeth. 'Anglo-Saxon Charters and the Historian'. Offprint from *Bulletin of the John Rylands Library*, Vol. XXII, no. 2. Manchester: The University Press, 1938, pp. 339-67.
      Notes: A copy was sent to Tolkien by the author, 22 November 1938.
      S.s.: Scull-Hammond (2017a), p. 238.

938. Harper, Carrie A. 'Carados and the Serpent'. MLN (*Modern Language Notes*), Vol. 13. 1898, pp. 209-16.
      P.s.: *Sir Gawain and the Green Knight* (1925), p. xxvi. Tolkien and Gordon write: 'For bibliography of the Irish and French analogues of *Sir Gawain*, see the bibliography in Kittredge's study'. [*NED*] In Kittredge's study, this article is mentioned in 'V. Le Livre de Caradoc' (p. 298).

939. Harris, Joel Chandler. *Uncle Remus and Brer Rabbit*. New York: Frederick A. Stokes, 1907.
      P.s. 1: *Dragons* (1938), p. 40.
      P.s. 2: *Tolkien On Fairy-stories* (2008) 'Manuscript B [MS. Tolkien 4, fols. 73-120]', p. 217.
      P.s. 3: *Tolkien On Fairy-stories* (2008) 'Manuscript B [MS. Tolkien 14, fol. 25]', p. 281.
      S.s.: Scull-Hammond (2006b), p. 820.

940. Harrison, William. *Elizabethan England: from 'A Description of England'*. Series: Scott Library, 50. Edited by Lothrop Withington with Introduction by Frederick James Furnivall. London: Walter Scott, 1921.
      S.s.: University of Leeds (1920), p. 147. English Language and Literature - Scheme A. Texts and Period selected for 1920-21. (b) Special period: 1557-1637. (c) Texts suggested for study with Special Period. Ordinary Degree of B.A. with Honours. Final Examination.

941. Harsley, Fred. *Eadwine's Canterbury Psalter*. Series: E.E.T.S. (Early English Text Society), OS 92. London: Published for the Early English Text Society by Kegan Paul, Trench, Trübner and Co., 1889.
      P.s. 1: MS. Tolkien A 12/1 *Commentary on Sir Gawain, lines 37-1987* fol. 33. [Tolkien Papers, Bodleian Library, Oxford].
      P.s. 2: MS. Tolkien A 21/13 fol. 119. Note by Tolkien, 'Books in Exeter Library useful', with shelfmarks, on back of photostat reading list dated October 1913. Tolkien writes: 'All EETS publications'. [Tolkien Papers, Bodleian Library, Oxford].

942. Harte, Bret. *The Society upon the Stanislaus*. 1868.
      P.s.: *Letters* 53 (1943). To Christopher Tolkien. Tolkien writes: 'nearly curled up on the floor, and the subsequent proceedings interested me no more' from Harte's strophe 'curled up on the floor, and the subsequent proceedings interested him no more.'

943. Hart, Elizabeth M. 'The Heaven of Virgins'. MLN (*Modern Languages Notes*), Vol. 42, no. 2 February 1927, pp. 113-15.
      P.s.: MS. Tolkien A 35 *Pearl* fol. 114. [Tolkien Papers, Bodleian Library, Oxford].

944. Hartland, Edwin Sidney. *English Fairy and Other Folk Tales*. London: Walter Scott, 1893.
      Description: Tolkien requested the book on 27 February 1939 (MS. Library Records b. 618). Weston Library (Oxford), 930 e.175.

945. Hartmann, von Aue. *Iwein* [Middle High German verse romance].

P.s.: 'Middle English 'Losenger'' (1953), p. 66 n. 1.

946. *Hatton Gospels* [Bodleian Library, as MS Hatton 38]
P.s.: MS. Tolkien A 13/2 *Notes and drafts of lectures on Chaucer: Pardoner's Tale* fol. 141. [Tolkien Papers, Bodleian Library, Oxford].

947. Hauser, Otto (Edited by). *Die Edda*. Weimar: Alexander Duncker Verlag, 1926.
Description: Autographed on front flyleaf.
Collection: Tolkien's personal Celtic library, preserved at the Weston library under the auspices of the English Faculty Library (Oxford).
P.s.: *The Legend of Sigurd & Gudrún* (2009), pp. 368-77.
S.s. 1: Scull-Hammond (2017a), p. 143.
S.s. 2: McIlwaine (2018), no. 84.

948. *Havelok the Dane* about 1300. [Middle English romance, see Holthausen, Skeat].
P.s. 1: MS. Tolkien A 21/13 *The English MSS.* fol. 203. [Tolkien Papers, Bodleian Library, Oxford].
P.s. 2: 'Chaucer as a Philologist: *The Reeve's Tale*' (1934), p. 134.
S.s.: Scull-Hammond (2017a), p. 46. April 1913: Tolkien will need to become familiar with a range of literary and philological subjects and set texts as prescribed in the Oxford Regulations of the Board of Studies, knowing that he may be examined on them in ten papers at the end of *Trinity Term 1915*: Middle English texts.

949. Hawks, Ellison. *The Starry Heavens*. London: Thomas Nelson & Sons Ltd, 1933.
S.s. Scull-Hammond (2006b), p. 877.

950. Hayashi, Shigeru. *Unended wandering: A selection of verse*. Tokio: Shigeru Hayashi, 1970.
Description: Presentation copy to J.R.R. Tolkien from the author inscribed on front endpaper: 'With best wishes to Mr. J.R.R. Tolkien | 14th June 1971 | Shigeru Hayashi'. And in ink on front free endpaper: 'J.R.R. Tolkien'. Includes a label added by Stan Revell to books owned by Tolkien, 'From the Library of J.R.R. Tolkien', on front cover.
Collection: Marion E. Wade Center, Wheaton College (Wheaton, Illinois).

951. Hayens, Herbert. *Scouting for Buller*. London: Thomas Nelson and Sons, 1902.
Notes: Tolkien gives this book to the King Edward's School in Birmingham in 1911.
S.s.: Scull-Hammond (2017a), p. 31.
Reading period: 1908 – 1910 (S.s.: Scull-Hammond (2017c), p. 1054)

952. *Heart of a Monkey*. [Swahili fairy tale, see Lang].
P.s. 1: *On Fairy-stories* (1947), p. 46.
P.s. 2: *Tolkien On Fairy-stories* (2008) 'Manuscript A. [MS Tolkien 4, fols. 59-77]', p. 280.

953. Hecht, Hans; Julius Zupitza and Henry Johnson (Edited by). *Bischof Wærferth von Worcesters Übersetzung der Dialoge Gregors des Grossen*. Series: Bibliothek der angelsächsischen Prosa, 5. Leipzig: Georg H. Wigand, 1900.
Description: Autographed and dated on front flyleaf: '1920'. Also in pencil on front flyleaf: 'badly penciled | marked and scored | a few ink markings, | under purchased'. Messily annotated in pencil by a previous owner.
Collection: Tolkien's personal Celtic library, preserved at the Weston library under the auspices of the English Faculty Library (Oxford).
P.s. 1: MS. Tolkien A 12/3 *Rough text of a lecture on Sir Gawain*, 1965 fols. 17-59. [Tolkien Papers, Bodleian Library, Oxford].
P.s. 2: *Sigelwara land* (1934), p. 111.
P.s. 3: *The Old English Exodus* (1982), p. 41.

Section A

954. Heinrich, von dem Türlin. *Diu crône*. Series: Blibliothek des Literarischen Vereins in Stuttgart, XXVII. Edited by Gottlob Heinrich Friedrich Scholl. Stuttgart: Litterarischen Verein, 1852.
    P.s. 1: *Sir Gawain and the Green Knight* (1925), p. xxvi. Tolkien and Gordon write: 'For bibliography of the Irish and French analogues of *Sir Gawain*, see the bibliography in Kittredge's study'. [*NED*] In Kittredge's study, this article is mentioned in 'VI. La Mule sanz Frain' (p. 299).
    P.s. 2: *Sir Gawain and the Green Knight* (1967) 'Select Bibliography', p. 154.

955. Heinzel, Otto. *Kritische Entstehungsgeschichte des ags. interlinear-Psalters*. Series: Palaestra 151. Leipzig: Mayer and Müller, 1926.
    Collection: Tolkien's personal Celtic library, preserved at the Weston library under the auspices of the English Faculty Library (Oxford).
    P.s.: *Sigelwara land* (1932), p. 185 n. 1; p. 186 n. 1.

956. Heinzel, Richard. *Ueber die französischen Gralromane*. Series: Denkschriften der Kaiserlichen Akademie der Wissenschaften in Wien., Philosophisch-historische Classe, 40.3. Wien: Denkschriften 1891.
    P.s.: *Sir Gawain and the Green Knight* (1925), p. xxvi. Tolkien and Gordon write: 'For bibliography of the Irish and French analogues of *Sir Gawain*, see the bibliography in Kittredge's study'. [*NED*] In Kittredge's study, this article is mentioned in 'V. Le Livre de Caradoc' (p. 298).

957. Helgason, Jón (Edited by). *Heiðreks saga: Hervarar saga ok Heiðreks Konungs*. Kobenhavn: Jorgensen And Co, 1924.
    Description: Signed by Tolkien in pencil to the front free endpaper.
    Collection: Private [TolkienLibrary.com, Sold on Ebay 17 July 2012].
    P.s.: *The Legend of Sigurd & Gudrún* (2009), p. 323

958. Helten, Willem Lodewijk van. *Die Altostniederfrankischen Psalmenfragmente, die Lipsius'schen Glossen*, Vol. I. Texte, Glossen und Indices. Groningen: J. B. Wolters, 1902.
    P.s.: 'Middle English 'Losenger'' (1953), p. 74 n. 1.

959. _____. *Die Altostniederfrankischen Psalmenfragmente, die Lipsius'schen Glossen*, Vol. II. Die Grammatiken. Groningen: J. B. Wolters, 1902.
    P.s.: 'Middle English 'Losenger'' (1953), p. 74 n. 1.

960. Hempel, Heinrich. *Nibelungenstudien*, Vol. I. Nibelungenlied Thidrikssaga und Balladen. Neidelberg: Carl Winters Universitätsbuchhandlung, 1926.
    Description: Autographed on front flyleaf.
    Collection: Tolkien's personal Celtic library, preserved at the Weston library under the auspices of the English Faculty Library (Oxford).
    P.s.: *The Legend of Sigurd & Gudrún* (2009), p. 325.

961. Henderson, George (Edited with translation, introduction and notes by). *Fled Bricrend. The Feast of Briciu. An Early Gaelic Saga Transcribed from Older MSS. Into the Book of the Dun Cow, by Moelmuiri Mac Mic Cuinn Na M-Bocht*. Series: Irish Text Society, II. London: Published for the Irish Texts Society by David Nutt, 1899.
    P.s. 1: *Sir Gawain and the Green Knight* (1925), p. xii line 1;p. xxvi. Tolkien and Gordon write: 'For bibliography of the Irish and French analogues of *Sir Gawain*, see the bibliography in Kittredge's study'. In Kittredge's study, this article is mentioned in 'I. Fled Bricrend' (p. 290 n. 3).
    P.s. 2: *Sir Gawain and the Green Knight* (1967) 'Select Bibliography', p. 154. Ch. 39 on *Gawain*. (pp. 97-101, 117-29).

962. Henry, Francoise. *Early Christian Irish Art*. Translated by Máire MacDermott.

Dublin: Three Candles, 1963.
: Collection: Tolkien's personal Celtic library, preserved at the Weston library under the auspices of the English Faculty Library (Oxford).

963. Henry VIII. *An acte for certayne ordinaunces in the Kinges maiesties dominion and principalitie of Wales.* 1562.
: P.s.: *English and Welsh* (1963), p. 4.

964. Herbert, Frank. *Dune.* Chilton Books, 1965.
: P.s. 1: Tolkien's unpublished letter to Sterling Lanier, 29 September 1965. Tolkien writes: 'Dear Mr. Lanier, I received your book *Dune* just before I went abroad for a short while. Hence the delay in acknowledging it. I don't think I shall have time to read it until I next get a holiday.'
: P.s. 2: Tolkien's unpublished letter to John Bush, 12 March 1966. Tolkien writes: 'Thank you for sending me a copy of *Dune*. I received one last year from Lanier and so already know something about the book. It is impossible for an author still writing to be fair to another author working along the same lines. At least I find it so. In fact I dislike *DUNE* with some intensity, and in that unfortunate case it is much the best and fairest to another author to keep silent and refuse to comment. Would you like me to return the book as I already have one, or to hand it on?'

965. Herbert, James (Edited by). *The French Text of the Ancrene Riwle.* Series: E.E.T.S. (Early English Text Society), OS 219. London: Published for the Early English Text by H. Milford, Oxford University Press, 1944.
: Description: Marked with green crayon. Annotated in pencil. Bookmark at pages 166, 167.
: Collection: Tolkien's personal Celtic library, preserved at the Weston library under the auspices of the English Faculty Library (Oxford).
: S.s.: McIlwaine (2018), no. 84.

966. Herbert, John Alexander. *Catalogue of romances in the Department of manuscripts in the British museum*, Vol. III. London: Printed by order of the Trustees, 1910.
: P.s.: *Sir Gawain and the Green Knight* (1925), p. xxvi. Tolkien and Gordon write: 'For bibliography of the Irish and French analogues of *Sir Gawain*, see the bibliography in Kittredge's study'. [*NED*] In Kittredge's study, this article is mentioned in 'XII. The Exempla' (p. 305).

967. Hermannsson, Halldór. *Bibliography of the mythical-heroic sagas.* Series: Islandica, an Annual Relating to Iceland and the Fiske Icelandic Collection in Cornell University Library, 5. New York: Cornell University Library, 1912.
: Collection: Tolkien's personal Celtic library, preserved at the Weston library under the auspices of the English Faculty Library (Oxford).

968. _____. *Icelandic manuscripts.* Series: Islandica, an Annual Relating to Iceland and the Fiske Icelandic Collection in Cornell University Library, 19. New York: Cornell University Library, 1929.
: Description: Autographed on cover.
: Collection: Tolkien's personal Celtic library, preserved at the Weston library under the auspices of the English Faculty Library (Oxford).

969. _____. *The Sagas of the Kings (Konunga Sögur) and the mythical-heroic sagas (Fornaldar Sögur). Two bibliographical supplements.* Series: Islandica, an Annual Relating to Iceland and the Fiske Icelandic Collection in Cornell University Library, 26. New York: Cornell University Press, 1937.
: Collection: Tolkien's personal Celtic library, preserved at the Weston library under the auspices of the English Faculty Library (Oxford).

970. Herrick, Robert. *Hesperides.* Edited by Frederic William Moorman. Oxford: At

the Clarendon Press, 1915.
> S.s.: University of Leeds (1921), p. 154. English Language and Literature - Scheme A. Texts and Period selected for 1921-22. (d) Texts suggested for study with Special Period 1637-1700. Ordinary Degree of B.A. with Honours. Final Examinations.

971. _____ (Edited by). *Welsh Writers: Life and Letters and the London Mercury*. Series: Welsh Writers, Vol. 52, no. 115. Brendin Publishing Company, March 1947.
> Notes: Contains *The Modernity of Beowulf* by Francis Berry (pp. 19-26) in which Tolkien is mentioned: 'Unfortunately, as J.R.R. Tolkien points out, it is the history and the linguistics that have received examination to the neglect of the monsters which are the real excuse for the poem'. (p. 20)
> Collection: Tolkien's personal Celtic library, preserved at the Weston library under the auspices of the English Faculty Library (Oxford).

972. Herrtage, Sidney John Hervon. *Catholicon Anglicum, an English-Latin wordbook, dated 1483*. Series: E.E.T.S. (Early English Text Society), OS 75. London: Published for the Early English Text Society by Kegan Paul, Trench, Trübner and Co., 1881.
> Description: Autographed on front flyleaf, and autographed on page after front flyleaf: 'John Reuel Tolkien | 1922'.
> Collection: Tolkien's personal Celtic library, preserved at the Weston library under the auspices of the English Faculty Library (Oxford).
> P.s. 1: MS. Tolkien A 21/13 fol. 119. Note by Tolkien, 'Books in Exeter Library useful', with shelfmarks, on back of photostat reading list dated October 1913. Tolkien writes: 'All EETS publications'. [Tolkien Papers, Bodleian Library, Oxford].
> P.s. 2: *A Middle English Vocabulary* (1922). Tolkien refers to the Layamon on the term 'Coker' (*coker*, autumnarius).
> P.s. 3: 'Chaucer as a Philologist: *The Reeve's Tale*' (1934), p. 146.

973. _____. *English Charlemagne Romances*, Pt. IV. The taill of Rauf Coilzear: (about 1475 A.D.); (from the unique copy of Lekpreuik's ed. of 1572); with the fragments of Roland and Vernagu and Otuel (from the unique Auchinleck MS., about 1330 A.D.). Series: E.E.T.S. (Early English Text Society), OS 37, 1882.
> P.s. 1: MS. Tolkien A 21/13 fol. 119. Note by Tolkien, 'Books in Exeter Library useful', with shelfmarks, on back of photostat reading list dated October 1913. Tolkien writes: 'All EETS publications'. [Tolkien Papers, Bodleian Library, Oxford].
> P.s. 2: *Sir Gawain and the Green Knight* (1925), p. xxvi. Tolkien and Gordon write: 'For bibliography of the Irish and French analogues of *Sir Gawain*, see the bibliography in Kittredge's study'. [*NED*] In Kittredge's study, this article is mentioned in 'XIII. Rauf Coilyear' (p. 306).

974. Herzfeld, George (Edited by). *An Old English Martyrology*. Series: E.E.T.S. (Early English Text Society), OS 116. London: Published for the Early English Text Society by Kegan Paul, Trench, Trübner and Co., 1900.
> P.s. 1: MS. Tolkien A 21/13 fol. 119. Note by Tolkien, 'Books in Exeter Library useful', with shelfmarks, on back of photostat reading list dated October 1913. Tolkien writes: 'All EETS publications'. [Tolkien Papers, Bodleian Library, Oxford].
> P.s. 2: *Sigelwara land* (1932), p. 188 n. 4.
> P.s. 3: *Sigelwara land* (1934), pp. 101; 106 n. 2.
> P.s. 4: *The Old English Exodus* (1982), p. 42.

975. Hessels, John Henry. (Edited by). *An eight-century Latin-Anglo-Saxon glossary. Preserved in the library of Corpus Christi College, Cambridge. (MS. no. 144)*. Cambridge: The Cambridge University Press, 1890.
    Description: Signed by Tolkien 'J.R.R. Tolkien 1919' on front free endpaper.
    Collection: Private [Sold by Simon Finch Rare Books Ltd.].
    S.s.: Finch (2002), p. 52.

976. Heusler, Andreas. *Deutsche Versgeschichte*, Vol. I, Pt. I-II: Einführendes, Grundbegriffe der Verslehre, Der altgermanische Vers: Mit Einschluss des altenglischen und altnordischen Stabreimverses. Series: Grundriss der germanischen Philologie, 8.1. Berlin: Walter de Gruyter, 1925.
    Description: Ex Libri J.R.R. Tolkien. Autographed: 'J.R.R. Tolkien'.
    Collection: Taylor Institution Library, Bodleian Libraries (Oxford).

977. _____. *Deutsche Versgeschichte*, Vol. I, Pt. III: Der altdeutsche Vers: Mit Einschluss des altenglischen und altnordischen Stabreimverses. Series: Grundriss der germanischen Philologie, 8.2. Berlin: Walter de Gruyter, 1927.
    Collection: Taylor Institution Library, Bodleian Libraries (Oxford).

978. _____. *Deutsche Versgeschichte*, Vol. III, Pt. IV-V: Der frühneudeutsche Vers; Der neudeutsche Vers: Mit Einschluss des altenglischen und altnordischen Stabreimverses. Series: Grundriss der germanischen Philologie, 8.3. Berlin: Walter de Gruyter, 1929.
    Collection: Taylor Institution Library, Bodleian Libraries (Oxford).

979. _____ and Wilhelm Ranisch. *Eddica Minora: Dichtungen eddischer Art aus den Fornaldarsögur und anderen Prosawerken*. Dortmund: W. Ruhfus, 1903.
    P.s.: *Sir Gawain and the Green Knight* (1925), p. 102, line 1255 *garysoun uper golde*. Tolkien and Gordon quote: '*gulli ok gorsimum*' (36/16).

980. Heyne, Moritz (Edited by). *Beowulf. Mit ausfürlichem glossar herausgegeben*. Revised by Levin Ludwig. Schucking: Paderborn, 1908.
    Description: Inscribed: 'J. Pym St. Hugh's', with a few Tolkien's annotations.
    Collection: Weston Library, Bodleian Libraries (Oxford).

981. _____ (Edited by). *Beowulf. Mit ausfürlichem glossar*. Series: Bibliothek der ältesten deutschen Literatur-Denkmäler, 3. Paderborn: Ferdinand Schöningh, 1913.
    Description: Autographed on front flyleaf and on next page.
    Collection: Tolkien's personal Celtic library, preserved at the Weston library under the auspices of the English Faculty Library (Oxford).
    S.s.: McIlwaine (2018), no. 84.

982. _____ (Edited by). *Hêliand*. Paderborn: Ferdinand Schönigh, 1905 (4nd ed.).
    Collection: Tolkien's personal Celtic library, preserved at the Weston library under the auspices of the English Faculty Library (Oxford).

983. Hichens, Jacobine Napier. *Noughts and Crosses. A novel*. London: Putnam, 1952.
    P.s.: Tolkien's unpublished letter to Miss Stanley-Smith, 22 November 1956. Tolkien writes: 'Wonder if Mrs Lionel Hichens is the mother of Miss Phoebe Hichens, whom I have met, since my daughter knows her. She was, I think, the cousin (?) of the woman novelist of the same name (*Noughts & Crosses ... etc.*)'.

984. Hickes, George and Andrew Fountaine. *De Antiquæ Litteraturæ Septentrionalis*

Utilitate, Sive De Linguarum Veterum Septentrionalium Usu Dissertatio Epistolaris, Ad Bartholomæum Showere. Numismata Anglo-Saxonica & Anglo-Danica. Oxford: E. Theatro Sheldoni, 1703.
>P.s.: *Beowulf* (2002) 'Version A', p. 42.

985. _____ with Runólfur Jónsson, Humphrey Wanley and Andrew Fountaine. *Linguarum Vett. septentrionalium thesaurus grammatico-criticus et archæologicus*, Vol. I. Oxford: E. Theatro Sheldoni, 1703.
>P.s. 1: *Sigelwara land* (1934), p. 98 n. 1, 3.
>P.s. 2: *Finn and Hengest* (1982), p. 9 n. 3.

986. _____ with Runólfur Jónsson, Humphrey Wanley and Andrew Fountaine. *Linguarum Vett. septentrionalium thesaurus grammatico-criticus et archæologicus*, Vol. II. Oxford: E. Theatro Sheldoni, 1705.
>P.s. 1: *Beowulf* (1937), p. 4.
>P.s. 2: *Beowulf* (2002) 'Version A', p. 42. Tolkien quotes the text 'In hoc libro qui Poeseos Anglosaxonicæ egregium est exemplum descripta videntur bella quae Beowulfus quidam Danus ex regio Scyldingorum stirpe ortus gessit contra Sueciae regulos'; and he points to page 218, but in the volume the page is 129.

987. Highfield, John Roger Loxdale. 'The Green Squire'. *Medium Ævum*, Vol. 22, No. 1, 1953, pp. 18-23.
>P.s.: MS. Tolkien A 35 *Pearl* fol. 24. [Tolkien Papers, Bodleian Library, Oxford].

988. Higham, T. F. and Cecil Maurice Bowra (Edited by). *The Oxford Book of Greek Verse in Translation*. Oxford: At the Clarendon Press, 1938.
>Description: On p. viii: 'Professor J.R.R. Tolkien and Mr. W. H. Shewing in the second part of Introduction.'
>S.s.: Scull-Hammond (2017a), p. 225.

989. Hildebert of Lavardin. *Oratio ad Dominum*.
>P.s.: *Letters* 267 (1965). From a letter to Michael Tolkien. Tolkien quotes: 'In hac urbe lux solemnis'.

990. Hildebrand, Karl (Edited by). *Die Lieder der Älteren Edda* (Sæmundar Edda). Translated by Hugo Gering. Paderborn: Ferdinand Schöningh, 1922 (4th ed.).
>Description: Autographed in pencil on front flyleaf. Bookmark at pp. 380, 381.
>Collection: Tolkien's personal Celtic library, preserved at the Weston library under the auspices of the English Faculty Library (Oxford).

991. Hill, John. *An history of animals: containing descriptions of the birds, beasts, fishes, and insects, of the several parts of the world, and including accounts of the several classes of animalcules, visible only by the assistance of microscopes.*
>P.s.: MS. Tolkien A 19/3 *Etymologies or history of Walrus* fols. 162-195 [Tolkien Papers, Bodleian Library, Oxford].
>S.s.: Tolkien, *Family Album* (1992), p. 42.
>*NED*: #2 i. | 'W' (1928), p. 58 'Walrus, 1.' 1752 – 'The Phoca, with the canine teeth exerted. The Walrus' (p. 555).

992. Hill, Raymond Thompson. 'Boleslas Orlowski, La Damoisele a la Mule, Conte en vers par Pairn de Maisières'. *The Romanic Review*, Vol. IV, 1913, pp. 392-95.
>P.s.: *Sir Gawain and the Green Knight* (1925), p. xxvi. Tolkien and Gordon write: 'For bibliography of the Irish and French analogues of *Sir Gawain*, see the bibliography in Kittredge's study'. [*NED*] In Kittredge's study, this article is mentioned in 'VI. La Mule sanz Frain' (p. 299).

993.   Hillmann, (Sister) Mary Vincent. *The Pearl*. New York: College of Saint Elizabeth Press, 1961.
   P.s.: *Sir Gawain and the Green Knight* (1967) 'Select Bibliography', p. 153.

994.   _____. *La mule sanz frain, an Arthurian romance by Paiens de Maisieres*. Thesis presented to the Faculty of the Graduate School of Yale University in candidate for the Degree of Doctor of Philosophy. Edited with introduction, notes and glossary by Raymond Thompson Hill. Baltimore: J. H. Furst Company, 1911.
   P.s. 1: *Sir Gawain and the Green Knight* (1925), pp. xiii; xxvi. Tolkien and Gordon write: 'For bibliography of the Irish and French analogues of *Sir Gawain*, see the bibliography in Kittredge's study'. In Kittredge's study, this article is mentioned in 'VI. La Mule sanz Frain' (p. 298).
   P.s. 2: *Sir Gawain and the Green Knight* (1967) 'Select Bibliography', p. 155.

995.   Hirt, Hermann Alfred. *Handbuch der Greichischen Laut- und Formenlehre eine Einführung in das Sprachwissenschaftliche Studium des Griechischen*. Heidelberg: Carl Winter's Universitätsbuchhandlung, 1912.
   Description: Tolkien's signature with a few light pencil annotations throughout.
   Collection: Private [Sold by Simon Finch Rare Books Ltd.].
   S.s.: Finch (2002), p. 53.

996.   _____. *Der Indogermanische Ablaut, vornehmlich in seinem Verhältnis zur Betonung*. Strassburg: Karl J. Trübner, 1900.
   Description: The contents are described as a: 'classic work of Indo-Germanic philology'. And has Tolkien's ownership signature to the front free endpaper and his annotations to pages 2, 11, 33, 77, 147, 224. Includes a label added by Stan Revell to books owned by Tolkien, 'From the Library of J.R.R. Tolkien'.
   Collection: Private [Sold by Christie's, 22 June 2010].

997.   _____. *Indogermanische Grammatik*, Vol. I. Einleitung: I. Etymologie. II. Konsonantismus. Heidelberg: Carl Winters Universitätsbuchhandlung, 1927.
   Description: Tolkien heavily annotated chapter twenty, 'Die Lautverschiebung.' In these annotations, Tolkien actually corrects Hirt on what he has to say about Grimm's Law. This is, apparently, a subject about which Tolkien feels very passionately – parts of his annotations read: 'probably wrong,' 'most unlikely!' and 'nonsense!' (Keyser 2012).
   Collection: The Science Fiction and Fantasy Research Collection of the Cushing Memorial Library and Archives at Texas A&M University.

998.   _____. *Indogermanische Grammatik*, Vol. II. Der indogermanische Vokalismus. Heidelberg: Carl Winters Universitätsbuchhandlung, 1927.
   Collection: The Science Fiction and Fantasy Research Collection of the Cushing Memorial Library and Archives at Texas A&M University.

999.   _____. *Indogermanische Grammatik*, Vol. III. Das Nomen. Heidelberg: Carl Winters Universitätsbuchhandlung, 1927.
   Collection: The Science Fiction and Fantasy Research Collection of the Cushing Memorial Library and Archives at Texas A&M University.

1000.   _____. *Indogermanische Grammatik*, Vol. IV. Doppelung Zusammensetzung Verbum. Heidelberg: Carl Winters Universitätsbuchhandlung, 1928.
   Collection: The Science Fiction and Fantasy Research Collection of the Cushing Memorial Library and Archives at Texas A&M University.

1001.   _____. *Indogermanische Grammatik*, Vol. V. Der Akzent. Heidelberg: Carl Winters Universitätsbuchhandlung, 1929.
   Collection: The Science Fiction and Fantasy Research Collection of the Cushing Memorial

Library and Archives at Texas A&M University.

1002. _____. *Indogermanische Grammatik*, Vol. VI. Syntax 1: syntaktische Verwendung der Kasus und der Verbalformen. Heidelberg: Carl Winters Universitätsbuchhandlung, 1934.
   Collection: The Science Fiction and Fantasy Research Collection of the Cushing Memorial Library and Archives at Texas A&M University.

1003. _____. *Indogermanische Grammatik*, Vol. VII. Syntax II: Die Lehre vom einfachen und zusammengesetzen Satz. Heidelberg: Carl Winters Universitätsbuchhandlung, 1937.
   Collection: The Science Fiction and Fantasy Research Collection of the Cushing Memorial Library and Archives at Texas A&M University.

1004. *History of Whittington*. [Characteral tale, see Lang].
   P.s.: Tolkien On Fairy-stories (2008) 'Manuscript A. [MS Tolkien 4, fols. 59-77]', p. 177.
   S.s.: Scull-Hammond (2017b), p. 611.

1005. Hobbes, Thomas. *Leviathan. Or The Matter, Forme, and Power of a Commonwealth Ecclesiasticall and Civill*. Oxford: J. Thornton, 1881.
   Description: Autographed on half title. Includes a label added by Stan Revell to books owned by Tolkien, 'From the Library of J.R.R. Tolkien'.
   S.s. 1: University of Leeds (1920), p. 139 English Language and Literature: English Literature. Text selected for 1920-21. Texts Selected for 1920-21. Ordinary Degree of B.A. with Honours. Final Course and Examination. Extracts cc. 1-13
   S.s. 2: University of Leeds (1921), p. 154. English Language and
   Literature - Scheme A. Texts and Period selected for 1921-22. (d) Texts suggested for study with Special Period 1637-1700. Ordinary Degree of B.A. with Honours. Final Examinations. Parts suggested I and II.

1006. Hobhouse, Leonard Trelawny. *The metaphysical theory of the state: a criticism*. London: George Allen & Unwin, 1918.
   Description: Tolkien requested the book on 12 May 1931 (MS. Library Records b. 640). Weston Library (Oxford), 24817 e.409 (ex S. Pol. Sci. 4t).

1007. Hodgkin, Robert Howard. *A History of the Anglo-Saxons*. London: Oxford University Press, 1935.
   P.s.: *Finn and Hengest* (1982), p. 66 n. 65.

1008. Hoffmann-Krayer, Eduard. 'Grundsätzliches über Ursprung und Wirkungen der Akzentuation'. *Beiträge zur Germanischen Sprachwissenschaft: Festschrift für Otto Behaghel* [A. 1045]. Heidelberg: Carl Winter, 1924.
   P.s.: *Philology: General Works* (V 1926, for 1924), pp. 35-36. Tolkien writes: 'The article by E. Hoffmann-Krayer on the origin and effects of accentuation is of considerable interest, but based as it is almost entirely on German dialects must be passed over.'

1009. Hoffman, Richard L. 'The Theme of 'Judgment Day II'. Offprint from *English Language Notes*, Vol. 6, no. 3. Boulder: University of Colorado, 1969, pp. 161-64.
   Notes: A copy was sent to Tolkien by the author.
   S.s.: Scull-Hammond (2017a), p. 781.

1010. Hogan, Jeremiah Joseph. *Text of introductory address delivered by Professor Jeremiah J. Hogan: On 20 July 1954 on the occasion of the conferring of an honorary Doctorate of Letters on Tolkien from the National University of Ireland*. National University of Ireland, 1954.

S.s.: Hostetter, *Vinyar Tengwar* (50, 2013), p. 11, n. 11.

1011. Holcot, Robertus. *Super librum Sapientiae*. 1506.
P.s.: MS. Tolkien A 12/1 *Commentary on Sir Gawain, lines 37-1987* fol. 24. [Tolkien Papers, Bodleian Library, Oxford].

1012. Holder, Alfred Theophil. *Alt-Celtischer Sprachschatz*, Vol. I 'A-H'. Leipzig: Teubner, 1896.
Collection: Tolkien's personal Celtic library, preserved at the Weston library under the auspices of the English Faculty Library (Oxford).

1013. _____. *Alt-Celtischer Sprachschatz*, Vol. II 'I-T'. Leipzig: Teubner, 1904.

1014. _____. *Alt-Celtischer Sprachschatz*, Vol. III 'U-Z'. Leipzig: Teubner, 1907.
Collection: Tolkien's personal Celtic library, preserved at the Weston library under the auspices of the English Faculty Library (Oxford).

1015. _____. *Beowulf. Herausgegeben*: Pt. I, Neue Billige Ausgabe. Freiburg: J. C. B. Mohr, 1895.
Collection: Weston Library, Bodleian Libraries (Oxford).

1016. Hollingshead, John (Edited by). *The illustrated catalogue of the industrial department. British Division*, Vol. II. London International Exhibition (1862). London: Printed for Her Majesty's Commissioners, 1862.
P.s.: MS. Tolkien A 19/3 *Etymologies or history of Walrus* fols. 162-195 [Tolkien Papers, Bodleian Library, Oxford].
S.s.:Tolkien, *Family Album* (1992), p. 42.
NED 1: #2 i. | 'W' (1928), pp. 57-58 'Walrus, 3. *attrib.* and *comb.*' 1862 – 'No. 4638, Patent walrus-hide belting' (Class XXVI, p. 12).
NED 2: #2 i. | 'W' (1928), p. 57 'Walnut, 4.' 1862 – 'A walnut sideboard, Renaissance style' (ch. xxx no. 5731).

1017. Holmqvist, Erik. *On the History of the English present inflections particularly -th and –s*. Series: Verlags, 1694. Heidelberg: Carl Winter's Universitätsbuchhandlung, 1922.
Description: Inscribed on the cover 'JRR Tolkien'.
Collection: Private [Tolkien Collector's Guide].

1018. Holthausen, Ferdinand. *Altfriesisches Wörterbuch*. Series: Germanische Bibliothek I. Abteilung, Sammlung germanischer Elementar- und Handbücher, 5. Heildelberg: Carl Winter, 1925.
P.s.: *Philology: General Works* (VI 1927, for 1925), p. 57.

1019. _____. *Altenglisches etymologisches Wörterbuch*. Series: Germanische Bibliothek, 1. Sammlung germanischer Elementar- und Handbücher, 4. Heidelberg: Carl Winter, 1932.
P.s. 1: MS. Tolkien A 12/3 *Rough text of a lecture on Sir Gawain*, 1965 fol. 70. [Tolkien Papers, Bodleian Library, Oxford].
P.s. 2: *Sigelwara land* (1934), p. 106 n. 3.

1020. _____. *Altenglisches etymologisches Wörterbuch*. Series: Germanische Bibliothek, 1. Sammlung germanischer Elementar- und Handbücher, 4. Heidelberg: Carl Winter, 1934.
P.s. 1: MS. Tolkien A 12/3 *Rough text of a lecture on Sir Gawain*, 1965 fol. 70. [Tolkien Papers, Bodleian Library, Oxford].

SECTION A

P.s. 2: *The Old English Exodus* (1982), p. 55.

1021. _____ (Edited by). *Die Ältere Genesis, mit Einleitung, Anmerkungen, Glossar und der lateinischen Quelle.* Series: Alt- und mittelenglische Texte, 7. Heidelberg: Carl Winter's Universitätsbuchhandlung, 1914.
    Description: Autographed and annotated in pencil on front flyleaf: 'First read Oct. 20th 1920'. Annotated in pencil.
    Collection: Tolkien's personal Celtic library, preserved at the Weston library under the auspices of the English Faculty Library (Oxford)

1022. _____. *Altisländisches Elementarbuch.* Series: Lehrbuch der altisländischen Sprache, 1. Weimar: Emil Felber, 1895.
    Description: Very decorative inscription in Latin. Annotated. Decoratively autographed and inscribed on front flyleaf: 'e | coll: exon: oxon: | mcmxiii | ex libris de litt: et plul: geni: | collect: | etc:'. Annotated in pencil and ink.
    Collection: Tolkien's personal Celtic library, preserved at the Weston library under the auspices of the English Faculty Library (Oxford).

1023. _____. *Beowulf nebst dem Finnesburg-Bruchstück*, Vol. I. Series: Alt- und Mittelenglische Texte, 3. Heidelberg: Carl Winter, 1905.
    P.s.: *Finn and Hengest* (1982), p. 86 n. 10.

1024. _____. *Beowulf nebst dem Finnesburg-Bruchstück*, Vol. II. Series: Alt- und Mittelenglische Texte, 3. Heidelberg: Carl Winter, 1906.
    P.s.: *Finn and Hengest* (1982), p. 86 n. 10.

1025. _____ (Edited by). *Beowulf. Nebst den kleineren Denkmälern der Heldensagen, mit Einleitung, Glossar und Anmerkungen. Herausgegeben*: Pt. I, Texte und Namenverzeichnis. Heidelber: Carl Winter, 1912.
    Description: Signed: '1913. | J.R.R. Tolkien bnd. | Sept. 1919' with a few Tolkien's annotations.
    Collection: Weston Library, Bodleian Libraries (Oxford).

1026. _____ (Edited by). *Beowulf. Nebst den kleineren Denkmälern der Heldensagen, mit Einleitung, Glossar und Anmerkungen. Herausgegeben*: Pt. II, Einleitung, Glossar und Anmerkungen. Heidelber: Carl Winter, 1913.
    Collection: Weston Library, Bodleian Libraries (Oxford).

1027. _____ (Edited by). *Havelok; mit Einleitung, Glossar und Anmerkungen.* Series: Alt- und mittelenglische Texte, 1. Heidelberg: Carl Winter, 1910.
    Description: Exeter College. Inscribe: 'John Reuel Tolkien. | Exeter College 1913. | ex libris de phil. et litt. Germanicus'. Extensively annotated [Judith Priestman 1994, revd. 2016].
    Collection: Weston Library, Bodleian Libraries (Oxford).
    P.s.: *A Middle English Vocabulary* (1922). Tolkien refers to the *Havelok* on the terms 'Criing, Criyng(e)' (*at one cri*, 2273),'spare' (*sparede he neyþer tos ne heles*, 898).
    S.s.: Scull-Hammond (2017a), p. 47. *Trinity Term 1913*: *Havelok*, on Thursdays at 10.00 a.m. in the Examination Schools, beginning 24 April.

1028. _____. 'Der König des Lebens: metrische Übersetzung'. *Probleme der Englischen Sprache und Kultur. Festschrift Johannes Hoops zum 60* [A. 1169]. Heidelberg: Carl Winter, 1925.
    P.s.: *Philology: General Works* (VI 1927, for 1925), p. 45. Tolkien writes: 'Professor Holthausen contributes not etymology but a metrical German version of the morality, *The Pride of Life*.'

1029. Homer. *Iliad*, Vol. I. Edited by David Binning Munro. Oxford: At the Clarendon Press, 1903.
> Description: King Edward's School. Inscribed variously: 'J.R.R. Tolkien. | September 5th 1908. | I KEHS' 'Ronald Tolkien' 'Birmingham I' 'RonaldTolkien'. Heavily annotated on pp 13; a few annotations after [Judith Priestman 1994, revd. 2016].
> Collection: Weston Library, Bodleian Libraries (Oxford).

1030. _____. *Iliad*, Vol. II. Edited by David Binning Munro. Oxford: At the Clarendon Press, 1906:
> Description: King Edward's School. Inscribed: 'J.R.R. Tolkien' 'J.R.R. Tolkien | September 1909 | K.E.S. Birmingham' 'J R R Tolkien' 'Ronald Tolkien' 'J R R Tolkien'. A few annotations [Judith Priestman 1994, revd. 2016].
> Collection: Weston Library, Bodleian Libraries (Oxford).

1031. _____. *The Odyssey of Homer*. Translated by Alexander Pope. Edinburgh: John Ross and Co., 1870.
> P.s.: MS. Tolkien A 13/1 *Draft of talk to the Oxford Dante Society: A neck-verse* (1947). Tolkien quotes 'brown evening' (Book xvii, 215).

1032. _____. *The Odysseys of Homer*, Vol. I. Translated by George Chapman, and Revised by Richard Hooper. London: Reeves & Turner, 1907.
> P.s. 1: *Beowulf* (1937), p. 25.
> P.s. 2: *English and Welsh* (1963), p. 38. Tolkien writes: 'The contemplation of the vocabulary in *A Primer of the Gothic Language* [A. 2548] was enough: a sensation at least as full of delight as first looking into Chapman's *Homer*'.
> S.s.: Scull-Hammond (2017a), p. 40. *Michaelmas Term 1912*: Tolkien probably attends lectures by L.R. Farnell on the *Odyssey* (Homer is a set author) on Mondays, Wensdays, and Fridays at 12.00 noon at Exeter College, beginning 14 October.

1033. _____. *The Odysseys of Homer*, Vol. II. Translated by George Chapman, and Revised by Richard Hooper. London: Reeves & Turner, 1907.
> P.s.: *English and Welsh* (1963), p. 38.
> S.s.: Scull-Hammond (2017a), p. 40. *Michaelmas Term 1912*: Tolkien probably attends lectures by L.R. Farnell on the *Odyssey* (Homer is a set author) on Mondays, Wensdays, and Fridays at 12.00 noon at Exeter College, beginning 14 October.

1034. Hooker, Richard. *The Laws of Ecclesiastical Polity*. Series: Everyman's library, 202. London: Joseph Malaby Dent, 1907.
> S.s.: University of Leeds (1920), p. 147. English Language and Literature - Scheme A. Texts and Period selected for 1920-21. (b) Special period: 1557-1637. (c) Texts suggested for study with Special Period. Ordinary Degree of B.A. with Honours. Final Examination.

1035. Hoops, Johannes. *Kommentar zum Beowulf*. Heidelberg: Carl Winters Universitätsbuchhandlung, 1932.
> P.s.: *Beowulf* (1937), p. 53 n. 39.

1036. _____ (Edited by). *Reallexikon der Germanischen Altertumskunde*, Vol. I. Strassburg: Trübner, 1911.
> S.s.: Mythopoeic Society, *Parma Eldalamberon* 20 (2012), pp. 6, 158.

1037. _____ (Edited by). *Reallexikon der Germanischen Altertumskunde*, Vol. II. Strassburg: Trübner, 1911.
> S.s.: Mythopoeic Society, *Parma Eldalamberon* 20 (2012), pp. 6, 158.

SECTION A

1038. _____ (Edited by). *Reallexikon der Germanischen Altertumskunde*, Vol. III. Strassburg: Trübner, 1911.
S.s.: Mythopoeic Society, *Parma Eldalamberon* 20 (2012), pp. 6, 158.

1039. _____ (Edited by). *Reallexikon der Germanischen Altertumskunde*, Vol. IV. Strassburg: Trübner, 1911.
Description: Documents written in early Elvish alphabets (published in Parma Eldalamberon 20) were found in this copy.
S.s.: Mythopoeic Society, *Parma Eldalamberon* 20 (2012), pp. 6, 158.

1040. _____. 'Werder, Rasen and Wisse. Eine Untersuchung zur germanischen Wortgeschichte'. *Anglica: Untersuchungen zur englischen Philologie: Alois Brandl zum 70. Geburtstage überreicht*, Vol. I [A. 30], 1925.
P.s.: *Philology: General Works* (VI 1927, for 1925), p. 34. Tolkien writes: 'Professor Hoops contributes Weltgeschichte – not Weltgeschichte as the table of contents (faulty in other particulars, see p. 39) has it, which would attribute to the author a theory of a wet green world for primitive Germans that is no part of his article'. And he writes: 'is an interesting etymological study, and an attempt to unravel the tangled connexions of a group of words represented in the title and in OE. *wær, waroð, wāse, wōs, wār, waru, weorð, wer* (weir)'.

1041. Hopkins, Gerard Manley and Richard Watson Dixon. *The Correspondence of Gerard Manley Hopkins and Richard Watson Dixon*. Translated and annotated by Claude Colleer Abbott. London: Oxford University Press, 1955.
P.s.: *Letters* 113 (1948). To C.S. Lewis. Tolkien writes: 'one works really for the one man who may rise to understand one' from this book (Letter 8 June 1878)'.

1042. Horace, *Ars Poetica*.
S.s. 1: University of Leeds (1921), p. 154. English Language and Literature - Scheme A. Texts and Period selected for 1921-22. (e) History of Criticism: Special Texts suggested for study. Ordinary Degree of B.A. with Honours. Final Examinations.
S.s. 2: Lewis (2009a), p. 991. Letter to Tolkien – 27 October 1949. Lewis writes: 'Ubi plura nitent in carmine non ego paucis offendo maculis' (351– 2: 'Indeed, when much glistens in a poem, I shall not be offended by a few blemishes').

1043. _____. *The Odes of Horace*. Translated by William Ewart Gladstone. London: John Murray, 1894.
P.s.: *Oxford University Press Archives* (Oxford). A slip written by Tolkien on the etymology of 'Wake' used ('W' p. 31) [A. 1721].
NED: #2 f. | 'W' (1928), p. 31 'Wake, 3.' 1894 – 'New contracts for new marbles thou dost make, But thou art near thy wake' (Ode xviii 'Philosophy of Life').

1044. Horn, Wilhelm. *Beiträge zur Germanischen Sprachwissenschaft: Festschrift für Otto Behaghel*. Series: Germanische Bibliothek, 2. Abteilung, Untersuchungen und Texte, 15. Heidelberg: Carl Winter, 1924.
Collection: Taylor Institution Library, Bodleian Libraries (Oxford).
P.s.: *Philology: General Works* (V 1926, for 1924), p. 34 n. 2, 35-36.

1045. _____. 'Beobachtungen über Sprachkörper und Sprachfunktion'. *Beiträge zur Germanischen Sprachwissenschaft: Festschrift für Otto Behaghel* [A. 1045]. Heidelberg: Carl Winter, 1924.
P.s.: *Philology: General Works* (V 1926, for 1924), p. 34.

1046. _____. 'Die Englische Sprachwissenschaft'. *Stand und Aufgaben der Sprachwissenschaft. Festschrift für Wilhelm Streitberg* [A. 726]. Heidelberg, Carl Winter, 1924.

P.s.: *Philology: General Works* (V 1926, for 1924), p. 45. Tolkien writes 'from its length and its wealth of bibliography alone, is testimony to the organization and intensity of study that are devoted to English subjects in Germany'.

1047. _____. 'Gepp, A Contribution to an Essex Dialect Dictionary'. *Beiblatt zur Anglia*, Vol. XXXIII, February 1922.
P.s.: *Philology: General Works* (IV 1924, for 1923), p. 26.

1048. _____ (Edited by). *Giessner Beiträge zur Erforschung der Sprache und Kultur. Englands und Nordamerikas*, Vol. I, Pt. I. Die Analyse im Formenbau d. engl. Namens by Hermann Düringer. Giessen Englisches Seminar der Universität Giessen, 1923.
P.s.: *Philology: General Works* (V 1926, for 1924), p. 34. Tolkie cites 'Neue Beobachtungen über Sprachkörper und Sprachfunktion im Englischen' by Horn: 'The two chief points now treated are the postulates that (i) if any part of a word, compound, or word-group becomes 'functionless' and emptied of all significance, then it is liable to specially rapid phonetic weakening or will disappear; (ii) that similar but less marked weakening will set in when the element is weak in 'function', though not robbed of all significance.'

1049. _____. *Sprachkörper und Sprachfunktion*. Series: Palaestra, 135. Berlin: Mayer & Müller, 1921.
P.s.: *Philology: General Works* (V 1926, for 1924), p. 34.

1050. _____. 'Zweck und Ausdruck in der Sprache: Die Verneinung im Englischen'. *Anglica: Untersuchungen zur englischen Philologie: Alois Brandl zum 70. Geburtstage überreicht*, Vol. I [A. 30], 1925.
P.s.: *Philology: General Works* (VI 1927, for 1925), p. 33. Tolkien writes: 'The article, which runs to less than eighteen pages, is not, of course, exhaustive or profound, but it deals with, or touches on, several points of interest...'

1051. Horstmann, Carl (Edited by). *Altenglische Legenden: Kindheit Jesu, Geburt Jesu, Barlaam und Josaphat und St Patrik's Fegefeuer*. Paderborn: Ferdinand Schöningh, 1875.
Collection: Tolkien's personal Celtic library, preserved at the Weston library under the auspices of the English Faculty Library (Oxford).

1052. _____ (Edited by). *Altenglische Legenden: I. Sammlung de MS. Vernon f. 89 ff., Bruchstück einer metrischen Uebertragung einzehner Legenden der Legenda Aurea; II. Einzellegenden*. Heilbronn: Verlag von gebr. Henninger, 1878.
Collection: Tolkien's personal Celtic library, preserved at the Weston library under the auspices of the English Faculty Library (Oxford).

1053. _____ (Edited by). *Altenglische Legenden: I. A Die nordenglische Legendensammlung des MS. Harl. 4196 (und Cott. Tib. E VII); I.B Aus Barbour's Legendensammlung: S. Machot, al. Moris; II. Einzellegenden*. Heilbronn: Verlag von gebr. Henninger, 1881.
Collection: Tolkien's personal Celtic library, preserved at the Weston library under the auspices of the English Faculty Library (Oxford).

1054. _____ (Edited by). *The Early South-English legendary, or lives of saints*. Series: E.E.T.S. (Early English Text Society), OS 87. London: Published for the Early English Text Society by Kegan Paul, Trench, Trübner and Co., 1887.
Collection: Tolkien's personal Celtic library, preserved at the Weston library under the auspices of the English Faculty Library (Oxford).
P.s. 1: MS. Tolkien A 21/13 fol. 119. Note by Tolkien, 'Books in Exeter Library useful', with

shelfmarks, on back of photostat reading list dated October 1913. Tolkien writes: 'All EETS publications'. [Tolkien Papers, Bodleian Library, Oxford].
P.s. 2: *Sir Gawain and the Green Knight* (1925), p. 95 line 774 *Sayn Gilyan*. Tolkien and Gordon cite p. 256'st. Julian the Confessor'.
S.s.: Shippey (1992), p. 300.

1055. _____. 'De Erkenwalde (S. Erkenwald tauft einen Leichnam) aus MS. Harl. 2250'. *Altenglische legenden*. Heilbronn: Gebr. Henninger, 1881, pp. 265-74.
Collection: Tolkien's personal Celtic library, preserved at the Weston library under the auspices of the English Faculty Library (Oxford).
P.s. 1: *Sir Gawain and the Green Knight* (1925), p. xxv.
P.s. 2: *Sir Gawain and the Green Knight* (1967) 'Select Bibliography', p. 153.

1056. _____. 'King Horn nach MS. Laud 108'. *Archiv für das Studium der neueren Sprachen und Literaturen*, Vol. L. Braunschweig: Druk und verlag von George Westermann, 1872, pp. 39-58.
P.s.: MS. Tolkien A 13/1 *annotated texts of King Horn* fol. 94. [Tolkien Papers, Bodleian Library, Oxford].

1057. _____. 'Die Legenden des MS. Laud 108'. *Archiv für das Studium der neueren Sprachen und Literaturen*, Vol. XLIX. Braunschweig: Druk und verlag von George Westermann, 1872, pp. 395-414.
P.s.: MS. Tolkien A 13/1 *annotated texts of King Horn* fol. 94. [Tolkien Papers, Bodleian Library, Oxford].

1058. _____. *The Minor poems of the Vernon MS.*, Vol. I. Series: E.E.T.S. (Early English Text Society), OS 98. Side-notes by Frederick J. Furnivall. London: Published for the Early English Text Society by Kegan Paul, Trench, Trübner and Co., 1892.
P.s. 1: MS. Tolkien A 21/13 fol. 119. Note by Tolkien, 'Books in Exeter Library useful', with shelfmarks, on back of photostat reading list dated October 1913. Tolkien writes: 'All EETS publications'. [Tolkien Papers, Bodleian Library, Oxford].
P.s. 2: *Sir Gawain and the Green Knight* (1925), p. 92 line 642 *þe fyue woundeȝ*. Tolkien and Gordon cite pp. 22, 48, 131; p. 111, line 1881 *þe more and þe mynne*.

1059. _____ (Edited by). *Yorkshire Writers: Richard Rolle of Hampole an English Father of the Church and his followers*, Vol. I. London: Swan Sonnenschein and Co., 1895.
Description: Autographed and dated on the back of the first blank page in ink: 'J.R.R. Tolkien | 1922'.
Collection: Private [Pieter Collier].

1060. _____ (Edited by). *Yorkshire Writers: Richard Rolle of Hampole an English Father of the Church and his followers*, Vol. II. London: Swan Sonnenschein and Co., 1895.
Collection: Private [Pieter Collier].

1061. Howard, Robert E. *Shadows in the Moonlight*.
S.s. 1: Rateliff (2005), p. 4 'de Camp: [Tolkien] said something casual to him about involvement with Howard's Conan stories [as an editor and author], and he said he 'rather liked them'. I don't know if he had read any other Conan besides'shadows in the moonlight' but I rather doubt it'.
S.s. 2: Scull-Hammond (2017c), p. 1058.

1062. How, Ruth W. *Adventures at Friendly Farm*. London: Hollis & Carter, 1948.

S.s.: Scull-Hammond (2017a), p. 375. [12 December 1949] For Christmas Tolkien sends his grandson, Michael George, two books 'Written by a very nice lady that I met at Sidmouth'. This is probably one of the two.

1063. _____. *The Friendly Farm*. London: Hollis & Carter, 1946.
S.s.: Scull-Hammond (2017a), p. 375. [12 December 1949] For Christmas Tolkien sends his grandson, Michael George, two books 'Written by a very nice lady that I met at Sidmouth'. This is probably one of the two.

1064. Hübner, Ernst Willibald Emil. *Inscriptiones Britanniae christianae*. Berolini: Georgium Reimerum; Londini: Williams et Norgate, 1876.
P.s.: *The Name 'Nodens'* (1932), p. 133. Tolkien quotes *Nudi Dumnogeni* from n. 209 p. 75.

1065. Huchon, René. *Histoire de la Langue anglaise*, Vol. I – Des Origines a la Conquéte normande (450-1066). Paris: Colin, 1923.
P.s.: *Philology: General Works* (IV 1924, for 1923), p. 34.

1066. Hughes, Arthur Montague d'Urban (Edited by). *Edmund Burke. Selections. With essays by Hazlitt*. Oxford: At the Clarendon Press, 1921.
S.s.: University of Leeds (1921), p. 141. English Literature, text selected for 1921-22. Ordinary Degree of B.A.; p. 190 English Language and Literature. Int. 1 Intermediate Course (Literature).

1067. _____. (Edited by). De necessariis observantiis scaccarii dialogus, commonly called Dialogus de scaccario, by Richard, son of Nigel, Treasurer of England and Bishop of London. Oxford: At the Clarendon Press, 1902.
Description: From flyleaf in Tolkien's hand: 'JRR Tolkien 1922 (from W. Warde Fowler's library)'. Collection: Private [Sold by Loome Theological Booksellers, 1993].

1068. Hugo, Victor. *Préface de 'Cromwell'*. Oxford: At the Clarendon Press, 1916.
S.s.: University of Leeds (1921), p. 141. English Literature, text selected for 1921-22. Ordinary Degree of B.A.; p. 154. English Language and Literature - Scheme A. Texts and Period selected for 1921-22. (e) History of Criticism: Special Texts suggested for study. Ordinary Degree of B.A. with Honours. Final Examinations.

1069. Hulbert, James R. 'The name of the Green Knight'. *The Manly Anniversary Studies in Language and Literature*. Chicago: The University of Chicago Press, 1923, pp. 12-19.
P.s.: *Sir Gawain and the Green Knight* (1925), p. 114, line 2445 Bercilak de Hautdesert.

1070. _____. 'Syr Gawayn and the Grene Knyȝt'. *Modern Philology*, Vol. XIII. Chicago: The University of Chicago Press, 1915-1916, pp. 433, 689.
P.s.: *Sir Gawain and the Green Knight* (1925), p. xxvi. Tolkien and Gordon write: 'For bibliography of the Irish and French analogues of *Sir Gawain*, see the bibliography in Kittredge's study'. [*NED*] In Kittredge's study, this article is mentioned in 'II. Gawain and the Green Knight' (p. 295).

1071. Humbert, Agnes. *Verbal Repetition in the Ancren Riwle*. Washington D.C.: Catholic University of America Press, 1944.
Collection: Tolkien's personal Celtic library, preserved at the Weston library under the auspices of the English Faculty Library (Oxford).

1072. Huon de Rotelande. *Ipomedon in drei englischen Bearbeitungen*. Edited by Eugen Kölbing. Breslau: W. Koebner, 1889.
P.s. 1: *Sir Gawain and the Green Knight* (1925), p. 100, line 1139 ff. Tolkien and Gordon cite lines 587-680.
P.s. 2: *Sir Gawain and the Green Knight* (1967) 'Select Bibliography: editions of texts quoted more than once in the notes', p. 156.

1073. Hutchinson, Thomas. *The History of the County of Cumberland: and some places adjacent, from the earliest accounts to the present time*, Vol. I. Carlisle: Printed by F. Jollie, 1794.

P.s.: *Sir Gawain and the Green Knight* (1925), p. 94 line 709. Tolkien and Gordon cite p. 512 'Parish of Hutton'.

1074. Huxley, Aldous. *Ends and means. An enquiry into the nature of ideals and into the methods employed for their realization*. London: Chatto & Windus, 1937.
P.s.: *Tolkien On Fairy-stories* (2008), p. 118.

1075. Huxley, Thomas Henry. *Physiography*. London: Macmillan and Co. Ltd., 1877.
P.s.: *The Notion Club Papers* (1945), p. 208. Tolkien quotes:'symmetrical solid shape assumed spontaneously by lifeless matter' (ch. iv p. 59).

1076. Hwon Holy *Chireche is Vnder Uote*. [Old English sermon, see R. Morris].
P.s.: MS. Tolkien A 21/7 fol. 47. [Tolkien Papers, Bodleian Library, Oxford].

1077. Imelmann, Rudolf. 'Beowulf' [Englische und romanische Philologie und Literaturgeschichte: Beowulf]. Review of Schücking's in *Deutsche Literaturzeitung für Kritik der internationalen Wissenschaft*, XXX. Berlin: Akademie Verlag, 1909, pp. 995-1000.
P.s.: *Finn and Hengest* (1982), p. 67 n. 65.

1078. Innocent III, Pope. *De Miseria Conditionis Humanae*.
P.s.: *A Middle English Vocabulary* (1922). Tolkien refers in the *Index of names* under 'Innocent, Pope'.

1079. Irving, Edward Burroughs (Edited by). *The Old English Exodus*. Series: Yale studies in English, 122. New Haven, Yale University Press, 1953.
P.s.: *The Old English Exodus* (1982), p. ix.

1080. _____ (Edited by). *The Old English Exodus. With supplementary bibliography*. Hamden, Conn: Archon Books, 1970.
P.s.: *The Old English Exodus* (1982), p. ix.

1081. Isidore of Seville, Saint. *Etymologiarum sive Originvm libri XX*. Edited by William Martin Lindsay. Oxonii: E typographeo Clarendoniano, 1911.
P.s.: *Sigelwara land* (1932), pp. 188 ff. n. 1. Tolkien cites: '*Arfaxat*' VII vi 21'; 191 'XII ii 39, 127, XIV v 14'; 192 'IX ii 127-9, XIV v 14-17'.

1082. *Jack and the Beanstalk*. [English fairy tale, see Jacobs].
P.s. 1: *Beowulf* (2002) 'Version A', p. 53.
P.s. 2: *Beowulf* (2002) 'Version B', p. 107.
P.s. 3: *Beowulf* (2002) 'Textual Notes A-Text', p. 331.
P.s. 4: *Beowulf* (2013), p. 12. Tolkien cites *Jack and the Beanstalk*.

1083. *Jack the Giant-Killer*. [English fairy tale, see Jacobs and Lang].
P.s.: MS. Tolkien A 12/1 *Commentary on Sir Gawain, lines 37-1987* fol. 34. Tolkien quotes: 'Fee, fi, fo, fum, I smell the blood of an Englishman'. [Tolkien Papers, Bodleian Library, Oxford].
S.s.: Scull-Hammond (2017b), p. 611

1084. Jackson, Issac. '*Sir Gawain and the Green Knight*. Considered as a *Garter Poem*'. *Anglia. Zeitschrift für Englische Philologie*, Vol. XXXVII. Halle: Max Niemeyer, 1913, pp. 393-423.
P.s.: *Sir Gawain and the Green Knight* (1925), p. xx line 1; p. xxvi. Tolkien and Gordon write: 'For bibliography of the Irish and French analogues of *Sir Gawain*, see the bibliography in Kittredge's study'. In Kittredge's study, this article is mentioned in 'II. *Gawain and the Green Knight*' (p. 296).

1085. Jacob, Henry. 'On Language Making'. Pamphlet printing of a paper read to the Philological Society on 6 February 1948. London: Dennis Dobson, 1948.
   Description: Inscribed by Tolkien 'Very interesting paper'. Includes a label added by Stan Revell to books owned by Tolkien, 'From the Library of J.R.R. Tolkien'.
   Collection: Private [Christina Scull & Wayne G. Hammond].
   S.s.: Scull-Hammond (2018a).

1086. Jacobs, Joseph. *Celtic Fairy Tales*. London: David Nutt, 1892.
   S.s.: *The Lay of Aotrou & Itroun* (2016), p. 32.

1087. _____. *English Fairy Tales*. London: David Nutt, 1890.
   P.s. 1: *Beowulf* (2013), p. 12. Tolkien cites *Jack and the Beanstalk*.
   P.s. 2: *On Fairy-stories* (1947), pp. 46, 48, 82 n. 3.
   P.s. 3: *Tolkien On Fairy-stories* (2008), pp. 36, 38, 76 n. 3.
   P.s. 4: *Tolkien On Fairy-stories* (2008) 'Manuscript A. [MS Tolkien 4, fols. 59-77]', p. 178.
   P.s. 5: *Tolkien On Fairy-stories* (2008) 'Manuscript B [MS. Tolkien 4, fols. 73-120]', pp. 217, 215, 218. 244.
   P.s. 6: *Tolkien On Fairy-stories* (2008) 'Manuscript B [MS. Tolkien 14, fol. 25]', p. 281.

1088. Jacobsohn, Hermann. 'Zum Vokalismus der germanischen und litanischen Lehnwörter im Ostseefinnischen'. *Streitberg-Festgabe* [A. 2228]. Leipzig: Market und Petter, 1924.
   P.s.: *Philology: General Works* (V 1926, for 1924).

1089. Jacobus de Voragine, *Legenda Aurea*.
   P.s.: *Sir Gawain and the Green Knight* (1925), p. 95, line 774 *Sayn Gilyan*. Olkien and Gordon cite '(Chap. XXX, I and iv)' 'De Sancto Juliano'.

1090. Jagger, Hubert. *Modern English*. University of London, 1925.
   P.s.: *Philology: General Works* (VI 1927, for 1925), p. 59 n. 18.

1091. Jakobsen, Jakob. *Færøske. Folkesagn og æventyr. Udgivne for Samfund til udgivelse af gammel nordisk litteratur*. Series: Samfund til udgivelse af gammel Nordisk literatur, 27. København: S. L. Møller, 1898-1901.
   Description: Inscribed: 'Helen Mc. H. Buckurst. | 1924.' Autographed and dated on front title page: '1933'.
   Collection: Tolkien's personal Celtic library, preserved at the Weston library under the auspices of the English Faculty Library (Oxford).

1092. James, Montague Rhodes. *Ghost-stories of an antiquary*. London: Edward Arnold, 1904.
   P.s.: *Tolkien On Fairy-stories* (2008) 'Manuscript B [MS. Tolkien 6, fol. 113]', p. 261.

1093. _____. *More ghost stories of an antiquary*. London: Edward Arnold, 1911.
   P.s.: *Tolkien On Fairy-stories* (2008) 'Manuscript B [MS. Tolkien 6, fol. 113]', p. 261.

1094. Jamieson, Robert. *Popular Ballads and Songs, from Tradition, Manuscripts, and scarce editions*, Vol. I. Edinburgh: A. Constable and Co., 1806.
   P.s.: *On Fairy-stories* (1947), p. 39.

1095. _____. *Popular Ballads and Songs, from Tradition, Manuscripts, and scarce editions*, Vol. II. Edinburgh: A. Constable and Co., 1806.
   P.s.: *On Fairy-stories* (1947), p. 39. Tolkien quotes: 'O see ye not yon narrow road ... Where thou and I this night maun gae' (p. 9).

Section A

1096. Jean, d'Arras. *Melusine*. Series: E.E.T.S. (Early English Text Society), OS 60. Edited by Alexander Karley Donald. London: Published for the Early English Text Society by Kegan Paul, Trench, Trübner and Co., 1895.
    P.s. 1: MS. Tolkien A 21/13 fol. 119. Note by Tolkien, 'Books in Exeter Library useful', with shelfmarks, on back of photostat reading list dated October 1913. Tolkien writes: 'All EETS publications'. [Tolkien Papers, Bodleian Library, Oxford].
    P.s. 2: *Tolkien On Fairy-stories* (2008) 'Manuscript A. [MS Tolkien 4, fols. 59-77]', p. 180.
    NED: #2 h. | 'W' (1928), p. 53 'Wallop v. I. 1. b.' – c 1500 'And thenne the Knight broched hys hors, and waloped toward hys felawes' (xxi, 130).

1097. Jean de Flagy. *Li romans de Garin le Loherain*, Vol. I. Edited by Paulin Paris. Series: Romans des douze pairs de France, 2. Paris: Techener, 1833.
    P.s.: *Sir Gawain and the Green Knight* (1925), p. 105, line 1412 ff. Tolkien and Gordon cite 'Livre V, Caps 2, 3, 4'; p. 108 line 1593 ff. T. and G. quote: 'Begues l'attent, … li fer passé'.

1098. Jeanroy, Alfred. *Les Origines de la poésie lyrique en France au Moyen Âge*. Paris: Hachette, 1889.
    P.s.: *Sir Gawain and the Green Knight* (1925), p. 81 line 43 *caroles*.

1099. Jenks, Edward. *The government of the British empire, as at the end of 1917*. London: J. Murray, 1918.
    Description: Tolkien requested the book on 6 February 1940 (MS. Library Records b. 629). Weston Library (Oxford), 227 e.162 (ex S. Hist. Eng. 32).

1100. Jennings, Elizabeth. *A Way of Looking*. London: André Deutsch, 1955.
    Notes: December 1955: A copy was sent to Tolkien by Jennings with dedication.
    P.s.: Tolkien's unpublished letter to Elizabeth Jennings, 2 December 1955. Tolkien congratulates Jennings on the publication of her poetry book *A Way of Looking* and discusses the merits of W. H. Auden's *Shield of Achilles*, and mentions the review of both books in *Time and Tide*.
    S.s.: Scull-Hammond (2017a), p. 506.

1101. Jespersen, Otto. *Growth and Structure of the English Language*. Leipzig: B. G. Teubner, 1912.
    P.s.: *Philology: General Works* (V 1926, for 1924), p. 52.
    S.s. 1: University of Leeds (1920), p. 182. English Language and Literature. F2. Final Course (English Literature and Language). Books reccomended.
    S.s. 2: University of Leeds (1921), p. 193 English Language and Literature. F2. Final Course (English Literature and Language). Books recommended; p. 192 English Language and Literature. Honours and M.A. Courses. A. Language. H1. First Year. Books Recommended.

1102. _____. *Mankind, nation and individual from a linguistic point of view*. Oslo, H. Aschehoug; Cambridge, Mass., Harvard University Press, 1925.
    P.s.: *Philology: General Works* (VI 1927, for 1925), p. 56.

1103. _____. *Menneskehed, nasjon, og individ i sproget*. Series: Instituttet for sammenlignende kulturforskning; Publikasjoner. Oslo: H. Aschehoug, 1925.
    P.s.: *Philology: General Works* (VI 1927, for 1925), p. 56 n. 12.

1104. _____. *Modersmålets fonetik*. København og Kristiania Gyldendalske Boghandel, 1922.
    Description: Autographed on front flyleaf.
    Collection: Tolkien's personal Celtic library, preserved at the Weston library under the auspices of the English Faculty Library (Oxford).

1105. _____. *The Philosophy of Grammar*. London: Allen and Unwin, 1925.
    P.s.: *Philology: General Works* (V 1926, for 1924), p. 28 n. 1.

1106. _____. *Phonetische Grundfragen*. Leipzig and Berlin: B. G. Teubner, 1904.
   Collection: The Science Fiction and Fantasy Research Collection of the Cushing Memorial Library and Archives at Texas A&M University.

1107. Joad, Cyril Edwin Mitchinson. *The Recovery of Belief*. London: Faber & Faber, 1952.
   Description: Tolkien attends Joad's lecture, 1943.
   P.s.: *Letters* 51 (1943). From a letter to Christopher Tolkien.

1108. Jocelin, de Brakelond. *Chronica Jocelini de Brakelond: de rebus gestis Samsonis abbatis monasterii Sancti Edmundi*.
   P.s.: *Sir Gawain and the Green Knight* (1925), p. 82 line 67. Tolkien and Gordon cite chapter 46.

1109. Jóhannesson, Jón (Edited by). *Austfirðinga sǫgur*. Series: Íslenzk fornrit, 11. Reykjavík: Hið íslenzka Fornritafélag, 1950.
   P.s.: *Finn and Hengest* (1982), p. 102 n. 43.

1110. Johns, Charles Alexander. *Flowers of the Field*. London: G. Routledge, 1908.
   P.s.: Tolkien's unpublished letter to Miss E. Byrne, 1 March 1968. Tolkien writes: '*Teenage* is a long period, and there is a vast gap between one's thirteenth birthday and one's twentieth. I can name no book that influenced me deeply as a book. I found certain elements in books that I liked and stored away in memory. During most of this period I was not interested in 'Literature'. In the early part of this period things I read with most pleasure were most scientific in reference, especially botany and astronomy. My most treasured volume was John's *Flowers of the Field*, an account of the flora of the British Isles'.
   S.s. 1: Scull-Hammond (2017a), p. 796.
   S.s. 2: Scull-Hammond (2006b), p. 877.

1111. Johnson, Samuel. *Lives of the English Poets*, Vol. I. Series: World's Classics, 83. London: H. Milford, Oxford University Press, 1920.
   S.s.: University of Leeds (1921), p. 141. English Literature, text selected (*Milton, Dryden* and *Swift*) for 1921-22. Ordinary Degree of B.A.; p. 145 (*Addison*); p. 190 English Language and Literature. Int. 1 Intermediate Course (Literature); p. 191 English Language and Literature. F1. Final Course (English Literature) (ii) The History of English Literature from 1700 to 1765.

1112. _____. *Lives of the English Poets*, Vol. II. Series: World's Classics, 83. London: H. Milford, Oxford University Press, 1920.
   S.s.: University of Leeds (1921), p. 141. English Literature, text selected (*Milton, Dryden* and *Swift*) for 1921-22. Ordinary Degree of B.A.; p. 145 (*Addison*); p. 190 English Language and Literature. Int. 1 Intermediate Course (Literature); p. 191 English Language and Literature. F1. Final Course (English Literature) (ii) The History of English Literature from 1700 to 1765.

1113. _____. *London: and The vanity of human wishes*. London: Longmans Green and Co., 1893.
   S.s.: University of Leeds (1921), p. 145. English Literature, text selected for 1921-22. Ordinary Degree of B.A.; p. 191 English Language and Literature. F1. Final Course (English Literature) (ii) The History of English Literature from 1700 to 1765.

1114. _____. *Preface to a Dictionary of the English Language*.
   S.s.: University of Leeds (1921), p. 145. English Literature, text selected for 1921-22. Ordinary Degree of B.A.; p. 156. English Language and Literature - Scheme B. Texts for 1921-22. (d) Outlines of the History of English Literature. Ordinary Degree of B.A. with Honours. Final Examinations; p. 191 English Language and Literature. F1. Final Course (English Literature) (ii) The History of English Literature from 1700 to 1765.

1115. _____. *The Preface to Shakespeare*.

S.s.: University of Leeds (1921), p. 145. English Literature, text selected for 1921-22. Ordinary Degree of B.A.; p. 154. English Language and Literature - Scheme A. Texts and Period selected for 1921-22. (e) History of Criticism: Special Texts suggested for study. Ordinary Degree of B.A. with Honours. Final Examinations; p. 156. English Language and Literature - Scheme B. Texts for 1921-22. (d) Outlines of the History of English Literature. Ordinary Degree of B.A. with Honours. Final Examinations; p. 191 English Language and Literature. F1. Final Course (English Literature) (ii) The History of English Literature from 1700 to 1765.

1116. _____. *The Six Chief Lives*. Edited by Matthew Arnold. London: Macmillan, 1908.
S.s. 1: University of Leeds (1921), p. 156. English Language and Literature - Scheme B. Texts for 1921-22. (d) Outlines of the History of English Literature. Ordinary Degree of B.A. with Honours. Final Examinations.
S.s. 2: Scull-Hammond (2017a), p. 52. *Michaelmas Term 1913*: Tolkien probably attends lectures on (Samuel) Johnson and His Friends on Wednesdays and Fridays at 11.00 a.m. in the Examination Schools, beginning 15 October.

1117. Johnston, Edward. *Writing & illuminating, & lettering*. London: J. Hogg, 1906.
P.s.: Tolkien owned a copy of Johnston's *Writing & Illuminating, & Lettering*, which was inherited by Christopher Tolkien. (see S.s. 2).
S.s. 1: Scull-Hammond (1998), p. 201.
S.s. 2: Scull-Hammond (2018b). Although he may well have used other manuals or instruction sheets, Tolkien certainly used Johnston's book. The design for the decorative title border of *The Front Door*, an illustration for *The Hobbit* (*Artist and Illustrator*, fig. 135; *Art of The Hobbit*, fig. 76), is adapted from *Writing & Illuminating, & Lettering*, fig. 87.

1118. Johnston, George Burke. *The Poetry of J.R.R. Tolkien*. Blacksburg: White Rhinoceros press, 1967.
P.s.: Tolkien's unpublished letter to George Burke Johnston, 24 May 1968. Tolkien responded with a thank you note and explained that in his youth 'root' was used as 'boot' is now, i.e. slang for 'kick'.

1119. Jonckbloet, Willem Jozef Andries. *Roman van Walewein*, Pt. II. Series: Vereeniging ter Bevordering der Oude Nederlandsche Letterkunde.; Werken. Leiden: Du Mortier, 1848.
P.s.: *Sir Gawain and the Green Knight* (1925), p. xxvi. Tolkien and Gordon write: 'For bibliography of the Irish and French analogues of *Sir Gawain*, see the bibliography in Kittredge's study'. [*NED*] In Kittredge's study, this article is mentioned in 'X. Le Chevalier à l'Épée' (p. 302).

1120. _____ (Edited by). *Roman van Lancelot (XIII eeuw.)*, Vol. II. s'Gravenhage: W. P. van Stockum, 1849.
P.s.: *Sir Gawan and the Green Knight* (1925), p. 115, line 2452 Morgene þe goddess.

1121. Jones, Alexander (Edited by). *The Jerusalem Bible*. London: Darton, Longman & Todd, 1966.
Description: Contains *Book of Jonah* edited by Tolkien.

1122. Jones, Edmund. *English Critical Essays: Nineteenth Century*. London: H. Milford, Oxford University Press, 1916.
S.s.: University of Leeds (1921), p. 156. English Language and Literature - Scheme B. Texts for 1921-22. (d) Outlines of the History of English Literature. Ordinary Degree of B.A. with Honours. Final Examinations.

1123. Jones, Gwyn. *The Buttercup Field and Other Stories*. Cardiff: Penmark Press, 1945.
Description: Inscribed on front flyleaf: 'J.R.R.T. | From | Gwyn Jones | whishing him | everything

that is good | 22ⁿᵈ Dec. 45.'
Collection: Tolkien's personal Celtic library, preserved at the Weston library under the auspices of the English Faculty Library (Oxford).
S.s. 1: Phelpstead (2011), p. 118.
S.s. 2: Scull-Hammond (2017a), p. 314.

1124. _____ (Translated by). *Sir Gawain and the Green Knight; a prose translation.* London: [C. Sandford at] the Golden Cockered Press, 1952.
P.s.: MS. Tolkien A 35 *Sir Gawain* fol. 75. [Tolkien Papers, Bodleian Library, Oxford].
S.s.: Scull-Hammond (2017a), p. 415. 25 November 1952 Tolkien writes to thank a Mr (Christopher) Sandford for the gift of the Golden Cockerel Press *Sir Gawain and the Green Knight: A Prose Translation*, with an introductory essay by Gwyn Jones (1952), which he received at the beginning of a troubled term. He apologizes for his delay in acknowledging it.

1125. _____ and Thomas Jones. *The Mabinogion.* Series: Everyman's Library. 97. London: J.M. Dent & Sons, 1949.
P.s.: *Sir Gawain and the Green Knight* (1967) 'Select Bibliography', p. 155.

1126. Jones, Owen (called Owain Myfyr); William Owen Pughe (called Idrison) and Edward Williams (called Iolo Morganwg) (Edited by). *The Myvyrian archaiology of Wales Collected out of Ancient Manuscripts.* Denbigh: T. Gee, 1870 (2ⁿᵈ ed.).
Collection: Tolkien's personal Celtic library, preserved at the Weston library under the auspices of the English Faculty Library (Oxford).
S.s.: Phelpstead (2011), p. 118.

1127. Jonson, Ben. *The Alchemist.*
S.s.: University of Leeds (1920), p. 147. English Language and Literature - Scheme A. Texts and Period selected for 1920-21. (b) Special period: 1557-1637. (c) Texts suggested for study with Special Period. Ordinary Degree of B.A. with Honours. Final Examination.

1128. _____. *Every man in his humour.*
S.s. 1: University of Leeds (1920), p. 147. English Language and Literature - Scheme A. Texts and Period selected for 1920-21. (b) Special period: 1557-1637. (c) Texts suggested for study with Special Period. Ordinary Degree of B.A. with Honours. Final Examination.
S.s. 2: University of Leeds (1923), p. 81. Ordinary Degree of B.A., Intermediate Course and Examination: English Literature. Text selected for 1923-24 (ii) Texts suggestes as part of a course of general rending in the period 1579-1645.

1129. _____. *Timber: or, Discoveries made upon men and matter.* Paris: Hachette, 1906.
S.s.: University of Leeds (1921), p. 154. English Language and Literature - Scheme A. Texts and Period selected for 1921-22. (e) History of Criticism: Special Texts suggested for study. Ordinary Degree of B.A. with Honours. Final Examinations.

1130. Jónsson, Finnur (Edited by). *Atlakviða.* København: Thieles Bogtrykkeri, 1912.
Notes: Tolkien translates two portions of the Old Norse poem *Atlakviða* into Old English. 'Ætla Guðhere ‖ ar onsend' on Attila's invitation to Gðhere, and 'Þa hlog Hagena ‖ þe man heortan scear' on the death of Guðhere, sometimes given the title *Gunnar's End*.
P.s. 1: *Beowulf* (2002) 'Version A', p. 50.

1131. _____ (Edited by). *Eddalieder. Altnordische Gedichte mythologischen und heroischen Inhalts*, Vol. I. Gedichte mythologischen inhalts. Halle: Max Niemeyer, 1888.
Description: Decoratively autographed and dated on front flyleaf: '1926'.
Collection: Tolkien's personal Celtic library, preserved at the Weston library under the auspices of the English Faculty Library (Oxford).

1132. _____ (Edited by). *Flateyjarbok. MS. no. 1005 f. in the old royal collection in the Royal Library of Copenhagen = Codex Flateyensis*. Series: Corpus Codicum Islandicorum Medii Avi, I. Copenaghen: Levin and Munksgaard, 1930.
   Description: Prospectus for CJ 200 [Cor] no. I.
   Collection: Tolkien's personal Celtic library, preserved at the Weston library under the auspices of the English Faculty Library (Oxford).

1133. _____ (Edited by). *Eddukvæði*, Vol. I. Akureyri: Íslendingasagnaútgáfan, 1954.
   P.s.: *Finn and Hengest* (1982), p. 47 n. 31; p. 84 n. 6; p. 133 n. 73; p. 142 n. 92.

1134. _____ (Edited by). *Eddukvæði*, Vol. II. Akureyri: Íslendingasagnaútgáfan, 1954.
   P.s.: *Finn and Hengest* (1982), p. 58 n. 51.

1135. _____ (Edited by). *Den Norsk-islandske skjaldedigtning*, Vol. I A. Tekst efter håndskrifterne I. København og Kristiania: Gyldendal, Nordisk forlag, 1912.
   P.s. 1: *Sigelwara land* (1934), p. 110.
   P.s. 2: *Finn and Hengest* (1982), p. 86 nos. 5, 8.

1136. _____ (Edited by). *Den Norsk-islandske skjaldedigtning*, Vol. II A. Tekst efter håndskrifterne II. [København og Kristiania: Gyldendal, Nordisk forlag, 1912.
   P.s.: Sigelwara land (1934), p. 110.

1137. _____ (Edited by). *Den Norsk-islandske skjaldedigtning*, Vol. III B. Rettet tekst I. København og Kristiania: Gyldendal, Nordisk forlag, 1915.
   P.s.: *Sigelwara land* (1934), p. 110.

1138. _____ (Edited by). *Den Norsk-islandske skjaldedigtning*, Vol. IV B. Rettet tekst II. [København og Kristiania: Gyldendal, Nordisk forlag, 1915.
   P.s.: Sigelwara land (1934), p. 110.

1139. _____ (Edited by). *Den Oldnorske og oldislandske litteraturs historie*, Vol. I. København: G. E. C. Gads Forlag, 1920.
   Description: Signed twice; once on the front pastedown and once on the verso of the front free end paper.
   Collection: Private [TolkienLibrary.com, Sold on Ebay 17 July 2012].

1140. _____ (Edited by). *Den Oldnorske og oldislandske litteraturs historie*, Vol. II. København: G. E. C. Gads Forlag, 1923.
   Description: Once on the front pastedown and once on the verso of the front free end paper.
   Collection: Private [TolkienLibrary.com, Sold on Ebay 17 July 2012].

1141. _____ (Edited by). *Den Oldnorske og oldislandske litteraturs historie*, Vol. III. København: G. E. C. Gads Forlag, 1924.
   Description: Once on the front pastedown and once on the verso of the front free end paper.
   Collection: Private [TolkienLibrary.com, Sold on Ebay 17 July 2012].

1142. _____ (Edited by). *Sæmundar-Edda: Eddukvæði*. Reykjavík: S. Kristjánsson, 1905.
   P.s. 1: 'Middle English 'Losenger'' (1953), p. Tolkien writes: 'seen in *björt í búri* 'bright in bower', in *Goðrúnarkviða* II'.
   P.s. 2: *Finn and Hengest* (1982), p. 47 n. 31; p. 84 n. 6; p. 133 n. 73; p. 142 n. 92.

1143. Jónsson, Guðni (Edited by). *Fornaldar Sögur Norðurlanda*, Vol. I. Reykjavík:

Íslendingasagnaútgáfan, 1954.
P.s.: *Finn and Hengest* (1982), p. 58 n. 54.

1144. _____. *Forníslenzk Lestrarbók*. Reykjavík: Sigfúsar Eymundssonar, 1933.
Description: Inscribed on front flyleaf: 'Professor J.R.R. Tolkien | Oxford | með kveðjn frà | Guðna Jonssyni'.
Collection: Tolkien's personal Celtic library, preserved at the Weston library under the auspices of the English Faculty Library (Oxford).

1145. Jónsson, Þórleifr. *Hænsa-Þóris saga*. Series: Islendinga sögur, 5. Reykjavík: Kristjánsson, 1892.
S.s. 1: Birkett (2014), p. 257 n. 5.
S.s. 2: Scull-Hammond (2017a), p. 162.

1146. Jordan, Richard. *Eigentümlichkeiten des anglischen wortschatzes. Eine wortgeographische Untersuchung mit etymologischen Anmerkungen*, Vol. I. Spezifisch anglische Worte. Series: Anglistische Forschungen, 17. Heidelberg: Carl Winter's Universitätsbuchhandlung, 1906.
P.s.: MS. Tolkien A 11 *Notes on Pearl* fol. 114. [Tolkien Papers, Bodleian Library, Oxford].

1147. _____. *Handbuch der Mittelenglische Grammatik*, Vol. I. *Lautlehre*. Heidelberg: Carl Winter's Universitätsbuchhandlung, 1925.
Description: Autographed on front flyleaf.
Collection: Tolkien's personal Celtic library, preserved at the Weston library under the auspices of the English Faculty Library (Oxford).
P.s. 1: *Ancrene Wisse and Hali Meiðhad* (1929), p. 108.
P.s. 2: 'Chaucer as a Philologist: *The Reeve's Tale*' (1934), p. 166 n. 78.

1148. Joseph, Bertram Leon. *Elizabethan Acting*. Series: Oxford English Monographs, 2. London Oxford University Press, 1951.
Notes: Tolkien was one of the General Editors for the series. In the Introduction Joseph thanks Tolkien for his: 'comment and encouragement'.

1149. Joyce, James. *Anna Livia Plurabelle. Fragment of work in progress*. Series: Criterion miscellany, 15. London: Faber & Faber, 1930.
P.s. 1: [Mythopoeic Society, *Parma Eldalamberon* 20 (2012), Q17 'Tolkien's Name and Address and Three Prayers', p. 88-89] Tolkien writes a transliterations into the Qenya of the name 'Livia Plurabelle' (on the deleted top line) (p. 89).
P.s. 2: *A Secret Vice* (2016), p. 91.

1150. _____. *Finnegan's Wake*. London: Faber and Faber, 1939.
Description: The MSS. *A Secret Vice*, contains two pages written by Tolkien. In the text, Tolkien quotes 'stream of consciousness', Gertrude Stein and Anna Livia Plurabelle, a protagonist of the book by Joyce.
P.s.: MSS. Tolkien 24. '(fols. 44-5) notes on *Finnegans' Wake*' in 'Collection: Taylor Institution Library, Bodleian Libraries (Oxford)'.
S.s.: Scull-Hammond (2006b), p. 817.

1151. *Judith*. [Old English poem]
Collection: Taylor Institution Library, Bodleian Libraries (Oxford).
P.s. 1: MS. Tolkien 16/2 *Notes and drafts concerning Judith*. [Tolkien Papers, Bodleian Library, Oxford].
P.s. 2: *Beowulf* (1937), p. 47 n. 20.

1152. Jung, Carl Gustav. *Psychology of the unconscious*. New York: Moffat, Yard and Co., 1916.

P.s.: *Tolkien On Fairy-stories* (2008), p. 129.

1153. Jusserand, Jean Jules. *A Literary History of the English People from the Origins to the Renaissance*. London: T. Fisher Unwin, 1895.
    P.s. 1: *Beowulf* (2002) 'Version A', pp. 48, 49, 53.
    P.s. 2: *Beowulf* (2002) 'Version B', pp. 92-94, 96, 106, 116.
    P.s. 3: *Beowulf* (2002) 'Textual Notes A-Text', p. 322. Tolkien quotes: 'they sacrifice their life in battle without a frown' (p. 56).

1154. Juvenal. *D. Iunii Iuvenalis Saturae XIV. Fourteen satires of Juvenal*. Edited by James D. Duff. Cambridge: The University Press, 1904.
    Description: King Edward's School. Some annotations, with notes on back end-paper and pastedown [Judith Priestman 1994, revd. 2016].
    Collection: Weston Library, Bodleian Libraries (Oxford).

1155. *Kalevala* [Finnish epic poem].
    For editions and translations of this work, see Kirby, Lönnrot.
    P.s. 1: *Letters* 1 (1914). To Edith Bratt. Tolkien ciets *Kullervo* (Runes 31-36)
    P.s. 2: *Letters* 74 (1944). To Christopher Tolkien. Tolkien cites Runo XX.
    P.s. 3: *Letters* 131 (1951). To Milton Waldman. Tolkien cites *The Tale of Kullervo*
    P.s. 4: *Letters* 163 (1955). To W. H. Auden.
    P.s. 5: *Letters* 257 (1964). To Christopher Bretherton.
    P.s. 6: *The Story of Kullervo* (2016).

1156. Kane, Elisha Kent. *Arctic explorations: the second Grinnell expedition in search of Sir John Franklin, 1853, '54, '55*, Vol. I. Philadelphia: Childs & Peterson, 1856.
    P.s.: MS. Tolkien A 19/3 *Etymologies or history of Walrus* fols. 162-195. [Tolkien Papers, Bodleian Library, Oxford].
    S.s.: Tolkien, *Family Album* (1992), p. 42.
    NED: #2 i. | 'W' (1928), p. 58 'Walrus, 1.' 1856 – 'The last remnant of walrus did not leave us until … the temperature had sunk below zero' (ch. xiii, p. 140); 3. *attrib*. and *comb*. 1856 – 'Laden with … as much walrus-beef … as would pay for their board' (p. 366).

1157. *Kari Woodengown*. [Norwegian fairy tale, see Lang].
    P.s.: *Tolkien On Fairy-stories* (2008) 'Manuscript A. [MS Tolkien 4, fols. 59-77]', p. 179.

1158. Karsten, Torsten Evert. *Die Germanen: eine Einführung in die Geschichte ihrer Sprache und Kultur*. Series: Grundriss der germanischen Philologie, 9. Berlin: Walter de Gruyter, 1928.
    Description: Ex Libris J.R.R. Tolkien. Autographed: 'J.R.R. Tolkien'.
    Collection: Taylor Institution Library, Bodleian Libraries (Oxford).

1159. Karstien, Carl. 'Altgermanische Dialekte'. *Stand und Aufgaben der Sprachwissenschaft. Festschrift für Wilhelm Streitberg* [A. 726]. Heidelberg, Carl Winter, 1924.
    P.s.: *Philology: General Works* (V 1926, for 1924), p. 44.

1160. _____. *Die Reduplizierten Perfekta des Nord- und Westgermanischen*. Giessen: Vlg. v. Münchow'sche Universitäts-Druckerei, 1921.
    Collection: The Science Fiction and Fantasy Research Collection of the Cushing Memorial Library and Archives at Texas A&M University.

1161. Kasmann, Hans. 'Review of 'Ancrene Wisse'. Corpus Christi College Cambridge MS 402 edited by J.R.R. Tolkien' [E.E.T.S. 249]. Offprint from *Anglia, Zeitschrift fur englische Philologie*, Vol. LXXXI, Heft 3-4. Tubingen: Max Niemeyer, 1963.
    Collection: Tolkien's personal Celtic library, preserved at the Weston library under the auspices of

the English Faculty Library (Oxford).

1162. Kauffmann, Friedrich. *Deutsche Altertumskunde*, Vol. I. Von der Urzeit bis zur Völkerwanderung. Series: Handbuch des deutschen unterrichts an höheren schulen. München: Beck, 1913–1923.
    Collection: Taylor Institution Library, Bodleian Libraries (Oxford).

1163. _____. *Deutsche Altertumskunde*, Vol. II. Von der Völkerwanderung bis zur Reichsgründung. Series: Handbuch des deutschen unterrichts an höheren schulen. München: Beck, 1913–1923.
    Collection: Taylor Institution Library, Bodleian Libraries (Oxford).

1164. Keats, John. *Isabella and The eve of St Agnes*. Boston: Bartlett, 1908.
    S.s.: University of Leeds (1920), p. 135 English Literature. Texts Selected for 1920-21; p. 181. English Language and Literature. Int. I Intermediate Course (Literature).

1165. _____. *Odes*. London: University Tutorial Press, 1920.
    S.s.: University of Leeds (1921), p. 156. English Language and Literature - Scheme B. Texts for 1921-22. (d) Outlines of the History of English Literature. Ordinary Degree of B.A. with Honours. Final Examinations.

1166. Keightley, Thomas. *The Fairy Mythology. Illustrative of the romance and superstition of various countries*. London: G. Bell & Daldy, 1873.
    S.s.: *The Lay of Aotrou & Itroun* (2016), p. 32.

1167. Keller, Gottfried. *Der Grüne Heinrich 3 – Fragmente aus der ersten Fassung; Dramatische Fragmente*. Zürich and Berline: Atlantis Verlag, 1941.
    Description: Autographed: 'J.R.R. Tolkien', under the previous dedication with a name and: 'The Queen's College, Oxford'.
    Collection: Private [TolkienLibrary.com].

1168. Keller, Wolfgang. 'Keltisches im englischen Verbum'. *Anglica: Untersuchungen zur englischen Philologie: Alois Brandl zum 70. Geburtstage überreicht*, Vol. I [A. 30], 1925.
    P.s.: *Philology: General Works* (VI 1927, for 1925), p. 33. Tolkien writes: 'Professor Keller's article is none the less worthy of attention, especially in the matter of the forms in *b-* of the verb 'to be' in Old English' and 'The second part of the article ('Englisches und keltisches Gerundium') is not so striking'.

1169. _____. *Probleme der Englischen Sprache und Kultur. Festschrift Johannes Hoops zum 60. Geburtstag überreicht von Freunden und Kollegen*. Series: Germanische Bibliothek II Abteilung, 20. Heidelberg: Carl Winter, 1925.
    Description: This collection of essays (14 in German, 1 in English) was compiled to celebrate the 60th birthday of Johannes Hoops. He signed it on the first flyleaf as an ex-lbiris and made four corrections in the margin.
    Collection: Private [Tolkienshop].
    P.s.: *Philology: General Works* (VI 1927, for 1925), p. 32 n. 2, 45.

1170. Kelly, Francis Michael and Randolph Schwabe. *A short history of costume et armour: chiefly in England*, Vol. I. 1066-1485. London: Batsford, 1931.
    P.s.: *Sir Gawain and the Green Knight* (1967) 'Select Bibliography', p. 155.

1171. Kemble, John Mitchell (Edited by). *The Anglo-Saxon poems of Beowulf, the Travellers Song and the Battle of Finnesburh edited together with a Glossary of the more difficult words and an Historical Preface*. London: William Pickering, 1833.

SECTION A

P.s.: *Beowulf* (2002) 'Version A', p. 45.

1172. _____ (Edited by). *The Anglo-Saxon poems of Beowulf, the Travellers Song and the Battle of Finnesburh*. London: William Pickering, 1835 (2nd ed.).
P.s.: *Beowulf* (2002) 'Version A', p. 31 n. 1.

1173. _____. 'On Anglo-Saxon Runes'. *Archaeologia, or, Miscellaneous Tracts Relating to Antiquity*, Vol. 28, 1840, pp. 327-72.
P.s.: [Mythopoeic Society, *Parma Eldalamberon* 15 (2004), ER1 p. 95] 1918-1920, on a sheet of ruled paper Tolkien quotes: '*byð oferceald unʒemetum slidor ʒlisnaþ ʒlæshlúttur ʒimmum ʒelicust*' and 'Runic Poem. Kemble p. 341. (the poem is in Kluge, *Angel[sächsisches] Lesebuch*.)' [A. 1207].

1174. _____. *A Translation of the Anglo-Saxon Poem of Beowulf: With a Copious Glossary*. London: William Pickering, 1833 (2nd ed.).
P.s.: *Beowulf* (2002) 'Version A', p. 31 n. 1.

1175. Kendrick, Thomas Downing. *A History of the Vikings*. London: Methuen and Co. Ltd. 1930.
Collection: Taylor Institution Library, Bodleian Libraries (Oxford).

1176. Kennedy, Charles W. *Early English Christian Poetry*. Translated into alliterative verse with critical commentary. London: Hollis & Carter, 1952.
S.s.: Scull-Hammond (2017a), p. 414. [November 1952] a gift from a Professor Kennedy about which Tolkien writes a lengthy commentary and negative criticism.

1177. Ker, Neil Ripley. 'A. S. Napier, 1853-1916'. Offprint from *Philological Essays: Studies in Old and Middle English Literature in Honour of Herbert Dean Meritt*, 152-81. The Haguye, 1970.
P.s.: *Letters* 318 (1970). From a letter to Neil Ker.

1178. Ker, William Paton. *The Dark Ages*. New York: C. Scribner's sons, 1904.
P.s. 1: *Beowulf* (1937) p. 9.
P.s. 2: *Beowulf* (2002) 'Version A', p. 52. Tolkien quotes the passage from 'A reasonable view of the merit of *Beowulf*' to 'among the noblest authors' (252-53).

1179. _____. *The Dark Ages*. London: Thomas Nelson and Sons, 1955.
Description: Annotations in pencil by Tolkien. Includes a label added by Stan Revell to books owned by Tolkien, 'From the Library of J.R.R. Tolkien'. In frontespice: Tolkien written 'Correction | p. xv p. 217'. On page xv: '*Poésies populaires latines antérieures au douzième siècle*, 1843' > '*Poésies populaires latines antérieures au douzième siècle*, 1843'; on page 204: An annotation with reference to the works *Locksley Hall* by Alfred Tennyson and *A Toccata of Galuppi's* by Robert Browning; on page 217 'Gothshalk's' > 'Gottshalk's'; on page 224 'togeher' > 'together'. Collection: Private [Oronzo Cilli].

1180. _____. *English Literature: Medieval*. Series: Home University Library of Modern Knowledge. London: Williams & Norgate, 1912.
P.s.: *Beowulf* (1937), p. 47 n. 7.
S.s.: University of Leeds (1921), p. 192 English Language and Literature. F2. Final Course (English Literature and Language). Books recommended; p. 193 English Language and Literature. Honours and M.A. Courses. A. Language. H1. First Year. Books Recommended.

1181. _____. *Epic and romance: essays on medieval literature*. London: Macmillan and Co., 1897.
P.s. 1: *Exeter College library register*. Tolkien's borrowing record: *Summer 1919* from 22 May to 16 June; *Hilary Term 1920* from 21 January to 12 March.

P.s. 2: *Beowulf* (2002) 'Version B', p. 104.

1182. _____. *Essays and Studies by Members of the English Association*, Vol. III. Oxford: At the Clarendon Press, 1910.
S.s.: University of Leeds (1921), p. 154. English Language and Literature - Scheme A. Texts and Period selected for 1921-22. (d) Texts suggested for study with Special Period 1637-1700. Ordinary Degree of B.A. with Honours. Final Examinations. In particular *Address to the Reader*.

1183. Kiaer, Egil. *Garden Flowers in Colour*. Translated by Harry George Witham Fogg and illustrated by Verner Hancke. London: Brandford Press, 1959.
Description: Decoratively autographed on front flyleaf: 'E | * | From | R | Nov 1964'. [E = Edith and R = Ronald].
Collection: Private [Fr. Richard Aladics].

1184. Kidd, Mary Maytham. *Wild Flowers of the Cape Peninsula*. London: Oxford University Press, 1950.
Notes: 1969, A copy was sent to Tolkien by Any Ronald.
P.s.: *Letters* 312 (1969). From a letter to Amy Ronald.
S.s.: Scull-Hammond (2017a), p. 784.

1185. Kilby, Clyde (Edited by). *A Mind awake. An Anthology of C. S. Lewis*. London: Geoffrey Bles, 1968.
Notes: 13 April 1968: A copy was sent to Tolkien by the author.
S.s.: Scull-Hammond (2017a), p. 758.

1186. *King Alfred and the cakes*. [Legendary tale]
S.s.: Lee (2005), p. 9. Notes: In a note on 'Anglo-Saxon period' in history, Tolkien cites the stories of King Canute the Great, recorded in the 12th century by Henry of Huntingdon, and King Alfred and the Cakes: 'You can, if you like, speak of an 'Anglo-Saxon period' in history, before 1066. But it is not a very useful label. You might as well label all the jars on the top-shelf in your store cupboard as PRESERVE, and all the rest JAM. In actual fact, there was no such thing as a single uniform 'Anglo-Saxon' period: just a time when all men wore funny trousers with cross-straps, and ate too much pork and drank too much beer; a time whose chief events were the burning of some cakes by Alfred and the wetting of Canute's feet. That is a legendary time that never happened or existed, and it is not nearly as interesting as the real thing.' [MS. Tolkien A 30/1 *Lectures on Old English* fol. 70].

1187. *King Canute and the waves*. [Legendary tale]
S.s.: Lee (2005), p. 9. [A. 1186].

1188. *King Horn*. [Middle English romance, see Hall, Lumby and R. Morris].
P.s. 1: MS. Tolkien A 21/7 fol. 29. [Tolkien Papers, Bodleian Library, Oxford].
P.s. 2: MS. Tolkien A 21/13 *The English MSS*. fol. 203. [Tolkien Papers, Bodleian Library, Oxford].
P.s. 3: *Letters* 276 (1963). To Dick Plotz, 'Thain' of the Tolkien Society of America. Tolkien writes: 'I have often used Westernesse as a translation. This is derived from rare Middle English Westernesse (known to me only in MS. C of *King Horn*) where the meaning is vague, but may be taken to mean 'Western lands' as distinct from the East inhabited by the Paynim and Saracens.'

1189. Kingsley, Mary H. *West African Studies*. London: Macmillan and Co. Ltd., 1901 (2nd ed.).
P.s.: *Tolkien On Fairy-stories* (2008) 'Manuscript A. [MS Tolkien 4, fols. 59-77]', p. 182.

1190. Kington-Oliphant, Thomas Laurence. *The New English*, Vol. I. London: Macmillan and Co., 1886.
P.s.: *Exeter College library register*. Tolkien's borrowing record: *Summer 1919* from 22 May to 16 June; Long vacation 1919 from 18 June to 14 October.

Section A

1191. _____. *The New English*, Vol. II. London: Macmillan and Co., 1886.
P.s.: Exeter College library register. Tolkien's borrowing record: *Summer 1919* from 22 May to 16 June.

1192. Kipling, Rudyard. *Kim*. Doubleday: Page & Co., 1901.
P.s.: Tolkien's unpublished letter to Mr. Killion, 20 August 1913. In an interesting group of early Tolkien letters providing a highly detailed account of the tragedy that bestruck him while serving as a tutor to two young Mexican boys and their aunt in 1913. 'Rushing about sight-seeing or any obvious form of enjoyment is of course out of the questions for a while so I have tried to find out what the best, most readable, and best palpable 'instructive' of boys books they haven't read. Many of these I have got in cheap editions … such as *King Solomon's Mines*, *Kim* and so forth … [Jose] is now reading *The White Company*.' [Sold by Christie's, 8 April 2003].
S.s. 1: Scull-Hammond (2017a), p. 51.
S.s. 2: Scull-Hammond (2006b), p. 816.
Reading period: 1913 (S.s.: Scull-Hammond (2017c), p. 1054).

1193. _____. *Puck of Pook's Hill*. New York: Doubleday Page, 1906.
S.s.: Shippey (1992), p. 302.

1194. _____. *Rewards and Fairies*. New York: Doubleday Page, 1910.
S.s.: Shippey (1992), p. 302.

1195. Kirby, William Forsell (Translated by). *Kalevala, the land of heroes*, Vol. I. Series: Everyman's library, 259. London: Joseph Malaby Dent & Co., 1907.
P.s. 1: *Letters* 75 (1944). To Christopher Tolkien.
P.s. 2: *Letters* 131 (1951). To Milton Waldman.
P.s. 3: *Letters* 163 (1955). To W.H. Auden.
P.s. 4: *Letters* 257 (1964). To Christopher Bretherton. Tolkien writes: 'I was immensely attracted by something in the air of the *Kalevala*, even in Kirby's poor translation (1955)'.
P.s. 5: Carpenter (1977), p. 49. [1910s] 'And at about this time he discovered the Finnish *Kalevala* or Land or Heroes, the collection of poems which is the principal repository of Finland's mythology. Not long afterwards he wrote appreciatively of 'this strange people and these new gods, this race of unhypocritical lowbrow scandalous heroes', adding 'the more I read of it, the more I felt at home and enjoyed myself. He had discovered the *Kalevala* in W. H. Kirby's Everyman translation.'
P.s. 6: *The Story of Kullervo* (2016), p. 88.
S.s. 1: Shippey (1992), p. 300.
S.s. 2: Scull-Hammond (2017a), p. 24.
S.s. 3: Scull-Hammond (2006b), p. 440.

1196. _____ (Translated by). *Kalevala, the land of heroes*, Vol. II. Series: Everyman's library, 259L. London: Joseph Malaby Dent & Co., 1907.
Notes: In an entry from the Qenya Lexicon Tolkien writes 'Leminkainen 23'. For Christopher Tolkien 'the choice of '23' suggests that this was my father's age at the time, and that the book was begun therefore in 1915' (*Book of Lost Tales*, Vol. I (1992), p. 280) while 'Leminkainen' bears an uncanny resemblance to the name Lemminkäinen a 'reckless adventurer', as Kirby's glossary describes him (p. 282). (*Cfr.* Arden R. Smith (1989), p. 16; Mythopoeic Society, *Parma Eldalamberon* 12 (1998), p. 13).
P.s. 1: *Letters* 75 (1944). To Chrsitopher Tolkien.
P.s. 2: *Letters* 163 (1955). To W.H. Auden. Tolkien writes: 'I was immensely attracted by something in the air of the *Kalevala*, even in Kirby's poor translation'.
P.s. 3: Carpenter (1977), p. 49. [1910s].
P.s. 4: *The Story of Kullervo* (2016), p. 88.
S.s. 1: Shippey (1992), p. 300.
S.s. 2: Scull-Hammond (2017a), p. 24.
S.s. 3: Scull-Hammond (2006b), p. 440.

1197. Kircher, Athanasius. *Mundus subterraneus in XII libros digestus*, Vol. I.

Amsterdam: Joannem Janssonium a Waesberge, 1668.
>   P.s.: *Dragons* (1938), p. 61. Tolkien writes: 'Here is one from the *Mundus Subterraneus* of Fr Kirchner — showing a dragon of the caves of Mt Pilatus. It also shows what I rather suspect that dragons were on the dwindle'. The illustration is on page 94.

1198. Kirk, Robert. *The secret commonwealth of elves, fauns & fairies: a study in folk-lore & psychical research*. Introduction by Andrew Lang. London: David Nutt, 1893.
>   Description: Tolkien requested the book on 27 February 1939 (MS. Library Records b. 618). Weston Library (Oxford), 938 e.5.
>   P.s. 1: *Tolkien On Fairy-stories* (2008) 'Manuscript B [MS. Tolkien 6, fol. 113]', p. 260.
>   P.s. 2: #1 a. | *Tolkien On Fairy-stories* (2008) 'Manuscript A. [MS Tolkien 4, fols. 59-77]', p. 309.
>   S.s.: *The Lay of Aotrou & Itroun* (2016), p. 38-39.

1199. Kirtlan, Ernest J. B. *Sir Gawain and the Green Knight; rendered literally into modern English from the alliterative romance-poem of A.D. 1360, from Cotton Ms. Nero Ax in British Museum. With an introd. on the Arthur and Gawain sagas in early English literature.* London: C.H. Kelly, 1912.
>   P.s.: *Sir Gawain and the Green Knight* (1925), p. xxvi. Tolkien and Gordon write: 'For bibliography of the Irish and French analogues of *Sir Gawain*, see the bibliography in Kittredge's study'. [*NED*] In Kittredge's study, this article is mentioned in 'II. *Gawain and the Green Knight*' (p. 294).

1200. Kittredge, George Lyman. *A Study of Gawain and the Green Knight*. Cambridge: Harvard University Press, 1916.
>   P.s. 1: *Sir Gawain and the Green Knight* (1925), p. x (Tolkien and Gordon cite pp. 132, 136); p. xxvi. Tolkien and Gordon write: 'For bibliography of the Irish and French analogues of *Sir Gawain*, see the bibliography in Kittredge's study'.
>   P.s. 2: *Sir Gawain and the Green Knight* (1967) 'Select Bibliography', p. 154. Ch. 39 on *Gawain*.

1201. _____. 'Arthur and Gorlagon'. *Harvard studies and notes in philology and literature*, Vol. VIII, 1903, pp. 150-260.
>   P.s.: *Sir Gawain and the Green Knight* (1925), p. xxvi. Tolkien and Gordon write: 'For bibliography of the Irish and French analogues of *Sir Gawain*, see the bibliography in Kittredge's study'. [*NED*] In Kittredge's study, this article is mentioned in 'V. Le Livre de Caradoc' (p. 298), 'X. Le Chevalier à l'Épée' (p. 304).

1202. Klaeber, Frederick. 'Zu altenglischen Dichtung'. *Archiv Für das Studium der neueren Sprachen und Literaturen*, Vol. CXIII. Braunschweig: G. Westermann, 1904, pp. 146-49.
>   P.s.: *The Old English Exodus* (1982), p. ix.

1203. _____ (Edited by). *Beowulf and the Fight at Finnesburg*. London, D. C. Heath and Company, 1922.
>   Description: Some pencil notes. Loose leaves.
>   Collection: Weston Library, Bodleian Libraries (Oxford).
>   P.s. 1: *The Old English Exodus* (1982), p. ix.
>   P.s. 2: *Beowulf* (2002) 'Version A', p. 46.

1204. _____ (Edited by). *Beowulf and the Fight at Finnesburg*. London: D. C. Heath and Co., 1928.
>   P.s. 1: *The Old English Exodus* (1982), p. 34.
>   P.s. 2: *Finn and Hengest* (1982), p. 83 n. 1; p.138 n. 84.
>   P.s. 3: *Beowulf* (2002) 'Version A', p. 46
>   P.s. 4: *Beowulf* (2014), p. 114.

SECTION A

1205. _____ (Edited by). *Beowulf and the Fight at Finnesburg*. Boston: Houghton Mifflin Company, 1936.
> P.s. 1: *Beowulf* (1937), p. 29. Tolkien writes: 'The poem *lacks steady advance*: so Klaeber heads a critical section in his edition' (p. lvii).
> P.s. 2: *The Old English Exodus* (1982), pp. ix, 34.
> P.s. 3: *Finn and Hengest* (1982), p. 16 n. 18; p. 45 n. 27; p. 55 n. 45; p. 88 n. 14; p. 99 n. 29; p. 122 n. 65; p. 138 n. 84; p. 167 n. 11.
> P.s. 4: *Beowulf* (2014), p. 195. Tolkien quotes: 'One would like to know the origin of this quaint expression' (p. 138).

1206. _____. 'Concerning the relations between *Exodus* and *Beowulf*'. MLN (*Modern Language Notes*), Vol. 33. Baltimore: Johns Hopkins Press [etc.], 1918, pp. 218-24.
> P.s.: *The Old English Exodus* (1982), p. ix.

1207. Kluge, Friedrich. *Angelsächsisches Lesebuch. Zusammengestellt und mit Glossar versehen*. Halle: Max Niemeyer, 1888.
> P.s. 1: [*Parma Eldalamberon* 15 (2004), ER1 p. 95] 1918-1920, on a sheet of ruled paper Tolkien quotes: 'byð oferceald unʒemetum slidor ʒlisnap ʒlæshlúttur ʒimmum ʒelicust' (p. 135) and 'Runic Poem. Kemble p. 341 (the poem is in Kluge, *Angel[sächsisches] Lesebuch*.)'
> P.s. 2: *Sigelwara land* (1934), p. 102 n. 2. Tolkien writes that for the term *sigillum* s.v. *Siegel*.
> P.s. 3: *The Old English Exodus* (1982), p. x.

1208. _____. *Die Elemente des Gotischen: eine erste Einführung in die deutsche Sprachwissenschaft*. Berlin and Leipzig: Vereinigung Wissenschaftlichen, 1921.
> Description: Signed in the front by J.R.R. Tolkien and annotations in pencil.
> Collection: Private [Sold by Peter Harrington Antiquarian Bookseller].
> S.s.: Harrington (2003), p. 25.

1209. _____. *Etymologisches Wörterbuch der deutschen Sprache*. Strassburg: Karl Trübner, 1905.
> P.s.: *Sigelwara land* (1934), p. 109 n. 3.

1210. _____. *Urgermanisch, Vorgeschichte der altgermanischen Dialekte*. Series: Grundriss der germanischen Philologie, 2. Strassburg: K. J. Trübner, 1913.
> P.s.: *Sigelwara land* (1934), p. 105 n. 3.

1211. Knatchbull-Hugessen, Edward H. *Stories for my Children*. London: Macmillan, 1869.
> P.s.: *Letters*, 319 (1971). From a letter to Roger Lancelyn Green.
> S.s. 1: Anderson (2002), p. 83 n. 23; p. 279 n. 5.
> S.s. 2: Scull-Hammond (2017a), p. 6. 'Especially the tale of Puss-cat Mew'.
> S.s. 3: Scull-Hammond (2006b), p. 815.
> S.s. 4: *Tales before Tolkien* (2003), ch.
> Reading period: 1900 – 1906 (S.s.: Scull-Hammond (2017c), p. 1053)

1212. Knatchbull-Hugessen, Reginald. *Fairy Tales for My Grandchildren*. London: Simpkin, Marshall & Co., 1910.
> P.s.: # 1 *Tolkien On Fairy-stories* (2008), p. 308.

1213. Kneen, John Joseph. *Grammar of the Manx Language*. London: Oxford University Press, 1931.
> Description: Printed introduction to reviewers used as bookmark at pages 96, 97.
> Collection: Tolkien's personal Celtic library, preserved at the Weston library under the auspices of the English Faculty Library (Oxford).

1214. Knigge, Friedrich (Edited by). *Die Sprache des Dichters von Sir Gawain, und der sagen*. Marburg: Friderich, 1885.
   P.s.: *Sir Gawain and the Green Knight* (1925), p. xxvii.

1215. Knight, Damon (Edited by). *Orbit #2: The best new science fiction of the year*. G. P. Putnam's Sons, June 1967.
   P.s. 1: Tolkien's unpublished letter to Gene Wolfe, 7 November 1966 [Marion E. Wade Center, Wheaton College (Wheaton, Illinois)]: 'Dear Mr Wolfe, | Thank you very much for your letter. The etymology of words and names in my story has two sides: (1) their etymology within the story; and (2) the sources from which I, as an author, derive them. I expect you mean the latter. Orc I derived from Anglo-Saxon, a word meaning demon, usually supposed to be derived from the Latin Orcus -- Hell. But I doubt this, though the matter is too involved to set out here. Warg is simple. It is an old word for wolf, which also had the sense of an outlaw or hunted criminal. This is its usual sense in surviving texts.* I adopted the word, which had a good sound for the meaning, as a name for this particular brand of demonic wolf in the story. | Yours sincerely, | J.R.R. Tolkien. | *O.E. wearg | O. High German warg-- | O. Norse varg-r (also = 'Wolf', espec. of legendary kind)'.
   P.s. 2: *Letters* 297 (1967). Drafts for a letter to 'Mr Rang'. Tolkien mentions the term *Warg* present in *Trip, Trap* by Wolfe contained in this collection.

1216. Knott, Thomas A. 'The Text of *Sir Gawain and the Green Knight*'. *MLN (Modern Language Notes)*, Vol. 30, 102-108. Baltimore: Johns Hopkins Press, 1915.
   P.s.: *Sir Gawain and the Green Knight* (1925), p. xxvii.

1217. Koenders, J. A.-G. *Soeskie Tien Tien: Moi en bekente Siengi*. Paramaribo: Drukkerij Eben-Haëzer, 1944.
   Collection: Taylor Institution Library, Bodleian Libraries (Oxford).

1218. Kölbing, Eugen. *Arthour and Merlin, nach der Auchinleck-hs. Nebst zwei Beilagen*. Series: Altenglische Bibliothek, 4. Leipzig: Reisland, 1890.
   P.s. 1: *Sir Gawain and the Green Knight* (1925), p. 117, line 2523 *Brutus bokeʒ*.
   P.s. 2: *Sir Gawain and the Green Knight* (1967) 'Select Bibliography: editions of texts quoted more than once in the notes', p. 155.

1219. _____. *Englische studien: Organ für englische philologie unter mitberücksichtigung des englischen unterrichts auf höheren schulen*, Vol. XVI. Leipzig: O.R. Reisland, 1892.
   P.s.: *Exeter College library register*. Tolkien's borrowing record: *Michaelmas Term 1914* from 23 October to 11 November.

1220. _____. *Siege of Jerusalem*. Series: E.E.T.S. (Early English Text Society), OS 188. Edited by H. Harnelius. London: Published for the Early English Text Society by Kegan Paul, Trench, Trübner and Co., 1935.
   P.s.: *Sir Gawain and the Green Knight* (1967) 'Select Bibliography: editions of texts quoted more than once in the notes', p. 156.

1221. Konrad, von Würzburg. *Der Trojanische Krieg*. Edited by Johann Franz Roth. Series: Bibliothek des Litterarischen Verenis, XLIV. Stuttgart: Littearischen Verein, 1858.
   P.s.: 'Middle English 'Losenger'' (1953), p. 66 n. 1.

1222. Kottler, Barnet. *A concordance to five Middle English poems*. Pittsburgh: University of Pittsburgh Press, 1966.
   P.s.: *Sir Gawain and the Green Knight* (1967) 'Select Bibliography', p. 153.

1223. Krapp, George Philip. (Edited by). *Andreas and the Fates of the Apostles*.

Boston: Ginn & Co., 1906.
> P.s. 1: *A Middle English Vocabulary* (1922). Tolkien refers to the *Fates of Apostles* on the term 'Hom(e)' (*langne hām gesēcean*, 92).
> P.s. 2: *Sigelwara land* (1932), p. 193 n. 4.
> P.s. 3: *Beowulf* (2014), p. 310.

1224. _____. *The English Language in America*, Vol. I. New York and London: Century Co. and Oxford University Press, 1925.
> P.s.: *Philology: General Works* (VI 1927, for 1925), p. 64; 64 n. 25. Also, Tolkien cites the chapters: 'The Mother Tongue'; 'Vocabulary'; 'Proper Names'; 'Literary Dialects';'style'; 'American Spelling and American Dictionaries'.

1225. _____. *The English Language in America*, Vol. II. New York and London: Century Co. and Oxford University Press, 1925.
> P.s.: *Philology: General Works* (VI 1927, for 1925), p. 64; 64 n. 25. Also, Tolkien cites the chapters: 'Pronunciation', 'Unstressed syllables', 'Inflections and Sintax', 'Bibliography ('very extensive') and Index'.

1226. _____ (Edited by). *The Junius Manuscript*. Series: The Anglo-Saxon Poetic Records, 1. London: Routledge and Kegan Paul, 1931.
> P.s.: *Finn and Hengest* (1982), p. 99 n. 34.

1227. _____. *The Paris Psalter and the Meters of Boethius*. Series: The Anglo-Saxon Poetic Records, 5. London: Routledge and Kegan Paul, 1932.
> P.s. 1: MS. Tolkien A 12/3 *Rough text of a lecture on Sir Gawain*, 1965 fols. 17-59. [Tolkien Papers, Bodleian Library, Oxford].
> P.s. 2: *Finn and Hengest* (1982), p. 98 n. 27.

1228. _____ (Edited by). *The Vercelli Book*. Series: The Anglo-Saxon Poetic Records, 2. London: Routledge and Kegan Paul, 1932.

1229. _____ and Elliott van Kirk Dobbie (Edited by). *The Exeter Book*. Series: The Anglo-Saxon Poetic Records, 3. London: Routledge and Kegan Paul, 1936.
> P.s. 1: *Letters* 90 (1944). To Christopher Tolkien. Tolkien quotes: 'Is nu fela folca þætte fyrngewritu healdan wille, ac him hyge brosnað.' from 'Precepts', pp. 140-43.
> P.s. 2: *Finn and Hengest* (1982), p. 122 n. 66; p. 134 n. 76.
> P.s. 3: *Beowulf* (2002) 'Version A', p. 37.

1230. Kraufe, Wolfgang. *Die Frau In Der Altisländischen Familiengeschichten*. Göttingen: Vandenhoeck and Ruprecht, 1926.
> Description: Autographed on front flyleaf: '1926'.
> Collection: Tolkien's personal Celtic library, preserved at the Weston library under the auspices of the English Faculty Library (Oxford).

1231. Kretschmer, Paul. *Die Indogermanische Sprachwissenschaft: eine Einführung für die Schule*. Göttingen: Vandenhoeck and Ruprecht, 1925.
> Collection: Taylor Institution Library, Bodleian Libraries (Oxford).

1232. Kroesch, Samuel. *Germanic Words for 'deceive'. A Study in Semantics*. Series: Hesperia, 1. Göttingen: Vandenhoeck and Ruprecht, 1923.
> Description: Signed, including year: '1928'.
> Collection: Private.
> P.s.: *Philology: General Works* (IV 1924, for 1923), p. 20 n. 2.

1233. Kruisinga, Etsko. *A Handbook of Present-day English*, Vol. I. English Sounds.

Utrecht: Kemink en Zoon, 1922.
>P.s.: *Philology: General Works* (VI 1927, for 1925), p. 63.

1234. _____. *A Handbook of Present-day English*, Vol. II, Pt. I. English Accidence and Siyntax. Utrecht: Kemink en Zoon, 1922.
>P.s.: *Philology: General Works* (VI 1927, for 1925), p. 63.

1235. _____. *A Handbook of Present-day English*, Vol. II, Pt. II. English Accidence and Siyntax. Utrecht: Kemink en Zoon, 1922.
>P.s.: *Philology: General Works* (VI 1927, for 1925), p. 63.

1236. _____. *A Handbook of Present-day English*, Vol. II, Pt. III. English Accidence and Siyntax. Utrecht: Kemink en Zoon, 1922.
>P.s.: *Philology: General Works* (VI 1927, for 1925), p. 63.

1237. _____. *A Handbook of Present-day English*, Vol. I. English Sounds. Utrecht: Kemink en Zoon (4nd ed.), 1925.
>P.s.: *Philology: General Works* (VI 1927, for 1925), p. 63.

1238. _____. *A Handbook of Present-day English*, Vol. II, Pt. I. English Accidence and Siyntax. Utrecht: Kemink en Zoon (4th ed.), 1925.
>P.s.: *Philology: General Works* (VI 1927, for 1925), p. 63.

1239. _____. *A Handbook of Present-day English*, Vol. II, Pt. II. English Accidence and Siyntax. Utrecht: Kemink en Zoon (4th ed.), 1925.
>P.s.: *Philology: General Works* (VI 1927, for 1925), p. 63.

1240. _____. *A Handbook of Present-day English*, Vol. II, Pt. III. English Accidence and Siyntax. Utrecht: Kemink en Zoon (4th ed.), 1925.
>P.s.: *Philology: General Works* (VI 1927, for 1925), p. 63.

1241. Kurath, Hans. *Prospectus for the Linguistic Atlas of New England by Hans Kurath*. Providence: Rhode Island, 1938.
>Description: Annotated by Tolkien on one page. Includes a label added by Stan Revell to books owned by Tolkien, 'From the Library of J.R.R. Tolkien'.
>Collection: Private [Christina Scull & Wayne G. Hammond].
>S.s. Scull-Hammond (2018a).

1242. Kurschat, Friedrich. *Wörterbuch der Littauischen Sprache*, Vol. I. Halle: Waisenhaus, 1870.
>Description: Signed by Tolkien on front free endpaper and dated '1925'.
>Collection: Private [Sold by Simon Finch Rare Books Ltd.].
>S.s.: Finch (2002), p. 53.

1243. _____. *Wörterbuch der Littauischen Sprache*, Vol. II. Halle: Waisenhaus, 1883.
>Description: Signed by Tolkien on front free endpaper and dated '1925'.
>Collection: Private [Sold by Simon Finch Rare Books Ltd.].
>S.s.: Finch (2002), p. 53.

1244. Kurvinen, Auvo. *Sir Gawain and the Carl of Carlisle in two versions*. Series: Annales Academiae scientiarum Fennicae., Series B, 71, 2. Helsinki: Suomalainen tiedeakatemia, 1951.
>Description: On page 3, Kurvinen thanks Tolkien: 'My sincere thanks are due to Professor O. R. Reuter for encouragement, useful criticism, and valuable suggestions; to Professor J. R. R. Tolkien

for his ready advice and the generosity with which he allowed me to draw upon his outstanding knowledge of Middle English philology and literature while I was pursuing postgraduate studies at Oxford'.
Notes: Kurvinen had worked on the text as a B.Litt, student under Tolkien [See C. 35].
P.s. 1: MS. Tolkien A 12/2 *Commentary on Sir Gawain, lines 1999-2523* fol. 37. [Tolkien Papers, Bodleian Library, Oxford].
P.s. 2: *Sir Gawain and the Green Knight* (1967) 'Select Bibliography', p. 154.

1245. _____. 'The Source of Capgrave's *Life of St Katharine of Alexandria*'. Offprint from *Neuphilologische Mitteilungen*, Vol. 61, no. 3, 1960, pp. 268-324.
Description: Inscribed on the cover, in the upper right: 'To Professor J.R.R. Tolkien | with kindest wishes | Auvo Kurvinen'. Neither the title of the article nor the author's name appear on the cover, so J.R.R. Tolkien has handwritten on the cover in his typical red ink: 'A Kurvinen | Capgrave | S. Katharine'. Includes a label added by Stan Revell to books owned by Tolkien, 'From the Library of J. R.
Collection: Private [Worthpoint]

1246. La Villemarqué (Hersart de), Theodoré Claude Henri (Collected and edited by). *Barzaz-Breiz: Chants Populaires de la Bretagne*, Vol. I. Paris: Franck, 1846.
Description: Autographed and dated on front flyleaf: '1922'.
Collection: Tolkien's personal Celtic library, preserved at the Weston library under the auspices of the English Faculty Library (Oxford).
S.s. 1: Fimi (2007), p. 53.
S.s. 2: *The Lay of Aotrou & Itroun* (2016), pp. xvi-xvii, 25.
S.s. 3: Scull-Hammond (2017a), p. 126.

1247. _____ (Collected and edited by). *Barzaz-Breiz: Chants Populaires de la Bretagne*, Vol. II. Paris: Franck, 1846.
Description: Autographed and dated on front flyleaf: '1922'.
Collection: Tolkien's personal Celtic library, preserved at the Weston library under the auspices of the English Faculty Library (Oxford).
S.s. 1: Fimi (2007), p. 53.
S.s. 2: *The Lay of Aotrou & Itroun* (2016), pp. xvi-xvii, 25.
S.s. 3: Scull-Hammond (2017a), p. 126.

1248. _____ (Edited by). *Poèmes Bretons du moyen âge*. Paris: Didier, 1879.
Collection: Tolkien's personal Celtic library, preserved at the Weston library under the auspices of the English Faculty Library (Oxford).

1249. Laborde, Edward Dalrymple. *Byrhtnoth and Maldon*. London: Heinemann, 1936.
P.s. 1: *Beowulf* (1937), p. 48 n. 12. Tolkien quotes: 'hige sceal þe heardra, heorte þe cenre, mod sceal þe mare þe ure mægen lytlað' (vv. 312-3).
P.s. 2: *The Homecoming of Beorhtnoth Beorhthelm's Son* (1953), p. 1.

1250. Labriolle, Pierre Champagne de. *Histoire de la Litterature latine chretienne*. Paris: Les belles lettres, 1920.
Description: Signed by Tolkien in pencil to the front free endpaper. On page 499 this passage is underlined (it is presumable by Tolkien himself): 'Jérôme serait un saint hors cadre. Son imagination ardente, ses passions fougueuses, quoique disciplinées, sa nature violente et éruptive, le rattachent de toutes parts à l'humanité réelle. Il est profondément humain.'
Collection: Private [TolkienLibrary.com].

1251. Ladd, Charles Anthony. 'A Note on the Language of the Ancrene Riwle'. Offprint from *Notes and Queries*, no. 206. London: Oxford University Press, August 1961, pp. 288-90.

S.s.: Scull-Hammond (2017a), p. 608. 18 August 1961, Burchfield sends him a proof of an article by C.A. Ladd on the Ancrene Riwle which is to appear in Notes and Queries (August 1961), though he is not sure that Tolkien will agree with it. 20 August 1961, Tolkien reply to Burchfield and comments on Ladd's article.

1252.   Lamb, Charles. *Beauty and the Beast*. With an introduction by Andrew Lang. London: Field & Tuer, 1887.
P.s.: #1 a. | *Tolkien On Fairy-stories* (2008), p. 309. Tolkien refers to Lang introduction.

1253.   *Lambeth MS.* 187 1200. [Old English homilies, see R. Morris].
P.s.: MS. Tolkien A 21/13 *The English MSS.* fol. 203. [Tolkien Papers, Bodleian Library, Oxford].

1254.   *Lancelot and the Quest for the Holy Grail*. [Old French romance, see H.O. Sommer].
P.s.: MS. Tolkien A 21/13 *The English MSS.* fol. 203. [Tolkien Papers, Bodleian Library, Oxford].

1255.   *Land of Cokaygne* about 1300. [Middle English satirical piece].
P.s.: MS. Tolkien A 21/13 *The English MSS.* fol. 203. [Tolkien Papers, Bodleian Library, Oxford].

1256.   Laneham, Robert. *Robert Laneham's letter describing a part of the entertainment unto Queen Elizabeth at the castle of Kenilworth in 1575*. Edited with introduction by Frederick James Furnivall. London: Chatto & Windus, 1907.
S.s.: University of Leeds (1920), p. 147. English Language and Literature - Scheme A. Texts and Period selected for 1920-21. (b) Special period: 1557-1637. (c) Texts suggested for study with Special Period. Ordinary Degree of B.A. with Honours. Final Examination.

1257.   Lang, Andrew. *The Arabian Nights Entertainments*. London: Longmans Green & Co., 1898.
P.s.: # 1 *Tolkien On Fairy-stories* (2008), p. 308.

1258.   _____. *The Book of Dreams and Ghosts*. London: Longmans, Green, 1897.
Description: Tolkien requested the book on 27 February 1939, at 10:30am (MS. Library Records b. 618). Weston Library (Oxford), 937 e.14.
P.s.: # 1 *Tolkien On Fairy-stories* (2008), p. 308.

1259.   _____. *The Brown Fairy Book*. London: Longmans, Green & Co., 1904.
Description: Tolkien requested the book on 27 February 1939, at 10:30am (MS. Library Records b. 618). Weston Library (Oxford), 937 e.107.
P.s. 1: *On Fairy-stories* (1947), pp. 40, 59.
P.s. 2: *Tolkien On Fairy-stories* (2008), pp. 33, 51.

1260.   _____. *The Blue Fairy Book*. London: Longmans, Green, 1889.
Description: Tolkien made careful notes.
P.s. 1: *On Fairy-stories* (1947), pp. 43, 44, 59, 89, 243.
P.s. 2: *Tolkien On Fairy-stories* (2008), pp. 34, 43, 51, 84.
P.s. 3: *Tolkien On Fairy-stories* (2008) 'Manuscript A. [MS Tolkien 4, fols. 59-77]', pp. 177, 183, 185, 187, 189, 193, 194.
P.s. 4: *Tolkien On Fairy-stories* (2008) 'Manuscript B [MS. Tolkien 4, fols. 73-120]', pp. 213, 215, 244 Tolkien quotes: 'Seven long years I served for thee ... He heard and turned to her' (from 'Black Bull of Norroway', p. 384); 247.
S.s.: Scull-Hammond (2017b), p. 611 (*Jack the Giant-Killer, Dick Whittington, The Black Bull of Norroway* and *The Red Etin*).

1261.   _____. *The chronicles of Pantouflia: as notably the adventures of Prigio, prince of that country, and of his son, Ricard*. London: Arrowsmith, 1932.
P.s.: # 1 *Tolkien On Fairy-stories* (2008), p. 308.

Section A

1262. _____. *The Crimson Fairy Book*. London: Longmans, Green & Co., 1903.
Description: Tolkien requested the book on 27 February 1939, at 10:30am (MS. Library Records b. 618). Weston Library (Oxford), 93 e.103.
P.s. 1: *On Fairy-stories* (1947), pp. 40, 59.
P.s. 2: *Tolkien On Fairy-stories* (2008), pp. 33, 51.

1263. _____. *Custom and Myth*. London: Longmans, Green and Co., 1884.
P.s.: # 1 *Tolkien On Fairy-stories* (2008), p. 308.
S.s.: Flieger (2003), p. 28. Flieger writes: '[In *On Fairy-stories*] From Lang he took the idea of human maturation as the model for cultural evolution. This had led Lang to the conclusion that the matter of fairy-stories was *primitive* and the consequent assumption that the stories themselves were only fit for children, concepts he spelled out in one of his most widely read books, *Custom and Myth*'.

1264. _____. *Essays in Little*. Series: Whitefriars library of wit and humour. London: Henry and Co., 1891.
Description: Tolkien requested the book on 27 February 1939, at 11:30am (MS. Library Records b. 618). Weston Library (Oxford), 3962 e.20.
P.s.: # 1 *Tolkien On Fairy-stories* (2008), p. 308.

1265. _____. *The Gold of Fairnilee*. Bristol: J.W. Arrowsmith, 1888.
P.s.: # 1 *Tolkien On Fairy-stories* (2008), p. 308.

1266. _____. *The Green Fairy Book*. London: Longmans, Green & Co., 1892.
Description: Tolkien requested the book on 27 February 1939, at 10:30am (MS. Library Records b. 618). Weston Library (Oxford), 930 e.157.
P.s. 1: *On Fairy-stories* (1947), pp. 40, 59, 62 n. 1.
P.s. 2: *Tolkien On Fairy-stories* (2008), pp. 33, 51, 54
P.s. 3: *Tolkien On Fairy-stories* (2008) 'Manuscript A. [MS Tolkien 4, fols. 59-77]', p. 188
P.s. 4: *Tolkien On Fairy-stories* (2008) 'Manuscript B [MS. Tolkien 4, fols. 73-120]', p. 233.
P.s. 5: Tolkien On Fairy-stories (2008) 'Manuscript B [MS. Tolkien 14, fol. 36]', p. 293
P.s. 6: #1 a. | *Tolkien On Fairy-stories* (2008), p 308 Verlyn Flieger writes: 'In his notes, Tolkien listed four authors from *The Green Fairy Book*: 'Duelin. Kletke. Caylus. Sébillot.' More fully, these authors and their stories in this volume are: Charles Duelin, *The Enchanted Watch* and *The Little Soldier*; Hermann Kletke, *The Magic Swan* and *The Biter Bit*; the Comte de Caylus, *Rosanella, Sylvain and Jocosa, Fairy Gifts*, and *Heart of Ice*; and Paul Sébillot, *The Snuff Box, The Golden Blackbird*, and *The Dirty Shepherdess*.'

1267. _____. *The Grey Fairy Book*. London: Longmans, Green & Co., 1900.
P.s. 1: *On Fairy-stories* (1947), pp. 40, 59.
P.s. 2. *Tolkien On Fairy-stories* (2008), pp. 33, 51.

1268. _____. *The Lilac Fairy Book*. London: Longmans, Green, 1910.
Description: Tolkien requested the book on 27 February 1939, at 10:30am (MS. Library Records b. 618). Weston Library (Oxford), 93 e.410.
P.s. 1: *On Fairy-stories* (1947), pp. 40, 46, 59, 65.
P.s. 2: *Tolkien On Fairy-stories* (2008), pp. 33, 36, 51, 58.
P.s. 3: *Tolkien On Fairy-stories* (2008) 'Manuscript A. [MS Tolkien 4, fols. 59-77]', pp. 178, 190.
P.s. 4: *Tolkien On Fairy-stories* (2008) 'Manuscript B [MS. Tolkien 4, fols. 73-120]', p. 217.
P.s. 5: *Tolkien On Fairy-stories* (2008) 'Manuscript B [MS. Tolkien 14, fol. 25]', p. 280.

1269. _____. *The Magic Ring, and other stories from the Yellow and Crimson Fairy Books*. London: Longmans, Green, and Co., 1906.
Description: Tolkien requested the book on 27 February 1939, at 11:30am (MS. Library Records b. 618). Weston Library (Oxford), 93 e.119.
P.s.: # 1 *Tolkien On Fairy-stories* (2008), p. 308.

1270. _____. *Myth, Ritual, And Religion*, Vol. I. London: Longmans, Green and Co., 1887.
    P.s.: # 1 *Tolkien On Fairy-stories* (2008), p. 118; p. 308.

1271. _____. *Myth, Ritual, And Religion*, Vol. II. London: Longmans, Green and Co., 1887.
    P.s.: # 1 *Tolkien On Fairy-stories* (2008), p. 308.

1272. _____. 'Mythology and Fairy Tales'. *The Fortnightly Review*, Vol. XIII, N.S., January-June. London: Chapman and Hall, 1873, pp. 618-30.
    P.s.: # 1 *Tolkien On Fairy-stories* (2008), p. 118; p. 308.

1273. _____. *The Nursery Rhyme Book*. London: Frederick Warne & Co., 1897.
    P.s. 1: *On Fairy-stories* (1947), p. 40.
    P.s. 2: *Tolkien On Fairy-stories* (2008), p. 33.

1274. _____. *The Olive Fairy Book*. London: Longmans, Green & Co., 1907.
    Description: Tolkien requested the book on 27 February 1939, at 10:30am (MS. Library Records b. 618). Weston Library (Oxford), 93 e.124.
    P.s. 1: *On Fairy-stories* (1947), pp. 40, 59.
    P.s. 2: *Tolkien On Fairy-stories* (2008), pp. 33, 51.

1275. _____. *The Orange Fairy Book*. London: Longmans, Green & Co., 1906.
    Description: Tolkien made careful notes.
    P.s. 1: *On Fairy-stories* (1947), p. 40.
    P.s. 2: *Tolkien On Fairy-stories* (2008), p. 33.

1276. _____. *The Pink Fairy Book*. London: Longmans, Green & Co., 1897.
    Description: Tolkien made careful notes.
    P.s. 1: *On Fairy-stories* (1947), pp. 40, 59.
    P.s. 2: *Tolkien On Fairy-stories* (2008), pp. 33, 51.
    P.s. 3: *Tolkien On Fairy-stories* (2008) 'Manuscript B [MS. Tolkien 4, fols. 73-120]', p. 210.

1277. _____. *Prince Prigio*. Bristol: Arrowsmith, Bristol, 1889.
    P.s. 1: *On Fairy-stories* (1947), pp. 64, 82.
    P.s. 2: *Tolkien On Fairy-stories* (2008), pp. 57, 76.
    P.s. 3: *Tolkien On Fairy-stories* (2008) 'Manuscript B [MS. Tolkien 4, fols. 73-120]', pp. 235, 245.
    S.s.: Scull-Hammond (2006b), p. 815.
    Reading period: 1908 – 1910 (S.s.: Scull-Hammond (2017c), p. 1054).

1278. _____. *Prince Ricardo of Pantouflia*. Bristol: J. W. Arrowsmith, 1893.
    P.s. 1: *On Fairy-stories* (1947), p. 64.
    P.s. 2: *Tolkien On Fairy-stories* (2008), p. 57.
    P.s. 3: *Tolkien On Fairy-stories* (2008) 'Manuscript A. [MS Tolkien 4, fols. 59-77]', p. 190.
    P.s. 4: *Tolkien On Fairy-stories* (2008) 'Manuscript B [MS. Tolkien 4, fols. 73-120]', p. 236.
    S.s.: Scull-Hammond (2006b), p. 815.
    Reading period: 1908 – 1910 (S.s.: Scull-Hammond (2017c), p. 1054)

1279. _____. *The Princess Nobody: a tale of fairy land*. Series: Nineteenth Century Collections Online: Children's Literature and Childhood. London: Longmans, Green, and Company, 1884
    P.s.: # 1 *Tolkien On Fairy-stories* (2008); p. 308.

1280. _____. *The Red Fairy Book*. London: Longmans Green, 1890.
    Description: Tolkien made careful notes.
    P.s. 1: *On Fairy-stories* (1947), pp. 40, 48, 59.

P.s. 2: *Tolkien On Fairy-stories* (2008), pp. 33, 39, 51.
P.s. 3: *Tolkien On Fairy-stories* (2008) 'Manuscript A. [MS Tolkien 4, fols. 59-77]', p. 179.
S.s. 1: Scull-Hammond (2017a), p. 6. In particular *The Story of Sigurd* which fires his interest in dragons.
S.s. 2: Scull-Hammond (2006b), p. 815.
S.s. 3: Anderson (2002), p. 72 n. 16.
Reading period: 1900-1904 (S.s.: Scull-Hammond (2017c), p. 1053).

1281. _____. *Tales of a Fairy Court*. Series: Tales of children. London: Collins Clear-type, 1907.
P.s.: # 1 *Tolkien On Fairy-stories* (2008), p. 308.

1282. _____. *Tales of Troy and Greece*. London: Longmans, 1907.
P.s.: *Tolkien On Fairy-stories* (2008) ' MS. B', p. 243. Tolkien cites 'Perseus and Andromeda'.

1283. _____. *The Violet Fairy Book*. London: Longmans, Green & Co., 1901.
Description: Tolkien requested the book on 27 February 1939, at 10:30am (MS. Library Records b. 618). Weston Library (Oxford), 93 e.96.
P.s. 1: *On Fairy-stories* (1947), pp. 40, 59, 62 n. 1.
P.s. 2: *Tolkien On Fairy-stories* (2008), pp. 33, 51, 54.
P.s. 3: *Tolkien On Fairy-stories* (2008) 'Manuscript A. [MS Tolkien 4, fols. 59-77]', p. 188.
P.s. 4: Tolkien On Fairy-stories (2008) 'Manuscript B [MS. Tolkien 14, fol. 35]', p. 291.

1284. _____. *In the Wrong Paradise: And other Stories*. London: Kegan Paul & Co., 1886.
P.s.: *Valedictory Address* (1959), p. 237. Tolkien writes: 'As in Andrew Lang's fable a missionary turned on a critic with the words: 'Did Paul know Greek?' Some members of our School would probably have said: 'Did Paul know language?' 'Lang's fables is *The End of Phaecia*.

1285. _____. *The Yellow Fairy Book*. London: Longmans, Green & Co., 1894.
Description: Tolkien requested the book on 27 February 1939, at 10:30am (MS. Library Records b. 618). Weston Library (Oxford), 93 e.71.
P.s. 1: *On Fairy-stories* (1947), pp. 40, 59.
P.s. 2: *Tolkien On Fairy-stories* (2008), pp. 33, 51.
S.s.: Bodleian Libraries Blog (2017). December 2017, this book was called up from the closed stacks. In the book was found the last borrower had left their slip in there: Tolkien [JRR or Christopher?]. 'The slip we found was left in the book at the beginning of *The Dragon of the North* a story about a courageous youth who defeats a man-eating dragon. He manages this feat with a magic ring, stolen from a witch maiden. Amongst many of its powers, if placed on the third finger of the left hand, it turns the wearer invisible. In the end, the ring is too powerful, and the youth learns that 'ill-gotten gains never prosper' when the witch retrieves the ring and punishes him for his deception. There is a eucatastrophe- the term Tolkien coined to describe happy endings in Fairy Tales- as the youth is rescued and made king. It looks like Tolkien must have returned to consult *The Yellow Fairy Book* at least once more, as the slip suggests he sat in seat 23 of the Upper Reading Room- whereas the records from the 27th February state seat 22. He obviously liked that particular area of the reading room'.

1286. Lang, David. *Early popular poetry of Scotland and the northern border*, Vol. I. Series: Library of old authors. Edited by Carew William Hazlitt. London: Reeves and Turner, 1895.
P.s.: *Sir Gawain and the Green Knight* (1925), p. xxvi. Tolkien and Gordon write: 'For bibliography of the Irish and French analogues of *Sir Gawain*, see the bibliography in Kittredge's study'. [*NED*] In Kittredge's study, this article is mentioned in 'XIII. Rauf Coilyear' (p. 306).

1287. _____. *Select remains of the ancient popular poetry of Scotland*. Edinburgh: [Printed for Wm. and D. Laing by Balfour and Clarke], 1822.
P.s.: *Sir Gawain and the Green Knight* (1925), p. xxvi. Tolkien and Gordon write: 'For bibliography

of the Irish and French analogues of *Sir Gawain*, see the bibliography in Kittredge's study'. [*NED*] In Kittredge's study, this article is mentioned in 'XIII. Rauf Coilyear' (p. 305).

1288. _____. *Select remains of the ancient popular and romance poetry of Scotland*. Edited by John Small. Edinburgh and London: W. Blackwood and sons, 1885.
> P.s.: *Sir Gawain and the Green Knight* (1925), p. xxvi. Tolkien and Gordon write: 'For bibliography of the Irish and French analogues of *Sir Gawain*, see the bibliography in Kittredge's study'. [*NED*] In Kittredge's study, this article is mentioned in 'XIII. Rauf Coilyear' (p. 306).

1289. Lang, Leonora Blanche [Mrs. Andrew Lang] (Edited by). *The Red Book of Heroes*. London Longmans, Green, and Co., 1909.
> P.s.: #1 a. | *Tolkien On Fairy-stories* (2008), p. 309.

1290. _____ (Edited by). *The Strange Story Book*. London Longmans, Green, and Co., 1913.
> P.s.: #1 a. | *Tolkien On Fairy-stories* (2008), p. 309.

1291. Langebek, Jacob. *Scriptores rerum Danicarum medii aevi*, Vol. I. Hafniae: Godiche, 1772.
> P.s.: *Finn and Hengest* (1982), p. 55.

1292. Langland, William. *Parallel extracts from twenty-nine manuscripts of Piers Plowman: with comments, and a proposal for the Society's three-text edition of this poem*. Series: E.E.T.S. (Early English Text Society), OS 17. Edited by Walter William Skeat. London: Published for the Early English Text Society, by N. Trübner & Co., 1866.
> P.s. 1: *Exeter College library register*. Tolkien's borrowing record: *Hilary Term 1914* from 29 January to 18 February.
> P.s. 2: MS. Tolkien A 21/13 fol. 119. Note by Tolkien, 'Books in Exeter Library useful', with shelfmarks, on back of photostat reading list dated October 1913. Tolkien writes: 'All EETS publications'. [Tolkien Papers, Bodleian Library, Oxford].
> P.s. 3: *Sir Gawain and the Green Knight* (1967) 'Select Bibliography: editions of texts quoted more than once in the notes', p. 156.

1293. _____. *Parallel extracts from forty-five manuscripts of Piers Plowman, with notes upon their relation to the Society's three-text edition of this poem*. Series: E.E.T.S. (Early English Text Society), OS 17. Edited by Walter William Skeat. London: Published for the Early English Text Society, by N. Trübner & Co., 1905 (2nd ed.).
> P.s. 1: *Exeter College library register*. Tolkien's borrowing record: *Hilary Term 1914* from 29 January to 18 February.
> P.s. 2: MS. Tolkien A 21/13 fol. 119. Note by Tolkien, 'Books in Exeter Library useful', with shelfmarks, on back of photostat reading list dated October 1913. Tolkien writes: 'All EETS publications'. [Tolkien Papers, Bodleian Library, Oxford].

1294. _____. *Pierce the Ploughman's crede (about 1394 A.D.)*. Series: E.E.T.S. (Early English Text Society), OS 30. London: Published for the Early English Text Society, by N. Trübner & co., 1867.
> P.s. 1: MS. Tolkien A 21/13 fol. 119. Note by Tolkien, 'Books in Exeter Library useful', with shelfmarks, on back of photostat reading list dated October 1913. Tolkien writes: 'All EETS publications'. [Tolkien Papers, Bodleian Library, Oxford].
> P.s. 2: MS. Res. e. 308 *Sir Gawain and the Green Knight*. [Tolkien Papers, Bodleian Library, Oxford].
> P.s. 3: 'Chaucer as a Philologist: *The Reeve's Tale*' (1934), p. 137.

1295. _____. *The Vision of William concerning Piers the Plowman in three parallel texts: together with Richard the Redeless*, Vol. I. Text. Oxford: At the Clarendon Press, 1886.
> P.s. 1: *Exeter College library register*. Tolkien's borrowing record: *Hilary Term 1914* from 29 January to 18 February.
> P.s. 2: MS. Tolkien A 21/13 fol. 119. Note by Tolkien, 'Books in Exeter Library useful', with shelfmarks, on back of photostat reading list dated October 1913. [Tolkien Papers, Bodleian Library, Oxford].
> P.s. 3: MS. Res. e. 308 *Sir Gawain and the Green Knight*. [Tolkien Papers, Bodleian Library, Oxford].

1296. _____. *The Vision of William concerning Piers the Plowman in three parallel texts: together with Richard the Redeless*, Vol. II. Preface, notes and glossary. Oxford: At the Clarendon Press, 1886.
> P.s. 1: *Exeter College library register*. Tolkien's borrowing record: *Hilary Term 1914* from 29 January to 18 February.
> P.s. 2: MS. Tolkien A 21/13 fol. 119. Note by Tolkien, 'Books in Exeter Library useful', with shelfmarks, on back of photostat reading list dated October 1913. [Tolkien Papers, Bodleian Library, Oxford].
> P.s. 3: MS. Res. e. 308 *Sir Gawain and the Green Knight*. [Tolkien Papers, Bodleian Library, Oxford].

1297. _____. *The Vision of William concerning Piers Plowman: together with Vita de Dowel, Dobet, et Dobest, secundum Wit et Resoun*, Pt. I. 'Vernon' text, or text A. Series: E.E.T.S. (Early English Text Society), OS 28. Edited by Walter William Skeat. London: Published for the Early English Text Society, by N. Trübner & Co., 1867.
> P.s. 1: *Exeter College library register*. Tolkien's borrowing record: *Hilary Term 1914* from 29 January to 18 February.
> P.s. 2: MS. . Tolkien A 21/13 fol. 119. Note by Tolkien, 'Books in Exeter Library useful', with shelfmarks, on back of photostat reading list dated October 1913. [Tolkien Papers, Bodleian Library, Oxford].
> P.s. 3: MS. Tolkien A 21/13 fol. 119. Note by Tolkien, 'Books in Exeter Library useful', with shelfmarks, on back of photostat reading list dated October 1913. Tolkien writes: 'All EETS publications'. [Tolkien Papers, Bodleian Library, Oxford].

1298. _____. *The Vision of William concerning Piers Plowman: together with Vita de Dowel, Dobet, et Dobest, secundum Wit et Resoun*, Pt. II. 'Crowley' text, or text B. Series: E.E.T.S. (Early English Text Society), OS 38. Edited by Walter William Skeat. London: Published for the Early English Text Society, by N. Trübner & Co., 1869.
> P.s. 1: *Exeter College library register*. Tolkien's borrowing record: *Hilary Term 1914* from 29 January to 18 February; *Michaelmas Term 1919* from 14 October to 21 January 1920.
> P.s. 2: MS. Tolkien A 21/13 fol. 119. Note by Tolkien, 'Books in Exeter Library useful', with shelfmarks, on back of photostat reading list dated October 1913. [Tolkien Papers, Bodleian Library, Oxford].
> P.s. 3: MS. Tolkien A 21/13 fol. 119. Note by Tolkien, 'Books in Exeter Library useful', with shelfmarks, on back of photostat reading list dated October 1913. Tolkien writes: 'All EETS publications'. [Tolkien Papers, Bodleian Library, Oxford].

1299. _____. *The Vision of William concerning Piers Plowman: together with Vita de Dowel, Dobet, et Dobest, secundum Wit et Resoun*, Pt. III 'Whitaker' text, or text C, with Richard the Redeles, by Langland, and The Crowned King, by another hand Series: E.E.T.S. (Early English Text Society), OS 54. Edited by Walter William Skeat. London: Published for the Early English Text Society, by N. Trübner & Co.,

1873.
> P.s. 1: *Exeter College library register*. Tolkien's borrowing record: *Hilary Term 1914* from 29 January to 18 February.
> P.s. 2: MS. Tolkien A 21/13 fol. 119. Note by Tolkien, 'Books in Exeter Library useful', with shelfmarks, on back of photostat reading list dated October 1913. [Tolkien Papers, Bodleian Library, Oxford].
> P.s. 3: MS. Tolkien A 21/13 fol. 119. Note by Tolkien, 'Books in Exeter Library useful', with shelfmarks, on back of photostat reading list dated October 1913. Tolkien writes: 'All EETS publications'. [Tolkien Papers, Bodleian Library, Oxford].
> *NED*: #2 h. | 'W' (1928), p. 56. 'Walm, *v. Obs.* 1. *intr.* b. *fig.*' – 1399 'Þe wikkid werchage þat walmed in her daies, And ȝit woll here-after' (314).

1300. _____. *The Vision of William concerning Piers Plowman: together with Vita de Dowel, Dobet, et Dobest, secundum Wit et Resoun*, Pt. IV, general preface, notes and indexes [including glossary]. Series: E.E.T.S. (Early English Text Society), OS 67. Edited by Walter William Skeat. London: Published for the Early English Text Society, by N. Trübner & Co., 1877.
> P.s. 1: *Exeter College library register*. Tolkien's borrowing record: *Hilary Term 1914* from 29 January to 18 February.
> P.s. 2: MS. . Tolkien A 21/13 fol. 119. Note by Tolkien, 'Books in Exeter Library useful', with shelfmarks, on back of photostat reading list dated October 1913. [Tolkien Papers, Bodleian Library, Oxford].
> P.s. 3: MS. Tolkien A 21/13 fol. 119. Note by Tolkien, 'Books in Exeter Library useful', with shelfmarks, on back of photostat reading list dated October 1913. Tolkien writes: 'All EETS publications'. [Tolkien Papers, Bodleian Library, Oxford].

1301. _____. *The Vision of William concerning Piers the Plowman. According to the version revised and enlarged by the author about A.D. 1377*. Edited by Walter William Skeat. Oxford: At the Clarendon Press, 1869.
> P.s. 1: *Exeter College library register*. Tolkien's borrowing record: *Hilary Term 1914* from 29 January to 18 February.
> P.s. 2: MS. Tolkien A 21/13 fol. 119. Note by Tolkien, 'Books in Exeter Library useful', with shelfmarks, on back of photostat reading list dated October 1913. Tolkien writes: 'All EETS publications'. [Tolkien Papers, Bodleian Library, Oxford].

1302. _____. *The Vision of William concerning Piers the Plowman*. Edited by Walter William Skeat. Oxford: At the Clarendon Press, 1906 (9th rev.).
> Description: Decoratively autographed, dated on front flyleaf: 'Exeter College. Feb. 1914. | ex libris | coll. | de litt. | et phil. | germ. | etc'. Annotated in pencil on back flyleaf, and on text in pencil and ink.
> Collection: Tolkien's personal Celtic library, preserved at the Weston library under the auspices of the English Faculty Library (Oxford).
> P.s. 1: MS. Tolkien A 21/13 fol. 119. Note by Tolkien, 'Books in Exeter Library useful', with shelfmarks, on back of photostat reading list dated October 1913. Tolkien writes: 'All EETS publications'. [Tolkien Papers, Bodleian Library, Oxford].
> P.s. 2: *A Middle English Vocabulary* (1922). Tolkien refers to the *Piers Pl. B* XXI on the term 'Troteuale' (*walt(e)rot*, 146).
> P.s. 3: *Sir Gawain and the Green Knight* (1925), p. 89, line 331 *no fage*; p. 111, line 1881, *þe more and þe mynne*.
> P.s. 4: *Sir Gawain and the Green Knight* (1975), p. 21.
> S.s. 1: University of Leeds (1920), p. 139 English Language and Literature: English Language. Text selected for 1920-21. Texts Selected for 1920-21. Ordinary Degree of B.A. with Honours. Final Course and Examination. Extracts B. version, prologue and Passus i-v.; p. 182. English Language and Literature. F2. Final Course (English Literature and Language).
> S.s. 2: Ollscoil na h-Éireann G 259 (1949).
> *NED*: #2 i. | 'W' (1928), p. 57 'Walnut, 1.' 1377 – 'As on a walnot with-onte is a bitter barke, And after þat bitter barke … Is a kirnelle of conforte kynde to restore' (xi. 251-2).

1303. _____. *The vision of William concerning Piers the Plowman*. Edited by Walter William Skeat. Oxford: At the Clarendon Press, 1923.
>P.s.: MS. Res. e. 308 *Sir Gawain and the Green Knight*. [Tolkien Papers, Bodleian Library, Oxford].
>S.s.: #1 Holland (1949), p. 143. Appendix XI: Oxford Examinations for Prisoners of War. English B.2 Chaucer and his Contemporaries.

1304. *Language: Journal of the Linguistic Society of America*, Vol. 9, no. 3, September 1933. Complete issue.
>Description: Inscribed: 'JRRT'. In the table of contents, 'A Note on the Development of the Indo-European Dental Groups' by M.B. Emeneau is ticked, and 'The Germano-Celtic Vocabulary' by George S. Lane is underlined. Annotated by Tolkien on four pages (in the Lane article). Includes a label added by Stan Revell to books owned by Tolkien, 'From the Library of J.R.R. Tolkien'.
>Collection: Private [Christina Scull & Wayne G. Hammond].
>S.s.: Scull-Hammond (2018a).

1305. Lanier, Sterling E. *The war for the lot; a tale of fantasy and terror*. Chicago: Follett Pubb. Co, 1969.
>P.s.: Tolkien's unpublished letter to Lanier, 24 January 1973. Tolkien writes: 'Dear Lanier, thank you much for your letter and also for your book *The War for the lot*. I found this very original and quite unlike anything I had read before: in fact very frightening'.

1306. Lascelles, Mary. 'Alexander and the Earthly Paradise in Mediæval English Writings'. *Medium Ævum*, Vol. 5, no. 1 (February), pp. 31-48; no. 2 (June), pp. 79-104 and no. 3 (October), pp. 173-88, 1936.
>S.s.: Scull-Hammond (2017a), p. 148. 9 December 1926. The Applications Committee has appointed Tolkien and Gordon examiners of the B.Litt. thesis of Mary Lascelles of Lady Margaret Hall; p. 149 10 February 1927. Tolkien and George S. Gordon examine Mary Lascelles of Lady Margaret Hall viva voce on her B.Litt. thesis, *Alexander and the Earthly Paradise in Mediæval English Literature*, at 2.00 p.m. in the Examination Schools.

1307. Lattey, Cuthbert. *The New Testament in the Westminster Version of the Sacred Scriptures*. London: Sands & Co. Ltd., 1947.
>Description: The front free endpaper has a wonderful example of his signature, characterized by the three dots and underlying 'swoosh': 'J.R.R. Tolkien'. In the text block are numerous notes and bibliographical amendments. In some cases Professor Tolkien even corrects errors in the Bible's footnotes. There are numerous instances of burned spots from tobacco ash falling on the pages. A letter of provenance is included from a member of the family that previously owned this Bible, stating: 'This New Testament was handed down to me from my parents who had known the Tolkiens (in Bournemouth) since the sixties. They had often talked fondly about the time spent with them and used to say how they were very happy people who enjoyed the simple things in life like hearty conversation amongst friends. All the amendments within its pages are totally genuine as well as the tobacco as both my parents never smoked.' Different annotations and corrections in pencil and ink.
>Collection: Private [TolkienLibrary.com].

1308. *Laud. MS. 471* 1200. [Middle English homilies, see R. Morris].
>P.s.: MS. Tolkien A 21/13 *The English MSS*. fol. 203. [Tolkien Papers, Bodleian Library, Oxford].

1309. Lauder, William. *The Minor Poems of William Lauder*. Series: E.E.T.S. (Early English Text Society), OS 41. Edited by Frederick James Furnivall. London: Published for the Early English Text Society by Kegan Paul, Trench, Trübner and Co., 1870.
>Notes: In composite volume with: *Story of Genesis and Exodus* E.E.T.S. 7, 1865 [A. 1661] and *Lancelot of the Laik* E.E.T.S. 6, 1870 (2nd rev.) [A. 2115].
>Description: Inscribed on back of front flyleaf by JRRT: 'EETS O.S. 3. (Lauder) 7 (Gen and Ex)'.

And inscribed below, half rubbed out, the signature in pencil: 'W. Marty[n]'. Autographed and marked on next page: 'Leeds | October 1921'. Contents listed before half title page of first iten by JRRT. Annotated in pencil.
Collection: Tolkien's personal Celtic library, preserved at the Weston library under the auspices of the English Faculty Library (Oxford).
P.s.: MS. Tolkien A 21/13 fol. 119. Note by Tolkien, 'Books in Exeter Library useful', with shelfmarks, on back of photostat reading list dated October 1913. Tolkien writes: 'All EETS publications'. [Tolkien Papers, Bodleian Library, Oxford].

1310.   Lawrence, William Witherle. *Beowulf and Epic Tradition*. Cambridge, MA: Harvard University Press, 1928.
P.s.: *Beowulf* (2002) 'Version A', p. 46.

1311.   *Laws of Alfred and Ine. [King Alfred's code, including the laws of King Ine of Wessex]*
P.s.: 'Chaucer as a Philologist: *The Reeve's Tale*' (1934), p. 137. Tolkien refers to 'sect. 49'.

1312.   Layamon. *Layamon's Brut, Or Chronicle of Britain A Poetical Semi Saxon Paraphrase of the Brut of Wace. Now First Published from the Cottonian Manuscripts in the British Museum, Accompanied by a Literal Translation, Notes, and a Grammatical Glossary*, Vol. I. Edited by Frederic Madden. London: Published by the Society of Antiquaries of London, 1847.
P.s. 1: MS. Tolkien A 21/7 fol. 19. [Tolkien Papers, Bodleian Library, Oxford].
P.s. 2: MS. Tolkien A 21/13 *The English MSS*. fol. 203. [Tolkien Papers, Bodleian Library, Oxford].
P.s. 3: MS. Tolkien A 28/B Commentary on *Beowulf*, delivered as lectures at Oxford, fol. 171. [Tolkien Papers, Bodleian Library, Oxford].
P.s. 4: *Sir Gawain and the Green Knight* (1967) 'Select Bibliography: editions of texts quoted more than once in the notes', p. 156.
S.s. 1: University of Leeds (1923), pp. 135-37. Hb3. (Scheme A and B) Second and Third Year: Thursday 12.00: (ii) Second Year: Middle English Texts (*Layamon's Brut: Selections*).
S.s. 2: Scull-Hammond (2017a), p. 122. Leeds academic year 1920-1921. While at Leeds Tolkien will produce various duplicated or mimeographed pages to give to his students. The topics of such pages include the Phonology, and the Grammar of *Layamon's Brut* (November 1920); p. 135. Leeds academic year 1924-1925. Tolkien teaches Middle English Texts (*Layamon's Brut: Selections*) on Thursdays at 11.00 a.m.

1313.   _____. *Layamon's Brut, Or Chronicle of Britain A Poetical SemiSaxon Paraphrase of the Brut of Wace. Now First Published from the Cottonian Manuscripts in the British Museum, Accompanied by a Literal Translation, Notes, and a Grammatical Glossary*, Vol. II. Edited by Frederic Madden. London: Published by the Society of Antiquaries of London, 1847.
P.s. 1: MS. Tolkien A 21/7 fol. 19. [Tolkien Papers, Bodleian Library, Oxford].
P.s. 2: MS. Tolkien A 21/13 *The English MSS*. fol. 203. [Tolkien Papers, Bodleian Library, Oxford].
P.s. 3: *A Middle English Vocabulary* (1922). Tolkien refers to the *Layamon* on the term 'Biwyled'.
P.s. 4: *Sir Gawain and the Green Knight* (1925), p. 81 line 39 *þe Rounde Table*. Tolkien and Gordon cite p. 329, line 22685 ff.; p. 82 n. 73 *þe best burne ay abof*. T. and G. cite 22765 ff.; p. 109, line 1699 ff. T. and G. cite p. 451.
P.s. 5: *Sir Gawain and the Green Knight* (1967) 'Select Bibliography: editions of texts quoted more than once in the notes', p. 156.
S.s. 1: Scull-Hammond (2017a), p. 122. Leeds academic year 1920-1921. While at Leeds Tolkien will produce various duplicated or mimeographed pages to give to his students. The topics of such pages include the Phonology, and the Grammar of *Layamon's Brut* (November 1920).
S.s. 2: Scull-Hammond (2017a), p.135. Leeds academic year 1924-1925. Tolkien teaches Middle English Texts (*Layamon's Brut: Selections*) on Thursdays at 11.00 a.m.
S.s. 3: University of Leeds (1923), pp. 135-37. Hb3. (Scheme A and B) Second and Third Year: Thursday 12.00: (ii) Second Year: Middle English Texts (*Layamon's Brut: Selections*).
NED: #2 h. | 'W' (1928), p. 56. 'Walm, *sb*.²' – c 1205 'And wulc mon swa wurs dude þene þe

king hafde iboden he wolde bine ifusen to ane bare walme, and ȝif hit weore laæð mon he sculde hongie for þon' (22124).

1314. _____. *Layamon's Brut: Selections*. Edited with introduction, notes and glossary by Joseph Hall. Oxford: At the Clarendon Press, 1924.
Description: Autographed and dated on front flyleaf: '1924 | (from the Delegates)'.
Collection: Tolkien's personal Celtic library, preserved at the Weston library under the auspices of the English Faculty Library (Oxford).
P.s. 1: MS. Res. e. 308 *Sir Gawain and the Green Knight*. [Tolkien Papers, Bodleian Library, Oxford].
P.s. 2: *Sigelwara land* (1932), p. 192 n. 2.
P.s. 3: 'Chaucer as a Philologist: *The Reeve's Tale*' (1934), pp. 136-38. Tolkien writes: [*wanges* 110] 'To the examples quoted by the *N.E.D.* (from *Cursor Mundi, Alysoun, Sir Tristrem, Wyntoun*, and the *York Plays*, all northern except the second which is probably western in origin) I can only add *Layamon, Brut* 30268: *wete weren his wongen* (the earliest M.E. instance), and *Joseph of Arimathie* (an alliterative poem) 647: *I wepte water warm and wette my wonges*, both of which show the same formula.
P.s. 4: *On Fairy-stories* (1947), p. 48.
P.s. 5: *Tolkien On Fairy-stories* (2008), p. 39.
P.s. 6: *Tolkien On Fairy-stories* (2008) 'Manuscript A. [MS Tolkien 4, fols. 59-77]', p. 219.
P.s. 7: *The Fall of Arthur* (2013), p. 62
S.s.: Fitzgerald (2009), p. 53 n. 9.

1315. _____. *Layamon's Brut*, Vol. I. Text lines 1-8020. E.E.T.S. (Early English Text Society), OS 250. Edited by George Lesile Brook and Roy Francis Leslie. London: Univerity Press, 1963.
P.s.: *Sir Gawain and the Green Knight* (1967) 'Select Bibliography: editions of texts quoted more than once in the notes', p. 156.

1316. _____. *Selections from Layamon's Brut*. Series: Clarendon medieval and Tudor series. Oxford: At the Clarendon Press, 1963.
P.s.: *Sir Gawain and the Green Knight* (1967) 'Select Bibliography: editions of texts quoted more than once in the notes', p. 156.

1317. Least, Werner and Heinrich Spies. *Das Bahuvrihi-compositum im Altenglischen, Mittelenglischen und Neuenglischen*. Greifswald: Adler, 1925.
P.s.: *Philology: General Works* (VI 1927, for 1925), p. 62 n. 23.

1318. Lecky, William Edward Haitpole. *A History of England in the eighteenth century*, Vol. I. London: Longmans, Green & Co., 1907.
S.s.: University of Leeds (1921), p. 191 English Language and Literature. F1. Final Course (English Literature) For consultation on Special Period.

1319. _____. *A History of England in the eighteenth century*, Vol. II. London: Longmans, Green & Co., 1909.
S.s.: University of Leeds (1921), p. 191 English Language and Literature. F1. Final Course (English Literature) For consultation on Special Period.

1320. _____. *A History of England in the eighteenth century*, Vol. III. London: Longmans, Green & Co., 1913.
S.s.: University of Leeds (1921), p. 191 English Language and Literature. F1. Final Course (English Literature) For consultation on Special Period.

1321. Lee, Sidney and Frederick Samuel Boas (Edited by). *The Year's Work in English Studies 1920-1*. London: Oxford University Press, H. Milford, 1922.
Description: Contains a review by Margaret L. Lee, *Middle English* (41-54), on the book by

Kenneth Sisam, *Fourteenth-Century Verse and Prose*, In the first edition of 1921, it was expected the glossary compiled by Tolkien, but for a problem was entered only by the first reprint of 1922. On p. 42-43: 'It is unfortunate that this separate issue is unpaged, and that it should be entitled a Vocabulary on the cover and a Glossary within. But these small points do not obscure the fact that Mr. Tolkien has worthily completed a piece of work which can hardly he praised too highly by teachers whom experience has brought to realize the underlying unity of all literary and linguistic study worthy of the name. Mr. Tolkien gives 'exceptionally full treatment to what may rightly be called the backbone of the language', eg. he devotes much space and care to the various meanings of the prepositions to, and the various forms of the pronoun he, or the verb habben, rather than to suggested etymologies of the rare and obscure words contained in his texts. The result is a Vocabulary with exhaustive textual references, having a value independent of the extracts to which it is appended – comparable indeed in fullness and interest with Heyne's Glossary to Beowulf and a few others like it. The treatment of convertible symbols such as ʒ and g, þ and th, v I and y, is particularly to be commended.'
P.s.: *Philology: General Works* (VI 1927, for 1925), p. 46 n. 7.

1322. _____ and Frederick Samuel Boas (Edited by). *The Year's Work in English Studies 1922*. London: Oxford University Press and H. Milford, 1923.
P.s.: *Philology: General Works* (IV 1924, for 1923), p. 22. Tolkien cites 'II. Philology: General Works' by Hilda M. R. Murray.

1323. _____, Walter Alexander Raleigh and Charles Talbut Onions (Edited by). *Shakespeare's England*, Vol. I. An account of the life & manners of his age. Oxford: At the Clarendon Press, 1916.
S.s.: University of Leeds (1923), p. 81. Ordinary Degree of B.A., Intermediate Course and Examination: English Literature. Text selected for 1923-24. Note. – For a general view of the period of following books are recommended.

1324. _____,Walter Alexander Raleigh and Charles Talbut Onions (Edited by). *Shakespeare's England*, Vol. II. An account of the life & manners of his age. Oxford: At the Clarendon Press, 1916.
S.s.: University of Leeds (1923), p. 81. Ordinary Degree of B.A., Intermediate Course and Examination: English Literature. Text selected for 1923-24. Note. – For a general view of the period of following books are recommended.

1325. Leeds, Edward Thurlow. *The Archæology of the Anglo-Saxon settlements*. Oxford: At the Clarendon Press, 1913.
P.s.: *Finn and Hengest* (1982), p. 72 n. 73.
NED: #2 b. | 'W' (1928), p. 23. 'Waisted'. 1913 – 'A peculiar waisted beaker with rounded base often terminating in an excrescent knob' (ch. vii, p. 132).

1326. Legrand d'Aussy, Pierre Jean-Baptiste. *Fabliaux ou contes: fables et romans du XIIe et du XIIIe siècle*. Paris: Jules Renouard, Libraire, 1829 (3rd ed.).
P.s.: *Sir Gawain and the Green Knight* (1925), p. xxvi. Tolkien and Gordon write: 'For bibliography of the Irish and French analogues of *Sir Gawain*, see the bibliography in Kittredge's study'. [*NED*] In Kittredge's study, this article is mentioned in 'X. Le Chevalier à l'Épée' (p. 302).

1327. Lempriére, John. *Bibliotheca classica; or, A classical dictionary*. London: Printed for T Cadell, 1788.
P.s.: #1 a. | *Tolkien On Fairy-stories* (2008), p. 309.

1328. Leonhardi, Günther. *Kleinere angelsächsische Denkmäler*, Vol I. Das Laecebor Series: Bibliothek der angelsächsischen Prosa, 6. Hamburg: Henri Grand, 1905.
Description: Autographed on front flyleaf.
Collection: Tolkien's personal Celtic library, preserved at the Weston library under the auspices of the English Faculty Library (Oxford).

SECTION A

P.s.: *Sigelwara land* (1934), p. 97 n. 1.

1329. _____. *Kleinere angelsächsische Denkmäler*, Vol. II. Die Lacnunga mit grammatischer Einleitung Series: Bibliothek der angelsächsischen Prosa, 6. Hamburg: Henri Grand, 1905.
Description: Autographed on front flyleaf.
Collection: Tolkien's personal Celtic library, preserved at the Weston library under the auspices of the English Faculty Library (Oxford).
P.s.: *Sigelwara land* (1934), p. 97 n. 1.

1330. _____. *Kleinere angelsächsische Denkmäler*, Vol. III. Der Lorica-Hymnus mit der angelsächsischen Glossierung nebst einer Abhandlung über Text und Sprache des Denkmals Series: Bibliothek der angelsächsischen Prosa, 6. Hamburg: Henri Grand, 1905.
Description: Autographed on front flyleaf.
Collection: Tolkien's personal Celtic library, preserved at the Weston library under the auspices of the English Faculty Library (Oxford).
P.s.: *Sigelwara land* (1934), p. 97 n. 1.

1331. _____. *Kleinere angelsächsische Denkmäler*, Vol. IV. Das Lorica-Gebet und die Lorica-Namen. Series: Bibliothek der angelsächsischen Prosa, 6. Hamburg: Henri Grand, 1905.
Description: Autographed on front flyleaf.
Collection: Tolkien's personal Celtic library, preserved at the Weston library under the auspices of the English Faculty Library (Oxford).
P.s.: *Sigelwara land* (1934), p. 97 n. 1.

1332. Leprince de Beaumont, Jeanne-Marie. *Les Contes de fées*. Paris: Libraire Centrale, 1865.
P.s.: *Tolkien On Fairy-stories* (2008) 'Manuscript A. [MS Tolkien 4, fols. 59-77]', p. 177.

1333. Leskien, August. *Litauisches Lesebuch mit Grammatik und Wörterbuch*. Heidelberg: Carl Winter, 1919.
Collection: Taylor Institution Library, Bodleian Libraries (Oxford).

1334. Leslie, Shane. *An anthology of Catholic poets*. London: Macmillan, 1925.
P.s.: *Beowulf* (2002) 'Version A', p. 41. Tolkien writes: 'Thus the introduction to Mr. Shane Leslie's anthology of (I believe he said) Catholic poets speaks of 'Beowulf' 'as small beer'. I hope in depending on memory (for I do not possess the worthless book) I am not wrong in ascribing these introductory words to Mr. Chesterton. This ascription alone causes me to mention them. On such a matter Mr. Shane Leslie is of course already honoured more than he deserves by the mere mention of his name: his book includes what by its title seems intended for the 'Dream of the Rood' in translation, but in content is more wholly unlike that poem than the versions of plough-candidates in a provincial university. But Mr. Chesterton is difficult. Still one may guess he could not construe a line of the original and had depended on translation (if on anything but imagination). He might as well judge of English beer by visiting an American speak-easy. Old English verse - less perhaps in essence than because it is now strange and unfamiliar in metre and manner and methods of diction - does not unlock the treasures of its <u>word hord</u> readily, and least to the hasty and conceited'.

1335. Lessing, Gotthold Ephrain. *Hamburgische Dramaturgie*. Leipzig: Tempel, 1912.
S.s.: University of Leeds (1921), p. 154. English Language and Literature - Scheme A. Texts and Period selected for 1921-22. (e) History of Criticism: Special Texts suggested for study. Ordinary Degree of B.A. with Honours. Final Examinations.

1336. _____. *Laokoon*. Leipzig: Quelle & Meyer, 1907.
S.s.: University of Leeds (1921), p. 154. English Language and Literature - Scheme A. Texts and Period selected for 1921-22. (e) History of Criticism: Special Texts suggested for study. Ordinary Degree of B.A. with Honours. Final Examinations.

1337. Levens, Peter. *Manipulus vocabulorum. A dictionarie of English and Latine wordes*. Series: E.E.T.S. (Early English Text Society), OS 27. Edited, with an alphabetical index, by Henry B. Wheatley. London: Published for the Early English Text Society by Kegan Paul, Trench, Trübner and Co., 1867.
P.s.: MS. Tolkien A 21/13 fol. 119. Note by Tolkien, 'Books in Exeter Library useful', with shelfmarks, on back of photostat reading list dated October 1913. Tolkien writes: 'All EETS publications'. [Tolkien Papers, Bodleian Library, Oxford].
NED: #2 h. | 'W' (1928), p. 53 'Wallop v. I. 1. a.' – 1570 'To gallop, *fundere gradus*, to Wallop, *idem, cursitare*' (169/34).

1338. Lewis, Clive Staples. *The Abolition of Man*. Or, Reflections on education with special reference to the teaching of English in the upper forms of schools. London: Oxford University Press, 1943.
Description: Includes a label added by Stan Revell to books owned by Tolkien, 'From the Library of J.R.R. Tolkien'.
Collection: Marion E. Wade Center, Wheaton College (Wheaton, Illinois).

1339. _____. *The Allegory of Love. A Study in Medieval Tradition*. Oxford: At the Clarendon Press, 1936.
Description: Tolkien gives the book, with a dedication, to Simonne d'Ardenne.
Collection: Fonds J.R.R. Tolkien, Bibliothèque ALPHA principale, Université de Liège (Liège), Tol/049.
P.s.: *The Notion Club Papers* (1945), p. 219 n. 52.
S.s.: Scull-Hammond (2017a), p. 198.

1340. _____. *Beyond personality: the Christian idea of God*. London: Geoffrey Bles, The Centenary Press, 1944.
P.s.: *The Notion Club Papers* (1945), p. 149. Tolkien writes: 'Beyond Probability | or | Our of the Talkative Planet'. *Beyond Probability* is a pun on the title of Lewis's book *Beyond Personality* (Christopher Tolkien, p. 153 n. 6).

1341. _____. *Christian Behaviour*. London: Geoffrey Bles, 1943.
Description: Tolkien writes and keeps in his copy of the book a lengthy draft letter to Lewis commenting on and disagreeing with many of Lewis's views on the subject.
P.s.: *Letters* 49 (1943). To C.S. Lewis.
S.s.: Scull-Hammond (2017a), p. 277.

1342. _____. *The Discarded Image: An Introduction to Medieval and Renaissance Literature*. Cambridge: The University Press, 1963.
S.s.: Scull-Hammond (2017a), p. 201. Tolkien and Dagnall also discuss a *prolegomena* by C. S. Lewis which Allen & Unwin are interested in publishing as a text for students (probably his celebrated lectures 'Prolegomena to Medieval Poetry' begun in January 1932, much later partly the basis of his book *The Discarded Image*).

1343. _____. *English Literature in the Sixteenth Century: excluding Drama*. Series: Clark lectures, 1944; Oxford history of English literature, 3. Oxford: At the Clarendon Press, 1954.
P.s.: *Letters* 113 (1948). To C.S. Lewis.

1344. _____. *The Great Divorce*. London: Geoffrey Bles, 1945.
P.s. 1: *Letters* 60 (1944). To Christopher Tolkien. Tolkien writes: 'I did not think so well of the

concluding chapter of C.S.L's new moral allegory or 'vision', based on the mediaeval fancy of the Refrigerium, by which the lost souls have an occasional holiday in Paradise'.
P.s. 2: *Letters* 69 (1944). To Christopher Tolkien.
P.s. 3: *Letters* 72 (1944). To Christopher Tolkien. [Originally *Who Goes Home?*] 'a book on Hell, which I suggested should have been called rather *Hugo's Home.*' [Tolkien plays on the fact that the pronunciation of the Lewis title can mean both *Who Goes Home?* that *Hugo's Home.*]
S.s.: Scull-Hammond (2017a), pp. 284, 285, 290.

1345. _____. *Letters To An American Lady*. Grand Rapids, Michigan: William B. Eerdmans, 1966.
P.s.: Tolkien's unpublished letter to Roger Verhulst, 4 December 1967. Roger Verhulst (W. B. Eerdmans) sent him two copies. December 4, 1967, Tolkien writes appreciatively about C.S. Lewis's *Letters* to Verhulst: 'Thank you very much for your letter and also for fulfillment of your promise of two copies of LETTERS TO AN AMERICAN LADY which I gratefully received a few days ago. I have now for the first time had an opportunity of reading these letters continuously ad with full attention. I found them deeply interesting and very moving, and on certain points also to me enlightening.'
Collection: [Sold by Christie's, 28 November 2011].
S.s.: Scull-Hammond (2017a), p. 747.

1346. _____. *Letters to Malcolm: Chiefly on Prayer*. London: Geoffrey Bles, 1964.
Description: Tolkien bought the book just published. Inscribed: [That the book was not] 'about prayer, but about Lewis praying, [and] But the whole book is always interesting. Why? Because it is about Jack, by Jack, and that is a topic that no one who knew him well could fail to find interesting even when exasperating.'
Notes: Tolkien's reaction to Lewis's work, titled *The Ulsterior Motive*, was never published in its entirery, but it has survived and is currently a part of the Tolkien manuscript collection at the Bodleian Library, Oxford.
P.s.: *Letters* 265 (1964). From a letter to David Kolb, S.J.
S.s. 1: Carpenter (1979), p. 250.
S.s. 2: Scull-Hammond (2017a), p. 649.
S.s. 3: Scull-Hammond (2006b), p. 819.

1347. _____. *The Lion, the Witch and the Wardbrode*. Series: The Chronicle of Narnia, 1. London: Geoffrey Bless, 1950.
S.s. 1: Carpenter (1979), p. 222. One day in the early spring of 1949, Lewis began to read aloud to Tolkien the beginning of a new book he was writing; 223 Tolkien had said he [C. S. Lewis] 'disliked it intensely'. And when Green met Tolkien shortly afterwards, Tolkien said to him, 'I hear you 've been reading Jack's children's story. It really won't do, you know! '
S.s. 2: Scull-Hammond (2017a), p. 364

1348. _____. 'Myth Became Fact'. *World Dominion*, Vol. XXII, September-October, 1944, pp. 267-70.
P.s.: *Letters* 96 (1945). To Christopher Tolkien.

1349. _____. *Of Other Worlds: Essays and Stories*. Edited by Walter Hooper. London: Geoffrey Bles, 1966.
Notes: November 1966: A copy was sent to Tolkien by the editor.
P.s.: *Letters* 291 (1966). To Walter Hooper.

1350. _____. *Out of the Silent Planet*. The Space Trilogy, 1. London: John Lane, 1938.
Description: Tolkien gives the book, with a dedication, to Simonne d'Ardenne.
Collection: Fonds J.R.R. Tolkien, Bibliothèque ALPHA principale, Université de Liège (Liège), Tol/051.
P.s. 1: *Letters* 22 (1938). To C.A. Furth, Allen & Unwin.
P.s. 2: *Letters* 24 (1938). To Stanley Unwin. Tolkien writes: 'I read it, of course'.

P.s. 3: *Letters* 26 (1938). To Stanley Unwin.
P.s. 4: *Letters* 77 (1944). From a letter to Christopher Tolkien.
P.s. 5: *Letters* 276 (1965). To Dick Plotz, 'Thain' of the Tolkien Society of America.
P.s. 6: *Letters* 294 (1967). To Charlotte and Denis Plimmer.
S.s. 1: Scull-Hammond (2006b), p. 819.
S.s. 2: Scull-Hammond (2017a), p. 218.

1351. _____. *Perelandra*. The Space Trilogy, 2. London: The Bodley Head, 1943.
P.s. 1: *Letters* 77 (1944). From a letter to Christopher Tolkien.
P.s. 2: *Letters* 252 (1963); From a letter to Michael Tolkien.
P.s. 3: *Letters* 276 (1965). Dick Plotz, 'Thain' of the Tolkien Society of America.
P.s. 4: *The Notion Club Papers* (1945).
S.s. 1: Carpenter (1979), p. 182. When Tolkien's daughter Priscilla read *Perelandra*, she told her father that she thought the hero, the philologist Ransom who had also played a central part in *Out of the Silent Planet*, was surely meant to be a portrait of him. Tolkien replied: 'As a philologist, I may have some part in him, and recognize some of my opinions and ideas Lewisified in him'.
S.s. 2: Scull-Hammond (2006b), p. 819.

1352. _____. *The Pilgrim's Regress. An allegorical apology for Christianity, reason and romanticism*. London: Joseph Malaby Dent & Sons, 1933.
P.s. 1: *Letters* 257 (1964). To Christopher Bretherton. Tolkien writes: 'I read The Pilgrim's Regress in MS.'
P.s. 2: *Beowulf* (2002) 'Version A', p. 57.
S.s.: Carpenter (1979), p. 66. Tolkien recommended the book in warm terms to Stanley Unwin 'I read the story in the original MS.,' he told Unwin, 'and was so enthralled that I could do nothing else until I had finished it. My first criticism was simply that it was too short'. And Tolkien concluded: 'I at any rate should have bought this story at almost any price if I had found it in print'.

1353. _____. *The Problem of Pain*. London: The Centenary Press, 1940.
S.s. 1: Lewis (2009a), p. 289. Letter to his brother (W) – 19 November 1939. Lewis writes: 'On Thursday we had a meeting of the Inklings [...] The bill of fare afterwards consisted of a section of the new *Hobbit* book from Tolkien, a nativity play from Williams (unusually intelligible for him, and approved by all) and a chapter out of the book on the *Problem of Pain* from me'.
S.s. 2: Scull-Hammond (2017a), pp. 249, 252.

1354. _____. *Rehabilitations And Other Essays*. London: Oxford University Press, 1939.
P.s.: *English and Welsh* (1963), p. 2. Tolkien quotes: 'remains all his life a child among real students of English' (Lewis' book p. 92).

1355. _____. *Selected Literary Essays*. Edited by Walter Hooper. Cambridge: The University Press, 1969.
Notes: In his preface, Walter Hooper thanks Tolkien: 'My thanks to the friends who have helped me with this book are many and great. Professor J.R.R. Tolkien has given me much wise advice and permitted me to print part of a letter he wrote to me on page 18'.

1356. _____. *Studies in words*. Cambridge at the University Press, 1960.
Notes: 12 September 1960, a copy was sent to Tolkien.
P.s.: *Letters* 224 (1960). From a letter to Christopher Tolkien. Tolkien writes: 'I have just received a copy of C. S. L's latest: *Studies in Words*. Alas! His ponderous silliness is becoming a fixed manner. I am deeply relieved to find I am not mentioned. I wrote for him a long analysis of the semantics and formal history of BHŪ with special reference to φυ¬σις. All that remains is the first 9 lines of PHUSIS (pp. 33-34) with the characteristic Lewisian intrusion of 'beards and cucumbers'. The rest is dismissed on p. 36 with '*We* have not a shred of evidence'. He remains at

best and worst an Oxford 'classical' don – when dealing with words. I think the best bit is the last chapter, and the only really wise remark is on the last page: 'I think we must get it firmly fixed in our minds that the very occasions on which we should most like to write a slashing review are precisely those on which we had much better hold our tongues.' *Ergo silebo*'.
S.s.: Scull-Hammond (2017a), p. 592.

1357. _____. *The Screwtape Letters*. London: G. Bles, Centenary Press, 1942.
P.s. 1: *Letters* 96 (1945). To Christopher Tolkien. Tolkien writes: 'The minor imp of Slubgob's brood who specially attends to preventing C.S.L. and myself from meeting'.
P.s. 2: *Letters* 252 (1963). From a letter to Michael Tolkien.
P.s. 3: *Letters* 291 (1966). To Walter Hooper. Tolkien writes 'Too brief. But I am snowed up. I noticed, for the first time consciously, how dualistic Lewis' mind and imagination [were], though as a philosopher his reason entirely rejected this. So the pun Hierarchy Lowerarchy.'
P.s. 4: Tolkien's unpublished letter to George Sayer, 28 November 1963. 'But then Jack [C. S. Lewis] never sent me anything. Not even of Screwtape Letters which he dedicated to me (without permission). I was wryly amused to learn from the Daily Telegraph that 'Lewis was never (sic) himself very fond of this work'. I after/often [this word is especially hard to discern] wondered why the dedication was made. Now I know—or should'.
S.s.: Carpenter (1979), p. 174. A copy was sent to Tolkien by the author. Beneath the printed dedication, Lewis added in Tolkien's personal copy: 'In token payment of a great debt'.

1358. _____. 'Statius and Dante'. *Medium Ævum*, Vol. 35, 133-139. Cambridge, 1956.
S.s.: Scull-Hammond (2017a), p. 417. 10 February 1953: Tolkien attends a meeting of the Oxford Dante Society. C.S. Lewis reads a paper, *Statius and Dante*.

1359. _____. *Surprised by Joy: The Shape of My Early Life*. London: G. Bles, 1955.
S.s.: Sayer (1988), p. 133. In *Surprised by Joy*, he also mentions a few intermediate influences, notably, a midnight conversation with Hugo. Dyson and J.R.R. Tolkien.

1360. _____. *That Hideous Strength*. The Space Trilogy, 3. London: The Bodley Head, 1945.
P.s. 1: *Letters* 227 (1961). From a letter to Mrs E.C. Ossen Drijver.
P.s. 2: *Letters* 252 (1963). From a letter to Michael Tolkien.
P.s. 3: *Letters* 276 (1965). Dick Plotz, 'Thain' of the Tolkien Society of America.
S.s. 1: *The Notion Club Papers* (1945), Introduction by Christopher Tolkien, p. 153 n. 1. 'It may be mentioned here that my father had evidently discussed with Lewis the matter of 'true dreams': an important element in the plot of That Hideous Strength is Jane Studdock's 'tendency to dream real things', in the words of Miss Ironwood (Chapter 3, $iii), and this can hardly be a mere coincidence. It is presumably not coincidental either that there should be so many references to 'Numinor' in *That Hideous Strength* (published in 1945)'.
S.s. 2: Carpenter (1979), p. 198. [...] when Tolkien began to hear it read aloud by Lewis he thought it trivial. Yet when Tolkien had heard it right through he remarked that though it was scarcely a proper conclusion to Lewis's trilogy it was certainly 'good in itself.
S.s. 3: Lewis (2009a), p. 682. Letter to Dorothy L. Sayers – 14 December 1945. Lewis writes: 'Mr Bultitude is described by Tolkien as a portrait of the author, but I feel that is too high a compliment'.
S.s. 4: Scull-Hammond (2006b), p. 819.

1361. _____. *Till We Have Faces: A Myth Retold*. London: G. Bles, 1965.
S.s.: Lewis (2009b), p. 1647.

1362. Lewis, D. B. Wyndham, Charles Lee and Max Beerbohm. *The stuffed owl: an anthology of bad verse*. London: Joseph Malaby Dent and Sons, 1930.
P.s.: *Letters* 267 (1965). From a letter to Michael Tolkien. Tolkien writes 'stuffed owl'.

1363. Lewis, Glyn Cothi. *Gwaith Lewis Glyn Cothi: The Poetical works of Lewis Glyn Cothi. A celebrated bard who flourished in the reigns of Henry VI, Edward*

IV, Richard III and Henry VII. Edited by John Jones. Oxford: Council of the Cymmsodorion, 1837.
>Description: Autographed in pencil on inside front cover: 'W. J. Grffydd'. Contains page of Blackwell cat 520 for 1947 with a listing for this book circled, with in blue crayon marking, between pp. 124-25.
>Collection: Tolkien's personal Celtic library, preserved at the Weston library under the auspices of the English Faculty Library (Oxford).
>S.s. 1: Phelpstead (2011), p. 118.
>S.s. 2: Scull-Hammond (2017a), p. 332.

1364. Lewis, Harry Sinclair. *Babbitt*. New York: Harcourt, Brace, 1922.
>P.s. 1: MS. Tolkien A 13/1 *Draft of talk to the Oxford Dante Society: A neck-verse* (1947), fol. 169. Tolkien cites Vergil Gunch, a Zenith coal merchant and one of Babbitt's many friends and associates in the Zenith business community. [Tolkien Papers, Bodleian Library, Oxford].
>P.s. 2: Tolkien's unpublished letter to H. C. Bauer, 24 November 1966. 'After reading it I wonder whether Sinclair Lewis's <u>Babbitt</u> had not some part in the invention of this name: <u>hobbit</u>. I read all Sinclair Lewis's works'.
>P.s. 3: 'The Man Who Understands Hobbits' (1968), p. 32 Tolkien said: 'I don't know where the word came from. You can't catch your mind out. It might have been associated with Sinclair Lewis's Babbitt. Certainly not rabbit, as some people think. Babbitt has the same bourgeois smugness that hobbits do. His world is the same limited place'
>S.s.: Scull-Hammond (2017c), p. 1059.

1365. Lewis, Matthew Gregory. *Tales of Wonder*, Vol. I. London: Printed by W. Bulmer and Co. for the author; and sold by J. Bell, 1801.
>P.s.: *Beowulf* (2014), p. 208. Tolkien writes: 'And then we come to a new and very fascinating character, Unferth. To which book does he belong? *The Book of Kings*, or *Tales of Wonder*? [Tolkien could refer to Lord Dunsany's work *The Last Book of Wonder*, originally published as *Tales of Wonder*, but in my opinion the most probable reference consists in Lewis' works.] It is very difficult to decide – or Unferth is the actual link between the two worlds. He is balanced precisely between them.'

1366. _____. *Tales of Wonder*, Vol. II. London: Printed by W. Bulmer and Co. for the author; and sold by J. Bell, 1801.
>P.s.: Beowulf (2014), p. 208. [see A. 1365, P.s.]

1367. Lewis, Timothy. *A Glossary of Mediaeval Welsh Law Based Upon the Black Book of Chirk*. Manchester: The University Press, 1913.
>Description: Decoratively autographed and dated in red crayon on front flyleaf: '1924'.
>Collection: Tolkien's personal Celtic library, preserved at the Weston library under the auspices of the English Faculty Library (Oxford).
>S.s.: Phelpstead (2011), p. 119.

1368. Lewis, Warren Hamilton. *The Splendid Century. Some Aspects of French Life in the Reign of Louis XIV*. Eyre and Spottiswoode, 1953.
>P.s. 1: *Letters* 60 (1944). To Christopher Tolkien.
>P.s. 2: *Letters* 72 (1944). To Christopher Tolkien;
>P.s. 3: *Letters* 73 (1944). From a letter to Christopher Tolkien
>P.s. 4: *Letters* 81 (1944). To Christopher Tolkien.
>S.s.: Scull-Hammond (2017a), p. 285.

1369. Lexer, Matthias. *Mittelhochdeutsches Handwörterbuch*, Vol. I A-M. Leipzig: S. Hirzel, 1872.
>Description: Signed by Tolkien on front free endpaper.
>Collection: Private [Sold by Simon Finch Rare Books Ltd.].
>P.s.: 'Middle English 'Losenger'' (1953), p. 68 n. 1.
>S.s.: Finch (2002), p. 51.

1370. _____. *Mittelhochdeutsches Handwörterbuch*, Vol. II N-U. Leipzig: S. Hirzel, 1876.
   Description: Signed by Tolkien on front free endpaper.
   Collection: Private [Sold by Simon Finch Rare Books Ltd.].
   S.s.: Finch (2002), p. 53.

1371. _____. *Mittelhochdeutsches Handwörterbuch*, Vol. III V-Z. Leipzig: S. Hirzel, 1878.
   Description: Signed by Tolkien on front free endpaper.
   Collection: Private [Sold by Simon Finch Rare Books Ltd.].
   S.s.: Finch (2002), p. 53.

1372. Leyerle, John. 'Beowulf the Hero & the King' Offprint from *Medium Ævum*, Vol. 34, no. 2. Oxford: Basil Blackwell, 1963.
   Description: Inscribed on the front wrapper: 'For J.R.R. Tolkien | Whose work has | been seed and | nourishment for | this article and | its writer | John Leyerle | April 1967.'
   Collection: Private [Worthpoint].

1373. Liebermann, Felix. 'Die Abfassungszeit von 'Rectitudines singularum personarum' und ags *aferian*'. *Archiv für das Studium der neueren Sprachen und Literaturen*, Vol. CIX. Braunschweig: G. Westermann, 1902, pp. 73-82.
   P.s.: *The Devil's Coach-Horses* (1925), pp. 332 n. †; 333 n. ‡ Tolkien writes: 'For this point the present note is indebted to Liebremann's article'.

1374. _____ (Edited by). *Die Gesetze der Angelsachsen*, Vol. I. Text und Übersetzung. Halle: Max Niemeyer, 1903.
   P.s. 1: MS. Tolkien A 11 *Notes on Pearl* fol. 140. Tolkien refers to the word 'banweorc' on pages 244 [32,4]. [Tolkien Papers, Bodleian Library, Oxford].
   P.s. 2: *The Devil's Coach-Horses* (1925), p. 332.

1375. _____ (Edited by). *Die Gesetze der Angelsachsen*, Vol. II, Pt. I. Wörterbuch. Halle: Max Niemeyer, 1903.
   P.s.: *The Devil's Coach-Horses* (1925), p. 332.

1376. _____ (Edited by). *Die Gesetze der Angelsachsen*, Vol. II, Pt. II. Rechts-und Sachglossar. Halle: Max Niemeyer, 1903.
   P.s.: *The Devil's Coach-Horses* (1925), p. 332.

1377. _____ (Edited by). *Die Gesetze der Angelsachsen*, Vol. III. Einleitung zu jedem Stück: Erklärungen zu einzelnen Stellen. Halle: Max Niemeyer, 1903.
   P.s.: *The Devil's Coach-Horses* (1925), p. 332.

1378. _____. 'Zum deutsch-englischen Wörterbuch'. *Anglica: Untersuchungen zur englischen Philologie: Alois Brandl zum 70. Geburtstage überreicht*, Vol. I [A. 30], 1925.
   P.s.: *Philology: General Works* (VI 1927, for 1925), p. 35. Tolkien writes: 'is of interest primarily to Germans and secondarily to all lexicographers'

1379. _____ and Boehmer, Heinrich. *Texte und Forschungen zur englischen Kulturgeschichte: Festgabe für Felix Liebermann zum 20. Juli 1921*. Halle: Max Nemeyer, 1924.
   P.s.: *Philology: General Works* (IV 1924, for 1923), p. 22.

1380. *Life of St Margaret* 1210. [Middle English hagiography, see Cockayne].
   P.s.: MS. Tolkien A 21/13 *The English MSS*. fol. 203. [Tolkien Papers, Bodleian Library, Oxford].

1381. Liljegren, Sten Bodvar and Johan Melander (William Edward Collinson) (Edited by). *A Philological Miscellany Presented to Eilert Ekwall*. Uppsala: A.B. Lundequistska Bokhandeln, 1942.
    Notes: The volume includes an introductory note signed by J.R.R. Tolkien and others.

1382. Lindelöf, Uno Lorenz. *Engelska Språkets Ortografi i Historisk Belysning: föredrag vid finska vetenskaps-societetens sammanträde den 22 maj 1923*. Series: Årsbok. Societas scientiarum Fennica, 2, B, 1. Helsingfors Söderström, 1923.
    P.s.: *Philology: General Works* (IV 1924, for 1923), p. 33.

1383. _____ (Edited by). *Der Lambeth-Psalter*, Vol. I. *Text und Glossar*. Series: Suomen Tiedeseura; Acta Societatis Scientiarum Fennicae. Helsingfors: Druckerei der Finnischen Litteraturgesellschaft, 1909.
    P.s.: *Sigelwara land* (1932), p. 186 n. 1.

1384. _____. *Studien zu altenglischen Psalterglossen*. Series: Bonner Beiträge zur Anglistik, XIII. Bonn: P. Hanstein, 1904.
    P.s.: *Sigelwara land* (1932), p. 185 n. 1; p. 186 n. 1.

1385. Lindsay, David. *A Voyage to Arcturus*. London: Methuen and Co. Ltd., 1920.
    Description: Annotated by Tolkien on one page. Includes a label added by Stan Revell to books owned by Tolkien, 'From the Library of J.R.R. Tolkien'. Includes a fold-out map illustrating the use in New England of earthworm and its variants.
    Collection: Private [Christina Scull & Wayne G. Hammond].
    P.s. 1: *Letters* 26 (1938). To Stanley Unwin. Tolkien writes: 'I read with avidity'.
    P.s. 2: *The Notion Club Papers* (1945), p. 164.
    S.s.: Scull-Hammond (2018a).

1386. _____. *A Voyage to Arcturus*. Series: The connoisseur's library of strange fiction. London: V. Gollancz, 1946.
    Description: Includes a label added by Stan Revell to books owned by Tolkien, 'From the Library of J.R.R. Tolkien'.
    Collection: Private [Christina Scull & Wayne G. Hammond].
    P.s. 1: *On Fairy-stories* (1947), p. 68.
    P.s. 2: *Tolkien On Fairy-stories* (2008), pp. 60-61, 111.
    S.s. 1: Scull-Hammond (2017a), p. 228.
    S.s. 2: Scull-Hammond (2018a).

1387. Lindsay, Wallace Martin (Edited by). *The Corpus, Épinal, Erfurt and Leyden Glossaries*. Series: Philological Society, 8. London: Oxford University Press, 1921.
    Description: Signed on the first free end page in fountain pen with his ownership signature: 'J.R.R. Tolkien'.
    Collection: Private [Sold by Saleroom, 9 Apr. 2015].

1388. _____ (Edited by). *The Corpus Glossary with an Anglo-Saxon*. Index by Helen McMillan Buckhurst. Cambridge: The University Press, 1921.
    Description: Signed and annotated by Tolkien. Of particular relevance to Tolkien's creation of words and characters, the word 'Orcus' is underlined in the glossary and in the index.
    Collection: Private [Sold by Simon Finch Rare Books Ltd.].
    S.s.: Finch (2002), p. 52.

1389. Livingstone, David. *Missionary Travels And Researches In South Africa*. Cambridge: The University Press, 1857.
    P.s.: *Oxford University Press Archives* (Oxford). A slip written by Tolkien on the etymology of

'Wake' used ('W' p. 31) [A. 1721].
NED 1: #2 f. | 'W' (1928), p. 31 'Wake' 3. 1857 – 'A poor man and his wife were accused of having bewitched the man, whose wake was now held in the village' (p. 468).
NED 2: #2 c. | 'W' (1928), p. 27 'Wait-a-bit' a.' 1857 – 'The 'Wait-a-bit thorn', or *Acacia detinens*' (p. 61).

1390. Livingston, Margaret Vere (Farrington). *Fra Lippo Lippi: A Romance.*
S.s.: Ollscoil na h-Éireann G 101 (1949).

1391. Loewe, Richard. *Germanic Philology*: Edited and translated by John Jones. London: George Allen, 1913.
Description: Signed: 'J R R Tolkien'. With three short marginal notes on pages 4-5, also with briefer annotations in margins at pages 7-8, 16-18, 64-65.
Collection: Private [Worthpoint].

1392. _____. *Germanische Sprachwissenschaft*. Series: Sammlung Göschen, 238. Leipzig: G. J. Göschen'sche Verlagshandlung, 1911.
Description: Signed by Tolkien on the cover 'JRRT' and on top of the inside front page: 'J.R.R. Tolkien Exeter Coll'. Includes a label added by Stan Revell to books owned by Tolkien, 'From the Library of J.R.R. Tolkien', at the bottom left of the inside cover. Several pages with annotations in pencil (in the hand of Tolkien); pp. 80, 88, 101. Some small corrections added in black ink on page 133.
Collection: Private [TolkienLibrary.com].

1393. Lofting, Hugh. *Doctor Dolittle and the Green Canary*. Series: Doctor Dolittle, 11. New York: Friederick A. Stokes, 1950.
S.s.: Scull-Hammond (2006b), p. 820.

1394. _____. *Doctor Dolittle and the Secret Lake*. Series: Doctor Dolittle, 10. New York: Friederick A. Stokes, 1948.
S.s.: Scull-Hammond (2006b), p. 820.

1395. _____. *Doctor Dolittle in the Moon*. Series: Doctor Dolittle, 8. New York: Friederick A. Stokes, 1928.
S.s.: Scull-Hammond (2006b), p. 820.

1396. _____. *Doctor Dolittle Return*. Series: Doctor Dolittle, 9. New York: Friederick A. Stokes, 1933.
S.s.: Scull-Hammond (2006b), p. 820.

1397. _____. *Doctor Dolittle's Caravan*. Series: Doctor Dolittle, 6. New York: Friederick A. Stokes, 1926.
S.s.: Scull-Hammond (2006b), p. 820.

1398. _____. *Doctor Dolittle's Circus*. Series: Doctor Dolittle, 4. New York: Friederick A. Stokes, 1924.
S.s.: Scull-Hammond (2006b), p. 820.

1399. _____. *Doctor Dolittle's Garden*. Series: Doctor Dolittle, 7. New York: Friederick A. Stokes, 1927.
S.s.: Scull-Hammond (2006b), p. 820.

1400. _____. *Doctor Dolittle's Post Office*. Series: Doctor Dolittle, 3. New York: Friederick A. Stokes, 1923.
S.s.: Scull-Hammond (2006b), p. 820.

1401. _____. *Doctor Dolittle's Puddleby Adventures*. Series: Doctor Dolittle, 12. New York: Friederick A. Stokes, 1952.
S.s.: Scull-Hammond (2006b), p. 820.

1402. _____. *Doctor Dolittle's Zoo*. Series: Doctor Dolittle, 5. New York: Friederick A. Stokes, 1926.
S.s.: Scull-Hammond (2006b), p. 820.

1403. _____. *The Story of Doctor Dolittle*. Series: Doctor Dolittle, 1. New York: Friederick A. Stokes, 1920.
S.s.: Scull-Hammond (2006b), p. 820.

1404. _____. *The Voyages of Doctor Dolittle*. Series: Doctor Dolittle, 2. Philadelphia: J. B. Lippincott & Co., 1922.
S.s.: Scull-Hammond (2006b), p. 820.

1405. Longfellow, Henry Wadsworth. *The Song of Hiawatha*.
P.s. 1: Tolkien: *1964 BBC Interview*. Tolkien replied to Denys Gueroult: 'People remember Longfellow wrote *Hiawatha* and perhaps one or two other things and quite forget he was a Professor of Modern Languages.'
P.s. 2: *The Story of Kullervo* (2016). [Wanōna]
S.s. 1: Garth (2014).
S.s. 2: Scull-Hammond (2017c), p. 1055: 'In the essay Tolkien writes on the *Kalevala* in 1914-15 he demonstrates knowledge of Longfellow's *Song*, which uses the *Kalevala* metre'.
Reading period: 1900 – 1910 (S.s.: Scull-Hammond (2017c), p. 1055).

1406. Longinus. *On the sublime*. Edited by Robert Lowth. Oxford: At the Clarendon Press, 1906.
S.s.: University of Leeds (1921), p. 154. English Language and Literature - Scheme A. Texts and Period selected for 1921-22. (e) History of Criticism: Special Texts suggested for study. Ordinary Degree of B.A. with Honours. Final Examinations.

1407. Lönnrot, Elias; Robert Wilhelm Ekman and Kai Linnilä (Edited by). *Kalevala*. Helsinki: Tammi, 1849.
P.s.: *The Story of Kullervo* (2016), p. 111.

1408. Loomis, Roger Sherman. *Arthurian literature in the Middle Ages: a collaborative history*. Oxford: At the Clarendon Press, 1959.
P.s.: *Sir Gawain and the Green Knight* (1967) 'Select Bibliography', p. 154. Ch. 39 on Gawain.

1409. _____. *Arthurian tradition and Chrétien de Troyes*. New York: Columbia University Press, 1949.
P.s.: *Sir Gawain and the Green Knight* (1967) 'Select Bibliography', p. 154.

1410. _____. 'Bleheris and the Tristram Story'. MLN (*Modern Language Notes*), Vol. 39. Baltimore: The Johns Hopkins Press, 1924, pp. 319-29.
P.s.: *Sir Gawain and the Green Knight* (1925), p. xii line 2.

1411. _____. *Celtic myth and Arthurian romance*. Columbia University Press, 1927.
P.s.: *Sir Gawain and the Green Knight* (1967) 'Select Bibliography', p. 154.

1412. _____. *The development of Arthurian romance*. Series: Hutchinson university library: Modern languages and literature. New York: Harper & Row 1963.
P.s.: *Sir Gawain and the Green Knight* (1967) 'Select Bibliography', p. 154.

Section A

1413. _____. *Mélanges d'histoire du théatre du Moyen-Age et de la Renaissance offerts a Gustave Cohen Professeur Honoraire en Sorbonne par ses collègues, ses élèves et ses amis*. Paris: Librarie Nizet, 1950.
   Description: Presentation copy: 'To Professor Tolkien // with the esteem // and cordial regards // of Roger Loomis'.
   Collection: Private [Pieter Collier].

1414. _____. *Wales and the Arthurian Legend*. Cardiff: University of Wales, 1956.
   Collection: Tolkien's personal Celtic library, preserved at the Weston library under the auspices of the English Faculty Library (Oxford).
   P.s.: *Sir Gawain and the Green Knight* (1967) 'Select Bibliography', p. 154.
   S.s.: Phelpstead (2011), p. 119.

1415. _____ and Rudolph Willard. *Medieval English Verse and Prose in Modernized Versions*. New York: Appleton-Century Crofts, 1948.
   Description: Decoratively inscribed: 'Nevill K. Coghill. | Exeter Coll.' In ball point below on front flyleaf: 'from the library | of J.R.R. Tolkien.'
   Collection: Tolkien's personal Celtic library, preserved at the Weston library under the auspices of the English Faculty Library (Oxford).

1416. Lorenz, Konrad. *King Solomon's ring: new light on animal ways*. Translated by Marjorie Kerr Wilson. London: Methuen, 1955.
   Description: Inscribed: 'Daddy, with very much love from Prisca. Christmas, 1957'. Possible annotation by J.R.R. Tolkien on page 191.
   Collection: The Azusa Pacific University libraries, Inklings Collection.

1417. _____. *Man meets dog*. Translated by Marjorie Kerr Wilson. London: Methuen, 1955.
   Description: Inscribed: 'Daddy, with very much love from Prisca. Christmas, 1957'.
   Collection: The Azusa Pacific University libraries, Inklings Collection.

1418. Lot, Ferdinand. 'Caradoc et Saint Patern'. *Romania: Recueil trimestriel consacré a l'étude des langues et des literatures romanes*, Vol. XXVIII, 1899, pp. 568-78.
   P.s.: *Sir Gawain and the Green Knight* (1925), p. xxvi. Tolkien and Gordon write: 'For bibliography of the Irish and French analogues of *Sir Gawain*, see the bibliography in Kittredge's study'. [*NED*] In Kittredge's study, this article is mentioned in 'V. Le Livre de Caradoc' (p. 298).

1419. Loth, Joseph Marie (Edited by). *Les Mabinogion*, Vol. I. Du Livre rouge de Hergest avec les variantes du Livre blanc de Rhydderch. Paris: Fontemoing et cie, 1913 (2nd ed.), 1913.
   P.s.: *Sir Gawain and the Green Knight* (1925), p. xxvi. Tolkien and Gordon write: 'is more accurate and more fully annotated. [Tolkien had indicated '2nd edition, Paris 1912' but in that year, Loth had published only the first edition of *Contributions à l'étude des romans de la Table ronde* (Paris: Honoré Champion, 1912) that contains the chapter: 'IV. Remarques diverses aux Mabinogion: 1. Le nom de Mabinogi et Mabinogion. 2. Bledri (Berri). Blegobred. 3. La date de la composition de Kulhwch et Olwen, sa place et son importance parmi les Mabinogion et les romans arthuriens'.]

1420. _____ (Edited by). *Les Mabinogion*, Vol. II. Du Livre rouge de Hergest avec les variantes du Livre blanc de Rhydderch. Paris: Fontemoing et cie, 1913 (2nd ed.), 1913.
   P.s.: Sir Gawain and the Green Knight (1925), p. xxvi. [*Ibid.*]

1421. _____. *Vocabulaire Vieux-Breton avec commentaire*. Paris: F. Vieweg, 1884.
   Description: Decoratively autographed on front title page: 'John Reuel Tolkien | 1922'.

Collection: Tolkien's personal Celtic library, preserved at the Weston library under the auspices of the English Faculty Library (Oxford).
S.s.: Scull-Hammond (2017a), p. 126.

1422.   Lounsbury, Thomas R. *History of the English language*. New York: Henry Holl and Co., 1907.
S.s.: Scull-Hammond (2017a), p. 46. April 1913: Tolkien will need to become familiar with a range of literary and philological subjects and set texts as prescribed in the Oxford Regulations of the Board of Studies, knowing that he may be examined on them in ten papers at the end of Trinity Term 1915: Middle English texts.

1423.   Lovelich, Herry. *The History of the Holy Grail*, Vol. I. Series: E.E.T.S. (Early English Text Society), OS 20. Edited by Frederick J. Furnivall. London: Published for the Early English Text Society by Kegan Paul, Trench, Trübner and Co., 1874.
P.s.: MS. Tolkien A 21/13 fol. 119. Note by Tolkien, 'Books in Exeter Library useful', with shelfmarks, on back of photostat reading list dated October 1913. Tolkien writes: 'All EETS publications'. [Tolkien Papers, Bodleian Library, Oxford].

1424.   _____. *The History of the Holy Grail*, Vol. II. Series: E.E.T.S. (Early English Text Society), OS 24. Edited by Frederick J. Furnivall. London: Published for the Early English Text Society by Kegan Paul, Trench, Trübner and Co., 1875.
P.s.: MS. Tolkien A 21/13 fol. 119. Note by Tolkien, 'Books in Exeter Library useful', with shelfmarks, on back of photostat reading list dated October 1913. Tolkien writes: 'All EETS publications'. [Tolkien Papers, Bodleian Library, Oxford].
NED: #2 h. | 'W' (1928), p. 54. 'Walm *sb.*¹ *Obs.* 3. a.' – a 1450 'That water that Cold was before, Anon brennng hot it be-Cam thore, and with grete walmes it boyllede so faste, that the dewkes hondis it brende' (lxvi, 397).

1425.   _____. *The History of the Holy Grail*, Vol. III. Series: E.E.T.S. (Early English Text Society), OS 28. Edited by Frederick J. Furnivall. London: Published for the Early English Text Society by Kegan Paul, Trench, Trübner and Co., 1877.
P.s.: MS. Tolkien A 21/13 fol. 119. Note by Tolkien, 'Books in Exeter Library useful', with shelfmarks, on back of photostat reading list dated October 1913. Tolkien writes: 'All EETS publications'. [Tolkien Papers, Bodleian Library, Oxford].

1426.   _____. *The History of the Holy Grail*, Vol. IV. Series: E.E.T.S. (Early English Text Society), OS 30. Edited by Frederick J. Furnivall. London: Published for the Early English Text Society by Kegan Paul, Trench, Trübner and Co., 1877.
P.s.: MS. Tolkien A 21/13 fol. 119. Note by Tolkien, 'Books in Exeter Library useful', with shelfmarks, on back of photostat reading list dated October 1913. Tolkien writes: 'All EETS publications'. [Tolkien Papers, Bodleian Library, Oxford].

1427.   _____. *The History of the Holy Grail*, Vol. V. Series: E.E.T.S. (Early English Text Society), OS 95. Edited by Frederick J. Furnivall. London: Published for the Early English Text Society by Kegan Paul, Trench, Trübner and Co., 1905.
P.s.: MS. Tolkien A 21/13 fol. 119. Note by Tolkien, 'Books in Exeter Library useful', with shelfmarks, on back of photostat reading list dated October 1913. Tolkien writes: 'All EETS publications'. [Tolkien Papers, Bodleian Library, Oxford].

1428.   Lubovius, Louis. *First Introduction to German Philology*: Edinburgh: Wm. Blackwood, 1899.
S.s.: Scull-Hammond, *Chronology* (2017), p. 133.

1429.   Luick, Karl. 'Beiträge zur englischen Sprachgeschichte'. *Anglica: Untersuchungen zur englischen Philologie: Alois Brandl zum 70. Geburtstage*

SECTION A

überreicht, Vol. I [A. 30], 1925.
P.s.: *Philology: General Works* (VI 1927, for 1925), p. 35.

1430. _____. 'Experimentalphonetik und Sprachwissenschaft. Lecture delivered at the Österreichische Gesellschaft für experimentelle Phonetik, March 6, 1923'. *Germanisch-romanische Monatsschrift*, Vol. XI. Heidelberg: Carl Winter, Sept-Oct. 1923, pp. 257-70.
P.s.: *Philology: Genral Works*, 1924, p. 33.

1431. _____. 'Geschichte der Heimischen Versarten'. Offprint from *Grundriss der germanischen Philologie*, 3. Strassburg: K. J. Trübner, 1905, pp. 141-80.
Description: Autographed decoratively on front flyleaf.
Collection: Tolkien's personal Celtic library, preserved at the Weston library under the auspices of the English Faculty Library (Oxford).
P.s.: *Sir Gawain and the Green Knight* (1925), p. xxvii.

1432. _____. *Historische Grammatik der englischen Sprache*, Vol. I, Pt. I. Leipzig: C. H. Tauchnitz, 1921.
Description: two copies.
Collection: Tolkien's personal Celtic library, preserved at the Weston library under the auspices of the English Faculty Library (Oxford).

1433. _____. *Historische Grammatik der englischen Sprache*, Vol. I, Pt. II. Leipzig: C. H. Tauchnitz, 1921.
Collection: Tolkien's personal Celtic library, preserved at the Weston library under the auspices of the English Faculty Library (Oxford).

1434. _____ (Edited by). *Neusprachliche Studien: Festgabe Karl Luick zu seinem 60. Geburtstag dargebracht von Freunden und Schülern*. Series: Die Neuren Sprachen, 6. Beiheft. Marburg a. d. Lahn: Elwert, 1925.
P.s.: *Philology: General Works* (VI 1927, for 1925), p. 32 n. 4.

1435. _____. 'Über einige Zukunftsaufgaben der englischen Sprachwissenschaft'. Offprnt from *Germanisch-Romanische Monatsschrift*, Vol. XVIII. Heidelberg: Carl Winters, September-October 1930, pp. 364-76.
Description: Autographed on front cover by Luick. Red ball pen gives description of contents.
Collection: Tolkien's personal Celtic library, preserved at the Weston library under the auspices of the English Faculty Library (Oxford).

1436. Lumby, Joseph Rawson. *[i.e. Ðe] Be Domes dæge. De die judicii, an Old English version of the Latin poem ascribed to Bede*. Series: E.E.T.S. (Early English Text Society), OS 65. London: Published for the Early English Text Society by Kegan Paul, Trench, Trübner and Co., 1876.
Description: Engraved label on front flyleaf: 'J. G. Ronksley | no. 349'. Inside front flyleaf autographed and dated: '1923'. Some pencil notes on text.
Collection: Tolkien's personal Celtic library, preserved at the Weston library under the auspices of the English Faculty Library (Oxford).
P.s.: MS. Tolkien A 21/13 fol. 119. Note by Tolkien, 'Books in Exeter Library useful', with shelfmarks, on back of photostat reading list dated October 1913. Tolkien writes: 'All EETS publications'. [Tolkien Papers, Bodleian Library, Oxford].

1437. _____ (Edited by). *Bernardus De cura rei familiaris. With some early Scottish prophecies. From a MS. KK. 1. 5. in the Cambridge University Library*. Series: E.E.T.S. (Early English Text Society), OS 42. London: Published for the Early

English Text Society by Kegan Paul, Trench, Trübner and Co., 1870.
: Collection: Tolkien's personal Celtic library, preserved at the Weston library under the auspices of the English Faculty Library (Oxford).
: P.s.: MS. Tolkien A 21/13 fol. 119. Note by Tolkien, 'Books in Exeter Library useful', with shelfmarks, on back of photostat reading list dated October 1913. Tolkien writes: 'All EETS publications'. [Tolkien Papers, Bodleian Library, Oxford].

1438. _____ (Edited by). *King Horn, Floriz and Blauncheflur, The Assumption of Our Lady*. Series: E.E.T.S. (Early English Text), OS 14. London: Published for the Early English Text Society, by Trübner & Co., 1866.
: P.s. 1: MS. Tolkien A 21/13 fol. 119. Note by Tolkien, 'Books in Exeter Library useful', with shelfmarks, on back of photostat reading list dated October 1913. Tolkien writes: 'All EETS publications'. [Tolkien Papers, Bodleian Library, Oxford].
: P.s. 2: MS. Tolkien A 12/1 *Commentary on Sir Gawain, lines 37-1987* fol. 9. Tolkien quotes: 'a mantyl of Scarlet' from *Floriz and Blauncheflur*. [Tolkien Papers, Bodleian Library, Oxford].
: P.s. 3: MS. Tolkien A 13/1 *annotated texts of King Horn* fol. 94. [Tolkien Papers, Bodleian Library, Oxford].

1439. _____ (Edited by). *Polychronicon Ranulphi Higden monachi Cestrensis; together with the English translations of John Trevisa and of an unknown writer of the fifteenth century*, Vol. I. Series: Rerum Britannicarum Medii Ævi Scriptores, or Chronicles and Memorials of Great Britain and Ireland during the Middle Ages. London: Longman & Co., 1865.
: P.s.: MS. Tolkien A 21/13 *Chronological Library Table of Middle English* fol. 202. [Tolkien Papers, Bodleian Library, Oxford].

1440. _____ (Edited by). *Polychronicon Ranulphi Higden monachi Cestrensis; together with the English translations of John Trevisa and of an unknown writer of the fifteenth century*, Vol. II. Series: Rerum Britannicarum Medii Ævi Scriptores, or Chronicles and Memorials of Great Britain and Ireland during the Middle Ages. London: Longman & Co., 1869.
: P.s. 1: MS. Tolkien A 21/13 *Chronological Library Table of Middle English* fol. 202. [Tolkien Papers, Bodleian Library, Oxford].
: P.s. 2: 'Chaucer as a Philologist: *The Reeve's Tale*' (1934), p. 111. Tolkien quotes: '*scharp, slyttyng, andfrotyng, and unschape*' (p. 163).
: *NED*: #2 h. | 'W' (1928), p. 54. 'Walm *sb.*¹ *Obs.* 2.' – 1387 'In þe welmes ofter þan ones Is y-founde reed splekked stones ; In tokene of [þe] blood reed, Þat þe mayde Wynefrede Schadde at þat putte' (429).

1441. _____ (Edited by). *Polychronicon Ranulphi Higden monachi Cestrensis; together with the English translations of John Trevisa and of an unknown writer of the fifteenth century*, Vol. III. Series: Rerum Britannicarum Medii Ævi Scriptores, or Chronicles and Memorials of Great Britain and Ireland during the Middle Ages. London: Longman & Co, 1871.
: P.s.: MS. Tolkien A 21/13 *Chronological Library Table of Middle English* fol. 202. [Tolkien Papers, Bodleian Library, Oxford].

1442. _____ (Edited by). *Polychronicon Ranulphi Higden monachi Cestrensis; together with the English translations of John Trevisa and of an unknown writer of the fifteenth century*, Vol. IV. Series: Rerum Britannicarum Medii Ævi Scriptores, or Chronicles and Memorials of Great Britain and Ireland during the Middle Ages. London: Longman & Co. et alii, 1872.
: P.s.: MS. Tolkien A 21/13 *Chronological Library Table of Middle English* fol. 202. [Tolkien Papers, Bodleian Library, Oxford].

Section A

1443. _____ (Edited by). *Polychronicon Ranulphi Higden monachi Cestrensis; together with the English translations of John Trevisa and of an unknown writer of the fifteenth century*, Vol. V. Series: Rerum Britannicarum Medii Ævi Scriptores, or Chronicles and Memorials of Great Britain and Ireland during the Middle Ages. London: Longman & Co. et alii, 1874.
    P.s.: MS. Tolkien A 21/13 *Chronological Library Table of Middle English* fol. 202. [Tolkien Papers, Bodleian Library, Oxford].

1444. _____ (Edited by). *Polychronicon Ranulphi Higden monachi Cestrensis; together with the English translations of John Trevisa and of an unknown writer of the fifteenth century*, Vol. VI. Series: Rerum Britannicarum Medii Ævi Scriptores, or Chronicles and Memorials of Great Britain and Ireland during the Middle Ages. London: Longman & Co. et alii, 1876.
    P.s.: MS. Tolkien A 21/13 *Chronological Library Table of Middle English* fol. 202. [Tolkien Papers, Bodleian Library, Oxford].

1445. _____ (Edited by). *Polychronicon Ranulphi Higden monachi Cestrensis; together with the English translations of John Trevisa and of an unknown writer of the fifteenth century*, Vol. VII. Series: Rerum Britannicarum Medii Ævi Scriptores, or Chronicles and Memorials of Great Britain and Ireland during the Middle Ages. London: Longman & Co. et alii, 1879.
    P.s.: MS. Tolkien A 21/13 *Chronological Library Table of Middle English* fol. 202. [Tolkien Papers, Bodleian Library, Oxford].

1446. _____ (Edited by). *Polychronicon Ranulphi Higden monachi Cestrensis; together with the English translations of John Trevisa and of an unknown writer of the fifteenth century*, Vol. VIII. Series: Rerum Britannicarum Medii Ævi Scriptores, or Chronicles and Memorials of Great Britain and Ireland during the Middle Ages. London: Longman & Co. et alii, 1882.
    P.s.: MS. Tolkien A 21/13 *Chronological Library Table of Middle English* fol. 202. [Tolkien Papers, Bodleian Library, Oxford].

1447. _____ (Edited by). *Polychronicon Ranulphi Higden monachi Cestrensis; together with the English translations of John Trevisa and of an unknown writer of the fifteenth century*, Vol. IX. Series: Rerum Britannicarum Medii Ævi Scriptores, or Chronicles and Memorials of Great Britain and Ireland during the Middle Ages. London: Longman & Co. et alii, 1886.
    P.s.: MS. Tolkien A 21/13 *Chronological Library Table of Middle English* fol. 202. [Tolkien Papers, Bodleian Library, Oxford].

1448. _____ (Edited by). *Ratis raving, and other moral and religious pieces, in prose and verse*. Series: E.E.T.S. (Early English Text Society), OS 43. London: Published for the Early English Text Society by Kegan Paul, Trench, Trübner and Co., 1870.
    Collection: Tolkien's personal Celtic library, preserved at the Weston library under the auspices of the English Faculty Library (Oxford).
    P.s.: MS. Tolkien A 21/13 fol. 119. Note by Tolkien, 'Books in Exeter Library useful', with shelfmarks, on back of photostat reading list dated October 1913. Tolkien writes: 'All EETS publications'. [Tolkien Papers, Bodleian Library, Oxford].

1449. Lydgate, John. *Lydgate's Troy book. A.D. 1412-20*, Vol. I. Series: E.E.T.S. (Early English Text Society), ES 97. Edited by Henry Bergen. London: Published for the Early English Text Society by Kegan Paul, Trench, Trübner and Co., 1906.
    P.s. 1: MS. Tolkien A 21/13 fol. 119. Note by Tolkien, 'Books in Exeter Library useful', with

shelfmarks, on back of photostat reading list dated October 1913. Tolkien writes: 'All EETS publications'. [Tolkien Papers, Bodleian Library, Oxford].
P.s. 2: *Sir Gawain and the Green Knight* (1967) 'Select Bibliography: editions of texts quoted more than once in the notes', p. 156.

1450. _____. *Lydgate's Troy book. A.D. 1412-20*, Vol. II. Series: E.E.T.S. (Early English Text Society), ES 103. Edited by Henry Bergen. London: Published for the Early English Text Society by Kegan Paul, Trench, Trübner and Co., 1910.
P.s. 1: MS. Tolkien A 21/13 fol. 119. Note by Tolkien, 'Books in Exeter Library useful', with shelfmarks, on back of photostat reading list dated October 1913. Tolkien writes: 'All EETS publications'. [Tolkien Papers, Bodleian Library, Oxford].
P.s. 2: *Oxford University Press Archives* (Oxford). A slip written by Tolkien on the etymology of 'Wake' used ('W' p. 31) [A. 1721].
P.s. 3: *Sir Gawain and the Green Knight* (1967) 'Select Bibliography: editions of texts quoted more than once in the notes', p. 156.
NED: #2 f. | 'W' (1928), p. 31 'Wake, 3.' 1412-20 – 'What shulde I now any lenger dwelle ... for to telle ... of þe pleies called palestral, Nor be wrastelyng þat was at þe wake?' (book iv, vv. 3251-3261, pp. 559-660).

1451. _____. *Lydgate's Troy book. A.D. 1412-20*, Vol. III. Series: E.E.T.S. (Early English Text Society), ES 106. Edited by Henry Bergen. London: Published for the Early English Text Society by Kegan Paul, Trench, Trübner and Co., 1910.
P.s.: *Sir Gawain and the Green Knight* (1967) 'Select Bibliography: editions of texts quoted more than once in the notes', p. 156.

1452. Lye, Eduardo. *Dictionarium saxonico et gothico-latinum*, Vol. I. London: Allen, 1772.
Description: Inscribed in pencil on front flyleaf: 'John Reuel Tolkien | 1922'.
Collection: Private.

1453. Lyly, John. *Campaspe*.
S.s.: University of Leeds (1920), p. 147. English Language and Literature - Scheme A. Texts and Period selected for 1920-21. (b) Special period: 1557-1637. (c) Texts suggested for study with Special Period. Ordinary Degree of B.A. with Honours. Final Examination.

1454. _____. *Euphues*.
S.s.: University of Leeds (1920), p. 147. English Language and Literature - Scheme A. Texts and Period selected for 1920-21. (b) Special period: 1557-1637. (c) Texts suggested for study with Special Period. Ordinary Degree of B.A. with Honours. Final Examination.

1455. Lyndesay, David. *The Monarche and Other Poems*, Pt. I. Series: E.E.T.S. (Early English Text Society), OS 19. Edited by Fitzedward Hall. London: Published for the Early English Text Society by Kegan Paul, Trench, Trübner and Co., 1865.
P.s.: MS. Tolkien A 21/13 fol. 119. Note by Tolkien, 'Books in Exeter Library useful', with shelfmarks, on back of photostat reading list dated October 1913. Tolkien writes: 'All EETS publications'. [Tolkien Papers, Bodleian Library, Oxford].
NED: #2 h. | 'W' (1928), p. 53 'Wallop v. I. 1. b.' – 1529 'And sum, to schaw thare courtlie corsis, Wald ryid to leith, and ryn thare borssis, And wychtlie wallope ouer the sandis' (p. 179).

1456. Lyngbye, Hans Christian and Peter Erasmus Müller (Edited by). *Færøiske Qvæder om Sigurd Fofnersbane og hans Æt: med et anhang*. Randers: S. Elmenhoff, 1822.
Collection: Tolkien's personal Celtic library, preserved at the Weston library under the auspices of the English Faculty Library (Oxford).

1457. Lyons, Albert Neil. *Arthur's: the romance of a coffee stall*. London and New York: John Lane, 1915.
P.s.: *Philology: General Works* (IV 1924, for 1923), p. 28.

1458. *Mabinogion* [Middle Welsh collection of tales].
For editions and translations of this work, see Edwards, Evans (John), Guest, Loth, Meyer, Mühlhausen, Rhys.

1459. Macaulay, Thomas Babington. *History of England: Ch.s I-III*. Edited by William Fiddian Reddaway. Cambridge: The University Press, 1914.
S.s.: University of Leeds (1921), p. 154. English Language and Literature - Scheme A. Texts and Period selected for 1921-22. (d) Texts suggested for study with Special Period 1637-1700. Ordinary Degree of B.A. with Honours. Final Examinations.

1460. _____. *Lays of ancient Rome*. London: Longmans, Green and Co., 1888.
Notes: Tolkien's poem *The Battle of the Eastern Field* [B. 4], is the parody of *The Battle of Lake Regillus*, which is one of Macaulay's *Lays of Ancient Rome*.
S.s.: Scull-Hammond (2017c), p. 995.
Reading period: 1910 ca. (S.s.: Scull-Hammond (2017c), p. 995).

1461. Macbain, Alexander. *Gaelic reader with outlines of grammar. For use in higher classes of schools in the Highlands*. Enverness: 'Northern Chronicle' Office, 1920 (3rd ed.).
Description: Autographed and dated on front flyleaf: '1922'.
Collection: Tolkien's personal Celtic library, preserved at the Weston library under the auspices of the English Faculty Library (Oxford).

1462. _____. *Place-names, Highlands and Islands of Scotland*. Stirling: Mackay, 1923.
P.s.: *Philology: General Works* (IV 1924, for 1923), p. 30.

1463. _____ and John White. *How to learn Gaelic, orthographical instructions, grammar*. Enverness: 'Northern Chronicle' Office, 1906 (4th ed.).
Description: Autographed and dated upside down on front flyleaf '1922'.
Collection: Tolkien's personal Celtic library, preserved at the Weston library under the auspices of the English Faculty Library (Oxford).

1464. MacCracken, Henry Noble. 'Concerning Huchown'. PMLA (*Publications of the Modern Language Association of America*), Vol. XXV, no. 3. Edited by Charles H. Grandgent. Baltimore: J. H. Furst Company, 1910, pp. 507-34.
P.s.: *Sir Gawain and the Green Knight* (1925), p. xvii line 2.

1465. MacDonald, Alexander. *The Lost Explorers: A Tale of the Trackless Desert*. London: Blackie and son, limited, 1906.
Notes: Tolkien gives this book to the King Edward's School in Birmingham in 1911.
S.s. 1: Garth (2003), p. 79.
S.s. 2: Rateliff (2012), p. 147.
S.s. 3: Scull-Hammond (2017a), p. 31.
Reading period: 1908 – 1910 (S.s.: Scull-Hammond (2017c), p. 1054).

1466. MacDonald, George. *A Dish of Orts: Chiefly Papers on the Imagination, and on Shakespere*. London: Sampson, Low, Marston, 1893.
P.s.: *Tolkien On Fairy-stories* (2008), p. 98. Tolkien refers to MacDonald introduction 'The Fantastic Imagination'.

1467. _____. *Dealings with the fairies*. London: Alexander Strahan, 1867.
P.s. 1: *Tolkien On Fairy-stories* (2008) 'Manuscript A. [MS Tolkien 4, fols. 59-77]', pp. 248-308.
P.s. 2: #1 a. | *Tolkien On Fairy-stories* (2008), p. 309. Tolkien refers to MacDonald tale 'The Golden Key'.

1468. _____. 'The Giant's Heart'. In *Adela Cathcart*. Boston: Loring, 1864.
P.s.: *Tolkien On Fairy-stories* (2008) 'Manuscript B [MS. Tolkien 4, fols. 73-120]', p. 217.

1469. _____. *The Golden Key*.
P.s. 1: MS. Tolkien 9-13. 'b (fols. 5-12) Notes on George Macdonald's *The Golden Key*, c. 1965'. [Tolkien Papers, Bodleian Library, Oxford].
P.s. 2: *On Fairy-stories* (1947), p. 55.
P.s. 3: *Letters* 262 (1964). To Michael di Capua.
P.s. 4: *Smith of Wootton Major* (2005), pp. 71-6 'Tolkien's draft introduction to *The Golden Key*'
P.s. 5: *Tolkien On Fairy-stories* (2008) 'Manuscript B [MS. Tolkien 4, fols. 73-120]', pp. 242, 250. Tolkien writes that it 'is not for children though children do read it with pleasure'.
S.s.: Scull-Hammond (2006b), p. 821.

1470. _____. *Lilith*. London: Chatto and Windus, 1895.
P.s. 1: *On Fairy-stories* (1947), p. 55.
P.s. 2: *Tolkien On Fairy-stories* (2008), p. 45.
P.s. 3: *Tolkien On Fairy-stories* (2008) 'Manuscript A. [MS Tolkien 4, fols. 59-77]', p. 242.
S.s.: Scull-Hammond (2006b), p. 820.

1471. _____. *Orts*. London: S. Low. Marston, Searle & Rivington, 1882.
P.s.: *Tolkien On Fairy-stories* (2008), p. 98.

1472. _____. *Phantastes. A faerie romance for men and women*.
P.s. 1: Tolkien's unpublished letter to L. M. Cutts, 26 October 1958. Tolkien writes: 'Ents is also an ancient English word (for a giant); but the Ent of my world I suppose are entirely 'original' creatures, so far as that can be said of any human work. If you like, they are a mythological form taken by my life long love for trees, with perhaps some remote influence from George MacDonald's *Phantastes* (a work I do not much like), and certainly a strong (twist?) given my deep disappointment with Shakespeare's *Macbeth*...'
P.s. 2: *Tolkien On Fairy-stories* (2008) 'Manuscript B [MS. Tolkien 4, fols. 73-120]', p. 207.
S.s. 1: Shippey (1992), p. 300.
S.s. 2: Scull-Hammond (2006b), p. 821. For Tolkien, the book 'afflicted me with profound dislike'.

1473. _____. *The Princess and Curdie*. London: Strahan and Co.
P.s.: *Tolkien On Fairy-stories* (2008) 'Manuscript B [MS. Tolkien 4, fols. 73-120]', pp. 242, 250.
S.s. 1: Shippey (1992), p. 301.
S.s. 2: Scull-Hammond (2017a), p. 6.
S.s. 3: Scull-Hammond (2006b), p. 815.
S.s. 4: Anderson (2002), p. 6.
Reading period: 1900 – 1906 (S.s.: Scull-Hammond (2017c), p. 1053).

1474. _____. *The Princess and the Goblin*. London: Strahan and Co.
P.s.: *Tolkien On Fairy-stories* (2008) 'Manuscript B [MS. Tolkien 4, fols. 73-120]', pp. 231, 250.
S.s. 1: Shippey (1992), p. 301.
S.s. 2: Scull-Hammond (2017a), p. 6.
S.s. 3: Scull-Hammond (2006b), p. 815.
S.s. 4: Anderson (2002), p. 6.
Reading period: 1900 – 1906 (S.s.: Scull-Hammond (2017c), p. 1053).

1475. MacDougall, James and George Calder. *Folk tale and fairy lore in Gaelic and English. Collected from oral tradition*. Edinburgh: John Grant, 1910.
P.s. 1: *On Fairy-stories* (1947), p. 89.
P.s. 2: *Tolkien On Fairy-stories* (2008), p. 84.
P.s. 3: *Tolkien On Fairy-stories* (2008) 'Manuscript A. [MS Tolkien 4, fols. 59-77]', p. 176.

1476. Maceachen, Ewan. *Gaelic-English Dictionary*. Inverness: Northern Counties, 1922 (4th ed.).
Description: Autographed and dated on front flyleaf: '1922'.

Collection: Tolkien's personal Celtic library, preserved at the Weston library under the auspices of the English Faculty Library (Oxford).

1477. MacFarlane, Malcom. *An Comh-threaiche*. Stirling: Eaneas Mackay, 1913.
Description: Autographed and dated on front page.
Collection: Tolkien's personal Celtic library, preserved at the Weston library under the auspices of the English Faculty Library (Oxford).

1478. _____. *The Phonetics of the Gaelic Language. With an exposition of the current orthography and a system of phonography*. Edinburgh: Parlane, Paisley, 1889.
Description: Autographed decoratively on front flyleaf: 'JRR Tolkien | 1922'.
Collection: Tolkien's personal Celtic library, preserved at the Weston library under the auspices of the English Faculty Library (Oxford).

1479. MacFayden, John. *Companach Na Cloinne. Leabhran sgoil anns am bheil sgeoil thaitneach*. Stirling: Eaneas Mackay, 1913.
Description: Autographed on front page.
Collection: Tolkien's personal Celtic library, preserved at the Weston library under the auspices of the English Faculty Library (Oxford).

1480. Mack, Frances May (Edited by). *English Text of the Ancrene Riwle, British Museum MS. Cotton Titus D. xviii and the Lanhydrock Fragment, Bodleian MS. Eng. the. c. 70* (edited by Arne Zettersten). Series: E.E.T.S. (Early English Text Society), OS 252. London: Oxford University Press, 1963.
S.s. 1: Scull-Hammond (2017a), pp. 607-09. 'Oxford University Press sent to Tolkien for comments, several proof copies on signatures: B-C (18 July 1961); D (14 September 1961); O (15 September 1961); E-G (16 September 1961) and H (22 September 1961). Last, proofs of the preliminaries, table of contents, and introductions (4 October 1962)'.
S.s. 2: Scull-Hammond (2017c), p. 1238. 'In August 1961 Tolkien, who had been sent proofs of Frances M. Mack's edition of *Ancrene Riwle* (B.M. MS Cotton Titus D.XVIII), wrote to Burchfield that he had read the first section with care, 'as befits one who has received many valuable suggestions from other members of the Council' (Tolkien Papers, Bodleian Library, Oxford)'.

1481. _____ (Edited and revised by). *Seinte Marherete þe Meiden ant Martyr*. Series: E.E.T.S. (Early English Text Society), OS 193. London: Oxford University Press, 1934.
Description: Inscribed on front flyleaf in pencil:'s. d'Ardenne | 1934'. Underlined in red crayon. Annotated in pencil.
Collection: Tolkien's personal Celtic library, preserved at the Weston library under the auspices of the English Faculty Library (Oxford).

1482. Mackail, John William. *The life of William Morris*, Vol. I. London: Longmans, Green and Co., 1907.
S.s.: Mathews (2002), p. 87. Richard Mathews writes: '[Christopher Tolkien] In a subsequent letter, he listed 11 titles of Morris's books of poems, translations, and fantasies that his father bequeathed to him, including *The House of the Wolfings*, *The Roots of the Mountains*, and *The Sundering Flood*, plus J. W. Mackail's two-volume *Life of William Morris* and A. Clutton-Brock's *William Morris: His Work and Influence*. Tolkien had begun collecting and reading Morris–even reading Morris aloud to his son–at a time when his popularity and critical reputation were at an all-time low and his work had been eclipsed by World War I and the onward rush of technology and current events.' (Christopher Tolkien to the author).

1483. _____. *The life of William Morris*, Vol. II. London: Longmans, Green and Co., 1907.
S.s.: Mathews (2002), p. 87. [see A. 1482, S.s.].

1484. Mackenzie, Barbara Alida. *The Early London Dialect. Contributions to the history of the dialect of the Middle English period*. Oxford: At the Clarendon Press, 1928.
> Description: Inscribed on front flyleaf with autograph below: 'C. L. Peacock'.
> Collection: Tolkien's personal Celtic library, preserved at the Weston library under the auspices of the English Faculty Library (Oxford).

1485. Macleod, Fiona. *The divine adventure: Iona: By sundown shores, studies in spiritual history by Fiona Macleod*. Edited by William Sharp, London: Chapman and Hall, 1900.
> Description: Tolkien requested the book on 27 February 1939 (MS. Library Records b. 618). Weston Library (Oxford), 930 e.256.

1486. Madden, Frederic (Edited by). *Syr Gawayne. A collection of ancient romance-poems by Scotish and English authors relating to that celebrated knight of the Round Table*. London: Bannatyne Club, 1839.
> P.s. 1: *Sir Gawain and the Green Knight* (1925), p. xxvi. Tolkien and Gordon write: 'For bibliography of the Irish and French analogues of *Sir Gawain*, see the bibliography in Kittredge's study'. [*NED*] In Kittredge's study, this article is mentioned in 'II. Gawain and the Green Knight' (pp. 293, 294), 'III. The Green Knight' (p. 296). 'IV. The Turk and Gawain' (p. 297), 'V. Le Livre de Caradoc' (p. 298), 'IX. The Carl of Carlisle' (p. 301); p. vii.
> P.s. 2: *Sir Gawain and the Green Knight* (1967) 'Select Bibliography', p. 153.

1487. Madeleva, Mary (Sister). *Pearl: a study in spiritual dryness*. New York & London: D. Appleton and Co., 1925. Notes: Thesis (Ph. D. in English), University of California, Berkeley, May 1925.
> P.s.: MS. Tolkien A 35 *Pearl* fol. 114. [Tolkien Papers, Bodleian Library, Oxford].

1488. Maeterlinck, Maurice. *The Blue Bird. A fairy play in six acts*. New York: Dodd, Mead and Co., 1911.
> P.s. 1: *On Fairy-stories* (1947), p. 65.
> P.s. 2: *Tolkien On Fairy-stories* (2008), p. 57.
> P.s. 3: *Tolkien On Fairy-stories* (2008) 'Manuscript A. [MS Tolkien 4, fols. 59-77]', p. 190.
> S.s.: Scull-Hammond (2006b), p. 820.

1489. Magner, James Edmund, Jr. *Toiler of the sea*. Francestown, New Hampshire: The Golden Quill press, 1965.
> Description: Not signed by J.R.R. Tolkien, but with a long note by James Edmund Magner, Jr. 'July 18, 1965 | John Carroll University | to you Professor Tolkein, | with my respect, | warm regards | and my wish | for your | personal fulfillment. | James Edmund Magner.'
> Collection: Private [Pieter Collier]

1490. Malone, Kemp. 'Anglist and Anglicist'. Offprint from *Studies in honor of Hermann Collitz. Presented by a group of his pupils and friends on the occasion of his seventy-fifth birthday, February 4, 1930*. Baltimore: John Hopkins Press, 1930, pp. 324-29.
> Description: Includes a label added by Stan Revell to books owned by Tolkien, 'From the Library of J.R.R. Tolkien', on front cover.
> Collection: Marion E. Wade Center, Wheaton College (Wheaton, Illinois).

1491. _____. *Chapters on Chaucer*. Baltimore: John Hopkins Press, 1951.
> Description: Inscribed on front flyleaf: 'Ronald Tolkien | with the regards of | Kemp Malone'.
> Collection: Tolkien's personal Celtic library, preserved at the Weston library under the auspices of the English Faculty Library (Oxford).

SECTION A

1492. _____. 'From Academic Darkness'. PMLA (*Publications of the Modern Language Association of America*), Vol. LXXVIII, no. 1, 1963 (March), pp. 1-7.
   Description: Annotations by Tolkien.
   Collection: Private.
   S.s.: Waterfield (1980), item 712.

1493. _____. *The Semantics of Toast*. Amsterdam: Swets & Zeitlinger, 1949.
   Description: Includes a label added by Stan Revell to books owned by Tolkien, 'From the Library of J.R.R. Tolkien', on front cover.
   Collection: Marion E. Wade Center, Wheaton College (Wheaton, Illinois).

1494. _____. 'The terminology of Anglistics'. Reprinted for private circulation from *The English Journal* (College Edition), XIX, 8 October, 1930. [S.l.]: *The English Journal*, 1930.
   Description: Includes a label added by Stan Revell to books owned by Tolkien, 'From the Library of J.R.R. Tolkien', on front cover.
   Collection: Marion E. Wade Center, Wheaton College (Wheaton, Illinois).

1495. Malory, Thomas. *Le Morte d'Arthur. The original edition of William Caxton*, Vol. I. Texte. Foreword and Glosses by Heinrich Oskar Sommer and with Andrew Lang's essay. London: D. Nutt, 1889.
   Description: Tolkien's copy, signed bequeathed to him by G. B. Smith. Signed 'Geoffrey B. Smith January 1910'; with a note beneath in Tolkien's hand 'left by will to JRRT'.
   Collection: Private [Sold by Simon Finch Rare Books Ltd.].
   P.s. 1: *Sir Gawain and the Green Knight* (1925), p. 82, line 90 ff.
   P.s. 2: *The Fall of Arthur* (2013), p. 94.
   S.s. 1: Finch (2002), p. 51.
   NED: #2 h. | 'W' (1928), p. 53 'Wallop *sb*. 1. a.'' – 1470-85 'So he rode a grete wallop tyll he cam to the fontayne' (p. 69).

1496. _____. *Le Morte d'Arthur. Sir Thomas Malory's book of King Arthur and of his noble knights of the round table*. Series: The Globe. Edited by Edward Strachey. London: Macmillan, 1919.
   S.s.: University of Leeds (1920), p. 135. English Literature. Texts Selected for 1920-21; p. 180. English Language and Literature. Int. I Intermediate Course (Literature). Extracts Book VI.

1497. _____. *The Works of Sir Thomas Malory*, Vol. I. Edited by Eugéne Vinaver. Oxford: At the Clarendon Press, 1947.
   P.s. 1: *Sir Gawain and the Green Knight* (1967) 'Select Bibliography: editions of texts quoted more than once in the notes', p. 156.
   P.s. 2: *The Fall of Arthur* (2013), p. 85 [C. T.].
   S.s.: Scull-Hammond (2017a), p. 336. C. S. Lewis has already bought the three-volume set and sells his review copies received by the *Times Literary Supplement* to Tolkien.

1498. _____. *The Works of Sir Thomas Malory*, Vol. II. Edited by Eugéne Vinaver. Oxford: At the Clarendon Press, 1947.
   P.s.: *Sir Gawain and the Green Knight* (1967) 'Select Bibliography: editions of texts quoted more than once in the notes', p. 156.
   S.s.: Scull-Hammond (2017a), p. 336. C. S. Lewis has already bought the three-volume set and sells his review copies received by the *Times Literary Supplement* to Tolkien.

1499. _____. *The Works of Sir Thomas Malory*, Vol. III. Edited by Eugéne Vinaver. Oxford: At the Clarendon Press, 1947.
   P.s.: *Sir Gawain and the Green Knight* (1967) 'Select Bibliography: editions of texts quoted more than once in the notes', p. 156.
   S.s.: Scull-Hammond (2017a), p. 336. C. S. Lewis has already bought the three-volume set and

sells his review copies received by the *Times Literary Supplement* to Tolkien.

1500. Manchon, Joseph. *Le Slang, lexique de l'anglais familier et vulgaire*. Paris: Payot, 1923.
    P.s.: *Philology: General Works* (IV 1924, for 1923), p. 28 n. 10.

1501. Mandeville, John. *Mandeville's Travels, from MS. Cotton Titus C.xvi*, Vol. I. Series: E.E.T.S. (Early English Text Society), OS 153. Edited by H. Harnelius. London: Published for the Early English Text Society by Kegan Paul, Trench, Trübner and Co., 1919.
    P.s. 1: MS. Tolkien A 35 *Pearl* fol. 111. [Tolkien Papers, Bodleian Library, Oxford].
    P.s. 2: *Sir Gawain and the Green Knight* (1925), p. 82 line 77 *Tarse*. Tolkien and Gordon cite 'marcheth toward the west unto the kingdom of Tarse' (ch. XXVII).
    P.s. 3: *Sir Gawain and the Green Knight* (1967) 'Select Bibliography: editions of texts quoted more than once in the notes', p. 156.
    S.s.: #1 Holland (1949), p. 144. Appendix XI: Oxford Examinations for Prisoners of War. English B.2 Chaucer and his Contemporaries.

1502. _____. *Mandeville's Travels, from MS. Cotton Titus C.xvi*, Vol. II. Series: E.E.T.S. (Early English Text Society), OS 154. Edited by H. Harnelius. London: Published for the Early English Text Society by Kegan Paul, Trench, Trübner and Co., 1923.
    P.s. 1: MS. Tolkien A 35 *Pearl* fol. 111. [Tolkien Papers, Bodleian Library, Oxford].
    P.s. 2: *Sir Gawain and the Green Knight* (1967) 'Select Bibliography: editions of texts quoted more than once in the notes', p. 156.

1503. Mannying, Robert. *Handlyng Synne*, Pt. I. Series: E.E.T.S. (Early English Text Society), OS 119. Edited by Frederick James Furnivall. London: Published for the Early English Text Society by N. Trübner, 1901.
    P.s. 1: MS. Tolkien A 21/13 fol. 119. Note by Tolkien, 'Books in Exeter Library useful', with shelfmarks, on back of photostat reading list dated October 1913. Tolkien writes: 'All EETS publications'. [Tolkien Papers, Bodleian Library, Oxford].
    P.s. 2: MS. Tolkien A 11 *Notes on Pearl* fols. 38-9. [Tolkien Papers, Bodleian Library, Oxford].

1504. _____. *Handlyng Synne*, Pt. II. Series: E.E.T.S. (Early English Text Society), OS 119. Edited by Frederick J. Furnivall. London: Published for the Early English Text Society by N. Trübner, 1901.
    P.s. 1: MS. Tolkien A 21/13 fol. 119. Note by Tolkien, 'Books in Exeter Library useful', with shelfmarks, on back of photostat reading list dated October 1913. Tolkien writes: 'All EETS publications'. [Tolkien Papers, Bodleian Library, Oxford].
    P.s. 2: MS. Tolkien A 11 *Notes on Pearl* fols. 38-9. [Tolkien Papers, Bodleian Library, Oxford].

1505. _____. *The Story of England by Robert Manning of Brunne, AD 1338*, Vol. I. Series: Cambridge library collection, Rolls. Edited by Frederick J. Furnivall. Cambridge: The University Press, 1887.
    P.s. 1: MS. Tolkien A 11 *Notes on Pearl* fol. 58. [Tolkien Papers, Bodleian Library, Oxford].
    P.s. 2: *Sir Gawain and the Green Knight* (1925), p. 90 line 568 ff.
    P.s. 3: 'Chaucer as a Philologist: *The Reeve's Tale*' (1934), p. 131. Tolkien writes: 'fonne 169 ... The simple fon is found, in Manning' (4051).

1506. Mansfield, Robert Blachford. *New and Old Chips from an Old Block*. London: J. Blackwood & Co., 1896.
    P.s.: *Oxford University Press Archives* (Oxford). In a slip written by Tolkien on the etymology of 'Waistcoated' not used, and reads: '(waistcoated) | 2. Comb. esp. white-waistcoated: | Weaning a white waistcoat, also applied to | birds with white plumage on the beast'.

> *NED*: #2 b. | 'W' (1928), p. 23 'Waistcoated, *b.*' 1896 – 'Magpies ... the black-coated and white-waistcoated gentry. (p. 224)'

1507. Mansion, Joseph. 'L'Ancien néerlandais d'Aprés les noms propres'. *Bullettin de la Société de Linguistique de Paris*, Vol. XXVI, 1-2, no. 79. Paris: Librairie Ancienne Honoré Champion, 1925, pp. 67-97.
> P.s.: 'Middle English 'Losenger'' (1953), p. 74 n. 2.

1508. _____. *Oud-gentsche naamkunde: bijdrage tot de kennis van het oud-nederlandsch*. S'Gravenhage: M. Nijhoff, 1924.
> Collection: Taylor Institution Library, Bodleian Libraries (Oxford).

1509. Manzalaoui, Mahmoud. 'Lydgate and English Prosody'. Offprint from *Cairo Studies in English*. Cairo: Costa Tsoumas, 1960, pp. 87–104.
> Notes: A copy was sent to Tolkien by the author.
> S.s.: Scull-Hammond (2017a), pp. 620-21. 6 March 1962:

1510. _____. 'Rasselas and some mediaeval ancillaries'. Offprint from *Bicentenary Essays on Rasselas* by Magdi Wahba. Cairo: Société Orientale de Publicité, 1959, pp. 59-73.
> Collection: From the library of Dr J.D. Fleeman, University of St Andrews Library (St Andrews)
> Description: Bookplate of J.R.R. Tolkien. Inscribed 'Very interesting. A copy from an Egyptian Arab of great intelligence' in an unknown hand, in ink, on front cover. '£15 40/Can' inscribed in pencil on p. [59].

1511. Mapes, Walter. *The Latin Poems Commonly Attributed to Walter Mapes*, Vol. I. Collected and edited by Thomas Wright. London: Printed for the Camden Society by J. B. Nichols, 1841.
> Description: Autographed on frontispiece and dated: '1923'.
> Collection: Private [Bloomsbury Auctions].

1512. _____. *The Latin Poems Commonly Attributed to Walter Mapes*, Vol. II. Collected and edited by Thomas Wright. London: Printed for the Camden Society by J. B. Nichols, 1850.
> Description: Autographed on front flyleaf and dated: '1923'.
> Collection: Private [Bloomsbury Auctions].

1513. *Marche romane*. Cahiers de l'A.R.U.Lg. (Association des romanistes de l'Université de Liège). Liège: Université de Liège. Association des romanistes, Juin 1951. Complete issue.
> Description: Includes a label added by Stan Revell to books owned by Tolkien, 'From the Library of J.R.R. Tolkien'.
> Collection: Private [Christina Scull & Wayne G. Hammond].
> S.s.: Scull-Hammond (2018a).

1514. Marie de France. *Die Fabeln der Marie de France*. Edited by Warnke Karl. Halle: Max Niemeyer, 1898.
> Description: Autographed on front flyleaf.
> Collection: Tolkien's personal Celtic library, preserved at the Weston library under the auspices of the English Faculty Library (Oxford).

1515. _____. *Die Lais der Marie de France*. Edited by Karl Warnke. Halle: Max Niemeyer, 1900.
> Description: Autographed and dated at first in pencil, notes inked in, on front flyleaf: 'sept. 1920'.

Annotated in ink. Underlined in red crayon.
Collection: Tolkien's personal Celtic library, preserved at the Weston library under the auspices of the English Faculty Library (Oxford).
S.s. 1: Fimi (2007), p. 53.
S.s. 2: *The Lay of Aotrou & Itroun* (2016), p. 24.

1516. _____. *Die Lais de Marie de France*. Edited by Karl Warnke. Halle: Max Niemayer, 1925.
Description: Signed by Tolkien on front free endpaper.
Collection: Private [Sold by Simon Finch Rare Books Ltd.].
S.s.: Finch (2002), p. 53.

1517. Maritain, Jacques. *An Introduction to Philosophy*. Translated by Edward Ingram Watkin. London: Sheed & Ward, 1942 (7th impr.).
Description: Inscribed in pencil on front flyleaf: 'J.R.R. Tolkien | 1944'. Contains a handwritten note about setting an RAF cadet examination: "R.N and R.A.F. Cadets | History of the English Language | These copies of the Extracts (Old and Middle English) and Texts are for use in Papers I and II Monday morning, 11 September; and Tuesday morning, 12 September. They should not be marked, and should be returned with the answer-paper at the end of the morning Session on 12 September. The passage set for translation in The Reeve's Tale (170-206) will be found on page 9 Thise sely clerks, to page 10 as is your guise! The passage set from Sir Orfeo is page 7 Oway to the last line of the page (234-264)."
Collection: Private [Charles Styles, book given to him by John and Hilary Haddleton who knew Tolkien].

1518. Marlowe, Christopher. *Edward II*.
S.s.: University of Leeds (1920), p. 147. English Language and Literature - Scheme A. Texts and Period selected for 1920-21. (b) Special period: 1557-1637. (c) Texts suggested for study with Special Period. Ordinary Degree of B.A. with Honours. Final Examination.

1519. _____. *The Tragical history of Dr Faustus*. London: Routledge, 1910.
S.s. 1: University of Leeds (1920), p. 147. English Language and Literature - Scheme A. Texts and Period selected for 1920-21. (b) Special period: 1557-1637. (c) Texts suggested for study with Special Period. Ordinary Degree of B.A. with Honours. Final Examination.
S.s. 2: University of Leeds (1923), p. 81. Ordinary Degree of B.A., Intermediate Course and Examination: English Literature. Text selected for 1923-24 (ii) Texts suggestes as part of a course of general rending in the period 1579-1645.

1520. Marsh, Edward Howard (Edited by). *Georgian Poetry 1911-1912*. London: The Poetry Booshop, 1912.
S.s. 1: Scull-Hammond (2006b), p. 819. 'If he followed G.B. Smith's advice in July 1915, he bought and read all of Rupert Brooke's poems [A. 222], and at least one of the volumes of *Georgian Poetry*.'
S.s. 2: Drout (2007), p. 367.

1521. Marstrander, Carl Johan Sverdrup. *Observations sur les présents indo-européens à nasale infixée en celtique*. Series: Videnskapsselskapets Skrifter, II. Hist.-Filos. Klasse. 1924. no. 4. Christiania: Jacob Dybwad, 1924.
Description: Autographed on front flyleaf.
Notes: Bound together with A. 1522.
Collection: Tolkien's personal Celtic library, preserved at the Weston library under the auspices of the English Faculty Library (Oxford).

1522. _____. *Une Correspondence germano-celtique*. Series: Videnskapsselskapets Skrifter, 8. Christiania: Jacob Dybwad, 1924.
Description: Autographed on front flyleaf.
Notes: Bound together with A. 1521
Collection: Tolkien's personal Celtic library, preserved at the Weston library under the auspices of the English Faculty Library (Oxford).

1523. Marvell, Andrew. *Satires*. London: A. H. Bullen, 1901.
S.s.: University of Leeds (1921), p. 154. English Language and Literature - Scheme A. Texts and Period selected for 1921-22. (d) Texts suggested for study with Special Period 1637-1700. Ordinary Degree of B.A.

with Honours. Final Examinations.

1524. Masefield, John. *A Letter from Pontus and other verse*. London: William Heinmann and Sons, 1936.
S.s.: Scull-Hammond (2017a), p. 234. 11 August 1938 Tolkien writes to John Masefield. He enjoyed hearing his *Letter from Pontus* which Masefield read in the Summer Diversions, as well as the prologue and epilogues. He asks for a copy of them.

1525. _____. *Reynard the Fox*. New York: Macmillan, 1921.
P.s. 1: *On Fairy-stories* (1947), p. 46.
P.s. 2: 'Nomenclature of *The Lord of the Rings*' (1966), p. 758 '*Isengrim*.'
P.s. 3: *Tolkien On Fairy-stories* (2008), p. 36.
P.s. 4: *Tolkien On Fairy-stories* (2008) 'Manuscript B [MS. Tolkien 4, fols. 73-120]', p. 217.
P.s. 5: *Tolkien On Fairy-stories* (2008) 'Manuscript B [MS. Tolkien 14, fol. 25]', p. 281.

1526. Maskell, William. *Ivories ancient and mediæval*. London: Chapman and Hall, 1875.
P.s.: MS. Tolkien A 19/3 *Etymologies or history of Walrus* fols. 162-195. [Tolkien Papers, Bodleian Library, Oxford].
S.s.: Tolkien, *Family Album* (1992), p. 42.
NED: #2 i. | 'W' (1928), pp. 57-8 'Walrus, 3. *attrib.* and *comb.*' 1875 – 'In quality and beauty of appearance walrus ivory scarcely yields to that of the elephant' (p. 2).

1527. Mason, William Shaw. *A Statistical Account, Or Parochial Survey of Ireland: Drawn Up from the Communications of the Clergy*, Vol. I. Dublin: Printed by Graisberry and Campbell, 1814.
P.s.: *Oxford University Press Archives* (Oxford). A slip written by Tolkien on the etymology of 'Wake' used ('W' p. 31) [A. 1721].
NED: #2 f. | 'W' (1928), p. 31 'Wake, 3.' 1814 – 'The Presbyterian wake is conducted with profound silence and great decorum … The wakes of the members of the established church differ little from those in other parts of Ireland' (p. 596).

1528. Massingham, Harold John. *A Treasury of Seventeenth Century English Verse from the Death of Shakespeare to the restoration (1616-1660)*. London: Macmillan, 1920.
S.s.: University of Leeds (1920), p. 139 English Language and Literature: English Literature. Text selected for 1920-21. Texts Selected for 1920-21. Ordinary Degree of B.A. with Honours. Final Course and Examination

1529. Matthes, Henrich Christoph. 'Das Orrmulum und die Frage der intonationsgerechten Orthographie'. Offprint from *Anglia, Zeitschrift fur englische Philologie*, Vol. LV, 1931, pp. 400-11.
Description: Inscribed on front cover: 'Ergebenst überreicht | vom verfasser'. Beneath this in pencil: 'to H. C. K. Wyld | to me | JRRT'. Contains visiting card of Dr Heinrich Matthes.
Collection: Tolkien's personal Celtic library, preserved at the Weston library under the auspices of the English Faculty Library (Oxford).

1530. Matthew, Arnold. *Essays in criticism*. Second Series. London: Macmillan, 1913.
S.s.: University of Leeds (1921), p. 141. English Literature, text selected for 1921-22. Ordinary Degree of B.A.; p. 154. English Language and Literature - Scheme A. Texts and Period selected for 1921-22. (e) History of Criticism: Special Texts suggested for study. Ordinary Degree of B.A. with Honours. Final Examinations.

1531. Mätzner, Eduard. *Altenglische Sprachproben: Nebst einem Wörterbuche*, Vol. I. Berlin: Weidmann'sche Buchhandlung, 1867.
P.s.: MS. Tolkien A 13/1 *annotated texts of King Horn* fol. 94. [Tolkien Papers, Bodleian Library, Oxford].

1532. Mawer, Allen. *The place-names of Northumberland and Durham*. Cambridge: The University Press, 1920.
P.s.: 'Chaucer as a Philologist: *The Reeve's Tale*' (1934), p. 150. Tolkien quotes: 'The Durham area … patrimonium Sancti Cuthberti' (p. xiii).

1533. _____. 'Some place-name identifications in the Anglo-Saxon chronicles'. *Anglica:*

Untersuchungen zur englischen Philologie: Alois Brandl zum 70. Geburtstage überreicht, Vol. I [A. 30], 1925.
    P.s.: *Philology: General Works* (VI 1927, for 1925), p. 50.

1534. _____ and Frank Merry Stenton (Edited by). *Introduction to the Survey of English place-names*, Vol. I, Pt. I. Introduction to the survey of English place-names. Cambridge: The University Press, 1924.
    P.s. 1: *Philology: General Works* (V 1926, for 1924), p. 55 n. 13, 56, 64.
    P.s. 2: *Finn and Hengest* (1982), p. 67 n. 65.

1535. _____ and Frank Merry Stenton (Edited by). *Introduction to the Survey of English place-names*, Vol. I, Pt. II. The chief elements used in English place-names. Cambridge: The University Press, 1924.
    P.s.: *Philology: General Works* (V 1926, for 1924), p. 55 n. 13.

1536. _____ and Frank Merry Stenton (Edited by). *The place-names of Buckinghamshire*. English Place-name Society, 2. Cambridge: The University Press, 1925.
    P.s.: *Philology: General Works* (V 1926, for 1924), p. 48 n. 8.

1537. Mayer, Charles-Joseph (Edited by). *Cabinet des fées, ou, Collection choisie des contes des fées et autre contes merveilleux*, Vol. 1. Précis de la vie et des ouvrages de Charles Perrault, avec l'analyses de ses contes – Contient aussi: 'Contes des fées' par Charles Perrault; 'Nouveaux contes des fées', par madame la comtesse de Murat, comprenant: 'Le parfait amour. Anguillette. Jeune et belle. Le palais de la vengeance. Le prince des feuilles. L'heureuse peine'. Amsterdam; Paris, 1785.
    P.s. 1: *Tolkien On Fairy-stories* (2008) 'Manuscript A. [MS Tolkien 4, fols. 59-77]', p. 188 'But in general I disliked most of the more fairyish fairy stories (to which I vastly preferred novels: stories of my own day). the children and was I was most attracted by the older tales that hat not come through the frippery and folly/finery of *Cabinet*.'
    P.s. 2: *Tolkien On Fairy-stories* (2008) 'Manuscript B [MS. Tolkien 4, fols. 73-120]', p. 214 'I have never had much affection for even Perrault. For so powerful has been influence of Charles Perrault dince his *Contes de ma Mére L'Oye* was first Englished (in the eighteenth century), and of such other excerpts from the vast sorehouse of the *Cabinet de Fées* as have become wellknown, that still, I suppose, fi anyone were asked to name at random a typical 'fairy-story', he would name one of these French things such a *Puss-in-Boots, Cinderella, Red Ridding Hood*.'; p. 235 'I preferred the older tales that had not acquired the frippery and finery of the *Cabinet des Fées*.'; p. 251.
    P.s. 3: #1 a. | *Tolkien On Fairy-stories* (2008), p. 309.

1538. _____ (Edited by). *Cabinet des fées, ou, Collection choisie des contes des fées et autre contes merveilleux*, Vol. 2. Contes des fées, par madame la comtesse d'Aulnoy. Amsterdam; Paris, 1785.
    P.s.: *Tolkien On Fairy-stories* (2008) [see A. 1537, P.s. 1, P.s. 2, P.s. 3].

1539. _____ (Edited by). *Cabinet des fées, ou, Collection choisie des contes des fées et autre contes merveilleux*, Vol. 3. La suite des contes des fées, par madame la comtesse d'Aulnoy – Contient aussi: 'Les fées à la mode' du même auteur. Amsterdam; Paris, 1785.
    P.s.: *Tolkien On Fairy-stories* (2008) [see A. 1537, P.s. 1, P.s. 2, P.s. 3].

1540. _____ (Edited by). *Cabinet des fées, ou, Collection choisie des contes des fées et autre contes merveilleux*, Vol. 4. La suite des fées à la mode, par madame la comtesse d'Aulnoy. Amsterdam; Paris, 1785.

P.s.: *Tolkien On Fairy-stories* (2008) [see A. 1537, P.s. 1, P.s. 2, P.s. 3].

1541. _____ (Edited by). *Cabinet des fées, ou, Collection choisie des contes des fées et autre contes merveilleux*, Vol. 5. Les illustres fées. – Par la comtesse d'Aulnoy, d'après Barbier; attribué aussi à Louis de Mailly ou à madame d'Auneuil. – Contient aussi: 'La tyrannie des fées détruite', par madame la comtesse d'Auneuil; 'Les contes moins contes que les autres' par Jean de Préchac, comprenant: 'Sans parangon' et 'La reine des fées'. Amsterdam; Paris, 1785.
    P.s.: *Tolkien On Fairy-stories* (2008) [see A. 1537, P.s. 1, P.s. 2, P.s. 3].

1542. _____ (Edited by). *Cabinet des fées, ou, Collection choisie des contes des fées et autre contes merveilleux*, Vol. 6. Fées, contes des contes: Plus belle que fée, Persinette, L'enchanteur, Tourbillon, Vert et Bleu, Le pays des délices, La puissance d'amour, La Bonne Femme, par mademoiselle de Laforce. – Contient aussi: 'Les chevaliers errants et le génie familier' par la comtesse d'Auneuil. Amsterdam; Paris, 1785.
    P.s.: *Tolkien On Fairy-stories* (2008) [see A. 1537, P.s. 1, P.s. 2, P.s. 3].

1543. _____ (Edited by). *Cabinet des fées, ou, Collection choisie des contes des fées et autre contes merveilleux*, Vol. 7. Les mille et une nuits, contes arabes, traduits en françois par M. Galland. Amsterdam; Paris, 1785.
    P.s. 1: *Tolkien On Fairy-stories* (2008) [see A. 1537, P.s. 1, P.s. 2, P.s. 3].
    P.s. 2: *Tolkien On Fairy-stories* (2008) 'Manuscript A. [MS Tolkien 4, fols. 59-77]', p. 184.

1544. _____ (Edited by). *Cabinet des fées, ou, Collection choisie des contes des fées et autre contes merveilleux*, Vol. 8. Les mille et une nuits, contes arabes, traduits en françois par M. Galland. Amsterdam; Paris, 1785.
    P.s. 1: *Tolkien On Fairy-stories* (2008) [see A. 1537, P.s. 1, P.s. 2, P.s. 3].
    P.s. 2: *Tolkien On Fairy-stories* (2008) 'Manuscript A. [MS Tolkien 4, fols. 59-77]', p. 184.

1545. _____ (Edited by). *Cabinet des fées, ou, Collection choisie des contes des fées et autre contes merveilleux*, Vol. 9. Les mille et une nuits, contes arabes, traduits en françois par M. Galland. Amsterdam; Paris, 1785.
    P.s. 1: *Tolkien On Fairy-stories* (2008) [see A. 1537, P.s. 1, P.s. 2, P.s. 3].
    P.s. 2: *Tolkien On Fairy-stories* (2008) 'Manuscript A. [MS Tolkien 4, fols. 59-77]', p. 184.

1546. _____ (Edited by). *Cabinet des fées, ou, Collection choisie des contes des fées et autre contes merveilleux*, Vol. 10. Les mille et une nuits, contes arabes, traduits en françois par M. Galland. Amsterdam; Paris, 1785.
    P.s. 1: *Tolkien On Fairy-stories* (2008) [see A. 1537, P.s. 1, P.s. 2, P.s. 3].
    P.s. 2: *Tolkien On Fairy-stories* (2008) 'Manuscript A. [MS Tolkien 4, fols. 59-77]', p. 184.

1547. _____ (Edited by). *Cabinet des fées, ou, Collection choisie des contes des fées et autre contes merveilleux*, Vol. 11. Les mille et une nuits, contes arabes, traduits en françois par M. Galland. Amsterdam; Paris, 1785.
    P.s. 1: *Tolkien On Fairy-stories* (2008) [see A. 1537, P.s. 1, P.s. 2, P.s. 3].
    P.s. 2: *Tolkien On Fairy-stories* (2008) 'Manuscript A. [MS Tolkien 4, fols. 59-77]', p. 184.

1548. _____ (Edited by). *Cabinet des fées, ou, Collection choisie des contes des fées et autre contes merveilleux*, Vol. 12. La tour ténébreuse et les jours lumineux [Texte imprimé], contes anglois, par mademoiselle L'Héritier. – Contient aussi: 'Les aventures d'Abdalla, fils d'Hanif, ou son voyage à l'île de Borico' par l'abbé Bignon. Amsterdam; Paris, 1785.

P.s.: *Tolkien On Fairy-stories* (2008) [see A. 1537, P.s. 1, P.s. 2, P.s. 3].

1549. _____ (Edited by). *Cabinet des fées, ou, Collection choisie des contes des fées et autre contes merveilleux*, Vol. 13. La suite des aventures d'Abdalla, fils d'Hanif, ou son voyage à l'île de Borico. – Par l'abbé Jean-Paul Bignon, d'après la Bibliographie du genre romanesque français, 1751-1800. Amsterdam; Paris, 1785.
P.s.: *Tolkien On Fairy-stories* (2008) [see A. 1537, P.s. 1, P.s. 2, P.s. 3].

1550. _____ (Edited by). *Cabinet des fées, ou, Collection choisie des contes des fées et autre contes merveilleux*, Vol. 14. Les mille et un jours, contes persans, traduits en français par M. Petis de La Croix. Amsterdam; Paris, 1785.
P.s.: *Tolkien On Fairy-stories* (2008) [see A. 1537, P.s. 1, P.s. 2, P.s. 3].

1551. _____ (Edited by). *Cabinet des fées, ou, Collection choisie des contes des fées et autre contes merveilleux*, Vol. 15. Les mille et un jours, contes persans, traduits en français par M. Petis de La Croix. Amsterdam; Paris, 1785.
P.s.: *Tolkien On Fairy-stories* (2008) [see A. 1537, P.s. 1, P.s. 2, P.s. 3].

1552. _____ (Edited by). *Cabinet des fées, ou, Collection choisie des contes des fées et autre contes merveilleux*, Vol. 16. L'histoire de la sultane de Perse et des visirs [sic], contes turcs, composés en langue turque par Chec Zadé et traduite en français par M. Galland. – Contient aussi: 'Les voyages de Zulma dans le pays des fées' par l'abbé Nadal, d'après Barbier. Amsterdam; Paris, 1785.
P.s.: *Tolkien On Fairy-stories* (2008) [see A. 1537, P.s. 1, P.s. 2, P.s. 3].

1553. _____ (Edited by). *Cabinet des fées, ou, Collection choisie des contes des fées et autre contes merveilleux*, Vol. 17. Les contes et fables indiennes de Bidpai et de Lokman, traduites d'Ali Tchélébi ben Saleh, auteur turc. Oeuvre posthume par M. Galland – Trad. d'après la version turque 'Ali-Tchelebi ibn-Salih; la trad. commencée par Antoine Galland a été continuée et finie par Denis-Dominique Cardonne. Amsterdam; Paris, 1785.
P.s.: *Tolkien On Fairy-stories* (2008) [see A. 1537, P.s. 1, P.s. 2, P.s. 3].

1554. _____ (Edited by). *Cabinet des fées, ou, Collection choisie des contes des fées et autre contes merveilleux*, Vol. 18. Suite des contes et fables indiennes de Bidpaï et de Lokman, traduits d'Ali-Tchélébi-ben-Saleh, auteur turc. – Trad. d'après la version turque d'Ali-Tchelebi ibn-Salih; la trad. commencée par Antoine Galland a été continuée et finie par Denis-Dominique Cardonne. – Contient aussi: 'Fables et contes composés pour l'éducation de feu monseigneur le duc de Bourgogne' par Fénelon; 'Boca, ou La vertu récompensée' par Françoise Le Marchand. Amsterdam; Paris, 1785.
P.s.: *Tolkien On Fairy-stories* (2008) [see A. 1537, P.s. 1, P.s. 2, P.s. 3].

1555. _____ (Edited by). *Cabinet des fées, ou, Collection choisie des contes des fées et autre contes merveilleux*, Vol. 19. Les contes chinois, ou Les aventures merveilleuses du mandarin Fum-Hoam, par Gueulette. – Contient aussi: 'Florine, ou La belle Italienne'. Titre alternatif: Les aventures merveilleuses du mandarin Fum-Hoam. Amsterdam; Paris, 1785.
P.s.: *Tolkien On Fairy-stories* (2008) [see A. 1537, P.s. 1, P.s. 2, P.s. 3].

1556. _____ (Edited by). *Cabinet des fées, ou, Collection choisie des contes des fées et autre contes merveilleux*, Vol. 20. Le bélier, Fleur-d'Épine, Les quatre Facardins,

par M. le comte Hamilton. Amsterdam; Paris, 1785.
   P.s.: Tolkien On Fairy-stories (2008) [see A. 1537, P.s. 1, P.s. 2, P.s. 3].

1557. _____ (Edited by). *Cabinet des fées, ou, Collection choisie des contes des fées et autre contes merveilleux*, Vol. 21. Les mille et un quart [sic] d'heure, contes tartares, par M. Gueulette. Amsterdam; Paris, 1786.
   P.s.: Tolkien On Fairy-stories (2008) [see A. 1537, P.s. 1, P.s. 2, P.s. 3].

1558. _____ (Edited by). *Cabinet des fées, ou, Collection choisie des contes des fées et autre contes merveilleux*, Vol. 22. La suite des mille et un quart [sic] – d'heure, contes tartares, par M. Gueulette. – Contient aussi: 'Les sultanes de Guzaratte, ou Les songes des hommes éveillés' du même auteur. Amsterdam; Paris, 1786.
   P.s.: Tolkien On Fairy-stories (2008) [see A. 1537, P.s. 1, P.s. 2, P.s. 3].

1559. _____ (Edited by). *Cabinet des fées, ou, Collection choisie des contes des fées et autre contes merveilleux*, Vol. 23 La suite des sultanes de Guzaratte, ou Les songes des hommes éveillés, contes mogols, par M. Gueullette. Amsterdam; Paris, 1786.
   P.s.: Tolkien On Fairy-stories (2008) [see A. 1537, P.s. 1, P.s. 2, P.s. 3].

1560. _____ (Edited by). *Cabinet des fées, ou, Collection choisie des contes des fées et autre contes merveilleux*, Vol. 24 Le prince des Aigues-Marines, et Le prince invisible [Texte imprimé], par madame L'Evêque. – Contient aussi: 'Les féeries nouvelles', par le comte de Caylus. Amsterdam; Paris, 1786.
   P.s.: Tolkien On Fairy-stories (2008) [see A. 1537, P.s. 1, P.s. 2, P.s. 3].

1561. _____ (Edited by). *Cabinet des fées, ou, Collection choisie des contes des fées et autre contes merveilleux*, Vol. 25 Les nouveaux contes orientaux, par M. le comte de Caylus. – Contient aussi: 'Tout vient à point qui peut attendre, ou Cadichon et Jeannette' du même auteur; les 'Contes des fées' par François-Augustin Paradis de Moncrif. Amsterdam; Paris, 1786.
   P.s.: Tolkien On Fairy-stories (2008) [see A. 1537, P.s. 1, P.s. 2, P.s. 3].

1562. _____ (Edited by). *Cabinet des fées, ou, Collection choisie des contes des fées et autre contes merveilleux*, Vol. 26. La reine Fantasque, par J. J. Rousseau. – Contient aussi: 'La Belle et la Bête' par madame de Villeneuve; 'Les veillées de Thessalie' par mademoiselle de Lussan. Amsterdam; Paris, 1786.
   P.s.: Tolkien On Fairy-stories (2008) [see A. 1537, P.s. 1, P.s. 2, P.s. 3].

1563. _____ (Edited by). *Cabinet des fées, ou, Collection choisie des contes des fées et autre contes merveilleux*, Vol. 27. La suite des veillées de Thessalie, par mademoiselle de Lussan. – Contient aussi: 'Histoire du prince Titi' par Thémiseul de Saint-Hyacinthe. Amsterdam; Paris, 1786.
   P.s.: Tolkien On Fairy-stories (2008) [see A. 1537, P.s. 1, P.s. 2, P.s. 3].

1564. _____ (Edited by). *Cabinet des fées, ou, Collection choisie des contes des fées et autre contes merveilleux*, Vol. 28. La suite de l'histoire du prince Titi, par S. Hyacinthe. – Comporte une conclusion par Charles-Joseph Mayer, d'après la Bibliographie du genre romanesque français 1751-1800. Amsterdam; Paris, 1786.
   P.s.: Tolkien On Fairy-stories (2008) [see A. 1537, P.s. 1, P.s. 2, P.s. 3].

1565. _____ (Edited by). *Cabinet des fées, ou, Collection choisie des contes des*

fées et autre contes merveilleux, Vol. 29. Les contes des génies, ou Les charmantes leçons d'Horam, fils d'Asmar ... par sir Charles Morell. – Trad. de 'The tales of the Genii or The delightful lessons of Horam, the son of Asmar'. Amsterdam; Paris, 1786.
  P.s.: *Tolkien On Fairy-stories* (2008) [see A. 1537, P.s. 1, P.s. 2, P.s. 3].

1566. _____ (Edited by). *Cabinet des fées, ou, Collection choisie des contes des fées et autre contes merveilleux*, Vol. 30. Les contes des génies, ou Les charmantes leçons d'Horam, fils d'Asmar ... par sir Charles Morell. – Trad. de 'The tales of the Genii or The delightful lessons of Horam, the son of Asmar'. Amsterdam; Paris, 1786.
  P.s.: *Tolkien On Fairy-stories* (2008) [see A. 1537, P.s. 1, P.s. 2, P.s. 3].

1567. _____ (Edited by). *Cabinet des fées, ou, Collection choisie des contes des fées et autre contes merveilleux*, Vol. 31. Funestine, par Beauchamps. – Contient aussi: 'Nouveaux contes de fées' attribués à Louis de Mailly, comprenant: 'La petite grenouille verte. Les perroquets. Le Navire volant. Le prince Perinet ou L'origine des pagodes. Incarnat, blanc, et noir. Le buisson d'épines fleuries. Alphinge ou Le singe vert. Kadour. Le médecin de satin. Le prince Arc-en-ciel'; 'Le loup galeux' et 'Bellinette' par le comte de Caylus. Amsterdam; Paris, 1786.
  P.s.: *Tolkien On Fairy-stories* (2008) [see A. 1537, P.s. 1, P.s. 2, P.s. 3].

1568. _____ (Edited by). *Cabinet des fées, ou, Collection choisie des contes des fées et autre contes merveilleux*, Vol. 32. Les soirées bretonnes, dédiées à monseigneur le Dauphin. Par M. Gueulette. – Contient aussi: 'Trois nouveaux contes des fées' par madame de Lintot, comprenant: 'Timandre et Bleuette; le prince Sincer; Tendrebrun et Constance'; 'Les aventures de Zeloïde et d'Amanzarifdine, contes indiens' par M. de Moncrif. Amsterdam; Paris, 1786.
  P.s.: *Tolkien On Fairy-stories* (2008) [see A. 1537, P.s. 1, P.s. 2, P.s. 3].

1569. _____ (Edited by). *Cabinet des fées, ou, Collection choisie des contes des fées et autre contes merveilleux*, Vol. 33. Trois contes, de mademoiselle de Lubert. – Comprend: 'La princesse Lionnette et le prince Coquerico. Le prince Glacé et la princesse Étincelante. La princesse Camion'. – Contient aussi: 'Nourjahad', trad de: 'The history of Nourjahad' par Frances Sheridan. Amsterdam; Paris, 1786.
  P.s.: *Tolkien On Fairy-stories* (2008) [see A. 1537, P.s. 1, P.s. 2, P.s. 3].

1570. _____ (Edited by). *Cabinet des fées, ou, Collection choisie des contes des fées et autre contes merveilleux*, Vol. 34. La bibliothèque des fées et des génies recueillie par l'abbé de La Porte. – Réunit: 'Les contes' de M. Pajon comprenant: 'Eritzine et Parelin', 'L'enchanteur ou La bague de puissance' et 'Histoire des trois fils d'Hali Bassa de la mer, et des filles de Siroco, gouverneur d'Alexandrie'; 'La princesse Minon-Minette' et 'Aphranor et Bellanire', par le comte de Caylus; 'Merveilleux et Charmante', 'Grisdelin et Charmante', 'Le prince Ananas' par des auteurs inconnus; 'Cornichon et Toupette' par mademoiselle de Lubert. Amsterdam; Paris, 1786.
  P.s.: *Tolkien On Fairy-stories* (2008) [see A. 1537, P.s. 1, P.s. 2, P.s. 3].

1571. _____ (Edited by). *Cabinet des fées, ou, Collection choisie des contes des fées et autre contes merveilleux*, Vol. 35. Minet-bleu et Louvette [Texte imprimé], par madame Fagnan. – Contient aussi: 'Acajou et Zirphile' par Charles Duclos; 'Aglaé ou Nabotine' par Charles-Antoine Coypel; 'Contes des fées' par Jeanne-

Marie Leprince de Beaumont; 'Le prince Désiré' par; 'Contes choisis, extraits de différents recueils'. Amsterdam; Paris, 1786.
P.s.: *Tolkien On Fairy-stories* (2008) [see A. 1537, P.s. 1, P.s. 2, P.s. 3].

1572. _____ (Edited by). *Cabinet des fées, ou, Collection choisie des contes des fées et autre contes merveilleux*, Vol. 36. Les aventures merveilleuses de Don Silvio de Rosalva, traduites de l'allemand de M. Wieland par Madame d'Ussieux. – Publié en 1770 sous le titre: 'Le nouveau don Quichotte'. – Trad. de: 'Der Sieg der Natur über die Schwärmerey oder Die Abenteuer des Don Sylvio von Rosalva' par Louis d'Ussieux ou madame d'Ussieux d'après la Bibliographie du genre romanesque français 1751-1800. Amsterdam; Paris, 1786.
P.s.: Tolkien On Fairy-stories (2008) [see A. 1537, P.s. 1, P.s. 2, P.s. 3].

1573. _____ (Edited by). *Cabinet des fées, ou, Collection choisie des contes des fées et autre contes merveilleux*, Vol. 37. Notice des auteurs qui ont écrit dans le genre des contes de fees. – Contient aussi la liste complète des ouvrages de la collection Amsterdam; Paris, 1786.
P.s.: *Tolkien On Fairy-stories* (2008) [see A. 1537, P.s. 1, P.s. 2, P.s. 3].

1574. _____ (Edited by). *Cabinet des fées, ou, Collection choisie des contes des fées et autre contes merveilleux*, Vol. 38. Suite des Mille et une nuits, contes arabes, traduits par dom Chavis et M. Cazotte – A paru aussi en 1788-1789 sous le titre: 'Continuation des Mille et une nuits'. Amsterdam; Paris, 1788.
P.s.: *Tolkien On Fairy-stories* (2008) [see A. 1537, P.s. 1, P.s. 2, P.s. 3].

1575. _____ (Edited by). *Cabinet des fées, ou, Collection choisie des contes des fées et autre contes merveilleux*, Vol. 39. Suite des Mille et une nuits, contes arabes, traduits par dom Chavis et M. Cazotte – A paru aussi en 1788-1789 sous le titre: 'Continuation des Mille et une nuits'. Amsterdam; Paris, 1788.
P.s.: *Tolkien On Fairy-stories* (2008) [see A. 1537, P.s. 1, P.s. 2, P.s. 3].

1576. _____ (Edited by). *Cabinet des fées, ou, Collection choisie des contes des fées et autre contes merveilleux*, Vol. 40. Suite des Mille et une nuits, contes arabes, traduits par dom Chavis et M. Cazotte – A paru aussi en 1788-1789 sous le titre: 'Continuation des Mille et une nuits'. Amsterdam; Paris, 1788.
P.s.: *Tolkien On Fairy-stories* (2008) [see A. 1537, P.s. 1, P.s. 2, P.s. 3].

1577. Mayhew, Anthony Lawson. *A concise dictionary of Middle English from A.D. 1150 to 1580*. Oxford: At the Clarendon Press, 1888.
P.s.: MS. Res. e. 308 *Sir Gawain and the Green Knight*. [Tolkien Papers, Bodleian Library, Oxford].

1578. _____ (Edited by). *The Promptorium Parvulorum. The first English-Latin dictionary*. Series: E.E.T.S. (Early English Text Society), ES 102. London: Published for the Early English Text Society by Kegan Paul, Trench, Trübner and Co., 1908.
Description: Inscribed on front cover in pencil: 'Tolkien | 15'.
Collection: Tolkien's personal Celtic library, preserved at the Weston library under the auspices of the English Faculty Library (Oxford).
P.s. 1: MS. Tolkien A 21/13 fol. 119. Note by Tolkien, 'Books in Exeter Library useful', with shelfmarks, on back of photostat reading list dated October 1913. Tolkien writes: 'All EETS publications'. [Tolkien Papers, Bodleian Library, Oxford].
P.s. 2: MS. Tolkien A 11 *Notes on Pearl* fol. 124. [Tolkien Papers, Bodleian Library, Oxford].
P.s. 3: *A Middle English Vocabulary* (1922). Tolkien refers to the *Promptorium Parvulorum* on

the terms 'Balȝ' (*balwe*, planus), 'Coffes' (*cuffe*, glove or meteyne), 'Cokeres' (*cocur*, cothurnus).
P.s. 4: 'Chaucer as a Philologist: *The Reeve's Tale*' (1934), pp. 133, 137
S.s.: Fitzgerald (2009), p. 53 n. 9.

1579.   Maynader, Howard. *The wife of Bath's tale; its sources and analogues*. Series: Grimm library, 13. London. David Nutt, 1901.
P.s.: *Sir Gawain and the Green Knight* (1925), p. xxvi. Tolkien and Gordon write: 'For bibliography of the Irish and French analogues of *Sir Gawain*, see the bibliography in Kittredge's study'. [*NED*] In Kittredge's study, this article is mentioned in 'II. Gawain and the Green Knight' (p. 293 n. 2).

1580.   McCallum, Ronald Buchanan. *Public Opinion and the Last Peace*. London: Oxford University Press, 1944.
Notes: McCallum writes: 'My colleague, Professor J.R.R. Tolkien, has suggested that there is an important connection between the word *pacifist* and the term *passive-resistance*. It is partly a mere suggestion of sound, as both words begin with the same syllable, however different they may be etymologically. There is also the historical fact that *passive resistance* has been used as a method of opposing governments armed with force, as for instance the '*passive resisters*' who refused to pay rates under the Balfour Education Bill of 1902 and the passive resistance to which. Mr. Gandhi from time to time summons his followers in India' (p. 174).

1581.   McIntosh, Angus. *Introduction to a survey of Scottish dialects*. Edinburgh: Thomas Nelson, 1952.
Description: Inscribed on front flyleaf: 'To J.R.R. Tolkien | with greetings and good wishes | from | Angus McIntosh.'
Collection: Tolkien's personal Celtic library, preserved at the Weston library under the auspices of the English Faculty Library (Oxford).
P.s.: *Philology: General Works* (V 1926, for 1924), p. 55 n. 13.

1582.   McLaughlin, John C. *A graphemic-phonemic study of a Middle English manuscript*. The Hague: Mouton, 1963.
P.s.: *Sir Gawain and the Green Knight* (1967) 'Select Bibliography', p. 154.

1583.   Meissner, Albert L. *The Public School German Grammar*. London and Paris, 1908.
Description: King Edward's School. Inscribed by Dr Meissner: 'J.R.R. Tolkien in der erste Klasse der Königedwardschüle Birmingham England eine deutsche Grammatik von Dr Meissner.' Inscribed by Tolkien: 'J.R.R. Tolkien I K.E.H.S. 1908'. Some annotations. Loose leaf and another loose leaf still between pp. 290-91 [Judith Priestman 1994, revd. 2016].
Collection: Weston Library, Bodleian Libraries (Oxford).
S.s.: Zettersten (2011), p. 78 'During my last visit to the Tolkien Collection at the Bodleian Library, Oxford, I went through Tolkien's books in his private library from his school time, which his family had donated to the Bodleian in July 1982.'

1584.   Mellersh, Harold Edward Leslie. *Soldiers of Rome*. London: Robert Hale Ltd, 1964.
Description: Written on M.H.R. personal book label (on the front flyleaf) 'from: Daddy and Mummy. | Michael H.R. Tolkien | Cleveleys | October 22nd 1964'.
Collection: Private [Pieter Collier].

1585.   Menner, Robert James. 'The Anglian vocabulary of the Bickling homilies'. Offprint from *Philologica: the Malone anniversary studies* edited by Thomas Austin Kirby. Baltimore: Johns Hopkins Press, 1949, pp. 56-64.
Description: In manuscript on front: 'To Professor Tolkien from R.J. Menner'. Includes a label added by Stan Revell to books owned by Tolkien, 'From the Library of J.R.R. Tolkien'.
Collection: John J. Burns Special Collections Library, Boston College (Chestnut Hill, Massachusetts).

1586. _____. 'Middle English *lagmon* (*Gawain* 1729) and Modern English lag'. *Philological Quarterly: a journal devoted to scholarly investigation in the classical and modern languages and literatures*, Vol. 10. Iowa: University of Iowa, 1931, pp. 163-68.
- P.s. 1: *Sir Gawain and the Green Knight* (1936, 3rd ed.), p. 110, line 1729 lad hem bi lagmon.
- P.s. 2: MS. Tolkien A 12/1 *Commentary on Sir Gawain, lines 37-1987* fol. 100. [Tolkien Papers, Bodleian Library, Oxford].

1587. _____. 'Two Old English words' (1. 'Old Anglian *(ge)strynd*' And 2. 'OE *gullisc*'). Offprint from MLN (*Modern Language Notes*), Vol. 59, no. 2, February 1944, pp. 106-112.
- Description: In manuscript on front: 'OE gestrynd gullisc R.J. Menner'. Includes a label added by Stan Revell to books owned by Tolkien, 'From the Library of J.R.R. Tolkien'.
- Collection: John J. Burns Special Collections Library, Boston College (Chestnut Hill, Massachusetts).

1588. _____ (Edited by). *Purity; a Middle English poem*. New Haven: Yale University Press, 1920.
- Description: Annotated in pencil.
- Collection: Tolkien's personal Celtic library, preserved at the Weston library under the auspices of the English Faculty Library (Oxford).
- P.s. 1: *Sir Gawain and the Green Knight* (1925), p. xxv.
- P.s. 2: *Sir Gawain and the Green Knight* (1930 2nd ed.), p. 114, line 2329 *fermed*.
- P.s. 3: *Sir Gawain and the Green Knight* (1967) 'Select Bibliography', p. 153.

1589. Méon, Dominique Martin. *Nouveau recueil de fabliaux et contes inédits des poètes français des XIIe, XIIIe, XIVe et XVe siecles*, Vol. I. Paris: Chasseriau, 1823.
- P.s.: *Sir Gawain and the Green Knight* (1925), p. xxvi. Tolkien and Gordon write: 'For bibliography of the Irish and French analogues of *Sir Gawain*, see the bibliography in Kittredge's study'. [NED] In Kittredge's study, this article is mentioned in 'VI. La Mule sanz Frain' (p. 298), 'X. Le Chevalier à l'Épée' (p. 302).

1590. Meriton, George. *George Meriton's A Yorkshire dialogue* (1683). Edited by Arthur C. Cawley. Series: Yorkshire Dialect Society reprint, 2. Kendal: Titus Wilson, 1959.
- Description: In manuscript on inside front cover: 'To Professor J.R.R. Tolkien with good wishes from A.C. Cawley June 1959.' Includes a label added by Stan Revell to books owned by Tolkien, 'From the Library of J.R.R. Tolkien'.
- Collection: John J. Burns Special Collections Library, Boston College (Chestnut Hill, Massachusetts).

1591. Merz, John Theodore. *Leibniz*. Edinburgh: Blackwood, 1884.
- Description: Tolkien requested the book on 12 May 1931 (MS. Library Records b. 640). Weston Library (Oxford), 26681 fol. 4 (ex S. Phil. Gen. 44h).

1592. Mesqua, Mari de. *Comedia Famosa del Esclavo del Demonio (Barcelona 1612)*. Edited, with an introduction and notes by Milton A. Buchanan. Baltimore: J. H. Furst, 1906.
- Description: Signed in the front by J.R.R. Tolkien and annotations in pencil.
- Collection: Private [Sold by Peter Harrington Antiquarian Bookseller].
- S.s.: Harrington (2003), p. 25

1593. Messenius, Johannis. *Scondia illustrata: seu Chronologia de rebus Scondiæ, hoc est, Sueciæ, Daniæ, Norvegiæ, atque una Islandiæ, Gronlandiæque, tam ecclesiasticis quam politicis; â mundi cataclysmo, usque annum Christi MDCXII*

gestis, Vol. I. Stockholm: Typis O. Enæi, 1700.
: P.s.: *Finn and Hengest* (1982), p. 58. Tolkien translates from Messenius' Latin 'Lotherus igitur Danorum Rex, ab Othino, vehementer infestatus, & ope fuorum propter nimiam destitutus tyrannidem, supeatusque in Jutiam profugit' (p. 5): 'therefore Lotherus, King of the Danes, bereft of his wealth because of his *excessive tyranny*, and defeated, *fled into Jutia*'.

1594. Metcalfe, William Musham. *Specimens of Scottish literature, 1325-1835*. Glasgow: Blackie, 1913.
: S.s. 1: University of Leeds (1920), p. 139 English Language and Literature: English Language. Text selected for 1920-21. Texts Selected for 1920-21. Ordinary Degree of B.A. with Honours. Final Course and Examination. Extracts pp. 42-57, 65-66; p. 182. English Language and Literature. F2. Final Course (English Literature and Language). Extracts pp. 42-57, 65-66.
: S.s. 2: University of Leeds (1921), p. 153. English Language and Literature - Scheme A. Text selected for 1921-22. Ordinary Degree of B.A. with Honours. Extracts pp. 34-38; 42-57 and 65-68; p. 192 English Language and Literature. Honours and M.A. Courses. A. Language. H1. First Year. Extracts pp. 34-38; 42-57 and 65-68.

1595. *Metrical Life of St. Cuthbert* (c. 1430).
: P.s.: 'Chaucer as a Philologist: *The Reeve's Tale*' (1934), p. 150.

1596. Meyer, Kuno (Edited by). *Aislinge Meic Conglinne* (The vision of MacConglinne: a Middle-Irish wonder tale). London: David Nutt, 1892.
: Collection: Tolkien's personal Celtic library, preserved at the Weston library under the auspices of the English Faculty Library (Oxford).

1597. _____ (Translated by). *Cáin Adamnáin. An Old-Irish treatise on the law of Adamnan*. Series: Anecdota oxoniensia, Mediaeval and modern series, 12. Oxford: At the Clarendon Press, 1905.
: Description: two same books. Autographed in pencil a front cover.
: Collection: Tolkien's personal Celtic library, preserved at the Weston library under the auspices of the English Faculty Library (Oxford).

1598. _____ (Edited by). *The Cath Finntrága or Battle of Ventry*. Oxford: At the Clarendon Press, 1885.
: Collection: Tolkien's personal Celtic library, preserved at the Weston library under the auspices of the English Faculty Library (Oxford).

1599. _____. 'The Edinburgh Gaelic Manuscript, XL'. *The Celtic magazine; a monthly periodical devoted to the literature, history, antiquities, folk lore, traditions, and the social and material interests of the Celt at home and abroad*, Vol. XII, 1887, pp. 208-18.
: P.s.: *Sir Gawain and the Green Knight* (1925), p. xxvi. Tolkien and Gordon write: 'For bibliography of the Irish and French analogues of *Sir Gawain*, see the bibliography in Kittredge's study'. [NED] In Kittredge's study, this article is mentioned in 'I. Fled Bricrend' (p. 291).

1600. _____. 'The Edinburgh version of the *Cennach in Rúanado*'. *Revue Celtique*, Vol. XIV, 1893, pp. 450-58.
: P.s.: *Sir Gawain and the Green Knight* (1925), p. xxvi. Tolkien and Gordon write: 'For bibliography of the Irish and French analogues of *Sir Gawain*, see the bibliography in Kittredge's study'. [NED] In Kittredge's study, this article is mentioned in 'I. Fled Bricrend' (p. 291).

1601. _____. *Peredur ab Efrawc* (Pt. of *Mabinogion*). Leipzig: Hirzel, 1887.
: Description: Autographed and dated on front flyleaf: 'Oct. 1920'. Annotated in pencil.
: Collection: Tolkien's personal Celtic library, preserved at the Weston library under the auspices of the English Faculty Library (Oxford).
: S.s. 1: Fimi (2007), p. 66 n. 1.

S.s. 2: Phelpstead (2011), p. 119, p. 60: 'Has annotations that indicate it was read carefully against the manuscript facsimile edited by Rhŷs and Evans'.

1602. Meyer-Lübke, Wilhelm. *Historische Grammatik der französischen Sprache von W. Meyer-Lübke*. Erster Teil: Laut- und Flexionslehre. 2.und 3.durchgesehene Aufl. Series: Sammlung romanischer Elemantar- un Handbücher. I Reihe: Grammatiken, 2. Heildelberg: Carl Winter's Universitätsbuchhandlung, 1913.
Description: In ink, on front endpaper, in Tolkien's hand: "J.R.R.Tolkien".
Collection: Private [Pieter Collier].

1603. _____. *Romanisches etymologisches Wörterbuch*. Series: Sammlung romanischer Elementar- und Handbücher, 3. Heidelberg: Carl Winter, 1911.
P.s. 1: *Sigelwara land* (1934), p. 105 n. 2.
P.s. 2: 'Middle English 'Losenger'' (1953), p. 68.

1604. Meynell, Everard. *The Life of Francis Thompson*. London: Burns & Oates Ltd., 1913.
P.s.: *The Book of Lost Tales*, Vol. I (1992) p. 335 n. 14.
S.s.: Drout (2007), p. 220.

1605. Michel, Francisque (Edited by). *Charlemagne. An Anglo-Norman Poem of the Twelfth Century, Now first published with an introduction and glossarial index*. London: William Pickering; Paris: Techener, 1836.
Description: Signed by Tolkien on front free endpaper. Armorial bookplate of Charles Lawrence; quote from Hallam's Literature of Europe written in contemporary hand to verso of front free endpaper with catalogue entry concerning the 1488 edition pasted below, and next to it, a handwritten note'sold at Bright's library sale, Feb 1845'.
Collection: Private [Sold by Simon Finch Rare Books Ltd.].
S.s.: Finch (2002), p. 53.

1606. _____ (Edited by). *Horn et Rimenhild. Recueil de ce qui reste des poëmes relatifs à leurs aventures composés en françois, en anglois, et en écossois dans le treizième, quatorzième, quinzième, et seizième siècles. Publié d'Après les manuscrits de Londres, de Cambridge, d'Oxford, et d'Edinburgh*. Series: Bannatyne Club, 80. Paris: Imprimé pour le Bannatyne Club par Maulde et Renou, 1845.
P.s.: MS. Tolkien A 13/1 *annotated texts of King Horn* fol. 94. [Tolkien Papers, Bodleian Library, Oxford].

1607. Microw, Charles Christopher (Translated by). *The Gothic history of Jordanes*. Princeton: The University Press, 1915.
S.s.: Shippey (1992), p. 301.

1608. Migliorini, Bruno. *Storia della lingua italiana*. Firenze: G. C. Sansoni, 1971.
Description: Inscribed on front free endpaper: (Monogram) 'MHRT | XI/76' | Michael H. R. Tolkien | Waddington | November 26th 1976'.
Notes: A copy was sent to J.R.R.T. by the author.
Collection: Private [Oronzo Cilli].

1609. Migne, Jacques-Paul (Edited by). *Patrologiae cursus completus LXXIX. Sive biblioteca universalis, integra uniformis, commoda, oeconomica, omnium SS. Patrum, doctorum scriptorumque eccelesiasticorum qui ab aevo apostolico ad usque Innocentii III tempora*. Paris: Migne, 1849.
P.s.: *The Devil's Coach-Horses* (1925), p. 332. Tolkien quotes: 'Jumenta quippe in stercore suo putrescere est, carnales homines in fetore luxuriæ vitam finire. Bene ergo jejunamus quando hoc mortale corpus a luxuriæ putredine per continentiæ condimentum custodimus' [*Liber De*

Expositione Veteris Ac Novi Testamenti (S. Gregorii v.), p. 1008].

1610. *Milk-white Doo*. [Scottish popular rhyme, see R. Chambers].
P.s.: *Tolkien On Fairy-stories* (2008) 'Manuscript A. [MS Tolkien 4, fols. 59-77]', p. 179.

1611. Mills, Stella Marie (Translated by). *The Saga of Hrolf Kraki*. Oxford: B. H. Blackwell, 1933.
Notes: The volume is dedicated to E.V. Gordon, J.R.R. Tolkien, and C.T. Onions.
S.s. 1: Shippey (1992), p. 73. Tom Shippey writes of the influence of Böðvar Bjarki, hero appearing in tales of Hrólf Kraki's Saga, on the character of Beorn in *The Hobbit*.
S.s. 2: Anderson (2002), p. 165 n. 5.

1612. Milne, Alan Alexander. *Toad of Toad hall. A play from Kenneth Grahame's book*. New York: Scribner, 1929.
P.s. 1: *On Fairy-stories* (1947), p. 85.
P.s. 2: *Tolkien On Fairy-stories* (2008), p. 79.

1613. Milton, John. *Areopagitica*.
S.s. 1: University of Leeds (1920), p. 139 English Language and Literature: English Literature. Text selected for 1920-21. Texts Selected for 1920-21. Ordinary Degree of B.A. with Honours. Final Course and Examination.
S.s. 2: University of Leeds (1921), p. 154. English Language and Literature - Scheme A. Texts and Period selected for 1921-22. (d) Texts suggested for study with Special Period 1637-1700. Ordinary Degree of B.A. with Honours. Final Examinations; p. 156. English Language and Literature - Scheme B. Texts for 1921-22. (d) Outlines of the History of English Literature. Ordinary Degree of B.A. with Honours. Final Examinations.

1614. _____. *Comus*.
S.s. 1: University of Leeds (1920), p. 139 English Language and Literature: English Literature. Text selected for 1920-21. Texts Selected for 1920-21. Ordinary Degree of B.A. with Honours. Final Course and Examination.
S.s. 2: Scull-Hammond (2017a), p. 74.

1615. _____. *Milton: Poetry & Prose*. Edited by Arthur Montagne d'Urban Hughes. Oxford: At the Clarendon Press, 1920.
S.s. 1: University of Leeds (1920), p. 135 English Literature. Texts Selected for 1920-21. Text suggested: Paradise Lost, Book 1.
S.s. 2: University of Leeds (1921), p. 141. English Literature, text selected for 1921-22. Ordinary Degree of B.A.; p. 189 English Language and Literature. Int. 1 Intermediate Course (Literature).

1616. _____. *Paradise Lost*.
P.s. 1: MS. Tolkien A 13/1 *Draft of talk to the Oxford Dante Society: A neck-verse* (1947) fol. 171. Tolkien quotes 'brown as evening'.
P.s. 2: *Philology General Works* (V 1926, for 1924), p. 33. Tolkien quotes: 'Beelzebub than whom, Satan excepted, none higher sat '
S.s. 1: University of Leeds (1920), p. 139 English Language and Literature: English Literature. Text selected for 1920-21. Texts Selected for 1920-21. Ordinary Degree of B.A. with Honours. Final Course and Examination. Extracts: Books i and ii; p. 181. English Language and Literature. Int. I Intermediate Course (Literature).
S.s. 2: Ollscoil na h-Éireann G 101; G 258 (1949).
S.s. 3: Scull-Hammond (2017a), p. 74.

1617. _____. *Paradise Regained*.
S.s. 1: University of Leeds, *Calendar 1921-22*, p. 154. English Language and Literature - Scheme A. Texts and Period selected for 1921-22. (d) Texts suggested for study with Special Period 1637-1700. Ordinary Degree of B.A. with Honours. Final Examinations.
S.s. 2: Ollscoil na h-Éireann G 101, G 258 (1949).

SECTION A

1618. _____. *Poems*. Edited by Walter Alexander Raleigh. London: Blackie, 1905.
   S.s. 1: University of Leeds (1921), p. 154. English Language and Literature - Scheme A. Texts and Period selected for 1921-22. (d) Texts suggested for study with Special Period 1637-1700. Ordinary Degree of B.A. with Honours. Final Examinations.
   S.s. 2: University of Leeds (1923), p. 81. Ordinary Degree of B.A., Intermediate Course and Examination: English Literature. Text selected for 1923-24 (ii) Texts suggestes as part of a course of general rending in the period 1579-1645.

1619. _____. *The Poetical works of John Milton*. Series: Everyman's library. London: Joseph Malaby Dent, 1909.
   P.s.: *Valedictory Address* (1959), p. 235.

1620. _____. *Of Reformation touching Church-Discipline in England*. Edited by Will T. Hale. New Haven: Yale University Press, 1916.
   S.s.: University of Leeds (1921), p. 154. English Language and Literature - Scheme A. Texts and Period selected for 1921-22. (d) Texts suggested for study with Special Period 1637-1700. Ordinary Degree of B.A. with Honours. Final Examinations.

1621. _____. *Samson Agonistes*. Oxford: At the Clarendon Press, 1889.
   S.s. 1: University of Leeds (1920), p. 139 English Language and Literature: English Literature. Text selected for 1920-21. Texts Selected for 1920-21. Ordinary Degree of B.A. with Honours. Final Course and Examination.
   S.s. 2: University of Leeds (1921), p. 156. English Language and Literature - Scheme B. Texts for 1921-22. (d) Outlines of the History of English Literature. Ordinary Degree of B.A. with Honours. Final Examinations.
   S.s. 3: University of Leeds (1923), p. 81. Ordinary Degree of B.A., Intermediate Course and Examination: English Literature. Text selected for 1923-24 (i) For detailed study.

1622. Minot, Laurence. *The Poems of Laurence Minot*. Edited with introduction and notes by Joseph Hall. Oxford: At the Clarendon Press, 1914 (rev.).
   P.s. 1: MS. Res. e. 308 *Sir Gawain and the Green Knight*. [Tolkien Papers, Bodleian Library, Oxford].
   P.s. 2: 'Chaucer as a Philologist: *The Reeve's Tale*' (1934), p. 150. Tolkien quotes: 'þe Scottes with þaire ... Cros law gan þai lout' (33-62),

1623. Mirk, John. *Instructions for parish priest*. Series: E.E.T.S. (Early English Text Society), OS 31. Edited by Edward Peacock. London: Published for the Early English Text Society by Kegan Paul, Trench, Trübner, 1868.
   P.s. 1: MS. Tolkien A 21/13 fol. 119. Note by Tolkien, 'Books in Exeter Library useful', with shelfmarks, on back of photostat reading list dated October 1913. Tolkien writes: 'All EETS publications'. [Tolkien Papers, Bodleian Library, Oxford].
   P.s. 2: 'Chaucer as a Philologist: *The Reeve's Tale*' (1934), p. 131. Tolkien writes: '*fonne* 169 ... The simple *fonne* is found, in Mirk' (358, 1668)

1624. Mitchell, Bruce. 'Until the Dragon comes.' some thoughts on *Beowulf*. Offprint from *Neophilologus*, Vol. 47, no. 1. Berlin and Heidelberg: Springer, 1963, pp. 126-138.
   S.s.: Scull-Hammond (2006b), p. 605. 16 May 1963, Mitchell, who had not been invited to contribute to the seventieth birthday *Festschrift*, writes to Tolkien. He encloses an offprint of his article as a personal tribute to Tolkien.

1625. Mitchison, Naomi. *To the Chapel Perilous*. London: George Allen and Unwin, 1955.
   Notes: 29 July 1955: a copy was sent to Tolkien by the publisher.
   S.s.: Scull-Hammond (2017a), p. 488.

1626. Mogk, Eugen. *Festschrift für Eugen Mogk zum 70. Geburtstag: 19. Juli 1924.* Edited by Elisabeth Karg-Gasterstädt. Halle: Verlag von Max Niemeyer, 1924.
P.s.: *Philology: General Works* (V 1926, for 1924), p. 34 n. 2.

1627. _____. *Geschichte der Norwegisch-Isländischen Literatur. Sonderdruck aus der zweiten Auflage von Pauls Grundriss der germanischen Philologie.* Strassburg: K. J. Trübner, 1904.
Description: Autographed on front flyleaf. Uncut pages.
Collection: Tolkien's personal Celtic library, preserved at the Weston library under the auspices of the English Faculty Library (Oxford).

1628. Molee, Elias. *Pure Saxon English.* Chicago: Rand, 1890.
P.s.: *A Secret Vice* (2016), p. 71.

1629. Mollegen Smith, Anne. *Redbook. The Magazine for Young Adults*, Vol. 130, no. 2. New York McCall Corporation, December 1967.
Notes: 23 November 1967, Joy Hill sent him a copy.
S.s.: Scull-Hammond (2017a), p. 746. 1967. Contains *Smith of Wootton Major* by Tolkien (pp. 58-61; 101-107).

1630. Mommsen, Theodor. *Chronica Minora Saec. IV, V, VI, VII*, Vol. III. Berolini: apvd Weidmannos, 1898.
P.s.: *Finn and Hengest* (1982), pp. 46, 50 n. 37, p. 69 n. 69. Tolkien cites 'Historia Brittonum cum additamentis Nenni'.

1631. Moore, Arthur William and Sophia Morrison (with the co-operation of Edmund Goodwin) (Edited by). *A Vocabulary of the Anglo-Manx Dialect.* London: Oxford University Press, 1924.
Collection: Tolkien's personal Celtic library, preserved at the Weston library under the auspices of the English Faculty Library (Oxford).
P.s.: *Philology: General Works* (V 1926, for 1924), p. 47 n. 7.

1632. Moore, Samuel. *Historical outlines of English phonology and morphology.* Ann Arbor: Wahr, 1929.
Description: Inscribed on front free endpaper: 'J.R.R. Tolkien'. Includes a label added by Stan Revell to books owned by Tolkien, 'From the Library of J.R.R. Tolkien'.
Collection: Marion E. Wade Center, Wheaton College (Wheaton, Illinois).
P.s.: *Philology: General Works* (VI 1927, for 1925), p. 61. Tolkien cites the parts: 'Modern English Sounds'; 'The History of English Sound'; 'Historical Development of Modern English Inflections'; 'Modern English Dialects'; 'The Language of Chaucer'; 'Historical Development of Modern English Inflections.

1633. _____. *Historical outlines of English sounds and Middle English grammar. For courses in Chaucer, Middle English, and the history of the English language.* Ann Arbor, Michigan: George Wahr, 1919.
P.s.: *Philology: General Works* (VI 1927, for 1925), p. 61.

1634. Moorman, Frederic William. *Yorkshire Dialect Poems (1673-1915) and Traditional Poems.* London Published for the Yorkshire Dialect Society, by Sidgwick and Jackson Ltd., 1917.
S.s. 1: University of Leeds (1920), p. 180. English Language and Literature. Int. I Intermediate Course (Literature).
S.s. 2: University of Leeds (1921), p. 156. English Language and Literature - Scheme B. Texts for 1921-22. (d) Outlines of the History of English Literature. Ordinary Degree of B.A. with Honours. Final Examinations.

1635. *Moral Ode (or Poema Morale)* 1200. [Early Middle English moral poem, see R. Morris].
    P.s. 1: MS. Tolkien A 21/7 fol. 27. [Tolkien Papers, Bodleian Library, Oxford].
    P.s. 2: MS. Tolkien A 21/13 *The English MSS.* fol. 203. [Tolkien Papers, Bodleian Library, Oxford].
    S.s.: Scull-Hammond (2017a), p. 46. April 1913: Tolkien will need to become familiar with a range of literary and philological subjects and set texts as prescribed in the Oxford Regulations of the Board of Studies, knowing that he may be examined on them in ten papers at the end of Trinity Term 1915: Middle English texts.

1636. More, Thomas (Saint). *The dialogue concerning Tyndale by Sir Thomas More: reproduced in black letter facsimile from the collected edition (1557) of More's English works*. Edited by William Edward Campbell and Arthur William Reed. London: Eyre & Spottiswoode, 1927.
    P.s.: *Sir Gawain and the Green Knight* (1930, 2nd ed.), p.117, line 2123 as … halydam. Tolkien and Gordon quote: 'My lordes, as help me God and halidome, master doctor here said'.

1637. Morey, Adrian. *Bartholomew of Exeter, Bishop and Canonist. A Study in the Twelfth Century*. Cambridge: The University Press, 1937.
    S.s.: Scull-Hammond (2017a), p. 199. Include the text of the Anglo-Saxon 'Our Father' by Tolkien.

1638. Morgan, William. *Y Beibl Cyssegr-lan: sef yr Hen Destament, a 'r Newydd*. Imprinted at London: by the deputies of Christopher Barker, printer to the Queenes most excellent Maiestie, 1588.
    P.s.: *English and Welsh* (1963), p. 4. Tolkien writes: 'But fortunately in the Bible of 1588, by Dr William Morgan, most of Salesbury's pedantries were abandoned. Among these was Salesbury's [A. 1980] habit of spelling words of Latin origin (real or supposed) as if they had not changed: as, for example, *eccles* for *eglwys* from *ecclēsia*.'

1639. Morlini, Girolamo. *Hieronymi Morlini Parthenopei novellæ, fabulæ, comœdia [from the ed. of 1520]*. Paris: Apud P. Jannet, 1855.
    P.s.: MS. Tolkien A 13/2 *Notes and drafts of lectures on Chaucer: Pardoner's Tale* fol. 79. [Tolkien Papers, Bodleian Library, Oxford].

1640. Morris, Richard. *The Blickling homilies of the tenth century, from the Marquis of Lothian's unique ms. A.D. 971*. Series: E.E.T.S. (Early English Text Society), OS 73. London: Published for the Early English Text Society by Kegan Paul, Trench, Trübner, 1880.
    P.s. 1: MS. Tolkien A 21/13 fol. 119. Note by Tolkien, 'Books in Exeter Library useful', with shelfmarks, on back of photostat reading list dated October 1913. Tolkien writes: 'All EETS publications'. [Tolkien Papers, Bodleian Library, Oxford].
    P.s. 2: MS. Tolkien A 11 *Notes on Pearl* fol. 140. Tolkien quotes 'him wæs æghweþer on weorce ge þæt' (p. 225 v. 28). [Tolkien Papers, Bodleian Library, Oxford].

1641. _____ (Edited by). *Cursor mundi: a Northumbrian poem of the XIVth century edited from British Museum ms. Cotton Vespasian A. III, Bodleian ms., Fairfaix 14, Göttingen university library ms. Theol. 107, Trinity college Cambridge ms. R. 3. 8., Pt. I*. Series: E.E.T.S. (Early English Text Society), OS 57. London: Published for the Early English Text Society by Kegan Paul, Trench, Trübner and Co., 1874.
    Description: Decoratively autographed on page before half title page: 'John Reuel Tolkien | 1921'. Blank bookmark at pp. 102, 103.
    Collection: Tolkien's personal Celtic library, preserved at the Weston library under the auspices of the English Faculty Library (Oxford).
    P.s. 1: MS. Tolkien A 21/13 fol. 119. Note by Tolkien, 'Books in Exeter Library useful', with shelfmarks, on back of photostat reading list dated October 1913. Tolkien writes: 'All EETS publications'. [Tolkien Papers, Bodleian Library, Oxford].

P.s. 2: MS. Tolkien A 12/1 *Commentary on Sir Gawain, lines 37-1987* fol. 144. [Tolkien Papers, Bodleian Library, Oxford].
P.s. 3: *Foreword to A New Glossary of the Dialect of Huddersfield District* (1928), p. xviii. Tolkien quotes 'Thar-by growse sum apell-tre | Wit appuls selcut fair to se, | Quen thai ar in hand, als a fisebal | To poudir wit a stink thai fal.' (p. 172, vv. 2877-2880).
P.s. 4: 'Chaucer as a Philologist: *The Reeve's Tale*' (1934), p. 131. Tolkien quotes: 'thre thinges þam es witjn' (354).
P.s. 5: *Sir Gawain and the Green Knight* (1967) 'Select Bibliography: editions of texts quoted more than once in the notes', p. 156.
NED: #2 c. | 'W' (1928), p. 29 'Waiting, *vbl. sb. obs.*' 1300 – 'Ilk man gaue he [sc. Abraham's servant, Gen. xxiv. 53] sumkin thing, And batuel made fair waiting [*Gölt.* gestning]' (v. 3344).

1642. _____ (Edited by). *Cursor mundi: a Northumbrian poem of the XIVth century edited from British Museum ms. Cotton Vespasian A. III, Bodleian ms., Fairfaix 14, Göttingen university library ms. Theol. 107, Trinity college Cambridge ms. R. 3. 8, Pt. II.* Series: E.E.T.S. (Early English Text Society), OS 59. London: Published for the Early English Text Society by Kegan Paul, Trench, Trübner and Co., 1875.
Description: Decoratively autographed on page before half title page: '1921'.
Collection: Tolkien's personal Celtic library, preserved at the Weston library under the auspices of the English Faculty Library (Oxford).
P.s. 1: MS. Tolkien A 21/13 fol. 119. Note by Tolkien, 'Books in Exeter Library useful', with shelfmarks, on back of photostat reading list dated October 1913. Tolkien writes: 'All EETS publications'. [Tolkien Papers, Bodleian Library, Oxford].
P.s. 2: MS. Tolkien A 12/1 *Commentary on Sir Gawain, lines 37-1987* fol. 144. [Tolkien Papers, Bodleian Library, Oxford].
P.s. 3: 'Chaucer as a Philologist: *The Reeve's Tale*' (1934), p. 160 n. 15.
P.s. 4: *Sir Gawain and the Green Knight* (1967) 'Select Bibliography: editions of texts quoted more than once in the notes', p. 156.
NED: #2 c. | 'W' (1928), p. 29 'Waiting, *vbl. sb. obs.*' 1300 – 'Ai quen iosep was wont at weind, Til ani waiting wit sum frend, His suns war ai wit him bun' (v. 12544).

1643. _____ (Edited by). *Cursor mundi: a Northumbrian poem of the XIVth century edited from British Museum ms. Cotton Vespasian A. III, Bodleian ms., Fairfaix 14, Göttingen university library ms. Theol. 107, Trinity college Cambridge ms. R. 3. 8, Pt. III.* Series: E.E.T.S. (Early English Text Society), OS 59. London: Published for the Early English Text Society by Kegan Paul, Trench, Trübner and Co., 1876.
Description: Decoratively autographed on page before half title page: '1921'.
Collection: Tolkien's personal Celtic library, preserved at the Weston library under the auspices of the English Faculty Library (Oxford).
P.s. 1: MS. Tolkien A 21/13 fol. 119. Note by Tolkien, 'Books in Exeter Library useful', with shelfmarks, on back of photostat reading list dated October 1913. Tolkien writes: 'All EETS publications'. [Tolkien Papers, Bodleian Library, Oxford].
P.s. 2: MS. Tolkien A 12/1 *Commentary on Sir Gawain, lines 37-1987* fol. 144. [Tolkien Papers, Bodleian Library, Oxford].
P.s. 3: 'Chaucer as a Philologist: *The Reeve's Tale*' (1934), p. 160 n. 15; pp. 137-38.
P.s. 4: *Sir Gawain and the Green Knight* (1967) 'Select Bibliography: editions of texts quoted more than once in the notes', p. 156.

1644. _____ (Edited by). *Cursor mundi: a Northumbrian poem of the XIVth century edited from British Museum ms. Cotton Vespasian A. III, Bodleian ms., Fairfaix 14, Göttingen university library ms. Theol. 107, Trinity college Cambridge ms. R. 3. 8, Pt. IV.* Series: E.E.T.S. (Early English Text Society), OS 66. London: Published for the Early English Text Society by Kegan Paul, Trench, Trübner and Co., 1877.
Description: Decoratively autographed on page before half title page: '1921'.
Collection: Tolkien's personal Celtic library, preserved at the Weston library under the auspices of the English Faculty Library (Oxford).

P.s. 1: MS. Tolkien A 21/13 fol. 119. Note by Tolkien, 'Books in Exeter Library useful', with shelfmarks, on back of photostat reading list dated October 1913. Tolkien writes: 'All EETS publications'. [Tolkien Papers, Bodleian Library, Oxford].
P.s. 2: MS. Tolkien A 12/1 *Commentary on Sir Gawain, lines 37-1987* fol. 144. [Tolkien Papers, Bodleian Library, Oxford].
P.s. 3: 'Chaucer as a Philologist: *The Reeve's Tale*' (1934), p. 160 n. 15.
P.s. 4: *Sir Gawain and the Green Knight* (1967) 'Select Bibliography: editions of texts quoted more than once in the notes', p. 156.

1645. _____ (Edited by). *Cursor mundi: a Northumbrian poem of the XIVth century edited from British Museum ms. Cotton Vespasian A. III, Bodleian ms., Fairfaix 14, Göttingen university library ms. Theol. 107, Trinity college Cambridge ms. R. 3. 8*, Pt. V. Series: E.E.T.S. (Early English Text Society), OS 68. London: Published for the Early English Text Society by Kegan Paul, Trench, Trübner and Co., 1878.
Description: Decoratively autographed on page before half title page: '1921'.
Collection: Tolkien's personal Celtic library, preserved at the Weston library under the auspices of the English Faculty Library (Oxford).
P.s. 1: MS. Tolkien A 21/13 fol. 119. Note by Tolkien, 'Books in Exeter Library useful', with shelfmarks, on back of photostat reading list dated October 1913. Tolkien writes: 'All EETS publications'. [Tolkien Papers, Bodleian Library, Oxford].
P.s. 2: MS. Tolkien A 12/1 *Commentary on Sir Gawain, lines 37-1987* fol. 144. [Tolkien Papers, Bodleian Library, Oxford].
P.s. 3: 'Chaucer as a Philologist: *The Reeve's Tale*' (1934), p. 160 n. 15.
P.s. 4: *Sir Gawain and the Green Knight* (1967) 'Select Bibliography: editions of texts quoted more than once in the notes', p. 156.

1646. _____ (Edited by). *Cursor mundi: a Northumbrian poem of the XIVth century edited from British Museum ms. Cotton Vespasian A. III, Bodleian ms., Fairfaix 14, Göttingen university library ms. Theol. 107, Trinity college Cambridge ms. R. 3. 8*, Pt. VI. Series: E.E.T.S. (Early English Text Society), OS 99. London: Published for the Early English Text Society by Kegan Paul, Trench, Trübner and Co., 1892.
Description: Decoratively autographed on page before half title page: '1921'. Contains loose hal-page of notes, crossed out, as bookmark at pp. 1690, 1691 from brigdom to certain.
Collection: Tolkien's personal Celtic library, preserved at the Weston library under the auspices of the English Faculty Library (Oxford).
P.s. 1: MS. Tolkien A 21/13 fol. 119. Note by Tolkien, 'Books in Exeter Library useful', with shelfmarks, on back of photostat reading list dated October 1913. Tolkien writes: 'All EETS publications'. [Tolkien Papers, Bodleian Library, Oxford].
P.s. 2: MS. Tolkien A 12/1 *Commentary on Sir Gawain, lines 37-1987* fol. 144. [Tolkien Papers, Bodleian Library, Oxford].
P.s. 3: 'Chaucer as a Philologist: *The Reeve's Tale*' (1934), p. 160 n. 15.
P.s. 4: *Sir Gawain and the Green Knight* (1967) 'Select Bibliography: editions of texts quoted more than once in the notes', p. 156.

1647. _____ (Edited by). *Cursor mundi: a Northumbrian poem of the XIVth century edited from British Museum ms. Cotton Vespasian A. III, Bodleian ms., Fairfaix 14, Göttingen university library ms. Theol. 107, Trinity college Cambridge ms. R. 3. 8*, Pt. VII. Series: E.E.T.S. (Early English Text Society), OS 101. London: Published for the Early English Text Society by Kegan Paul, Trench, Trübner and Co., 1893.
Description: Decoratively autographed on page before half title page: '1921'.
Collection: Tolkien's personal Celtic library, preserved at the Weston library under the auspices of the English Faculty Library (Oxford).
P.s. 1: MS. Tolkien A 21/13 fol. 119. Note by Tolkien, 'Books in Exeter Library useful', with shelfmarks, on back of photostat reading list dated October 1913. Tolkien writes: 'All EETS publications'. [Tolkien Papers, Bodleian Library, Oxford].
P.s. 2: MS. Tolkien A 12/1 *Commentary on Sir Gawain, lines 37-1987* fol. 144. [Tolkien Papers,

Bodleian Library, Oxford].
P.s. 3: 'Chaucer as a Philologist: *The Reeve's Tale*' (1934), p. 160 n. 15.
P.s. 4: *Sir Gawain and the Green Knight* (1967) 'Select Bibliography: editions of texts quoted more than once in the notes', p. 156.

1648. _____ (Edited by). *Dan Michel's Ayenbite of Inwyt; or, Remorse of conscience. In the Kentish dialect, 1340 A.D.* Series: E.E.T.S. (Early English Text Society), OS 23. London: Published for the Early English Text Society by Kegan Paul, Trench, Trübner and Co., 1866.
   Description: Autographed on front flyleaf and dated in pencil: 'Oxford 1919'. Annotated in pencil. Collection: Tolkien's personal Celtic library, preserved at the Weston library under the auspices of the English Faculty Library (Oxford).
   P.s.: MS. Tolkien A 21/13 fol. 119. Note by Tolkien, 'Books in Exeter Library useful', with shelfmarks, on back of photostat reading list dated October 1913. Tolkien writes: 'All EETS publications'. [Tolkien Papers, Bodleian Library, Oxford].
   S.s.: Scull-Hammond (2017a), p. 46. April 1913: Tolkien will need to become familiar with a range of literary and philological subjects and set texts as prescribed in the Oxford Regulations of the Board of Studies, knowing that he may be examined on them in ten papers at the end of Trinity Term 1915: Middle English texts. Particularly: Paternoster, Ave Maria, and Credo.

1649. _____ (Introduction, notes, and glossary). *Early English alliterative poems in the West-Midland dialect of the fourteenth century. Copied and edited from a unique manuscript in the library of the British Museum, Cotton, Nero A. X.* Series: E.E.T.S. (Early English Text Society), OS 1. London: Published for the Early English Text Society by Kegan Paul, Trench, Trübner and Co., 1864.
   Description: Contains *Pearl, Cleanness (Purity), and Patience*.
   P.s. 1: MS. Tolkien A 21/13 fol. 119. Note by Tolkien, 'Books in Exeter Library useful', with shelfmarks, on back of photostat reading list dated October 1913. Tolkien writes: 'All EETS publications'. [Tolkien Papers, Bodleian Library, Oxford].
   P.s. 2: *Pearl* (1953), p. xi n. 1.
   P.s. 3: *Sir Gawain and the Green Knight* (1967) 'Select Bibliography', p. 153.

1650. _____ (Introduction, notes, and glossary). *Early English alliterative poems in the West-Midland dialect of the fourteenth century. Copied and edited from a unique manuscript in the library of the British Museum, Cotton, Nero A. X.* Series: E.E.T.S. (Early English Text Society), OS 1. London: Published for the Early English Text Society by Kegan Paul, Trench, Trübner and Co., 1867.
   Notes: Contains *Pearl, Cleanness (Purity), and Patience*.
   P.s. 1: MS. Tolkien A 21/13 fol. 119. Note by Tolkien, 'Books in Exeter Library useful', with shelfmarks, on back of photostat reading list dated October 1913. Tolkien writes: 'All EETS publications'. [Tolkien Papers, Bodleian Library, Oxford].
   P.s. 2: *Sir Gawain and the Green Knight* (1925), p. xxv.

1651. _____ (Introduction, notes, and glossary). *Early English alliterative poems in the West-Midland dialect of the fourteenth century. Copied and edited from a unique manuscript in the library of the British Museum, Cotton, Nero A. X.* Series: E.E.T.S. (Early English Text Society), OS 1. London: Published for the Early English Text Society by Kegan Paul, Trench, Trübner and Co., 1869 (2nd ed.).
   Notes: Contains *Pearl, Cleanness (Purity), and Patience*.
   P.s. 1: MS. Tolkien A 21/13 fol. 119. Note by Tolkien, 'Books in Exeter Library useful', with shelfmarks, on back of photostat reading list dated October 1913. Tolkien writes: 'All EETS publications'. [Tolkien Papers, Bodleian Library, Oxford].
   P.s. 2: *Sir Gawain and the Green Knight* (1925), pp. vii, xxii, xxv Tolkiena and Gordon write: 'God text, the apparatus somewhat but of date', xxvii T. and G. write: 'Morris's views on the dialect of the poems were sound'.
   P.s. 3: *Sir Gawain and the Green Knight* (1967) 'Select Bibliography', p. 153.

1652. _____ (Edited by). *Old English Homilies and homiletic treatises. Sawles warde, and Þe wohunge of Ure Lauerd: Ureisuns of Ure Louerd and of Ure Lefdi, etc.) of the twelfth and thirteenth centuries.* Series: E.E.T.S. (Early English Text Society), OS 29. London: Published for the Early English Text Society by Kegan Paul, Trench, Trübner and Co., 1868.

> Description: Contains four sheets of JRRT's notes inside front cover. Annotated in pencil. Inside front cover, bookplate showing arms and name of J. T. Micklethwaite. Autographed on page after front flyleaf, and dated:'sept. 1920'.
> Collection: Tolkien's personal Celtic library, preserved at the Weston library under the auspices of the English Faculty Library (Oxford).
> P.s. 1: MS. Tolkien A 21/13 fol. 119. Note by Tolkien, 'Books in Exeter Library useful', with shelfmarks, on back of photostat reading list dated October 1913. Tolkien writes: 'All EETS publications'. [Tolkien Papers, Bodleian Library, Oxford].
> P.s. 2: *Some Contributions to Middle-English Lexicography* (1925), p. 213.
> P.s. 3: *Sir Gawain and the Green Knight* (1925), p. 102, line 1255 garysoun oþer golde. Tolkien and Gordon cite Wohunge of Ure laverd.
> P.s. 4: Ancrene Wisse and Hali Meiðhad (1929), p. 119
> P.s. 5: *'Iþþlen' in Sawles Warde* (1947), p. 168 n. 1.
> P.s. 6: *Studia Neophilologica* (1948), p. 71.
> *NED*: #2 h. | 'W' (1928), p. 54. 'Walm sb.[1] Obs. 2.' – c117S 'Þe stan to-chan and fouwer walmes of watere sprungen ut þer of' (141).

1653. _____ (Introduction and glossary). *An Old English Miscellany; containing a Bestiary, Kentish Sermons, Proverbs of Alfred, Religious Poems of the thirteenth century: from manuscripts in the British Museum, Bodleian Library, Jesus College Library, etc.* Series: E.E.T.S. (Early English Text Society), OS 49. London: Published for the Early English Text Society, by N. Trübner & Co., 1872.

> Description: Annotated in pencil.
> Collection: Tolkien's personal Celtic library, preserved at the Weston library under the auspices of the English Faculty Library (Oxford).
> P.s. 1: MS. Tolkien A 21/13 fol. 119. Note by Tolkien, 'Books in Exeter Library useful', with shelfmarks, on back of photostat reading list dated October 1913. Tolkien writes: 'All EETS publications'. [Tolkien Papers, Bodleian Library, Oxford].
> P.s. 2: *Exeter College library register*. Tolkien's borrowing record: Long vacation 1914 from 19 January to 14 October; *Hilary Term 1915* from 19 January to 1 March 1915.
> P.s. 3: *A Middle English Vocabulary* (1922). Tolkien refers to the *Old English Miscellany* on the term 'Gryed' (*gryd and wept*, 160).
> P.s. 4: 'Chaucer as a Philologist: *The Reeve's Tale*' (1934), p. 158. Tolkien writes: '*A Song on the Passion* (MS. Egerton G 13) in *O.E. Miscellany*, p. 199'.
> S.s.: Scull-Hammond (2017a), p. 46. April 1913: Tolkien will need to become familiar with a range of literary and philological subjects and set texts as prescribed in the Oxford Regulations of the Board of Studies, knowing that he may be examined on them in ten papers at the end of *Trinity Term 1915*: Middle English texts. Particularly *A Bestiary (The Lion, The Eagle, The Serpent, The Ant, The Hart, The Fox, The Spider, The Whale, The Elephant, The Panther and The Dove); Old Kentish sermons; and Miscellaneous from Jesus College (Oxford) MS*. I. (I-XXIX).

1654. _____. *Old English Homilies of the Twelfth Century*. Series: E.E.T.S. (Early English Text Society), OS 34. London: Published for the Early English Text Society by Kegan Paul, Trench, Trübner and Co., 1873.

> Description: Autographed and dated on front flyleaf: '1920'. Contains two strips of notes in ink (poo. Used as bookmarks) in front of book.
> Collection: Tolkien's personal Celtic library, preserved at the Weston library under the auspices of the English Faculty Library (Oxford).
> P.s. 1: MS. Tolkien A 21/13 fol. 119. Note by Tolkien, 'Books in Exeter Library useful', with shelfmarks, on back of photostat reading list dated October 1913. Tolkien writes: 'All EETS publications'. [Tolkien Papers, Bodleian Library, Oxford].
> P.s. 2: *Some Contributions to Middle-English Lexicography* (1925), p. 213.

1655. _____ (Edited by). *Sir Gawayne and the Green Knight*. Series: E.E.T.S. (Early English Text Society), OS 4. Revised by Israel Gollancz. London: Published for the Early English Text Society by Kegan Paul, Trench, Trübner and Co., 1864.
> Description: Decoratively initialed in pencil on front flyleaf. Old English word on front flyleaf in pencil. Annotated in ink and pencil. Notes pinned on pages 28 – 40, from line 859 '& vnder fete, on þe flet, of folʒande sute' to line 921 'Þat such a gest as Gawan grauntez vus to haue.'
> Collection: Tolkien's personal Celtic library, preserved at the Weston library under the auspices of the English Faculty Library (Oxford).
> P.s. 1: MS. Tolkien A 21/13 fol. 119. Note by Tolkien, 'Books in Exeter Library useful', with shelfmarks, on back of photostat reading list dated October 1913. Tolkien writes: 'All EETS publications'. [Tolkien Papers, Bodleian Library, Oxford].
> P.s. 2: *Exeter College library register*. Tolkien's borrowing record: *Michaelmas Term 1919* from 14 October to 21 January 1920; *Hilary Term 1920* from 21 January to 12 March.
> P.s. 3: *Sir Gawain and Green Knight* (1925), p. xxv. Tolkien and Gordon write: 'Corrects some of the errors of Madden's text. There are a few notes and a glossary (incomplete of little value)'; p. xxvi. Tolkien and Gordon write: 'For bibliography of the Irish and French analogues of *Sir Gawain*, see the bibliography in Kittredge's study'. In Kittredge's study, this article is mentioned in 'II. Gawain and the Green Knight' (p. 294).
> P.s. 4: *Sir Gawain and the Green Knight* (1967) 'Select Bibliography', p. 153.

1656. _____ (Edited by). *Sir Gawayne and the Green Knight*. Series: E.E.T.S. (Early English Text Society), OS 4. Revised by Israel Gollancz. London: Published for the Early English Text Society by Kegan Paul, Trench, Trübner and Co., 1869 (2nd rev.).
> Description: Label on front flyleaf, engraved: 'J. G. Ronksley | no. 345.' Autographed on back of front flyleaf.
> Collection: Tolkien's personal Celtic library, preserved at the Weston library under the auspices of the English Faculty Library (Oxford).
> P.s. 1: MS. Tolkien A 21/13 fol. 119. Note by Tolkien, 'Books in Exeter Library useful', with shelfmarks, on back of photostat reading list dated October 1913. Tolkien writes: 'All EETS publications'. [Tolkien Papers, Bodleian Library, Oxford].
> P.s. 2: *Sir Gawain and the Green Knight* (1925), p. xxvi. Tolkien and Gordon write: 'For bibliography of the Irish and French analogues of *Sir Gawain*, see the bibliography in Kittredge's study'. [*NED*] In Kittredge's study, this article is mentioned in 'II. Gawain and the Green Knight' (p. 294).

1657. _____ (Edited by). *Sir Gawayne and the Green Knight*. Series: E.E.T.S. (Early English Text Society), OS 4. Revised by Israel Gollancz. London: Published for the Early English Text Society by Kegan Paul, Trench, Trübner and Co., 1893.
> P.s. 1: MS. Tolkien A 21/13 fol. 119. Note by Tolkien, 'Books in Exeter Library useful', with shelfmarks, on back of photostat reading list dated October 1913. Tolkien writes: 'All EETS publications'. [Tolkien Papers, Bodleian Library, Oxford].
> P.s. 2: *Sir Gawain and the Green Knight* (1925), p. xxvi. Tolkien and Gordon write: 'For bibliography of the Irish and French analogues of *Sir Gawain*, see the bibliography in Kittredge's study'. [*NED*] In Kittredge's study, this article is mentioned in 'II. Gawain and the Green Knight' (p. 294).

1658. _____ (Edited by). *Sir Gawayne and the Green Knight*. Series: E.E.T.S. (Early English Text Society), OS 4. Revised by Israel Gollancz. London: Published for the Early English Text Society by Kegan Paul, Trench, Trübner and Co., 1897.
> P.s. 1: MS. Tolkien A 21/13 fol. 119. Note by Tolkien, 'Books in Exeter Library useful', with shelfmarks, on back of photostat reading list dated October 1913. Tolkien writes: 'All EETS publications'. [Tolkien Papers, Bodleian Library, Oxford].
> P.s. 2: *Sir Gawain and Green Knight* (1925), pp. xxv; xxvi. Tolkien and Gordon write: 'For bibliography of the Irish and French analogues of *Sir Gawain*, see the bibliography in Kittredge's study'. In Kittredge's study, this article is mentioned in 'II. Gawain and the Green Knight' (p. 294).
> P.s. 3: *Sir Gawain and the Green Knight* (1967) 'Select Bibliography', p. 153.

SECTION A

1659. _____ (Edited by). *Sir Gawayne and the Green Knight*. Series: E.E.T.S. (Early English Text Society), OS 4. Revised by Israel Gollancz. London: Published for the Early English Text Society by Kegan Paul, Trench, Trübner and Co., 1912.
    P.s. 1: MS. Tolkien A 21/13 fol. 119. Note by Tolkien, 'Books in Exeter Library useful', with shelfmarks, on back of photostat reading list dated October 1913. Tolkien writes: 'All EETS publications'. [Tolkien Papers, Bodleian Library, Oxford].
    P.s. 2: *Sir Gawain and the Green Knight* (1925), p. xxv.
    P.s. 3: *Sir Gawain and the Green Knight* (1967) 'Select Bibliography', p. 153.

1660. _____ (Edited by). *Sir Gawayne and the Green Knight*. Series: E.E.T.S. (Early English Text Society), OS 4. Revised by Israel Gollancz. London: Published for the Early English Text Society by Kegan Paul, Trench, Trübner and Co., Oxford University Press, 1919.
    Description: Autographed in pencil on front flyleaf. Annotated in pencil, ink and red crayon. Contains two loose sheets of JRRT's notes.
    Collection: Tolkien's personal Celtic library, preserved at the Weston library under the auspices of the English Faculty Library (Oxford).
    P.s. 1: MS. Tolkien A 21/13 fol. 119. Note by Tolkien, 'Books in Exeter Library useful', with shelfmarks, on back of photostat reading list dated October 1913. Tolkien writes: 'All EETS publications'. [Tolkien Papers, Bodleian Library, Oxford].
    P.s. 2: MS. Tolkien A 12/1 *Commentary on Sir Gawain, lines 37-1987* fol. 144. [Tolkien Papers, Bodleian Library, Oxford].
    S.s. 1: University of Leeds (1921), p. 153. English Language and Literature - Scheme A. Texts and Period selected for 1921-22. (a) Selected Texts in Old and Middle English. Ordinary Degree of B.A. with Honours. Final Examinations.
    S.s. 2: University of Leeds (1923), p. 94. English Language and Literature. Scheme A. Degree of B.A. with Honours. Texts and Period selected for 1923-24 (a).

1661. _____. *Story of Genesis and Exodus*. Series: E.E.T.S. (Early English Text Society), OS 7. London: Published for the Early English Text Society by Kegan Paul, Trench, Trübner and Co., 1865.
    Notes: In composite volume with: *The Minor Poems of William Lauder* E.E.T.S. 41, 1870 [A. 1309] and *Lancelot of the Laik* E.E.T.S. 6, 1870 (2nd rev.) [A. 2115].
    Description: Inscribed on back of front flyleaf by JRRT: 'EETS O.S.3. (Lauder) 7 (Gen and Ex)'. And inscribed below, half rubbed out, the signature in pencil: 'W. Marty[n]'. Autographed and marked on next page: 'Leeds | October 1921'. Contents listed before half title page of first iten by JRRT. Annotated in pencil.
    Collection: Tolkien's personal Celtic library, preserved at the Weston library under the auspices of the English Faculty Library (Oxford).
    P.s. 1: MS. Tolkien A 21/13 fol. 119. Note by Tolkien, 'Books in Exeter Library useful', with shelfmarks, on back of photostat reading list dated October 1913. Tolkien writes: 'All EETS publications'. [Tolkien Papers, Bodleian Library, Oxford].
    P.s. 2: Tolkien's copy of *Studien zu den Skalden des 9. und 10. Jahrhunderts* (1928) by Konrad Reichardt, contains a page of notes on the verso of Tolkien's dining expenses from Pembroke College during the week of 29 November 1928; the notes refer to the *Genesis* and *Exodus* poems – Old English poetry which Tolkien would used while working on Cynewulf's *Crist*.
    P.s. 3: 'Chaucer as a Philologist: *The Reeve's Tale*' (1934), p. 134.

1662. _____ and Walter William Skeat (Edited by). *Specimens of Early English. With introductions, notes, and glossarial index*. Pt. I from 'Old English homilies' to 'King Horn': A.D. 1150-A.D. 1300. Oxford: At the Clarendon Press, 1885 (2nd ed.).
    P.s.: MS. Res. e. 308 *Sir Gawain and the Green Knight*. [Tolkien Papers, Bodleian Library, Oxford].
    S.s. 1: Scull-Hammond (2017a), p. 46. April 1913: Tolkien will need to become familiar with a range of literary and philological subjects and set texts as prescribed in the Oxford Regulations of the Board of Studies, knowing that he may be examined on them in ten papers at the end of Trinity Term 1915: Middle English texts. Particularly nos.: V. *The Ormulum: Jewish and Christian*

Offerings; VI. *Layamon's Brut: Hengest and Horsa*; VIII. *The Life of St Juliana* (Two Texts); IX. *The Ancren Riwle (Rule of Nuns): The Seven Deadly Sins and Directions how a Nun should live*; XI. *A Bestiary: Nature of the Lion, Nature of the Eagle and Nature of the Ant*; XIII. *Old Kentish Sermons: Sermo in die Epiphaniæ* (Matt. ii. I), *Dominica Secunda post Octavam Epiphaniæ* (John ii. I); XV. *English Version of Genesis and Exodus: Passages in the Life of Joseph*; XVII. *A Moral Ode: Jesus MS. and Trin. MS.*; XIX. *King Horn*.
S.s. 2: Scull-Hammond (2017a), p. 52. *Michaelmas Term 1913*: Tolkien probably attends lectures by A.S. Napier on Morris and Skeat's Specimens of Early English on Mondays at 12.00 noon in the Examination Schools, beginning 20 October.
S.s. 3: Scull-Hammond (2017a), p. 56. *Hilary Term 1914*: Tolkien probably attends lectures on Morris and Skeat's Specimens, on Thursdays at 12.00 noon in the Examination Schools.

1663. _____ and Walter William Skeat (Edited by). *Specimens of Early English. With introductions, notes, and glossarial index*. Pt. I from 'Old English homilies' to 'King Horn': A.D. 1150-A.D. 1300. Oxford: At the Clarendon Press, 1935 (Reprint 1885).
Description: Signed by Tolkien, apparently the third owner of the book. It is covered with a lot of notes, especially the chapter 'The Ancren Riwle', but generally from the hands of students. On page 63: 'Sisam Rev. of. Eng. Studies. – Vol. 9. pp. 1-12' [A. 2104].
Collection: Private [Yvan Strelzyk].
P.s.: MS. Res. e. 308 *Sir Gawain and the Green Knight*. [Tolkien Papers, Bodleian Library, Oxford].

1664. _____ and Walter William Skeat (Edited by). *Specimens of Early English. With introductions, notes, and glossarial index*. Pt. II from Robert of Gloucester to Grower: A.D. 1298-A.D. 1393. Oxford: At the Clarendon Press, 1898 (4nd ed.).
P.s.: MS. Res. e. 308 *Sir Gawain and the Green Knight*. [Tolkien Papers, Bodleian Library, Oxford].
S.s. 1: Scull-Hammond (2017a), p. 46. Particularly nos.: I. *Robert of Gloucester:* (a) *Reign of William the Conqueror* and (b) *Life of St Dunstan*; VII. *Cursor Mundi, or Cursur þe Werld: The Visit of the Magi, and the Flight into Egypt*; X. *Richard Rolle de Hampole: Extracts from 'The Pricke of Conscience'*; XV. *William Langland, or Langley: Piers the Plowman (Earliest Version, or A-text): Prologues, The same: Passus* I, *The same: part of Passus* II, *The same: part of Passus* III *and The same: Passus* V; XVI. *John Barbour: The Bruce: Extracts from Book VII*.
S.s. 2: Scull-Hammond (2017a), p. 52. *Michaelmas Term 1913*: Tolkien probably attends lectures by A.S. Napier on Morris and Skeat's Specimens of Early English on Mondays at 12.00 noon in the Examination Schools, beginning 20 October.
S.s. 3: Scull-Hammond (2017a), p. 56. *Hilary Term 1914*: Tolkien probably attends lectures on Morris and Skeat's Specimens, on Thursdays at 12.00 noon in the Examination Schools.

1665. Morris, William. (Edited by). *The Defence of Guenevere: and other poems*. London: Longmans, Green, 1916.
P.s.: 'Chaucer as a Philologist: *The Reeve's Tale*' (1934), p. 139.
S.s.: Scull-Hammond (2006b), p. 819.

1666. _____. *The Earthly Paradise. A Poem*, Pt. III. Series: The Collected Works of William Morris, Vol. V. With Introductions by his Daughter May Morris. London: Longmans, Green and Co., 1911.
Notes: [22 August 1916] Wade-Gery presents to Tolkien.
S.s. 1: Garth (2003), p. 185. Garth wites: '[G. B.] Smith and Tolkien ate a last meal together at Bouzincourt with Wade-Gery, the Oxford don-turned-captain, who (probably on this occasion) presented Tolkien with a volume of William Morris's *The Earthly Paradise*.'
S.s. 2: Scull-Hammond (2017a), p. 96.

1667. _____. *The Life and Death of Jason*. Oxford: At the Clarendon Press, 1914.
Description: Tolkien bought this book with his Skeat Prize money in spring 1914.
S.s. 1: Scull-Hammond (2006b), p. 816

S.s. 2: Garth (2014), p. 26.
S.s. 3: Scull-Hammond (2017a), p. 58.
Reading period: 1914 (S.s.: Scull-Hammond (2017c), p. 1055)

1668. _____. *News from Nowhere*. London: Reeves and Turner, 1891.
P.s. 1: *Prefatory Remarks on Prose Translation of 'Beowulf'* (1940), p. xx. Tolkien writes: 'To render *leode* 'freemen, people' by leeds (favoured by William Morris) fails both to translate the Old English and to recall *leeds* to life'.
P.s. 2: *The Notion Club Papers* (1945), p. 172.
S.s.: Scull-Hammond (2006b), p. 818.

1669. _____. *The Roots of the Mountains*. London: Longmans, 1906.
P.s.: *Letters* 226 (1960). From a letter to Professor L.W. Forster.
S.s. 1: Shippey (1992), p. 300.
S.s. 2: Anderson (2002), p. 243 n. 4.
S.s. 3: Mathews (2002), p. 87. Richard Mathews writes: '[Christopher Tolkien] In a subsequent letter, he listed 11 titles of Morris's books of poems, translations, and fantasies that his father bequeathed to him, including *The House of the Wolfings, The Roots of the Mountains,* and *The Sundering Flood,* plus J. W. Mackail's two-volume *Life of William Morris* and A. Clutton-Brock's *William Morris: His Work and Influence.* Tolkien had begun collecting and reading Morris–even reading Morris aloud to his son–at a time when his popularity and critical reputation were at an all-time low and his work had been eclipsed by World War I and the onward rush of technology and current events.' (Christopher Tolkien to the author).
S.s. 4: Gilliver-Marshall-Weiner (2006), p. 96.

1670. _____. *Some Hints on Pattern Designing: A Lecture Delivered at the Working Men's College, London, on December 10, 1881*. London: Longmans, 1899.
Description: Autographed: 'J.R.R. Tolkien'. With a footnote. An Exeter College Prize copy linking two of its best-known graduates.
Collection: Private [Bonhams, 12 Nov 2013, London]

1671. _____. *The Story of the Glittering Plain*. London: Reeves and Turner, 1891.
S.s.: Shippey (1992), p. 301.

1672. _____ (Translated by). *Grettis Saga: The Story of Grettir the strong* (With Eiríkr Magnússon). London: F. S. Ellis, 1869.
P.s.: *Finn and Hengest* (1982), p. 44 n. 24.
S.s.: Scull-Hammond (2006b), p. 601

1673. _____ (Translated by). *The Story of Howard the Halt. The Story of the Banded Men. The Story of Hen Thorir* (With Eiríkr Magnússon). Series: The Saga Library, 1. London: Bernard Quaritch, 1891.
P.s.: *Beowulf* (2002), 'Version B', p. 97. Tolkien writes: [Morris] 'In his dealings with Beowulf he was perhaps not so fortunate in his crib as in his (still somewhat casual) dealing with Icelandic through Magnússon'.
S.s.: *King Edward's School Chronicle* (March 1911), p. 19. The Völsunga Saga is but one of many: for instance, the story of Burnt Njal, the longest of them all and one of the very best; and "Howard the Halt," the best of the shorter ones.' (*Cfr.* Anderson, *The Annotated Hobbit* 2002, p. 3).

1674. _____. *The Story of Sigurd the Volsung and the Fall of the Niblungs*. Series: The Collected Works of William Morris, Vol. XII. With Introduction by his Daughter May Morris. London: Green and Company, 1912.
Notes: Tolkien's scheduled lecture for Michaelmas Term (1941).
P.s. 1: *Dragons* (1938), p. 54.
P.s. 2: *Beowulf* (2002) 'Version A', p. 34.
P.s. 3: *The Legend of Sigurd & Gudrún* (2009), p. 196.

Reading period: 1900 – 1904 (S.s.: Scull-Hammond (2017c), p. 1053).

1675. _____. *The Sundering Flood*. London: Longmans, Green and Co., 1898.
S.s.: Mathews (2002), p. 87. Richard Mathews writes: '[Christopher Tolkien] In a subsequent letter, he listed 11 titles of Morris's books of poems, translations, and fantasies that his father bequeathed to him, including *The House of the Wolfings, The Roots of the Mountains*, and *The Sundering Flood*, plus J. W. Mackail's two-volume *Life of William Morris* and A. Clutton-Brock's *William Morris: His Work and Influence*. Tolkien had begun collecting and reading Morris–even reading Morris aloud to his son–at a time when his popularity and critical reputation were at an all-time low and his work had been eclipsed by World War I and the onward rush of technology and current events.' (Christopher Tolkien to the author).

1676. _____. *A Tale of the House of the Wolfings and All the Kindreds of the Mark*. Roberts Brothers, 1890.
Description: Tolkien bought this book with his Skeat Prize money in spring 1914.
P.s. *Letters* 226 (1960) From a letter to Professor L.W. Forster. Tolkien writes: 'The Dead Marshes and the approaches to the Morannon owe something to Northern France after the Battle of the Somme. They owe more to William Morris and his Huns and Romans, as in *The House of the Wolfings* or *The Roots of the Mountains*.'
S.s. 1: Shippey (1992), p. 300.
S.s. 2: Mathews (2002), p. 87. Richard Mathews writes: 'Christopher Tolkien recently recalled that his father owned nearly all of Morris's works and said that he has a distant but clear recollection of having been read *The House of the Wolfings* by his father' (Christopher Tolkien to the author 7 January 1990).
S.s. 3: Scull-Hammond (2006b), p. 816.
S.s. 4: Garth (2014), p. 26.
S.s. 5: Scull-Hammond (2017a), p. 58.
Reading period: 1914 (S.s.: Scull-Hammond (2017c), p. 1055).

1677. _____ (Translated by) *The Tale of Beowulf, sometime king of the folk of the Weder Geats*. London: Longman & Co., 1898.
P.s.: *Exeter College library register*. Tolkien's borrowing record: Easter vacation 1914 from 1 January to 17 June.

1678. _____. *Three Northern Love Stories the Tale of Beowulf*. Series: The Collected Works of William Morris, Vol. X. With Introductions by his Daughter May Morris. London: Green and Company, 1911.
P.s.: *Beowulf* (2002) 'Version B', p. 97. Tolkien writes: [Morris] 'In his dealings with Beowulf he was perhaps not so fortunate in his crib as in his (still somewhat casual) dealing with Icelandic through Magnússon.'
S.s.: Gilliver-Marshall-Weiner (2006), p. 221. 'Although *wyrmtunga* [Grima's nickname] is not attested in the Old English manuscripts, it can hardly be a coincidence that Old Norse *Ormstunga* 'Worm's tongue' is found as a nickname – in particular as the nickname of the subject of *Gunnlaugssaga Ormstungu* (The Saga of Gunnlaur Wormtongue), one of the sagas translated by William Morris in *Three Northern Love-Stories*.'

1679. _____ (Translated by). *The Völsunga Saga. The story of the Volsungs and Niblungs, with certain songs from the Elder Edda*. With Eiríkr Magnússon. London: Norroena Soc., 1870.
Description: Tolkien bought this book with his Skeat Prize money in spring 1914.
P.s. 1: *Letters* 240 (1962). To Mrs Pauline [Baynes] Gash. Tolkin writes: 'the otter's whisker sticking out of the gold, from the Norse Nibelung legends'.
P.s. 2: *English and Welsh* (1963), p. 38.
P.s. 3: *Tolkien On Fairy-stories* (2008) 'Manuscript A. [MS Tolkien 4, fols. 59-77]', p. 188.
P.s. 4: *Tolkien On Fairy-stories* (2008) 'Manuscript B [MS. Tolkien 4, fols. 73-120]', p. 235.
P.s. 5: *The Legend of Sigurd & Gudrún* (2009), p. 13. Christopher Tolkien remember: 'Many years ago my father referred to the words of William Morris concerning what he called 'the Great Story

of the North', which, he insisted, should be to us 'What the Tale of Troy was to the Greeks', and which far in the future'should be to those that come after us no less than the Tale of Troy has been to us.' On this my father observed: 'How far off and remote spund now the words of William Morris! The Tale of Troy has been falling into oblivion since that time with surprising rapidity. But the Völsunga have not taken its place.' (JRRT's reference is found in the Magnússon and Morris' preface, p. xi).

S.s. 1: *King Edward's School Chronicle* (March 1911), pp. 18-19. A report of Tolkien reading a paper on 'Norse Sagas' to the Literary Society at King Edward's School, Birmingham: [For Tolkien] 'One of the best (and indeed it is distinct from all the rest) is the Völsunga Saga–a strange and glorious tale. It tells of the oldest of treasure hunts: the quest of the red gold of Andvari, the dwarf. It tells of the brave Sigurd Fafnirsbane, who was cursed by the possession of this gold, who, in spite of his greatness, had no happiness from his love for Brynhild. The Saga tells of this and many another strange and thrilling thing. It shows us the highest epic genius struggling out of savagery into complete and conscious humanity. Though inferior to Homer in most respects, though as a whole the Northern epic has not the charm and delight of the Southern, yet in a certain bare veracity it excels it and also in the story of the Völsunga in the handling of the love interest. There is no scene in Homer like the final tragedy of Sigurd and Brynhild. The Völsunga Saga is but one of many: for instance, the story of Burnt Njal, the longest of them all and one of the very best; and "Howard the Halt," the best of the shorter ones.' (*Cfr.* Anderson, *The Annotated Hobbit* 2002, p. 3).

S.s. 2: Garth (2014), p. 26.

S.s. 3: Scull-Hammond (2017a), p. 28: According to the *King Edward's School Chronicle*, he considers the *Völsunga Saga* one of the best of the sagas, and though it is inferior to Homer in most respects, in some it excels: 'There is no scene in Homer like the final tragedy of Sigurd and Brynhild' ('Literary Society', n.s. 26, no. 186 (March 1911), p. 19); p. 46. April 1913: Tolkien will need to become familiar with a range of literary and philological subjects and set texts as prescribed in the Oxford Regulations of the Board of Studies, knowing that he may be examined on them in ten papers at the end of *Trinity Term 1915*. In addition, Tolkien will have to choose a Special Subject on which he will be examined separately. He will choose Scandinavian Philology, which according to the *Regulations* will have special reference to Icelandic, together with a special study of the *Snorra Edda*. (ch.s 13-31); p. 58.

S.s. 4: Scull-Hammond (2006b), p. 815.

1680. _____. *The Water of the Wondrous Isles*. London: Longmans, Green and Co., 1897.
S.s.: Anderson (2002), p. 243 n. 4.

1681. _____. *The Well at the World's End: a Tale*, Vol I. London: Longmans, Green and Co, 1896.
Notes: In December 1912, Tolkien made a drawing entitled End of the World that shows an apparently carefree man stepping out from a cliff into an abyss. On page 342 on the tale, William Morris writes: '"Of us none knoweth surely," said Otter; "whiles I deem that if one were to get to the other side there would be a great plain like to this: whiles that there is naught save mountains beyond, and yet again mountains, like the waves of a huge stone sea. Or whiles I think that one would come to an end of the world, to a place where is naught but a ledge, and then below it a gulf filled with nothing but the howling of winds, and the depth of darkness. Moreover this is my thought, that all we of these parts should be milder men and of better conditions, if yonder terrible wall were away. It is as if we were thralls of the great mountains"'.

1682. _____. *The Well at the World's End: a Tale*, Vol II. London: Longmans, Green and Co, 1896.

1683. _____. *The Wood beyond the World*. London: Lawrence and Bullen, 1895.
S.s.: Anderson (2002), p. 243 n. 4.

1684. _____ and Alfred John Wyatt (Translated by). *The Tale of Beowulf*. Hammersmith: Kelmscott Press, 1895.
P.s. 1: *Exeter College library register*. Tolkien's borrowing record: Easter vacation 1914 from 1

January to 17 June.
P.s. 2: *Beowulf* (2002) 'Version B', p. 97. Tolkien writes: 'The 'Morris and Wyatt' translation of *Beowulf* remains an oddity—quite outside the main line of development' [of Beowulf criticism].

1685. Morris-Jones, John. *A Welsh Grammar, Historical and Comparative. Phonology and Accidence*. Oxford: At the Clarendon Press, 1913.
> Description: Decoratively initialed and marked in blu crayon on front flyleaf: 'Coll. Exon. Oxon. | 1914'. Also, in pencil, marked:'skeat Prize. | 3'. and autographed fainthy in pencil. Pencilled annotations. Tolkien bought this book with his Skeat Prize money in spring 1914. Tolkien added several marginal notes and corrections. On page 33, Tolkien noted: 'I have heard it in 1920'. in reaction to Morris-Jones's remark that while the spelling ychain for Welsh ychen ('oxen') is wrongly derived, the form ychain can be heard in Gwynedd.
> Collection: Tolkien's personal Celtic library, preserved at the Weston library under the auspices of the English Faculty Library (Oxford).
> P.s. 1: *Sir Gawain and the Green Knight* (1925), p. 80 line 25 Bretaygne. Tolkien and Gordon cite pp.3, 157.
> P.s. 2: *English and Welsh* (1963), p. 38.
> P.s. 3: *Letters* 241 (1962). From a letter to Jane Neave
> S.s. 1: Rhys Roberts (1925), p. 59 n. 20. Rhys Roberts writes: 'Professor Tolkien suggests that "senior quidam" may be the Welsh *henddyn*, the typical wise old man; and, following Morris-Jones's *Welsh Grammar*, § 155 iii (2), p. 261, he would identify with *henddyn* the *Hending* who is represented as the author of a collection of traditional proverbial wisdom in South-West Midland Middle English, each proverb ending with "quoth Hending".'
> S.s. 2: Phelpstead (2011), p. 119.
> S.s. 3: Scull-Hammond (2006b), p. 816. Garth writes: 'With his £5 prize Tolkien also bought J. Morris-Jones's new A Welsh Grammar'.
> S.s. 4: Scull-Hammond (2017a), p. 58.
> S.s. 5: McIlwaine (2018), no. 84.
> Reading period: 1910 - 1913 (S.s.: Scull-Hammond (2017c), p. 214).

1686. _____ and John Rhys (Edited by). *The Elucidarium and other tracts in Welsh from Llyvyr agkyr Llandewivrevi A.D. 1346 Jesus college MS. 119*. Series: Anecdota oxoniensia. Mediaeval and modern series, 6. Oxford: At the Clarendon Press, 1894.
> Collection: Tolkien's personal Celtic library, preserved at the Weston library under the auspices of the English Faculty Library (Oxford).
> S.s.: Phelpstead (2011), p. 119.

1687. Morsbach, Lorenz. *Mittelenglische Grammatik*. Halle: Max Niemeyer, 1896.
> Description: Autographed and dated on front flyleaf: 'Oxford | 1920'.
> Collection: Tolkien's personal Celtic library, preserved at the Weston library under the auspices of the English Faculty Library (Oxford).
> P.s.: *A Middle English Vocabulary* (1922). Tolkien refers to the *Mittelenglische Grammatik* on the terms 'Cast(e)' (§ 87, n. 2), 'Do(n), Doo' (§ 130, n. 6), 'Wysty' (§ 109).

1688. _____. 'Prinzipielles zur modernen Syntaxforschung'. *Probleme der Englischen Sprache und Kultur. Festschrift Johannes Hoops zum 60* [A. 1169]. Heidelberg: Carl Winter, 1925.
> P.s.: *Philology: General Works* (VI 1927, for 1925), p. 45. Tolkien writes: 'Linguistically salutary is the article by Morsbach ... There are sound things said, which once would hardly have seemed necessary, in defence of the view of language as a tradition, and of the historical view generally.'

1689. Morse, Jedidiah. *The American Universal Geography, Or, A View of the Present State of All the Empires, Kingdoms, States, and Republics in the Known World, and of the United States in Particular*, Vol. II. Boston: Isaiah Thomas and Ebenezer T. Andrews, 1801.
> P.s.: MS. Tolkien A 19/3 *Etymologies or history of Walrus* fols. 162-195. [Tolkien Papers, Bodleian Library, Oxford].

S.s.: *Tolkien, Family Album* (1992), p. 42.
NED: #2 i. | 'W' (1928), p. 58 'Walrus, 1.' 1796 – 'The seals, walrosses, and cod, caught in the Russian seas, are likewise very important articles' (p. 75).

1690. *Morte Arthure* (Alliterative) 1360. [Middle English alliterative poem, see Brock and Perry].
P.s. 1: MS. Tolkien A 11 *Notes on Pearl* fol. 124. [Tolkien Papers, Bodleian Library, Oxford].
P.s. 2: MS. Tolkien A 21/13 *The English MSS.* fol. 203. [Tolkien Papers, Bodleian Library, Oxford].
P.s. 3: *Beowulf* (2014), p. 190. Tolkien writes: 'For the full vulgarity of shouting and overstatement you must look at the feast when in the alliterative Morte Arthure Arthur entertains the embassy of Rome' ['Sone the senator was sett …duellyde in erthe' (pp. 170-219).]

1691. *Morte d'Arthur* [Middle French poem, see Malory].
S.s.: Scull-Hammond (2017a), p. 122. Leeds academic year 1920-1921. Tolkien might also be responsible for the first few lectures in an introductory course on English Literature which begins with the *Morte d'Arthur*, Mondays and Wednesdays at 11.00 a.m.

1692. Morton, James and Francis Aidan Gasquet (Translated by). *The Nun's Rule, being the Ancren Riwle*. Series: The Medieval library, 18. London: Chatto & Windus, 1926.
P.s. 1: Tolkien annotated the informations on this book in *Specimens Of Early English* [A. 1663] on page 110 'Ancrene Riwle': 'Translation | Nun's Rule – Morton (Gasquet) | Chatto & Windus 1926 p. 156 + p. 316.'
P.s. 2: 'Chaucer as a Philologist: *The Reeve's Tale*' (1934), p. 153.

1693. Mroczkowski, Przemysław. *A lusty plain abundant of vitaille*. 1957.
Description: A typed essay by Polish professor and philologist Przemysław Mroczkowski on the second edition of the *Works of Geoffrey Chaucer*, edited by F. N. Robinson [A. 413]. The essay contains extensive suggested revisions and corrections by J.R.R. Tolkien, written in-line in red ink and pencil.
Collection: Literary and Historical Manuscripts, The Morgan Library & Museum (New York).
Notes: Tolkien has also given extensive commentary on Robinson's edition and on Mroczkowski's criticism of it in the margins and on the versos of some pages, and including general remarks on the incomplete nature of the Canterbury Tales; these notes are also written in red ink and pencil. This copy contains a letter from Tolkien to Mroczkowski dated "Midnight 9/10 Nov. 1957" (MA 7958.3). Hoping that his comments are legible and helpful, and remarking on Mroczkowski's style ('too many abstract nouns for my taste') and argument ('We don't agree, I think, on many points'). Tolkien notes that 'Red ink is used for changes and corrections which I propose to you seriously.' Remarking especially on the opening paragraph and generally advising Mroczkowski simplify his language.

1694. Mühlhausen, Ludwig (Edited by). *Die Vier Zweige des Mabinogi (Pedeir Ceinc y Maginogi). Mit Lesarten und Glossar*. Halle: Max Niemeyer, 1925.
Collection: Tolkien's personal Celtic library, preserved at the Weston library under the auspices of the English Faculty Library (Oxford).
S.s. 1: Fimi (2007), p. 51.
S.s. 2: Phelpstead (2011), p. 119.

1695. *Muliere Samaritana*. [Old English sermon, see R. Morris].
P.s.: MS. Tolkien A 21/7 fol. 44. [Tolkien Papers, Bodleian Library, Oxford].

1696. Müllenhoff, Karl. 'Der Mythus von Beowulf'. *Zeitschrift für deutsches Altertum*, Vol. VII. Wiesbaden: Steiner, 1849, pp. 419-41.
P.s.: *Beowulf* (2002) 'Version A', p. 48.

1697. _____. 'Sceáf und seine Nachkommen'. *Zeitschrift für deutsches Altertum*, Vol. VII. Wiesbaden: Steiner, 1849, pp. 410-19.

P.s.: *Beowulf* (2002) 'Version A', p. 48.

1698. _____. 'Zeugnisse und Excurse zur deutschen Heldensage'. *Zeitschrift für deutsches Altertum*, Vol. XII. Wiesbaden: Steiner, 1860, pp. 253-386.
P.s.: *Finn and Hengest* (1982), p. 51 n. 38.

1699. Müller, Friedrich Max. *Chips from a German Workshop*, Vol. I. Essays on the Science of Religion. London: Longmans, Green and Co., 1867 (2nd ed.).
P.s. 1: *Tolkien On Fairy-stories* (2008) 'Manuscript A. [MS Tolkien 4, fols. 59-77]', p. 182.
P.s. 2: #1 a. | *Tolkien On Fairy-stories* (2008), p. 310.

1700. _____. *Chips from a German Workshop*, Vol. II. Essays on Mythology, Traditions, and Customs. London: Longmans, Green and Co., 1868 (2nd ed.).
P.s. 1: *Tolkien On Fairy-stories* (2008) 'Manuscript A. [MS Tolkien 4, fols. 59-77]', p. 182.
P.s. 2: *Tolkien On Fairy-stories* (2008) 'Manuscript B [MS. Tolkien 4, fols. 73-120]', p. 241. Tolkien quotes: 'How came such a story ever to he invented? ... a frog and the daughter of a queen was absurd' (p. 246-7).
P.s. 3: #1 a. | *Tolkien On Fairy-stories* (2008), p. 310.

1701. _____. *Chips from a German Workshop*, Vol. III. Essays on Literature, Biography, and Antiquities. London: Longmans, Green and Co., 1870 (2nd ed.).
P.s. 1: *Tolkien On Fairy-stories* (2008) 'Manuscript A. [MS Tolkien 4, fols. 59-77]', p. 182.
P.s. 2: #1 a. | *Tolkien On Fairy-stories* (2008), p. 310.

1702. _____. *Chips from a German Workshop*, Vol. IV. Essays chiefly on the Science of Language. London: Longmans, Green and Co., 1875 (2nd ed.).
P.s. 1: *Tolkien On Fairy-stories* (2008) 'Manuscript A. [MS Tolkien 4, fols. 59-77]', p. 182.
P.s. 2: #1 a. | *Tolkien On Fairy-stories* (2008), p. 310.

1703. _____. *Comparative Mythology*. Series: Oxford essays, 2. London: John W. Parker and Son, 1856.
P.s.: *On Fairy-stories* (1949), p. 50. Tolkien writes: 'Philology has been dethroned from the high place it once had in this court of inquiry. Max Müller's view of mythology as a 'disease of language' can be abandoned without regret. Mythology is not a disease at all, though it may like all human things become diseased.'
S.s. 1: Flieger (2003), p. 28. Flieger writes: '[In *On Fairy-stories*] From Müller he took *nature myth, solar mythology*, and the concept of mythology as *a disease of language*, all of which were staples of Müller's groundbreaking first essay, *Comparative Mythology*, published in 1856'.
S.s. 2: Shippey (2004), p. 13 n. 5. 'Tolkien refers to Müller, while inverting the 'disease of language' thesis, in *On Fairy-Stories*.'

1704. _____. *The Science of Language*, Vol. I. London: Longmans, Green, and Co., 1891.
S.s.: Lewis (2009b), p. 140.

1705. _____. *The Science of Language*, Vol. II. London: Longmans, Green, and Co., 1891.
S.s.: Lewis (2009b), p. 140. Letter to Mr Kinter – 24 September 1951. Lewis writes: '[Tolkien] says he found that it was impossible to invent a language without at the same time inventing a mythology: he adds that Müller was wrong in calling mythology *a disease of language* and that it wd. be truer to say that language was a disease of mythology. I don't quite understand that'. The reference is at the paragraph 'The Mythic Period', pp. 454-56.

1706. Munch, Peter Andreas. *Saga Ólafs konúngs Tryggvasonar*. Series: Fornmanna sögur, 1. Kaupmannahøfn: Popp, 1825.
P.s. 1: *Dragons* (1938), p. 46. Tolkien writes: '[Dragon] Still the *Long Worm* does not sound

nowadays a good name for a ship: it suggests fishing rather than sailing. Nonetheless it was the name of one of the most famous ships of Northern history: *Ormurinn Langi* the ship of King Ólaf Tryggvason (who visited these shores in the 10th century, attacking London among other places).'
P.s. 2: *The Legend of Sigurd & Gudrún* (2009), p. 24. Tolkien quotes: '*at trúa á mátt sín ok megin* ['to trust in one's own might and main']' (p. 35).

1707. Mure, Geoffrey Reginald Gilchrist. *Retreat From Truth*. Oxford: Basil Blackwell, 1958.
Description: Inscribed by Tolkien on front free endpaper: 'given me by GRGM, | 1966 | JRRT'. Includes a label on the inner flap of the dust jacket added by Stan Revell to books owned by Tolkien, 'From the Library of J.R.R. Tolkien'.
Collection: Private [Sold by Maggs Bros. Ltd., London].

1708. Mürkens, Gerhard Hieronymus. 'Untersuchungen über das altenglische Exoduslied'. *Bonner Beiträge zur Anglistik*, Vol. II. Bonn: P. Hanstein's Verlag, 1899, pp. 62-117.
P.s. 1: *Sigelwara land* (1932), p. 195 n. 1.
P.s. 2: *The Old English Exodus* (1982), p. x.

1709. Murray, James Augustus Henry (Edited by). *A New English Dictionary on Historical Principles*, Vol. I 'A-B'. The Philological Society. Oxford: At the Clarendon Press, 1888.
Notes: Including parts or sections—now often called 'fascicles' originally published: A-Ant (1884), Ant-Batten (1885) and Batter-Boz (1888).
P.s. 1: MS. Tolkien A 21/13 fol. 119. Note by Tolkien, 'Books in Exeter Library useful', with shelfmarks, on back of photostat reading list dated October 1913. [Tolkien Papers, Bodleian Library, Oxford].
P.s. 2: *A Middle English Vocabulary* (1922). Tolkien cites the words: *Begger(e)* | *Bidene Bydene, Bedeyn* | *Bigge, Bygge* | *Bilt*.
P.s. 3: *The Devil's Coach-Horses* (1925), p. 333. Tolkien writes: 'For this word see *NED*, s.v. *Aver*, sb (sense 3). Evidence is there given for the existence of this word, especially in Northern and Scottish dialect, from Dunbar to Scott' [p. 582].
P.s. 4: 'Chaucer as a Philologist: *The Reeve's Tale*' (1934), pp. 112-13.
P.s. 5: *Farmer Giles of Ham* (1949), p. 15. Tolkien writes: 'A blunderbuss is a short gun with a large bore firing many balls or slugs, and capable of doing execution within a limited range without exact aim. (Now superseded in civilised countries by other firearms)'. the quotation from the *NED* (p. 947): 'Blunderbuss: 1. A short large-bored gun firing balls or slugs., and capable of doing execution within a limited range without exact aim (Now superseded in civilized countries by other fire-arms.).'

1710. _____ (Edited by). *A New English Dictionary on Historical Principles*, Vol. II 'C'. The Philological Society. Oxford: At the Clarendon Press, 1893.
Notes: Including parts or sections—now often called 'fascicles' originally published: C-Cass (1888), Cast-Clivy (1889), Clo-Consigner (1891), Consignificant-Crouching (1893) and Crouchmas-Czech (1893).
P.s. 1: MS. Tolkien A 21/13 fol. 119. Note by Tolkien, 'Books in Exeter Library useful', with shelfmarks, on back of photostat reading list dated October 1913. [Tolkien Papers, Bodleian Library, Oxford].
P.s. 2: *A Middle English Vocabulary* (1922). Tolkien cites the words: Caple | Chillyng | Coke | Coloppes.
P.s. 3: 'Chaucer as a Philologist: *The Reeve's Tale*' (1934), pp. 112-13.

1711. _____ (Edited by). *A New English Dictionary on Historical Principles*, Vol. III 'D-E'. The Philological Society. Oxford: At the Clarendon Press, 1897.
Notes: Including parts or sections—now often called 'fascicles' originally published: D-Deciet (1894), Deciet-Deject (1895), Deject-Depravation (1895), Deprative-Distrustful (1896), Distrustfully-Dziggetal (1897), E-Every (1891) and Everybody-Ezod (1894).

P.s. 1: MS. Tolkien A 21/13 fol. 119. Note by Tolkien, 'Books in Exeter Library useful', with shelfmarks, on back of photostat reading list dated October 1913. [Tolkien Papers, Bodleian Library, Oxford].

P.s. 2: *A Middle English Vocabulary* (1922). Tolkien cites the words: *Des | Deuelway | Deuise, -yes, Devise | Digge, Dyggen | Drynke(n) | Drone, Drowne | Endles(se)*.

P.s. 3: 'Chaucer as a Philologist: *The Reeve's Tale*' (1934), pp. 112-13.

1712. _____ and Henry Bradley (Edited by). *A New English Dictionary on Historical Principles*, Vol. IV 'F-G'. The Philological Society. Oxford: At the Clarendon Press, 1901.

Notes: Including parts or sections—now often called 'fascicles' originally published: F-Field (1895), Field-Frankish (1897), Frank law-Gain-coming (1898), Gaincope-Germanizing (1898), Germano-Glass-cloth (1899), Glass-coach-Graded (1900), Gradely-Greement (1900) and Green-Gyzzarn (1901)

P.s. 1: MS. Tolkien A 21/13 fol. 119. Note by Tolkien, 'Books in Exeter Library useful', with shelfmarks, on back of photostat reading list dated October 1913. [Tolkien Papers, Bodleian Library, Oxford].

P.s. 2: *A Middle English Vocabulary* (1922). Tolkien cites the words: *Gif(fe), Gyf(fe) | 3ede | 3emen | 3hernyng | 3iftis*.

P.s. 3: *Sir Gawain and the Green Knight* (1925), p. 86, line 211 *grayn*. Tolkien and Gordon cite *grain*.

P.s. 4: 'Chaucer as a Philologist: *The Reeve's Tale*' (1934), pp. 112-13.

P.s. 5: *Tolkien On Fairy-stories* (2008), pp. 66; 59. Entries for 'fairy', 'fairies', 'fantasy'.

P.s. 6: *Tolkien On Fairy-stories* (2008) 'Manuscript B [MS. Tolkien 4, fols. 73-120]', p. 208. Tolkien quotes the entry for "Fairy A. *sb*. 4.": 'supernatural beings of diminutive size, in popular belief supposed to possess magical powers and to have great influence for good or evil over the affairs of man'.

P.s. 7: *Tolkien On Fairy-stories* (2008) 'Manuscript B [MS. Tolkien 14, fols. 22-3]', p. 275. Tolkien writes: 'The *N.E.D.* under FANTASY notes in as Sense 4. Which is the same as that Imagination, is in early use not clearly distinguished from Sense 3: delusive imagination, hallucination – "an exercise of poetic imagination being conventionally regarded as accompanied by belief in the reality of what is imagined". I do not know wheter this convention ever really existed. There was a convention that a narrative-poem recounted either a "history" or a "dream".'

1713. _____ (Edited by). *A New English Dictionary on Historical Principles*, Vol. V 'H-K'. The Philological Society. Oxford: At the Clarendon Press, 1901.

Notes: Including parts or sections—now often called 'fascicles' originally published: H-Haversian (1898), Haversine-Heel (1898), Heel-Hood (1899), Hod-Horizontal (1899), Horizontality-Hywe (1899), I-In (1899) In-Infer (1900), Inferable-Inpushing (1900), Input-Invalid (1900), Invalid-Jew (1901), Jew-Karine (1901) and Kaiser-Kyx (1901).

P.s. 1: MS. Tolkien A 21/13 fol. 119. Note by Tolkien, 'Books in Exeter Library useful', with shelfmarks, on back of photostat reading list dated October 1913. [Tolkien Papers, Bodleian Library, Oxford].

P.s. 2: *A Middle English Vocabulary* (1922). Tolkien cites the words: *His(e) | Hoper*.

P.s. 3: 'Chaucer as a Philologist: *The Reeve's Tale*' (1934), pp. 112-13.

1714. _____. *A New English Dictionary on Historical Principles*, Vol. VI, Pt. I 'L-N'. The Philological Society. 'M' edited by Henry Bradley and 'N' edited by William A. Craigie. Oxford: At the Clarendon Press, 1908. Oxford: At the Clarendon Press, 1908.

Notes: Including parts or sections—now often called 'fascicles' originally published: L-Lap (1901), Lap-Leisurely (1902), Leisureness-Lief (1902), Lief-Lock (1903), Lock-Lyyn (1903), M-Mandragon (1904), Mandragora-Matter (1905), Matter-Mesnality (1906), Mesne-Misbirith (1907), Misbode-Monopoly (1907), Monopoly-Movemnent (1908), Movement-Myz (1906), N-Niche (1906) and Niche-Nywe (1907).

P.s. 1: MS. Tolkien A 21/13 fol. 119. Note by Tolkien, 'Books in Exeter Library useful', with shelfmarks, on back of photostat reading list dated October 1913. [Tolkien Papers, Bodleian Library, Oxford].

P.s. 2: *A Middle English Vocabulary* (1922). Tolkien cites the words: *Lascheth | Myke3*.
P.s. 3: 'Chaucer as a Philologist: *The Reeve's Tale*' (1934), pp. 112-13.

1715. _____. *A New English Dictionary on Historical Principles*, Vol. VII 'O-P'. The Philological Society. Oxford: At the Clarendon Press, 1909.
Notes: Including parts or sections—now often called 'fascicles' originally published: O-Onomonastic (1902), Onomonastical-Outing (1903), Oujet-Ozyat (1904), P-Pargeted (1904), Pargeter-Pennache (1905), Pennage-Pfenning (1905), Ph-Piper (1906), Piper-Polygenistic (1907), Polygenous-Premious (1908), Premisal-Prophesier (1909) and Prophesy-Pyxis (1909).
P.s. 1: MS. Tolkien A 21/13 fol. 119. Note by Tolkien, 'Books in Exeter Library useful', with shelfmarks, on back of photostat reading list dated October 1913. [Tolkien Papers, Bodleian Library, Oxford].
P.s. 2: *Oxford University Press Archives* (Oxford). In an 'office copy' of the OED (Vol. VII, O-P), Tolkien writes a marginal note about a sense *pass* (verb) on page 524: '1347 *Ayenbite vor to pasi þet*' (Of þe yſþe of red and virtue of merci). His quotation being added as an antedating '. (*Cfr* Gilliver-Marshall-Weiner 2006, pp. 34-5).
P.s. 3: *A Middle English Vocabulary* (1922). Tolkien cites the words: *Od | Part | Picche | Pike | Prece, Pres(s) | Prymer | Putte(n), Puit*.
P.s. 4: *Sir Gawain and the Green Knight* (1925), p. 107, line 1543 or. Tolkien and Gordon write: 'Or, adv.1, sense C 2 and C 3'.
P.s. 5: 'Chaucer as a Philologist: *The Reeve's Tale*' (1934), pp. 112-13.

1716. _____. *A New English Dictionary on Historical Principles*, Vol. VIII, Pt. I 'Q-R'. The Philological Society. 'Q-R' edited by William A. Craigie. Oxford: At the Clarendon Press, 1914.
Notes: Including parts or sections—now often called 'fascicles' originally published: Q (1902), R-Reactive (1903), Reactivel-Ree (1904), Ree-Reign (1905, Reign-Reserve (1906, Reserve-Ribaldously (1908), Robaldic-Romanite (1909), Romanity-Roundness (1910) and Roun-nose-Ryze (1910).
P.s. 1: MS. Tolkien A 21/13 fol. 119. Note by Tolkien, 'Books in Exeter Library useful', with shelfmarks, on back of photostat reading list dated October 1913. [Tolkien Papers, Bodleian Library, Oxford].
P.s. 2: *A Middle English Vocabulary* (1922). Tolkien cites the words: *Rapeled | Repe | Repleye | Restay | Ryste | Rowtyn*.
P.s. 3: 'Chaucer as a Philologist: *The Reeve's Tale*' (1934), pp. 112-13.

1717. _____. *A New English Dictionary on Historical Principles*, Vol. VIII, Pt. II 'S-Sh'. The Philological Society. 'S-Sh' edited by Henry Bradley. Oxford: At the Clarendon Press, 1914.
Notes: Including parts or sections—now often called 'fascicles' originally published: S-Sauce (1909), Sauce-along-Scouring (1910), Scouring-Sedum (1911), See-Senatory (1912), Senatory Several (1912), Several-Shaster (1913) and Shastri-Shyster (1914)
P.s. 1: MS. Tolkien A 21/13 fol. 119. Note by Tolkien, 'Books in Exeter Library useful', with shelfmarks, on back of photostat reading list dated October 1913. [Tolkien Papers, Bodleian Library, Oxford].
P.s. 2: *A Middle English Vocabulary* (1922). Tolkien cites the words: *Sche | Scornes | Shrewe*.
P.s. 3: 'Chaucer as a Philologist: *The Reeve's Tale*' (1934), pp. 112-13.

1718. _____. *A New English Dictionary on Historical Principles*, Vol. IX, Pt. I 'Si-St'. The Philological Society. 'Si-Sq' edited by William A. Craigie and 'St' edited by Henry Bradley. Oxford: At the Clarendon Press, 1919.
Notes: Including parts or sections—now often called 'fascicles' originally published: Si-Simple (1911), Simple-Sleep (1911), Sleep-Sniggle (1912), Sniggle-Sorrow (1913), Sorrow-Speech (1914), Speech-Spring (1914), Spring-Stead (1915), Standard-Stead (1915), Stead-Stillatim (1916), Stillation-Stratum (1916), Stratus-Styx (1918).
P.s. 1: MS. Tolkien A 21/13 fol. 119. Note by Tolkien, 'Books in Exeter Library useful', with shelfmarks, on back of photostat reading list dated October 1913. [Tolkien Papers, Bodleian

Library, Oxford].
P.s. 2: *A Middle English Vocabulary* (1922). Tolkien cites the words: *Spac | Steke*.
P.s. 3: *Sir Gawain and the Green Knight* (1925), p. 86, line 173 *sturtes*. Tolkien and Gordon cite Start; p. 86, line 1074 *spenne*. T. and G. write: '*spind* see *N.E.D, Spine, sb²* and compare *Sward*'.
P.s. 4: 'Chaucer as a Philologist: *The Reeve's Tale*' (1934), pp. 112-13.

1719. _____. *A New English Dictionary on Historical Principles*, Vol. IX, Pt. II 'Su-Th'. The Philological Society. 'Su-Sz' edited by Charles Talbut Onions and 'T-Th' edited by James A. H. Murray. Oxford: At the Clarendon Press, 1919.
Notes: Including parts or sections—now often called 'fascicles' originally published: Su-Subterraneous (1919), Subterraneously-Sullen (1919), Sullen-Supple (1919), Supple-Sweep (1919, Sweep-Szmikite (1919),
and T-Tealt (1912), Team-Tezkere (1912) and Th-Thyzle (1912).
P.s. 1: MS. Tolkien A 21/13 fol. 119. Note by Tolkien, 'Books in Exeter Library useful', with shelfmarks, on back of photostat reading list dated October 1913. [Tolkien Papers, Bodleian Library, Oxford].
P.s. 2: *A Middle English Vocabulary* (1922). Tolkien cites the words: *Swavnand | Tethee*.
P.s. 3: *Sir Gawain and the Green Knight* (1925), p. 86, line 1074 *spenne*. T. and G. write: '*spind* see *N.E.D, Spine, sb²* and compare *Sward*'.
P.s. 4: 'Chaucer as a Philologist: *The Reeve's Tale*' (1934), pp. 112-13.

1720. _____. *A New English Dictionary on Historical Principles*; Vol. X, Pt. I 'Ti-U'. The Philological Society. 'Ti' edited by James A. H. Murray and 'U' edited by William A. Craigie. Oxford: At the Clarendon Press, 1926.
Notes: Including parts or sections—now often called 'fascicles' originally published: Ti-Tombac (1914), Tombal-Trahysh (1914), Traik-Trinity (1914), Trink-Turn-Down (1921), Turndun-Tzirid (1921), Unforeseeing-Unright (1926) and Unright-Uzzle (1926).
P.s. 1: MS. Tolkien A 21/13 fol. 119. Note by Tolkien, 'Books in Exeter Library useful', with shelfmarks, on back of photostat reading list dated October 1913. [Tolkien Papers, Bodleian Library, Oxford].
P.s. 2: *A Middle English Vocabulary* (1922). Tolkien cites the words: *Toȝt | Þes | Þrestelcoc | Þrublet*.
P.s. 3: *Sir Gawain and the Green Knight* (1925), p. 82, line 77 *Tolouse*. Tolkien and Gordon cite *Turkestan*.
P.s. 4: 'Chaucer as a Philologist: *The Reeve's Tale*' (1934), pp. 112-13.

1721. _____. *A New English Dictionary on Historical Principles*, Vol. X, Pt. II 'V-Z'. The Philological Society. 'V' edited by William A. Craigie; 'W' edited by Charles Talbut Onions and W. A. Craigie; 'X, Y, Z' edited by C. T Onions. Oxford: At the Clarendon Press, 1928.
Notes: Including parts or sections—now often called 'fascicles' originally published: V-Vagabond (1920), Vagabond-Vanquish (1920), Vanquish-Verificative (1920), Verificatory-Visor (1920), Visor-Vywer (1920), W-Wash (October 1921), Wash-Wavy (May 1923), Wavy-Wezzon (August 1926), Wh-Whisking (1924), Whisking-Wilfulness (November 1924), Wilga-Wise (1924), Wise-Wyzen (1928) and X-Zyxt (1921).
Notes: Tolkien collaborated (1919-1920) on different words of the 'W': *Waggle* (noun and adjective); *Waggly*; *Wain*; *Waist*; *Waistband*; *Waist-cloth*; *Waistcoat*; *Waistcoated*; *Waistcoateer*; *Waisted*; *Waister*; *Waistless*; *Waist-rail*; *Waist-tree*; *Wait-a-bit*; *Waiter*; *Waitership*; *Waiting* (noun and adjective); *Waiting-maid*; *Waiting-man*; *Waiting-room*; *Waiting-woman*; *Waitress*; *Wake* (noun and verb); *Wake-robin*; *Wake-wort*; *Waldend*; *Wallop* (noun and verb); *Walloper*; *Walloping* (noun and adjective); *Walm* (noun and verb); *Walming*; *Walnut*; *Walrus*; *Wampum*; *Wampumpeag*; *Wan* (noun, adjective and verb); *Wander* (noun and adjective); *Wanderable*; *Wandered*; *Wanderer*; *Wandering* (noun and adjective); *Wanderment*; *Wander-year*; *Wandreth*; *Wane* (noun, adjective and verb); *Want* (noun and adjective); *Want-louse*; *Wariangle*; *Warlock* (noun and adjective); *Warlockry*; *Warm*; *Weald*; *Wealden*; *Wealding*; *Wield*; *Wild* and *Wold*.
With the reissue of X volumes in 1928, it assumes the definitive name by *The Oxford English Dictionary*.

Section A

P.s. 1: MS. Tolkien A 21/13 fol. 119. Note by Tolkien, 'Books in Exeter Library useful', with shelfmarks, on back of photostat reading list dated October 1913. [Tolkien Papers, Bodleian Library, Oxford].

P.s. 2: *Oxford University Press Archives* (Oxford). In a slip written by Tolkien on the etymology of 'Wain' used ('W' p. 19), reads: '[OE. wæᵹn, wǣn, str. masc. = OFris. wein str. masc. (mod. WFris. wein, woin, wīn, NFris. wein, wā(i)nj), ODu. reidi-waġen (Mou. waeġhen, Du. waġen). MLG., LG. waġen OHG. waġan str. masc. (MHG., G. waġen), ON. vagn str. masc. cart, barrow (Norw. vagn the Great Bear, vagn cart, Da. vogn, Sw. vagn cart) :— OTetit.' (*Cfr.* Gilliver-Marshall-Weiner (2006), fig. 4a p. 16).

P.s. 3: *Oxford University Press Archives* (Oxford). In different slips written by Tolkien on the etymology of 'Waistcoat' used ('W' p. 23), reads: no. 145: '(1.) d. [not used] Applied to any covering resembling a waistcoat (in being placed, as wound, about the middle of persons, or animals). obs' no. 148: '(1.) e. [not used] Applied to the garments of foreign peoples resembling, or thought to resemble, the contemporary waistcoat (in being worn about the upper part of the body.' no. 151: '(1.) f. [then used for 'e'] trans. Applied to the plumage of birds, or the coat of animals, about the breast or stomach, esp. where this is strikingly different in colour or marking from that of the rest of the body.' no. 153: 'g. [then used for 'c'] phr. Under one's waistcoat: in one's breast.' (*Cfr.* Gilliver-Marshall-Weiner (2006), fig. 5a p. 18); No, 194 [not used] '(waistcoat) 2. Comb. esp. white-waiscoated: weaning a white waistcoat; also applied to bird white plumage on the beast.' (*Cfr. Ivi*, fig. 5b p. 19).

P.s. 4: *Oxford University Press Archives* (Oxford). In a slip written by Tolkien on the etymology of 'Wake' used ('W' p. 31), reads: no. 287 '3. The watching (by esp. by night) of relatives and friends beside the body of a dead person from death to burial, or during a part of that time; the drinking, feasting, and other observances incidental to this. Now chiefly Anglo-Irish or with reference to Irish custom. Also applied to similar funeral customs in other times or among pagan peoples. Small | ~~This custom (of next sense) appears need to home been from frivolous or difonderly tendencies. It now survives most rigorously in Ireland, or colonies of Irish.~~' (*Cfr.* Gilliver-Marshall-Weiner (2006), fig. 6 p. 21).

P.s. 5: *Oxford University Press Archives* (Oxford). In a slip written by Tolkien on the etymology of 'Walnut' partly used ('W' p. 57), reads: no. 528 '(Walnut, sb.) [OE. walh-hnutu str. form. walnut(tres) = Mod WFris. walnut (NFris. walnödd, MDu. walnote, Kilian walnut), Du. walnoot, MLG. wallnot, -nut, LG. (Bremisch. Wörterb. wallnut) walnut, G. walnuss (earlier wallnuss), ON. valhnot str. fem. (Nonv. valnot, Sw. valnöt, Da valnød). The Compare also, with ME, walsch (welsch) note, Flem (Kilian) walsche not, MHG. wälhisch nuz, G (Southern) wälsche nuss […].

P.s. 6: MS. Tolkien A 19/3 *Etymologies or history of Walrus* fols. 162-195 [Tolkien Papers, Bodleian Library, Oxford].

P.s. 7: *Oxford University Press Archives* (Oxford). In a slip written by Tolkien on the etymology of 'Walrus' partly used ('W' p. 57), reads: 'Cf. also earlier G. roszwal, ruszwal. Norw. russhval ? OFr. rohal (rohart, later rochal by association with roche) walrus-ivory (but Du Cange rohanlum, –alum). | This formation has been interpreted as 'horse-whale' (which is zoologically [illegible] appears to be only one of the popular etymologies that have influenced the forms of the word. The existence of an ON. ~~horosshal~~ hrosshvalr a kind of whale (not walrus) way have assisted is and have been the origin even of the OE. form occurring as it does only in Ælfred's record of the Scandinavian Ohthere's report. An elemnt in ththe purple certains seems […] speakess of Southern Tut. Languages heand and confused this word with […].' (*Cfr.* McIlwaine (2018), p. 84). In the *OED* was published: 'The interpretation of formation (ii) as 'horse-whale' '(zoologically improbable) appears to be only one of the various popular etymologies that have influenced the forms of the word. Ultimately a confusion, either within or outside the Scandinavian languages, has perhaps taken place between ON. *hrosshvalr* a kind of whale, and *rosmhvalr* walrus. The latter is related obscurely to ON. *rosmall*, Norw. *rosmaal*, *rosmaar*, Da. *rosmaer*, *-er*, *-ar* walrus, whence the scientific specific name *rosmarus*. See Rosmasine. Some scholars have connected *rosm-* with ON., Icel. *Rostungr* walrus, and assumed relationship of both with ON. *Rautôr* Red. (*Cfr.* Roequal and OHG. *ros(a)mo* redness.) This is zoologically possible, but it seems more likely that *rosm-* is a corruption of some non-Teut. word: cf. Morse.] ('W' p. 57).

P.s. 8: *Oxford University Press Archives* (Oxford). In a slip written by Tolkien on the etymology of 'Warm' used ('W' p. 101), reads: no. 197 'Warm (wǫm), adj. [Com. Tent.: OE. wearm = OFris. warm (mod. WFris. waeym, NFris. wāram), MDu., Du. warm, OS. warm (MLG. war(e)m, LG. warm), OHG. war(a)m (MHG., G. warm), ON. varmr (Norw., Sw., Da. varm), Goth, *warm-* in *warmjan* to warm, cherish:—OTeut. *warmo-*, also *werm-* (in ON. verme wk. masc. warmth,

OHG. wirma, MHG. wirm(e) fern, warmth). The further relationship of this word is somewhat doubtful. In spite of the certain difficulties attending such an etymology it is probably to be composed with Pre-Tent. identified with Indogermanic * g^whormō-, or * g^whermō- found in Skr.gharmá heat, Avesta garamō- hot, Gr. ζεστός.6s hot, L. formus warm, O Prussian gorme heat, Albanian zjarm heat, Armenian jerm warm, derivatives of *g^w 'her- with a radical sense of heat. For another possible example of initial w- in Tent. from *g^wh- or *ģhw- see Wild adj. Compare also the similar phonetic phenomena in Latin whereby older g^w- gave ģ- before u and consonants, v before other vowels (e. g. gurgēs, vorāre).' (Cfr. Gilliver-Marshall-Weiner (2006), fig. 2 p. 10).

P.s. 9: *A Middle English Vocabulary* (1922). Tolkien cites the words: *Ybilt | Yei | Yone*.

P.s. 10: *Sir Gawain and the Green Knight* (1925), p. 99, line 1008-9. Tolkien and Gordon cite *Yet*.

P.s. 11: 'Chaucer as a Philologist: *The Reeve's Tale*' (1934), pp. 112-13; pp. 136-38. Tolkien writes: '[*wanges* 110] To the examples quoted by the *N.E.D.* (from *Cursor Mundi, Alysoun, Sir Tristrem, Wyntoun*, and the *York Plays*, all northern except the second which is probably western in origin) I can only add *Layamon, Brut* 30268: *wete weren his wongen* (the earliest M.E. instance), and *Joseph of Arimathie* (an alliterative poem) 647: *I wepte water warm and wette my wonges*, both of which show the same formula.'

S.s. 1: Gilliver (2002), pp. 1-3.

S.s. 2: Gilliver-Marshall-Weiner (2006).

1722. _____; Henry Bradley; William A. Craigie; Charles Talbut Onions and Robert William Burchfield (Edited by). *The Oxford English Dictionary*, Vol. I 'A-B'. The Philological Society. Oxford: At the Clarendon Press, 1933.
Notes: Tolkien collaborated (1919-1920) to 10 volume on different words of the 'W'. With the reissue of X volumes in 1928, it assumes the definitive name by *The Oxford English Dictionary* (previously *A New English dictionary on historical principles* 1888-1928). Description: 16 March 1933, Tolkien writes to Kenneth Sisam that he hopes to see him at his home at Boar's Hill, Oxford, on 18 March. Tolkien is very pleased because he has been given a complete set of the *Oxford English Dictionary*. The book set is in the new edition, with the thirteenth volume, Supplement, published the same year by the Clarendon Press.
S.s.: Scull-Hammond (2017a), p. 179.

1723. _____; Henry Bradley; William A. Craigie; Charles Talbut Onions and Robert William Burchfield (Edited by). *The Oxford English Dictionary*, Vol. II 'C'. The Philological Society. Oxford: At the Clarendon Press, 1933.
S.s.: Scull-Hammond (2017a), p. 179.

1724. _____; Henry Bradley; William A. Craigie; Charles Talbut Onions and Robert William Burchfield (Edited by). *The Oxford English Dictionary*, Vol. III 'D-E'. The Philological Society. Oxford: At the Clarendon Press, 1933.
S.s.: Scull-Hammond (2017a), p. 179.

1725. _____; Henry Bradley; William A. Craigie; Charles Talbut Onions and Robert William Burchfield (Edited by). *The Oxford English Dictionary*, Vol. IV 'F-G'. The Philological Society. Oxford: At the Clarendon Press, 1933.
S.s.: Scull-Hammond (2017a), p. 179.

1726. _____; Henry Bradley; William A. Craigie; Charles Talbut Onions and Robert William Burchfield (Edited by). *The Oxford English Dictionary*, Vol. V 'H-K'. The Philological Society. Oxford: At the Clarendon Press, 1933.
S.s.: Scull-Hammond (2017a), p. 179.

1727. _____; Bradley, Henry; William A. Craigie; Charles Talbut Onions and Robert William Burchfield (Edited by). *The Oxford English Dictionary*, Vol. VI 'L-M'. The Philological Society. Oxford: At the Clarendon Press, 1933.
S.s.: Scull-Hammond (2017a), p. 179.

1728. _____; Henry Bradley; William A. Craigie; Charles Talbut Onions and Robert William Burchfield (Edited by). *The Oxford English Dictionary*, Vol. VII 'N-Poy'. The Philological Society. Oxford: At the Clarendon Press, 1933.
   S.s.: Scull-Hammond (2017a), p. 179.

1729. _____; Henry Bradley; William A. Craigie; Charles Talbut Onions and Robert William Burchfield (Edited by). *The Oxford English Dictionary*, Vol. VIII 'Poy-Ry'. The Philological Society. Oxford: At the Clarendon Press, 1933.
   S.s.: Scull-Hammond (2017a), p. 179.

1730. _____; Henry Bradley; William A. Craigie; Charles Talbut Onions and Robert William Burchfield (Edited by). *The Oxford English Dictionary*, Vol. IX, Pt. I 'S-Soldo'. The Philological Society. Oxford: At the Clarendon Press, 1933.
   S.s.: Scull-Hammond (2017a), p. 179.

1731. _____; Henry Bradley; William A. Craigie; Charles Talbut Onions and Robert William Burchfield (Edited by). *The Oxford English Dictionary*, Vol. IX, Pt. II 'Sole-Sz'. The Philological Society. Oxford: At the Clarendon Press, 1933.
   S.s.: Scull-Hammond (2017a), p. 179.

1732. _____; Henry Bradley; William A. Craigie; Charles Talbut Onions and Robert William Burchfield (Edited by). *The Oxford English Dictionary*, Vol. X, Pt. I 'T-U'. The Philological Society. Oxford: At the Clarendon Press, 1933.
   S.s.: Scull-Hammond (2017a), p. 179.

1733. _____; Henry Bradley; William A. Craigie; Charles Talbut Onions and Robert William Burchfield (Edited by). *The Oxford English Dictionary*, Vol. X, Pt. II 'V-Z'. The Philological Society. Oxford: At the Clarendon Press, 1933.
   S.s.: Scull-Hammond (2017a), p. 179.

1734. _____; Henry Bradley; William A. Craigie; Charles Talbut Onions and Robert William Burchfield (Edited by). *The Oxford English Dictionary*, Vol. XI, Supplement and Bibliography. The Philological Society. Oxford: At the Clarendon Press, 1933.
   P.s. 1: *The Notion Club Papers* (1945), p. 225.
   P.s. 2: *On Fairy-stories* (1947), p. 39.
   P.s. 2: 'Nomenclature of *The Lord of the Rings*' (1966), p. 764 '*Took*'.
   P.s. 3. *Tolkien On Fairy-stories* (2008), p. 28.
   S.s.: Scull-Hammond (2017a), p. 179.

1735. Mustanoja, Tauno F. *A Middle English syntax*. Series: Mémoires de la société néophilologique de Helsinki, 23. Helsinki: Societe Neophilologique, 1960.
   P.s.: *Sir Gawain and the Green Knight* (1967) 'Select Bibliography', p. 154.

1736. Nansen, Fridtjof. *In Northern Mists Arctic Exploration in Early Times*, Vol. I. London: William Heinemann, 1911.
   P.s.: #1 a. | *Tolkien On Fairy-stories* (2008), p. 310.
   S.s.: Scull-Hammond (2006b), p. 820.

1737. _____. *In Northern Mists Arctic Exploration in Early Times*, Vol. II. London: William Heinemann, 1911.
   P.s. 1: *On Fairy-stories* (1947), p. 40 n. 2. Tolkien writes: 'For the probability that the Irish *Hy Breasail* played a part in the naming of Brazil see Nansen, *In Northern Mists*, ii, 223-30'.
   P.s. 2: *Tolkien On Fairy-stories* (2008), p. 29 n. 2.

S.s.: Scull-Hammond (2006b), p. 820.

1738. Napier, Arthur Sampson. 'Contributions to Old English lexicography'. Offprint from *Transactions of the Philological Society 1903-1906*. Hertford: Stephen Austin and Sons, 1906, pp. 265-359.
>Description: Autographed in pencil on front flyleaf. Contains loose photograph labeled in red crayon: 'Prof. A. S. Napier | (undated) | given me in 1944 by | Prof. H. G. Fielder | JRRT'.
>Collection: Tolkien's personal Celtic library, preserved at the Weston library under the auspices of the English Faculty Library (Oxford).
>P.s.: *The Devil's Coach-Horses* (1925), p. 332.

1739. _____. 'A Fragment of the Ancren Riwle'. *JGP (The Journal of Germanic Philology)*, Vol. 2, no. 2, 1898, pp. 199-202.
>P.s.: MS. Tolkien A 21/13. [Tolkien Papers, Bodleian Library, Oxford].

1740. _____ (Edited by). *History of the Holy Rood-Tree*. Series: E.E.T.S. (Early English Text Society), OS 103. London: Published for the Early English Text Society by Kegan Paul, Trench, Trübner and Co., 1894.
>Collection: Tolkien's personal Celtic library, preserved at the Weston library under the auspices of the English Faculty Library (Oxford).
>P.s.: MS. Tolkien A 21/13 fol. 119. Note by Tolkien, 'Books in Exeter Library useful', with shelfmarks, on back of photostat reading list dated October 1913. Tolkien writes: 'All EETS publications'. [Tolkien Papers, Bodleian Library, Oxford].

1741. _____ (Edited by). *Iacob and Ioseph. A Middle English poem of the thirteenth century*. Oxford: At the Clarendon Press, 1916.
>Collection: Tolkien's personal Celtic library, preserved at the Weston library under the auspices of the English Faculty Library (Oxford).
>P.s.: MS. Res. e. 308 *Sir Gawain and the Green Knight*. [Tolkien Papers, Bodleian Library, Oxford].

1742. _____. 'Notes on the Orthography of the Ormulum'. *Transactions of the Philological Society* 1891-4. Oxford, 1893.
>Description: Inscribed: 'J. R. Reuel Tolkien'.
>Collection: Weston Library, Bodleian Libraries (Oxford).
>S.s. 1: Scull-Hammond (2017a), p. 52. *Michaelmas Term 1913*: He definitely attends Napier's lectures on English Historical Grammar on Tuesdays and Fridays at 12.00 noon in the Examination Schools, beginning 21 October; p. 56. Hilary Term 1914: Tolkien probably also attends A.S. Napier's continuation of his lectures on English Historical Grammar, on Mondays, Tuesdays, and Fridays at 12.00 noon in the Examination Schools, beginning 23 January.
>S.s. 2: Lapidge (2002), p. 104. [Napier] Cyclostyled sheets for distribution on Ancren Riwle, Ayenbite, Robert of Gloucester, Ormulum, OE dialects, OE verbal declensions, and a reading list for Historical English Grammar: these bear dates from 1904 to 1914 and, Sisam tells me, 'Were distributed (or most them) at the Historical English Grammar course'.

1743. _____. 'The Old English *Exodus*, Vol. II, 63-134'. MLR (*The Modern Language Review*), Vol. 6.2. Belfast: Modern Humanities Research Association, April 1911, pp. 165-68.
>P.s.: *The Old English Exodus* (1982), p. x.

1744. _____. 'An Old English vision of Leofric, Earl of Mercia'. *Transactions of the Philological Society*, 1907-10. London: Kegan Paul, Trench, Trübner & Co., 1908, pp. 180-88.
>P.s.: *Some Contributions to Middle-English Lexicography* (1925), p. 210.

1745. _____ (Edited by). *Old English Glosses*. Series: Anecdota oxoniensia,

Mediæval and modern series. Oxford: At the Clarendon Press, 1900.
  Description: Autographed and marked in blue crayon on front flyleaf: 'from W. A. Craigie | 1920'.
  Collection: Tolkien's personal Celtic library, preserved at the Weston library under the auspices of the English Faculty Library (Oxford).
  P.s. 1: *Sigelwara land* (1932), p. 189 n. 3.
  P.s. 2: *The Old English Exodus* (1982), p. 56.
  S.s.: Scull-Hammond (2017a), p. 52. *Michaelmas Term 1913*: Tolkien probably attends Napier's lectures on Old English Dialects on Thursday at 12.00 noon in the Examination Schools, beginning 23 October.

1746. _____ and John Evans. 'On Barnstaple as a Minting-Place'. Offprint from *Numismatic Chronicle*, Series 3, Vol. XVIII. London: The Numismatic Chronicle, 1898.
  Description: Autographed on cover.
  Collection: Tolkien's personal Celtic library, preserved at the Weston library under the auspices of the English Faculty Library (Oxford).

1747. _____; Walter William Skeat; Frederick James Furnivall and William Paton Ker (Edited by). *An English Miscellany. Presented to Dr. Furnivall in Honour of His Seventy-fifth Birthday*. Oxford: At the Clarendon Press, 1901.
  Collection: Library, Exeter College (Oxford).
  S.s.: Simmonet (2014).

1748. Nash, Thomas. *Have with you to Saffron-Walden*, 1596.
  P.s.: *English and Welsh* (1963), p. 25. Tolkien quotes: 'Fy fa fum, I smell the blood of an Englishman'.

1749. _____. *The Unfortunate Traveller; or, The life of Jack Wilton*.
  S.s.: University of Leeds (1920), p. 147. English Language and Literature - Scheme A. Texts and Period selected for 1920-21. (b) Special period: 1557-1637. (c) Texts suggested for study with Special Period. Ordinary Degree of B.A. with Honours. Final Examination.
  NED: #2 a. | 'W' (1928), p. 14 'Waggle, *v*. 1. *trans. a*.'. 1594 – 'A third [man] wauerd & wagled his head, like a proud horse playing with his bridle.'

1750. Naunton, Robert. *Fragmenta Regalia*. Printed from the Third Posthumous edition of 1653 by Edward Arber.
  S.s.: University of Leeds (1920), p. 147. English Language and Literature - Scheme A. Texts and Period selected for 1920-21. (b) Special period: 1557-1637. (c) Texts suggested for study with Special Period. Ordinary Degree of B.A. with Honours. Final Examination.

1751. Neckel, Gustav. *Walhall. Studien über germanischen Jenseitsglauben*. Dortmund: Fr. Wilh Ruhfus, 1913.
  Description: Decoratively autographed on front cover: 'C. J. R. Tolkien'. Pencil marks in margins. Inscribed on title page: 'B. J. Timmer | Wageringen | Julie 1931.' Bookplate on inside front cover, inscribed: 'Ex Libris Dr. B. J. Timmer.'
  Collection: Tolkien's personal Celtic library, preserved at the Weston library under the auspices of the English Faculty Library (Oxford).

1752. Neilson, William Allan and Kenneth Grant Tremayne Webster (Edited by), joint ed. Chief British poets of the fourteenth and fifteenth centuries. Boston: Houghton Mifflin Company, 1916.
  P.s.: *Sir Gawain and the Green Knight* (1925), p. xxvi. Tolkien and Gordon write: 'For bibliography of the Irish and French analogues of *Sir Gawain*, see the bibliography in Kittredge's study'. [*NED*] In Kittredge's study, this article is mentioned in 'II. Gawain and the Green Knight' (p. 294).

1753. Nelson, William (Edited by). *The Life of St George by Alexander Barclay*.

Series: E.E.T.S. (Early English Text Society), OS 230, London: Oxford University Press, 1955.
:   P.s.: MS. Tolkien A 13/2 *Notes and drafts of lectures on Chaucer: Pardoner's Tale* fol. 126. The MS. contains the Frontispice. [Tolkien Papers, Bodleian Library, Oxford].

1754. Nennius. *Historia Brittonum.* [see Faral].
:   P.s.: *Finn and Hengest* (1982), p. 45 n. 28, p. 46 n. 30, p. 50.

1755. Nerman, Birger. *The Poetic Edda in the light of Archæology.* Series: Viking Society for Northern Research, E.S. IV, 32. Coventry: Curtis and Beamish Ltd., 1931.
:   P.s.: *Sigelwara land* (1934), p. 104 n. 2.

1756. _____. *Det Svenska Rikets Uppkomst.* Series: Föreningen för Svenska Kulturhistoria Böcker, 6. Stockholm: Generalstabens Litogrufiska Anstalt, 1925.
:   P.s. 1: *Beowulf* (2002) 'Version A', p. 43
    P.s. 2: *Beowulf* (2002) 'Version B', p. 104.

1757. Nesbit, Edith. *Five Children – and It.* London: T. Fisher Unwin, 1902.
:   S.s.: Scull-Hammond (2006b), p. 815.
    Reading period: 1908 – 1910 (S.s.: Scull-Hammond (2017c), p. 1054)

1758. _____. *The Phoenix and the Carpet.* London: Macmillan, 1904.
:   P.s.: *Tolkien On Fairy-stories* (2008) 'Manuscript B [MS. Tolkien 4, fols. 73-120]', pp. 249, 251.
    S.s.: Scull-Hammond (2006b), p. 815.
    Reading period: 1908 – 1910 (S.s.: Scull-Hammond (2017c), p. 1054).

1759. _____. *The Story of the Amulet.* London: Macmillan, 1906.
:   P.s.: *Tolkien On Fairy-stories* (2008) 'Manuscript B [MS. Tolkien 4, fols. 73-120]', pp. 249, 251.
    S.s.: Scull-Hammond (2006b), p. 815.
    Reading period: 1908 – 1910 (S.s.: Scull-Hammond (2017c), p. 1054).

1760. Newby, Percy Howard. *Picnic at Sakkara.* London: Jonathan Cape, 1955.
:   Notes: A copy was sent to Tolkien by the author.
    S.s. 1: Scull-Hammond (2017a), p. 479.
    S.s. 2: Scull-Hammond (2006b), p. 818.

1761. Newell, Peter (Illustrated by). *Favourite Fairy Tales (Fairy tales retold).* The Childhood Choice of Representative Men and Women. Decorative bordes by Francis Bennett. New York and London: Harper & Brothers Publishers, 1907.
:   Description: Tolkien requested the book on 27 February 1939 (MS. Library Records b. 618). Weston Library (Oxford), 93 e.123.

1762. Newman, Ernest. *A Study of Wagner.* London: Bertram Dobell, 1899.
:   P.s. 1: *Beowulf* (2002) 'Version A', p. 55. 'There is of course, a value in heroic tales of divided allegiance and unacknowledged defeat. But it is not the only mode of imagination. Almost an element of cant creeps in, as if such things had a mysterious, almost magical virtue. The musical critic Ernest Newman I remember once commented on a similar superstition that there was something inexplicable by analysis, inimitable, about old traditional'airs' - remarking that any competent modern musician with any melodic invention could turn them out by the score to defeat the powers of discrimination of their most enthusiastic admirers. He may or may not have been right. But I feel it is true at any rate of these 'heroic-tales'.
    P.s. 2: *Beowulf* (2002) 'Transcription of Legibile Portions of Folios 71-81: Notes and Jottings', pp. 425-26. Tolkien writes: 'Ernest Newman once remarked on the superstition that there was something inseplicable, invaluable about [illegible] with folk lay'.

Section A

1763. Newman, John Henry. *Apologia pro vita sua*. Series: Everyman's library. London: Joseph Malaby Dent, 1912.
    P.s.: *Valedictory Address* (1959), p. 238. Tolkien writes: 'I have not made any effective *apologia pro consulatu meo*, for none is really possible'. With *apologia*, it is also possible that Tolkien referred to Owen Wilfred's poem, *Apologia Pro Poemate Meo*.

1764. _____. *The Dream of Gerontius, and other poems*. London: Humphrey Milford, 1914.
    S.s.: Ollscoil na h-Éireann G 259 (1949).

1765. Niedermann, Max and Eduard Hermann. *Historische Lautlehre des Lateinischen*. Heidelberg: Carl Winter's Universitätsbuchhandlung, 1907.
    Description: Two signatures. The first is an early ink signature, undoubtedly an ownership signature, penned on the first free end page; Tolkien adds a date of 1912 and a second date of 1919. The second signature is written in pencil on the second free end page - it is a much later signature and Tolkien adds. 'Exeter Coll.'
    Collection: Private [RR Auction, Item 1321, June 1997].

1766. Nitze, William Albert. *The Old French Grail romance Perlesvaus: a study of its principal sources*. Baltimore: J. Murphy Co., 1902.
    P.s.: *Sir Gawain and the Green Knight* (1925), p. xxvi. Tolkien and Gordon write: 'For bibliography of the Irish and French analogues of *Sir Gawain*, see the bibliography in Kittredge's study'. [*NED*] In Kittredge's study, this article is mentioned in 'V. Le Livre de Caradoc' (p. 298), 'VII. Perlesvaus' (p. 300).

1767. _____ and T. Atkinson Jenkins. *Perlesvaus. Le haut livre du Graal*, Vol. I. Text, variants, and glossary. Series: The Modern Philology Monographs. Chicago: The University of Chicago Press, 1932.
    P.s.: *Sir Gawain and the Green Knight* (1967) 'Select Bibliography', p. 155.

1768. _____ and T. Atkinson Jenkins. *Perlesvaus. Le haut livre du Graal*, Vol. II. Commentary and notes. Series: The Modern Philology Monographs. Chicago: The Univiversity. of Chicago Press, 1937.
    P.s.: *Sir Gawain and the Green Knight* (1967) 'Select Bibliography', p. 155.

1769. Nordal, Sigurður. *Íslenzk Lestrarbók, 1400-1900*. Reykjavík: Sigfúsar Eymundssonar, 1924.
    Description: Autographed on page after front flyleaf: 'JRR Tolkien | (from E. V. G. 1928)'.
    Collection: Tolkien's personal Celtic library, preserved at the Weston library under the auspices of the English Faculty Library (Oxford).

1770. _____. *Íslenzk menning*, Vol. I. Reykjavík: E. Munksgaards, 1942.
    Description: Inscribed in front cover: 'Prófessor J.R.R. Tolkien | með – – (illegible) | Sigurður Nordal.' Contains bookmark at pp. 56-57.
    Collection: Tolkien's personal Celtic library, preserved at the Weston library under the auspices of the English Faculty Library (Oxford).

1771. _____. *Snorri Sturluson*. Reykjavík: Þór. B. Þorláksson, 1920.
    Description: Autographed in pencil inside front cover and dated: 'from EVG | 1935'. [E. V. Gordon].
    Collection: Tolkien's personal Celtic library, preserved at the Weston library under the auspices of the English Faculty Library (Oxford).

1772. Noreen, Adolf Gotthard. *Altisländische und altnorwegische Grammatik. Altnordische Grammatik*, Vol. I. Series: Sammlung Kurzer Grammatiken

Germanischer Dialecte, 4. Halle: Max Niemeyer, 1884.
: Description: Inscribed on front cover: 'W. I., Stevenson Dec. 14, 1884 'Autographed on front flyleaf. Contains two loose pages of JRRT's notes and bookmark at pp. 14-15 (*Lautlehere. I Abschnitt. Einleitendes über schrift un aussprache*. Kap. 1. Die runen, 13-22.)
: Collection: Tolkien's personal Celtic library, preserved at the Weston library under the auspices of the English Faculty Library (Oxford).

1773. _____. *Altschwedische grammatik, mit einschluss des altgutnischen*. Halle: Max Niemeyer, 1904.
: Description: Original cloth. Signed in ink on the end paper.
: Collection: Private [TolkienLibrary, Sold on Ebay 17 July 2012].

1774. Norman, Friederick and Peter Felix Ganz (Edited by). *Proceedings of the seventh International Congress of Linguistic*. London: Titus Wilson, 1956.
: Description: Proceedings of the seventh International Congress of Linguistic, London September 1-6, 1952. Tolkien did not attend the conference, as he explained in a letter to Rayner Unwin (August 29, 1952), but is mentioned in the Organizing Committee on p. x: 'Prof. J.R.R. Tolkien, M. A.'

1775. Northall, G. F. (Edited by). *A Warwickshire Word-book: Comprising Obsolescent and Dialect Words, Colloquialisms*. London: Pub. for the English dialect society by H, Frowde, 1896.
: S.s.: Gilliver-Marshall-Weiner (2009), p. 92
: NED: #2 h. | 'W' (1928), p. 53 'Wallop *sb*. 3. b.' – 1896 'He *went wallop* = he fell down all of a heap'.

1776. Norton, Charles Eliot. *Letters of Charles Eliot Norton*, Vol. II. Edited by Sara Norton and Mary Anthony De Wolfe Howe. London: Costable & Co., 1913.
: P.s.: *Oxford University Press Archives* (Oxford). A slip written by Tolkien on the etymology of 'Wake' used ('W' p. 31) [A. 1721].
: NED: #2 f. | 'W' (1928), p. 31 'Wake, 3.' 1874 –'sumner is dead. We have had a great wake over him, and the echoes of it have scarcely yet died away' (p. 42).

1777. Norton, Mary. *The Borrowers*. London: Joseph Malaby Dent, 1952.
: S.s.: Scull-Hammond (2006b), p. 820. His own copy of which Tolkien lent to his granddaughter, Joanna.

1778. _____. *The Borrowers Afield*. London: Joseph Malaby Dent, 1955.
: S.s.: Scull-Hammond (2006b), p. 820. His own copy of which Tolkien lent to his granddaughter, Joanna.

1779. _____. *The Borrowers Afloat*. London: Joseph Malaby Dent, 1959.
: S.s.: Scull-Hammond (2006b), p. 820. His own copy of which Tolkien lent to his granddaughter, Joanna.

1780. _____. *The Borrowers Aloft*. London: Joseph Malaby Dent, 1961.
: S.s.: Scull-Hammond (2006b), p. 820. His own copy of which Tolkien lent to his granddaughter, Joanna.

1781. _____. *Poor Stainless: A new story about the Borrowers*. London: Joseph Malaby Dent, 1966.
: S.s.: Scull-Hammond (2006b), p. 507 Tolkien lent to his granddaughter, Johanna.

1782. Norton, Thomas and Thomas Sackville Dorset. *Ferrex and Porrex; or Gorboduc*.
: S.s.: Ollscoil na h-Éireann G 101 (1949).

SECTION A

1783. _____ with Thomas Sackville Dorset; George Peele; Thomas Kyd; Ashley Horacee Thorndike; Nicholas Udall; John Lyly and Robert Green (Edited by). *The Minor Elizabethan Drama,* Vol. I, Pre-Shakespearean Tragedies. Series: Everyman's library, 491. London: Joseph Malaby Dent & Sons Ltd., 1917.
    S.s.: University of Leeds (1923), p. 81. Ordinary Degree of B.A., Intermediate Course and Examination: English Literature. Text selected for 1923-24 (ii) Texts suggests as part of a course of general rending in the period 1579-1645. Texts suggested: *Arden of Feversham* and *David and Bethsabe* by George Peele; p. 85. Ordinary Degree of B.A., Final Course and Examination. I. Principal Subjects, studied for Two Years. English Language and Literature: English Literature. Period selected for 1923-24: 1579-1645. Texts selected for 1923-24.

1784. _____ with Thomas Sackville Dorset et alii (Edited by). *The Minor Elizabethan Drama,* Vol. II, Pre-Shakespearean Comedies. Series: Everyman's library, 492. London: Joseph Malaby Dent & Sons Ltd., 1917.
    S.s.: University of Leeds (1923), p. 85. Ordinary Degree of B.A., Final Course and Examination. I. Principal Subjects, studied for Two Years. English Language and Literature: English Literature. Period selected for 1923-24: 1579-1645. Texts selected for 1923-24.

1785. O'Domhnuill, Huilliam. *An Tiomna Nuadh ar dTíghearna agus ar Slanuightheóra Iosa Criosd.* London: Bagster and Thoms for the British and Foreign Bible Society, 1827.
    Description: Autographed on front flyleaf. On next pages is some pencil and ink using now illegible and partly rubbed out. Inscribed on following page: 'Margaret (rubbed out) | December 15th 1830' | 'A. W. Skreane, Nov. 1901 | E [dono?] A.J. Wallis.' On 4 pages following the vocabulary are penciled writings in Irish.
    Collection: Tolkien's personal Celtic library, preserved at the Weston library under the auspices of the English Faculty Library (Oxford).

1786. O'Growney, Eugene. *Simple Lessons in Irish. Giving the Pronunciation of Each Word Pts I-V* (5 vols in 1, 8th ed.). Dublin: Gaelic League, 1912.
    Description: Autographed and dated in pencil on front flyleaf: 'Dublin | 1949'.
    Collection: Tolkien's personal Celtic library, preserved at the Weston library under the auspices of the English Faculty Library (Oxford).

1787. O'Keeffe, James George (Edited by). *Buile Suibhne (The Frenzy of Suibhne). Being the adventures of Subhne Geilt, a Middle Irish romance.* Series: Irish Texts Society, XII, 1910. London: Published from the Irish Texts Society by David Nutt, 1913.
    Collection: Tolkien's personal Celtic library, preserved at the Weston library under the auspices of the English Faculty Library (Oxford).
    S.s.: McIlwaine (2018), no. 84.

1788. O'Neill, Joseph. *Land under England.* London: Victor Gollancz Ltd., 1935.
    P.s.: *Letters* 26 (1938). To Stanley Unwin. Tolkien writes: 'I am extremely fond of the genre, even having read 'Land' with some pleasure (though it was a weak example, and distasteful to me in many points).'
    S.s.: Scull-Hammond (2017a), p. 228.

1789. Oakden, James Parker. *Alliterative poetry in Middle English,* Vol. I. Series: Publications of the University of Manchester. English series, 19. Manchester: The University Press, 1930.
    P.s.: *Sir Gawain and the Green Knight* (1967) 'Select Bibliography', p. 154.

1790. _____. *Alliterative poetry in Middle English,* Vol. II. Series: Publications of the University of Manchester. English series, 22. Manchester: The University Press,

1935.
>P.s.: *Sir Gawain and the Green Knight* (1967) 'Select Bibliography', p. 154.

1791. Oesterley, William Oscar Emil. *The evolution of the messianic idea, a study in comparative religion*. New York: Edward Payson Dutton & Co. 1908.
>Description: Tolkien requested the book on 27 February 1939 (MS. Library Records b. 618). Weston Library (Oxford), 93 e.126.

1792. Offord, Marguerite Yvonne (Edited by). *The Parlement of the Thre Ages*. Series: E.E.T.S. (Early English Text Society), OS 246. London: Oxford University Press, 1959.
>Notes: 27 November 1940 Tolkien certifies that M. Y. Offord (nee Pickard) is qualified to be a B.Litt. student. Her thesis will be an edition of *The Parlement of the Thre Ages*. 2 October 1948 Tolkien attends an Early English Text Society Committee meeting at Magdalen College, Oxford. M. Y. Offord, his former B.Litt. student, is given permission to submit her B.Litt. thesis, *The Parlement of the Thre Ages*, for consideration. (It will be published in 1959).
>P.s.: *Sir Gawain and the Green Knight* (1967) 'Select Bibliography: editions of texts quoted more than once in the notes', p. 156.

1793. Öfverberg, William. *The Inflections of the East Midland dialects in Early Middle English: Substantives adjectives, numerals and pronouns*. Lund: Hakan Ohlsson, 1924.
>Description: Autographed on front flyleaf.
>Collection: Tolkien's personal Celtic library, preserved at the Weston library under the auspices of the English Faculty Library (Oxford).

1794. _____. *Verbal Inflections of the East Midland dialects in Early Middle English*. Lund: Hakan Ohlsson, 1924.
>Description: Autographed on front cover.
>Collection: Tolkien's personal Celtic library, preserved at the Weston library under the auspices of the English Faculty Library (Oxford).

1795. Ogden, Margaret (Edited by). *Cyrurgie of Guy de Chauliac*, Vol. I. Text. Series: E.E.T.S. (Early English Text Society), OS 265. London: Oxford University Press, 1971.
>Description: Contains three pages of JRRT's loose notes.
>Collection: Tolkien's personal Celtic library, preserved at the Weston library under the auspices of the English Faculty Library (Oxford).

1796. *Old English Homilies* 1150. [Collection of homilies in Old English, see R. Morris].
>P.s.: MS. Tolkien A 21/13 *The English MSS*. fol. 203. [Tolkien Papers, Bodleian Library, Oxford].

1797. *Old Kentish Sermons*. [Preserved in Laud. MS. 471, see R. Morris].
>P.s.: MS. Tolkien A 21/13 *The English MSS*. fol. 203. [Tolkien Papers, Bodleian Library, Oxford].

1798. Olrik, Axe. *A Book of Danish ballads*. Princeton: University Press, 1939.
>S.s.: Shippey (1992), p. 299.

1799. Ólsen, Björn Magnússon. *Um Sturlungu*, Vol. III. Kaupmannahöfn: S. L. Møller, 1897.
>Description: Autographed on front flyleaf.
>Collection: Tolkien's personal Celtic library, preserved at the Weston library under the auspices of the English Faculty Library (Oxford).

1800. Oman, Charles Williams Chadwick. *The Art of War in the Middle Ages, A.D.*

378-1515. Oxford: B. H. Blackwell, 1885.
   S.s.: Shippey (2005), p. 9.

1801. *On Ilkla Moor baht 'at* [Dialect Song from the West Riding of Yorkshire].
   P.s.: *Philology: General Works* (VI 1927, for 1925), p. 38.

1802. Onions, Charles Talbut. 'Breche in *The Owl and the Nightingale*, line 14', *A Grammatical Miscellany Offered to Otto Jespersen on his Seventieth Birthday*. Copenhagen, Levin og Munksgaard; London, Allen and Unwin, 1930, pp. 105-08.
   Collection: Weston Library, Bodleian Libraries (Oxford).

1803. _____. 'Letter: Sir Gawayne and the Green Knight, II, 530'. *The Times Literary Supplement*, 16 August 1923.
   P.s.: *Sir Gawain and the Green Knight* (1925), p. 89, line *no fage*. Tolkien and Gordon write: 'This emendation was made by C. T. Onions in a letter published in the Times Literary Supplement of August 16, 1923, and defended in the issue of September 20. For evidence of the phrase *no fage* in Middle English see these two letters'.

1804. _____. 'Letter: Sir Gawayne and the Green Knight, II, 530'. *The Times Literary Supplement*, 20 September 1923.
   P.s.: *Sir Gawain and the Green Knight* (1925), p. 89, line *no fage*. Tolkien and Gordon write: 'This emendation was made by C. T. Onions in a letter published in the Times Literary Supplement of August 16, 1923, and defended in the issue of September 20. For evidence of the phrase *no fage* in Middle English see these two letters'.

1805. _____. 'Middle English *Ord and ende*'. Offprint from MLR (*The Modern Language Review*), Vol 24, no. 4, October 1929.
   Description: Includes a label added by Stan Revell to books owned by Tolkien, 'From the Library of J.R.R. Tolkien'.
   Collection: John J. Burns Special Collections Library, Boston College (Chestnut Hill, Massachusetts).

1806. _____. 'Middle English (i) Wite God, Wite Crist, (ii) God It Wite'. *The Review of English Studies*, Vol. 4, no. 16. London: Oxford University Press, July 1928, pp. 334-37.
   S.s.: Scull-Hammond (2017a), p. 1 48. '?1927-early 1928 Tolkien draws the attention of C.T. Onions to the use in *The Owl and the Nightingale* of a phrase about which Onions is writing an article for the *Review of English Studies* ('Middle English (i) *Wite God, Wite Crist*, (ii) *God It Wite*, July 1928).'

1807. _____. *Modern English Sintax*. Revised by Brian Donald Hewens Miller. London: Routledge & Kegan Paul, 1971.
   P.s.: Tolkien's unpublished letter to Miller, 21 June 1971. Tolkien writes: 'Thank you very much for sending me a copy of your revision of Onions"syntax'. I have never possessed a copy before'.

1808. _____. *A Shakespeare glossary*. Oxford: At the Clarendon Press, 1941 (2nd rev.).
   Descriptin: Includes a label added by Stan Revell to books owned by Tolkien, 'From the Library of J.R.R. Tolkien', on front pastedown.
   Collection: Private [Sold by Bloomsbury Auctions, 2 February 2006].

1809. _____. *The Shorter Oxford English Dictionary On Historical Principles*, Vol. I 'A-Markworthy'. Oxford: At the Clarendon Press, 1956 (rev. repr. of 3rd ed.).
   Description: Signed by Tolkien on front free end-paper with occasional annotations. Tolkien adds an entry of his own: 'Bag-end 'As' a cul-de-sac or a house that stands at the closed end of one' (p.

137); he notes the plural form of 'elf' as 'elves' (p. 593) and he provides additional information on 'fairy' (p. 669).
Collection: Private [Sold by Sotheby's, 13 December 2001].

1810. _____. *The Shorter Oxford English Dictionary On Historical Principles*, Vol. II 'Marl-Z' with Addenda. Oxford: At the Clarendon Press, 1956 (rev. repr. of 3rd ed.).
Description: Signed by Tolkien on front free end-paper with occasional annotations. Tolkien annotates 'rune' (p. 1770).
Collection: Private [Sold by Sotheby's, 13 December 2001].

1811. *Only English proclamation of Henry III* 1258. [Thirteenth-century celebrative poem, see Ellis].
P.s.: MS. Tolkien A 21/13 *The English MSS.* fol. 203. [Tolkien Papers, Bodleian Library, Oxford].

1812. *Orison of Our Lord*, 1210. [Middle English poems, see R. Morris].
P.s.: MS. Tolkien A 21/13 *The English MSS.* fol. 203. [Tolkien Papers, Bodleian Library, Oxford].

1813. Orlowski, Boleslaw Kamil. *Le demoiselle à la mule (Le mule sanz frain): conte en vers du cycle Arthurien par Païen de Maigiere*. Paris: H. Champion, 1911.
P.s. 1: *Sir Gawain and the Green Knight* (1925), pp. xiii; xxvi. Tolkien and Gordon write: 'For bibliography of the Irish and French analogues of *Sir Gawain*, see the bibliography in Kittredge's study'. In Kittredge's study, this article is mentioned in 'VI. La Mule sanz Frain' (p. 298).
P.s. 2: *Sir Gawain and the Green Knight* (1967) 'Select Bibliography', p. 155.

1814. *Ormulum* 1200. [Middle English exegetical poem, see Burchfield and Sweet].
P.s. 1: MS. Tolkien A 21/7 fol. 16. [Tolkien Papers, Bodleian Library, Oxford].
P.s. 2: MS. Tolkien A 21/13 *The English MSS.* fol. 203. [Tolkien Papers, Bodleian Library, Oxford].
P.s. 3: 'Chaucer as a Philologist: *The Reeve's Tale*' (1934), p. 134.
P.s. 4: *Foreword to A New Glossary of the Dialect of Huddersfield District* (1928), p. xv.

1815. Orosius, Paulus Alfred. *Extracts from Alfred's Orosius*. Edited by Henry Sweet. Oxford: At the Clarendon Press, 1893 (2nd ed.).
Description: Signature in pencil on front free endpaper: 'J.R.R. Tolkien'. A few annotations to text at beginning and library book-label on front pastedown.
Collection: Private [Sold by Bloomsbury Auctions, 6 December 2007].
P.s. 1: *Some Contributions to Middle-English Lexicography* (1925), p. 211.
P.s. 2: *Finn and Hengest* (1982), p. 60 n. 57.

1816. _____. *King Alfred's Orosius*. Series: E.E.T.S. (Early English Text Society), OS 79. Edited by Henry Sweet. London: Published for the Early English Text Society by Kegan Paul, Trench, Trübner and Co., 1883.
P.s. 1: MS. Tolkien A 21/13 fol. 119. Note by Tolkien, 'Books in Exeter Library useful', with shelfmarks, on back of photostat reading list dated October 1913. Tolkien writes: 'All EETS publications'. [Tolkien Papers, Bodleian Library, Oxford].
P.s. 2: MS. Tolkien A 19/3 *Etymologies or history of Walrus* fols. 162-195. [Tolkien Papers, Bodleian Library, Oxford].
P.s. 3: MS. Tolkien A 12/3 *Rough text of a lecture on Sir Gawain*, 1965 fols. 17-59. [Tolkien Papers, Bodleian Library, Oxford].
P.s. 4: *Finn and Hengest* (1982), p. 99 n. 32, p. 108 n. 49.
S.s.: *Tolkien, Family Album* (1992), p. 42.
NED: #2 i. | 'W' (1928), pp. 57-58 'Walrus, 1.' 1883 (c893 Aelfred Oros. 1. i. § 15 For þæm horschwælum for ðæm hie habbaþ swíðe æðele bán on heora tóþum.

1817. _____. *King Alfred's Anglo-Saxon version of the Compendious History of the World*. Translated by Joseph Bosworth; edited by Robert Thomas Hampson. London: Longman, Brown, Green, 1859.
P.s.: *Finn and Hengest* (1982), p. 99 n. 32, p. 108 n. 49.
S.s. 1: #1 Holland (1949), p. 140. Appendix XI: Oxford Examinations for Prisoners of War.
B.1 Old English: 'He sæde ðæt Norðmanna ... hergiað on ða Norðmen' (from 'The Voyages of

Ohthere and Wulfstan').

S.s. 2: Scull-Hammond (2017a), p. 46. April 1913: Tolkien will need to become familiar with a range of literary and philological subjects and set texts as prescribed in the Oxford Regulations of the Board of Studies, knowing that he may be examined on them in ten papers at the end of Trinity Term 1915: Old English texts. […] 'The Amazons (I, 10) and 'The Voyages of Ohthere and Wulfstan'.

1818. Orton, Harold. *Phonology of a South Durham Dialect. Descriptive, historical, and comparative*. London: Kegan Paul, Trench, Trübner, 1933.
Description: Autographed in pencil on front flyleaf: 'JRR Tolkien | from author | April | 1946'. Decorative note on front flyleaf.
Collection: Tolkien's personal Celtic library, preserved at the Weston library under the auspices of the English Faculty Library (Oxford).

1819. Osgood, Charles Grosvenor (Edited by). *The Pearl*. Boston and London: Health, 1906.
Description: Inscribed [by E. V. Gordon?]: 'livre de J. P. [?] | and E. V. Gordon. | Univ. Coll. Oxon 1915'. Annotations [by E.V. Gordon?] [Judith Priestman 1994, revd. 2016].
Collection: Weston Library, Bodleian Libraries (Oxford).
P.s. 1: *Sir Gawain and the Green Knight* (1925), p. xxv.
P.s. 2: *Sir Gawain and the Green Knight* (1967) 'Select Bibliography', p. 153.

1820. _____ (Edited by). *The Pearl*. Boston and London: Health, 1910.
Description: Exeter College. Tolkien inscribed: 'John Reuel Tolkien | e Coll. | exon oxon Easter mcmxiii. | ex libris de litt et phil germ Coll.' And in Latin form the date: 'Easter 1913'. And its location in his libraryInscribed. Extensively annotated; one page of notes tipped-in at pp. 26-27. Loose leaves (letter to Tolkien from Ida Gordon, 1947-50).
Collection: Weston Library, Bodleian Libraries (Oxford).

1821. Osterley, Hermann. *A Hundred Merry Tales*. London: J. R. Smith, 1866.
P.s.: *Letters* 241 (1962). From a letter to Jane Neave.

1822. Otway, Thomas. *The Best Plays of Thomas Otway*. Series: Mermaid. Edited by Roden Noel. London: Fisher Unwyn, 1903.
S.s.: University of Leeds (1921), p. 154. English Language and Literature - Scheme A. Texts and Period selected for 1921-22. (d) Texts suggested for study with Special Period 1637-1700. Ordinary Degree of B.A. with Honours. Final Examinations.

1823. Ovid. *Metamorphoses. Shakespeare's Ovid: being Arthur Golding's translation of the Metamorphoses*. Translated by Arthur Golding and edited by William Henry Denham Rouse. London: At the De La More Press, 1904.
P.s.: *Sigelwara land* (1932), p. 194 n. 1. Tolkien cites lines 235-6.
NED: #2 h. | 'W' (1928), p. 53 'Wallop sb. 2. a' – 1565 'The medicine seething all the while a wallop in a pan Of brasse, to spirt and leape a loft and gather froth began' (1593, p. 160).

1824. Owen, Dora. *The Book of Fairy Poetry*. London and New York: Longmans and Green and Co., 1920.
Notes: Tolkien's poem *Goblin Feet* is included (pp. 177-78).
S.s.: Scull-Hammond (2017a), p. 121.

1825. Owen, Douglas David Roy. 'Burlesque Tradition and Sir Gawain and the Green Knight'. Offprint from MLN (*Modern Language Notes*), Vol. IV, no. 2, Aprile 1968, pp. 125-145.
P.s.: Tolkien's unpublished letter to Dr. Owen, 24 May 1968. 'I find it most interesting, though I haven't yet had time to study it with care, as I have just returned to Oxford after some absence and am in the middle of arranging a removal.'

1826. Owen, Edward. 'A note on the identification of the *Bleheris* of Wauchier de Denain'. *Revue Celtique*, Vol. XXXII. Dirigée par Joseph Marie Loth, Georges

Dottin, Emilie Ernault and Joseph Vendryes. Paris: Librairie Honoré Champion, 1911, pp. 5-16.
>P.s.: *Sir Gawain and the Green Knight* (1925), p. xii line 2.

1827. *Owl and the Nightingale* 1246-50. [Middle English poem, see Onions, Stevenson, Wells, Hodgson].
>P.s.: MS. Tolkien A 21/13 *The English MSS*. fol. 203. [Tolkien Papers, Bodleian Library, Oxford].
>S.s.: Lewis (2009a), p. 75. Letter to his Brother Warren – 8 Aprile 1932. Lewis writes: 'I have read very little but middle english texts since I last wrote: specially the *Owl and the Nightingale* which you must read in Tolkien's translation some day.'

1828. Paget, Richard. *Babel. Or, the past, present, and future of human speech.* London: K. Paul, Trench, Trubner & Co., 1930.
>P.s.: *A Sceret Vice* (2016), p. 68.

1829. _____. *Human speech. Some observations, experiments, and conclusions as to the nature, origin, purpose and possible improvement of human speech.* London: K. Paul, Trench, Trubner & Co., 1930.
>P.s.: *A Secret Vice* (2016), p. 68.

1830. Palgrave, Francis Turner. *The Golden Treasury of the best songs and lyrical poems. With Additional Poems*. Series: World's classics, 133. London: H. Milford, Oxford University Press, 1920.
>S.s. 1: University of Leeds (1920), p. 135 English Literature. Texts Selected for 1920-21; p. 180. English Language and Literature. Int. I Intermediate Course (Literature).
>S.s. 2: University of Leeds (1921), p. 141. English Literature, text selected for 1921-22. Ordinary Degree of B.A.; p. 156. English Language and Literature - Scheme B. Texts for 1921-22. (d) Outlines of the History of English Literature. Ordinary Degree of B.A. with Honours. Final Examinations; p. 190 English Language and Literature. Int. 1 Intermediate Course (Literature).

1831. Palmer, Harold Edward. *English Intonation with Systematic Exercise.* Cambridge: W. Heffer, 1922.
>P.s.: *Philology: General Works* (V 1926, for 1924), p. 32.

1832. _____. *Everyday sentences in spoken English. In phonetic transcription with intonation mark* (For the use of Foreign Students). Cambridge: Heffer, 1922.
>S.s.: Hime (1980), p. 6.

1833. _____. *A Grammar for Spoken English on a strictly phonetic basis*. Cambridge: W. Heffer, 1924.
>P.s.: *Philology: General Works* (V 1926, for 1924), pp. 28, 32.

1834. Panzer, Friedrich Whilelm. *Studien zur germanischen sagengeschichte*, Vol. I. Beowulf. München: C. H. Beck (O. Beck), 1910.
>P.s.: *Beowulf* (2002) 'Version B', p. 104.

1835. _____. *Studien zur germanischen sagengeschichte*, Vol. II. Sigfrid. München: C. H. Beck (O. Beck), 1912.
>P.s.: *Beowulf* (2002) 'Version B', p. 104.

1836. Paris, Gaston. 'Caradoc et le Serpent'. *Romania: Recueil trimestriel consacré a l'étude des langues et des literatures romanes*, Vol. XXVIII, 1899, pp. 214-31.
>P.s.: *Sir Gawain and the Green Knight* (1925), p. xxvi. Tolkien and Gordon write: 'For bibliography of the Irish and French analogues of *Sir Gawain*, see the bibliography in Kittredge's study'. [*NED*] In Kittredge's study, this article is mentioned in 'V. Le Livre de Caradoc' (pp. 297, 298).

1837. _____. 'La Mule sans Frein'. *Histoire littéraire de la France*, Vol. XXX, 1888, pp. 68-69.
    P.s.: *Sir Gawain and the Green Knight* (1925), p. xxvi. Tolkien and Gordon write: 'For bibliography of the Irish and French analogues of *Sir Gawain*, see the bibliography in Kittredge's study'. [*NED*] In Kittredge's study, this article is mentioned in 'VI. La Mule sanz Frain' (p. 299), 'VIII. Humbaut' (p. 301), 'IX. The Carl of Carlisle' (p. 302).

1838. Partridge, Eric. *A Dictionary of Slang and Unconventional English*. London: Routledge & Kegan Paul Ltd., 1923, p. 975.
    P.s.: *Letters* 83 (1944). From a letter to Christopher Tolkien.

1839. Patmore, Coventry. *The wedding sermon*. London: Burns & Oates, 1911.
    Description: Includes a label added by Stan Revell to books owned by Tolkien, 'From the Library of J.R.R. Tolkien'.
    Collection: Private.
    S.s. Scull-Hammond (2018a).

1840. Paul, Hermann. *Grundriss der germanischen Philologie*, Vol. I Begriff und Geschichte der Germanischen Philologie, Methodenlehre, Schriftkunde, Sprachjeschichte, Mythologie. Strassburg: Karl J. Trübner, 1891.
    P.s.: *Exeter College library register*. Tolkien's borrowing record: *Hilary Term 1914* from 29 January to 10 March.

1841. _____. *Grundriss der germanischen Philologie*, Vol. II Heldensage, Literaturgeschichte, Metrik. Strassburg: Karl J. Trübner, 1893.
    P.s. 1: *Exeter College library register*. Tolkien's borrowing record: *Hilary Term 1914* from 29 January to 10 March; Easter vacation 1914 from 1 January to 17 June; Hilary Term 1915 from 28 January to 1 March 1915.
    P.s. 2: *Beowulf* (2002) 'Version B', p. 103.

1842. _____. *Mittelhochdeutsche Grammatik*. Halle: Max Niemeyer, 1904.
    Description: Signed in the front by J.R.R. Tolkien and annotations in pencil.
    Collection: Private [Sold by Peter Harrington Antiquarian Bookseller].
    S.s.: Harrington (2003), p. 25.

1843. Paul the Apostle. *Epistle to the Philippians* [early 2nd century, see Wycliffe IV]
    P.s.: MS. Tolkien A 13/2 *Notes and drafts of lectures on Chaucer: Pardoner's Tale* fol. 159. [Tolkien Papers, Bodleian Library, Oxford]. Tolkien refers to Philippians 3:18-19 [18 For, as I have often told you before and now tell you again even with tears, many live as enemies of the cross of Christ. 19 Their destiny is destruction, their god is their stomach, and their glory is in their shame. Their mind is set on earthly things.]

1844. Paul the Deacon, *Historia Langobardorum*. Edited by Ludvig Konrad Bethmann and Georg Waitz. Hannoverae Impensis Bibliopolii Hahniani, 1878.
    S.s.: Shippey (2005), p. 9.

1845. Pauphilet, Albert. *La Queste del Saint Graal: roman du XIII Siecle*. Paris E. Champion, 1923.
    P.s.: *Sir Gawain and the Green Knight* (1925), p. 82, line 90 ff.

1846. Peacock, William. *Selected English essays*. Series: World's Classics, 32. With notes by Charles Bickersteth Wheeler. London: H. Milford and Sons and Oxford University Press.
    S.s.: University of Leeds (1920), p. 181. English Language and Literature. Int. I Intermediate Course (Literature).

1847.   *Pearl* [Middle English dream vision poem].
   For editions and translations of this poem, see Gollancz, Gordon E. V., Osgood, Tolkien.
   P.s. 1: MS. Tolkien A 13/1 *Draft of talk to the Oxford Dante Society: A neck-verse* (1947) fol. 171. Tolkien quotes 'Sone Þe worlde ... hit wex late' (vv. 537-38).
   P.s. 2: *Foreword to A New Glossary of the Dialect of Huddersfield District* (1928), p. xvi.

1848.   Pedersen, Holger. *Vergleichende Grammatik der keltischen Sprachen*, Vol. I. Einleitung und Lautlehre. Göttingen: Vandenhoeck und Ruprecht, 1909.
   Description: Autographed on front flyleaf: 'John Reuel Tolkien'. Annotated in pencil. V. I. – page after front flyleaf, decoratively drawn 'Ex Libris Johannis Tolkien'.
   Collection: Tolkien's personal Celtic library, preserved at the Weston library under the auspices of the English Faculty Library (Oxford).

1849.   _____. *Vergleichende Grammatik der keltischen Sprachen*, Vol. II. Bedeutungslehre (Wortlehre). Göttingen: Vandenhoeck und Ruprecht, 1913.
   Description: Autographed on front flyleaf.
   Collection: Tolkien's personal Celtic library, preserved at the Weston library under the auspices of the English Faculty Library (Oxford).

1850.   Peek, Hedley and Frederick George Aflalo. *The Encyclopaedia of Sport*, Vol. I. London: Lawrence and Bullen, Ltd., 1897.
   P.s.: *Oxford University Press Archives* (Oxford). In a slip written by Tolkien on the etymology of 'Waggle' reads: 'Waggle, sb. [f. Waggle v.]' [...] 'act of waggling; spec. in Golf (see quoted 1897)'.
   NED: #2 a. | 'W' (1928), p. 14 'Waggle, *v.* 1. *trans.* a.' 1897 – '(Golf) In taking aim or addressing the ball, it is the almost invariable practice to pass or flourish the club head a few times backwards and forwards over the top of the ball in the direction of the proposed stroke. This is called the 'Waggle'. (p. 464).

1851.   Pennant, Thomas. *Synopsis of quadrupeds*. Chester: printed by J. Monk, Ann Arbor, 1771.
   P.s.: MS. Tolkien A 19/3 *Etymologies or history of Walrus* fols. 162-195. [Tolkien Papers, Bodleian Library, Oxford].
   S.s.: *Tolkien, Family Album* (1992), p. 42.
   NED: #2 i. | 'W' (1928), pp. 57-58 'Walrus, 2. *obs.*' 1771 – 'Indian Walrus' (p. 338).

1852.   Pennock, South Helen (Edited by). *The Proverbs of Alfred*. New York City: New York University, 1931.
   Description: Autographed in pencil on front flyleaf.
   Collection: Tolkien's personal Celtic library, preserved at the Weston library under the auspices of the English Faculty Library (Oxford).

1853.   *Pepys MS. 2498*. [Contains *Ancrene Wisse*].
   P.s.: MS. Tolkien A 21/13 *The English MSS*. fol. 197. [Tolkien Papers, Bodleian Library, Oxford].

1854.   Pepys, Samuel. *The Diary of Samuel Pepys*, Vol. I. Edited by Mynors Bright. London: J. M Dent & Sons, 1906.
   P.s.: MS. Tolkien A 13/2 *Notes and drafts of lectures on Chaucer: Pardoner's Tale* fol. 141. [Tolkien Papers, Bodleian Library, Oxford].
   S.s. 1: University of Leeds (1920), p. 139 English Language and Literature: English Literature. Text selected for 1920-21. Texts Selected for 1920-21. Ordinary Degree of B.A. with Honours. Final Course and Examination. Extracts 1659-June 30, 1661 pp. 1-262.
   S.s. 2: University of Leeds (1921), p. 154. English Language and Literature - Scheme A. Texts and Period selected for 1921-22. (d) Texts suggested for study with Special Period 1637-1700. Ordinary Degree of B.A. with Honours. Final Examinations.
   NED 1: #2 b. | 'W' (1928), p. 23 'Waist-cloth' 1.' 1660, 16 May – We ... had our guns ready to fire, and our scarlet waist-cloathes out and silk pendants.'

SECTION A

NED 2: #2 b. | 'W' (1928), p. 23 'Waistcoat' colloq. or vulgar. 1.' 1666 – '20 June, I have of late taken too much cold by washing my feet and going tn a thin silke waistcoate, without any other coate over it, and open-breasted.'

1855. _____. *The Diary of Samuel Pepys*, Vol. II. Edited by Mynors Bright. London: J. M Dent & Sons, 1906.
    P.s.: MS. Tolkien A 13/2 *Notes and drafts of lectures on Chaucer: Pardoner's Tale* fol. 141. [Tolkien Papers, Bodleian Library, Oxford].

1856. Percy, Thomas. *Bishop Percy's Folio Manuscript: Ballads and Romances*, Vol. II. Edited by Frederick James Furnivall and John Wesley Hales. London: N. Trübner & Co., 1868.
    P.s.: *Sir Gawain and the Green Knight* (1925), p. xxvi. Tolkien and Gordon write: 'For bibliography of the Irish and French analogues of *Sir Gawain*, see the bibliography in Kittredge's study'. [*NED*] In Kittredge's study, this article is mentioned in 'III. The Green Knight' (p. 296), 'IV. The Turk and Gawain' (p. 297), 'IX. The Carl of Carlisle' (p. 301).

1857. _____. *The Percy folio of old English ballads and romances*, Vol. II. Edited by Frederick James Furnivall and John Wesley Hales. London: N. Trübner & Co., 1906.
    P.s.: *Sir Gawain and the Green Knight* (1925), p. xxvi. Tolkien and Gordon write: 'For bibliography of the Irish and French analogues of *Sir Gawain*, see the bibliography in Kittredge's study'. [*NED*] In Kittredge's study, this article is mentioned in 'III. The Green Knight' (p. 296).

1858. Perrault, Charles *Beauty and the Beast.*
    P.s. 1: *On Fairy-stories* (1947), p. 48.
    P.s. 2: *Tolkien On Fairy-stories* (2008), p. 38
    P.s. 3: *Tolkien On Fairy-stories* (2008) 'Manuscript A. [MS Tolkien 4, fols. 59-77]', p. 177.
    P.s. 4: *Tolkien On Fairy-stories* (2008) 'Manuscript B [MS. Tolkien 4, fols. 73-120]', p. 218.

1859. _____. *Les Contes de ma mère l'Oye*. Paris: E. Dentu, 1879.
    P.s. 1: *On Fairy-stories* (1947), p. 43.
    P.s. 2: *Tolkien On Fairy-stories* (2008), p. 33.
    P.s. 3: *Tolkien On Fairy-stories* (2008) 'Manuscript A. [MS Tolkien 4, fols. 59-77]', p. 186.
    P.s. 4: *Tolkien On Fairy-stories* (2008) 'Manuscript B [MS. Tolkien 4, fols. 73-120]', pp. 214, 231.
    S.s.: Scull-Hammond (2006b), p. 820.

1860. _____. *Histoires ou Contes du Temps Passé, avec des Moralités*. Paris: Claude Barbin, 1697.
    P.s.: #1 a. | *Tolkien On Fairy-stories* (2008), p. 310. Includes 'Little Red Riding Hood' and 'Puss-in-Boots',

1861. _____. *Little Red Riding-Hood*
    P.s.: *Tolkien On Fairy-stories* (2008) 'Manuscript A. [MS Tolkien 4, fols. 59-77]', p. 191.

1862. _____. *The Master Cat, or, Puss in Boots.*
    P.s. 1: *On Fairy-stories* (1947), p. 69.
    P.s. 2: *Tolkien On Fairy-stories* (2008), p. 62

1863. _____. *Perrault's Popular Tales*. Series: The Fairy Book series. With an introduction by Andrew Lang. Oxford. The Clarendon Press, 1888.
    Description: Tolkien requested the book on 27 February 1939, at 11:30am (MS. Library Records b. 618). Weston Library (Oxford), 930 e.82.
    .s.: #1 a. | *Tolkien On Fairy-stories* (2008), p. 310. Tolkien refers to Lang introduction.

1864. _____ *The Sleeping Beauty in the Wood.*

P.s.: *Tolkien On Fairy-stories* (2008) 'Manuscript B [MS. Tolkien 4, fols. 73-120]', p. 215

1865. Perry, George Gresley (Edited by). *English prose treatises of Richard Rolle de Hampole: who died A.D. 1349*. Series: E.E.T.S. (Early English Text Society), OS 20. London: Published for the Early English Text Society by Kegan Paul, Trench, Trübner and Co., 1866.
    Description: Inside front cover, engraved bookplate featuring derù-lion couchant inside badge of an order, featuring motto:'sub Rovere Virtus'. Stamped into front flyleaf, a shield showing two lions rampant and three fleur de lys with motto below and derù-lion rampant above. Inscribed: 'H. W. Carey'. Penciled annotations on flyleaf.
    Collection: Tolkien's personal Celtic library, preserved at the Weston library under the auspices of the English Faculty Library (Oxford).
    P.s.: MS. Tolkien A 21/13 fol. 119. Note by Tolkien, 'Books in Exeter Library useful', with shelfmarks, on back of photostat reading list dated October 1913. Tolkien writes: 'All EETS publications'. [Tolkien Papers, Bodleian Library, Oxford].

1866. Perry, Thomas Sergeant. *English literature in the eighteenth century*. New York: Harper, 1883.
    Description: Tolkien requested the book on 23 February 1921 (MS. Library Records b. 667). Weston Library (Oxford), 258 b.274.

1867. *Perseus and Andromeda*. [Greek Mythological Story, see Lang].
    P.s.: *Tolkien On Fairy-stories* (2008) 'Manuscript B [MS. Tolkien 4, fols. 73-120]', p. 243.

1868. Persson, Per. *Studien zur Lehre: von der Wurzelerweiterung und Wurzelvariation*. Upsala: Academiska Boktryckeriet, 1891.
    Description: Autographed on front flyleaf: 'J.R.R. Tolkien | 1926'. Note illegible on p. 50; a note in Greek on p. 130: 'x ιολὺς - σιολυς - ιολυς by dissim. = ῖλύς. | cf [deleted ιχθυς] ισχὺς - σισχυς = ισχυς by dissim'. with a 'X' on left (note 20 [: *sl-u-* klebrig sein: gr. ἰλῦς Schlamm a. *$zl\bar{u}s$ nach Thurneysen (K. Z. XXX, 352), wo auch lat *polluo*, *lŭ-tum*, gr, *λῦ-μα* Schmutz u.s.w.herangezogen warden, mhd. *Sliere slier* schmierige, Klebrige Masse, *slie-me* dünne Haut, Netzhaut (s. Schade s.s.): *sel- sl-i** (s. p. 110)]); a greek word on right p. 157; and a note in end-paper: 'for βλεμεαινω connected with βλύω cf. glu- and | glomus (Ger klemmen = glomjan)'.
    Collection: Taylor Institution Library, Bodleian Libraries (Oxford).

1869. Phaedrus. *Vulpes et Draco*. [Fable].
    P.s.: *Dragons* (1938), p. 46. Tolkien writes: 'Phaedrus tells fable of a fox that in burrowing came to the inmost cave of a *draco* that was guarding hidden treasure'. Tolkien cites the fable XIX, *Vulpes et Draco*.

1870. Phebus, Gaston. *La Livre de la Chace*. [1401-1500]
    P.s.: *Sir Gawain and the Green Knight* (1925), p. 105, line 1436 þe blodhoundeȝ.

1871. Phillips, Hubert. *The Book of Indoor Games*. London: Faber & Faber Limited, 1933.
    Description: Inscribed in pencil on half title page: 'J.R.R. Tolkien'. On front free endpaper: 'Pd.D. Bliss | Sep/42'. Contains annotations on pages 250, 254, 276, 327-329. Includes a label added by Stan Revell to books owned by Tolkien, 'From the Library of J.R.R. Tolkien', on inside front cover.
    Collection: Marion E. Wade Center, Wheaton College (Wheaton, Illinois).

1872. Pierquin, Hubert. *Recueil Général des Chartes Anglo-Saxonnes les Saxons en Angleterre*. Paris: Alphonse Picard & Fils, 1912.
    Description: Signed by Tolkien on front free endpaper, with one emendation.
    Collection: Private [Sold by Simon Finch Rare Books Ltd.].
    S.s.: Finch (2002), p. 54.

1873. *Piers Plowman* 1362. [Middle English allegorical narrative poem, see Plowman and Skeat].
    P.s. 1: MS. Tolkien A 21/7 fol. 33. [Tolkien Papers, Bodleian Library, Oxford].
    P.s. 2: MS. Tolkien A 21/13 *Chronological Library Table of Middle English* fol. 202. [Tolkien Papers, Bodleian Library, Oxford].

1874. *Piers Plowman* Text B 1377. [Middle English allegorical narrative poem, see Plowman and Skeat].
    P.s.: MS. Tolkien A 21/13 *Chronological Library Table of Middle English* fol. 202. [Tolkien Papers, Bodleian Library, Oxford].

1875. Pinder, Moritz and Gustav Parthey (Edited by). *Ravennatis Anonymi Cosmographia et Gvidonis Geographica*. Berolini: in aedibus Friderici Nicolai, 1860.
    P.s.: *Finn and Hengest* (1982), p. 14 n. 13.

1876. Plancé, James Robinson (Edited by). *A Cyclopædia of costume*, Vol. I. Dictionary. London: Chatto and Windus, 1876.
    P.s.: *Sir Gawain and the Green Knight* (1925), p. xxvii.

1877. _____ (Edited by). *A Cyclopædia of costume*, Vol. II. A General History of Costume in Europe. London: Chatto and Windus, 18768.
    P.s.: *Sir Gawain and the Green Knight* (1925), p. xxvii.

1878. Pokorny, Julius. *Altirische Grammatik*. Series: Sammlung Göschen, 896. Berlin and Leipzig: W. de Gruyter, 1925.
    Collection: Tolkien's personal Celtic library, preserved at the Weston library under the auspices of the English Faculty Library (Oxford).

1879. _____ (Edited by). *A Historical Reader of Old Irish*. Halle: Max Niemeyer, 1923.
    Description: Personal copy.
    Collection: Tolkien's personal Celtic library, preserved at the Weston library under the auspices of the English Faculty Library (Oxford).

1880. Pollard, Albert Frederick (Introduction by). *Tudor Tracts 1532-1588*. Series: An English Garner. Westminster: A. Constable and Co., 1903.
    S.s.: University of Leeds (1920), p. 147. English Language and Literature - Scheme A. Texts and Period selected for 1920-21. (b) Special period: 1557-1637. (c) Texts suggested for study with Special Period. Ordinary Degree of B.A. with Honours. Final Examination. Extracts 13, 14.

1881. Pollard, Alfred William. *Chaucer*. London: Macmillan, 1919.
    S.s.: University of Leeds (1921), p. 193 English Language and Literature. Honours and M.A. Courses. A. Language. H1. First Year. Books Recommended.

1882. _____. *English miracle plays, moralities and interludes: specimens of the pre-Elizabethan drama*. Oxford: At the Clarendon Press, 1923 (7th ed.).
    P.s.: MS. Res. e. 308 *Sir Gawain and the Green Knight*. [Tolkien Papers, Bodleian Library, Oxford].

1883. *Polychronicon* 1352. [Latin version].
    P.s.: MS. Tolkien A 21/13 *The English MSS.* fol. 203. [Tolkien Papers, Bodleian Library, Oxford].

1884. *Polychronicon. John of Trevisa's transltation Ranulf of Higden's Polychronicon* 1387. [Middle English encyclopedical treatise in prose and verse, see Lumby].

P.s.: MS. Tolkien A 21/13 *Chronological Library Table of Middle English* fol. 202. [Tolkien Papers, Bodleian Library, Oxford].

1885. Pons, Emilie. *Sire Gauvain et le Chevalier vert, poème anglais du XIVe siècle*. Series: Bibliothèque de philologie germanique., 9. Paris, Aubier, Éditions Montaigne, 1946.
P.s.: *Sir Gawain and the Green Knight* (1967) 'Select Bibliography', p. 153.

1886. Poole, Austin Lane. *Medieval England*. Oxford: Oxford University Press, 1958.
P.s.: *Sir Gawain and the Green Knight* (1967) 'Select Bibliography', p. 155. (Chapters on archtecture, costume, armour etc.)

1887. Poole, Jacob and William Barnes (Edited by). *A Glossary with some Pieces of Verse of the Old Dialect of the English Colony in the Forth and Bargy County of Wexford Ireland*. London: J. Russel Smith, 1867.
Description: Decoratively autographed and dated on front flyleaf: '1923'.
Collection: Tolkien's personal Celtic library, preserved at the Weston library under the auspices of the English Faculty Library (Oxford).

1888. Pope, Alexander. *The Complete poetical works of Alexander Pope*. Edited by Henry Walcott Boynton. Boston: Houghton Mifflin Company, 1903.
P.s.: *Letters* 89 (1944). To Christopher Tolkien. Tolkien quotes: 'the feast of reason and flow of soul' from *The first Satire of the Second Book of Horace*, p. 184.
S.s. 1: University of Leeds (1920), p. 135 English Literature. Texts Selected for 1920-21. Text suggested: The Rape of the Lock; p. 181. English Language and Literature. Int. I Intermediate Course (Literature).
S.s. 2: University of Leeds (1921), p. 144. English Literature, text selected (Essay on Criticism, Essay on Man, I. Epistle to Dr. Arbuthond) for 1921-22. Ordinary Degree of B.A.

1889. _____. *The Poetical Works of Alexander Pope*. Series: The Globe edition. London: MaCmillan, 1917.
S.s.: University of Leeds (1921), p. 141. English Literature, text selected (*Pastorals, Essay on Criticism* and *Epistle to Dr. Arbuthnot*) for 1921-22. Ordinary Degree of B.A.; p. 190 English Language and Literature. Int. 1 Intermediate Course (Literature) (*Pastorals, Essay on Criticism* and *Epistle to Dr. Arbuthnot*); p. 191 English Language and Literature. F1. Final Course (English Literature) (ii) The History of English Literature from 1700 to 1765 (*Essay on Criticism, Essay on Man*, I, *Epistle to Dr. Arbuthnot*).

1890. Potter, Beatrix. *The Tale of Benjamin Bunny*. London: Frederick Warne & Co., 1904.
P.s.: *Dragons* (1938), p. 40.

1891. _____. *The Tailor of Gloucester*. London: Frederick Warne and Co., 1903
P.s. 1: *On Fairy-stories* (1947), p. 46 n. 1.
P.s. 2: *Tolkien On Fairy-stories* (2008), p. 36 n. 2.
P.s. 3: *Tolkien On Fairy-stories* (2008) 'Manuscript B [MS. Tolkien 4, fols. 73-120]', p. 217
P.s. 4: *Tolkien On Fairy-stories* (2008) 'Manuscript B [MS. Tolkien 14, fol. 25]', p. 281.
S.s.: Scull-Hammond (2006b), p. 820.

1892. _____. *The Tale of Jemima Puddle-Duck*. New York: F. Warne and Co, 1908.
P.s.: *Tolkien On Fairy-stories* (2008) 'Manuscript B [MS. Tolkien 4, fols. 73-120]', p. 217.

1893. _____. *The Tale of Peter Rabbit*. London: Frederick Warne and Co.
P.s. 1: *Dragons* (1938), p. 40.
P.s. 2: *On Fairy-stories* (1947), p. 46.
P.s. 3: *Tolkien On Fairy-stories* (2008), p. 36.

P.s. 4: *Tolkien On Fairy-stories* (2008) 'Manuscript B [MS. Tolkien 4, fols. 73-120]', p. 217
P.s. 5: *Tolkien On Fairy-stories* (2008) 'Manuscript B [MS. Tolkien 14, fol. 25]', p. 281.
S.s.: Scull-Hammond (2006b), p. 820.

1894. _____. *The Tale of Mrs Tiggy-winkle*. London: Frederick Warne and Co.
P.s. 1: *Letters* 190 (1956). From a letter to Rayner Unwin.
P.s. 2: *On Fairy-stories* (1947), p. 46 n. 1.
P.s. 3: *Tolkien On Fairy-stories* (2008), p. 36 n. 2.
P.s. 4: *Tolkien On Fairy-stories* (2008) 'Manuscript B [MS. Tolkien 4, fols. 73-120]', p. 217.
P.s. 5: *Tolkien On Fairy-stories* (2008) 'Manuscript B [MS. Tolkien 6, fols. 6-8]', p. 256.
S.s.: Scull-Hammond (2006b), p. 820.

1895. _____. *The Tale of Mr. Tod.* New York: F. Warne and Co, 1912.
P.s.: *Tolkien On Fairy-stories* (2008) 'Manuscript B [MS. Tolkien 4, fols. 73-120]', p. 217.

1896. Powell, Edgar (Edited by). *A Suffolk Hundred in the Year 1283*. Includes 38 folded sheets of addenda (tax sheets from different locations) Cambridge: University Press Cambridge by John Clay, 1910.
Description: Signed on the front flyleaf "J.R.R.Tolkien"
Collection: Private [Pieter Collier].

1897. Prellwitz, Walther. *Etymologisches Wörterbuch der griechischen Sprache.* Göttingen: Vandenhoeck und Ruprecht, 1905.
P.s.: MS. Tolkien A 21/13 fol. 119. Note by Tolkien, 'Books in Exeter Library useful', with shelfmarks, on back of photostat reading list dated October 1913. [Tolkien Papers, Bodleian Library, Oxford].

1898. Procopius. *History of the wars*, Vol. V. Gothic War (continued). Series: The Loeb Classic Library. Translated by Henry Bronson Dewing. London: Heinemann, 1928.
P.s.: *Finn and Hengest* (1982), 11 n. 7. Tolkien quotes: 'The island of Brittia is inhabited by three very numerous nations, each having one king over it. And the names of these nations are Anglii, Frissones and Brittones, the last being named from the island itself.'

1899. Proudfit, S. V. 'The Hobyahs: A Scotch Nursery Tale'. *The Journal of American Folklore*, Vol. 4. The Journal of American Folklore, April 1891, pp. 173-74.
S.s.: Anderson (2002), p. 24 n. 12.

1900. *Proverbs of Alfred* 1246-50. [Collection of early Middle English sayings, see R. Morris and Th. Wright *Rel. Ant.*].
P.s. 1: MS. Tolkien A 21/7 fol. 48. [Tolkien Papers, Bodleian Library, Oxford].
P.s. 2: MS. Tolkien A 21/13 *The English MSS.* fol. 203. [Tolkien Papers, Bodleian Library, Oxford].

1901. Pucci, Antonio. 'Canzone morale'. *L'Etruria: studi di filologia, di letteratura, di pubblica istruzione e di belle arti,* Vol. 2, 1852, pp. 124-27.
P.s.: *Sir Gawain and the Green Knight* (1925), p. xxvi. Tolkien and Gordon write: 'For bibliography of the Irish and French analogues of *Sir Gawain*, see the bibliography in Kittredge's study'. [*NED*] In Kittredge's study, this article is mentioned in 'XI. The Canzoni' (p. 304).

1902. Quiller-Couch, Arthur Thomas. *The Oxford Book of English verse, 1250-1900.* London: Oxford Univeristy Press, 1900.
P.s.: *On Fairy-stories* (1947), p. 39. Tolkien recites the verses from the 'Thmas the Rhymer': O see ye not yon narrow road... Where thou and I this night maun gae.

1903. Raffel, Burton. *Poems from the Old English.* University of Nebraska Press,

1961 (2nd rep.).
>   Description: Inscribed by the author: '17 March 1963. | To J.R.R. Tolkien, Old English recreations for a far greater re-creator, | whose hobbit-lore has bewitched my whole family. | Burton Raffel' [Judith Priestman 1994, revd. 2016].
>   Collection: Weston Library, Bodleian Libraries (Oxford).
>   S.s. 1: Scull-Hammond (2017a), p. 583. Early 1960s Raffel sends Tolkien an inscribed copy.
>   S.s. 2: Lee (2005), p. 214: In his justifiable attack on translations published by Burton Raffel Tolkien stated: [in *The Wanderer*] 'anhaga does not mean just 'lonely one', but refers to a man living in special conditions and is not applicable (for instance) to a man in a boat' [MS. Tolkien A 30/1 *Lectures on Old English* fol. 113].
>   S.s. 3: Scull-Hammond (2017c), pp. 999-1000. He makes extensive critical comments. Extract 'The making of translations should be primarily for private amusement, and profit. The profit, at any rate, will be found in the increased and sharpened understanding of the language of the original which the translator will acquire in the process ... [f]irst of all by absolute allegiance to the thing translated: to its meaning, its style, technique, and form. The language used in translation is, for this purpose, merely an instrument, that must be handled so as to reproduce, to make audible again, as nearly as possible, the antique work. Fortunately modern (modern literary, not present-day colloquial) English is an instrument of very great capacity and resources, it has long experience not yet forgotten, and deep roots in the past not yet all pulled up. It can, if asked, still play in modes no longer favoured and remember airs not now popular; it is not limited to the fashionable cacophonies. I have little sympathy with contemporary theories of translation, and no liking for their results. In these the allegiance is changed. Too often it seems given primarily to 'contemporary English', the present-day colloquial idiom as if being 'contemporary', that most evanescent of qualities, by itself guaranteed its superiority. In many the primary allegiance of the 'translator' is to himself, to his own whims and notions, and the original author is evidently considered fortunate to have aroused the interest of a superior writer. This attitude is often a mask for incompetence, and for ignorance of the original idiom; in any case it does not encourage close study of the text and its language, the laborious but only sure way of acquiring a sensitive understanding and appreciation, even for those of poetic temperament, who might have acquired them, if they had started with a more humble and loyal allegiance. [MS. Tolkien A 30/1 *Lectures on Old English* fols. 107-109].'

1904.   *Ragnarssona þáttr* (Tale of Ragnar's Sons).
>   P.s.: *Dragons* (1938), p. 45.

1905.   Raith, Joseph (Edited by). *Die Altenglishe version des Halitgar'schen bussbuches*. Series: Bibliothek der angelsächsischen Prosa, 18. Hamburg: Henri Grand, 1933.
>   Description: Autographed on front cover.
>   Collection: Tolkien's personal Celtic library, preserved at the Weston library under the auspices of the English Faculty Library (Oxford).

1906.   Rajna, Pio. 'Intorno a due canzoni gemelle di materia cavalleresca' (23.2.1877). *Zeitschrift für romanische Philologie*, Vol. I. Halle: Max Niemeyer, 1877, pp. 381-86.
>   P.s.: *Sir Gawain and the Green Knight* (1925), p. xxvi. Tolkien and Gordon write: 'For bibliography of the Irish and French analogues of *Sir Gawain*, see the bibliography in Kittredge's study'. [*NED*] In Kittredge's study, this article is mentioned in 'XI. The Canzoni' (p. 304).

1907.   Raleigh, Walter Alexander. *The Last fight of the Revenge at sea. Under the command of Sir Richard Grenville: on the 10-11th of September 1591*. Edited by Edward Arber. Westmister: A. Constable and Co., 1895.
>   S.s.: University of Leeds (1923), p. 81. Ordinary Degree of B.A., Intermediate Course and Examination: English Literature. Text selected for 1923-24 (ii) Texts suggestes as part of a course of general rending in the period 1579-1645.

1908.   _____. *Raleigh's Selections. From his Historie of the World, his Letters &c.*

SECTION A

Oxford: At the Clarendon Press, 1917.
> S.s.: University of Leeds (1920), p. 147. English Language and Literature - Scheme A. Texts and Period selected for 1920-21. (b) Special period: 1557-1637. (c) Texts suggested for study with Special Period. Ordinary Degree of B.A. with Honours. Final Examination.

1909. _____. *Shakespeare*. Series: English Men of Letters. London: Macmillan and Co., Ltd., 1907.
> P.s.: *Exeter College library register*. Tolkien's borrowing record: Trinity Term 1915 from 15 May to 16 June 1915.

1910. _____. *Shakespeare*. Series: The Eversley Edition (Pocket edition). London: Macmillan and Co., Ltd., 1909.
> P.s.: *Exeter College library register*. Tolkien's borrowing record: Trinity Term 1915 from 15 May to 16 June 1915.

1911. _____. *Style*. London: E. Arnold, 1918.
> S.s.: University of Leeds (1921), p. 191 English Language and Literature. F1. Final Course (English Literature) Books recommended.

1912. _____. *Some gains of the war: An address to the Royal Colonial Institute*, delivered February 13, 1918. New York: George H. Doran Company, 1918.
> P.s.: *Philology: General Works* (VI 1927, for 1925), p. 65.

1913. Ranisch, Wilhelm. *Eddalieder. Mit Grammatik, Übersetzung und Erläuterungen*. Series: Sammlung Göschen, 171. Berlin: W. de Gruyter, 1920.
> Description: Autographed in pencil on front flyleaf.
> Collection: Tolkien's personal Celtic library, preserved at the Weston library under the auspices of the English Faculty Library (Oxford).
> P.s.: *Beowulf* (2014), p. 330 n. 3.

1914. Ransome, Arthur. *Swallows and Amazons*. London: Jonathan Cape, 1930.
> S.s.: Scull-Hammond (2006b), p. 820.

1915. Raspe, Rudolph Erich. *Tales from the travels of Baron Munchhausen*. Series: Books for the Bairns, 23. London: Review of Reviews, 1926.
> P.s. 1: *On Fairy-stories* (1947), p. 44.
> P.s. 2: *Tolkien On Fairy-stories* (2008) 'Manuscript B [MS. Tolkien 4, fols. 73-120]', p. 215.
> S.s.: Scull-Hammond (2006b), p. 820.

1916. Ray, John *et alii*. *Synopsis methodica animalium quadrupedum et serpentini generis*.
> P.s.: MS. Tolkien A 19/3 *Etymologies or history of Walrus* fols. 162-195 [Tolkien Papers, Bodleian Library, Oxford].
> S.s.: *Tolkien, Family Album* (1992), p. 42.
> NED: #2 i. | 'W' (1928), p. 58 'Walrus, 1.' 1693 – 'Anglis Mors à Russis mutuato nomine, Belgis Walrus ... The Morse or Sea-Horse' (p. 191).

1917. _____. *A collection of English words not generally used, with their significations and original, in two alphabetical catalogues: the one of such as are proper to the northern, the other to the southern counties*. London: Printed by H. Bruges for Tho. Burrell, 1674.
> P.s.: 'Chaucer as a Philologist: *The Reeve's Tale*' (1934), p. 137. Tolkien writes: '['wang-tōþ'] is fairly widely distributed in Middle English and is still preserved in the dialects of recent times (though the last reference in *N.E.D.* is from Ray's collection of north-country words, 1674)'.
> NED: #1 a. | 'W' (1928), p. 98 'Wariangle, 1.' 1674 – 'The great Butcher-bird called in the Peak of Derbyshire Wirrangle, Lanius cincreas major'. (p. 82-3)

1918.   Ready, William Bernard. *The Poor Hater: a novel*. Chicago: Henry Regnery Co., 1958.
Collection: British Library (St Pancras, London).
Description: With a newspaper cutting of an article by the author on the works of J.R.R. Tolkien and a MS.
Notes: Ready sent a copy of his novel to Tolkien; the latter sent him a letter of thanks.
P.s.: Tolkien's unpublished letter to William Ready, 5 March 1959. [Having received a copy of Ready's novel *The Poor Hater* just before his collapse, he hopes] 'to recover sufficient concentration soon to be able to read it, among other things'.
S.s.: Scull-Hammond (2017a), p. 568.

1919.   _____. *The Tolkien Relation [Understanding Tolkien, and, the Lord of the ring]*. New York: Warner Books, 1968.
P.s.: Tolkien's unpublished letter to Clyde S. Kilby, 4 June 1968. Tolkien writes: 'William Ready had 'the impertinence' to send him an inscribed copy of his book, *The Tolkien Relation*. He refutes Ready's claim that he spent hours interviewing Tolkien. He made only a short visit, and talked mainly about himself. 'I have now made up my mind not to see anybody from your country whom I do not already know, nor anybody from any Press in any country.' [Marion E. Wade Center, Wheaton College (Wheaton, Illinois). A part of this letter was published in *The Letters of J.R.R. Tolkien* (*Letters* n. 304)].

1920.   *Red Etin*. [Fairy tale, see Jacobs and Lang].
S.s.: Scull-Hammond (2017b), p. 611.

1921.   Reeves, James. *A Short History of English Poetry 1340-1940*. London: Heinemann, 1961.
Description: In the acknowledgments (p. 224): 'Thanks are due also to Professor J.R.R. Tolkien for permission to quote from his version of *Sir Gawain and the Green Knight.*' Includes Stanza 32 from Tolkien's Modern English translation of the Middle English poem *Sir Gawain and the Green Knight*. (see p. 7) The text as printed here contains a number of minor variations compared to the text published in *Sir Gawain and the Green Knight, Pearl* and *Sir Orfeo* (1975). 'By a mount in the morning merrily he riding | into a forest that was deep and fearsomely wild; | high hills at each hand, and hoar wood under them | of aged oaks and huge by the hundred together; | the hazel and hawthorn were huddled and tangled | with rough ragged moss around them trailing, | while many birds blieakly on the bare twigs sat | and piteously piped there for pain of the cold. | The good man on Gringolet goes now beneath them | through many marshes and mires, a man all alone, | troubled lest a truant at that time he should prove, | from the service of the sweet Lord, who that on that selfsame night | of a maid became man our mourning to conquer. | And therefore sighing he said; 'I beseech thee, O Lord, | and Mary, who is the mildest of mother most dear, | for some harbour where with honour I might hear Mass, |and thy Matins tomorrow. This meekly I ask, | and thereto promptly I pray with Pater and Ave | and Creed. | In payer he now did ride, | Lamenting his misdeed; | He blest him oft and cried, | The cross of Christ me speed!'

1922.   Reichardt, Konrad. *Studien zu den Skalden des 9. und 10. Jahrhunderts*. Palaestra, Vol. 159. Leipzig: Mayer & Müller, 1928.
Description: Tolkien's signature dated '1928' on top right hand corner of front wrap; one leaf laid in with Tolkien's battels and notes. One page of notes on the verso of Tolkien's dining expenses from Pembroke College during the week of 29 November 1928; the notes refer to the *Genesis* and *Exodus* poems – Old English poetry which Tolkien would used while working on Cynewulf's *Crist*.
Collection: Private [Sold by Simon Finch Rare Books Ltd.].
S.s.: Finch (2002), p. 52.

1923.   Reid, Duncan. *A Course of Gaelic grammar*. Glasgow: Sinclair, 1908 (3rd ed.).
Description: Autographed and dated on front flyleaf: '1922'.

Section A

Collection: Tolkien's personal Celtic library, preserved at the Weston library under the auspices of the English Faculty Library (Oxford).

1924. Reitz, Johann Ernst. *Svenskt Dialect-Lexicon eller Ordbok öfver Svenska allmogespraket*. Lund: C. W. K. Gleerups Förlag, 1877.
Description: Signed twice by Tolkien; first on front free endpaper, the second signature (on title) occurs next to a former owner's signature and read: 'John Reuel Tolkien 1922'.
Collection: Private [Sold by Simon Finch Rare Books Ltd.].
S.s.: Finch (2002), p. 54.

1925. Renault, Mary. *The Bull from the Sea*. London: Longmans, 1962.
P.s.: *Letters* 294 (1967). To Charlotte and Denis Plimmer. Tolkien writes: 'I was recently deeply engaged in the books of Mary Renault; especially the two about Theseus, *The King Must Die*, and *The Bull from the Sea*. A few days ago I actually received a card of appreciation from her; perhaps the piece of 'Fan-mail' that gives me most pleasure.'
S.s.: Scull-Hammond (2006b), p. 819.

1926. _____. *The King Must Die*. London: Longmans, 1958.
P.s.: *Letters* 294 (1967). To Charlotte and Denis Plimmer. Tolkien writes: 'I was recently deeply engaged in the books of Mary Renault; especially the two about Theseus, *The King Must Die*, and *The Bull from the Sea*. A few days ago I actually received a card of appreciation from her; perhaps the piece of 'Fan-mail' that gives me most pleasure.'
S.s.: Scull-Hammond (2006b), p. 819.

1927. Rhys, Ernest. *'Everyman'. With other interludes, including eight miracle plays*. London: Joseph Malaby Dent & Co., 1909.
S.s. 1: University of Leeds (1920), p. 135 English Literature. Texts Selected for 1920-21. Extracts *The Wakefield Second Shepherds' Play* and *Everyman*; p. 180. English Language and Literature. Int. I Intermediate Course (Literature).
S.s. 2: Scull-Hammond (2017a), p. 122. Leeds academic year 1920-1921. Tolkien might also be responsible for the first few lectures in an introductory course on English Literature which begins with the *Everyman*, Mondays and Wednesdays at 11.00 a.m.

1928. _____. *Fairy Gold: a Book of Old English Fairy Tales*. London: J. M. Dent & Co., 1907.
Description: Weston Library, Special Collections (Oxford), MS. Library Records b. 618 'Entry Book - Camera Basement and Underground Bookstore Volumes fetched for Bodleian Readers, Sept. 1938 - 930 f.103.'. Tolkien requested the book on 27 February 1939, at 11:30am.

1929. Rhys, John (Edited by). *Celtic Britain*. London: Society for Promoting Christian Knowledge, 1882.
P.s.: *Letters* 324 (1971). From a letter to Graham Tayar.
S.s. 1: Hammond-Scull (2014), p. 18.
S.s. 2: Scull-Hammond (2017a), p. 818.
Reading period: 1904 - 1910 (S.s.: Scull-Hammond (2017b), p. 214).

1930. _____. *Celtic Folklore: Welsh and Manx*, Vol. I. Oxford: At the Clarendon Press, 1901.

1931. _____. *Celtic Folklore: Welsh and Manx*, Vol. II. Oxford: At the Clarendon Press, 1901.
P.s.: *Sir Gawain and the Green Knight* (1925), p. xxvi. Tolkien and Gordon write: 'For bibliography of the Irish and French analogues of *Sir Gawain*, see the bibliography in Kittredge's study'. In Kittredge's study, this article is mentioned in 'V. Le Livre de Caradoc' (p. 298).
S.s.: *The Lay of Aotrou & Itroun* (2016), p. 25.

1932. _____. and John Gwenogvryn Evans (Edited by). *The Text of the Mabinogion: and other Welsh tales from the Red Book of Hergest.* Oxford: Evans, 1887.
>Description: Inscribed on half title page: 'W. Llewllyn Williams | Brasenose College | Oxford'. Decoratively autographed and dated '1922' below. Annotations in pencil and ink.
>Collection: Tolkien's personal Celtic library, preserved at the Weston library under the auspices of the English Faculty Library (Oxford).
>P.s. 1: MS. Tolkien A 12/2 *Commentary on Sir Gawain, lines 1999-2523* fol. 37. Tolkien cites 'Peredur'. [Tolkien Papers, Bodleian Library, Oxford].
>P.s. 2: *The Name 'Nodens'* (1932), p. 133.
>S.s. 1: Phelpstead (2011), p. 119.
>S.s. 2: Scull-Hammond (2017a), p. 126; p. 56. *Hilary Term 1914*: Tolkien possibly attends as well lectures by Sir John Rhys on Welsh: *The Mabinogion* on Tuesdays and Fridays at 6.00 p.m. at Jesus College, beginning 23 January.

1933. _____ and John Gwenogvryn Evans (Edited by). *The Text of the Bruts from the Red Book of Hergest.* Oxford: Evans, 1890.
>Description: Inscribed on half title page: 'W. Llewllyn Williams'. Decoratively autographed and dated below: '1922'. Annotated in pencil.
>Collection: Tolkien's personal Celtic library, preserved at the Weston library under the auspices of the English Faculty Library (Oxford).
>P.s.: MS. Tolkien A 12/2 *Commentary on Sir Gawain, lines 1999-2523* fol. 37. Tolkien cites 'Peredur'. [Tolkien Papers, Bodleian Library, Oxford].
>S.s.: Scull-Hammond (2017a), p. 126.

1934. _____ and John Gwenogvryn Evans (Edited by). *Y Elyvyr Coch o Ergest. The Text of the Bruts from the Red Book of Hergest.* Oxford, 1890.
>Description: Autographed and dated on frontispiece: 'J.R.R. Tolkien 1922'.
>Collection: Taylor Institution Library, Bodleian Libraries (Oxford).
>S.s.: Phelpstead (2011), p. 119.

1935. *Richard the Redeless* 1399. [Middle English Alliterative poem, see Plowman and Skeat].
>P.s.: MS. Tolkien A 21/13 *Chronological Library Table of Middle English* fol. 202. [Tolkien Papers, Bodleian Library, Oxford].

1936. Richardson, S. *Pamela.* Series: Everyman's library, 683. Edited by George Saintsbury. London: Joseph Malaby Dent, 1914.
>S.s.: University of Leeds (1921), p. 145. English Literature, text selected for 1921-22. Ordinary Degree of B.A.; p. 191 English Language and Literature. F1. Final Course (English Literature) (ii) The History of English Literature from 1700 to 1765.

1937. _____. *Pamela*, Vol. II. Series: Everyman's library, 63. Edited by George Saintsbury. London: Joseph Malaby Dent, 1914.
>S.s.: University of Leeds (1921), p. 145. English Literature, text selected for 1921-22. Ordinary Degree of B.A.; p. 191 English Language and Literature. F1. Final Course (English Literature) (ii) The History of English Literature from 1700 to 1765.

1938. Richmond, Ian Archibald and Osbert Guy Stanhope Crawford. *The British section of the Ravenna Cosmography.* Oxford: Society of Antiquaries of London, 1949.
>P.s.: *Finn and Hengest* (1982), p. 69 n. 69.

1939. Richthofen, Karl Otto Johannes Theresius freiherr von. *Altfriesisches Wörterbuch.* Göttingen: Dieterichsche Buchhandlung, 1840.
>Notes: Tolkien requested the book on 25 January 1919 (MS. Library Records b. 638). Weston Library (Oxford), 303 u.125 (ex S. Lang. Fris. 07).

Description: Autographed on front flyleaf 'J.R.R. Tolkien'. Dated 1926 or 1928. In front page there is an ex libris 'Taylor Institution Library | Oxford | Presented by | The executors of | Professor | J.R.R. Tolkien'.
Collection: Taylor Institution Library's Frisian Collection, Bodleian Libraries (Oxford).
P.s.: *Philology: General Works* (VI 1927, for 1925), p. 57 n. 14.

1940. Rickert, Edith. *The Romance of Emaré*. Series: E.E.T.S. (Early English Text Society), ES 99. Edited by David Donaldson and George A. Panton. London: Trübner, 1908.
P.s. 1: MS. Tolkien A 21/13 fol. 119. Note by Tolkien, 'Books in Exeter Library useful', with shelfmarks, on back of photostat reading list dated October 1913. Tolkien writes: 'All EETS publications'. [Tolkien Papers, Bodleian Library, Oxford].
P.s. 2: *Sir Gawain and the Green Knight* (1967) 'Select Bibliography: editions of texts quoted more than once in the notes', p. 156.

1941. Rieger, Max. 'Die Alt- und angelsächsische verskunst'. *Zeitschrift für deutsche Philologie*, Vol. II, pp. 1-64. Halle: Erich Schmidt Verlag, 1876.
P.s.: *The Old English Exodus* (1982), p. x.

1942. Rietz, Johan Ernst. *Svenskt Dialekt-Lexikon eller Ordbok öfver Svenska Allmogespråket*. Lund: C. W. K. Gleerup, 1877.
Description: Dated '1922'.
S.s.: Scull-Hammond (2017a), p. 126.

1943. Rieu, Emilie Victor (Edited by). *Essays by Divers Hands, Behind the Transactions of the Royal Society of Literature*, Vol. 29. London: Oxford University Press, 1958.
P.s.: Tolkien's letter to Canon N. S. Power, MA, Lady wood Vicarage, Birmingham – 8 July 1973 (Letter published in *Mallorn*, 9, 1975, p. 19). Tolkien writes: 'I send you a copy. It is a spare copy and I would be pleased if you would accept it.'
S.s.: Scull-Hammond (2017a), p. 739. 2 August 1967. Tolkien writes to the Royal Society of Literature to obtain another copy of their *Essays* which contains an essay by Morchard Bishop, 'John Inglesant and Its Author'.

1944. Ritson, Joseph. *Ancient English Metrical Romanceës*, Vol. II. London: Printed by W. Bulmer and Company, for G. and W. Nicol, 1802.
P.s.: MS. Tolkien A 13/1 *annotated texts of King Horn* fol. 94. [Tolkien Papers, Bodleian Library, Oxford].

1945. Ritter, Otto. 'Lauthistorisches zum namen *Don Adriano de Armado*'. *Probleme der Englischen Sprache und Kultur. Festschrift Johannes Hoops zum 60* [A. 1169]. Heidelberg: Carl Winter, 1925.
P.s.: *Philology: General Works* (VI 1927, for 1925), p. 45.

1946. Robbins, Rossell Hope. *Historical poems of the XIVth and XVth centuries*, no. 38. New York: Columbia University Press, 1959.
P.s.: *Sir Gawain and the Green Knight* (1967) 'Select Bibliography: editions of texts quoted more than once in the notes', p. 156. 'Summer Sunday'.

1947. *Robert of Gloucester Chronicle* 1298. [Middle English Chronicle, see Robert of Gloucester].
P.s.: MS. Tolkien A 21/13 *The English MSS*. fol. 203. [Tolkien Papers, Bodleian Library, Oxford].

1948. Robert, de Boron. *Joseph of Arimathie: Otherwise Called The Romance of the Seint Graal, Or Holy Grail: an Alliterative Poem Written about A.D. 1350*. Series:

E.E.T.S. (Early English Text Society), OS 44. Edited by Walter William Skeat. London: Published for the Early English Text Society by Kegan Paul, Trench, Trübner and Co., 1871.
> P.s. 1: MS. Tolkien A 21/13 fol. 119. Note by Tolkien, 'Books in Exeter Library useful', with shelfmarks, on back of photostat reading list dated October 1913. Tolkien writes: 'All EETS publications'. [Tolkien Papers, Bodleian Library, Oxford].
> P.s. 2: MS. Tolkien A 21/13 *The English MSS*. fol. 203. [Tolkien Papers, Bodleian Library, Oxford].
> P.s. 3: 'Chaucer as a Philologist: *The Reeve's Tale*' (1934), pp. 136-38. Tolkien writes: [*wanges* 110] 'To the examples quoted by the *N.E.D.* (from *Cursor Mundi, Alysoun, Sir Tristrem, Wyntoun*, and the *York Plays*, all northern except the second which is probably western in origin) I can only add *Layamon, Brut* 30268: *wete weren his wongen* (the earliest M.E. instance), and *Joseph of Arimathie* (an alliterative poem) 647: *I wepte water warm and wette my wonges*, both of which show the same formula.'

1949. _____. *Merlin, roman en prose du 13e siècle*, Vol. I. Series: Société des anciens textes français. Edited by Paulin Paris and Jakob Ulrich. Paris: Librairie de Firmin Didot, 1886.
> P.s. 1: *Sir Gawain and Green Knight* (1925), p. 113 line 2102 Hestor; p. 116 line 2460.
> P.s. 2: *Sir Gawain and the Green Knight* (1967) 'Select Bibliography', p. 155

1950. _____. *Merlin, roman en prose du 13e siècle*, Vol. II. Series: Société des anciens textes français. Edited by Paulin Paris and Jakob Ulrich. Paris: Librairie de Firmin Didot, 1886.
> P.s. 1: MS. Tolkien A 12/1 *Commentary on Sir Gawain, lines 37-1987* fol. 8. [Tolkien Papers, Bodleian Library, Oxford].
> P.s. 2: *Sir Gawain and Green Knight* (1925), p. 113 line 2102 Hestor.
> P.s. 3: *Sir Gawain and the Green Knight* (1967) 'Select Bibliography', p. 155

1951. _____. *The Metrical Chronicle of Robert of Gloucester. Rerum Britannicum Medii Aevi Scriptores*, Vol. I. Edited by William Aldis Wright. London: Printed for H.M. Stationery Off by Eyre & Spottiswoode, 1887.
> Description: Tolkien's signature to front free endpaper, with a few scattered marginal emphases.
> Collection: Private [Sold by Simon Finch Rare Books Ltd.].
> S.s.: Finch (2002), p. 54.

1952. _____. *The Metrical Chronicle of Robert of Gloucester. Rerum Britannicum Medii Aevi Scriptores*, Vol. II. Edited by William Aldis Wright. London: Printed for H.M. Stationery Off by Eyre & Spottiswoode, 1887.
> Description: Tolkien's signature to front free endpaper, with a few scattered marginal emphases.
> Collection: Private [Sold by Simon Finch Rare Books Ltd.].
> P.s.: *Sir Gawain and Green Knight* (1925), p. 88 line 477 *heng vp þyn ax*. Tolkien and Gordon cite 'Ich mai hoge vp min ax' (p. 767, line 11771).
> S.s.: Finch (2002), p. 54.

1953. Roberts, Ruby. 'A New Collation of the Vespasian Psalter and Hymns'. *Leeds Studies in English*, Vol. I. Leeds: The University of Leeds, 1932, pp. 22-23.
> Collection: Taylor Institution Library, Bodleian Libraries (Oxford).
> P.s. 1: MS. Tolkien 16/1 *Notes and drafts concerning the Vespasian Psalter*. [Tolkien Papers, Bodleian Library, Oxford].
> P.s. 2: *Sigelwara land* (1932), p. 190 n. 1.

1954. Roberts, Samuel. *Gwaith Samuel Roberts (S.R.)*. Edited by Owen M. Edwards. Llanuwchllyn: Ab Owen, 1906.
> Description: Inscribed on back of frontespice: 'Geoffrey Bache Smth' | 'left by will | to | J.R.R. Tolkien.' written below by JRRT.
> Collection: Tolkien's personal Celtic library, preserved at the Weston library under the auspices of

the English Faculty Library (Oxford).
S.s. 1: Garth (2003), p. 357.
S.s. 2: Fimi (2007), p. 67 n. 6.
S.s. 3: Phelpstead (2011), p. 119.
S.s. 4: Scull-Hammond (2017c), p. 1212.

1955. Robertson, Jean. 'George Gascoigne and *The Noble Arte of Venerie and Hunting*'. MLR (*The Modern Language Review*), Vol. XXXVII, no. 4, October 1942, pp. 484-85.
P.s.: *Sir Gawain and the Green Knight* (1967) 'Select Bibliography', p. 155.

1956. Robertson Nicoll, William. *The Seven Words of the Cross*. Series: Little books on religion. London: Hodder and Stoughton, 1903 (4th ed.).
S.s.: Scull-Hammond (2017a), p. 23: 26 March 1910 (Easter Saturday) With the permission of Father Francis, Ronald writes a long letter to Edith. [...] He encloses two devotional pamphlets, *The Stations of the Cross* [A. 2189] and *The Seven Words of the Cross*.

1957. *Robin Hood* (Tales, see Clawson).
P.s. 1: *Beowulf* (2002) 'Version A', p. 51.
P.s. 2: *Beowulf* (2002) 'Textual Notes A-Text', p. 329

1958. *Robin Hood and Guy of Gisborne*. [Robin Hood ballads, see Percy and Child (v)].
P.s.: *Philology: General Works* (VI 1927, for 1925), p. 32. Tolkien cites the incipit: 'when shaws be sheen and shrads full fair and leaves both large and long'.

1959. Robinson, John. A. T. *Honest to God*. Philadelphia: Westminster Press, 1963.
P.s.: *Letters* 306 (1968). From a letter to Michael Tolkien.

1960. Robinson, William Heath [Introduction and postscript]. *Heath Robinson's Book of Goblins: A Collection of Folk-lore and Fairy Tales*. London: Hutchinson, 1934.
P.s.: #1 a. | *Tolkien On Fairy-stories* (2008), p. 310. Tolkien refers to introduction and postscript.

1961. Robson, John (Edited by). *Three early English metrical romances: with an introduction and glossary: from a ms. in the possession of J.I. Blackburne*. Series: Camden Society, 18. London: Camden Society by John Bowyer Nichols and Son, 1842.
P.s. 1: *Sir Gawain and the Green Knight* (1925), p. xxii line 1. Tolkien and Gordon cite 'Description of the Manuscript' (pp.xxxvii-xlv); p. 105 line 1412 ff. T. and G. cite Stanzas III-XVII.
P.s. 2: *Sir Gawain and the Green Knight* (1967) 'Select Bibliography: editions of texts quoted more than once in the notes', p. 155. 'The Avouwynge of King Arther'.

1962. Roget, Peter Mark. *Thesaurus of English Words and Phrases*. Edited by John Lewis Roger. New edition. London: Longmans, 1925 (rev. ed.).
P.s.: *Philology: General Works* (VI 1927, for 1925), p. 58 n. 16.

1963. Rolle, Richard of Hampole. *The Pricke of Conscience (Stimulus conscientiæ): a Northumbrian poem*. Edited by Richard Morris. Berlin: Published for the Philological Society by A. Asher, 1863.
P.s.: MS. Tolkien A 21/13 *The English MSS*. fol. 203. [Tolkien Papers, Bodleian Library, Oxford].
S.s.: Scull-Hammond (2017a), p. 46. April 1913: Tolkien will need to become familiar with a range of literary and philological subjects and set texts as prescribed in the Oxford Regulations of the Board of Studies, knowing that he may be examined on them in ten papers at the end of Trinity Term 1915: Middle English texts.

1964. _____. *The Psalter of the Psalms of David and certain canticles with a translation and exposition in English*. Edited by Henry Ramsden Bramley. Oxford: At the Clarendon Press, 1884.
   P.s.: MS. Tolkien A 11 *Notes on Pearl* fol. 124. Tolkien quotes Psalm XXXVII, 2. 'Quoniam sagitte tue infixe sunt michi: & confirmasti super me manum tuam'. [Tolkien Papers, Bodleian Library, Oxford].

1965. Rook, Alan. *These Are My Comrades*. London: Routledge, 1943.
   Notes: A copy was sent to Tolkien by Alan Rook. Tolkien writes to him, thanking him for sending the book April 21, 1943: 'I hope you may manage one day to paint a | the great picture. I don't perceive the philosophy of it yet or the technique – but how should one from the note-book. You are certainly perfecting a poignant 'snap' technique: Aeroplane (no 2) is (if I may be allowed to say so) an almost flawless example'.

1966. Ros, Amanda McKittrick. *Irene Iddesleigh. A novel*. Belfast: Printed by W. & G. Baird, 1897.
   S.s. 1: Carpenter (1979), p. 226. [...] sometimes Lewis would take Amanda Ros's eccentric novel *Irene Iddesleigh* from the shelves and set a competition to see who could read the longest passage without breaking into helpless laughter.
   S.s. 2: Scull-Hammond (2017a), p. 249. The book was read by members of the Inklings during their meetings in late 1930. 'According to Walter Hooper, it became a customary feature of Inklings meetings to bet that no one could read a passage from the writings of Ros, the 'World's Worst Writer', with a straight face.

1967. *Ruin*. [a fragmentary poem found in the Exeter Book, see Krapp and Dobbie]
   S.s.: Scull-Hammond (2017a), p. 46. April 1913: Tolkien will need to become familiar with a range of literary and philological subjects and set texts as prescribed in the Oxford Regulations of the Board of Studies, knowing that he may be examined on them in ten papers at the end of Trinity Term 1915: Old English texts.

1968. Ruskin, John. *Unto this last*. London: Joseph Malaby Dent & sons, 1921.
   S.s.: University of Leeds (1921), p. 156. English Language and Literature - Scheme B. Texts for 1921-22. (d) Outlines of the History of English Literature. Ordinary Degree of B.A. with Honours. Final Examinations.

1969. *Ruthwell Cross* [cross bearing an important runic inscription in the Old English]
   P.s.: 'Chaucer as a Philologist: *The Reeve's Tale*' (1934), p. 135.

1970. Rypins, Stanley (Edited by). *Three Old English prose texts in MS. Cotton Vitellius A XV*. Series: E.E.T.S. (Early English Text Society), OS 161. London: Published for the Early English Text Society by H. Milford, Oxford University Press, 1924.
   P.s.: *Sigelwara land* (1932), p. 189 n. 1.

1971. Sæmundsson, Sjéra Tómas et alii. 'Fjölnir'. *Fjölnir: Ársrit handa Íslendingum*, Vol. I, 1835, pp. 1-17.
   P.s.: *English and Welsh* (1963), p. 6. Tolkien quotes: 'Málin eru höfuðeínkenni þjóðanna...' on page 11.

1972. Saintsbury, George Edward Bateman. *Dryden*. Series: English Men of Letters. Dryden. London: Macmillan and Co., 1881.
   P.s.: *Exeter College library register*. Tolkien's borrowing record: *Trinity Term 1915* from 4 May to 15 May 1915.

1973. _____. *Historical Manual of English Prosody*. London: Macmillan, 1914.
   S.s.: University of Leeds (1921), p. 191 English Language and Literature. F1. Final Course

SECTION A

(English Literature) Books recommended.

1974. _____. *A Short History of English Literature*. London: Macmillan, 1913.
S.s.: University of Leeds (1921), p. 191 English Language and Literature. F1. Final Course (English Literature) Books recommended.

1975. Saki [H. H. Munro]. *Beasts and super-beasts*. London: John Lane Co., 1914.
P.s.: *Letters* 232 (1961). From a letter to Joyce Reeves.

1976. _____. *The Chronicles of Clovis*. London: John Lane The Bodley Head, 1912.
P.s.: *Letters* 232 (1961). From a letter to Joyce Reeves.

1977. _____. *The Novels and Plays of Saki*, Vol. I. London: John Lane The Bodley Head, 1912.
P.s.: *Letters* 232 (1961). From a letter to Joyce Reeves.

1978. _____. *The Short Stories of Saki*. London: John Lane The Bodley Head, 1913.
P.s.: *Letters* 232 (1961). From a letter to Joyce Reeves.

1979. Salesbury, William. *A Dictionary in Englyshe and Welshe*. Pts I, II, III, IV. London: for the Cymmrodorion society by T. Richards, 1877.
Description: Included on facsimile of the original title page and an inscription by a previous owner: 'From T. Shankland | May. 9. 1907.' Contains a page of manuscript notes translating the opening of the Welsh prologue, between pp. 3-4, but the pages of the dictionary proper remain uncut.
Collection: Tolkien's personal Celtic library, preserved at the Weston library under the auspices of the English Faculty Library (Oxford).
P.s.: *English and Welsh* (1963), p. 3.
S.s. 1: Scull-Hammond (2006a), p. 12.
S.s. 2: Phelpstead (2011), p. 119: 'Notes in pencil and ink on a loose calendar page for 9-15 August 1954 and translating the opening of the Welsh preface are inserted'.
Reading period: 1924 - 1925 (S.s.: Scull-Hammond (2017c), p. 215).

1980. _____. *Testament Newydd ein arglwydd Jesu Christi Gwedy ei dynnu*. London: Henry Denham at the cost and charges of Humfrey Toy, 1567.
P.s.: *English and Welsh* (1963), p. 4. Tolkien writes: 'The Welsh New Testament played a considerable part in preserving to recent times, as a literary norm above the colloquial and the divergent dialects, the language of an earlier age. But fortunately in the Bible of 1588, by Dr William Morgan [A. 1638], most of Salesbury's pedantries were abandoned. Among these was Salesbury's habit of spelling words of Latin origin (real or supposed) as if they had not changed: as, for example, *eccles* for *eglwys* from *eclēsia*.'

1981. _____. *Y Llyfr Gweddi Gyffredin*. London: Henry Denham at the cost and charges of Humfrey Toy, 1567, 1586.
P.s.: *English and Welsh* (1963), p. 4; p. 40. Tolkien quotes: 'Gogoniant i 'r Tad ac i' r Mab ac i 'r Ysbryd Glân, | megis yr oedd yn y dechrau, y mae 'r awr hon, ac y | bydd yn wastad, yn oes oesoedd. Amen'.

1982. Salu, Mary (Translated in Modern English by). *The Ancrene Riwle* (*The Corpus MS.*: Ancrene Wisse). With an Introduction by Dom Gerard Sitwell, O.S.B., and a Preface by J.R.R. Tolkien. London: Burns & Oates, [November] 1955.

1983. Sapir, Edward. *Language: An Introduction to the Study of Speech*. Harcourt Brace and Company, 1921.
P.s. 1: *Philology: General Works* (VI 1927, for 1925), p. 52. Tolkien writes: '[Vendryes] we note (and heartily agree) signalizes Sapir's book (1921), of the same title, as one of first-rate

importance—it is now regrettably out of print.'
P.s. 2: *Tolkien On Fairy-stories* (2008), p. 98.

1984. _____. 'A Study in phonetic symbolism'. *Journal of Experimental Psychology*, Vol. 12, no. 3, Jun 1929. Lancaster: American Psychological Association, 1929, pp. 225-39.
P.s.: *A Secret Vice* (2016), p. 64.

1985. Sarrazin, G. 'Der Balder-kultus in Lethra'. *Anglia, Zeitschrift für englische Philologie*, Vol. XIX. Tübingen: Max Niemeyer, 1897, pp. 392-97.
P.s.: *Finn and Hengest* (1982), p. 58 n. 56.

1986. Saussure, Ferdinand de. *Cours de linguistique générale*. Lausanne & Paris: Librairie Payot & Cie, 1916.
P.s.: *Philology: General Works* (VI 1927, for 1925), p. 53

1987. Savage, Henry Lyttleton. 'Brow or Brawn?'. MLN (*Modern Language Notes*), Vol. 52, no. 1, January 1937, pp. 36-38.
P.s.: MS. Tolkien A 12/1 *Commentary on Sir Gawain, lines 37-1987* fol. 78. [Tolkien Papers, Bodleian Library, Oxford].

1988. _____. 'A Note on Parlement of the Thre Ages 38'. Offprint from MLN (*Modern Language Notes*), Vol. 43, no. 3, March 1928, pp. 177-79.
Description: Inscribed by the author: 'With the author's greetings'.
Collection: Private [Christina Scull & Wayne G. Hammond].
S.s. Scull-Hammond (2018a).

1989. _____. 'A Note on Parlement of the Thre Ages, 220'. Offprint from MLN (*Modern Language Notes*), Vol. 46, no. 3, March 1930, pp. 169-70.
Description: Inscribed by author, but with most of the inscriptions cut away.
Collection: Private [Christina Scull & Wayne G. Hammond].
S.s. Scull-Hammond (2018a).

1990. _____. 'Notes on the Prologue of "The Parlement of the Thre Ages"'. Offprint from the *Journal of English and Germanic Philology*, Vol. 29, no. 1, January 1930, pp. 74-82.
Description: Inscribed by Tolkien: 'JRRT Savage – Notes on Parlement of the Thre Ages'. Includes a label added by Stan Revell to books owned by Tolkien, 'From the Library of J.R.R. Tolkien'.
Collection: Private [Christina Scull & Wayne G. Hammond].
S.s. Scull-Hammond (2018a).

1991. _____. 'Sir Gawain "Fer ouer þe French flod"'. Offprint from the *Journal of English and Germanic Philology*, Vol. 47, no. 1, January 1948, pp. 44-52.
Description: Inscribed by author: 'With the author's good whishes, H.L.S.' Includes a label added by Stan Revell to books owned by Tolkien, 'From the Library of J.R.R. Tolkien'.
Collection: Private [Christina Scull & Wayne G. Hammond].
S.s. Scull-Hammond (2018a).

1992. _____. *The Gawain-Poet: studies in his personality and background*. Chapel Hill: University of North Carolina Press, 1956.
P.s.: *Sir Gawain and the Green Knight* (1967) 'Select Bibliography', p. 154.

1993. _____. (Introduction, notes and glossary). *St. Erkenwald, a middle English poem*. London: H. Milford, Oxford University Press, 1926.
P.s.: *Sir Gawain and the Green Knight* (1967) 'Select Bibliography', p. 153.

1994. Savile, George. *The Complete works of George Savile, first Marquess of Halifax*. Edited by Walter Alexander Raleigh. Oxford: At the Clarendon Press, 1912.
    S.s.: University of Leeds (1921), p. 154. English Language and Literature - Scheme A. Texts and Period selected for 1921-22. (d) Texts suggested for study with Special Period 1637-1700. Ordinary Degree of B.A. with Honours. Final Examinations. Parts suggested: *Advice to a Daughter* and *The Character of a Trimmer*.

1995. Savonarola, Jerome. *The Lord's Prayer and the Angelical Salutation*. London: Catholic Truth Society, 1899.
    Description: On first front flyleaf: 'Mabel Tolkien' and on another page: '25 Stirling Road | B 'ham | Tolkien J.R.R. | II | English Div II'.
    Collection: Library of the Oratory of Saint Philip Neri (Birmingham).

1996. *Sawles Warde* 1210. [Alliterative prose allegorical work, see Colborn, N.R. Ker, R. Morris, Tolkien-d'Ardenne, and Wilson].
    P.s.: MS. Tolkien A 21/13 *The English MSS.* fol. 203. [Tolkien Papers, Bodleian Library, Oxford].

1997. *Seven Sages* 1320-50. [Middle English collection of tales, see Campbell and Wright].
    P.s.: MS. Tolkien A 21/13 *The English MSS.* fol. 203. [Tolkien Papers, Bodleian Library, Oxford].

1998. Saxo, Grammaticus. *The First nine books of the Danish history of Saxo Grammaticus*. Edited by Oliver Elton and Frederick York Powell. London: David Nutt, 1894.
    P.s.: *Finn and Hengest* (1982), p. 55 n. 45; p. 58 n. 53; p. 76 n. 80; p. 90 n. 17; p. 133 n. 72; p. 167 n. 11.
    S.s.: Shippey (1992), p. 301.

1999. _____. *Saxonis Grammatici Gesta Danorvm*. Edited by Alfred Theophil Holder. Strassburg: K. J. Trübner, 1886.
    P.s.: *Finn and Hengest* (1982), p. 58 n. 53; p. 76 n. 80; p. 90 n. 17; p. 133 n. 72; p. 167 n. 11.

2000. _____. *Saxonis Grammatici Historia Danica*, Vol. I, Pt. I. Edited by Hans Mattias Velschow and Peter Erasmus Müller. Havniæ: Sumtibus Librariæ Gyldendalianæ, 1839.
    P.s. 1: *Finn and Hengest* (1982), p. 58 n. 53; p. 76 n. 80; p. 90 n. 17; p. 133 n. 72; p. 134 n. 74.
    P.s. 2: *Beowulf* (2014), p. 154 n. 3; p. 167 n. 11.

2001. _____. *Saxonis Grammatici Historia Danica*, Vol. I, Pt. II. Edited by Hans Mattias Velschow and Peter Erasmus Müller. Havniæ: Sumtibus Librariæ Gyldendalianæ, 1839.
    P.s. 1: *Finn and Hengest* (1982), p. 58 n. 53; p. 76 n. 80; p. 90 n. 17; p. 133 n. 72; p. 134 n. 74.
    P.s. 2: *Beowulf* (2014), p. 154 n. 3; p. 167 n. 11.

2002. _____. *Saxonis Grammatici Historia Danica*, Vol. II. Edited by Hans Mattias Velschow and Peter Erasmus Müller. Havniæ: Sumtibus Librariæ Gyldendalianæ, 1858.
    P.s. 1: *Finn and Hengest* (1982), p. 58 n. 53; 90 n. 17 133 n. 72; 134 n. 74.
    P.s. 2: *Beowulf* (2014), p. 154 n. 3; 167 n. 11.

2003. Sayers, Dorothy L. *Busman's Honeymoon*. Series: Lord Peter Wimsey, 11. London: Victor Gollancz, 1937.
    P.s.: *Letters* 71 (1944). To Christopher Tolkien.
    S.s.: Scull-Hammond (2006b), p. 818. In 1944, Tolkien confessed not to appreciate this.

2004. _____. *Clouds of Witness*. Series: Lord Peter Wimsey, 2. London: T. Fisher Unwin, 1926.
   P.s.: *Letters* 71 (1944). To Christopher Tolkien.
   S.s.: Scull-Hammond (2006b), p. 818.

2005. _____. *et alii*. *Essays presented to Charles Williams*. London: Oxford University Press, 1947.
   Description: Tolkien gives the book, with a dedication, to Simonne d'Ardenne.
   Collection: Fonds J.R.R. Tolkien, Bibliothèque ALPHA principale, Université de Liège (Liège), Tol/058.
   S.s.: Lewis (2009a), p. 817. Letter to Owen Barfield – 16 December 1947. Lewis writes: 'Your essay ['Poetic Diction and Legal Fiction' pp. 106-27] is magnificent and I don't know why you are disappointed with it. Tolkien thinks the same & has read it twice'.

2006. _____. *et alii*. *Essays presented to Charles Williams*. Grand Rapids: W. Eerdmans Publishing Co., 1966.
   P.s.: Tolkien's unpublished letter to William B. Eerdmans Publishing Co., 3 May 1966. Tolkien writes: 'Thank you very much for the copy in your edition, which I received today'.

2007. _____. *Five Red Herrings*. Series: Lord Peter Wimsey, 6. London: Victor Gollancz, 1931.
   P.s.: *Letters* 71 (1944). To Christopher Tolkien.
   S.s.: Scull-Hammond (2006b), p. 818.

2008. _____. *Gaudy Night*. Series: Lord Peter Wimsey, 10. London: Victor Gollancz, 1935.
   P.s.: *Letters* 71 (1944). Tolkien, though he liked Dorothy Sayers personally, wrote of it and its hero Lord Peter Wimsey: 'I could not stand *Gaudy Night*. I followed P. Wimsey from his attractive beginnings so far, by which time I conceived a loathing for him not surpassed by any other character in literature known to me, unless by his Harriet'.
   S.s. 1: Carpenter (1979), p. 189.
   S.s. 2: Scull-Hammond (2006b), p. 818.

2009. _____. *Have His Carcase*. Series: Lord Peter Wimsey, 7. London: Victor Gollancz, 1932.
   P.s.: *Letters* 71 (1944). To Christopher Tolkien.
   S.s.: Scull-Hammond (2006b), p. 818

2010. _____. *The Man Born to be King: a play-cycle on the life of our Lord and Saviour Jesus Christ*. London: Victor Gollancz Ltd., 1943.
   Description: Bookplate: Woman in window with manuscript 'Michael H.R. Tolkien, 22 October, 1948, from his father JRRT' in JRRT's hand.
   Collection: Private.
   S.s.: Carpenter (1979), p. 189. Lewis and Tolkien greatly admired *The Man Born to be King*.

2011. _____. *Murder Must Advertise*. Series: Lord Peter Wimsey, 8. London: Victor Gollancz, 1933.
   P.s.: *Letters* 71 (1944). To Christopher Tolkien.
   S.s.: Scull-Hammond (2006b), p. 818.

2012. _____. *Strong Poison*. Series: Lord Peter Wimsey, 5. London: Victor Gollancz, 1931.
   P.s.: *Letters* 71 (1944). To Christopher Tolkien.
   S.s.: Scull-Hammond (2006b), p. 818.

2013. _____. *The Nine Tailors*. Series: Lord Peter Wimsey, 9. London: Victor

Gollancz, 1934.
> P.s.: *Letters* 71 (1944). To Christopher Tolkien.
> S.s.: Scull-Hammond (2006b), p. 818.

2014. _____. *The Unpleasantness at the Bellona Club*. Series: Lord Peter Wimsey, 4. London: Ernest Benn, 1928.
> P.s.: *Letters* 71 (1944). To Christopher Tolkien.
> S.s.: Scull-Hammond (2006b), p. 818.

2015. _____. *Whose Body?* Series: Lord Peter Wimsey, 1. London: T. Fisher Unwin, 1923.
> P.s.: *Letters* 71 (1944). To Christopher Tolkien.
> S.s.: Scull-Hammond (2006b), p. 818.

2016. Schaubert, Else von. 'Der Englische Ursprung von *Syr Gawayn and the Grene Knyzt*'. *Englische Studien. Organ für englische Philologie unter Mitberücksichtigung des englischen Unterrichts auf höheren Schulen*, Vol. LVII. Edited by Johannes Hoops. Leipzig: O. R. Reisland, 1923, pp. 330-446.
> P.s.: *Sir Gawain and the Green Knight* (1925), pp. xiii, xxvi. Tolkien and Gordon cite specifically Pt. IV. 'Widerlegung der von einer französischen Gesamtvorlage ausgehenden Ansichten' (pp. 394-415).

2017. Schick, Joseph. 'Indische Quellen zu Longfellow's *Kavanagh*'. *Probleme der Englischen Sprache und Kultur*. Festschrift Johannes Hoops zum 60 [A. 1169]. Heidelberg: Carl Winter, 1925.
> P.s.: *Philology: General Works* (VI 1927, for 1925), p. 45. Tolkien writes: 'different and quite unexpectedly entertaining is J. Schick's Indische, which affords a rare mixture of Longfellow, Sanskrit, and some easy simple and quadratic equations'.

2018. Schiller, Friedrich. *Geschichte des Dreissigjährigen Kriegs*. Stuttgart: Cotta'schen Buchhandlung, 1862.
> Description: King Edward's School with seal stamp on upper board. Inscribed: 'German Division I. | Midsummer 1910. | Ronald Tolkien' [Judith Priestman 1994, revd. 2016].
> Collection: Weston Library, Bodleian Libraries (Oxford).
> S.s.: Zettersten (2011), p. 78 'During my last visit to the Tolkien Collection at the Bodleian Library, Oxford, I went through Tolkien's books in his private library from his school time, which his family had donated to the Bodleian in July 1982.'

2019. Schipper, Jacob (Edited by). *König Alfreds übersetzung von Bedas Kirchengeschichte*, Vol. I. Series: Bibliothek der angelsächsischen Prosa, 4. Leipzig: Heorg H. Wigand, 1897.
> Description: Autographed and dated on front flyleaf: 'Oxford | 1920'.
> Collection: Tolkien's personal Celtic library, preserved at the Weston library under the auspices of the English Faculty Library (Oxford).
> P.s. 1: *Sigelwara land* (1934), p. 101.
> P.s. 2: *The Old English Exodus* (1982), p. 37 n. 14.
> S.s.: McIlwaine (2018), no. 84.

2020. Schlutter, Otto (Edited by). *Das Epinaler Und Erfurter Glossar*. Hamburg: Verlag van Henri Grand, 1912.
> Description: Autographed on front flyleaf.
> Collection: Tolkien's personal Celtic library, preserved at the Weston library under the auspices of the English Faculty Library (Oxford).
> P.s.: *Sigelwara land* (1934), p. 103 n. 1. Tolkien writes that for the term *sigillum* s.v. *seglgerd*.

2021. Schmidt-Petersen, Jürgen. *Die Orts- und Flurnamen Nordfrieslands*. Husum: C. F. Delff, 1925.
　　Description: Tolkien's signature to front free endpaper.
　　Collection: Private [Sold by Simon Finch Rare Books Ltd.].
　　S.s.: Finch (2002), p. 54.

2022. Schneider, Hermann. *Germanische Heldensage*, Vol. I. *Einleitung: Ursprung und Wesen der Heldensage*. Deutsche Heldensage. Series: Grundriss der germanischen Philologie, 10.1. Berlin: Mouton de Gruyter, 1928.
　　Description: Inscribed on front flyleaf: 'Presented by the executors of Professor J.R.R. Tolkien'.
　　Collection: Taylor Institution Library, Bodleian Libraries (Oxford).
　　S.s.: Shippey (1992), p. 16.

2023. _____. *Germanische Heldensage*, Vol. II, Pt. I. *Nordgermanische Heldensage*. Series: Grundriss der germanischen Philologie, 10.2. Berlin: Mouton de Gruyter, 1934.
　　Description: Inscribed on front flyleaf: 'Presented by the executors of Professor J.R.R. Tolkien'.
　　Collection: Taylor Institution Library, Bodleian Libraries (Oxford).
　　S.s.: Shippey (1992), p. 16.

2024. _____. *Germanische Heldensage*, Vol. II, Pt. II. *Festländische Heldensage in nordgermanischer und englischer Überlieferung. Verlorene Heldensage*. Series: Grundriss der germanischen Philologie, 10.3. Berlin: Mouton de Gruyter, 1934.
　　Description: Inscribed on front flyleaf: 'Presented by the executors of Professor J.R.R. Tolkien'.
　　Collection: Taylor Institution Library, Bodleian Libraries (Oxford).
　　S.s.: Shippey (1992), p. 16.

2025. Schofield, William Henry. *English literature, from the Norman conquest to Chaucer*. London: Macmillan and Co., 1906.
　　P.s.: *Sir Gawain and the Green Knight* (1925), p. xxvi. Tolkien and Gordon write: 'For bibliography of the Irish and French analogues of *Sir Gawain*, see the bibliography in Kittredge's study'. [*NED*] In Kittredge's study, this article is mentioned in 'II. Gawain and the Green Knight' (p. 294).

2026. _____. 'The nature and fabric of *The Pearl* with an appendix concerning the source of the poem'. PMLA (*Publications of the Modern Language Association of America*), Vol. XIX, no. 1, 1904, pp. 154-215.
　　P.s. 1: MS. Tolkien A 35 *Pearl* fol. 114. [Tolkien Papers, Bodleian Library, Oxford].
　　P.s. 2: *Pearl* (1953), p. xi. 'The personal interpretation was first questioned in 1904 by W. H. Schofield, who argued that the maiden of the poem was an allegorical figure of a kind usual in medieval vision-literature, an abstraction representing 'clean maidenhood' (Schofield's book p. 174).
　　P.s. 3: *Sir Gawain and the Green Knight* (1975), p. 18. Tolkien writes ... [see P.s. 1].

2027. _____. 'Symbolism, Allegory, and Autobiography in *The Pearl*'. PMLA (*Publications of the Modern Language Association of America*), Vol. XXIV, No. 4, 1909, pp. 585-675.
　　P.s.: MS. Tolkien A 35 *Pearl* fol. 114. [Tolkien Papers, Bodleian Library, Oxford].

2028. Schröer, Arnold. (Edited by). *Die Angelsächsischen Prosabearbeitungen der Benedictinerregel*. Series: Bibliothek der angelsächsischen Prosa, 2. Kassel: Georg H. Wigand, 1885-1888.
　　Description: Autographed on front flyleaf.
　　Collection: Tolkien's personal Celtic library, preserved at the Weston library under the auspices of the English Faculty Library (Oxford).
　　P.s.: *Finn and Hengest* (1982), p. 99 n. 35.

SECTION A

2029. _____. 'Das Problem und die Darstellung des'standard of Spoken English'. Vom Standpunkte der Sprachgeschichte und der Praxis'. Offprint from *Germanisch-romanische Monatsschrift*, Vol. IV. Edited by Heinrich Schröder. Heidelberg: Carl Winter's Universitätsbuchhandlung, April-May 1912.
   Description: A few annotations.
   S.s.: Hime (1980), p. 6.

2030. Schück, Henrik. 'Inbjudningsskrift till åhörande af den offentliga föreläsning med hvilken professorn i kemi Oskar Widman tillträder sitt embete'. *Studier i Ynglingatal*, Vol. I. Series: Uppsala Universitet.; Inbjudningsskrift till åhörande av de offentliga föreläsningar, 1. Upsala: Berling, 1905.
   Description: Tolkien's signature to front wrapper, with date in Tolkien's hand '1905'.
   Collection: Private [Sold by Simon Finch Rare Books Ltd.].
   S.s.: Finch (2002), p. 54.

2031. _____. 'Inbjudningsskrift till åhörande af den offentliga föreläsning med hvilken professorn i civilrätt Alfred Ossian Winroth tillträder sitt embete'. *Studier i Ynglingatal*, Vol. II. Series: Uppsala Universitet.; Inbjudningsskrift till åhörande av de offentliga föreläsningar, 2. Upsala: Berling, 1906.
   Description: Tolkien's signature to front wrapper, with date in Tolkien's hand '1906'.
   Collection: Private [Sold by Simon Finch Rare Books Ltd.].
   S.s.: Finch (2002), p. 54.

2032. _____. 'Inbjudningsskrift till åhörande af den offentliga föreläsning med hvilken professorn i matematik Anders Wiman tillträder sitt embete'. *Studier i Ynglingatal*, Vol. III. Series: Uppsala Universitet.; Inbjudningsskrift till åhörande av de offentliga föreläsningar, 3. Upsala: Berling, 1907.
   Description: Tolkien's signature to front wrapper, with date in Tolkien's hand '1907'.
   Collection: Private [Sold by Simon Finch Rare Books Ltd.].
   S.s.: Finch (2002), p. 54.

2033. _____. 'Inbjudningsskrift till åhörande af den öffentliga föreläsning, med hvilken professorn i pedagogik Bertil Hammer tillträder sitt ämbete'. *Studier i Ynglingatal*, Vol. IV. Series: Uppsala Universitet.; Inbjudningsskrift till åhörande av de offentliga föreläsningar, 4. Upsala: Almqvist & Wiksell, 1910.
   Description: Tolkien's signature to front wrapper.
   Collection: Private [Sold by Simon Finch Rare Books Ltd.].
   S.s.: Finch (2002), p. 54.

2034. Scoresby, William. *An Account of the Arctic Regions with a History and Description of the Northern Whale-fishery*, Vol. II. Edinburgh: A. Constable & Co., 1820.
   P.s.: MS. Tolkien A 19/3 *Etymologies or history of Walrus* fols. 162-195. [Tolkien Papers, Bodleian Library, Oxford].
   S.s.: *Tolkien, Family Album* (1992), p. 42.
   NED: #2 i. | 'W' (1928), pp. 57-58 'Walrus, 3. *attrib.* and *comb.*' 1820 – 'Walrus-fishing in succeeding years in high northern latitudes' (p. 5).

2035. Scott, Herbert S. *Anglo-Catholicism & Re-Union*. London: R. Scott, 1923.
   Description: The original paper cover of this book is gone, and in its place in a manilla colored cover that is handwritten by Tolkien himself: 'Anglo-Catholicism | & | Re-Union | S. H. Scott | (of Addington)'. On the second page is Tolkiens signature with the inscription: 'given to me by Rev. S H Scott | in the old'Newman Bookshop' | at that time in Beaumont | Street, Oxford'.
   Collection: Private [Tolkien Collector's Guide].

2036.	Scott, Walter. *Marmion*.
P.s.: *Letters* 319 (1971). From a letter to Roger Lancelyn Green.Tolkien writes 'Oh what a tangled web they weave who try a new word to conceive!' while the original verse is 'Oh! What a tangled web we weave | When first we practise to deceive!' (Canto VI, vv. 532-3).

2037.	*Seafarer*. [Old English poem preserved in the *Exeter Book*, see Krapp and Dobbie]
Collection: Taylor Institution Library, Bodleian Libraries (Oxford).
P.s. 1: *Beowulf* (1937), p. 39.
P.s. 2: *Valedictory Address* (1959), p. 239. Tolkien recites: 'Nearon nú cyningas ne cáseras | ne goldgiefan swylce iú wæron!' [Tolkien's translation] 'There are not now any kings or emperors, nor any patrons giving gifts of gold, such as once there were!'
P.s. 3: *Beowulf* (2002) 'Textual Notes A-Text', p. 346.
S.s.: Lee (2009), p. 194-5. Notes: In the Bodleian Library, Oxford, its preserved the note on *The Wanderer* and *The Seafarer*. Extract from Tolkien's notes: [MS. Tolkien A 30/1 *Lectures on Old English* fol. 33.] 'These are the words of men who knew the northern seas in small boats. Anglo-Saxon verse has many echoes of the cold waves, and the cry of the seabirds. It is, perhaps, not surprising that the reflective poetry of a people with the traditions of the cold north seas, frozen in winter, should show two elegiac poems, in which the sorrows of the lonely seafarer are a leading theme, and a symbol of desolation of spirit. These two remarkable poems of individual sentiment, are also preserved in the *Exeter Book*, and are now usually known as the *Wanderer* and *Seafarer*.'

2038.	Searle, William George. *Anglo Saxon Bishops Kings and Nobles. The Succession of the Bishops and the Pedigrees of the Kings and Nobles*. Cambridge: The University Press, 1899.
Description: Tolkien's signature with annotations, mainly to genealogical tables.
Collection: Private [Sold by Simon Finch Rare Books Ltd.].
S.s.: Finch (2002), p. 53.

2039.	_____. *Onomasticon Anglo-Saxonicum. A list of Anglo-Saxon proper names from the time of Beda to that of King John*. Cambridge: The University Press, 1897.
Description: Tolkien's signature dated 1921 on the front free endpaper with annotations, mainly to the introduction.
Collection: Private [Sold by Simon Finch Rare Books Ltd.].
P.s.: *Finn and Hengest* (1982), p. 31 n. 7; p. 39 n. 15.
S.s.: Finch (2002), p. 53.

2040.	Sébillot, Paul. *Revieu des Traditions Populaires*, Vols. 1-34, 1886-1919.
P.s.: #1 a. | *Tolkien On Fairy-stories* (2008), p. 310. Tolkien writes: 'Sébillot articles'.

2041.	*Second Shepherds' Play* (Medieval mystery play, see Rhys].
S.s.: Scull-Hammond (2017a), p. 122. Leeds academic year 1920-1921. Tolkien might also be responsible for the first few lectures in an introductory course on English Literature which begins with the Second Shepherd's Play, Mondays and Wednesdays at 11.00 a.m.

2042.	Sedgefield, Walter John. *Anglo-Saxon Verse-Book*. Series: Publications of the University of Manchester. English series, 13. Manchester: The University Press, 1922.
Description: Autographed in front flyleaf and marked in pencil: 'From the M. Univ. Press. 'Annotated in pencil. Bookmark at pp. 68-69. [From lines 603 of *Beowulf: The Giant Sword dissolves in the Monster's blood*, 'ðonne forstes bend Fæder onlæteð', to line 41 of *The Battle of Brunanburh*, 'frēonda gefylled on folcstede,']
Collection: Tolkien's personal Celtic library, preserved at the Weston library under the auspices of the English Faculty Library (Oxford).
P.s. 1: *Letters* 90 (1944). To Christopher Tolkien. Tolkien writes: 'Is nu fela folca þætte fyrngewritu healdan wille, ac him hyge brosnað.' from 'V. Miscellaneous. 21. Gnomic and

Didactic' v. 245-6, p. 111.
P.s. 2: *The Old English Exodus* (1982), p. x.
S.s.: McIlwaine (2018), no. 84.

2043. _____. *Beowulf*. Manchester: The University Press, 1910.
P.s.: *Finn and Hengest* (1982), p. 88 n. 14.

2044. _____. *Beowulf*. Manchester: The University Press, 1935 (3rd ed.).
P.s.: *Finn and Hengest* (1982), p. 94 n. 20.

2045. Seebohm, Frederic. *The Tribal System in Wales. Being part of an inquiry into the structure and methods of tribal society*. London: Longmans, Green and Co., 1904 (2nd ed.).
Description: Decoratively autographed, also initialed and dated on front flyleaf: 'JRRT | 1922'.
Collection: Tolkien's personal Celtic library, preserved at the Weston library under the auspices of the English Faculty Library (Oxford).
S.s. 1: Phelpstead (2011), p. 119.
S.s. 2: Scull-Hammond (2017a), p. 126.

2046. Sehrt, Edward Henry. *Vollständiges Wörterbuch zum Heliand und zur altsächsischen Genesis*. Göttingen: Vandenhoek and Ruprecht, 1925.
P.s.: *Philology: General Works* (VI 1927, for 1925), p. 57 n. 15.

2047. _____. *Zur Geschichte der westgermanischen Konjunktion 'und'*. Series: Hesperia. Schriften zur germanischen Philologie, 8. Göttingen: Vandenhoeck & Ruprecht; Baltimore: The Johns Hopkins Press, 1916.
Description: Signed in the front by J.R.R. Tolkien and annotations in pencil.
Collection: Private [Sold by Peter Harrington Antiquarian Bookseller].
S.s.: Harrington (2003), p. 25.

2048. Senff, Herbert. *Die Nominalflexion in Ayenbite of Inwyt*. Jena: Frommannschen Buchhandlung Walter Biedermann, 1937.
Description: Uncut pages.
Collection: Tolkien's personal Celtic library, preserved at the Weston library under the auspices of the English Faculty Library (Oxford).

2049. Serjeantson, Mary S. 'The Dialect of the Earliest Complete English Prose Psalter'. Offprint from *English Studies*, Vol. 6, n. 1-6. Amsterdam: 1924, pp. 177-99.
Description: Inscribed by Tolkien:'serjeantson E.E. Prose Psalter'. Includes a label added by Stan Revell to books owned by Tolkien, 'From the Library of J.R.R. Tolkien'.
Collection: Private [Christina Scull & Wayne G. Hammond].
S.s. Scull-Hammond (2018a).

2050. Severius, Sulpicius. *St. Martin of Tours: the chronicles of Sulpicius Severus done into English from the French of Paul Monceaux and with an introduction by him*. London: Sands, 1928.
P.s.: *Beowulf* (2002) 'Textual Notes A-Text', p. 339.

2051. Shakespeare, William. *Antony and Cleopatra*.
S.s.: Scull-Hammond (2017a), p. 46. April 1913: Tolkien will need to become familiar with a range of literary and philological subjects and set texts as prescribed in the Oxford Regulations of the Board of Studies, knowing that he may be examined on them in ten papers at the end of *Trinity Term 1915*: Middle English texts.

2052. _____. *Hamlet. Coriolanus. Twelfth night.* Series: Plays of Shakespeare. Edited by George Stuart Gordon. Oxford: At the Clarendon Press, 1912.
S.s. 1: University of Leeds (1921), p. 141. English Literature, text selected for 1921-22 (*Coriolanus*); p. 155. English Language and Literature - Scheme B. Texts for 1921-22. (d) Outlines of the History of English Literature (*Twelfth night*). Ordinary Degree of B.A. with Honours. Final Examinations; p. 189 English Language and Literature. Int. 1 Intermediate Course (Literature).
S.s. 2: Ollscoil na h-Éireann G 257 (1949).
S.s. 3: Scull-Hammond (2017a), p. 46. April 1913: Tolkien will need to become familiar with a range of literary and philological subjects and set texts as prescribed in the Oxford Regulations of the Board of Studies, knowing that he may be examined on them in ten papers at the end of *Trinity Term 1915*: Middle English texts.

2053. _____. *Hamlet.*
P.s. 1: *Sir Gawain and the Green Knight* (1953), p. 72.
P.s. 2: *Beowulf* (2002) 'Version A', p. 38.

2054. _____. *King Henry IV.*
P.s.: *Letters* 326 (1971). To Carole Batten-Phelps (draft). Tolkien writes 'uneasy lies the head that wears the father's bowler'. The original verse is 'Uneasy lies the head that wears a crown'.
S.s.: Scull-Hammond (2017a), p. 46. April 1913: Tolkien will need to become familiar with a range of literary and philological subjects and set texts as prescribed in the Oxford Regulations of the Board of Studies, knowing that he may be examined on them in ten papers at the end of Trinity Term 1915: Middle English texts. Pt. I and Pt. II.

2055. _____. *King Henry V.*
P.s. 1: *Beowulf* (2002) 'Version A', p. 55.
P.s. 2: *Beowulf* (2002) 'Textual Notes A-Text', p. 332.

2056. _____. *King Henry VIII.*
P.s.: *Sir Gawain and the Green Knight* (1925), p. 85, line 137 *on þe most on þe mode*. Tolkien and Gordon write: '... and still survived in Shakespeare's time, e.g. Henry VIII, II. iv, 48 *one the wisest prince*'. In *Fourteenth century verse & prose* (1921), Kennet Sisam writes: [*Sir Gawain*] '294-5. 'And truly you seem to me the most faultless man that ever walked on foot.' The ME. construction, *on þe fautlest*, where on 'one' strengthens the superlative, is found in Chaucer, *Clerk's Tale* 212: *Thanne was she oon thefaireste under sonne*, and still survives in Shakespeare's time, e.g. Henry VIII, n. iv. 48 f. *one the wisest prince*' (p. 223).
S.s.: Ollscoil na h-Éireann G 257 (1949).

2057. _____. *King Lear.*
P.s. 1: *Beowulf* (1937), p. 11.
P.s. 2: *On Fairy-stories* (1947), p. 48.
P.s. 3: 'Middle English 'Losenger'' (1953), p. 75.
P.s. 4: *Sir Gawain and the Green Knight* (1953), p. 72.
P.s. 5: *English and Welsh* (1963), p. 25. Tolkien quotes: 'Child Rowland to the dark tower came, | His word was stil: Fie, foh, and fum, | I smell the blood of a British man' (Act III, scene iv),
P.s. 6: *Beowulf* (2002) 'Version A', p. 55.
P.s. 7: *Beowulf* (2002) 'Textual Notes A-Text', p. 332.
P.s. 8: #1 a. | *Tolkien On Fairy-stories* (2008), p. 310.
P.s. 9: *Beowulf* (2014), p. 170.
S.s. 1: University of Leeds (1921), p. 155. English Language and Literature - Scheme B. Texts for 1921-22. (d) Outlines of the History of English Literature. Ordinary Degree of B.A. with Honours. Final Examinations.
S.s. 2: Ollscoil na h-Éireann G 257 (1949).

2058. _____. *Love's Labour's Lost.*
S.s.: Scull-Hammond (2017a), p. 46. April 1913: Tolkien will need to become familiar with a range of literary and philological subjects and set texts as prescribed in the Oxford Regulations of the Board of Studies, knowing that he may be examined on them in ten papers at the end of Trinity

Term 1915: Middle English texts.

2059. _____. *Macbeth.*
P.s. 1: *On Fairy-stories* (1947), p. 69.
P.s. 2: *Letters* 163 (1955). To W.H. Auden. [Shakespeare] 'Which I disliked cordially'.
P.s. 3: Tolkien's unpublished letter to L. M. Cutts, 26 October 1958. Tolkien writes: 'Ents is also an ancient English word (for a giant); but the Ent of my world I suppose are entirely 'original' creatures, so far as that can be said of any human work. If you like, they are a mythological form taken by my life long love for trees, with perhaps some remote influence from George MacDonald's Phantastes (a work I do not much like), and certainly a strong (twist ?) given my deep disappointment with Shakespeare's Macbeth … '
P.s. 4: 'Nomenclature of *The Lord of the Rings*' (1966), p. 758 '*Crack of Doom*.' Tolkien cites *Macbeth* IV, i, 117.
P.s. 5: *Beowulf* (2002) 'Version A', p. 55.
P.s. 6: *Beowulf* (2002) 'Textual Notes A-Text', p. 332.
P.s. 7: #1 a. | *Tolkien On Fairy-stories* (2008), p. 310.
P.s. 8: *Beowulf* (2014), p. 168.
S.s.1: University of Leeds (1920), p. 135 English Literature. Texts Selected for 1920-21; p. 181. English Language and Literature. Int. I Intermediate Course (Literature).
S.s. 2: Hammond-Scull (2014), p. 89.

2060. _____. *The Merchant of Venice.*
P.s. 1: *Beowulf* (2002) 'Version A', p. 53.
P.s. 2: *Beowulf* (2014), p. 337.
S.s.: Hammond-Scull (2014), p. 160. Hammnd and Scull write: 'All that is gold does not glitter' [FoTR, X] Compare the traditional saying all that glitters is not gold (in Shakespeare's *Merchant of Venice*, 'All that glisters is not gold').

2061. _____. *Midsummer Night's Dream.*
P.s. 1: *Letters* 219 (1959). From a letter to Allen & Unwin. Tolkien writes: 'My only comment is that of Puck upon mortals', quoting Puck who speaks to Oberon: 'Lor, what fools these mortal be!' (Scene 2, v. 115).
P.s. 2: #1 a. | *Tolkien On Fairy-stories* (2008), p. 310.
S.s. 1: University of Leeds (1920), p. 135 English Literature. Texts Selected for 1920-21; p. 180. English Language and Literature. Int. I Intermediate Course (Literature).
S.s. 2: Lewis (2009a), p. 349. Letter to his brother Warren – 18 February 1940. Lewis writes: 'believe I forgot to mention in my last week's letter the really excellent performance of a *Midsummer Nights Dream* which Tolkien and I saw at the Playhouse '

2062. _____. *Richard II.*
S.s.: University of Leeds (1921), p. 155. English Language and Literature - Scheme B. Texts for 1921-22. (d) Outlines of the History of English Literature. Ordinary Degree of B.A. with Honours. Final Examinations.

2063. _____. *Romeo and Juliet.*
S.s.: University of Leeds (1923), p. 81. Ordinary Degree of B.A., Intermediate Course and Examination: English Literature. Text selected for 1923-24 (ii) Texts suggests as part of a course of general rending in the period 1579-1645.

2064. _____. *Shakespeare's As you Like it.* Edited by George Stuart Gordon. Oxford: At the Clarendon Press, 1920.
P.s.: 'Nomenclature of *The Lord of the Rings*' (1966), p. 758 '*Gamling (the Old)*.'
S.s. 1: University of Leeds (1921), p. 141. English Literature, text selected for 1921-22; p. 189 English Language and Literature. Int. 1 Intermediate Course (Literature).
S.s. 2: Lewis (2009b), p. 1382. Letter to Tolkien – 20 November 1962. Lewis writes: 'I am, if not a lean, at least a slippered, pantaloon'. Lewis refers: II, vii, 157–9: 'The sixth age shifts | Into the lean and slippered pantaloon | With spectacles on nose and pouch on side…'

2065. _____. *Ein Sommernachtstraum (Midsummer Night's Dream)*. Translated by Christopher Martin Wieland, 1764.
    P.s. 1: *On Fairy-stories* (1947), p. 40 n. 3. Tolkien writes: '…German *Elf, Elfe* appears to be derived from *A Midsummer-night's Dream*, in Wieland's translation (1764).
    P.s. 2: 'Nomenclature of *The Lord of the Rings*' (1966), p. 756 '*Elven-smiths*.' Tolkien writes: With regard to German: I would suggest with diffidence that *Elf, elfen* are perhaps to be avoided as equivalents of *elf, elven*. *Elf* is, I believe, borrowed from English, and may retain some of the associations of a kind that I should particularly desire not to be present (if possible): for example those of Drayton or of *A Midsummer Night's Dream* (in the translation of which, I believe, *Elf* was first used in German).

2066. _____. *The Tempest*. London: MacMillan, 1921.
    S.s.: Ollscoil na h-Éireann G 107 (1949).

2067. _____. *The Tragedy of Julius Cæsar*. Series: The Warwick Shakespeare 1. Edited by Arthur Donald Innes. London: Backie & Son Ltd., 1906.
    Description: On first front flyleaf: 'J.R.R. Tolkien | Class IV. Div II English | Div II French. Set. BIV | Summer Trim | 1906 | King Edward High School | B 'ham [New Street]'.
    Collection: Library of the Oratory of Saint Philip Neri (Birmingham).

2068. _____. *Winter's Tale*.
    S.s.: University of Leeds (1923), p. 81. Ordinary Degree of B.A., Intermediate Course and Examination: English Literature. Text selected for 1923-24 (ii) Texts suggestes as part of a course of general rending in the period 1579-1645.

2069. Sharp, Elizabeth A. and John Matthay (Edited by). *Lyra Celtica. An anthology of representative Celtic poetry*. Edinburgh: John Grant, 1924 (2nd ed.).
    Collection: Tolkien's personal Celtic library, preserved at the Weston library under the auspices of the English Faculty Library (Oxford).
    Notes: The book was featured in the exhibition *Tolkien: Maker of Middle-earth* at the Weston Library in Oxford (June-October 2018).

2070. Shelley, Percy Bysshe. *Adonais*. London: Humphrey Milford and Oxford University Press, 1913.
    S.s. 1: University of Leeds (1920), p. 135 English Literature. Texts Selected for 1920-21; p. 181. English Language and Literature. Int. I Intermediate Course (Literature).
    S.s. 2: University of Leeds (1921), p. 156. English Language and Literature - Scheme B. Texts for 1921-22. (d) Outlines of the History of English Literature. Ordinary Degree of B.A. with Honours. Final Examinations.
    S.s. 3: Ollscoil na h-Éireann G 258 (1949).

2071. _____. *Alastor; or, The spirit of solitude, and other poems*. London: Published for the Shelley Society by Reeves and Turner, 1895.
    S.s.: Ollscoil na h-Éireann G 258 (1949).

2072. _____. *Arethusa* [Poem].
    S.s.: Garth (2014), p. 33. Garth writes: ['The Voyage of Earendel the Evening Star' (1914)] 'Tolkien also closely echoed the metre and rhyme scheme of Shelley's 'Arethusa', a retelling of the Greek myth about the origin of a Sicilian stream:'

2073. _____. *A Defence of Poetry*. Oxford: B. H. Blackwell, 1921.
    S.s.: University of Leeds (1921), p. 141. English Literature, text selected for 1921-22. Ordinary Degree of B.A.; p. 154. English Language and Literature - Scheme A. Texts and Period selected for 1921-22. (e) History of Criticism: Special Texts suggested for study. Ordinary Degree of B.A. with Honours. Final Examinations.

SECTION A

2074. Sheridan, Richard Brinsley. *The Rivals*.
S.s.: Scull-Hammond (2017a), p. 37. 21 December 1911 Sheridan's *The Rivals* is performed under the auspices of the King Edward's School Musical and Dramatic Society. According to the King Edward's School Chronicle: 'the performance was a thorough success both artistically and financially ... J.R.R. Tolkien's *Mrs Malaprop* was a real creation, excellent in every way and not least so in make-up. ['The Musical and Dramatic Society', n.s. 27, no. 191 (March 1912), p. 10].

2075. Shetelig, Haakon and Hjalmar Falk. *Scandinavian Archaeology*. Translated by Eric Valentine Gordon. Oxford: At the Clarendon Press, 1937.
Description: With a typed notes: 'With the compliments of Professor E.V. Gordon'. Signed in pencil on the end paper with the additional note in Tolkien's hand: 'from EVG'.
Collection: Private [TolkienLibrary.com, Sold on Ebay 17 July 2012].

2076. Shideler, Mary McDermott. *Charles Williams: A Critical Essay*. William B. Eerdmans, 1966.
Notes: 2 March 1966: A proof copy was sent to Tolkien by the publisher Roger Verhulst (provisory title *Charles Williams in Christian Perspective*).
P.s.: Tolkien's unpublished letter to Roger Verhulst, 9 March 1966. Tolkien writes: 'Thank you for sending me the uncorrected proof copy of the pamphlet by Mary McDermott Shideler' [Sold by Christie's, 28 November 2011].
S.s.: Scull-Hammond (2017a), p. 691.

2077. Shippey, Tom. 'The Author as Philologist', 1969.
P.s.: Tolkien's unpublished letter to Tom Shippey, 12 April 1970. Comments on Shippey's paper 'The Author as Philologist '

2078. Shorthouse, Joseph Henry. *John Inglesant, a romance*, Vol. I. London: Macmillan and Co, 1881.
P.s. 1: *Letters* 257 (1964). To Christopher Bretherton.
P.s. 2: Tolkien's letter to Canon N. S. Power, MA, Lady wood Vicarage, Birmingham – 8 July 1973 (Letter published in *Mallorn*, 9, 1975, p. 19).
S.s. 1: Scull-Hammond (2017a), p. 739.
S.s. 2: Scull-Hammond (2006b), p. 816.
Reading period: 1908 – early 1910 (S.s.: Scull-Hammond (2017c), p. 1054).

2079. _____. *John Inglesant, a romance*, Vol. II. London: Macmillan and Co, 1882.
P.s. 1: *Letters* 257 (1964). To Christopher Bretherton.
P.s. 2: Tolkien's letter to Canon N. S. Power, MA, Lady wood Vicarage, Birmingham – 8 July 1973 (Letter published in *Mallorn*, 9, 1975, p. 19).
S.s.: Scull-Hammond (2017a), p. 739.
Reading period: 1908 – early 1910 (S.s.: Scull-Hammond (2017c), p. 1054).

2080. Shub, Elizabeth. *An Adventure in Translation*. Boston: The Horn Book, 1971.
Description: Inscribed on front cover: 'J.R.R. T.' Contains annotations on title page and page 336 of index. Includes a label added by Stan Revell to books owned by Tolkien, 'From the Library of J.R.R. Tolkien', on slip inserted prior to title page.
Collection: Marion E. Wade Center, Wheaton College (Wheaton, Illinois).

2081. Sidgwick, Arthur. *Introduction to Greek prose composition; with exercises*. Boston: Ginn and Company, 1902.
Description: Inscribed by Tolkien with many youthful variants of his signature and accompanying dates: 'J.R.R. Tolkien | Class II KEMS | January 22. 1909'. [KEMS is King Edward's Musical Society]. On front flyleaf: 'e. coll: | exon: oxon 1911 | tandem A. G. Cox e Coll. Vig. Oxon'. In following page, thre different autographs with indicated King's Edward Class. Dates between September 1907 and January 1910. Inscribed a Notes: 'K.E.M.S. January 1907'.
Collection: Private [Bonhams, 13 Nov. 2012].

2082. Sidney, Philip. *Astrophel and Stella*.
S.s.: University of Leeds (1920), p. 147. English Language and Literature - Scheme A. Texts and Period selected for 1920-21. (b) Special period: 1557-1637. (c) Texts suggested for study with Special Period. Ordinary Degree of B.A. with Honours. Final Examination.

2083. _____. *Defence of Poesy: or, An apology for poetry*. Edited by Albert Feuillerat. Cambridge: The University Press, 1912.
S.s. 1: University of Leeds (1920), p. 147. English Language and Literature - Scheme A. Texts and Period selected for 1920-21. (b) Special period: 1557-1637. (c) Texts suggested for study with Special Period. Ordinary Degree of B.A. with Honours. Final Examination.
S.s. 2: University of Leeds (1921), p. 154. English Language and Literature - Scheme A. Texts and Period selected for 1921-22. (e) History of Criticism: Special Texts suggested for study. Ordinary Degree of B.A. with Honours. Final Examinations.
S.s. 3: Scull-Hammond (2017a), p. 77.

2084. Sievers, Eduard. *Abriss der Angelsächsischen Grammatik*. Halle: Max Niemeyer, 1895.
P.s. 1: MS. Tolkien A 21/13 fol. 119. Note by Tolkien, 'Books in Exeter Library useful', with shelfmarks, on back of photostat reading list dated October 1913. [Tolkien Papers, Bodleian Library, Oxford].
P.s. 2: MS. Tolkien A 12/3 *Rough text of a lecture on Sir Gawain*, 1965 fol. 70. [Tolkien Papers, Bodleian Library, Oxford].

2085. _____. *Altgermanische Metrik*. Series: Sammlung kurzer Grammatiken germanischer Dialekte, B., Ergänzungsreihe, 2. Halle: Max Niemeyer, 1893.
Collection: Exeter College, Oxford.
P.s. 1: MS. Tolkien A 21/13 fol. 119. Note by Tolkien, 'Books in Exeter Library useful', with shelfmarks, on back of photostat reading list dated October 1913. [Tolkien Papers, Bodleian Library, Oxford].
P.s. 2: *Beowulf* (2002) 'Version B', p. 103.
S.s.: Simmonet (2014).

2086. _____. *An Old English Grammar*. Boston and Co.,1903.
Description: Exeter College. Inscribed: 'John Reuel Tolkien | Exeter Coll. Oxford. | ex libris Coll. de litt and phil German' [Judith Priestman 1994, revd. 2016].
Collection: Weston Library, Bodleian Libraries (Oxford).

2087. _____. 'Zu Codex Junius XI'. Beiträge zur Geschichte der älteren Deutschen Litteratur, Vol. X. Bonn: E. Weber, 1855, pp. 195-99.
P.s.: *The Old English Exodus* (1982), p. x.

2088. _____ (Edited by). *Germanica: Eduard Sievers zum 75. Geburtstage*. Halle: Max Niemeyer, 1925.
P.s.: *Philology: General Works* (VI 1927, for 1925), p. 32 n. 3, 36-39, 43.

2089. _____. *Grundzüge der Phonetik zur Einführung in das Studium der Lautlehre der Indogermanischen Sprachen*. Leipzig: Breitkopf and Härtel, 1885 (3rd ed.).
Collection: The Science Fiction and Fantasy Research Collection of the Cushing Memorial Library and Archives at Texas A&M University.

2090. _____. 'Zur Rhythmik des germanischen alliterationsverses'. *Beiträge zur Geschichte der älteren Deutschen Literatur*, Vol. X. Bonn: E. Webber, 1885, pp. 451-545.
P.s.: *The Old English Exodus* (1982), p. x.

2091. _____. *Ziele und Wege der Schallanalyse*. Series: Germanische Bibliothek.

Heidelberg: Carl Winter, 1924.
:::
Description: On this book, Cecil Lewis of the Lincoln College, Oxford, sent to Tolkien a letter dated July 5, 1926 (Collection: Private: Oronzo Cilli).
P.s.: *Philology: General Works* (V 1926, for 1924), p. 40.
:::

2092. _____ and Karl Brunner. *Altenglische Grammatik nach der angelsächsisches Grammatik*. Halle: Max Niemeyer, 1942.
:::
P.s.: *The Old English Exodus* (1982), p. x.
:::

2093. Sigart, Joseph Désiré. *Glossaire étymologique montois; ou, Dictionnaire du Wallon de Mons et de la plus grande partie du Hainaut*. Bruxelles: F. Claassen, 1870.
:::
NED: #2 h. | 'W' (1928), p. 53 'Wallop'.
:::

2094. Sigurðsson, Jón and Jón Þorkelsson for Íslenska Bókmenntafélag. *Diplomatarium Islandicum: Íslenzkt Fornbréfasafn, sem hefir inni a halda bréf og gjörninga, dóma og máldaga, og arar skrár, er snerta Ísland eða íslenzka Menn*, Vol. I 834 – 1264 Kaupmannohöfn. Reykjavik: Kaupmannahöfn Reykjavík Fél. prentsmiðjan, 1857-76.
:::
Description: Bound in contemporary half calf. With the bookplate of the historian Charles Plummer. This book belonged to Charles Plummer and was bought by J.R.R. Tolkien. Tolkien's note reads in ink: 'bt from. | by J.R.R. Tolkien'. Loosely inserted are a couple of scraps of paper with notes by Tolkien. Loose leaves: 'The appearance of the _Ethiopians_ at this point in the account is clearly, in part at least, due to a comparison of Psalm lxxiii with the book of Exodus. It is probable too that v. 16 of the psalm ('The day is thine, the night also is thine: thou hast prepared the light and the sun') was brought into relation with the mention, in Exod. xiii 21, of the pillars of cloud and fire immediately after _Etham_.' | ' _byrig_ is probably plural, as noted above: 'the cities of the region of Etham'. See quot. in note p. 32. In any case, of course, _Etham_ (_Æthan_) is taken not as a city or place, but a region; _Æthanes byrig_ in O.E. does not mean 'the city of Etham', where city = Etham, but 'the city belonging to or in Etham'.' | '67 _mearelandum ón ...:_ a good example of a manuscript accent indicating emphasis and stress (here properly borne by the 'postponed' _on_ in archaic word order) and not quantity. The words render _in extremis finibus solitudinis_. [Vulgate Exodus 13:20]' | '68 _nearwe genyddon ...:_ it is a little difficult to interpret these words with'.
Collection: Private [TolkienLibrary.com, Sold on Ebay 17 July 2012].
:::

2095. Sijmons, Barend and Hugo Gering. *Kommentar zu den Lieder der Edda*, Vol. I. Series: Germanistische Handbibliothek, 7, 3, 2. Halle: Saale Das Waisenhaus, 1927.
:::
P.s.: *Sigelwara land* (1934), p. 104 n. 2.
:::

2096. _____. *Kommentar zu den Lieder der Edda*, Vol. II. Series: Germanistische Handbibliothek, 7, 3, 2. Halle: Saale Das Waisenhaus, 1931.
:::
P.s.: *Sigelwara land* (1934), p. 104 n. 2.
:::

2097. *Sinners Beware*. [Homiletic poem, see R. Morris].
:::
P.s.: MS. Tolkien A 21/7 fol. 43. [Tolkien Papers, Bodleian Library, Oxford].
:::

2098. *Sir Eglamour of Artois* [Middle English verse romance, see Halliwell-Phillipps]
:::
P.s.: 'Chaucer as a Philologist: *The Reeve's Tale*' (1934), p. 139. Tolkien quotes: 'as wyght as any roo' (261).
:::

2099. *Sir Gawain and the Green Knight* [Middle English romance].
:::
For editions and translations of this poem, see Gollancz, Jones (Gwyn), Madden, Morris R., Tolkien and Gordon E. V., Tolkien.
P.s. 1: MS. Tolkien A 28/B Commentary on *Beowulf*, delivered as lectures at Oxford, fol. 169. [Tolkien Papers, Bodleian Library, Oxford].
:::

P.s. 2: *Foreword to A New Glossary of the Dialect of Huddersfield District* (1928), p. xvi.
P.s. 3: 'Chaucer as a Philologist: *The Reeve's Tale*' (1934), p. 143.
P.s. 4: *Letters* 25 (1938) To the editor of the *Observer*. Tolkien writes: '*Beowulf* is among my most valued sources'.
P.s. 5: *Letters* 61 (1944) From a letter to Christopher Tolkien. Tolkien writes: 'If the censor (and you) will permit me to quote an ancient English poet – and I can't help thinking it comes better from father to son, than from young Beowulf, about your age, to old greybeard Hrothgar!'
P.s. 6: *Letters* 92 (1944) From a letter to Christopher Tolkien. Tolkien writes: 'I have been getting a lot of new ideas about Prehistory lately (via *Beowulf* and other sources of which I may have written) and want to work them into the long shelved time-travel story I began.'
P.s. 7: *Letters* 122 (1949). To Naomi Mitchison.
P.s. 8: *Letters* 156 (1954) To Robert Murray, SJ. (draft)
P.s. 9: *Letters* 183 (1956) Notes on W. H. Auden's review of *The Return of the King*
P.s. 10: *Letters* 235 (1961) From a letter to Mrs Pauline Gasch (Pauline Baynes). Tolkien writes: '*iúmonna gold galdre bewunden*', 'the gold of men of long ago enmeshed in enchantment' (3052).
P.s. 11: *Letters* 236 (1961) To Rayner Unwin. Tolkien writes: 'In all Old English poetry 'elves' (ylfe) occurs once only, in *Beowulf*, associated with trolls, giants, and the Undead, as the accursed offspring of Cain.'
P.s. 12: *Letters* 289 (1966) From a letter to Michael George Tolkien. Tolkien writes: [*Mirkwood*] 'or rather *gloomy*, only in *Beowulf* 1405 *ofer myrcan mor*: elsewhere only with the sense *murky* > wicked, hellish'.
P.s. 13: *Tolkien On Fairy-stories* (2008), pp. 33, 83.
P.s. 14: *Tolkien On Fairy-stories* (2008) 'Manuscript A. [MS Tolkien 4, fols. 59-77]', p. 184.
P.s. 15: *Tolkien On Fairy-stories* (2008) 'Manuscript B [MS. Tolkien 4, fols. 73-120]', p. 227.
P.s. 16: *The Fall of Arthur* (2013), p. 19, vv. 44-50. Christopher Tolkien writes: 'Several of these knights appear in *Sir Gawain and the Green Knight*: Lionel, Bors, Bedivere, Errac, Iwain son of Urien (in my father's translation, stanzas 6 and 24)' [p. 61].
P.s. 17: *Beowulf* (2014), p. 190. Tolkien quotes: 'Now wyl I of hor seruise ... wont þat þer were' (130-1); pp. 280-81. Tolkien quotes: 'If ȝe wyl lysten þis ... hatȝ ben longe' (30-6).
S.s. 1: University of Leeds (1923), pp. 135-37. Hb3. (Scheme A and B) Second and Third Year: Thursday 12.00: (i) Third Year: Middle English Texts (*Sir Gawain and the Green Knight*).
S.s. 2: Scull-Hammond (2017a), p.135. Leeds academic year 1924-1925. Tolkien teaches Middle English Texts (*Sir Gawain and the Green Knight*) on Thursdays at 12.00 noon.

2100. *Sir Orfeo* [Middle English romance].
For editions and translations of this poem, see Bliss, Tolkien.

2101. *Sir Tristram,* 1230. [Middle English romance, see Zupitza].
P.s. 1: MS. Tolkien A 21/13 The English MSS. fol. 203. [Tolkien Papers, Bodleian Library, Oxford].
P.s. 2: 'Chaucer as a Philologist: *The Reeve's Tale*' (1934), p. 137. Tolkien quotes: 'þe king biheld þat old, Hou his wonges were wcte.' (732).

2102. Sisam, Celia. 'The Scribal Tradition of the Lambeth Homilies'. *The Review of English Studies*, Vol. 2, N.E., no. 6. London: Oxford University Press, April 1951, pp. 105-13.
Description: Article related to her B.Litt. thesis [C. 5]. With Tolkien's detailed corrections, some in pen, some in pencil, on the first 8 pp. ALS from Sisam to Tolkien loosely inserted. Uundated: 'Dear Professor Tolkien, Here are the proofs of my article – the spare copy – so that you can see the worst before it is published ... I hope the new house turns out well. It was nice of you to see me in the middle of moving in. yours sincerely, Celia Sisam'.
Collection: Private [Sold by Loome Theological Booksellers, 1993]
S.s.: Scull-Hammond (2017a), p. 383.

2103. Sisam, Kenneth. 'Mss. Bodley 340 and 342: Ælfric's Catholic Homilies'. *The Review of English Studies*, Vol. 8, no. 29. London: Oxford University Press, January 1932, pp. 51-68.
P.s.: *Sigelwara land* (1932), p. 187 n. 5.

2104. _____. 'Mss. Bodley 340 and 342: Ælfric's Catholic Homilies'. *The Review of English Studies*, Vol. 9, no. 33. London: Oxford University Press, January 1933, pp. 1-12.

P.s.: Tolkien annotated on page 63 of the *Specimens of Early English* by Richard Morris [A. 1663]: 'Sisam Rev. of. Eng. Studies. – Vol. 9. pp. 1-12'.

2105. _____. 'The Cædmonian Exodus 492'. MLN (*Modern Language Notes*), Vol. 32, no. 1. January, 1917.
P.s.: *The Old English Exodus* (1982), p. 73.

2106. _____. *Cynewulf and his poetry*. Sir Israel Gollancz Memorial Lecture, British Academy 1932. Series: Proceedings of the British Academy, 18. London: Milford, 1932.
P.s.: *Sigelwara land* (1934), p. 99 n. 2.

2107. _____ (Edited by). *Fourteenth Century Verse and Prose*. Oxford: At the Clarendon Press, 1921.
Description: Inscribed: 'J.R.R. Tolkien | Oct. 1921 | from the C. Press'. A few annotations, notes (for review?) on back endpaper and pastedown. Loose leaves [Judith Priestman 1994, revd. 2016].
Collection: Weston Library, Bodleian Libraries (Oxford).
Notes: Sisam writes: 'to Mr. J.R.R. Tolkien who has undertaken the preparation of the Glossary, the most exacting part of the apparatus' (p. xliii).
P.s. 1: MS. Res. e. 308 *Sir Gawain and the Green Knight*. [Tolkien Papers, Bodleian Library, Oxford].
P.s. 2: MS. Tolkien A 12/2 *Commentary on Sir Gawain, lines 1999-2523* fol. 33. [Tolkien Papers, Bodleian Library, Oxford].
P.s. 3: *Sir Gawain and the Green Knight* (1925), p. xxv; p. 99, line 1049 *toun*. Tolkien and Gordon quote 'Lenten ys come wiþ loue to toune' (B. Spring, MS. Harley 2253, line 1, p. 164) [Tolkien and Gordon cite Sisam's *Fourteenth Century Prose and Verse* instead of the correct title *Fourteenth Century Verse and Prose* in *Sir Gawain* editions: 1925, 1930, 1936, 1946, 1949, 1960, 1969.]
P.s. 4: *Sigelwara land* (1932), p. 185 n. 1.
S.s. 1: University of Leeds, *Calendar 1923-24*, p. 94. English Language and Literature. Scheme A. Degree of B.A. with Honours. Texts and Period selected for 1923-24 (a). General reading. Especially extracts i, ii, iii, vi, viii, ix, x, xia, xiii, xiv, xv, xvii.
S.s. 2: Ollscoil na h-Éireann G 259 (1949): *The Blacksmiths*, British Museum MS. Arundel 292 (about 1425-50), f. 71 b.

2108. _____ (Edited by). *Fourteenth Century Verse and Prose*. Glossary by J.R.R. Tolkien. Oxford: At the Clarendon Press, 1922.
Description: Bound with J.R.R. Tolkien *A Middle English Vocabulary*. Inscribed: 'J.R.R. Tolkien | From the C. P.' A few annotations, notes (see'sir Orpheo') amd notes on the *Vocabulary*. Loose leaves (letter from Sisam) [Judith Priestman 1994, revd. 2016].
Collection: Weston Library, Bodleian Libraries (Oxford).

2109. Skeat, Walter William. *A Concise Etymological Dictionary of the English Language*. Oxford: At the Clarendon Press, 1924.
P.s.: *Philology: General Works* (V 1926, for 1924), p. 50.

2110. _____. *Early English proverbs, chiefly of the thirteenth and fourteenth centuries, with illustrative quotations*. Oxford: At the Clarendon Press, 1910.
P.s.: MS. Res. e. 308 *Sir Gawain and the Green Knight*. [Tolkien Papers, Bodleian Library, Oxford].

2111. _____. *The Holy Gospels in Anglo-Saxon, Northumbrian, and Old Mercian versions, synoptically arranged: with collations exhibiting all the readings of all the MSS.: together with the early Latin version as contained in the Lindisfarne MS., collated with the Latin version in the Rushworth MS.*, Vol. I. St Matthew. Cambridge: The University Press, 1871.

P.s.: MS. Tolkien A 21/13 fol. 119. Note by Tolkien, 'Books in Exeter Library useful', with shelfmarks, on back of photostat reading list dated October 1913. [Tolkien Papers, Bodleian Library, Oxford].

2112. _____. *The Holy Gospels in Anglo-Saxon, Northumbrian, and Old Mercian versions, synoptically arranged: with collations exhibiting all the readings of all the MSS.: together with the early Latin version as contained in the Lindisfarne MS., collated with the Latin version in the Rushworth MS.*, Vol. II. St Mark. Cambridge: The University Press, 1871.
    P.s.: MS. Tolkien A 21/13 fol. 119. Note by Tolkien, 'Books in Exeter Library useful', with shelfmarks, on back of photostat reading list dated October 1913. [Tolkien Papers, Bodleian Library, Oxford].

2113. _____. *The Holy Gospels in Anglo-Saxon, Northumbrian, and Old Mercian versions, synoptically arranged: with collations exhibiting all the readings of all the MSS.: together with the early Latin version as contained in the Lindisfarne MS., collated with the Latin version in the Rushworth MS.*, Vol. III. St Luke. Cambridge: The University Press, 1874.
    P.s. 1: MS. Tolkien A 21/13 fol. 119. Note by Tolkien, 'Books in Exeter Library useful', with shelfmarks, on back of photostat reading list dated October 1913. [Tolkien Papers, Bodleian Library, Oxford].
    P.s. 2: 'Middle English 'Losenger'' (1953), p. 68 n. 1. Tolkien writes: 'in the Gothic Gospel of St. Luke we find lausjan used = to exact a tax-payment.'

2114. _____. *The Holy Gospels in Anglo-Saxon, Northumbrian, and Old Mercian versions, synoptically arranged: with collations exhibiting all the readings of all the MSS.: together with the early Latin version as contained in the Lindisfarne MS., collated with the Latin version in the Rushworth MS.*, Vol. IV. St John. Cambridge: The University Press, 1878.
    P.s.: MS. Tolkien A 21/13 fol. 119. Note by Tolkien, 'Books in Exeter Library useful', with shelfmarks, on back of photostat reading list dated October 1913. [Tolkien Papers, Bodleian Library, Oxford].

2115. _____ (Edited by). *Lancelot of the Laik: a Scottish metrical romance (about 1490-1500 A.D.)*. Edited by Walter W. Skeat. Series: E.E.T.S. (Early English Text Society), OS 6. London: Published for the Early English Text Society by Kegan Paul, Trench, Trübner and Co., 1870 (2nd rev.).
    Notes: In composite volume with: *Story of Genesis and Exodus* E.E.T.S. 7, 1865 [A. 1661] and *The Minor Poems of William Lauder* E.E.T.S. 41, 1870 [A. 1309].
    Description: Inscribed on back of front flyleaf by JRRT: 'EETS 0.S.3. (Lauder) 7 (Gen and Ex)'. And inscribed below, half rubbed out, the signature in pencil: 'W. Marty[n]'. Autographed and marked on next page: 'Leeds | October 1921'. Contents listed before half title page of first iten by JRRT. Annotated in pencil.
    Collection: Tolkien's personal Celtic library, preserved at the Weston library under the auspices of the English Faculty Library (Oxford).
    P.s.: MS. Tolkien A 21/13 fol. 119. Note by Tolkien, 'Books in Exeter Library useful', with shelfmarks, on back of photostat reading list dated October 1913. Tolkien writes: 'All EETS publications'. [Tolkien Papers, Bodleian Library, Oxford].

2116. _____ (Edited by). *The Lay of Havelok the Dane*. London: Kegan Paul Trench & Trübner & Co., 1868.
    Description: Signed 'J R R Tolkien bud. Sept. 1919'.
    Collection: Private [Sold by Simon Finch Rare Books Ltd.].
    S.s.: Finch (2002), p. 53.

SECTION A

2117. _____ (Edited by). *The Lay of Havelok the Dane*. Oxford: At the Clarendon Press, 1902.
> Description: Exeter College. Inscribed: 'John Reuel Tolkien. | coll. exon oxon. | April 1913. | ex libris de phil. germ. collect.' A few annotations [Judith Priestman 1994, revd. 2016].
> Collection: Weston Library, Bodleian Libraries (Oxford).

2118. _____ (Edited by). *The Lay of Havelok the Dane*. Revised by Kenneth Sisam. Oxford: At the Clarendon Press, 1915 (2nd ed.).
> Description: Exeter College. Inscribed: 'J.R.R. Tolkien. | Exeter Coll. 2/5/19'. Annotated throughout; some not by Tolkien. Loose leaf [Judith Priestman 1994, revd. 2016].
> Collection: Weston Library, Bodleian Libraries (Oxford).

2119. _____ (Edited by). *The Lay of Havelok the Dane*. Revised by Kenneth Sisam. Oxford: At the Clarendon Press, 1923.
> P.s.: MS. Res. e. 308 *Sir Gawain and the Green Knight*. [Tolkien Papers, Bodleian Library, Oxford].

2120. _____ (Edited by). *The Proverbs of Alfred*. Oxford: At the Clarendon Press, 1907.
> P.s. 1: MS. Res. e. 308 *Sir Gawain and the Green Knight*. [Tolkien Papers, Bodleian Library, Oxford].
> P.s. 2: *Finn and Hengest* (1982), p. 119 n. 61.

2121. _____ (Edited by). *The romance of William of Palerne: (otherwise known as the romance of 'William and the werwolf')*. Series: E.E.T.S. (Early English Text Society), ES 1. London: Published for the Early English Text Society, by N. Trübner & Co., 1867.
> P.s. 1: MS. Tolkien A 12/1 *Commentary on Sir Gawain, lines 37-1987* fol. 2. Tolkien quotes: 'ȝifter-neue' (2160). [Tolkien Papers, Bodleian Library, Oxford].
> P.s. 2: MS. Tolkien A 12/2 *Commentary on Sir Gawain, lines 1999-2523* fol. 33. [Tolkien Papers, Bodleian Library, Oxford].
> P.s. 3: MS. Tolkien A 21/13 fol. 119. Note by Tolkien, 'Books in Exeter Library useful', with shelfmarks, on back of photostat reading list dated October 1913. Tolkien writes: 'All EETS publications'. [Tolkien Papers, Bodleian Library, Oxford].
> P.s. 4: *Sir Gawain and the Green Knight* (1967) 'Select Bibliography: editions of texts quoted more than once in the notes', p. 156.

2122. _____. *A rough list of English words found in Anglo-French, especially during the thirteenth and fourteenth centuries: with numerous references*. London: Published for the Philological Society by Trübner & Co., 1882.
> P.s.: MS. Tolkien A 21/13 fol. 119. Note by Tolkien, 'Books in Exeter Library useful', with shelfmarks, on back of photostat reading list dated October 1913. [Tolkien Papers, Bodleian Library, Oxford].

2123. _____ (Edited with notes and a glossarial index by). *The tale of Gamelyn. From the Harleian MS. no. 7334, collated with six other MSS*. Oxford: At the Clarendon Press, 1884.
> P.s. 1: MS. Res. e. 308 *Sir Gawain and the Green Knight*. [Tolkien Papers, Bodleian Library, Oxford].
> P.s. 2: 'Chaucer as a Philologist: *The Reeve's Tale*' (1934), p. 136.
> P.s. 3: 'Nomenclature of *The Lord of the Rings*' (1966), p. 758 '*Gamling (the Old)*.'

2124. _____ (Edited by). *The wars of Alexander*. Series: E.E.T.S. (Early English Text Society), ES 47. London: Published for the Early English Text Society by Kegan Paul, Trench, Trübner and Co., 1886.

P.s. 1: MS. Tolkien A 21/13 fol. 119. Note by Tolkien, 'Books in Exeter Library useful', with shelfmarks, on back of photostat reading list dated October 1913. Tolkien writes: 'All EETS publications'. [Tolkien Papers, Bodleian Library, Oxford].
P.s. 2: MS. Tolkien A 11 *Notes on Pearl* fols. 40-1. [Tolkien Papers, Bodleian Library, Oxford].
P.s. 3: MS. Tolkien A 12/2 *Commentary on Sir Gawain, lines 1999-2523* fol. 33. [Tolkien Papers, Bodleian Library, Oxford].
P.s. 4: *Sir Gawain and Green Knight* (1925), p. 96, line 847; p. 112, line 1964.
P.s. 5: Foreword to *A New Glossary of the Dialect of Huddersfield District* (1928), p. xvi.
P.s. 6: *Sir Gawain and Green Knight* (1930 2nd ed.), p. 111, line 1853 *hapel under heuer.*
P.s. 7: 'Chaucer as a Philologist: *The Reeve's Tale*' (1934), p. 143.
P.s. 8: *Sir Gawain and the Green Knight* (1967) 'Select Bibliography: editions of texts quoted more than once in the notes', p. 156.

2125. Skelton, John. *Magnyfycence*.
P.s.: MS. Tolkien A 11 *Notes on Pearl* fol. 124. Tolkien cites 'I wolde haunke whylest my hede dyd warke' (v. 1581). [Tolkien Papers, Bodleian Library, Oxford].

2126. _____. *Phyllyp Sparowe*.
P.s.: *Oxford University Press Archives* (Oxford). A slip written by Tolkien on the etymology of 'Wake' used ('W' p. 31) [A. 1721].
NED: #2 f. | 'W' (1928), p. 31 'Wake, 3.' 1529 – 'The gose and the gander, The ducke and the drake, Shall watche at this wake' (vv. 435-7).

2127. Small, Andrew. *Interesting Roman antiquities recently discovered in Fife ascertaining the site of the great battle fought betwixt Agricola and Galgacus; with the discovery of the position of five Roman towns, and of the site and names of upwards of seventy Roman forts: also observations regarding the ancient palaces of the Pictish kings in the town of Abernethy, and other local antiquities.* Edinburgh: Printed for the author and sold by J. Anderson, 1823.
P.s.: *Sir Gawain and the Green Knight* (1925), p. xxvi. Tolkien and Gordon write: 'For bibliography of the Irish and French analogues of *Sir Gawain*, see the bibliography in Kittredge's study'. [*NED*] In Kittredge's study, this article is mentioned in 'XIII. Rauf Coilyear' (p. 306).

2128. Smith, Albert Hugh. *English Place-Name Elements*, Pt. I. Introduction Bibliography The Elements A-IW, Maps. Series: English Place-Name Society, 25. Cambridge: The University Press, 1956.
P.s.: *Sir Gawain and the Green Knight* (1967) 'Select Bibliography', p. 154.

2129. _____. *English Place-Name Elements*, Pt. II. The Elements JAFN-YTRI Index and Maps. Series: English Place-Name Society, 26. Cambridge: The University Press, 1956.
P.s.: *Sir Gawain and the Green Knight* (1967) 'Select Bibliography', p. 154.

2130. _____. *The place-names of the East Riding of Yorkshire and York*. Series: English Place-Name Society, 14. Cambrdge: The University Press, 1937.
P.s.: MS. Tolkien A 12/1 *Commentary on Sir Gawain, lines 37-1987* fol. 53. [Tolkien Papers, Bodleian Library, Oxford].

2131. _____. *The place-names of the North Riding of Yorkshire*. Series: English Place-Name Society, 5. Nottingham: English Place Name Society, 1928.
P.s.: 'Chaucer as a Philologist: *The Reeve's Tale*' (1934), p. 168 n. 92.

2132. _____. *The place-names of Gloucestershire*, Vol. XXXVIII, Pt. I. River and Road-Names; The East Cotswolds. Cambridge: The University Press, 1964.
P.s.: *Letters* 324 (1971). From a letter to Graham Tayar.

Section A

2133. _____. *The place-names of Gloucestershire*, Vol. XXXIX, Pt. II. The North and West Cotswolds. Cambridge: The University Press, 1964.
P.s.: *Letters* 324 (1971). From a letter to Graham Tayar.

2134. _____. *The place-names of Gloucestershire*, Vol. XL, Pt. III. The Lower Seven Valley and the Forest of Dean. Cambridge: The University Press, 1964.
P.s.: *Letters* 324 (1971). From a letter to Graham Tayar.

2135. _____. *The place-names of Gloucestershire*, Vol. XLI, Pt. IV. Introduction. Cambridge: The University Press, 1965.
P.s.: *Letters* 324 (1971). From a letter to Graham Tayar.

2136. _____. 'The place-names Jervaulx, Ure, and York'. *Anglia, Zeitschrift fur englische Philologie*, Vol. XLVIII (N. F. 36), pp. 291-96. Berlin: W. De Gruyte, 1924.
P.s.: *Philology: General Works* (V 1926, for 1924), p. 55.

2137. _____. 'Some place-names and the Etymology of *She*'. *The Review of English Studies*, Vol. I. London: Sidgwick & Jackson, October 1925, pp. 437-40.
P.s.: *Philology: General Works* (VI 1927, for 1925), p. 52.

2138. _____ and John Leslie Noble O'Loughlin. *Odhams dictionary of the English language*. London: Odhams Books, 1965.
P.s.: Tolkien's unpublished letter to O'Loughlin, 30 October 1965. Tolkien has read article by O'Loughlin, which he finds plausible, but does not have time to comment on it in detail.

2139. Smith, Charlotte Turner. *The young philosopher: A Novel*, Vol. I.
P.s.: *Oxford University Press Archives* (Oxford). In a slip written by Tolkien on the etymology of 'Waistcoated' not used, and reads: '(waistcoated) | 2. Comb. esp. white-waistcoated: | Weaning a white waistcoat, also applied to | birds with white plumage on the beast'.
NED: #2 b. | 'W' (1928), p. 23 'Waistcoated, *a.*' 1798 – 'He ... was pantalooned and waistcoated after the very newest fashion.'

2140. Smith, David Nichol. *Characters from the histories and memoirs of the seventeenth century*. Oxford: At the Clarendon Press, 1920.
S.s. 1: University of Leeds (1920), p. 139 English Language and Literature: English Literature. Text selected for 1920-21. Texts Selected for 1920-21. Ordinary Degree of B.A. with Honours. Final Course and Examination; p. 147. English Language and Literature - Scheme A. Texts and Period selected for 1920-21. (b) Special period: 1557-1637. (c) Texts suggested for study with Special Period. Ordinary Degree of B.A. with Honours. Final Examination. Extracts Nos. 1-18.
S.s. 2: University of Leeds (1921), p. 154. English Language and Literature - Scheme A. Texts and Period selected for 1921-22. (d) Texts suggested for study with Special Period 1637-1700. Ordinary Degree of B.A. with Honours. Final Examinations; p. 155. English Language and Literature - Scheme B. Texts for 1921-22. (d) Outlines of the History of English Literature. Ordinary Degree of B.A. with Honours. Final Examinations.

2141. Smith, George Gregory. *Elizabethan Critical Essays*, Vol. I. Oxford: At the Clarendon Press, 1904.
S.s.: University of Leeds (1920), p. 147. English Language and Literature - Scheme A. Texts and Period selected for 1920-21. (b) Special period: 1557-1637. (c) Texts suggested for study with Special Period. Ordinary Degree of B.A. with Honours. Final Examination. Extracts: Spenser-Harvey Correspondence 1579-80.

2142. _____. *Specimens of Middle Scots*. London: W. Blackwood and Sons, 1902.
Description: Autographed on front flyleaf: 'John Reuel Tolkien. | Exeter Coll. | March 1914'.

Collection: The Fellows' Library, Jesus College (Oxford).

2143. Smith, Logan Pearsall. *The English language*. Series: Home University Library of Modern Knowledge. London: William and Norgate, 1912.
> S.s. 1: University of Leeds (1920), p. 180. English Language and Literature. Int. 2 Intermediate Course (Composition). Text-books recommended.
> S.s. 2: University of Leeds (1921), p. 190 English Language and Literature. Int. 2 Intermediate Course (Composition).

2144. _____. *Words and Idioms: Studies in the English Language*. London: Constable & Co., 1925.
> P.s.: *Philology: General Works* (VI 1927, for 1925), p. 58 n. 17. Tolkien cites the chapters 'English Words Abroad' And 'Four Romantic Words'.

2145. Smith, Lucy Toulmin (Edited by). *York Plays: The Plays Performed by the Crafts Or Mysteries of York, on the Day of Corpus Christi in the 14th and 16th centuries*. Oxford: At the Clarendon Press, 1885.
> P.s. 1: MS. Res. e. 308 *Sir Gawain and the Green Knight*. [Tolkien Papers, Bodleian Library, Oxford].
> P.s. 2: 'Chaucer as a Philologist: *The Reeve's Tale*' (1934), pp. 135; 138. Tolkien quotes: 'Thy wordis makis me my wangges to wete.' (x, 275).

2146. Smith, Thomas. *De recta et emendata linguae anglicae scriptione Dialogus.* (1568). Edited by Otto Deibel. Halle: Max Niemeyer, 1913.
> Description: Tolkien added his calligraphic fountain pen signature, 'JRR Tolkien' below this, followed by, 'from E.V. Gordon. | April | 1933' adding his three-dot symbol beneath the date. The fountain pen signature and note were written over an earlier, faded signature and note in pencil, also in Tolkien's hand: 'JRR Tolkien | From EVG | 1933 | .' [EVG = Eric Valentine Gordon].
> Collection: Private [Pieter Collier].

2147. Smith, William. *Latin-English Dictionary: Based Upon the Works of Forcellini and Freund*. London: John Murray, 1857.
> Description: Inscribed on the title page with: 'John Ronald Reuel Tolkien'. And the initials and date written underneath: 'K.E.S 1908'.
> Collection: Special Collections, Liverpool Hope University (Liverpool).

2148. Solano, E. John (Edited by). *Signalling: Morse, Semaphore, Station Work, Despatch Riding, Telephone Cables, Map Reading*. London: John Murray, 1915.
> S.s.: Scull-Hammond (2017a), p. 79. Tolkien, who served as a signals officer, studied this book in 1915.

2149. Sommer, Heinrich Oskar. *The Vulgate version of the Arthurian romances*, Vol. I. *Lestoire del Saint Graal*. Series: Carnegie institution of Washington, 74. Washington: The Carnegie institution of Washington, 1909.
> P.s. 1: *Sir Gawain and the Green Knight* (1925), p. 89, line 552 *Doddinaual de Sauage*. Tolkien and Gordon write: 'according to *Lestoire de Merlin* and *Le Roman de Lancelot* (the so-called Vulgate versions edited by Dr Sommer) the duke of Clarence was named Galshin, cousin, according to the former, brother, according to the latter, of Sir Dodinel'.
> P.s. 2: *Sir Gawain and the Green Knight* (1967) 'Select Bibliography', p. 155.

2150. _____. *The Vulgate version of the Arthurian romances*, Vol. II. Lestoire de Merlin. Series: Carnegie institution of Washington, 74. Washington: The Carnegie institution of Washington, 1909.
> P.s. 1: *Sir Gawain and the Green Knight* (1925), p. 89, line 552 *Doddinaual de Sauage* [A. 2149].
> P.s. 2: *Sir Gawain and the Green Knight* (1967) 'Select Bibliography', p. 155.

Section A

2151. _____. *The Vulgate version of the Arthurian romances*, Vol. III, Pt. I. Le Livre de Lancelot du Lac. Series: Carnegie institution of Washington, 74. Washington: The Carnegie institution of Washington, 1910.
   P.s. 1: *Sir Gawain and the Green Knight* (1925), p. 89, line 552 *Doddinaual de Sauage* [A. 2149].
   P.s. 2: *Sir Gawain and the Green Knight* (1967) 'Select Bibliography', p. 155.

2152. _____. *The Vulgate version of the Arthurian romances*, Vol. IV, Pt. II. Le Livre de Lancelot du Lac. Series: Carnegie institution of Washington, 74. Washington: The Carnegie institution of Washington, 1911.
   P.s. 1: *Sir Gawain and the Green Knight* (1925), p. 89, line 552 *Doddinaual de Sauage* [A. 2149]; p. 116, line 2460. Tolkien and Gordon cite p. 124.
   P.s. 2: *Sir Gawain and the Green Knight* (1967) 'Select Bibliography', p. 155.

2153. _____. *The Vulgate version of the Arthurian romances*, Vol. V, Pt. III. Le Livre de Lancelot du Lac. Series: Carnegie institution of Washington, 74. Washington: The Carnegie institution of Washington, 1912.
   P.s. 1: *Sir Gawain and the Green Knight* (1925), p. 89, line 552 *Doddinaual de Sauage* [A. 2149].
   P.s. 2: *Sir Gawain and the Green Knight* (1967) 'Select Bibliography', p. 155.

2154. _____. *The Vulgate version of the Arthurian romances*, Vol. VI. Les aventures ou la queste del Saint Graal. La mort le roi Artus. Series: Carnegie institution of Washington, 74. Washington: The Carnegie institution of Washington, 1913.
   P.s. 1: *Sir Gawain and the Green Knight* (1925), p. 89, line 552 *Doddinaual de Sauage* [A. 2149].
   P.s. 2: *Sir Gawain and the Green Knight* (1967) 'Select Bibliography', p. 155.

2155. _____. *The Vulgate version of the Arthurian romances*, Vol. VII. Supplement: Le livre d'Artus, with glossary. Series: Carnegie institution of Washington, 74. Washington: The Carnegie institution of Washington, 1913.
   P.s. 1: MS. Tolkien A 12/2 *Commentary on Sir Gawain, lines 1999-2523* fol. 54. [Tolkien Papers, Bodleian Library, Oxford].
   P.s. 2: *Sir Gawain and the Green Knight* (1925), p. 89, line 552 *Doddinaual de Sauage* [A. 2149]; p. 116, line 2460. Tolkien and Gordon cite p. 135.
   P.s. 3: *Sir Gawain and the Green Knight* (1967) 'Select Bibliography', p. 155.

2156. _____. *The Vulgate version of the Arthurian romances*, Vol. VIII. *Index of names and places to v. I-VIII*. Series: Carnegie institution of Washington, 74. Washington: The Carnegie institution of Washington, 1916.
   P.s. 1: *Sir Gawain and the Green Knight* (1925), p. 89, line 552, Doddinaual de Sauage [A. 2149].
   P.s. 2: *Sir Gawain and the Green Knight* (1967) 'Select Bibliography', p. 155.

2157. *Song against the King of Almaigne* 1264. [Middle English song, see Wells].
   P.s.: MS. Tolkien A 21/13 *The English MSS.* fol. 203. [Tolkien Papers, Bodleian Library, Oxford].

2158. Sommer, Ferdinand. *Handbuch der lateinischen Laut- und Formenlehre: eine Einführung in das sprachwissenschaftliche Studium des Lateins*. Series: Indogermanische Bibliothek. Abt. 1: Sammlung indogermanischer Lehr- u. Handbücher. 1. Reihe: Grammatiken, 3. Heidelberg: Winter's Universitätsbuchhandlung 1914.
   Description: Signed in the front by J.R.R. Tolkien and annotations in pencil.
   Collection: Private [Sold by Peter Harrington Antiquarian Bookseller].
   S.s.: Harrington (2003), p. 25.

2159. Sonnenschein, Edward Adolf. *A Greek Grammar for Schools*. London: Swan Sonnenschein, 1906.

Description: King Edward's School. Hilary Tolkien's book, inscribed: 'H. A. R. Tolkien'. With some notes and doodles by him [Judith Priestman 1994, revd. 2016].
Collection: Weston Library, Bodleian Libraries (Oxford).
S.s.: Zettersten (2011), p. 78 'During my last visit to the Tolkien Collection at the Bodleian Library, Oxford, I went through Tolkien's books in his private library from his school time, which his family had donated to the Bodleian in July 1982.'

2160. Sophocles. *The Electra*. Edited by Richard Claverhouse Jebb. London: Rivingtons, 1870 (2nd ed. rev.).
P.s.: *Exeter College library register*. Tolkien's borrowing record: *Michaelmas Term 1912* from 16 November 5 December; Hilary Term 1913 from 17 January to 4 February.

2161. _____. *The Electra of Sophocles*. With a commentary abridged from the larger edition of Richard Claverhouse Jebb by Gilbert A. Davis. Cambridge: The University Press, 1908.
P.s.: *Exeter College library register*. Tolkien's borrowing record: *Michaelmas Term 1912* from 16 November 5 December; *Hilary Term 1913* from 17 January to 4 February.
S.s. 1: Garth (2014), p. 23. Garth writes: [1913] 'With a mere six weeks left before the exams, a flurry of library borrowings - Sophocles' *Oedipus Tyrannus* and *Electra* and Aeschylus' *Eumenides*, *Agamennon* and *Choephoroe* - suggest he was far from familiar with the set texts'.
S.s. 2: Scull-Hammond (2017a), p. 44. 27 February 1913: The First Public Examination for the Honour School of Greek and Latin Literature (Honour Moderations) begins. He is also examined on four Greek plays, *Oedipus Tyrannus* and *Elektra* by Sophocles, *Agamemnon* by Aeschylus, and the *Bacchæ* by Euripides, with special attention to *Oedipus Tyrannus*.

2162. _____. *The Oedipus Tyrannus of Sophocles*. Series: Pitt Press Series. Edited by Richard Claverhouse Jebb. Cambridge: The University Press, 1885.
P.s.: *Exeter College library register*. Tolkien's borrowing record: *Michaelmas Term 1912* from 16 October to 5 December; *Hilary Term 1913* from 17 January to 4 February.
S.s. 1: Garth (2014), p. 23. Garth writes: [1913] 'With a mere six weeks left before the exams, a flurry of library borrowings - Sophocles' *Oedipus Tyrannus* and *Electra* and Aeschylus' *Eumenides*, *Agamennon* and *Choephoroe* - suggest he was far from familiar with the set texts'.
S.s. 2: Scull-Hammond (2017a), p. 44. 27 February 1913: The First Public Examination for the Honour School of Greek and Latin Literature (Honour Moderations) begins. He is also examined on four Greek plays, *Oedipus Tyrannus* and *Elektra* by Sophocles, *Agamemnon* by Aeschylus, and the *Bacchæ* by Euripides, with special attention to *Oedipus Tyrannus*.

2163. _____. *The Oedipus tyrannus*. Series: Pitt Press Series. Edited with introduction and notes by Richard Claverhouse Jebb. Cambridge: The University Press, 1897.
P.s.: *Exeter College library register*. Tolkien's borrowing record: *Michaelmas Term 1912* from 16 October to 5 December; *Hilary Term 1913* from 17 January to 4 February.

2164. _____. *The plays and fragments*, Pt. I. The Oedipus Tyrannus. With Critical Notes, Commentary, and Translation in English Prose by Richard Claverhouse Jebb. Cambridge: The University Press, 1887 (2nd ed.).
P.s.: *Exeter College library register*. Tolkien's borrowing record: *Michaelmas Term 1912* from 16 October to 5 December; *Hilary Term 1913* from 17 January to 4 February.

2165. _____. *The plays and fragments*, Pt. I. The Oedipus Tyrannus. With Critical Notes, Commentary, and Translation in English Prose by Richard Claverhouse Jebb. Cambridge: The University Press, 1900 (3rd ed.).
P.s.: *Exeter College library register*. Tolkien's borrowing record: *Michaelmas Term 1912* from 16 October to 5 December; *Hilary Term 1913* from 17 January to 4 February.

2166. *Soria Moria Castel*. [Norwegian fairy tale, see Dasent].
P.s.: *Letters* 297 (1967). Drafts for a letter to 'Mr Rang'.

SECTION A

2167. Southey, Robert. *The Story of the Three Bears*. London: Porter and Wright, 1837.
P.s.: #1 a. | *Tolkien On Fairy-stories* (2008), p. 310.

2168. Spenser, Edmund. *Epithalamion*.
S.s.: University of Leeds (1920), p. 135 English Literature. Texts Selected for 1920-21; p. 181. English Language and Literature. Int. I Intermediate Course (Literature).

2169. _____. *Two Cantos of Mutability*.
S.s.: University of Leeds (1923), p. 81. Ordinary Degree of B.A., Intermediate Course and Examination: English Literature. Text selected for 1923-24 (i) For detailed study.

2170. _____. *The Faerie Queene*, Book I. The Legend of the Knight of the Red Cross, or of Holinesse.
P.s.: *Tolkien On Fairy-stories* (2008) 'Manuscript A. [MS Tolkien 4, fols. 59-77]', p. 175.
S.s.: University of Leeds (1920), p. 147. English Language and Literature - Scheme A. Texts and Period selected for 1920-21. (b) Special period: 1557-1637. (c) Texts suggested for study with Special Period. Ordinary Degree of B.A. with Honours. Final Examination.

2171. _____. *The Faerie Queene*, Book II. The Legend of Sir Guyon, or of Temperance. Edited by George William Kitchin and Anthony Lawson Mayhew. Oxford: At the Clarendon Press, 1932.
Description: Annotated by J.R.R. Tolkien. Includes a label added by Stan Revell to books owned by Tolkien, 'From the Library of J.R.R. Tolkien'.
Collection: Lilly Library, Indiana University (Bloomington).

2172. _____. *The Faerie Queene* Book III. The Legend of Britomartis, or of Chastity. Edited by Alfred Bradly Gough. Oxford: At the Clarendon Press, 1918.
S.s. 1: University of Leeds (1923), p. 85. Ordinary Degree of B.A., Final Course and Examination. I. Principal Subjects, studied for Two Years. English Language and Literature: English Literature. Period selected for 1923-24: 1579-1645. Texts selected for 1923-24.
S.s. 2: Hammond-Scull (2014), p. 160. Hammnd and Scull write: '*From the ashes afire shall be woken*' [*FotR*, X] For this Tom Shippey has suggested an inspiration by Spenser's *Faerie Queene*: 'There shall a sparke of fire, which hath long-while | Bene in his ashes raked up and hid | Be freshly kindled …'

2173. _____. *The Faerie Queene* Book IV. The Legend of Cambel and Telamond, or of friendship.
P.s.: #1 a. | *Tolkien On Fairy-stories* (2008), p. 310.

2174. _____. *The Faerie Queene* Book V. The Legend of Artegal, or of Justice. Edited by Alfred Bradly Gough. Oxford: At the Clarendon Press, 1918.
P.s.: *The Notion Club Papers* (1945), p. 161. Tolkien writes: 'After F. had read a poem (later again) called *The Chronicle of Artegall* they parted'.
S.s. 1: University of Leeds (1921), p. 141. English Literature, text selected for 1921-22. Ordinary Degree of B.A.; p. 189 English Language and Literature. Int. 1 Intermediate Course (Literature).

2175. _____. *The Faerie Queene* Book VI. The Legend of Calidore, or of Courtesie.
P.s.: #1 a. | *Tolkien On Fairy-stories* (2008), p. 310.

2176. _____. *Four hymns on earthly and heavenly love & beauty*. London: London County Council Central School of Arts and Crafts, 1912; colophon 1913.
S.s.: University of Leeds (1920), p. 147. English Language and Literature - Scheme A. Texts and Period selected for 1920-21. (b) Special period: 1557-1637. (c) Texts suggested for study with Special Period. Ordinary Degree of B.A. with Honours. Final Examination.

2177. _____. *Shepheards Calendar. Containing Twelve Eclogues Proportionable to the Twelve Months*. Edited by Charles Harold Herford. London: Macmillan and Co., 1895.
   S.s. 1: University of Leeds (1920), p. 147. English Language and Literature - Scheme A. Texts and Period selected for 1920-21. (b) Special period: 1557-1637. (c) Texts suggested for study with Special Period. Ordinary Degree of B.A. with Honours. Final Examination.
   S.s. 2: University of Leeds (1921), p. 155. English Language and Literature - Scheme B. Texts for 1921-22. (d) Outlines of the History of English Literature. Ordinary Degree of B.A. with Honours. Final Examinations.
   S.s. 3: University of Leeds (1923), p. 81. Ordinary Degree of B.A., Intermediate Course and Examination: English Literature. Text selected for 1923-24 (ii) Texts suggestes as part of a course of general rending in the period 1579-1645.

2178. _____. *A View of the Present State of Ireland*.
   S.s.: University of Leeds (1920), p. 147. English Language and Literature - Scheme A. Texts and Period selected for 1920-21. (b) Special period: 1557-1637. (c) Texts suggested for study with Special Period. Ordinary Degree of B.A. with Honours. Final Examination.

2179. Sperber, Hans. *Einführung in die Bedeutungslehre*. Bonn and Leipzig: Schroder, 1923.
   P.s.: *Philology: General Works* (IV 1924, for 1923), p. 20 n. 1.

2180. Spies, Heinrich. *Kultur und Sprache im neuen England*. Leipzig: Teubner, 1925.
   P.s.: *Philology: General Works* (VI 1927, for 1925), p. 60 n. 19.

2181. Spurrell, William. *An English-Welsh Pronouncing Dictionary*. Caerfyrddin: W. Spurrel, 1909.
   Description: Inscribed in back of flyleaf: 'G. B. Smith | [T. T. Tb. Eng. Essay, 1913.]'. Pencilled annotation on title page. In pencil and ink in Welsh and English.
   Collection: Tolkien's personal Celtic library, preserved at the Weston library under the auspices of the English Faculty Library (Oxford).
   S.s. 1: Garth (2003), p. 357.
   S.s. 2: Fimi (2007), p. 67 n. 6.
   S.s. 3: Phelpstead (2011), p. 119.

2182. *St. Juliana*. [Middle English hagiography, see Krapp and Dobbie].
   P.s. 1: MS. Tolkien A 21/7 fol. 6. [Tolkien Papers, Bodleian Library, Oxford].
   P.s. 2: *Holy Maidenhood* (1923), p. 281.
   NED: #2 h. | 'W' (1928), p. 54. 'Walm *sb*.¹ *Obs.* 5.' – a 1225 'He het fecchen a ueat and wið pich fullen, and wallen hit walmhat'.

2183. Stammler, Wolfgang. *Mittelniederdeutsches Lesebuch*. Hamburg: P. Hartung, 1921.
   Collection: Taylor Institution Library, Bodleian Libraries (Oxford).

2184. Standen, Anthony. *Science is a sacred cow*. New York: E. P. Dutton and Co., Inc., 1950.
   Notes: A copy was sent to Tolkien by Clyde Kilby in the early months of 1967.
   S.s.: Scull-Hammond (2017a), p. 724.

2185. Stanley, Eric Gerald. 'Old English Poetic Diction'. Offprint from *Anglia, Zeitschrift fur englische Philologie*, Vol. LXXVIII, 1955, pp. 413-66.
   Description: Inscribed on title page: 'To Professo C. L. Wrenn | with best wishes | E. G. Stanley'. Tolkien has written in ball print pen: 'STANLEY'.
   Collection: Tolkien's personal Celtic library, preserved at the Weston library under the auspices of the English Faculty Library (Oxford).

SECTION A

2186. _____. *The owl and the nightingale*. London: 1960.
P.s.: *Sir Gawain and the Green Knight* (1967) 'Select Bibliography: editions of texts quoted more than once in the notes', p. 156.

2187. Stapledon, Olaf. *Last and First Man*. London: Methuen and Co. Ltd. 1930.
P.s.: *Tolkien On Fairy-stories* (2008) 'Manuscript A. [MS Tolkien 4, fols. 59-77]', p. 178.

2188. _____. *Last Men in London*. London: Methuen Publishing, 1932.
P.s.: *The Notion Club Papers* (1945), p. 175.
S.s.: Scull-Hammond (2006b), p. 818.

2189. *Stations of the Cross, The*. [Liturgical text]
S.s.: Scull-Hammond (2017a), p. 23: 26 March 1910 (Easter Saturday) With the permission of Father Francis, Ronald writes a long letter to Edith. [...] He encloses two devotional pamphlets, *The Stations of the Cross* and *The Seven Words of the Cross* [A. 1956].

2190. Steere, Edwin. *Swahili tales: as told by natives of Zanzibar*. London: Bell & Daldy, 1870.
P.s.: #1 a. | *Tolkien On Fairy-stories* (2008), p. 310.

2191. Steinbeck, John. *The Grapes of Wrath*. New York: The Viking Press-James Lloyd, 1939.
S.s.: Scull-Hammond (2006b), p. 818.

2192. Stene, Aasta. *English Loan-Words in Modern Norwegian. A study of Linguistic Borrowing in the Process*. London: Oxford University Press, 1945.
Collection: Tolkien's personal Celtic library, preserved at the Weston library under the auspices of the English Faculty Library (Oxford).

2193. Stenton, Frank Merry. *Anglo-Saxon England*. Oxford: At the Clarendon Press, 1943.
P.s.: *Letters* 95 (1945). From a letter to Christopher Tolkien. Tolkien writes: 'I read till 11.50, browsing through the packed and to me enthralling pages of Stenton's *Anglo Saxon England*'.

2194. Step, Edward. *Animal life of the British Isles: a Pocket Guide to the Mammals, Reptiles and Batrachians of wayside and woodland*. Series: Wayside and woodland series. London: Frederick Warne & Co Ltd., 1927.
Description: Inscribed: 'Michael Tolkien | from Father | Oxford: Oct. 22nd 1928'.
Collection: Private [Pieter Collier].

2195. Stern, Ludwig Christian. 'Fled Bricrend nach dem Codex Vossianus'. *Zeitschrift für celtische Philologie*, Vol. IV, 1903, pp. 143-77.
P.s.: *Sir Gawain and the Green Knight* (1925), p. xxvi. Tolkien and Gordon write: 'For bibliography of the Irish and French analogues of *Sir Gawain*, see the bibliography in Kittredge's study'. [*NED*] In Kittredge's study, this article is mentioned in 'I. Fled Bricrend' (p. 291 n. 1).

2196. _____. 'Le manuscript irlandais de Leide'. *Revue Celtique*, Vol. XIII, 1892, pp. 1-31.
P.s.: *Sir Gawain and the Green Knight* (1925), p. xxvi. Tolkien and Gordon write: 'For bibliography of the Irish and French analogues of *Sir Gawain*, see the bibliography in Kittredge's study'. [*NED*] In Kittredge's study, this article is mentioned in 'I. Fled Bricrend' (p. 291 n. 1).

2197. Stevens, Edward James. *Field telephones for army use, including an elementary course in electricity and magnetism*. London: Crosty Lockwood & Son, 1916 (3rd

ed.).
: Collection: Weston Library, Bodleian Libraries (Oxford).
: Notes: The book was featured in the exhibition *Tolkien: Maker of Middle-earth* at the Weston Library in Oxford (June-October 2018).

2198. Stevenson, Joseph. *The Owl and the Nightingale: a poem of the twelfth century: Now first printed from manuscripts in the Cottonian Library and at Jesus College Oxford, with an introduction and glossary.* London, Printed by S. Bentley, 1838.
: P.s. 1: MS. Tolkien A 12/2 *Commentary on Sir Gawain, lines 1999-2523* fol. 6. [Tolkien Papers, Bodleian Library, Oxford].
: P.s. 2: MS. Tolkien A 21/6. [Tolkien Papers, Bodleian Library, Oxford].

2199. _____ and George Waring (Edited by). *The Lindisfarne and Rushworth Gospels: Now first printed from the original manuscripts in the British Museum and the Bodleian Library,* Pt IV. Durham: Published for the Society by G. Andrews, 1865.
: Description: Signed 'JRR Tolkien | 1923'.
: Collection: Private [Pieter Collier].

2200. Stevenson, Robert Louis. *The strange case of Dr Jekyll and Mr. Hyde.*
: P.s. 1: *Letters* 111 (1947). From a letter to Sir Stanley Unwin.
: P.s. 2: *Valedictory Address* (1959), p. 230.

2201. _____. *Treasure Island.* London: Cassell and Company, 1883.
: P.s. 1: *On Fairy-stories* (1947), p. 63.
: P.s. 2: *Tolkien On Fairy-stories* (2008), p. 55.
: S.s.: Scull-Hammond (2017a), p. 6. In later life, he will note that he did not enjoy of this book.
: Reading period: 1900 – 1906 (S.s.: Scull-Hammond (2017c), p. 1053).

2202. _____ and Fanny van de Grift Stevenson. *The Dynamiter.* London: William Heinemann, 1885.
: P.s.: *Oxford University Press Archives* (Oxford). In a slip written by Tolkien on the etymology of 'Waggle' reads: 'Waggle, sb. [f. Waggle v.]…'
: *NED*: #2 a. | 'W' (1928), p. 14 'Waggle, *v.* 1. *trans.* a.' 1885 – 'With a friendly waggle of the hand.' (p. 199).

2203. Stevenson, William Henry. 'Some Old-English words omitted or imperfectly explained in dictionaries'. *Transactions of the Philological Society* 1895-8. Oxford: B. H. Blackwell, 1898, pp. 528-42.
: P.s.: 'Chaucer as a Philologist: *The Reeve's Tale*' (1934), p. 167 n. 91.

2204. _____ (Edited by). *Records of the borough of Nottingham: being a series of extracts from the archives of the Corporation of Nottingham,* Vol. III. King Henry VII to King Henry VIII 1485-1547. London: Bernard Quaritch, 1885.
: P.s.: MS. Tolkien A 12/2 *Commentary on Sir Gawain, lines 1999-2523* fol. 5. Tolkien refers to page 375. [Tolkien Papers, Bodleian Library, Oxford].
: *NED*: #2 b. | 'W' (1928), p. 23 'Waistcoat, *colloq.* or *vulgar.* 1.' 1519 – 'For makyng of a waste cotte.' (p.354).

2205. _____ (Edited by). *Records of the borough of Nottingham: being a series of extracts from the archives of the Corporation of Nottingham,* Vol. IV King Edward VI to King James I, 1547-1625. London: Bernard Quaritch, 1889.
: P.s.: MS. Tolkien A 12/2 *Commentary on Sir Gawain, lines 1999-2523* fol. 5. Tolkien refers to page 375. [Tolkien Papers, Bodleian Library, Oxford].

SECTION A

2206. Stjerna, Knut. *Essays on Questions connected with the Old English Poem of 'Beowulf'*. Translated by John R. Clark-Hall. Coventry: Viking Club Society for Northern Research, 1912.
P.s.: *Beowulf* (2002) 'Versione B', p. 104.

2207. Stokes, Whitley (Edited by). 'The Breton glosses at Orleans'. From *Transactions of the Philological Society*, September 1886, pp. 539-618.
Collection: Tolkien's personal Celtic library, preserved at the Weston library under the auspices of the English Faculty Library (Oxford).

2208. _____. 'The Eulogy of Cúrói (Amra Chonrói)'. *Ériu: The Journal of the School of Irish Learning, Dublin*, Vol. II, 1905, pp. 1-14.
P.s.: *Sir Gawain and the Green Knight* (1925), p. xxvi. Tolkien and Gordon write: 'For bibliography of the Irish and French analogues of *Sir Gawain*, see the bibliography in Kittredge's study'. [*NED*]
In Kittredge's study, this article is mentioned in 'II. Gawain and the Green Knight' (p. 293).

2209. _____ (Edited by). *The Life of Saint Meriasek, bishop and confessor: a Cornish drama*. London: Trübner & Co., 1872.
Description: Decoratively autographed and dated on front flyleaf: '1922'. Contains 14 pages of errata, sticked together, but net part of the main book, inside front cover. Some uncut pages.
Collection: Tolkien's personal Celtic library, preserved at the Weston library under the auspices of the English Faculty Library (Oxford).

2210. _____ (Edited by). *The Old-Irish glosses at Würzburg and Carlsruhe*. Pt. I. The glosses and translation. [Codex Paulinus, Codex Augustini, Codex Prisciani, and Codex Bedae]. Hertford: Austin, 1887.
Description: Autographed on front flyleaf. Some uncut pages.
Collection: Tolkien's personal Celtic library, preserved at the Weston library under the auspices of the English Faculty Library (Oxford).

2211. _____ (Edited by). *The Saltair na rann: a collection of early Middle Irish poems*. Oxford: At the Clarendon Press, 1883.
Description: Pencil note on back flyleaf.
Collection: Tolkien's personal Celtic library, preserved at the Weston library under the auspices of the English Faculty Library (Oxford).

2212. _____ and Ernst Windisch. *Irische Texte mit Übersetzungen Wörterbuch*, Vol. I. Leipzig: S. Hirzel, 1880.
Collection: Tolkien's personal Celtic library, preserved at the Weston library under the auspices of the English Faculty Library (Oxford).
P.s.: *Sir Gawain and the Green Knight* (1925), p. xxvi. Tolkien and Gordon write: 'For bibliography of the Irish and French analogues of *Sir Gawain*, see the bibliography in Kittredge's study'. [*NED*]
In Kittredge's study, this article is mentioned in 'I. Fled Bricrend' (p. 290 n. 1).

2213. _____ and Ernst Windisch. *Irische Texte mit Übersetzungen Wörterbuch*, Vol. II. Leipzig: S. Hirzel, 1880.
Collection: Tolkien's personal Celtic library, preserved at the Weston library under the auspices of the English Faculty Library (Oxford).

2214. _____ and Ernst Windisch. *Irische Texte mit Übersetzungen Wörterbuch*, Vol. III. Leipzig: S. Hirzel, 1880.
Collection: Tolkien's personal Celtic library, preserved at the Weston library under the auspices of the English Faculty Library (Oxford).

2215. _____ and Ernst Windisch. *Irische Texte mit Übersetzungen Wörterbuch*, Vol.

III, Pt. I-II. *Mit Wörterbuch*. Leipzig: S. Hirzel, 1897.
>Description: Contains Cóir Anmann (Fitness of Names) Edited by Stoke and Tochmarc Ferbe Edited by E. Windisch.
>P.s.: *The Name 'Nodens'* (1932), p. 134.

2216. _____ and Ernst Windisch. *Irische Texte mit Übersetzungen Wörterbuch*, Vol. IV, Pt. I. Leipzig: S. Hirzel, 1900.
>Collection: Tolkien's personal Celtic library, preserved at the Weston library under the auspices of the English Faculty Library (Oxford).

2217. _____ and Windisch, Ernst. *Irische Texte mit Übersetzungen Wörterbuch*, Vol. IV, Pt. II. Leipzig: S. Hirzel, 1909.
>Collection: Tolkien's personal Celtic library, preserved at the Weston library under the auspices of the English Faculty Library (Oxford).

2218. Story, Graham. M. and Helen Gardner (Edited by). *The Sonnets of William Alabaster*. Series: Oxford English Monographs, 7. London: Oxford University Press, 1959.
>Notes: Tolkien was one of the General Editors for the series.

2219. Strachan, John. *An Introduction to Early Welsh*. Series: Celtic, 1. Manchester: The University Press, 1909.
>Description: Autographed and dated in pencil on front flyleaf: '1926'.
>Collection: Tolkien's personal Celtic library, preserved at the Weston library under the auspices of the English Faculty Library (Oxford).
>S.s.: Phelpstead (2011), p. 119.

2220. Stratmann, Francis Henry. *A Dictionary of the Old English Language, compiled from writings of the XII, XIII, XIV and XV Centuries*. London: Krefeld and Trübner and Co: London, 1873 (2nd ed.).
>P.s.: *Exeter College library register*. Tolkien's borrowing record: Long vacation 1919 from 18 June to 14 October; *Michaelmas Term 1919* from 14 October to 21 January 1920; *Hilary Term 1920* from 21 January to 12 March.

2221. _____. *A Dictionary of the Old English Language, compiled from writings of the XII, XIII, XIV and XV Centuries*. Printed for the author: Krefeld, 1878 (3rd ed.).
>P.s.: *Exeter College library register*. Tolkien's borrowing record: Long vacation 1919 from 18 June to 14 October; *Michaelmas Term 1919* from 14 October to 21 January 1920; *Hilary Term 1920* from 21 January to 12 March.

2222. _____. *A Dictionary of the Old English Language, compiled from writings of the XII, XIII, XIV and XV Centuries*. Printed for the author: Krefeld, 1881 (3rd ed.).
>P.s.: *Exeter College library register*. Tolkien's borrowing record: Long vacation 1919 from 18 June to 14 October; *Michaelmas Term 1919* from 14 October to 21 January 1920; *Hilary Term 1920* from 21 January to 12 March.

2223. _____. *A Dictionary of the Old English Language, compiled from writings of the XII, XIII, XIV and XV Centuries*. Printed for the author: Krefeld, 1867.
>P.s.: *Exeter College library register*. Tolkien's borrowing record: Long vacation 1919 from 18 June to 14 October; *Michaelmas Term 1919* from 14 October to 21 January 1920; *Hilary Term 1920* from 21 January to 12 March.

2224. _____. *A Middle English Dictionary*. Revised and enlarged by Henry Bradley. London: Oxford University Press, 1891.
>Description: Inscribed: 'J.R.R. Tolkien. | March 24th 1920'. Annotations throughout. Loose

leaves [Judith Priestman 1994, revd. 2016].
Collection: Weston Library, Bodleian Libraries (Oxford).
P.s. 1: MS. Tolkien A 12/3 *Rough text of a lecture on Sir Gawain*, 1965 fols. 17-59.
P.s. 2: MS. Res. e. 308 *Sir Gawain and the Green Knight*. [Tolkien Papers, Bodleian Library, Oxford].
P.s. 3: *The Devil's Coach-Horses* (1925), p. 331.

2225. Strecker, Karl. *Ekkehards Waltharius*. Berlin: Weidmann, 1924 (2nd ed.).
P.s.: *Finn and Hengest* (1982), p. 87 n. 12.

2226. Streitberg, Wilhelm. *Die Gotische Bibel*. Series: Germanische Bibliothek. Abt. 2. Bd. 3. Heidelberg: Carl Winter, 1919.
P.s.: *Sigelwara land* (1934), p. 100 n. 1.

2227. _____. *Gotisches Elementarbuch*. Series: Germanische Bibliothek. Abteilung 1, Sammlung germanischer Elementar- und Handbücher. Reihe 1, Grammatiken, 2. Heidelberg: Carl Winter, 1920.
P.s.: *Sigelwara land* (1934), p. 100 n. 1.

2228. _____. *Streitberg-Festgabe. Herausgegeben von der Direktion der vereinigten Sprachwissenschaftlichen Institute an der Universität zu Leipzig*. Leipzig: Market und Petter, 1924.
Description: Autographed on front flyleaf: 'J.R.R. Tolkien'. A few annotations in pencil pp. xv, 79, 156, 419.
Collection: Private (Carl F. Hostetter).
P.s.: *Philology: General Works* (V 1926, for 1924), p. 34 n. 3, 36-38.

2229. _____ and Victor Michels. *Die Erforschung der indogermanischen Sprachen*, Vol. II. Germanisch. Berlin and Leipzig: Walter De Gruyter, 1927.
Collection: The Science Fiction and Fantasy Research Collection of the Cushing Memorial Library and Archives at Texas A&M University.
P.s.: *Sigelwara land* (1934), p. 104 n. 1.

2230. Strong, Archibald. *Beowulf. Translated into Modern English Rhymed Verse, with Introduction and Notes*. Foreword by Raymond Wilson Chambers. London: Constable, 1925.
P.s. 1: *Beowulf* (1937), p. 11 Tolkien cites Chambers's Foreword, *Beowulf and the Heroic Age*, as: 'the most significant essay on the poem that I know'.
P.s. 2: *Prefatory Remarks on Prose Translation of 'Beowulf'* (1940), p. xxviii n. 1.
P.s. 3: *Beowulf* (2002) 'Version A', p. 33 n. 2, pp. 60-61. Tolkien quotes: 'Yet professor Chadwick has shown us know a study of *Beowulf* ... put spear in the rest' (pp. vii-xxxii).
S.s. Scull-Hammond (2018a).

2231. _____. *A Short History of English Literature*. London: Oxford University Press, 1921.
Description: Includes a label added by Stan Revell to books owned by Tolkien, 'From the Library of J.R.R. Tolkien'.
Collection: Private.
P.s. 1: *Beowulf* (1937), p. 47 n. 4.
P.s. 2: *Beowulf* (2002) 'Version A', p. 35.
P.s. 3: *Beowulf* (2002) 'Textual Notes A-Text', p. 312.

2232. Stuart, John (Edited by). *The Book of Deer*. Edinburgh: Clark for the Spalding Club, 1869.
Description: Decoratively autographed and dated on front flyleaf: '1922'.
Collection: Tolkien's personal Celtic library, preserved at the Weston library under the auspices of

the English Faculty Library (Oxford).

2233. Sturluson, Snorri. *Edda Snorra Sturlusonar*. Edited by Finnur Jónsson. København: Gyldendalske boghandel, 1931.
    P.s.: *Finn and Hengest* (1982), p. 48 n. 34; p. 165 n. 10.

2234. _____. *Edda Snorra Sturlusonar. Eða Gylfaginníng, Skáldskaparmál og Háttatal*. Edited by Sveinbjörn Egilsson. Reykjavik: Prentuð i prentsmiðjulandsins, af prentara H. Helgasyni, 1848.
    P.s. 1: *Sigelwara land* (1932), p. 193 n. 1. Tolkien cites '*Múspells megir*' and translates into English the piece: '*Ok svo sem hon er sterk, þá mun hon brotna, þá er Múspells megir fara ok ríða hana, ok svima hestar þeirra ifir stórar ár; svo koma þeir frara. Þá mælti Gángleri: eigi þótti mér goðin gera af trúnaði brúna, er hon skal brotna mega, er þau megu gera, sem þau vilja. Þá mælti Hár: eigi eru goðin hallmælis verð firir þessa smið; góð brú er Bifröst, en engi lutr er sá i þessum heimi, er sér megi treystast.* [p. 8]'. With: 'First there was that region in the South which is called Múspell; it is bright and hot. That quarter is flaming and burning, and impassable for those that are aliens and have not there their native land. He is named Surtr who dwells there on the borders for the land's defense; he has a flaming sword and at the end of the world he will come and invade with war and vanquish all the gods and burn all the earth with fire.'
    P.s. 2: *The Hobbit* (1937). The dwarf-names.
    P.s. 3: *Beowulf* (2014), p. 283.
    S.s.: Scull-Hammond (2017a), p. 46. April 1913: Tolkien will need to become familiar with a range of literary and philological subjects and set texts as prescribed in the Oxford Regulations of the Board of Studies, knowing that he may be examined on them in ten papers at the end of Trinity Term 1915. In addition, Tolkien will have to choose a Special Subject on which he will be examined separately. He will choose Scandinavian Philology, which according to the Regulations will have special reference to Icelandic, together with a special study of the *Snorra Edda*. (ch.s 20-54); p. 52. *Michaelmas Term 1913*: Tolkien probably attends lectures on Gylfaginning on Thursdays at 5.00 p.m. in the Taylor Institution, beginning 16 October.

2235. _____. *The Heimskringla: or, Chronicle of the kings of Norway*, Vol. I. Translated by Samuel Laing. London: Longman, Brown, Green, and Longmans, 1844.
    Collection: Private (Sold on Ebay).

2236. _____. *The Heimskringla: or, Chronicle of the kings of Norway*, Vol. II. Translated by Samuel Laing. London: Longman, Brown, Green, and Longmans, 1844.
    Collection: Private (Sold on Ebay).

2237. _____. *The Heimskringla: or, Chronicle of the kings of Norway*, Vol. III. Translated by Samuel Laing. London: Longman, Brown, Green, and Longmans, 1844.
    Collection: Private (Sold on Ebay).

2238. _____. *Heimskringla*, Vol. I. Series: Íslenzk fornrit, 26. Edited by Bjarni Adalbjarnarson. Reykjavík: Hið Íslenzka Fornritafélag, 1941.
    P.s.: *Finn and Hengest* (1982), p. 90 n. 18; p. 134 nos. 75, 76.

2239. _____. *Heimskringla*, Vol. II. Series: Íslenzk fornrit, 27. Edited by Bjarni Adalbjarnarson. Reykjavík: Hið Íslenzka Fornritafélag, 1945.
    P.s.: *Finn and Hengest* (1982), p. 90 n. 18; p. 134 nos. 75, 76.

2240. _____. *Heimskringla*, Vol. III. Series: Íslenzk fornrit, 28. Edited by Bjarni Adalbjarnarson. Reykjavík: Hið Íslenzka Fornritafélag, 1951.

P.s.: *Finn and Hengest* (1982), p. 90 n. 18; p. 134 nos. 75, 76.

2241. _____ and Sigurður Nordal. *Egils saga Skalla-grímssonar.* Series: Islenzk fornrit v. 2. Reykjavík; Hið Íslenzka Fornritfélag, 1933.
: Description: On cover 'Professor J.R.R. Tolkien | Með vináttu frá | Sigurd Nordal', tiny notes on p. IX, inserted 3 tiny pages of notes on 'Egla Verse' (in between pp. 128-29).
Collection: Private [Pieter Collier].

2242. Stürzinger, Johann Jakob and Hermann Breuer. *Hunbaut: altfranzösischer Artusroman des XIII. Jahrhunderts*. Series: Gesellschaft für romanische Literatur, 35. Dresden and Halle: Gesellschaft für romanische Literatur and Max Niemeyer, 1914.
: P.s. 1: *Sir Gawain and the Green Knight* (1925), pp. xiii; xxvi. Tolkien and Gordon write: 'For bibliography of the Irish and French analogues of *Sir Gawain*, see the bibliography in Kittredge's study'. In Kittredge's study, this article is mentioned in 'VIII. Humbaut' (p. 301).
P.s. 2: *Sir Gawain and the Green Knight* (1967) 'Select Bibliography', p. 154.

2243. Suchier, Hermann. *La Chançun de Guillelme: Französisches Volksepos des XI. Jahrhunderts kritisch*. Series: Bibliotheca normannica, 8. Halle: Max Niemeyer, 1911.
: Description: J.R.R. Tolkien's copy, with his signature on the front free endpaper and with his extensive annotations in both ink and (mostly) pencil on pp. 1-76 of the text proper, plus a few other checkmarks and marked passages in the historical preface and in the 50-p. glossary at the back.
Collection: Private [Sold by Rulon-Miller Books].

2244. Suhm, Peter Friedrich. *Geschichte der Dänen*. Translated by Friedrich Dav. Gräter. Leipzig: Heinrich Gräft, 1803.
: P.s.: *Beowulf* (2002) 'Version A', p. 44.

2245. Suzuki, Shigetake. 'Ancrene Riwle – A Study in the MS. Readings'. Offprint from *Studies in English. Language and Literature*, Vol. V. Tokyo: Metropolitan University, 1957.
: Collection: Tolkien's personal Celtic library, preserved at the Weston library under the auspices of the English Faculty Library (Oxford).

2246. _____. 'Biblical Latin Quotations in Ancrene Wisse'. Offprint from *Studies in English. Language and Literature*, Vol. V. Tokyo: Metropolitan University, 1960.
: Collection: Tolkien's personal Celtic library, preserved at the Weston library under the auspices of the English Faculty Library (Oxford).

2247. _____. *The Language of the Ancrene Wisse*. Tokyo: Metropolitan University, 1967.
: Description: Contains loose letter from the author to JRRT, 4.8.1967.
Collection: Tolkien's personal Celtic library, preserved at the Weston library under the auspices of the English Faculty Library (Oxford).

2248. Sveinsson, Benedikt (Edited by). *Bandamanna saga*. Series: Íslendinga sögur, 30. Rejkyavik: Sigurður Kritjánsson, 1901.
: Description: Initialled on front cover. Annotated in pencil.
Collection: Tolkien's personal Celtic library, preserved at the Weston library under the auspices of the English Faculty Library (Oxford).
S.s.: Scull-Hammond (2017a), pp. 152, 162.

2249. _____ (Edited by). *Hávarðs saga Ísfirðings*. Series: Islendinga sögur, 15.

Reykjavík: Kristjánsson, 1896.
>S.s. 1: Birkett (2014), p. 257 n. 5.
>S.s. 2: Scull-Hammond (2017a), p. 162.

2250. _____ (Edited by). *Kormáks saga.* Íslendinga sögur, 6. Rejkyavik: Sigurður Kritjansson, 1893.
>Description: Autographed in pencil inside front cover. Annotated in pencil on front flyleaf and text. Contains 4 photographs (? of Iceland) at title page to Hrafnkels saga Freysgoða.
>Notes: Four volumes bound together: spine marked 6, 8 [A. 56], 9 [A. 55], 17 [A. 2252].
>Collection: Tolkien's personal Celtic library, preserved at the Weston library under the auspices of the English Faculty Library (Oxford).

2251. _____ (Edited by). *Kormáks saga.* Íslendinga sögur, 6. Rejkyavik: Sigurður Kristjánsson, 1916.
>Description: Uncut pages.
>Collection: Tolkien's personal Celtic library, preserved at the Weston library under the auspices of the English Faculty Library (Oxford).

2252. _____. *Þorskfirðinga saga.* Íslendinga sögur, 17. Rejkyavik: Sigurður Kritjansson, 1924.
>Notes: Four volumes bound together: spine marked 6 [A. 2250], 8 [A. 56], 9 [A. 55], 17.
>Collection: Tolkien's personal Celtic library, preserved at the Weston library under the auspices of the English Faculty Library (Oxford).

2253. Sweet, Henry. *An Anglo-Saxon Primer. With grammar, notes and glossary.* Oxford: At the Clarendon Press, 1905.
>Collection: Exeter College, Oxford.
>S.s. 1: University of Leeds (1920), p. 139 English Language and Literature: English Language. Text selected for 1920-21. Texts Selected for 1920-21. Ordinary Degree of B.A. with Honours. Final Course and Examination; p. 182. English Language and Literature. F2. Final Course (English Literature and Language).
>S.s. 2: University of Leeds (1921), p. 145. English Language, text selected for 1921-22. Ordinary Degree of B.A.; p. 153. English Language and Literature - Scheme A. Text selected for 1921-22. Ordinary Degree of B.A. with Honours; p. 192 English Language and Literature. F2. Final Course (English Literature and Language); p. 192 English Language and Literature. Honours and M.A. Courses. A. Language. H1. First Year.
>S.s. 3: University of Leeds (1923), p. 93. English Language and Literature. Scheme A. Degree of B.A. with Honours.
>S.s. 4: Simmonet (2014).

2254. _____. *An Anglo-Saxon Reader in Prose and Verse. With grammar, metre, notes and glossary.* Oxford: At the Clarendon Press, 1908 (8th ed.).
>Description: Exeter College. Inscribed: 'J.R.R. Tolkien | e coll. Exon. Oxon. | Michaelmas 1911 | EB | Ex libris de Iitt phll germ'. Extensive annotations [Judith Priestman 1994, revd. 2016].
>Collection: Weston Library, Bodleian Libraries (Oxford).
>P.s. 1: *Dragons* (1938), p. 49. Tolkien writes: *Draca sceal on hlæwe*: these words stand in an ancient English or Anglo-Saxon poem, and mean in full '*the right place to look for a dragon is in a burial mound*'. Tolkien quotes 'Gnomic Verse' XXVI, 26.
>P.s. 2: *Letters* 163 (1955). To W.H. Auden. Tolkien writes: 'But looking back analytically I should say that Ents are composed of philology, literature, and life. They owe their name to the *eald enta geweorc* of Anglo-Saxon, and their connexion with stone' from of the *Wanderer*, 'eald enta geweorc ídlu stódon' (v. 87, p. 177).
>P.s. 3: *English and Welsh* (1963), p. 24. Tolkien quotes: 'ne mihte gebigan his spraece to Norðhymbriscum swa hraþe þa git' from 'Ælfric's Life of King Oswald', 57-58, p. 100.
>S.s. 1: University of Leeds (1920), p. 139 English Language and Literature: English Language. Text selected for 1920-21. Texts Selected for 1920-21. Ordinary Degree of B.A. with Honours. Final Course and Examination. Extracts ii (*On the State of Learning in England*), viii (*Alfred's*

Wars with the Dunes) and xxv (*Selections from the Riddles of Cynewulf*; p. 182. English Language and Literature. F2. Final Course (English Literature and Language). Extracts ii, viii, xxv.
S.s. 2: Scull-Hammond (2017a), p. 46. April 1913: Tolkien will need to become familiar with a range of literary and philological subjects and set texts as prescribed in the Oxford Regulations of the Board of Studies, knowing that he may be examined on them in ten papers at the end of *Trinity Term 1915*: Old English texts. [...] comprise 'Cynewulf and Cyneheard' And 'On the State of Learning in England' from King Alfred's preface to the West-Saxon version of Gregory's *Cura Pastoralis (Pastoral Care)*; 'Wulfstan's address to the English'; Selection 1-34; 'The Battle of Ashdown'; 'Alfred and Godrum' and 'Alfred's Wars with the Danes'; 'The Martyrdom of Ælfeah'; 'Eustace at Dover, and the Outlawry of Godwine'; 'Charms'; 'Beowulf and Grendel's Mother'; 'The Battle of Maldon'; 'The Fall of the Angels'; Judith; 'The Happy Land' from The Phoenix'; 'The Dream of the Rood'; 'The Wanderer'; 'A selection from the Riddles of Cynewulf'; 'Gnomic Verses' and 'The Seafarer'; p. 47. Trinity Term 1913: During this term Kenneth Sisam gives the following classes: on Sweet's *Anglo-Saxon Reader* (prose), on Mondays at 10.00 a.m. in the Examination Schools, beginning 28 April. And Sweet's *Anglo-Saxon Reader* (verse), on Fridays at 10.00 a.m. in the Examination Schools, beginning 25 April; p. 56. *Hilary Term 1914*: Kenneth Sisam continues to teach the *Anglo-Saxon Reader* (Prose), *Elementary Historical Grammar*, *Havelok*, and the *Anglo-Saxon Reader* (Verse).

2255. _____. *An Anglo-Saxon Reader in Prose and Verse. With Grammar, Metre, Notes and Glossary.* Edited by Charles Talbut Onions. Oxford: At the Clarendon Press, 1922 (9th ed.).
Description: Inscribed: 'J.R.R. Tolkien [1922] | from the C. Press'. A few annotations. Loose leaves [Judith Priestman 1994, revd. 2016].
Collection: Weston Library, Bodleian Libraries (Oxford).
S.s.: University of Leeds (1923), p. 93. English Language and Literature. Scheme A. Degree of B.A. with Honours. Extracts I, ii, iv, ix, xv, xxiii, xxvi; p. 94. Texts and Period selected for 1923-24 (a).

2256. _____ (Edited by). *First Middle English Primer. Extracts from the Ancren Riwle and Ormulum with Grammar and Glossary.* Oxford: At the Clarendon Press, 1884.
Description: Pencil notes in Tolkien's hand between pp. 7-12. Signed by Tolkien on front free endpaper. The notes are in Tolkien's mature hand, while his signature, though undated, is clearly juvenile and suggests that Tolkien owned this book very close to the time when he first became acquainted With Middle English in his senior year at King Edward's school.
Collection: Private [Sold by Simon Finch Rare Books Ltd.].
P.s. 1: *Exeter College library register.* Tolkien's borrowing record: *Summer term 1913* from 3 May to 12 January; *Hilary Term 1920* from 21 January to 12 March.
P.s. 2: MS. Res. e. 308 *Sir Gawain and the Green Knight.*[Tolkien Papers, Bodleian Library, Oxford].
S.s.: Finch (2002), p. 51.

2257. _____ (Edited by). *First Middle English Primer. Extracts from the Ancren Riwle and Ormulum with Grammar and Glossary.* Oxford: At the Clarendon Press, 1891 (2nd ed.).
P.s.: *Exeter College library register*. Tolkien's borrowing record: *Summer term 1913* from 3 May to 12 January; *Hilary Term 1920* from 21 January to 12 March.

2258. _____ (Edited by). *First steps in Anglo-Saxon.* Series: Clarendon Press series. Oxford: At the Clarendon Press, 1897.
Description: Autographed on front flyleaf: 'J.R.R. Tolkien | Exeter College | Oxford'. Annotations in pencil pp. vii, ix, 2, 3, 5, 9, 10, 11, 12, 13, 14, 15, 16, 23, 24, 26, 28, 33, 35, 36, 39, 41, 50, 51, 52, 59, 64, 65, 71, 78, 84, 87.
Collection: Private (Carl F. Hostetter).

2259. _____ (Edited by). *A History of English Sounds from the earliest period,* including an investigation of the general laws of sound change, and full word lists. (From the *Transactions of the Philological Society* for 1873-4). Series: English Dialect Society publications, 9. Preface by Walter William Skeat. London: Published for the English Dialect Society by Trübner & Co., 1874.

> P.s.: *Exeter College library register.* Tolkien's borrowing record: *Hilary Term 1914* from 29 January to 10 March; *Michaelmas Term 1914* from 5 November to 16 January 1915; *Hilary Term 1915* from 19 January to 1 March.

2260. _____ (Edited by). *A History of English Sounds from the earliest period, including an investigation of the general laws of sound change, and full word lists.* Oxford: At the Clarendon Press, 1888.

> P.s.: MS. Tolkien A 21/13 fol. 119. Note by Tolkien, 'Books in Exeter Library useful', with shelfmarks, on back of photostat reading list dated October 1913. [Tolkien Papers, Bodleian Library, Oxford].
> S.s.: Garth (2014), p. 39 n. 26. Garth writes: 'Tolkien knew it from Henry Sweet's *History of English Sounds* in the college library. He had borrowed it in January and did so again two days after the debate - for four months' [The Rector and Dr Marett lead a discussion of 'superman and International Law' to which Tolkien also contributes (27 October 1914)].

2261. _____ (Edited by). *King Alfred's West-Saxon Version of Gregory's Pastoral Care (Cura Pastoralis)*, Vol. I. Series: E.E.T.S. (Early English Text Society), OS 45. Published for the Early English Text Society, by N. Trübner & Co., 1871.

> P.s. 1: MS. Tolkien A 21/13 fol. 119. Note by Tolkien, 'Books in Exeter Library useful', with shelfmarks, on back of photostat reading list dated October 1913. Tolkien writes: 'All EETS publications'. [Tolkien Papers, Bodleian Library, Oxford].
> P.s. 2: *Philology: General Works* (VI 1927, for 1925), p. 38.
> S.s.: Scull-Hammond (2017a), p. 46. April 1913: Tolkien will need to become familiar with a range of literary and philological subjects and set texts as prescribed in the Oxford Regulations of the Board of Studies, knowing that he may be examined on them in ten papers at the end of *Trinity Term 1915*: Old English texts. [...] 'On the State of Learning in England' from King Alfred's preface to the West-Saxon version of Gregory's *Cura Pastoralis (Pastoral Care)*.
> *NED*: #2 h. | 'W' (1928), p. 54. 'Walm sb.¹ Obs. 2.' – 'He drincð of ðæm wielme his aȝnes pyttes' (p. 373).

2262. _____ (Edited by). *King Alfred's West-Saxon Version of Gregory's Pastoral Care (Cura Pastoralis)*, Vol. II. Series: E.E.T.S. (Early English Text Society), OS 50. Published for the Early English Text Society, by N. Trübner & Co., 1871.

> P.s. 1: MS. Tolkien A 21/13 fol. 119. Note by Tolkien, 'Books in Exeter Library useful', with shelfmarks, on back of photostat reading list dated October 1913. Tolkien writes: 'All EETS publications'. [Tolkien Papers, Bodleian Library, Oxford].
> P.s. 2: *Philology: General Works* (VI 1927, for 1925), p. 38.
> S.s.: Scull-Hammond (2017a), p. 46. April 1913: Tolkien will need to become familiar with a range of literary and philological subjects and set texts as prescribed in the Oxford Regulations of the Board of Studies, knowing that he may be examined on them in ten papers at the end of *Trinity Term 1915*: Old English texts. [...] 'On the State of Learning in England' from King Alfred's preface to the West-Saxon version of Gregory's *Cura Pastoralis (Pastoral Care)*.

2263. _____. *The Oldest English texts*. Series: E.E.T.S. (Early English Text Society), OS 83. London: Published for the Early English Text Society by Kegan Paul, Trench, Trübner and Co., 1885.

> P.s. 1: MS. Tolkien A 21/13 fol. 119. Note by Tolkien, 'Books in Exeter Library useful', with shelfmarks, on back of photostat reading list dated October 1913. Tolkien writes: 'All EETS publications'. [Tolkien Papers, Bodleian Library, Oxford].
> P.s. 2: *Finn and Hengest* (1982), p. 30 n. 5; p. 40 n. 33.

2264. _____. *The Practical study of languages. A guide for teachers and learners.*

London: Oxford University Press, 1899.
   P.s.: *A Secret Vice* (2016), p. 71.

2265. _____. *A Primer of Historical English Grammar*. Series: Clarendon Press Series. Oxford: At the Clarendon Press, 1902.
   P.s.: *Exeter College library register*. Tolkien's borrowing record: *Hilary Term 1914* from 26 January to 11 March; *Hilary Term 1920* from 21 January to 12 March.

2266. _____. *A second Anglo-Saxon Reader archaie and dialectal*. Oxford: At the Clarendon Press, 1887.
   Description: Inscribed: 'J.R.R. Tolkien, 1919'. A few annotations. Loose leaves [Judith Priestman 1994, revd. 2016].
   Collection: Weston Library, Bodleian Libraries (Oxford).
   P.s.: Notes on *The Wanderer* supplementing Tolkien's lecture on 'The Verse of Sweet's *Anglo-Saxon Reader*' for Oxford's English Faculty (1926 — *Hilary Term 1927*). Contents: MS. Tolkien A 38 fols. 1-8 — typed up version of MS. Tolkien A 38 fols. 22-25 | MS. Tolkien A 38 fols. 9-12 — later general statements about *The Wanderer* (?1940s) | MS. Tolkien A 38 fols. 13-15 — a translation of *The Wanderer* | MS. Tolkien A 38 fols. 16-21 — lecture list for 1927 (notes not directly related to *The Wanderer*) | MS. Tolkien A 38 fols. 22-25 — introductory remarks on *The Wanderer* | MS. Tolkien A 38 fols. 26-39 — word by word notes on *The Wanderer*. Extracts: [MS. Tolkien A 38 *Papers relating to Old and Middle English: The Wanderer* fol. 3]: 'The chief reason for studying Old English, must always remain Old English. There is a kinship, in spite of all the remoteness and the strangeness, in Old English verse with Modern English: it is definitely part of the history of the mind and mood of England and the English. The men who made it walked this soil and under this sky. All the immense changes of life here in more than a thousand years have not yet made the end entirely foreign to the beginning.' Quote in Lee (2005), p. 19. [MS. Tolkien A 38 *Papers relating to Old and Middle English: The Wanderer* fol. 9 On *wyrd*:]: 'What is *wyrd*? History. [This] can be viewed as an ineluctable series of events that has marched, and will march on and over Man, without regard to any man, Cæsar or churl; or as a flowing stream of things that can be by some great men, or by many men united in some hope or passion, be turned this way or that: yet even so it runs down inevitably to the Great Sea at last.' (*Cfr*. Lee (2005), p. 214 and in *J.R.R. Tolkien and 'The Wanderer'* (Lee, 2009, p. 201). [MS. Tolkien A 38 *Papers relating to Old and Middle English: The Wanderer* fol. 9 On *paganism*:]: 'Past beliefs cast their shadow behind: the mood long outlives them. The dominant note of paganism is regret, or indeed despair. It may have fair gods or foul gods (or both); but at any rate it has little hope.' (*Cfr. J.R.R. Tolkien and 'The Wanderer'* (Lee 2009, p. 201). [MS. Tolkien A 38 *Papers relating to Old and Middle English: The Wanderer* fol. 12. A sideswipe at some unnamed critics of elegiac sentiment:] '[In *The Wanderer*] [w]e have, it is nonetheless murmured, the hackneyed hour before dawn; the same old generous patron (the *goldwine*); the wintry sea, of course; the crumbling ruin, alas!; the transitiveness of earth, yes, yes. But why not? These things are fundamental at all times; and they must have touched very near the heart in England (especially the North of England) round about the year A.D. 800.' (*Cfr. J.R.R. Tolkien and 'The Wanderer'* (Lee 2009, pp. 201-02). [MS. Tolkien A 38 *Papers relating to Old and Middle English: The Wanderer* fol. 12. On contemporary events:] 'I at least find more sustenance and support in *The Wanderer*, amid the present catastrophe (which seems likely to leave Europe in ruins whichever way it turns) than in all the pretty prattle ... There is no happy ending to cyningas or caseras 'of this world', whichever new names they may give themselves, and whichever side they may be on, left or right, black or white \[interlinear gloss:] red or white' ... The Old English poets knew that at any rate.' (*Cfr. J.R.R. Tolkien and 'The Wanderer'* (Lee 2009, pp. 205-06). [MS. Tolkien A 38 *Papers relating to Old and Middle English: The Wanderer* fol. 36. On the famous lines of *The Wanderer* — 'Where is the horse gone', etc:] '[these lines] were deservedly famous. One of the best expressions of this motive in literature ... we do not gain much from the argument of scholars as to whether it is a native or a learned motive. We might say it is a human motive! ... And the question 'Where are' of the departed has been asked (as one might expect) in many languages.' [Tolkien Papers, Bodleian Library, Oxford]. (*Cfr. J.R.R. Tolkien and 'The Wanderer'* (Lee 2009, p. 189.
   S.s. 1: *Tolkien* (2014), p. 67.
   S.s. 2: Scull-Hammond (2017a), p. 46. April 1913: Tolkien will need to become familiar with a range of literary and philological subjects and set texts as prescribed in the Oxford Regulations of

the Board of Studies, knowing that he may be examined on them in ten papers at the end of Trinity Term 1915: Old English texts. 'Northumbrian fragments'; 'Mercian hymns'; 'Kentish charters'; the *Codex Aureus* inscription and a Kentish psalm.

2267. _____ (Edited by). *Second Middle English primer: extracts from Chaucer: with grammar and glossary*. Series: Clarendon Press Series. Oxford: At the Clarendon Press, 1886.
> P.s. 1: *Exeter College library register*. Tolkien's borrowing record: *Summer term 1913* from 3 May to 12 January; *Hilary Term 1920* from 21 January to 12 March.
> P.s. 2: MS. Res. e. 308 *Sir Gawain and the Green Knight*. [Tolkien Papers, Bodleian Library, Oxford].

2268. _____ (Edited by). *A Short Historical English Grammar*. Oxford: At the Clarendon Press, 1892.
> Description: Autographed on front flyleaf in pencil. Some pencil note eg. pp. 81, 82, 85, 143.
> Collection: Tolkien's personal Celtic library, preserved at the Weston library under the auspices of the English Faculty Library (Oxford).
> P.s. 1: *Exeter College library register*. Tolkien's borrowing record: *Summer term 1913* from 3 May to 12 January; *Hilary Term 1914* from 26 January to 11 March.
> P.s. 2: MS. Tolkien A 21/13 fol. 119. Note by Tolkien, 'Books in Exeter Library useful', with shelfmarks, on back of photostat reading list dated October 1913. [Tolkien Papers, Bodleian Library, Oxford].
> S.s. 1: Scull-Hammond (2017a), p. 47. *Trinity Term 1913*: Elementary Historical Grammar, on Tuesdays at 10.00 a.m. in the Examination Schools, beginning 22 April.
> S.s. 2: McIlwaine (2018), no. 84.

2269. _____ (Edited by). *A Short Historical English Grammar*. Oxford: At the Clarendon Press, 1893.
> P.s.: *Exeter College library register*. Tolkien's borrowing record: *Summer term 1913* from 3 May to 12 January; *Hilary Term 1914* from 26 January to 11 March.

2270. _____. *The Student's Dictionary of Anglo-Saxon*. London: Oxford University Press, 1911.
> Description: [King Edward's School] and Exeter College. Inscribed: 'Library of German philolo. | No[.] V. | 1910'. With Anglo-Saxon inscription on half-title. Losse leaves [Judith Priestman 1994, revd. 2016].
> Collection: Weston Library, Bodleian Libraries (Oxford).
> P.s. 1: *Philology: General Works* (V 1926, for 1924), p. 46.
> P.s. 2: *A Secret Vice* (2016), p. 71.
> S.s.: Zettersten (2011), p. 78 'During my last visit to the Tolkien Collection at the Bodleian Library, Oxford, I went through Tolkien's books in his private library from his school time, which his family had donated to the Bodleian in July 1982.'

2271. Swift, Jonathan. *Gulliver's Travels*.
> P.s. 1: *On Fairy-stories* (1947), p. 44. [A Voyage to Lilliput].
> P.s. 2: *Tolkien On Fairy-stories* (2008) 'Manuscript B [MS. Tolkien 6, fol. 14]', pp. 264-65.
> P.s. 3: #1 a. | *Tolkien On Fairy-stories* (2008), p. 310. [A Voyage to Lilliput]
> P.s. 4: *A Secret Vice* (2016).
> S.s. 1: University of Leeds (1921), p. 141. English Literature, text selected (Pts III and IV) for 1921-22. Ordinary Degree of B.A.; p. 190 English Language and Literature. Int. 1 Intermediate Course (Literature) (Pts III and IV). pp. 86-87.
> S.s. 2: Michael G.R. Tolkien (1989). Michael G.R. Tolkien writes: 'I remember his saying to me several times that one of Swift's great contributions to the language was his invention of a new sound in the word 'Yahoo' to describe the humanoid apes of Gulliver's Travels, Book IV' [A Voyage to the Land of the Houyhnhnms].
> S.s. 3: Scull-Hammond (2017a), p. 645.
> S.s. 4: Scull-Hammond (2006b), pp. 684, 820.

2272. _____. *Miscellanies, in prose and verse*, Vol. V. London: Printed for Charles Davis, 1735.
  P.s.: *Oxford University Press Archives* (Oxford). A slip written by Tolkien on the etymology of 'Wake' used ('W' p. 31) [A. 1721].
  NED: #2 f. | 'W' (1928), p. 31 'Wake, 3.' 1724 – 'When he was cut down, the Body was carried through the whole City to gather Contributions for his Wake (From 'An Account of Wood's Execution')

2273. _____. *A Voyage to Lilliput* [see Lang and Swift].
  P.s. 1: *On Fairy-stories* (1947), p. 44.
  P.s. 2: *Tolkien On Fairy-stories* (2008) 'Manuscript B [MS. Tolkien 4, fols. 73-120]', p. 215.

2274. _____. *The Works of Jonathan Swift*.
  S.s.: University of Leeds (1921), p. 144. English Literature, text selected (*Tale of a Tub, Battle of the Books, Letter to a Young Clergyman* and *Letter of Advice to a Young Poet*) for 1921-22. Ordinary Degree of B.A.; p. 191 English Language and Literature. F1. Final Course (English Literature) (ii) The History of English Literature from 1700 to 1765 (*Tale of a Tub, Battle of the Books, Letter to a Young Clergyman* and *Letter of Advice to a Young Poet*).

2275. Symons, Barend. *Kudrun*. Series: Altdeutsche Textbibliothek, herausgegeben von H; Paul Nr.5. Halle: Max Niemeyer, 1914.
  Description: Signed in pencil 'JRR Tolkien' on flyleaf.
  Collection: Private [Sold by Loome Theological Booksellers, Sold by Gabriel Books, Pieter Collier].

2276. Tacitus, Cornelius. *Annals of Tacitus*, Vol. I. Book I-VI Edited by Henry Furneaux. Oxford: At the Clarendon Press, 1896.
  S.s.: Scull-Hammond (2017a), p. 39. *Trinity Term 1912*: Tolkien attends lectures on the authors set for Honour Moderations: Annals I and II of Tacitus (set texts), on Wednesdays and Fridays at 12.00 noon, beginning 1 May.

2277. _____. *Annals of Tacitus*, Vol. II. Book XI-XVI Edited by Henry Furneaux. Oxford: At the Clarendon Press, 1907.
  S.s.: Scull-Hammond (2017a), p. 39. *Trinity Term 1912*: Tolkien attends lectures on the authors set for Honour Moderations: Annals I and II of Tacitus (set texts), on Wednesdays and Fridays at 12.00 noon, beginning 1 May.

2278. _____. *Corneli Taciti de Origine et Situ Germanorum*. Edited by John George Clark Anderson. Oxford: At the Clarendon Press (2nd ed.), 1938.
  P.s. 1: *Finn and Hengest* (1982), p. 11 n. 6.
  P.s. 2: *Beowulf* (2014), p. 191. Tolkien quotes: 'auspicia sortesque ut qui maxime observant' (ch. x).

2279. _____. *Historiae*.
  P.s.: *Sir Gawain and the Green Knight* (1925), p. 83, line 109 *Gawan*. Tolkien and Gordon cite the name Volaginius in Book II, 75.

2280. *Taill of Rauf Coilyear* [Scottish dialect Middle English poem].
  S.s.: Scull-Hammond (2017a), p. 46. April 1913: Tolkien will need to become familiar with a range of literary and philological subjects and set texts as prescribed in the Oxford Regulations of the Board of Studies, knowing that he may be examined on them in ten papers at the end of *Trinity Term 1915*: Middle English texts.

2281. Tait, James. 'The Feudal Element'. *Introduction to the Survey of English place-names*, Vol. I, Pt. I [A. 1534]. Cambridge: The University Press, 1924.

P.s.: *Philology: General Works* (V 1926, for 1924), p. 60.

2282.   *Tale of a Youth who Set out to Learn what Fear Was, The*. [German folktale, see Grimm and Lang]
P.s.: *Tolkien On Fairy-stories* (2008) 'Manuscript B [MS. Tolkien 4, fols. 73-120]', p. 247.

2283.   Taylor, A. B. 'On the History of Old English *ēa, ēo* in Middle Kentish'. MLR (*The Modern Language Review*), Vol. 19.1, pp. 1–10. Belfast: Modern Humanities Research Association, 1924.
P.s.: *Philology: General Works* (IV 1924, for 1923), p. 25.

2284.   Taylor, Jeremy. *A Discourse of the Liberty of Prophesying*. London: Joseph Rickerby, 1836.
S.s.: University of Leeds, *Calendar 1921-22*, p. 154. English Language and Literature - Scheme A. Texts and Period selected for 1921-22. (d) Texts suggested for study with Special Period 1637-1700. Ordinary Degree of B.A. with Honours. Final Examinations.

2285.   Taylor, Paul Beekman and Wystan Hugh Auden (Edited by). *The Elder Edda: a selection*. London: Faber & Faber, 1969.
Notes: Their book is dedicated to Tolkien, an honor he well deserves.
P.s. 1: *Letters* 295 (1967). To W.H. Auden.
P.s. 2: *The Legend of Sigurd & Gudrún* (2009), p. 6.
S.s. 1: Shippey (1992), p. 297.
S.s. 2: Scull-Hammond (2017a), p. 729.

2286.   Taylor, Tom. *Ballads and Songs of Brittany*. Translated from the *Barzaz-Breiz* of Vicomte H. de la Villemarqué. London: Macmillan and Co., 1865.
S.s. 1: Fimi (2007), p. 52.
S.s. 2: *The Lay of Aotrou & Itroun* (2016), p. 25.

2287.   Temple, William. *Miscellanea. The Second Part in Four Essays*.
S.s.: University of Leeds (1921), p. 154. English Language and Literature - Scheme A. Texts and Period selected for 1921-22. (d) Texts suggested for study with Special Period 1637-1700. Ordinary Degree of B.A. with Honours. Final Examination.

2288.   ten Brink, Bernhard Egidius Konrad. *History of English Literature*, Vol. I. Translated by Horace M. Kennedy. London: George Bell and Sons, 1895.
P.s.: *Beowulf* (2002) 'Version A', p. 33.

2289.   Tennyson, Alfred 1st Baron Tennyson. *In Memoriam*. London: Macmillan, 1906.
S.s. 1: University of Leeds (1921), p. 156. English Language and Literature - Scheme B. Texts for 1921-22. (d) Outlines of the History of English Literature. Ordinary Degree of B.A. with Honours. Final Examinations.
S.s. 2: Ollscoil na h-Éireann G 101 (1949).

2290.   _____. *Poems of Tennyson 1829-1868*. London: Oxford University Press, 1929.
P.s.: [Mythopoeic Society, *Parma Eldalamberon* 18 (2009), PF20 p. 113] Tolkien writes in ink on one side of a sheet of 'Oxford paper' a text in Pre-Fëanorian characters and quotes 'Break, break, break on thy cold grey stones, o sea', an excerpt from the first verse of 'Break, Break, Break' (p. 226).

2291.   *Terrible Head, The*. [Fairy tale, see Lang]
P.s. 1: *On Fairy-stories* (1947), p. 243.
P.s. 2: *Tolkien On Fairy-stories* (2008), p. 84.

SECTION A

2292. Thacker, Eric and Anthony Ernshaw. *Musrum*. London: Jonathan Cape, 1968.
   Notes: A copy was sent to Tolkien by the publisher Jonathan Cape. Tolkien does not like the book at all, and has had difficulty in writing a reply which does not seem rude. He asks Joy's opinion of a noncommittal reply that the book: 'is quite outside the range of my interests and I do not feel moved to say anything at all about it'.
   S.s.: Scull-Hammond (2017a), p. 769.

2293. Thackeray, William Makepeace. *The rose and the ring, or, The history of Prince Giglio and Prince Bulbo: a fire-side pantomime for great and small children.* London: Smith, Elder, and Co., 1858 (3rd ed.).
   P.s. 1: *On Fairy-stories* (1947), p. 82 n. 1.
   P.s. 2: *Tolkien On Fairy-stories* (2008), p. 76 n. 1.
   S.s.: Scull-Hammond (2006b), p. 820.

2294. Thomas Aquinas, Saint. *Summa Theologica*, Tomus primus complectens primam partem. Venice: Cudebat Simon Occhi, 1787.
   Description: Two autographed on a first white page: 'John Knott, M.D. | John Reuel Tolkien'. Christopher Tolkien says that his father bought these volumes in the 1920s. It is of particular note that within this Summa there are many notes in pencil (gray, blue and red) and in purple ink.
   Collection: Private (Claudio Testi)

2295. _____. *Summa Theologica*. Tomus secundus complectens primam secundæ. Venice: Cudebat Simon Occhi, 1787.
   Description: It is of particular note that within this Summa there are many notes in pencil (gray, blue and red) and in purple ink.
   Collection: Private (Claudio Testi)

2296. _____. *Summa Theologica*. Tomus tertius complectens Secundae secundae priores quaestiones C. Venice: Cudebat Simon Occhi, 1787.

2297. _____. *Summa Theologica*. Tomus quartus complectens secundæ secundæ reliquas supra c. quæstiones. Venice: Cudebat Simon Occhi, 1787.
   Description: It is of particular note that within this Summa there are many notes in pencil (gray, blue and red) and in purple ink.
   Collection: Private (Claudio Testi).

2298. _____. *Summa Theologica*. Tomus quintus complectens partem tertiam. Venice: Cudebat Simon Occhi, 1787.

2299. _____. *Summa Theologica*. Tomus sextus complectens supplementum partis tertiæ. Venice: Cudebat Simon Occhi, 1787.
   Description: It is of particular note that within this Summa there are many notes in pencil (gray, blue and red) and in purple ink.
   Collection: Private (Claudio Testi).

2300. _____. *Summa Theologica*. Tomus septimus complectens indices, & D. Thomæ sermones. Venice: Cudebat Simon Occhi, 1787.

2301. Thomas of Erceldoune. *Sir Tristrem; a metrical romance of the thirteenth century*. Edited by Walter Scott. Series: Works of Walter Scott, 6. Edinburgh: A Constable and Company, 1811 (3rd ed.).
   P.s.: *Sir Gawain and the Green Knight* (1925), p. 568 ff.

2302. _____. *Sir Tristrem*. Series: Scottish Text Society. Edited by George P. McNeill. Edinburgh and London: Printed for the Society by W. Blackwood and sons, 1886.

P.s. 1: *Sir Gawain and the Green Knight* (1925), p. 100 line 1139 ff. Tolkien and Gordon cite line 441-528.
P.s. 2: *Sir Gawain and the Green Knight* (1967) 'Select Bibliography: editions of texts quoted more than once in the notes', p. 156.

2303. Thomas, Joseph. *Randigal rhymes and a glossary of Cornish words*. Penzance: F. Rodda, 1895.
Collection: Tolkien's personal Celtic library, preserved at the Weston library under the auspices of the English Faculty Library (Oxford).

2304. Thomas, Martha Carey. *Sir Gawayne and the green knight, a comparison with the French Perceval*. Zürich: Printed by Orell Füssli & Co., 1883.
P.s.: *Sir Gawain and the Green Knight* (1925), p. xxvi. Tolkien and Gordon write: 'For bibliography of the Irish and French analogues of *Sir Gawain*, see the bibliography in Kittredge's study'. [*NED*] In Kittredge's study, this article is mentioned in 'II. Gawain and the Green Knight' (p. 294), 'V. Le Livre de Caradoc' (p. 298).

2305. Thomas, P. G. 'The Middle English Alliterative Poem *Sir Gawayne the Green Knight*'. *Englische Studien. Organ für englische Philologie unter Mitberücksichtigung des englischen Unterrichts auf höheren Schulen*, Vol. XLVII. Leipzig: O. R. Reisland, 1913, pp. 311-13.
P.s.: *Sir Gawain and the Green Knight* (1925), p. 86, line 160 *scholes*. Tolkien and Gordon cite page 312; p. 87 line in fere. T. and F. cite p. 250.

2306. Thompson, Ashley Horace (Edited by). *Bede: his life, times and writings: Essays in Commemoration of the Twelfth Centenary of His Death*. Oxford: At the Clarendon Press, 1935.
P.s.: *Beowulf* (1937), p. 49 n. 17.

2307. _____ (Edited by). *Military Architecture in England during the Middle Ages*. London: Oxford University Press, 1912.
P.s.: *Sir Gawain and the Green Knight* (1925), p. xxvii.

2308. Thompson, Francis. *A Renegade poet and other essays*. Boston: The Ball Publishing Co., 1910.
P.s.: *The Story of Kullervo* (2016), p. 114.

2309. _____. *The Works of Francis Thompson*, Vol. I. Poems. London: Burns & Oates Ltd., 1913.
P.s.: *The Book of Lost Tales*, Vol. I (1992), p. 21. Christopher Tolkien writes: 'My father acquired *The Works of Francis Thompson* in 1913 and 1914'.
S.s.: Scull-Hammond (2006b), p. 819.
Bought period: 1913-14 (S.s.: Scull-Hammond (2017c), p. 1059).

2310. _____. *The Works of Francis Thompson*, Vol. II. Poems. London: Burns & Oates Ltd., 1913.
P.s.: *The Book of Lost Tales*, Vol. I (1992), p. 21. Christopher Tolkien writes: 'My father acquired *The Works of Francis Thompson* in 1913 and 1914'.
S.s.: Scull-Hammond (2006b), p. 819.
Bought period: 1913-14 (S.s.: Scull-Hammond (2017c), p. 1059).

2311. _____. *The Works of Francis Thompson*, Vol. III. Prose. London: Burns & Oates Ltd., 1913.
P.s.: *The Book of Lost Tales*, Vol. I (1992), p. 21. Christopher Tolkien writes: 'My father acquired *The Works of Francis Thompson* in 1913 and 1914'.

S.s.: Scull-Hammond (2006b), p. 819.
Bought period: 1913-14 (S.s.: Scull-Hammond (2017c), p. 1059).

2312. _____ and Nora Kershaw Chadwick (Edited by). *Transactions 1940-1946 – Yorkshire Celtic Studies III*. Leeds: University of Leeds, 1940-1946.
> Contains: 'The Irish Language Revival' by G. Thomson and 'The Celtic Background of Anglo-Saxon England' by N. Kershaw Chadwick.
> Collection: Tolkien's personal Celtic library, preserved at the Weston library under the auspices of the English Faculty Library (Oxford).

2313. Thompson, Whitney Meredith (Edited by). *Þe wohunge of Ure Lauerd*. Series: E.E.T.S. (Early English Text Society), OS 241. London: Oxford University Press, 1958.
> Notes: In his prefatory notes, W. M. Thompson thanks Tolkien: 'For this edition I am indebted to the kind unfailing stimulus and advice of Professor J. R. R. Tolkien, who, wearing his own ring of power, is present in most of its best parts only.'
> S.s. 1: Scull-Hammond (2017a), p. 232. July-13 August 1938 Tolkien works with W. Meredith Thompson from Winnipeg on Wohunge and related Middle English manuscripts.
> S.s. 2: Scull-Hammond (2017c), p. 1238. 'At a meeting of 23 March 1956 J.A.W. Bennett and C. L. Wrenn reported on Meredith Thompson's edition of *Þe Wohunge ure Lauerd* and other pieces, presumably expressing some qualifications about accepting it, as Tolkien said that he thought that the edition should be accepted, and offered to read through its notes and help Thompson (a friend) make them conform to the requirements of the Society'.

2314. Thomson, John. *The Complete poetical works of James Thomson*. London: H. Frowde, Oxford University Press, 1908.
> S.s.: University of Leeds (1921), p. 144. English Literature, text selected for 1921-22. Ordinary Degree of B.A. (*Winter* and *The Castle of Indolence*); p. 191 English Language and Literature. F1. Final Course (English Literature) (ii) The History of English Literature from 1700 to 1765 (*Winter* and *The Castle of Indolence*).

2315. Thorkelin, Grímur Jónsson. *De Danorum rebus gestis secul. III & IV*. Poëma Danicum Dialecto Anglosaxonica [i.e. the Anglo-Saxon poem *Beowulf*] Ex Bibliotheca Cottoniana Musei Britannici. Havniæ: Th. E. Rangel, 1815.
> P.s. 1: *Beowulf* (1937), p. 4.
> P.s. 2: *Beowulf* (2002) 'Version A', p. 43.
> S.s.: Scull-Hammond (2017a), p. 132. [14 December 1923] Tolkien has been lucky enough to acquire a copy of Thorkelin's *Beowulf* (the first full edition of that poem) for seven shillings.

2316. Thoroddsen, Þorvaldur. *Geschichte der Isländischen geographie*, Vol. I. Bis zum Sclusse des 16. Jahrunderts. Translated by August Gebhardt. Leipzig: Teubner, 1897.
> Collection: Tolkien's personal Celtic library, preserved at the Weston library under the auspices of the English Faculty Library (Oxford).

2317. _____. *Geschichte der Isländischen geographie*, Vol. II. Von 17 bis 18 Jahrhunderts. Translated by August Gebhardt. Leipzig: Teubner, 1898.
> Collection: Tolkien's personal Celtic library, preserved at the Weston library under the auspices of the English Faculty Library (Oxford).

2318. Þórólfsson, Björn Karel (Edited by). *Hávarðar saga Ísfirðings: udgivet for Samfund til udgivelse af gammel nordisk litteratur*. København: Trykt hos. J. Jørgensen, 1923.
> Description: The book was released in 1923 and also shows a typical 1923-24 autograph by J.R.R. Tolkien. Next to that the books contains numerous notes in pencil in the sideline of the text in the hand of J.R.R. Tolkien. This was clearly a working copy and part of Tolkien's personal library

Collection: Private [TolkienLibrary.com, Sold on Ebay 17 July 2012].

2319. _____. *Um Íslenskar orðmyndir á 14 og 15 öld og breytingar þeirra úr fornmálinu*. Reykjavik: Fjelagsprentsmiðjan, 1925.
    Description: Inscribed on front cover: 'J.R.R. Tolkien'. Includes a label added by Stan Revell to books owned by Tolkien, 'From the Library of J.R.R. Tolkien', on inside front cover.
    Collection: Marion E. Wade Center, Wheaton College (Wheaton, Illinois).

2320. Thorpe, Benjamin. *The Anglo-Saxon poems of Beowulf, the Scôp or Gleeman's tale and the fight at Finnesburg: With a literal transl., notes, glossary, etc.* Oxford: Parker, 1855.
    P.s.: *Beowulf* (2002) 'Transcription of Legibile Portions of Folios 71-81: Notes and Jottings', p. 431.

2321. _____. *The Anglo-Saxon poems of Beowulf, the Scôp or Gleeman's tale, and the fight at Finnesburg*. London: Smith, 1875.
    P.s.: *Beowulf* (2002) 'Transcription of Legibile Portions of Folios 71-81: Notes and Jottings', p. 431.

2322. _____. *The Anglo-Saxon Chronicle*, Vol. I. Original texts. London: Longman, Green, Longman and Roberts, 1861.
    P.s. 1: MS. Tolkien A 12/2 *Commentary on Sir Gawain, lines 1999-2523* fol. 32. [Tolkien Papers, Bodleian Library, Oxford].
    P.s. 2: *Finn and Hengest* (1982), p. 13 n. 9.
    P.s. 3: *The Fall of Arthur* (2013), p. 224.
    S.s. 1: Scull-Hammond (2017a), pp. 156, 468.
    S.s. 2: Scull-Hammond (2017b), pp. 61, 455.

2323. _____. *The Anglo-Saxon Chronicle*, Vol. II. Translations. London: Longman, Green, Longman and Roberts, 1861.
    P.s.: *The Fall of Arthur* (2013), p. 224.
    S.s. 1: Scull-Hammond (2017a), pp. 156, 468.
    S.s. 2: Scull-Hammond (2017b), pp. 61, 455.

2324. _____. *Cædmon's metrical paraphrase of parts of the Holy Scriptures in Anglo-Saxon*. Cædmon Society of Antiquaries of London, 1832.
    P.s.: MS. Tolkien A 12/2 Commentary on Sir Gawain, lines 1999-2523 fol. 32. [Tolkien Papers, Bodleian Library, Oxford].

2325. _____. *Florentii Wigorniensis monachi Chronicon*, Vol. II. 1152-1295. Londini, Sumptibus societatis, 1848.
    P.s.: *Finn and Hengest* (1982), p. 61 n. 63.

2326. _____. *Libri Psalmorum versio antiqua Latina. Cum paraphrasi Anglo-Saxonica, partim soluta oratione, partim metrice composita; nunc primum e Cod. MS. in Bibl. Regia Parisiensi adservato*. Oxford: E Typographeo Academico, 1835.
    P.s.: *Sigelwara land* (1932), p. 184 n. 2.

2327. *Thousand and one nights, Or The Arabian Nights*. New York: International Book Company, 1892.
    P.s. 1: *Tolkien On Fairy-stories* (2008) 'Manuscript A. [MS Tolkien 4, fols. 59-77]', p. 184.
    P.s. 2: *Tolkien On Fairy-stories* (2008) 'Manuscript B [MS. Tolkien 4, fols. 73-120]', p. 215 [*Aladdin and The Forty Thieves*], p. 227 [*Prince Ahmed and the Fairy Paribanon*]

2328. *Three Little Pigs* [Fable]

P.s.: #1 a. | *Tolkien On Fairy-stories* (2008), p. 311.

2329. Thucydides. *The Fifth Book of Thucydides*. Edited by Charles Edward Graves. London: Macmillan, 1899.
   Description: Tolkien dated: '12 June 1910'. and he wrote in gothic: 'I read the words of these books of Greek history ('year-writing') in the sixth month of this year: thousand, nine hundreds, ten, of Our Lord: in order to gain the prize given every year to the boy knowing most about Thucydides, and this I inscribed in my books on the twelfth of the sixth (month) after I had already? First read through all the words carefully'.
   P.s.: *Letters* 272 (1965). From a letter to Zillah Sherring.
   S.s. 1: Scull-Hammond (2017a), pp. 23, 675.
   S.s. 2: Scull-Hammond (2006b), p. 822.

2330. _____. *Thucydides Book I*, Vol. I Introduction and text. Edited with introduction and notes by William Henry Forbes. Oxford: At the Clarendon Press, 1895.
   Description: Tolkien requested the book on 9 December 1930 (MS. Library Records b. 640). Weston Library (Oxford), 2353 e.119 (ex SCI Gr. 222s).

2331. _____. *Thucydides Book I*, Vol. II Notes. Edited with introduction and notes by William Henry Forbes. Oxford: At the Clarendon Press, 1895.
   Description: Tolkien requested the book on 9 December 1930 (MS. Library Records b. 640). Weston Library (Oxford), 2353 e.119 (ex SCI Gr. 222s).

2332. _____. *Thucydides: Book VI*. Edited by Albert William Spratt. Cambridge: The University Press, 1905.
   Description: Signed twice on the front free endpaper by Tolkien, once in brown ink and once in green ink, the second written underneath with English and Greek: 'May 1911 K. E. S'.
   Collection: Private [Sold by Bloomsbury Auctions, 18 March 2004].

2333. Thumb, Albert. *Handbuch des sanskrit, mit texten und glossar; eine einführung in das sprachwissenschaftliche studium des altindischen*, Vol. II. Texte und Glossar. Heidelberg: Carl Winter, 1905.
   Description: Autographed in ink: 'J.R.R. Tolkien'.
   Collection: J.R.R. Tolkien Collection, Department of Special Collections and University Archives, Raynor Memorial Libraries, Marquette University (Milwaukee).

2334. Thurneysen, Rudolf (Edited by). *Cōic Conara Fugill: die fünf Wege zum Urteil*. Series: Abhandlungen der Preussischen Akademie der Wissenschaften. Jahrg. 1925. Phil.-hist. Klasse, 7. Berlin: Akademie der Wissenschaften, 1926.
   Collection: Tolkien's personal Celtic library, preserved at the Weston library under the auspices of the English Faculty Library (Oxford).

2335. _____. *Handbuch Des Alt-Irischen*, Vol. I. Grammatik. Heidelberg: Carl Winter, 1909.
   Description: Decoratively autographed and inscribed on front flyleaf: 'e. coll. exon. oxon. | Feb. mcmxiv'. Annotated in pencil. Contains empty envelope addressed by JRRT, 12.8.1934, and 8 pages of penciled vocabulary notes 3 made by JRRT.
   Collection: Tolkien's personal Celtic library, preserved at the Weston library under the auspices of the English Faculty Library (Oxford).

2336. _____. *Handbuch Des Alt-Irischen*, Vol. II. Texte mit Wörterbuch. Heidelberg: Carl Winter, 1909.
   Description: Decoratively inscribed: 'J.R.R. Tolkien. | Exeter College: Oxford: | Feb. 1914 | AMDG | EMB'. Annotated in pencil.
   Collection: Tolkien's personal Celtic library, preserved at the Weston library under the auspices of the English Faculty Library (Oxford).

2337. _____. *Zu Irischen Handschriften und Litteraturdenkmälern*. Berlin: Weldmannsche buchharndlung, 1912.
>Description: Autographed and inscribed: 'from K. Sisam | April 23rd | 1922.' On front flyleaf. On title page:'sisam | London'.
>Collection: Tolkien's personal Celtic library, preserved at the Weston library under the auspices of the English Faculty Library (Oxford).

2338. _____. 'Zui irischen Texten: 1. Die Überlieferung der Fled Bricenn. 2. Zum Gedicht von St. Paul II'. *Zeitschrift für celtische Philologie*. Vol. IV, 1902, pp. 193-207.
>P.s.: *Sir Gawain and the Green Knight* (1925), p. xxvi. Tolkien and Gordon write: 'For bibliography of the Irish and French analogues of *Sir Gawain*, see the bibliography in Kittredge's study'. [NED] In Kittredge's study, this article is mentioned in 'I. Fled Bricrend' (p. 292).

2339. _____. 'Nachträge zur Sage von CuRoi'. *Zeitschrift für celtische Philologie*, Vol. IX, 1913, pp. 336-37.
>P.s.: *Sir Gawain and the Green Knight* (1925), p. xxvi. Tolkien and Gordon write: 'For bibliography of the Irish and French analogues of *Sir Gawain*, see the bibliography in Kittredge's study'. [NED] In Kittredge's study, this article is mentioned in 'II. Gawain and the Green Knight' (p. 293).

2340. _____. 'Die Sage von CuRoi'. *Zeitschrift für celtische Philologie*, Vol. IX, 1913, pp. 189-234.
>P.s.: *Sir Gawain and the Green Knight* (1925), p. xxvi. Tolkien and Gordon write: 'For bibliography of the Irish and French analogues of *Sir Gawain*, see the bibliography in Kittredge's study'. [NED] In Kittredge's study, this article is mentioned in 'II. Gawain and the Green Knight' (p. 293).

2341. _____. *Sagen aus dem alten Irland*. Berlin: Wiegandt & Grieben, 1901.
>P.s.: *Sir Gawain and the Green Knight* (1925), p. xxvi. Tolkien and Gordon write: 'For bibliography of the Irish and French analogues of *Sir Gawain*, see the bibliography in Kittredge's study'. [NED] In Kittredge's study, this article is mentioned in 'I. Fled Bricrend' (p. 291).

2342. Tilander, Gunnar. *Boke of huntyng*. Series: Cynegetica, 11. Karlshamn: E. G. Johansson, 1964.
>P.s.: *Sir Gawain and the Green Knight* (1967) 'Select Bibliography', p. 155.

2343. _____. *Essais d'étymologie cynégétique*. Series: Cynegetica, 1. Lund: H. Ohlssons Boktryckeri, 1953.
>P.s.: *Sir Gawain and the Green Knight* (1967) 'Select Bibliography', p. 155.

2344. _____. *La Chace dou cerf*. Series: Cynegetica, 7. Stockholm: Offset-Lito, 1960.
>P.s.: *Sir Gawain and the Green Knight* (1967) 'Select Bibliography', p. 155.

2345. Tolkien, Christopher J. R. (Edited by). *The Saga of King Heidrek the Wise*. London: Thomas Nelson & Sons (Icelandic Texts), 30 June 1960.

2346. _____. *Hervarar Saga ok Heidreks Konungs*. B. Litt. Thesis. (Oxford University, Trinity College), 1953-4. [Year uncertain].

2347. Tolkien, J. R. R. 'Chaucer as a Philologist: *The Reeve's Tale*'. Offprint from *The Philological Society's Transactions*, Oxford: The Philological Society, 1934, pp. 1-70.
>Description 1: A presentation copy inscribed by Tolkien to G. H. Cowling, 'G. H. C. | from | JRRT', on the front wrapper and with text corrections by the author on pages 6 ('little of his origins' >

'little of the origins'), 20 ('*himseluen serue pat*' > '*himseluen serue þat*'), 36 ('L Hl *þeir*(e)' > '*þeir*(e) L Hl'), 38 ('be assumed unproven' > 'be assumed unproved'), and 47 ('especially ll. 36 ff.' > 'especially lll. 56 ff.'; '*William of Palerne* 12443' > *William of Palerne* 1243'; 'hurtled to þe grounde' > 'hurled to þe grounde'). Collection: Private [Peter Harrington, London]
Description 2: Inscribed by Tolkien to David Nichol Smith, 'D.NiS | with greetings | from | J.R.R.T'. Accompanied by a letter from the author. Collection: National Library of Australia, Special Collections Reading Room.
Description 3: Inscribed by Tolkien to Angus McIntosh, 'A. McIntosh | from | JRRT.' Collection: Private [Tolkien Books].

2348. _____. *The English Text of the Ancrene Riwle: Ancrene Wisse. Edited from MS. Corpus Christi College Cambridge 402*. Series: E.E.T.S. (Early English Text Society), OS 249. London: Oxford University Press, 1962.
Description: Autographed on front flyleaf.
Collection: Tolkien's personal Celtic library, preserved at the Weston library under the auspices of the English Faculty Library (Oxford).
P.s.: *Letters* 240 (1962). To Mrs Pauline [Baynes] Gash. Tolkin writes: 'the three places for gossip, smithy, mill, and cheaping (market), from a mediaeval instructive work that I have been editing!'.

2349. _____. *Farmer Giles of Ham*. London: Allen and Unwin, 1949.
Description: Inscribed by Tolkien to his son John: 'Fileo mio primo & perdilecto Johanni Francisco Josepho | in confinibus Regni minimi de nutrito huc libello dat pater et auctor. | Vadi Bovini xvi novebris mcmxlix.'
Collection: Taylor Institution Library, Bodleian Libraries (Oxford).

2350. _____. *The Hobbit, Or, There and Back Again*. London: George Allen & Unwin, 1942.
Description: Author's copy, signed on half title: 'J.R.R. Tolkien'. Extensively Annotated in ballpoint and pencil on pages 17, 27, 30, 31, 35, 53, 63, 64, 82, 85, 86, 87, 88. 89, 90, 91, 94, 95, 104, 210, 215, 240, 273 and 294.
Collection: Private [Christie's]

2351. _____. *The Lord of the Rings – The Fellowship of the Ring*. Proof copy of the first edition. London: Jarrold and Sons Limited for George Allen & Unwin Ltd., 1953.
Description: (A few leaves lightly marked, pp. 32-33 slightly affected by adhesive.) Original brown paper wrappers, the upper wrapper with pasted-on typewritten lettering-piece reading '*THE FELLOWSHIP OF THE RING*, by J.R.R. Tolkien', and ink inscription 'Not less than 21/-, nor more than 25/-'. In this copy the number '12' on p. 21 has been corrected in pencil, and the uncorrected errors on p. 48, ll. 13-14, p. 166, l. 41, and p. 197, l. 40 have been retained. The illustrations which occur on pp. 59, 319 and 333 of the first edition have been omitted.
Collection: Private [Sold by Christie's, 16 November 2001].

2352. _____. *The Lord of the Rings – The Return of the King*. Proof copy of the first edition, the Appendices corrected throughout by Tolkien. London: *The Return of the King*. London: Jarrold and Sons Limited for George Allen & Unwin Ltd., 1954.
Description: Circa 295 loose galley sheets, printed on rectos only, and the loose galley sheets of the Appendices, calligraphic manuscript title '*The Return of the King*. Appendices, pp. 313-416' in Tolkien's hand, paginated 313-416, pp. 379-83 and 401-03 in Tolkien's hand, corrected by Tolkien in red, blue and black inks, the first leaf with printer's inkstamp dated 29 June 1955 and dated by Tolkien 'received July 2'. (Some leaves a little frayed or occasionally torn and marked, p. 360 erroneously inserted between pp. 377 and 378) The main text in loose sheets, the Appendices held together with a paper fastener.
Collection: Private [Sold by Christie's, 16 November 2001].

2353. _____. *The Lord of the Rings – The Two Towers*. Proof copy of the first edition. London: Jarrold and Sons Limited for George Allen & Unwin Ltd., 1954.

Description: (Short tear affecting text on 6/1, short marginal tears on 19/7, 21/3-4 and 22/8.) Original brown paper wrappers, with two typewritten lettering-pieces pasted onto upper wrapper, reading 'about 21s.' and '*THE TWO TOWERS*, by J.R.R. Tolkien' (corners slightly frayed, short tears at head and tail of spine). This copy has the incorrect 'all the season of the year' reading on p. 111, l. 34, but the correct 'may like' reading on p. 350, l. 31 (misprinted as 'maylike' in the first edition).
Collection: Private [Sold by Christie's, 16 November 2001].

2354. _____. 'Middle English 'Losenger': sketch of an etymological and semantic enquiry'. Offprint from *Essais de philologie modern*. Paris: Société d'édition Les Belles lettres, 1953.
Description: Inscribed in pencil on p. 63: '[From Prof. Tolkien's Library]'. Includes a label added by Stan Revell to books owned by Tolkien, 'From the Library of J.R.R. Tolkien'.
Collection: Marion E. Wade Center, Wheaton College (Wheaton, Illinois).

2355. _____. *A Middle English Vocabulary*. Oxford: At the Clarendon Press, 1922.
Description: Some annotation and notes on vocabulary. Autographed: 'J.R.R. Tolkien. | From the C. P.' [Clarendon Press]
S.s. 1: Priestman (1992), p. 39 no. 68.

2356. _____. *Sir Orfeo*. Oxford: The Academic Office, 1944.
Description: He has made 3 holograph corrections and numbered the lines to 340.
S.s.: Hime (1980), p. 10.

2357. _____. *The Reeve's Tale*. Oxford, 1939.
Description: Version prepared for recitation at the 'summer diversions' Oxford: 1939. Cover title: Edited and introduced by J.R.R. Tolkien [Judith Priestman 1994, revd. 2016].
Collection: Weston Library, Bodleian Libraries (Oxford).

2358. _____. 'Some Contributions to Middle-English Lexicography'. Offprint from *The Review of English Studies*, Vol. 1, no. 2. London: Sidgwick & Jackson, April 1925.
Description: Tolkien has pencilled a note on the outer margin to page 5, where is inscribed his consideration of the word 'suti' (in modern form sooty) thus: 'Though ON sút may be concerned in some cases | There are clear cases in 'AB' of sút=dirt.' Includes a label added by Stan Revell to books owned by Tolkien, 'From the Library of J.R.R. Tolkien', to the inside from cover. Revell has also loosely inserted's a note:'sole copy with Tolkien's MS Notes - NOT FOR SALE'.
S.s.: Blackwell's Rare Books (2012), pp. 81-82.
Collection: Private.

2359. _____ and Eric Valentine Gordon (Edited by). *Sir Gawain and the Green Knight*. Oxford: At the Clarendon Press, 1925.
Description: Inscribed: 'J.R.R. Tolkien'. Annotations throughout [Judith Priestman 1994, revd. 2016].
Collection: Weston Library, Bodleian Libraries (Oxford).
P.s.: *Sir Gawain and the Green Knight* (1967) 'Select Bibliography', p. 153.

2360. _____ and Eric Valentine Gordon (Edited by). *Sir Gawain and the Green Knight*. Oxford: At the Clarendon Press, 1930 (impression of above).
Description: Inscribed: 'J.R.R. Tolkien 1932 | JRRT'. Annotations throughout. Loose leaves [Judith Priestman 1994, revd. 2016].
Collection: Weston Library, Bodleian Libraries (Oxford).
Notes: Tolkien gives a copy, with a dedication, to Simonne d'Ardenne [Fonds J.R.R. Tolkien, Bibliothèque ALPHA principale, Université de Liège (Liège), Tol/057].

2361. _____ and Eric Valentine Gordon (Edited by). *Sir Gawain and the Green*

Knight. Oxford: At the Clarendon Press, 1946 (4th ed.).
   Description: Annotated in pencil and ink.
   Collection: Private.

2362. _____ and Eric Valentine Gordon (Edited by). *Sir Gawain and the Green Knight*. Edited by Norman Davis. London: Oxford University Press, 1968.
   Description: Signed by the author on half-title: 'J.R.R. Tolkien'.
   Collection: Private [Bloomsbuty Auctions].
   P.s.: MS. Tolkien A 34/3 Texts for the BBC radio presentation of the translation of *Sir Gawain and the Green Knight*, 1953 fol.f. 221. [Tolkien Papers, Bodleian Library, Oxford].

2363. _____, Eric Valentine Gordon *et alii*. *Songs for the Philologists*. Privately printed in and for the Department of English at University College, London, 1936.
   Description: Tolkien's personal copy with handwritten notes and corrections.
   Collection: J.R.R. Tolkien Collection, Department of Special Collections and University Archives, Raynor Memorial Libraries, Marquette University (Milwaukee).

2364. Tonndorf, M. *The taill of Rauf Coilyear; mit lierarhistorischer, grammatischer und metrischer Einleitung*. Berlin: C. Vogt's Verlag, 1894.
   P.s.: *Sir Gawain and the Green Knight* (1925), p. xxvi. Tolkien and Gordon write: 'For bibliography of the Irish and French analogues of *Sir Gawain*, see the bibliography in Kittredge's study'. [*NED*] In Kittredge's study, this article is mentioned in 'XIII. Rauf Coilyear' (p. 306).

2365. Torp, Alf. *Nynorsk Etymologisk Ordbok*. Kristiana: H. Aschehoug, 1919.
   P.s.: *Sigelwara land* (1934), p. 109 n. 3.

2366. Tottel, Richard; Henry Howard; Thomas Wyatt; Nicholas Grimald *et alii*. *Tottel's Miscellany: Songs and Sonettes*. Edited by Edward Arber. London: A. Constable and Co., 1903.
   S.s.: University of Leeds (1920), p. 147. English Language and Literature - Scheme A. Texts and Period selected for 1920-21. (b) Special period: 1557-1637. (c) Texts suggested for study with Special Period. Ordinary Degree of B.A. with Honours. Final Examination.

2367. Trethewey, William H. (Edited by). *The French Text of the Ancrene Riwle. Trinity College Cambridge MS. R. 14.7*. Series: E.E.T.S. (Early English Text Society), OS 240. London: Oxford University Press, 1958.
   Description: Contains bookmark at pp. xxvi-xxvii.
   Collection: Tolkien's personal Celtic library, preserved at the Weston library under the auspices of the English Faculty Library (Oxford).
   S.s.: McIlwaine (2018), no. 84.

2368. Trounce, Allan McIntyre (Edited by). *Athelston: A Middle English Romance*. Series: Philological Society, XI. London: Oxford University Press, H. Milford, 1933.
   Description: On p. vi: 'This edition is substantially the work presented as a Dissertation for the degree of Bachelor of Letters in the University of Oxford, the examiners being Professor J.R.R. Tolkien and Mr. C. L. Wrenn, to whom thanks are due for criticisms made in the course of the viva-voce examination.'
   S.s.: Scull-Hammond (2017a), pp. 172-73.

2369. _____. 'The English Tail-Rhyme Romances'. Offprint from *Medium Ævum*, Vol. 1, no. 2. Oxford: Basil Blackwell, 1932, pp. 87-108.
   P.s.: 'Chaucer as a Philologist: *The Reeve's Tale*' (1934), p. 165 n. 57.

2370. Turberville, George. *The Noble Art of Venerie or Hunting. (Turberville's Booke of hunting)* Reprint of 1576. Series: Tudor & Stuart library; Library of English literature. Oxford: At the Clarendon Press, 1908.

P.s. 1: *Sir Gawain and the Green Knight* (1925), p. xxvii. p. 104, line 1334 *and lere of þe knot*; line 1337-8; line 1355 *þe corbels*.

P.s. 2: *Sir Gawain and the Green Knight* (1967) 'Select Bibliography', p. 155.

NED 1: #2 h. | 'W' (1928), p. 53 'Wallop *sb*. 2. a' – 1576 'Put a glasse full of white wine to them, and let them boyle therein, a whalme or a wallop in a pewter pot' (lxxix, p. 230).

NED 2: #2 h. | 'W' (1928), p. 54. 'Walm *sb.*¹ *Obs*. 3. c.' – 1575 'Let them boyle two or three whalmes vpon the fire' (ch. 79, p. 231-2).; 'Let them boyle therein, a whalme or a wallop in a pewter pot' (p. 232)

2371. Turnbull, William Braclay (Edited by). *Arthour and Merlin: a metrical romance. Now first edited from the Auchinleck MS*. Edinburgh, Abbotsford club, 1838.

P.s. 1: MS. Tolkien A 12/1 *Commentary on Sir Gawain, lines 37-1987* fol. 20. [Tolkien Papers, Bodleian Library, Oxford].

P.s. 2: 'Chaucer as a Philologist: *The Reeve's Tale*' (1934), p. 152.

2372. Turner, Sharon. *The History of the Anglo-Saxons*, Vol. I. London: Longman Hurst, Rees & Orme, 1807 (2nd ed.).

P.s. 1: *Beowulf* (2002) 'Version A', p. 44.

P.s. 2: *Beowulf* (2002) 'Textual Notes A-Text', p. 322.

2373. _____. *The History of the Anglo-Saxons*, Vol. II. London: Longman Hurst, Rees & Orme, 1807 (2nd ed.).

P.s. 1: *Beowulf* (2002) 'Version A', p. 44.

P.s. 2: *Beowulf* (2002) 'Textual Notes A-Text', p. 322.

2374. Turville-Petre, Edward Oswald Gabriel (Edited by). *Hervarar Saga ok Heidreks*. Introduction by Christopher J. R. Tolkien. London: University College London, for the Viking Society for Northern Research, 1956.

2375. _____ (Edited by). *Víga-Glúms Saga*. Series: Oxford English Monographs, 1. London: Oxford University Press, 1940.

S.s.: Scull-Hammond (2006b), p. 728: was originally a thesis produced under Tolkien's supervision. Tolkien was one of the General Editors for the series. In the introduction Turville-Petre says: 'It would be difficult to overestimate all that I owe to Professor Tolkien; his sympathy and encouragement have been constant and, throughout the work I have had the benefit of his wide scholarship.'

2376. _____ and Joan Elizabeth. 'Studies in the *Ormulum* MS.' *The Journal of English and Germanic Philology*, Vol. 43, no. 1, 1947, pp. 1-27.

Collection: Taylor Institution Library, Bodleian Libraries (Oxford).

P.s.: MS. Tolkien 10/2 'Offprint of J. E. Turville-Petre,'studies on the *Ormulum* MS.' (1947).' [Tolkien Papers, Bodleian Library, Oxford].

2377. Twemlow, Jesse Alfred (Edited by). *Liverpool Town Books, proceedings of assemblies, common councils, Portmoot courts, [etc.], 1550-1862*, Vol. I. Liverpool: University Press, 1918.

P.s.: *Sir Gawain and the Green Knight* (1925), p. 112, line 2004 *wapped*. Tolkien and Gordon quote: 'the snowe dryvyng and wappyng to and froe' ('John Cross, Mayor, 1565-1566', p. 292).

2378. Twici, Guillaume. *La vénerie de Twiti; le plus ancien traité de chasse écrit en Angleterre, la version anglaise du même traité et Craft of venery*. Eited by Gunnar Tilander. Series: Cynegetica, 2. Uppsala: Almqvist & Wiksell, 1956.

P.s.: *Sir Gawain and the Green Knight* (1967) 'Select Bibliography', p. 155.

Section A

2379. Ulrich von Zatzikhoven. *Lanzelet: a romance of Lancelot*. Series: Records of civilization, sources and studies, 47. Edited and translated by Roger Sherman Loomis and K.G. T. Webster.New Yor: Columbia University Press, 1951.
   P.s.: *Sir Gawain and the Green Knight* (1967) 'Select Bibliography', p. 155.

2380. Ungnad, Arthur. *Babylonisch-Assyrische Grammatik. Mit Übungsbuch (in Transskription)*. Series: Clavis linguarum semiticarum, 2. München: C. H. Beck'sche Verlagsbuchhandlung, 1926 (3rd ed.).
   Collection: The Science Fiction and Fantasy Research Collection of the Cushing Memorial Library and Archives at Texas A&M University.
   S.s.: Birns (2012), p. 66.

2381. University of Oxford. *Speech delivered for the presentation of the Honorary Degree of Doctor of Letters to Professor John Ronald Reuel Tolkien*. Oxford: 3 June, 1972.
   Description: Single leaf printed recto, in Latin. Tolkien's own copy of the speech delivered by the Public Orator on the occasion of his honorary Doctorate, which was awarded by Oxford for his contribution to Anglo Saxon scholar ship and Philology: The speech was read by his old friend Colin Hardie.
   Collection: Private [Sold by Simon Finch Rare Books Ltd.].
   S.s.: Finch (2002), p. 54.

2382. Untermeyer, Bryna Ivens and Untermeyer, Louis. *The Children's Treasury of literature in colour*. London: Hamlyn, 1966.
   S.s.: Scull-Hammond (2017a), p. 719 Joy Hill has sent him a copy of *The Children's Treasury of English Literature*, published by Paul Hamlyn, an anthology which includes the first chapter of *The Hobbit*.; p. 720. Tolkien writes to Joy Hill on 5 January, 1967: Tolkien thinks a great many of the illustrations are very good, including some of the modern ones. Illustrations to *The Hobbit* extract seem to him the worst of all, vulgar, stupid, and entirely out of keeping with the text.

2383. Unwin, Stanley. *Truth About Publishing*. London: George Allen & Unwin.
   P.s.: *Letters* 257 (1964). To Christopher Bretherton.

2384. Vachell, Horace Annesley. *The Hill. A romance of friendship*. London: John Murray, 1923.
   P.s.: *Philology: General Works* (IV 1924, for 1923), p. 29.

2385. Valladares Nuñez, Marcial. *Diccionario gallego-castellano*. Santiago [de Compostela]: Impr. del Seminario Conciliar Central, 1884.
   Collection: Taylor Institution Library, Bodleian Libraries (Oxford).

2386. van Langenhove, George. *On the Origin of the Gerund in English* (Phonology). Gand: Van Rysselberghe and Rombaut, 1925.
   Description: Autographed on front cover.
   Collection: Tolkien's personal Celtic library, preserved at the Weston library under the auspices of the English Faculty Library (Oxford).
   P.s.: *Philology: General Works* (VI 1927, for 1925), p. 62.

2387. Vendryes, Joseph. *Language: a Linguistic Introduction to History*. Translated by Paul Radin. London: Kegan Paul Trench, Trübner & Co. Ltd., 1925.
   P.s.: *Philology: General Works* (VI 1927, for 1925), p. 52 n. 9.

2388. Verdaguer, Joaquin. *The art of pipe smoking*. London: Curlew Press, 1958.
   Collection: Private [Sold by Thornton's of Oxford]

2389. Verdeyen, René. 'Le Flaman'. *Encyclopédie belge*. Bruxelles: La Renaissance du Livre, 1933.
    P.s.: 'Middle English 'Losenger'' (1953), p. 74 n. 2.

2390. Vernaleken, Theodor. *In the Land of Marvels: Folk-tales from Austria and Bohemia*. Preface by Edwin Johnson. London: Swan Sonnenschein & Co., 1884.
    P.s.: *Tolkien On Fairy-stories* (2008) 'Manuscript A. [MS Tolkien 4, fols. 59-77]', p. 182. In his preface, Johnson writes: 'in Nature could ever wear a personal significance or glory not cast upon it from the human spirit itself, the one theatre and focus of all marvels' (p. 12). While Tolkien writes, in quotation marks: "in Nature could wear a personal significance or glory if it were not cast upon it from the human spark itself, the one that is the form of all marvels".

2391. *Vernon MS. Bodleian*. [Contains *Ancrene Riwle*].
    P.s.: MS. Tolkien A 21/13 *The English MSS*. fol. 197. [Tolkien Papers, Bodleian Library, Oxford].

2392. Villari, Pasquale. *Life and times of Girolamo Savonarola*, Vol. I. Translated by Linda Villari. London: Fisher Unwin, 1888.
    Description: Tolkien requested the book on 1 May 1931 (MS. Library Records b. 626). Weston Library (Oxford), 1190 d.6 (ex S. Hist. It. 2b might be S. Hist. It. 25?).

2393. _____. *Life and times of Girolamo Savonarola*, Vol. II. Translated by Linda Villari. London: Fisher Unwin, 1888.
    Description: Tolkien requested the book on 1 May 1931 (MS. Library Records b. 626). Weston Library (Oxford), 1190 d.6 (ex S. Hist. It. 2b might be S. Hist. It. 25?).

2394. Virgil. *The Aeneid of Virgil*, Vol. I. Translated into Scottish verse by Gavin Douglas. Edinburgh: T. Constable, 1839.
    P.s.: *Sir Gawain and the Green Knight* (1925), p. 111, line 1881 *þe more and þe mynne*. Tolkien and Gordon cite 87/24.

2395. _____. *The Aeneid*. Edited by John William Mackail. Oxford: At the Clarendon Press, 1930.
    P.s. 1: *Beowulf* (1937), p. 24.
    P.s. 2: *Beowulf* (2002) 'Version B', pp. 124-25. Tolkien quoting lines 600-665 ('per sidera testor … latera ardua tinxit') from Book III.

2396. _____. *P. Vergilii Maronis opera*, Vol. I. With introduction and English notes by Arthur Sidgwick. Cambridge: The University Press, 1897.
    Description: King Edward's School and Exeter College. Inscribed: 'J.R.R. Tolkien Class (i). | King Edward's School Verg. Oper. Text. | Oct first 1907' | 'J.R.R. Tolkien | King Edward's School. | Cl. l, Mar. 7. 1910' | 'J.R.R. Tolkien.' With Anglo-Saxon inscription on half-title, followed by: 'J.R.R. Tolkien Exeter Coll. Oxford'. Back paste down annotated: 'J. R. Reuel Tolkien. | Exeter Coll. Oxford. | Michaelmas 1911'. A few annotations [Judith Priestman 1994, revd. 2016].
    Collection: Weston Library, Bodleian Libraries (Oxford).
    P.s.: *Beowulf* (2002) 'Textual Notes B-Text', p. 411. Tolkien quotes: 'Cithara crinitus iopas … unde imber et ignis' (740-43).
    S.s.: Zettersten (2011), p. 78 'During my last visit to the Tolkien Collection at the Bodleian Library, Oxford, I went through Tolkien's books in his private library from his school time, which his family had donated to the Bodleian in July 1982.'

2397. _____. *P. Vergilii Maronis opera*, Vol. II. Notes. With introduction and English notes by Arthur Sidgwick. Cambridge: The University Press, 1897.
    Description: Inscribed (right fore-edge): 'JRRT'. And (bottom fore-edge): 'Ronald Tolkien'. Flyleaf inscribed: 'J.R.R. Tolkien. | Class I King Edward's School | Oct first 1907 | Verg. Oper. Notes'. | 'J.R.R. Tolkien | Exeter Coll. Oxford' [Judith Priestman 1994, revd. 2016].

Collection: Weston Library, Bodleian Libraries (Oxford).

2398. Vising, Johan. *Anglo-Norman language and literature*. London: Oxford University Press, 1923.
    Notes: On page 114, Tolkien is cited among contributors of the *The Oxford Language and Literature Series*.

2399. _____. *Mélanges de philologie offerts á M. Johan Vising. Par ses élèves et ses amis scandinaves à l'occasion du soixante-dixième anniversaire de sa naissance le 20 avril 1925*. Göteborg and Paris: Gumperts and Champion, 1925.
    Notes: Limited to 250 copies.
    P.s.: *Philology: General Works* (VI 1927, for 1925), p. 32 n. 5, 47.

2400. Vleeskruyer, Rudolf (Edited by). *The life of St Chad: an old English homily*. Amsterdam: North-Holland Pub. Co., 1953.
    Description: The book is the Thesis D.Phil of Vleeskruyer. Tolkien was his supervisor. In his preface, Vleeskruyer thanks Tolkien and C.L. Wrenn: 'I owe much to the wise criticism and the generous advice of Professor C.L. Wrenn, and have been fortunate in profiting by the learning of Professor J.R.R. Tolkien' (p. viii).

2401. Vočadlo, Otakar. 'Anglo-Saxon Terminology'. From *Studies in English by Members of the English Seminar at the Charles University, Prague, 4th*. Praha: Charles Press, 1933, pp. 61-85.
    Description: Inscribed on the cover: "Prof Tolkien with the author's compliments | Oxford 14/6/46'.
    Notes: A copy was sent to Tolkien by the author. Uncut and presumably unread, in original wrappers.
    Collection: Private [Sold by Loome Theological Booksellers, 1993]

2402. *Völundarkviða* [Mythological poems, see Poetic Edda].
    S.s.: Michael G.R. Tolkien (1989). Michael G. R. cites a letter from his grandfather JRR.

2403. von Wartburg, Walter. *Französisches etymologisches Wörterbuch*, Vol. III D-F. Bâle: Zbinden Dr. u. Verl., 1934.
    P.s.: 'Middle English 'Losenger'' (1953), p. 66 n. 1.

2404. Wace, Robert. *Le Roman de Brut*, Vol. I. Publié pour la première fois d'Apres les Manuscrits des Bibliotheques de Paris avec un commentaire et des notes par le roux de lincy. Rouen: Eduard Frere, 1836.
    Description: Signed by Tolkien.
    Collection: Private [Sold by Simon Finch Rare Books Ltd.].
    P.s.: MS. Tolkien A 21/13 *The English MSS*. fol. 203. [Tolkien Papers, Bodleian Library, Oxford].
    S.s.: Finch (2002), p. 53.

2405. _____. *Le Roman de Brut*, Vol. II. Publié pour la première fois d'Apres les Manuscrits des Bibliotheques de Paris avec un commentaire et des notes par le roux de lincy. Rouen: Eduard Frere, 1838.
    Description: Signed by Tolkien.
    Collection: Private [Sold by Simon Finch Rare Books Ltd.].
    P.s.: MS. Tolkien A 21/13 *The English MSS*. fol. 203. [Tolkien Papers, Bodleian Library, Oxford].
    S.s.: Finch (2002), p. 53.

2406. _____. *Le Roman de Brut*, Vol. I. Edited by Ivor Arnold. Paris: Societe des

anciens textes francais, 1938.
> P.s.: *Sir Gawain and the Green Knight* (1967) 'Select Bibliography', p. 155.

2407. _____. *Le Roman de Brut*, Vol. II. Edited by Ivor Arnold. Paris: Societe des anciens textes francais, 1940.
> P.s.: *Sir Gawain and the Green Knight* (1967) 'Select Bibliography', p. 155.

2408. Wadstein, Elis. 'The Beowulf Poem as an English National Epos'. Offprint from *Acta Philologica Scandinavica*, 8, 1931–2, pp. 273–91.
> Description: Inscribed by the author: 'With the author's compliments'. Inscribed by Tolkien: 'Beowulf a National Wadstein'. Includes a label added by Stan Revell to books owned by Tolkien, 'From the Library of J.R.R. Tolkien'.
> Collection: Private [Christina Scull & Wayne G. Hammond].
> S.s. Scull-Hammond (2018a).

2409. Wagner, Felix. *Les poemes mythologiques de l'Edda*. Traduction française d'Après le texte original islandais accompagnée de notices interprétatives et précédée d'un exposé général de la mythologie Scandinave basé sur les sources primitives. Paris: Éditions Droz (Bibliothèque de la Faculté de philosophie et des lettres de l'Université de Liège), Fasc. LXXI, 1936.
> P.s.: Tolkien's unpublished letter to Simonne d'Ardenne, 1938-39. Tolkien writes: 'You have rightly erred on the side of compliment and civility. I have not myself read the work thoroughly, but only a rapid glance recent Mr. Wagner as insufficient in control of the language and philology of Scand. (and English) or Germanic in general. I add a few notes simply on yours review' [Fonds J.R.R. Tolkien, Bibliothèque ALPHA principale, Université de Liège (Liège)].
> S.s.: Scull-Hammond (2017a), p. 237. 10 October 1938: Simonne d'Ardenne writes to Tolkien. She encloses a copy of her review of *Les poemes mythologiques de l'Edda*, translated by Felix Wagner (1936) and asks if Tolkien approves of it.

2410. Wagner, Richard. *Der Ring des Nibelungen*, Vol. I. Das Rheingold: Vorspiel.
> S.s.: Scull-Hammond (2017a), p. 841. '26 March 1934 Tolkien and the Lewis brothers met regularly in early 1934 to read the four operas of Wagner's *Der Ring des Nibelungen*, in preparation for a planned attendance of the complete cycle at Covent Garden in London along with their friends Owen Barfield and Cecil Harwood. In the event, Harwood failed to book their seats. Priscilla Tolkien recalls, however, that her father and C.S. Lewis once attended a performance of one of the operas, possibly Siegfried, at Covent Garden, where they found themselves to be almost the only members of the audience in their part of the theatre not in evening dress.'

2411. _____. *Der Ring des Nibelungen*, Vol. II. Die Walküre: Erster Tag.
> S.s.: Scull-Hammond (2017a), p. 841 [see A. 2410, S.s.].

2412. _____. *Der Ring des Nibelungen*, Vol. III. Siegfried: Zweiter Tag.
> S.s.: Scull-Hammond (2017a), p. 841 [see A. 2410, S.s.].

2413. _____. *Der Ring des Nibelungen*, Vol. IV. Götterdämmerung: Dritter Tag.
> S.s.: Scull-Hammond (2017a), p. 841 [see A. 2410, S.s.].

2414. Wahba, Magdi. *Cairo Studies in English* (Periodical). Cairo: Costa Tsoumas & Co., 1959.
> Description: Presentation copy to J.R.R. Tolkien from Geoffrey Bullough, inscribed in red pen on cover: 'Geoffrey Bullough'. And in pencil on title page: 'J.R.R. Tolkien'. and contains pencilled markings on table of contents page. Includes a label added by Stan Revell to books owned by Tolkien, 'From the Library of J.R.R. Tolkien', on front cover. Autographed: 'J.R.R. Tolkien'.
> Collection: Marion E. Wade Center, Wheaton College (Wheaton, Illinois).

2415. Wainwright, Frederick Threlfall (Edited by). *The Problem of the Picts*.

Section A

Edinburgh: Nelson, 1955.
>Description: Contains a few pencilled annotations and invoice for purchase of the book used as marked at p. 35.
>Collection: Tolkien's personal Celtic library, preserved at the Weston library under the auspices of the English Faculty Library (Oxford).
>P.s.: *English and Welsh* (1963), p. 11 n 1. Tolkien cites discussion of Professor Jackson in chapter vi; p. 16 Tolkien quotes: 'Which so far as language goes formed a single linguistic province from Dumbarton and Edinburgh to Cornwall and Kent' (p. 156).

2416. Waitz, Hugo. *Die Fortsetzungen von Chrestiens' Perceval le Gallois nach den Pariser Handschriften.* Strassburg: K.J. Trübner, 1890.
>P.s.: *Sir Gawain and the Green Knight* (1925), p. xxvi. Tolkien and Gordon write: 'For bibliography of the Irish and French analogues of *Sir Gawain*, see the bibliography in Kittredge's study'. [*NED*] In Kittredge's study, this article is mentioned in 'V. Le Livre de Caradoc' (p. 298).

2417. Walde, Alois (Edited by). *Lateinisches Etymologisches Woerterbuch.* Heidlberg: Carl Winter, 1910.
>P.s. 1: *The Devil's Coach-Horses* (1925), p. 335.
>P.s. 2: *Sigelwara land* (1934), p. 108 n. 1; p. 110 n. 4.
>P.s. 3: *Beowulf* (2014), p. 269.

2418. _____. *Über älteste sprachliche Beziehungen zwischen Kelten und Italikern.* Innsbruch: R. Kiesel, 1917.
>Collection: Tolkien's personal Celtic library, preserved at the Weston library under the auspices of the English Faculty Library (Oxford).

2419. _____ and Julius Pokorny. *Vergleichendes Wörterbuch der indogermanischen Sprachen*, Vol. I. Berlin: de Gruyter, 1926.
>P.s.: *Sigelwara land* (1934), p. 108 n. 1; p. 109 n. 3; p. 110 n. 4.

2420. _____ and Julius Pokorny. *Vergleichendes Wörterbuch der indogermanischen Sprachen*, Vol. II. Berlin: de Gruyter, 1927.
>P.s.: *Sigelwara land* (1934), p. 105 n. 3.

2421. *Waldere* [Old English poem, edited in The Anglo-Saxon Minor Poems, see Krapp]
>S.s. 1: University of Leeds (1920), pp. 182-84. H2. (Scheme A and B) Second Year: Monday 10.00: Old English Verse with a special study of *Waldere*.
>S.s. 2: University of Leeds (1921), (pp. 192-94), University of Leeds (1922), (pp. 133-35) and University of Leeds (1923) (pp. 133-35). H2. (Scheme A nd B) Second and Third Year: Monday 10.00: Old English Verse with a special study of *Waldere*.
>S.s. 3: Scull-Hammond (2017a), p. 46. April 1913: Tolkien will need to become familiar with a range of literary and philological subjects and set texts as prescribed in the Oxford Regulations of the Board of Studies, knowing that he may be examined on them in ten papers at the end of *Trinity Term 1915*: Old English texts.
>S.s. 4: Scull-Hammond (2017a). Leeds academic years 1920-1921 (p. 122); 1921-22 (p. 125) and 1923-24 (p. 131). Lists several lectures or classes to take place during the year for which Tolkien may have responsibility: *Waldere* on Mondays at 10.00 a.m.

2422. Walker, Hugh. *Selected English short stories* (nineteenth century). Series: World's Classic, 193. London: H. Milford, Oxford University Press, 1914.
>S.s.: University of Leeds (1920), p. 135 English Literature. Texts Selected for 1920-21; p. 181. English Language and Literature. Int. I Intermediate Course (Literature).

2423. Wallenberg, Johannes Knut. *Kentish place-names. A topographical and etymological study of the place-name material in Kentish charters dated before the*

conquest. Uppsala: Lundequist, 1931.
Collection: Private [Sold by Bloomsbury Auctions, 13 March 2008].
P.s.: Tolkien's unpublished letter to Robert W. Burchfield, 11 June 1972. Tolkien writes: 'In unpacking my books I discovered this book which belongs to you. You lent it me a long while ago'.
S.s.: Scull-Hammond (2017a), p. 802.

2424. _____. *The Vocabulary of Dan Michel's Ayenbite of Inwyt*. Uppsala: Appelbergs Botryckeri Aktiebolag, 1923.
Description: Autographed in red crayon on front flyleaf. annotated in ink and pencil.
Collection: Tolkien's personal Celtic library, preserved at the Weston library under the auspices of the English Faculty Library (Oxford).
P.s. 1: MS. Tolkien A 12/2 *Commentary on Sir Gawain, lines 1999-2523* fol. 11. [Tolkien Papers, Bodleian Library, Oxford].
P.s. 2: *Philology: General Works* (IV 1924, for 1923), p. 23 n. 7.
S.s.: Zettersten (2011), p. 139.

2425. Walton, Izaak. *The Lives of Donne, Wotton, Hooker, Hebert, and Sanderson*. Series: The Standard Library. London: William Smith, 1843.
S.s.: University of Leeds (1921), p. 154. English Language and Literature - Scheme A. Texts and Period selected for 1921-22. (d) Texts suggested for study with Special Period 1637-1700. Ordinary Degree of B.A. with Honours. Final Examinations.

2426. *Wanderer*. [Old English poem preserved in the Exeter Book, see Krapp and Dobbie]
P.s. 1: *Valedictory Address* (1959), p. 239. Tolkien recites: 'fród in ferðe' and 'Hwǽr cwóm mearh, hwǽr cwóm mago? Hwér cwóm máððumgyfa? | Hwǽr cwóm symbla gesetu? Hwǽr sindon seledréamas? | Éalá, beorht bune! Éalá, byrnwiga! | Éalá, þéodnes þrym! Hú seo þrág gewát, | genáp under niht-helm, swá heo nó wǽre!' [Tolkien's translation] 'Where is the horse gone, where the young rider? Where now the giver of gifts? Where are the seats at the feasting gone? Where are the merry sounds in the hall? Alas, the bright goblet! Alas, the knight and his hauberk! Alas, the glory of the king! How that hour has departed, dark under the shadow of night, as had it never been!' In *The Lord of the Rings*, in chapter six of *The Two Towers*, Aragorn sings a song of Rohan, remember these lines: 'Where now the horse and the rider? [...] Or behold the flowing years from the Sea returning? '
P.s. 2: Lee (2005), p. 214 n. 1: In his justifiable attack on translations published by Burton Raffel [A. 1903] Tolkien stated: 'anhaga does not mean just 'lonely one', but refers to a man living in special conditions and is not applicable (for instance) to a man in a boat' [MS. Tolkien A 30/1 *Lectures on Old English* fol. 113]; p. 215 n. 2 Tolkien writes: 'Hwǽr cwóm mearh, hwǽr cwóm mago? Hwér cwóm máððumgyfa? | Hwǽr cwóm symbla gesetu? Hwǽr sindon seledréamas? | Éalá, beorht bune! Éalá, byrnwiga! | Éalá, þéodnes þrym! Hú seo þrág gewát, | genáp under niht-helm, swá heo nó wǽre!' [Tolkien's translation] 'Where now the horse, | where now the man, | where now the giver of gold? | Where now the places of feasting? | Where are the glad voices of the hall? | Alas, the bright goblet! | Alas, the mail-clad knight! | Alas, the glory of the King! | How that hour hath passed dark under night-shade, | as had it never been!' (MS. Tolkien A 30/1 *Lectures on Old English* fol. 33ff., lecture on 'Anglo-Saxon Verse'). [Tolkien Papers, Bodleian Library, Oxford].
P.s. 3: *J.R.R. Tolkien and 'The Wanderer'* (Lee 2009), p. 204-205 n. 1: Tolkien clarifies the reference to the lines 92-97: 'I must protest that I have never attempted to 're-create' anything. My aim has been the basically more modest, and certainly the more laborious one of trying to make* something new. No one would learn anything valid about the 'Anglo-Saxons' from any of my lore, not even that concerning the Rohirrim; I never intended that they should. Even the lines beginning 'Where now the horse and the rider,' though they echo a line in 'The Wanderer', are indeed not much further removed from it verbally, metrically, or in sentiment than are parts of Raffel's 'translation', are certainly not a translation, re-creative or otherwise. They are integrated (I hope) in something wholly different, the only excuse for the borrowing: they are particular in reference, to a great hero and his renowned horse, and they are supposed to be part of the song of a minstrel of a proud and undefeated people in a hall still populous with men. Even the sentiment is different:

it laments the ineluctable ending and passing back into oblivion of the fortunate, the full-lived, the unblemished and the beautiful. To me that is more poignant than any particular disaster, from the cruelty of men or the hostility of the world. But if I were to venture to translate 'The Wanderer' — the lament of the lonely man withering away in regret, and the poet's reflexions upon it — I would not dare to intrude any sentiment of my own, not to disarrange the order of word and thought in the old poem, in an impertinent attempt to make it more pleasing to myself, and perhaps to others. That is not 're-creation' but destruction. At best a foolish misuse of a talent for personal poetic expression; at worst the unwarranted impudence of a parasite.' '*I might say'sub-create', indicating that if successful the result may be new (in art), though all its material is given.' [MS. Tolkien A 30/1 *Lectures on Old English* fol. 121.]. Pages 194-5. Notes 2: In the Bodleian Library, Oxford, its preserved the note *On The Wanderer and The Seafarer*. Extract from Tolkien's notes: [MS. Tolkien A 30/1 *Lectures on Old English* fol. 33.] 'These are the words of men who knew the northern seas in small boats. Anglo-Saxon verse has many echoes of the cold waves, and the cry of the seabirds. It is, perhaps, not surprising that the reflective poetry of a people with the traditions of the cold north seas, frozen in winter, should show two elegiac poems, in which the sorrows of the lonely seafarer are a leading theme, and a symbol of desolation of spirit. These two remarkable poems of individual sentiment, are also preserved in the *Exeter Book*, and are now usually known as the *Wanderer* and *Seafarer*. In *The Wanderer* the poet passes before the end of the poem to the vision of a ruin, and a lament for the days devoured by time, a poignant expression of a dominant Anglo-Saxon mood: with this epitaph on antiquity, I will end this brief echo of the now long-vanished Anglo-Saxon days.' Pages 199-200. Notes 3: '[The] *Wanderer*, and *Seafarer* all seem to be concerned with nameless 'types'. No names are at any rate mentioned. But 'types' are derived from individuals, known by expression or from report and story, and it is by no means certain that these pieces had not, or at least that the material they adapted had not, at one time recognizable references to actual named figures of story: \e.g./ *Seafarer* to a mariner-adventurer a northern Ulysses-like character in his old age: *Wanderer* to an exile-survivor of a national disaster, sole champion of a King's *gesiþas* to escape …' | '… the *eardstapa* is not identical with the *anhaga* of line 1: he is a similar case introduced as an illustration … the general *oratio recta* of the piece is interrupted in lines 88-95b to introduce the similar case of the *anhaga* who finds his situation of (?) and persecutions in his own land insupportable … I personally believe that the *eardstapa* and his reported lament ends probably at *wynnum* 29a where *ic/me* gives way to *se/he*, and certainly goes no further than *wynn eal gedreas* [36b]. The *anhaga* of 40 is the *anhaga* of 1.' [MS. Tolkien A 30/1 *Lectures on Old English* fol. 152.]. Pages [Tolkien Papers, Bodleian Library, Oxford]. S.s.: #1 Holland (1949), p. 140. Appendix XI: Oxford Examinations for Prisoners of War. B.1 Old English: vv. 6-24.

2427. Ward, Adolphus William. '*Sir Gawain and the Green Knight*, and other similar English poems'. *Catalogue of Romances in the Department of Manuscripts in the British Museum*, Vol. 1, 1883.

P.s.: *Sir Gawain and the Green Knight* (1925), p. xxvi. Tolkien and Gordon write: 'For bibliography of the Irish and French analogues of *Sir Gawain*, see the bibliography in Kittredge's study'. [*NED*] In Kittredge's study, this article is mentioned in 'II. Gawain and the Green Knight' (p. 293).

2428. _____ and Alfred Rayney Waller. *The Cambridge History of English Literature*, Vol. I From the Beginnings to the Cycles of Romance. Cambridge: At the University Press, 1907.

P.s. 1: MS. Tolkien A 21/13 fol. 119. Note by Tolkien, 'Books in Exeter Library useful', with shelfmarks, on back of photostat reading list dated October 1913. [Tolkien Papers, Bodleian Library, Oxford].

P.s. 2: *Exeter College library register*. Tolkien's borrowing record: *Trinity Term 1915* from 27 April to 31 May 1915; Long vacation 1919 from 18 June to 14 October; *Hilary Term 1920* from 21 January to 12 March.

P.s.: *Sir Gawain and the Green Knight* (1925), p. xxvi. Tolkien and Gordon write: 'For bibliography of the Irish and French analogues of *Sir Gawain*, see the bibliography in Kittredge's study'. [*NED*] In Kittredge's study, this article is mentioned in 'II. Gawain and the Green Knight' (p. 294).

2429. _____ and Alfred Rayney Waller. *The Cambridge History of English Literature*, Vol. II The End Of The Middle Ages. Cambridge: At the University Press, 1908.

P.s. 1: *Exeter College library register*. Tolkien's borrowing record: *Trinity Term 1915* from 15 May to 16 June 1915; Long vacation 1919 from 18 June to 14 October; *Hilary Term 1920* from 21 January to 12 March.
P.s. 2: MS. Tolkien A 21/13 fol. 119. Note by Tolkien, 'Books in Exeter Library useful', with shelfmarks, on back of photostat reading list dated October 1913. [Tolkien Papers, Bodleian Library, Oxford].

2430. _____ and Alfred Rayney Waller. *The Cambridge History of English Literature*, Vol. III Renascence and Reformation. Cambridge: At the University Press, 1908.
P.s. 1: *Exeter College library register*. Tolkien's borrowing record: *Trinity Term 1915* from 31 May to 16 June; *Hilary Term 1920* from 21 January to 12 March.
P.s. 2: MS. Tolkien A 21/13 fol. 119. Note by Tolkien, 'Books in Exeter Library useful', with shelfmarks, on back of photostat reading list dated October 1913. [Tolkien Papers, Bodleian Library, Oxford].

2431. _____ and Alfred Rayney Waller. *The Cambridge History of English Literature*, Vol. V The Drama to 1642: Pt. I. Cambridge: At the University Press, 1909.
P.s.: MS. Tolkien A 21/13 fol. 119. Note by Tolkien, 'Books in Exeter Library useful', with shelfmarks, on back of photostat reading list dated October 1913. [Tolkien Papers, Bodleian Library, Oxford].

2432. _____ and Alfred Rayney Waller. *The Cambridge History of English Literature*, Vol. VI The Drama to 1642: Pt. II. Cambridge: At the University Press, 1910.
P.s.: MS. Tolkien A 21/13 fol. 119. Note by Tolkien, 'Books in Exeter Library useful', with shelfmarks, on back of photostat reading list dated October 1913. [Tolkien Papers, Bodleian Library, Oxford].

2433. _____ and Alfred Rayney Waller. *The Cambridge History of English Literature*, Vol. VII Cavalier and Puritan. Cambridge: At the University Press, 1910.
P.s.: MS. Tolkien A 21/13 fol. 119. Note by Tolkien, 'Books in Exeter Library useful', with shelfmarks, on back of photostat reading list dated October 1913. [Tolkien Papers, Bodleian Library, Oxford].

2434. _____ and Alfred Rayney Waller. *The Cambridge History of English Literature*, Vol. VIII The Age of Dryden. Cambridge: At the University Press, 1910.
P.s.: MS. Tolkien A 21/13 fol. 119. Note by Tolkien, 'Books in Exeter Library useful', with shelfmarks, on back of photostat reading list dated October 1913. [Tolkien Papers, Bodleian Library, Oxford].

2435. _____ and Alfred Rayney Waller. *The Cambridge History of English Literature*, Vol. IX From Steele and Addison to Pope and Swift. Cambridge: At the University Press, 1912.
P.s.: MS. Tolkien A 21/13 fol. 119. Note by Tolkien, 'Books in Exeter Library useful', with shelfmarks, on back of photostat reading list dated October 1913. [Tolkien Papers, Bodleian Library, Oxford].

2436. _____ and Alfred Rayney Waller. *The Cambridge History of English Literature*, Vol. X The Age of Johnson. Cambridge: At the University Press, 1913.
P.s.: MS. Tolkien A 21/13 fol. 119. Note by Tolkien, 'Books in Exeter Library useful', with shelfmarks, on back of photostat reading list dated October 1913. [Tolkien Papers, Bodleian Library, Oxford].

2437. Warnatsch, Otto. *Der Mantel, Bruchstück eines Lanzeletromans des Heinrich von dem Türlin, nebst einer Abhandlung über die Sage vom Trinkhorn und Mantel und die Quelle der Krone*. Series: Germanistische Abhandlungen, II. Breslan: Wilhelm Kocebner, 1883.

P.s.: *Sir Gawain and the Green Knight* (1925), p. xxvi. Tolkien and Gordon write: 'For bibliography of the Irish and French analogues of Sir Gawain, see the bibliography in Kittredge's study'. [*NED*] In Kittredge's study, this article is mentioned in 'V. Le Livre de Caradoc' (p. 298).

2438. Warner, Rubie (Edited by). *Early English Homilies from the Twelfth-Century MS. Vespasian D. xiv*. Series: E.E.T.S. (Early English Text Society), OS 152. London: Published for the Early English Text Society by Kegan Paul, Trench, Trübner and Co., 1927.
Description: Penciled annotations in front flyleaf.
Collection: Tolkien's personal Celtic library, preserved at the Weston library under the auspices of the English Faculty Library (Oxford).

2439. Warrack, John. *Carl Maria von Weber*. New York: Macmillan Co., 1968.
P.s.: *Tolkien in Oxford* (BBC, 1968), 22':36".
S.s.: Scull-Hammond (2006b), p. 617.

2440. Watson, E. W. 'The Age of Bede'. *Bede: his life, times and writings* [A. 2306]. Oxford: At the Clarendon Press, 1935.
P.s.: *Beowulf* (1937), p. 49 n. 17. Tolkien cites 'The Age of Bede' by E. W. Watson (pp. 39-59) and he writes [*Beowulf* is an historical document] 'It is, for instance, dismissed cursorily, and somewhat contemptuously in the recent (somewhat contemptuous) essay of Dr Watson'.

2441. Watson, George. *The Roxburghshire Word-Book. Being a record of the special vernacular vocabulary of the County of Roxburgh*. Series: Transaction of the Scottish Dialects Committee. Oxford: At the Clarendon Press, 1923.
P.s.: *Philology: General Works* (IV 1924, for 1923), p. 25 n. 9.

2442. Watt. John A.; John B. Morral and Francis Xavier Martin (Edited by). *Medieval Studies Presented to Aubrey Gwynn*. Dublin: Lochlainn, 1961.
Collection: Tolkien's personal Celtic library, preserved at the Weston library under the auspices of the English Faculty Library (Oxford).

2443. Way, Albertus (Edited by). *Promptorium Parvulorum Sive Clericorum Dictionarius Anglo-Latinus Princeps*. London: Published for the Camden Society by Longmans, Green, 1865.
P.s.: *A Middle English Vocabulary* (1922). Tolkien refers to the *Promptorium Parvulorum* on the terms 'Balʒ' (*balwe*, planus), 'Coffes' (*cuffe*, glove or meteyne), 'Cokeres' (*cocur*, cothurnus).
NED 1: #2 h. | 'W' (1928), p. 53 'Wallop v. I. 1. a.' – c 1440 'Waloppōn, as horse, *volopto*' (p. 514/2).
NED 2: #2 l. | 'W' (1928), p. 54. 'Walloping, *vbl, sb.*' – c 1440 'Waloppynge, of horse, *voloptacio*' (514/2).
NED 3: #2 h. | 'W' (1928), p. 57. 'Walming, vbL *sb.² Obs*.' – c1440 'Walmynge, of the stomake … nausea' (p. 514/2).

2444. Wayn, John. *Mixed Feelings. Nineteen Poems*. Reading, Berkshire: School of Art, University of Reading, 1951.
Description: 'List of subscribers before publication' (p. 6) includes: Nevill Coghill, H.V.D. Dyson, Roger Lancelyn Green, R.E. Havard, C.S. Lewis, Warren Lewis, J.R.R. Tolkien.
S.s.: Scull-Hammond (2017a), p. 393. [1951] Tolkien subscribes to Mixed Feelings: Nineteen Poems.

2445. Webster, Kenneth Grant Tremayne and Milton Price Webster. *Guinevere: A Study of Her Abductions*. Massachusetts: The Turtle Press, 1951.
Description: Inscribed on the title page in pen and ink: 'Professor Tolkien | from Deborah and Deborah Webster | with our admiration and respect'. Weston with her own line drawings illustrating the text; privately printed by The Turtle Press, Milton, Massachusetts. Separate typed

letter is inserted, not addressed to Tolkien personally, but stating: 'I am sending you this copy of Professor Webster's GUINEVERE with my compliments, because I think he would have wished to send it to you, had he lived to see it in print.' 'This is a covering letter, with the typed date'september, 1951' corrected in pen and ink to 'Oct '52'. The book was sold by Thornton's, in Oxford, to academic scholar prof. Michael Bath for his own research purposes in then late-1970s when he was doing the research for his book *The Image of the Stag: Iconographic Themes in Western Art* (Baden-Baden: Koerner Verlag, 1992), and he made a few scholarly annotations in pencil on pp. 19, 74, 98, 104, 109 - Webster has a whole chapter on 'The White Hart' which is a key motif in prof. Baths' Stag book. These are brief annotations in pencil by an academic scholar who was responding to some of Webster's discoveries in the course of research that fed into another scholarly publication directly related to the medieval and Arthurian interests that both authors shared in their published writing with Tolkien himself.'
Collection: Private [TolkienLibrary.com].

2446. Weekley, Ernest. *A Concise Etymological Dictionary of Modern English*. New York: E. P. Dutton and Co., 1924.
P.s.: *Philology: General Works* (V 1926, for 1924), p. 50 n. 10.

2447. Weir, Elizabeth. *German-English English-German Dictionary*. London: Cassell and Company, Limited, 1906.
Description: King Edward's School. Inscribed: 'Bought in School-days. J.R.R. Tolkien. re-bound 1926' [Judith Priestman 1994, revd. 2016].
Collection: Weston Library, Bodleian Libraries (Oxford). [Lacks title-page].
S.s.: Zettersten (2011), p. 78 'During my last visit to the Tolkien Collection at the Bodleian Library, Oxford, I went through Tolkien's books in his private library from his school time, which his family had donated to the Bodleian in July 1982.'

2448. Wells, Herbert George. *The First Men in the Moon*. London: G. Newnes, limited, 1901.
P.s. 1: *The Notion Club Papers* (1945), 165
P.s. 2: *On Fairy-stories* (1947), p. 44.
P.s. 3: *Tolkien On Fairy-stories* (2008), p. 34.
P.s. 4: *Tolkien On Fairy-stories* (2008) 'Manuscript B [MS. Tolkien 4, fols. 73-120]', p. 215.
P.s. 5: *Tolkien On Fairy-stories* (2008) 'Manuscript B [MS. Tolkien 14, fol. 25]', p. 280.
S.s.: Scull-Hammond (2006b), p. 818.

2449. _____. *The History of Mr. Polly*.
S.s.: Michael G.R. Tolkien (1995). Michael G.R. Tolkien writes: [JRRT] 'he was fascinated by the miraculous capacity of small and insignificant people (like H.G.Wells's Mr Polly)'.

2450. _____. *The Plattner story*. In *The Plattner story and others*. London: Methuen and Co. Ltd. 1897.
P.s.: *Tolkien On Fairy-stories* (2008), p. 111.

2451. _____. *The Time Machine*. London: William Heinemann, 1895.
P.s. 1: *The Notion Club Papers* (1945), p. 165
P.s. 2: *Letters* 109 (1947). TO Sir Stanley Unwin.
P.s. 3: *On Fairy-stories* (1947), p. 44.
P.s. 4: *Tolkien On Fairy-stories* (2008), p. 34.
P.s. 5: *Tolkien On Fairy-stories* (2008) 'Manuscript A. [MS Tolkien 4, fols. 59-77]', p. 178.
P.s. 6: *Tolkien On Fairy-stories* (2008) 'Manuscript B [MS. Tolkien 4, fols. 73-120]', p. 215.
P.s. 7: *Tolkien On Fairy-stories* (2008) 'Manuscript B [MS. Tolkien 14, fol. 25]', p. 280.
S.s.: Scull-Hammond (2006b), p. 818.

2452. Wells, John Edwin (Edited by). *A Manual of the Writings in Middle English 1050-1400*. London and Oxford: Humphrey Milford and University Press, 1916.
P.s. 1: *Holy Maidenhood* (1923), p. 281.

P.s. 2: *Sir Gawain and the Green Knight* (1925), p. xxvi Tolkien and Gordon write: 'For bibliograp of the Middle English texts referred to in this edition'; p. 84, line 109 *Gawan*; p. 89. line 553 *Lancelot*. T. and G. write: 'Later in *La Chevalier de la Charrette* Lancelot is the chief knight of Arthur's court, and he now appears also as Guinevere's lover'. Wells write: 'But in Chretien's still later *La Chevalier de la Charrette* he is Gawain's superior, and his relations with Guinevere as lover are the central theme' (p. 45).
S.s.: #1 Holland (1949), p. 144. Appendix XI: Oxford Examinations for Prisoners of War. English B.2 Chaucer and his Contemporaries. It is cited [*Piers Plowman*] 'Actual figures out of the roads, the ale-houses, the marts, the churches, the law-courts enter into the allegory'; also [Gower's *Confesio Amantis*] 'His narrative is interesting, simple, lucid, and often notably picturesque'.

2453. _____ (Edited by). *A Manual of the Writings in Middle English 1050-1400*. (supplement). New Haven: The Connecticut Academy of Arts and Sciences, 1919.
P.s. 1: *Holy Maidenhood* (1923).
P.s. 2: *Sir Gawain and the Green Knight* (1925), p. xxvi.

2454. _____ (Edited by). *A Manual of the Writings in Middle English 1050-400*. (supplement). New Haven: Yale University Press, 1923.
P.s.: *Sir Gawain and the Green Knight* (1925), p. xxvi.

2455. _____ (Edited by). *The Owl and the Nightingale*. Boston and London: D. C. Health and Co., 1907.
Description: Exeter College. Inscribed: 'John Ronald Tolkien. | Exeter Coll. Oxford. | Ascension Day mcmxiii. | Ex libris de litt. et phil germ Coll.' Annotations throughout [Judith Priestman 1994, revd. 2016].
Collection: Weston Library, Bodleian Libraries (Oxford).
P.s.: *Some Contributions to Middle-English Lexicography* (1925), p. 213.
S.s.: Scull-Hammond (2017a), p. 46. April 1913: Tolkien will need to become familiar with a range of literary and philological subjects and set texts as prescribed in the Oxford Regulations of the Board of Studies, knowing that he may be examined on them in ten papers at the end of *Trinity Term 1915*: Middle English texts.

2456. _____ (Edited by). *The Owl and the Nightingale*. Boston and London: D. C. Health and Co., 1907.
Description: Exeter College. Inscribed: 'J R R Tolkien'. Annotations throughout. Loose leaves; has notes on pronunciation of 'Legolas' (*The Lord of the Rings*) [Judith Priestman 1994, revd. 2016].
Collection: Weston Library, Bodleian Libraries (Oxford).
P.s.: MS. Tolkien A 12/2 *Commentary on Sir Gawain, lines 1999-2523* fol. 6. [Tolkien Papers, Bodleian Library, Oxford].

2457. Wernher der Gartenaere. *Meier Helmbrecht*. Edited by Friedrich Whilelm Panzer. Halle: Max Niemeyer, 1911.
P.s.: 'Middle English 'Losenger'' (1953), p. 66 n. 1.

2458. Weston, Jessie Laidlay. *The Legend of Sir Gawain; studies upon its original scope and significance*. London: David Nutt, 1898.
P.s.: *Sir Gawain and the Green Knight* (1925), p. xxvi. Tolkien and Gordon write: 'For bibliography of the Irish and French analogues of *Sir Gawain*, see the bibliography in Kittredge's study'. [*NED*] In Kittredge's study, this book (ch. X) is mentioned in 'I. Fled Bricrend' (p. 293); 'II. Gawain and the Green Knight' (pp. 294, 295), 'V. Le Livre de Caradoc' (p. 298).

2459. _____. *The Legend of Sir Perceval: studies upon its origin, development, and position in the Arthurian cycle*, Vol. I. Chrétien de Troyes and Wauchier de Denain. Series: Grimm Library, 17. London: David Nutt, 1906.
P.s.: *Sir Gawain and the Green Knight* (1925), p. xii line 2. Tolkien and Gordon cite chapter 12.

2460. _____. *The Legend of Sir Perceval: studies upon its origin, development, and position in the Arthurian cycle*, Vol. II. The Prose Perceval according in the Modena MS. Series: Grimm Library, 19. London: David Nutt, 1909.
P.s.: *Sir Gawain and the Green Knight* (1925), p. xii line 2. Tolkien and Gordon cite page 12.

2461. Whealley, Henry Benjamin. *Merlin Or the Early History of King Arthur: A Prose Romance (about 1450 - 1460 A. D.): from the Unique Ms. in the University Library, Cambridge*, Vol. I. Series: E.E.T.S. (Early English Text Society), OS 10. London: Published for the Early English Text Society by Kegan Paul, Trench, Trübner and Co., 1865.
P.s.: MS. Tolkien A 21/13 fol. 119. Note by Tolkien, 'Books in Exeter Library useful', with shelfmarks, on back of photostat reading list dated October 1913. Tolkien writes: 'All EETS publications'. [Tolkien Papers, Bodleian Library, Oxford].
NED: #2 h. | 'W' (1928), p. 53 'Wallop *sb.* 1. a." – c 1450 'And than he rode a walop after Vlfyn, gripynge his spere' (p. 127).

2462. Wheeler, Timothy J. *Rally*, Vol. 1 no. 0. Milwaukee: Rally, August 1966.
P.s. 1: Tolkien's unpublished letter to Timothy J. Wheeler, 1 August 1966. Tolkien writes: 'Thank you so much for sending me the copy of *RALLY*'.
P.s. 2: Tolkien's unpublished letter from Timothy J. Wheeler, 22 August 1966. Wheeler writes: 'I have forwarded the August *RALLY*, in which I call your attention to Jared Lobdell's review of *LOTR* on page 24'.

2463. Wheleer, Charles Bickersteth. *Six plays by contemporaries of Shakespeare*. Series: World's classics, 199. London: H. Milford, Oxford University Press, 1915.
S.s.: University of Leeds (1920), p. 147. English Language and Literature - Scheme A. Texts and Period selected for 1920-21. (b) Special period: 1557-1637. (c) Texts suggested for study with Special Period. Ordinary Degree of B.A. with Honours. Final Examination.

2464. White, Robert Meadows. *The Ormulum*. Oxford: At the University Press, 1852.
P.s.: *Sir Gawain and the Green Knight* (1967) 'Select Bibliography: editions of texts quoted more than once in the notes', p. 156.

2465. _____. *The Ormulum*. With the notes and glossary by Robert Holt. Oxford: At the University Press, 1878 (revd.).
P.s.: *Sir Gawain and the Green Knight* (1967) 'Select Bibliography: editions of texts quoted more than once in the notes', p. 156.

2466. White, Terence Hanbury. *The Sword in the Stone*. London: Collins, 1938.
S.s.: Scull-Hammond (2006b), p. 818.

2467. *Widsith* [Old English poem, see R. W. Chambers].
P.s. 1: *Beowulf* (1937), pp. 10; 18: Tolkien quotes: 'Lif is læne, eal sæceð leoht and lif somod' (vv. 141-2).
P.s. 2: *Finn and Hengest* (1982).
P.s. 3: *The Fall of Arthur* (2013), p. 227.
P.s. 4: *Beowulf* (2014), p. 239.
S.s. 1: University of Leeds (1921) (pp. 192-94), University of Leeds (1922), (pp. 133-35) and University of Leeds (1923) (pp. 133-35). H2. (Scheme A and B) Second Year: Monday 10.00: Old English Verse with a special study of *Widsith*.
S.s. 2: #1 Holland (1949), p. 139. Appendix XI: Oxford Examinations for Prisoners of War. B.1 Old English.
S.s. 3: Scull-Hammond (2017a). Leeds academic years 1920-1921 (p. 122); 1921-22 (p. 125) and 1923-24 (p. 131). Lists several lectures or classes to take place during the year for which Tolkien may have responsibility: *Widsith* on Mondays at 10.00 a.m.

2468. Wieland, Christopher Martin. *Oberon: ein romantisches Heldengedicht*

in zwölf Gesängen. Series: Graesers Schulausgaben klassischer Werke. Neue Taschenausgabe, ausgewählt, revidiert und eingeleitet von Dr. Franz Deibel. Die Zeichnung des Titels und Einbandes ist von W. Tiemann. Leipzig: Insel-Verl., 1905.
    P.s. 1: *On Fairy-stories* (1947), p. 39.
    P.s. 2: *Tolkien On Fairy-stories* (2008), p. 29.

2469. Wiessner, Erich. *Wortweiser (Index verborum) zu den bisher erschienenen Teilen der Historischen Grammatik der englischen Sprache von Dr. Karl Luick*. Paper covers, reproduced from typescript, 33 cms. Wien: Kommissionverlag Gerold und Co., 1934.
    Collection: Tolkien's personal Celtic library, preserved at the Weston library under the auspices of the English Faculty Library (Oxford).

2470. *Wife's Complaint*. [Old English poem preserved in the Exeter Book, see Krapp and Dobbie]
    S.s.: Scull-Hammond (2017a), p. 46. April 1913: Tolkien will need to become familiar with a range of literary and philological subjects and set texts as prescribed in the Oxford Regulations of the Board of Studies, knowing that he may be examined on them in ten papers at the end of *Trinity Term 1915*: Old English texts.

2471. Wiget, Wilhelm. 'Die Endung der weiblichen germanischen Lehnwörter im Finnischen'. *Streitberg-Festgabe* [A. 2228]. Leipzig: Market und Petter, 1924.
    P.s.: *Philology: General Works* (V 1926, for 1924).

2472. Wiklund, Karl Bernhard. 'Zur Frage vom germanischen in den Lehnwörter im Finnischern und Lappischen'. *Streitberg-Festgabe* [A. 2228]. Leipzig: Market und Petter, 1924.
    P.s.: *Philology: General Works* (V 1926, for 1924).

2473. Wildhagen, Karl. (Edited by). *Der Cambridger Psalter*. Series: Bibliothek der angelsächsischen Prosa, 7. Hamburg: Henri Grand, 1910.
    Description: Autographed in pencil on front flyleaf: 'John Reuel Tolkien'.
    Collection: Tolkien's personal Celtic library, preserved at the Weston library under the auspices of the English Faculty Library (Oxford).
    P.s.: *Sigelwara land* (1932), p. 186 n. 1.

2474. _____. *Der Psalter des Eadwine von Canterbury*. Halle: Max Niemeyer, 1905.
    P.s.: *Sigelwara land* (1932), p. 186 n. 1; p. 191 n. 2.

2475. Wilken, Ernst (Edited by). *Die Prosaische Edda im Auszuge, nebst Volsungasaga und Nornagests-þáttr*, Vol. I. Text. Series: Bibliothek der ältesten deutschen Literatur-Denkmäler, 11. Paderborn: Ferdinand Schöningh, 1912, p. 288.
    P.s.: *Beowulf* (1937), p. 15. Tolkien quotes: 'hans nafn mun uppi medan veröldin stendr'.

2476. Wilkes, Lyall and Keith Briant (Edited by). *Would I Fight?* Oxford: Basil Blackwell, 1938.
    Description: Inscribed in pencil on fly leaf 'Prize given for best reading at a meeting of the "Cave". The prize to be the worst book which could be found! Awarded to L. R-O. [Leonard Rice-Oxley]' followed by penciled signature of 11 member of the Oxford English Faculty: J.R.R. Tolkien, H.F. Brett-Smith, Elaine Grifiths, Leonard Rice-Oxley, Dorothy Whitelock, F.C. Horwood, C.L. Morrison, Charles Wrenn, Joan Blomfield, Dorothy Everett, and finally C.S. Lewis.
    Collection: Private.
    S.s. 1: Scull-Hammond (2017a), p. 225.
    S.s. 2: Scull-Hammond (2017c), pp. 1232-33.

2477.   William of Malmesbury. *De Gestis Regum Anglorum libri quinque: Historiae novellae libri tres*, Vol. I. Series: Cambridge library collection. Rolls. Edited by William Stubbs. Cambridge: The University Press, 1887.
 P.s. 1: *English and Welsh* (1963), p. 29. Tolkien writes: 'William of Malmesbury in his *Gesta Regum* says that Exeter was divided between the English and the Welsh as late as the reign of Athelstan' (Lib. Ii, p. 214).
 P.s. 2: *Sir Gawain and the Green Knight* (1967) 'Select Bibliography', p. 155.

2478.   _____. *De Gestis Regum Anglorum libri quinque: Historiae novellae libri tres*, Vol. II. Series: Cambridge library collection. Rolls. Edited by William Stubbs. Cambridge: The University Press 1889.
 P.s. 1: *English and Welsh* (1963), p. 29.
 P.s. 2: *Sir Gawain and the Green Knight* (1967) 'Select Bibliography', p. 155.

2479.   *William of Palerne* 1353. [Middle English romance, see Skeat].
 P.s. 1: MS. Tolkien A 21/13 *The English MSS*. fol. 203. [Tolkien Papers, Bodleian Library, Oxford].
 P.s. 2: 'Chaucer as a Philologist: *The Reeve's Tale*' (1934), p. 140.
 NED: #2 h. | 'W' (1928), p. 53 'Wallop *sb*. 1. a." – c 1350 'þei went a-wai a wallop as þei wod semed'

2480.   Williams, Charles. *Arthurian Torso. Containing the Posthumous Fragment of the Figure of Arthur. A Commentary on the Arthurian Poems of Charles Williams by C. S. Lewis*. London: Geoffrey Cumberlege, Oxford University Press, 1948.
 Notes: *Introduction* by C. S. Lewis, p. 2. Lewis writes: 'Chapters IV and V of his work I saw for the first time when Mrs. A. M. Hadfield sent me a typed copy of them. The two first chapters had been read aloud by the author to Professor Tolkien and myself. It may help the reader to imagine the scene; or at least it is to me both great pleasure and great pain to recall. Picture to yourself, then, an upstairs sittingroom with windows looking north into the 'grove' of Magdalen College on a sunshiny Monday Morning in vacation at about ten o 'clock. The Professor and I, both on the chesterfield, lit our pipes and stretched out our legs. Williams in the arm-chair opposite to us threw his cigarette into the grate, took up a pile of the extremely small, loose sheets on which he habitually wrote —they came, I think, from a twopenny pad for memoranda, and began as follows:—'. On page 15, Williams writes: 'It was this communion which was referred to in the Lord's Prayer. St Cyril of Jerusalem wrote: '*Give us this day our substantial bread*: Common bread is not substantial, but this holy bread is substantial. ... It is imparted to your whole system for the benefit of body and soul.' In a Williams' note: 'Quoted in *A History of the Doctrine of the Holy Eucharist*: Darwell Stone; from which the other quotations are taken— C. W.' And Lewis added: 'Beside this footnote Williams has pencilled'Tolkien'. This means that Professor Tolkien here raised some philological questions about the meaning of ἐπιούσιον (Matt. vi. 11) and, probably that Williams intended to discuss the matter with him more fully on some later occasion—C. S. L.'
 S.s.: Carpenter (1979), p. 197. [*The Figure of Arthur*] On a couple of Monday mornings he read aloud what he had written to Tolkien and Lewis. Tolkien recalled of one of these morning sessions: 'It was a bright morning, and the mulberry tree in the grove outside Lewis's window shone like fallow gold against the cobalt blue sky' (*Letters* 89, 1944, to Christopher Tolkien).

2481.   _____. *The Figure of Beatrice. A study in Dante*. London: Faber & Faber, 1943.
 P.s.: Tolkien's unpublished letter to Roger Verhulst, 9 March 1966. Tolkien writes: 'I did, however, hear some of his work read aloud, in various stages, the novel ultimately called *All Hallows' Eve*, large parts of the Arthurian matter and *The Figure of Beatrice*'.
 S.s.: Carpenter (1979), p. 187. In the summer of 1943 Williams's book was published. Tolkien wrote: 'The sales of Charles Williams | Leapt up by millions, | When a reviewer surmised | He was only Lewis disguised'.

2482.   _____. *All Hallows' Eve*. London: Faber & Faber, 1945.

P.s. 1: *Letters* 259 (1964). From a letter to Anne Barrett.
P.s. 2: Tolkien's unpublished letter to Roger Verhulst, 9 March 1966. Tolkien writes: 'I did, however, hear some of his work read aloud, in various stages, the novel ultimately called *All Hallows' Eve*, large parts of the Arthurian matter and *The Figure of Beatrice*'.
S.s. 1: Carpenter (1979), p. 194. [Williams] was reading the new draft aloud to the Inklings in November 1943. 'I heard two chapters of a new novel by Charles Williams, read by him, this morning' Tolkien told his son Christopher. Years later he recalled of those readings: 'I was in fact a sort of assistant midwife at the birth of *All Hallows' Eve*, read alound to us as it was composed, but the very great changes made in it were I think mainly due to C. S. L.'
S.s. 2: Scull-Hammond (2017a), p. 280.

2483. _____. *The Place of the Lion*. London: Mundanus ltd., V. Gollancz, 1931.
S.s. 1: Lewis (2009a), p. 183. Letter to Williams – 11 March 1936. Lewis writes: 'I have just read your Place of the Lion and it is to me one of the major literary events of my life […] I have put on Tolkien (the Professor of Anglo Saxon and a papist)'.
S.s. 2: Scull-Hammond (2017a), p. 196. [Early March 1936] Tolkien reads the book which C. S. Lewis has recommended.

2484. _____. *The Region of the Summer Stars*. London: Editions Poetry, 1944.
P.s.: Tolkien's unpublished letter to Roger Verhulst, 9 March 1966. Tolkien writes: 'I did, however, hear some of his work read aloud, in various stages, the novel ultimately called *All Hallows' Eve*, large parts of the Arthurian matter and *The Figure of Beatrice*'.
S.s.: Scull-Hammond (2006b), p. 819.

2485. _____. *Seed of Adam and other plays*. Edited by Anne Ridler. London: Geoffrey Cumberlege, Oxford University Press, 1948.
S.s.: Lewis (2009b), p. 288-9. Letter to his brother (W) – 19 November 1939. Lewis writes: 'On Thursday we had a meeting of the Inklings […] The bill of fare afterwards consisted of a section of the new *Hobbit* book from Tolkien, a nativity play from Williams (unusually intelligible for him, and approved by all) [*The hous by the Stable*] and a chapter out of the book on the *Problem of Pain* from me'.

2486. _____. *Taliessin through Logres*. London: Oxford University Press, 1938.
P.s.: Tolkien's unpublished 9 March 1966 letter to Roger Verhulst. Tolkien writes: 'I did, however, hear some of his work read aloud, in various stages, the novel ultimately called *All Hallows' Eve*, large parts of the Arthurian matter and *The Figure of Beatrice*'.
S.s. 1: Carpenter (1979), p. 124 n. 4. Tolkien's poem about Charles Williams ('Our dear Charles Williams many guises show…', pp. 123-26). Tolkien quotes The Throne, the war-lords etc.: reminiscent of Williams's poem 'The Vision of the Empire' in *Taliessin through Logres*, except of course that to Williams these things are pleasing.
S.s. 2: Scull-Hammond (2006b), p. 819.

2487. _____. *Terror of Light*. 1940. Collected Plays by Charles Williams. Edited by John Heath-Stubbs. London: Oxford University Press, 1963.
S.s. 1: Lewis (2009b), p. 410. Letter to his brother Warren – 4 May 1940. Lewis writes: 'We had an unusually good Inklings on Thursday at wh. Charles Williams read us a Whitsun play, a mixture of very good stuff and some deplorable errors in taste.
S.s. 2: Scull-Hammond (2017a), p. 255. [2 May 1940] Williams reads his play at a meeting of the Inklings in C. S. Lewis's rooms in Magdalen College. The play has been published in *Collected plays*, edited by John Heath-Stubbs.

2488. Williams, John (Ab Ithel). *Annales Cambriæ*. Series: Rerum Britannicarum Medii Ævi Scriptores, or Chronicles and Memorials of Great Britain and Ireland during the Middle Ages. London: Longman, Green, Longman and Roberts, 1860.
Description: Autographed and dated on front title page: '1922'.
Collection: Tolkien's personal Celtic library, preserved at the Weston library under the auspices of the English Faculty Library (Oxford).

S.s. 1: Phelpstead (2011), p. 119.
S.s. 2: Scull-Hammond (2017a), p. 126.

2489. _____ (Translated by). *Barddas*, Vol. I. Llandovery: Roderic, 1862.
Description: Stamped: 'C. J. Evans'. inscribed in blue crayon: 'Bt. From Siad Thannen | TRef. yghnys Aug 05 | Geo GT Tickene'. Decoratively autographed and dated: '1923'. Also JRRT's writing: 'bt. of G. Harding | London.' All these inscriptions on front flyleaf.
Collection: Tolkien's personal Celtic library, preserved at the Weston library under the auspices of the English Faculty Library (Oxford).
S.s.: Scull-Hammond (2017a), p. 129.

2490. _____ (Translated by). *Barddas*, Vol. II. *Or A Collection of Original Documents, Illustrative of the Theology, Wisdom, and Usages of the Bardo-Druidic System of the Isle of Britain with Translations and Notes*. London: Longman and Co., 1874.
Description: Stamped: 'C. J. Evans'. Inscribed in blue crayon: '141 | Bt. From Siad Thannen | Geo GT Tickene | TRef.yghnys | Aug 05'. Decoratively autographed and dated: '1923'. Also JRRT's writing: 'from. Geo. Harding | London.' All these inscriptions on front flyleaf. At p. 168 contains loose letter, George Harding to JRRT '4.1.1923'.
Collection: Tolkien's personal Celtic library, preserved at the Weston library under the auspices of the English Faculty Library (Oxford).
S.s. 1: Phelpstead (2011), p. 119.
S.s. 2: Scull-Hammond (2017a), p. 152, 162.

2491. _____. *Brut y Tywysogion. Or the Chronicle of the Princes [of Wales]*. Series: Rerum Britannicarum Medii Ævi Scriptores, or Chronicles and Memorials of Great Britain and Ireland during the Middle Ages. London: Longmans, Green, Longman and Roberts, 1860.
Description: Autographed and dated on front flyleaf: 'March 1922'.
Collection: Tolkien's personal Celtic library, preserved at the Weston library under the auspices of the English Faculty Library (Oxford).
S.s. 1: Phelpstead (2011), p. 119.
S.s. 2: Scull-Hammond (2017a), p. 126.

2492. Williams, Mary Rhiannon. *Essai sur la Composition du Roman Gallois de Peredur. Thèse présentée à la Faculté des Lettres de Paris, pour le doctorat d'université*. Paris: H. Champion, 1909.
Description: Autographed inside front flyleaf: 'Geoffrey B. Smith'.
Collection: Tolkien's personal Celtic library, preserved at the Weston library under the auspices of the English Faculty Library (Oxford).
S.s. 1: Garth (2003), p. 357.
S.s. 2: Fimi (2007), p. 67 n. 6.
S.s. 3: Phelpstead (2011), p. 119.
S.s. 4: Scull-Hammond (2017c), p. 1212.

2493. _____ (Edited by). 'Llyma Vabinogi Iessu Grist'. Offprint from *Revue Celtique*, Vol. XXXIII, Nos. 2-3. Paris: H. Champion, 1912, pp. 184-248.
Collection: Tolkien's personal Celtic library, preserved at the Weston library under the auspices of the English Faculty Library (Oxford).
S.s.: Phelpstead (2011), p. 119.

2494. Williams, Robert (Edited by). *Selections from the Hengwrt MSS preserved in the Peniarth Library*, Vol. I Y Seint Greal: being the adventures of King Arthur's knights of the Round Table, in the quest of the Holy Greal, and on other occasions; originally written about the year 1200. London: T. Richards, 1876.
Collection: Tolkien's personal Celtic library, preserved at the Weston library under the auspices

of the English Faculty Library (Oxford).
P.s.: *Sir Gawain and the Green Knight* (1925), p. xxvi. Tolkien and Gordon write: 'For bibliography of the Irish and French analogues of *Sir Gawain*, see the bibliography in Kittredge's study'. [NED] In Kittredge's study, this article is mentioned in 'VII. Perlesvaus' (p. 300).
S.s.: Phelpstead (2011), p. 119.

2495. _____ (Edited by). *Selections from the Hengwrt MSS preserved in the Peniarth Library*, Vol. II Containg Campu Charlymain, Purdan Padric, Buchedd Meir Wyry, Evengyt, Nicodemus, Y Groglith, Breuddwyt Pawl, Seith Doethion Ruvein, Ipotis Yspryt Awl, Luidsarius, Ymborth Yr Eneit, etc. London: T. Richards, 1892.
Collection: Tolkien's personal Celtic library, preserved at the Weston library under the auspices of the English Faculty Library (Oxford).
S.s.: Phelpstead (2011), p. 119.

2496. Williams, Robert Allan. *The Finn Episode in Beowulf: An Essay on Interpretation*. Cambridge: The University Press, 1924.
Description: Autographed with three point on front free endpaper: 'Tolkien'. Under the signature, in pencil: 'A very bad book'.
Collection: Private [The Tolkien Bookshelf].
P.s.: *Finn and Hengest* (1982), p. 38 n. 13; p. 95 n. 22; p. 99 n. 36; p. 105 n. 44; p. 108 n. 48; p. 115 n. 57; p. 119 n. 62; p. 122 nos. 64, 65; p. 136 nos. 79-81; p. 141 n. 91.

2497. Williams, Taliesin. *Iolo Manuscripts*. A selection of ancient Welsh manuscripts, in prose and verse, from the collection made by the late Edward Williams, Iolo Morganwg, for the purpose of forming a continuation of the Myfyrian archaiology; and subsequently proposed as materials for a new history of Wales Translated and notes. Series: Society for the Publication of Ancient Welsh Manuscripts (Abergavenny, Wales). Liverpool: I. Foulkes, 1888 (2nd ed.).
Description: Decoratively autographed and dated on front flyleaf: '1922'. Inside front cover written in pencil: 'Wales'. Inscribed on back of frontispiece: 'JG. WW. 1896'. followed by a word in ink, underlined and new rubbed out. An inscription in ink at the top of title page has been stuck cover with gummed paper.
Collection: Tolkien's personal Celtic library, preserved at the Weston library under the auspices of the English Faculty Library (Oxford).
S.s. 1: Phelpstead (2011), p. 119.
S.s. 2: Scull-Hammond (2017a), p. 126.

2498. Williamson, F. 'Glossary of words used by Derbyshire lead-miners during the past 250 years'. *Journal of the Derbyshire Archaeological and Natural History Society*, Vol. 46. Kendal: Titus Wilson and Son, 1924, pp. 1-55.
P.s.: *Philology: General Works* (V 1926, for 1924), p. 46.

2499. Wilmotte, Maurice. *Études de Philologie Wallone*. Paris: Librairie E. Droz, 1932.
Description: Signed in the front by J.R.R. Tolkien and annotations in pencil.
Collection: Private [Sold by Peter Harrington Antiquarian Bookseller].
S.s.: Harrington (2003), p. 25.

2500. Wilson, Herbert Wingley. *With the flag to Pretoria. A History of the Boer War of 1899-1900*. Vol. I. London: Harmsworth Bros, 1900.
P.s.: *Letters* 183 (1956). Notes on W.H. Auden's review of *The Return of the Ring*. Tolkien writes:'some critics seem determined to represent me as a simple-minded adolescent, inspired with, say, a With-the-flag-to-Pretoria spirit, and wilfully distort what is said in my tale.'

2501. _____. *With the flag to Pretoria. A History of the Boer War of 1899-1900*. Vol. II. London: Harmsworth Bros, 1902.
   P.s.: *Letters* 183 (1956). Notes on W.H. Auden's review of *The Return of the Ring*. Tolkien writes:'some critics seem determined to represent me as a simple-minded adolescent, inspired with, say, a With-the-flag-to-Pretoria spirit, and wilfully distort what is said in my tale.'

2502. Wilson, John Dover. *Life in Shakespeare's England. A book of Elizabethan prose*. Cambridge: The University Press, 1920.
   S.s.: University of Leeds (1923), p. 81. Ordinary Degree of B.A., Intermediate Course and Examination: English Literature. Text selected for 1923-24. Note. – For a general view of the period of following books are recommended.

2503. Wilson, Robert M. *Early Middle English Literature*. London: Metheun and Co, 1939.
   Description: Complimentary copy. Signed on front flyleaf in ink perhaps written by his son, Christopher. 'JRRT'.
   Collection: Private [Sold by Loome Theological Booksellers, formerly 'Greg Miller collection']

2504. _____ (Edited by). *The English Text of the Ancrene Riwle. Edited from Gonville and Caius College MS. 234-120*. Series: E.E.T.S. (Early English Text Society), OS 229. London: Geoffrey Cumberlege, Oxford University Press, 1954.
   Description: Underlined in purple crayon. Annotated in pencil. Bookmark at pp. 70, 71. Letter from Neil Ker as bookmark between XIV and p. 1.
   Collection: Tolkien's personal Celtic library, preserved at the Weston library under the auspices of the English Faculty Library (Oxford).

2505. _____. *The Lost literature of medieval England*. London: Methuen and Co. Ltd., 1952.
   S.s.: Shippey (1992), 301.

2506. _____ (Edited by). *Sawles Warde*. Leeds: Monograph, III, 1938.
   Description: A few annotations.
   Collection: Weston Library, Bodleian Libraries (Oxford).
   P.s. 1: MS. Tolkien A 11 *Notes on Pearl* fols. 40-1. [Tolkien Papers, Bodleian Library, Oxford].
   P.s. 2: *'Iþþlen' in Sawles Warde* (1947), p. 168 n. 1.
   P.s. 3: *Studia Neophilologica* (1948), p. 71.
   P.s. 4: *The Old English Exodus* (1982), p. 54.

2507. _____. 'Some Lost Saint's Lives in Old and Middle English'. MLR (*The Modern Language Review*), Vol. 36, no. 2, pp. 161-72. April 1941.
   S.s.: Shippey (1992), p. 315 n. 12.

2508. Wimberly, Lowry Charles. *Folklore in the English and Scottish ballads*. The University of Chicago Press, 1928.
   S.s.: Shippey (1992), p. 299.

2509. Wimmer, Ludvig Frands Adalbert. *Oldnordisk læsebog med anmærkninger og ordsamling*. København: Jespersen og Pios, 1929.
   Description: Inscribed on front flyleaf: 'Tolkien | 1930'.
   Collection: Tolkien's personal Celtic library, preserved at the Weston library under the auspices of the English Faculty Library (Oxford).

2510. _____ and Finnur Jónsson. *Håndskriftet nr. 2365 4 to gl. kgl. samling på det store Kgl. bibliothek i København: (Codex regius af den aeldre Edda) i fotypisk og diplomatisk gengivelse*. København: S. L. Møllers bogtrykkeri, 1891.
   P.s.: *The Legend of Sigurd & Gudrún* (2009), p. 199.

2511. Windisch, Ernst. *Die Altirische Heldensage, Táin bó Cúalnge*. Series: Irische Texte mit Übersetzungen und Wörterbuch, extraband zu serie I bis IV. Leipzig: S. Hirzel, 1905.
>Description: A few pencilled annotations.
>Collection: Tolkien's personal Celtic library, preserved at the Weston library under the auspices of the English Faculty Library (Oxford).

2512. _____. *Kurzgefasste Irische Grammatik: mit Lesestücken*. Leipzig: Hirzel, 1879.
>Description: Inscribed on front flyleaf: 'G. D.' Also decoratively autographed and dated: '1926'. Pencilled annotation p. 15.
>Collection: Tolkien's personal Celtic library, preserved at the Weston library under the auspices of the English Faculty Library (Oxford).

2513. Wisse, Claus and Colin Philipp. *Parzifal* (1331-1336). Edited by Karl Schorbach. Strassburg: Karl J. Trübner, 1888.
>P.s.: *Sir Gawain and the Green Knight* (1925), p. xxvi. Tolkien and Gordon write: 'For bibliography of the Irish and French analogues of *Sir Gawain*, see the bibliography in Kittredge's study'. [NED] In Kittredge's study, this article is mentioned in 'V. Le Livre de Caradoc' (p. 298).

2514. Wodehouse, Pelham Grenville. *The Man with two left feet*. London: Methuen and Co. Ltd. 1917.
>P.s.: *Farmer Giles of Ham* (2014), p. 200.

2515. Wodron, George. *A description of the Isle of Man: with some useful and entertaining reflections on the laws, customs, and manners of the inhabitants*. Series: Manx Society series, 11. Edited by William Harrison. Douglas: Printed for the Manx Society, 1865.
>P.s.: *Oxford University Press Archives* (Oxford). A slip written by Tolkien on the etymology of 'Wake' used ('W' p. 31) [A. 1721].
>*NED*: #2 f. | 'W' (1928), p. 31 'Wake, 3.' 1726-31 – 'When a person dies, several of his acquaintance come to sit up with him, which they call the Wake' (p. 60).

2516. Wolfe, Humbert. *London Sonnets*. Oxford: Blackwell, 1920.
>Description: On front flyleaf: 's. R. T. Because he doesn't, | either to you or me, | I do to you | J. R. T. 22.2.20'.
>S.s.: Beahm (2004), p. 154.

2517. Wolff, Eduard. *Tacitus' Germania*. Leipzig: B. G. Teubner, 1907.
>P.s.: *Beowulf* (2014), p. 191.

2518. Wollheim, Donald A. and Arthur W. Saha. *The 1972 Annual World's Best SF*. New York: Daw Books, 1972.
>P.s.: Tolkien's unpublished letter to Lanier, 24 January 1973. Tolkien writes: 'I received four copies of Daw Books (publisher Donald A. Wollheim)'.

2519. Wood, Francis Asbury. *Indo-European ax: axi: axu: A study in ablaut and in word formation*. Strassburg: K. J. Trübner, 1905.
>Collection: Taylor Institution Library, Bodleian Libraries (Oxford).

2520. Woodward, John. *An Attempt Towards a Natural History of the Fossils of England*, Vol. I, Pt. I.
>P.s.: MS. Tolkien A 19/3 *Etymologies or history of Walrus* fols. 162-195 [Tolkien Papers, Bodleian

Library, Oxford].
S.s.: *Tolkien, Family Album* (1992), p. 42.
NED: #2 i. | 'W' (1928), p. 58 'Walrus, 1.' 1728 – 'A Tusk of the Morse, or Walrous, call'd by some the Sea-Horse' ('Bones, Teeth, &c. of Fishes', p. 22).

2521. Wordsworth, William. *Lines a few miles above Tintern Abbey*. New York: Adams Press, 1907.
S.s.: University of Leeds (1920), p. 135 English Literature. Texts Selected for 1920-21; p. 181. English Language and Literature. Int. I Intermediate Course (Literature).

2522. _____. *Michael: A Pastoral Poem*.
S.s.: University of Leeds, *Calendar 1920-21*, p. 135 English Literature. Texts Selected for 1920-21; p. 181. English Language and Literature. Int. I Intermediate Course (Literature).

2523. _____ and Samuel Taylor Coleridge. *The Lyrical Ballads 1798-1805*. Edited by George Sampson. London: Methuen & Co., 1914.
S.s.: University of Leeds (1921), p. 141. English Literature, text selected for 1921-22. Ordinary Degree of B.A.; p. 154. English Language and Literature - Scheme A. Texts and Period selected for 1921-22. (e) History of Criticism: Special Texts suggested for study. Ordinary Degree of B.A. with Honours. Final Examinations. Parts suggested: Preface and Appendices; p. 156. English Language and Literature - Scheme B. Texts for 1921-22. (d) Outlines of the History of English Literature. Ordinary Degree of B.A. with Honours. Final Examinations; p. 190 English Language and Literature. Int. 1 Intermediate Course (Literature).

2524. Worm, Ole. *Museum Wormianum, seu, Historia rerum rariorum, tam naturalium, quam artificialium, tam domesticarum, quam exoticarum, quae Hafniae Danorum in aedibus authoris servantur*.
P.s.: MS. Tolkien A 19/3 *Etymologies or history of Walrus* fols. 162-195 [Tolkien Papers, Bodleian Library, Oxford].
S.s.: *Tolkien, Family Album* (1992), p. 42.
NED: #2 i. | 'W' (1928), p. 58 'Walrus, 1.' 1653 – 'Animal ... quod Anglis &. Russis Walrus, aliis Mors, Danis & Islandis Rosmarus vocatur' ('De Delphino, Pristi, Phoca, Rosmaro', chapter xv, p. 289).

2525. Wrede, Ferdinand. 'Sprachliche Adoptivformen'. *Beiträge zur Germanischen Sprachwissenschaft: Festschrift für Otto Behaghel* [A. 1045]. Heidelberg: Carl Winter, 1924.
P.s.: *Philology: General Works* (V 1926, for 1924), p. 36.

2526. Wrenn, Charles Leslie. (Edited by). *Beowulf: with the Finnesburg fragment*. London: George G. Harrap, 1953.
Description: Tolkien's copy contains autograph letter signed from him, two autograph letters signed & a postcard signed from Lewis; autograph letter signed from Christopher Tolkien; typed letter signed by Wrenn and a note and draft letter by Robert Burchfield.
Notes: In his preface, Charles Wrenn thanks Tolkien: 'While acknowledging my vast indebtedness to all my predecessor in the appropriate places I obviously owe a deeper and more general debt to them which cannot be effectively indicated. Most of all I am conscious of owing what is valuable in my approach to Beowulf to the late Professor R. W. Chambers, of University College, London, and to Professor J.R.R. Tolkien, my predecessor in the Chair of Anglo-Saxon at Oxford.'
Collection: Private [Sold by Bloomsbury Auctions, 13 March 2008].

2527. _____. 'Late Old English Rune-Names'. *Medium Ævum*, Vol. 1, 1932. Oxford: Basil Blackwell, 1932, pp. 24-34.
P.s.: *Sigelwara land* (1934), p. 98 n. 2, 4.

2528. Wright, David. *Beowulf*. London: Penguin Books, 1957.
Description: On p. 12: 'For the poem is a bit of a rag-bag as well, stuffed with fragments from

the history of Scandinavian tribes, and spilling over with untidy-looking references to apparently irrelevant events and legends. But Professor J.R.R. Tolkien, in his famous essay, *Beowulf: The Monsters and the Critics*, was one of the first to show that the construction of the poem was rather more subtle than had been thought. He pointed out that it depended, like the alliterative measure in which the poem is written, on a balance – thesis and antithesis – rather than straightforward narrative. Thus the poem begins, and ends, with a funeral; and the first part, which tells of the hero's youth, is in contrast to the second, which deals with his old age.'

2529. Wright, Elizabeth Mary. *The Life of Joseph Wright*, Vol. 1. London: Oxford University Press, 1932.

2530. _____. *The Life of Joseph Wright*, Vol. 2. London: Oxford University Press, 1932.
 Notes: Includes extracts from a letter by Tolkien to Joseph Wright dated 26 January 1925.

2531. _____. 'The Word *Abloy* in *Sir Gawayne and the Green Knight*, L. 1174'. Offprint from MLR (*The Modern Language Review*), Vol. 18, no. 1. Cambridge: The Univeristy Press, January 1923, pp. 86-87.
 Notes: 13 February 1923: A copy was sent to Tolkien by the author.
 P.s. 1: *Letters* 6 (1923) To Mrs E. M. Wright. Tolkien writes: 'I am very grateful to you for the offprint'.
 P.s. 2: *Sir Gawain and the Green Knight* (1925), p. 101, line 1174 abloy.
 S.s.: Scull-Hammond (2017a), p. 129.

2532. Wright, Joseph. *Comparative Grammar of the Greek language*. London: Oxford University Press and H. Frowde, 1912.
 P.s.: *Letters* 308 (1969). To Christopher Tolkien.
 S.s.: Scull-Hammond (2017a), pp. 37-38. *Hilary Term 1912*: Tolkien again has a choice of lectures on the various Greek and Latin authors set for Honour Moderations, and will attend Joseph Wright's lectures on Comparative Greek Grammar on Tuesdays and Thursdays at 12.15 pm. in the Taylor Institution, beginning 24 January; p. 39: *Trinity Term 1912*: Tolkien attends Joseph Wright's continuing lectures on Comparative Greek Grammar on Tuesdays and Thursdays at 12.15 Pm- in the Taylor Institution, beginning 2 May.

2533. _____. *The English Dialect Dictionary*, Vol. I, 'A-C'. London: Oxford University Press, 1898.
 P.s. 1: MS. Tolkien A 11 *Notes on Pearl* fol. 124. [Tolkien Papers, Bodleian Library, Oxford].
 P.s. 2: *Philology: General Works* (V 1926, for 1924), p. 47.
 P.s. 3: *Sir Gawain and the Green Knight* (1925), p. 87, line 296 barlay. Tolkien and Gordon write:'scott's Waverley: a proper lad of his quarters that will not cry barley in a bruilʒie (=broil, fight) = quoted in E.D.D.' [voice Barley, p. 167].
 P.s. 4: Foreword to *A New Glossary of the Dialect of Huddersfield District* (1928), p. xiv.
 S.s.: Scull-Hammond (2006b), p. 1125.

2534. _____. *The English Dialect Dictionary*, Vol. II, 'D-G'. London: Oxford University Press, 1900.
 P.s. 1: MS. Tolkien A 11 *Notes on Pearl* fol. 124. [Tolkien Papers, Bodleian Library, Oxford].
 P.s. 2: *Philology: General Works* (V 1926, for 1924), p. 47.
 P.s. 3: Foreword to *A New Glossary of the Dialect of Huddersfield District* (1928), p. xiv.
 S.s.: Scull-Hammond (2006b), p. 1125.

2535. _____. *The English Dialect Dictionary*, Vol. III, 'H-L'. London: Oxford University Press, 1902.
 P.s. 1: MS. Tolkien A 11 *Notes on Pearl* fol. 124. [Tolkien Papers, Bodleian Library, Oxford].
 P.s. 2: *Philology: General Works* (V 1926, for 1924), p. 47.
 S.s.: Scull-Hammond (2006b), p. 1125.

2536. _____. *The English Dialect Dictionary*, Vol. IV, 'M-Q'. London: Oxford University Press, 1903.
    P.s. 1: MS. Tolkien A 11 *Notes on Pearl* fol. 124. [Tolkien Papers, Bodleian Library, Oxford].
    P.s. 2: *Philology: General Works* (V 1926, for 1924), p. 47.
    P.s. 3: Foreword to *A New Glossary of the Dialect of Huddersfield District* (1928), p. xiv.
    S.s.: Scull-Hammond (2006b), p. 1125.

2537. _____. *The English Dialect Dictionary*, Vol. V, 'R-S'. London: Oxford University Press, 1904.
    P.s. 1: MS. Tolkien A 11 *Notes on Pearl* fol. 124. [Tolkien Papers, Bodleian Library, Oxford].
    P.s. 2: *Philology: General Works* (V 1926, for 1924), p. 47.
    P.s. 3: Foreword to *A New Glossary of the Dialect of Huddersfield District* (1928), p. xiv.
    S.s.: Scull-Hammond (2006b), p. 1125.

2538. _____. *The English Dialect Dictionary*, Vol. VI, 'T-Z'. London: Oxford University Press, 1905.
    P.s. 1: MS. Tolkien A 11 *Notes on Pearl* fol. 124. [Tolkien Papers, Bodleian Library, Oxford].
    P.s. 2: *Philology: General Works* (V 1926, for 1924), p. 47.
    P.s. 3: Foreword to *A New Glossary of the Dialect of Huddersfield District* (1928), p. xiv.
    S.s.: Scull-Hammond (2006b), p. 1125.
    NED 1: #2 h. | 'W' (1928), p. 54 'Wallop v. III. 4. b.' – Tolkien cites E.D.D. (English Dialect Dictionary): Picken, Ebenezer. *Miscellaneous poems, songs, &c. partly in the Scottish dialect, with a glossary*, Vol. I. Edinburgh: Printed by James Clarke, 1813, p. 407. 'Whan the tide o youthfu' bluid Thro' a' yer heartstrings wallops'.
    NED 2: #2 h. | 'W' (1928), p. 53 'Wallop sb. 3. b.' – Tolkien cites E.D.D. (English Dialect Dictionary): 1885, Towes, Walter. *Poems, Songs, and Ballads*. Glasgow: A. Bryson & Co., 1885. 'Souple Tarn Gaed wallop ower the stile' (p. 182).; 1766 Nicol, Alexander. *Poems on several subjects: both comical and serious*, Edinburgh: Printed for the Author, 1766. 'My heart will., wallop'.
    NED 3: #2 l. | 'W' (1928), p. 54. 'Walloper, *colloq.* or *jocular*. 2. *dial*.' – 'Anything strikingly large or big; a 'thumper', 'whopper'; e.g. an astounding lie. (See *Eng. Dial. Diet.*).'

2539. _____. *The English Dialect Grammar. Comprising the dialects of England, of the Shetland and Orkney islands, and of those parts of Scotland, Ireland & Wales where English is habitually spoken.* Oxford: H. Frowde, 1905.
    P.s.: *Exeter College library register*. Tolkien's borrowing record: *Michaelmas Term 1911* from 25 November to 5 December.
    S.s. 1: Garth (2014), p. 21.
    S.s. 2: Scull-Hammond (2017a), p. 36.

2540. _____. *Grammar of the Gothic language, and the Gospel of St. Mark; selections from the other Gospels, and the Second Epistle to Timothy, with notes and glossary.* Oxford: At the Clarendon Press, 1910.
    P.s.: *Letters* 308 (1969). To Christopher Tolkien.
    S.s. 1: University of Leeds (1921), p. 155. English Language and Literature - Scheme B. Texts for 1921-22. (b) Gothic. Ordinary Degree of B.A. with Honours. Final Examinations; p. 193 English Language and Literature. Honours and M.A. Courses. A. Language. H7. (Scheme B) Second Year. Text-book.
    S.s. 2: Scull-Hammond (2017a), p. 40. *Michaelmas Term 1912*: Tolkien having chosen Comparative Philology as his Special Subject, he attends lectures by Joseph Wright on Gothic Grammar with Translation of the Gospel of St Mark, at 12.15 p.m. on Tuesdays and Thursdays in the Taylor Institution, beginning 19 October.

2541. _____. *Grammar of the Gothic Language*. Oxford: At the Clarendon Press, 1954 (2nd ed.).
    P.s.: *Letters* 272 (1965). From a letter to Zillah Sherring.

2542. _____. *A Grammar of the dialect of Windhill, in the West Riding of Yorkshire.* Series: E.D.S. (English Dialect Society). London: K. Paul, Trench, Trübner, 1892.
   Description: Annotated: 'presented me by J. Wright | shortly before his death'.
   Collection: Tolkien's personal Celtic library, preserved at the Weston library under the auspices of the English Faculty Library (Oxford).
   S.s.: McIlwaine (2018), no. 84.

2543. _____. *A Help to Latin Grammar.* Cambridge: Macmillan, 1855.
   P.s.: *Letters* 308 (1969). To Christopher Tolkien.

2544. _____. *A Middle High German Primer, with grammar, notes, and glossary.* Oxford: At the Clarendon Press, 1888.
   P.s.: *Exeter College library register.* Tolkien's borrowing record: *Michaelmas Term 1912* from 25 October to 5 December.

2545. _____. *A Middle High German Primer, with grammar, notes, and glossary.* Oxford: At the Clarendon Press, 1899 (2nd ed.).
   P.s.: *Exeter College library register.* Tolkien's borrowing record: *Michaelmas Term 1912* from 25 October to 5 December.

2546. _____. *A Middle High German Primer, with grammar, notes, and glossary.* Oxford: At the Clarendon Press, 1917 (3rd ed.).
   P.s.: *Exeter College library register.* Tolkien's borrowing record: *Michaelmas Term 1912* from 25 October to 5 December.

2547. _____. *A Primer of the Gothic Language: containing the gospel of St. Mark, selections from the other gospels, and the second epistel to Timothy with grammar, notes and glossary.* Series: Clarendon Press. Oxford: At the Clarendon Press, 1892.
   S.s. 1: Priestman (1992), p. 24 no. 35.
   S.s. 2: Scull (1993), p. 51. Scull writes: 'The exhibition displayed books from Tolkien's library which showed his interest in languages, including Joseph Wright's *A Primer of the Gothic Language*'.

2548. _____. *A Primer of the Gothic Language with grammar and glossary.* Oxford: At the Clarendon Press, 1899 (2nd ed.).
   Description: One of Tolkien's school-friends bought this book at a missionary sale, thinking it a Bible Society product. The friend, not happy with the book, sold it to Tolkien between 1908 and 1909.
   P.s. 1: *Letters* 272 (1965). From a letter to Zillah Sherring.
   P.s. 2: *English and Welsh* (1963), p. 38. Tolkien writes: 'The contemplation of the vocabulary in *A Primer of the Gothic Language* was enough: a sensation at least as full of delight as first looking into Chapman's *Homer*' [A. 1033].

2549. _____. *Old English Grammar.* London: Oxford University Press, 1914.
   P.s.: *Philology: General Works* (IV 1924, for 1923), p. 33.
   S.s.: University of Leeds (1921), p. 193 English Language and Literature. Honours and M.A. Courses. A. Language. H1. First Year. Books Recommended.

2550. _____ and Elizabeth Mary Wright. *An Elementary historical new English grammar.* London: H. Milford, Oxford University Press, 1924.
   P.s.: *Philology: General Works* (V 1926, for 1924), p. 52.

2551. _____ and Elizabeth Mary Wright. *An Elementary Old English Grammar.* London: Oxford University Press, 1923.
   P.s.: *Philology: General Works* (IV 1924, for 1923), p. 33.

2552. Wright, Thomas. *Political Poems and Songs Relating to English History*, Vol. I. London: Longman, Green, and Roberts, 1859.
: Description: Signed by Tolkien on front free endpaper and dated '1923'.
: Collection: Private [Sold by Simon Finch Rare Books Ltd.].
: S.s.: Finch (2002), p. 54.

2553. _____. *Political Poems and Songs Relating to English History*, Vol. II. London: Longman, Green, and Roberts, 1861.
: Description: Signed by Tolkien on front free endpaper and dated '1923'.
: Collection: Private [Sold by Simon Finch Rare Books Ltd.].
: S.s.: Finch (2002), p. 54.

2554. _____. *The seven ages. Percy Society: Early English Poetry*, Vol. XVI. London: Printed for the Percy Society by T. Richards, 1845.
: P.s. 1: MS. Tolkien A 11 *Notes on Pearl* fol. 58. [Tolkien Papers, Bodleian Library, Oxford].
: P.s. 2: MS. Tolkien A 21/13 *The English MSS*. fol. 203. [Tolkien Papers, Bodleian Library, Oxford].
: *NED*: #2 h. | 'W' (1928), p. 54. '*Walm sb*.¹ Obs. 3. a.' – c 1425 'Thys sevene walmes sygnyfye Seven devels in thy Companye, That ben thy seven clerkys' (2363).

2555. _____. *Specimens of lyric poetry, composed in England in the reign of Edward the First. Ed. from ms. Harl. 2253, in the British museum.* Series: Percy Society. London: Printed for the Percy society by T. Richards, 1842.
: P.s. 1: MS. Tolkien A 11 *Notes on Pearl* fol. 124. [Tolkien Papers, Bodleian Library, Oxford].
: P.s. 2: 'Chaucer as a Philologist: *The Reeve's Tale*' (1934), p. 137. Tolkien quotes: 'Nihtes when y wende ant wake, for-thi myn wonges waxeth won' (vi, p. 28).

2556. _____ and Richard Paul Wülcker (Edited by). *Anglo-Saxon and Old English vocabularies*, Vol. I. Vocabularies. London: Trübner & Co., 1884 (2nd ed.).
: Description: Inscribed in pencil on front flyleaf: 'J. Mowak | 1884'. Autographed and dated on front flyleaf: '1922'.
: Collection: Tolkien's personal Celtic library, preserved at the Weston library under the auspices of the English Faculty Library (Oxford).
: P.s. 1: *Sigelwara land* (1934), p. 96 n. 2; p. 101 n. 2.
: P.s. 2: *English and Welsh* (1963), p. 27 n. 1. Tolkien quotes: '*jus quiritium*, weala sunderriht' (p. 115).
: *NED*: #2 g. | 'W' (1928), p. 57 'Walnut, 1.' c 1050 – '*Nux*, hnutbeam oðð e walhhnutu' (p. 452/34).

2557. _____ and Richard Paul Wülcker (Edited by). *Anglo-Saxon and Old English vocabularies*, Vol. II. Indices. London: Trübner & Co., 1884 (2nd ed.).
: Description: Inscribed in pencil on front flyleaf: 'J. Mowak | 1884'. Autographed and dated on front flyleaf: '1922'.
: Collection: Tolkien's personal Celtic library, preserved at the Weston library under the auspices of the English Faculty Library (Oxford).

2558. _____ and James Orchard Halliwell-Phillipps (Edited by). *Reliquiae Antiquae: Scraps from Ancient Manuscripts, Illustrating Chiefly Early English Literature and the English Language*, Vol. I. London: John Russel Smith, 1845.
: P.s. 1: MS. Tolkien A 11 *Notes on Pearl* fol. 124. Tolkien refers 'Medical Receipts' on page 51. [Tolkien Papers, Bodleian Library, Oxford].
: P.s. 2: *A Middle English Vocabulary* (1922). Tolkien refers to the *Rel. Ant.* on the word 'Blew' (*clothe here well yn Stafford blewe* on page 29).
: *NED*: #2 h. | 'W' (1928), p. 54. '*Walm sb*.¹ Obs. 1. a. (In OE. only.).' – c 1325 Tolkien cites: 'An Old English Song' 'Me is wo so is þe be þat belles in þe walmes' (p. 292).

2559. Wright, William Aldis. (Edited by). *Generydes, a romance in seven-line stanzas*. Series: E.E.T.S. (Early English Text Society), OS 70. London: Published for the

Early English Text Society by Kegan Paul, Trench, Trübner and Co., 1878.
> P.s.: MS. Tolkien A 21/13 fol. 119. Note by Tolkien, 'Books in Exeter Library useful', with shelfmarks, on back of photostat reading list dated October 1913. Tolkien writes: 'All EETS publications'. [Tolkien Papers, Bodleian Library, Oxford].
> *NED*: #2 h. | 'W' (1928), p. 53 'Wallop *v*. I. 1. b.' – c 1440 'He founde anon The kyng of kynggez vppe and down ndeng, And he anon to hym com waloping' (3325).

2560. Wülfing, J. Ernest. *Die Syntax in den Werken Alfreds des Grossen*, Vol I Huptwort, Artikel, Eigenschaftswort, Zahlwort und Fürwort. Bonn: P. Hanstein, 1894.
> P.s.: MS. Tolkien A 21/13 fol. 119. Note by Tolkien, 'Books in Exeter Library useful', with shelfmarks, on back of photostat reading list dated October 1913. [Tolkien Papers, Bodleian Library, Oxford].

2561. _____. *Die Syntax in den Werken Alfreds des Grossen*, Vol II Zeitwort, Adverb, Präpositionen, Konjunktionen und Interjektionen. Bonn: P. Hanstein, 1901.
> P.s.: MS. Tolkien A 21/13 fol. 119. Note by Tolkien, 'Books in Exeter Library useful', with shelfmarks, on back of photostat reading list dated October 1913. [Tolkien Papers, Bodleian Library, Oxford].

2562. Wulfstan, Archbishop of York. *The Homilies of Wulfstan*. Edited by Dorothy Bethurum. Oxford: At the Clarendon Press, 1957.
> P.s.: *Finn and Hengest* (1982), p. 98 n. 26.

2563. _____. *Sermo Lupi ad Anglos*. Edited by Dorothy Whitelock. London: Methuen and Co. Ltd., 1939.
> P.s.: *English and Welsh* (1963), p. 21

2564. _____.*Wulfstan: Sammlung der ihm zugeschriebenen homilien nebst Untersuchungen über ihre Echtheit*. Edited by Arthur Sampson Napier. Berlin: Weidmann, 1883.
> P.s. 1: *Sigelwara land* (1934), p. 101.
> P.s. 2: *Beowulf* (2014), p. 168. Notes: The reference written by Tolkien'so Wulfstan couples *wiccan* (witches) and *wælcyrian* (valkyries)', is on page 165 of the book by Wulfstan.

2565. _____. *Wulfstan's Canons of Edgar*. Series: E.E.T.S. (Early English Text Society), 266. Edited by Roger Fowler. London: Oxford University Press, 1972.
> Collection: Tolkien's personal Celtic library, preserved at the Weston library under the auspices of the English Faculty Library (Oxford).

2566. Wülker, Richard Paul (Edited by). *Anglia: Zeitschrift für englische Philologie*, Vol. IX. Tübingen: Max Niemeyer, 1886.
> P.s.: *Exeter College library register*. Tolkien's borrowing record: *Michaelmas Term 1914* from 23 October to 11 November.

2567. _____. *Das Beowulfslied nebst den kleineren epischen, lyrischen, didaktischen und geschichtlichen Stücken*. Series: Bibliothek der angelsächsischen Poesie. Begründet von Christian Wilhelm Michael Grein. Leipzig: Kassel George H. Wigand, 1883.
> P.s.: *Exeter College library register*. Tolkien's borrowing record: Easter vacation 1914 from 1 January to 17 June; Long vacation 1914 from 19 January to 14 October.

2568. _____. *Grundriss zur Geschichte der angelsächsischen Litteratur: mit einer Übersicht der angelsächsischen Sprachwissenschaft*. Leipzig: von Veit & Comp.,

1885.
>Description: Tolkien's signature to front free endpaper, pencil annotations, and marginal emphases.
>Collection: Private [Sold by Simon Finch Rare Books Ltd.].
>P.s.: *Exeter College library register*. Tolkien's borrowing record: Easter vacation 1914 from 1 January to 17 June.
>S.s.: Finch (2002), p. 53.

2569. _____. *Die Verceller Handschrift, die Handschrift des Cambridger Corpus Christi Collegs CCI, die Gedichte der Sogen. Cædmonhandscrift, Judith, der Hymnus Cædmons, Heiligenkalender, nebst kleineren geistlichen Dichtungen.* Series: Bibliothek der angelsächsischen Poesie. Begründet von Christian Wilhelm Michael Grein. Leipzig: Kassel George H. Wigand, 1894.
>P.s.: *Exeter College library register*. Tolkien's borrowing record: Long vacation 1914 from 19 January to 14 October.

2570. Wyatt, Alfred John. *An Anglo-Saxon Reader*. Cambridge: The University Press, 1919.
>P.s.: *Some Contributions to Middle-English Lexicography* (1925), p. 212. Tolkien cites Exeter Book Gnomic Verses, 64.
>S.s.: University of Leeds (1921), p. 153. English Language and Literature - Scheme A. Text selected for 1921-22. Ordinary Degree of B.A. with Honours. Extracts: i. *The Chronicle* (755-897 A.D.), ii. *Alfred's Orosius*, iii. *Cura Pastoralis*, iv. *Apolonnius of Tyre*, v. *Ælfric's Colloquy*, xviii. *Preface of Alfred's Blooms*, xx. *Riddles*, xxii. *Déor* and xxv. *Waldere*; p. 192 English Language and Literature. Honours and M.A. Courses. A. Language. H1. First Year. Extracts i-v, xviii, xx, xxii, xxv; p. 193 English Language and Literature. Honours and M.A. Courses. A. Language. H2. (Scheme A and B) Second and Third Year (*Waldere* and *Déor's Lament*).

2571. _____ (Edited by). *Beowulf. With the Finnsburg fragment*. With introduction by Raymond Wilson Chambers. Cambridge: The University Press, 1914.
>P.s.: *Finn and Hengest* (1982), p. 98 n. 24; p. 114 n. 56.
>S.s.: University of Leeds (1921), p. 193 English Language and Literature. Honours and M.A. Courses. A. Language. H2. (Scheme A and B) Second and Third Year.

2572. _____. *Old English Riddles*. London: D.C. Health & Co., 1912.
>P.s.: MS. Tolkien A 11 *Notes on Pearl* fol. 140. Tolkien quotes 'weocr þrōwade, earfoða dæl' (*Riddle* 71, p. 50). [Tolkien Papers, Bodleian Library, Oxford].

2573. Wycherley, William. *The Complete Plays of William Wycherley*. Series: Mermaid. Edited by William C. Ward. London: E. Benn, 1920.
>S.s.: University of Leeds (1921), p. 154. English Language and Literature - Scheme A. Texts and Period selected for 1921-22. (d) Texts suggested for study with Special Period 1637-1700. Ordinary Degree of B.A. with Honours. Final Examinations.

2574. Wycliffe, John. *The Holy Bible*, Vol. I. Cointaining The Old and New Testament, with the Aprocryphal Books, in the earliest English version made from the Latin Vulgate by John Wycliffe and his Followers. Edited by Josiah Forshall and Frederic Madden. Oxford: At the University Press, 1850.
>P.s. 1: MS. Tolkien A 21/13 *Chronological Library Table of Middle English* fol. 202. [Tolkien Papers, Bodleian Library, Oxford].
>P.s. 2: MS. Tolkien A 12/1 *Commentary on Sir Gawain, lines 37-1987* fol. 33. [Tolkien Papers, Bodleian Library, Oxford].
>P.s. 3: 'Chaucer as a Philologist: *The Reeve's Tale*' (1934), p. 131. Tolkien writes: *'fonne* 169 ... The derivative fonned is found, contemporary with Chaucer, in Wyclif or Wycliffite writings' [pp. 31-32, 235, 545]; p. 137. Tolkien quotes the word '*wang-töp*' (p. 657).

2575. _____. *The Holy Bible*, Vol. II. Cointaining The Old and New Testament,

with the Aprocryphal Books, in the earliest English version made from the Latin Vulgate by John Wycliffe and his Followers. Edited by Josiah Forshall and Frederic Madden. Oxford: At the University Press, 1850.
>P.s.: MS. Tolkien A 21/13 *Chronological Library Table of Middle English* fol. 202. [Tolkien Papers, Bodleian Library, Oxford].
>*NED*: #2 c., d., e. | 'W' (1928), p. 27 'Waiter, 1. *obs.*' 1382 – 'And the child weyter [Vulg. *puer speculator*] heuede vp his eyen, and bihelde' [from *II. Kings* xiii, 34 by John Wyclif. In *NED* is written '2. Sam. xiii, 34' for '2. Kings'].

2576. _____. *The Holy Bible*, Vol. III. Cointaining The Old and New Testament, with the Aprocryphal Books, in the earliest English version made from the Latin Vulgate by John Wycliffe and his Followers. Edited by Josiah Forshall and Frederic Madden. Oxford: At the University Press, 1850.
>P.s. 1: MS. Tolkien A 21/13 *Chronological Library Table of Middle English* fol. 202. [Tolkien Papers, Bodleian Library, Oxford].
>P.s. 2: 'Chaucer as a Philologist: *The Reeve's Tale*' (1934), p. 137. Tolkien quotes the word '*wang-töþ*' (p. 49).
>*NED*: #2 c., d., e. | 'W' (1928), p. 27 'Waiter, 1. *obs.*' c 1420 –'sophonyas the wayter [L. *speculator*] and the knowerof the priuetees of the Lord, herith a cry' (*Prefatory Epistles of St Jerome*, pp. 70-71).

2577. _____. *The Holy Bible*, Vol. IV. Cointaining The Old and New Testament, with the Aprocryphal Books, in the earliest English version made from the Latin Vulgate by John Wycliffe and his Followers. Edited by Josiah Forshall and Frederic Madden. Oxford: At the University Press, 1850.
>P.s. 1: MS. Tolkien A 21/13 *Chronological Library Table of Middle English* fol. 202. [Tolkien Papers, Bodleian Library, Oxford].
>P.s. 2: MS. Tolkien A 12/1 *Commentary on Sir Gawain, lines 37-1987* fol. 33. [Tolkien Papers, Bodleian Library, Oxford].
>P.s. 3: *A Middle English Vocabulary* (1922). Tolkien refers to the Wycliffe version on the term 'Platen' (Matt. xxvi 15, &c., p. 73).
>P.s. 4: 'Chaucer as a Philologist: *The Reeve's Tale*' (1934), p. 137. Tolkien quotes the word '*wang-töþ*' (p. 746).

2578. Wyke-Smith, Edward Augustine. *Marvellous Land of Snergs*. London: Benn, 1927.
>P.s. 1: *Letters* 163 (1955). To W.H. Auden. Tolkien writes:'seeing the date I should say that this was probably an unconscious source-book! For the Hobbits, not of anything else'.
>P.s. 2: *Tolkien On Fairy-stories* (2008) 'Manuscript B [MS. Tolkien 4, fols. 73-120]', pp. 249-50. Tolkien writes: 'I should like to record my own love and my children's love of E.A. Wyke-Smith's *Marvellous Land of Snergs*, at any rate of the Snerg-element in that tale, and of Gorbo the gem of dunderheads, jewel of a companion in an escapade.'
>S.s. 1: Scull-Hammond (2006b), p. 820.
>S.s. 2: Anderson (2002), pp. 6-7.

2579. Wyld, Henry Cecil Kennedy. *A History of Modern Colloquial English*. London: Fisher, 1920.
>P.s.: *Philology: General Works* (V 1926, for 1924), p.

2580. _____. 'Place-name and English Linguistic Studies'. With the assistance of Mary S. Serjeantson. *Introduction to the Survey of English place-names*, Vol. I, Pt. I [A. 1534]. Cambridge: The University Press, 1924.
>P.s.: *Philology: General Works* (V 1926, for 1924).

2581. _____. *Short History of English*. London: John Murray (2nd ed.), 1921.
>P.s.: 'Chaucer as a Philologist: *The Reeve's Tale*' (1934), p. 170 n. 119.

2582. _____. *Short History of English. With a bibliography of recent books on the subject, and lists of texts and editions*. London: John Murray, 1914.
    Description: Autographed on front flyleaf. Some pencil note eg. pp. 63, 83, 86.
    Collection: Tolkien's personal Celtic library, preserved at the Weston library under the auspices of the English Faculty Library (Oxford).
    S.s.: University of Leeds (1921), p. 193 English Language and Literature. Honours and M.A. Courses. A. Language. H2. (Scheme A and B) Second and Third Year.

2583. _____. *Studies in English Rhymes from Surrey to Pope, a chapter in the History of English*. London: Murray, 1923.
    P.s.: *Philology: General Works* (IV 1924, for 1923), p. 33 n. 15.

2584. _____. 'Studies in the diction of Layamon's Brut'. Offprint from *Language*, Vol. 6, no. 1, March 1930, pp. 1-24.
    Description: Library copy inscribed to J.R. Tolkien. Includes a label added by Stan Revell to books owned by Tolkien, 'From the Library of J.R.R. Tolkien' on page [1] of wrappers.

2585. Young, Williams Thomas. *An Anthology of the poetry of the age of Shakespeare*. Cambridge: The University Press, 1910.
    S.s.: University of Leeds (1923), p. 85. Ordinary Degree of B.A., Final Course and Examination. I. Principal Subjects, studied for Two Years. English Language and Literature: English Literature. Period selected for 1923-24: 1579-1645. Texts selected for 1923-24.

2586. *Ywain and Gawain* [Middle English Arthurian verse].
    P.s.: 'Chaucer as a Philologist: *The Reeve's Tale*' (1934), p. 141.

2587. Zachrisson, Robert Eugen. 'English place-names in -ing of Scandinavian origin'. *Språkvetenskapliga Sällskapets i Uppsala Förhandlingar*, Vol. 4. Uppsala: Almqvist och Wiksells boktryckeri, 1922, pp. 107-30.
    P.s.: *Philology: General Works* (V 1926, for 1924), p. 55.

2588. _____. 'The French Element'. *Introduction to the Survey of English place-names*, Vol. I, Pt. I [A. 1532]. Cambridge: The University Press, 1924.
    P.s.: *Philology: General Works* (V 1926, for 1924), p. 60.

2589. Zettersten, Arne. *Studies in the Dialect and Vocabulary of the Ancrene Riwle*. Lund: Hkan Ohlssons Boktryckeri, 1965.
    Description: Inscribed on front cover: 'To Professor J.R.R. Tolkien | with the author's compliments'. Uncut pages.
    Collection: Tolkien's personal Celtic library, preserved at the Weston library under the auspices of the English Faculty Library (Oxford).

2590. Zeuss, Johann Caspar (Edited by). *Grammatica celtica e monumentis vetustis tam hibernicae linguae quam britannicae dialecti, cambricae, cornicae, armoricae nec non e gallicae priscae reliquiis*, Vol. I. Lipsiae: Weidman, 1853.
    Collection: Tolkien's personal Celtic library, preserved at the Weston library under the auspices of the English Faculty Library (Oxford).

2591. _____ (Edited by). *Grammatica celtica e monumentis vetustis tam hibernicae linguae quam britannicae dialecti, cambricae, cornicae, armoricae nec non e gallicae priscae reliquiis*, Vol. II. Lipsiae: Weidman, 1853.
    Collection: Tolkien's personal Celtic library, preserved at the Weston library under the auspices of the English Faculty Library (Oxford).

SECTION A

2592. Zimmer, Heinrich (Edited by). *Glossae Hibernicae e codicibus wirziburgensi, carolisruhensibus, aliis, adiuvante Academiae Regiae berolinensis liberali tate.* Berolini: Weidman, 1881.
    Description: Decoratively autographed and dated: '1923'. Inscribed on title page and p. v in red crayon: 'H.8'.
    Collection: Tolkien's personal Celtic library, preserved at the Weston library under the auspices of the English Faculty Library (Oxford).
    Notes: It is probable that Tolkien referred to 'Honours and M.A. Course. B. Literature. H8. (Scheme A and B) First Year: Essays and discussions. In tutorial groups and time to be arranged' S.s.: University of Leeds (1924), p. 134.

2593. _____. 'Der Kampf des Wettergottes mit der Schlange Illujankaš. Ein hethitischer Mythus'. *Streitberg-Festgabe* [A. 2228]. Leipzig: Market und Petter, 1924.
    P.s.: *Philology: General Works* (V 1926, for 1924).

2594. _____. 'Keltische Studien. 5. Ueber den compilatorischen charakter der irischen sagen texte im sogenannten Lebor na hUidre'. *Zeitschrift für vergleichende Sprachforschung auf dem Gebiete der Indogermanischen Sprachen*, Vol. XXVIII, No. 5, 1887, pp. 417-689.
    P.s.: *Sir Gawain and the Green Knight* (1925), p. xxvi. Tolkien and Gordon write: 'For bibliography of the Irish and French analogues of *Sir Gawain*, see the bibliography in Kittredge's study'. [*NED*] In Kittredge's study, this article is mentioned in 'I. Fled Bricrend' (p. 290 n. 3).

2595. Zoëga, Geir T.; Richard Cleasby and Guðbrandur Vigfússon (Edited by). *A Concise Dictionary of Old Icelandic.* Oxford: At the Clarendon Press, 1910.
    P.s.: *A Middle English Vocabulary* (1922), Note.

2596. Zupitza, Julius (Edited by). *Beowulf. Autotypes of the unique Cotton MS. Vitellius A 15 in the British Museum.* Series: E.E.T.S. (Early English Text Society), OS 77. London Published for the Early English Text Society by N. Trübner, 1882.
    P.s.: MS. Tolkien A 21/13 fol. 119. Note by Tolkien, 'Books in Exeter Library useful', with shelfmarks, on back of photostat reading list dated October 1913. Tolkien writes: 'All EETS publications'. [Tolkien Papers, Bodleian Library, Oxford].

2597. _____. *The Romance of Guy of Warwick: the second or fifteenth-century version I and II.* Series: E.E.T.S. (Early English Text Society), SS 25. London: Oxford University Press, 1875.
    P.s. 1: MS. Tolkien A 12/1 *Commentary on Sir Gawain, lines 37-1987* fol. 8. [Tolkien Papers, Bodleian Library, Oxford].
    P.s. 2: MS. Tolkien A 21/13 fol. 119. Note by Tolkien, 'Books in Exeter Library useful', with shelfmarks, on back of photostat reading list dated October 1913. Tolkien writes: 'All EETS publications'. [Tolkien Papers, Bodleian Library, Oxford].
    P.s. 3: *A Middle English Vocabulary* (1922). Tolkien refers to the *Guy of Warwick* (15th c.) on the term 'Fine' (Afine, Fyn, 9083 note).
    P.s. 4: *Sir Gawain and the Green Knight* (1925), p. 105, line 1412 ff. Tolkien and Gordon cite vv. 6417-60 'They enturde into a wylde foreste ... And Gye with hye horne blewe a blaste.' (pp. 184-85).
    NED: #2 h. | 'W' (1928), p. 54. 'Walm *sb.*¹ *Obs.* 2.' – 'Al to-hewe was his helme, þe blod ran out als a welme' (3592).

2598. _____. *The Romance of Guy of Warwick*, Pt. II. Series: E.E.T.S. (Early English Text Society), SS 26. London: Oxford University Press, 1876.
    P.s. 1: MS. Tolkien A 12/1 *Commentary on Sir Gawain, lines 37-1987* fol. 8. [Tolkien Papers,

Bodleian Library, Oxford].
P.s. 2: MS. Tolkien A 21/13 fol. 119. Note by Tolkien, 'Books in Exeter Library useful', with shelfmarks, on back of photostat reading list dated October 1913. Tolkien writes: 'All EETS publications'. [Tolkien Papers, Bodleian Library, Oxford].

2599. _____ and Norman Davis (Edited by). *Beowulf: facsimile of BM MS. Cotton Vitellius A xv*. Series: E.E.T.S. (Early English Text Society), OS 245. London: Oxford University Press, 1959 (2nd ed.).
S.s.: Scull-Hammond (2017a), p. 542.

*'My library is now in order;
and nearly all the things that I thought were lost
have turned up.'*

J.R.R. Tolkien to Christopher Tolkien
(2 January 1969)

The published writings of J.R.R. Tolkien
1910 - 1972

Listed here are the books by Tolkien and his contributions to periodicals published during his lifetime[1].

– 1910 –

1. 'Debating Society' [Report]. *King Edward's School Chronicle*. Birmingham, Vol. 25, no. 183 (November), pp. 68-71.
   Notes: Unsigned.

2. 'Debating Society' [Report]. *King Edward's School Chronicle*. Birmingham, Vol. 25, no. 184 (December), pp. 94-95.
   Notes: Unsigned.

– 1911 –

3. 'Acta Senatus'. *King Edward's School Chronicle*. Birmingham, Vol. 26, no. 186 (March), pp. 26-27.
   Notes: Unsigned report in Latin. The article does not appear to be a simple translation of Debating Society report, rather it seems to be more dramatic and written in the style of the Acta Diurna (the official notices of the Roman Republic). The names of participants in the debate are in Latin, being translations of names or nicknames, interests or plays on words. John Garth identifies T. Portorius Acer Germanicus as being Tolkien [Toll Keen].

4. 'The Battle of the Eastern Fields'. *King Edward's School Chronicle*. Birmingham, Vol. 26, no. 186 (March), pp. 22-26.
   Notes: Poem. Reprinted in *Mallorn*, no. 12 (1978), pp. 24-28.

5. 'Debating Society' [Report]. *King Edward's School Chronicle*. Birmingham, N.S., Vol. 26, no. 185 (February), pp. 5-9.
   Notes: Unsigned.

6. 'Debating Society' [Report]. *King Edward's School Chronicle*. Birmingham, N.S., Vol. 26, no. 187 (June), pp. 42-45.
   Notes: Unsigned.

7. 'Editorial'. *King Edward's School Chronicle*. Birmingham, Vol. 26, no. 187 (June), pp. 33-34.
   Notes: Unsigned.

8. 'Editorial'. *King Edward's School Chronicle*. Birmingham, Vol. 26, no. 188 (July), pp. 53-54.
   Notes: Unsigned.

---

1. The information for the notes in this section have been taken from TolkienBooks and Åke Bertenstam.

– 1913 –

9. 'From the many-willow 'd margin of the immemorial Thames'. *The Stapeldon Magazine*. Oxford, Vol. 4, no. 20 (December), p. 11.
   Notes: Poem signed 'J.' Reprinted in *Tolkien and The Great War* (2003) by John Garth.

– 1915 –

10. 'Goblin Feet'. *Oxford Poetry* 1915. Cole, G. D. H. and Earp, T. W (Edited by). Oxford: B. H. Blackwell, pp. 66-65.
    Notes: Reprinted in Anderson, *The Annotated Hobbit*, p. 77. The first two verses are reprinted in Carpenter's *Biography*, while the second, third and fourth verses are reprinted in *Tolkien and the Great War*.

– 1918 –

11. 'Prefatory note'. Smith, Geoffrey Bache. *A Spring Harvest*. London: Erskine Macdonald, [June or July].
    Notes: The note, signed 'JRRT', appears on p. 7.

– 1920 –

12. 'The Happy Mariners'. *The Stapeldon Magazine*. Oxford, Vol. 5, no. 26 (June), pp. 69-70.
    Notes: Poem, signed 'JRRT' Reprinted as *Tha Eadigan Saelidan: The Happy Mariners* in *A Northern Venture*, pp 273-274 and in *The Book of Lost Tales*, Vol. II, pp. 273-274 under the original title. In the latter a later version is also given (pp. 275-276).

– 1922 –

13. 'The Clerke's Compleinte'. *The Gryphon*. Leeds, Vol. 4, no. 3 (December), p. 95.
    Notes: A poem written in Middle English, signed 'N.N.'

14. *A Middle English Vocabulary*. Oxford: At the Clarendon Press, [11 May] p.168.
    Notes: A glossary of Middle English words and names compiled by Tolkien between 1919 and 1922. After it was published were bound with Sisam's book, *Fourteenth Century Verse & Prose*.

– 1923 –

15. 'The Cat and the Fiddle: A Nursery Rhyme Undone and its Scandalous Secret Unlocked'. *Yorkshire Poetry*. Leeds, Vol. 2, no. 19 (October-November).
    Notes: Poem. Reprinted in *The Return of the Shadow*, pp. 145-147. Revised version printed in *The Lord of the Rings*, Book One, chapter 9 and as *The Man in the Moon Came Down Too Soon* in *The Adventures of Tom Bombadil*.

16. 'The City of the Gods'. *Microcosm*. Leeds, Vol. 8, no. 1 (Spring), p. 8.
    Notes: Poem, The poem is reprinted in *The Book of Lost Tales*, Vol. I (1983), p. 136, and in *Tolkien and the Great War* with the title *Kôr: In a City Lost and Dead* - this was the title Tolkien gave to the poem when it was composed in 1915.

17. 'Tha Eadigan Saelidan: The Happy Mariners'. *A Northern Venture: Verses by Members of the University of Leeds University English School Association*. Leeds: At the Swan Press, [June], pp. 15-16.
    Notes: This poem is a slightly revised version of that published in *The Stapeldon Magazine* in 1920 and later in *Tolkien and the Great War*. The 1920 version is also reprinted in *The Book of Lost Tales*, Vol. II (1984) along with a later revision.

18. 'Enigmata Saxonica Nuper Inventa Duo'. *A Northern Venture: Verses by Members of the University of Leeds University English School Association*. Leeds: At the

Swan Press, [June], pp. 17-19.
> Notes: This riddle-poem is reprinted in Anderson (2nd Edition only). An earlier variant is reproduced under the title *Enigma Saxonicum Nuper Inventum* in *The Oxford Inklings*.

19. 'Henry Bradley: 3 Dec., 1845-23 May, 1923'. *Bulletin of the Modern Humanities Research Association*. London, no. 20 (October 1923), pp. 4-5.
> Notes: Obituary signed 'JRRT' that ends in a 13-line poem written in Old English.

20. 'Holy Maidenhood'. *The Times Literary Supplement*. London, no. 1110 (26 April), p. 281.
> Notes: A unsigned review of *Hali Meidenhad*, edited by F.J. Furnivall (Early English Text Society), Original series; 18).

21. 'Iúmonna Gold Galdre Bewunden'. *The Gryphon*. Leeds, Vol. 4, no. 4 (January), p. 130.
> Notes: The poem, inspired by line 3052 in *Beowulf*, was later reprinted in Anderson, *The Annotated Hobbit*, pp. 288-289. Both the 1923 and 1937 versions are reprinted in *Beowulf and the Critics* along with an intermediate version (printed twice, the first time without the final stanza). Later revised and printed in *Oxford Magazine* as The Hoard in *The Adventures of Tom Bombadil*.

22. 'Philology: General Works'. *The Year's Work in English Studies*. London, Vol. IV, pp. 20-37.
> Notes: Review essay. This covers philological books and articles published in 1923. It includes a fairly lengthy discussion of two newly published sections of the *OED* (*Wash-Wavy* and *Wh-Whisky*) which may include some words that Tolkien worked on during his time at the Dictionary.

23. 'Why the Man in the Moon Came Down Too Soon'. *A Northern Venture: Verses by Members of the University of Leeds University English School Association*. Leeds: At the Swan Press, [June].
> Notes: The poem appears on pp. 17-19. Reprinted in *The Book of Lost Tales*, Vol. I, pp. 204-206. A revised version was printed as The Man in the Moon Came Down Too Soon in *The Adventures of Tom Bombadil*.

– 1924 –

24. 'An Evening in Tavrobel'. *Leeds University Verse 1914-1924*. Leeds: At the Swan Press.
> Notes: The poem appears on p. 56.

25. 'The Lonely Isle'. *Leeds University Verse 1914-1924*. Leeds: At the Swan Press.
> Notes: The poem appears on p. 57.

26. 'Philology: General Works'. *The Year's Work in English Studies*. London, Vol. V, pp. 26-65.
> Notes: Review essay. This covers philological books and articles published in 1924. In his introduction Tolkien comments on the increasing number and scope of philological publications and blurring of the lines between philology and related disciplines. As with the previous volume, Tolkien discusses the latest section of the *OED* to be published (*Whisking-Wilfulness*) which includes some of the words he worked on during his time at the Dictionary.

27. 'The Princess Ní'. *Leeds University Verse 1914-1924*. Leeds: At the Swan Press.
> Notes: The poem appears on p. 58. A revised version was printed as 'Princess Mee' in *The Adventures of Tom Bombadil*.

SECTION B

– 1925 –

28. 'The Devil's Coach-Horses'. *The Review of English Studies*. London, Vol. 1, no. 3 (July), pp. 331-336.
    Notes: The essay discusses *eaueres*, a word found in the 1922 Early English Text Society Edition of *Hali Meidenhad*. Tolkien suggests that rather than meaning boar, the word should be translated as *draught horse*.

29. 'Light as Leaf on Lindentree'. *The Gryphon*. Leeds, Vol. 6, no. 6 (June) p. 217.
    Notes: Poem. Reprinted in *The Lays of Beleriand*, pp. 108-111 as a poem inserted into *The Lay of the Children of Húrin* and with its introductory lines in alliterative verse printed on p. 120. A revised version is to be found in *The Lord of the Rings*, Book 1, chapter 11.

30. 'Philology: General Works'. *The Year's Work in English Studies*. London, Vol. VI, pp. 32-66.
    Notes: Review essay. This covers the plethora of philological books and articles published in 1925.

31. *Sir Gawain and the Green Knight*. Tolkien, J.R.R. and Eric Valentine Gordon (Edited by). London: Oxford University Press, [23 April], pp. [iii]-xxvii, [i], 211, [1], [2] plates.
    Notes: Revised edition, edited by Norman Davis. Oxford: At the Clarendon Press, [October] 1967, pp. xxvii + 232, plates.

32. 'Some Contributions to Middle-English Lexicography'. *The Review of English Studies*. London, Vol. 1, no. 2 (April), pp. 210-215.
    Notes: Pt. I: Tolkien discusses aspects of a variety of Middle English words and their Modern English meanings. Pt. II: consists of a series of notes on the glossary to the Early English Text Society Edition of *Hali Meidenhad*.

– 1927 –

33. 'Adventures in Unnatural History and Medieval Metres: being The Freaks of Fisiologus (i): Fastitocalon'. *Stapeldon Magazine*. Oxford, Vol. 7, no. 40 (June), pp. 123-125.
    Notes: Poem, signed 'Fisiologus'. Printed in a revised version as *Fastitocalon* in *The Adventures of Tom Bombadil*.

34. 'Adventures in Unnatural History and Medieval Metres: being The Freaks of Fisiologus (ii): Iumbo, or, Ye Kind of Ye Oliphaunt'. *Stapeldon Magazine*. Oxford, Vol. 7, no. 40 (June), pp. 125-127.
    Notes: Poem, signed 'Fisiologus'. Despite its title this poem bears almost no resemblance to the one recited by Sam in *The Lord of the Rings*, Book IV, chapter 3 and reprinted as *Oliphaunt* in *The Adventures of Tom Bombadil*.

35. 'The Grey Bridge of Tavrobel'. *Inter-University Magazine*. Oxford, Vol. 8, No 5 [May], p. 82.
    Notes: Poem, four of the six stanzas are reprinted in *Tolkien and the Great War*.

36. 'The Nameless Land'. *Realities: An Anthology of Verse*. Tancred, G. S (Edited by). Leeds: At the Swan Press, p. 31.
    Notes: The poem appears on pp. 24-25. Reprinted in *The Lost Road*, pp. 98-100 (with later versions entitled *The Song of Ælfwine* given on pp. 100-103).

37. 'Tinfang Warble'. *Inter-University Magazine*. Oxford, Vol. 8, No 5 [May], p. 63.
    Notes: Poem, reprinted in *The Book of Lost Tales*, Vol. I, and also in *Tolkien and the Great War*, minus the first three and last two lines.

– 1928 –

38. 'Foreword'. *A New Glossary of the Dialect of the Huddersfield District.* Haigh, Walter E (Edited by). London: Oxford University Press, [12 January].
   Notes: The foreword appears on pp. [xiii]-xviii. In his preface, Walter Haigh thanks Tolkien: 'In the first place I would sincerely thank Professor J.R.R. Tolkien, formerly Professor in Leeds University, now Professor of Anglo-Saxon at Oxford. Not only has he almost from the first shown his warm approval of the work, and befriended me with ever-ready advice and encouragement throughout, but he has also generously contributed a valuable Foreword to the Glossary.'

– 1929 –

39. 'Ancrene Wisse and Hali Meiðhad'. *Essays and Studies by members of the English Association.* Oxford, Vol. XIV, pp. 104-126.
   Notes: In this essay Tolkien contends that the languages used in the original versions of the Middle English texts *Ancrene Wisse* and *Hali Meiðhadare* one and the same – a language that he dubbed 'language (AB)'.

– 1930 –

40. 'At the Tabacconist's' (Record code: EC.20.E). *Linguaphone: Conversational Course: English.* Edited by Arthur Lloyd James. London, The Linguaphone Institute [June].
   Notes: Tolkien reads the introduction and plays the part of the shop owner in the following dialogue with a customer played by Lloyd James. Whether the text Tolkien read was written by him and/or whether he supervised its writing is unknown.

41. 'Wireless' (Record code: EC.30.E). *Linguaphone: Conversational Course: English.* Edited by Arthur Lloyd James. London, The Linguaphone Institute [June].
   Notes: Tolkien plays the part of a the owner of a radio set explaining to Lloyd James what stations he can receive and how great this modern technology is! Whether the text Tolkien read was written by him and/or whether he supervised its writing is unknown.

42. 'The Oxford English School'. *The Oxford Magazine.* Oxford, Vol. 48, no. 21 (29 May), pp. 778-782.
   Notes: Essay. discusses the divide between 'language' and 'literature' and the failings of the English syllabus; he goes on to suggest improvements.

– 1931 –

43. 'Progress in Bimble Town' (Devoted to the Mayor and Corporation). *The Oxford Magazine.* Oxford, Vol. 50, no. 1 (15 October), p. 22.
   Notes: Poem, signed 'K. Bagpuize'. It was later reprinted in Anderson, *The Annotated Hobbit*, p. 212.

– 1932 –

44. 'Appendix I: The Name *Nodens*'. Wheeler, R. E. M. and Wheeler, T. V. *Report on the Excavation of the Prehistoric, Roman, and Post-Roman Site in Lydney Park, Gloucestershire.* Oxford: Printed at the University Press for The Society of Antiquaries, [July]. pp. [iii]-viii + 142, plates. (Reports of the Research Committee of the Society of Antiquaries of London; 9).
   Notes: Essay, printed on pp. 132-137. The word Nodens appears in three inscriptions found at the excavations in Lydney Park and appears to be the name of an otherwise unrecorded god. Tolkien links the name to the Old Irish *Núadu* and Welsh *Nudd*. Núadu was the King of the Túatha dé Danann, the one time rulers of Ireland. Tolkien goes on to trace the name in other ancient languages and finally comes to the conclusion that the name means either 'the catcher', 'the snarer' or 'the hunter'.

45. 'A Philologist on Esperanto'. *The British Esperantist*. Butler, M. C. (Edited by). London, *The British Esperanto Association*, Vol. 28 [May], p. 182.
   Notes: Extracts from a letter written to the secretary of the Education Committee of the British Esperanto Association.

46. 'Sigelwara land I'. *Medium Aevum*. Oxford, Vol. 1, no. 3 (December), pp. 183-196.
   Notes: Essay. In the essay Tolkien discusses the etymology of *Sigelwaran* (and the more usual form *Sigelhearwan*) - the Old English word for Ethiopians.

– 1933 –

47. 'The Educational Value of Esperanto'. *The British Esperantist*. Butler, M. C. London, *The British Esperanto Association*, Vol. 29 [May], p. 182.
   Notes: Appeal. Tolkien is among the twenty signatories of the document.

48. 'Errantry'. *The Oxford Magazine*. Oxford, Vol. 52, no. 5 (9 November), p. 180.
   Notes: Poem. Reprinted in *The Adventures of Tom Bombadil*. Concerning its complicated textual history and gradual development into 'The Lay of Eärendil' (*The Lord of the Rings*, Book II, chapter 1) see The Treason of Isengard, chapter V: 'Bilbo's Song at Rivendell: *Errantry* and *Eärendil linwë*', pp. 81-109.

– 1934 –

49. 'The Adventures of Tom Bombadil'. *The Oxford Magazine*. Oxford, Vol. 52, no. 13 (13 February), pp. 464-465.
   Notes: Poem. Reprinted in *The Adventures of Tom Bombadil*.

50. 'Chaucer as a Philologist: *The Reeve's Tale*'. Transactions of the Philological Society. London, pp. 1-70.
   Notes: Essay, read before the society in 1931. (Its reading is reported in the *Annual Report for 1931* in the *Transactions for 1931-32*. It was read on 16th May 1931 in Oxford and presented under the title Chaucer's Use of Dialects).

51. 'Firiel'. *The Chronicle of the Convent of the Sacred Heart*. Roehampton, 4, pp. 30-32: ill.
   Notes: Poem. Printed in a revised version as 'The Last Ship' in *The Adventures of Tom Bombadil*. The phrase 'Unione Fortior' on the upper cover seems to be a motto – 'strength in Union'.

52. 'Looney'. *The Oxford Magazine*. Oxford, Vol. 52, no. 9 (18 January), p. 340.
   Notes: Poem. Printed in a revised version as 'The Sea-Bell' in *The Adventures of Tom Bombadil*.

53. 'Sigelwara land II'. *Medium Aevum*. Oxford, Vol. 3, no. 2 (June), pp. 95-111.
   Notes: Essay, continuation of *Sigelwara land I* above.

– 1936 –

54. 'Bagme Bloma'. *Songs for the Philologists*. Tolkien, J.R.R. and Eric Valentine Gordon *et alii* (Edited by). London: Privately printed in the Department of English at University College.
   Notes: Poem in Gothic, printed on p. 12. Reprinted, together with a prose translation ('Flower of the Trees') in Shippey (1982, pp. 227-228; 1992, pp. 303-304).

55. 'Éadig Béo þu!' *Songs for the Philologists*. Tolkien, J.R.R. and Eric Valentine Gordon *et alii* (Edited by). London: Privately printed in the Department of English at University College.
   Notes: Poem in Old English, printed on p. 13. Reprinted, together with a prose translation ('Good Luck to You') in Shippey (1982, pp. 228-229; 1992, pp. 304-305).

56. *An Edition of Þe Liflade ant te Passiun of Seinte Iuliene*. [An Edition of The Life and the Passion of Saint Juliana]. d'Ardenne, S. R. T. O. [and Tolkien, J.R.R.] ed. Liége and Paris, Bibliothéque de la Faculté de Philosphie et Lettres de l'Université de Liége (Fasc. LXIV). Faculté de Philosphie et Lettres and Librarie E. Droz.
    Notes: D'Ardenne admitted privately that Tolkien should have been credited as a joint editor. It was published solely under d'Ardenne's name as a thesis that enabled her to be elected as a professor at the University of Liége.

57. 'Frenchmen Froth'. *Songs for the Philologists*. Tolkien, J.R.R. and Eric Valentine Gordon *et alii* (Edited by). London: Privately printed in the Department of English at University College.
    Notes: Poem, printed on pp. 24-25.

58. 'From One to Five'. *Songs for the Philologists*. Tolkien, J.R.R. and Eric Valentine Gordon *et alii* (Edited by). London: Privately printed in the Department of English at University College.
    Notes: Poem, printed on p. 6.

59. 'I Sat upon a Bench'. *Songs for the Philologists*. Tolkien, J.R.R. and Eric Valentine Gordon *et alii* (Edited by). London: Privately printed in the Department of English at University College.
    Notes: Poem, printed on p. 17.

60. 'Ides Ælfscýne'. *Songs for the Philologists*. Tolkien, J.R.R. and Eric Valentine Gordon *et alii* (Edited by). London: Privately printed in the Department of English at University College.
    Notes: Poem in Old English, printed on pp. 10-11. Reprinted, together with a prose translation ('Elf-fair Lady') in Shippey (1982, pp. 229-231; 1992, pp. 306-307).

61. 'La Húru'. *Songs for the Philologists*. Tolkien, J.R.R. and Eric Valentine Gordon *et alii* (Edited by). London: Privately printed in the Department of English at University College.
    Notes: Poem, printed on p. 16.

62. 'Lit' and 'Lang'. *Songs for the Philologists*. Tolkien, J.R.R. and Eric Valentine Gordon *et alii* (Edited by). London: Privately printed in the Department of English at University College.
    Notes: Poem, printed on p. 27.

63. 'Natura Apis: Morali Ricardi Eremite'. London: Privately printed in the Department of English at University College.
    Notes: Poem, printed on p. 18.

64. 'Noel'. *The 'Annual' of Our Lady's School, Abingdon*. Abingdon, Our Lady's School.
    Notes: Poem.

65. 'Ofer Wídne Gársecg'. *Songs for the Philologists*. Tolkien, J.R.R. and Eric Valentine Gordon *et alii* (Edited by). London: Privately printed in the Department of English at University College.
    Notes: Poem in Old English, printed on pp. 14-15. Reprinted, together with a prose translation ('Across the Broad Ocean') in Shippey (1982, pp. 231-233; 1992, pp. 308-309).

66. 'The Root of the Boot'. *Songs for the Philologists*. Tolkien, J.R.R. and Eric Valentine Gordon *et alii* (Edited by). London: Privately printed in the Department of English at University College.
   Notes: Poem, printed on pp. 20-21. Reprinted in Anderson, *The Annotated Hobbit*, p. 45 and in *The Return of the Shadow*, p. 143 (slightly corrected). Later revised and printed in *The Lord of the Rings*, Book One, chapter 12 and as 'The Stone Troll' in *The Adventures of Tom Bombadil*.

67. 'Ruddoc Hana'. *Songs for the Philologists*. Tolkien, J.R.R. and Eric Valentine Gordon *et alii* (Edited by). London: Privately printed in the Department of English at University College.
   Notes: Poem in Old English, a rendering of 'Who Killed Cock Robin', printed on pp. 8-9.

68. 'The Shadow Man'. *The 'Annual' of Our Lady's School, Abingdon*. Abingdon, Our Lady's School, no. 12.
   Notes: Poem, reprinted in a revised form 'Shadow-Bride' in *The Adventures of Tom Bombadil*.

69. 'Syx Mynet'. *Songs for the Philologists*. Tolkien, J.R.R. and Eric Valentine Gordon *et alii* (Edited by). London: Privately printed in the Department of English at University College.
   Notes: Poem in Old English, a rendering of 'I Love Sixpence', printed on p. 7.

– 1937 –

70. *Beowulf: The Monsters and the Critics*. London: Humphrey Milford [1 July], p.56.
   Notes: Also issued in the *Proceedings* of the British Academy (Vol. 22, 1936, pr. 1937, pp. [245]-295). This essay is a revised version of a much longer work, *Beowulf and the Critics*.

71. 'The Dragon's Visit'. *The Oxford Magazine*. Oxford, Vol. 55, no. 14 (4 February), p.342.
   Notes: Poem. Reprinted in Anderson, *The Annotated Hobbit*, and in a revised form in Winter's *Tales for Children* Vol. I and *The Young Magicians*.

72. *The Hobbit, or, There and Back Again*. London: George Allen & Unwin [21 September], plate.
   Notes: Revised editions: The second edition appeared in 1951 and the third in 1966. Further corrections have been made in later editions. An annotated edition was published on 28th October 1988: Anderson, *The Annotated Hobbit*. Introduction and notes by Douglas A. Anderson. Boston. Houghton Mifflin Company. Pp. x, [i], 335. J.R.R. Tolkien's own recording of the second edition version of chapter V: 'Riddles in the Dark' was released on J.R.R. Tolkien reads and sings his *The Hobbit* and *The Fellowship of the Ring* (New York: Cædmon Records, 1975, TC 1477).

73. 'Iumonna Gold Galdre Bewunden'. *The Oxford Magazine*. Oxford, Vol. 55, no. 15 (4 March), p. 473.
   Notes: Revised version of a poem earlier published in *The Gryphon*. The poem was later reprinted in Anderson, *The Annotated Hobbit*, pp. 288-289. Both the 1923 and 1937 versions are reprinted in Beowulf and the Critics along with an intermediate version (printed twice, the first time without the final stanza). Later revised and printed in *The Oxford Magazine* as 'The Hoard' in *The Adventures of Tom Bombadil*.

74. 'Knocking at the Door: Lines induced by sensations when waiting for answer at the door of an Exalted Academic Person'. *The Oxford Magazine*. Oxford, Vol. 55, no. 13 (18 February), p. 403.
   Notes: Poem. Reprinted as 'The Mewlips' in *The Adventures of Tom Bombadil*.

– 1938 –

75. 'Letter to the editor'. *The Observer*. London, 20 February, p. 9.
    Notes: This is a reply to a letter by 'Habit' published on 16 January 1938. Tolkien sent a short reply to be published in the newspaper, and a longer letter to be forwarded on to 'Habit'. The longer reply was published without Tolkien's permission.

– 1939 –

76. *The Reeve's Tale: version prepared for recitation at the 'summer diversions*. Oxford, p. 14.
    Notes: Prepared by Tolkien to accompany his performance on 28 July 1939 of Chaucer's *The Reeve's Tale* at the 'summer Diversions' - a festival of recitals, plays and ballet. Includes a two-page introduction by Tolkien to a slightly reworked version of the text of *The Reeve's Tale* by Chaucer as printed by Skeat. The changes to the text seem to have been made for length and to cut out some of the bawdier elements that may have offended at a public performance.

– 1940 –

77. 'Prefatory Remarks on Prose Translation of *Beowulf*'. *Beowulf and the Finnesburg Fragment. A Translation into Modern English Prose by John R. Clark Hall. New ed., completely revised, with notes and an Introduction by C.L. Wrenn, [and] with Prefatory Remarks by J.R.R. Tolkien*. London: George Allen & Unwin [16 July].
    Notes: Essay, printed on pp. [viii]-xli. Tolkien's essay was reprinted in *The Monsters and the Critics and Other Essays* (1983) as *On Translating Beowulf*.
    S.s.: Lewis (2009a), p. 349. Letter to Michael Thwaites – 22 April 1945. Lewis writes: 'Whether you can begin O.E. poetry on your own I don't know. But try getting Klaeber's or Chamber's ed. of *Beowulf*: and with it Clark Hall's trans. ed. by Wrenn with preface by Tolkien (Allen & Unwin, 1940). This edition is essential for it is Tolkien's part of metre wh. is essential. (O.E. verse uses both quality and accent, and your ear is prob. ruined, as mine was, by the false way they teach Latin metre at schools–drastic re-education is required. You were prob. never taught to pronounce the double l in *ille* like the double l in palely. It matters enormously).'

– 1944 –

78. *Sir Orfeo*. Oxford: The Academic Copying Office, p. 18.
    Notes: Although the booklet does not identify Tolkien's editorship, a copy held by the Bodleian Library in Oxford includes a note in Tolkien's hand which states that it was prepared for a naval cadets' course in English that ran from 1943-1944. Edition of a Middle English poem. Tolkien's translation of it was later published in *Sir Gawain and the Green Knight, Pearl*, and *Sir Orfeo*.

– 1945 –

79. 'The Lay of Aotrou and Itroun'. *The Welsh Review*. Cardiff, Vol. 4, no. 4 (December), pp. 254-266.
    Notes: Poem.

80. 'Leaf by Niggle'. *Dublin Review*. London, 432 (January), pp. 46-61.
    Notes: Short story. Later reprinted in *Tree and Leaf*.

81. 'The Name Coventry'. *Catholic Herald*. London, 23 February, p. 2.
    Notes: Letter to the editor, written in response to a query by 'H.D.' concerning the etymology of Coventry.

– 1946 –

82. 'Research v. literature'. *The Sunday Times*. London, April 14.
    Notes: Review of E. K. Chambers, *English literature at the close of the Middle Ages*.

– 1947 –

83. 'Iþþlen in Sawles Warde'. *English Studies*. S.R.T.O. d'Ardenne, J.R.R. Tolkien. Amsterdam, Vol. 27, no. 6 (December), pp. 168-170.
   Notes: The essay discusses a corrupted or misread word in printed editions of an early manuscript of the Middle English homily *Sawles Warde*.

84. 'On Fairy-Stories'. *Essays presented to Charles Williams*. Sayers, D. L. Tolkien, J.R.R. Lewis, C. S. Barfield, A. O. Mathew, Gervase and Lewis. W. H. London: Oxford University Press [December].
   Notes: Essay, printed on pp. [38]-89. Printed in revised version in *Tree and Leaf*.

– 1948 –

85. 'MS Bodley 34: A re-collation of a collation'. S.R.T.O. d'Ardenne, J.R.R. Tolkien. *Studia Neophilologica*. Uppsala, Vol. 20, no. 1-2, pp. 65-72.
   Notes: Essay. Comments to Ragnar Furuskog: *A Collation of the Katherine Group* (MS Bodley 34) (idem, Vol. 19, no. 1-2 (1946-47, pr. 1946), pp. [119]-166)

– 1949 –

86. *Farmer Giles of Ham*. Embellished by Pauline Baynes. London: George Allen & Unwin [October].
   Notes: The 50th anniversary of the publishing of this book was celebrated with a new edition, edited by Christina Scull and Wayne G. Hammond: London: HarperCollins*Publishers*, [October] 1999. Pp. [6], xii, 7-127, 2 plates. (ISBN 0-261-10377-6). In this new edition the first manuscript version of *Farmer Giles of Ham* is given as well the fragmentary sequel to the story.

– 1953 –

87. 'Form and Purpose'. *Pearl*. Gordon, Ida (Edited by). Oxford: At the Clarendon Press [11 June], plate.
   Notes: This text, appearing on pp. xi-xix, forms part of the introduction (pp. [ix]-lii). Reprinted as part III of the Introduction to *Sir Gawain and the Green Knight, Pearl*, and *Sir Orfeo* (pp. 18-23).

88. 'A Fourteenth-Century Romance'. *Radio Times*. London, 4 December, p. 9.
   Notes: Article written in connection with the performance of Tolkien's translation of *Sir Gawain and the Green Knight*. Regional editions of *Radio Times* were issued in different parts of the country to reflect local programming. Tolkien's essay appears only in the London edition.

89. 'The Homecoming of Beorhtnoth, Beorhthelm's Son'. *Essays and Studies by members of the English Association*. London, Vol. 6, pp. 1-18.
   Description: Consists of three parts: 'Beorhtnoth's Death' (essay), 'The Homecoming of Beorhtnoth, Beorhthelm's Son' (dramatic dialogue in rhyming verse), and 'Ofermod' (essay). Reprinted in *The Tolkien Reader, Tree and Leaf; Smith of Wootton Major; The Homecoming of Beorhtnoth, Beorthelm's Son*, and *Poems and Stories*.
   Notes: It has also been published separately: *Pinner: Anglo-Saxon Books*, 1991. P. 28 (A limited edition of 300 numbered copies published to commemorate the 1000th anniversary of the Battle of Maldon.) Tolkien made a recording of the poem, which has never been commercially released, but copies of it on cassette tapes were given by the Tolkien Estate to the participants of the J.R.R. Tolkien Centenary Conference, held in Oxford in August 1992.

90. 'Middle English 'Losenger': Sketch of an etymological and semantic enquiry'. *Essais de philologie moderne (1951): Communications présentées au Congrès International de Philologie Moderne, réuni à Liège du 10 au 13 septembre 1951, à l'occasion du LXe Anniversaire des Sections de Philologie germanique et de Philologie romane de la Faculté de Philosophie et Lettres de l'Université de Liège*. Paris: Les Belles Lettres [before 13 October]. (Bibliothèque de la Faculté de

Philologie et Lettres de l'Université de Liège).
Notes: Tolkien's essay appears on pp. 63-76.

– 1954 –

91. *The Fellowship of the Ring: Being the First Pt. of The Lord of the Rings*. London: George Allen & Unwin [29 July].

92. *The Two Towers: Being the Second Pt. of The Lord of the Rings*. London: George Allen & Unwin [11 November].

– 1955 –

93. *The Return of the King: Being the Third Pt. of The Lord of the Rings*. London: George Allen & Unwin [20 October].

94. 'Imram'. *Time and Tide*. With two illustrations by Robert Gibbings. London, 3 December, p. 1561.
Notes: Poem. Reprinted in *Sauron Defeated*, pp. 296-299 (an earlier version, part of 'The Notion Club Papers' and entitled 'The Death of St Brendan' is printed on pp. 295-296).

95. 'Preface'. *The Ancrene Riwle (The Corpus MS.*: Ancrene Wisse). Translated in Modern English by Mary Salu. With an Introduction by Dom Gerard Sitwell, O.S.B., and a Preface by J.R.R. Tolkien. London: Burns & Oates [November].
Notes: The preface is printed on p. v. The two-paragraph preface discusses the version of the *Ancrene Riwle* chosen for translation by Salu.

– 1958 –

96. 'Prefatory Note'. *The Old English Apollonius of Tyre*. Goolden, Peter (Edited by). Oxford: Oxford University Press.
Notes: Contains a one paragraph prefatory note by Tolkien explaining the delay in publishing Goolden's edition and justifying its publication despite the appearance of Dr Josef Raith's edition in 1956.

– 1960 –

97. 'Letter to the editor'. *Triode*. Manchester, no. 18 (May), p. 27.
Notes: Comments to Arthur R. Weir, *No Monroe in Lothlorien!* (idem, no. 17 (January 1960), p. 31-33). Tolkien is of the opinion that only considerable financial reward could compensate an author for the horrors involved in the adaption of a book.

– 1962 –

98. *The Adventures of Tom Bombadil and Other Verses from the Red Book*. With illustrations by Pauline Baynes. London: George Allen & Unwin [22 November].
Notes: Contains 16 poems. Six of these were read by J.R.R. Tolkien on *Poems and Songs of Middle Earth* (New York: Cædmon Records, © 1967, TC 1231). (*Cfr. The Road Goes Ever On.*)

99. *The English Text of the Ancrene Riwle: Ancrene Wisse*. Edited from MS. Corpus Christi College. Cambridge 402. With an Introduction by N.R. Ker. London: Published for the Early English Text Society by the Oxford University Press [7 December].

– 1963 –

100. 'English and Welsh'. *Angles and Britons: O'Donnell Lectures*. Cardiff: University of Cardiff Press [8 July].

Notes: Essay, printed on pp. [1]-41. The lecture was delivered on 21 October 1955 at the Examination Schools in Oxford.

– 1964 –

101. *Tree and Leaf*. London: Unwin Books [28 May].
Notes: Reprints of 'On Fairy-Stories' (revised version of the text published in *Essays Presented to Charles Williams*) and 'Leaf by Niggle'. The second edition, issued by Unwin Hyman on 25th August 1988 (p. 101; ISBN 0-04-440254-6) also contains the poem 'Mythopoeia'.

– 1965 –

102. 'The Dragon's Visit'. *Winters' Tales for Children*. Willier, Caroline (Edited by). Marshall, Hugh. ill. London: Macmillan [October].
Notes: The poem appears on p. 84. An earlier version appeared in 1937. Reprinted in Anderson, *The Annotated Hobbit*, pp. 262-263.

103. 'Once Upon a Time'. *Winters Tales for Children*. Willier, Caroline (Edited by). Marshall, Hugh. ill. London: Macmillan [October].
Notes: The poem appears on p. 56.

– 1966 –

104. 'Jonah'. *The Jerusalem Bible*. Jones, Alexander (Edited by). London, Darton, Longman & Todd.

– 1967 –

105. 'For W.H.A.' *Shenandoah*. Lexington, Vol. 18, no. 2 (Winter), pp. 96-97.
Notes: Poem dedicated to W.H. Auden. It appears in two versions: In Old English (signed 'Ragnald Hrædmóding') and in English (signed 'JRRT')

106. *The Road Goes Ever On: A Song Cycle*. Poems by J.R.R. Tolkien and Music by Donald Swann with decorations by J.R.R. Tolkien. Boston: Houghton Mifflin Company [31 October].
Notes: Music for six poems from *The Lord of the Rings* ('The Road Goes Ever on', 'Upon the Hearth the Fire is Red', 'In the Willow-meads of Tasarinan', 'In Western Lands', 'Namárië', 'I Sit beside the Fire', 'A Elbereth Gilthoniel') and one from *The Adventures of Tom Bombadil* ('Errantry') together with notes on and translations of 'A Elbereth Gilthoniel' and 'Namárië'. A recording of the music, with William Elvin as vocalist, appeared under the title *Poems and Songs of Middle Earth*. This record also contains readings from *The Adventures of Tom Bombadil* by J.R.R. Tolkien. Second edition: London: George Allen & Unwin, [October] 1978. Pp. ix, 75, [1]. In the revised edition a setting of 'Bilbo's Last Song (at the Grey Havens)' has been added.

107. *Smith of Wootton Major*. Baynes, Pauline. ill. London: George Allen & Unwin [9 November].

– 1972 –

108. 'Beautiful Place because Trees are Loved'. *Daily Telegraph*. London, 4 July, p. 16.
Notes: Letter to the editor in response to an editorial ('Forestry and Us', idem, 29 June 1972, p. 18). Printed in *Letters*, no. 339.

Interviews & Reviews

1. Auden, Wystan Hugh. 'A World Imaginary, but Real'. *Encounter*, 3 November 1954, pp. 59-62. [Review of The Fellowship of the Ring].
   S.s.: Scull-Hammond (2017a), p. 469. Tolkien writes to Katherine Farrer and 'he returns a copy of a work by C.S. Lewis which Farrer had lent him, and a copy of Encounter with W.H. Auden's review of *The Fellowship of the Ring*.'

2. _____. 'At the End of the Quest, Victory'. *The New York Times*, 22 January 1955 [Review of *The Return of the King*].
   P.s. 1: *Letters* 163 (1955) To W. H. Auden.
   P.s. 2: *Letters* 183 (1956) Notes on W. H. Auden's review of *The Return of the King*.
   S.s.: Scull-Hammond (2017a), p. 511.

3. Brace, Keith. 'In the Footsteps of the Hobbits'. Birmingham Post, 25 May 1968 [Interview].
   S.s.: Scull-Hammond (2017a), p. 758.

4. Breit, Harvey. 'Oxford Calling'. *New York Times Book Review*. 5 June 1955, p. 8 [Interview].
   S.s.: Scull-Hammond (2017a), p. 478.

5. Brober, Jan. '*Sagan om ringen* ingen allegori: ff-författaren vill ge avkoppling'. *Kvällsposten*, 27 July 1961 [Interview].

6. Cater, Bill (William). 'The Lord of the Legends: A Birthday Tribute to the Creator of *The Hobbit*'. *The Sunday Times Magazine*, 2 January 1972 [Interview].

7. _____. 'Lord of the Hobbits'. *Daily Express*, 22 November 1966 [Interview].
   S.s.: Scull-Hammond (2017a), p. 699.

8. _____. 'More and More People are Getting the J.R.R. Tolkien Habit'. *Los Angeles Times*, 9 April 1972, pp. 14, 18 [Interview].
   P.s.: *Letters* 330 (1971) From a letter to William Cater.
   S.s.: Scull-Hammond (2017a), p. 705.

9. Castell, Daphne. 'The Realm of Tolkien' *New Worlds*, Vol. 50, November 1966, p. 144 [Interview].

10. Chambers, Raymond Wilson. Review of 'Beowulf: The Monsters and the Critics' by J.R.R. Tolkien. MLR (*The Modern Language Review*), Vol. 33, 1938, pp. 272-3.
    S.s.: Scull-Hammond (2017a), p. 221.

11. Chaudry, Athar. 'Tolkien Seeks the Quiet Life in Oxford'. *Oxford Mail*, 22 March 1972 [Interview].

12. Cherryman, A. E. (pseudonym by Bernard Levin) 'Myth-Maker'. *Truth*, 6 August 1954. [Review of *The Fellowship of the Rings*].

P.s. *Letters* 149 (1954) From a letter to Rayner Unwin. Tolkien writes: 'Cherryman in Truth and Howard Spring in C. Life were pleasing to one's vanity, and also Cherryman's ending: that he would turn eagerly to the second and third volumes!'

13. Curtis, Anthony. 'Hobbits and Heroes'. *The Sunday Telegraph*, 10 November 1963. [Interview extract].
    S.s.: Scull-Hammond (2017a), pp. 643, 644.

14. Dempsey, David. 'The Candy Covered Copyright'. *Saturday Review*, 2 October 1965 [Ace Books affair].
    S.s.: Scull-Hammond (2017a), p. 678.

15. Don Chapman (pseudonym by Anthony Wood). 'Fireworks for the Author'. *Oxford Mail*, 9 February 1968 [Interview].
    S.s.: Scull-Hammond (2017a), p. 752.

16. Duggan, Alfred. 'Middle Earth Verse'. *Time Literary Supplement*, 23 November 1962, p. 892 [Review of Adventures of Tom Bombadil].
    P.s.: *Letters* 242 (1962) From a letter to Sir Stanley. Tolkien writes: 'I have so far seen two reviews of Tom Bombadil: T. Litt. Suppl. and Listener: 1 I was agreeably surprised: I expected remarks far more snooty and patronizing. Also I was rather pleased, since it seemed that the reviewers had both started out not wanting to be amused, but had failed to maintain their Victorian dignity intact'.
    S.s.: Scull-Hammond (2017a), p. 633.

17. Ezard, John. 'Successor to the Hobbits at Last'. *Oxford Mail*, 11 February 1966 [Interview].
    S.s.: Scull-Hammond (2017a), pp. 704, 705.

18. _____. 'Writers Talking-1: The Hobbit Man'. *The Oxford Times*, 3 August 1966 [Interview].
    S.s.: Scull-Hammond (2017a), p. 687.

19. Fawcett, H. l'A. 'Review of *The Fellowship of the Rings*'. *Manchester Guardian*, 20 August 1954.
    P.s. *Letters* 149 (1954) From a letter to Rayner Unwin. Tolkien writes: 'Fawcett was complimentary in brief'.

20. Foster, William. 'A Benevolent and Furry-footed People'. *The Scotsman*, 25 March 1967 [Interview].
    P.s.: *Letters* 293 (1966) From a letter to William Foster.
    S.s.: Scull-Hammond (2017a), pp. 718, 719.

21. _____. 'An Early History of the Hobbits'. *Edinburgh Scotsman*, 5 February 1972 [Interview].
    S.s.: Scull-Hammond (2017a), pp. 718, 719.

22. Fuller, Edmund. 'Of Frodo and Fantasy'. *Wall Street Journal*, 4 January 1966, p. 14 [Review of *The Lord of the Rings*].
    S.s.: Scull-Hammond (2017a), p. 686.

23. Green, Peter. 'Outward Bound by Air to an Inappropriate Ending'. *Daily Telegraph*, 27 August 1954, p. 8 [Review of *The Fellowship of the Rings*].
    P.s. *Letters* 149 (1954) From a letter to Rayner Unwin. Tolkien writes: 'I must say that I was unfortunate in coming into the hands of the D. Telegraph, during the absence of Betjeman. My

work is not in his line, but he at any rate is neither ignorant nor a gutterboy. Peter Green seems to be both. I do not know him or of him, but he is so rude as to make one suspect malice'.

24. Green, Roger Lancelyn. 'Slicing a Magical Cake'. *Sunday Telegraph*, 3 December 1967 [Review of *Smith of Wootton Major*].
    P.s.: *Letters* 299 (1967) To Roger Lancelyn Green. Tolkien writes: 'Thank you for your most gracious review (esp. for comment on the search for source of bounce!). Though I have been much better treated than I expected'.
    S.s.: Scull-Hammond (2017a), p. 748.

25. Gustafsson, Lars. 'Den besynnerlige professor Tolkien'. *Dagens Nyheter*, 21 August 1961 [Interview].

26. Hudson, C. H. Review of *The Fellowship of the Ring*. *The Oxford Times*, 13 August 1954.
    P.s. *Letters* 149 (1954) From a letter to Rayner Unwin. Tolkien writes: 'was especially interested by a long notice in the *The Oxford Times* (by the editor himself) in being by one quite outside the ring, and he seemed to have enjoyed himself'.

27. Hughes, Richard. 'Books for Pre-Adults'. *New Statesman and Nation*, 14, 4 December 1937, pp. 944, 946 [Review of The Hobbit].
    P.s.: *Letters* 17 (1937) To Stanley Unwin, Chairman of Allen & Unwin.
    S.s.: Scull-Hammond (2017a), p. 217.

28. Lambert, Jack Walter. 'New Fiction'. *The Sunday Times*, 8 August 1954, p. 3 [Review of *The Fellowship of the Ring*].
    P.s. *Letters* 149 (1954) From a letter to Rayner Unwin.
    S.s.: Scull-Hammond (2017a), p. 460.

29. Lewis, Clive Staples. (unsigned). 'A world for children: J. R. R. Tolkien'. *Times Literary Supplement*, 2 October 1937, p. 714 [Review of *The Hobbit*].
    P.s. 1: *Letters* 14 (1937) To Allen & Unwin.
    P.s. 2: *Letters* 26 (1938) To Allen & Unwin.
    S.s.: Scull-Hammond (2017a), p. 216.

30. _____. (unsigned). 'Professor Tolkien's "Hobbit"'. *Times*, 8 October 1937, p. 20 [Review of *The Hobbit*].
    P.s.: *Letters* 26 (1938) To Allen & Unwin.
    S.s.: Scull-Hammond (2017a), p. 216.

31. _____. 'The Dethronement of Power'. *Time and Tide*, 22 October 1955, p. 1373 [Review of *The Fellowship of the Ring*].
    S.s.: Scull-Hammond (2017a), p. 506.

32. _____. 'The Gods Return to Earth'. *Time and Tide*, 14 August 1954, p. 1082 [Review of *The Fellowship of the Ring*].
    S.s.: Scull-Hammond (2017a), p. 461.

33. Manzalaoui, Mahmoud. 'A Fantasy based on Ancient Myths'. *Egyptian Gazette*, 20 April 1961, p. 2. [Review of *The Lord of the Rings*].
    S.s.: Scull-Hammond (2017a), p. 610.

34. Mitchison, Naomi. 'One Ring to Bind Them'. *New Statesman and Nation*, 48, 18 September 1954, p. 33 [Review of *The Fellowship of the Ring*].
    P.s. *Letters* 154 (1954) To Naomi Mitchison. Tolkien writes: 'You have been most kind and

encouraging to me, and your generous and perceptive review puts me in your debt.'

35. Muir, Edwin. 'A Boy's World'. *Sunday Observer*, 27 November 1955, p. 11 [Review of *The Return of the King*].
    P.s. *Letters* 177 (1955) From a letter to Rayner Unwin. Tolkien writes: 'Blast Edwin Muir and his delayed adolescence. He is old enough to know better. It might do him good to hear what women think of his knowing about women, especially as a test of being mentally adult. If he had an M.A. I should nominate him for the professorship of poetry – a sweet revenge.'

36. _____. 'Strange Epic'. *The Observer*, 22 August 1954, p. 7 [Review of *The Fellowship of the Rings*].
    P.s. *Letters* 149 (1954) From a letter to Rayner Unwin.

37. _____. 'The Ring'. *The Observer*, 11 November 1954, p. 9 [Review of *The Two Towers*].
    P.s. *Letters* 157 (1954) From a letter to Katherine Farrer.

38. Norman, Philip. 'The Hobbit Man'. *Sunday Times Magazine*, 15 January 1967 [Interview].
    S.s.: Scull-Hammond (2017a), pp. 706, 709.

39. _____. 'The Prevalence of Hobbits'. *The New York Times Magazine*, 15 January 1967 [Interview].
    S.s.: Scull-Hammond (2017a), p. 720.

40. Plimmer, Charlotte & Denis. 'The Man Who Understands Hobbits'. *The Daily Telegraph Magazine*, 22 March 1968 [Interview].
    P.s.: *Letters* 294 (1967) To Charlotte and Denis Plimmer
    S.s.: Scull-Hammond (2017a), pp. 715, 716, 721-724, 756.

41. Plotz, Richard. 'J.R.R. Tolkien Talks about the Discovery of Middle-earth, the Origins of Elvish'. *Seventeen*, 17 January 1967 [Interview].
    S.s.: Scull-Hammond (2017a), pp. 710, 712, 713.

42. Price, Anthony. 'Fairy Story for Grown Ups Too'. *Oxford Mail*, 16 September 1954 [Review of *The Fellowship of the Ring*].
    S.s.: Scull-Hammond (2017a), p. 462.

43. _____. 'With Camera and Pen'. *The Oxford Times*, 27 January 1956, p. 8. [Interview].
    S.s.: Scull-Hammond (2017a), p. 508.

44. Resnik, Henry. 'An Interview with Tolkien'. *Niekas*, Vol. 18, Late Spring 1967 [Interview].
    S.s.: Scull-Hammond (2017a), p. 691.

45. _____. 'The Hobbit-forming World of J.R.R. Tolkien'. *Saturday Evening Post*, 2 July 1967 [Interview].
    S.s.: Scull-Hammond (2017a), p. 691.

46. Richardson, Maurice. 'New Novels'. *New Statesman and Nation*, 18 December 1954, pp. 835-6. [Review of *The Two Towers*].
    P.s. *Letters* 163 (1955) To W. H. Auden. Tolkien writes: 'Except for a few deliberately disparaging reviews – such as that of Vol. II in the *New Statesman*, in which you and I were both scourged with

such terms as 'pubescent' and 'infantilism'.'

47. Spring, Howard. Review of 'The Fellowship of the Rings'. *Country Life*, 26 August 1954.
   > P.s. *Letters* 149 (1954) From a letter to Rayner Unwin. Tolkien writes: 'Cherryman in Truth and Howard Spring in C. Life were pleasing to one's vanity'.

48. Straight, Michael. 'Fantastic World of Professor Tolkien'. *New Republic*, 134. 16 January 1956, p. 26-26 [Review of *The Lord of the Rings*].
   > P.s.: *Letters* 181 (1956) To Michael Straight.
   > S.s.: Scull-Hammond (2017a), p. 505.

49. Thwaite, Anthony. 'Hobbitry'. *The Listener*, 22 November 1962, p. 831 [Review of *The Adventures of Tom Bombadil*].
   > P.s.: *Letters* 242 (1962) From a letter to Sir Stanley. Tolkien writes: 'I have so far seen two reviews of *Tom Bombadil*: *T. Litt. Suppl.* and *Listener*: 1 I was agreeably surprised: I expected remarks far more snooty and patronizing. Also I was rather pleased, since it seemed that the reviewers had both started out not wanting to be amused, but had failed to maintain their Victorian dignity intact'.
   > S.s.: Scull-Hammond (2017a), p. 633.

50. [Tolkien, J.R.R.]. 'Tolkien on Tolkien'. *Diplomat*, Vol. 18, no. 197, October 1966, p. 39.
   > Notes: Article with autobiographical elements.

J. R. R. Tolkien: Supervisor and Examiner
1929-1960

Listed below are J.R.R. Tolkien's research students, the Colleges, Oxford theses examined by him, with the dates of commencement enclosed in parentheses.

1. Aitken, Daniel Ferguson (Balliol College). *A Study of the English Romance of Sir Tristrem in Relation to Its Sources*. University of Oxford, Thesis (B.Litt.), (?)-1927.
    Examiners: J.R.R. Tolkien and Eugene Vinaver.
    S.s.: Scull-Hammond (2017a), pp. 150, 152.

2. Bennett, Jack Arthur Walter. (Merton College). *The History of Old English and Old Norse Studies in England from the Time of Junius till the End of the Eighteenth Century*. University of Oxford, Thesis (D.Phil.), (1936)-1938.
    Examiners: J.R.R. Tolkien and David Nicol Smith.
    S.s.: Scull-Hammond (2017a), pp. 200, 229, 231.
    Location: Bodleian Library, MS. D.Phil. d.287.

3. Bishop, Ian B. (Queen College). *The structure of 'Pearl': The Interrelations between 'Liturgical' and 'Poetic' Elements*. [Originally *The 'Pearl' poem considered in relation to thirteenth—-and fourteenth—century ideals of poetry*]. University of Oxford, Thesis (M.Litt.), (1949)-1952.
    Supervisor: J.R.R. Tolkien replace Gervase Mathew.
    S.s. 1: Scull-Hammond (2017a), pp. 392, 395, 400, 404, 406.
    S.s. 2: Ryan (2002), p. 57.
    Location: Bodleian Library, MS. M.Litt. c.108.

4. Bliss, Alan Joseph. *Sir Orfeo: edited, with introduction, parallel texts, commentary and glossary*. University of Oxford, Thesis (M.Litt.), (1946)-1948 [A. 162].
    Supervisor: J.R.R. Tolkien.
    S.s. 1: Scull-Hammond (2017a), pp. 329, 332, 334, 343, 346, 348, 349.
    S.s. 2: Ryan (2002), p. 57.
    Location: Bodleian Library, MS. M.Litt. d.343.

5. Blomfield, Joan E. (Somerville College). *The Origins of Old English Orthography, with Special Reference to the Representation of the Spirants and W*. University of Oxford, Thesis (M.Litt.), (1933)-1935.
    Supervisor: J.R.R. Tolkien.
    S.s. 1: Scull-Hammond (2017a), pp. 182, 183, 184, 186, 187, 188.
    S.s. 2: Ryan (2002), p. 56.
    Location: Bodleian Library, MS. M.Litt. d.263.

6. Briggs, K.M. (Lady Margaret Hall). *Folk Lore in Jacobean Literature*. University of Oxford, Thesis (M.Litt.), (1946)-?
    S.s. Ryan (2002), p. 57. 'Supervised by Miss Seaton but encouraged by Tolkien'.

7. Brooks, Kenneth Robert. (Merton College). *An edition of the Anglo-Saxon poem 'Andreas': with introduction, notes, glossary, and appendices [etymological,*

grammatical, metrical, and related texts]. University of Oxford, Thesis (D.Phil.), (1937)-1941 [A. 224].
>Supervisor: J.R.R. Tolkien. Examiners: J.R.R. Tolkien and C.T. Onions.
>S.s. 1: Ryan (2002), p. 56.
>S.s. 2: Scull-Hammond (2017a), pp. 218, 226, 229, 237, 240, 242, 248, 252, 255, 260, 262, 263, 268.
>Location: Bodleian Library, MS. D.Phil. d.400-2.

8. Brown (later Dronke), Ursula Mary (Somerville College). *An edition of the Saga of Þorgils and Hafliði (from Sturlungasaga)*. University of Oxford, Thesis (M.Litt.), (?)-1949.
>Supervisor: J.R.R. Tolkien.
>Examiners: J.R.R. Tolkien and Alistair Campbell.
>S.s.: Scull-Hammond (2017a), pp. 367, 372, 373.
>Location: Bodleian Library, MS. M.Litt. d.352.

9. Buckhurst, H. M. (St Hugh College). *The Historical Grammar of Old Icelandic*. University of Oxford, (1927)-?.
>Supervisor: J.R.R. Tolkien.
>S.s.: Scull-Hammond (2017a), p. 152.

10. Burchfield, R. W. (Magdalen College). *The Vocabulary and Phonology of the Ormulum*. University of Oxford, Thesis (D.Phil.), (1951)-?1957.
>Supervisor: J.R.R. Tolkien.
>S.s. 1: Ryan (2002), p. 57.
>S.s. 2: Scull-Hammond (2017a), pp. 400, 403 'Burchfield will later recall that during his postgraduate work he saw Tolkien: 'at weekly intervals in the academic years 1951-2 and 1952-3, sometimes in Merton College, sometimes at his home in Holywell. He puffed at his pipe while I told him of my work. He made many acute observations. I followed them all up. He beamed when I made some discoveries. Now and then he mentioned the hobbits, but he didn't press them on me, spotting that my interest lay in the scraped out o's and doubled consonants of the Ormulum rather than in the dwarves ... Orcs, and Mr Bilbo Baggins. The two years passed all too quickly and then I was swept into fulltime teaching at Christ Church and afterwards into lexicography. My work on the Ormulum had to be put aside.' [*The Independent Magazine*, 4 March 1989, p. 50]', 404, 406, 412, 416, 421, 435-6, 444, 450.

11. Campbell, Alistair (Balliol College). *The Production of Dipthongs by Breaking in Old English from c. 700-900*. University of Oxford, Thesis (M.Litt.), (?)-1931.
>Examiners: J.R.R. Tolkien and C.T. Onions.
>S.s.: Scull-Hammond (2017a), pp. 168, 169.
>Location: Bodleian Library, MS. M.Litt. d.226-7.

12. Carroll, Mary Elizabeth (St Hilda College). *The Phonology of Hampshire Place-Name Forms, Particularly as Found in Documents of the Thirteenth and Fourteenth Centuries, Compared with That of the Usages of Winchester, and of Other Texts for Which a Hampshire Origin Has Been Suggested*. University of Oxford, Thesis (B.Litt.), (?)-1933.
>Examiners: J.R.R. Tolkien and Dorothy Everett.
>S.s.: Scull-Hammond (2017a), pp. 177, 179.

13. Colborn, A. F. (St Edmund Hall). *A Critical Text of Hali Meidhad Together with a Grammar and Glossarial Note*. University of Oxford, Thesis (B.Litt.), (1931)-1934 [A. 463].
>Supervisor: J.R.R. Tolkien.
>S.s. 1: Ryan (2002), p. 56.
>S.s. 2: Scull-Hammond (2017a), pp. 171, 172, 182, 184.

SECTION D

14. Corlett, A. C. (St Edmund Hall). *The Phonology of the Vowels in the Poems of B. Mus. MS Nero Ax (Sir Gawain, Pearl, Patience, Purity) with Special Reference to the Treatment of Middle English*. University of Oxford, Thesis (B.Litt.), (1927)-1929.
    Supervisor: J.R.R. Tolkien.
    S.s.: Scull-Hammond (2017a), pp. 149, 152, 159.

15. Crook, Ruth A. (Somerville College). *An Edition of the Prose Life of St Margaret (Seinte Marherete), based on MS. Bodley 34 and MS. Reg. 17. A. XXVII, with a Grammar and a Glossary which will consider Parallels in other Texts of the Same Group*. University of Oxford, Thesis (M.Litt.), (1926)-1929.
    Supervisor: J.R.R. Tolkien.
    S.s.: Scull-Hammond (2017a), pp. 147, 149, 159.

16. Dobson, E. J. (Merton College). *English Pronunciation 1500-1700. According to the Evidence of the English Orthoepists*. University of Oxford, Thesis (D.Phil.), (1949)-1951.
    Examiners: J.R.R. Tolkien and C.L. Wrenn.
    S.s.: Scull-Hammond (2017a), pp. 372, 384, 392.
    Location: Bodleian Library, MS. D.Phil. c.245-8.

17. Evans, G. M. G. (St Hugh College). *An edition of the fable of 'The Fox and the Wolf' from MS Digby 86*. University of Oxford, Thesis (B.Litt.), (1950)-?1956.
    Supervisor: J.R.R. Tolkien.
    S.s. 1: Ryan (2002), p. 57.
    S.s. 2: Scull-Hammond (2017a), pp. 390, 393, 394, 400, 400, 404, 406, 412, 416, 421, 435, 444, 450, 464, 502, 510, 517, 523.

18. Evans, W. O. (Merton College). *The Five Virtues of Gawain's shield and their contemporary equivalents*. Oxford of University, Thesis (M.Litt.), (1955)-1959.
    Supervisor: J.R.R. Tolkien.
    S.s. 1: Ryan (2002), p. 58.
    S.s. 2: Scull-Hammond (2017a), pp. 503, 510, 517, 519, 523, 528, 532, 540, 547, 562, 567, 573.
    Location: Bodleian Library, MS. M.Litt. d.728.

19. Glanville, Lucia. (Somerville College). *A new edition of the Middle English romance 'The weddyng of Syr Gawen and Dame Ragnell'*. Oxford of University, Thesis (M.Litt.), (1954)-1958.
    Supervisor: J.R.R. Tolkien.
    S.s. 1: Ryan (2002), p. 58.
    S.s. 2: Scull-Hammond (2017a), pp. 465, 471, 475, 478, 502, 510, 517, 523, 528, 532, 540, 547, 562.
    Location: Bodleian Library, MS. MS. M.Litt. d.728.

20. Goolden, Peter (Trinity College). *Apollonius of Tyre: a parallel edition of the Old English translation and the underlying Latin version of the story of Apollonius of Tyre, together with an introduction, commentary and glossary*. University of Oxford, Thesis (M.Litt.), (1950)-1953 [A. 811].
    Supervisor: J.R.R. Tolkien, after C.L. Wrenn.
    S.s.: Scull-Hammond (2017a), pp. 383, 384, 385.
    Location: Bodleian Library, MS. M.Litt. d.167-8.

21. Grace, Thomas J. (Campion Hall). *A study of the ascetical elements in Piers Plowman and their bearing on the structure and meaning of the poem: with special*

reference to the B-text. University of Oxford, Thesis (D.Phil.) (?)-1951.
   Examiners: J.R.R. Tolkien and Nevill Coghill.
   S.s.: Scull-Hammond (2017a), p. 400.
   Location: Bodleian Library, MS. D.Phil. d.1059.

22. Green, Roger Lancelyn (Merton College). *Andrew Lang as a writer of fairy stories and romances*. University of Oxford, Thesis (M.Litt.), (1941)-1944.
    Supervisor: J.R.R. Tolkien replacing David Nichol Smith.
    Examiners: J.R.R. Tolkien and David Nichol Smith.
    S.s. 1: Lewis (2009a), p. 1039. '*Andrew Lang as a Writer of Fairy Stories and Romances* (1944), was supervised by Professor J. R. R. Tolkien, who became another lifelong friend.'
    S.s. 2: Ryan (2002), p. 56.
    S.s. 3: Scull-Hammond (2017a), pp. 274, 276, 277, 278, 280, 282, 283.
    Location: Bodleian Library, MS. M.Litt. d.336.

23. Griffiths, M. Elaine. (Society of Oxford Home-Students). *Notes and Observations on the Vocabulary of Ancrene Wisse MS CCCC. 402*. University of Oxford, Thesis (B.Litt.), (1933)-1936.
    Supervisor: J.R.R. Tolkien.
    S.s. 1: Ryan (2002), p. 56.
    S.s. 2: Scull-Hammond (2017a), pp. 178, 182, 183, 184, 185, 186, 187, 189, 191, 195, 196.

24. Haworth, J. C. (St Hilda College). *The Icelandic Episode in the Life and Work of William Morris*. University of Oxford, Thesis (M.Litt.), (1952)-1953.
    Supervisor: J.R.R. Tolkien.
    S.s.: Scull-Hammond (2017a), pp. 407, 412, 416, 421, 435, 444, 450, 464, 471.

25. Haworth, Peter (University College). *An Edition of British Museum MS Harley 2257*. University of Oxford, Thesis (D.Phil.), (?)-1928.
    Examiners: J.R.R. Tolkien and Kenneth Sisam.
    S.s. 1: Ryan (2002), p. 58.
    S.s. 2: Scull-Hammond (2017a), p. 157.

26. Heywood, John. *A dialogue of proverbs*. University of Oxford, Thesis (D.Phil.), (?)-1959.
    S.s.: Scull-Hammond (2017a), p. 587. 1 May 1960 Robert Burchfield, Early English Text Society, writes to Tolkien. He encloses a memo about Heywood's *Dialogue of Proverbs* (possibly being considered as a future Society publication).
    Location: Bodleian Library, MS. D.Phil. d.2195.

27. Horgan, A. D. (New College). *The vocabulary of the Cursor mundi, with principal reference to MS. Cotton Vesp. A3*. University of Oxford, Thesis (D.Phil.), (1953)-1957.
    Supervisor: J.R.R. Tolkien.
    S.s. 1: Ryan (2002), p. 58.
    S.s. 2: Scull-Hammond (2017a), pp. 416, 421, 435, 444, 447, 450, 451, 471, 478, 502, 510, 517, 523, 527, 532, 540.

28. Inokuma, Y. (University of the Sacred Heart). *The Characteristics of English Children's Literature*. University of Oxford, (1957)-1958.
    Supervisor: J.R.R. Tolkien, later C.L. Morrison.
    S.s.: Scull-Hammond (2017a), pp. 536, 543.

29. Jones, L. E. (Lady Margaret Hall). *An Edition of British Museum MS Harley 2372*. University of Oxford, Thesis (B.Litt.), (?)-?1933.
    Examiners: J.R.R. Tolkien and C.T. Onions.

S.s.: Scull-Hammond (2017a), pp. 165, 167, 182.

30. Jones, R. J. (St Hugh College). *Sir Kaye in Medieval Arthurian Literature*. University of Oxford, Thesis (B.Litt.), (1958)-?.
    Supervisor: J.R.R. Tolkien.
    S.s.: Scull-Hammond (2017a), pp. 562, 567.

31. Keays-Young, Julia Maud (Society of Oxford Home-Students). *England and the English in the Icelandic Sagas*. University of Oxford, Thesis (B.Litt.), (1925)-1928.
    Supervisor: J.R.R. Tolkien.
    Examiners: J.R.R. Tolkien and E.V. Gordon.
    S.s.: Scull-Hammond (2017a), pp. 142, 147, 152, 154.
    Location: Bodleian Library, MS. M.Litt. c.148.

32. Ker, N. R. (Magdalen College). *A Study of the Additions and Alterations in MSS Bodley 340 and 342*. University of Oxford, Thesis (M.Litt.), (?)-1933.
    Examiners: J.R.R. Tolkien and Kenneth Sisam.
    S.s.: Scull-Hammond (2017a), p. 179.
    Location: Bodleian Library, MS. M.Litt. d.243.

33. Kiteley, J. F. (Wadham College). *Characterisation in Sir Gawain and the Green Knight*. University of Oxford, Thesis (M.Litt.), (1957)-1958.
    Examiners: J.R.R. Tolkiena and U.M. Brown.
    S.s.: Scull-Hammond (2017a), p. 531, 547.
    Location: Bodleian Library, MS. M.Litt. d.715.

34. Kolve, V. A. (Jesus College). *Religious grotesque in the Middle English drama cycles*. University of Oxford, Thesis (M.Litt.), (1957)-?.
    Supervisor: J.R.R. Tolkien, later K.M. Lea.
    S.s. 1: Ryan (2002), p. 58.
    S.s. 2: Scull-Hammond (2017a), pp. 540, 543, 562, 567.

35. Kurvinen, Auvo (St Anne). *Syre Gawene and the Carle of Carelyle*. University of Oxford, Thesis (B.Litt.), (1947)-1949 [A. 1244].
    Supervisor: J.R.R. Tolkien.
    S.s. 1: Ryan (2002), p. 57.
    S.s. 2: Scull-Hammond (2017a), pp. 344, 348, 352, 361, 365, 369.
    Location: Bodleian Library, MS. M.Litt. c.104.

36. _____. *The Life of St Catharine of Alexandria in Middle English prose*. University of Oxford, Thesis (D.Phil.), (1955)-?1960.
    Supervisor: J.R.R. Tolkien.
    S.s. 1: Ryan (2002), p. 57.
    S.s. 2: Scull-Hammond (2017a), pp. 465, 471, 478, 502, 510, 517, 523, 527, 532, 540, 547, 562, 567, 571.
    Location: Bodleian Library, MS. D.Phil. d.2381.

37. Lascelles, Mary M. (Lady Margaret Hall). *Alexander and the Earthly Paradise in Medieval English Literature Writings*. University of Oxford, Thesis (B.Litt.), (?)-1927.
    Examiners: Tolkien and George S. Gordon.
    S.s.: Scull-Hammond (2017a), pp. 148, 149.

38. Lawlor, John J. (Magdalen College). *The Revelations of Dame Juliana of Norwich edited from the Manuscripts with Introduction, Notes, and Glossary*. University of

Oxford, Thesis (B.Litt.), (1946)-?.
: Supervisor: J.R.R. Tolkien.
S.s. 1: Ryan (2002), p. 57.
S.s. 2: Scull-Hammond (2017a), p. 317 'Lawlor will later comment about Tolkien as his supervisor: 'My first and abiding impression was one of immediate kindness. Tutored [as an undergraduate] by [C.S.] Lewis I had expected to be tested with a few falls, so to speak. But the gentle creature who sucked his pipe and gazed meditatively along its stem seemed interested only in what he could do to help' (Lawlor, *C.S. Lewis: Memories and Reflections* (1998), pp. 30-1)', 319, 329, 332.

39. Levinson, D. C. (St Anne College). *Studies in the treatment of Old Testament themes in the poems of MS. Junius 11, Pt. 1*. University of Oxford, Thesis (M.Litt.), (1954)-1957.
: Supervisor: J.R.R. Tolkien in place of C.L. Wrenn.
S.s. 1: Ryan (2002), p. 58.
S.s. 2: Scull-Hammond (2017a), pp. 475, 478, 482, 502, 510, 523, 528.
Location: Bodleian Library, MS. M.Litt. d.593.

40. Llewellyn, Evan Clifford (Jesus College). *The Influence of Middle Dutch and Middle Low German on English Speech*. University of Oxford, Thesis (B.Litt.), (?)-1930.
: Examiners: J.R.R. Tolkien and C.L. Wrenn.
S.s.: Scull-Hammond (2017a), pp. 163, 164.

41. Martin, V. M. (St Hilda College). *An Edition of the Minor Pieces of MS Nero A14*. University of Oxford, Thesis (B.Litt.), (1951)-1956.
: Supervisor: J.R.R. Tolkien.
S.s. 1: Ryan (2002), p. 57.
S.s. 2: Scull-Hammond (2017a), pp. 394, 395, 400, 403, 404, 406, 412, 421, 436, 444, 464, 471, 478, 502, 210, 517.

42. McEldowney, Mary M. (Society of Oxford Home-Students). *The Fairy Tales and Fantasies of George MacDonald*. University of Oxford, Thesis (B.Litt. thesis, supervised by C.S. Lewis, and examined by Tolkien), (1933)-1934.
: Examiners: J.R.R. Tolkien and M.R. Ridley.
P.s.: #1 a. | *Tolkien On Fairy-stories* (2008), p. 309.
S.s. 1: Ryan (2002), p. 56.
S.s. 2: Scull-Hammond (2017a), p. 186.
Location: Bodleian Library, Mss B.Litt. d.257.

43. Miller, B. D. H. (New College). *Dame Sirith*. University of Oxford, Thesis (D.Phil.), (1952)-1956.
: Supervisor: J.R.R. Tolkien.
Examiners: J.R.R. Tolkien and G.V. Smithers.
S.s. 1: Ryan (2002), p. 57.
S.s. 2: Scull-Hammond (2017a), pp. 404, 406, 412, 416, 421, 435, 444, 450, 464, 471, 477, 502, 503, 505, 512.
Location: Bodleian Library, MS. M.Litt. c.121.

44. Monaghan, Thomas J. A. (Exeter College). *Thomas Tyrwhitt (1730-1786) and his contribution to English Scholarship*. University of Oxford, Thesis (D.Phil.), (1943)-1947.
: Supervisor: J.R.R. Tolkien, in place of David Nichol Smith.
S.s. 1: Ryan (2002), p. 57.
S.s. 2: Scull-Hammond (2017a), pp. 314, 316, 319, 329, 332, 334, 336.
Location: Bodleian Library, MS. D.Phil. c.190.

45. Morton, A. M. (St Hugh College). *William Morris's Treatment of His Icelandic Sources. [researching under C. S. Lewis]*. University of Oxford, Thesis (M.Litt.), (1932)-1935.
    Examiners: J.R.R. Tolkien and C.L. Wrenn.
    S.s. 1: Ryan (2002), p. 56.
    S.s. 2: Scull-Hammond (2017a), pp. 190, 191.
    Location: Bodleian Library, MS. M.Litt. d.274.

46. Olszewska, E. (Lady Margaret Hall). *A History of the Scandinavian Influence on the English Language*. University of Oxford, Thesis (D.Phil.), (?)-1934.
    Supervisor: J.R.R. Tolkien.
    S.s.: Scull-Hammond (2017a), p. 151.
    Location: Bodleian Library, MS. MS. M.Litt. d.261.

47. O'Neill, Michael J. *Lennox Robinson : playwright of a changing Ireland*. University College Dublin, Thesis (M.A.), (?)-1950.
    P.s.: Tolkien's unpublished letter to O'Neill, 20 September 1950. [Special Collections Research Center Morris Library Southern Illinois University, 1/4/MSS 082].

48. Pickard, M. Y. (Lady Margaret Hall). *An Edition of the Parlement of the Three Ages*. Oxford, Thesis (M.Litt.), (1941)-1946.
    Supervisor: J.R.R. Tolkien.
    S.s. 1: Ryan (2002), p. 56.
    S.s. 2: Scull-Hammond (2017a), pp. 260, 261, 262, 264, 266, 269, 270, 273, 275, 277, 279, 282, 287, 299, 304, 309, 312.

49. Reeves, Joseph (non-collegiate student). *An Edition of the Vernon Text of the Ancrene Riwle and a Study of Its Relation to the Other MSS*. Oxford, Thesis (M.Litt.), (?)-1926.
    Examiners: J.R.R. Tolkien and C.T. Onions.
    S.s.: Scull-Hammond (2017a), p. 144, 146.

50. Richardson, R. E. (St Hugh College). *An edition of 'sir Eglamour of Artois'*. University of Oxford, Thesis (M.Litt.), (1955)-1957.
    Supervisor: J.R.R. Tolkien.
    S.s. 1: Ryan (2002), p. 58.
    S.s. 2: Scull-Hammond (2017a), pp. 505, 510, 517, 523, 527, 532, 534.
    Location: Bodleian Library, MS. M.Litt. d.634.

51. Rogers, D. J. (Jesus College). *The Syntax of 'Cursor Mundi'*. University of Oxford, Thesis (D.Phil.), (?)-1932.
    Examiners: J.R.R. Tolkien and C.L. Wrenn.
    S.s.: Scull-Hammond (2017a), pp. 175, 176.

52. Ross, J. (St Anne College). *A critical edition of the Middle English poem 'On God Ureisun of Ure Lefdi' from MS Cotton Nero A. XIV, with a study of the earliest English Marian poetry*. University of Oxford, Thesis (B.Litt.), (1955)-1959.
    Supervisor: J.R.R. Tolkien, in C.L. Wrenn's absence.
    S.s. 1: Ryan (2002), p. 58.
    S.s. 2: Scull-Hammond (2017a), pp. 527, 532, 540, 547, 562, 567, 571.

53. Salu, Mary B. (Lady Margaret Hall). *Grammar of Ancrene Wisse (Phonology and Accidence)*. University of Oxford, Thesis (M.Litt.), (1941)-1949.
    Supervisor: J.R.R. Tolkien.
    S.s. 1: Ryan (2002), p. 56.

S.s. 2: Scull-Hammond (2017a), pp. 266, 269, 270, 273, 275, 277, 279, 282, 286, 287, 299, 301, 304, 309, 312, 316, 319, 320, 329, 332, 334, 343, 348, 352, 361, 365.
Location: Bodleian Library, MS. M.Litt. d.550.

54. Seymour, M. C. (St Edmund Hall). *A Study of the Interrelationship of the English Versions of Mandeville's Travels.* University of Oxford, Thesis (D.Phil.), (1957)-1960.
    Supervisor: J.R.R. Tolkien.
    S.s. 1: Ryan (2002), p. 58.
    S.s. 2: Scull-Hammond (2017a), pp. 541, 543, 562, 567, 571.
    Location: Bodleian Library, MS. D.Phil. d.2276-9.

55. Sisam, Celia (Lady Margaret Hall). *A Text of the 'Lambeth Homilies' with a select glossary, critical notes and a linguistic introduction.* University of Oxford, Thesis (B.Litt.), (1947)-1951 [A. 2102].
    Supervisor: J.R.R. Tolkien.
    S.s. 1: Ryan (2002), p. 57.
    S.s. 2: Scull-Hammond (2017a), pp. 344, 348, 352, 361, 365, 369, 371, 382, 390, 393.

56. Stormon, E. J. (Campion Hall). *A Study of the Symbolism of Spiritual Renewal with Special Reference to The Pearl and The Final Plays of Shakespeare.* University of Oxford, Thesis (D.Phil.), (1949)-1956.
    Supervisor: J.R.R. Tolkien.
    S.s. 1: Ryan (2002), p. 57.
    S.s. 2: Scull-Hammond (2017a), pp. 380, 382, 390, 393, 403, 404, 406, 412, 421, 435, 444, 450, 464, 471, 478, 502.

57. Tittensor, D. J. (Merton College). *Middle English philology subject.* University of Oxford, Thesis (B.Litt.), (1958)-?.
    Supervisor: J.R.R. Tolkien.
    S.s. 1: Ryan (2002), p. 58.
    S.s. 2: Scull-Hammond (2017a), pp. 562, 567, 571, 573.

58. Trounce, Allan McIntyre (St Catherine Society). *An Edition of the Middle English Romance of 'Athelston' with historical, literary and linguistic introduction, notes and a glossary.* University of Oxford, Thesis (M.Litt.), (?)-1931.
    Examiners: J.R.R. Tolkien and C.L. Wrenn.
    S.s.: Scull-Hammond (2017a), pp. 172, 173, 174.
    Location: Bodleian Library, MS. M.Litt. c.63.

59. Turville-Petre. Edward Oswald Gabriel. (Christ Church). *An Edition of 'Viga-Glums Saga' from the Manuscripts, with Introduction and Notes.* University of Oxford, Thesis (B.Litt.), (1931)-1934.
    Supervisor: J.R.R. Tolkien.
    S.s. 1: Ryan (2002), p. 56.
    S.s. 2: Scull-Hammond (2017a), pp. 171, 174, 180, 182, 185.

60. Tuve, Rosemond. (Somerville College). *Seasons and months: studies in a tradition of Middle English poetry.* University of Oxford, Thesis (PH.D), (1928)-1931.
    Supervisor: J.R.R. Tolkien.
    S.s.: Scull-Hammond (2017a), p. 157.
    Location: Bodleyan Library, 2792 d.26.

61. Vleeskruyer, R. (St Catherine College). *The Old English Life of St Chad.* University of Oxford, Thesis (B.Litt.), (1949)-1951.

Supervisor: J.R.R. Tolkien.
S.s. 1: Ryan (2002), p. 57.
S.s. 2: Scull-Hammond (2017a), pp. 385, 390, 393, 395.
Location: Bodleian Library, MS. M.Litt. c.107.

62. Voitl, H. J. O. (Freiburg). *History of the development of the English language with special reference to the 15th, 16th & 17th centuries.* University of Oxford, Thesis (D.Phil.), (1957)-?.
    Supervisor: J.R.R. Tolkien, later E.J. Dobson.
    S.s.: Scull-Hammond (2017a), pp. 530, 543.

63. Wakefield, Anne. (St. Hilda's College). *Some new words and word-patterns in early Modern English.* University of Oxford, Thesis (B.Litt.), (1949)-?
    Supervisor: J.R.R. Tolkien.
    S.s. 1: Ryan (2002), p. 57.
    S.s. 2: Scull-Hammond (2017a), pp. 365, 369, 371, 382, 390, 393, 395, 400, 404.

64. Ward, A. W. (St Edmund Hall). *Some Problems in the English Orthoepists.* University of Oxford, Thesis (B.Litt.), (?)-1952.
    Examiners: J.R.R. Tolkien and G.V. Smithers.
    S.s.: Scull-Hammond (2017a), pp. 404, 407.

65. Watt, F. W. (Queen College). *Dialogue in Chaucer.* University of Oxford, Thesis (B.Litt.), (?)-1954.
    Examiners: J.R.R. Tolkien and G.V. Smithers.
    S.s.: Scull-Hammond (2017a), pp. 451, 456.

66. Whalley, E. M. (St Anne College). *The Rise of the English Original Fairy-Story 1800-1865.* University of Oxford, Thesis (B.Litt.), (?)-1953.
    Examiners: J.R.R. Tolkien and Mary Lascelles.
    S.s.: Scull-Hammond (2017a), pp. 412, 422.

67. Williams, E. V. (Jesus College). *The Phonology and Accidence of the [Old English] Glosses in MS Cotton Vespasian A.i (Vespasian Psalter).* University of Oxford, Thesis (B.Litt.), (1930)-1935.
    Supervisor: J.R.R. Tolkien, later C.L. Wrenn.
    Examiners: J.R.R. Tolkien and C.T. Onions.
    S.s.: Scull-Hammond (2017a), pp. 153, 165, 168, 189, 192.

68. Woolf, Rosemary (St Hugh College). *An Edition of the Old English Julian.* University of Oxford, Thesis (B.Litt.), (?)-1949.
    Examiners: J.R.R. Tolkien and Alistair Campbell.
    S.s.: Scull-Hammond (2017a), pp. 362, 365.

'Still what we read and when goes, like the people we meet, by fate.'

J.R.R. Tolkien to Mrs M. Wilson (11 April 1956)

Tolkien and Early English Text Society
1938-1972

1. Baugh, Albert Croll (Edited by). *English Text of the Ancrene Riwle: BM MS. Royal c. VI.* E.E.T.S. OS 232, 1956 [Reprinted 1999].

2. Bazire, Joyce (Edited by). *The Metrical Life of St Robert of Knaresborough (and other Middle English pieces) from BM MS. Egerton 3143.* E.E.T.S. OS 228, 1953 [Reprinted 1968].

3. Blake, Norman Francis (Edited by). *The History of Reynard the Fox translated from the Dutch Original by William Caxton*, E.E.T.S. OS 263, 1970.

4. Bühler, Curt Ferdinand (Edited by). *The Epistle of Othea translated from the French text of Christine de Pisan by Stephen Scrope.* E.E.T.S. OS 264, 1970.

5. _____ (Edited by). *Dicts and Sayings of the Philosophers.* E.E.T.S. OS 211, 1941 [Reprinted 2000].

6. d'Evelyn Charlotte and Anna Jean Mill (Edited by). *The South English Legendary*, Vol. I Text. E.E.T.S. OS 235, 1956 [Reprinted 2004].

7. _____ (Edited by). *The South English Legendary*, Vol. II Text. E.E.T.S. OS 236, 1956 [Reprinted 2008].

8. _____ (Edited by). *The South English Legendary*, Vol. III Introduction and glossary. E.E.T.S. OS 244, 1959 [Reprinted 1963].

9. Davis, Norman (Edited by). *Non-Cycle Plays and Fragments.* E.E.T.S. S.S. 1, 1970.

10. Dobson, Eric John (Edited by). *The English Text Ancrene Riwle BM MS. Cotton Cleopatra C vi.* E.E.T.S. OS 267, 1972.

11. _____ (Edited by). *The Phonetic Writings of Robert Robinson.* E.E.T.S. OS 238, 1957.

12. Eccles, Mark (Edited by). *The Macro Plays.* E.E.T.S. OS 262, 1969.

13. Fisher, John Hurt (Edited by). *The Tretyse of Loue.* E.E.T.S. OS 223, 1951 [Reprinted 1970].

14. Flower, Robin and Albert Hugh Smith (Edited by). *Parker Chronicle and Laws: facsimile of CCCC MS 173.* E.E.T.S. OS 208, 1941 [Reprinted 1972].

15. Fowler, Roger G. (Edited by). *Wulfstan's Canons of Edgar.* E.E.T.S. OS 266, 1972.

16. Friedman, Albert Barron (Edited by). *Ywain and Gawain.* E.E.T.S. OS 254, 1964.

Section E

17. Greg, Walter Wilson (Edited by). *Respublica: an interlude for Christmas 1553 attributed to Nicholas Udall.* E.E.T.S. OS 226, 1952 [Reprinted 1970].

18. Henel, Heinrich (Edited by). *Ælfric's De Temporibus Anni.* E.E.T.S. OS 213, 1942.

19. Hitchcock, Elsie Vaughan and Philip E. Hallent (Edited by). *The Lyfe of Syr Thomas More.* E.E.T.S. OS 222, 1950 [Reprinted 1996].

20. Hodgson, Phyllis (Edited by). *Deonise hid Diuinite.* E.E.T.S. OS 231, 1955 [Reprinted 2006].

21. _____ (Edited by). *The Cloud of Unknowing and The Book of Privy Counselling.* E.E.T.S. OS 218, 1944 [Reprinted 1981].

22. _____ and Gabriel Michael Liegey (Edited by). *The Orcherd of Syon*, Vol. I Text. E.E.T.S. OS 258, 1966.

23. Ker, Neil Ripley (Edited by). *Facsimile of MS. Bodley 34: St Katherine, St Juliana, Hali Meidhad, Sawles Warde.* E.E.T.S. OS 247, 1960 [Reprinted 2006].

24. _____ (Edited by). *The Owl and the Nightingale: facsimile of Jesus College MS 29 & BM Cotton Caligula A.IX.* E.E.T.S. OS 251, 1963.

25. _____ (Intro.) *Facsimile of British Museum MS. Harley 2253* (Reprinting). E.E.T.S. OS 255, 1965.

26. Leach, MacEdward (Edited by). *Paris and Vienne translated from the French and printed by William Caxton.* E.E.T.S. OS 234, 1957 [Reprinted 1970].

27. Macrae-Gibson, Osgar Duncan (Edited by). *Of Arthour and of Merlin*, Vol. I Text. E.E.T.S. OS 268, 1973.

28. Meech, Sanford Brown (Edited by). *The Book of Margery Kempe*, Vol I Text E.E.T.S. OS 212, 1940 [Reprinted 1997].

29. Miller, Clarence H. (Edited by). *The Praise of Folie by Sir Thomas Chaloner.* E.E.T.S. OS 257, 1965.

30. Mills, Maldwyn (Edited by). *Lybeaus Desconus.* E.E.T.S. OS 261, 1969.

31. Offord, Marguerite Yvonne (Edited by). *The Book of the Knight of the Tower translated by William Caxton.* E.E.T.S. S.S. 2, 1971.

32. Ogden, Margaret Sinclair (Edited by). *The Liber de Diversis Medicinis in the Thornton Manuscript.* E.E.T.S. OS 207, 1938 [Reprinted 1970].

33. Pope, John Collins (Edited by). *Homilies of Ælfric*, Vol. I A Supplementary Collection. E.E.T.S. OS 259, 1967.

34. _____ (Edited by). *Homilies of Ælfric*, Vol. II A Supplementary Collection. E.E.T.S. OS 260, 1968.

35. Richardson, Frances E. (Edited by). *Sir Eglamour of Artois*. E.E.T.S. OS 256, 1965.

36. Ross, Woodburn O. (Edited by). *Middle English Sermons*. E.E.T.S. OS 209, 1940 [Reprinted 1998].

37. Serjeantson, Mary S. (Edited by). *Osborn Bokenham: Legendys of Hooly Wummen*. E.E.T.S. OS 206, 1938 [Reprinted 1997].

38. Seymour, Maurice Charles (Edited by). *The Bodley Version of Mandeville's Travels*. E.E.T.S. OS 253, 1963.

39. _____ (Edited by). *The Metrical Version of Mandeville's Travels*. E.E.T.S. OS 269, 1973.

40. Sisam, Celia and Kenneth Sisam (Edited by). *The Salisbury Psalter*. E.E.T.S. OS 242, 1959 [Reprinted 1961].

41. Smithers, Geoffrey Victor (Edited by). *Kyng Alisaunder*, Vol I Text. E.E.T.S. OS 227, 1952 [Reprinted 1963].

42. _____ (Edited by). *Kyng Alisaunder*, Vol II: *Introduction, commentary and glossary*. E.E.T.S. OS 237, 1957 [Reprinted 1970].

43. Steele, Robert (Edited by). *Charles of Orleans: The English Poems II*. E.E.T.S. OS 220, 1946 [See OS 215]

44. _____ and Mabel Day (Edited by). *Charles of Orleans: The English Poems*. E.E.T.S. OS 215 & 220, 1941 [Reprinted 1970].

45. Sylvester, Richard Standish (Edited by). *The Life and Death of Cardinal Wolsey by George Cavendish*. E.E.T.S. OS 243, 1959 [Reprinted 1969].

46. Welson Francis, Winthrop (Edited by). *Book of Vices and Virtues*. E.E.T.S. OS 217, 1940 [Reprinted 1999].

47. Wright, Herbert Gladstone (Edited by). *Forty-Six Lives translated from Boccaccio's De Claris Mulieribus by Henry Parker, Lord Morley*. E.E.T.S. OS 214, 1943 [Reprinted 1970].

Tolkien's Lectures 1920-1959

University of Leeds Leeds Lectures and Classes given by J. R. R. Tolkien, *Reader in English Language*					
1920-1921[1] 4 Oct. 21 Dec. 11 Jan. 23 Mar. 21 Apr. 2 Jul.	A. Lang.	History of English Language to the Close of the Fourteenth Century, and the special study of West Saxon Texts and the Language of Chaucer	Mon/Fri Thu	3 p.m. 11.30 a.m.	H1. 1st Yr
		Prologue to the Canterbury Tales, the *Second Shepherd's Play*, *Everyman*, and *Morte d'Arthur*, and then moves on to Shakespeare	Mon. Wed.	11 a.m.	
		Old English Verse with a special study of *Beowulf*, *The Fight at Finnesburg*, *Widsith*, *Waldere*, and *Déor's Lament*	Mon	10 a.m.	H2. (Scheme A and B) 2nd Yr
		The History of Modern English. Old and Middle English texts.	Wed	10 a.m.	H3. (Scheme A and B) 2nd and 3rd Yr
		Old and Middle English Dialects	Fri	12 noon	H4. (Scheme B) 2nd Yr
		Gothic	Tue	2 p.m.	H5. (Scheme B) 2nd Yr
	B. Lit.	Early English Literature	Mon	12 noon	H7. (Scheme A and B) 2nd Yr
		Chaucer	Weekly at an hour to be arranged		H8. (Scheme A and B) 3rd Yr
		Essay Class The work will take the form of discussions, following upon papers read by students to the Class. Subject for 1920-21: Early English Literature and Civilization.	Weekly at an hour to be arranged		H12. (Scheme B) 3rd Yr

While at Leeds Tolkien will produce various duplicated or mimeographed pages to give to his students: *Ancrene Riwle* (October 1920) and Phonology, and the Grammar of *Layamon's Brut* (November 1920).

1921-1922[2] 3 Oct. 20 Dec. 12 Jan. 22 Mar. 20 Apr. 1 Jul.	A. Lang.	History of the English Language to the Close of the Fourteenth Century, and the special study of West Saxon Texts and of the Language of Chaucer	Mon/Fri	3 p.m.	H1. 1st Yr
		Old English Verse with a special study of *Beowulf*, *The Fight at Finnesburg*, *Widsith*, *Waldere*, *Déor's Lament*	Mon	10 a.m.	H2. (Scheme A and B) 2nd and 3rd Yr
		The History of English	Wed	10 a.m.	H3. (Scheme A and B) 2nd and 3rd Yr
		Old and Middle English texts	Mon	12 noon	H4. (Scheme B) 2nd and 3rd Yr
		Old and Middle English Dialects	Fri (fortnightly)	12 noon	H5. (Scheme B) 2nd and 3rd Yr
		Introduction to Germanic Philology, with special reference to Old English	Wed	11 a.m.	H6. (Scheme B) 3rd Yr
		Gothic	Tue	2 p.m.	H.7. (Scheme B) 2nd Yr
	B. Lit.	Early English Literature	Thu	11 a.m.	H9. (Scheme A and B) 3rd Yr
		Chaucer	Weekly at an hour to be arranged		H10. (Scheme A and B) 3rd Yr

		Essay Class. The work will take the form of discussions, following upon papers read by students to the Class. Subject for 1921-22: Early English Literature and Civilization.	Fri (fortnightly)	12 noon	H.14. (Scheme B) 3rd Yr
1922-23 2 Oct. 20 Dec. 10 Jan. 21 Mar. 19 Apr. 30 Jun.	A. Lang.	History of the English Language to the Close of the Fourteenth Century, and the special study of West Saxon Texts and of the Language of Chaucer.	Mon/Fri Thu	3 p.m. 12 noon	H1. 1st Yr
		Old English Verse with a special study of *Beowulf, The Fight at Finnesburg, Widsith, Waldere, Déor's Lament*.	Mon	10 a.m.	H2. (Scheme A and B) 2nd and 3rd Yr
		Old and Middle English texts	Mon	12 noon	H4. (Scheme A and B) 2nd and 3rd Yr
		Old and Middle English Dialects	Fri (fortnightly)	12 noon	H5. (Scheme B) 2nd and 3rd Yr
		Introduction to Germanic Philology, with special reference to Old English	Wed	11 a.m.	H2. (Scheme B) 3rd Yr
	B. Lit.	Early English Literature	Thu	11 a.m.	H.10. (Scheme A and B) 3rd Yr
		Chaucer	Thu	12 noon	H.11. (Scheme A and B) 2nd Yr
		Essay Class The work will take the form of discussions, following upon papers read by students to the Class. Subject for 1922-23: Early English Literature and Civilization.	Fri (fortnightly)	12 noon	H.15. (Scheme B) 3rd Yr
		While at Leeds Tolkien will produce various duplicated or mimeographed pages to give to his students: Kentish Dialect (Middle English) (27 January 1923); and the Development of Old English to Middle English (14 October 1923).			

1. University of Leeds (1920). Leeds: Jowett & Sowry Ltd., 1920, pp. 182-84.
2. University of Leeds (1921). Leeds: Jowett & Sowry Ltd., 1921, pp. 192-94.

SECTION F

University of Leeds
Leeds Lectures and Classes given by J. R. R. Tolkien, *Professor in English Language*

Period	Section	Course	Day	Time	Code
1923-1924[3] 1 Oct. 19 Dec. 10 Jan. 20 Mar. 24 Apr. 5 Jul.	A. Lang.	History of the English Language to the Close of the Fourteenth Century, and the special study of West Saxon Texts and of the Language of Chaucer	Mon/Fri Thu	3 p.m. 12 noon	H1. 1st Yr
		Old English Verse with a special study of *Beowulf, The Fight at Finnesburg, Widsith, Waldere, Déor's Lament*.	Mon	10 a.m.	H2. (Scheme A and B) 2nd and 3rd Yr
		The History of English	Wed	10 a.m.	H3. (Scheme A and B) 2nd and 3rd Yr
		Old and Middle English Texts	Mon	12 noon	H4. (Scheme A and B) 2nd and 3rd Yr
		Old and Middle English Dialects	Fri (fortnightly)	12 noon	H5. (Scheme B) 2nd and 3rd Yr
		Introduction to Germanic Philology, with special reference to Old English	Wed	11 a.m.	H6. (Scheme B) 3rd Yr
		Special Subject (Gothic, Old Icelandic, etc.)	Tue	2 p.m.	H7. (Scheme B) 2nd Yr
	B. Lit.	Early English Literature	Thu	11 a.m.	H10. (Scheme A and B) 3rd Yr
		Chaucer	Thu	12 noon	H11. (Scheme A and B) 2nd Yr
		Essay Class. The work will take the form of discussions, following upon papers read by students to the Class. Subject for 1923-24: Early English Literature and Civilization.	Fri (fortnightly)	12 noon	H15. (Scheme B) 3rd Yr
1924-1925[4] 1 Oct. 20 Dec. 13 Jan. 25 Mar. 25 Apr. 4 Jul.	A. Lit.	Essays and Discussions	In tutorial groups at times to be arranged		H*a*1. (Scheme A and B) 1st Yr
		Essays and Discussions	In tutorial groups at times to be arranged		H*a*2. (Scheme A and B) 2nd Yr
		Early English Literature	Thu	11 a.m.	H*a*3. (Scheme A and B) 3rd Yr
		Chaucer	Thu	12 noon	H*a*4. (Scheme A and B) 2nd Yr
	B. Lang.[5]	The History of English	Mon/Wed	12 noon	H*b*1. (Scheme A and B) 2nd Yr
		Old and Middle English Readers	Mon	10 a.m.	H*b*2. (Scheme A and B) 2nd Yr
		Middle English Texts. (i) Scheme A and B: Third Year: *Sir Gawain and the Green Knight*	Thu.	12 noon	H*b*3. (Scheme A and B) 2nd and 3rd Yr
		(ii) Scheme B: Second Year. *Layamon's Brut* (Selections)	Thu	11 a.m.	
		Old English Heroic Poetry, with special study of *Beowulf*	Mon/Wed	12 noon	H*b*4. (Scheme A and B) 3rd Yr
		Linguistic Study of Old and Middle English Texts	Fri	11 a.m.	H*b*5. (Scheme B) 3rd Yr
		Introduction to Germanic Philology	Thu	10 a.m.	H*b*6. (Scheme B) 3rd Yr
		Old Icelandic (Second Year)	Fri	2 p.m.	H*b*7. (Scheme B) 2nd and 3rd Yr
		Gothic	Thu	10 a.m.	H*b*8. (Scheme B) 2nd and 3rd Yr

3. University of Leeds (1923). Leeds: Jowett & Sowry Ltd., 1923, pp. 133-35.
4. University of Leeds (1924). Leeds: Jowett & Sowry Ltd., 1924, pp. 135-36.
5. Ivi., p. 95. 'Note :— Students are requested to give notice of their choice of subject, or subjects, not later than the beginning of their second year. Courses in Old Icelandic and Gothic are given in the department each year ; courses in any other of the above subjects may be arranged through Mr. Tolkien.'

		Pembroke Lectures and Classes given by J. R. R. Tolkien while Rawlinson and Bosworth Professor of Anglo-Saxon (1925–45 [46])[6]				
1925-26	MICHAELMAS 11 Oct. 12 Dec.	*Anglo-Saxon Reader* (Selected Extracts, for those who have already acquired the elements of Old English)	Fortnightly on Fri./Sat.	10 a.m.	16 Oct.	Examination Schools
		Beowulf (Text)		11 a.m.		
	HILARY 17 Jan. 13 Mar.	Germanic Philology	Tue.	10 a.m.	19 Jan.	Examination Schools
		Beowulf (Text)	Tue./Thu.	11 a.m.	21 Jan.	
		Anglo-Saxon Reader	Thu.	10 a.m.	21 Jan.	
	TRINITY 25 Apr. 19 Jun.	*Beowulf* (Text, continued)	Tue./Fri.	11 a.m.	27 Apr.	Examination Schools
		Anglo-Saxon Reader (selected extracts)	Tue./Fri.	10 a.m.	29 Apr.	
		Introduction to Germanic Philology	Thu.	11 a.m.	29 Apr.	
1926-27	MICHAELMAS 17 Oct. 11 Dec.	Old English *Exodus*	Tue.	10 a.m.	19 Oct.	Examination Schools
		Gothic	Tue.	5.30 p.m.	19 Oct.	TBCA
		The Verse of Sweet's *Anglo-Saxon Reader*	Thu.	10 a.m.	21 Oct.	Examination Schools
		Old English Philology	Thu.	11 a.m.	21 Oct.	Examination Schools
		Old Icelandic Texts (Class)	Thu.	5.30 p.m.	21 Oct.	TBC
		King Horn	Fri.	11 a.m.	22 Oct.	Examination Schools
		Icelandic Discussion Class	Fri.	5.30 p.m.	22 Oct.	TBC
	HILARY 23 Jan. 19 Mar.	Old English *Exodus*	Tue.	10 a.m.	25 Jan.	Examination Schools
		Gothic (Class, continued)	Tue.	5.30 p.m.	25 Jan.	Pembroke College
		The Verse of Sweet's *Anglo-Saxon Reader*	Thu.	10 a.m.	27 Jan.	Examination Schools
		Old English Philology (Morphology and Vocabulary)	Thu.	11 a.m.	27 Jan.	Examination Schools
		Volsunga Saga	Thu.	5.30 p.m.	27 Jan.	Pembroke College
		King Horn (Textual and Dialectical Comparisons of the Manuscripts)	Fri.	11 a.m.	28 Jan.	Examination Schools
		Discussion Class (continued)	Fri.	5.15 p.m.	28 Jan.	Examination Schools
	TRINITY 1 May 25 Jun.	*Judith*	Thu.	10 a.m.	5 May	Examination Schools
		Beowulf (lines 1251-1650)	Thu.	10 a.m.	5 May	
		Old English Philology	Thu.	11 a.m.	5 May	
		The Heroic Poems of the *Elder Edda*	Fri.	11 a.m.	6 May	

Section F

1927-28	MICHAELMAS 16 Oct. 10 Dec.	*Beowulf and The Fight at Finnesburg*	Tue./Thu.	11 a.m.	18 Oct.	Examination Schools
		The Prose of Sweet's *Anglo-Saxon Reader*	Thu.	10 a.m.	20 Oct.	Examination Schools
		Germanic Philology (Class)	Fri.	12 noon	21 Oct.	Pembroke College
	HILARY 22 Jan. 17 Mar.	*Beowulf and The Fight at Finnesburg*	Tue./Thu.	11 a.m.	24 Jan.	Examination Schools
		The Prose of Sweet's *Anglo-Saxon Reader*	Thu.	10 a.m.	26 Jan.	
		Germanic Philology (Class)	Fri.	12 noon	27 Jan.	
	TRINITY 29 Apr. 23 Jun.	The Legendary Traditions in *Beowulf* and *Déor's Lament*	Tue./Thu.	11 a.m.	1 May	Examination Schools
		The Fight at Finnesburg and the 'Finn Episode'	Thu.	10 a.m.	3 May	
		The Mythological Poems of the *Elder Edda*	Fri.	12 noon	4 May	
1928-29	MICHAELMAS 14 Oct. 8 Dec.	The Battle of Maldon, Brunanburh, and verse from the *Chronicle*	Tue.	10 a.m.	16 Oct.	Examination Schools
		Old English *Exodus*	Tue.	11 a.m.	16 Oct.	
		Old English Verse (Miscellaneous Pieces)	Thu.	11 a.m.	18 Oct.	
		The *Volsunga Saga* and Related Lays	Fri.	12 noon	19 Oct.	
		The Germanic Verb	Thu.	10 a.m.	18 Oct.	
	HILARY 20 Jan. 16 Mar.	Old English *Exodus* (continued)	Tue.	11 a.m.	22 Jan.	Examination Schools
		Old English Verse (Miscellaneous Pieces)	Thu.	10 a.m.	24 Jan.	
		Volsunga Saga and Related Lays	Fri.	12 noon	25 Jan.	
		Legends of the Goths	Tue.	10 a.m.	22 Jan.	
		The Germanic Verb (continued)	Thu.	11 a.m.	24 Jan.	
	TRINITY 28 Apr. 22 Jun.	Old English Verse (Miscellaneous Pieces)	Thu./Tue.	10 a.m.	2 May	Examination Schools
		(Old Norse) *Carmina Scaldica*	Thu.	11 a.m.	30 Apr.	
1929-30	MICHAELMAS 6 Oct. 30 Nov.	The Common Germanic Consonant-Changes	Tue.	10 a.m.	15 Oct.	Examination Schools
		Beowulf	Tue.	11 a.m.	15 Oct.	
		Baldrs Draumar, Atlakviða and *Guðrunarkvida enforna*	Thu.	10 a.m.	17 Oct.	

Year	Term	Lecture	Day	Time	Date	Location
	HILARY 12 Jan. 8 Mar.	Problems of Old English Philology	Tue.	10 a.m.	21 Jan.	Examination Schools
		Beowulf	Tue.	11 a.m.	21 Jan.	Examination Schools
		Baldrs Draumar, Atlakviða, Bandamanna Saga, Hænsa-Þóris saga, and Hávarðs saga Halta	Thu.	10 a.m.	23 Jan.	Examination Schools
		Old Norse Texts (Class)	TBC	TBC	TBC	TBC
	TRINITY 27 Apr. 21 Jun.	Finn and Hengest: The Problem of the Episode in Beowulf and the Fragment	Tue.	11 a.m.	29 Apr.	Examination Schools
		Germanic Numerals	Tue.	12 noon	29 Apr.	
		Déor's Lament, Waldere, and Runic Poem	Thu	11 a.m.	1 May	
1930-31	MICHAELMAS 12 Oct. 6 Dec.	Elene		11 a.m. 12 noon	14 Oct.	Examination Schools
		Old English Minor Poems (including The Wanderer, The Seafarer, The Dream of the Rood, and The Battle of Maldon)	Tue./Thu.			
	HILARY 18 Jan. 14 Mar.	Old English Minor Poems (continued): Judith, Riddles, and The Battle of Brunanburh	Tue.	11 a.m.	20 Jan.	Examination Schools
		Old English Exodus	Tue.	12 noon	20 Jan.	Examination Schools
		Gothic Traditions	Thu.	11 a.m.	22 Jan.	Examination Schools
		Carmina Scaldica: Introduction to Reading of Scaldic Poetry	TBC	TBC	TBC	TBC
		Old English Textual Criticism	Day TBC	TBC	TBC	TBC
	TRINITY 26 Apr. 20 Jun.	The Battle of Brunanburh	Tue.	11 a.m.	28 Apr.	Examination Schools
		Old English Exodus (continued)	Thu.	10 a.m.	30 Apr.	
		Old English Textual Criticism (continued)	Thu.	11 a.m.	30 Apr.	
		The Germani: Problems of Gothic Philology	not given			
		Introduction to the Elder Edda.	not given			
1931-32	MICHAELMAS 11 Oct. 5 Dec.	Beowulf	Tue./Thu.	11 a.m.	13 Oct.	Examination Schools
		Gubrunarkvida en forna	Tue.	12 noon	13 Oct.	
		Problems of Old English Philology	Thu.	12 noon	15 Oct.	
	HILARY 17 Jan. 12 Mar.	Beowulf (continued)	Tue.	11 a.m.	19 Jan.	Examination Schools
		Atlakviða and Baldrs Drau-mar	Thu.	12 noon	21 Jan.	Examination Schools
		The Language of the Vespasian Psalter Glosses	Tue.	12 noon	19 Jan.	Taylor Institution
		Problems of Old English Philology	Fri.	12 noon	22 Jan.	Taylor Institution

SECTION F

	TRINITY 24 Apr./18 Jun.	*Finn and Hengest*: The Fragment and the Episode (Textual Study and Reconstruction)	Tue./Thu.	11 a.m.	26 Apr.	Examination Schools
		Déor's Lament and *Waldere*	Tue.	12 noon	26 Apr.	
		Volundarkvida	Thu.	12 noon	28 Apr.	
1932-33	MICHAELMAS 9 Oct. 3 Dec.	*Elene*	Tue./Thu.	11 a.m.	11 Oct.	Examination Schools
		Old English Philology	Tue.	12 noon	11 Oct.	
		Old English Prosody	Thu.	12 noon	13 Oct.	
		Völuspá	Fri.	12 noon	14 Oct.	
	HILARY 15 Jan. 11 Mar.	*Elene* (continued) and *The Vision of the Cross* (i.e. *The Dream of the Rood*)	Tue./Thu.	11 a.m.	17 Jan.	Examination Schools
		Old English Textual Criticism	Tue.	12 noon	17 Jan.	
		Volsunga Saga	Thu.	12 noon	19 Jan.	
		The Language of the Vespasian Psalter Glosses	Fri.	12 noon	20 Jan.	
	TRINITY* 23 Apr. 17 Jun.	Old English Verse Texts (for those beginning the Honour Course)	Tue./Thu.	11 a.m.	25 Apr.	Examination Schools
		The Germani	Tue.	12 noon	25 Apr.	
		Prolegomena to the Study of Old English and Old Norse Poetry	Thu.	12 noon	27 Apr.	
		* E. O. G. Turville-Petre is to teach a class in Old Norse on behalf of Tolkien.				
1933-34	MICHAELMAS 8 Oct. 2 Dec.	*Beowulf*: General Criticism	Tue.	11 a.m.	10 Oct.	Examination Schools
		The Origins of the English Language	Tue.	12 noon	10 Oct.	
		Old English Prose Pieces (Cynewulf and Cyneheard, Ohthere and Wulfstan, *Sermo Lupi ad Anglos*)	Thu.	11 a.m.	12 Oct.	
		The Historical and Legendary Traditions in *Beowulf* and Other Old English Poems	Thu./Fri.	12 noon	12 Oct.	
	HILARY 14 Jan. 10 Mar.	*Waldere* and *Déor's Lament*, together with the Old Norse *Volun-darkvida*	Tue.	11 a.m.	16 Jan.	Examination Schools
		The Historical and Legendary Traditions in *Beowulf* and Other Old English Poems (continued)	Tue./Thu.	12 noon		

	TRINITY 22 Apr. 16 Jun.	Old English Verse (for those beginning the Honour Course)	Tue.	11 a.m	24 Apr.	Examination Schools
		Volun-darkvida, Atlakviða, and *Atlamdl*	Tue.	11 a.m.		
		The Fight at Finnesburg (continued; probably a further continuation of The Historical and Legendary Traditions in *Beowulf* and Other Old English Poems)	Tue./Thu.	12 noon		
1934-35	MICHAELMAS 14 Oct 8 Dec.	*Beowulf*: General Criticism	Tue.	11 a.m.	16 Oct.	Examination Schools
		Elene and *The Vision of the Cross*	Tue./Thu.	12 noon		
		Outlines of the History of English (Old English Period)	Tue.	12 noon		
	HILARY 20 Jan. 16 Mar.	*Elene* (concluded) and the Old English Exodus	Tue./Thu.	11 a.m.	22 Jan.	Examination Schools
		Grammar of the Vespasian Psalter Glosses	Tue.	12 noon	22 Jan.	
		The Principal Problems of Old English Phonology	Thu.	12 noon	24 Jan.	
	TRINITY 28 Apr. 16 Jun.	Introduction to the *Poetic Edda*	Thu.	11 a.m.	2 May	Examination Schools
		Grimm's Law	Thu.	12 noon	2 May	
		Introduction to Old English Verse (for those beginning the Honours Course)	Fri.	12 noon	30 Apr.	
1935-36	MICHAELMAS 13 Oct 7 Dec.	*Beowulf*: Text	Tue.	11 a.m.	15 Oct.	Examination Schools
		Finn and Hengest	Tue./Thu.	12 noon	15 Oct.	
		Old English Texts (Paper B2)	Thu.	11 a.m.	17 Oct.	
	HILARY* 19 Jan. 14 Mar.	The Legend of Wayland the Smith, followed by a study of the text of *Déor's Lament* and of *Volundarkvida*	Tue./ Thu.	11 a.m.	21 Jan.	Examination Schools
		Atlakviða * These are probably cancelled, however, after Tolkien injures his leg on 1 February; he will offer them as classes at his home in Northmoor Road in Trinity Term 1936.	Tue./ Thu.	12 noon		

6. Scull-Hammond (2017a).

SECTION F

Merton Lectures and Classes given by J. R. R. Tolkien, while *Merton Professor of English Language* (1946–59)[7]						
1946-47	MICHAELMAS 13 Oct 7 Dec.	*Ormulum* and *Ancrene Wisse*	Wed.	12 noon	16 Oct.	Examination Schools
		Sir Gawain and the Green Knight	Fri.		18 Oct.	
	HILARY 19 Jan. 15 Mar.	*Sir Gawain and the Green Knight* (continued)	Wed.	11 a.m.	22 Jan.	Examination Schools
		Ancrene Wisse and *Ormulum*	Wed.	12 noon		
	TRINITY 27 Apr. 21 Jun.	Middle English (Seminar)	Tue.	5.30 p.m.	29 Apr.	Merton College
		Ormulum	Wed.	11 a.m.	30 Apr.	Examination Schools
		Germanic Philology (Seminar)	Thu.	5.30 p.m.	1 May	Merton College
		[Another series of lectures to be arranged on Fridays at 11 a.m. in the Examination Schools, beginning 2 May]				
1947-48	MICHAELMAS 12 Oct 6 Dec.	Seminar (Middle English)	Tue./Thu.	5.30 p.m.	14 Oct.	Merton College
		Outline of the History of English	Wed.	11 a.m.	15 Oct.	Examination Schools
		Chaucer: the *Clerk's Tale* and the *Pardoner's Tale*	Wed./Fri.	12 noon	15 Oct.	Examination Schools
	HILARY 18 Jan. 13 Mar.	Outline of the History of English (continued)	Wed.	11 a.m.	21 Jan.	Examination Schools
		Chaucer's *Parlement of Foules*	Wed./Fri.	12 noon	21 Jan.	Examination Schools
		Seminar (Middle English)*	Thu.	5.30 p.m.		Merton College
		*Sir Orfeo***	Sat.	11 a.m.		
		* Seminar conducted by Tolkien and Angus McIntosh ** Given by A. J. Bliss for the Merton Professor of English Language and Literature.				
	TRINITY 25 Apr. 19 Jun.	Outline of the History of English Language (contined)	Thu./Fri.	12 noon		Examination Schools
		The West Saxon Dialect in Middle English*	Wed.	12 noon		
		*Given by A. J. Bliss for the Merton Professor of English Language and Literature.				

1948-49	MICHAELMAS 10 Oct 4 Dec.	The Influence of Latin upon English	Wed.	12 noon	13 Oct.	Examination Schools
		Sir Gawain and the Green Knight	Fri.	12 noon	15 Oct.	Examination Schools
		Middle English Philology (Seminar)	Fri.	5.30 p.m.	15 Oct.	Merton College
		Language and Literature*	20 Nov.	11 a.m.		Examination Schools
		*For the course 'The Study of Literature'.				
	HILARY 16 Jan. 12 Mar.	The Language of the Ayenbyte of Inwit	Wed.	12 noon	19 Jan.	Examination Schools
		Sir Gawain and the Green Knight	Fri.	12 noon	21 Jan.	Examination Schools
		English Philology (Seminar)	Fri.	5.30 p.m.	21 Jan.	Merton College
	TRINITY 24 Apr. 18 Jun.	Sawles Warde	Wed.	11 a.m.	21 Apr.	Examination Schools
1949-50	MICHAELMAS 9 Oct 3 Dec.	Tolkien is on sabbatical leave.				
	HILARY 15 Jan. 11 Mar.	Tolkien is on sabbatical leave.				
	TRINITY 23 Apr. 17 Jun.	Outlines of English Linguistic History	Wed./Fri.	11 a.m.	26 Apr.	Examination Schools
1950-51	MICHAELMAS 8 Oct 2 Dec.	Sir Gawain and the Green Knight	Wed.	11 a.m.	11 Oct.	Examination Schools
		Outlines of English Linguistic History (continued): The Foreign Elements	Fri.	11 a.m.	13 Oct.	Examination Schools
		Philology: Discussion Class	Tue.	5.30 p.m.	17 Oct.	Merton College
	HILARY 14 Jan. 10 Mar.	Sir Gawain and the Green Knight (continued)	Wed.	12 noon	17 Jan.	Examination Schools
		Philology: Discussion Class	Thu.	5.15 p.m.	18 Jan.	Merton College
		Middle English	Fri.	12 noon	19 Jan.	Examination Schools
	TRINITY 22 Apr. 16 Jun.	Ormulum and Ayenbite of Inwit	Wed./Fri.	12 noon	25 Apr.	Examination Schools
		Sir Gawain and the Green Knight	Fri.	11 a.m.	27 Apr.	
1951-52	MICHAELMAS 14 Oct 8 Dec.	Pardoner's Tale by Chaucer	Wed.	12 noon	17 Oct.	Examination Schools
		Philology: Outlines of History of English	Fri.	12 noon	19 Oct.	
	HILARY 20 Jan. 15 Mar.	Pardoner's Tale by Chaucer (continued)	Wed.	12 noon	23 Jan.	Examination Schools
		Philology: Outlines of History of English (continued)	Fri.	12 noon	25 Jan.	

Section F

	TRINITY 27 Apr. 21 Jun.	Philology: Outlines of the History of English Accidence (concluded)	Wed.	12 noon	30 Apr.	Examination Schools
		Ayenbite of Inwit	Fri.	12 noon	2 May	
1952-53	MICHAELMAS 12 Oct 6 Dec.	*Sir Gawain and the Green Knight*	Wed.	12 noon	15 Oct.	Examination Schools
		Philology: English Orthography	Fri.	11 a.m.	17 Oct.	
		Ayenbite of Inwit	Fri.	12 noon	17 Oct.	
	HILARY 18 Jan. 14 Mar.	*Sir Gawain and the Green Knight* (continued)	Wed.	11 a.m.	21 Jan.	Examination Schools
		The Language of the *Ayenbite of Inwit* (continued)	Fri.	11 a.m.	23 Jan.	
		Pardoner's Tale by Chaucer	Fri.	12 noon	23 Jan.	
	TRINITY 26 Apr. 20 Jun.	*Sir Gawain and the Green Knight* (concluded)	Wed.	12 noon	29 Apr.	Examination Schools
		The Language of the *Ancrene Wisse*	Fri.	12 noon	1 May	
1953-54	MICHAELMAS 11 Oct 5 Dec.	*Pardoner's Tale* and Prologue by Chaucer	Mon.	11 a.m.	12 Oct.	Examination Schools
		The Owl and the Nightingale	Mon./Wed.	12 a.m.		
	HILARY 17 Jan. 13 Mar.	*The Owl and the Nightingale*	Mon.	11 a.m.	18 Jan.	Examination Schools
		Pardoner's Tale by Chaucer	Wed.	11 a.m.	20 Jan.	
	TRINITY 15 Apr. 19 Jun.	*Pardoner's Tale*: The Legend	Wed.	11 a.m.	28 Apr.	Examination Schools
		The Owl and the Nightingale	Fri.	11 a.m.	30 Apr.	
1954-55	MICHAELMAS 10 Oct 4 Dec.	*Sir Gawain and the Green Knight*	Wed.	11 a.m.	13 Oct.	Examination Schools
		Ayenbite of Inwit	Wed.	12 noon	13 Oct.	
		Philology: Outline of the History of English Accidence	Fri.	11 a.m.	15 Oct.	
	HILARY 16 Jan. 12 Mar.	*Sir Gawain and the Green Knight*	Wed.	11 a.m.	19 Jan.	Examination Schools
		Ayenbite of Inwit	Wed.	12 noon	19 Jan.	
		Philology: History of English Accidence	Fri.	12 noon	21 Jan.	
	TRINITY 24 Apr. 18 Jun.	*Sir Gawain and the Green Knight*	Wed.	12 noon	27 Apr.	Examination Schools
		Ayenbite of Inwit	Thu.	12 noon	28 Apr.	
1955-56	MICHAELMAS 9 Oct 3 Dec.	Phonology: English Verbs	Wed.	11 a.m.	12 Oct.	Examination Schools
		The Owl and the Nightingale	Thu.	12 noon	13 Oct.	
		Pardoner's Tale and Prologue by Chaucer	Fri.	12 noon	14 Oct.	
	HILARY 15 Jan. 10 Mar.	*Pardoner's Tale* and Prologue by Chaucer	Wed.	12 noon	18 Jan.	Examination Schools
		The Owl and the Nightingale	Wed.	12 noon		

	TRINITY 22 Apr. 16 Jun.	*Sawles Warde*	Wed.	12 noon	25 Apr.	Examination Schools
		Pardoner's Tale by Chaucer (concluded)	Fri.	12 noon	27 Apr.	
1956-57	MICHAELMAS 14 Oct 8 Dec.	*Sir Gawain and the Green Knight*	Wed.	11 a.m.	17 Oct.	Examination Schools
	HILARY 20 Jan. 16 Mar.	*Sir Gawain and the Green Knight* (continued)	Wed.	11 a.m.	23 Jan.	Examination Schools
		Old English *Exodus*	Thu.	11 a.m.	24 Jan.	
	TRINITY 28 Apr. 22 Jun.	Old English *Exodus*	Wed.	11 a.m.	1 May	Examination Schools
		The Language of Chaucer	Fri.	11 a.m.	3 May	
1957-58	MICHAELMAS 13 Oct 7 Dec.	*Sawles Warde*	Wed.	11 a.m.	16 Oct.	Merton College
		Some Middle English Dialects	Fri.	11 a.m.	18 Oct.	
	HILARY 19 Jan. 15 Mar.	Tolkien has no lectures this term, as he is on sabbatical leave.					
	TRINITY 27 Apr. 21 Jun.	Tolkien has no lectures this term, as he is on sabbatical leave.					
1958-59	MICHAELMAS 12 Oct 6 Dec.	*Sir Gawain and the Green Knight*	Wed.	11 a.m.	15 Oct.	Examination Schools
	HILARY 18 Jan. 14 Mar.	*Sawles Warde*	Fri.	11 a.m.	23 Jan.	Examination Schools
	TRINITY 26 Apr. 20 Jun.	*Sawles Warde*	Wed.	11 a.m.	29 Apr.	Examination Schools
	5 Jun.	Tolkien delivers his valedictory address to the University of Oxford at 5 p.m. in the Hall at Merton College, to a capacity audience. Tolkien enters in full spate, shouting the opening lines of *Beowulf*.					

7. Scull-Hammond (2017a).

Bibliography

Following is a list of the books, articles, Web pages, and other materials used in the writing of *Tolkien's Library*.

Tolkien Papers
(Bodleian Library, Oxford)

MS. Tolkien 10/2 *Drafts of articles or lectures, and rough notes on Ormulum*

MS. Tolkien A 11 *Notes on Pearl* fols. 38-9, 40-1, 58, 59, 114, 124, 140, 143

MS. Tolkien A 12/1 *Commentary on Sir Gawain*, lines 37-1987 fols. 1, 2, 8, 9, 11, 20, 24, 33, 53, 78, 100, 102, 103, 106, 108, 109, 144

MS. Tolkien A 12/2 *Commentary on Sir Gawain*, lines 1999-2523 fols. 2, 5, 6, 7, 11, 12, 16, 31, 32, 33, 37, 54

MS. Tolkien A 12/3 *Rough text of a lecture on Sir Gawain*, 1965 fols. 17-59, 62-74, 70

MS. Tolkien A 13/1 *Annotated texts of King Horn* fol. 94

MS. Tolkien A 13/1 *Draft of talk to the Oxford Dante Society: A neck-verse* (1947), fols. 169, 170, 171, 172

MS. Tolkien A 13/2 *Notes and drafts of lectures on Chaucer: Pardoner's Tale* fols. 141, 159, 160, 163, 178.

MS. Tolkien A 13/2 *Notes and drafts of lectures on Chaucer: Clerk's Tale*

MS. Tolkien 16/2 *Notes and drafts concerning Andreas*

MS. Tolkien 16/2 *Notes and drafts concerning Elene*

MS. Tolkien 16/2 *Notes and drafts concerning Judith*

MS. Tolkien A 19/3 *Etymologies or history of Walrus* fols. 162-195

MS. Tolkien A 21/6 fol. 1.

MS. Tolkien A 21/7 fols. 6, 16, 19, 27, 29, 30, 31, 32, 33, 35, 43, 44, 47, 48.

MS. Tolkien A 21/13 fols. 119, 197, 202, 203.

MS. Tolkien A 28/B Commentary on *Beowulf*, delivered as lectures at Oxford, fols. 169, 171.

MS. Tolkien A 29(a) *Lecture notes, 1920s-1930s, on prose extracts and poems from Sweet's* fol. 93

MS. Tolkien A 30/1 *Lectures on Old English* fols. 33, 70, 107-9, 113, 121, 152

MS. Tolkien A 34/3 Texts for the BBC radio presentation of the translation of *Sir Gawain and the Green Knight*, 1953 fol. 221.

MS. Tolkien A 35 *Pearl* fols. 11, 24, 75, 111, 112, 113, 114.

MS. Tolkien A 38 *Papers relating to Old and Middle English: The Wanderer* fols. 3, 9, 12, 36

MS. Res. e. 308 *Sir Gawain and the Green Knight*.

Tolkien's letters unpublished in *Letters* by Humphrey Carpenter:

Bauer, H. C. (24 November 1966)
Bratt, Edith (1920s)
Brett, Cyril (24 August 1924)
Burchfield, Robert W. (11 June 1972)
Bush, John (12 March 1966)
Byrne, E. (1 March 1968)
Colborn, A. F. (21 July 1938)
Cowling, G. H. (23 December 1934)
Cutts, L. M. (26 October 1958)
d'Ardenne, Simonne (1938-39)
Eerdmans, William B. Publishing Co. (3 May 1966)
Jennings, Elizabeth (2 December 1955)
Johnston, George Burke (24 May 1968)
Kilby, Clyde S. (4 June 1968)
Killion Mr (20 August 1913)
Lanier, Sterling E. (24 January 1973)
Lanier, Sterling E. (29 September 1965)
Miller, Brian (21 June 1971)
O'Loughlin, J. L. N. (30 October 1965)
O'Neill, Timothy R. (20 September 1950)
Owen Dr (24 May 1968)
Ready, William (5 March 1959)
Sayer, George (28 November 1963)
Shippey, Tom (12 April 1970)
Sibley, Jane T. (30 May 1959)
Stanley-Smith Miss (22 November 1956)
Verhulst, Roger (4 December 1967)

Verhulst, Roger (9 March 1966)
Wheeler, Timothy J. (1 August 1966)
Wheeler, Timothy J. (22 August 1966)

Works By J. R. R. Tolkien

1922 *A Middle English Vocabulary*. Oxford and London: At the Clarendon Press and Oxford University Press.

1923 'Henry Bradley. 3 Dec., 1843 – 23 may, 1923' in *Bulletin of the Modern Humanities Research Association*. no. 20, October. Cambridge: The University Press. pp. 4-5.

1923 'Holy Maidenhood'. *The Times Literary Supplement*. London, n. 1110, April 26, p. 281.

1924 'Philology: General Works'. *The Year's Work in English Studies* 1923, Edited by Sir Sidney Lee and F. S. Boas, Vol. IV. London: The English Association and Oxford University Press, pp. 20-44.

1925 *Sir Gawain and the Green Knight*. Edited with E.V. Gordon. London: Oxford University Press.

1925 'Some Contributions to Middle-English Lexicography'. *The Review of English Studies: A Quarterly Journal of English Literature and the English Language*. Edited by R. B. McKerrow. Vol. 1, no. 2. London: Sidgwick & Jackson, April. pp. 210-215.

1925 'The Devil's Coach-Horses'. *The Review of English Studies: A Quarterly Journal of English Literature and the English Language*. Edited by R. B. McKerrow. Vol. 1, no. 3. London: Sidgwick & Jackson, July, pp. 331-336.

1926 'Philology: General Works'. *The Year's Work in English Studies* 1924, Edited by F. S. Boas and C. H. Herford, Vol. V. London: The English Association and Oxford University Press, pp. 26-65.

1927 'Philology: General Works'. *The Year's Work in English Studies* 1925, Edited by Sir Sidney Lee and F. S. Boas, Vol. VI. London: The English Association and Oxford University Press, pp. 32-66.

1928 'Foreword'. *A New Glossary of the Dialect of the Huddersfield District*. Edited by Walter E. Haigh. London: Oxford University Press.

1929 'Ancrene Wisse and Hali Meiðhad'. *Essays and Studies by Members of the English Association*. Collected by H. W. Gerrod. Vol. XIV. London and Oxford: At the Clarendon Press and Oxford University Press, 1929, pp. 104-126.

1930   *Sir Gawain and the Green Knight*. Edited with E.V. Gordon. 2nd ed. reprinted with corrections. London: Oxford University Press.

1932   'The Name 'Nodens'. *Report on the Excavation of the Prehistoric, Roman and Post-Roman Site in Lydney Park, Gloucestershire*. Edited by R. E. M. Wheeler and T. V. Wheeler, Reports of the Research Committee of the Society of the Antiquaries of London, no. IX. London: Oxford University Press for the Society of the Antiquaries, pp. 132-137.

1932   'Sigelwara land'. *Medium Ævum*, Vol. 1, no. 3. Edited by C. T. Onions. Oxford: Basil Blackwell. December, pp. 183-96.

1934   'Sigelwara land'. *Medium Ævum*, Vol. 3, no. 2. Edited by C. T. Onions. Oxford: Basil Blackwell. June, pp. 95-111.

1934   'Chaucer as a Philologist: *The Reeve's Tale*'. *Tolkien Studies*, Vol. 5 (2008), pp. 109-171 [First edition in *Transactions of the Philological Society* 1934. Edited by Professor G. E. K. Braunholtz, London: David Nutt (A. G. Berry), pp. 1-70.]

1936   *Sir Gawain and the Green Knight*. Edited with E.V. Gordon. 3rd ed. reprinted with corrections London: Oxford University Press.

1937   *Beowulf: The Monsters and the Critics*. Sir Israel Gollancz Memorial Lecture British Academy 1936, London: H. Milford for the British Academy.

1938   *Dragons. J.R.R. Tolkien The Hobbit 1937-2017*. A commemorative booklet celebrating the 80th anniversary written by Christina Scull & Wayne G. Hammond. London: HarperCollins*Publisher*, pp. 39-62.

1940   'Prefatory Remarks on Prose Translation of '*Beowulf*'. *Beowulf and the Finnsburg Fragment*. Translated by John R. Clark Hall, Notes and Introduction by C. L. Wrenn. London: George Allen and Unwin, Revised Edition, pp. ix-xliii.

1945   *The Notion Club Papers. The History of Middle-earth* Pt. Two, Vol. IX, *Sauron Defeated*. Edited by Christopher Tolkien. London: HarperCollins*Publisher*, 2002.

1946   'Research v. literature'. *The Sunday Times*. London, April 14.

1947   'On Fairy-stories'. *Essays Presented to Charles Williams*. Edited by C. S. Lewis. London: Oxford University Press, pp. 38-89.

1947   '*Iþþlen*' in *Sawles Warde*'. Written together with S. R. T. O. d'Ardenne. *English Studies*, Vol. XXVIII, no. 6, edited by R. W. Zandvoort, Amsterdam: Swets & Zeitlinger. December, pp. 168-70.

1948   'MS. Bodley 34: A re-collation of a collation'. Written together with S. R. T. O. d'Ardenne. *Studia Neophilologica*. Vol. XX no. 1-2. Edited by Paul Falk John Holmberg and S. B. Liljegren. Uppsala: A.-B. Lundequistska Bokhandeln, pp. 65-72.

1949 *Farmer Giles of Ham*. London: George Allen & Unwin.

1953 'Sir Gawain and the Green Knight'. *The Monsters and the Critics and Other Essays*. Edited by Christopher Tolkien. London: George Allen & Uniwin, 1983, pp. 72-108.

1953 'Form and Purpose'. *Pearl*, Edited by Eric Valentine Gordon. London: Oxford University Press, pp. xi-xix.

1953 'Middle English '*Losenger*''. *Essais de Philologie Moderne* (1951). Paris: University of Liege, pp. 63-76.

1953 'The Homecoming of Beorhtnoth Beorhthelm's Son'. *Essays and Studies* Edited by Geoffrey Bullough. London: John Murray (Publishers) Ltd., pp. 1-18.

1959 'Valedictory Address'. *The Monsters and the Critics and Other Essays.* Edited by Christopher Tolkien. London: George Allen & Uniwin, 1983, pp. 224-40.

1963 'English and Welsh'. *O'Donnell Lectures: Angles and Britons*. Edited by Henry Lewis. Cardiff: University of Wales, pp. 1-41.

1966 'Nomenclature of *The Lord of the Rings*'. *The Lord of the Rings: A Reader's Companion*. Edited by Wayne G. Hammond and Christina Scull. London: HarperCollinsPublishers, pp. 750-782.

1967 *Sir Gawain and the Green Knight*. 2nd edition edited by Norman Davis. Oxford: Oxford University Press.

1975 *Sir Gawain and the Green Knight, Pearl, Sir Orfeo*. Translated by J. R. R. Tolkien, edited by Christopher Tolkien. London: George Allen & Unwin.

1981 *The Letters of J.R.R. Tolkien*. A selection edited by Humphrey Carpenter with assistance of Christopher Tolkien. London: George Allen & Unwin.

1982 *Finn and Hengest. The Fragment and the Episode*. Edited by Alan Bliss. London: George Allen & Unwin.

1983 *The Monsters and the Critics and Other Essays*. Edited by Christopher Tolkien. Contains '*Beowulf*: The Monsters and the Critics', 'On Translating *Beowulf*', 'Sir Gawain and the Green Knight', 'On Fairy-Stories', 'English and Welsh', 'A Secret Vice', and 'Valedictory Address to the University of Oxford'. London: George Allen & Unwin.

1992 *The Book of Lost Tales*, Vol. I. Edited by Christopher Tolkien. Boston: Ballantine Books.

1992 *The Book of Lost Tales*, Vol. II. Edited by Christopher Tolkien. Boston: Ballantine Books.

2002   *Beowulf and the Critics*. Edited by Michael Drout. Tempe: Arizona Centre for Medieval and Renaissance Studies.

2005   *Smith of Wootton Major*. Edited by Verlyn Flieger. London: HarperCollins*Publisher*.

2008   *On Fairy-stories*. Expanded edition, with commentary and notes. Edited by Verlyn Flieger and Douglas A. Anderson. London: HarperCollins*Publisher*.

2009   *The Legend of Sigurd & Gudrún*. Edited by Christopher Tolkien. London: HarperCollins*Publisher*.

2013   *The Fall of Arthur*. Edited by Christopher Tolkien. London: HarperCollins*Publisher*.

2014   *Beowulf. A Translation and Commentary. Together with Sellic Spel*l. Edited by Christopher Tolkien. London: HarperCollins*Publisher*.

2014   *Farmer Giles of Ham*. Edited by Christina Scull and Wayne G. Hammond. London: HarperCollins*Publisher*.

2015   *The Story of Kullervo*. Edited by Verlyn Flieger. London: HarperCollins*Publisher*.

2016   *A Secret Vice. Tolkien on invented languages*. Edited by Dimitra Fimi & Andrew Higgins. London: HarperCollins*Publisher*.

2016   *The Lay of Aotrou & Itroun*. Edited by Verlyn Flieger. London: HarperCollins*Publisher*.

Secondary Sources

ANDERSON, Douglas A. (Edited by)
2002   *The Annotated Hobbit*. Revised and expanded edition. London: HarperCollinsPublisher.
2006a   'Personal Library'. *The J.R.R. Tolkien Encyclopedia: Scholarship and Critical Assessment*. Edited by Michael D. C. Drout. New York: Routledge.
2006b   'R. W. Chambers and *The Hobbit*'. *Tolkien Studies*, no. 3, pp. 137-147. Edited by Douglas A. Anderson, Michael D. C. Drout and Verlyn Flieger. West Virginia University.

BEAHM, George W.
2004   *The Essential J.R.R. Tolkien Sourcebook: A Fan's Guide to Middle-earth and Beyond*. Career Press.

BIRKETT, Tim
2014 'Old Norse'. *A companion to J.R.R. Tolkien*. Edited by Stuart Lee. Chichester, West Sussex Wiley Blackwell Chichester, West Sussex Wiley Blackwell, pp. 244-58.

BIRNS, Nicholas
2012 'The Stones and the Book: Tolkien, Mesopotamia, and Biblical Mythopeia'. *Tolkien and the Study of His Sources: Critical Essays*. Edited by Jason Fisher. Jerson, North Carolina, and London: McFarland & Company, pp. 45-68.

BLACKWELL'S RARE BOOKS
2012   Catalogue B172.

BRITISH RED CROSS SOCIETY
1942 *Prisoners of War News*. Printed at the University Press, Aberdeen, Vol. III, April, p. 137.
1943 *Prisoners of War News*. Printed at the University Press, Aberdeen, Vol. V, March, p. 112.

CARPENTER, Humphrey
1977 *J.R.R. Tolkien: A Biography*. London: George Allen & Unwin.
1979 *The Inklings: C. S. Lewis, J.R.R. Tolkien, Charles Williams and Their Friends*. Boston: Houghton Mifflin Company.

D'ENTRÉVES, Alessandro Passerin
1952 *Dante as a Political Thinker*. Oxford: At the Clarendon Press.
1955 *Dante politico e altri saggi*. Torino: Einaudi Editore.

DROUT, Michael D. C.
2007 *J.R.R. Tolkien Encyclopedia: Scholarship and Critical Assessment*. Abingdon: Taylor & Francis.

EDWARDS, Raymond
2014 *Tolkien*. London: Robert Hale.

FIMI, Dimitra
2007 'Tolkien's Celtic type of legends: Merging Traditions'. *Tolkien Studies*, no. 4, pp. 51-71. Edited by Douglas A. Anderson, Michael D. C. Drout and Verlyn Flieger. West Virginia University.

FINCH [Simon] Rare Books Ltd.

2002   *Modern Books*. Catalogue 53.

FISHER, Jason
   The J.R.R. Tolkien Collection in the Cushing Memorial Library and Archives at Texas A&M University. [unpublished].
2012   *Tolkien and the Study of His Sources: Critical Essays*. Jerson, North Carolina, and London: McFarland & Company.

FITZGERALD, Jill
2009   *A 'Clerkes Compleinte': Tolkien and the Division of Lit. and Lang. Tolkien Studies*. Vol. 6, pp. 45-57.

FLIEGER, VERLYN
2001   *A Question of Time: J.R.R. Tolkien's Road to Faërie*. Kent: Kent State University Press.
2003   "There would always be a fairy-tale': J. R. R. Tolkien and the folklore controversy'. *Tolkien the medievalist*. Edited by Jane Chance. London; New York: Routledge, 2003, pp. 26-35.
2004   'Do the Atlantis story and abandon Eriol-Saga'. *Tolkien Studies*, Vol. 1, pp. 43-68.

GARTH, John
2003   *Tolkien and the Great War*. The Threshold of Middle-earth. Boston: Houghton Mifflin.
2014   *Tolkien at Exeter College: How an Oxford undergraduate created Middle-earth*. Oxford: Exeter College.
2014   "The road from adaptation to invention: How Tolkien Came to the Brink of Middle-earth in 1914'. *Tolkien Studies*, no. 11, pp. 1-44. Edited by Michael D. C. Drout, Verlyn Flieger and David Bratman. West Virginia University

GILLIVER, Peter M.
2002   *Oxford English Dictionary News*. Oxford: Oxford University Press. Series 2, no. 21, June.

GILLIVER, Peter; MARSHALL, Jeremy H.; WEINER, Edmund
2009   *The Ring of Words. Tolkien and the Oxford English Dictionary*. Oxford: University Press.

GOODKNIGHT, Glen H.
1982   'Tolkien in Translation'. *Mythlore* 32 (Summer), pp. 22-27.

GREEN, Lancelyn Roger
1980 'Recollections'. *Amon Hen,* Vol. 44, May, pp. 6-8.

GUEROULT, Denis
1964 BBC Interview.

GUNSTON, D. J.
1943 'Studying in Prison Camps'. *Chambers's Journal*, Orr and Smith, p. 305.

HAMMOND, Wayne G. & SCULL, Christina
2014 *The Lord of the Rings. A Reader's Companion.* London: HarperCollinsPublisher.

HARRINGTON [Peter] Antiquarian Bookseller
2003 *The 2003 New York Antiquarian Book Fair.* Catalogue.

HIME, Melissa & Mark
1980 *Eorclanstanas: or The Hobbitianahe Hobbitiana.* (Catalogue). Idyllwild, CA, USA.

HOLLAND, Robert W. (Compiled and Edited by)
1949 *Adversis Major. A Short of the Educational Books Scheme of the Prisoners of War Department of the British Red Cross Society and Order of St. John of Jerusalem.* London: Staples Press Limited.

HOSTETTER, Carl F.
2013 *Vinyar Tengwar,* Number 50, March.

KERRY, Paul E. (Edited by)
2011 *The Ring and the Cross: Christianity and the Writings of J.R.R. Tolkien.* Teaneck: Fairleigh Dickinson University Press.

KING EDWARD'S SCHOOL CHRONICLE
1911 'Speech Day'. no. 189. October
1911 'Literary Society', 26 no. 2, March, pp. 18-19

LAPIDGE, Michael (editor)
2002 *Interpreters of Early Medieval Britain.* Oxford: The British Academy & Oxford University Press.

LEE, D. Stuart (with Elizabeth SOLOPOVA)
2005 *The Keys of Middle-earth.* Basingstoke: Palgrave Macmillan.
2009 'J.R.R. Tolkien and 'The Wanderer': From Edition to Application'.

Tolkien Studies. Vol. 6, pp. 189-211.

LEWIS, Clive Staples
2009a *Collected Letters Books, Broadcasts and War, 1931–1949*. Edited by Walter Hooper. London: HarperCollins*Publisher*.
2009b *Collected Letters Volume Three: Narnia, Cambridge and Joy 1950–1963*. Edited by Walter Hooper. London: HarperCollins*Publisher*.

LOBDELL, Jared
1981 *England and Always: Tolkien's World of the Rings*. Grand Rapids: W.B. Eerdmans Pub. Co., 1981.

MANDER, Geoffrey
1949 'Educational work in the British prisoner of war camps in enemy territory'. *Rewley House Papers*, Vol. 2. University of Oxford, pp. 189-191.

MATHEWS, Richard
2002 *Fantasy: The Liberation of Imagination*. Psychology Press (repr.).

MCILWAINE, Chaterine
2018 *Tolkien: Maker of Middle-earth*. Oxford: Bodleian Library.

MILLETT, Bella
1996 *Ancrene Wisse, the Katherine Group, and the Wooing Group*. Vol. 2 of Annotated bibliographies of Old and Middle English literature. Woodbridge: Boydell & Brewer.

MURRAY, James Augustus Henry
1928 *A New English Dictionary on Historical Principles* IX Pt. II'su-Th'. The Philological Society. 'Su-Sz' edited by Charles Talbut Onions and 'T-Th' edited by James A. H. Murray. Oxford: At the Clarendon Press.
1928 *A New English Dictionary on Historical Principles*, Vol. X Pt. II 'V-Z'. The Philological Society. 'V' edited by William A. Craigie; 'W' edited by Charles Talbut Onions and W. A. Craigie; 'X, Y, Z' edited by C. T Onions. Oxford: At the Clarendon Press.

MYTHOPOEIC SOCIETY
1998 Mythopoeic Society, *Parma Eldalamberon* 12: 'Qenyaqetsa: The Qenya Phonology and Lexicon by J.R.R. Tolkien'. Edited by Christopher Gilson, Carl F. Hostetter, Patrick H. Wynne and Arden R. Smith.
2004 Mythopoeic Society, *Parma Eldalamberon* 15:'sí Qente Feanor and

Other Elvish Writings by J.R.R. Tolkien'. Edited by Christopher Gilson, Arden R. Smith, Patrick H. Wynne and Bill Welden.
2009   Mythopoeic Society, *Parma Eldalamberon* 18: 'Tengwesta Qenderinwa and Pre-Fëanorian Alphabets Pt. 2 by J.R.R. Tolkien'. Edited by Christopher Gilson, Arden R. Smith and Patrick H. Wynne.
NELSON, Dale
2004   'Possible Echoes of Blackwood and Dunsany in Tolkien's Fantasy'. *Tolkien Studies*, Vol. 1, pp. 177-181.

OLLSCOIL NA H-ÉIREANN (The National University of Ireland – University of Galway)
1949   *Summer Examinations, 1949 – Pass.* B.A. Degree and B.A. Sussidiary. English, Fourth Paper. Professor J.R.R. Tolkien & Professor Murphy, G 101.
1949   *Summer Examinations, 1949 – Pass.* First University Examination in Arts, Commerce and Science. English, First Paper. Professor J.R.R. Tolkien & Professor Murphy, G 107.
1949   *Autumn Examinations, 1949 – Honours.* B.A. Degree Examination. English, First Paper. Professor J.R.R. Tolkien & Professor Murphy, G 257.
1949   *Autumn Examinations, 1949 – Honours.* B.A. Degree Examination. English, Second Paper. Professor J.R.R. Tolkien & Professor Murphy, G 258.
1949   *Autumn Examinations, 1949 – Honours.* B.A. Degree Examination. English, Third Paper. Professor J.R.R. Tolkien & Professor Murphy, G 259.
1949   *Autumn Examinations, 1949 – Honours.* B.A. Degree Examination. English, Fourth Paper. Professor J.R.R. Tolkien & Professor Murphy, G 260.

PHELPSTEAD, Carl
2011   *Tolkien and Wales: Language, Literature and Identity.* Cardiff: University of Wales Press.

PLIMMER, Charlotte & Denis
1968   'The Man Who Understands Hobbits'. *London Daily Telegraph Magazine*, March 22, pp. 31-32, 35.

PRIESTMAN, Judith
1992   *J.R.R. Tolkien: Life and Legend. An Exhibition to commemorate the Centenary of the Birth of J.R.R. Tolkien (1892 – 1973).* (Catatlogue of the Exhibition to commemorate the Centenary of the Birth of J.R.R. Tolkien, 1892 - 1973). Oxford: Bodleian Library, p. 96.
1994 (Compiled by) A list of the Papers of J.R.R. Tolkien. Oxford: Bodleian Library. Revised (25 April 2016).

POWER, N.S.

1975   'Tolkien's Walk (An unexpected personal link with Tolkien)'. *Mallorn*, 9. Tolkien Society, pp. 16-19.

RATELIFF, John D.
1981   'She and Tolkien'. *Mythlore* 28 (Summer), pp. 6-8.
2005   'Letter'. *Beyond Bree*, no. 4 March.
2012   '*She* and Tolkien, Revisited'. *Tolkien and the Study of His Sources: Critical Essays*. Edited by Jason Fisher. Jerson, North Carolina, and London: McFarland & Company, pp. 145-161.

RED CROSS AND ST. JOHN WAR ORGANISATION – PRISONERS OF WAR DEPARTMENT
1944   *Results of Examinations. Prisoners of war camps. 1st July to 31st December 1943*. New Bodleian Library, p. 34.

RESNIK, Henry
1967   'An Interview with Tolkien'. *Niekas* Issue 18, Late Spring, pp. 37-43. Center Harbour: Niekas Publication.

RHYS ROBERTS, William
1925   'Gerald of Wales on the Survival of Welsh'. *The Transactions of the Honourable Society of Cymmrodorion. Session 1923-24*. Edited by Sir E. Vincent Evans. London: The Honourable Society of Cymmrodorion, pp. 46-60.

RYAN, J. S.
2002   'J.R.R. Tolkien's Formal Lecturing and Teaching at the University of Oxford, 1929-1959'. *SEVEN: An Anglo-American Literary Review*, Vol. 19. Marion E. Wade Center of Wheaton College, pp. 45-62.

SAYER, GEORGE
1988   *Jack. C. S. Lewis and his Time*. London: Macmillan.

SCULL, Christina
1993   Review: 'J.R.R. Tolkien: Life and Legend. An Exhibition to commemorate the Centenary of the Birth of J.R.R. Tolkien (1892 - 1973). Compiled by Dr. Judith Priestman.' *Mallorn*, 30, pp. 50-52.

SCULL, Christina; HAMMOND, G. Wayne
1998   *J.R.R. Tolkien: Artist & Illustrator*. London: HarperCollin*Publisher*.
2006a   *The J.R.R. Tolkien Companion and Guide: Chronology*. London: HarperCollins*Publisher*.
2006b   *The J.R.R. Tolkien Companion and Guide: Reader's Guide*. London:

HarperCollins*Publisher*.
2017a *The J.R.R. Tolkien Companion and Guide: Chronology*. London: HarperCollins*Publisher*.
2017b *The J.R.R. Tolkien Companion and Guide: Reader's Guide I A-M*. London: HarperCollins*Publisher*.
2017c *The J.R.R. Tolkien Companion and Guide: Reader's Guide II N-Z*. London: HarperCollins*Publisher*.

SHIPPEY, Tom
1992 *The Road to Middle-earth*. London: Grafton.
2004 'Light-elves, Dark-elves, and Others: Tolkien's Elvish Problem'. *Tolkien Studies*, Vol. 1, pp. 1-15.
2005 *La Via per la Terra di Mezzo*. Genova-Milano: Marietti *1820*.
2007 'Buchan, John (1875-1940)'. *J.R.R. Tolkien Encyclopedia: Scholarship and Critical Assessment*. Abingdon: Taylor & Francis, pp. 77-8.
2014 *J.R.R. Tolkien: Author of the Century*. Reprint. Boston: Houghton Mifflin Harcourt.

SIMMONET, Olivier
2014 *A la recherche du Hobbit*. Documentary film in 5 parts. Author: Yannis and Alexis Metzinger, Olivier Simonnet, John Howe. CERIGO Films, Arte, WDR and Mirabelle TV.

SMITH, Arden Ray
1989 '23 and 31: Problematic Numbers in Elvish'. Mythopoeic Society, *Parma Eldalamberon* 8. Edited by Christopher Gilson. Berkeley: Elvish Linguistic Fellowship.
2012 Mythopoeic Society, *Parma Eldalamberon* 20. The Mythopoeic Society.

TOLKIEN, John & Priscilla
1992 *The Tolkien Family Album*. London: HarperCollins*Publisher*.

UNIVERSITY OF LEEDS
1920 University of Leeds, *Calendar 1920-21*. Leeds: Jowett & Sowry Ltd.
1921 University of Leeds, *Calendar 1921-22*. Leeds: Jowett & Sowry Ltd.
1922 University of Leeds, *Calendar 1922-23*. Leeds: Jowett & Sowry Ltd.
1924 University of Leeds, *Calendar 1924-25*. Leeds: Jowett & Sowry Ltd.

WATERFIELD, Robin (Edited by)
1980 *Catalogue 40: English Literature*. Oxford: Robin Waterfield Ltd.

WEST, Richard

1981   *Tolkien Criticism: An Annotated Checlist*. The Kent State University Press.

ZETTERSTEN, Arne
2011   *J.R.R. Tolkien's Double Worlds and Creative Process: Language and Life*, Springer.

Web Sources (Accessed January 2019)

ALADICS, Fr. Ricard
Friend with Christ (http://friendswithchrist.blogspot.com/)

BERTENSTAM, Åke
2015   *A Chronological Bibliography of the Writings of J.R.R. Tolkien* (www.forodrim.org/bibliography/tbchron.html)

BODLEIAN LIBRARIES
SOLO   (http://solo.bodleian.ox.ac.uk/primo_library/libweb/action/search.do?vid=OXVU1)
Special Collection J.R.R. Tolkien (www.bodleian.ox.ac.uk/weston/finding-resources/guides/literary)

BODLEIAN LIBRARIES WEBLOG
2017   *A piece of Bodleian History: Clues from the Stacks*. By Whiteg. 21 December.
        (http://blogs.bodleian.ox.ac.uk/oxfordtrainees/2017/12/21/a-piece-of-bodleian-history-clues-from-the-stacks/)

BOSTON COLLEGE
Burns Library (https://library.bc.edu/)

CILLI, Oronzo
Tolkieniano Collection (http://tolkieniano.blogspot.com/)

KEYSER, Madeline J.
2012   *Sixteen Philological Books and Notes from the Library of J.R.R. Tolkien*. TolkienLibrary.com   (http://www.tolkienlibrary.com/press/1066-Sixteen-philological-books-notes-library-of-Tolkien.php#footnotes).

EDEN, Bradford Lee
2015   'Michael H.R. Tolkien (1920-84): a research travelogue'.

Journal of Tolkien Reasearch, Vol. 2, no. 1. (https://scholar.valpo.edu/journaloftolkienresearch/vol2/iss1/7/)

FISHER, Jason

2015   *Scattered leaves* (http://lingwe.blogspot.com/2015/10/scattered-leaves.html)

HUDSON, Anne

2015   'Early English Text Society'. *Early English Text Society. List of publications 2015*. (http://users.ox.ac.uk/~eets/list-of-all publications-2015.pdf)

LIVERPOOL HOPE UNIVERSITY, SPECIAL COLLECTIONS

2017   'Signed Tolkien book discovered in Liverpool Hope Special Collections'. Friday 11 November (www.hope.ac.uk/news/newsitems/signedtolkienbookdiscoveredinliverpoolhopespecialcollections.html)

MARQUETTE UNIVERSITY

J.R.R. Tolkien Collection Manuscripts, circa 1930-1955 printed literature & secondary works, 1910- (http://www.marquette.edu/library/archives/Mss/JRRT/)

SCULL, Christina; HAMMOND, G. Wayne

2018a (5 May) *From Tolkien's Library*, (https://wayneandchristina.wordpress.com/2018/05/05/from-tolkiens-library/)

2018b (16 September) *The J.R.R. Tolkien Companion and Guide: Reader's Guide* I A-M. Addenda & Corrigenda (http://www.hammondandscull.com/addenda/guide_by_date2.html)

TOLKIEN, Michael George Reuel

1989   Lecture on J.R.R. Tolkien given to the University of St. Andrews Science Fiction and Fantasy Society on 2nd May. (http://www.michaeltolkien.com/page74.html)

1995   Autobiographical essay on my grandfather, J.R.R. Tolkien, based on a public talk requested by The Leicester Writers' Club at College of Adult Education, Wellington Street October 19th. (http://www.michaeltolkien.com/page73.html)

TOLKIEN BOOKS

An Illustrated Tolkien Bibliography (www.tolkienbooks.net)

TOLKIEN GATEWAY

List of books in Tolkien's library (http://tolkiengateway.net/wiki/List_of_

books_in_Tolkien's_library)

TOLKIEN LIBRARY
Collecting Tolkien owned books (www.tolkienlibrary.com/reviews/tolkienownedbooks.htm)

TOLKIEN SHOP
Tolkien autographs (www.tolkienshop.com/contents/en-uk/d228.html)

WHEATON CENTER
J.R.R. Tolkien Library (www.wheaton.edu/~/media/Files/Centers-and-Institutes/Wade-Center/RR-Docs/Non-archive-Listings/Tolkien_Library.pdf)

Archival Sources

Azusa Pacific University (Azusa)
Bodleian Library (Oxford)
Boston College (Chestnut Hill)
British Library (London)
Cardiff University Archives
Center Morris Library (Southern Illinois)
Exeter College (Oxford)
Indiana University (Bloomington)
James Joyce Library (University College Dublin)
Jesus College (Oxford)
Liverpool Hope University (Liverpool)
Marion E. Wade Center, Wheaton College (Wheaton, Illinois)
Marquette University (Milwaukee)
Merton College (Oxford)
Morgan Library & Museum (New York)
Oratory of Saint Philip Neri (Birmingham)
Oxford University Press Archives (Oxford)
Taylor Institution Library (Oxford)
Texas A&M University (College Station)
Université de Liège (Liège)
University of St Andrews Library (St Andrews)
Weston Library (Oxford)

Private collections

[I have also consulted online sites of auction houses (Bonhams, Christie's,

Worthpoint, The Saleroom, RR Auction, Dreweatts & Bloomsbury Auctions, Simon Finch, Invaluable), private collections, collectors sites (Tolkien Library, Tolkien Collector's Guide) and rare book dealers, where letters, inscribed copies, and other items by Tolkien are occasionally offered (Loome Theological Booksellers, Thornton's Bookshop, Tolkienshop, The Tolkien Bookshelf, Peter Harrington Rare Books and St Philip's Books).]

[SECTION A]

INDEX OF AUTHORS AND EDITORS

A

Aasen, Ivar Andreas 1
Abbott, Claude Colleer 127
Adalbjarnarson, Bjarni 278, 279
Adamnan, Saint 1
Adams, Joseph Quincy 1
Adington, William 6
Adshead, Gladys L. 1
Ælfric, Abbot of Eynsham 1, 2
Aeschylus 2, 3, 82, 270
Aflalo, Frederick George 232
Ahlqvist, August 3
Albrecht, William Price 3
Alighieri, Dante 3, 4
Allen, Hope Emily 5
Alois, Brandl 5
Ammianus, Marcellinus 5
Amours, François Joseph 5
Anderson, John George Clark 285
Andler, Charles 6
Andrews, Albert Le Roy 6
Anwyl, Edward 6
Appel, Carl 6
Appelöf, Jakob Johan Adolf 6
Apuleius 6
Arber, Edward 6, 7, 221, 238, 295
Aristophanes 7
Armstrong, Edward Cooke 7
Arngrimur Jónsson 7
Arnold, Ivor 300
Arnold, Thomas 74
Ascham, Roger 7
Ásmundarson, Valdimar 7, 8, 9
Asser, John 9
Assmann, Bruno 9
Auden, Wystan Hugh 9, 10, 286
Auerbach, Erich 10
Augustine, Saint 10
Aulnoy, Madame d' 10
Austin, Thomas 10
Avicenna 10, 50

B

Bach, Adolf 11
Bach, Herbert Ernest 11
Bacon, Francis 11
Baillie-Grohman, William Adolph 11
Baist, Gottfried 11
Baker, Augustine 11
Baker, George P. 12
Banks, Mary Macleod 12
Barbier, Paul 12
Barbour, John 12

Barfield, Owen 13
Barners, Juliana 13
Barnes, William 236
Barrie, James Matthew 13
Barth, Karl 14
Baskervill, William Malone 14
Bateson, H. 14
Bauer, Harry C. 14
Baynes, Thomas Spencer 14
Beaumont, Francis 14
Bede, the Venerable Saint 15
Beerbhon, Max 165
Belfour, Algernon Ikey 16
Bell, Charles 16
Belloc, Hilaire 16
Bellows, Henry Adams 16
Benedict, Saint 16
Benediktsson, Jakob 7
Bennett, Francis 222
Bennett, Jack Arthur Walter 17
Benson, Larry Dean 17
Bentcliffe, Eric 17
Benz, Richard 17
Bergen, Henry 175, 176
Bergin, Osborn Joseph 17
Bernardi, Theodor von 18
Berry, Francis 119
Berry, Wendell 18
Bertelsen, Henrik 18
Best, Richard Irvine 18
Bethge, Richard 70
Bethmann, Ludvig Konrad 231
Beveridge, Erskine 18
Bignon, Jean-Paul 188
Binz, Gustav 18
Birch, Walter de Gray 19
Birney, Earle 19
Bishop, Edmund 93
Bishop, Ian 19, 344, 440
Bjarnarson, Birkir 20
Björkman, Erik 20
Blackburn, Francis Adalbert 20
Blackwood, Algernon 21
Blades, William 13
Blakeley, Lesley 21
Blake, William 21
Blanch, Robert J. 22
Bliss, Alan J. 22
Blöndal, Sigfús 22
Bloomfield, Morton Wilfred 22
Blümel, Rudolf 22
Boas, Frederick Samuel 159, 160
Boccaccio, Giovanni 22

386

Böddeker, Karl 22
Bodley, John Eduard Courtenay 23
Bodmer, Frederick 23
Boer, Richard Constant 23
Boethius 23, 147, 419, 425
Bohnenberger, Karl 23
Boileau Despréaux, Nicolas 23
Bolingbroke, Henry Saint-John 23
Bonjour, Adrien 23, 24
Bonner, Arthur 102
Boorde, Andrew 24
Borgström, Edward 24
Borowski, Bruno 24
Borroff, Marie 24
Boswell, James 24, 25
Bosworth, Joseph 25, 228
Bouterwek, Heinrich 25
Bouterwek, Karl Wilhelm 25, 26
Bowcock, Elijah Wood 26
Bowra, Cecile Maurice 121
Boynton, Henry Walcott 236
Bradley, Andrew Cecil 26
Bradley, George Granville 26
Bradley, Henry 26, 214, 215, 218, 219
Brady, Caroline 27
Bramley, Henry Ramsden 27, 246
Brandl, Alois 27
Brate, Erik 27
Braune, Wilhelm 27
Brehier, Louis 27
Bremer, Otto 27, 70
Brett, Cyril 27, 28
Breuer, Hermann 28, 279
Brewer, John S. 96
Brewster, William Tenney 28
Briant, Keith 309
Bright, James Wilson 28
Bright, Mynors 232, 233
Brock, Edmund 28, 91, 211
Bromwich, Rachel 29
Brooke, Rupert 29
Brook, George Leslie 29, 159
Brooks, Harold. F. 29
Brooks, Kenneth Robert 29
Brown, Arthur C. 29, 30
Brown, Carleton 30
Browne, Thomas 30, 31
Browne, William Hand 31
Browning, Robert 31
Brown, Ursula 31
Bruce, Douglas, J. 31, 32
Brugmann, Karl 32, 33
Brunner, Karl 261
Buchan, John 33, 34
Buchanan, Milton A. 193
Buckhurst, Helen T. MacMillan 34, 168
Buckingham, George Villiers, Duke of 34
Budge, E. A. T. Wallis 34, 35
Buga, Kazimieras 35
Bugge, Sophus 35
Bülbring, Karl Daniel 35
Bullen, Arthur Henry 6

Bulwer-Lytton, Edward 35
Bunyan, John 36
Burchfield, Robert William 36, 218, 219, 228
Burke, Edmund 36
Burkitt, Miles Crawford 36
Burnet, Gilbert 36
Burnham, Josephine May 37
Burrow, John Anthony 37
Burton, Robert 37
Butcher, Samuel Henry 37
Butler, Florence Ruth 37
Butler, Samuel 37
Byrne, Evelyn B. 37

C

Cabrol, Fernand 37
Cædmon 25, 26, 38, 84, 98, 104, 290
Caesar, Julius 38
Calder, George 38, 178
Callaway, Canon [Henry] 38
Campbell, Alistair 38
Campbell, Joseph Francis 38, 39
Campbell, Killis 39
Campbell, Roy 39
Campbell, Thomas 39
Campbell, William Edward 199, 249
Capes, William Wolfe 39
Capgrave, John 40
Cardonne, Denis-Dominique 188
Carducci, Giosué 40
Carlyle, Alexander James 40
Carlyle, Robert Warrand 40
Carlyle, Thomas 40
Carmichael, Alexander 40
Carroll, Lewis 41
Carryl, Edward Charles 41
Cartellieri, Alexander 41
Casson, Leslie Frank 41
Castrén, Matthias Alexander 42
Cato, Dionysius 42
Cawley, Arthur C. 42, 193
Caxton, William 42
Cazotte, M. 191
Cecil, David 42
Chadwick, Hector Munro 42
Chadwick, Nora Kershaw 43
Chambers, Edmund Kerchever 43, 73
Chambers, Raymond Wilson 43, 44, 196, 277, 322
Chambers, Robert 44, 45
Chant, Joy (E. J. Rutter) 45
Chapman, Coolidge Otis 45
Chapman, George 126
Chapman, Robert William 25
Chase, Stanley Perkins 45
Chaucer, Geoffrey 45, 46, 47, 48, 49, 50, 51, 52, 53
Chesterton, Gilbert Keith 54, 55
Child, Francis James 55, 56, 68, 245
Chrétien de Troyes 56, 57, 170, 307
Christie, Agatha 57
Christie, William Dougal 74
Christopher, John 57

Cibber, Colley 57
Cicero, Marcus Tullius 57
Clarendon, Edward Hyde 57
Clark, Cecily 57
Clark-Hall, John R. 17, 142, 275
Classen, Ernest 57
Clawson, William Hall 58, 245
Cleasby, Richard 325
Clemoes, Peter 1
Clutton-Brock, Arthur 58
Cockayne, Thomas Oswald 58, 92, 167
Coghill, Nevil 49, 50
Colborn, A. F. 59, 249
Coleridge, Ernest Hartley 59
Coleridge, Samuel Taylor 59, 316
Colgrave, Bertram 86
Collingwood, Robin George 59
Collins, William 59
Collitz, Hermann 59
Colvin, Sidney 59
Compton-Ricket, Arthur 60
Conan Doyle, Arthur 60
Congreve, William 60
Conway, Robert Seymour 60
Conybeare, John Josias 60
Cook, Albert Stanborough 60, 61
Corelli, Marie 61
Cosijn, Pieter Jacob 61
Cotgrave, Rande 61
Coulton, George Gordon 61, 62
Courthorpe, William John 62
Coverdale, Miles 62
Coward, Thomas Alfred 63
Cowley, Abraham 63
Cowling, Harry Walter 52
Cowper, William 63
Cox, Marian Roalfe 63
Coypel, Charles-Antoine 190
Craigie, William Alexander 63, 109, 214, 215, 216, 218, 219
Crawford, Osbert Guy Stanhope 242
Crawford, Samuel Johnson 2
Crockett, Samuel Rutherford 63
Croker, Bithia Mary 64
Crombie, Max 64
Crossley-Holland, Kevin 64
Culley, Matthew Tewart 42
Cynewulf 49, 63, 64, 205, 240, 263, 281

D

d'Alòs-Moner, Ramon 64
D'Ancona, Alessandro 64
d'Arbois de Jubainville, Henry 64, 65
D'Arcy, Martin Cyril 65
d'Ardenne, S. R. T. O. 65, 66
d'Ardenne, Simonne 249
d'Entréves, Alessandro Passerin 66
D'Evelyn, Charlotte 66
d'Ussieux, Louis 191
Dal, Ingerid 66
Dalton, Ormonde Maddock 66, 106
Daniel, William 60

Dares Phrygius 67
Darmesteter, Arséne 67
Dasent, George Webbe 67, 271
Davis, Gilbert A. 270
Davis, Henry William Carless 67
Davis, Norman 14
Dawson, Christopher 67
Day, Mabel 67, 98, 99
de Camp, Lyon Sprague 68
De la Mare, Walter 68
de la Villemarqué, H. 286
de Moncrif, M. 190
de Saint-Amand, Imbert 68
de Saint-Hyacinthe, Thémiseul 189
De Wolfe Howe, Mary Anthony 224
Defoe, Daniel 68
Deibel, Otto 268
Dekker, Thomas 68
Demosthenes 68, 429
Deneke, Helena Clara 68
Denham, Michael Aislabie 69
Denham Rouse, William Henry 229
Deulin, Charles 69
Dewing, Henry Bronson 237
Dibelius, Wilhelm 69
Dickens, Charles 70
Dictys Cretensins 70
Diefenbach, Lorenz 70
Dieter, Ferdinand 70
Dietrich, Franz Eduard 70
Dillon, Myles 70
Dinneen, Patrick Stephen 71
Diodorus, Siculus 71
Dixon, Richard Watson 71, 72, 127
Dobbie, Elliott van Kirk 63, 69, 147, 246, 254, 272, 302, 309
Dobson, Eric John 66, 72
Donald, Alexander Karley 133
Donaldson, David 110, 111, 243
Donne, John 72
Dottin, Georges 73
Douglas, Gavin 298
Doutrepont, Auguste 73
Dowden, Edward 73
Draak, Maartje 73
Drayton, Michael 74
Drennan, Charles Maxwell 46
Dreyden, Alice 74
Dryden, Henry Edward Leigh 74
Dryden, John 74, 75
Du Bellay, Joachim 75
Duff, Annis 1
Duff, James D. 139
Dumas, Alexander 75
Du Méril, Édélestand Pontas 75
Dunne, John William 75, 76
Dunn, C. W. 94
Dunn, Joseph 76
Dunsany, Lord (E. J. M. D. Plunkett) 76
Düringer, Hermann 128
Duval, Amaury 76
Dyche, Lewis Lindsay 76

E

Earle, John 76, 77
Eddison, Eric Rücker 78
Edeyrn, Davod Aur 78
Edwards, John Morgan 78, 79
Edwards, Owen M. 244
Edwards, Thomas 79
Edwyn, Bevan 106
Egerton, Alix 48
Egilsson, Sveinbjörn 79, 278
Einenkel, Eugen 79
Ekman, Robert Wilhelm 170
Ekwall, Eilert 79, 80
Eliot, Charles Norton Edgecumbe 80
Elliott, Ralph Warren Victor 80
Ellis, Alexander John 80, 81
Ellis, Thomas Peter 81
Elton, Oliver 249
Emerson, Oliver Farrar 81
Endter, Wilhelm 81
England, George 81
English Association 82
Enlart, Camille 82
Erhardt-Siebold, Erika von 82
Ernault, Emilie 65, 82
Ernshaw, Anthony 287
Euripides 3, 82, 270, 406, 412
Evan, Thomas 79
Evans, Daniel Silvan 83
Evans, Joan 83
Evans, John Gwenogvryn 83, 84, 221, 242
Evans, Sebastian 84
Evans-Wentz, Walter Yeeling 84
Ewald, Alexander Charles 60
Ewert, Alfred 84

F

Falconer, John A. 85
Falk, Hjalmar 85, 259
Faral, Edmond 85, 222
Farrow, John 85
Fauriel, Claude Charles 85
Fehr, Bernhard 85
Feist, Sigmund 85, 86
Felix of Crowland 86
Ferri, Ferruccio 86
Feuillerat, Albert 260
Fiedler, Hermann George 87
Fielding, Henry 87
Finch, Rowland George 87
Findlater, Andrew 87
Firth, Charles Harding 74, 87
Fisher, Herbert Albert Laurens 87
Fletcher, Jefferson Butler 87
Fletcher, John 14
Flom, George T. 87
Fogg, Harry George Witham 142
Foncieux, Georges 87
Foote, Peter Godfrey 88
Forbes, Alexander Robert 88
Forbes, William Henry 291

Forchhammer, Jörgen 88
Forshall, Josiah 322, 323
Förstemann, Ernst Wilhelm 88
Förster, Max 88, 89
Fountaine, Andrew 120, 121
Fowler, Alastair 89
Fowler, Francis George 90
Fowler, Henry Watson 89, 90
Fowler, Joseph Thomas 1, 90
Fox, Adam 90
Franck, Johannes 90
Freston, Hugh Reginald 90
Friedrich, Johannes 90
Friedwagner, Mathias 90
Fry, Donald 91
Fryske Akademy 38
Fuller, Thomas 91
Funke, Otto 91
Furneaux, Henry 285
Furnivall, Frederick James 24, 40, 42, 45, 48, 49, 51, 91, 92, 114, 115, 150, 157, 172, 182, 221, 233
Furuskog, Ragnar 92

G

Galland, M. 187, 188
Gamillscheg, Ernst 92
Ganz, Peter Felix 224
Gard, Joyce 92
Gardner, Edmund 106
Gardner, Helen 92, 276
Garner, Alan 92
Garrett, Robert Max 92
Gasquet, Francis Aidan (Abbot) 93, 211
Gaston Paris, Bruno Paulin 93
Gay, John 93
Gebhardt, August 289
Gelzer, Heinrich 93
Geoffrey of Monmouth, Bishop of St Asaph 93, 94
Geoghegan, Joseph B. 94
Gepp, Edward 94
Gerbert, de Montreuil 94
Gering, Hugo 94, 121, 261
Gerrod, H. W. 94
Gessler, Jean 95
Gibb, Jocelyn 95
Gibbon, Edward 95, 96
Gibbs, Henry H. 96
Gildas 96
Giles, John A. 93
Gilson, Julius Parnell 96
Giovene, Andrea 96
Giraldus, Cambrensis 96
Girvan, Ritchie 97
Gislason, Konrad 97
Goates, Margery 97
Goethe, Johann Wolfgang von 97
Goffin, Raymond Cullis 53
Golding, Arthur 229
Golding, William 97
Goldsmith, Oliver 97
Goldthorpe, John 97

INDEX

Gollancz, Israel 98, 99, 100, 204, 205
Golther, Wolfgang 100
Gonçalves Viana, Aniceto dos Reis 100
Goodwin, Charles Wycliffe 86
Goodwin, Edmund 198
Goolden, Peter 100
Gordon, Eric Valentine 14, 100, 101, 259, 294, 295
Gordon, George Stuart 101, 256, 257
Gordon, Ida L. 101
Gordon, Robert Kay 101
Gottfried, von Strassburg 101
Götze, Alfred 101
Gough, Alfred Bradly 271
Gover, John Eric Bruce 101, 102
Gower, John 102
Gow, James 103
Graetz, Heinrich 103
Graf, Leopold 103
Grahame, Kenneth 103
Grammont, Maurice 104
Grandgent, Charles H. 177
Grant, David 104
Grattan, John Henry Grafton 104
Gray, Thomas 104
Graz, Friedrich 104
Great Britain Royal Commission on Historical Manuscripts 105
Green, Arthur Robert 105
Green, John Richard 105
Green, Robert 225
Green, Roger Lancelyn 105
Greene, Walter Kirkland 105
Greenhill, William Alexander 31
Greenhough, James Bradstreet 38
Gregory of Tours 106
Gregory, Pope 106
Grein, Christian Wilhelm Michael 17, 106, 107
Grierson, Herbert John Clifford 72, 73
Griffith Hartwell Jones 313
Grigson, Geoffrey 107
Grimald, Nicholas 295
Grimm, Jacob Ludwig 107, 108, 114, 286
Griscom, Acton 94
Gröber, Gustav 108, 109
Grote, George 109
Groth, Ernst Johann 109
Grundtvig, Nicolai Frederik Severin 109
Gualteruzzi, Carlo 109
Guðrundsson, Einar 109
Guest (Lady), Charlotte 110
Gueulette, M. 189
Guido delle Colonne 110, 111
Gummere, Francis Barton 111
Güntert, Hermann 111
Gurrey, P. 104
Güterbock, Bruno G. 111
Gutheil, Heinrich 111

H

Haggard, H. Rider 111, 112
Hahn, Johann Georg von 112

Haigh, Walter Edward 112
Hakluyt, Richard 112
Haldane, John Burdon Sanderson 113
Hale, Will T. 197
Hales, John Wesley 233
Hall, Fitzedward 176
Hall, John R. Clark 113, 114
Hall, Joseph 114, 159, 197
Halliwell-Phillipps, James Orchard 113, 261, 320
Hamilton, George Livingstone 114
Hampson, Robert Thomas 228
Hancke, Verner 142
Harbour, Jennie 114
Hardie, Colin 114
Hardwick, Carles 115
Hardy, James 69
Hargrove, Henry Lee 10
Harnelius, H. 100, 182
Harmer, Florence Elizabeth 57, 115
Harper, Carrie A. 115
Harris, Joel Chandler 115
Harrison, William 115, 315
Harsley, Fred 115
Harte, Bret 115
Hart, Elizabeth M. 115
Hartland, Edwin Sidney 115
Hartmann, Friedrich 70
Hartmann, von Aue 115
Hassall, Arthur 23
Hauser, Otto 116
Hawks, Ellison 116
Hayashi, Shigeru 116
Hayens, Herbert 116
Hazlitt, Carew William 153
Hecht, Hans 116
Heinrich, von dem Türlin 117
Heinzel, Otto 117
Heinzel, Richard 117
Helgason, Jón 117
Helten, Willem Lodewijk van 117
Hempel, Heinrich 117
Henderson, George 117
Henry, Francoise 117
Henry VIII 71, 118, 256, 274
Herbert, Frank 118
Herbert, James 118
Herbert, John Alexander 118, 119
Herford, Charles Harold 272
Hermann, Eduard 223
Hermannsson, Halldór 118
Herrick, Robert 118, 119
Herrtage, Sidney John Hervon 119
Herzfeld, George 119
Hessels, John Henry 120
Heusler, Andreas 120
Heyne, Moritz 120
Hewens, Brian Donald 227
Hichens, Jacobine Napier 120
Hickes, George 120, 121
Higham, T. F. 121
Highfield, John Roger Loxdale 121
Hildebert of Lavardin 121

390

Hildebrand, Karl 121
Hill, George Francis 106
Hill, John 121
Hill, Raymond Thompson 121, 122
Hillmann, (Sister) Mary Vincent 122
Hingeston, Francis Charles 40
Hirt, Hermann Alfred 122, 123
Hobbes, Thomas 123
Hobhouse, Leonard Trelawny 123
Hodgkin, Robert Howard 123
Hodgson, Phyllis 230
Hoffmann-Krayer, Eduard 123
Hoffmann, Johannes Baptista 90
Hoffman, Richard L. 123
Hogan, Jeremiah Joseph 123
Hogben, Lancelot 23
Holcot, Robertus 124
Holder, Alfred Theophil 124, 249
Holland, Philemon 5
Hollingshead, John 124
Holmqvist, Erik 124
Holthausen, Ferdinand 64, 116, 124, 125
Homer 67, 126, 209, 319
Hooker, Richard 126
Hooper, Walter 164
Hoops, Johannes 126, 127, 251
Hopkins, Gerard Manley 127
Horace xiii, 127, 236, 286
Horn, Wilhelm 90, 111, 127, 128
Horstmann, Carl 12, 40, 128, 129
Howard, Henry 295
Howard, Robert E. 129
How, Ruth W. 129, 130
Hübner, Ernst Willibald Emil 130
Huchon, René 130
Hughes, Arthur Montague d'Urban 101, 130
Hugo, Victor 130
Hulbert, James R. 130
Humbert, Agnes 130
Hunt, Marguerite 108
Huon de Rotelande 130
Hutchinson, Thomas 130
Huxley, Aldous 131
Huxley, Thomas Henry 131
Hwon Holy 131

I

Imelmann, Rudolf 131
Innes, Arthur Donald 258
Innocent III, Pope 131
Irving, Edward Burroughs 131
Isidore of Seville, Saint 131
Ivy, Robert H. 56

J

Jackson, Issac 131
Jacob, Henry 132
Jacobs, Joseph 131, 132, 240
Jacobsohn, Hermann 132
Jacobus de Voragine 132
Jagger, Hubert 132

Jakobsen, Jakob 132
James, Montague Rhodes 132
Jamieson, Robert 132
Jean, d'Arras 133
Jean de Flagy 133
Jeanroy, Alfred 133
Jebb, Richard Claverhouse 270
Jenkins, T. Atkinson, 223
Jenks, Edward 133
Jennings, Elizabeth 133
Jespersen, Otto 133
Jessopp, Augustus 91
Joad, Cyril Edwin Mitchinson 134
Jocelin, de Brakelond 134
Jóhannesson, Jón 134
Johns, Charles Alexander 134
Johnson, Edwin 298
Johnson, Henry 116
Johnson, Samuel 134, 135
Johnston, Edward 135
Johnston, George Burke 135
Jonckbloet, Willem Jozef Andries 135
Jones, Alexander 135
Jones, Edmund 135
Jones, Gwyn 135, 136
Jones, John 165, 169
Jones, Owen 136
Jones, Thomas 136
Jonson, Ben 136
Jónsson, Finnur 79, 136, 137, 278
Jónsson, Guðni 137, 138
Jónsson, Runólfur 121
Jónsson, Þorleifr 138
Jordan, Richard 138
Joseph, Bertram Leon 138
Joyce, James 138
Jung, Carl Gustav 138
Jusserand, Jean Jules 139
Juvenal 139

K

Kane, Elisha Kent 139
Karg-Gasterstädt, Elisabeth 198
Karl, Warnke 183
Karsten, Torsten Evert 139
Karstien, Carl 139
Kasmann, Hans 139
Kauffmann, Friedrich 140
Keats, John 140
Keightley, Thomas 140
Keller, Gottfried 140
Keller, Wolfgang 140
Kelly, Francis Michael 140
Kemble, John Mitchell 140, 141
Kendrick, Thomas Downing 141
Kennedy, Benjamin Hall 2
Kennedy, Charles W. 141
Kennedy, Horace M. 286
Ker, Neil Ripley 141, 249
Ker, William Paton 141, 142, 221
Keynes, Geoffrey 31

INDEX

Kiaer, Egil 142
Kidd, Mary Maytham 142
Kilby, Clyde 142
Kingsley, Mary H. 142
Kington-Oliphant, Thomas Laurence 142, 143
Kipling, Rudyard 143
Kirby, Thomas Austin 192
Kirby, William Forsell 143
Kircher, Athanasius 143
Kirk, Robert 144
Kirtlan, Ernest J. B. 144
Kitchin, George William 271
Kittredge, George Lyman 144
Klaeber, Frederick 17, 144, 145
Kluge, Friedrich 145
Knatchbull-Hugessen, Edward H. 145
Knatchbull-Hugessen, Reginald 145
Kneen, John Joseph 145
Knigge, Friedrich 146
Knight, Damon 146
Knott, Thomas A. 146
Koenders, J. A.-G. 146
Kölbing, Eugen 130, 146
Köler, Johann Jakob 106
Konrad, von Würzburg 146
Kottler, Barnet 146
Krapp, George Philip 63, 69, 146, 147, 246, 254, 272, 302, 309
Kraufe, Wolfgang 147
Kretschmer, Paul 147
Kroesch, Samuel 147
Kruisinga, Etsko 147, 148
Kurath, Hans 148
Kurschat, Friedrich 148
Kurvinen, Auvo 148, 149
Kyd, Thomas 224, 225

L

La Villemarqué (Hersart de), Theodoré Claude Henri 149
Laborde, Edward Dalrymple 14, 149
Labriolle, Pierre Champagne de 149
Ladd, Charles Anthony 149
Laing, Samuel 278
Lamb, Charles 150
Laneham, Robert 60, 150
Lang, Andrew 6, 63, 69, 108, 114, 123, 139, 144, 146, 150, 151, 152, 153, 181, 233, 234, 240, 285, 286
Lang, David 153, 154
Lang, Leonora Blanche 154
Langebek, Jacob 154
Langland, William 154, 155, 156
Lanier, Sterling E. 157
Lascelles, Mary 157
Lattey, Cuthbert 157
Lauder, William 157
Lawrence, William Witherle 158
Layamon 119, 158, 159, 206, 218, 244, 324
Le Marchand, Françoise 188
Least, Werner 159
Lecky, William Edward Haitpole 159
Leeds, Edward Thurlow 160

Lee, Charles 165
Lee, Sidney 159, 160
Legrand d'Aussy, Pierre Jean-Baptiste 160
Lempriére, John 160
Leonhardi, Günther 160, 161
Leprince de Beaumont, Jeanne-Marie 161, 190
Leskien, August 161
Leslie, Roy Francis 159
Leslie, Shane 161
Lessing, Gotthold Ephrain 161, 162
Levens, Peter 162
Lewis, Clive Staples 162, 163, 164, 165
Lewis, D. B. Wyndham 165
Lewis, Glyn Cothi 165
Lewis, Harry Sinclair 166
Lewis, Matthew Gregory 166
Lewis, Timothy 166
Lewis, Warren Hamilton 166
Lexer, Matthias 166, 167
Leyerle, John 167
Liebermann, Felix 167
Liljegren, Sten Bodvar 168
Lindelöf, Uno Lorenz 168
Lindsay, David 168
Lindsay, Wallace Martin 168
Lindsay, William Martin 131
Linnilä, Kai 170
Lisle, William 2
Livingstone, David 168
Livingston, Margaret Vere 169
Lloyd, John 81
Loewe, Richard 169
Lofting, Hugh 169, 170
Longfellow, Henry Wadsworth 170
Longinus 170
Lönnrot, Elias 170
Loomis, Roger Sherman 170, 171
Lorenz, Konrad 171
Lot, Ferdinand 171
Loth, Joseph Marie 171, 230
Lounsbury, Thomas R. 172
Lovelich, Herry 172
Lubovius, Louis 172
Ludwig, Levin 120
Luick, Karl 172, 173
Lumby, Joseph Rawson 142, 173, 174, 175, 235
Lydgate, John 175, 176
Lye, Eduardo 176
Lyly, John 176, 225
Lyndesay, David 176
Lyngbye, Hans Christian 176
Lyons, Albert Neil 176

M

Macaulay, George Campbell 102
Macaulay, Thomas Babington 177
Macbain, Alexander 177
MacCracken, Henry Noble 177
MacDermott, Máire 117
MacDonald, Alexander 177
MacDonald, George 177, 178

MacDougall, James 178
Maceachen, Ewan 178
MacFarlane, Malcom 179
MacFayden, John 179
Mackail, John William 179, 298
Mackenzie, Barbara Alida 180
Mack, Frances May 179
Macleod, Fiona 180
Macray, William Dunn 57
Madden, Frederic 158, 180, 322, 323
Madeleva, Mary (Sister) 180
Maeterlinck, Maurice 180
Magner, James Edmund, Jr. 180
Magnússon, Eiríkr 207, 208
Malone, Kemp 180, 181
Malory, Thomas 181, 211
Manchon, Joseph 182
Mandeville, John 182
Mannying, Robert 182
Mansfield, Robert Blachford 182
Mansion, Joseph 183
Manzalaoui, Mahmoud 183
Mapes, Walter 68, 183
Marie de France 183, 184
Maritain, Jacques 184
Marlowe, Christopher 184
Marsh, Edward Howard 184
Marstrander, Carl Johan Sverdrup 184
Martin, Francis Xavier 305
Marvell, Andrew 184
Masefield, John 184
Maskell, William 185
Mason, William Shaw 185
Massingham, Harold John 185
Matthey, John 258
Matthes, Henrich Christoph 185
Matthew, Arnold 185
Mätzner, Eduard 18, 185
Mawer, Allen 102, 185, 186
Mayer, Charles-Joseph 186, 187, 188, 189, 190, 191
Mayhew, Anthony Lawson 191, 271
Maynader, Howard 192
McCallum, Ronald Buchanan 192
McCann, Justine 11
McIntosh, Angus 192
McLaughlin, John C. 192
McManaway, James Gilmer 1
McNeill, George P. 288
Meissner, Albert L. 192
Melander, Johan 168
Mellersh, Harold Edward Leslie 192
Menner, Robert James 192, 193
Méon, Dominique Martin 193
Meriton, George 193
Merz, John Theodore 193
Mesqua, Mari de 193
Messenius, Johannis 193
Metcalfe, William Musham 194
Meyer, Kuno 194, 195
Meyer-Lübke, Wilhelm 195
Meynell, Everard 195
Michel, Francisque 195

Mierow, Charles Christopher 195
Migliorini, Bruno 195
Migne, Jacques-Paul 195
Miller, Thomas 15
Mills, Stella Marie 196
Milne, Alan Alexander 196
Milton, John 196, 197
Minot, Laurence 197
Mirk, John 197
Mitchell, Bruce 197
Mitchison, Naomi 197
Mogk, Eugen 198
Molee, Elias 198
Mollegen Smith, Anne 198
Momigliano, Attilio 4
Mommsen, Theodor 198
Moore, Arthur William 198
Moore, Samuel 198
Moorman, Frederic William 118, 198
More, Thomas (Saint) 199
Morell, Charles 190
Morey, Adrian 199
Morgan, Roscoe 57
Morgan, William 199
Morlini, Girolamo 199
Morral, John B. 305
Morris, May 206, 207, 208
Morris, Richard 17, 18, 22, 52, 64, 131, 142, 150, 157, 199, 200, 201, 202, 203, 204, 205, 206, 211, 226, 228, 237, 245, 249
Morris, William 206, 207, 208, 209
Morris-Jones, John 210
Morrison, Sophia 198
Morsbach, Lorenz 210
Morse, Jedidiah 210
Morton, James 211
Mroczkowski, Przemysław 211
Mühlhausen, Ludwig 211
Müllenhoff, Karl 211, 212
Müller, Friedrich Max 212
Müller, Peter Erasmus 176, 249
Munch, Peter Andreas 212
Mure, Geoffrey Reginald Gilchrist 213
Mürkens, Gerhard Hieronymus 213
Murray, Gilbert 83
Murray, James Augustus Henry 213, 214, 215, 216, 217, 218, 219
Mustanoja, Tauno F. 219
Myres, John Nowell Linton 59

N

Nansen, Fridtjof 219
Napier, Arthur Sampson 89, 220, 221
Nash, Thomas 221
Naunton, Robert 221
Neckel, Gustav 221
Neilson, William Allan 221
Nelson, William 221
Nennius 89, 222
Nerman, Birger 222
Newby, Percy Howard 222

Newell, Peter 222
Newman, Ernest 222
Newman, John Henry 223
Newmark, Leonard 22
Niedermann, Max 223
Nitze, William Albert 223
Noel, Roden 229
Nordal, Sigurður 223, 279
Noreen, Adolf Gotthard 223, 224
Norman, Friederick 224
Northall, G. F. 224
Norton, Charles Eliot 224
Norton, Mary 224
Norton, Sara 224
Norton, Thomas 224, 225
Nutt, Alfred Trübner 110

O

Oakden, James Parker 225
O'Domhnuill, Huilliam 225
Oesterley, William Oscar Emil 226
Offord, Marguerite Yvonne 226
Öfverberg, William 226
Ogden, Margaret 226
O'Growney, Eugene 225
O'Keeffe, James George 225
Olrik, Axe 226
Ólsen, Björn Magnússon 226
Olsen, Magnus 35
Oman, Charles Williams Chadwick 226
O'Neill, Joseph 225
Onions, Charles Talbut 160, 216, 218, 219, 227, 228, 230
Orlowski, Boleslaw Kamil 228
Orosius, Paulus Alfred 228
Orton, Harold 229
Osgood, Charles Grosvenor 229
Osthoff, Hermann 32
Osterley, Hermann 229
Otway, Thomas 229
Ovid 229
Owen, Dora 229
Owen, Edward 229

P

Paget, Richard 230
Palgrave, Francis Turner 230
Paley, Frederick Apthorp 68
Palmer, Harold Edward 230
Panton, George A. 110, 111, 243
Panzer, Friedrich Whilelm 230, 307
Paradis de Moncrif, François-Augustin 189
Paris, Gaston 230, 231
Paris, Paulin 133, 244
Parthey, Gustav 235
Partridge, Eric 231
Patmore, Coventry 231
Paton, Lucy Allen 94
Paul, Hermann 231
Paul the Apostle 231
Paul the Deacon 231
Pauphilet, Albert 231

Payne, Edward John 112
Peacock, Edward 197
Peacock, William 231
Pedersen, Holger 232
Peek, Hedley 232
Peele, George 224, 225
Pennant, Thomas 232
Pennock, South Helen 232
Penzler, Otto 37
Pepys, Samuel 232, 233
Percy, Thomas 233, 245
Perrault, Charles 233
Perry, George Gresley 234
Perry, Thomas Sergeant 234
Persson, Per 234
Petis de La Croix, M. 188
Phaedrus 234
Phebus, Gaston 234
Philipp, Colin 315
Phillips, Hubert 234
Pierquin, Hubert 234
Pinder, Moritz 235
Plancé, James Robinson 235
Plowman, Piers 235, 242
Plummer, Charles 15, 77
Pokorny, Julius 235
Pollard, Albert Frederick 235
Pollard, Alfred William 46, 50, 81, 235
Pons, Emilie 236
Poole, Austin Lane 236
Poole, Jacob 236
Pope, Alexander 126, 236
Potter, Beatrix 236, 237
Powell, Davidis 96
Powell, Edgar 237
Powell, Frederick York 249
Prellwitz, Walther 237
Pritchard, Mabel Henrietta 37
Procopius 237
Proudfit, S. V. 237
Pucci, Antonio 237
Pughe, William Owen 135, 136

Q

Quiller-Couch, Arthur Thomas 237

R

Radin, Paul 297
Raffel, Burton 237
Raith, Joseph 238
Rajna, Pio 238
Raleigh, Walter Alexander 160, 197, 238, 239, 249
Ranisch, Wilhelm 120, 239
Ransome, Arthur 239
Raspe, Rudolph Erich 239
Ray, John 239
Ready, William Bernard 240
Reddaway, William Fiddian 177
Reed, Arthur William 199
Reeves, James 1, 240
Reichardt, Konrad 240

Reid, Duncan 240
Reitz, Johann Ernst 241
Renault, Mary 241
Rhys, Ernest 241
Rhys, John 210, 241, 242, 254
Richardson, Octavia 42
Richardson, S. 242
Richmond, Ian Archibald 242
Richthofen, Karl Otto Johannes Theresius freiherr von 242
Rickert, Edith 243
Ridler, Anne 311
Rieger, Max 243
Rietz, Johan Ernst 243
Rieu, Emilie Victor 243
Ritson, Joseph 243
Ritter, Otto 243
Roach, William 56
Robbins, Rossell Hope 243
Robert, de Boron 244
Robert of Gloucester 243
Robertson, Jean 245
Robertson Nicoll, William 245
Roberts, Ruby 244
Roberts, Samuel 244
Robinson, Fred Norris 53
Robinson, John. A. T. 245
Robinson, William Heath 245
Robson, John 245
Roger, John Lewis 245
Roget, Peter Mark 245
Rolle, Richard of Hampole 27, 245, 246
Rook, Alan 246
Ros, Amanda McKittrick 246
Ruskin, John 246
Rypins, Stanley 246

S

Sackville Dorset, Thomas 224, 225
Sæmundsson, Sjéra Tómas 246
Saha, Arthur W. 315
Saintsbury, George Edward Bateman 74, 240, 246, 247
Salesbury, William 247
Salter, Frederick Millet 71
Salu, Mary 247
Sampson, George 316
Sampson, John 21
Sandys, John A. 68
Sapir, Edward 248
Sargeaunt, John 74
Sarrazin, G. 248
Saussure, Ferdinand de 248
Savage, Henry Lyttleton 248, 249
Savile, George 249
Savonarola, Jerome 249
Saxo, Grammaticus 249
Sayers, Dorothy L. 250, 251
Schaubert, Else von 251
Schick, Joseph 251
Schiller, Friedrich 251
Schipper, Jacob 251
Schlüter, Wolfgang 70
Schlutter, Otto 251
Schmidt-Petersen, Jürgen 252
Schneider, Hermann 252
Schofield, William Henry 252
Scholl, Gottlob Heinrich Friedrich 117
Schorbach, Karl 315
Schröder, Heinrich 253
Schröer, Arnold 16, 252, 253
Schück, Henrik 253
Schultz, Albert 94
Schwabe, Randolph 140
Scoresby, William 253
Scott, Herbert S. 254
Scott, Walter 254, 287
Searle, William George 254
Sébillot, Paul 254
Sedgefield, Walter John 23, 254, 255
Seebohm, Frederic 255
Sehrt, Edward Henry 255
Senff, Herbert 255
Serjeantson, Mary S. 99, 255
Severius, Sulpicius 255
Shakespeare, William 256, 257, 258
Sharp, Elizabeth A. 258
Sharp, William 180
Shelley, Percy Bysshe 258
Sheridan, Frances 190
Sheridan, Richard Brinsley 259
Shetelig, Haakon 259
Shideler, Mary McDermott 259
Shippey, Tom 259
Shorthouse, Joseph Henry 259
Shub, Elizabeth 259
Sidgwick, Arthur 3, 43, 259, 299
Sidney, Philip 260
Sievers, Eduard 260, 261
Sigart, Joseph Désiré 261
Sigtryggson, Sigurður 22
Sijmons, Barend 261
Sisam, Celia 262
Sisam, Kenneth 47, 262, 263, 265
Sitwell, Gerard 247
Skeat, Walter William 1, 47, 48, 49, 50, 51, 53, 116, 154, 155, 156, 157, 206, 221, 235, 242, 244, 263, 264, 265, 266, 282, 310
Skelton, John 266
Small, Andrew 266
Small, John 154
Smith, Albert Hugh 266, 267
Smith, Charlotte Turner 267
Smith, David Nichol 23, 267
Smith, George Gregory 267, 268
Smith, Logan Pearsall 268
Smith, Lucy Toulmin 268
Smith, Thomas 268
Smith, William 268
Smithers, Geoffrey Victor 30
Solano, E. John 268
Sommer, Ferdinand 269
Sommer, Heinrich Oskar 150, 181, 268, 269
Sonnenschein, Edward Adolf 270

Sophocles 2, 3, 82, 270
Southey, Robert 271
Spenser, Edmund 271, 272
Sperber, Hans 272
Spies, Heinrich 159, 272
Spratt, Albert William 291
Spurrell, William 272
Stallybrass, James Steven 107, 108
Stammler, Wolfgang 272
Standen, Anthony 272
Stanley, Eric Gerald 273
Stapledon, Olaf 273
Steere, Edwin 273
Steinbeck, John 273
Stene, Aasta 273
Stenton, Frank Merry 102, 186, 273
Step, Edward 273
Stern, Ludwig Christian 273
Stevens, Edward James 274
Stevenson, Joseph 274
Stevenson, Robert Louis 274
Stevenson, William Henry 9, 230, 274, 275
Stjerna, Knut 275
Stokes, Whitley 275, 276
Story, Graham. M. 276
Strachan, John 276
Strachey, Edward 181
Stratmann, Francis Henry 276, 277
Strecker, Karl 277
Streitberg, Wilhelm 32, 277
Strong, Archibald 277
Strunk, William 64
Stuart, John 278
Stubbs, William 310
Sturluson, Snorri 278, 279
Stürzinger, Johann Jakob 279
Suchier, Hermann 279
Suhm, Peter Friedrich 279
Suzuki, Shigetake 279
Sveinsson, Benedikt 279, 280
Sweet, Henry 14, 228, 280, 281, 282, 283, 284
Swift, Jonathan 284, 285
Symons, Barend 285

T

Tacitus, Cornelius 285
Tait, James 286
Taylor, A. B. 286
Taylor, Jeremy 286
Taylor, Paul Beekman 286
Taylor, Tom 286
Temple, William 286
ten Brink, Bernhard Egidius Konrad 286
Tennyson, Alfred 286
Thacker, Eric 287
Thackeray, William Makepeace 287
Thomas Aquinas, Saint 287
Thomas, Joseph 288
Thomas, Martha Carey 288

Thomas of Erceldoune 3, 287
Thomas, P. G. 288
Thompson, Ashley Horace 288
Thompson, Francis 288, 289
Thompson, Whitney Meredith 289
Thomson, John 289
Thorkelin, Grímur Jónsson 289
Thirndike, Ashley Horacee 225
Thoroddsen, Þorvaldur 289
Thorpe, Benjamin 2, 290
Thucydides 291
Thumb, Albert 291
Thurneysen, Rudolf 111, 291, 292
Tilander, Gunnar 292, 297
Tolkien, Christopher J. R. 49, 50, 292, 293, 294, 295
Tolkien, J. R. R. 65, 66, 101, 113, 114, 247, 263, 292, 293, 294, 295
Toller, T. Northcote 25
Tonndorf, M. 295
Þórólfsson, Björn Karel 289, 290
Torp, Alf 85, 295
Tottel, Richard 295
Townsend, John 88
Trethewey, William H. 295
Trounce, Allan McIntyre 295
Turberville, George 296
Turnbull, William Braclay 296
Turner, Sharon 296
Turville-Petre, Edward Oswald Gabriel 296
Twemlow, Jesse Alfred 296
Twici, Guillaume 297

U

Udall, Nicolas 225
Ulrich, Jakob 244
Ulrich von Zatzikhoven 297
Ungnad, Arthur 297
University of Oxford 297
Untermeyer, Bryna Ivens 297
Unwin, Stanley 297

V

Vachell, Horace Annesley 297
Valladares Nuñez, Marcial 297
van Langenhove, George 297
van Vijk, Nicolaas 90
Velschow, Hans Mattias 249
Vendryes, Joseph 297
Verdaguer, Joaquin 298
Verdeyen, René 298
Vernaleken, Theodor 298
Verrall, Arthur Woollgar 3
Vigfússon Guðbrandur 325
Villari, Linda 298
Villari, Pasquale 298
Vinaver, Eugéne 181
Virgil 4, 73, 298
Vising, Johan 299
Vleeskruyer, Rudolf 299

Vočadlo, Otakar 299
von Wartburg, Walter 299

W

Wace, Robert 299, 300
Wadstein, Elis 300
Waever, John Reginald Home 67
Wagner, Felix 300
Wagner, Richard 300
Wahba, Magdi 183, 300
Wainwright, Frederick Threlfall 301
Waitz, Georg 231
Waitz, Hugo 301
Walde, Alois 301
Walker, Hugh 301
Wallenberg, Johannes Knut 301, 302
Waller, Alfred Rayney 303, 304
Walton, Izaak 302, 303
Wanley, Humphrey 121
Ward, Adolphus William 303, 304
Waring, George 274
Warnatsch, Otto 304
Warner, Rubie 305
Warrack, John 305
Watkin, Edward Ingram 184
Watkinson, John 39
Watson, E. W. 305
Watson, George 305
Watt, John A. 305
Way, Albertus 305
Wayn, John 305
Weale, M. 100
Webster, Kenneth Grant Tremayne 221, 305
Weekley, Ernest 306
Weir, Elizabeth 306
Wells, Herbert George 306
Wells, John Edwin 306, 307
Wernher der Gartenaere 307
Westman, Karl Gustav 6
Weston, Jessie Laidlay 307, 308
Whealley, Henry Benjamin 308
Wheatley, Henry B. 162
Wheeler, Timothy J. 308
Wheleer, Charles Bickersteth 231, 308
White, Robert Meadows 308
White, Terence Hanbury 308
Whitelock, Dorothy 321
Wieland, Christopher Martin 258, 309
Wiessner, Erich 309
Wiget, Wilhelm 309
Wiklund, Karl Bernhard 309
Wildhagen, Karl 309
Wilken, Ernst 309
Wilkes, Lyall 309
Willard, Rudolph 171
William of Malmesbury 310
Williams, Charles 310, 311
Williams, Edward 136
Williams, John (Ab Ithel) 311, 312
Williams, Mary Rhiannon 94, 312
Williamson, F. xi, 313

Williams, Robert 312
Williams, Robert Allan 313
Williams, Taliesin 313
Wilmotte, Maurice 313
Wilson, Chambers, Raymond 249, 308
Wilson, Herbert Wingley 313, 314
Wilson, John Dover 314
Wilson, Marjorie Kerr 171
Wilson, Robert M. 100, 314
Wimberly, Lowry Charles 314
Wimmer, Ludvig Frands Adalbert 314
Windisch, Ernst 275, 276, 315
Winstanley, Lilian 51
Wisse, Claus 315
Withington, Lothrop 115
Wodehouse, Pelham Grenville 315
Wodron, George 315
Wolfe, Gene 146
Wolfe, Humbert 315
Wolff, Eduard 315
Wollheim, Donald A. 315
Wood, Francis Asbury 315
Woodward, John 315
Wordsworth, William 316
Worm, Ole 316
Wrede, Ferdinand 316
Wrenn, Charles Leslie 17, 113, 114, 316
Wright, David 317
Wright, Elizabeth Mary 317
Wright, Joseph 317, 318, 319
Wright, Thomas 18, 183, 237, 249, 320
Wright, William Aldis 244, 321
Wülfing, J. Ernest 321
Wulfstan, Archbishop of York 321
Wülker, Richard Paul 106, 107, 320, 321, 322
Wyatt, Alfred John 17, 46, 209, 322
Wyatt, Thomas 295
Wycherley, William 322
Wycliffe, John 24, 322, 323
Wyke-Smith, Edward Augustine 323
Wyld, Henry Cecil Kennedy 323, 324

Y

Young, Williams Thomas 324

Z

Zachrisson, Robert Eugen 324
Zettersten, Arne 324
Zeuss, Johann Caspar 324
Zimmer, Heinrich 325
Zoëga, Geir T. 325
Zupitza, Julius 18, 111, 116, 262, 325, 326

[SECTION A]

INDEX OF BOOKS

1914 and other poems (1914) 29
1972 Annual World's Best SF (1972) 315

A

A. S. Napier, 1853-1916 (1970) 141
Abers' and 'Invers' of Scotland (1923) 18
Abfassungszeit von 'Rectitudines ... 'aferian' (1902) 167
Abhandlungen aus dem Gebiete ... Hilfswissenschaften (1925) 64
Ablaut in Flussnamen (1924) 88
Abolition of Man (1943) 162
About the House (1966) 9
Abriss der Angelsächsischen Grammatik (1895) 260
Account of the Arctic Regions (1820) 253
Acte for certayne ordinaunces ... of Wales 118
Adonais (1913) 258
Advancement of Learning (1915) 11
Adventure in Translation (1971) 259
Adventures at Friendly Farm (1948) 129
Ælfric's Catholic homilies [1997] 1
Ælfric's Lives of Saints, Vol. I (1881) 1
Ælfric's Lives of Saints, Vol. II (1900) 1
Aeneid (1930) 298
Aeneid of Virgil, Vol. I (1839) 298
Agamemnon of Aeschylus (1882) 2
Agamemnon of Aeschylus (1889) 2
Age of Bede (1935) 305
Aislinge Meic Conglinne (1892) 194
Alastor; or, The spirit of solitude, and other poems (1895) 258
Alchemist (Jonson) 136
Alexander and the Earthly Paradise (1937) 348
Älfrik de Vetere et Novo Testamento, Vol. I (1872) 106
Alice through the Looking Glass 41
Alice's Adventures in Wonderland 41
All Hallows' Eve (1945) 311
Allegory of Love (1936) 162
Allegory of the Pearl (1921) 87
Alliterative poetry in Middle English, Vol. I (1930) 225
Alliterative poetry in Middle English, Vol. II (1935) 225
Alphabet of tales, Vol. I Pt. A-H (1904) 12
Alphabet of tales, Vol. II Pt. I-Z (1904) 12
Alt- und angelsächsische verskunst (1876) 243
Alt-Celtischer Sprachschatz, Vol. I A-H (1896) 124
Alt-Celtischer Sprachschatz, Vol. II I-T (1904) 124
Alt-Celtischer Sprachschatz, Vol. III U-Z (1907) 124
Altdeutsches Namenbuch, Vol. I (1856) 88
Altdeutsches Namenbuch, Vol. I (1900) 88
Altenglische Dichtungen des MS. Harley 2253 (1878) 22
Altenglische Grammatik nach der angelsächsisches Grammatik (1942) 261
Altenglische Legenden (1875) 128
Altenglische Legenden (1878) 128
Altenglische Legenden (1881) 128
Altenglische Sprachproben: Nebst einem Wörterbuche, Vol. I (1867) 185

Altenglischen Dichtung (1904) 144
Altenglisches Elementarbuch (1902) 35
Altenglisches etymologisches Wörterbuch (1932) 124
Altenglisches etymologisches Wörterbuch (1934) 124
Altenglishe version des Halitgar'schen bussbuches (1933) 238
Ältere Genesis, mit Einleitung, Anmerkungen, Glossar und der lateinischen Quelle (1914) 125
Altfranzösische Yderroman (1913) 93
Altfriesisches Wörterbuch (1840) 242
Altfriesisches Wörterbuch (1925) 124, 125
Altgermanische Dialekte (1924) 139
Altgermanische Metrik (1893) 260
Althochdeutsches Lesebuch (1921) 27
Altirische Grammatik (1925) 235
Altirische Heldensage, Táin bó Cúalnge (1905) 315
Altisländische und altnorwegische Grammatik (1884) 223
Altisländisches Elementarbuch (1895) 125
Altostniederfrankischen Psalmenfragmente, Vol. I (1902) 117
Altostniederfrankischen Psalmenfragmente, Vol. II (1902) 117
Altschwedische grammatik, mit einschluss des altgutnischen (1904) 224
American Universal Geography, Vol. II (1801) 210
An Edition of Þe Liflade ant te Passiun of Seinte Iuliene (1936) 65
An eight-century Latin-Anglo-Saxon glossary (1890) 120
Anatomy of Melancholy (1912) 37
Ancien néerlandais d'Aprés les noms propres (1925) 183
Ancien vers Breton (1912) 82
Anciens peuples de l'Europe (1916) 73
Ancient English Metrical Romanceës, Vol. II (1802) 243
Ancient Irish epic tale Táin bó Cúalnge (1914) 75
Ancrene Riwle | Ancrene Wisse 6
Ancrene Riwle – A Study in the MS. Readings (1957) 279
Andreas (1885) 14
Andreas and the Fates of the Apostles (1906) 146
Andreas and the Fates of the Apostles (1961) 29
Andrew Lang: a critical biography (1946) 105
Angelsächsische glosse (1853) 25
Angelsächsischen Prosabearbeitungen der Benedictinerregel (1888) 252
Angelsächsisches Glossar (1851) 25
Angelsächsisches Lesebuch (1888) 145
Anglia, Vol. IX (1886) 321
Anglia, Vol. XX (1898) 79
Anglian vocabulary of the Bickling homilies (1949) 192
Anglica: Untersuchungen zur englischen Philologie, Vol. I (1925) 5
Anglica: Untersuchungen zur englischen Philologie, Vol. II (1925) 5
Anglist and Anglicist (1930) 180
Anglo Saxon Bishops Kings and Nobles (1899) 254
Anglo-Catholicism & Re-Union (1923) 254
Anglo-Norman language and Literature (1923) 299
Anglo-Saxon and Norse poems (1922) 43
Anglo-Saxon and Old English vocabularies, Vol. I (1884) 320

Anglo-Saxon and Old English vocabularies, Vol. II (1884) 320
Anglo-Saxon Charters and the Historian (1938) 115
Anglo-Saxon Chronicle (1137-54) 6
Anglo-Saxon chronicle from the British Museum, Cotton MS., Tiberius B. IV (1926) 57
Anglo-Saxon Chronicle, Vol. I (1861) 290
Anglo-Saxon Chronicle, Vol. II (1861) 290
Anglo-Saxon dictionary (1897) 25
Anglo-Saxon dictionary: Supplement (1921) 25
Anglo-Saxon England (1943) 273
Anglo-Saxon Minor Poems (1942) 72
Anglo-Saxon Poems Exodus (1912) 28
Anglo-Saxon poems of Beowulf, the Travellers Song and the Battle of Finnesburh (1833) 140
Anglo-Saxon poems of Beowulf, the Travellers Song and the Battle of Finnesburh (1835) 141
Anglo-Saxon poems of Beowulf, the scôp or gleeman's tale and the fight at Finnesburg (1855) 290
Anglo-Saxon poems of Beowulf, the scôp or gleeman's tale and the fight at Finnesburg (1875) 290
Anglo-Saxon Poetry (1926) 101
Anglo-Saxon Primer (1905) 280
Anglo-Saxon Reader (1919) 322
Anglo-Saxon Reader in Prose and Verse (1908) 280
Anglo-Saxon Reader in Prose and Verse (1922) 281
Anglo-Saxon Runes (1840) 141
Anglo-Saxon Terminology (1933) 299
Anglo-Saxon Verse-Book (1922) 254
Anglo-Saxon version of the life of St Guthlac (1848) 86
Anglosaxonica, Vol. I (1894) 61
Anglosaxonica, Vol. II (1895) 61
Animal life of the British Isles (1927) 273
Anna Livia Plurabelle (1930) 138
Annales Cambriæ (1860) 311
Annals of Tacitus, Vol. I (1896) 285
Annals of Tacitus, Vol. II (1907) 285
Anthology of Catholic poets (1925) 161
Anthology of the poetry of the age of Shakespeare (1910) 324
Antiquæ Litteraturæ Septentrionalis Utilitate (1703) 120
Antony and Cleopatra 256
Apologia Pro Poemate Meo 223
Apologia pro vita sua (1912) 223
Apology for the life of Mr. Colley Cibber, Vol. I (1899) 57
Arabian Nights Entertainments (1898) 150
Archæology of Roman Britain (1930) 59
Archæology of the Anglo-Saxon settlement (1913) 160
Arctic explorations (1856) 139
Areopagitica (1911) 196
Arethusa 258
Aristotle's theory of poetry and fine art: with a critical text and translation of the Poetics (1920) 37
Arngrimi Jonae Opera Latine conscripta Vol. I (1950) 7
Arngrimi Jonae Opera Latine conscripta Vol. II (1951) 7
Arngrimi Jonae Opera Latine conscripta Vol. III (1952) 7
Arngrimi Jonae Opera Latine conscripta Vol. IV (1957) 7
Ars Poetica (1877) 127
Art and Artifice in the Divina Commedia (1965) 84
Art and tradition in Sir Gawain and the Green Knight (1965) 17
Art of Hunting (1843) 74
Art of Hunting (1908) 74
Art of pipe smoking (1958) 298
Art of War in the Middle Ages, A.D. 378-1515 (1885) 226

Art poétique (1919) 23
Arthour and Merlin (1838) 296
Arthour and Merlin (1890) 146
Arthur and Gorlagon (1903) 144
Arthur's: the romance of a coffee stall (1915) 176
Arthurian literature in the Middle Ages (1959) 170
Arthurian Torso (1948) 310
Arthurian tradition and Chrétien de Troyes (1949) 170
Asser's Life of King Alfred (1904) 9
Astrophel and Stella 260
Athelston: A Middle English Romance (1933) 295
Atlakviða 9
Atlakviða (1912) 136
Attacks of taste (1971) 37
Attempt Towards a Natural History, Vol. I, Pt. 1 (1728) 315
Auraicept Na N-éces (1917) 38
Austfirðinga Sǫgur (1950) 134
Author as Philologist (1969) 259
Awntyrs off Arthure 10
Ayenbite of Inwyt 11
Ayesha: the return of She (1905) 111

B

Babbitt (1922) 166
Babes in the Wood 11
Babes in the wood: a romance of the jungles (1910) 64
Babees Book: Early English Meals and Manners (1868) 91
Babel (1930) 230
Babylonian story of the Deluge and the Epic of Gilgamish (1920) 34
Babylonisch-Assyrische Grammatik (1926) 297
Bacchae of Euripides (1913) 82
Baedae Opera Historica (1896) 15
Bahuvrihi-compositum im Altenglischen, Mittelenglischen und Neuenglischen (1925) 159
Balder-kultus in Lethra (1897) 248
Ballad of the White Horse (1911) 54
Ballads and Songs of Brittany (1865) 286
Bandamanna saga (1901) 279
Barbour's Des schottischen Nationaldichters Legendensammlung (1881) 12
Barddas, Vol. I (1862) 312
Barddas, Vol. II (1874) 312
Barnstaple as a Minting Place (1898) 221
Bartholomew of Exeter, Bishop and Canonist (1937) 199
Barzaz-Breiz: Chants Populaires de la Bretagne, Vol. I (1846) 149
Barzaz-Breiz: Chants Populaires de la Bretagne, Vol. II (1846) 149
Battle of Brunanburh 14
Battle of Maldon 14
Battle of Maldon (1937) 100
Beasts and super-beasts (1914) 247
Beauty and the Beast (1887) 150
Beauty and the Beast 233
Bede: his life, times and writings (1935) 288
Beggar's opera (1920) 93
Beibl Cyssegr-lan: sef yr Hen Destament, a 'r Newydd (1588) 199
Beiträge zur englischen Sprachgeschichte (1925) 172
Beiträge zur textkritik der sogenannten Cædmon's-chen Dichtungen (1895) 104
Beobachtungen über Sprachkörper und Sprachfunktion (1924) 127

Beovulf nebst den fragmenten Finnsburg und Valdere in kritisch (1867) 106
Beowulf 17
Beowulf. Autotypes of the unique Cotton MS. Vitellius A 15 in the British Museum (1882) 325
Beowulf. Herausgegeben: Pt. I (1895) 124
Beowulf. Mit ausfürlichem glossar herausgegeben (1908) 120
Beowulf (1909) 131
Beowulf (1910) 255
Beowulf. Nebst den kleineren Denkmälern der Heldensagen, mit Einleitung, Glossar und Anmerkungen. Herausgegeben: Pt. I (1912) 125
Beowulf. Nebst den kleineren Denkmälern der Heldensagen, mit Einleitung, Glossar und Anmerkungen. Herausgegeben: Pt. II (1913) 125
Beowulf. Mit ausfürlichem glossar herausgegeben (1913) 120
Beowulf. With the Finnsburg fragment (1914) 322
Beowulf. Translated into Modern English Rhymed Verse, with Introduction and Notes (1925) 277
Beowulf (1935) 255
Beowulf (1957) 317
Beowulf: facsimile of BM MS. Cotton Vitellius A xv. (1959) 326
Beowulf (1968) 64
Beowulf and Epic Tradition (1928) 158
Beowulf and the Fight at Finnburg (1922) 144
Beowulf and the Fight at Finnesburg 17
Beowulf and the Fight at Finnsburg (1928) 144
Beowulf and the Fight at Finnsburg (1936) 145
Beowulf and the Finnesburg fragment (1911) 113
Beowulf and the Finnesburg fragment (1940) 113
Beowulf and the Finnsburg fragment (1950) 114
Beowulf and the seventh century: language and content (1935) 97
Bêowulf-Materialien zum Gebrauch bei Vorlesungen (1900) 88
Beowulf nebst dem Finnsburg-Bruchstück, Vol. I (1905) 125
Beowulf nebst dem Finnsburg-Bruchstück, Vol. II (1906) 125
Beowulf Poem as an English National Epos (1931–2) 300
Beowulf Poet (1968) 91
Beowulf the Hero & the King (1963) 163
Beowulf with the Finnesburg fragment (1953) 316
Beowulf, and Judith (1953) 72
Beowulf, The Fight at Finnesburg 17
Beowulf. An introduction to the study of the poem (1921) 43
Beowulf. An introduction to the study of the poem (1932) 43
Beowulfslied nebst den kleineren epischen (1883) 321
Bernardus De cura rei famuliaris (1870) 173
Bertram's Hotel (1965) 57
Best Plays of Thomas Otway (1903) 229
Bestiary (1240-50) 18
Betydningslær (Semasiologi) (1920) 85
Bevis of Hampton (1320) 18
Beyond personality (1944) 162
Biblia (1535) 62
Biblical Latin Quotations in Ancrene Wisse (1960) 279
Bibliography of the mythical-heroic sagas (1912) 118
Bibliotheca classica; or, A classical dictionary (1788) 160
Bibliotheca Historica of Diodorus Siculus, Vol. I (1956) 71
Bibliotheca Historica of Diodorus Siculus, Vol. II (1963) 71
Bibliothek der Angelsächsischen Poesie, Vol. I (1857) 106
Bibliothek der Angelsächsischen Poesie, Vol. II (1894) 106
Bibliothek der Angelsächsischen Poesie, Vol. III (1898) 107
Bibliothek der Angelsächsischen Poesie, Vol. IV (1900) 107
Bibliothek der Angelsächsischen Poesie, Vol. V (1921) 107

Biographia literaria (1905) 59
Bjowulfs Drape (1820) 109
Birds of Aristophanes 7
Birds of the British Isles and their eggs (1919) 63
Bischof Wærferth von Worcesters Übersetzung der Dialoge Gregors des Grossen (1900) 116
Bishop Percy's Folio Manuscript: Ballads and Romances, Vol. II (1868) 233
Black Book of Carmarthen (1907) 83
Black Book of Carmarthen (Facsimile) (1888) 83
Black Douglas (1899) 63
Blanket of the dark (1931) 33
Bleheris and the Tristram Story (1924) 170
Blickling homilies of the tenth century (1880) 199
Blue Bird (1911) 180
Blue Fairy Book (1889) 150
Blyssen (The Five Joys of the Virgin) 22
Boke of huntyng (1964) 292
Boke of Saint Albans (1901) 13
Boke of the Duchesse 45
Boleslas Orlowski: La Damoisele a la Mule (1913) 121
Book of Proverbs 24
Book of Danish ballads (1939) 226
Book of Deer (1869) 278
Book of Dragons (1970) 105
Book of Dreams and Ghosts (1897) 150
Book of Fairy Poetry (1920) 229
Book of Indoor Games (1933) 234
Book of Sansevero (1970) 96
Book of Taliesín (1910) 83
Book of Wonder (1912) 76
Borrowers (1952) 224
Borrowers Afield (1955) 224
Borrowers Afloat (1959) 224
Borrowers Aloft (1961) 224
Bósa saga ok Herrauds 24
Bosworth Psalter (1908) 93
Breche in The Owl and the Nightingale, line 14 (1930) 227
Breton glosses at Orleans (1866) 275
British section of the Ravenna Cosmography (1949) 242
Broomsticks & Other Tales (1925) 68
Brow or Brawn? (1937) 248
Brown Fairy Book (1904) 150
Bruce (Barbour) 12
Brut y Tywysogion (1860) 312
Buile Suibhne (The frenzy of Suibhne) (1910) 225
Bull from the Sea (1962) 241
Busman's Honeymoon (1937) 250
Buttercup Field and Other Stories (1945) 135
Byrhtnoth and Maldon (1936) 149

C

Cabinet des fees, Vol. 1 (1785) 186
Cabinet des fees, Vol. 2 (1785) 186
Cabinet des fees, Vol. 3 (1785) 186
Cabinet des fees, Vol. 4 (1785) 186
Cabinet des fees, Vol. 5 (1785) 187
Cabinet des fees, Vol. 6 (1785) 187
Cabinet des fees, Vol. 7 (1785) 187
Cabinet des fees, Vol. 8 (1785) 187
Cabinet des fees, Vol. 9 (1785) 187

Cabinet des fees, Vol. 10 (1785) 187
Cabinet des fees, Vol. 11 (1785) 187
Cabinet des fees, Vol. 12 (1785) 187
Cabinet des fees, Vol. 13 (1785) 188
Cabinet des fees, Vol. 14 (1785) 188
Cabinet des fees, Vol. 15 (1785) 188
Cabinet des fees, Vol. 16 (1785) 188
Cabinet des fees, Vol. 17 (1785) 188
Cabinet des fees, Vol. 18 (1785) 188
Cabinet des fees, Vol. 19 (1785) 188
Cabinet des fees, Vol. 20 (1785) 188
Cabinet des fees, Vol. 21 (1786) 189
Cabinet des fees, Vol. 22 (1786) 189
Cabinet des fees, Vol. 23 (1786) 189
Cabinet des fees, Vol. 24 (1786) 189
Cabinet des fees, Vol. 25 (1786) 189
Cabinet des fees, Vol. 26 (1786) 189
Cabinet des fees, Vol. 27 (1786) 189
Cabinet des fees, Vol. 28 (1786) 189
Cabinet des fees, Vol. 29 (1786) 189
Cabinet des fees, Vol. 30 (1786) 190
Cabinet des fees, Vol. 31 (1786) 190
Cabinet des fees, Vol. 32 (1786) 190
Cabinet des fees, Vol. 33 (1786) 190
Cabinet des fees, Vol. 34 (1786) 190
Cabinet des fees, Vol. 35 (1786) 190
Cabinet des fees, Vol. 36 (1786) 191
Cabinet des fees, Vol. 37 (1786) 191
Cabinet des fees, Vol. 38 (1788) 191
Cabinet des fees, Vol. 39 (1788) 191
Cabinet des fees, Vol. 40 (1788) 191
Cædmon (1865) 70
Cædmon Manuscript of Anglo-Saxon Biblical Poetry, Junius XI in the Bodleian Library (1927) 98
Cædmon's des Angelsachsen biblische Dichtungen (1849) 25
Cædmon's des Angelsachsen biblische Dichtungen (1854) 25
Cædmon's Hymn 38
Cædmon's metrical paraphrase of parts of the Holy Scriptures in Anglo-Saxon (1832) 290
Cædmonian Exodus 492 (1917) 293
Caesar's Gallic war (1898) 38
Cáin Adamnáin (1905) 224
Cairo Studies in English (1959) 330
Cambriæ Description 96
Cambridge History of English Literature, Vol. I (1907) 333
Cambridge History of English Literature, Vol. II (1908) 333
Cambridge History of English Literature, Vol. III (1908) 334
Cambridge History of English Literature, Vol. IV (1909) 334
Cambridge History of English Literature, Vol. V (1909) 334
Cambridge History of English Literature, Vol. VI (1910) 334
Cambridge History of English Literature, Vol. VII (1910) 334
Cambridge History of English Literature, Vol. VIII (1910) 334
Cambridge History of English Literature, Vol. IX (1912) 334
Cambridge History of English Literature, Vol. X (1913) 334
Cambridge MS. (University library, Gg. 4.27) (1879) 45
Cambridger Psalter (1910) 309
Campaspe 176
Cannibalism and Arctic Exploration (1884) 39
Canon medicinae, Vol. I 10
Canon's Yeoman's Tale 46
Canterbury Tales, Vol. I (1907) 46
Canterbury Tales, Vol. II (1907) 46

Canzone morale (1852) 237
Caradoc et le Serpent (1899) 230
Caradoc et Saint Patern (1899) 171
Carados and the Serpent (1898) 115
Carl Maria von Weber (1968) 305
Cartularium Saxonicum, Vol. I (1885) 19
Cartularium Saxonicum, Vol. II (1887) 19
Cartularium Saxonicum, Vol. III (1893) 19
Cartularium Saxonicum, Vol. IV (1899) 19
Castle Gay (1930) 33
Castrén's Ethnologische Vorlesungen (1857) 42
Catalogue of romances in the Department of manuscripts in the British museum, Vol. III (1910) 118
Cath Finntrága or Battle of Ventry (1885) 224
Catholicon Anglicum, an English-Latin wordbook, dated 1483 (1881) 119
Caxton's Blanchardyn and Eglantine c. 1489 (1890) 42
Caxton's Eneydos (1890) 42
Celtes (1904) 64
Celtic Background of Anglo-Saxon England (1946) 289
Celtic Britain (1882) 241
Celtic Fairy Tales (1892) 132
Celtic Folklore: Welsh and Manx, Vol. I (1901) 241
Celtic Folklore: Welsh and Manx, Vol. II (1901) 241
Celtic myth and Arthurian romance (1927) 170
Celtica, Vol. I (1839) 70
Celtica, Vol. II (1840) 70
Centenary Essays on Dante (1965) 114
Chace dou cerf (1960) 292
Chambers's Etymological Dictionary of the English language (1882) 87
Chançun de Guillelme (1911) 279
Chants Populaires de la Grece Moderne, Vol. I (1824) 85
Chants Populaires de la Grece Moderne, Vol. II (1825) 85
Chapel Perilous (1955) 197
Chapters on Chaucer (1951) 180
Characters from the histories and memoirs of the seventeenth century (1920) 267
Characters of the reformation (1936) 16
Charlemagne. An Anglo-Norman Poem of the Twelfth Century (1836) 195
Charles Dickens (1906) 54
Charles Lamb: Prose & Poetry (1921) 101
Charles Williams: A Critical Essay (1966) 259
Chaucer (1919) 235
Chaucer and his England (1909) 61
Chaucer as a Philologist: The Reeve's Tale (1934) 292
Chaucer: The Pardoner's Tale (1911) 46
Chaucer's Canterbury tales: The Prologue (1920) 46
Cheddar, its gorge and caves (1947) 11
Chevalier à l'Épée; an old French poem (1900) 7
Chief British poets of the fourteenth and fifteenth centuries (1916) 221
Children's Treasury of literature in colour (1966) 297
Chips from a German Workshop, Vol. I (1867) 212
Chips from a German Workshop, Vol. II (1868) 212
Chips from a German Workshop, Vol. III (1870) 212
Chips from a German Workshop, Vol. IV (1875) 212
Chireche is Vnder Uote 131
Chirk codex of the Welsh laws (Facsimile) (1909) 83
Choephoroi (1892) 3
Choephoroi (1893) 3

Christian Behaviour (1943) 162
Chronica Jocelini de Brakelond 134
Chronica Minora Saec. IV, V, VI, VII, Vol. III (1898) 198
Chronicle of England (1858) 40
Chronicles of Clovis (1912) 247
Chronicles of Pantouflia (1932) 150
Ciento nouelle antike (1525) 109
Cinderella (1893) 63
Cleanness (1922) 98
Clef d'Amors: texte critique avec introduction, appendice et glossaire (1890) 73
Clerk's Tale 46
Clerkes Tale of Oxenford (1923) 47
Cloud of unknowing and other treatises (1952) 11
Clouds of Witness (1926) 250
Codex Junius XI (1855) 260
Cōic Conara Fugill die fünf Wege zum Urteil (1926) 291
Collation of the Katherine Group (MS Bodley 34) (1946-47) 92
Collection of English words not generally used (1674) 239
Collection of Popular Tales from the Norse and North German (1906) 67
Colonisation germanique dans la Gaule du Nord (1953) 92
Coloured Lands (1938) 54
Comedia Famosa del Esclavo del Demonio (1906) 193
Comh-threaiche (1913) 179
Companach Na Cloinne (1913) 179
Companion to school classics (1896) 103
Comparative grammar of the Greek language (1912) 317
Comparative Mythology (1856) 212
Complaynt of Scotland (1548) 60
Complete Plays of William Congreve (1912) 60
Complete Plays of William Wycherley (1920) 322
Complete poetical works of Alexander Pope (1903) 236
Complete poetical works of James Thomson (1908) 289
Complete works of Geoffrey Chaucer, Vol. I (1894) 47
Complete works of Geoffrey Chaucer, Vol. II (1900) 47
Complete works of Geoffrey Chaucer, Vol. III (1900) 47
Complete works of Geoffrey Chaucer, Vol. IV (1894) 47
Complete works of Geoffrey Chaucer, Vol. V (1894) 47
Complete works of Geoffrey Chaucer, Vol. VI (1894) 48
Complete works of Geoffrey Chaucer, Vol. VII (1897) 48
Complete works of George Savile, first Marquess of Halifax (1912) 249
Complete works of John Gower, Vol. I (1901) 102
Complete works of John Gower, Vol. II (1901) 102
Complete works of John Gower, Vol. III (1901) 102
Complete works of John Gower, Vol. IV (1902) 102
Composition und Alter der altenglischen (angelsächsischen) Exodus (1883) 109
Comus 196
Concerning Certain Great Teachers of the English Language (1923) 43
Concerning Huchown (1910) 177
Concerning the relations between Exodus and Beowulf (1918) 145
Concessive Constructions in Old English Prose (1911) 37
Concise Anglo-Saxon Dictionary (1916) 114
Concise dictionary of Middle English from A.D. 1150 to 1580 (1888) 191
Concise Dictionary of Old Icelandic (1910) 325
Concise Encyclopaedia of Modern World Literature (1963) 107
Concise Etymological Dictionary of Modern English (1924) 306

Concise Etymological Dictionary of the English Language (1924) 263
Concordance to five Middle English poems (1966) 176
Contes de fées (1865) 161
Contes de ma mère l'Oye (1879) 233
Continuation de Perceval, Vol. I (1922) 94
Continuations of the Old French Perceval of Chrétien de Troyes, Vol. I (1949) 56
Continuations of the Old French Perceval of Chrétien de Troyes, Vol. II (1950) 56
Continuations of the Old French Perceval of Chrétien de Troyes, Vol. III, Pt. I (1952) 56
Continuations of the Old French Perceval of Chrétien de Troyes, Vol. III, Pt. II (1955) 56
Contributions to Old English lexicography (1906) 220
Corneli Taciti de Origine et Situ Germanorum (1938) 285
Corpus Glossary with an Anglo-Saxon (1921) 168
Corpus MS. (Corpus Christi coll., Oxford) (1868) 48
Corpus, Epinal, Erfurt and Leyden Glossaries (1921) 168
Correspondence germano-celtique (1924) 214
Correspondence of Gerard Manley Hopkins and Richard W. Dixon (1955) 127
Cours de linguistique générale (1916) 248
Course of Gaelic grammar (1908) 240
Cowley's Essays 63
Crimson Fairy Book (1903) 151
Crisis of Our Civilization (1937) 16
Crist 63
Cuckoo Song (1240) 64
Cursor Mundi (1320) 64
Cursor Mundi, Vol. I (1874) 199
Cursor Mundi, Vol. II (1875) 200
Cursor Mundi, Vol. III (1876) 200
Cursor Mundi, Vol. IV (1877) 200
Cursor Mundi, Vol. V (1878) 201
Cursor Mundi, Vol. VI (1892) 201
Cursor Mundi, Vol. VII (1893) 201
Custom and Myth (1884) 151
Cycles of the Kings (1946) 70
Cyclopaedia of costume, Vol. I (1876) 235
Cyclopaedia of costume, Vol. II (1876) 235
Cyclopædia of English literature, Vol. I (1906) 44
Cyclopædia of English literature, Vol. II (1906) 44
Cyclopædia of English literature, Vol. III (1906) 44
Cynewulf and his poetry (1932) 263
Cynewulf's Elene (1914) 64
Cyrurgie of Guy de Chauliac, Vol. I (1971) 226

D

D. Iunii Iuvenalis Saturae XIV (1904) 139
Dialogues of Saint Gregory, surnamed the Great (1911) 106
Dancing Floor (1926) 33
Danorum rebus gestis secul. III & IV (1815) 289
Dansk Sproghistorisk Læsbog, Vol. I (1905) 18
Dansk Sproghistorisk Læsbog, Vol. II (1905) 18
Danton: a study (1899) 16
Daretis Phrygii de excidio Trojae historia 67
Dark ages (1904) 141
Dark ages (1955) 141
De Bello Troiano 70
De Fem första sångerna af Kalevala med svensk ordbok (1853) 3

De Miseria Conditionis Humanae 131
De Monarchia 3
De Vulgari Eloquentia 3
Dealings with the fairies (1867) 177
Death of Grass (1956) 57
Debate of the Body and the Soul (1300) 68
Debate of the Body and the Soul (1888) 55
Decline and Fall of the Roman Empire, Vol. I 95
Decline and Fall of the Roman Empire, Vol. II 95
Decline and Fall of the Roman Empire, Vol. III 95
Decline and Fall of the Roman Empire, Vol. IV 95
Decline and Fall of the Roman Empire, Vol. V 95
Decline and Fall of the Roman Empire, Vol. VI 95
Decline and Fall of the Roman Empire, Vol. VII 95
Decline and Fall of the Roman Empire, Vol. VIII 95
Decline and Fall of the Roman Empire, Vol. IX 95
Decline and Fall of the Roman Empire, Vol. X 95
Decline and Fall of the Roman Empire, Vol. XI 96
Decline and Fall of the Roman Empire, Vol. XII 96
Deeds of Beowulf (1892) 76
Defence of Guenevere: and other poems (1916) 206
Defence of Pearl (1907) 62
Defence of Poesy (1912) 260
Defence of Poetry (1921) 258
Deffence et illustration de la langue francoyse (1904) 75
Definition des Begriffes 'Eigenname' (1925) 91
Deirdire, and Lay of the Children of Uisne (1914) 40
Demoiselle à la mule (1911) 228
Denham Tracts, Vol. I (1895) 69
Denham Tracts, Vol. II (1895) 69
Déor's Lament 69
Description of the Isle of Man (1865) 315
Deutsche Altertumskunde, Vol. I (1913-1923) 140
Deutsche Altertumskunde, Vol. II (1913-1923) 140
Deutsche Siedlungsnamen in genetisch-wortgeographischer Betrachtung (1924) 11
Deutsche Versgeschichte, Vol. I, Pt. I-II (1925) 120
Deutsche Versgeschichte, Vol. II, Pt. III (1927) 120
Deutsche Versgeschichte, Vol. III, Pt. IV-V (1929) 120
Deutsch-englischen Wörterbuch (1925) 167
Development of Arthurian romance (1963) 170
Devil's Spout (1946) 65
Dialect of the Earliest Complete English Prose Psalter (1924) 255
Dialogue concerning Tyndale (1927) 199
Diary of Samuel Pepys, Vol. I (1906) 232
Diary of Samuel Pepys, Vol. II (1906) 233
Diccionario gallego-castellano (1884) 297
Dictionarie of the French and English Tongues (1611) 61
Dictionarium saxonico et gothico-latinum, Vol. I (1772) 176
Dictionary in Englyshe and Welshe (1877) 247
Dictionary of archaic and provincial words, Vol. I (1847) 113
Dictionary of archaic and provincial words, Vol. II (1847) 113
Dictionary of National Biography 1912-1921 (1927) 67
Dictionary of Slang and Unconventional English (1923) 231
Dictionary of the Old English Language (1867) 276
Dictionary of the Old English Language (1873) 276
Dictionary of the Old English Language (1878) 276
Dictionary of the Old English Language (1881) 276
Die Handschrift von Exeter, Metra des Boetius, Salomo und Saturn, die Psalmen (1894) 9
Diplomatarium Islandicum: Íslenzkt Fornbréfasafn, Vol. I (1857) 261

Discarded Image (1963) 162
Discourse of the Liberty of Prophesying (1836) 286
Disgression in Beowulf (1950) 23
Dish of Orts (1893) 177
Disticha de moribus ad filium 42
Diu crône (1852) 117
Divina Commedia 4
Divina Commedia – Inferno (1945) 4
Divina Commedia – Purgatorio (1946) 4
Divina Commedia – Paradiso (1947) 4
Divine adventure: Iona (1900) 180
Doctor Dolittle and the Green Canary (1950) 169
Doctor Dolittle and the Secret Lake (1948) 169
Doctor Dolittle in the Moon (1928) 169
Doctor Dolittle Return (1933) 169
Doctor Dolittle's Caravan (1926) 169
Doctor Dolittle's Circus (1924) 169
Doctor Dolittle's Garden (1927) 169
Doctor Dolittle's Post Office (1923) 169
Doctor Dolittle's Puddleby Adventures (1952) 170
Doctor Dolittle's Zoo (1926) 170
Domes dæge (1876) 173
Donne's Sermons: selected passages (1919) 72
Dosparth Edeyrn Davod Aur (1861) 78
Dr Karl Barth and The War, A Letter to a French Pastor (1940) 14
Dream of Gerontius (1914) 223
Dream of the Rood (1942) 29
Dress in mediaeval France (1952) 83
Dryden 74
Dryden (1881) 246
Dryden's Plays (1904) 74
Dryden's Poems (1913) 74
Duchess of Berry and the Revolution of 1830 (1892) 68
Dune (1965) 118
Dynamiter (1885) 274

E

E and Æ in the Vespasian Psalter (1901) 35
Eadwine's Canterbury Psalter (1889) 115
Early Christian Irish Art (1963) 117
Early English alliterative poems in the West-Midland dialect of the fourteenth century (1864) 202
Early English alliterative poems in the West-Midland dialect of the fourteenth century (1867) 202
Early English alliterative poems in the West-Midland dialect of the fourteenth century (1869) 202
Early English Christian Poetry (1952) 141
Early English Homilies from the Twelfth-Century (1927) 305
Early English Lyrics: Amorous, Divine, Moral & Trivial (1921) 43
Early English pronunciation, Pt. III (1871) 80
Early English proverbs (1910) 263
Early Irish Reader (1927) 43
Early London Dialect (1928) 180
Early Middle English Literature (1939) 314
Early popular poetry of Scotland and the northern border, Vol. I (1895) 153
Early South-English legendary, or lives of saints (1887) 128
Earthly Paradise. A Poem, Pt. III (1911) 206
Ecclesiastical History of the English People (1935) 15
Edda 77

Edda (1926) 116
Edda Snorra Sturlusonar (1848) 278
Edda Snorra Sturlusonar (1931) 278
Eddalieder (1920) 239
Eddalieder, Vol. I (1888) 138
Eddalieder, Vol. II (1890) 139
Eddica Minora (1903) 120
Eddukvæði, Vol. I (1954) 137
Eddukvæði, Vol. II (1954) 137
Edinburgh Gaelic Manuscript, XL (1887) 194
Edinburgh version of the Cennach in Rúanado (1893) 194
Edmund Burke: Selections (1921) 130
Education of Uncle Paul (1909) 21
Edward II 184
Egil's saga, done into English out of the Icelandic (1930) 78
Egils saga Skalla-Grimssonar (1933) 279
Egyptian Reading Book for Beginners (1896) 34
Eigentümlichkeiten des anglischen wortschatzes, Vol. I (1906) 138
Einführung in das Gotische (1922) 85
Einführung in die Bedeutungslehre (1923) 272
Eiríks saga Rauða ok Graenlendinga þattr (1902) 7
Ekkehards Waltharius (1924) 277
Elder Edda: a selection (1969) 286
Electra of Euripides (1910) 82
Electra of Sophocles (1870) 270
Electra of Sophocles (1908) 270
Elementary Grammar of Old Icelandic (1925) 34
Elementary historical new English grammar (1924) 319
Elementary Old English grammar (1923) 319
Elemente des Gotischen (1921) 145
Elizabethan Acting (1951) 138
Elizabethan Critical Essays, Vol. I (1904) 267
Elizabethan England (1921) 115
Ellesmere Chaucer reproduced in facsimile (1911) 48
Ellesmere MS. of Chaucer's Canterbury Tales (1879) 48
Elucidarium and other tracts in Welsh from Llyvyr agkyr Llandewivrevi A.D. 1346 Jesus college MS. 119 (1894) 210
Elyvyr Coch o Ergest (1890) 242
Encyclopaedia Britannica, Vol. XXIV (1888) 14
Encyclopaedia of Sport, Vol. I (1897) 232
Ends and means (1937) 131
Endung der weiblichen germanischen Lehnwörter im Finnischen (1924) 309
Engelska Språkets Ortografi i Historisk Belysning. 168
England before the Norman Conquest (1926) 43
Englische Cato und Ilias-Glossen des 12. Jahrhunderts (1906) 89
Englische Literatur (1893) 27
Englische Ortsnamenforschung (1925) 79
Englische Sprachwissenschaft (1924) 127
Englische studien, Vol. XVI (1892) 146
Englische Ursprung von Syr Gawayn and the Grene Knyzt (1923) 251
Englischen Namenkunde (1912) 20
English and Scottish popular ballads, Vol. I Pt. I (1882) 55
English and Scottish popular ballads, Vol. I Pt. II (1884) 55
English and Scottish popular ballads, Vol. II Pt. I (1885) 55
English and Scottish popular ballads, Vol. II Pt. II (1886) 55
English and Scottish popular ballads, Vol. III Pt. I (1888) 55
English and Scottish popular ballads, Vol. III Pt. II (1889) 55
English and Scottish popular ballads, Vol. IV Pt. I (1890) 55

English and Scottish popular ballads, Vol. IV Pt. II (1892) 56
English and Scottish popular ballads, Vol. V Pt. I (1894) 56
English and Scottish popular ballads, Vol. V Pt. II (1898) 56
English and Welsh Dictionary, Vol. I (1852) 83
English and Welsh Dictionary, Vol. II (1858) 83
English Charlemagne Romances, Pt. IV (1882) 119
English Critical Essays: Nineteenth Century (1916) 135
English Dialect Dictionary, Vol. I (1898) 317
English Dialect Dictionary, Vol. II (1900) 317
English Dialect Dictionary, Vol. III (1902) 317
English Dialect Dictionary, Vol. IV (1903) 317
English Dialect Dictionary, Vol. V (1904) 318
English Dialect Dictionary, Vol. VI (1905) 318
English Dialect Grammar (1905) 318
English Fairy and Other Folk Tales (1893) 115
English Fairy Tales (1890) 132
English History in English Poetry (1911) 87
English Influence on the French Vocabulary Pt. I (1922) 12
English Influence on the French Vocabulary Pt. II (1923) 12
English Intonation with Systematic Exercise (1922) 230
English Irony before Chaucer (1937) 19
English language (1912) 141
English Language in America, Vol. I (1925) 147
English Language in America, Vol. II (1925) 147
English Literature at the Close of the Middle Ages, Vol. II Pt. II (1945) 43
English literature in the eighteenth century (1883) 234
English Literature in the Sixteenth Century: excluding Drama (1954) 162
English literature, from the Norman conquest to Chaucer (1906) 252
English Literature: Medieval (1912) 141
English Loan-Words in Modern Norwegian (1945) 273
English miracle plays, moralities and interludes (1923) 235
English Miscellany (1901) 35
English Place-Name Elements, Pt. I (1956) 266
English Place-Name Elements, Pt. II (1956) 266
English place-names in –ing (1923) 80
English place-names in -ing of Scandinavian origin (1922) 324
English Poem on a Sacred Subject (1929) 90
English pronunciation 1500-1700, Vol. I (1957) 72
English pronunciation 1500-1700, Vol. II (1957) 72
English prose treatises of Richard Rolle de Hampole: who died A.D. 1349 (1866) 234
English Tail-Rhyme Romances (1932) 295
English Text of Ancrene Riwle (1963) 179
English Text of the Ancrene Riwle (1952) 67
English Text of the Ancrene Riwle (1954) 314
English Text of the Ancrene Riwle: Ancrene Wisse (1962) 293
English-Welsh Pronouncing Dictionary (1909) 272
Entstehung des englischen Participium Praesentis auf –ing (1952) 66
Epic and romance (1897) 141
Epinaler Und Erfurter Glossar (1912) 251
Epistle to Cangrande 5
Epistle to the Philippians 231
Epithalamion 271
Erewhon (1872) 37
Erforschung der indogermanischen Sprachen, Vol. II (1927) 277
Eric Brighteyes (1891) 111

Erkenwalde (1881) 129
Eros and Psyche 6
Essai sur la Composition du Roman Gallois de Peredur (1909) 312
Essais d'étymologie cynégétique (1953) 292
Essay of dramatic poesy (1918) 74
Essays (1765) 97
Essays and Studies, Vol. III (1910) 142
Essays and Studies, Vol. XIV (1929) 94
Essays by Divers Hands (1958) 243
Essays in criticism (1913) 185
Essays in Little (1891) 151
Essays of Joseph Addison (1920) 105
Essays presented to Charles Williams (1947) 250
Essays presented to Charles Williams (1966) 250
Essex Dialect Dictionary (1923) 94
Ethnographie der germanischen Stämme (1904) 27
Études de Philologie Wallone (1932) 313
Etymologiarum sive Originvm libri XX (1911) 131
Étymologie Bretonne (1914) 82
Etymologisch woordenboek der Nederlandsche taal (1912) 90
Etymologisches Wörterbuch der deutschen Sprache (1905) 145
Etymologisches Wörterbuch der gotischen Sprache (1909) 86
Etymologisches Wörterbuch der gotischen Sprache (1923) 86
Etymologisches Wörterbuch der griechischen Sprache (1905) 237
Eulogy of Cúrói (1905) 275
Eumenides of Aeschylus (1908) 3
Euphues 176
Everlasting Man (1925) 54
Every man in his humour 136
Everyday sentences in spoken English (1922) 230
Everyman (1909) 241
Evolution of Arthurian romance, Vol. I (1928) 31
Evolution of Arthurian romance, Vol. II (1928) 32
Evolution of the messianic idea, a study in comparative religion (1908) 226
Exameron Anglice (1921) 2
Excidio et conquestu Britanniae 96
Exeter Book (1864) 98
Exeter Book (1936) 147
Exodus 84
Exodus and Daniel (1907) 20
Experiment with Time (1934) 76
Experimentalphonetik und Sprachwissenschaft (1923) 173
Extra day (1915) 21
Extracts from Alfred's Orosius (1893) 228

F

Fabeln der Marie de France (1898) 183
Faerie Queene Book I 271
Faerie Queene Book II (1932) 271
Faerie Queene Book III (1918) 271
Faerie Queene Book IV 271
Faerie Queene Book V (1918) 271
Faerie Queene Book VI 271
Færøiske Qvæder om Sigurd Fofnersbane og hans Æt: med et anhang (1822) 176
Færøske Folkesagn og æventyr (1898-1901) 132
Fairy Gold: a Book of Old English Fairy Tales (1907) 243
Fairy Mythology (1873) 140
Fairy Tale Book (1934) 114

Fairy Tales for My Grandchildren (1910) 145
Fairy Tales of Madame d'Aulnoy (1892) 10
Fairy-Faith in Celtic Countries (1911) 84
Far islands (1899) 33
Favourite Fairy Tales (1907) 222
Felix's Life of Saint Guthlac (1956) 86
Ferrex and Porrex; or Gorboduc 224
Festschrift für Berthold Delbrück (1912-1913) 32
Festschrift für Eugen Mogk zum 70. Geburstag (1924) 198
Festschrift für Otto Behaghel (1924) 127
Feudal Element (1924) 285
Few notes on English etymology and word-history (1918) 80
Field telephones for army use (1916) 273
Fifth Book of Thucydides (1899) 291
Fighting Kings of Wessex (1931) 12
Figure of Beatrice (1943) 310
Filostrato 22
Finn Episode in Beowulf (1924) 313
Finnegan's Wake (1939) 138
Finnish Grammar (1890) 80
First Introduction to German Philology (1899) 172
First Men in the Moon (1901) 306
First Middle English Primer (1884) 281
First Middle English Primer (1891) 281
First nine books of the Danish history of Saxo Grammaticus (1894) 249
First steps in Anglo-Saxon (1897) 281
First Whispers of 'The Wind in the Willows' (1944) 103
Fish Dinner in Memison (1941) 78
Five Children – and It (1902) 222
Five Red Herrings (1931) 250
Fjölnir (1835) 246
Flaman (1933) 298
Flaming Terrapin (1924) 39
Flateyjarbok (1930) 137
Fled Bricrend: the feast of Briciu (1899) 117
Florentii Wigorniensis monachi Chronicon, Vol. II (1848) 290
Flowering Rifle (1939) 39
Flowers of the Field (1908) 134
Flussname Themse (1941) 88
Flying Inn (1914) 54
Folk tale and fairy lore in Gaelic and English (1910) 178
Folklore in the English and Scottish ballads (1928) 314
Fornaldar Sögur Norðurlanda, Vol. I (1954) 137
Forníslenzk Lestrarbók (1933) 138
Fóstbræðra saga (1852) 97
Fóstbræðra saga (1899) 7
Four hymns on earthly and heavenly love & beauty (1913) 271
Four orations of Cicero against Catiline (1879) 57
Fourteenth Century Verse and Prose (1921) 263
Fourteenth Century Verse and Prose (1922) 263
Fra Lippo Lippi: A Romance 169
Frage vom germanischen in den Lehnwörter im Finnischern und Lappischen (1924) 309
Fragment of the Ancren Riwle (1898) 220
Fragmenta Regalia (1653) 221
Fragmente des Trojanerkrieges, Vol. II (1882) 12
France (1907) 23
Frankeleyns Tale 48
Französierung des Englischen Personennamenschatzes (1925) 89
Französisches etymologisches Wörterbuch, Vol. III D-F

405

(1934) 299
Frau In Der Altisländischen Familiengeschichten (1926) 147
French Element (1924) 324
French Text of the Ancrene Riwle (1944) 118
French Text of the Ancrene Riwle (1958) 295
Freske Riim en Tractatus Alvinus (1952) 38
Friar's Tale 48
Friendly Farm (1946) 130
Frithegodi monachi Breviloquium vitae Beati Wilfredi et Wulfstani cantoris Narratio metrica de Sancto Swithuno (1950) 38
From Academic Darkness (1963) 181
Fyrst boke of the introduction of knowledge made by Andrew Boorde (1870) 24

G

Gaelic reader with outlines of grammar (1920) 177
Gaelic-English Dictionary (1922) 178
Galfredi Monumetensis Historia Britonum. Nunc primum in Anglia, novem codd. msstis collatis (1844) 93
Garden Flowers in Colour (1959) 142
Gaudy Night (1935) 250
Gawain-Poet: studies in his personality and background (1956) 248
Generydes (1878) 320
Gentilesse 48
Geoffrey of Monmouth (1903) 93
George Bernard Shaw (1909) 54
George Gascoigne and The Noble Arte of Venerie and Hunting (1942) 245
George Meriton's A Yorkshire dialogue (1683) (r1959) 193
Georgian Poetry 1911-1912 (1912) 184
Gepp, A Contribution to an Essex Dialect Dictionary (1922) 128
Germanen und Kelten in der antiken Überlieferung (1927) 86
Germanen: eine Einführung in die Geschichte ihrer Sprache und Kultur (1928) 139
German-English English-German Dictionary (1906) 306
Germanic Philology (1913) 169
Germanic Words for 'deceive' (1923) 147
Germanica: Eduard Sievers zum 75. Geburtstage (1925) 260
Germanische Heldensage, Vol. I (1925) 252
Germanische Heldensage, Vol. II Pt. I (1934) 252
Germanische Heldensage, Vol. II Pt. II (1934) 252
Germanische Sprachwissenschaft (1911) 169
Germanische Suffix –ingô (1907) 11
Geschichte der Dänen (1803) 279
Geschichte der Deutschen Sprache, Vol. I (1848) 108
Geschichte der Deutschen Sprache, Vol. II (1848) 108
Geschichte der Englischen Sprache (1916) 79
Geschichte der Heimischen Versarten (1905) 173
Geschichte der Isländischen geographie, Vol. I (1897) 289
Geschichte der Isländischen geographie, Vol. II (1898) 289
Geschichte der Norwegisch-Isländischen Literatur (1904) 198
Geschichte der westgermanischen Konjunktion 'und' (1916) 255
Geschichte des Dreissigjährigen Kriegs (1862) 251
Gesetze der Angelsachsen, Vol. I (1903) 167
Gesetze der Angelsachsen, Vol. II Pt. II (1903) 167
Gesetze der Angelsachsen, Vol. II, Pt. I (1903) 167
Gesetze der Angelsachsen, Vol. III (1903) 167

Gest hystoriale of the destruction of Troy, Vol. I (1869) 110
Gest hystoriale of the destruction of Troy, Vol. II (1874) 111
Gestis Regum Anglorum, Vol. I (1887) 309
Gestis Regum Anglorum, Vol. II (1889) 310
Giant's Heart (1864) 177
Giessner Beiträge zur Erforschung der Sprache und Kultur. Englands und Nordamerikas, Vol. I Pt. 1 (1923) 128
Glamour of the Snow 21
Glossae Hibernicae e codicibus wirziburgensi, carolisruhensibus, aliis, adiuvante Academiae Regiae berolinensis liberalitate (1881) 324
Glossaire étymologique montois (1870) 261
Glossaire Moyen-Breton, Vol. II (1895) 65
Glossar zu den Liedern der Edda (Saemundar Edda) (1896) 94
Glossar zu den Liedern der Edda (Saemundar Edda) (1923) 94
Glossary of mediaeval Welsh Law (1913) 166
Glossary of the Old Northumbrian Gospels (1894) 60
Glossary of words used by Derbyshire lead-miners during the past 250 years (1924) 313
Glossary with some pieces of verse of the Old dialect of the English colony in the forth and bargy county of Wexford Ireland (1867) 236
Goethes Faust (1900) 97
Golagros and Gawain 97
Gold of Fairnilee (1888) 151
Golden Key 178
Golden Treasury of the best songs and lyrical poems (1920) 230
Good short debate between Winner and Waster (1920) 98
Good short debate between Winner and Waster (1931) 98
Ghost-stories of an antiquary (1904) 132
Gothic history of Jordanes (1915) 195
Gotische Bibel (1919) 277
Gotisches Elementarbuch (1920) 277
Gottfried's von Monmouth Historia regum Britanniae mit literar-historischer Einleitung und äusführlichen Anmerkungen (1854) 94
Government of the British empire, as at the end of 1917 (1918) 133
Grace abounding to the chief of sinners (1905) 36
Grace Hadow (1946) 68
Grammar for Spoken English on a strictly phonetic basis (1924) 230
Grammar of Basque 103
Grammar of Danish 103
Grammar of Hungarian 103
Grammar of Irish 103
Grammar of Japanese 104
Grammar of Polish 104
Grammar of Roumanian 104
Grammar of Sanskrit 104
Grammar of Swedish 104
Grammar of the dialect of Windhill, in the West Riding of Yorkshire (1892) 318
Grammar of the Gothic Language (1910) 318
Grammar of the Gothic Language (1954) 318
Grammar of the Manx Language (1931) 145
Grammar of Turkish 104
Grammatica celtica e monumentis ... reliquiis, Vol. I (1853) 324
Grammatica celtica e monumentis ... reliquiis, Vol. II (1853) 324

Grapes of Wrath (1939) 273
Graphemic-phonemic study of a Middle English manuscript (1963) 192
Gratiosum lumen rationis (1952) 66
Great Divorce (1945) 162
Great Expectations 70
Greek Grammar for Schools (1906) 269
Green Fairy Book (1892) 151
Greenmantle (1925) 33
Grettis saga Ásmundarsonar (1900) 23
Grey Fairy Book (1900) 151
Griechische und Albanesische Märchen (1864) 112
Grimm's Household Tales, Vol. I (1884) 108
Grimm's Household Tales, Vol. II (1884) 108
Gringolet, Gawain's, Horse (1907-8) 98
Growth and Structure of the English Language (1912) 133
Grundbedingungen der quantitierenden und der akzentuierende Dichtung (1924) 22
Grundfrage der Sprachwissenschaft (1925) 111
Grundlage der Phonetik (1924) 88
Grundriss der germanischen Philologie, Vol. I (1891) 231
Grundriss der germanischen Philologie, Vol. II (1893) 231
Grundriss der romanischen philologie, unter mitwirkung, Vol. I (1886) 108
Grundriss der romanischen philologie, unter mitwirkung, Vol. II Pt. I (1902) 109
Grundriss der romanischen philologie, unter mitwirkung, Vol. II Pt. II (1902) 109
Grundriss der romanischen philologie, unter mitwirkung, Vol. II Pt. III (1902) 109
Grundriss zur Geschichte der angelsächsischen Litteratur (1885) 321
Grundsätzliches über Ursprung und Wirkungen der Akzentuation (1924) 123
Grundzüge der Phonetik zur Einführung in das Studium der Lautlehre der Indogermanische Sprachen (1885) 260
Grüne Heinrich (1941) 140
Guide to the mediaeval antiquities and objects (1924) 66
Guinevere: A Study of Her Abductions (1951) 305
Guls Hornbook: and The belman of London in two parts (1905) 68
Gulliver's Travels 284
Gunnlaugs saga Ormstungu (1911) 8
Guy of Warwick 111
Gwaith Lewis Glyn Cothi The Poetical works of Lewis Glyn Cothi (1837) 165
Gwaith Samuel Roberts (1906) 244
Gwaith Twm o 'r Nant (1909) 79

H

Hálfs saga ok Hálfsrekka (1909) 6
Hali Meidenhad: An Alliterative Homily of the Thirteenth Century (1922) 92
Hali meiðhad (1940) 59
Hallfreðar saga (1901) 8
Hamburgische Dramaturgie (1912) 161
Hamlet 256
Hamlet. Coriolanus. Twelfth night (1912) 256
Hand: its mechanism and vital endowments as evincing design (1834) 16
Handbook of Present-day English, Vol. I (1922) 147

Handbook of Present-day English, Vol. II Pt. I (1922) 148
Handbook of Present-day English, Vol. II Pt. II (1922) 148
Handbook of Present-day English, Vol. II Pt. III (1922) 148
Handbook of Present-day English, Vol. I (1925) 148
Handbook of Present-day English, Vol. II Pt. I (1925) 148
Handbook of Present-day English, Vol. II Pt. II (1925) 148
Handbook of Present-day English, Vol. II Pt. III (1925) 148
Handbuch der Greichischen Laut- und Formenlehre eine Einführung in das Sprach wissenschaftliche Studium des Griechischen (1912) 122
Handbuch der lateinischen Laut- und Formenlehre (1914) 269
Handbuch der Mittelenglischen Grammatik (1925) 138
Handbuch Des Alt-Irischen, Vol. I (1909) 291
Handbuch Des Alt-Irischen, Vol. II (1909) 291
Handbuch des sanskrit, mit texten und glossar; eine einführung in das sprach wissenschaftliche studium des altindischen, Vol. II (1905) 291
Handlyng Synne (1303) 114
Handlyng Synne, Pt. I (1901) 182
Handlyng Synne, Pt. II (1901) 182
Handschrift von Exeter (1894) 9
Håndskriftet nr. 2365 4 ... (Codex regius af den aeldre Edda) (1891) 314
Hanes A Chan (Story and Song) (1908) 78
Hansel and Gretel 114
Harleian MS.7334 (1885) 49
Harley lyrics: the Middle English lyrics of Ms. Harley 2253 (1956) 29
Hatton Gospels 116
Hávarðar saga Ísfirðings: udgivet for Samfund til udgivelse af gammel nordisk litteratur (1923) 289
Hávarðs saga Ísfirðings (1896) 279
Have His Carcase (1932) 250
Have with you to Saffron-Walden 221
Havelok (1910) 125
Havelok the Dane (about 1300) 116
Heart of a Monkey 116
Heath Robinson's Book of Goblins (1934) 245
Heaven of Virgins (1927) 115
Heiðreks Saga (1924) 117
Heimskringla, Vol. I (1844) 278
Heimskringla, Vol. II (1844) 278
Heimskringla, Vol. III (1844) 278
Heimskringla, Vol. I (1941) 278
Heimskringla, Vol. II (1945) 278
Heimskringla, Vol. III (1951) 278
Hêliand (1905) 120
Help to Latin Grammar (1855) 319
Hengwrt MS. of Chaucer's Canterbury Tales (1868) 49
Heretics (1908) 54
Hervarar Saga ok Heidreks (1956) 296
Hervarar Saga ok Heidreks Konungs (1953-54) 292
Hesperides (1915) 118
Heu-Heu or The Monster (1924) 111
Hidden Wound (1970) 18
Hydriotaphia, Urn Burial 30
Hieronymi Morlini Parthenopei novellæ, fabulæ, comœdia (1855) 199
High History of the Holy Graal (1913) 84
High History of the Holy Graal, Vol. I (1898) 84
High History of the Holy Graal, Vol. II (1898) 84
Hill (1923) 297

Hirtenbriefe Ælfrics in altenglischer und lateinischer Fassung (1914) 85
Histoire Anonyme de la Première Croisade (1924) 27
Histoire de la Langue anglaise, Vol. I (1923) 130
Histoire de la Litterature latine chretienne (1920) 149
Histoires ou Contes du Temps Passé (1697) 233
Histoiries of the Kings of Britain (1912) 94
Histoiries of the Kings of Britain (1958) 94
Historia Brittonum 222
Historia Ecclesiastica Gentis Anglorum, Vol. I (1896) 15
Historia Ecclesiastica Gentis Anglorum, Vol. II (1896) 15
Historia Langobardorum (1878) 231
Historia von D. Johann Fausten dem weitbeschreyten zauberer und schwarzkünstler (1911) 17
Historiae (Tacitus) 285
Historical Manual of English Prosody (1914) 246
Historical outlines of English phonology and morphology (1929) 198
Historical outlines of English sounds and Middle English grammar (1919) 198
Historical poems of the XIVth and XVth centuries (1959) 243
Historical Reader of Old Irish (1923) 235
Historische Grammatik der englischen Sprache, Vol. I Pt. I (1921) 173
Historische Grammatik der englischen Sprache, Vol. I Pt. II (1921) 173
Historische Grammatik der französischen Sprache von W. Meyer-Lübke (1913) 195
Historische Lautlehre des Lateinischen (1907) 223
Historische neuenglische Laut- und Formenlehre (1914) 80
Historische neuenglische Laut- und Formenlehre (1922) 80
History of Mr. Polly 306
History of animals (1752) 121
History of England in the eighteenth century, Vol. I (1907) 159
History of England in the eighteenth century, Vol. II (1909) 159
History of England in the eighteenth century, Vol. III (1913) 159
History of England: Ch.s I-III (1914) 177
History of English Literature, Vol. I (1895) 286
History of English Literature (1912) 60
History of English Poetry, Vol. I (1895) 62
History of English Poetry, Vol. II (1897) 62
History of English Poetry, Vol. III (1903) 62
History of English Poetry, Vol. IV (1903) 62
History of English Poetry, Vol. V (1905) 62
History of English Poetry, Vol. VI (1910) 62
History of English Sounds (1874) 281
History of English Sounds (1888) 282
History of Europe (1938) 87
History of Greece, Vol. V (1851) 109
History of His Own Time 36
History of mediaeval political theory in the West, Vol. I (1903) 40
History of mediaeval political theory in the West, Vol. II (1909) 40
History of mediaeval political theory in the West, Vol. III (1916) 40
History of mediaeval political theory in the West, Vol. IV (1922) 40
History of Modern Colloquial English (1920) 323
History of Old English and Old Norse studies in England (1938) 17
History of Old English ēa, ēo in Middle Kentish (1924) 286
History of the Adventures of Joseph Andrews, and his friend Mr. Abraham Adams (1920) 87
History of the Anglo-Saxons (1935) 123
History of the Anglo-Saxons, Vol. I (1807) 296
History of the Anglo-Saxons, Vol. II (1807) 296
History of the Church of England, Vol. I (1895) 71
History of the Church of England, Vol. II (1895) 71
History of the Church of England, Vol. III (1895) 71
History of the Church of England, Vol. IV (1895) 71
History of the Church of England, Vol. V (1902) 71
History of the Church of England, Vol. VI (1902) 71
History of the County of Cumberland, Vol. I (1794) 130
History of the English language (1907) 172
History of the English present inflections particularly -th and –s (1922) 124
History of the Franks, Vol. I (1927) 106
History of the Holy Grail, Vol. I (1874) 172
History of the Holy Grail, Vol. II (1875) 172
History of the Holy Grail, Vol. III (1877) 172
History of the Holy Grail, Vol. IV (1877) 172
History of the Holy Grail, Vol. V (1905) 172
History of the Holy Rood-Tree (1894) 220
History of the Rebellion and civil wars in England begun in the year 1641, Vol. I (1888) 57
History of the Rebellion and civil wars in England begun in the year 1641, Vol. II (1888) 57
History of the Vikings (1930) 141
History of the wars, Vol. V (1928) 237
History of Whittington 123
Hobbit (1942) 293
Hobyahs: A Scotch Nursery Tale (1891) 237
Hænsa-Þóris saga (1892) 138
Holy Bible, Vol. I (1850) 322
Holy Bible, Vol. II (1850) 322
Holy Bible, Vol. III (1850) 322
Holy Bible, Vol. IV (1850) 322
Holy Gospels in Anglo-Saxon, Vol. I (1871) 263
Holy Gospels in Anglo-Saxon, Vol. II (1871) 264
Holy Gospels in Anglo-Saxon, Vol. III (1874) 264
Holy Gospels in Anglo-Saxon, Vol. IV (1878) 264
Holy War (1901) 36
Homilien und Heiligenleben (1889) 9
Homilies of the Anglo-Saxon Church, Vol. I (1884) 2
Homilies of the Anglo-Saxon Church, Vol. II (1884) 2
Homilies of Wulfstan (1957) 321
Honest to God (1963) 245
Horn Book Magazine (1971) 92
Horn et Rimenhild (1845) 195
House of Fame in three books (1893) 49
House of the Four Winds (1935) 33
How to learn Gaelic, orthographical instructions, grammar (1906) 177
Hrafnkels saga Freysgoða (1911) 8
Hudibras (1905) 37
Human speech (1930) 230
Hunbaut: altfranzösischer Artusroman des XIII. Jahrhunderts (1914) 279
Hundred Merry Tales (1866) 229
Huntingtower (1922) 33
Hymn to the Virgin (1955) 72

I

Iacob and Ioseph (1916) 220
Icelandic manuscripts (1929) 118
Iliad, Vol. I (1903) 126
Iliad, Vol. II (1906) 126
Ilkla Moor baht 'at 227
Illustrated catalogue of the industrial department, Vol. II (1862) 124
Illustrations of Anglo-Saxon (1826) 60
Indebtedness of Chaucer's Troilus and Criseyde to Guido delle Colonne's Historia trojana (1903) 114
Indices glossarum et vocabulorum hibernicorum quae in Grammaticae celticae editione altera explanantur (1881) 111
Indische Quellen zu Longfellow's Kavanagh (1925) 251
Indo-European ax: axi: axu: (1905) 315
Indogermanen und Germanen (1924) 86
Indogermanische Ablaut, vornehmlich in seinem Verhältnis zur Betonung (1900) 122
Indogermanische Grammatik, Vol. I (1927) 122
Indogermanische Grammatik, Vol. II (1927) 122
Indogermanische Grammatik, Vol. III (1927) 122
Indogermanische Grammatik, Vol. IV (1928) 122
Indogermanische Grammatik, Vol. V (1929) 122
Indogermanische Grammatik, Vol. VI (1934) 123
Indogermanische Grammatik, Vol. VII (1937) 123
Indogermanische Sprachwissenschaft: eine Einführung für die Schule (1925) 147
Infidel Grape: An Anthology in Miniature in Praise of Wine (1940) 64
Inflections of the East Midland dialects in Early Middle English (1924) 226
Inheritance of Poetry (1948) 1
Innere Sprachform (1924) 91
Inscriptiones Britanniae christianae (1876) 130
Instructions for parish priest (1868) 197
Interesting Roman antiquities recently discovered in Fife (1823) 266
Interversion (1924) 104
Intorno a due canzone gemelle di materia cavalleresca (1877) 238
Introduction a l'etude de la litterature celtique (1883) 65
Introduction to a survey of Scottish dialects (1952) 192
Introduction to Early Welsh (1909) 276
Introduction to Philosophy (1942) 184
Introduction to Greek prose composition; with exercises (1902) 259
Introduction to Old Norse (1927) 100
Introduction to the Survey of English place-names, Vol. I Pt. I (1924) 186
Introduction to the Survey of Survey of English place-names, Vol. I Pt. II (1924) 186
Iolo Manuscripts (1888) 313
Ipomedon in drei englischen Bearbeitungen (1889) 130
Irene Iddesleigh (1897) 246
Irische Texte, Vol. I (1880) 275
Irische Texte, Vol. II (1880) 275
Irische Texte, Vol. III (1891) 275
Irische Texte, Vol. III Pt. I-II (1897) 275
Irische Texte, Vol. IV Pt. I (1900) 276
Irische Texte, Vol. IV Pt. II (1909) 276
Irischen handschriften und litteraturdenkmälern (1912) 292

Irischen Texten (1902) 292
Irish Language Revival (1946) 289
Irish-English Dictionary (1904) 71
Isabella and The eve of St Agnes (1908) 140
Islandsk-dansk ordbog, Vol. I (1920) 22
Islandsk-dansk ordbog, Vol. II (1920) 22
Íslenskar orðmyndir á 14 og 15 öld og breytingar þeirra úr fornmálinu (1925) 290
Íslenzk Lestrarbók, 1400-1900 (1924) 223
Íslenzk menning, Vol. I (1942) 223
Italic dialects, Vol. I (1897) 60
Italic dialects, Vol. II (1897) 60
Iþþlen in Sawles Warde (1947) 66
Itinerarium Cambriae (1804) 96
Ivories ancient and mediæval (1875) 185
Iwain: A Study in the Origins of Arthurian Romance (1903) 30
Iwein 115

J

Jack and the Beanstalk 131
Jack the Giant-Killer 131
Jacobean Shakespeare and Measure for Measure (1937) 44
Jaufre: ein altprovenzalischer Abenteuerroman des XIII. Jahrhunderts (1925) 28
Jerusalem Bible (1966) 135
John Dryden, Vol. I (1920) 75
John Inglesant and Its Author (1958) 243
John Inglesant, a romance, Vol. I (1881) 259
John Inglesant, a romance, Vol. II (1882) 259
Johnny Nut and the Golden Goose (1887) 69
Joseph Quincey Adams memorial studies (1948) 1
Journal of a Tour to the Hebrides with Samuel Johnson (1920) 24
Juifs d'Espagnes 945 – 1205 (1872) 103
Juliana of Cynewulf (1904) 64
Junius Manuscript (1931) 147

K

Kalevala (1849) 170
Kalevala, the land of heroes, Vol. I (1907) 143
Kalevala, the land of heroes, Vol. II (1907) 143
Kampf des Wettergottes mit der Schlange Illujankaš. Ein hethitischer Mythus (1924) 325
Kari Woodengown (1924) 139
Keats (1887) 59
Keltische Studien (1887) 325
Keltisches im englischen Verbum (1925) 140
Keltisches Wortgut im Englischen (1921) 89
Kentish place-names (1931) 301
Kim (1901) 143
Kinder- und Hausmärchen, Vol. I (1888) 108
Kinder- und Hausmärchen, Vol. II (1888) 108
King Alfred and the cakes 142
King Alfred's Anglo-Saxon version of the Compendious History of the World (1859) 228
King Alfred's Old English of Boethius De Consolatione Philosophiae (1899) 23
King Alfred's Old English version of St. Augustine's Soliloquies (1902) 10

INDEX

King Alfred's Orosius (1883) 228
King Alfred's West-Saxon Version of Gregory's Pastoral Care, Vol. I (1871) 282
King Alfred's West-Saxon Version of Gregory's Pastoral Care, Vol. II (1871) 282
King Canute and the waves 142
King Henry IV 256
King Henry V 256
King Henry VIII 256
King Horn 142
King Horn nach MS. Laud 108 (1872) 129
King Horn, Floriz and Blauncheflur, The Assumption of Our Lady (1866) 174
King Horn: a Middle English romance (1901) 114
King Lear 256
King Must Die (1958) 241
King Solomon's Mines (1886) 112
King Solomon's ring: new light on animal ways (1955) 171
King's English (1920) 90
Kleinere angelsächsische Denkmäler (1905) 160
Knight of the Lion (1905) 29
Knight's Tale 49
Kommentar zu den Lieder der Edda, Vol. I (1927) 261
Kommentar zu den Lieder der Edda, Vol. II (1931) 261
Kommentar zum Beowulf (1932) 126
König Alfreds des Grossen Bearbeitung der Soliloquien des Augustinus (1922) 81
König Alfreds übersetzung von Bedas Kirchengeschichte, Vol. I (1897) 251
König des Lebens: metrische Übersetzung (1925) 125
Kormáks saga (1893) 280
Kormáks saga (1916) 280
Kritische Entstehungsgeschichte des ags. interlinear-Psalters (1926) 117
Kudrun (1914) 285
Kultur und Sprache im neuen England (1925) 272
Kurze vergleichende Grammatik der indogermanischen Sprachen (1904) 32
Kurzgefasste Irische Grammatik: mit Lesestücken (1879) 315

L

Lais de Marie de France (1925) 184
Lais der Marie de France (1900) 183
Lambeth MS. 187 (1200) 150
Lambeth-Psalter, Vol. I (1909) 168
Lancelot and the Quest for the Holy Grail 150
Lancelot of the Laik: a Scottish metrical romance (about 1490-1500 A.D.) (1870) 264
Land of Cokaygne (a. 1300) 150
Land of Marvels: Folk-tales from Austria and Bohemia (1884) 298
Land under England (1935) 225
Landwirtschaftliches im altenglischen Wortschatze (1909) 103
Language Making (1948) 132
Language of the Ancrene Wisse (1967) 279
Language: a Linguistic Introduction to History (1925) 297
Language: An Introduction to the Study of Speech (1921) 247
Language: Journal of the Linguistic Society of America (Sep. 1933) 157
Langue gauloise: grammaire, textes et glossaire (1920) 73
Lansdowne MS. (No. 851) (1868) 49

Lanzelet: a romance of Lancelot (1951) 297
Laokoon (1907) 162
Last and First Man (1930) 273
Last fight of the Revenge at sea (1895) 238
Last Men in London (1932) 273
Late Old English Rune-Names (1932) 316
Lateinischen Rätsel der Angelsachsen (1925) 82
Lateinisches Etymologisches Woerterbuch (1910) 301
Latin Poems Commonly Attributed to Walter Mapes, Vol. I (1841) 183
Latin Poems Commonly Attributed to Walter Mapes, Vol. II (1850) 183
Latin Prose Composition (1902) 26
Latin Text of the Ancrene Riwle (1944) 66
Latin-English Dictionary (1857) 268
Laud. MS. 471 (1200) 157
Laut- und Formenlehre der altgermanischen Dialekte: zum Gebrauch für Studierende (1898) 70
Lautdubletten im Altenglischen (1924) 24
Lauthistorisches zum namen Don Adriano de Armado (1925) 243
Laws of Alfred and Ine 158
Laws of Ecclesiastical Polity (1907) 126
Lay of Havelok the Dane (1868) 264
Lay of Havelok the Dane (1902) 265
Lay of Havelok the Dane (1915) 265
Lay of Havelok the Dane (1923) 265
Layamon's Brut, Vol. I (1847) 158
Layamon's Brut, Vol. II (1847) 158
Layamon's Brut, Vol. I (1963) 159
Layamon's Brut: Selections (1924) 159
Lays of ancient Rome (1888) 177
Leechdoms, wortcunning, and starcraft of early England, Vol. I (1864) 58
Leechdoms, wortcunning, and starcraft of early England, Vol. II (1865) 58
Leechdoms, wortcunning, and starcraft of early England, Vol. III (1866) 58
Légende arthurienne, Vol. I (1929) 85
Légende arthurienne, Vol. II (1929) 85
Légende arthurienne, Vol. III (1929) 85
Legend of Good Women (1889) 49
Legend of Sir Gawain (1898) 307
Legend of Sir Perceval, Vol. I (1906) 307
Legend of Sir Perceval, Vol. II (1909) 307
Legenda Aurea 132
Legenden des MS. Laud 108 (1872) 129
Leibniz (1884) 193
Letter from Pontus and Other Verse (1936) 185
Letters of Charles Eliot Norton, Vol. II (1913) 224
Letters on the Spirit of Patriotism and on the Idea of a Patriot King (1917) 23
Letters to An American Lady (1966) 163
Letters to Malcolm: Chiefly on Prayer (1964) 163
Leviathan (1881) 123
Lexicon Poeticum Antiquæ Linguae Septentrionalis (1860) 79
Lexicon Poeticum Antiquæ Linguae Septentrionalis (1931) 79
Library of Henry Savile of Banke (1908) 96
Libri Psalmorum versio antiqua Latina (1835) 290
Libro di nouelle, et di bel parlar gentile (1572) 109

Lieder der Älteren Edda (Sæmundar Edda) (1922) 121
Life and Death of Jason (1914) 206
Life and death of Mr. Badman (1905) 36
Life and Strange Surprising Adventures of Robinson Crusoe 68
Life and times of Girolamo Savonarola, Vol. I (1888) 298
Life and times of Girolamo Savonarola, Vol. II (1888) 298
Life in Shakespeare's England (1920) 314
Life of Francis Thompson (1913) 195
Life of Joseph Wright, Vol. I (1932) 317
Life of Joseph Wright, Vol. II (1932) 317
Life of Richard Nash 97
Life of Saint Katherine (1884) 79
Life of Saint Meriasek, bishop and confessor: a Cornish drama (1872) 275
Life of Samuel Johnson, Vol. I 24
Life of St Chad: an old English homily (1953) 299
Life of St George by Alexander Barclay (1955) 221
Life of St Katharine of Alexandria (1893) 40
Life of St Margaret (1210) 167
Life of William Morris, Vol. I (1907) 179
Life of William Morris, Vol. II (1907) 179
Liflade ant Te Passiun of Seinte Iuliene (1961) 66
Liflade of St Juliana (1882) 58
Light on C. S. Lewis (1965) 95
Lilac Fairy Book (1910) 151
Lilith (1895) 178
Limits of literary criticism (1956) 92
Lindisfarne and Rushworth Gospels (1865) 274
Lindisfarne s/ð Problem (1949-50) 21
Lines a few miles above Tintern Abbey (1907) 316
Linguarum Vett. septentrionalium thesaurus grammatico-criticus et archæologicus, Vol. I (1703) 121
Linguarum Vett. septentrionalium thesaurus grammatico-criticus et archæologicus, Vol. II (1705) 121
Linguistic introduction to the history of English (1963) 22
Lion, the Witch and the Wardbrode (1950) 163
Litauisches Lesebuch mit Grammatik und Wörterbuch (1919) 161
Literary History of the English People (1895) 139
Literary Middle English Reader (1915) 61
Littérature française au Moyen Âge 11e-14e siècle (1905) 93
Littérature française au Moyen Âge 11e-14e siècle (1914) 93
Little Red Riding-Hood 233
Liverpool Town Books, Vol. I (1918) 296
Lives of Donne, Wotton, Hooker, Hebert, and Sanderson (1843) 302
Lives of the English Poets, Vol. I (1920) 134
Lives of the English Poets, Vol. II (1920) 134
Livre de la Chace (1401-1500) 234
Livre des mestiers de Bruges et ses dérivés: Quatre anciens manuels de conversation (1931) 95
Llyfr Gweddi Gyffredin 247
Llyma Vabinogi Iessu Grist (1912) 312
Loathly Lady in 'Thomas of Erceldoune' (1954) 3
London and The vanity of human wishes (1893) 134
London Sonnets (1920) 315
Loom of Language (1943) 23
Lord of the Flies (1954) 97
Lord of the Rings – The Fellowship of the Ring (Proof, 1953) 293
Lord of the Rings – The Two Towers (Proof, 1954) 293

Lord of the Rings – The Return of the King (Proof, 1954) 293
Lord's Prayer and the Angelical Salutation (1899) 249
Lost Explorers: A Tale of the Trackless Desert (1906) 177
Lost literature of medieval England (1952) 314
Love's Labour's Lost 256
Ludus Coventriæ (1841) 113
Lusty plain abundant of vitaille (1957) 211
Lydgate and English Prosody (1960) 183
Lydgate's Troy book, Vol. I (1906) 175
Lydgate's Troy book, Vol. II (1910) 176
Lydgate's Troy book, Vol. III (1910) 176
Lyra Celtica (1924) 258
Lyrical Ballads 1798-1805 (1914) 316

M

Mabinogion 177
Mabinogion (1877) 110
Mabinogion (1913) 110
Mabinogion (1921) 79
Mabinogion (1929) 81
Mabinogion (1949) 136
Mabinogion, mediaeval Welsh romances (1910) 110
Mabinogion, Vol. I (1849) 110
Mabinogion, Vol. II (1849) 110
Mabinogion, Vol. III (1849) 110
Mabinogion, Vol. I (1913) 171
Mabinogion, Vol. II (1913) 171
Mac Flecknoe; or, A satyr upon the True-Blew-Protestant Poet 75
Macbeth 257
Magic Ring, and other stories from the Yellow and Crimson Fairy Books (1906) 151
Magnyfycence 266
Maitresse volage et le chien fidèle (1893) 87
Making of English (1904) 26
Making, Knowing and Judging (1956) 10
Man Born to be King (1943) 250
Man meets dog (1955) 171
Man of Law's Tale (1969) 49
Man Who Was Thursday (1908) 54
Man with two left feet (1917) 315
Man's Unconquerable Mind (1939) 44
Mandeville's Travels, Vol. I (1919) 182
Mandeville's Travels, Vol. II (1923) 182
Manipulus vocabulorum. A dictionary of English and Latine words (1867) 162
Mankind, nation and individual from a linguistic point of view (1925) 133
Mantel, Bruchstück eines Lanzeletromans des Heinrich von dem Türlin (1883) 304
Manual of the Writings in Middle English 1050-1400 (1916) 305
Manual of the Writings in Middle English 1050-1400 (1919) 306
Manual of the Writings in Middle English 1050-1400 (1923) 306
Manuel d'Archeologie, Vol. III (1916) 82
Manuel d'Irlandais Moyen, Vol. I (1913) 73
Manuel d'Irlandais Moyen, Vol. II (1913) 73
Manuscript irlandais de Leide (1892) 273
Marche romane (Juin 1951) 183

Marmion 254
Marvellous Land of Snergs (1927) 323
Master Cat, or, Puss in Boots 233
Master Gamer the oldest English book on hunting (1904) 11
Master Gamer the oldest English book on hunting (1909) 11
Medieval England (1958) 236
Medieval English Verse and Prose in Modernized Versions (1948) 171
Medieval Studies Presented to Aubrey Gwynn (1961) 305
Meier Helmbrecht (1911) 307
Mélanges d'histoire du théatre du Moyen-Age et de la Renaissance offerts a Gustave Cohen (1950) 171
Mélanges de Littérature et de philologie germaniques offerts á Charles Andler (1924) 6
Mélanges de philologie offerts á M. Johan Vising (1925) 299
Melusine (1895) 133
Memoriam of Tennyson (1906) 286
Men of the Moss-Hags (1895) 63
Menneskehed, nasjon, og individ i sproget (1925) 133
Merchant of Venice 257
Merlin Or the Early History of King Arthur, Vol. I (1865) 308
Merlin, roman en prose du 13e siècle, Vol. I (1886) 244
Merlin, roman en prose du 13e siècle, Vol. II (1886) 244
Metaphysical theory of the state: a criticism (1918) 123
Metrical Chronicle of Robert of Gloucester, Vol. I (1887) 244
Metrical Chronicle of Robert of Gloucester, Vol. II (1887) 244
Metrical life of St Cuthbert (1910) 90
Mezentian Gate (1958) 78
Michael: A Pastoral Poem 316
Michel's Ayenbite of Inwyt; or, Remorse of conscience. In the Kentish dialect, 1340 A.D (1866) 202
Microcosmography 77
Middle English (i) Wite God, Wite Crist, (ii) God It Wite (1928) 227
Middle English 'losenger': sketch of an etymological and semantic enquiry (1953) 294
Middle English Alliterative Poem Sir Gawayne the Green Knight (1913) 288
Middle English Dictionary (1891) 276
Middle English Iagmon (Gawain 1729) and Modern English Iag (1931) 193
Middle English Ord and ende (1929) 227
Middle English Reader (1905) 81
Middle English Reader (1919) 81
Middle English syntax (1960) 219
Middle English Vocabulary (1922) 294
Middle High German Primer (1888) 319
Middle High German Primer (1899) 319
Middle High German Primer (1917) 319
Midsummer Night's Dream 257
Midwinter: certain travellers in old England (1923) 33
Military Architecture in England during the Middle Ages (1912) 288
Milk-white Doo 196
Miller's Tale 50
Milton: Poetry & Prose (1920) 196
Mimesis (1953) 10
Mind awake (1968) 142
Minor Elizabethan Drama, Vol. I (1917) 225
Minor Elizabethan Drama, Vol. II (1917) 225
Minor Poems (1888) 50
Minor poems of the Vernon MS., Vol. I (1892) 129

Minor Poems of William Lauder (1870) 157
Mirour de l'Omme (1899) 102
Miscellanea of Temple 286
Missionary Travels And Researches In South Africa (1857) 168
Mistress (1905) 63
Mistress of Mistresses (1935) 78
Mittelenglische Grammatik (1896) 210
Mittelhochdeutsche Grammatik (1904) 231
Mittelhochdeutsches Handwörterbuch, Vol. I A-M (1872) 166
Mittelhochdeutsches Handwörterbuch, Vol. II N-U (1876) 166
Mittelhochdeutsches Handwörterbuch, Vol. III V-Z (1878) 167
Mittelniederdeutsches Lesebuch (1921) 272
Mixed Feelings. Nineteen Poems (1951) 305
Modern English (1925) 132
Modern English Sintax (1971) 227
Modern Languages and the Recent Reform in Dutch Universities (1925) 85
Modersmålets fonetik (1922) 133
Monarche and Other Poems, Pt. I (1865) 176
Monk's Tale 50
Monsters Crouching and Critics Rampant: Or the Beowulf Dragon Debated (1953) 24
Moral Ode (1200) 199
More ghost stories of an antiquary (1911) 132
Morphologische Untersuchungen ... indogermanischen Sprachen, Vol. I (1878) 32
Morphologische Untersuchungen ... indogermanischen Sprachen, Vol. II (1879) 32
Morphologische Untersuchungen ... indogermanischen Sprachen, Vol. III (1880) 32
Morphologische Untersuchungen ... indogermanischen Sprachen, Vol. IV (1881) 32
Morphologische Untersuchungen ... indogermanischen Sprachen, Vol. V (1890) 33
Morte Arthure (1865) 28
Morte Arthure (1915) 20
Morte Arthure (Alliterative) (1360) 211
Morte d'Arthur 211
Morte d'Arthur (1919) 181
Morte d'Arthur, Vol. I (1899) 181
Most Pleasant and Delectable Tale of the Marriage of Cupid and Psyche (1887) 6
Mss. Bodley 340 and 342: Ælfric's Catholic Homilies (1932) 262
Mss. Bodley 340 and 342: Ælfric's Catholic Homilies (1933) 262
Mule sans Frein (1888) 231
Mule sans Frein, par Paiens de Maisière (1838) 76
Mule sanz Frain (1911) 122
Muliere Samaritana. 211
Mundus subterraneus, Vol. I (1668) 143
Murder Must Advertise (1933) 250
Museum Wormianum 316
Musrum (1968) 287
My friend Mr. Leakey (1937) 113
Myndir úr Menningarsögu Íslands á Lidnum Öldum (1929) 22
Myth Became Fact (1944) 163
Myth, Ritual and Religion, Vol. I (1887) 152
Myth, Ritual and Religion, Vol. II (1887) 152
Mythology and Fairy Tales (1873) 152

Mythus von Beowulf (1849) 211
Myvyrian archaiology of Wales (1870) 136

N

Nachträge zur Sage von CuRoi (1913) 292
Name of the Green Knight (1923) 130
Napoleon of Notting Hill 54
Narratiunculae Anglice conscriptae (1861) 58
Natura Deorum 57
Nature and fabric of the Pearl (1904) 252
Nature of belief (1931) 65
Necessariis observantiis scaccarii dialogus (1902) 130
Neue Beobachtungen über Sprachkörper und Sprachfunktion im Englischen (1923) 128
Neusprachliche Studien: Festgabe Karl Luick zu seinem 60. Geburtstag dargebracht von Freunden und Schülern (1925) 173
New and Old Chips from an Old Block (1896) 182
New Collation of the Vespasian Psalter and Hymns (1932) 244
New English Dictionary, Vol. I A-B (1888) 213
New English Dictionary, Vol. II C (1893) 213
New English Dictionary, Vol. III D-E (1897) 213
New English Dictionary, Vol. IV F-G (1901) 214
New English Dictionary, Vol. V H-K (1901) 214
New English Dictionary, Vol. VI L-N (1908) 214
New English Dictionary, Vol. VII O-P (1909) 215
New English Dictionary, Vol. VIII Pt I Q-R (1914) 215
New English Dictionary, Vol. VIII Pt. II S-Sh (1914) 215
New English Dictionary, Vol. IX Pt. I Si-St (1919) 215
New English Dictionary, Vol. IX Pt. II Su-Th (1919) 216
New English Dictionary, Vol. X Pt. I Ti-U (1926) 216
New English Dictionary, Vol. X Pt. II V-Z (1928) 216
New English, Vol. I (1886) 142
New English, Vol. II (1886) 143
New Glossary of the Dialect of the Huddersfield District (1928) 112
New Testament in the Westminster Version of the Sacred Scriptures (1947) 157
News from Nowhere (1891) 207
Nibelungenstudien, Vol. I (1926) 117
Nine Tailors (1934) 251
Noble Art of Venerie or Hunting (1908) 295
Nominalflexion in Ayenbite of Inwyt (1937) 255
Nordische lehnwörter im Orrmulum (1884) 27
Nordische Literaturgeschichte, Vol. I (1921) 100
Nordische Personennamen in England in alt- und frühmittel-englischer Zeit (1910) 20
Norges Indskrifter med de aeldre Runer, Vol. I (1891) 35
Norges Indskrifter med de aeldre Runer, Vol. II (1903) 35
Norges Indskrifter med de aeldre Runer, Vol. III (1924) 35
Norsk ordbog med dansk forklaring (1873) 1
Norsk-islandske skjaldedigtning, Vol. I (1912) 137
Norsk-islandske skjaldedigtning, Vol. II (1912) 137
Norsk-islandske skjaldedigtning, Vol. III (1912) 137
Norsk-islandske skjaldedigtning, Vol. IV (1912) 137
Northern Mists Arctic Exploration in Early Times, Vol. I (1911) 219
Northern Mists Arctic Exploration in Early Times, Vol. II (1911) 219
Northern research, Vol. II. Icelandic (1968) 88
Note on Parlement of the Thre Ages 38 (1928) 248
Note on Parlement of the Thre Ages, 220 (1930) 248
Note on the Language of the Ancrene Riwle (1961) 149
Notes on "Cleanness" and "Sir Gawayne" (1915) 28
Notes on Passages of Old and Middle English (1919) 28
Notes on Sir Gawain and the Green Knight (1922) 81
Notes on Sir Gawayne and the Green Knight (1913) 27
Notes on the Cædmonian Exodus (1902) 28
Notes on the Orthography of the Ormulum (1893) 220
Notes on the Prologue of 'The Parlement of the Thre Ages' (1930) 248
Notes on the script of Labor na hUidre (1912) 18
Noughts and Crosses (1952) 120
Nouveau recueil de fabliaux et contes inédits des poètes français des XIIe, XIIIe, XIVe et XVe siecles, Vol. I (1823) 193
Novel and the fairy tale (1931) 33
Novels and Plays of Saki, Vol. I (1912) 247
Numbered sections in Old English poetical MSS (1915) 26
Numerical Symbolism in Dante and the Pearl (1939) 45
Nun's Priest's Tale (1915) 50
Nun's Priest's Tale (1959) 50
Nun's Rule, being the Ancren Riwle (1926) 211
Nursery Rhyme Book (1897) 152
Nursery tales (1868) 38
Nymphidia 74
Nynorsk Etymologisk Ordbok (1919) 295

O

Oberon 308
Observations sur les présents indo-européens à nasale infixée en celtique (1924) 184
Odes by Collins 59
Odes by Keats 140
Odes of Horace (1894) 127
Odhams dictionary of the English language (1965) 267
Odysseys of Homer (1870) 126
Odysseys of Homer, Vol. I (1907) 126
Odysseys of Homer, Vol. II (1907) 126
Oedipus Tyrannus of Sophocles (1885) 270
Oedipus Tyrannus of Sophocles (1897) 270
Old English Apollonius of Tyre (1958) 100
Old English Ballads (1899) 111
Old English Exodus 84
Old English Exodus (1953) 131
Old English Exodus (1970) 131
Old English Exodus ll. 63-134 (1911) 220
Old English glosses (1900) 220
Old English Grammar (1903) 260
Old English Grammar (1914) 319
Old English Grammar (1959) 38
Old English Homilies (1150) 226
Old English Homilies and homiletic treatises (1868) 203
Old English Homilies of the Twelfth Century (1873) 203
Old English inscription on the Brussels cross (1939) 65
Old English Martyrology (1900) 119
Old English Miscellany (1872) 203
Old English Nominal Compounds in –rád (1952) 27
Old English Poetic Diction (1955) 272
Old English Riddles (1912) 322
Old English version of Bede's Ecclesiastical history of the English people, Vol. I Pt. I (1890) 15
Old English version of Bede's Ecclesiastical history of the

English people, Vol. I Pt. II (1891) 15
Old English version of Bede's Ecclesiastical history of the English people, Vol. II Pt. I (1898) 15
Old English version of Bede's Ecclesiastical history of the English people, Vol. II Pt. II (1898) 15
Old English version of the Heptateuch Ælfric's treatise on the Old and New Testament and his preface to Genesis (1922) 2
Old English vision of Leofric, Earl of Mercia (1908) 220
Old French Grail romance Perlesvaus (1902) 223
Old Kentish Sermons 226
Old King Coel: A Rhymed Tale in four Books (1937) 90
Old Vicarage, Grantchester (1916) 29
Oldest English texts (1885) 282
Old-Irish glosses at Würzburg and Carlsruhe, Pt. I (1887) 275
Oldnordisk læsebog med anmærkninger og ordsamling (1929) 314
Oldnorske og oldislandske litteraturs historie, Vol. I (1920) 137
Oldnorske og oldislandske litteraturs historie, Vol. II (1923) 137
Oldnorske og oldislandske litteraturs historie, Vol. III (1924) 137
Olive Fairy Book (1907) 152
Oliver Twist (1898) 70
On the Sublime (1906) 170
Only English proclamation of Henry III (1258) 228
Only English proclamation of Henry III., 18 October 1258 (1868) 81
Onomasticon Anglo-Saxonicum (1897) 254
Orange Fairy Book (1906) 152
Oratio ad Dominum 121
Orbit #2 (1967) 146
Origin of the English Nation (1907) 42
Origin of the Gerund in English (Phonology) (1925) 297
Original Chronicle of Andrew of Wyntoun (1906) 5
Originals and analogues of some of Chaucer's Canterbury tales (1888) 91
Origines de la poésie lyrique en France au Moyen Âge (1889) 133
Orison of Our Lord (1210) 228
Ormulum (1200) 228
Ormulum (1852) 308
Ormulum (1878) 308
Orrmulum und die Frage der intonationsgerechten Orthographie (1931) 185
Orthodoxy (1908) 54
Orts by G. MacDonald (1882) 178
Orts- und Flurnamen Nordfrieslands (1925) 252
Other Worlds: Essays and Stories (1966) 163
Oud-gentsche naamkunde: bijdrage tot de kennis van het oud-nederlandsch (1924) 183
Our Living Language: a new guide to English grammar (1925) 104
Out of the Silent Planet (1938) 163
Outline of Anglo-Saxon grammar (1911) 28
Outline of Sanity (1926) 55
Ovid's Metamorphoses 229
Owl and the Nightingale (1246-50) 230
Owl and the Nightingale (1838) 274
Owl and the Nightingale (1907) 307
Owl and the nightingale (1960) 273

Oxford Book of English verse, 1250-1900 (1900) 237
Oxford Book of Greek Verse in Translation (1938) 121
Oxford English Dictionary, Vol. I (1933) 218
Oxford English Dictionary, Vol. II (1933) 218
Oxford English Dictionary, Vol. III (1933) 218
Oxford English Dictionary, Vol. IV (1933) 218
Oxford English Dictionary, Vol. V (1933) 218
Oxford English Dictionary, Vol. VI (1933) 218
Oxford English Dictionary, Vol. VII (1933) 219
Oxford English Dictionary, Vol. VIII (1933) 219
Oxford English Dictionary, Vol. IX Pt. I (1933) 219
Oxford English Dictionary, Vol. IX Pt. II (1933) 219
Oxford English Dictionary, Vol. X Pt. I (1933) 219
Oxford English Dictionary, Vol. X Pt. II (1933) 219
Oxford English Dictionary, Vol. XI (1933) 219
Oxford Lectures on Poetry (1909) 26

P

Pageant of the Popes (1943) 85
Pamela (1914) 242
Pamela, Vol. II (1914) 242
Paradise Lost 196
Paradise Regained 196
Parallel extracts from forty-five MS. of Piers Plowman (1905) 154
Parallel extracts from twenty-nine MS. of Piers Plowman (1866) 154
Pardoner's Prologue and Tale (1902) 50
Paris Psalter and the Meters of Boethius (1932) 147
Parlement of Foules 51
Parlement of the Thre Ages (1959) 226
Parson's Tale 51
Path of the King (1923) 34
Patience, a West Midland poem of the fourteenth century (1912) 14
Patience, a West Midland poem of the fourteenth century (1918) 14
Patience: an alliterative version of Jonah (1924) 99
Patience: an alliterative version of Jonah (1913) 98
Patrologiae cursus completus, LXXIX (1849) 195
Parzifal (1331-1336) (1888) 315
Peace of Aristophanes 7
Pearl 232
Pearl (1906) 229
Pearl (1910) 229
Pearl (1953) 101
Pearl (1961) 122
Pearl in Its Setting (1968) 19
Pearl, Cleanness, Patience and Sir Gawain, reproduced in facsimile from the unique MS. Cotton Nero A.x in the British Museum (1923) 99
Pearl. Sir Gawain and the Green Knight (1962) 42
Pearl: a new interpretation (1925) 105
Pearl: a study in spiritual dryness (1925) 180
Pearl: An English Poem of the 14th Century (1891) 99
Pearl: an English poem of the 14th century (1897) 99
Pearl: An English Poem of the 14th Century (1921) 99
Pearl: and interpretation (1918) 92
Pearl: the 14th century English poem rendered in modern verse (1932) 45
Pedeir Kainc y Mabinogi, Breuddwyd Maxe, Lludd a

Llevelys (1905) 83
Pepysian Gospel Harmony (1922) 97
Perceval le Gallois ou le Conte du Graal, Vol. I (1866) 56
Perceval le Gallois ou le Conte du Graal, Vol. III (1866) 56
Percevalroman (1932) 57
Percy folio of old English ballads and romances, Vol. II (1906) 233
Peredur ab Efrawc (1887) 194
Perelandra (1943) 164
Perlesvaus. Le haut livre du Graal, Vol. I (1932) 223
Perlesvaus. Le haut livre du Graal, Vol. II (1937) 223
Perrault's Popular Tales (1888) 233
Perseus and Andromeda 234
Peter and Wendy (1912) 13
Peter Pan in Kensington Gardens 13
Peterborough Chronicle 1070-1154 (1958) 54
Petworth MS. (1868) 51
Phantastes 178
Philaster 14
Philological Miscellany Presented to Eilert Ekwall (1942) 168
Philosophical Survey of the South of Ireland (1778) 39
Philosophy of Grammar (1925) 133
Phoenix and the Carpet (1904) 222
Phonetics of the Gaelic Language (1889) 179
Phonetische Grundfragen (1904) 134
Phonology of a South Durham Dialect (1933) 229
Phyllyp Sparowe 266
Physiography (1877) 131
Picnic at Sakkara (1955) 222
Pied Piper of Hamelin (1845) 31
Pierce the Ploughman's crede (1867) 154
Piers Plowman (1362) 235
Piers Plowman Text B (1377) 235
Pilgrim's progress (1917) 36
Pilgrim's Regress (1933) 164
Pilgrims of the Rhine (1834) 35
Pink Fairy Book (1897) 152
Place of the Lion (1931) 311
Place-name and English Linguistic Studies (1924) 323
Place-name Tests of Racial Mixture in Northern England (1924) 87
Place-names Jervaulx, Ure, and York (1924) 267
Place-names of Buckinghamshire (1925) 186
Place-names of Devon, Pt. 1 (1931) 101
Place-names of Devon, Pt. 2 (1932) 101
Place-names of Gloucestershire, Vol. XXXVIII, Pt. I (1964) 266
Place-names of Gloucestershire, Vol. XXXIX, Pt. II (1964) 267
Place-names of Gloucestershire, Vol. XL, Pt. III (1964) 267
Place-names of Gloucestershire, Vol. XLI, Pt. IV (1965) 267
Place-names of Lancashire (1922) 80
Place-names of Northamptonshire (1933) 101
Place-names of Northumberland and Durham (1920) 185
Place-names of Skye and adjacent Islands (1923) 98
Place-names of Surrey (1934) 102
Place-names of the East Riding of Yorkshire and York (1937) 266
Place-names of the North Riding of Yorkshire (1928) 266
Place-names, Highlands and Islands of Scotland (1923) 177
Plattner story (1897) 306
Plays and fragments, Pt. I (1887) 270
Plays and fragments, Pt. I (1900) 270

Pocket Oxford Dictionary of Current English (1924) 90
Pocket volume of selections from the poetical works of Robert Browning (1898) 31
Poem on the times of Edward the second (1849) 115
Poèmes Bretons du moyen âge (1879) 149
Poemes mythologiques de l'Edda (1936) 300
Poems by Dixon (1909) 72
Poems by Gray (1915) 104
Poems by Milton (1905) 197
Poems from the Old English (1961) 237
Poems of John Donne, Vol. II (1901) 72
Poems of John Donne, Vol. I (1912) 72
Poems of John Donne, Vol. II (1912) 73
Poems of Laurence Minot (1914) 197
Poems of Samuel Taylor Coleridge (1927) 59
Poems of Tennyson 1829-1868 (1929) 286
Poems of To-day (1916) 82
Poesia popolare di Antonio Pucci (1909) 86
Poésies populaires latines antérieures au douzième siècle (1843) 75
Poetic Diction (1928) 13
Poetic Edda (1923) 16
Poetic Edda in the light of Archæology (1931) 222
Poetical Works of Alexander Pope (1917) 236
Poetical Works of John Dryden (1920) 75
Poetical works of John Milton (1909) 197
Poetical works of William Blake (1913) 21
Poetry for Pleasure (1938) 90
Poetry in the Red Book of Hergest (1911) 84
Poetry of J.R.R. Tolkien (1967) 135
Political Poems and Songs Relating to English History, Vol. I (1859) 319
Political Poems and Songs Relating to English History, Vol. II (1861) 320
Polychronicon (1352) 235
Polychronicon. John Trevisa's translation (1387) 235
Polychronicon Ranulphi Higden monachi Cestrensis, Vol. I (1865) 174
Polychronicon Ranulphi Higden monachi Cestrensis, Vol. II (1869) 174
Polychronicon Ranulphi Higden monachi Cestrensis, Vol. III (1871) 174
Polychronicon Ranulphi Higden monachi Cestrensis, Vol. IV (1872) 174
Polychronicon Ranulphi Higden monachi Cestrensis, Vol. V (1874) 175
Polychronicon Ranulphi Higden monachi Cestrensis, Vol. VI (1876) 175
Polychronicon Ranulphi Higden monachi Cestrensis, Vol. VII (1879) 175
Polychronicon Ranulphi Higden monachi Cestrensis, Vol. VIII (1882) 175
Polychronicon Ranulphi Higden monachi Cestrensis, Vol. IX (1886) 175
Poor Hater: a novel (1958) 240
Poor Stainless: A new story about the Borrowers (1966) 224
Popular Ballads and Songs, Vol. I (1806) 132
Popular Ballads and Songs, Vol. II (1806) 132
Popular rhymes of Scotland (1874) 45
Popular Tales from the Norse (1859) 67
Popular Tales of the West Highlands, Vol. I (1890) 39
Popular Tales of the West Highlands, Vol. II (1890) 40

Popular Tales of the West Highlands, Vol. III (1892) 40
Popular Tales of the West Highlands, Vol. IV (1893) 40
Portugais; phonétique et phonologie, morphologie, texts (1903) 100
Posthumous papers of the Pickwick club (1837) 70
Practical study of languages (1899) 282
Préface de 'Cromwell' (1916) 130
Preface to a Dictionary of the English Language 134
Preface to Shakespeare 134
Preface to the Fables (1912) 75
Prehistory: A Study of Early Cultures in Europe and the Mediterranean Basin (1925) 36
Pricke of Conscience (1863) 275
Primer of Historical English Grammar (1902) 283
Primer of the Gothic language (1892) 319
Primer of the Gothic language (1899) 319
Prince Prigio (1899) 152
Prince Ricardo of Pantouflia (1893) 152
Princess and Curdie 178
Princess and the Goblin 178
Princess Nobody: a Tale of Fairy Land (1884) 152
Prinzipielles zur modernen Syntaxforschung (1925) 210
Prioress's Tale, The tale of Sir Thopas (1922) 51
Prioresses Tale, Sir Thopas, the Monkes Tale, the Clerkes Tale, the Squieres Tale (1880) 51
Proben eines englischen Eigennamen-Wörterbuches (1923) 89
Problem of Pain (1940) 164
Problem of the Picts (1955) 300
Problem und die Darstellung des 'standard of Spoken English' (1912) 253
Probleme der Englischen Sprache und Kultur (1925) 41
Proceedings of the seventh International Congress of Linguistic (1956) 224
Progress & Religion: An Historical Enquiry (1929) 67
Prologue and Three Tales (1934) 52
Prologue to the Canterbury Tales 51
Prologue to the Canterbury Tales (1897) 51
Prologue, The Knights Tale, The Nonne Preestes Tale (1885) 52
Promptorium Parvulorum Sive Clericorum Dictionarius Anglo-Latinus Princeps (1865) 305
Promptorium Parvulorum. The first English-Latin dictionary (1908) 191
Prosaische Edda, Vol. I (1912) 309
Prospectus for the Linguistic Atlas of New England (1938) 148
Provenzalische Chrestomathie (1920) 6
Proverbs of Alfred (1246-50) 237
Proverbs of Alfred (1907) 265
Proverbs of Alfred (1908) 24
Proverbs of Alfred (1931) 232
Psalm LXXXV 9 (1920) 26
Psalter des Eadwine von Canterbury (1905) 309
Psalter of the Psalms of David (1884) 27
Psalter, or Psalms of David and certain canticles (1884) 246
Pseudodoxia Epidemica 30
Psychology of the unconscious (1916) 138
Public Opinion and the Last Peace (1944) 192
Public School German Grammar (1908) 192
Puck of Pook's Hill (1906) 143
Pure Saxon English (1890) 198
Purity; a Middle English poem (1920) 193

Q

Qautrefoil of Love (1935) 100
Quest of Beauty and Other Poems (1915) 90
Queste del Saint Graal (1923) 231
Questions connected with the Old English Poem of 'Beowulf' (1912) 275

R

Ragnarssona þáttr 238
Raleigh's Selections 238
Rally, Vol. I (1966) 308
Randigal rhymes and a glossary of Cornish words (1895) 288
Rare Use of the Preposition 'to' (1925) 63
Rasselas and some mediaeval ancillaries (1959) 183
Ratis raving, and other moral and religious pieces, in prose and verse (1870) 175
Ravennatis Anonymi Cosmographia et Gvidonis Geographica (1860) 235
Readers of Literature (1973) 89
Reading of Sir Gawain and the Green Knight (1965) 37
Reallexikon der Germanischen Altertumskunde, Vol. I (1911) 126
Reallexikon der Germanischen Altertumskunde, Vol. II (1911) 126
Reallexikon der Germanischen Altertumskunde, Vol. III (1911) 127
Reallexikon der Germanischen Altertumskunde, Vol. IV (1911) 127
Records of the borough of Nottingham, Vol. III (1885) 274
Records of the Borough of Nottingham, Vol. IV (1889) 274
Recovery of Belief (1952) 134
Recta et emendata linguae anglicae scriptione Dialogus (1913) 268
Recueil Général des Chartes Anglo-Saxonnes les Saxons en Angleterre (1912) 234
Red Book of Heroes (1909) 154
Red Etin 240
Red Fairy Book (1890) 152
Red Moon and Black Mountain (1970) 45
Redbook (1967) 198
Reduplizierten Perfekta des Nord- und Westgermanischen (1921) 139
Reeve's Tale 52
Reeve's Tale (1939) 294
Reflections on the French Revolution (1910) 36
Reformation touching Church-Discipline in England (1916) 197
Region of the Summer Stars (1944) 311
Rehabilitations And Other Essays (1939) 164
Rehearsal (1914) 34
Religio medici 31
Religio medici, Letter to a friend &c., and Christian morals (1889) 31
Religious Lyrics of the Fourteenth Century (1923) 30
Religious Lyrics of the XIVth century (1952) 30
Reliquiae Antiquae, Vol. I (1845) 320
Renegade poet, and other essays (1910) 288
Report on Manuscripts in the Welsh Language, Vol. I (1898) 105
Report on Manuscripts in the Welsh Language, Vol. II Pt.

I (1902) 105
Report on Manuscripts in the Welsh Language, Vol. II Pt. II (1902) 105
Retreat From Truth (1958) 213
Review of Ancrene Wisse (1963) 139
Rewards and Fairies (1910) 143
Reynard the Fox (1921) 185
Rhyme? and reason? 41
Rhythmik des germanischen alliterationsverses (1885) 260
Richard II 257
Richard Löwenherz (1925) 41
Richard the Redeless (1399) 242
Right Pleasant and Goodly Historie of the Foure Sonnes of Aymon, Pt. I (1884) 42
Rime of Dante Alighieri 4
Rime di m. Cino da Pistoia e d'altri del secolo XIV (1852) 40
Ring des Nibelungen, Vol. I. Das Rheingold: Vorspiel 300
Ring des Nibelungen, Vol. II. Die Walküre: Erster Tag 300
Ring des Nibelungen, Vol. III. Siegfried: Zweiter Tag 300
Ring des Nibelungen, Vol. IV. Götterdämmerung: Dritter Tagise and Rivals by Sheridan 300
Robert Laneham's letter (1907) 150
Robert of Gloucester Chronicle (1298) 243
Robin Hood 245
Robin Hood and Guy of Gisborne 245
Roman Britain and the English Settlements (1936) 59
Roman de Brut, Vol. I (1836) 299
Roman de Brut, Vol. II (1838) 299
Roman de Brut, Vol. I (1938) 299
Roman de Brut, Vol. II (1840) 300
Roman Historie (1609) 5
Roman History (1879) 39
Roman Missal in Latin and English (1921) 37
Roman van Lancelot (XIII, eeuw.), Vol. II (1849) 135
Roman van Walewein, Pt. II (1848) 135
Romance of Cheuelere Assigne (1868) 96
Romance of Guy of Warwick I and II (1875) 325
Romance of Guy of Warwick, Pt. II (1876) 325
Romance of William of Palerne (1867) 265
Romanisches etymologisches Wörterbuch (1911) 195
Romans de Garin le Loherain, Vol. I (1833) 133
Romaunt of the Rose (1360) 52
Romance of Emaré (1908) 243
Romance of Sir Degrevant (1949) 41
Romeo and Juliet 257
Roots of the Mountains (1906) 207
Rose and the Ring (1855) 287
Rosemounde. A Balade 52
Rough list of English words found in Anglo-French (1882) 265
Roxburghshire Word-Book (1923) 305
Ruin 246
Runes. An Introduction (1959) 80
Ruthwell Cross 246

S

Sacre rappresentazioni dei secoli XIV, XV e XVI, Vol. II (1872) 64
Sæmundar-Edda: Eddukvæði (1905) 137
Saga of Hrolf Kraki (1933) 196
Saga of King Heidrek the Wise (1960) 292
Saga of the Volsungs (1965) 87
Saga Ólafs konúngs Tryggvasonar (1825) 212
Sagas of the Kings (Konunga Sögur) and the mythical-heroic sagas (Fornaldar Sögur) (1937) 118
Sage von CuRoi (1913) 292
Sagen aus dem alten Irland (1901) 292
Saint Denis portant sa téte sur la potrine (1891) 65
Saint Erkenwald (1922) 99
Saltair na rann: a collection of early Middle Irish poems (1883) 275
Same Scourge (1954) 97
Samson Agonistes (1889) 197
Sartor resartus (1905) 40
Satires of Marvell (1901) 184
Sawles Warde (1210) 249
Sawles Warde (1938) 314
Saxon treatise concerning the Old and New Testament (1623) 2
Saxonis Grammatici Gesta Danorvm (1886) 249
Saxonis Grammatici Historia Danica, Vol. I Pt. I (1839) 249
Saxonis Grammatici Historia Danica, Vol. I Pt. II (1839) 249
Saxonis Grammatici Historia Danica, Vol. II (1858) 249
Scandinavian Archaeology (1937) 259
Sceáf und seine Nachkommen (1849) 211
Scholemaster 7
School of John Donne (1912) 73
Schwache Präteritum und seine Vorgeschichte, Vol. I (1912) 59
Science is a sacred cow (1950) 272
Science of Language, Vol. I (1891) 212
Science of Language, Vol. II (1891) 212
Scondia illustrata, Vol. I (1700) 193
Scottish Alliterative Poems (1897) 5
Scouting for Buller (1902) 116
Screwtape letters (1942) 165
Scribal Tradition of the Lambeth Homilies (1951) 262
Scriptores rerum Danicarum medii aevi, Vol. I (1772) 154
Seafarer 254
Seafarer (1960) 101
Second Anglo-Saxon Reader (1887) 283
Second Middle English primer (1886) 284
Second Shepherds' Play 254
Secret Commonwealth of Elves, Fauns & Fairies (1893) 144
Seed of Adam and other plays (1948) 311
Scintc Katerine (1981) 66
Seinte Marherete the meiden ant martyr, in Old English (1866) 58
Seinte Marherete þe Meiden ant Martyr (1934) 179
Selbaständigkeitsbewegung in den englischen Kolonien (1925) 69
Select private Orations of Demosthenes. Pt. I (1885) 68
Select private Orations of Demosthenes. Pt. II (1886) 68
Select remains of the ancient popular and romance poetry of Scotland (1885) 154
Select remains of the ancient popular poetry of Scotland (1822) 153
Selected English essays 231
Selected English short stories (nineteenth century) (1914) 301
Selections from Confessio Amantis (1903) 102
Selections from Early Middle English, 1130-1250, Vol. I (1920) 114
Selections from Early Middle English, 1130-1250, Vol. II (1920) 114

Selections from James Boswell's Life of Samuel Johnson (1919) 25
Selections from Layamon's Brut (1963) 159
Selections from the Hengwrt MSS. preserved in the Peniarth library, Vol. I (1876) 312
Selections from the Hengwrt MSS. preserved in the Peniarth library, Vol. II (1892) 313
Semantics of Toast (1949) 181
Sermo Lupi ad Anglos (1939) 321
Seven ages (1845) 320
Seven Sages (1320-50) 249
Seven Words of the Cross 245
Sgéalaigheacht Chéitinn (1930) 17
Shadows in the Moonlight 129
Shakespeare glossary (1941) 227
Shakespeare's As you Like it (1920) 257
Shakespeare's England, Vol. I (1916) 160
Shakespeare's England, Vol. II (1916) 160
Shakespearean Tragedy (1904) 26
She and Allan (1921) 112
She: A history of adventure (1887) 112
Shepheards Calendar (1895) 272
Shield of Achilles (1955) 10
Short Historical English Grammar (1892) 284
Short Historical English Grammar (1893) 284
Short history of costume et armour, Vol. I (1931) 140
Short History of English (1914) 323
Short History of English (1921) 323
Short History of English Literature (1913) 247
Short History of English Literature (1921) 277
Short History of English Poetry 1340-1940 (1961) 240
Short History of the English People (1907) 105
Short Stories of Saki (1913) 247
Shorter Elizabethan Poems (1903) 6
Shorter Oxford English Dictionary, Vol. I (1956) 227
Shorter Oxford English Dictionary, Vol. II (1956) 228
Shrine: a collection of occasional papers on dry subjects (1864) 58
Shropshire place-names (1923) 26
Siege and conquest of the North Pole (1910) 76
Siege of Jerusalem (1935) 146
Sign of Four (1890) 60
Signalling: Morse, Semaphore, Station Work, Despatch Riding, Telephone Cables, Map Reading (1915) 268
Significance of the 'Garlande Gay' in the Allegory of Pearl (1957) 19
Silver Trumpet (1925) 13
Simple Lessons in Irish (1912) 225
Sinners Beware 261
Sir Eglamour of Artois 261
Sir Gawain 'Fer ouer þe French flod' (1948) 248
Sir Gawain and the Carl of Carlisle in two versions (1951) 148
Sir Gawain and the Green Knight 261
Sir Gawain and the Green Knight (1912) 144
Sir Gawain and the Green Knight (1925) 294
Sir Gawain and the Green Knight (1930) 294
Sir Gawain and the Green Knight (1940) 99
Sir Gawain and Pearl. Critical Essays (1968) 295
Sir Gawain and the Green Knight (1946) 294
Sir Gawain and the Green Knight, and other similar English poems (1883) 303
Sir Gawain and the Green Knight. Considered as a Garter Poem (1913) 131
Sir Gawain and the Green Knight; a prose translation (1952) 136
Sir Gawain and the Green Knight; a stylistic and metrical study (1962) 24
Sir Gawayne and the Green Knight (1864) 204
Sir Gawayne and the Green Knight (1869) 204
Sir Gawayne and the green knight (1883) 288
Sir Gawayne and the Green Knight (1893) 204
Sir Gawayne and the Green Knight (1897) 204
Sir Gawayne and the Green Knight (1912) 205
Sir Gawayne and the Green Knight (1919) 205
Sir Gawayne and the Green Knight, Lines 697-702 (1907) 44
Sir Orfeo 262
Sir Orfeo (1944) 294
Sir Orfeo (1954) 22
Sir Orfeo (1966) 22
Sir Thopas Tale 52
Sir Tristrem (1230) 262
Sir Tristrem (1811) 287
Sir Tristrem (1886) 287
Sire Gauvain et le Chevalier vert, poème anglais du XIVe siècle (1946) 236
Six Chief Lives (1908) 135
Six plays by contemporaries of Shakespeare (1915) 308
Skotlands Rímur: Icelandic Ballads on the Gowrie Conspiracy (1908) 109
Slang, lexique de l'anglais familier et vulgaire (1923) 182
Sleeping Beauty in the Wood 233
Snorri Sturluson (1920) 223
Society of Oxford Home-Students: retrospects and recollections (1879-1921) (1930) 37
Society upon the Stanislaus (1868) 115
Soeskie Tien Tien: Moi en bekente Siengi (1944) 146
Soldiers of Rome (1964) 192
Some Contributions to Middle-English Lexicography (1925) 294
Some gains of the war (1918) 239
Some Hints on Pattern Designing (1899) 207
Some Lost Saint's Lives in Old and Middle English (1941) 314
Some Old-English words omitted or imperfectly explained in dictionaries (1898) 274
Some place-name identifications in the Anglo-Saxon chronicles (1925) 185
Some place-names and the Etymology of 'she' (1925) 267
Somer soneday (1929) 30
Song against the King of Almaigne (1264) 269
Song of Hiawatha 170
Songs for the Philologists (1936) 295
Sonnets of William Alabaster (1959) 276
Soria Moria Castel 270
Source of Capgrave's Life of St Katharine of Alexandria (1960) 149
Source of Scribal Error in Early Middle English MSS. (1953) 36
Spätaltenglische Übersetzung der Pseudo-Anselmschen Marienpredigt (1925) 89
Specimens of Early English (1885) 205
Specimens of Early English (1898) 206
Specimens of Early English: with introductions, notes, and glossarial index (1935) 206

Specimens of lyric poetry (1842) 320
Specimens of Middle Scots (1902) 267
Specimens of Modern English Literary Criticism (1919) 28
Specimens of Scottish literature, 1325-1835 (1913) 194
Speech delivered for the presentation of the Honorary Degree of Doctor of Letters to Professor John Ronald Reuel Tolkien (1972) 297
Speech on American Taxation (1905) 36
Splendid Century (1953) 166
Split Infinitive (1923) 90
Sprache des Dichters von Sir Gawain, und der sagen (1885) 146
Sprachkörper und Sprachfunktion (1921) 128
Sprachkörper und Sprachfunktion im englischen (1923) 111
Sprachliche Adoptivformen (1924) 316
Sprachschatz der Angelsächsischen Dichter (1912) 106
Squire's Tale 52
St. Erkenwald, a middle English poem (1926) 248
St. Francis of Assisi (1923) 54
St. Juliana 272
St. Martin of Tours (1928) 255
Stand und Aufgaben der Sprachwissenschaft (1924) 90
Starry Heavens (1933) 116
Stations of the Cross 273
Statistical Account, Or Parochial Survey of Ireland (1814) 185
Statius and Dante (1956) 165
Storia della lingua italiana (1971) 195
Stories for my Children 145
Story of Doctor Dolittle (1920) 170
Story of England by Robert Manning of Brunne, AD 1338, Vol. I (1887) 182
Story of Burnt Njal (1861) 67
Story of Genesis and Exodus (1865) 157
Story of Grettir the strong (1869) 207
Story of Howard the Halt. The Story of the Banded Men. The Story of Hen Thorir (1891) 207
Story of Sigurd the Volsung and the fall of the Niblunges (1912) 207
Story of the Amulet (1906) 222
Story of the Glittering Plain (1891) 207
Story of the Three Bears (1837) 271
Strange case of Dr Jekyll and Mr. Hyde 274
Strange Story Book (1913) 154
Streitberg-Festgabe (1924) 277
Strong Poison (1931) 250
Stuart Tracts 1603-1693 (1903) 87
Student's Chaucer (1894) 52
Student's Dictionary of Anglo-Saxon (1911) 284
Studien zu altenglischen Psalterglossen (1904) 168
Studien zu den Skalden des 9. und 10. Jahrhunderts (1928) 240
Studien zur germanischen sagengeschichte, Vol. I. Beowulf (1910) 230
Studien zur germanischen sagengeschichte, Vol. II. Sigfrid (1912) 230
Studien zur Lehre: von der Wurzelerweiterung und Wurzelvariation (1891) 234
Studier i Ynglingatal, Vol. I (1905) 253
Studier i Ynglingatal, Vol. II (1906) 253
Studier i Ynglingatal, Vol. III (1907) 253
Studier i Ynglingatal, Vol. IV (1910) 253
Studies in English Rhymes from Surrey to Pope, a Ch. in the History of English (1923) 324

Studies in the Dialect and Vocabulary of the Ancrene Riwle (1965) 324
Studies in the diction of Layamon's Brut (1930) 324
Studies in the Ormulum MS. (1947) 296
Studies in words (1960) 164
Study in phonetic symbolism (1929) 248
Study of Gawain and the Green Knight (1916) 144
Study of Wagner (1899) 222
Stuffed owl (1930) 165
Sturlunga saga, Vol. I (1908) 20
Sturlunga saga, Vol. II (1909) 20
Sturlunga saga, Vol. III (1913) 20
Sturlunga saga, Vol. IV (1915) 20
Sturlungu, Vol. III (1897) 226
Style of Raleigh (1918) 239
Styrbjörn the Strong (1926) 78
Suffolk Hundred in the Year 1283 (1910) 237
Summa Theologica, Vol. I (1787) 287
Summa Theologica, Vol. II (1787) 287
Summa Theologica, Vol. III (1787) 287
Summa Theologica, Vol. IV (1787) 287
Summa Theologica, Vol. V (1787) 287
Summa Theologica, Vol. VI (1787) 287
Summa Theologica, Vol. VII (1787) 287
Sundering Flood (1898) 208
Sundials: Incised Dials or Mass-Clocks (1926) 105
Super librum Sapientiae (1506) 124
Surprised by Joy (1955) 165
Svenska Rikets Uppkomst (1925) 222
Svenskt Dialect-Lexicon eller Ordbok öfver Svenska allmogespraket (1877) 241
Sveriges förkristna konungalängd (1910) 6
Swahili tales: as told by natives of Zanzibar (1870) 273
Swallows and Amazons (1930) 239
Swift's Miscellanies, in prose and verse, Vol. V (1735) 284
Sword in the Stone (1938) 308
Swords & Sorcery (1963) 68
Sylvie and Bruno 41
Sylvie and Bruno Concluded 41
Symbolism, Allegory, and Autobiography in The Pearl (1909) 252
Synopsis methodica animalium quadrupedum (1693) 239
Synopsis of quadrupeds (1771) 232
Syntax des Einfachen Satzes im Indogermanischen (1925) 32
Syntax in den Werken Alfreds des Grossen, Vol I (1894) 321
Syntax in den Werken Alfreds des Grossen, Vol II (1901) 321
Syr Gawayn and the Grene Knyʒt (1915-1916) 130
Syr Gawayne (1839) 180

T

Tacitus' Germania (1907) 315
Taill of Rauf Coilyear 285
Taill of Rauf Coilyear (1894) 295
Taill of Rauf Coilyear: a Scottish metrical romance of the fifteenth century (1903) 31
Tailor of Gloucester (1903) 236
Tale of a Youth who Set out to Learn what Fear Was 286
Tale of Benjamin Bunny (1904) 236
Tale of Beowulf (1895) 209
Tale of Beowulf (1898) 208
Tale of Gamelyn (1884) 265

Tale of Jemima Puddle-Duck (1908) 236
Tale of Mr. Tod (1912) 237
Tale of Mrs Tiggy-winkle 237
Tale of Peter Rabbit 236
Tale of the House of the Wolfings and All the Kindreds of the Mark (1890) 208
Tale of the Man of Lawe; The Pardoneres Tale; The Second Nonnes Tales; The Chanouns Yemannes Tale (1897) 53
Tales from the travels of Baron Munchhausen (1926) 239
Tales of a Fairy Court (1907) 153
Tales of Troy and Greece (1907) 153
Tales of Wonder, Vol. I (1801) 166
Tales of Wonder, Vol. II (1801) 166
Taliessin through Logres (1938) 313
Task: A Poem, in Six Books 63
Technicalities 84
Tellers of Tales (1953) 105
Tempest of Shakespeare 258
Ten Thousand Miles away (1897) 94
Terminology of Anglistics (1930) 181
Terms Briton, British, Britisher; preposition at end (1923) 26
Terrible Head 286
Terror of Light (1940) 311
Testament Newydd ein arglwydd Jesu Christi Gwedy ei dynnu 247
Teutonic Mythology, Vol. I (1883) 107
Teutonic Mythology, Vol. II (1883) 107
Teutonic Mythology, Vol. III (1888) 107
Teutonic Mythology, Vol. IV (1882) 108
Text of introductory address delivered by Professor Jeremiah J. Hogan (1954) 123
Text of Sir Gawain and the Green Knight (1915) 146
Text of the Bruts from the Red book of Hergest (1890) 242
Text of The Canterbury tales by John M. Manly and Edith Rickert (1940) 30
Text of the Mabinogion: and other Welsh tales from the Red Book of Hergest (1887) 242
Texte und Forschungen zur englischen Kulturgeschichte: Festgabe für Felix Liebermann (1924) 167
Textkritik der angelsächsischen Dichter (1865) 106
That Hideous Strength (1945) 165
Theme of 'Judgment Day II' (1969) 123
Thesaurus of English Words and Phrases (1925) 245
These Are My Comrades (1943) 246
Thirteenth-Century Manuscript from Llanthony Priory (1928) 30
Thomas More (1935) 44
Þorfinns saga Hvita (1902) 8
Þorfinns saga Karlsefnis (1902) 8
Þorgils Saga ok Hafliða (1952) 31
Thornton romances: Early English Metrical Romances of 'Perceval', 'Isumbras', 'Eglamour' and 'Degrevant' (1844) 113
Thousand and one nights (1892) 290
Three Early English Metrical Romances (1842) 245
Three Little Pigs 290
Three Musketeers 75
Three Northern Love Stories the Tale of Beowulf (1911) 208
Three Old English prose texts in MS. Cotton Vitellius A XV (1924) 246
Through the crack (1925) 21
Thucydides Book I, Vol. I (1895) 291

Thucydides Book I, Vol. II (1895) 291
Thucydides: Book VI (1905) 291
Time Machine (1895) 306
Timber: or, Discoveries made upon men and matter (1906) 136
Tiomna Nuadh ar dTighearna agus ar Slanuightheóra Iosa Criosd (1827) 225
Toad of Toad hall (1929) 196
Toiler of the sea (1965) 180
Tolkien Relation (1968) 240
Tottel's Miscellany (1903) 295
Towneley plays (1907) 81
Tragedy of Julius Cæsar (1906) 258
Tragic Death of Cúrói mac Dári (1905) 18
Tragical history of Dr Faustus (1910) 184
Transcripts and Studies (1896) 73
Translation of the Anglo-Saxon Poem of Beowulf: With a Copious Glossary (1833) 141
Treasure Island (1883) 274
Treasury of Seventeenth Century English Verse (1920) 185
Tribal system in Wales (1904) 255
Triode, no. 18 (1960) 17
Trioedd Ynys Prydein (1951) 29
Tristan 101
Troilus and Criseyde 53
Troilus and Criseyde (1935) 53
Trojanische Krieg (1858) 176
Truth About Publishing 297
Truth of Chaucer 53
Tudor Tracts 1532-1588 (1903) 235
Twelfth Century Homilies in MS. Bodley 343 (1909) 16
Two Cantos of Mutability 271
Two fifteenth-century cookery-books (1888) 10
Two of the Saxon Chronicles Parallel (787-1001 A.D.) (1920) 77
Two of the Saxon Chronicles Parallel, Vol. I (1929) 77
Two of the Saxon Chronicles Parallel, Vol. II (1929) 77
Two Old English words (1944) 193
Two Problems of the German Preterite-Present Verbs (1928) 87
Two Quiet Lives: Dorothy Osborne, Thomas Gray (1948) 42

U

Über älteste sprachliche Beziehungen zwischen Kelten und Italikern (1917) 301
Über einige Zukunftsaufgaben der englischen Sprachwissenschaft (1930) 173
Ueber die französischen Gralromane (1891) 117
Uncle Remus and Brer Rabbit (1907) 115
Unended wandering: A selection of verse (1970) 116
Unfortunate Traveller 221
Unpleasantness at the Bellona Club (1928) 251
Untersuchungen über das altenglische Exoduslied (1899) 213
Until the Dragon comes ... some thoughts on Beowulf (1963) 197
Unto this last (1921) 246
Urgermanisch, Vorgeschichte der altgermanischen Dialekte (1913) 145

V

Vénerie de Twiti (1956) 296

Vengeance Raguidel: altfranzösischer Abenteurroman (1909) 90
Verbal Inflections of the East Midland dialects in Early Middle English (1924) 226
Verbal Repetition in the Ancren Riwle (1944) 130
Verceller Handschrift (1894) 322
Vercelli Book (1932) 147
Vercelli-Homilien, Vol. I (1932) 89
Vergilii Maronis opera, Vol. I (1897) 298
Vergilii Maronis opera, Vol. II (1897) 298
Vergleichende Grammatik der keltischen Sprachen, Vol. I (1909) 232
Vergleichende Grammatik der keltischen Sprachen, Vol. II (1913) 232
Vergleichendes Wörterbuch der indogermanischen Sprachen, Vol. I (1926) 301
Vergleichendes Wörterbuch der indogermanischen Sprachen, Vol. II (1927) 301
Vergleichendes Wörterbuch der indogermanischen Sprachen, Vol. III (1874) 86
Vernon MS. Bodleian 298
Vicar of Wakefield (1910) 97
Vie de Saint Patrice: mystère Breton en trois actes (1909) 76
Vie des mots étudiée dans leurs significations (1887) 67
Vier Zweige des Mabinogi (Pedeir Ceinc y Maginogi) (1925) 211
View of the Present State of Ireland 272
Vigá-Glúms saga (1897) 9
Víga-Glúms Saga (1940) 296
Violet Fairy Book (1901) 153
Virgil of Salzburg versus 'Aethicus Ister' (1959) 73
Vision of William concerning Piers Plowman, Pt. I (1867) 155
Vision of William concerning Piers Plowman, Pt. II (1869) 155
Vision of William concerning Piers Plowman, Pt. III (1873) 155
Vision of William concerning Piers Plowman, Pt. IV (1877) 156
Vision of William concerning Piers the Plowman (1906) 156
Vision of William concerning Piers the Plowman (1923) 157
Vision of William concerning Piers the Plowman in three parallel texts, Vol. I (1886) 155
Vision of William concerning Piers the Plowman in three parallel texts, Vol. II (1886) 155
Vision of William concerning Piers the Plowman. According to the version revised and enlarged by the author about A.D. 1377 (1869) 156
Vita nova 4
Vita S. Columbae (1920) 1
Vocabulaire Vieux-Breton (1884) 171
Vocabulary of Dan Michel's Ayenbite of Inwyt (1923) 302
Vocabulary of the Anglo-Manx Dialect (1924) 198
Vokalismus der germanischen und litanischen Lehnwörter im Ostseefinnischen (1924) 132
Volksmährchen und epische Dichtung (1871) 18
Vollständiges Wörterbuch zum Heliand und zur altsächsischen Genesis (1925) 255
Völsunga Saga (1870) 208
Völundarkviða 299
Vorgeschichte der aistischen (baltischen) Stömme in Lichte der Ortsnamenforschung (1924) 35
Voyage to Arcturus (1920) 168
Voyage to Arcturus (1946) 168
Voyages of Doctor Dolittle (1922) 170
Voyages of the Elizabethan seamen 112
Vulgate version of the Arthurian romances, Vol. I (1909) 268
Vulgate version of the Arthurian romances, Vol. II (1908) 268
Vulgate version of the Arthurian romances, Vol. III Pt. I (1910) 269
Vulgate version of the Arthurian romances, Vol. IV Pt. II (1911) 269
Vulgate version of the Arthurian romances, Vol. V Pt. III (1912) 269
Vulgate version of the Arthurian romances, Vol. VI (1913) 269
Vulgate version of the Arthurian romances, Vol. VII (1913) 269
Vulgate version of the Arthurian romances, Vol. VIII (1916) 269
Vulpes et Draco 234

W

Waes (1968) 104
Waldere 301
Wales and the Arthurian Legend (1956) 171
Walhall. Studien über germanischen Jenseitsglauben (1913) 221
Walloping window-blind (1885) 41
Walrus Hunting in the arctic (1896) 76
Wanderer 302
Wanderer's Necklace (1914) 112
War for the lot (1969) 157
War Nennius ein Ire? (1925) 89
Wars of Alexander (1886) 265
Warwickshire Word-book (1896) 224
Well at the World's End, Vol. I (1896) 209
Well at the World's End, Vol. II (1896) 209
Water of the Wondrous Isles (1897) 209
Way of Looking (1955) 133
Way of the World 60
Wedding sermon (1911) 231
Weingarten und Weinberg in deutschen Ortsnamen (1924) 101
Weirdstone of Brisingamen: A Tale of Alderley (1960) 92
Welsh grammar for Schools (1907) 6
Welsh Grammar, Historical and Comparative (1913) 210
Welsh Writers: Life and Letters and the London Mercury (1947) 119
Wendigo (1910) 21
West African Studies (1901) 142
White Book of Mabinogion (1907) 84
White Company (1895) 60
Whose Body? (1923) 251
Widsith 308
Widsith (1912) 44
Wife of Bath's Tale 53
Wife of Bath's tale (1901) 192
Wild Flowers of the Cape Peninsula (1950) 142
Wild Goose Chase 55
William Morris: his work and influence (1914) 58
William of Palerne (1353) 310
Willows (1907) 21
Wind in the Willows (1908) 103
Winteney-Version der Regula S. Benedicti (1888) 16
Winter's Tale 258
Wisdom's daughter (1923) 112
Wise words and quaint counsels of Thomas Fuller (1892) 91

Witch Wood (1927) 34
With the flag to Pretoria, Vol. I (1900) 313
With the flag to Pretoria, Vol. II (1902) 313
Wohunge of Ure Lauerd (1958) 289
Wood beyond the World (1895) 209
Woorroo (1961) 92
Word Abloy in sir Gawayne and the Green Knight. 1174 (1923) 317
Words and Idioms: Studies in the English Language (1925) 268
Words with a bibliographic provenience (1966) 14
Works of Francis Thompson, Vol. I (1913) 288
Works of Francis Thompson, Vol. II (1913) 288
Works of Francis Thompson, Vol. III (1913) 288
Works of Geoffrey Chaucer (1957) 53
Works of Jonathan Swift 285
Works of Oliver Goldsmith, Vol. II (1907) 97
Works of Sir Thomas Browne, Vol. III (1928) 31
Works of Sir Thomas Malory, Vol. I (1947) 181
Works of Sir Thomas Malory, Vol. II (1947) 181
Works of Sir Thomas Malory, Vol. III (1947) 181
Worm Ouroboros (1922) 78
Wörterbuch der Littauischen Sprache, Vol. I (1870) 148
Wörterbuch der Littauischen Sprache, Vol. II (1883) 148
Wortschatz der Germanischen Spracheinheit (1909) 85
Wortweiser (Index verborum) zu den bisher erschienenen Teilen der Historischen Grammatik der englischen Sprache von Dr. Karl Luick (1934) 309
Would I Fight? (1938) 309
Writing & illuminating, & lettering (1906) 135
Writings ascribed to Richard Rolle (1927) 5
Wrong Paradise: And other Stories (1886) 153
Wulfstan (1883) 321
Wulfstan's Canons of Edgar (1972) 321

Y

Year's Work in English Studies 1920-1 (1922) 159
Year's Work in English Studies 1922 (1923) 160
Yellow Fairy Book (1894) 153
York Plays (1885) 268
Yorkshire Celtic Studies, Vol. III (1946) 289
Yorkshire dialect poems (1673-1915) and traditional poems (1917) 198
Yorkshire Writers: Richard Rolle of Hampole an English Father of the Church and his followers., Vol. I (1895) 129
Yorkshire Writers: Richard Rolle of Hampole an English Father of the Church and his followers, Vol. II (1895) 129
Young philosopher: A Novel, Vol. I 267
Ywain and Gawain 324

Z

Zeitschrift für romanische Philologie, Vol. XXXI (1926) 109
Zeugnisse und Excurse zur deutschen Heldensage (1860) 212
Zeugnisse zur germanischen Sage in England (1895) 18
Ziele und Wege der Schallanalyse (1907) 260
Ziska; the problem of a wicked soul (1897) 61
Zur den Ortsnamen (1925) 23

[SECTION B]

INDEX of J. R. R. TOLKIEN'S WRITINGS

Acta Senatus (1911) 328

Adventures in Unnatural History and Medieval Metres: being The Freaks of Fisiologus (i): Fastitocalon (1927) 331

Adventures in Unnatural History and Medieval Metres: being The Freaks of Fisiologus (ii): Iumbo, or, Ye Kind of Ye Oliphaunt (1927) 331

Adventures of Tom Bombadil (1934) 333

Adventures of Tom Bombadil and Other Verses from the Red Book (1962) 338

An Edition of Þe Liflade ant te Passiun of Seinte Iuliene (1936) 334

Ancrene Wisse and Hali Meiðhad (1929) 332

Ancrene Wisse: The English Text of the Ancrene Riwle (1962) 338

Appendix I: The Name 'Nodens' (1932) 332

At the Tabacconist's (1930) 332

Bagme Bloma (1936) 333

Battle of the Eastern Fields (1911) 328

Beautiful Place because Trees are Loved (1972) 339

Beowulf: The Monsters and the Critics (1937) 335

Cat and the Fiddle: A Nursery Rhyme Undone and its Scandalous Secret Unlocked (1923) 329

Chaucer as a Philologist: The Reeve's Tale (1934) 333

City of the Gods (1923) 329

Clerke's Compleinte (1922) 329

Debating Society [KES] (November 1910) 328

Debating Society [KES] (December 1910) 328

Debating Society [KES] (February 1911) 328

Debating Society [KES] (June 1911) 328

Devil's Coach-Horses (1925) 331

Dragon's Visit (1937) 335

Dragon's Visit (1965) 339

Éadig Béo þu! (1936) 333

Eadigan Saelidan: The Happy Mariners (1923) 329

Editorial [KES] (June 1911) 328

Editorial [KES] (July 1911) 328

Educational Value of Esperanto (1933) 333

English and Welsh (1963) 338

Enigmata Saxonica Nuper Inventa Duo (1923) 329

Errantry (1933) 333

Evening in Tavrobel (1924) 330

Farmer Giles of Ham (1949) 337

Fellowship of the Ring (1954) 338

Firiel (1934) 333

For W.H.A. (1967) 339

Foreword [A New Glossary of the Dialect of the Huddersfield District] (1928) 332

Form and Purpose [Pearl] (1953) 337

Fourteenth-Century Romance (1953) 337

Frenchmen Froth (1936) 334

From One to Five (1936) 334

From the many-willow 'd margin of the immemorial Thames (1913) 329

Goblin Feet (1915) 329

Grey Bridge of Tavrobel (1927) 331

Happy Mariners (1920) 329

Henry Bradley: 3 Dec., 1845-23 (1923) 330

Hobbit, or, There and Back Again (1937) 335

Holy Maidenhood (1923) 330

Homecoming of Beorhtnoth, Beorhthelm's Son (1953) 337

I Sat upon a Bench (1936) 334

Ides Ælfscýne (1936) 334

Imram (1955) 338

Iþþlen in Sawles Warde (1947) 337

Iúmonna Gold Galdre Bewunden (1923) 330

Iumonna Gold Galdre Bewunden (1937) 335

Jonah [The Jerusalem Bible] (1966) 339

Knocking at the Door: Lines induced by sensations when waiting for answer at the door of an Exalted Academic Person (1937) 335

La Húru (1936) 334

Lay of Aotrou and Itroun (1945) 336

Leaf by Niggle (1945) 336

Letter to the editor of The Observer (1938) 336

Letter to the editor of Triode (1960) 338

Light as Leaf on Lindentree (1925) 331

Lit and Lang (1936) 334

Lonely Isle (1924) 330

Looney (1934) 333

Middle English 'Losenger' (1953) 337

Middle English Vocabulary (1922) 329

MS Bodley 34: A re-collation of a collation (1948) 337

Name Coventry (1945) 336

Nameless Land (1927) 331

Natura Apis: Morali Ricardi Eremite (1936) 334

Noel (1936) 334

423

Ofer Wídne Gársecg (1936) 334
On Fairy-Stories (1947) 337
Once Upon a Time (1965) 339
Oxford English School (1930) 332
Philologist on Esperanto (1932) 333
Philology: General Works, Vol. IV 1923 (1924) 330
Philology: General Works, Vol. V 1924 (1926) 331
Philology: General Works, Vol. VI 1925 (1927)
Preface [The Ancrene Riwle] (1955) 338
Prefatory note [A Spring Harvest] (1918) 329
Prefatory Note [The Old English Apollonius of Tyre] (1958) 338
Prefatory Remarks on Prose Translation of Beowulf [Beowulf and the Finnesburg Fragment] (1940) 336
Princess Ni (1924) 330
Progress in Bimble Town (1931) 332
Reeve's Tale (1939) 336
Research v. literature (1946) 336
Return of the King (1955) 338
Road Goes Ever On: A Song Cycle (1967) 339
Root of the Boot (1936) 335
Ruddoc Hana (1936) 335
Shadow Man (1936) 335
Sigelwara Land I (1932) 333
Sigelwara Land II (1934) 333
Sir Gawain and the Green Knight (1925) 331
Sir Orfeo (1944) 336
Smith of Wootton Major (1967) 339
Some Contributions to Middle-English Lexicography (1925) 331
Syx Mynet (1936) 335
Tinfang Warble (1927) 331
Tree and Leaf (1964) 339
Two Towers (1954) 338
Why the Man in the Moon Came Down Too Soon (1923) 330
Wireless (1930) 332

[SECTION C]

INDEX of AUTHORS

Auden, Wystan Hugh 340
Brace, Keith 340
Breit, Harvey 340
Brober, Jan 340
Cater, Bill 340
Castell, Daphne 340
Chambers, Raymond Wilson 340
Chaudry, Athar 340
Cherryman, A. E. (Bernard Levin) 340
Curtis, Anthony 341
Dempsey, David 341
Don Chapman (Anthony Wood) 341
Duggan, Alfred 341
Ezard, John 341
Fawcett, H. l'A. 341
Foster, William 341
Fuller, Edmund 341
Green, Peter 341
Green, Roger Lancelyn 342
Gustafsson, Lars 342
Hudson, C. H. 342
Hughes, Richard 342
Lambert, Jack Walter 342
Lewis, Clive Staples 342
Manzalaoui, Mahmoud 342
Mitchison, Naomi 342
Muir, Edwin 343
Norman, Philip 343
Plimmer, Charlotte & Denis 343
Plotz, Richard 343
Price, Anthony 343
Resnik, Henry 343
Richardson, Maurice 343
Spring, Howard 344
Straight, Michael 344
Thwaite, Anthony 344

[SECTION C]

INDEX of INTERVIEWS & REVIEWS

Interviews

1955 – Oxford Calling 340
1956 – With Camera and Pen 343
1961 – Den besynnerlige professor Tolkien 342
1961 – Sagan om ringen ingen allegori: ff-författaren vill ge avkoppling 340
1963 – Hobbits and Heroes 341
1966 – Lord of the Hobbits 340
1966 – Successor to the Hobbits at Last 341
1966 – The Realm of Tolkien 340
1966 – Writers Talking-1: The Hobbit Man 341
1966 – Tolkien on Tolkien 344
1967 – A Benevolent and Furry-footed People 341
1967 – An Interview with Tolkien Late Spring 343
1967 – J.R.R. Tolkien Talks about the Discovery of Middle-earth, the Origins of Elvish 343
1967 – The Hobbit Man 343
1967 – The Hobbit-forming World of J.R.R. Tolkien 343
1967 – The Prevalence of Hobbits 343
1968 – Fireworks for the Author 341
1968 – In the Footsteps of the Hobbits 340
1968 – The Man Who Understands Hobbits 343
1972 – An Early History of the Hobbits 341
1972 – More and More People are Getting the J.R.R. Tolkien Habit 340
1972 – The Lord of the Legends: A Birthday Tribute to the Creator of The Hobbit 340
1972 – Tolkien Seeks the Quiet Life in Oxford 340

Reviews of *The Hobbit*

1937 – Books for Pre-Adults 342
1937 – Professor Tolkien's Hobbit 342
1937 – A world for children: J. R. R. Tolkien 342

Review of *Beowulf: The Monsters and the Critics*

1938 – Review 340

Reviews of *The Fellowship of the Ring*

1954 – Fairy Story for Grown Ups Too 343

1954 – The Gods Return to Earth 342
1954 – Myth-Maker 340
1954 – New Fiction 342
1954 – One Ring to Bind Them 342
1954 – Outward Bound by Air to an Inappropriate Ending 341
1954 – Review of *The Fellowship of the Ring (Country Life)* 344
1954 – Review of *The Fellowship of the Ring (Manchester Guardian)* 341
1954 – Review of *The Fellowship of the Ring (Oxford Times)* 342
1954 – Strange Epic 343
1954 – A World Imaginary, but Real 340
1955 – The Dethronement of Power 342

Reviews of *The Two Tower*

1954 – The Ring 343
1954 – New Novels 343

Reviews of *The Return of the King*

1955 – At the End of the Quest, Victory 340
1955 – A Boy's World 343

Reviews of *The Lord of the Rings*

1956 – Fantastic World of Professor Tolkien 344
1961 – A Fantasy based on Ancient Myths 342
1966 – Of Frodo and Fantasy 341

Ace Books affair

1965 – The Candy Covered Copyright 341

Reviews of *Adventures of Tom Bombadil*

1962 – Hobbitry 344
1962 – Middle Earth Verse 341

Review of *Smith of Wootton Major*

1967 – Slicing a Magical Cake 342

[SECTION D]

INDEX of STUDENTS

Aitken, Daniel Ferguson 345
Bennett, Jack Arthur Walter 345
Bishop, Ian B. 345
Bliss, Alan Joseph 345
Blomfield, Joan E 345
Briggs, K.M. 345
Brooks, Kenneth Robert 345
Brown (later Dronke), Ursula Mary 346
Buckhurst, Helen Therese McMillan 346
Burchfield, Robert William 346
Campbell, Alistair 346
Carroll, Mary Elizabeth 346
Colborn, A. F. 346
Corlett, A. C. 347
Crook, Ruth A. 347
Dobson, Eric John 347
Evans, G. M. G. 347
Evans, W. O. 347
Glanville, Lucia 347
Goolden, Peter 347
Grace, Thomas J. 347
Green, Roger Lancelyn 348
Griffiths, M. Elaine 348
Haworth, J. C. 348
Haworth, Peter 348
Heywood, John 348
Horgan, A. D. 348
Inokuma, Y. 348
Jones, L. E. 348
Jones, R. J. 349
Keays-Young, Julia Maud 349
Ker, N. R. 349
Kiteley, J. F. 349
Kolve, V. A. 349
Kurvinen, Auvo 349
Lascelles, Mary M. 349
Lawlor, John J. 349
Levinson, D. C. 350
Llewellyn, Evan Clifford 350
Martin, V. M. 350
McEldowney, Mary M. 350
Miller, B. D. H. 350
Monaghan, Thomas J. A. 350
Morton, A. M. 351

Olszewska, E. O'Neill, Michael J. 351
O'Neill, Michael J. 351
Pickard, M. Y. 351
Reeves, Joseph 351
Richardson, R. E. 351
Rogers, D. J. 351
Ross, J. 351
Salu, Mary B. 351
Seymour, M. C. 352
Sisam, Celia 352
Stormon, E. J. 352
Tittensor, D. J. 352
Trounce, Allan McIntyre 352
Turville-Petre, Edward Oswald Gabriel 352
Tuve, Rosemond 352
Vleeskruyer, R. 352
Voitl, H. J. O. 353
Wakefield, Anne 353
Ward, A. W. 353
Watt, F. W. 353
Whalley, E. M. 353
Williams, E. V. 353
Woolf, Rosemary 353

[SECTION D]

INDEX of THESES

Alexander and the Earthly Paradise in Medieval English Literature Writings (1927) 349
Andrew Lang as a writer of fairy stories and romances (1944) 348
Apollonius of Tyre (1953) 347
Characterisation in Sir Gawain and the Green Knight (1958) 349
Characteristics of English Children's Literature (1958) 348
Critical edition of the Middle English poem 'On God Ureisun of Ure Lefdi' from MS Cotton Nero A. XIV (1959) 351
Critical Text of Hali Meidhad (1934) 346
Dame Sirith (1956) 350
Dialogue in Chaucer (?-1954) 353
Dialogue of proverbs (?-1959) 348
Edition of 'sir Eglamour of Artois' (1957) 351
Edition of 'Viga-Glums Saga' from the Manuscripts (1934) 352
Edition of British Museum MS Harley 2257 (1928) 348
Edition of British Museum MS Harley 2372 (?-1933) 348
Edition of the Anglo-Saxon poem 'Andreas' (1941) 345
Edition of the fable of 'The Fox and the Wolf' from MS Digby 86 (1956) 347
Edition of the Middle English Romance of 'Athelston' (1931) 352
Edition of the Minor Pieces of MS Nero A14 (1956) 350
Edition of the Old English Julian (1949) 353
Edition of the Parlement of the Three Ages (1946) 351
Edition of the Prose Life of St. Margaret (1929) 347
Edition of the Saga of Þorgils and Hafliði (?-1949) 346
Edition of the Vernon Text of the Ancrene Riwle and a Study of Its Relation to the Other MSS (1926) 351
England and the English in the Icelandic Sagas (1928) 349
English Pronunciation 1500-1700 (1951) 347
Fairy Tales and Fantasies of George MacDonald (1934) 350
Five Virtues of Gawain's shield and their contemporary equivalents (1959) 347
Folk Lore in Jacobean Literature (1946-?) 345
Grammar of Ancrene Wisse (1949) 351
Historical Grammar of Old Icelandic 346
History of Old English and Old Norse Studies in England from the Time of Junius till the End of the Eighteenth Century (1938) 345
History of the development of the English language with special reference to the 15th, 16th & 17th centuries (1957-?) 353
History of the Scandinavian Influence on the English Language (1934) 351
Icelandic Episode in the Life and Work of William Morris (1953) 348
Influence of Middle Dutch and Middle Low German on English Speech (1930) 350
Lennox Robinson : playwright of a changing Ireland (1950) 351
The Life of St Catharine of Alexandria in Middle English prose (1960) 349
Middle English Philology subject (1958-?) 352
New edition of the Middle English romance 'The weddyng of Syr Gawen and Dame Ragnell' (1958) 347
Notes and Observations on the Vocabulary of Ancrene Wisse MS CCCC. 402 (1936) 348
Old English Life of St Chad (1951) 352

Origins of Old English Orthography, with Special Reference to the Representation of the Spirants and W. (1935) 345
Phonology and Accidence of the [Old English] Glosses in MS Cotton Vespasian A.i (1935) 353
Phonology of Hampshire Place-Name Forms (?-1933) 346
Phonology of the Vowels in the Poems of B. Mus. MS Nero Ax (1929) 347
Production of Dipthongs by Breaking in Old English from c.700-900 (?-1931) 346
Religious grotesque in the Middle English drama cycles (1957-?) 349
Revelations of Dame Juliana of Norwich (1946-?) 349
Rise of the English Original Fairy-Story 1800-1865 (?-1953) 353
Seasons and months: studies in a tradition of Middle English poetry (1931) 352
Sir Kaye in Medieval Arthurian Literature (1958-?) 349
Sir Orfeo (1948) 345
Some new words and word-patterns in early Modern English (1949-?) 353
Some Problems in the English Orthoepists (?-1952) 353
Structure of 'Pearl': The Interrelations between 'Liturgical' and 'Poetic' Elements (1952) 345
Studies in the treatment of Old Testament themes in the poems of MS. Junius 11, part 1 (1957) 350
Study of the Additions and Alterations in MSS Bodley340 and 342 (1933) 349
Study of the ascetical elements in Piers Plowman (1951) 347
Study of the English Romance of Sir Tristrem in Relation to Its Sources (1927) 345
Study of the Interrelationship of the English Versions of Mandeville's Travels (1960) 352
Study of the Symbolism of Spiritual Renewal with Special Reference to The Pearl and The Final Plays of Shakespeare (1956) 352
Syntax of 'Cursor Mundi' (1932) 351
Syre Gawene and the Carle of Carelyle (1949) 349
Text of the 'Lambeth Homilies' (1951) 352
Thomas Tyrwhitt (1730-1786) (1947) 350
Vocabulary and Phonology of the Ormulum (1957)-?1957 346
Vocabulary of the Cursor mundi, with principal reference to MS. Cotton Vesp. A3 (1957) 348
William Morris's Treatment of His Icelandic Sources (1935) 351

[SECTION E]

INDEX of EDITORS

Baugh, Albert Croll 354
Bazire, Joyce 354
Blake, Norman Francis 354
Bühler, Curt Ferdinand 354
d'Evelyn Charlotte 354
Davis, Norman 354
Day, Mabel 356
Dobson, Eric John 354
Eccles, Mark 354
Fisher, John Hurt 354
Flower, Robin 354
Fowler, Roger G. 354
Friedman, Albert Barron 354
Greg, Walter Wilson 355
Hallent, Philip E. 355
Henel, Heinrich 355
Hitchcock, Elsie Vaughan 355
Hodgson, Phyllis 355
Ker, Neil Ripley 355
Leach, MacEdward 355
Liegey, Gabriel Michael 355
Macrae-Gibson, Osgar Duncan 355
Meech, Sanford Brown 355
Mill, Anna Jean 354
Miller, Clarence H. 355
Mills, Maldwyn 355
Offord, Marguerite Yvonne 355
Ogden, Margaret Sinclair 355
Pope, John Collins 355
Richardson, Frances E. 356
Ross, Woodburn O. 356
Serjeantson, Mary S. 356
Seymour, Maurice Charles 356
Sisam, Celia 356
Sisam, Kenneth 356
Smith, Albert Hugh 354
Smithers, Geoffrey Victor 356
Steele, Robert 356
Sylvester, Richard Standish 356
Welson Francis, Winthrop 356
Wright, Herbert Gladstone 356

[SECTION E]

INDEX of EARLY ENGLISH TEXT SOCIETY PUBLICATIONS

Ælfric's De Temporibus Anni, OS 213 (1942) 355
Arthour and of Merlin, Vol I text, OS 268 (1973) 355
Bodley Version of Mandeville's Travels, OS 253 (1963) 356
Book of Margery Kempe, Vol I Text, O.S.212 (1940) 355
Book of the Knight of the Tower, S.S. 2 (1971) 355
Book of Vices and Virtues, O.S.217 (1940) 356
Charles of Orleans: The English Poems, OS 215 & 220 (1941) 356
Charles of Orleans: The English Poems II, OS 220 (1946) 356
Cloud of Unknowing and The Book of Privy Counselling, OS 218 (1944) 355
Deonise hid Diuinite, OS 231 (1955) 355
Dicts and Sayings of the Philosophers, OS 211 (1941) 354
English Text Ancrene Riwle BM MS Cotton Cleopatra c VI, OS 267 (1972) 354
English Text of the Ancrene Riwle: BM MS Royal c VI, OS 232 (1956) 354
Epistle of Othea translated from the French text of Christine de Pisan by Stephen Scrope, OS 264 (1970) 354
Facsimile of British Museum MS Harley 2253, OS 255 (1965) 355
Facsimile of MS Bodley 34: St Katherine, OS 247 (1960) 355
Forty-Six Lives translated from Boccaccio's De Claris Mulieribus by Henry Parker, OS 214 (1943) 356
History of Reynard the Fox, OS 263 (1970) 354
Homilies of Ælfric, Vol I, OS 259 (1967) 355
Homilies of Ælfric, Vol II, OS 260 (1968) 355
Kyng Alisaunder, Vol I, OS 227 (1952) 356
Kyng Alisaunder, Vol II, OS 237 (1957) 356
Liber de Diversis Medicinis in the Thornton Manuscript, OS 207 (1938) 355
Life and Death of Cardinal Wolsey by George Cavendish, OS 243 (1959) 356
Lybeaus Desconus, OS 261 (1969) 355
Lyfe of Syr Thomas More, OS 222 (1950) 355
Macro Plays, OS 262 (1969) 354
Metrical Life of St Robert of Knaresborough from BM MS Egerton 3143, OS 228 (1953) 354
Metrical Version of Mandeville's Travels, OS 269 (1973) 356
Middle English Sermons, OS 209 (1940) 356
Non-Cycle Plays and Fragments, S.S. 1 (1970) 354
Orcherd of Syon, Vol I Text, OS 258 (1966) 355
Osborn Bokenham: Legendys of Hooly Wummen, OS 206 (1938) 356
Owl and the Nightingale: facsimile of Jesus College MS 29 & BM Cotton Caligula AIX, OS 251 (1963) 355
Paris and Vienne translated from the French and printed by William Caxton, OS 234 (1957) 355
Parker Chronicle and Laws: facsimile of CCCC MS 173, OS 208 (1941) 354
Phonetic Writings of Robert Robinson, OS 238 (1957) 354
Praise of Folie by Sir Thomas Chaloner, OS 257 (1965) 355
Respublica: an interlude for Christmas 1553 attributed to Nicholas Udall, OS 226 (1952) 355
Salisbury Psalter, OS 242 (1959) 356
Sir Eglamour of Artois, OS 256 (1965) 356
South English Legendary, Vol I, OS 235 (1956) 354
South English Legendary, Vol II, OS 236 (1956) 354

South English Legendary, Vol III, OS 244 (1959) 354
Tretyse of Loue, OS 223 (1951) 354
Wulfstan's Canons of Edgar, OS 266 (1972) 354
Ywain and Gawain, OS 254 (1964) 354

www.ingramcontent.com/pod-product-compliance
Lightning Source LLC
Chambersburg PA
CBHW081226080526
44587CB00022B/3841